Philanthropy in England
1480–1660

by the same author

THE DEVELOPMENT OF RELIGIOUS TOLERATION
IN ENGLAND

1 *From the beginning of the English Reformation
to the death of Queen Elizabeth*

2 *From the Accession of James I to the Convention
of the Long Parliament, 1603–1640*

3 *From the Convention of the Long Parliament
to the Restoration, 1640–1660*

4 *Attainment of the theory and accommodations in
Thought and Institutions, 1640–1660*

THE CHARITIES OF LONDON, 1480–1660

THE CHARITIES OF RURAL ENGLAND, 1480–1660

Philanthropy in England
1480–1660

A STUDY OF THE CHANGING PATTERN
OF ENGLISH SOCIAL ASPIRATIONS

BY

W. K. JORDAN

President of Radcliffe College
Professor of History, Harvard University

RUSSELL SAGE FOUNDATION

NEW YORK, N.Y. 10017

FIRST PUBLISHED IN 1959

SECOND IMPRESSION 1964

PRINTED IN GREAT BRITAIN
in 10 on 11 point Plantin type
BY OFFSET
UNWIN BROTHERS LIMITED
WOKING AND LONDON

FOR

F. R. J.

Animae dimidium meae

———

PREFACE

This is the first of a series of volumes dealing with the changing pattern of men's aspirations for their society during a long and critical period in the history of western Europe. The present volume is an essay commenting on the subject and presenting conclusions drawn from a considerable mass of available evidence. In the very nature of the case the whole of the research had to be completed and the later volumes written in first draft before it was possible to undertake this essay. The second projected volume will deal in some detail with the philanthropic impulse in the English urban society, attention being confined to London, where a rich, an incredibly generous, and a most articulate merchant aristocracy was in the course of our period to lay solidly the foundations of liberal institutions not only in the metropolis but throughout England. The third volume will consider at length the changing structure of men's aspirations in rural England, with documentation supplied from a sampling of counties in various parts of the realm. There will remain studies of several additional rural counties and of Bristol, an urban complex second in importance only to London. It is hoped that these may be published separately in appropriate periodicals.

Many years have elapsed since this study was begun under the kindly auspices of a grant from the John Simon Guggenheim Memorial Foundation. The work has been sustained through the years by most helpful subventions from the American Philosophical Society, Harvard University, and Radcliffe College. More recently it has been brought to completion with the help of a generous grant from the Ford Foundation which made it possible to complete the research, to assemble and assess the materials, and to reduce the data to statistical order. These volumes will record the benefactions of many men of an earlier age; the author's experience would suggest that even the slow and fumbling efforts of the student of history are not without their support by equally generous donors in these later days.

The gathering of the materials for these volumes has required work in the principal libraries and archives in England and the United States, where in every instance the author has met with courteous and patient treatment. The work has imposed particularly heavy burdens on the staffs of Somerset House, York Minster, and many district registries, and for their most helpful assistance we would express our deepest gratitude.

W. K. J.

Cambridge, Massachusetts

January, 1958

P.E. I—I*

BIBLIOGRAPHICAL NOTE

The bibliographical citations in this work are necessarily very heavy, particularly in the later volumes. Hence no formal bibliography will be presented, but a full reference will be supplied in the instance of the first citation of a printed or manuscript source.

It has been our intention to render all quotations exactly as written or printed, save that capitalization has in all cases been modernized.

CONTENTS

I

The Conception

I esteeme wills . . . to be of the noblest sort of recordes; for yt they
acquaint us wth more circumstances (and at the least wth no lesse
certainty) then other recordes comonly do. As namely, the substance of the deceased especially in his personall estate, his wife,
children, kindred, servants and his esteemed freindes (for of such
consist his executors, supervisers, and legatees) his inclinations to
piety, charity and bounty, the circumstantiall time (for the most
part) of his death and the place of buriall; all wch give much light
and satisfaction to such as listen after the memory of their ancestors.

Gervase Holles, *Memorials of the Holles family*
(A. C. Wood, ed.) (L., 1937), 20.

This study is concerned with men's aspirations for their own age and
for generations yet to come; with their heroic effort to shape the course of
history by creating enduring social institutions which would contribute
significantly, often decisively, in determining the structure and nature
of the society just then coming into being. It has been our purpose to
record every gift and bequest made to charities, quite broadly defined,
during the period 1480–1660 in a selected and, it is hoped, representative group of ten English counties, which probably included about one-
third of the population and somewhat more than half of the disposable
wealth of the entire realm. The broad objective of the study is to trace
with care the changing aspirations of English society as reflected in the
benefactions of the age. The period with which we are to deal is long,
extending as it does for very nearly two centuries. It is likewise an era
of great importance in the history of thought and institutions, witnessing
as it did the collapse of the mediaeval society and the rise of the modern
era, the triumph of a strong monarchy on the ruins of the feudal polity,
the revolutionary impact of that complex movement which we call the
Reformation, the emergence of a powerful and responsible gentry, and
the swift rise of a principally Puritan urban aristocracy—the merchants
—to the seats of economic power. A detailed examination of the benefactions of this momentous period provides a sensitive and surely an
accurate barometer of powerful forces of historical change at work in the
English society and affords us a most intimate understanding of the

shifting morphology of aspirations which were producing changes that were in their total effect revolutionary.

Very broadly, it may be said that this study documents, though certainly imperfectly, one of the few great cultural revolutions in western history: the momentous shift from men's primarily religious preoccupations to the secular concerns that have moulded the thought and institutions of the past three centuries. This profoundly important metamorphosis in the nature and quality of men's aspirations for their society is quite perfectly mirrored in their benefactions. When men come to draw their wills they express their aspirations with a kind of ultimate honesty, and when they leave charitable bequests they arm these aspirations with effective and enduring sanctions. The drafting of a will is for any human being a final and a solemn stocktaking not only of his personal estate, but if he be charitably disposed, of the world around him and of the world as he would like it to become.

'*In Dei nomine Amen.*' With this sonorous and solemn phrase almost every will drawn before 1640 was prefaced, suggesting not only the sentiments of the age but the historical and social sanctity and honesty of these documents. Men drew their wills in the name of God and in the face of God. A will in our period was quite as much a testament of faith as a secular document disposing of goods and chattels. Almost every will begins with a carefully considered and eloquently elaborated confession of faith, in which the testator earnestly strives to set out the nature of his beliefs, to confess his own inadequacies, to confirm his confidence in the mercy of God, and to prepare himself for a death which he believes to be imminent. Wills in this age of profound faith were mirrors of men's souls as truly as they were mirrors of their mundane aspirations. They were intensely personal documents, as well, for relatively few betray the cold hand of the lawyer or notary in the language and form of their composition. And they are completely honest documents, since men examined their consciences and defined their aspirations with searching of soul and in the sight of God, as they came at last to order their charitable dispositions, to project, as it were, their convictions and their fondest hopes for the earthly society from which they must now reluctantly depart.

The wills of our period, then, were made in full contemplation of death, and they were ordinarily drawn in the immediate presence of death. They were literally last wills and testaments. An extensive sampling would suggest that for wills proved in the Prerogative Court of Canterbury in the earlier years of our period only two months intervened between the drafting of the median will and its admission to probate; that not as much as three months elapsed during the early Elizabethan period; and almost exactly four months in the early Stuart era.[1] These wills brought at last into formal language and decision matters of personal and social significance on which the testator had long brooded and towards which the slope of his aspirations had run for many years past. These were not 'ad hoc' or tentative determinations, but rather the ultimate and irrevocable dispositions of men of some substance towards their families, their friends, and their society. They accordingly possess great dignity, great poignancy, and great clarity with respect to the ultimate aspirations of the testator.

These, then, are in large part the documents from which our evidence will be drawn. The benefactions made by men of our period bear eloquent witness to a profoundly significant, a truly revolutionary, shift in the nature and structure of men's aspirations: to the rapid withering of the religious preoccupation as the secular needs of humanity came, well before our period was out, to absorb the concern and the fortunes of men who were laying most securely and solidly the *Grundlagen* of a new civilization. This study will be concerned with an examination of the striking change in the pattern of men's attitude towards the problems of poverty, misery, and ignorance. The Middle Ages were acutely sensitive to the spiritual needs of mankind while displaying only scant, or ineffectual, concern with the alleviation or cure of the ills that beset the bodies of so large a mass of humanity. The mediaeval system of alms, administered principally by the monastic foundations, was at once casual and ineffective in its incidence, never seeking to do more than relieve conspicuous and abject suffering. This is probably the most significant reason why benefactions to monastic foundations had so sharply declined prior to 1480 in England and why they literally dried up well before their properties were expropriated by the Crown in the fourth and fifth decades of the sixteenth century.

Poverty was first systematically attacked in the sixteenth century with gifts for the outright relief of the poor and then later in our period with really massive endowments designed to eradicate its causes by a great variety of undertakings, among which the extension of educational opportunities was not the least. These efforts, so important in the development of the ethic as well as the institutions of the liberal society,

---

[1] Some further details on this point may be of interest. A long sampling of wills proved in the Prerogative Court of Canterbury for the years 1504 and 1517 yields an average interval of 106 days between the drafting of the will and its probate, the more meaningful median figure being 59 days. The range of time extends from 6 days to 2 years, 2 months, and 11 days. A similar sampling for the years 1558 and 1564, with a range of from 6 days to 3 years and 14 days, gives an average interval of 158 days and a median of 81. For the years 1617 and 1637 the average was 273 days, while the median figure was 121 days, and the range from 3 days to 7 years, 6 months, and 1 day. Less extensive samplings made of wills proved at York for these same years yielded substantially similar results.

were implemented by Elizabethan and Jacobean legislation planned to make each parish responsible for its poor and to separate the employable from the unemployable poor. But it is clear that the constructive effort, as well as most of the funds, flowed from private endowments rather than from the mechanism contemplated by legislation.

This study, then, will trace out from the wealth of detail available the development of moral and social responsibility in the English society. Many factors, it is clear, account for the almost precocious maturity of this attitude in the late Tudor and the early Stuart reigns. The Tudor sovereigns had given England a long and stern tuition in local administrative responsibility. The gentry, raised up to political and economic strength by Henry VIII and Elizabeth, assumed new and heavy public burdens with grace and considerable skill. At the same time, Calvinism was in England sublimated into a sensitive social conscience that was secular in its aspirations and fruits even when the animating impulse may have been religious. Two classes of men, the gentry and the newer urban aristocracy of merchants, assumed an enormous measure of responsibility for the public welfare while rapidly and most effectively translating their ideals for society into a new philosophy of the state which we denominate liberalism.

The whole realm stirred as men began to discover that they could create institutions of social change and reformation with their own wealth and charity. Well before our period was finished, a veritable transformation had occurred in the social and cultural institutions of the realm, the artifact, in large part, of a relatively small group of rich, aggressive, and generous men who were creating a society in the image of their own aspirations. In this essentially revolutionary process, they received full encouragement from the masterful Tudors, perhaps the most secular as well as the most enlightened of all English sovereigns. The tide of philanthropic change mounted into a flood during the early years of the Stuart age, completing a social revolution intimately connected with a more dramatic, though in ultimate terms less effective, religious and political revolution which occurred directly a bewildered royal prerogative was thrown across the course of historical change.

It is likewise clear that it was the mercantile aristocracy of London which came in the course of our period to exercise a dominant influence on the moulding of national aspirations and on shaping and endowing the institutions required to translate aspirations into enduring reality. These Londoners, who were very rich and almost incredibly generous, spread the pervasive pattern of their giving across the whole face of England. The focus of their attack was on the ancient evil of poverty. But they were prescient enough to sense that poverty could never be destroyed unless the ignorance in which it spawns was relieved. Such men scorned and discarded alms, the mechanism of mediaeval charity, since they were profoundly persuaded that casual, undisciplined charity was as ineffective as it was wasteful. The great and effective instrument which the mercantile aristocracy, whether of London, Bristol, or Norwich, developed to secure the translation of their aspirations into historical reality was the charitable trust, which was to be classically defined and most powerfully encouraged by the great Elizabethan statute of charitable uses.

It is not too much to say that the gentry and the merchants assumed a very large measure of social responsibility in England early in the Tudor period, which during the Elizabethan era was so expanded that it became dominant. Older classes of men, and most particularly the nobility and clergy, were quietly withdrawing from the tasks of responsibility, while these new and intensely aggressive classes were moving in to fill the vacuum of social and historical responsibility and power. In part, as we shall later note in detail, this cession of responsibility, whether among noblemen or husbandmen, can be explained by economic difficulties in which the older social groups found themselves, but far more important is the undoubted fact that the whole tendency of Tudor policy, so warmly espoused by the gentry and by their urban counterparts, was viewed with suspicion if not disfavour by the older and once powerful rural classes. We shall have occasion to observe that the gentry itself was fragmented as a consequence of Tudor policy, an historically decisive alliance having been forged between the rising mercantile aristocracy and the 'new gentry' which had its origin in the redistribution of monastic properties and in the speculative opportunities available to daring landed entrepreneurs throughout most of the sixteenth century. Various classes of men, then, responded in quite different ways to the dominant forces of sixteenth century history. One can perhaps more accurately say that they responded with differing degrees of willingness, for, as we shall see, the merchants and the gentry were with an immense generosity and a sureness of aspiration establishing social and cultural institutions, a whole pattern of civilization, all over England long before other and more reluctant classes of men made grudging concession that the mediaeval world was at an end.

With the accession of Queen Elizabeth, it is possible to say that the whole tone of social and cultural aspirations is secular. At about this date the historical commitment was made which over the next century was to lead to the foundation and the endowment of the whole complex structure of institutions which undergird the liberal society. The state lent little direct aid to this process of change, the ultimate effect of which was revolutionary, save by the tone of its policy and the great codifications of laws which defined the nature of the responsibility of the modern state towards poverty and which charted those regions of social need to be occupied and won by charitably disposed men armed with that most effective of social mechanisms, the charitable trust. But this was not all. The state, as personified by the great Queen, bestowed an even more effective kind of aid by the steady support which it lent to secularism in English life and even in the English church. This secularism of the Queen, always decently disguised when possible, was cold, efficient, and complete.

The secularism of this great and remarkable woman proceeded, we may believe, from complex sources. Policy encouraged it; the determination to protect the state against religious zeal and the fragmentation of sects dictated it; a prescient understanding of the slope of modern policy suggested it. But it ran deeper than that, for at the bottom of the unfathomable personality and genius of the Queen there seems to have been a religious indifference which was itself a kind of innate secularism. This mood of the woman who ruled England so firmly, translated as it was into brilliant policy, fitted precisely and effectively the aspirations of those classes which were moulding English institutions with their charitable wealth. Their mood, too, was intensely and irrevocably secular, as we shall have many occasions to point out. Yet it must be said that their immense secular bias sprang from quite different roots from that of the Queen. Most of these donors were deeply pious men; in fact, a very large proportion of the most effectively munificent among them were Puritans. They were simply moving in directions, often suggested by their own piety, in which the church was either unprepared or unfitted to move. Early in our period there is abundant evidence that they distrusted the church as feoffee for social change and amelioration because they knew that the ancient church had been in the generation just prior to the Reformation an inefficient, they rather said faithless, custodian of social wealth and because in certain areas of need, as, for example, education, it had stubbornly resisted progress. Much of this odium which these men attached to the mediaeval church their grandsons, particularly if they were Puritan, attached as well to the established church of the realm. But even more significantly, the broadening spectrum of social and cultural aspirations in the sixteenth and seventeenth centuries simply transcended and overran those areas of responsibility which the church was prepared or competent to undertake. Broadly speaking, therefore, the church and its needs, much less its social services and competences, came to be regarded as irrelevant. But at the same time the institutions founded by these donors, and the very content of their intense secularism, not infrequently sprang from sources of deep and moving piety.

Queen Elizabeth ruled so strongly and well because her aspirations for the English polity were so closely in attunement with the aspirations and interests of the dominant classes of the realm. We have observed that this sympathy, this synchronization of aspirations, lent profoundly

important support to the amazing accomplishments of private benefactors throughout her reign. A social and historical momentum
gathered force during her long reign which burst out into an immense
outpouring of principally secular charitable dispositions in the early
Stuart era. The power, the velocity, and the direction of movement,
which was ordering the basic social institutions of the modern world,
were so mighty that they could neither be controlled nor diverted to
causes which both James and Charles would have preferred. James was
bewildered and his son was not a little alarmed by the vast power and
social effectiveness of the huge and carefully devised charitable endowments of the age which were creating an England they did not understand, an England at bottom inimical to their conception of the state.
In particular, they both were aghast at the intense secularism explicit in
this tidal flow of funds which was moulding a society which they were
not competent either to rule or to administer. Archbishop Laud, always
expressing the half-formed views of his sovereign, made an heroic,
indeed, a tragic, effort first to discipline and then to order the social
forces of the age, but this interesting essay of policy had no other considerable effect than to hasten the outbreak of civil war. The Stuarts did
not understand England, its constitution, or its social institutions. Nor
did they understand the aspirations of men who with their own substance were creating a society of which we are still the inheritors. It is
with these great forces of social change that we are concerned in this
study.

## II

The Method

1. *Wills as sources*

This volume is an essay, which will undertake to comment rather generally on a considerable body of evidence to be more fully presented in the subsequent volumes comprising this work. In the later volumes we shall deal with the development of charitable institutions in the several counties included in this study, while in the present volume we shall be concerned with the interpretation of data aggregated from the individual counties and described conveniently, if inexactly, as applying to England as a whole. We should now, however, discuss the historical and statistical method employed in the accumulation, the aggregating, and the interpretation of the large mass of somewhat unruly evidence on which the study rests.

Our principal source has been the many thousands of wills proved in England during the period 1480–1660 and since 1858 most conveniently gathered in several repositories. By far the most important body of these materials are those to be found at Somerset House, these being wills proved in the Prerogative Court of Canterbury. Though any precise statement must be inexact, we may say that broadly speaking any will in which the testator possessed property in more than one diocese of the Province of Canterbury, or made bequests in more than one diocese, or was possessed of considerable property, would be proved in this archiepiscopal court. In this same great collection, moreover, are to be found wills proved in England during the years 1653–1660, when the Protectorate, among its many important reformations, not only withdrew the probate of wills from ecclesiastical hands but consolidated their probate for the entire nation.

A similar repository for the northern reaches of the realm is to be found at York, where, beginning in 1389, wills of persons dying within that province were proved if their property and dispositions fell within the roughly outlined categories mentioned above. The Prerogative Courts of Canterbury and of York, then, granted probate and became the repositories of the wills of most persons disposing substantial estates and, for us more pertinently, those bequeathing considerable sums for charitable uses. We have accordingly examined the wills of all testators dying during our period in the ten counties with which we are concerned and have assembled the particulars concerning the charitable dispositions of those who left such bequests.[1]

A very large proportion, upwards of 94 per cent, of charitable benefactions made by will are to be found in these two great repositories, where the wills of almost all men of considerable substance had necessarily to come for probate. But we are likewise deeply interested in the changing social aspirations of humble men whose wills, when they made them at all, only uncommonly possessed complications which would bring them to York or Canterbury. These wills were ordinarily proved in a diocesan court, or in a subordinate jurisdiction of the diocese, and were, for the most part, ultimately deposited in various district registries, where they may now be consulted.

There are few classes of historical records for whose preservation men show such tender concern as the wills of their ancestors. We may, consequently, assume with some confidence that we have found and recorded the charitable contributions of almost all men who within our period and region left charitable bequests. Such benefactions comprised a large proportion of the total sum given for charitable uses in the ten counties with which we are concerned, amounting in fact to almost two-thirds (63·17 per cent) of the aggregate. The proportion thus dis-

---

[1] The Prerogative Court of Canterbury normally embraced all testators dying within the Province of Canterbury who left *bona notabilia* of more than £5 value in more than one diocese of the province, and all estates of persons dying overseas. In many cases, however, executors preferred to prove wills in the prerogative court even if all goods fell within a single diocese. The PCC was not fully organized with its own officers until 1443, though the functions were certainly exercised at a much earlier date.

Under the prerogative courts, whether of Canterbury or York, were the bishops' consistory courts holding jurisdiction over an entire diocese, the archdeaconry courts, the peculiar courts, as well as manorial and local courts, such as the Court of Husting in London, in which many wills, usually of humble testators, might be proved.

When ecclesiastical jurisdiction over probate was abolished in 1858, wills from the two great prerogative courts were gathered in Somerset House in London and in York, while most, but by no means all, wills to be found in the lesser ecclesiastical jurisdictions were assembled in the various district probate registries. Thus at the Norwich District Probate Registry will be found wills proved in the Consistory Court of Norwich as well as wills formerly in the Court of the City of Norwich. G. W. Marshall's *Handbook to the ancient courts of probate* (L., 1895) is the only convenient guide to the various repositories, but, having been published two generations ago, is not reliable because of the steady progress that has been made in consolidating wills in the district registries. A study of this matter, and a published handlist, would be valuable, as would a thorough treatment of the history of probate during the unsettled years of the Civil War and the era of revolutionary government.

posed ranges from the inexplicably low figure of 27·60 per cent for Buckinghamshire to the very high proportion of 70·37 per cent and 77·75 per cent in the great urban centres of London and Bristol respectively.

2. *Living gifts as sources*

But we have likewise endeavoured to record every known gift for charitable purposes made during a donor's lifetime, whether that amount was disposed as an income or a capital sum. As has just been suggested, rather more than a third of the total sum was so given, though we remain uncomfortably certain that despite a diligent search many small income gifts have eluded us and that many more were never recorded at all. We have sought to work through all possibly relevant county, borough, and parochial records, for it does remain true that a really large number of such benefactions, even when quite casually made, somehow found their way into preserved historical materials. One may be reasonably confident that all the larger gifts made by living donors have been found if they were in capital form—and very few were not—because such benefactions almost invariably were or became trusts which in turn created an historical record. But the casual gift for alms, the spontaneous gift of a coin for a beggar, the modestly cloaked aid given to a worthy but needy householder—such gifts which reveal so much of the spirit of a man and of his age—are elusive and are probably wholly unrecorded. It seems certain indeed that we are here describing a relatively very small and statistically unimportant range of charitable gifts, yet we have found enough of them to know that they possess a virtue and a human significance far transcending their statistical importance.

We have been greatly assisted in our search by the fact that a large proportion of all charitable benefactions made in our period were in the enduring form of capital. As we shall have later occasion to observe, these endowments took many forms, but they did necessarily create a legal and an historical record. Of the total sums given for charitable uses in England, slightly more than 82 per cent was capital.[1] The proportion of funds established as endowments, whether by bequest or living gifts, was remarkably similar in all the counties examined, falling within the very tight range of from 76·83 per cent for Lancashire to the 91 per cent so constituted by the always prudent benefactors of Bristol.[2] In all counties the amounts left for educational purposes, for almshouses, and the various institutions created for the social rehabilitation

---

[1] We ask indulgence here and subsequently for quite inexactly, but most conveniently, using the term 'England' to describe the sampling of ten counties with which we deal.

[2] See table opposite.

of the poor were almost wholly in the form of endowments, while such secular uses as the household relief of the poor, the care of roads, and other public works received considerable support from outright gifts for immediate use. So too the various religious needs were heavily sustained by outright gifts, though the range in the several counties is wide, with the one exception of funds left or given for the support of lectureships, which, Bristol and Kent aside, were almost wholly endowed.

3. The principle of county selection

It being impossible, and probably unnecessary, to record the charities for all counties in the realm, some principle of selection had to be evolved, be it said after a number of false starts. It seemed most important that the group of counties should be as representative as possible, always subject to the pragmatic consideration of the availability of reasonably complete county, borough, and parochial records. It was also thought to be desirable that the counties should differ one from another in respects important to our study, and on these grounds Surrey was not included as being too similar to Kent and Westmorland as too similar to Yorkshire, after the research for these two counties was well along. It was necessary, too, to include socially and economically retarded counties with others at once prosperous and advanced, since England during most of our period was far from being a culturally homogeneous nation and the velocity of social change varied most remarkably from region to region. As importantly, it was necessary to include London (Middlesex), wherein so evidently the centre of gravity of wealth, social progress, and cultural power reposed, as well as one other important urban complex (Bristol), which was building its own social institutions and which stood reasonably free of the immense influence of the capital. It was desirable, too, to include a number of essentially agricultural counties with no considerable urban centres, as well as others with a more evenly mixed economy and population. Finally, it became very clear as the work progressed that, so dominant were London's aspirations in determining the social development of the entire realm, it was important to secure a range of counties reflecting these influences on a scale extending from the overwhelming consequences of London's charitable wealth in Kent to the relatively inde-

The proportion of capital gifts in relation to the total of charitable funds in the several counties is as follows:

	per cent		per cent
Bristol	91·00	London	82·60
Buckinghamshire	82·40	Norfolk	80·96
Hampshire	80·09	Somerset	80·86
Kent	81·35	Worcestershire	80·51
Lancashire	76·83	Yorkshire	82·17

pendent development of social institutions in that almost truculently proud county, Norfolk.

Accordingly, the counties included in our sample are: Bristol, Buckinghamshire, Hampshire, Kent, Lancashire, Middlesex (London), Norfolk, Somerset, Worcestershire, and Yorkshire. It is hoped that those so chosen fully meet the criteria of selection, though there are at least a few more which might well have been included in an ideal sample. Possibly another Midland county might have been added; the cultural and economic isolation of Dorset invites attention; the remarkably intimate ties binding Shropshire to London deserve even more study than has been given to them in our discussion of London; and another county in the northern reaches of the realm would have provided a better geographical representation had it met the other criteria being imposed.

4. *Population and wealth*

The general conclusions of this work resting as they do upon a sampling of the counties of the realm, a number of relevant and extremely difficult questions must be considered. The first of these is, of course, the relation of the population of our group of counties to that of the realm at large. Here we are in an area of conjecture, though recent scholars have, it would seem, reached a reasonably close agreement on at least one element of this mooted question. Responsible estimates of the population of England in *ca.* 1600 range from Thorold Rogers' certainly low figure of about 2,500,000 to Usher's suggestion of something like 4,460,000, while the more reliable of the seventeenth- and eighteenth-century estimates range from 3,500,000 to Gregory King's suggestion of 4,885,696. Our own very rough calculation is something like 4,200,000 as the probable order of population for England in 1600, since a fairly detailed study of relevant data in the ten counties would incline us towards supporting the higher estimates of Professor Usher and of Father Hughes, the latter having set forward a figure of about 4,000,000.[1]

If the whole question of the population of the realm at any given date in the Tudor and Stuart periods is uncertain and subject to wide differences of speculative judgment, the population of the several counties

---

[1] Rogers, J. E. T., *Six centuries of work and wages* (N.Y., 1884), 463; Darby, H. C., ed. *An historical geography of England before A.D. 1800* (Camb., 1951), 435; Usher, A. P., *An introduction to the industrial history of England* (Boston, 1920), 89; Hughes, Philip, *The Reformation in England* (3 vols., N.Y., 1951–1954), I, 32. A. M. Carr-Saunders (*Population*, L., 1925, 7) sets the estimate at 5,000,000 in 1603 for England and Wales, with which A. L. Rowse (*The England of Elizabeth*, L., 1951, 218) seems inclined to agree. A careful and an ambitious attack on the problem of population ought in all conscience to be made.

comprising the realm is a subject which has received very little even of speculative enquiry. Yet certainly no defensible estimate of the population of the whole can be presented without estimates of the population of the parts. We have necessarily devoted considerable attention to this difficult question, depending heavily upon parochial and diocesan materials in an effort to arrive at tentative estimates of the growth of population during our period in the several counties with which we are concerned. These estimates will be more fully set out in the subsequent volumes, but we should here present our judgment with respect to the population figures as they stood in 1600. It would seem probable that the population of our ten counties at this date was of the order of 1,389,000, which in turn suggests that our sampling of counties includes almost exactly one-third of the population of the entire realm.[1]

Interestingly enough, the regions with which we are concerned likewise comprised almost exactly a third (32·68 per cent) of the whole of the land mass of England. More significantly, the counties in our group included about a third (32·54 per cent) of all the parishes in England in 1600, or, more accurately, a third of the organized places of worship in the realm. Our count of the parochial units, made as near 1600 as possible, would suggest that there were in England at this time 9321 places of organized worship, of which 3033 were to be found in the counties included in our sample.[2] In several important particulars,

[1] For the individual counties our estimates of population are as follows:

Bristol	16,000
Buckinghamshire	55,000
Hampshire	135,000
Kent (16th century boundaries)	155,000
Lancashire	105,000
Middlesex (outside Greater London)	45,000
Greater London (1603)	225,000
Norfolk	180,000
Somerset	115,000
Worcestershire	58,000
Yorkshire	300,000
	1,389,000

This figure represents 33·07 per cent of our estimate of the population of the whole of England in 1600.

[2] No two counts can ever be quite the same. For one thing, as we shall mention in detail in our discussion of the individual counties, the parochial structure of the realm was not complete even in 1600, and the number was, on balance, steadily increasing. But more importantly, no two students can quite agree on what constituted a parish. Our count includes all places of settled and organized worship, the number consequently being somewhat larger than would result if the census were limited to parishes in the strict and legal sense of the term. Sir Thomas Wilson (*The state of England, anno dom. 1600*, F. J. Fisher, ed., L., 1936, 11) believed that there were 9725 parish churches in England (and Wales ?)

therefore, we would seem to be justified in assuming that we are dealing in this study with something like one-third of the realm at large.

But we are concerned not so much with the population base as with wealth, reflecting itself in generosity, of men and of regions. Thus the city of Bristol gave substantially more to charitable causes during the course of our period than did the county of Hampshire, though without any doubt the population of the latter county was something like eight times as great in say 1600. In these most relevant terms, our sampling of counties is by no means representative, principally because of the immense wealth of London and almost as significantly because of the effective quality of that wealth. We have dealt with this subject in some detail in our discussion of the individual counties, but it may be said here with fair certainty that the ten counties comprehended in our study disposed something over 50 per cent of the total wealth of the

in 1600; William Camden reckoned that there were 9284 in 1603, his count following a considerably earlier census made by Archbishop Parker (*Britain*, L., 1637, 161–162); John Weever (*Ancient funerall monuments*, L., 1631, 183) gives the same estimate; Sir Edward Coke reckoned the number at 8803 at the outset of the seventeenth century, but since he excluded cities and boroughs from his count, the total would be very close indeed to our own estimate; while a late sixteenth-century manuscript count of the parsonages and vicarages in England and Wales 'extracted out of records of first fruits and tenths in the Exchequer' (*BM Royal MSS.*, 18 D. III, f. 3) gives the total of strictly defined parishes as 8736, the accurate addition of the colums being, however 8733. The details of our own count, as compared with Camden's, may be of some interest:

County	Year	No. of parishes	No. of fully organized chapelries	Total places of organized worship	Camden's count	Camden's comments
Bristol	1600	17		17	17	
Buckinghamshire	1600	210		210	185	'and mercate
Hampshire	1600	320*		320	253	towns 18'
Kent	1600	395*		395	398	[36] 'beside
Lancashire	1650	64	118	182	[182]	very many
Middlesex						Chappels'
(outside						
London)	ca. 1600	76*		76	73	
London	ca. 1600	117*		117	121	
Norfolk	1600	581*		581	660	
Somerset	1560	395	74	469	385	'very many
Worcestershire	1600	196*		196	152	Chappels'
Yorkshire	ca. 1600	314	156	470	459	
		2685		3033	2885	

* Chapelries included.

realm and at least 60 per cent of the charitable wealth provided by the whole of England during the long period under investigation.[1] The disproportionate wealth, both total and charitable, disposed by the counties comprised in our sample is, as has been suggested, principally explained by the vast riches of London, but it should likewise be remarked that they included certainly six, and more probably seven, of the ten largest cities in the England of our age, and among them the four ranking cities of the realm: London, Bristol, Norwich, and York. And mercantile wealth in the second half of our period was not only very great, but, more significantly, it was largely disposable and it was incredibly generous and socially effective.

5. The historical intervals

We should also explain that in the key tables on which this study rests we have been obliged for statistical reasons to follow quite arbitrary conventions which do some violence not only to the usual chronological divisions but also to historical fact. The period covered extends from 1480 through 1660, beginning some years before the triumph of Henry Tudor and including as well some few months of the period after the restoration of the monarchy. This was regarded as essential for statistical and comparative purposes, since thereby the accumulation of benefactions and their analysis could be made in decade intervals for the whole of the long era under review. This quite inflexibly imposed convention required us, in the event a donor made charitable gifts in more than one decade, or, as was more commonly the case, made a gift in one decade and left a charitable bequest in a later decade, to divide the total contribution of the donor and to assign the correct portion to the proper decade. Similarly, charitable dispositions made prior to 1480 by donors who also made contributions in or after that year have been only in part recorded, as have the gifts of donors made after 1660, only the contributions prior to the Restoration having been counted. In a fair number of cases it proved to be impossible accurately to date a gift, though the total of such contributions amount to the statistically insignificant proportion of no more than 0·26 per cent of the *corpus* of charitable funds in our era. After some uncertainty, the whole of these gifts have arbitrarily been assigned to the interval 1641–1660, to which,

---

[1] These estimates represent amendments of the most valuable comments of Thorold Rogers and E. J. Buckatzsch ('The geographical distribution of wealth in England 1086–1843', *Econ. Hist. Rev.*, 2d. ser., III (1950), 180–202) on this subject. The estimate of the proportion of charitable wealth contributed by group of counties is derived principally from extensive samplings of the charitable gifts made in all other English counties as related to the presumably complete data for the counties under discussion. These samplings, however, were confined to the materials available in the PCC and PCY.

it seems likely, the largest proportion of the money total, though not of the donors, properly belongs.

Useful as are the decade intervals in which we have assembled our data, they are relatively unimportant as compared with the more generally recognized historical periods of our era into which our material has also been aggregated and among which useful and most revealing comparisons and changes may be observed. But since the decade intervals must be kept intact, we have necessarily in this basic scheme of organization done considerable violence not only to convention but to fact. The period 1480–1540 has been called with reasonable chronological accuracy 'The Pre-Reformation Era' and, as with the other periods, will ordinarily be mentioned without repeated and certainly monotonous reference to the dates with which it is defined. The years 1541–1560 have been described somewhat inexactly as 'The Age of the Reformation', while 'The Age of Elizabeth' has been foreshortened to the four decades, 1561–1600. The period 1601–1640 has been regarded as 'The Early Stuart Period', while the remaining two decades have been described as 'The Revolutionary Era'. These divisions, in addition to being methodologically desirable, have the further merit, for purposes of statistical convenience, of establishing successive chronological units of 60, 20, 40, 40, and 20 years, which may, of course, be easily and accurately compared in various ways.[1]

6. Units of reckoning

Convenience rather than strict accuracy must also be pleaded in explaining still another methodological decision. The smallest monetary unit carried into our many tables is the shilling, since it seemed desirable to avoid inconvenience and inaccuracy in arriving at totals and percentages if pence and their fractions were included. It should be emphasized, however, that all gifts of less than a shilling have been separately carried in working sheets and then aggregated to the nearest shilling and that some thousands of very small donors accordingly appear in our various tables only as 'aggregated individuals'. But the totals are believed to be correct. Moreover, all benefactions of £1 or more have been entered to the nearest shilling, without more precise regard for the pence, in a large number of early benefactions, when the mark was a common unit of bequest or gift. Since the number of benefactions runs into many thousands, there is statistical assurance that no mensurable inaccuracy has been introduced into our calculations by the convention of reckoning, shall we say, two marks as £1 7s 0d and four marks as £2 13s 0d.

---

[1] Reference to Table I (Appendix) will more clearly and succinctly suggest the chronological method followed.

B. FRAILTIES OF THE METHOD

The statistical method, on which this study so heavily depends, has no more than a limited utility to the historian, since most of the data with which he is necessarily concerned cannot be accurately measured. This is not to say that historians have not for too long neglected the methods and the instruments so elaborately and competently evolved by the statisticians, but it does suggest that these convenient and valuable tools must be used with great discretion. Such discretion is especially important because statistical results have an almost hypnotic effect in the beauty and rigour of their apparent accuracy. The mathematical result may all too often mask the unreliability or the inexactness of the raw data from which it was originally compiled. The facts, the truths, of history are elusive, incomplete, and lie subject to the interpretation of the historian, their assembling and elucidation being at least partially dependent on his judgment, his experience, and an artistry which remains an essential element of the method of his craft. These cautions should run for all the social scientists who inevitably deal with data as frail as they are fallible, but lie with particular force on the method and the conclusions of the historians who, happily, have thus far seemed indisposed to adduce an imagined infallibility of knowledge from data at once fallible and incomplete. This in no sense means that the historian cannot learn a great deal about the past of man, that his knowledge may not be far more complete and his conclusions far more correct than those once possessed by the men of the age with which he deals. But he dare not venture arrogantly into the claims of infallibility. The historian mixes in his method the rigorous disciplines of the scientist with the almost intuitive skill of the artist, but his conclusions remain tentative, suggestive, and humble, since he has at least learned that the image of truth in any age is indistinct, inexact, and all too often fractured.

These cautions we must apply with particular emphasis to the findings on which this work are based. We have, we believe, examined all the available evidence. We have, we trust, recorded it correctly, reckoned it exactly, and interpreted it with care. But, in dealing with huge totals aggregated from relatively tiny sums, we have been inevitably too much moved by the apparent exactness of great totals carried out to the delicate mensuration of a shilling, and above all by percentages carried out to the second decimal place, a measure of refinement competent ordinarily even for the physicist and mathematician. Yet, it must be said, that these findings are not exact, that they derive in some measure from human judgment compounded by human error, as it has dealt with sources very often difficult to assess and which in their totality omit many other sources now lost or which simply never existed at all in recorded form. We have, then, confessed sins of commission and sins of omission, which as we understand the orthodox canons comprise the generality of sins. To complete this confession, we should in all candour estimate that the significant findings, as for example the totals of charitable funds given during our entire period in the counties under examination, may well be in error within a range of from 10 per cent to 15 per cent either way, and that this error is probably on the side of understatement.

The doubts and cautions which we have tried to express have thus far been somewhat general in nature. We should now set out in detail the more specific frailties of method inherent in the research underlying this work, employing as it does a quite rigorously statistical method. Thus among the most tediously difficult of our problems has been the necessity of assigning some value to the gifts in kind so frequently left to charity by humble donors, particularly in the early decades of our period. The total value of all such gifts was certainly not relatively very important, but they tended to come from classes of men and to be given for charitable causes that interest us a great deal, and hence values have whenever possible been assigned. They were of many kinds: a ewe, a fat bullock, a hive of bees, a quiver of arrows, a handkerchief, a quantity of corn, or of lead, or of iron, or a specified number of trees of unspecified size which were to be employed for some worthy use on the local bridge or church. Such gifts in kind have been converted into monetary amounts, employing the price data so laboriously and so helpfully assembled by economic historians during the past two generations and more. But our own research has taught us that there were more complex variables of price in the England of our period than the economic historians have recognized, for price was above all else affected by costs of transportation, and hence we cannot be certain that the price of a fat ewe in Smithfield had any real relation to the value of the particular ewe, which was in any case probably a scrawny beast, which the executors of John Amys cut out from that husbandman's flock in his remote North Riding village in 1503 to be delivered up for the support of the worship of God in the testator's parish church. Fortunately, however, the guidance which Rogers, Beveridge, and others have given us has usually been supplemented by the careful disposition of other donors in the same parish in or near the same year to set in their wills a value on the same gift in kind, thereby most appreciably relieving this particular problem. There is one exception: the gifts in kind which humble women were all too likely to leave for pious purposes—the coverlets, the frocks, the silks, and the wedding rings which they loved to dispose and which quite defy valuation, particularly when they are described as 'my second best'. Women have complicated as they have graced the course of history.

More substantial and sophisticated donors have also caused us difficulty by the terms of their bequests and have doubtless in some cases led us into quite erroneous conclusions. In a few cases the enthusiasm of donors outran their estates, or an estate melted away in adversity, fire, or mismanagement between the date when the will was drafted and the time of probate. In fewer cases, one has reason to believe that the charitable enthusiasm of the testator was not unmixed with confusion of mind, since patently the estate could not possibly bear the charitable burdens laid against it. But in any event there is a small fraction of wills in which the charitable bequests failed for these or other reasons. We are fairly sure that there are a sufficient number of checks of subsequent historical record to justify some confidence that we have not been ensnared by such optimism in substantial charitable estates, though such checks do not exist in all cases when bequests failed in small estates.

Similar uncertainty can on occasion arise when a testator after setting out his schedule of bequests, some often being charitable, leaves the whole or a fraction of the residue of his estate for one or a group of charitable causes. Fortunately, this was rather uncommonly done, for tracing down the facts regarding such ultimate distributions can be most time-consuming, but in these cases the document itself provides a note of caution for the historian. The value of the charitable estate has in most of these instances been accurately determined and in the others has been assessed with at least a reasonably satisfactory approximation.

Charitable donors were also prone to leave land and other real property of unspecified worth for one or another charitable cause. Land so left was almost invariably described in terms of location and extent, while messuages, cottages, barns, mills, and other buildings of every conceivable type were almost always sufficiently described to make it possible to identify them in later records or judicial proceedings. Happily, almost all real property so disposed was settled in endowments, which makes it possible to assign a value at least at a relatively early subsequent date, though we should note that in Kent alone there were seven different pieces of real property the value of which could not be established until after lapses of from 61 to 128 years. Relatively rarely, real property was to be sold and the proceeds used for indicated purposes, and in these cases the problem of assigning values can be very difficult indeed. Usually the amount will appear in the churchwardens' accounts, the record books of a school foundation, in borough accounts, or in some other place of record, though on occasion we have had no other recourse than to assign a value which is certainly quite arbitrary and which may also be quite inexact.

In another area our difficulties in determining the amount of a charitable benefaction have been even greater. In point of fact, the data assembled under the head of *Church Building* have seemed so inexact as to make it desirable to designate this category of contribution as *'Estimated Church Building'* in every county. The subject has interested us because the curve of voluntary gifts for this purpose provides one of several clear indications of the mounting secularism of aspirations in England, but it has been necessary to present the data in a most tentative form. The costs of church building in England during our period were borne in several ways, for example, by local rates, by voluntary contributions, and, not uncommonly, by a mixture of charitable and non-charitable funds. Our interest has, of course, been wholly in the voluntary contributions made for the purpose and we have reasonable confidence that this line of distinction has at least been kept clear. In most cases, too, it has been possible to arrive either at an exact or at least a reasonably exact cost for construction carried forward by voluntary effort, though there is always some risk that certain contributions were not recorded by those in charge of the undertaking. There remain, as well, and it is here that our difficulties have been unresolved, a fair number of churches, or more commonly, chapels, which we know were built wholly or in part by charitable contributions, for which we have been able to find no cost figures whatsoever. In other cases we have found what are evidently no more than fragmentary records of contributions to work which involved a major outlay with no indication in the relevant parochial or diocesan records that the construction was in part financed from non-charitable sources. In other instances we have perhaps rashly undertaken to supply estimates of costs based on the approximate cube of the structure and the known costs of roughly similar construction in the same county and in the same general period.

Not only this study, but the whole economic history of our period, is likewise fallible in a statistical sense because we know so little regarding the true curve of the purchasing power of money during this era of almost two centuries. The presentation of our statistical data is, then, static, assuming as it were a level curve of prices because we are unable to adjust our decade and period totals to any index of price movements. The want of such information has troubled the economic historian, but it seems probable that our knowledge in this important area will remain as incomplete as it is unsatisfactory. We do know that a profoundly important inflationary process got under way in western Europe at about the beginning of our period which in a broad sense has persisted to our own generation. This inflationary process was relatively gradual during most of the era with which we are concerned, though its cumulative consequences were very important indeed and were fully recognized, though hardly understood, by contemporary social and economic theorists. At the same time, however, certain elements of cost, as for example wages, rose slowly if at all through most of the age, while some commodities were rising very rapidly in cost. The upward movement of prices, with its inevitable peaks and valleys, was then an uncoordinated, creeping, and exceedingly complex phenomenon. The state, moreover, tended to set its policy squarely against the entire process of inflation, particularly in its efforts to control wage costs and the costs of foodstuffs, with rather more success than has commonly been supposed.

In the course of this study we have amassed a vast store of material relating to the history of prices in the ten regions with which we have been concerned. Though we hope to put this material to some subsequent use, it is all too clear that these data will contribute little towards what this perhaps overly precise generation of scholars wishes it had, a curve of prices accurately reflecting the facts concerning the national economy. It is our impression that such a curve can never be constructed, not so much for want of data but because of the complex nature of the data. The basic difficulty is that we simply do not know how to construct an index properly weighted to reflect the needs, the aspirations, and the strivings of a nation and a culture as it was three or four centuries ago. This problem is difficult enough as we seek to measure purchasing power in our own society, but when we endeavour to do so in this much earlier age we tend inevitably to seek to measure not what men of the sixteenth century wanted but what we think they should have wanted. Further, the sixteenth century society was in so many ways far more complex than our own, for it was at once intensely parochial and highly stratified in all matters involving consumption and standard of living. Tastes, aspirations, and the definition of necessaries have become increasingly, perhaps dangerously, homogeneous since the Industrial Revolution, but our attitudes and preoccupations in these matters have little relevance for the sixteenth century.

The complexity of this problem is further enhanced by the fact that prices and values in one English region in say the late sixteenth century bore almost no relation to prices in another. Such fragmentary indexes as have been compiled for the period have largely, and inevitably, been constructed on prices at central market points, or, more exactly, for centres where there was a sustained and considerable consumption of goods and commodities. But such data have only limited utility and meaning when we examine prices in remote parts of the realm. Costs of transport were enormous in relation to the then value of most commodities, while, even more relevantly, the total absence of the possibility of transport did strange things indeed to prices in local areas. There was simply no system of national distribution of many commodities; local scarcities did not necessarily mean national scarcities; and local prices are no measure of national prices.

We have dealt at length with the reasons for our failure to adjust our data to the price changes of this long historical period. But perhaps one more comment may be made on the whole subject of the difficulties of assembling not only price data but statistical data generally. We are concerned with an age which possessed very little statistical sense or interest; this may in fact be argued to be one of the glories of the age. We are dealing with an age when a mayor in solemn address before the Queen could say that the number of unemployed cloth-workers in his city considerably exceeded what we know was the total population of the community. It is an age that dealt grandly in round numbers, when population estimates reflected little more than the then mood of the witness. There is, indeed, an almost poetic quality in the attitude of men of this era towards numbers: they were meant to have a broad and occasionally an heroic effect. All this was understood and accepted, and surely it could not have mattered much. In the course of this work we have added many thousands of estate inventories, and these were legal documents, and have come to the conclusion that when the totals are exactly accurate we have witnessed an instance of the inscrutable workings of the law of probability. Churchwardens had their difficulties with their quite simple accounts, but then so did the archbishop when he sought to tally the number of parishes in his province. These small and certainly unimportant errors are easily resolved, but what they betray is a want of statistical interest which in broader and more important areas of knowledge and fact has created a vacuum of information about matters we regard as important but which the age with which we are dealing largely ignored.

If we have found it impossible to adjust our data to the rising curve of prices in the course of our period, we have regarded it as at once impossible and unprofitable even to attempt to do so in relation to the purchasing power of money in our own age. There is simply no basis for comparison, not only because of the insoluble statistical problems involved but because such an effort seeks to compare scales of values which are wholly incomparable. Just one appealing and arguable constant seems to us to be available, the wages which unskilled and skilled labour received then and now in order to maintain life and some increment of decency in standard of living, though this last element in our statement introduces a variable of enormous importance that is statistically unreliable. But it still may be recorded that for a very long working day an ordinary farm labourer, when employed, late in our period (1647), received, without sustenance, from 5d to 6d *per diem* and that his modern English counterpart receives about £1 3s od; that a master mason or carpenter would then have been paid about 12d and now something like £1 16s od; and that a collier working at the coal face would then have had 10d, whereas his modern counterpart would be certain of £1 14s 1d. These are but fragile and partially unreliable comparisons, but they do suggest the enormous depreciation that has occurred in the purchasing power of money.[1] They suggest, too, that the historian of the sixteenth and seventeenth centuries must learn to think wholly in terms of the age in which he works, to accept its values, and gain by a process of absorption 'the feel' of a society and an economy that was very dissimilar to our own. Hence it is that we understand that a yeoman's legacy of £1 for the poor householders of his parish was by no means a socially insignificant sum; that an endowment of £50 established to provide care for the poor of a rural parish might in fact be quite sufficient for that purpose; or that £100 to £150 was quite enough capital to secure the founding and the endowment of a school or an almshouse in a small market town. Men of this age wrought mightily with instruments which seem puny indeed to us.

Still another statistical frailty has been occasioned by the inflexible requirements of the statistical method itself. In all cases it has been necessary to convert into capital amounts income gifts made in perpetuity, such as rent-charges which were expressed only in terms of annual worth. In other instances we have no certain clue to the precise capital worth of an endowment, consisting let us say of a tract of land or urban houses, though we are given the then income value of the property in question. These conversions have been made by applying a constant multiplier, which is in effect an estimate of the level rate of interest on trusteed funds throughout our period. The determination of this multiplier was made late in the course of our study, not in fact until large masses of material had been accumulated which would throw some degree of light on this whole obscure question. The decision was then reached to multiply all income amounts, yielded of course by capital assets, by a factor of 20, thus assuming a yield value of 5 per cent on trusteed funds in the several counties. These values have without exception, therefore, been recorded as capital sums, and we have ordinarily so rendered them in describing individual benefactions rather than explaining each time the procedure just discussed.

The whole question of the interest rate prevailing on trusteed funds is, of course, of much wider importance than the quite narrow question with which we are concerned. We shall later show that the massive accumulations of capital gradually gathered by trustees must have been one of the most important of all sources of credit in this period of the

---

[1] J. E. T. Rogers (*A history of agriculture and prices in England*, 7 vols., Oxford, 1866–1902) provides the largest mass of data available on this matter, though, as several commentators have pointed out, his conclusions must be used with caution. He suggests, for example, that for the period 1401–1582 the curve of prices for grain rose from a base of 1·00 to 2·40, while wages rose from 1·00 to 1·60 in the same interval (IV, 718–719). He would hold that prices rose much more steeply in the next interval, 1583–1642, for grains from 1·00 as a new base to 2·22, and for labour much more slowly in a range of 1·00 to 1·04 for the wages of carpenters and 1·00 to 1·65 for plumbers (V, 787–792).

early but rapid growth of capitalistic enterprise. The legal rate of interest was reduced from 10 per cent to 8 per cent in 1624 and again lowered to 6 per cent in 1651, though these figures supply no more than evidence of a slowly declining rate of interest during the course of our period for mercantile and entrepreneurial credit. The huge holdings of capital administered by charitable feoffees, particularly in London, had to be invested as cautiously as possible in what may well be described as prime securities. This normally meant that land, urban improvements on land, or mortgages secured by land were purchased by the charitable trustees, undoubtedly lending most substantial support to the structure of land values throughout our period. But larger risks were often taken both in London and in smaller communities when charitable capital was lent directly to responsible borrowers at rates of return rather higher than might be gained by investment in land. Normally a bond was required binding the borrowers to repayment under penalties, while not infrequently a co-signature was likewise demanded. Such secured loans were especially common in cloth towns and market towns throughout England, evidently constituting an important source of local entrepreneurial credit.[1] As we shall later point out, a large pool of charitable capital was also provided during our period quite specifically to serve as loan funds either for young men just beginning their callings or for responsible but needy persons who might thereby be relieved and rehabilitated. These funds, too, constituted a not unimportant source of credit, either at uneconomic interest rates or with no interest charge at all, though their purpose was of course wholly philanthropic. We shall see that very little indeed of the investment made by charitable trustees was lost, they with remarkably few exceptions having been prudent in their outlays and vigilant in the protection of their capital.

These trustees, then, took few speculative risks, with the consequence that the yield on charitable funds administered by them was much lower than might be supposed. We have particulars regarding the interest rate on £238,671 6s of trusteed funds, spread, it should be said, over our whole long period, which would suggest an average rate of return on such prime investments of 5·368 per cent for all England. These rates of return, it will be observed, varied rather widely from an average yield of 5·026 per cent for London and 5·16 per cent for Bristol to the 6·84 per cent which Lancastrian trustees found it possible, and prudent, to secure.[2] In many cases, particularly in London, large donors would

---

[1] *Vide* F. G. James, 'Charity endowments as sources of local credit in seventeenth and eighteenth century England', *Journal of Economic History*, VIII (1948), 153–170, for a brief but interesting discussion of an aspect of this question.

[2] Our present interest in this matter is of course narrowly restricted, though we do hope at a later time to deal more fully with this important question. The following table presents the data in hand for the several counties included in this

themselves prescribe at least the initial rate of prudent return on their benefactions by requiring their trustees to invest a given sum, usually in land, to yield a stated return, which in almost every case was exactly 5 per cent. These capital totals have not been included in our computations unless we are certain that the trustees abided by the injunctions of the testators, but so general was this practice as to suggest that 5 per cent was regarded by experienced and substantial men as a safe and reasonable return on such funds. This convention and this assumption we have likewise followed in translating income values into capital estimates, though, as has been observed, by a factor which almost certainly slightly underestimates the total worth of the charitable funds in question.

Certain difficulties in method had also to be resolved in determining to which county a particular benefaction should be credited. Normally, of course, a benefactor made his charitable dispositions in and to the county where he lived and died. The place of residence of the donor is an important element in the decision, but not infrequently substantial benefactors, particularly in London, divided their bequests between the county of their residence and still another county, usually of their birth. In all such cases the benefactions have been credited to the county or counties benefitting, though for statistical reasons we have tried to make certain that the donor was counted but once, and then in the county of his residence. In a few cases, the nobility and the upper clergy being mostly involved, it has been difficult indeed to determine the true, the sentimental, place of residence of the donor, and in these instances we have quite arbitrarily assigned the donor to the county in which the bulk of his wealth was seated, while the benefactions have been credited to the counties benefitting. There has, we fear, been some 'spilling over' of donors from one county to another and hence some

study. It should be noted that loan fund capital is not listed. The average yield given is for our whole period, though a more detailed analysis would reveal a steadily declining rate of return on trusteed funds down to about 1640.

	Capital £			Income £			Yield Per cent
Bristol	8709	8	0	449	12	0	5·16
Buckinghamshire	3260	0	0	174	4	0	5·34
Hampshire	15,040	0	0	842	4	0	5·60
Kent	11,989	8	0	646	4	0	5·39
Lancashire	23,779	2	0	1626	10	0	6·84
London	113,560	0	0	5708	0	0	5·026
Norfolk	33,230	16	0	1766	16	0	5·32
Somerset	8320	0	0	467	16	0	5·62
Worcestershire	5600	0	0	310	8	0	5·54
Yorkshire	15,182	12	0	820	16	0	5·41
All counties	£238,671	6	0	£12,812	10	0	5·368

little multiple counting, but we are reasonably confident that the benefactions themselves have been sorted out into the proper counties.
There is one important, and necessary, exception to these rules regarding the distribution of charitable bequests across county lines. We are
concerned with but ten counties, and it is to them and in them that the
rules apply. When a donor, and this almost invariably meant a London
donor, made a charitable benefaction to a county not included in our
group, this benefaction has been credited to the county in which the
donor resided, though rather detailed tables in the several counties
treated set out the full and somewhat complicated particulars. These
possibly elaborate conventions have seemed necessary in the interests
of accuracy, and most particularly to avoid counting the same benefaction twice, once in the county of residence and then in the county
benefitting from the charitable bequest.

C. THE GREAT CHARITABLE HEADS

We should in concluding these notes on method comment on the
scheme of distributing and grouping benefactions among the various
charitable uses. The great charitable heads, so perfectly and classically
defined in the preamble of the famous Elizabethan statute establishing
the law of charitable trusts, were all well developed and recognized
many years before the close of our period and, so constant are the needs
and aspirations of men, would seem most adequate for a classification
of charities in our own age. We are in this study, in point of fact, principally concerned with the profoundly important shift in men's aspirations and interests within this frame of charitable causes. None the less,
it has seemed advisable and convenient somewhat to extend and to
regroup the charitable heads as defined by the Elizabethan statute.

The first of the large groupings we have entitled simply *The Poor*, the
charitable causes comprising it having all been dedicated to the direct
and immediate relief of the needy. Included in this group of charities
is a principal head, or use, which we have somewhat unsatisfactorily
entitled *Household Relief*, or, alternately, *Outright Relief*. A great variety
of benefactions have been so grouped. Thus in the early decades of our
period the direct gift of alms, funeral doles, and testamentary outright
distributions to named or unnamed poor have been aggregated under
this head. But as time went on, benefactions for household relief tended
to be much more carefully devised and prudently administered, with
capital gifts, or endowments, replacing the earlier and more casual doles
or gifts for immediate use. The income from such funds was distributed
by responsible and named persons to the poor of a defined area or community under carefully regulated conditions which, as we shall later
observe, included a bewildering variety of provisions, definitions, and

prescriptions. But however constituted, and whether as doles or more carefully regulated stipends, benefactions of this kind were dedicated to the relief of existing poverty, to the prevention of vagabondage and social ruin, and to maintaining poor families at least at the level of subsistence in their own homes. Many, perhaps most, of the enormous number of gifts for these worthy purposes were quite unsophisticated, but they betoken in their ever-swelling number and amount an aroused social conscience and a determination to sustain men, and especially worthy men, who simply could not provide for their own support.

In almost all these benefactions there is expressed the implicit, and very often, the explicit, hope that by such outright alms families might during a season of unemployment or personal catastrophe be sustained until they had righted their affairs and found it possible to become self-supporting once more in an increasingly complex and competitive economy. Hence most of the endowments devoted to this use sought to differentiate, as did all legislation of the era, between the worthy poor and those who were believed to be either vicious or incorrigibly lazy. But there was an ever-growing realization that some men, whether because of age, injury, infirmity, or simple incompetence, had in fact been overwhelmed and must accordingly be either permanently sustained or allowed to starve. It was for the saving of such men that a mounting flood of capital gifts for the founding or endowment of *Almshouses* was dedicated in the course of our age. We shall be much concerned with rapidly spreading interest in these foundations, which by the close of our period formed a veritable network of carefully ordered institutions offering sanctuary to the socially and economically derelict. It must be remarked here that these almshouses were applauded by the best and socially most sensitive men of the era and that they made an immensely important contribution not only to the relief of abject poverty but also to the dignity and temper of an age. That noble term, *Almshouse,* which constitutes our second and important charitable head, was not to acquire the unfortunate connotation which it still possesses for us until several generations after our period had closed.

A third charitable head within this grouping we have somewhat ambiguously described as *Charity General*. These were funds, for the most part capital, left by donors for quite broadly defined charitable uses, or to be employed for worthy purposes at the discretion of the feoffees, named parishes, or municipal officers. Such income was of course applied for a variety of purposes, but it was so heavily concentrated during our whole period on the needs of the poor that we have thought it best to regard the use as falling wholly within this great charitable category. These funds represent a most interesting development, since their unrestricted nature made them especially effective. These accumulations were, however, derived from two different kinds of donors. Many of them, mostly in small amount, came into being because the donor had drawn his will or deed of gift so inexpertly and vaguely as to make any very specific interpretation impossible by his executors and, less importantly, by us. Certain others, however, including the great bequest of Henry Smith, a London merchant, were among the most sophisticated and carefully ordered of all the philanthropies of the age, these donors wisely holding the view that the social utility of their benefactions might be limited in future generations by too precise restrictions. But whatever the source and whatever the motives, these endowments were in fact largely employed during the age with which we are concerned for the relief of poverty.

The last of the charitable heads within the grouping of *The Poor* we have described as *The Aged*. These were funds given under most specific restrictions in order to secure the care of poor men and women simply because they were old rather than because they were at once aged and poor. These charities were concerned, then, with the amelioration of age itself; we can perhaps accurately say that they represent very early experiments in geriatrics. The whole *corpus* of these endowments was relatively small, representing only 0·17 per cent of the whole of charitable funds of the age, but does none the less constitute a clearly defined charitable use. It should, however, be emphasized that these sums by no means represent the extent of the concern of the era with the problems of the old. The fact of age and the fact of poverty bore a very close correlation during the whole of our period, and the aged poor are mentioned and are included in almost every fund established to secure some measure of help for the poor. In most instances, nomination for admission to almshouses was limited to the aged, while in many endowments for household relief a careful preference was expressed for the care of men and women who because of the infirmities of their years could no longer carry on with useful and remunerative tasks.

We have gathered a considerable number of additional and distinct charitable uses within a second grouping which we have called *Social Rehabilitation*. These were also benefactions which were directed towards the plight of the poor, but from a refreshingly and effectively different point of view. The massive funds which were slowly being gathered for the care of the poor were designed to secure no more than the amelioration of poverty, surely the first task in any socially responsible community, while those with which we are now concerned were dedicated to a frontal assault on the very sources of poverty. These were lively, hopeful, and experimental undertakings into which a great deal of wealth was poured, principally by urban donors, in an impressive effort to get at the roots of the problem. For the most part, the various experiments in social rehabilitation were developed in the course of our era and were to contribute significantly to the adoption of a new and much more hopeful attitude towards a grim and endemic evil which had throughout history sickened and weakened the western society. These ventures, many of which were as naïve as they were courageous, represent, so to speak, the risk capital which bold and certainly enlightened men provided in an heroic effort to bring about the cure of poverty.

Among the charitable heads included within this great grouping is the *Relief of Prisoners*. As we shall have later occasion to point out, the state during the whole of our period assumed little responsibility for the care of prisoners beyond administering their incarceration. In part, consequently, the benefactions given for this purpose were designated for no other end than to ensure at least the subsistence of poor prisoners who had no resources for their own care. But most of the considerable total of endowments established were designed to secure the release of men being held prisoners for debt. The laws respecting imprisonment for debt were at once harsh and rigid, with the consequence that an imprisoned debtor, save for the occasional gaol deliveries, might be held indefinitely unless he possessed some outside assistance. The endowments for this purpose were in the main established in order to gain the redemption of such prisoners being held for small sums and to restore them to useful and self-supporting lives.

Much larger sums were accumulated during the course of our period which may most exactly be described as *Loan Funds*. These capital amounts were established under a bewildering variety of deeds of gift, usually with most elaborate administrative provisions, and they were dedicated to several somewhat different purposes. Certain of them were carefully limited to small loans made without interest to respectable and responsible householders who were temporarily distressed. Other, and very large funds, were established to provide initial working capital for young men who had just completed their apprenticeships and who were ready to take up their callings as artisans, tradesmen, or merchants. This was a particularly critical stage in the life of any poor and ambitious youth, and there is abundant evidence that these loan stipends were immensely important as agencies of social and economic mobility during the second half of our period. Still other funds were established to provide loans for merchants, tradesmen, or craftsmen who had fallen upon evil times or who had met with financial reverses, so that they might be restored to their calling. Such loan funds, whether for young men beginning their careers or for older men who needed help in order to continue, almost invariably required some measure of security for the loan, while the interest rate was modest, if interest was imposed at all. Still another substantial total of loan funds we have after some hesitation regarded as more properly to be listed and discussed under other charitable heads. In these instances, the deed of gift provided that full security be required and that an economic rate of interest be imposed, the income to be distributed for specified charitable purposes to which we have likewise assigned the capital. The intentions of the donor in such cases were undoubtedly mixed, but his prime concern seems to have been in the charitable employment of the income, whatever the form that these funds took and whatever purpose they were established to serve. We are struck by the amazing powers of survival displayed by these revolving funds, sustained as they were by uneconomic interest rates and subject always to the hazards of failure, death, or dishonesty on the part of the borrowers. While reserving a fuller discussion of this matter to later pages, it may at least be said here that this proud record exhibits at once the care which feoffees took with such funds and the social needs which these loans served.

Another of the interesting and fruitful experiments undertaken by our age in the social rehabilitation of the poor were the *Workhouses and Stocks for the Poor* established by private donors. Fairly substantial amounts were dedicated to this purpose in every county with which we have been concerned. The enthusiasm for this charitable use was of course stimulated by legislative efforts to secure the setting up of workhouses in all parts of the realm, though it should be remarked that the earliest and most successful of these undertakings were launched either by private efforts or by forward-looking municipalities. We shall see that these experiments took many forms, but they were all founded in the conviction that some agency must be created which would provide not only sustenance but the possibility of rehabilitation for the poor. Some were designed to force the unruly and unworthy poor to work for their bread, while hoping that disciplined activity and instruction might mend the moral flaw which it was believed was the source of incorrigible poverty, while others were planned to provide useful and honourable employment for householders who simply could not find work for a season. In some cases these undertakings were elaborately housed and financed in institutions which partook of the nature of both a prison and a competently staffed and disciplined factory. More commonly, these benefactions did no more than provide stocks of materials on which the industrious poor could employ themselves in their own homes. It is most difficult to estimate the social value of these schemes, so varied were they and so differing in their success, but we can at least suggest that they betoken a lively, a sensitive, and a responsible concern of high-minded and courageous men who were seeking by every sensible means to secure the prevention as well as the relief of poverty.

Even larger capital sums were poured by benefactors into *Apprenticeship Schemes* in every part of England. These were of all sorts and for many purposes, but they were in every instance planned to provide a reasonable range of opportunity and training for boys and girls who would otherwise almost predictably have become public charges. Many of these endowments were organically connected with school and alms-house foundations, being designed to secure necessary training for a worthy boy or girl to whom the rudiments of an education had been given. Others provided a mechanism and the funds for the selection of apt and poor boys in remote rural regions for the inestimable benefits of an apprenticeship in London, in Bristol, or in Norwich. Some were modest indeed, undertaking no more than the binding out under responsible arrangements of destitute boys and girls in order to give them training in humble skills. But they were all intended to enlarge the ambit of opportunity for children possessing no resources and very little hope. There is abundant and most eloquent testimony that these foundations served an enormously fruitful purpose and that they gained for the realm new sources of human strength which would otherwise have been swallowed up in the slough of destitution.

The ends of social rehabilitation were likewise well served by the large endowments vested for the founding and support of *Hospitals and the Care of the Sick*. We have endeavoured to restrict the term 'hospital' to the meaning and function it was only just acquiring, though these institutions in the sixteenth century still on occasion served quite mixed purposes. Great sums were in the course of our period to be dedicated to the institutional care of the sick, the infirm, the crippled, and even the mentally ill. These donors and the foundations which they estab-lished were concerned with the rehabilitation of the stricken, in the first tentative assumption by society of a broad area of responsibility which even now in many western countries has not been fully embraced. But much of the capital included under this charitable head was more simply and perhaps less effectively vested, providing income for the care of the sick in their own households, while at the same time protecting such families from the poverty which so often marched in the train of illness. Great beginnings were made in this vast area of need by private donors during our period, by men who valiantly undertook to raise up at least some bulwarks to lend protection to the dignity of the human body and spirit.

Finally, we have included under the broad grouping of social re-habilitation those funds given to secure *Marriage Subsidies* for poor but respectable young women. These were of many sorts, and were usually cluttered with particularly complicated instructions and restrictions, but they were all designed to provide a small dowry for girls who were either orphans or whose families were destitute. The amounts given were usually modest but were none the less in average terms sufficient to enable a young woman to bring to her marriage the essentials required for her furnishings and her clothing. These gifts were intended to pro-vide a young couple, otherwise without means, with at least a respect-able start in life, and there is extensive evidence to suggest that certain of these funds made most substantial social contributions to the age. But they came to be less favoured during the closing decades of our period, especially by merchant donors, who were perplexed by the problems of administration inherent in such foundations. They were regarded, however, with more slowly diminishing enthusiasm by the gentry in the counties, who doubtless could supervise the distributions with greater prudence and who in any case seem to have taken a more pleasantly sentimental view of life and the problems of their age.

We tend to forget how narrowly the functions of government, whether national or local, were defined in the Tudor and Stuart periods. Broadly speaking, government was concerned with the maintenance of order, the administration of justice, and with the defence of the polity. Even the great Elizabethan poor laws, opening as up they did a new and a vastly important additional area of responsibility, sprang at least in part from the intense Tudor preoccupation with the maintenance of order and were set upon sound bases of responsibility only after the Tudor society had struggled valiantly for three generations to deny that there was even a problem with which government could or need be concerned. Just as private charity first assumed an ever-expanding social responsibility for the broad range of problems that cluster around the harsh reality of poverty, so did it first move into other areas of social need wholly or largely ignored by government. These charitable heads we have treated under a large grouping perhaps best described as *Municipal Betterments*.

The first of these heads we have called *General Municipal Uses*, including a great variety of benefactions designed to make a community a more comfortable and efficient place in which to live and work. A surprisingly high proportion of these benefactions, ranging from about 72 per cent to 99 per cent in the several counties, were settled in the form of endowments in order permanently to provide the benefits which the donor intended. They were of many sorts. Thus it was private generosity which ordinarily built, furnished, and kept in repair the municipal buildings of any town or city in this age. Plate, ceremonial vessels, regalia, and funds to defray the cost of the elaborate dinners so beloved by men of this period were bestowed upon the municipal officers and their successors. Markets and shambles were built and the title vested in the municipality, with the income often being assigned for general municipal purposes. Rudimentary fire-fighting apparatus was most often provided by private charity. Very substantial endowments were frequently established in order to pay all or part of local rates or national taxes that might be levied, particularly those falling on poor householders. Rather impressive and certainly useful endowments were vested in municipalities by private donors, the income of which was to be employed for the general uses of the communities thus favoured. These are but a few of the many charitable uses gathered under this head, all of which, however, bespeak the pride which the mercantile aristocracy felt for the cities in which they had prospered and which they had usually helped to govern.

It has likewise seemed best to include under the great grouping of *Municipal Betterments* those funds left to the merchant *Companies for the Public Benefit*. As one would expect, a large proportion of such charitable accumulations (93·17 per cent) were to be vested in the powerful livery companies of London, though lesser associations of this kind in London and in the provinces were also to benefit. The London livery companies in the course of our period were to become experienced, adept, and most responsible charitable trustees, administering enormous sums vested in them for many charitable causes. Here it should be made clear that none of these trusts is included in the funds now being briefly described. But the companies were also accumulating funds in their own right under trust obligations for their own or the public interest. Members almost by custom came to leave at least modest legacies for such purposes. Special endowments for the maintenance of their halls were built up, bequests to provide dinners and other entertainments were not uncommon, while still other funds were given to the companies with the instruction that the income was to be used for some designated civic purpose. Even more importantly, the companies gradually accumulated large endowments in return for their services as charitable trustees, a residue or an indicated amount being provided by the will of the donor for the pains to be taken in the administration of a charitable fund. The companies were, then, well before our period was out, taking on many of the attributes of the quasi-municipal bodies which they were to become in the course of another century.

We have also included under municipal betterments a very small charitable head which we have entitled *Public Parks and Recreation*, for which we have recorded no more than nominal contributions. None the less, one does sense at least an emerging concern on the part of men of the age with these ultimate ameliorations of urban life.

Finally, and most importantly, all the bequests and gifts dedicated to the improvement of public works have been gathered under a head which we have inexactly but persistently described as *Roads and Bridges*. Many thousands of donors made contributions for this general purpose, nearly all of them small and for immediate use. The limited responsibility assumed by government, both national and local, is most fully documented by these benefactions and the improvement which they sought to effect in the basic instrumentalities of community life. In our detailed discussion of the various counties, we shall have occasion to mention at least the principal of these gifts, though the great range of interest which they expressed can at least be summarized here. The largest in amount were the gifts for the building and repair of highways, provided particularly by merchants and clothiers, who had no doubt for many years cursed evil stretches of road which as the last action of their lives they determined to mend. We have noted as well many bequests for the maintenance, the sweeping, and the general betterment of streets, and even a few for street lighting. We have recorded some hundreds of bequests for the building or the maintenance of bridges, ranging from those over tiny streams to some that represented great engineering achievements for this period. Bequests for the repair of city walls, for the building of dikes and causeways, the digging of drainage canals, and the building of waterworks have all been gathered under this commodious heading. So too have benefactions for the construction of wharves and docks, and even for the cleansing of harbours, the building of jetties and breakwaters, as private benefactors sought to prod the central government to carry forward needed projects for the assistance of navigation. The whole sweep of these benefactions, mounting as they do during our long period, conveys the sense of a busy, an aggressive, and a sanguine age in which men were moulding the physical shape of the countryside and of their communities, just as with their larger benefactions they were fabricating the basic social and cultural institutions of the realm.

Under *Education* we have grouped a number of charitable uses to which men of the age made massive and permanently effective contribution. It is not too much to say that during the course of our period the basic educational institutions of the realm were founded and endowed. The determination of donors to extend and strengthen educational opportunity displays an almost obsessive confidence that thereby the ignorance from which poverty sprang might be dispelled, that youth might be encouraged, and that a way might be cleared for all men of talent and ambition. We shall later have occasion to comment at length on these sentiments and on the immense achievement wrought by benefactors who were determined to create a new England by freeing the mind of its youth. But here we may at least suggest that these men brought about a quiet revolution whose consequences were as apparent as they were beneficent well before our period had closed. Certainly it can be said that in 1660 educational opportunities were more widespread and stronger than they had ever been before or than were ever to be again until well into the nineteenth century.

The great and continuous flow of the charitable funds that were to accomplish this noble work of social betterment was directed principally towards the founding and endowment of *Schools*. Though we may on occasion have used the term 'grammar schools' loosely rather than precisely, it should be emphasized that under the head of *Schools* we have included all educational institutions offering instruction of an elementary or secondary nature. Thus we have been quite as much interested in the elementary schools as in those of a more advanced grade, though, unfortunately, few of the former were to be endowed and hence have on the whole escaped us. We have likewise included essentially technical or trade schools of several sorts within this head, almost all of which, it might be added, offered in their curricula at least some of the elements of the liberal disciplines. Most of the schools with which we are concerned were, it is true, grammar schools, but they constitute only part of an immense edifice of education which was being reared across the whole of the realm. Our census of these schools is of course by no means complete, since we are concerned only with those which were founded or endowed by private charity or which were in part supported by voluntary contributions. Our survey, then, includes no more than the structure of free education as it developed during this period of incredible generosity with which we are concerned.

Though the great weight of the effort to create an educational system in England was very properly and most fruitfully directed towards the needs of elementary and secondary education, almost exactly half as much charitable wealth was directed towards the needs of the *Colleges and Universities*. Here we are of course principally concerned with the impressive and the continuous flow of new and revivifying wealth to Oxford and Cambridge, but we have included as well other and most interesting educational experiments of an advanced nature such as, for example, Gresham College and the ill-fated Chelsea College. Benefactions of many kinds made for the support of the universities have been included under this head, whether for the founding of new colleges, the building or betterment of fabric, the endowment needs, the creation of professorships, or the strengthening of the libraries of the universities and their colleges. In assembling and aggregating these many and rich benefactions we have thought it desirable to depart from the rule normally followed in crediting charitable gifts.[1] These benefactions for the universities were national in their significance and consequence and hence had no specific efficacy in or meaning for the counties in which the two great foundations happened to be situated. Hence we have in every case credited such gifts within the county in which the donor was resident.

Both the schools and the universities were greatly strengthened during our period by the large sums given by private donors for *Scholarships and Fellowships*. It is particularly interesting, and important, to observe how benefactions were binding the schools to the universities by an intricate and well-considered system of endowed scholarships, offering to able youths the opportunity to proceed from a favoured school

[1] *Vide ante*, 39–40, for a fuller discussion of the scheme normally prevailing.

directly to the university. Many, perhaps most, of the university scholarships founded in this age were restricted to students from a prescribed geographical area, if not from particular schools, with the result that an impressive and most complex fabric of educational opportunity was extended across the whole country. Fellowship endowments were more commonly vested in the favoured college without geographical restrictions, donors being disposed, however, to express a preference if not a restriction with respect to the area of knowledge with which the fellow would be concerned.

Finally, under the great grouping of *Education* we have listed gifts made for the foundation and support of *Libraries,* not including, of course, those larger amounts designated for the strengthening of the libraries of the universities. The libraries were of several sorts, including, it may be said, the earliest of the truly public and free libraries of England. Some were connected with schools, rather more were housed in churches, and still others were provided with their own quarters. But whatever the nature of their organization and government, they too bespeak the thirst for knowledge and the tremendous confidence of an age which with private funds created more effective and widely available educational opportunities than the world had ever known before.

The last of our great groupings of charitable uses may simply and accurately be entitled *Religion.* There were many gifts which in an ever-decreasing volume flowed from benefactors for the support of the church, for its many needs and services. So complex were these needs and the structure of support that we have gathered such benefactions under several appropriate heads. We should, however, mention at this point that, though gifts for monastic uses will be separately and quite fully discussed in the several counties, they have for statistical purposes been distributed to the several more general heads included under *Religion.* This has seemed desirable not only because of the disappearance of the whole institution of monasticism rather early in the course of our period but, even more pertinently, because, whether in terms of the aspirations of the donor or the religious effectiveness of the gift, such benefactions cannot sensibly be differentiated from the larger complex of the religious institution and its work.

Under the head of *Church General* we have gathered many thousands of benefactions, for the most part small and outright, which were dedicated to the general support of the church and its worship. Under this heading are recorded all gifts and bequests to a particular church which were evidently unrestricted in their nature. Here too are aggregated the innumerable gifts for lights, for altars, for images, and for the general maintenance of worship and the sacramental system. The church depended heavily on the flow of such benefactions for the support of its complex ministry. The curve of these gifts, as we shall repeatedly suggest, may well constitute the most sensitively reliable index available to us of the intensity of the religious aspiration and the warmth of the devotion which men lent to their church.

After some hesitation we decided to regard as charitable gifts the large sums which were given or bequeathed to secure *Prayers* for the repose of the souls of the dead. These include many chantry foundations with considerable endowments, lending support to a large number of stipendiary priests. Included as well are smaller capital gifts left to secure in perpetuity or for a prescribed period of years obits, anniversary masses, and other carefully arranged masses for the soul of a deceased testator. There remain a host of outright gifts and bequests left by humbler, or more sceptical, men for a single mass, an anniversary dirge, or a trental of masses. But the question remains whether such gifts and bequests were in fact charitable at all. Strictly speaking, they doubtless were on balance not charitable in intent, though we believe that they were in effect. These celebrations were interwoven with the life and the worship of the church, and we may with some certainty believe that the interesting and very specific theological questions involved were in consequence obscure. It should also be noted that in most chantry foundations a usually tiny proportion of the income was set aside for charitable uses, while in a few at least the stipendiary priest was charged with educational duties. Moreover, the whole chantry system supported a considerable body of clergy, the stipendiary priests, whose duties and spiritual contributions, usually despite the relevant deeds of gift, extended far beyond their precisely defined spiritual obligations. It may in point of fact be well argued that the whole complex system of endowed prayers was brought under suspicion and some measure of disrepute long before the Reformation just because the church absorbed this huge aggregate of wealth for larger uses and needs, thereby in effect converting such endowments to charitable ends. The church did not follow this path of policy because it was faithless or corrupt, but because it was not an impressively vigilant trustee and because inevitably the larger needs came to absorb the lesser. It was quite uncommon for a chantry to survive at all for more than a century or so; it was even more unlikely that the carefully prescribed stipulations of a donor were fully honoured for more than a generation. With the Reformation there came a total conversion of such of these assets as survived; a not wholly unrelated conversion had been going on for many generations earlier.

A great variety of gifts have been gathered under the head of *Church Repairs*, or more exactly, we should perhaps say, church repairs and decorations. These were ordinarily intensely personal and parochial gifts made by men who loved and took pride in their parish church. By church repairs we have meant the ordinary care of the fabric, modest improvements and amendments of that fabric; in a word, the whole of the contributon made towards the maintenance of the religious structure of a community. But under this head we have included as well gifts and bequests made for the embellishment of the fabric and the services of the church: the sacred vessels, the crosses, the cloths, the vestments, the fonts, the antiphonaries, and a host of other articles.

Still another important category of contribution to the needs of the church and its offices we have described as *Maintenance of the Clergy*. These gifts were of two easily differentiated kinds. The first were the gifts and bequests made outright towards the support of named clergy or for the clergy of a district or of a monastery. Such benefactions were, prior to the Reformation, a by no means unimportant source of clerical income, as, we might add, were the many fees imposed by law and custom, which we have not, of course, included in our reckoning. More important, and we shall deal with this subject at length in later pages, were the endowments created by pious men in order to secure the augmentation of clerical stipends in particular parishes. The great bulk of the benefactions included under this head were of this type, representing in their totality an important effort to lend to the clergy of the realm a greater dignity of status and to attract to the calling men of more impressive attainments.

One aspect of this effort was so important both in its religious and political consequences that we have dignified it as a separate head, namely the large and most effective endowments accumulated for the founding of *Puritan Lectureships*. These funds were for the most part ultimately to be absorbed by the established church, but during our period they possessed not only a Puritan bias but an extraordinary prestige and an impressive spiritual power. This whole subject, indeed, deserves a far more detailed and comprehensive treatment than is possible within the limits of this study.

Finally, under *Religion* we have included an important category which has been most cautiously described as *Estimated Church Building*. We have had occasion to comment on the statistical difficulties involved in gathering the sums included under this use, but must once more say that the data represent no more than our best and probably conservative estimates.[1] By church building we have meant the building or rebuilding of churches and chapels, major enlargements of existing churches, and in a few instances the carrying forward of repairs so extensive as to amount to a rebuilding of a decayed structure. It should again be stressed that we have meant to include only those undertakings financed in whole or in part by voluntary subscriptions or gifts, which in a fair number of instances means that we have endeavoured to separate charitable gifts from sums provided by rates when mixed funds were used for building purposes.

[1] *Vide ante,* 33–34.

We have described the five great charitable heads and the twenty-four categories under which we have assembled and have sought to analyse a very large mass of data, data which on occasion were not wholly tractable even within an unfortunately elaborate scheme of organization. We have commented as well on the methods which we have employed and have endeavoured to deal fully and critically with the frailties which we observe in the method. There remains one certain and inherent frailty which we can confess but which we cannot cure. We are dealing with the aspirations of men, with the flux which we find in their sentiments, their intentions, and their vision of the world as they would like it. Their aspirations must at points engage our own even across the span of centuries, just as their prejudices must on occasion fortify our own. The scheme of attack and of analysis we believe to be rigorously objective; the interpretation we can only hope will be honest if it cannot be objective.

III

The Need

We are not directly concerned with the history of poverty during our era or with the measures taken by a vigilant society to effect its relief and cure. We are rather concerned with the rapidly changing structure of philanthropic aspirations during this period of almost two centuries; with documenting a momentous shift of these aspirations towards an all but complete secularism which almost incidentally brought the age-old problem of poverty under careful examination and which created amazingly effective provisions for its amelioration. Yet it must also be said that the question of poverty, its causes and its cure, was a central preoccupation of the social conscience of the sixteenth and seventeenth centuries and that a very considerable proportion of the huge aggregate of charitable wealth provided was dedicated in one way or another to laying this ancient spectre.

It must be emphasized that poverty, wide-scale and endemic poverty, did not burst unannounced on the early modern world. To a degree the nature of poverty was to change, but more importantly men's sensitivity to the fact and social threat of poverty was to be enormously sharpened and enhanced in the course of the period under review. We would agree with Professor Thorndike's wise comment that there have been three broadly held historical attitudes towards poverty in the Christian world. In the first poverty itself was idealized, possibly because its amelioration lay wholly beyond the resources of the society, and the obligation of alms was taught as an intrinsic and significant part of the Christian social duty. Such almsgiving was direct, spontaneous, and expressed the sentiment of true charity, the giver sharing vicariously in the poverty and need of the recipient. The second historical stage was much longer and far more complex, extending in point of fact until late in the sixteenth century. During this age no great virtue was argued for the fact of poverty, which came rather to be increasingly regarded as a social cancer which, while it could not be eradicated, must be treated with all the means available. The relief of the poor, then, became a social as well as a religious duty, which until about the time of the Reformation was largely assigned to the willing but almost wholly ineffectual agencies of the church and afterwards was undertaken principally by private and secular charity. These two first stages of development are not cleanly separable nor, certainly, does the third break sharply from that which had preceded it. In the final historical stage, which may be said to extend to our own day, a distinction is drawn between the employable poor and the derelict, society undertaking by a variety of measures to provide training, employment, and opportunity for those able and willing to work and decent economic sanctuary for those who are permanent casualties in an increasingly complex and competitive economy.[1]

Poverty, then, was not new. It was endemic in all of western Europe throughout the Middle Ages and in times of wide-scale warfare, plague, or regional crop failures could lash out in benumbing and killing epidemic form. In part, the terrible scourge of poverty in the earlier Middle Ages was a consequence of poor transport and the absence of strong central governments able and willing to act; in part, it was an aspect of the intense regionalism of mediaeval life. Many men died of hunger, but on the whole they died quietly. The economy possessed elements of great strength, but it was perenially vulnerable to poverty occasioned by local disaster, with the consequence that, if the serf died, his lord had at least gone very hungry and so had his parish priest. But England after the beginning of the fourteenth century was becoming a much more complex society, not only in the countryside at large but in the rapidly growing and prospering towns. Various ecclesiastical institutions, and most particularly the monasteries and the many hospitals, began to assume a larger role in the relief of at least conspicuous indigence, while in the towns the craft guilds in their various forms, undertook, usually under ecclesiastical auspices, the most effective social insurance and concern that the mediaeval world was to know. Then came the immense disaster accompanying the decline of the mediaeval society, resulting in a steady decay of institutions and of social attitudes, a process not yet complete as our period began. The decay of manors, the savage and destructive waves of plague, foreign and internecine wars, and the slow erosion of civil and economic order not only vastly worsened the problem of poverty but spawned a new kind of poor with which the sixteenth century sought to deal in an amazed and awkward incertitude. So convulsive was this long period that a once stable society was torn apart and masses of men—the dispossessed, the masterless, and the incompetent— were literally set in motion by irresistible forces as they sought first

[1] Thorndike, Lynn, ' The historical background', in *Intelligent philanthopy* (Chicago, 1930), 27–31; Birnie, Arthur, *An economic history of the British Isles* (L., 1955), 110; and *vide* Troeltsch's careful and thoughtful comments on early Christian and medieval charity (Troeltsch, Ernst, *The social teaching of the Christian churches*, Olive Wyon, trans., 2 vols., N.Y., 1931, I, 135–137, 303–305).

work that was not to be had and then alms which society was neither equipped nor disposed to give.

The problem which we have been sketching so generally and briefly possessed an almost cosmic significance. The particulars may differ, but throughout western Europe its broad outlines were much the same in say 1450 or in 1500. 'Economic causes were producing unemployment and in consequence vagrancy, and traditional methods of relieving the needy were proving insufficient.'[1] The collapse of a civilization brought in its train social consequences of stark severity which staggered men in their immensity and which found them without instrumentalities for alleviation, much less for correction. Moreover, as we shall point out in some detail, the church, so long charged by mankind with a general and somewhat vaguely defined area of responsibility, was itself in process of decay. Its once numerous hospitals and almshouses were in large part to disappear in the ruin of the fifteenth century, while the slender resources of those that survived were principally consumed by the tasks of administration and the obligations of pious observance; the monasteries were in a state of visible and rapid decline, suspect when they were not neglected by the society, and were lending, long before their dissolution, no more than token contribution towards the amelioration of a social crisis in which they were themselves engulfed; the craft guilds, perhaps the most effective of all mediaeval agencies for the care of the poor, were in process of dissolution for economic reasons and their charitable function had withered well before the Reformation ended it. The English society stood, then, as our study begins, with few organized, disciplined, and effective resources with which to meet a spreading and a blighting evil. We are concerned with the slow accumulation of new resources and with the fashioning of competent instrumentalities for the care and cure of poverty. The conscience of mankind during the course of our period was for the first time honestly and resolutely to embrace the problem of the poor.

B. THE PROBLEM OF POVERTY IN THE SIXTEENTH CENTURY

1. *Increasing sensitivity to suffering and want*

This is in very broad outlines the genesis of the problem of poverty in the acute and pressing forms in which the early modern world was obliged to deal with it. Poverty, want, and starvation were present, critically so, in the English society in 1480 and had evidently been somewhat abated, principally by the restoration of order and the revival of trade, in the first half-century of Tudor rule. Yet we tend to yield to

---

[1] Elton, G. R., 'An early Tudor poor law', *Econ. Hist. Rev.*, 2d. Ser., VI (1953), 55; and Chadwick, W. E., *The church, the state, and the poor* (L., 1914), 95–96.

an illusion of the increase of poverty in England for a full century after our period begins, chiefly because men of the age were preoccupied with the problem, were earnestly engaged in trying to deal with it, and were for the first time coming to possess some knowledge of the facts. The stern reality of need remained, though gradually diminishing, throughout our long period, but these two centuries were even more significantly marked by a very rapidly growing, a burgeoning, perception of that need. We shall be much occupied with mankind's increasing sensitivity to want, to acute suffering, and to the ignorance and hopelessness from which they spring. The sixteenth century was deeply concerned with the problem of poverty; its literature and documents are filled with the question; its discussion of causes, of extent, and of methods of action mount steadily as the century wears on. When men address themselves with such persistence, such eloquence, and on occasion with such exaggeration to a great social problem, the cure itself is close at hand. There was, we are confident, no real increase in poverty in England during the sixteenth century. Men were at last doing something about it. Thus it was that while the fierce and accusatory literature blasting the depopulation of villages rose to its effective height in the generation after 1517, it appears certain that the historical and economic forces which had brought ruin and death to many scores of Midland villages had in truth run their course well before 1485.[1] But this literature of protest and of reform none the less remains important and intensely relevant. Men were taking the shaping of their society into their own hands, were beginning to build it to a pattern supplied by their own aspirations. The doubtless tragic and perhaps unnecessary disappearance of unnumbered mediaeval villages had passed all but unnoticed in the fourteenth and fifteenth centuries; merely the threat of such social disaster was in the mid-sixteenth century sufficient to call down the moving and wholly persuasive wrath of a Latimer or a Lever. Conscience had been quickened, aspirations had been formed, and men were moving out into a new and unexplored terrain of social responsibility.

Such dramatic events as the dissolution of the monasteries or even the triumph of Protestantism in England seem to have had very little to do with this momentous course of change, save as they were themselves perhaps the consequence of the revolution which was so irresistibly under way. Neither of these events, for example, had any considerable connection with the extent of poverty or the slow mustering by the society of the immensely powerful forces which were brought to bear in the frontal assault that was to be made on poverty and want of opportunity. What did happen, with results persisting to our own generation, was the steady secularization of men's aspirations as they came to address themselves with wholly courageous spirit to the great

[1] Beresford, Maurice, *The lost villages of England* (N.Y., 1954), 137 ff.

problems that were at hand. Perhaps it is not too much to say that the expropriation of the monastic properties was no more than an early but effective instance of this profoundly important shift in the structure of men's aspirations for the world about them and the world of the future as they imagined it.

We would not, of course, suggest that the historical and economic forces of the early modern era did not create new and on occasion critical causes for poverty, even though it seems certain that such social losses were being rapidly offset by the gains of this remarkable period. There were sharp dislocations in the economy and the society, particularly in the first half of the sixteenth century, which undoubtedly bred poverty and which we should not at least briefly assess.

2. *The social consequences of the monastic expropriations*

It was that great nineteenth-century publicist, William Cobbett, who set firmly in our social tradition the notion that the dissolution of the monasteries was a principal cause for the prevalence of poverty in the sixteenth century. Interestingly enough, this view seems to have proceeded from his burning anger with Henry VIII and his advisers, not for having expropriated these foundations, but for having failed to devote the spoils to completely secular and charitable purposes. These judgments Cobbett preached with the moral earnestness and persuasiveness of a Ridley; his eloquence persuades us still, though his facts were wrong and his opinions uninformed.

We know relatively little regarding the role of the mediaeval monasteries in alleviating poverty in the areas in which they were situated, though it is at least clear that contemporary opinion regarded them as important defences against poverty and as rendering extremely useful services in succouring the transient poor. Even more significantly, most of the almshouses, hospitals, lazar-houses, and other charitable institutions of the age had been founded and administered either directly or indirectly by the monasteries, and there is no doubt whatever that these foundations carried on an extremely valuable social and healing function until they, with the monasteries, began slowly to decay at about the middle of the fourteenth century.[1]

This long and inexorable process of the deterioration of monasticism was far advanced well before the advent of the Reformation. This was true throughout western Europe, but perhaps most dramatically so in England where, almost a generation prior to the Dissolution, the fabric was in decay, contributions were drying up, and many foundations were so reduced in numbers that the spiritual offices required by the rule could not be maintained. Moreover, the historic role of these foundations in the distribution of alms had steadily declined and had become

[1] Steinbicker, C. R., *Poor-relief in the sixteenth century* (Washington, 1937), 33.

by the time of the Expropriation relatively insignificant, not, it seems clear, because of corruption or deliberate violations of trust covenants, but rather because of the wastage of estates, the ever-rising costs of administration, and simply befuddled mismanagement. We shall deal in some detail with these matters in our treatment of the several counties, but it may be said here that Savine's careful analysis of the *Valor Ecclesiasticus* lends full support to the inferences which may be drawn from extensive contemporary literature.[1] It would seem that 323 foundations, and including all the larger monasteries which enjoyed a total gross income of about £112,000 p.a., were just prior to the Dissolution distributing in alms under obligations of trust no more than £2700 p.a., or a scant 2·4 per cent of the whole of their available income. It is true that the commissioners were exacting in their definitions of both alms and trusts. When we take into account what we know of mediaeval gifts and bequests to the monasteries, however, it is abundantly clear that there had been an immense erosion of the admitted charitable responsibilities of these foundations. Many trusts had been diverted to other uses; many more, it seems probable, had simply been forgotten with the passage of time. We have much sparser data, whether from the *Valor Ecclesiasticus* or elsewhere, regarding the amounts distributed as voluntary alms by this group of foundations, together disposing almost 70 per cent of the monastic wealth of the realm. But there are sufficiently numerous instances where we have the amounts disbursed both under trusts and voluntarily to permit a statistical projection and to warrant the reasonably reliable estimate that these monasteries did not dispose in alms an amount exceeding £6500 p.a., requiring the income on capital of perhaps £130,000 in value. Within a period of forty years in our ten counties alone, the whole of this social capital had been restored by secular donors, being carefully vested for the relief of the poor. We may reasonably assume that at least twice as large a capital had been so disposed as a bulwark against poverty in the realm as a whole.

The charitable burden borne by the monasteries was, then, relatively slight, though in an age when £2 10s would sustain a human being at the level of subsistence for a year, it cannot be dismissed as without importance. It must be said, however, that the quality of monastic alms was even less impressive than the quantity. The number of poor corrodiers kept was few, and they were to be found in only relatively few houses. Most monastic alms were distributed as outright doles on holidays and commemorative days to beggars who thronged from house to house to piece together a scant living in which the acceptance of alms was not unmixed with periods of criminality. The monks cannot at this distance be blamed for the fact that their alms on the whole probably

---

[1] Savine, Alexander, *English monasteries on the eve of the Dissolution* (Oxford, 1909), 229–241, *et passim*.

created far more beggary than they cured. Their prime office was not the systematic care of the poor, they were engulfed by the begging flotsam thrown up by the great social catastrophe of the preceding century, and they were, in any case, imbued with a conception of the nature of alms that was as old as the Christian past. But it just happened that this conception of alms was not effective in dealing with the problem of poverty as it existed in western Europe at the turn of the sixteenth century, even if the monasteries had possessed sufficient resources for really generous distributions.[1]

There remains a more important consequence of the dissolution of the monasteries in relation to the problem of poverty. These expropriations, proceeding rapidly and ruthlessly as they did, represented still another in a train of social and economic dislocations which had beset the English society for a period of well over a century. Not many poor, particularly deserving poor, were deprived of sustenance, but some thousands of men and women were made poor, or faced the threat of poverty, because this great redistribution of national wealth had taken place. The monks were pensioned or absorbed into the fabric of the priesthood, but many of their tenants, their servants, and certain of their lay administrators were thrown upon a labour market already saturated. The new proprietors of the monastic lands managed them with far greater efficiency than the monks could ever contrive, but it was precisely here that the pinch of social distress occurred, especially in the north of England. The very mismanagement which had created an administrative hierarchy and a lightly exploited lay labour pool, thereby so seriously diminishing the funds left in monastic coffers for charitable uses, had in fact created substantial employment. Tudor literature is full of complaints, often by men themselves sternly Protestant, of the grasping quality of the too great efficiency of the new proprietors. Thus Becon wisely tells us that these men 'abhor the names of monks, friars, canons, nuns . . . but their goods they greedily gripe. And yet, where the cloisters kept hospitality, let out their farms at a reasonable price', they do 'none of all these things'.[2] These purchasers

---

[1] Dietz, F. C., *English government finance 1485–1558* (Urbana, Illinois, 1921), 123–124; Coulton, G. G., *Five centuries of religion* (4 vols., Cambridge, 1923–1950), IV, 713–723; Garnier, R. M., *History of the English landed interest* (L., 1892), 281 (Garnier believed, however, that slight as was the contribution of the monasteries, their sudden withdrawal created a crisis which compelled the state to intervene); Slater, Gilbert, *Poverty and the state* (L., 1930), 8–10; Hewins, W. A. S., 'The problem of pauperism' in *Social England* (H. D. Traill and J. S. Mann, eds.) (L., 1901, 6 vols.), III, 360; Webb, Sidney and Beatrice, *The old poor law* (L., 1927), 18–19; Gray, B. K., *A history of English philanthropy* (L., 1905), 9–13; Ashley, W. J., *An introduction to English economic history and theory* (2 vols., N. Y., 1888, 1893), II, 312–317.

[2] Becon, Thomas, 'The jewel of joy' (1553), in *The Catechism* (John Ayre, ed.), (Cambridge, 1844), 435.

of abbey lands were men, by and large, who understood that land when exploited as capital could found new fortunes and create a new aristocracy. They were men who knew what they wanted, who were quick to introduce new methods, and who became the exemplars of the enclosers, the sheep graziers, and the rent raisers so detested by the sixteenth century moralists.[1] Thus it was that around each destroyed foundation a tiny social dislocation occurred, unimportant in itself save in human terms, but which as it extended across the length and breadth of the realm enmeshed to form a major dislocation in a society only just beginning to find firm footing in a new and very complex world.

3. Agricultural changes and the increase of poverty

The problem of dealing with poverty in England was also very considerably complicated by the great agrarian revolution which had begun a century earlier but which continued throughout the sixteenth century. The driving force of that revolution was a changing attitude on the part of owners towards their land, which increasingly they came to regard and to exploit as a species of capital. Much land passed into the hands of new and vigorous men who were sensitive to the economic realities and who were wholly prepared to convert their holdings from arable to grazing or to reconstitute the semi-communal and wasteful open-field system still prevailing in many parts of England, if means could be found to gain their ends. Many of these proprietors, as we have noted, gained control of former monastic lands, with the result that the social dislocation resulting from expropriation was often compounded by the improving dispositions made by the new owners. It appears reasonably certain that the most sweeping of these agricultural changes, at least in terms of the actual depopulation of communities, were over by 1500, but they were none the less continuous throughout the Tudor period and in the view of all contemporary observers, including the three great and certainly unsentimental Tudor monarchs, worked real hardship on the landless agricultural labourers, some portion of whom now possessed no more than marginal and seasonal utility. It must be remembered, too, that the agrarian society was still most conservative and that any change wrought genuine injury on its weakest members, who simply did not have the capacities of adaptability required in finding new employment elsewhere.[2] This remains true even though we are describing a movement of change which was at once relatively slow and on the whole regional in its character. The most trustworthy estimates would

[1] Cheyney, E. P., *Social changes in England in the sixteenth century* (Boston, 1895), 67.

[2] Tawney, R. H., *The agrarian problem in the sixteenth century* (L., 1912), 263–265; Ernle, R. E. P., *English farming past and present* (L., 1919), 56–58; Gray, *History of philanthropy*, 2–3.

suggest that not much more than 1200 square miles of agricultural land was enclosed in the long interval 1455–1637 and that these changes probably did not result in the dispossession and possibly the unemployment of more than 35,000 families.[1]

Paradoxically enough, the rapid spread of sheep-farming in the first half of the sixteenth century, while undoubtedly creating rural unemployment in certain areas, was itself supporting the industrial prosperity of the woollen manufacturing regions, which certainly absorbed a much larger labour force than that which the sheep had dispossessed. But the difficulty was that these dislocations were local, or at most regional, and the labour dispossessed lacked both the mobility and the skill to effect a theoretically possible and desirable translation. Human beings are like that, whether we are speaking of a Yorkshire cottager in the sixteenth century or a Welsh coal miner in the twentieth century. Some thousands of men, consequently, who had been bound to particular stretches of land by ties which generations had forged suddenly became landless, rootless men. The Tudors as a result, in a period of expanding national prosperity, found themselves faced with a new and a pressing problem of vagrancy and genuine unemployment. It was with the definition and resolution of this problem that Parliament was to wrestle for a full two generations and it was to this problem that private charity was to address itself with such admirable pertinacity.[2] The particular crisis was spent by the close of the sixteenth century, in any case, when a great shift from grazing to arable farming set in, but it had occasioned great suffering and had taught England something of the sterner realities of the modern economic world.[3]

It is very possible that both sixteenth century moralists and twentieth century social historians have been so deeply moved by the undoubted though limited evils of depopulation as a result of enclosures for sheep-farming that we have devoted too little attention to the almost certainly more important sources of rural unemployment, the rise of the yeoman farmer and 'the squire who farmed like a yeoman'. Valuable insight provided by Professor Mildred Campbell and others, and their own account books, wills, and inventories, suggest that these aggressive, intelligent, and profit-minded men who farmed their own land were rapidly reducing the wasteful increments of labour undoubtedly borne by the manorial system. The labour which they employed was landless,

---

[1] Gay, E. F., 'Inclosures in England in the sixteenth century', *Quarterly Journal of Economics*, XVII (1903), 576–597; Johnson, A. H., *The disappearance of small landowners* (Oxford, 1909), 48, 58.

[2] Professor Tawney's comments on this general problem (*Agrarian problem*, 265–280) are wise and illuminating.

[3] Holdsworth, W. S., *A history of English law* (12 vols., L., 1922–1938), IV, 388–402; Palmer, R. L., *English social history in the making* (L., 1934), 58–59; Ashley, W. J., *The economic organisation of England* (L., 1949), 115.

disciplined, and in large part seasonal. The proprietors of this class were throughout the sixteenth century the most efficient farmers in England, and rural unemployment followed in the train of their very efficiency.

4. *Demographic factors*

Extensive work in local materials has also persuaded us that probably the most important of all the causes for rural poverty in our era was the steady and relatively steep increase in population which appears to have set in just a little while before the beginning of our period and which continued unabated to its close. There are many reasons for believing that the rural population of the realm was growing more rapidly than a tightening and somewhat harassed agrarian system could possibly absorb, and likewise faster than the mobile elements of this increase could be absorbed by a very rapidly expanding industrial and commercial economy. It is probable that the population of the realm increased by as much as 40 per cent between 1500 and 1600 and by another 30 per cent in the first four decades of the seventeenth century. Dramatic as was the increase in urbanization, it could not keep pace with this enormous and spiralling rise in population. Even the most casual examination of parish records, particularly in the southern and Midland counties, suggests all too clearly that rural parishes were seriously and heavily overpopulated from about 1550 onwards in terms of any reasonable assessment of available arable lands and of known local industries. Parishes such as these, and there were thousands of them, fed men and youths by the tens of thousands into that inexhaustible maw which was London, but never quite as rapidly as the parishes produced them and always a little faster than London could absorb them. The simple fact is that there was a substantial labour surplus, both rural and urban, during almost the whole of our period.

5. *The protest of conscience*

There were, then, complex economic and demographic forces which were at once producing a long period of agricultural prosperity for most classes of landowners and misery and ejection for the marginal elements of the agrarian community. Men of the sixteenth century did not understand the forces at work, but they feared them, and they were certainly warmly articulate in their denunciation of the social evils which ensued. There is a vast literature of social protest through the whole of the sixteenth century, of which the Tudors were not unmindful as they struggled to find ways and means to remedy ills which in a true sense their own wise economic policies had made inevitable. At least a few selected examples may be noted.

John Bayker, who represented himself as an artificer who had travelled through much of England, in *ca.* 1538 made bold to warn the

King of the decay of houses and villages throughout the realm. All this, he felt, could be corrected if vacant land were brought under tillage, if landlords were forbidden to raise rents and impose excessive fines, and if every dispossessed poor man might have but 'one lythyll howsse or cotage to inhabyt and but a lytyl garden grownde wythe all'.[1] Nostalgically, the great Latimer could recall his yeoman father who 'had no landes of hys owne, onlye he had a farme of iii or iiii pound by yere at the uttermost, and here upon he tilled so much as kept halfe a dosen men. He had walke for a hundred shepe, and my mother mylked xxx kyne. . . . He kept me to schole, or elles I had not bene able to haue preached before the Kinges maiestie now. . . . He kept hospitalitie for his pore neighbours. And sum almes he gaue to the poore, and all thys dyd he of the sayd farme', whereas the present owner could not afford 'a cup of drincke to the pore'.[2] What had happened? Graziers, enclosers, the shepherd and his dog, had destroyed a pastoral society, said Latimer, and with him all the sixteenth century moralists most vehemently agreed. Thomas Becon, who had been deeply influenced by Latimer while at Cambridge, writing a little later, denounced as sons of Satan those ambitious landlords who 'not only link house to house, but, when they have gotten many houses and tenements into their hands, yea, whole townships, they suffer the houses to fall into utter ruin and decay; so that by this means whole towns are become desolate, and like unto a wilderness, no man dwelling there, except it be the shepherd and his dog'. The encloser and the grazier have brought calamity on the rural poor and ruin to whole stretches of the kingdom. They are as evil as they are heartless, consigning the poor 'to starve and perish for hunger'.[3]

The rural ills which Latimer had observed in Leicestershire and Becon in Norfolk were with equal eloquence described by an anonymous writer who in *ca.* 1550 drew his knowledge from Oxfordshire. There was real dearth in England, he held, caused by the enclosures being made for sheep grazing. He testified that in Oxfordshire alone forty ploughs had disappeared during the reign of Henry VIII and that each plough provided sustenance for a household of six persons. These families were dispossessed and had no place to go because this corrosive process of change was to be found in every part of the realm. Hence they have gone 'forth from shire to shire and . . . be scattered thus abroad within the king's majesty's realm, where it shall please almighty God; and for lack of masters, by compulsion driven, some of them to beg and some

---

[1] *S.P. Henry VIII*, CXLI, 134-135, quoted in *Tudor economic documents* (R. H. Tawney and Eileen Power, eds.) (3 vols., L., 1951), II, 302-305.

[2] Latimer, Hugh, *The fyrste sermon . . . before the Kinges Maiestie* (L., 1549), no pagin.

[3] Becon, *Catechism*, 434.

to steal'.[1] These same ills had been noted through all the Midland counties and brooded on by John Hales, appointed in 1548 to the commission to redress enclosures. Writing perhaps two years later, Hales complains of dearth, of rising prices, and of enclosures which have driven away forty families from areas where 'nowe one man . . . and his shepherd hathe all'. The enclosures to make arable farming more profitable, already proceeding in several counties, do no harm to the economy or to the society, Hales tells us, but those which favour wool against grain are a scourge in the land of England.[2]

These rural dislocations were coming to an end towards the close of the sixteenth century as, on balance, land was returning to the plough in England. But even the troubled debates from which the great Elizabethan poor laws were to issue echoed the deep conviction that enclosures and land laid down to grazing were the prime cause of poverty in the realm. This persuasion had taken on the status of a national myth which, with alterations, has perpetuated itself down to our own century. Henry Arthington, writing in 1597, laid the blame for rural poverty principally on those proud and wasteful landowners who rack their tenants in order to maintain an indecently high standard of living. The enclosers, the covetous landlords, and the ruthless corn merchants he held to be the 'poor makers' of the age.[3] In the same year, the recently installed Dean of Durham, William James, complained repeatedly to Lord Burghley of the decay of tillage and of rural poverty in the North. In the bishopric, he held, at least 500 ploughs had decayed in the past half-century with the result that in an area where 8000 acres were once corn land, hardly 160 acres remained in tillage. 'Want and waste have crept into Northumberland, Westmoreland, and Cumberland', where one might travel for twenty miles and see no inhabitants. In Northumberland, James added, great villages had been depopulated, and there being 'no man to stop the enemy's attempt . . . people are driven to the poor port towns'.[4]

The great Tudor monarchs were almost intuitively sensitive to social criticism and were deeply concerned with economic dislocations which might lead to the subversion of the public order they were so grimly resolved to maintain. The Crown was accordingly troubled by these forces of rural change which were clearly under way and which evidently had some uncertainly defined connection with agrarian unemployment and unsettlement. The problem was not easy of solution.

[1] *Certain causes gathered together wherein is showed the decay of England* (L., [1550–1553]), in Dunham, William H., Jr., and Stanley Pargellis, eds., *Complaint and reform in England 1436–1714* (N. Y., 1938), 135–136, 138.

[2] Hales, John, *A discourse of the common weal of this realm of England* (Elizabeth Lamond, ed.) (Cambridge, 1893), 15, 18, 33, 37, 53, 66, 88–89, 97, 112–125.

[3] Arthington, Henry, *Provision for the poore* (L., 1597), no pagin.

[4] *S.P. Dom.*, 1597, CCLXII, 10, 11.

Tudor policy consistently favoured the very classes that were acquiring land and exploiting its ownership, while Tudor legislation quite as consistently sought to protect the smallholder and the rural wage earner from the consequences of that exploitation. The weight of law and of administration was consequently employed to retard and to control the progress of an agricultural revolution which was regarded as inevitable and desirable in the scale of national interests but which must be accomplished gradually lest the society itself be too severely strained. Accordingly, the whole temper of law and of policy were at once conservative and restraining throughout our period, as the government sought with a considerable measure of success to guide and to control the necessary process of agrarian change. From 1488 (4 *Henry VII*, *c.* 19) onwards until the last days of the Protectorate, there was constant concern and steady intervention in the agrarian problem, no fewer than twelve major statutes, seven royal commissions, many proclamations, and the steady attention of the Privy Council and the Court of Star Chamber attesting to the discipline with which the Crown ordered the rise of the gentry to the seats of economic power.[1]

6. *Urbanization and the new poverty*

The great and silent changes taking place in agriculture were, as we have seen, moderately paced and were subject to the constant and on the whole the wise restraining policy of the state. These agricultural dislocations bred poverty among rural groups now marginal in their economic utility and, connected as they were with a steadily increasing population, fed with surplus labour another great and more rapid revolutionary change under way in the economy of the nation. Professor Nef and other economic historians of our generation have traced out the principal lines of an early industrial and commercial revolution which occurred within the term of our study and which was profoundly to alter the whole shape of the English economy and society.[2] The rapid spread of industry, the closely connected growth of principally industrial urban communities, and the rise of new classes of employers who possessed no clearly held sense of social responsibility nurtured by tradition or by law vastly aggravated the whole problem of poverty during the sixteenth and seventeenth centuries. More specifically, industrialization and urbanization were to spawn a new kind of poor, workers dependent on specialized skills, cut off from the ever-sustaining resources of an uncomplicated rural parish, and living at the mercy of an employment subjected to periodic intervals of slump or complete

---

[1] Holdsworth, *English law*, IV, 362–373; Tawney, *Agrarian problem*, 313–317.
[2] Nef, J. U., *Industry and government in France and England 1540–1640* (Philadelphia, 1940) and the same author's masterly *The rise of the British coal industry* (2 vols., L., 1932).

stagnation. The always perceptive Eden has well said that 'manufactures and commerce are the true parents of our national poor'.[1]

The whole weight of the evidence which will be fully discussed in later volumes suggests that it was urban poverty which created the most serious and the most difficult problems for the society with which we are concerned. Men of the age, as we have seen, were principally preoccupied with the rural poor, and the great Elizabethan poor laws were to be framed principally to help them, though the peculiarly intransigent and sharp distress was to be found in the cities, the wool towns, and the commercial centres around which trade and industry clustered. In sixteenth century England a total want of employment in a rural area remained almost unknown, or at least contemporary observers viewed the possibility with incredulity; to put it with harsh but more pertinent accuracy, starvation was scarcely possible or tolerated in the still quite uncomplicated and amazingly stable society which rural England remained despite the dislocations to which it had been subjected. But in the urban and industrial complexes growing so rapidly in so many parts of the realm, men found themselves subject to the wholly unpredictable scourges of seasonal unemployment and, even worse, to cyclical periods of severe economic depression when work could not be gained even by the most desperately willing artisan. This was a development which was simply not comprehended by the English society until well into the seventeenth century, and then most grudgingly, because the whole frame of historical and economic reference remained agrarian in an economy undergoing an industrial revolution. It was to this great need, to this social crisis, that private charity addressed itself with such pertinacious concern, thereby relieving a need and a social tension of the utmost gravity. So too, as we shall see, the Elizabethan poor laws, passed as they were by men principally preoccupied with agrarian poverty, were in fact to have their first substantial application in the relief of urban, of industrial, poverty.

Thus it was that the industrial and commercial revolution which so quickly and so effectively created new opportunities for employment, which so enormously increased the value of the national product of the realm, and which steadily absorbed the ever-mounting population of rural England spawned the new and dreadful blight of industrial, of urban, poverty, a poverty which western society has only very recently been able to bring under relatively firm control. It is quite impossible to measure the extent of urban poverty at any time, but it may most confidently be said that it was endemic during the last century of our period and that it flared up on occasion in dreadful and epidemic out-

[1] Eden, F. M., *The state of the poor* (A. G. L. Rogers, ed.) (L., 1928), 3–4. This great work remains valuable for any student of English social and economic history.

bursts. In 1595, a year of great scarcity, the Lord Mayor of London reckoned that there were 4132 stricken householders in the city, which would suggest that possibly as much as 10 per cent of the whole population were at or below the line of pauperism, if allowances are made for aged and youthful dependents of these families. A recent writer, using Gregory King's figures for Lichfield, compiled just a century later, believes that at that date probably 16·8 per cent of the whole population of that provincial city were paupers,[1] while an anonymous author writing in 1641 certainly too pessimistically suggests that a quarter of the population of the realm was made up of 'miserable poor people'.[2] Though we shall deal with the subject in more detail in later pages, it may be appropriately said here that an extensive study of parochial records for the certainly critical period 1601–1640 would lead us to believe that something like 8 per cent of the population of any urban and industrial complex in England were quite chronically at or below the line of poverty as then most harshly defined, while in periods of trade depression or pestilence this proportion could rise, and that very quickly, to as much as 20 per cent of the population.

The truth is that in the towns as in the country areas there was a labour surplus through the whole of the last century of our period. This fact tended not only to keep wages depressed but likewise to make marginal or unemployable whole segments of the population which could have found at least partial employment under more stable rural conditions. It has been most pertinently pointed out that in seventeenth century England 'the labour force of the community was characterized by a relatively short span of working life at maximum productive efficiency'.[3] Such labour was discarded easily and quickly, particularly as an unending flow of youth poured into London, or Halifax, or Coventry in search of employment. This labour force was subjected, as well, to the necessity of supporting a large body of minor dependents resulting from a very high birth rate and the even heavier burden of lending sustenance to those whom an urban society declared to be aged. These burdens neither the labour force nor the municipalities involved could possibly bear alone. Here again private charity, mustered in enormous and disciplined aggregates, intervened quickly and with fair efficiency to save the society from what might easily have been a disastrous collapse.

The rise of industry in our period had many aspects and extended into many fields of endeavour, but the most important single develop-

---

[1] Coleman, D. C., 'Labour in the English economy of the seventeenth century', *Econ. Hist. Rev.*, 2d. ser., VIII (1956), 280–295.

[2] *Considerations touching trade, with the advance of the King's revenue* (L., 1641), 15.

[3] Coleman, in *Econ. Hist. Rev.*, 2d ser., VIII (1956), 285.

ment was without doubt in the cloth trade. The growth of the industry was very rapid, though our detailed examination of the counties suggests that the great prosperity attained and the mass employment resulting in certain areas such as the West Riding and the west of England was at the expense of much older, tradition-ridden, and now inefficient producing regions scattered all over the south and east of England. The new industry lay at particular hazard because its prosperity was so heavily dependent on the export market, while those employed were especially vulnerable because of the high degree of technical specialization which characterized cloth manufacturing. The clothier, the key figure in the industry, had only a relatively small capital commitment in his inventory or in forward purchases, with the result that he could and did adjust his business quite accurately to current demand and simply withdrew from the market and closed down an entire industry at will. Hence it was that 'we do not hear of the poor merchant' or the 'poor clothier' in the seventeenth century, while the 'poor spinner, weaver, dresser, and so on, was a continual object of concern'.[1] The industry was particularly subject to troughs of unemployment and remained throughout our period a breeder of poverty, even though it had come to be the employers of many thousands of persons.

The cloth industry, undoubtedly over-extended and with too large capacity for production, was in a generally unhealthy state in the long interval 1620–1640, having literally collapsed in 1621–1623 and suffering another serious depression in 1630–1631.[2] The complex reasons for this collapse of an industry which was the largest single industrial employer of labour in the realm have been carefully and expertly studied in recent years, the consensus being that the export market had by 1620 been largely lost to England. Spreading unemployment from this industry involved other artisan groups, with the result that England found herself, without experience or preparation, faced with her first major crisis of industrial depression. As we shall later note in some detail, the government found itself obliged to intervene vigorously and persistently, with, among other results, the first serious effort being made to secure a general and strict application of the Elizabethan poor laws. The Privy

---

[1] Hinton, R. W. K., 'The mercantile system in the time of Thomas More', Econ. Hist. Rev., 2d ser., VII (1955), 280; vide Stone, Lawrence, 'State control in sixteenth century England,' Econ. Hist. Rev., XVII (1947), 103. Stone holds that the state felt it necessary to intervene with controls as the economy became more complex, since 'the propertied classes of the Elizabethan period were faced with a turbulent and unruly proletariat, half industrial workers, half professional unemployed'. It was fear of disorder that made the propertied classes willing to accede to increasingly significant forms of state intervention.

[2] Hewins, W. A. S., 'Pauperism and the poor laws', in Social England, IV, 196–197; MacInnes, C. M., An introduction to the economic history of the British Empire (L., 1935), 21–22.

Council was deeply troubled by reports pouring in of distress and disorder in many parts of the realm, of which that from the High Sheriff of Somerset may be taken as typical. A 'tumultuous assembly of poor' in the eastern part of the county had been quieted, but he must warn the Council 'that there are such a multytude of poor cottages builte uppon the highwaies and odd corners in every country parishe within this countye and so stufte with pore people that in many of those parishes there are three or fower hundred poore . . . that did gett most of their lyvinge by spinninge, carding and such imployments aboute wooll and cloath'. Trade was dead, there was no reserve for these people, who 'are for the most parte without worke and knowe not how to live'.[1]

The High Sheriff of Somerset was troubled, and so was the Council as similar reports sifted in to them from affected areas all over England. Letters were despatched to the justices in all the cloth counties in 1622 requiring them to compel the clothiers to assume a larger measure of social responsibility. The Council would not endure 'that clothiers . . . should at their pleasure . . . dismiss their work folks, who, being many in number and most of them of the poorer sort, are in such cases likely by their clamours to disturb the quiet and government of those parts wherein they live'. In consequence, the wool growers, the clothiers, and the merchants who had profited greatly in good times, 'must now in the decay of trade . . . bear a part of the public losses as may best conduce to the good of the public and the maintenance of general trade'. But the industrial crisis was too severe, its economic and social consequences too widespread for this fiat of sovereignty to have much more than moral meaning. The state quickly found that words were not enough; it was itself soon deeply involved in a prolonged and arduous effort to stay the decay of the whole social fabric of the realm which was threatened by this first major episode of industrial depression.

In discussing the causes for the increase of poverty in England, we have laid frequent emphasis on the undoubted factor of a steep and continuously rising curve of population through the whole course of our period.[2] We have estimated, probably quite conservatively, that the population of the realm increased by as much as 40 per cent during the sixteenth century and then very steeply by another 30 per cent in the first four decades of the seventeenth century. Almost as certainly, the population of the kingdom was somewhat more than doubled in the course of our whole period. This was a very substantial increase for an economy with relatively modest resources of production and distribution, and for one still remarkably stable and conservative in its whole social and economic structure.[3] There was, as we have so often stressed,

---

[1] *S.P. Dom.*, 1622, CXXX, 73 (May 14).   [2] *Vide ante*, 26–29, 63.
[3] Barrington, Daines, *Observations on the more ancient statutes* (L., 1796), 536–537.

a major expansion of industry and of commerce under way which went far towards absorbing the ever-mounting store of labour available, but the whole social problem was not easily resolved because the marginal elements of the labour force were neither mobile nor skilled and because the economy itself was ill-proportioned and somewhat inelastic. The consequence was an undoubted labour surplus first in agrarian England and later in urban England, which was to create great hardship.for classes of men quite defenceless against change and also most difficult social problems for a government not fully comprehending the essentially revolutionary shifts that were under way. Broadly speaking, the whole era with which we are concerned was one in which prosperity and productivity were increasing both rapidly and generally, but not in such wise as to comprehend all elements that went to make up the realm. Much of the really widespread poverty and suffering which might have occurred was, as we shall see, to be relieved or prevented by an immense outpouring of private charity, supplemented modestly towards the close of our era by direct governmental intervention through the taxing power.

The fact of the increasing weight of population on the resources of the realm was well understood by contemporary opinion after about 1580, even by this age which was so happily disinterested in all matters statistical. We need here only mention the stream of publications dealing with the problem of overpopulation, usually closely connected with propaganda urging emigration to colonies either projected or recently founded.[1] In their search for arguments certain of these writers doubtless exaggerated the common conviction that the realm had become overpopulated and that much of existing poverty flowed from the fact, yet it seems quite clear that they were appealing to sentiments very widely held. In fact, the whole colonial movement of the early seventeenth century gained much of its impetus from this concern. Perhaps at least one of these writers might be briefly heard.

Richard Eburne, a Somerset clergyman, in 1624 published a systematic and eloquent plea for colonial emigration, especially in the interests of the Newfoundland plantation in which nearby Bristol had a considerable financial stake. In his preface he tells us that he is addressing himself to the poorer and meaner sort, whom he exhorts to 'looke upon the miserie and want wherein you doe, and abiding in England, you cannot but live'. God has offered, almost miraculously, a means of relief from the poverty which assails England, and it would be sinful indeed not to accept it. This poverty, the author believes, is principally occasioned by the fact that England has for long been spared from war and plague, 'the two great deuourers of mankinde', with the result that the realm swarms with a 'multitude and plentie of people'. It is this

[1] Wright, L. B., *Religion and empire* (Chapel Hill, N.C., 1943).

overplus, this marginal population, which should be sent abroad. It is in fact intolerable 'what a number in euery towne and citie, yea in euery parish and village, doe abound' who cannot be sustained save at damaging cost to the whole society. Such needed translations of people, he recognized, would not be easily effected, 'Englishmen especially, and of them, most of all the in-land sort' being 'wedded to their natiue soile'. Eburne would therefore use compulsion to secure the transportation first of the vagrants and then of those guilty of minor offences, often inspired by want. He would then sweep up the homeless men and squatters, that 'superfluous crue' who had always plagued the quiet of the realm. To these he would add pressed troops for garrison duty and then for colonization and lastly the children of paupers who would be bound to fruitful trades in the colonies. These were the marginal, the impoverished groups, which Eburne would have constituted as the mud sills of his colonial society, he having been fully confident that the needed farmers, artisans, and craftsmen could be induced to follow by the economic and social opportunities available in the new world. Ideally, he would wish to see about 16,000 persons emigrate each year from England, two for each parish, which would feed numbers in needed fashion to the new world and restore the stability of population so required in England if the problem of poverty was to be solved at all.[1]

7. The erosion of inflation

We have likewise stressed at several points in our earlier discussion the serious consequences of a steadily spiralling inflationary process on the society of the age.[2] We have suggested that it is probably impossible to construct a reliable index of prices that would have valid national meaning in our period, but we can most assuredly state that the rising curve of commodity prices, the cost of necessaries, steadily outstripped the curve of wages.[3] And it is precisely here that poverty was engendered and deepened by the inflationary process. Valiant, if largely ineffective, efforts were made by the central government to control the prices of necessaries, particularly in times of extreme dearth, but the powerful economic forces at work in the society simply could not be stilled by fiat. At the same time, steady and on the whole remarkably successful efforts were undertaken to retard the curve of wages, assisted no doubt by the fact of a labour surplus, with the result that quite unintended social injury resulted. One authority, indeed, would go so far as to maintain that the crisis of poverty in the sixteenth and seventeenth centuries was

---

[1] Eburne, Richard, *A plaine path-way to plantations* (L., 1624), 9, 59–62, 72–75.

[2] *Vide ante*, especially 34–37, 65–66.

[3] Beer, M., *Early British economics* (L., 1938), 82–99; Rogers, *Agriculture and prices*, IV, 716–719; V, 787–792.

principally due to the fact that wages did not rise as rapidly as did prices.[1] The government and responsible opinion generally were deeply concerned because of the eroding social effects of a gradually mounting inflation, but could never quite diagnose either the nature of the economic malady or set forth the appropriate remedies. Everyone in the society, a contemporary informs us, blamed everyone else: 'Some thought the husbandmen were guilty who charged high prices for victuals, whereupon the husbandmen said the fault was with the noblemen who raised the rents and . . . [made] enclosures. Noblemen said the fault was with the merchants and artificers for selling everything dearer than in past times.'

The economic processes which we have so briefly described undoubtedly condemned whole classes of men to a life without margins of safety, to a standard of living only scantly above the line of subsistence even in normal times. This was true in a long period which may generally be described as very prosperous indeed, when most classes of men were without doubt enjoying a rapid and visible increase at once in their standard of living and in the margins of their security. This everspreading gulf between classes troubled the whole society and was a principal factor in evoking the great charitable outpouring which characterizes the age under review. It is also responsible for a considerable exaggeration of the whole problem and fact of poverty in the realm, for it evoked a reaction in the conscience of certain classes of men who were prospering conspicuously because of the inflationary process. The fact and the fear of poverty were, then, present at all times among the rootless and the unskilled, and had, as it were, become endemic in the new society of the sixteenth century. But in periods of economic crisis, when there were widespread and successive crop failures, particularly if conjoined with industrial unemployment, the whole society found itself on the brink of frightful and almost paralysing disaster. This fear was to be demonstrated by almost every writer dealing with the social and economic problems of the era, but Eburne, whom we have just been citing in another connection, comes to mind. He complained that prices had risen steeply in the past generation with the result that the helpless poor had been pressed deeper and deeper into want and enjoyed an ever-smaller share in the necessaries of life. If steps were not at once taken to relieve the pressure on foodstuffs, war and pestilence would, he held, be the inevitable result. His over-simple cure was, of course, 'the diminution of the people, which reduced to such a competent number, as the land it selfe can well maintaine, would easily cause, not onely the excessiue height of fines and rents, but also the prices of all things else, to fall of themselues, and stay at . . . [a] reasonable . . . rate'.[2]

[1] Rogers, *Work and wages*, 427–430.   [2] Eburne, *Plaine path-way*, 10.

These all too frequent intervals of dearth the government sought to control and to alleviate by direct, sweeping, and angry interventions in the economic process which it is evident enjoyed the full support of the dominant elements in the society. There are literally hundreds of these interventions in which the whole administrative mechanism of the realm was charged with controlling the prices of necessaries by fiat and with arranging for the better distribution of commodities in short supply in order to relieve panic and afford some measure of protection for the poor. The government was searching for a way to master economic forces which even now we cannot fully control. It was hungry for information, for enlightenment. Thus it wished the deputy lieutenants of Hertfordshire to inform it of the reasons for the continuance there of high prices of grain. Wheat, the Council was told, was better in quality, though the yield was small, while barley 'carries a higher price, as the poor who were wont to feed upon wheat and rye are driven to it'. The county was seeking to supply itself from 'more fruitful shires', but was troubled by 'the higglers of Middlesex, and other purveyors for London' who scoured the county for its scant food resources. 'It is pitiful to consider the great multitude of poor in most of the towns of the shire, who having the last year spent the greatest part of their substance, are now driven to live upon relief.'[1] In such crises as this, and there were many of them, the whole weight of sovereignty was thrown quickly, aggressively, and on the whole effectively on the side of the poor and for the preservation of social order.[2] This fact in itself constitutes one of the greatest of the gains that men had thus far made in ordering their affairs and in assuming full responsibility in broad areas of social need.

8. *The scourge of epidemics*

There remains still another principal cause of poverty in the age with which we are concerned, the heavy and wholly unpredictable incidence of epidemic diseases which so plagued the whole of the western world from the middle of the fourteenth century until just past the middle of the seventeenth. The whole course of this strange visitation has been well traced out, though we remain uncertain of mortality rates until the late sixteenth century. It is clear that England was never wholly free of these scourges at any time, that rather limited areas tended to be

---

[1] *S.P. Dom.*, 1595, CCLIV, 10.

[2] Countless examples might be given. Typical are interventions in Buckinghamshire and Nottinghamsire in 1623 when, as we have earlier suggested, there was widespread dearth and suffering in both rural and urban communities (*S.P. Dom.*, 1623, CXL, 10, 19). Certain of the justices of Nottinghamshire reported that they had ordered the churchwardens and overseers to set the poor on work and to relieve the impotent, 'but the poverty of the country is generally soe great that it will bee a thinge of no small difficulty suffitiently to provide for them'.

affected at any given moment, and that the mortality rate, particularly in congested urban areas, was in the worst of these epidemics so staggeringly high as to cripple the normal functioning of an entire community and most severely to restrict its economic activity. From 1480 onwards there appear to have been seven outbreaks of bubonic plague or other epidemic diseases of major proportions in England, while in more than half the years included in this study at least localized epidemics have been noted.[1] The most feared of all circumstances was when, in a period of dearth or widespread unemployment, a visitation of the plague simply wiped out the always slender resources of the poorer classes, among whom in any case these epidemic diseases moved with a particularly savage virulence. Under such conditions whole areas became disaster regions in which all the resources that could be mustered by the region and often by the central government had to be mobilized to prevent starvation on a wide scale.[2]

England learned much about the whole intricate matter of poor relief in the course of protecting the society from the secondary consequences of such epidemics. One will observe in later pages that in many parishes the first experience in administering poor relief was gained in such periods of local disaster, while in most rural parishes throughout our period the poor laws were never fully applied save under these conditions. In really severe and protracted epidemics collections for relief were ordered to be taken throughout the realm for the sustenance of the poor in the afflicted communities, while poor rates, sometimes doubled or trebled, were imposed in such communities, often by the direct command of the central government.[3] These frightful visitations of epidemic taught the nation much regarding its own resources and disciplined it in the understanding that the poverty bred by plague must be instantly relieved lest even more terrible social consequences should ensue. Indeed, it is not too much to say that men had come to understand that poverty was itself a kind of plague, epidemic in the industrial society. But this plague of poverty, as we shall now observe, men discovered they could control and even possibly cure.

We have endeavoured to treat at least briefly the principal sources of poverty in the period with which we are concerned. They were numerous, they were interrelated, and they raised difficult and complex problems for the English society as it sought to grapple with them. Quite inevitably, we have doubtless sketched a more morbid picture of

---

[1] The statement is based on Creighton, Charles, *A history of epidemics in England* (2 vols., Cambridge, 1891), and Mullett, C. F., *The bubonic plague and England* (Lexington, Kentucky, 1956).

[2] Ewich, Johannes, *Of the duetie of a magistrate in the time of the plague* (L., 1583).

[3] *S.P. Dom.*, 1625, V, 34, for one example.

the age than actually existed. The whole subject of poverty in the early modern period has been too often treated with what can only be described as sentimentality, whether we are moved by the warm eloquence of a Latimer or some historian of our own age. The fact is that widespread poverty had cursed the western society long before the opening of our period and that on balance the expanding economy which marks the whole of our era itself relieved ever larger segments of the society from the fear of abject poverty. Poverty was slowly yielding to a more general prosperity than England had ever known, while an ever-quickening concern of responsible classes of men with the social and moral consequences of disabling poverty was to ensure its relief, if not its cure. Men in our age were moved by new and powerful aspirations for their world and among the strongest and most effective of them was the determination to root out and destroy this ancient evil.

## IV

The Mechanisms

A. SOCIAL REFORM AS AN ASPECT OF PUBLIC ORDER

The whole of the sixteenth century is remarkable for the cautious but progressive experimentation by the state with measures designed to secure the control and relief of poverty. We shall first be concerned with tracing out the development of poor-law legislation brought into a great statutory *corpus* at the very end of the Elizabethan era, though we shall treat this subject relatively briefly since it has been most competently described by authorities in whose debt we stand. Of even greater significance to us, and we believe for the relief of poverty, was a roughly parallel development of the law of charitable trusts and the evolution, and, at the close of the century, the perfection, of the charitable trust as a great and most effective mechanism for those who wished to perpetuate their philanthropic aspirations.

It may safely be said that the steady concern of the Tudors with the problem of poverty flowed from the almost obsessive preoccupation of these great rulers with the question of public order. Henry VII, his son, and his granddaughter all shared an intuitive sensitivity in this matter and were quick to lash out when the slightest threat to public security appeared in any part of the realm. This concern was surely part of their jealous conception of the meaning of sovereignty and their abiding resolution to secure the realm and their throne from the chronic disorder of the preceding century. We may well believe that these monarchs were not moved by sentiments of piety or of pity as they resolutely addressed themselves to the problem of poverty, but they were at the same time deeply persuaded that unrelieved and uncontrolled poverty was the most fertile breeding ground for local disorders which might by a kind of social contagion flame across the whole realm. Hence it was that the immense power of the Crown was steadily addressed to the problem of poverty.

Nor was their view without real justification. We sometimes forget how essentially insecure the Tudor political society really was and how awkwardly ineffective was the central power in dealing with purely local disturbances. Social discontent and occasionally the harsh reality of agrarian poverty were in some measure involved in the Pilgrimage of

Grace, in the rural risings in the South, in Kent, and in Essex in 1549–50, and in Wyatt's rebellion in 1554. There were enclosure riots in Derbyshire and Oxfordshire during the Elizabethan period and similar and more serious disturbances in the Midland counties shortly after the accession of James I. As Professor Tawney has so well said, these disturbances were essentially conservative in their nature, for they protested the whole course of agricultural change, which was producing an ever-increasing national wealth but also extensive poverty among marginal classes of men. The steady sympathy of the Tudors ran with these protesters and the whole weight of legislation sought to remedy their case. But the Tudors moved quickly and savagely when social protest gave way to riotous courses.[1]

B. THE PROBLEM OF VAGRANCY

The most immediate and pressing concern of government during our whole period, but particularly for something more than a century (*ca.* 1520–1640), was with the problem of vagrancy. There is no doubt whatever that vagabondage was widespread, that it was organized, and that it imposed on rural and village communities burdens and dangers with which they could not cope. The evidence is abundantly clear that this class was feared by all elements in the society and that the incredibly harsh penalties laid against it were to a large degree justified. Well before the beginning of the sixteenth century it is evident that these rootless beggars were a social nuisance, that very shortly afterwards they had become 'a chronic plague'.[2] These men comprised a fairly numerous class, the usually careful Harrison estimating their number as 10,000,[3] which seems to have appeared in every western European country at about the same time. They moved across the countryside in droves, swarming in to funerals for doles, infesting cities, and living in many cases by alms supplemented by a beggary tinged with criminality.[4] This class seems principally to have recruited itself from the agricultural displacements of the early sixteenth century, but drew as well from the general and persistent migratory movement, earlier described, from overpopulated rural areas to the rising urban centres. The vagabonds were, then, flotsam from the migratory movements of the period, who had settled into a rootless and wandering life from which they came in time to have no desire to be redeemed. They represented a social phenomenon with which the age was quite unprepared to deal and which it

[1] Tawney, *Agrarian problem*, 343–346.

[2] Leonard, E. M., *The early history of English poor relief* (Cambridge, 1900), 10.

[3] Harrison, William, *An historicall description of the islande of Britayne* (L., 1577), in *New Shakespeare Soc. Pub.*, 6th ser., I, 218.

[4] Gray, *English philanthropy*, 4–5.

could never quite stamp out. There is abundant evidence, too, that this class was to a remarkable degree self-perpetuating and that finally a breed of men, their women and their children, had insulated themselves from a society of which they were no more than a festering part.[1]

As we shall shortly note, the state in a continuous stream of statutes and proclamations sought to stamp out this social evil by penalties which were always harsh and on occasion brutal. These measures, however, enjoyed the universal approbation of all Englishmen of the age because the vagrants were hated with a detestation born of fear. Two contemporary comments, rather widely spaced in time, will perhaps suffice to give some sense of solid and conservative opinion on the matter. Thomas Harman, in a treatise published in 1564 and addressed to the Countess of Shrewsbury, announced that his purpose was 'to acquaynte your goodness with the abhominable, wicked, and detestable debauch of . . . these ragged rabblement of rakehelles that under the pretence of great misery . . . do wyn great almes . . . to the utter deludinge of the good gevers'. Their worst sin is that by their skilful arts the true and worthy poor are defrauded of their proper alms. They plague the state, disorder the whole society, and live as beasts from their own choice.[2] More than a generation later, an equally angry writer held that vagrancy could be stamped out only by punishment and strictly enforced labour. He tells us that unnamed 'counsellors of state' reckoned that there were as many as 80,000 idle vagrants who lived as an immense charge on the whole community. Those who obdurately refused to work should be shipped to sea or simply 'sold to the English plantations, to see whether God will turne their hearts and amend their lives'. This is a class which must be wiped out. It is, he reminded his readers, 'the generall rule of all England . . . to whip and . . . brand the wandring beggars . . . and so mark them with such a note of infamie', while no private person dared give them labour, even forced labour. The problem and its cure, he submitted, was so grave that it could only be met by the whole state using all its resources.[3]

The preoccupation of the sixteenth century with the acute but limited problem of vagrancy resulted in an inevitable but none the less

---

[1] Webb, *Old poor law*, 42–43.

[2] Harman, Thomas, *A caveat . . . for . . . vagabones* [sic] (L., 1564), no pagin.

[3] *Stanley's remedy* (L., 1646), 1–5. Aydelotte believes that vagabondage began to yield to controls after 1572–1575, when the fear of houses of correction did what the danger of severe corporal punishment failed to do (Aydelotte, Frank, *Elizabethan rogues and vagabonds*, Oxford, 1913, 69–70). In the cities, and especially in London, they were skilfully separated from the poor by the close of the century and were either set at work or pressed into the army. It is significant that the rogues and vagabonds, universally feared and hated during the sixteenth century, began after about 1600 to become romantic figures in literature.

most unfortunate confusion as men of the age tried to come to grips with the infinitely larger and more important problem of poverty. Much of Tudor legislation was aimed at vagrancy and the disorders accompanying it, tending to assume that poverty and vagrancy were synonymous. The notion persisted that hungry men were simply invincibly idle men, that poverty was a consequence of a moral fault. It was only slowly that this view yielded to the patent realities of the sixteenth century economy; that men even in Parliament came to understand and then to admit that much poverty, very real and killing poverty, flowed from the economic and social dislocations of the era. Perhaps the most difficult of all the social and legislative admissions which the Tudors had to make was that there was genuine unemployment in the realm and that whole classes of men were from time to time and from place to place literally thrust down well below the line of subsistence by forces with which they were powerless to contend. We shall observe that Parliament and opinion generally came slowly and reluctantly, but at last cleanly, to sort out the kinds of poverty that afflicted the realm and to take measures at least crudely appropriate to the circumstances. Perhaps the most significant of all the social gains of the century was made when it came generally to be understood that not all men who were forced to beg were actually or potentially vagrants of criminal disposition.

1. *The parish as the unit of responsibility*

Principally as a consequence of the fear of vagrancy, too, the whole weight of Tudor legislation and policy was directed towards the sealing off of poverty within the parish in which the poor man was resident. We have seen that both the state and beleaguered communities feared these wandering bands of idle rogues because there was neither administrative nor police machinery competent to deal with them. Vagrancy could neither be cured nor controlled until it could be brought to rest and then dispersed. Hence steady and really heroic efforts were made to declare the parish of birth or residence to be responsible and to force all poor men to remain in their home parish or to return there. This line of policy was both inevitable and correct, though it failed to take into account the fact that the most serious forms of unemployment, of true poverty, were regional. None the less, all the prescriptions of law ran against the man who left his native parish in search of work in another. He must bear a licence from his former employer, he must have funds, and he must be in a position to prove that he was on his way to arranged employment, or the conclusion of law as well as of local opinion was that he was a vagrant.[1] The preoccupation with the evils and dangers of

---

[1] Steinbicker, *Poor-relief*, 164-168; Tawney, R. H., *Agrarian problem*, 272; *Religion and the rise of capitalism* (N.Y., 1926) 217-218; Aschrott, P. F., *The English poor law system* (H. Preston-Thomas, trans.) (L., 1888), 2-3.

vagrancy on occasion almost made the poor laws unworkable, since a single critical and dramatic aspect of a policy question of vast and complex dimensions too consistently coloured men's thinking and decisions. In fact, as we have pointed out, the sixteenth century society was characterized by a really extraordinary mobility, derived its economic strength from this fact, and gained the self-cure of most regional poverty as a consequence. The law stood as an impediment to policy, but the social and economic realities were happily to prevail.

Yet there were sound and old precedents which undergirded Tudor policy in vesting in the parish such a large measure of responsibility for the care and administration of poor relief. In the earlier Middle Ages the tradition prevailed that a portion of all parochial tithes belonged to the poor, though there is little persuasive evidence that the realities ran with the tradition. But in any event the impropriation of tithes to the monastic foundations, with ultimately such disastrous consequences to the parochial clergy, was in full sway by the beginning of the twelfth century and had, broadly speaking, robbed the church of its possibility of meeting the traditional responsibility for the care of the poor long before the advent of the Reformation.[1] These wholesale impropriations, weakening as they did the fabric of parochial life, were steadily opposed by the bishops for a variety of cogent reasons and were as consistently, and as ineffectually, condemned by Parliament, principally on the ground that they robbed the poor of their due rights. Thus in 1391 the House of Commons complained to the King that impropriations were 'cruelly destroying and subtracting from the poor and needy', to which the King responded by ordering that a proper sum should annually be paid by impropriators for the relief of the poor and the support of vicars.[2] These complaints in Parliament were chronic throughout the fifteenth century, particularly since the practice of farming out tithes and rights of presentation on a frankly commercial basis had become widespread and since the endemic poverty with which the sixteenth century had to deal had already made its grim appearance. The bishops were by this time engaged in a defensive action to force from the impropriators some proportion of tithes adequate to pay the priests and maintain the fabric, while Parliament was seeking to find a way to secure a fraction of such tithes for the discharge of an obligation of alms within the parish. One authority, lending careful attention to twelve impropriated parishes in the fifteenth century, suggests that no more than 2 per cent of the whole of tithes were in fact made available

---

[1] *Vide* Coulton's discussion of this question in *Five centuries of religion*, III, 149–171. *Vide* also Ashley, *English economic history*, II, 308–311; Dowell, Stephen, *History of taxes in England* (4 vols., L., 1876–1884), I, 311–312; and Clarke, H. W., *A history of tithes* (L., 1894), 123–124.

[2] *Rot. Parl.* III, 293b; *15 Ric. II, c. 6*; *4 Henry IV, c. 12* (1402).

for alms in the parishes in question.[1] This may very well be near the mark for the possibly 40 per cent of all parishes whose tithes had by this date been swallowed up in monastic and other impropriations. But, none the less, an abiding tradition, or perhaps more accurately, an ideal, remained of parochial responsibility for the care of the poor.

But poor as most English parishes were, hard pressed as they were to maintain the essential services and offices of the church, they turned well before the advent of our period to an assumption of some measure of responsibility for the care of their poor. Relatively few church-wardens' accounts or other useful parochial documents survive from the fifteenth century, but, as we shall point out in our study of the several counties with which we are concerned, the earliest of surviving records make it clear that in most cases at least humble beginnings had been made towards building up modest endowments, of a most bewildering variety, as well as establishing the tradition of outright gifts or bequests for distribution to the poor. Church ales and other 'benefits' were also widely held in late mediaeval times, the profits being employed as income gifts for the succour of the parish poor. It should be emphasized here, as it will be documented later, that these parochial dispositions were very modest indeed, but at the same time they were widespread and had served well before the reign of Henry VIII to establish firmly and generally the tradition of parochial responsibility.

This preparatory stage of parochial development did not alter the essentially ecclesiastical nature of the parish, for this quite informal and rather crude system of alms remained within the structure of ecclesiastical organization and direction. The parish in 1480 had few links indeed with secular government, none at all with the central government, and hence remained free to develop intensely local and customary ways of doing things, subject always to the discipline of a normally remote ecclesiastical authority. An instrument of administration was at hand which the Tudors, geniuses as they were in the arts of administration, arrogated for secular uses and most particularly for the care of the poor. A long series of statutes, beginning in the reign of Henry VIII, assigned increasingly complex and important duties to the parish as a secular unit of administration, while the Elizabethan poor laws were to fix the status of the parish as a unit of secular government. This cumulative body of law established in the parish an organized mechanism for administering the affairs of the poor and entrusted it, ultimately, with the power and responsibility of levying local rates. At the same time, Tudor law most wisely left the parish free to manage these important affairs in its own way, subject only to the supervision of the local justices, with the result that local tradition and custom were respected

[1] Hartridge, R. A. R., *A history of vicarages in the Middle Ages* (Cambridge, 1930), 156 ff.

and maintained. 'The character of some of the measures needed to alleviate the prevailing distress suggested an ecclesiastical organization as an appropriate channel of relief, while the magnitude of the problem necessitated a national scheme controlled by the state.'[1] An entirely new group of trusted and responsible local officials was raised up by Tudor law and policy, thereby extending the fingers of administration from Westminster out to the remotest parishes of the realm. Whether it was intended or not, the inevitable and quick result was the secularization of the parish, and, for that matter, of the realm, for the central government had assumed vast social responsibilities which, in so far as they had been discharged at all in earlier generations, were universally regarded as an aspect of mankind's religious obligations.

C. THE POOR: THE GRADUAL ASSUMPTION OF NATIONAL RESPONSIBILITY

1. Early Tudor legislation

The great *corpus* of Tudor legislation dealing with the complex problems connected with poor relief was formed slowly, cautiously, and experimentally. There had been, it is true, mediaeval precedents stretching back to 1349 when as a consequence of the disorders attending the Black Death, a prohibition was laid against dispensing alms to able-bodied beggars who should rather be compelled to labour for their sustenance.[2] Later in the century, further efforts were made to restrain the migratory tendencies of labour, set in motion by the economic forces attending the deterioration of the manorial system, when in the reign of Richard II statutes of great severity were laid against vagabonds and all migratory beggars and labourers, while stating the obligation to provide relief for those unable to work. All men wishing to leave their place of abode were required to carry certificates, which should be freely granted to those who could prove certain employment in another community.[3] The extreme rigour of these laws against vagabondage, long unenforced and in fact unenforceable, was revived in 1495 when all local authorities from the sheriff down to the petty constables were ordered to search out vagabonds and other idle persons and, after placing them in stocks with only bread and water for three days and two nights, to send them on, each man to repair within six weeks to his own hundred, 'where he last dwelled, or . . . where he is best known or born', and there to remain without begging outside the hundred of his legal residence.[4]

---

[1] Holdsworth, *English law*, IV, 160. This paragraph owes much to Holdsworth's discussion, IV, 151–163.

[2] *36 Edw. III, c. 8.*   [3] *7 Ric. II, c. 5; 12 Ric. II, c. 3, c. 7.*

[4] *11 Henry VII, c. 2.*

The whole problem of poverty was first taken up with some freshness and originality in 1531, without doubt, because of Henry VIII's concern for the state of public order in his realm. England's alliance with France in 1528 had precipitated an economic crisis, since the cloth trade with Flanders was paralysed, resulting in serious unemployment in several populous areas, the situation being further worsened by a general dearth occasioned by bad harvests. The government intervened directly to compel the clothiers in several counties to maintain employment,[1] while strong measures were taken to regulate the price of the food grains. The statute of 1531 stemmed from this dislocation and is important in being the first to separate the worthy poor from the mendicants and to lay down quite different prescriptions for the handling of the two groups. Vagrants and unruly persons were to be whipped and then returned to their homes, while the impotent poor were to be licensed to beg in their own community. Heavy penalties were laid against begging by un-licensed persons, and private citizens were forbidden under pain of fine to extend alms to the unlicensed.[2]

It was soon evident that there were grave deficiencies in the statute of 1531, particularly since no provision whatever was made for the sustenance of the impotent poor save by reducing them to beggary. But that there was considerable discussion of the whole and now pressing problem of poverty is suggested by the draft of a statute apparently prepared in 1531, very possibly by one of the retinue of humanist re-formers surrounding Thomas Cromwell. A recent commentator has pointed out that the preamble of the document carefully distinguished between the 'strong valiaunt beggars' who waste the commonwealth and 'olde sicke lame feble and impotent persones not able to labour for ther livyng . . . dryuen of necessite to procure thalmes and charitie of the people'.[3] Certain of these poor are undoubtedly vicious, but others are poverty-stricken through no personal fault, and still others have had no opportunity ever to become self-supporting. The unknown author then proposed to solve the problem of unemployment by an elaborate programme of public works on roads, harbours, forts, and rivers. Due notice was to be provided throughout the kingdom of work made avail-able, while all able-bodied unemployed were to report for labour at reasonable wages, under pain of arrest and forced work with possible penalty of felony for refusal. This great undertaking was to be financed by royal bounty, rather vaguely defined taxes on income, and contri-butions gathered in the parish churches. There remained the poor who were too old or too infirm to work. The realities here should be accepted,

[1] Leonard, *English poor relief*, 46–48.
[2] *22 Henry VIII, c. 12.*
[3] *Econ. Hist. Rev.*, 2d. ser., VI (1953), 57. Elton follows *BM Royal MSS.* 18, C. vi.

two responsible men being appointed in each parish to separate the helpless from the idle but able-bodied poor. The truly impotent poor were to be sustained by public alms in their parishes, while their children should be apprenticed. Even these poor were to be forbidden to beg in the parish, save that they might be required to solicit gifts of food and alms for distribution by the appointed parochial authorities. Sermons were to be appointed to be read, exhorting each parish to take up the local burden of alms, while the collections made were to be assigned to the properly constituted parish officers for distribution.

The important statute of 1536 evidently owed something to this draft, though it failed to establish the contemplated administrative machinery and completely ignored the certainly grandiose recommendations for a national system of public works.[1] The act of 1536 described all earlier statutes as defective because they had made no provision for the unemployable poor, though it, too, in fact failed most significantly in this very respect. But it did open a long period of legislative and administrative experimentation by ordering the parish or municipal authorities to assume full responsibility for the impotent poor so that they would not be compelled to range abroad as beggars. The law sought to freeze the poor in the local area where they belonged, since all persons save beggars with certificates, mendicant friars, and servants seeking employment with letters explaining the circumstances were subject to its provisions. The children of the poor were to be taught a trade and set on work; alms were to be raised by voluntary means in each parish for the support of the helpless poor; while casual alms, so typical of mediaeval piety, were now declared to be harmful and were carefully restricted. In this statute, the broad outlines of later and more effective legislation begin to emerge, though no adequate provision was made either for financing poor relief or for its administration. The act fails, too, to do more than formally to distinguish between the derelict and the incorrigibly idle and vagrant. Underlying the statute one still sees the stubbornly held persuasion that there were no genuine unemployed and that vagrancy and beggary could be driven from the realm by the application of the criminal law.[2]

That the principal concern of the Crown and of informed political opinion was still with the troubled problem of vagrancy is clearly sug-

[1] Elton believes that the draft may have been prepared by William Marshall, who was close to Cromwell and who had recently translated and published the famous poor-relief ordinances of Ypres (1525–1529) under the title, *The manner of subuention of poore people* (L., 1535).
[2] *27 Henry VIII, c. 25.* For other comments on the statutes, *vide* Ashley, *Economic organisation,* 109; Leonard, *English poor relief,* 53; Holdsworth, *English law,* IV, 392; Nicholls, George, *A history of the English poor law* (3 vols., L., 1898), I, 124; Lipson, E., *The economic history of England* (3 vols., L., 1929–1931), III, 417.

gested by a statute passed in Edward VI's first regnal year. This act introduced really ferocious penalties against the vagrant poor, prescribing servitude for two years upon first conviction and penalties leading to lifelong slavery or a felon's death for those who proved to be intractable. The children of beggars were to be forcibly apprenticed, while if they ran away servitude might be imposed. At the same time, the pious wish was expressed that individual communities would erect houses for the reception of the impotent poor, and the clergy were once more admonished to exhort their flocks to give alms for their care.[1] Very shortly afterwards, Parliament confessed that the rigour of the first Edwardian law outran public sentiment, for, though 'wholesome' in its intent, it had not been enforced because of its 'extremity'. Accordingly, the statute was repealed, and that of *22 Henry VIII, c. 12* was reinstated in its stead.[2] This re-establishment was confirmed late in Edward's reign when the larger question of the plight of the impotent poor was taken under fresh review. This act enjoined the parochial clergy and officers to compile a census of the derelict poor and each year to ensure the election of two able men who should assume responsibility for the collection and distribution of alms. The poor might no longer beg openly, but were to be regarded as the responsibility of the whole parish. A hint of compulsion, of sanctions, followed in the prescription that any person, being able to do so, who refused to make due voluntary contribution for poor relief should, after local exhortation, be reported to the bishop who should then 'indue and persuade by charitable ways and means'.[3]

2. Early Elizabethan legislation

Parliament was moving cautiously in this new and uncharted field of legislation, being most reluctant to accept the consequences of the fact that there were deserving poor who were neither impotent nor vagrant rogues. This extreme caution doubtless arose from the immensely troubled question of how an extensive system of poor relief could be financed. In the last Edwardian statute it is evident that Parliament was edging close indeed to the frontiers of compulsion, being determined to screw the meaning of voluntary alms down just as far as the definition would hold. This statute was passed in a decade characterized by great political and economic dislocations and one, too, in which there was a remarkable body of literature urging social reform on a broad and bold scale. That the public conscience was all but prepared to undertake the burden of responsibility for the sustenance of the poor is, as we shall later see, impressively documented by the marked increase during this decade in the scale and quality of private giving dedicated to this pur-

---

[1] *1 Edw. VI, c. 3* (1547).   [2] *3 and 4 Edw. VI, c. 16* (1549–1550).
[3] *5 and 6 Edw. VI, c. 2* (1551–1552).

pose. Certain classes of men were, then, in fact already assuming social responsibility in a large area into which the state could move only by reluctant but still steady process of change. So, too, the principal commercial cities of the realm, dominated as they were by the mercantile élite who were also setting the pattern of private charitable aspirations, had by 1560 moved out far in advance of the national system. While reserving a full discussion of this remarkable phenomenon to later volumes, it may be said here that London had as early as 1533 arranged a system for the collection and distribution of voluntary alms and had in 1547 boldly embraced the principle of a compulsory poor-rate. Its great charitable institutions and its hospitals likewise date principally from this period, establishing as they did a structure of charitable institutions which was to be imitated all over the realm. Norwich was only a little behind London, for there a compulsory rate was sanctioned in 1549, while in 1570 a most elaborate and successful municipal assault was made on the whole complex problem of urban poverty. So, too, Bristol and York were in the vanguard of experimentation, with numerous other provincial cities in their train.

Still another reluctant step in the direction of an imposed rate was taken early in Elizabeth's reign, when Parliament ordained compulsion after the gentle and charitable pleas of the churchwardens, the clergymen, and the bishop had failed to persuade a stubborn parishioner to contribute voluntarily towards poor relief in his community. The bishop might in that event bind the recalcitrant over to the justices in the amount of £10, while the justices, after earnest efforts to persuade, might then levy a 'sesse' on him which must be paid in weekly instalments under penalty of imprisonment.[1]

The whole body of experience gained over more than a generation in dealing with the problems of the poor, or perhaps more accurately with categories of the poor, was brought under full discussion and to a quite new resolution in a very important codification of law made in 1572. The subject was first debated in Parliament in 1571, when a member attacked the whole law of vagabondage as being so 'over-sharp' as to be unenforceable. This member, Sandys, held that if the justices of the peace would carry out their legal and moral duties, as had been done in Worcestershire, most of the difficulties with which the realm had borne so long in handling vagrants would disappear. He was supported by another member, Knollys, who argued, as subsequent history was to prove with good reason, that the cure of vagrancy was to be gained by instituting houses of correction in every town, which he believed could be maintained by fines laid against the keepers of public houses.[2] That

---

[1] 5 Eliz., c. 3.
[2] D'Ewes, Symonds, The journals of all the parliaments, during the reign of Queen Elizabeth (L., 1682), 165.

this debate had its effect is evident in the act passed in the next year, when for the first time a clear and workable line of definition was drawn between vagabonds (the professional poor) and the impotent poor.[1]

This great act, *14 Eliz., c. 5*, defined as vagrants all able-bodied men without land or master who could not explain the source of their livelihood, all such men who declined to accept employment, and by prescription certain classes of men, such as peddlers, tinkers, and minstrels, who all too often had proved to be vagrants. The law was drawn to run heavily against the 'professional poor', for vagabondage and begging were outlawed under pain of whipping and boring through the ear for a first offence, unless the culprit would enter service for a period of one year, and then as a felony in the event of a third conviction. This class having been separated, the justices were to require in each parish the compilation of a register of the true poor, they being defined as the impotent and the aged, and to arrange for their relief, though always only in the home parish to which they were to repair and where they were to remain. The justices for the counties and mayors for the towns were further empowered to levy rates on all persons in weekly assessments to meet the needs of the lawful poor, with power to remand to gaol those who after due persuasion declined to pay the prescribed tax. All begging was prohibited by law even by the true poor, save in those instances when the parish found itself unable to maintain its own charges, while any tax surpluses remaining were to be paid over to the county which should provide places of correction and forced labour for all rogues and vagabonds. Finally, the act formally established the office of overseers of the poor in each parish, they being appointed annually by the justices of the peace from the substantial householders of the parish. These important local officials were unpaid, might not refuse to serve, and in general were to aid the constables and churchwardens in the discharge of their now greatly enlarged duties. Quite clearly the office regularized formally the important role heretofore played by the collectors of parochial alms required by earlier statutes. These powers and responsibilities were to be steadily increased, and for more than two centuries the overseers were to bear almost sole local responsibility for the care of the poor.[2]

Clear, courageous, and well drawn as was this statute, it still failed to meet the central problem of poverty as it had come to exist in the

[1] Peyton, S. A., 'The houses of correction at Maidstone and Westminster', *Eng. Hist. Rev.*, XLII (1927), 251-261.

[2] *14 Eliz., c. 5*. For significant discussion of this statute, *vide* Leonard, *English poor relief*, 69-72; Webb, Sidney and Beatrice, *English local government* (8 vols., L., 1906-1922), I, 31; Tate, W. E., *The parish chest* (Cambridge, 1946), 30; Cox, J. C., *Three centuries of Derbyshire annals* (2 vols., L., 1890), II, 140; Nicholls, *Poor law*, I, 163; Lipson, *Economic history*, III, 429.

modern world: the undoubted fact that there were genuinely unemployed men seeking work which was not to be found. Such unemployed persons were the special concern of private philanthropy, but it still remained true that a kind of poverty, scarcely admitted by a cautious government, existed which in the want of adequate and rehabilitating policy tended to plunge such men below the line of respectability and to make them either derelict or vagrants. Very cautious progress in facing this reality was made by Parliament in 1575–6, in an act really supplementing the great statute of 1572. This law had several important facets. Charitably disposed men were encouraged to leave property in trust for the founding of houses of correction without having to incur the trouble or expense of securing a licence in mortmain. Bastard children, a troublesome social problem in all parishes, were given some degree of protection by a provision declaring the mother and the reputed father to be wholly responsible for their support. More importantly, it was ordered that stocks of raw materials, wool, flax, iron, and the like, were to be maintained in every city, borough, and market town, on which vagrants could be compelled to work, young people trained in useful and gainful skills, 'and . . . other poore and needye persons being willinge to worcke maye bee set on worcke'. These stocks for the poor were somewhat optimistically supposed to be self-supporting and were to afford employment for those industrious poor who found themselves without occupations. In addition, houses of correction were once more ordered erected in each county for the reception and reform of the truly idle, the incorrigible vagabonds, who were simply to be compelled to submit to forced labour under possible pain of felony.

It may be said, then, that after 1572 England possessed a reasonably comprehensive and possibly a workable statutory provision for a national system of poor relief, but there is no evidence that the plan was given extensive or significant trial. The vast administrative powers of the Privy Council were simply not employed to breathe life into the statute. In the interval 1530–1597 there were eighteen proclamations dealing with various aspects of the problem of the poor, of which all save five were issued in the Elizabethan age. It is instructive to note that thirteen of them were concerned with the vexed problem of vagrancy, while two more ordered administrative action in the closely related subject of wandering beggars. Two conferred governmental blessing on specific charitable undertakings, such as granting permission to collect contributions for hospitals in Wales (1560). Only one, and that rather late in the reign (1593), was significantly concerned with the larger and more pressing problem of poverty, and even it was principally directed towards expelling vagrants and maimed soldiers from London.[1] It is likewise significant that Lambard in his valuable and much used hand-

[1] *An order for avoydyng of all kinds of beggars* (April 17, 1593).

books for justices of the peace and local officials was content with merely sketching the statutory provisions in effect after 1572, without affording any suggestion that there was life in the law or that it was being generally applied.[1]

All too frequently in the Elizabethan period we tend to confuse the careful prescriptions of law with the realities as they may be observed out in the provinces. Thus any student reading and reflecting on the laws as they stood on the statute books for the control of evangelical Roman Catholicism could only conclude that an active and a general persecution of the faith was steadily under way, whereas in fact the laws were seldom rigorously enforced during the reign. Elizabeth and her advisers wished the armoury of law to be well stocked, but they drew on that armoury most prudently. This in part explains the fact that the poor laws of England appear remote and non-existent when we examine the local evidence for their enforcement. The laws were held in reserve against social and economic emergencies of a most compelling order which did not in fact arise until the very close of the reign. It is also most important to observe that the flow of private charitable funds, much being directly addressed to poor relief, was increasing with great rapidity during this reign, with every encouragement from the state, and, as we shall later note, that these ever-swelling funds were almost sufficient to meet the more pressing needs in all save industrialized parishes in particularly difficult periods of economic depression. Most of the Elizabethan era was hopeful, prosperous, and confident, and there is abundant reason for believing that men still hoped that they might be able to grapple with the forces of poverty with their own essentially local strength, a view which the canny and cautious Elizabethan government blessed and fostered. This meant in turn that there was until the closing years of this great reign no insistent, no frightened, demand from the realm at large that the state intervene to implement and strengthen its own statutes; and this was a government ever sensitive to regional and group opinion and advice. The Queen was prepared, was armed, to move, but had no intention of moving into a vast and wholly uncharted area of social responsibility until the stern logic of events should compel her.

At the same time, this period of almost a generation was one in which there was active and most intelligent experimentation in all phases of poor relief in the principal urban centres of the realm. In the main these measures, which will be discussed in some detail in later volumes, were financed by private benefactions from the mercantile aristocracy which had moved with a singular dedication to the attack on the whole complex problem of poverty and the want of opportunity which bred it. In

[1] Lambard, William, *Eirenarcha: or the office of the justices of peace* (L., 1581), and *The duties of constables* (L., 1584).

the last quarter of the century at least twenty-two boroughs were experimenting with stocks for the unemployed poor, many more were actively administering apprenticeship schemes for the children of destitute parents, and bridewells had been established in at least fourteen communities as well as in three or four counties. Many more towns, especially those depending principally on a single dying industry, made systematic attempts to attract new industries with offers of tax abatement and capital assistance. There were many of these local ventures in the Elizabethan period, which when taken together constitute a most impressive annal of the effort of the burgher aristocracy to bring the wasting forces of poverty under control.[1]

3. The great Elizabethan code

a. The problem of poverty reaches a crisis

But the problem of poverty was in truth national and the resilient government, informed as it was by long legislative experimentation and the vast body of experience accumulated by private charity, stood ready to embrace resolute policy when regional and private devices should be unable to deal with emergency on a national scale. This emergency developed late in the Queen's reign. In 1596 Edward Hext, a respected justice of the peace in Somerset and a Member of Parliament, warned Lord Burghley that even rural communities could no longer cope with their social and economic responsibilities. In the recent quarter sessions in his county, 183 idle and unemployed poor had been set at liberty

[1] Though the discussion of these municipal undertakings is more properly reserved for later volumes, we might here mention at least one very interesting document which reveals the advanced social thinking and the deep concern of London 'for the reliefe of the poore so as they shall not nede to randge abroade in begginge'. These 'orders' provided that in each ward a 'grave and godlie man' be chosen as treasurer to receive legacies and gifts for the poor quite beyond the amounts raised by rates in the various parishes. Distributions were to be made by eight collectors in each ward. A careful census of the poor was to be made and kept, setting out the number who were for whatever reasons impotent, as well as to note those who 'can by labour get something to their relief', in order accurately to assess the need. All preachers were to exhort their flocks to contribute towards the maintenance of a stock for the poor, 'to the end that no poor should stray abroad begging'. Further, in every ward from £50 to £60 was to be made available 'by suche as may be conferred [?] withall havinge habillytie to set the poore on worke', these funds also to be raised by private subscription. The good work which London had undertaken, it was urged on the Council, would be of no effect unless means were found to rid the outlying urban and suburban areas of the wandering poor who so persistently filtered into London, recognizing perhaps unconsciously that the problem with which London grappled so intelligently and vigorously was in fact national in scope and required remedies nationally imposed. (*S.P. Dom.*, 1577 [?] CXX, 50.)

when it appeared that no one could be found who would take them into service. The social deterioration of these men had proceeded so far, 'by reason their sinews are so benumbed and stiff through idleness that as their limbs being put to any hard labour, will grieve them above measure: so as they will rather hazard their lives than work'. These men, Hext strongly argued, were derelict, for as a magistrate he had observed that they would rather risk their lives on a false plea of felony than be sent to a house of correction, even when one was available. In Somerset alone, £73 had been spent in sustaining these people in gaol at 6d a man. Nor will juries any longer convict really dangerous vagrants for felony, for 'most commonly the most simple country man and woman . . . are of opinion that they would not procure any man's death for all the goods in the world'.[1] Hext wrote from a region in which real suffering was widespread and from near a locality in Oxfordshire where the magistrates were dealing with what can only be described as insurrection induced by poverty. He wrote as a responsible man whose fright and perplexity still animate his letters. This was one of the many advices that the Queen and her Council were receiving in this troubled year, and the Tudors acted instantly when they sensed even the danger of disorder abroad in the realm.

In 1594 a severe economic depression began in England, on this occasion spreading through both urban and agricultural regions. There were heavy and unseasonable rains for some years beginning in 1594, with the result that harvests were poor for five consecutive years. The whole economy was in any event strained by the continuing war with Spain. The worst year was 1596, when it seems certain that the dearth of necessaries was so great, prices so high, and unemployment so general that numerous regions were really threatened by famine.[2] Despite the sternest efforts of the government to control prices and to relieve communities where the scarcities were greatest, the price of bread grains rose wildly to such figures as 9s a bushel for wheat in Devon in midsummer, 10s a bushel in London, 12s to 15s in Bristol, and in Shrewsbury to 18s.[3] Suffering was widespread, responsible magistrates such as Hext were frightened, and there is evidence that there were instances of outright starvation in England in the black summer of 1596. The government moved with great vigour in its efforts to prevent hoarding, to move supplies, and to control prices, while the gentry were ordered to depart from London to their estates to assume their responsibilities for hospitality and the maintenance of public order. The clergy were instructed to preach against forestalling and to encourage almsgiving,

[1] Strype, John, Annals of the Reformation (4 vols., L., 1725–1731), IV, 255–304.

[2] Strype, Annals, IV, 294–295; Camden, William, The history of the . . . Princess Elizabeth (L., 1688), 506; Stow, John, Annals (L., 1631), 783.

[3] Cheyney, E. P., History of England (2 vols., L., 1926), II. 6–8.

while observing two fast days each week and encouraging their congregations to follow their example.[1] Very rigid prohibitions were laid down against the export of any food-stuffs, while huge importations of grain were made from abroad, principally, it may be observed, by charitably disposed merchants, the enormous total of 888,660 bushels clearing the port of London alone in a period of seven months in 1596–1597.[2]

The turbulence so feared by the Tudors spread across the realm.in the wake of hunger. Bread riots occurred in the capital in 1595, while grain shipments in Norfolk were attacked by rioters in three communities. We have seen that the magistrates of Somerset were deeply troubled in 1596, the severity of their course being suggested by the fact that forty persons were put to death in the county upon conviction for felonies. The Privy Council was most gravely concerned, particularly when evidence of a planned uprising in Oxfordshire was disclosed.The ringleaders, Bartholomew Steere, a carpenter, and about twenty others, mostly artisans and labourers, were speedily arrested and executed, but the government feared that spontaneous insurrections might break out in almost any part of the realm. The government was likewise compelled by its observation and experience during these unhappy months to recognize that there were many thousands of able-bodied and wholly responsible men, in both urban and rural areas, who were desperately anxious to work for whom no work could be provided.[3] Harsh but persuasive reality had at last driven lines of separation and recognition among the several classes of poor—the genuinely unemployed, the impotent, and the vagrant. In two full generations Parliament had been moving grudgingly and slowly towards this admission which undergirds the great legislative measures of 1597–1601.

b. *The great debate*

When Parliament was convened in October, 1597, it passed quickly to a full debate of the whole problem of poverty and its relief. While, unfortunately, only sparse records of this great discussion have survived, it is clear indeed that the members had come up to Westminster gravely concerned by the recent, and current, disturbances and with an almost intuitive sense that they must come to grips with a pervading social problem which could in critical periods threaten the stability of the basic institutions of the nation. It is most significant that the dominant landed interest in the House of Commons moved with such enlightened and determined vigour to lay great responsibilities on themselves and on their land, though it was generally recognized that the poverty

[1] *Acts of the Privy Council* [1596–1597] n.s., XXVI (L., 1902) 95, 96, 380–383; Strype, John, *The life and acts of John Whitgift* (L., 1718), 490.

[2] Cheyney, *History of England*, II, 19.

[3] Ashley, *Economic organisation*, 110.

flowing from unemployment was principally an industrial, an urban, phenomenon.[1] All aspects of the problem of poverty were fully and intelligently debated. Sir Francis Bacon was especially concerned with the blighting effect of enclosures, which he said bred idleness, the decay of tillage, grievous poverty, and a substantial impoverishment of the realm.[2] Another member spoke with great eloquence of 'the extream and miserable estate of the godly and honest sort of the poor subjects of this realm', the undoubted sufferings and restlessness of whom had served so to move the House to action.[3] Sir Francis Hastings complained that far too much time and consideration were being given to the old and worn subjects of enclosures and tillage, to the neglect of the more pertinent and pressing problems of vagrancy and the plight of the true poor.[4] In all, seventeen separate bills were introduced, of which eleven dealt quite specifically with the problem of poor relief,[5] the confused legislative process being finally ordered and disciplined by the appointment of a powerful committee for consideration which included such parliamentary leaders as Sir Francis Bacon, Sir Nicholas Bacon, Sir Thomas Cecil, Sir Robert Wroth, a most persuaded proponent of bold legislation, and Edward Hext, whose earlier letter to the Privy Council on the deteriorating situation in Somerset has already been cited.

Meanwhile, in the Lords earnest debate ranged over these same grave matters, the preparation of legislation being referred to a committee of eminent peers which included Lord Burghley and Archbishop Whitgift. One bill, having been heavily amended in the House of Lords, was sent down to the Commons, a committee of the lower house, of which Sir Walter Raleigh was the spokesman, moving angrily to an obscure claim of privilege when the Lords somewhat peremptorily declined the usual form of conference for the reconciliation of differences in detail.[6] This bill was accordingly rejected by the Commons by a vote of 106 to 66, just as the flow of the great measures codifying and extending the poor law began to reach the floor from the committee of the Commons which had been meeting in Middle Temple Hall.[7]

c. *The framing of the law*

The first of this notable and carefully articulated series of statutes sought to deal severely and finally with the 'professional poor', the rogues, vagabonds, and sturdy beggars with whom the central government and Parliament had struggled so manfully for three generations. The act empowered the justices of the peace to erect houses of correction

[1] Garnier, *English landed interest*, 284.
[2] D'Ewes, *Journals*, 551.
[3] *Ibid.*, 552.
[4] *Ibid.*, 555.
[5] *Ibid.*, 561.
[6] *Ibid.*, 579–582.
[7] Rowse, *England of Elizabeth*, 355.

for this segment of the poor in each county and city in the realm. Vagabondage was once more carefully and accurately defined, while such persons were to be arrested, whipped until bloody, and then returned by a direct route to the parish of their birth or legal residence. They were to be whipped again in every parish where they tarried. The law further provided that upon reaching their home parish they were to be placed in service, if able-bodied; committed to gaol or a convenient house of correction if need be; and if adjudged incapacitated they were to be lodged in an almshouse. All really incorrigible and dangerous vagabonds were to be banished 'out of this realm' or committed 'perpetually to the galleys of this realm', and were to suffer death as felons if they should return.[1]

The old and troubled question of agrarian change and dislocation was treated in two connected statutes which dealt fully and somewhat sentimentally with a problem in fact no longer particularly urgent because tillage was tending to replace grazing in most parts of England. None the less, the *Act against the decaying of towns and houses of husbandry* recited the decay of husbandry that had occurred, whereby in many regions 'a great number of poor people are become wanderers, idle and loose, which is the cause of infinite inconvenience'. It was accordingly ordered that, castles and manor houses excepted, any house 'that now hath or heretofore hath had' twenty acres or more of land attached was to be 'adjudged a house of husbandry forever'. All such houses 'decayed or wasted' since the beginning of the reign, or half the number if forty acres of land were provided, were to be restored and so maintained. It was further and somewhat weakly stipulated that the assize justices were to be empowered 'to inquire of, hear and determine all said defaults and offences'.[2]

The related *Act for the maintenance of husbandry and tillage* in a magnificently eloquent preamble set forth the view that the strength and well-being of the realm are 'greatly upheld and advanced by the maintenance of the plough and tillage, being the occasion of the increase and multiplying of people . . . [and] a principal means that people are set on work and thereby withdrawn from idleness, drunkenness, unlawful gains, and all other lewd practices'. By tillage, too, the people were 'preserved from extreme poverty' and the wealth of the state healthfully 'dispersed and distributed in many hands . . . for the service of the realm'. The act recited the steady effort of law and policy since Henrician times to maintain 'a certain quantity and proportion of land' permanently in tillage, but confessed that depopulations attending 'turning tillage into pasture' had continued, to the great detriment of the whole

[1] *39 Eliz.*, *c. 4* (continued as *43 Eliz.*, *c. 9*; amended by *1 Jac. I*, *c. 7*; continued by *1 Jac. I*, *c. 25* and *21 Jac. I*, *c. 28*).
[2] *39 Eliz.*, *c. 1* (continued by *43 Eliz.*, *c. 9*; *1 Jac. I*, *c. 25*).

society. Accordingly, it was ordered that all grazing lands which were arable for a period of twelve years continuously prior to 1558 should before May 1, 1599 be restored to tillage and so maintained, while existing tillage land, which had been so employed for twelve years past, might under no circumstance be converted to grazing.[1]

The acts thus far discussed had sought to proscribe vagabondage and incorrigible idleness by cleanly separating out the vagrants and then in related statutes to protect and preserve an agrarian system which had rather more nostalgic meaning than economic reality. The processes of rural change, as we have seen, were slow, immutable, and on balance distinctly salutary, though they had for many years past caused social dislocations, migratory movements, and some real suffering among marginal labour groups. The intent of this last statute was to freeze the agrarian economy as it existed at the beginning of the century and to lend as effective protection as might be possible to the rural poor, to the landless men. Sharp questions were raised in Parliament regarding the efficacy of this legislation, but it was passed by men against whose own self-interest its prescription ran, surely with full knowledge that it was unenforceable.

The great central statute in this Elizabethan code of social legislation was entitled simply *An act for the relief of the poor*. This act contained little that was really novel or bold, but it gathered the legislative and administrative experience of almost a century in a most carefully drafted instrument which was meant to deal honestly and competently with a grave social problem heretofore never faced quite squarely. It is significant that the act bears no pious and eloquent Elizabethan preamble, but moves almost brusquely to the heart of the matter by establishing and defining the duties of the overseers of the poor. In every parish the churchwardens and 'four other substantial householders' should as overseers have power, with the consent of two or more justices, to set at work children whose parents could not provide for them, as well as all other persons 'having no means to maintain them'. Power was conferred to raise by the 'taxation of every inhabitant and every occupier of lands in the . . . parish' amounts sufficient to provide a convenient stock of commodities on which the poor should be set at work and also 'for the necessary relief of the lame, impotent, old, blind, and such other among them being poor and not able to work', as well as to bind out poor children as apprentices and do 'all other things' necessary to give such relief as might be required.

This provision was clear, unequivocal, and legally sufficient. It recognized the fact of unemployment and it made specific provision for the care and sustenance of the unemployable. The statute went on very carefully to outline the functions and responsibilities of the overseers,

[1] *39 Eliz.*, c. *2* (continued by *43 Eliz.*, c. *9*; *1 Jac. I*, c. *25*).

on whom it laid such heavy and, as time was to show, permanent tasks. They were required to meet monthly and each year should submit to two justices of the peace a full account of their activities and finances, a fine of £1 being imposed for unexcused absences from each monthly meeting or for being negligent in duty. If the justices 'do perceive' that any parish was economically unable to raise the necessary sums by taxation, the required rates should then be spread over the hundred, and if that should not prove sufficient, the justices in quarter sessions were instructed to rate other parishes of the county in order to ensure the purposes of the statute. Power was given to distrain and sell the goods of any rated inhabitant of a parish, while 'in defect of such distress' any two justices of the peace might commit such a recalcitrant person to prison until his tax was paid. The overseers were likewise vested with power to bind any poor boy as an apprentice until he had reached the age of twenty-four and any girl until she was twenty-one years of age. Suitable dwelling places for the poor might be built with funds raised by taxation. The parish, having been vested with these extensive powers and responsibilities, was to rid itself completely and forever of beggary, since it was ordered that 'no person shall go wandring abroad and beg in any place whatsoever, by licence or without, upon pain to be taken and punished as a rogue', save only for poor inhabitants of a parish who might, upon the determination of the overseers, be permitted within that parish to 'ask relief of victuals'. It was further provided that rated sums were to be levied on all parishes by the justices for the relief of prisoners of the King's Bench and Marshalsea, and support should be given to such almshouses as might need aid in each county. If, after these numerous obligations had been discharged, any surplus remained in the funds of the county, the justices in quarter session should bestow the amount for such charitable needs as they might find desirable.[1]

This great statute, passed to relieve an economic crisis already improving, though containing little that was either bold or original, clearly defined and cleanly delineated the nature of responsibility for the unemployed and the unemployable poor. It was amended in unimportant details in 1601 and then remained, with numerous reaffirmations and quite minor amendments, the central law of the land relating to poor relief for very nearly two and one-half centuries. It fixed the parish as the unit of ultimate responsibility not only because the facts regarding poverty were best known there, but probably more importantly, because the whole scheme of poor relief rested on the assumption that a stable society, a non-migratory society, offered fewer social perils to the state. An efficient and an important parochial mechanism for the administration of a wide area of social responsibility had likewise been established by law, linked. however, by carefully graduated degrees with the

[1] 39 Eliz., c. 3.

county and ultimately to Westminster itself. The act also represents the complete vesting of charitable responsibility in secular hands—neither church nor churchman is mentioned in the law—thus finally marking the completion of a translation of responsibility which, as we shall later observe in detail, had been steadily in progress from the beginning of our period. One of the most significant of all the steps in the social history of the modern world had been taken with, we believe, a full understanding of the meaning of what had been done.[1]

There remain two more statutes which completed the great design of Tudor social legislation gathered into a code by Parliament in 1597. Both these laws lend emphasis to the fact that the government and the dominant political classes in Parliament acknowledged the immense responsibility already being assumed by private charity in the care of the poor and sought means which would substantially encourage and enlarge the flow of such funds. As we shall later point out, the major responsibility continued to be borne by ever-expanding charitable endowments during the whole of our period, the great legislative undertakings having been regarded essentially as emergency measures to be employed when periods of economic crisis imposed greater burdens than private funds and voluntary institutions could assume. The greater of these statutes, *39 Eliz., c. 10* and *43 Eliz., c. 4*, which had the effect of creating and defining the law of charitable trusts, we must reserve for consideration in a more appropriate connection.[2] The *Act for erecting of hospitals or abiding and working houses for the poor* was in its effect supplementary, since it had as its purpose the encouragement of private benefactors who might wish to found and endow almshouses, houses of correction, and similar institutions for the care of the derelict or the social rehabilitation of the unfortunate. Power was given to such donors to give or bequeath lands or other resources in fee simple by the uncomplicated action of enrolling a deed in Chancery without the necessity of securing a special royal licence or act of Parliament to achieve the incorporation. It was further provided that such foundations must be effectively endowed with property of the clear annual value of at least £10.[3]

[1] For comment on the act, *vide* Cheyney, *History of England*, II, 270, 413; Webb, *Old poor law*, 61–65; Burn, Richard, *The history of the poor laws* (L., 1764), 104–134; Coate, Mary, *Social life in Stuart England* (L., 1924), 114–115; Eden, *State of the poor*, 19–20; Wickwar, W. H. and K. M., *The social services* (L., 1936), 21–23; Slater, *Poverty and the state*, 53–56; Aschrott, *English poor law*, 6–8; Hník, F. M., *The philanthropic motive in Christianity* (M. and R. Weatherall, trans.) (Oxford, 1938), 225–226.   [2] *Vide post*, 109–117.

[3] *39 Eliz., c. 5*. This statute was made permanent by *21 Jac. I, c. 1*: 'That all hospitals, maisons de diew, and abiding places for the poor, lame, maimed or impotent people or houses or correction at any time hereafter to be founded, shall be incorporated and have perpetual succession' (*House of Lords MSS.*, February 24, 1623–4).

d. *Pride of achievement*

The passage of the legislation of 1597 and its reaffirmation in the statutes of 1601 excited general interest and popular discussion which affords us some sense of how the great steps taken were viewed and understood by contemporaries. We may draw on two of these writings for some illustrations of public sentiment. Henry Arthington, writing in 1597, submitted that the care of the poor had throughout Scripture been the work of the good man. Yet for too long the poor of England have not been properly regarded. It is true, he maintained, that most poor men were themselves at fault, for they 'woulde not worke . . . in the time of abundance' and have been great wasters. Nor have private men met their obligations of charity fully, for 'some are willing to supply their wants, and do it in some places to God's glorie and their own comfort, but others (alas) are too hardhearted'. Neither law nor the process of charity has operated evenly in England, there being many regions where the scantest of responsibility is taken and other communities, like his own Wakefield, where, though 'the poor be . . . many and needy', none is left to penury and want.

Further, Arthington maintained, there are most evidently several kinds of poor men among whom careful discrimination must be made, if measures for relief are not to do more harm than good. There are first of all the impotent poor, those who simply cannot support themselves because of age, sickness, bodily injury, or extreme youth. 'All these . . . must be maintained in the whole.' Far more difficult to sort out and assist are the poor who are quite able to work, for they fall into numerous groups and tend to shift from one group to another. Those who are able and willing to support themselves but simply cannot find employment must be assisted, as, the writer seems to suggest, should those who 'bee overcharged with children' and who must support them by physical labour, and 'such as fall to decay in their workes'. But the beggars, the idle, the wasters deserve no help and must be firmly dealt with because they menace the whole society and consume resources needed for the help of the true poor. Writing very shortly before the passage of the great poor law, Arthington maintained that there were already in force sufficient and wholly worthy statutes for the relief of the great penury of the time, if they were rigorously enforced. He believed, in fact, that only a moral reformation which brought all men back into their parish churches, which softened the hearts of the rackers of rents, the enclosers, and the engrossers would provide the moral climate in which poverty might be relieved and very possibly cured.[1]

Quite different from Arthington's somewhat cloudy sentimentality and pious confusion were the pragmatic jottings in an anonymous

---

[1] Arthington, *Provision for the poore*, no pagin.

pamphlet entitled *An ease for overseers of the poore*, designed, the author says, to assist these officers in their new and important tasks. There is much that is statutory and as much that is gratuitous in this interesting work. England, he held, has found it necessary to legislate charity because 'men in this iron age have no devotion to doe good, [for] it falleth out, that where one dies as a benefactor to a town-stocke, many thousands die and bequeath all to their own stocke'.[1] It is still to be hoped that private charity can again be persuaded to assume its proper burdens. In the good old days of Edward VI, the author maintained with blissful historical inaccuracy, men did give 'according to their degrees and devotions', but in this 'obdurate age of ours, neither godly perswasions of the pastors, or pitifull exclamations of the poore, can move any to mercie: unless there were a lawe made to compell them'.[2] Until godly and charitable times have been restored, then, the overseers and their parishes must carry out the prescribed work of relieving the poor.

The overseers must be men of some wealth and station who may command the wholesome respect of the poor. All rates should be assessed carefully according to wealth and should be instantly discontinued in time of plenty, for 'contributions are not given to make or multiplie poore but to mitigate poverty'.[3] In so far as possible local employers, such as clothiers, should be assisted in accepting apprentices and temporary helpers, rather than undertaking to create work with elaborate and expensive stocks of materials. The statutes wisely limit stocks to simple commodities that can be worked by relatively unskilled men and women, and the overseers should use every inducement to have the finished goods sold locally, 'seeing it is for the benefit of their towne'.[4]

Then there are the impotent poor who must be provided with full care, including the very old, the very young, the blind, the dumb, the idiots, and the sick. The duty to these helpless people is clear and it is now statutory, but even so money is to be given them only as a last resort, for 'such as be chargeable to the towne which can live in some measure either of their labours or otherwise, are no better than theeves; for they take it from others, to whome it justly belongeth and those which give it, are guiltie as accessaries with them, if they knowe they may forbeare it'.[5] Every effort should be made to encourage gifts and bequests to ease the burdens of both the poor and the parish. At last vagrancy and idleness have really been proscribed by law, with the result that now those who give will know that they aid in relieving the really worthy poor. Rates should be assessed with great caution and in terms of the exact needs of the poor, for if too much is given 'you

[1] *An ease for overseers of the poore* (Cambridge, 1601), 16–17.   [2] *Ibid.*, 22.
[3] *Ibid.*, 15.   [4] *Ibid.*, 21.   [5] *Ibid.*, 26.

shall increase the number', since 'to enquire after poore is the next way to procure poore'.[1] England, the author evidently believed, could now face the future with cautious optimism, since agencies for reformation as well as relief had been competently fashioned and universally accepted.

e. Problems of administration

The knowledgeable though unknown author of *An ease for overseers* confessed that the problem of levying rates fairly within each parish was difficult, and he might well have added, the statute itself was probably purposefully vague in laying down the method. For the act of 1597/1601 opened up an almost wholly uncharted area of local taxation. The statute provided that the parish would 'raise weekly or otherwise, by taxations of every inhabitant, parson, vicar and other, and every occupier of landed houses tithes impropriate or impropriations of tithes, colemynos or saleable underwoods' such sums as might be required to give effect to the law's requirement. It is clear that the churchwardens and overseers were to set the rates under the supervision of the justices of the peace; power to collect by distraint was provided; and an appeal against an improper assessment might be taken to the justices of the peace in their quarter sessions. This was as far as the statutory instructions went, possibly because Parliament fully understood the great variety of local traditions and experience in raising modest sums for parochial uses.

Parliament also clearly intended that these assistance moneys should be raised by rates, that is, by the determination of an aggregate sum by competent authorities in each parish to be raised by dividing the total by some reasonable assessment among those subject to taxation. Something like this plan had been followed as early as 1531 when the Statute of Bridges[2] arranged for the assessment of lump sums on particular communities, leaving it to local authority and common sense to apportion the tax among the inhabitants. Somewhat more precise instructions were given in an act in the next year for raising money in twenty-five counties for the building of gaols, when the tax was to be levied on residents in proportion to the value of their income.[3] It seems certain, too, that Parliament intended in the poor law of 1572 that assessments should be made in relation to the wealth, the ability, of the inhabitants, rather than by the easier device of taxing the value of the land, or premises, occupied by the person being rated.[4] In most parishes in the older and the institutionally mature parts of the realm there was also long and

---

[1] *An ease for overseers of the poore*, 29.   [2] *22 Henry VIII, c. 5.*
[3] *23 Henry VIII, c. 2.*
[4] Cannan, Edwin, *History of local rates in England* (L., 1912), 54, 68–69.

relevant experience in levying church rates at vestry meetings, which by a not unreasonable extension was employed for the review if not the assessment of poor-rates. In such parishes the rates were levied by the churchwardens, overseers, and constables, subject to the review of the vestry, which also exercised a review of the details of the expenditures incurred under the statute. The vestry likewise exerted a very real, if indirect, control over the mechanism of taxation, since it also chose the churchwardens and in most cases the overseers, while, of course, the whole disposition was subject to the review of the justices of the peace.[1] That this was the method usually employed is further suggested by the fact that the records of assessments and outlays are most commonly to be found mingled with other parochial records.

The statute was imprecise with respect to both the administration of the assessment and the basis of taxation, though it carefully included all 'inhabitants' and all 'occupiers' of property in the parish. The whole question of the basis of the taxation had in fact to be adjudicated, a stream of appeals and complaints flowing from the parishes where the act was given local effect. Indeed, one of the most reliable ways of determining when a parish was first taxed under the poor law is to watch carefully for the arrival of the first angry protestations in the quarter-sessions records of the county. In most communities the tendency was for the overseers to lay the assessments by the value of pound rents, that is, by 'levies and payments according to the true value of the lands' of the parish, which of course threw the burden of taxation rather more on the occupiers of real property than on the owners. Lambard discussed the problem at length in his 1599 edition of the *Eirenarcha*, though he offered no clear instructions to the many overseers who bought his book because no body of judicial decisions had as yet accumulated. The even more ubiquitous *Countrey justice*, in commenting on the problem of the rating base a generation later, concluded, we think correctly, that Parliament intended two merged systems of assessment: on every inhabitant who could be rated at all, and on the known annual value of all property within the parish.[2] This view likewise enjoyed the cautious support of Sir Robert Heath, the Chief Justice, who in 1633 prepared an informal opinion to be used by the judges on circuit in dealing with the innumerable questions advanced by the uncertain and harassed justices of the peace. It was Heath's view that all land in each parish was to be taxed at a level rate, 'that

[1] Tate, *Parish chest*, 14-17.

[2] Dalton, Michael, *The countrey justice* (L., 1635), 94: 'In these taxations there must consideration be had, first to equality and then to estates. Equality, that men be equally rated with their neighbours, and according to an equal proportion. Estates, that men be rated according to their estates of goods known, or according to the known yearly value of their lands, farms, or occupyings, and not by estimation, supposition, or report.'

there may be an addition for the personal visible ability of the parishioners within that parish' which the overseers should take fully into account
in preparing the schedule of rates.

The fact is that each parish was left with almost complete autonomy
in determining not only the method by which the rates should be levied
and expended, but, and more importantly, whether one should be
ordered at all. We shall later point out that relatively few parishes felt
it necessary to apply this statute for almost a generation after its passage and that a great many never did so before the Restoration. The
judges and the justices of the peace permitted a quite bewildering
variety of local and traditional usages to persist among those parishes
which were rated, tending to intervene only on angry appeal from a
taxpayer and then almost invariably lending support to the local
authorities whose harassed life and responsibility commanded their
sympathy. This was doubtless sound practice, and it was certainly as
Parliament meant it to be. No systematic body of judicial decisions on
the matter of ratings under the statute is to be found prior to the
restoration of the monarchy.[1]

The *corpus* of law dealing with the whole complex range of problems
that centres around poverty stood very nearly complete for our period,
and, indeed, for a very long time afterwards, with the passage of the
great measures at the close of Queen Elizabeth's reign. A famous divine,
discussing the evils of beggary and vagabondage, could well speak for
the realm in the conviction that this legislation was 'in substance the
very lawe of God', which should never be repealed.[2] We shall now review briefly the refinements and additions made to the fabric of the
poor laws during the remainder of our era, leaving to later pages a discussion of the far more important subject of the administration and
enforcement of the laws.[3]

4. *Seventeenth century glosses on the law*

Even James I, so often nervously critical of the accomplishments of
his great predecessor, found little room for improvement on the code
which was his inheritance. A statute in his first regnal year provided
that in the event of plague a special rate might be levied not only on the

---

[1] An unsigned memorandum in the State Papers (1648–1649) complains of the
vagueness of the wording of *43 Eliz.*, *c. 2*. The writer suggested that it ought to
be amended significantly to make it clear that taxation should be based on the
value of property which any person held or occupied and also on the basis of his
known ability to pay. It should, however, be made clear that no man would be
taxed according to his 'ability' save in that parish where he maintained his chief
habitation. (*S.P. Dom.*, 1648–1649 [undated], DXX, 52).

[2] Perkins, William, *Works newly corrected according to his owne copies* (Cambridge, 1605), 910.

[3] *Vide post*, 126–142.

affected parish but likewise on the surrounding area.[1] A few years later, in 1609–1610, a bill which had failed of passage in 1597 was enacted into law requiring the justice of the peace to erect a house of correction in each county by rates, under penalty of a fine of £5 to be laid on each defaulting magistrate. The existing and fully competent laws against idle and disorderly persons were to be rigorously enforced, such vagabonds and malingerers to be placed in the contemplated houses of correction by the justices meeting in quarter-session, and while held there for amendment 'in no sort to be chargeable to the county for any allowance . . . but [to] have such allowance as they shall deserve by their own labour and work'.[2] The law cleanly and deliberately distinguished between the unemployed poor and the invincibly idle, whom earlier legislation had mixed in houses of correction with most unfortunate consequences. A further act was passed in 1621 which sought most severely to restrain agrarian migration to urban centres by requiring all persons who 'shall come to any city or town to dwell' to exhibit an estate to the value of £2 p.a. or goods to the worth of £5, unless they had served as apprentices in an 'art, mystery or manual occupation' for a term of at least seven years.[3] All persons removing to urban communities in violation of these provisions were to be returned at once to the parish of their origin. Shortly afterwards, an act of Parliament was passed lending further encouragement to those who desired to found and endow almshouses and houses of correction by specifying quite simple procedures of foundation and ensuring perpetuity to these incorporations.[4]

Charles I added no legislation of importance to the existing code of poor laws, though, as we shall later observe, the first really serious move to secure their administration was to be made in a remarkable and sustained effort in the course of his reign. In the early sessions of the Long Parliament, it is true, an interesting bill was drafted for the reform and administration of charitable institutions generally, though it seems never to have emerged from the committee of peers to which it was assigned in January, 1641, for further consideration. The draft memorandum pointed out that possible donors of endowments for almshouses, houses of correction, free schools, and other charitable institutions were discouraged because all too often their lands were leased out for very long terms in a time when 'the prices of all things [are] now risen above the rates of former ages'. It was accordingly proposed that no lease of property bearing a charitable use might be made for a term of more than twenty-one years or for three lives 'for a yearly rent of a full two-thirds of the true yearly value' of the property thus granted. It was further ordered that no master, governor, or adminis-

---

[1] 1 Jac. I, c. 31.
[2] 7 Jac. I, c. 4.
[3] Draft in House of Lords MSS., April 30, 1621.
[4] 21 Jac. I, c. 1.

trator of a charitable foundation might enjoy a stipend in excess of £30 p.a. or, if it be less, a sixth part of the total revenues, unless otherwise specifically appointed by the donor.[1]

A far more ambitious proposal was laid before the House of Lords which contemplated the revision and the redrafting of the Elizabethan poor laws. This memorandum was prepared by William Steele, a young lawyer who was subsequently to serve as Recorder of London and Lord Chancellor of Ireland. There is no evidence that this well-articulated proposal ever received serious legislative attention, but it none the less deserves at least brief comment here for the boldness and thoroughness of its recommendations. Basically, Steele proposed a shifting in the centre of gravity of social responsibility from the parish to the county, from the overseers to the justices of the peace, while leaving intact the administrative and taxing mechanism of the parish. A public stock, administered by a treasurer to be chosen by the general session of the justices, was to be created in each county, funds being supplied by taxation ordered by the justices, by all fines and penalties levied within the county, by contributions and bequests given for the use, and by any profits that might accrue from the workhouses of the county. The justices were in effect to be constituted as a charitable corporation and were within the county to have all powers heretofore vested in commissions of charitable uses for enforcing the charitable responsibilities imposed upon feoffees.

The county stock should be prudently employed for the erecting and maintenance of workhouses, for the support of derelict sailors and soldiers, and for providing stocks of goods on which the unemployed and needy might be set at useful and gainful employment. Rewards were to be paid from the stock for the apprehension of vagabonds and felons, while the proper charges of the justices, the overseers, and constables were also to be met from this treasury. The taxing power of the parish for the care of its poor was not to be disturbed, though the county would take over many of the responsibilities heretofore borne by the local unit. The overseers were to be directly responsible to the justices of the peace and the latter to the assize justices. Some assessment should be laid on all persons able to make contribution, and those not making payments should automatically be classified as poor who might be compelled to work. The old, the impotent, and the very young should, when there was clear need, be maintained by parish rates. The hopeless poor, then, were to be supported by the parish, the able-bodied but unemployed poor were to be assisted by works administered by the county, and 'all persons that can give no good account for their manner of living' and all wandering beggars were upon conviction to be sent to a county workhouse for a term of years or longer. Begging was

---

[1] *House of Lords MSS.*, January 2, 1640–1.

to be absolutely prohibited under penalties of transportation, while wandering persons were to be regarded as vagabonds and returned to their home parish for correction and cure. Each parish should bear, under supervision, the prime responsibility for the care of its own poor, but the whole system of relief and rehabilitation, Steele suggested, should be given a larger organization and support.[1]

The bold and original suggestions here advanced by Steele were, as we shall later notice, quite typical of a large body of reforming thought which made a significant contribution to the consideration of the whole problem of poverty and its relief. Yet, save for quite minor modifications, the Elizabethan *corpus* of legislation remained in force through the whole of the revolutionary era. Both the Commonwealth and Protectorate dealt most cautiously with this entire area of responsibility. There were nine ordinances in the period dealing specifically with problems created by the war itself and with the care of war casualties and there were ten which lent the sanction of the state to highly organized and worthy fund-raising efforts for the benefit of charitable needs in specified communities. We have likewise noted seven measures ordering the application of a proportion of confiscated properties to religious, educational, and other salutary purposes, though these ordinances can scarcely be regarded as having made substantial, much less permanent, contribution either to the purposes named or to the law relating to charitable responsibility. There are, however, a few ordinances in this troubled period which deserve some brief mention.

An ordinance dated May 28, 1647 had general application and significance, though its purpose was to afford relief for maimed soldiers and sailors and their dependents. Such needy persons were to be placed under the full protection of the statute of *43 Eliz., c. 2*, the parish of residence being declared responsible for their maintenance. Maimed soldiers were to be settled in the parish of their origin, while their widows and orphans were to be eligible for needed charitable relief 'besides such relief as they shall gain by their work and labour'.[2] This statute was amplified by a further ordinance in August, 1647, which required that a tax, to be approved by the justices, of from 3d to 2s 6d weekly be levied in each parish to carry out the intent of the law.[3]

It should also be noted that an important and, one must add, a

---

[1] 'Proposalls concerning ye maintenance of impotent and aged people and for imploying and punishing of beggars and vagabonds' (1641) (*House of Lords MSS.*, calendared in *Historical Manuscripts Commission, Fourth Report*, House of Lords, App. 114). Ludlow later described Steele as a 'man of great prudence and uncorrupted integrity'. There is a biographical notice in the *DNB*.

[2] Firth, C. H., and R. S. Rait, eds., *Acts and ordinances of the Interregnum* (3 vols., L., 1911), I, 938.

[3] *Ibid.*, I, 997. Another ordinance passed still later in the same year (1647) further amplified the law (*ibid.*, I, 1055).

much needed, act was passed by Parliament in 1649 discharging poor prisoners held for debt whose assets did not exceed £5 in value and who took the debtor's oath[1]; this was, however, subjected to subsequent review and suspension because of the difficulties found by the judges in its administration.[2] Special but important legislation, which will be considered in another connection, was passed dealing with the always urgent problem of the poor of London,[3] as was a carefully drafted act (September 26, 1649) for the reorganization and further maintenance of the school and almshouses in Westminster.[4] The important act passed in May, 1649, to enable the draining of the Great Level of the Fens professed to have as a central objective the enrichment of the commonwealth, the advancement of trade and agriculture, and the employment of the poor by the creation of opportunities for large-scale employment,[5] though the state itself carefully refrained from taking any of the considerable financial risk. Towards the end of the revolutionary era (June 9, 1657), an act was passed ordering that all wandering, idle, and vagrant persons, not found in their 'usual place of living or abode' be adjudged rogues under the statute of 39 Elizabeth, though it seems evident that the measure served rather to sharpen the memories of the law enforcement officers than to enlarge or modify the clear meaning of the earlier statute.[6] We may, in fact, say in summary that only inconsequential changes were made in the whole fabric of Elizabethan charitable legislation in the two generations that elapsed from the date of passage to the close of the period under review.

We have sketched the slow and somewhat reluctant development of a complex, an articulated, and a comprehensive code of legislation dealing with the problem of poverty. This was the work of the great Tudor sovereigns, who were neither sentimental nor tender towards their subjects, but who were ever prepared to face historical realities, who were jealous of the substance of their power, and who were almost intuitively sensitive to any dislocations or disorders which might erode the structure of their sovereignty. This great body of legislation may, then, be regarded as a mechanism competent to ensure the relief of poverty. It stood ready for enforcement in periods of economic distress and widespread poverty in any area of England, though, as we have so frequently said, there is no evidence that many communities undertook a serious or systematic application of the law until well into the seventeenth century. This legislation was at bottom prudential; it stood ready for enforcement in periods of crisis and national need. There was also implicit in the Tudor legislation the assumption that individual

---

[1] Firth and Rait, *Acts and ordinances*, II, 240–241, 321–324.
[2] *Ibid.*, II, 860–861 (1654).
[3] *Ibid.*, I, 1042–1045 (1647); *ibid.*, II, 104–110 (1649).
[4] *Ibid.*, II, 256–277.   [5] *Ibid.*, II, 130–139.   [6] *Ibid.*, II, 1098.

communities were themselves responsible for invoking the law when local need arose. The whole apparatus of law and the machinery of administration stood ready for use. But under Elizabeth at least the central government only rarely brought pressure to bear on the parish or the county. None the less, this *corpus* of legislation was of very great historical significance in that it represented the assumption by the state, in slow and ordered stages, of ultimate social responsibility for the care not only of those who were derelict but of those who were unemployed through no fault of their own. A great social floor at the level of subsistence had been laid under the Tudor society, and the morality as well as the practicality of this daring and enlightened commitment was generally accepted by the close of the great Queen's reign. An immense and an irreversible social gain had been made.

At the same time, however, the great legislative advance was possibly only because private men, by their own charities, had in fact already assumed an enormous and an ever-enlarging responsibility for the welfare and dignity of their society. The care of the poor, not to mention other equally important charitable outlays, throughout our period remained principally in the hands of private donors, who were creating with their wealth the great social institutions which may be said to frame and undergird the liberal society. The law, the use of the taxing power, was regarded, so to speak, as a kind of co-insurance against social disaster in the event the economy was overwhelmed by forces too powerful and too abrupt for private charity to master. It was the lively fear that such a period of disaster might be at hand which evoked the legislation of 1597 and which was to result in its first considerable enforcement about a generation later. But there remained the confidence that private charity, with its rapidly mounting resources, could not only bear the burdens of the society in normal times but could raise the level of opportunity throughout the realm so that poverty itself might be prevented. Accordingly, every encouragement was lent by the state through the whole course of the century to properly defined almsgiving, and a second great mechanism of social progress was gradually evolved in the shape of the charitable trust. It is most significant that the statute codifying and extending the legal meaning of charitable trusts was passed in the same year as the poor law. They were conjoined in the thinking of the legislature just as they were in the thinking of the community of the realm.

D. THE EVOLUTION AND MATURING OF THE CHARITABLE TRUST

1. *The historical and legal background*

The law of charitable trusts developed in step with the law of uses more generally, in the earlier stages without statutory definition and despite the clear meaning of common law and the intent of statute law. The trust was an invention of equity, affording a uniquely competent instrument for the distribution of private property and providing a quite perfect mechanism for the vesting of charitable endowments without the necessity of securing from the Crown or from Parliament charters of incorporation.[1] The development of the law of trusts in England owed its peculiar nature to the fact that there were separate courts of law and equity. Thus the law courts recognized though they would not enforce uses, while Chancery came rapidly to undertake responsibility not only for the enforcement of duties upon the legal owner but for the protection of the beneficiary in his interests in the trusteed property. Uses were so rapidly exploited as a means of creating estates because the mediaeval society was searching for some means of freeing itself from the strict rules of law and, as importantly, of escaping from the rigorous limitations imposed on the holders, one can scarcely say the owners, of property held under feudal tenure. Accordingly, 'the employment of the use or trust as a means of making testamentary disposition of land at a time when land was not devisable, and its employment to avoid the feudal claims of the overlord, were not condemned, since the courts recognized that these purposes were no longer against public policy, although they could not be accomplished under the old rules of the dying feudal system'.[2]

Some forms of uses extend far back in English history, though the great authority of Maitland would suggest that they were first generally and skilfully established in the thirteenth century when extensive endowments were placed under trusteeship by private donors for the benefit of the Franciscan order, which could not under its constitution hold property.[3] In the later fourteenth century private uses began to become very common indeed, though at some considerable hazard since the execution of the trust depended wholly on the good faith of the feoffee. But early in the fifteenth century Chancery had become an established court of the realm, and successive chancellors began to intervene to enforce on the trustee his duties and to protect uses in so

[1] Scott, A. W., *The law of trusts* (5 vols., Boston, 1956), I, 3–5. Our discussion of the development of private trusts depends heavily on this monumental work.
[2] *Ibid.*, I, 9.
[3] Maitland, F. W., *Equity* (Cambridge, 1910), 25; Tyssen, A. D., *The law of charitable bequests* (L., 1921), 1–2.

far as they did not lie athwart statute or public policy.[1] The development was rapid, uses becoming assignable, estates in uses being recognized, and the doctrine that uses descended by the same rules that applied to land having been sustained. These sophisticated arrangements with respect to property were throughout the century not only hastening the collapse of the whole system of feudal tenure but were being employed by the magnates during the tumultuous years of the War of the Roses to escape even the consequences of high treason.[2] Uses were also being employed to secure the effect of the devising of land, which ran wholly counter to the necessary assumptions of feudal tenure. But, even more importantly, the king was being injured not only because there was great confusion with respect to titles, but because it was no longer wholly clear where and to whom ran the lines of obligation for military service, taxes, and the ultimate responsibility for the ownership of property.

These abuses and obscurities Henry VIII sought to correct by the Statute of Uses in 1536. The King's agents on the floor of Parliament drove hard to secure this crown measure, which had in fact to be somewhat modified before men against whose personal and family interests it ran could be persuaded to effect its passage.[3] The preamble recited at length the abuses and national disadvantages flowing from the employment of uses, while the act cured the fault by the simple process of confirming the legal estate on the *cestui que use* (the person who had the use).[4] Thus the holder of the use was given title, it being intended that the use should no longer be an equitable interest protected by Chancery but should be dealt with by the ordinary law courts. Clearly, the intention was to join possession to the use and to annihilate the distinction between legal and beneficial ownership.[5] The statute, then, did not forbid uses, as the King would have preferred, but it rather vested the full responsibilities of ownership in the trust. The act had one further and perhaps not wholly intended effect in that it forbade the devising of freehold estates, a consequence which proved to be extremely unpopular among the gentry who had reluctantly passed *27 Henry VIII, c. 10*.[6] This grievance of the landowning class was redressed in the great Statute of Wills, passed a few years later, which by legalizing the devising of certain important categories of land relieved the most important of the social and human pressures which had led to the undisciplined development of the private trust.[7]

[1] Scott, *Trusts*, I, 15.   [2] *Ibid.*, I, 17.
[3] Holdsworth, *English law*, IV, 450–457.
[4] Tyssen, *Charitable bequests*, 4.
[5] Digby, K. E., *An introduction to the history of the law of real property* (Oxford, 1884), 302.
[6] Holdsworth, *English law*, IV, 464.
[7] *32 Henry VIII, c. 1*; in 1660, *12 Cha. II, c. 24*, made all lands devisable.

We may conclude, therefore, that the Statute of Uses did not destroy uses and that it remained possible to separate the beneficial interest from the legal title. It was held that when the trust was active, when real and active duties were vested in the trustee in relation to the beneficiary, the act did not prohibit, as was the construction of the statute when a use was established only for a term of years. The formidable ingenuity of the lawyers probed at the statute, until it was determined in Tyrrel's case (1557) that if a use be raised on a use, the first was illegal but the second held.[1] The effect of the statute as interpreted by the courts was, then, in no sense to destroy the instrumentality of the trust, but rather to clear away the thicket of abuse and legal evasion which had sprung up during the dying days of the mediaeval order. The main lines of development for the modern law of trusts had been clearly laid out, and most particularly for the rapid maturing of the great instrument of the charitable trust with which we are more immediately concerned.

In crude form at least the charitable trust was well known and extensively employed by donors long before the sixteenth century. Most mediaeval charitable dispositions were of course for religious purposes, and, though the common law held that unincorporated bodies might not hold property, the evident fact remained that many monasteries, churches, and other such bodies possessed very large properties indeed. Much of this wealth was, of course, held by religious bodies which were legally corporations and which were empowered to hold property by frank almoign, a licence in mortmain lending protection against possible forfeiture. Successive tightenings of the statute of mortmain were made, with the consequence that a second form of endowment developed which was in its legal structure a charitable trust. Property was conveyed to another person for the use of a named religious organization as beneficiary. When in the early fifteenth century the Chancellor began to intervene to enforce uses as part of his equitable jurisdiction, such trusts gained further protection and came gradually to be employed in the founding of secular as well as religious charities. As we shall later note in detail, the number and the value of charitable trusts increased enormously in the course of the sixteenth century, since from the time of the Reformation the Crown as well as Chancery lent all possible enforcement and protection to them. It was quickly established that a charitable use could be laid on property either by enfeoffment or by will.[2] The great transformation occurring in this century was, of course, the profoundly important shift from religious to secular aspirations, assisted somewhat by the Reformation statutes outlawing trusts

[1] Scott, *Trusts*, I, 22.
[2] Bristowe, L. S., *et al.*, *The law of charities . . . the fourth edition of Tudor's charitable trusts* (L., 1906), 3; Shelford, Leonard, *A practical treatise of the law of mortmain and charitable uses* (L., 1836), 44–45.

for superstitious purposes and outlawing endowments for prayers for the dead.[1] The ever-mounting flow of funds into charitable trusts was assisted as well by the disposition of the courts, after a momentary hesitation, to construe favourably all trusts created for charitable uses and, if any substantial difficulty appeared to intervene, by direct action to establish the trust legally and effectively.

2. *The Elizabethan codification*

The great Elizabethan statute of charitable trusts was notable, then, not because it created charitable uses, but rather because it codified a body of law badly wanting classical statement and because it vastly stimulated constructive and well considered charitable giving by lending full and most formidable protection to the aspirations of donors. It is, indeed, not too much to say that the essential features of the Elizabethan act were fully stated as early as the fourteenth century. In the *Vision of Piers Plowman* we observe that the troubled (and rich) merchants were counselled by *Truth* to gain full remission of sins and a happy death by the fruitful use of their fortunes:

> And therewith repair hospitals,
> help sick people,
> mend bad roads,
> build up bridges that had been broken down,
> help maidens to marry or to make them nuns,
> find food for prisoners and poor people,
> put scholars to school or to some other craft,
> help religious orders, and
> ameliorate rents or taxes.[2]

These are the good causes, religious orders aside, which achieved immortality of definition in the eloquent preamble to the Elizabethan act first passed in 1597 and with unimportant amendments gathered into the great code of social legislation in 1601.[3] The preamble undertook the recital of the proper objects of charitable interest and, for a society with limited resources, defined a very broad spectrum of responsibility and proclaimed a noble conception of what a society ought to be.[4] Thus it was recalled that wealth had been left by sovereigns and 'by sondrie other well disposed persons, some for releife of aged impotent and poore

[1] *23 Henry VIII, c. 10; 7 Edw. VI, c. 11; Adams v. Lambert, temp. Eliz., 4 co. 529.*

[2] Langland, William, *The vision of . . . Piers Plowman* (F. W. Skeat, ed.) (L., 1906), 80. My attention was first called to this passage by Mr Henry Moe, who includes it in his most persuasive *Guggenheim Foundation statement to Congressional Committee.*

[3] *39 Eliz., c. 6; 43 Eliz., c. 4.* Our references and discussion will be addressed to the latter statute.

[4] Gray, *English philanthropy,* 35.

people, some for maintenance of sicke and maymed souldiers and mar-
riners, schooles of learninge, free schooles and schollers in universities,
some for repaire of bridges portes havens causewaies churches seabankes and highwaies, some for education and preferments of orphans,
some for or towardes reliefe stocke or maintenance for howses of correction, some for mariages of poore maides, some for supportacion ayde
and helpe of younge tradesmen, handie-craftesmen and persons decayed, and others for releife or redemption of prisoners or captives,
and for aide or ease of any poore inhabitants concerning paymente of
fifteenes, [and] settinge out of souldiers and other taxes'.

The statute of 1601, as we shall date the law, secured the enforcement
of charitable uses by instructing the Chancellor to appoint commissions
to enquire into abuses, to take evidence, to impanel juries, and to hand
down decisions subject only to his own review. There remained as well
the possibility for a complainant to take a direct appeal to Chancery
against the abuses of feoffees, though this method gradually became
disused.[1] Though ostensibly concerned with no more than the correction
of existing abuses in charitable trusts and the encouragement of future
donors to raise up such charitable institutions, the statute became in
fact a great landmark in the development of the law of charitable trusts.
The statute remained unrepealed until 1888,[2] but even then the new
statute carefully preserved the preamble and its list of uses properly
defined as charitable. The recital in the preamble, it may be supposed,
was designed to be rather more hortatory than definitive, but none the
less the stamp of its eloquence upon law and aspirations has been such
that the courts of the United States as well as of Britain have tended to
be guided by its precepts. So, too, the precise word 'charitable' has
acquired a meaning that is anchored in the language of the preamble,
with the result that trusts have tended to fail when testators, and their
lawyers, have attempted to enlarge or refine the intention by some such
term as 'charitable and benevolent'.[3] The Nathan Committee on the Law
and Practice relating to Charitable Trusts, as recently as 1952, in commenting on the famous case of Diplock's will (1949) in which the
court held the will void for uncertainty because the words 'or benevolent' were appended after 'charitable', has ventured to propose legislation permitting the application of such estates to legal charities instead of permitting the complete frustration of the testator's intentions.[4]
It is interesting, however, to observe that this distinguished committee
would hesitate to broaden the definition of charitable purposes beyond

[1] Scott, *Trusts*, IV, 2564.
[2] Mortmain and Charitable Uses Act, *51 and 52 Victoria, c. 42*.
[3] Scott, A. W., 'Trusts for charitable and benevolent purposes', *Harvard Law Review*, LVIII (1945), 548 ff. This is a brilliant discussion of the matter.
[4] *The Economist* (January 10, 1953), 61.

Lord Macnaghten's modest rephrasing of the almost casual but beautiful wording of the Elizabethan preamble. These men in the Parliament of 1601 were drafting well and surely because they sought to state and to ennoble aspirations which had become and were to remain central to the structure of the liberal society.

One other aspect of the great Elizabethan statute deserves some comment. The conception and definition of charitable purposes here advanced was starkly and coldly secular, just as were the benefactions of the age. The only religious purpose mentioned at all was the repair of churches, and even this was quite inconspicuously tucked in between 'causewaies' and 'seabankes'. This omission was flagrantly deliberate, because the whole temper of the age had grown so completely secular and because the preoccupations of men had fastened so tenaciously on the many and pressing needs of the world and the society which they saw about them. In point of fact, even the repair of a parish church, very rarely undertaken in Elizabethan England, was itself a quasi-civic undertaking, the motives for which were quite as likely to proceed from local pride as from religious sentiment. But here the text of the law ran even more sternly secular than sentiment, for we have counted many scores of charitable trusts established for religious purposes between 1590 and 1639 which remained wholly unmolested, until in the latter year a judicial decision lent protection by ruling that a trust established to maintain a preaching minister was valid under the Elizabethan act.[1]

As we have suggested, the statute of 1601 was a great 'gathering act', bringing under codification a long development and a fruitful national experience in the growth of charitable trusts as instruments of social betterment. We should now review quite summarily the principal of these earlier statutes which had gradually opened as they had disciplined the flow of charitable funds into several deepening channels. Perhaps the first significant statute of this kind, offering protection to what can accurately be described as charitable trusts, was passed early in the reign of Henry V. The act recalled that there were many hospitals in the realm to which earlier founders had left their wealth for the sustenance of impotent persons, lazars, witless men, poor women with child, and the poor generally. A large number of these foundations had decayed or disappeared with resulting injury to the realm. It was consequently ordered that the appropriate ecclesiastical authorities enquire into the manner of founding of such institutions and take steps to secure such corrections and reparations as might be needed.[2] This law had the effect of creating a charitable commission with limited powers and instructions and of defining more precisely responsibilities and capacities already held by the ordinaries. There is, however, little evidence that the statute was given full effect or that the calamitous

[1] *Pember* v. *Inhabitants of Knighton.*   [2] *2 Henry V, c. 1* (1414).

decay of mediaeval charitable institutions, already far advanced, was significantly retarded.

The early Tudors, as we have observed, lent steady legislative and administrative support to the vesting of charitable endowments, though even prior to the Reformation the secular bias of their policy was only too evident. Considerable constraint was accordingly imposed on the creation of trusts for most religious purposes by an act passed in 1531–2. The statute recited the injury done to the king and realm when lands were alienated in mortmain to trusts created for the use of parish churches, chapels, guilds, brotherhoods, and for obits, whether perpetual or for a term of years. Such uses were prohibited and were to be without the effect of law, if they should be instituted for more than a term of twenty years, save that in cities and corporate towns where by ancient custom devises into mortmain had been permitted the act was not to prevail.[1] This statute, strengthened as it was by the whole weight of the Reformation legislation shortly to follow, was of considerable significance in drying up even further the rapidly diminishing flow of charitable funds to the various religious uses.

From this day forward, indeed, the whole weight of law as well as of policy was exerted to mould the charities of England to secular ends and to assist donors in creating the great charitable institutions which were so profoundly to alter the structure of the English society. Two examples will perhaps suffice. In 1572, in conjunction with the important poor law framed in this same session, an act was passed to encourage and assist benefactors who wished to found hospitals and almshouses. The great benefit that had flowed from the recent establishment and endowment of the four great London hospitals was cited and the hope expressed that there would in future years be many more benefactions for such worthy purposes. Many such gifts would be provided in wills, 'at which time for want of council and other opportunities, it may happen that the right names of the said corporations hath not or shall not be truly named or expressed', with resulting questions regarding the validity of the bequest. It was therefore enacted that such gifts or bequests left for the use of the poor in any hospital should be 'good and available in law' despite the 'misnaming, misreciting or not true naming or reciting' of the intended foundation.[2] Thus brusquely did Elizabeth seek to clear away legal niceties and flaws of instruction which ironically have for so long troubled the courts in the interpretation of the great statute passed in the closing years of her own reign. Of even greater significance was the enabling act passed in 1597 as part of the great code of social legislation enacted at that time. This act, it will be recalled, relieved founders of hospitals, almshouses, and houses of correction from the necessity of securing letters patent

[1] 23 Henry VIII, c. 10.   [2] 14 Eliz., c. 14.

and made it possible, by a deed enrolled in Chancery, to found such institutions so long as the yearly value of the endowment provided was at least £10.[1]

The requisite body of law and of experience for the founding and protection of charitable trusts stood substantially complete in 1597, and, as we shall shortly observe, an immense outlay of funds so constituted was to mark the social history of the next generation. One further statute, dealing with a single aspect of the whole broad range of charitable interests was, however, enacted in the early Stuart period. In 1610 Parliament turned specifically to the regulation and protection of the considerable sums being left for the support of apprenticeships. It was declared that 'experience whereof hath brought forth very great profit and commodity unto those cities, towns, and parishes where any parts of the said monies have been so given and employed'. At the same time, abuses had arisen in the rather random outlays made from such funds. It was accordingly enacted that in the future such sums were to be expended by the municipal authorities of the favoured towns and boroughs unless the instructions of the donor explicitly determined otherwise, while in unincorporated communities the outlays were to be made by the parish clergyman together with the churchwardens, the collectors, and the overseers of the poor. It was further ordered that masters taking apprentices should be bound to return the fees at the end of the period of service, with the intent that a revolving apprenticeship fund could thereby be established in each favoured community. Careful provision was also made to ensure that only the income on endowed apprenticeship funds might be expended, while enforcement of the act was to be obtained by inviting any person suspecting a breach of trust to petition Chancery for the appointment of a commission of enquiry with power to require restitution in the event of fraud or the impairment of funds.[2]

We have frequently noted that the poor laws were given full effect only very gradually and unevenly during the course of our period. In contrast, charitable trusts were lent formidable and most effective protection during the whole of the Tudor period and were subjected to periodic and competent review after the statute of 1601 had carefully delineated an impressively orderly scheme of commissions of enquiry.[3] We shall have occasion to mention many of these enquiries in our more detailed discussion of the counties under study and shall see that inquisitions into 'fraudes, breaches of truste, and negligence' could be instituted in a great variety of ways. Most commonly, responsible inhabitants of a parish simply complained of malfeasance to the bishop

---

[1] 39 *Eliz.*, c. 5. *Vide ante*, 94–98, for a fuller discussion in the context of related legislation.

[2] 7 *Jac. I*, c. 3.   [3] *Vide ante*, 113.

of the diocese, to a commission already in being, to the Lord Chancellor or Lord Keeper, or, and not infrequently, to the Privy Council. In other cases the institution of complaints has been noted from such persons as the clergyman, the vestry, the overseers, the municipal authorities, or a local justice of the peace. There are a number of instances, too, when descendants of the donor filed a complaint, and not a few in which a single and evidently humble petitioner set in motion the effective machinery of investigation. Finally, if a whole community was so negligent and dull as to fail to protect its self-interest, these commissions of enquiry could and did ferret out malfeasance and more often simply rural incompetence by regional enquiries designed to review the current status of all known charitable funds.[1] The consequence was that charitable funds were on the whole administered with quite astonishing probity and skill and that a tradition of the highest fidelity in the discharge of duty was quickly established. This fact in itself lent powerful encouragement to substantial men considering benefactions and accounts in no small part for the huge sums vested in charitable trusts during the last two generations of our period.

3. *Analysis of the achievement*

We have sought in all the counties under study to distinguish carefully between capital gifts (endowments) made for charitable uses and those benefactions which were made outright, that is for immediate expenditure of the whole of the gift or, and this rather uncommonly, the expenditure of the whole of the principal over a stated term of years. During the early decades of our period charitable benefactions tended to partake of the nature of alms and were most commonly made as outright gifts for immediate use. But from about 1520 onwards a steadily increasing proportion of donors were disposed to order charities in the form of endowments and a much larger proportion of the total of charitable sums was so disposed. With only minor and eccentric exceptions, these endowments were in legal form charitable trusts. The great Elizabethan statute ordering the structure of charitable trusts and

[1] A few examples of enquiries under the statute may be mentioned here: *S.P. Dom.*, 1616, LXXXVIII, 28; *Chancery Petty Bag*, Charity Inquisitions, Kent, C 93/7/7; *S.P. Dom.*, 1617, XCII; *S.P. Dom.*, 1621, XLII, 72; *S.P. Dom.*, 1634 [?], CCLXXXI, 49; *S.P. Dom.*, 1637, CCCLII, 78; *S.P. Dom.*, 1655, XCIX, 101–102; *S.P. Dom.*, 1656, CXXIV, 79.

A particularly valuable series of examples may be found in Herne, John, *Law of charitable uses* (L., 1663), 100 ff. Herne tells us in his preface that he had been present at hearings of many commissions 'grounded' on the Elizabethan statute. He had 'found the gentlemen . . . commissioners, jurors . . grown almost weary of well-doing . . . never cheerfully embraced these commissions . . . and many inquisitions and decrees have . . . miscarried'. He accordingly was hopeful that his book might secure the better observance and execution of the statute.

affording them effective and inexpensive protection was accordingly quite perfectly timed in relation to the historical realities, since it was in about 1590 that the immense outpouring of charitable funds for a great variety of secular uses set in. From that date forward to the close of our period, a very large proportion of all charitable benefactions was vested in the form of endowments, even relatively small sums having been given the dignity and protection of trusteeship.

Taking our whole period in view, the immense total of £2,551,880 19s was vested by donors in our ten counties as capital amounts under trusteeship of one kind or another. This sum constituted a not inconsiderable proportion of the capital wealth of the realm and must by the time of the Restoration have been yielding something like £127,600 p.a., which was being disposed for a great range of fruitful and greatly needed social purposes. The immense significance of the mechanism of the charitable trust is suggested when we reflect that upwards of 82 per cent of the huge aggregate of charitable sums disposed during our entire period was settled in the form of endowments. It is significant, too, that the proportion of total charities established in endowments was remarkably uniform in all the counties that we have examined, ranging from about 77 per cent in Lancashire to 91 per cent in Bristol.[1] Though the details may more appropriately be considered in our examination of the several counties, it may be suggested here that such great charitable needs as almshouses, loan funds, stocks, apprenticeship plans, and all the educational uses were almost wholly financed by the vesting of capital sums which would in perpetuity ensure the attainment of the aspirations of the donor.

The enormous capital which had by the close of our period been settled in charitable trusts possessed a qualitative as well as an overwhelming quantitative strength. Though, as we have seen, accounting for a very large proportion (82 per cent) of the total of charitable funds, this huge sum had been given by a relatively small group of 6328 individual donors, comprising no more than 18 per cent (18·1 per cent) of the whole number for our entire period. Accordingly, even the average worth of these trusts was the remarkably large sum of £403 5s 4d, an

[1] The proportions for the several counties are as follows:

	per cent
Bristol	91·00
Buckinghamshire	82·40
Hampshire	80·09
Kent	81·35
Lancashire	76·83
London	82·60
Norfolk	80·96
Somerset	80·86
Worcestershire	80·51
Yorkshire	82·17

amount, it must be noted, quite sufficient for the needs of most rural parishes for outright poor relief or to found a strongly endowed almshouse or grammar school. Even more importantly, these endowments were with few exceptions carefully and prudently ordered by their donors, with the result that they were well administered, carefully husbanded, and stood as open invitations to later benefactors to augment them as their enormous social value came to be recognized. With £403 5s 4d a late fifteenth century landed magnate could arrange funeral doles which were certain to attract unruly swarms of beggars from a half dozen nearby counties; with the same amount a Norwich merchant a century later could endow in perpetuity a social institution of great and abiding utility.

In our discussion of the development of the law of trusts, we suggested that historical fact was quite steadily outstripping law. Legal historians have tended to assume that the charitable trust was unimportant before 1597, or at the earliest 1572, though there were in fact some thousands of them in England and they had attained a relatively sophisticated development well before the close of the sixteenth century. The total of capital vested in charitable trusts in our ten counties, comprising, as we have estimated, perhaps half the wealth of England, had as early as 1600 reached the massive sum of £808,131 14s by gradual accumulations over the preceding decades. This capital amounted to 32 per cent (31·67 per cent) of the whole of the very large total to be vested in trusts during our entire period. At the same time, the Elizabethan legislation marking the close of the century lent even further stimulation to the flood of giving already well under way, with the consequence that the incredibly large proportion of almost 69 per cent of the whole was to be provided by donors in the course of the next two generations.

We have been discussing large capital sums settled in upwards of 6000 trusts over a period of almost two centuries. In many cases we know little about these trusts save for scant information provided by the will of the donor, the deed of gift, or the findings of a later commission of enquiry. In a far greater number of cases we know a fair amount regarding the circumstances of the founding of the trust but very little about its subsequent history. There remain a surprising number of instances when we have been able not only to secure quite full particulars regarding the establishment of the trust, but to trace its subsequent history to a fairly recent date. This group of trusts we should now examine in some detail.

There are in all 2121 of these trusts about which we have comfortably complete historical knowledge, these comprising almost exactly a third (33·51 per cent) of the total number which we know to have been vested in the course of our long period. This group of trusts possessed an original, a founding, worth of £727,590 of capital value, assuming always, as we have earlier explained, a level interest rate of 5 per cent on trusteed funds. These trusts were substantial, the average working out to £343 0s 10d, this being capital wholly adequate for the endowment of an ambitious apprenticeship scheme or for the founding of an excellent provincial school. When one examines the evidence in county terms, however, very marked differences in the average worth of these trusts appear, ranging from £116 18s 7d in Worcestershire to the really amazingly high average of £616 13s 4d for Bristol and £634 11s for London.[1] We are, then, dealing with trusts of considerable size and very great social significance, though it must be stressed that any discussion of averages always conceals the interesting complexities on the fringes of the data. Thus it seems quite astonishing that a fifth of the trusts in this group, 435 in all, were in fact established with capital sums of £20 or less. Even when we take into account the immense erosion that has occurred in the purchasing power of money, these remain very small legal entities indeed to have been vested with the full powers, and responsibilities, which accrue to trusteed funds.

It is also interesting to observe that in this group of trusts approximately the same proportion of the total capital had been vested prior to 1601 as was the case for the whole *corpus* of endowed funds in the counties under study. In all, 749 of these endowments were constituted before the close of the sixteenth century, this representing slightly more than 35 per cent (35·31 per cent) of the whole number, while the £212,430 of capital disposed by these trusts accounted for about 29 per cent of the entire sum to be accumulated in these endowments during our entire period. There are, it should be noted, rather marked differences in the proportion of trusteed funds vested before 1601 when we

[1]

	Average worth of trusts			Number of trusts	Number of trusts with capital of £20 or less
	£				
Bristol	616	13	4	42	6
Buckinghamshire	312	1	4	105	40
Hampshire	231	18	3	104	32
Kent	191	1	1	436	112
Lancashire	449	4	9	97	6
London	634	11	0	542	67
Norfolk	203	1	4	263	45
Somerset	332	15	6	102	13
Worcestershire	116	18	7	184	60
Yorkshire	264	14	0	246	54
Totals	343	0	10	2121	435
					(20·51 per cent of total number)

examine the county particulars, ranging from not much more than 12 per cent for Hampshire to the remarkably high proportion of almost 40 per cent. for Bristol.[1] It is quite clear that the sophisticated device of the charitable trust was first extensively employed by knowledgeable urban donors, men who could command expert legal counsel, a fact which would become even clearer if the heavy endowments dispersed to, and counted in, the counties by London donors were separated for detailed comment.

We have also been interested in attempting to sort at least into very roughly defined categories the bewildering variety of trusteeships constituted by these donors, one would suppose on the whole with little or no legal counsel. The largest number, 471 in all, comprising somewhat more than a fifth (22·21 per cent) of the group, were established in trust as rent-charges on real property, with fixed sums to be paid annually to indicated charities, parish officials, municipalities, or other agents. These trust arrangements may well have seemed prudent when concluded, but they have, of course, fared very badly indeed historically as the purchasing power of money has declined. In numerous cases, and particularly in urban communities, fluid capital was gained and more advantageously invested by the redemption of these charges, often, it would seem, without the formal approbation of Chancery or the courts. But in the main these foundations, which were in most cases slight in total capital worth, gradually declined in social utility.[2]

[1]

	Original worth	Total no. trusts	Total pre-1601	Total no. 1601–1600	Total worth of trusts founded pre-1601	Per cent of original worth of all trusts
	£				£	per cent
Bristol	25,900	42	16	26	10,164	39·24
Buckinghamshrie	32,767	105	22	83	9,569	29·20
Hampshire	24,119	104	18	86	2,998	12·43
Kent	83,322	436	166	270	19,711	23·66
Lancashire	43,576	97	22	75	8,757	20·10
London	343,925	542	291	251	108,759	31·62
Norfolk	53,407	263	90	173	18,053	33·80
Somerset	33,943	102	29	73	12,884	37·96
Worcestershire	21,515	184	35	149	5,960	27·70
Yorkshire	65,116	246	60	186	15,575	23·92
Totals	727,590	2121	749 (35·31 per cent)	1372 (64·69 per cent)	212,430 (29·20 per cent)	(29·20 per cent)

[2] It should perhaps be said here that a much larger number of capital gifts were made in the form of rent-charges which were not charitable trusts, the owner of the land having simply a legal obligation to pay the prescribed sum annually to a prescribed charitable cause or charitable trustee.

A second and also a large group of these charitable trusts were vested in private trustees under almost every conceivable kind of constitution and arrangement for securing the perpetuation of the feoffees. There were in all 402 of these trusts, or 18·95 per cent of the whole number, in which the details of trusteeship were set out in the will or the deed of gift. The original trustees were normally named by the donor, in number from two persons to one vast assembly of forty-seven, with careful provisions for new appointments when the number had dwindled to a prescribed level. Most of the large foundations were of this general type, while the trustees were not uncommonly at the same time responsible for the actual administration of the school, the almshouse, or some other institution founded under the deed of gift.

We have been most arbitrary in our definition of the next type of trusteeship, to which we have assigned almost as many, 397, of the trusts in the group under consideration. These were trusts in which the parish officers, the clergymen, and 'substantial inhabitants' of the parish were named as feoffees in an almost infinite variety of combinations. The parish itself, or, more accurately, its most respected and competent officers, was in these instances considered to be a corporaton on which the trust might be imposed. In another 173 cases, or 8·16 per cent of the whole number, the municipal officers, in various combinations, were vested as feoffees in larger corporate towns and cities.

In our discussion of London we shall have occasion to deal at length with the extraordinary competence displayed by its livery companies as trustees of charitable funds. It is noteworthy that about 40 per cent of all London trusts included within the group under consideration were so vested, while the value of these funds amounted to almost 60 per cent of the total worth. By no means all the charitable estates so disposed were the gifts of donors who were also members of the livery, while thirty-two of these were trusts from other counties, accepted by the companies under trust covenants. In all, therefore, 253, or 11·93 per cent of the whole number of trusts in our group designated the highly skilled and the already notably responsible city companies as feoffees.

It seems rather surprising that in only thirty instances were existing charitable institutions, such as the universities or the great London hospitals, to undertake trust responsibilities for purposes or for beneficiaries lying outside their own sphere of activity and responsibility. The pressure on such famous and generally respected institutions was heavy to accept such responsibility, the prospective donor usually baiting his proposal with a suggested subsidiary gift or rent-charge, but save for these few instances such requests were declined. There remain 395 trusts, 18·62 per cent of the whole number, regarding which we have reasonably full historical particulars but for which we cannot speak with certainty respecting the original trust constitution as arranged by the donor.[1]

This large group of trusts is in average terms well over three centuries old. For the most part, the trust instruments were drawn before the law of charitable trusts was well formulated and before men of the western world had gained much experience in the administration of this extraordinary legal and social instrumentality. Most of these trusts were relatively quite small, many very small indeed, and most of them were entrusted to laymen possessed of no particular administrative experience or financial sagacity. None the less, so important has society conceived their purposes to be, so competent were the safeguards erected by the Elizabethan legislation, and so faithful has been the unbroken succession of unpaid and almost unnoticed feoffees that over this long span of time only 174 of the total number of these trusts have been lost, through negligence, or malfeasance, or merger with other funds. This means, of course, that only 8 per cent (8·20 per cent) of these trusts have disappeared; that perpetuity has in fact been largely achieved even for the smallest and most eccentric of these many endowments. But this presentation in fact exaggerates the inevitable, if nominal, losses that have occurred as a consequence of the erosion of time against human institutions, for those that have disappeared have on the whole been the small rent-charges and other funds almost too tiny to command fiduciary attention. When set out in capital terms, it may be said that of the original capital worth of £727,590, funds possessing an original value of only £11,702 1s have been lost, which of course means that only 1·61 per cent of the capital worth has not been faithfully

[1]		Trust types						
	Total no. trusts	Rent-charges	Private	Parish officers	Munici-palities	Livery cos.	Existing charitable corporations	Uncertain
Bristol	42	18	5	3	16	—	—	—
Buckinghamshire	105	15	32	17	7	—	14	20
Hampshire	104	23	10	10	13	3	—	45
Kent	436	130	89	114	36	16	2	49
Lancashire	97	15	46	11	3	1	2	19
London	542	105	44	108	8	221	3	53
Norfolk	263	25	59	41	40	4	4	90
Somerset	102	30	23	31	7	—	—	11
Worcestershire	184	20	22	22	17	4	—	99
Yorkshire	246	90	72	40	26	4	5	9
Totals	2121	471	402	397	173	253	30	395

preserved. In London, Bristol, and Yorkshire the record of fiduciary responsibility has approached absolute perfection, since in these three regions not as much as 1 per cent of the original capital has disappeared. In point of fact, we greatly exaggerate the incidence of loss, inconsequential as it was, for in a great many cases we can say with certainty that these usually small funds were with the passage of time merged without legal authority with other capital, usually held by parishes or municipalities, vested for similar charitable uses. We may say with full confidence that we deal here with the most amazing record of fiduciary responsibility that the western world has ever known.

But this is by no means the full annal of the proud and fruitful record which English feoffees of charitable trusts have attained. These trusts were in most cases required to pay out the whole of income received, they have not been wholly exempted from the weight of taxation, and they have been administered through three centuries marked not only by violent economic dislocations but by a steadily mounting spiral of inflation. None the less, the original capital worth of £727,590 for this group of charitable trusts had increased at their last reporting dates to the staggering total capital sum of £10,549,387, a gain of 14·5 times in worth, which very possibly is not far off from the factor of inflation obtaining over the course of this long interval.[1] This really incredible record has been achieved despite the fact that a considerable proportion of these trusts were unfortunately frozen in rent-charges and though the increase in three of the counties that have remained predominantly rural has been within the relatively modest range of 203 per cent to 275 per cent. In Bristol, on the other hand, the capital worth of these funds has increased eleven times over as urban real property has risen steadily in value, while in Yorkshire and Lancashire the increase has been of the order of twelve and eighteen times over respectively as lands originally of modest value have vaulted in worth, first as minerals were found and exploited and then as urbanization spread across these once predominantly rural areas. The sprawling encroachments of London have been principally responsible for lifting the value of Kentish trust funds in this group by 1251 per cent, not to mention the fact that sixteen of the endowments of this county had been entrusted to the skilled hands of the city companies. London itself has had the proudest record of trusteeship, the original worth of £343,925 for this group of its funds having increased to the immense total of £6,736,396, or a rise

---

[1] We should say that these reporting dates range from 1808 to 1955. Most of the values have been derived from the Parliamentary Charity Commissioners' Reports, though for the larger trusts it has been possible to gain much more recent figures. Only a few of the reports are more than a half-century old. We need scarcely point out that we are here concerned with only a fraction of the whole of the trust funds established during our period and which have been treated in other connections in our discussion.

of nearly twenty times over. This incredible accomplishment has been the consequence of investment policies, particularly by the livery companies, which exhibited prudence tempered with daring and has principally been gained by successive commitments in land just ahead of the ever-expanding growth of the city. It is an accomplishment all the more remarkable because a large proportion of the improvements on land originally held by these 542 trusts were destroyed in the Great Fire, literally extinguishing more than a score of these trusts and very seriously impairing the resources of many more. But fire, pestilence, wars, and panics have not over a long span of three centuries seriously impeded good and faithful men as they have discharged with brilliance and steady purposefulness social burdens laid on them by men they never knew, but who like them were charged with a vision of a fairer habitation for all mankind.[1]

[1]	Original worth	Latest worth	Per cent increase	Lost or merged	Original value lost	
	£	£	per cent		£	s
Bristol	25,900	289,389	1017	1	10	0
Buckinghamshire	32,767	99,395	203	10	1,005	0
Hampshire	24,119	78,756	227	16	1,079	0
Kent	83,322	1,125,583	1251	38	2,403	0
Lancashire	43,576	799,859	1736	8	562	0
London	343,925	6,736,396	1859	29	3,061	0
Norfolk	53,407	376,269	605	12	1,200	0
Somerset	33,943	127,446	275	11	791	0
Worcestershire	21,515	144,241	570	17	954	0
Yorkshire	65,116	772,053	1086	32	637	1
Totals	727,590	10,549,387	1350 per cent	174 (8·20 per cent of total number)	11,702 (1·61 per cent of whole)	1

V

Law and Reality

From 1572 onwards local authorities in England had been legally empowered to levy rates to provide for the care of the hopelessly poor, while from 1597 onwards they were by law required to lay such charges upon their community in discharging a social obligation which the society had now formally undertaken. But as was so often the case with Tudor legislation, the law as debated and then prescribed at Westminster bore no precise or necessary relation to the realities of its administration in the thousands of parochial entities of which England was comprised. The fact is that the great codification of poor laws passed in 1597, and restated in 1601, was essentially prudential, having been drafted and passed by a government which liked to be fore-armed against all emergencies and which had been seriously frightened by the distress and the attendant disorders just prior to the convention of Parliament in 1597. The law was carefully and unambiguously drafted; a brilliantly conceived system of administration was established in which the remotest parish was linked with Westminster; and the whole realm was declared to be a single community of responsibility for the relief of poverty which threatened to overwhelm the private resources of any single locality. But the mechanism of relief thus created was intended as a system of co-insurance, as it were, when the normal resources which could be marshalled in any community had failed. The central authority very wisely contented itself with arming the local authority which it had created with plenary powers of levying and collecting taxes for the succour of the poor, but it made clear that it had no intention of intervening so long as any community resolved its problems in its own way.

The immediate, and perhaps the expected, consequence of the passage of this great *corpus* of legislation was a notable increase in the flow of private charitable funds designed to provide relief for the truly derelict and to attack the whole problem of poverty frontally by creating institutions which would effect its cure. We shall deal with this remarkable and certainly most impressive flood of charitable giving fully in later pages, but it may here be suggested that in the one generation following the passage of the Elizabethan poor laws rather more was given for charitable uses than in the whole of the preceding four. A truly magnificent effort was undertaken by private charity in the six decades with which our period closes to raise up and endow institutions which would at last bring endemic poverty under control by effective relief and achieve its cure by an immense expansion of the area of social opportunity for all classes of men. The state stood poised for intervention after 1597, if the need should arise, but because of the prodigal generosity of private men who had assumed for themselves an heroic burden of social responsibility that intervention was in fact to be long delayed; delayed, it is fair to say, in its ultimately complete sense, until our own century.

Broadly speaking, therefore, the burden of social responsibility was to be borne by private charity in England throughout our period, the taxing power being reserved for emergency situations in areas overwhelmed by plague, local disaster, or acute economic stress. Save for one brief period, when, as we shall see, the Privy Council intervened with forceful but on the whole ineffectual activity, it may be said that no effort whatever was made to secure the general enforcement of the great statutes of 1597 and that in most regions of the realm the resources provided by private charity proved sufficient for the need. Since it has been commonly assumed that because the statute had been enacted it was generally enforced, we shall want here to deal with this matter at least briefly, while reserving a fuller discussion to a later study.

We may first review the interval 1572 to 1597 when, as we have seen, the parochial authorities possessed power to levy taxes for poor relief if compelling need should arise, though no fully articulated scheme of administration had as yet been arranged by law. The central authority was by no means disinterested in the problem of poverty during these years, having concerned itself quite steadily with efforts to control prices of the important food-stuffs, to secure the better distribution of staple foods in periods of shortage, and to conserve the national stock by setting fast days and discouraging conspicuous consumption.[1] Steady pressure was maintained on the local authorities to achieve the enforcement of the laws against vagabondage and begging, determined efforts were made to regularize and increase the voluntary collections for the poor ordered to be taken in every parish, and a stream of enquiry flowed out from the Council to the justices of the peace demanding information regarding the state of their poor and the measures being taken for their care.[2] But no general or sustained action was taken to require the local

[1] For instances, vide Acts of Privy Council, 1586–1587, 71–72; 1596–1597, 380–386; 1597–1598, 388–389; Yorkshire Archaeological Association, Record Series, III (1888), 84–87, 118.

[2] For examples, vide Hist. MSS. Comm., Salisbury Papers, VII, 118; XIV, 98–99.

authorities to resolve their problems by resort to the legally available solution of taxation.

An extensive study of parochial records in the ten counties with which we are concerned suggests that during this interval the ever-mounting flow of charitable benefactions for poor relief was the principal source of funds wherewith local needs were met, while in many parishes church ales, voluntary offerings, and incidental revenues were employed to buttress the system of household and almshouse relief so rapidly being formed by private generosity. When local disaster struck, whether because of bad harvest or outbreak of plague, the responsible authorities resorted to rates which they and those who paid them regarded as an emergency measure to carry the community through a period of crisis, also likely to be relieved by greatly increased private giving.[1]

An examination of all the overseers' accounts as well as churchwardens' accounts available to us for the whole of England, with, however, somewhat closer attention to the ten counties with which we are concerned in this study, suggests that tax levies to aid with poor relief were by no means uncommon in the long interval from about 1560, when such accounts first appear in systematic form, to 1600, which we have taken as the effective date for the great legislation of 1597–1601.[2]

[1] There are in fact numerous instances of such impositions well before 1572. Thus in Cambridge in 1556, when an epidemic followed in the train of a poor harvest, the municipal authorities assessed a poor rate on the town. The mayor and vice-chancellor levied the assessment arbitrarily, following the principle that the richer parishes should bear most of the burden for the poorer. (Hampson, E. M., *Poverty in Cambs.*, 6–7; *VCH, Cambs.*, II, 90–97.)

[2] We should here comment on the method employed for this survey and on our treatment of the findings. All known printed overseers' accounts as well as churchwardens' accounts have been examined as have certain relevant masses of material in the *State Papers Domestic* and in the *Lansdowne Manuscripts*. But yielding far more have been the overseers' accounts thus far gathered from the parishes into numerous county archives. In four counties an effort has been made to work directly in all the parishes known to hold such accounts, but we are by no means certain that all have been seen, for in many cases parish officers simply do not possess adequate knowledge of their own holdings. A careful and complete census of overseers' accounts available before 1660 is badly needed and such materials, if they are ever to be effectively calendared and studied, should, of course, be gathered into the several county archives.

In all, we have found and examined overseers' accounts in twenty-seven counties. Overseers' records for our period have been found for 288 parishes, of which fifty-one were urban, all these being found in London or Norwich, forty-eight were from thirty-one market towns, and 189 from rural parishes. Many of these accounts were kept for quite short intervals, during periods of acute distress, and others, though cited, were so crudely or imperfectly recorded as to be almost unintelligible. In total, for the period 1560–1660 we have recorded rates and distributions reflecting 2348 annual levies for these parishes, suggesting that in average terms a parish compelled to impose rates during our period did so for a term of about eight years.

It should be added that our figures as presented are not wholly accurate,

During this interval assessments were ordered by the local authorities in 424 instances, the number of such parochial levies averaging about 10·6 for each year in the period. A total of £12,649 17s was raised by the overseers from various sources during the course of these years, of which more than two-thirds (£8716 19s) was derived from rates, while £3190 was gained from uncertain sources, and the remainder from outright gifts or endowed income available to the parish officers. These cautious custodians of funds did not expend the whole of the moneys available, having disbursed £11,904 6s for poor relief in the various parishes whose accounts we have examined. By far the largest distributions were in market towns, where a total of 66 assessments had been made and where £6822 11s was disbursed, or an average of £103 7s 5d in each year in which a levy was ordered. There were relatively few assessments noted in urban parishes and a surprisingly modest average outlay of £18 19s 2d in these instances. The number of rural parishes in which rates are known to have been levied is much larger, there having been 129 such annual assessments, while the average distribution in these relatively simple and homogeneous communities was no more than £5 14s 9d annually.

It seems doubtful that there were many more rates levied for poor relief in this interval than those we have found, while the structure of the levies suggests that they were imposed only in periods of acute local distress. Rather more than a fourth of them were imposed in parishes in the ten counties with which we are concerned, and it is most significant that in almost all cases they were levied in communities as yet without strong and effective charitable endowments. Moreover, such help as was afforded to the poor was regarded only as a subsistence payment to aid in a moment of acute family distress. The record of disbursements is incomplete in most parishes, but we can say that of the whole amount disposed £1339 5s was provided to meet the needs of 2616 individual paupers over this period of about forty years, or an average payment of no more than 10s 3d in each year for the support of a family in extreme distress.[1] Clearly, these payments were made only under circumstances

being drawn as they are from a most confused body of sources. The overseers were singularly unskilled in the arts of book-keeping, they rarely added a column of figures correctly, and they struck balances where balances simply do not exist. More troublesome is the fact that among receipts are mingled funds certainly from rates with funds clearly from charitable sources, while the source of still other considerable amounts remains wholly uncertain. It should also be emphasized that the funds credited in our analysis as from charitable sources in almost all cases reflect only those charitable incomes vested by donors in the church-wardens or overseers or income amounts specifically payable to them for distribution, the larger mass of endowments having been vested in independent trustees and the income paid quite separately to the recipients.

[1] These average amounts are not far off from those found by Emmison in his study of two Bedfordshire parishes in which rates were levied for poor relief

of great urgency and were designed to do no more than supplement the aid now beginning to be disbursed in generous sums by private donors. There was real and there was widespread suffering in Elizabethan England, but in so far as it was relieved it was principally from the hands of private donors.

From 1597 onwards the great Elizabethan poor laws, passed after careful debate and confirmed once more in 1601, were on the statute books, but were to remain only lightly enforced for a full generation as the immense flow of private charity in this remarkable period sustained the increasing social needs of the nation. In 1598 the Privy Council reminded all the justices of the peace of the recent enactments, while assuming that the judges on their last circuits had informed them of the great importance of the measures taken and of the intention of the government that they be put into force. They were accordingly instructed to discuss at their next quarter session ways and means of lending effect to the statutes and were reminded of the high trust imposed in them. But despite these and later representations, the evidence is clear indeed that there was no more than a slight increase in the amounts raised by rates for poor relief and that in almost all communities every possible expedient was exhausted before such levies were imposed. Nor did the government move with more than hortatory persistence to secure the enforcement of the law so long as the flow of endowed income or voluntary contributions was sufficient to carry local burdens which became progressively heavier during the early Stuart period.

In 1607-1608 the harvests were poor, prices were very high, and there were local disturbances reflecting the hardships of these months. Even so, the Council contented itself with issuing orders authorizing the justices of the peace to regulate and control grain supplies and commanding them to request the clergy to exhort their parishioners 'that the poore may be served of corne at convenient & charitable prices'.[1] Nor was any substantial effort made to secure the enforcement of the poor laws when from 1619 to 1622 there were meagre harvests just as the cloth trade found itself in a most severe depression. Instead, the traditional measures of exhortation, regulation of prices, appeals for private intervention, and proclamations concerned with public order were employed in an attempt to hold the economy at least relatively stable until nature afforded better harvests and the now much weakened

in this period. Mr. Emmison's study is a most valuable and pioneering work in this whole field of investigation, while his gathering of parochial accounts into the admirable county archive which he administers in Essex has greatly assisted us in this analysis. Emmison, F. G., 'Poor relief accounts . . . in Bedfordshire, 1563-1598', *Econ. Hist. Rev.*, III (1931-1932), 102-116.

[1] *Orders appointed . . . for . . . remedyng . . . the dearth of graine* (L., 1608), 13.

cloth trade showed some measure of revival. Not only were few parishes rated, but one angry commentator held that 'there hath beene no collection for them [the poor], no not these seven yeares, in many parishes of this land, especiallie in counties townes; but many of those parishes turneth forth their poore, yea and their lustie labourers that will not worke, or for any misdemeanour want to worke, to begg, filch, and steale for their maintenance'.[1]

Though these were difficult years for many segments of the economy, years in which the new and dreadful phenomenon of industrial unemployment first made its appearance in England, they were also years of incredible charitable generosity. In the one generation, 1601–1630, as we shall later observe in detail, the climax of charitable giving in England was attained. During this brief interval upwards of £500,000 was provided in our ten counties for the various heads of poor relief alone, while very large amounts were also poured into a great variety of experiments seeking the social rehabilitation of the poor. There can be no doubt that it was this immense and fruitful flow of funds, largely vested in the enduring form of endowments, which carried the burden of poverty during these years and made it unnecessary to invoke generally the poor laws standing at hand in the event of national emergency.

This is not to say that rates were not levied on occasion in particularly distressed areas, usually to be suspended when an epidemic had passed or when the local economy had regained its stability. It is also apparent that through the course of this generation there was a gradual but a sustained recourse to taxation for poor relief, particularly in the market towns which suffered most from the collapse of the cloth trade. In the first decade (1601–1610) rates were imposed in 184 parishes for at least one year, a total of £8098 coming into the overseers' accounts, of which £6388 8s was certainly derived from taxation, £854 11s from charity, and £855 1s from uncertain sources. In these same parishes £7600 1s was disbursed by the overseers for poor relief, of which it may be noted a very large total (£5373 13s) was given out in the hard-pressed market towns. We can account in individual human terms for the disbursement of only a small proportion of the total paid out by the overseers from income in hand, this being the relatively small sum of £1553 3s which was disposed to 912 paupers, or a sharply higher average stipend of £1 14s 1d annually. This would suggest, of course, that, as a consequence of the Elizabethan poor law, in all the parishes in which overseers' accounts have been found and studied perhaps 4400 persons were in the course of this decade supported, if £1 14s 1d can be regarded as lending support against the wasting ravages of poverty.

In the second decade of the century the amounts received and dis-

[1] S[parke], M[ichael], *Greevous grones for the poor* (L., 1621), 14–15.

bursed by the overseers were substantially increased. The number of parishes imposing rates during these years range from sixteen in the first year (1611) to twenty-two in a year of rather acute economic un-settlement (1619) towards the end of the decade. In all, we have found overseers' accounts for 198 parishes in the course of this decade, of which eighteen were urban, ninety-nine market towns, and the remainder rural. A total of £11,970 4s was entered in overseers' accounts for this decade, of which by far the largest amount (£8393) was from parish rates, £2751 19s from charity, and £825 5s from uncertain sources. The overseers laid out payments for poor relief totalling £11,538 1s, of which £1039 13s was expended in the eighty-one rural parishes, the relatively very large total of £7921 14s in the ninety-nine market towns, and £2576 14s in the eighteen urban parishes. Once again, we can ac-count for the ultimate distribution of only a small proportion of the whole outlay, £2559 4s having, we know, been disbursed to 1029 poor householders. This works out to an average annual distribution of £2 9s 9d for each impoverished household, an amount markedly greater than that prevailing in the previous decade (£1 14s 1d). Our evidence would most strongly suggest that this was occasioned by the fact that an increasing number of aged persons, especially widows, were now being permanently admitted to parochial relief rolls as pen-sioners and that the average length of time during which the able-bodied poor found themselves unemployed rose sharply, particularly in the market towns, during these years.

The curve of recourse to taxation for the support of the really derelict poor projects itself steadily upwards once more in the third decade of the century, the amount received and disbursed by the overseers in the parishes under study having again increased by something like 40 per cent. Overseers' accounts have been found covering at least one year for 251 parishes, the lowest number of impositions having occurred in 1623 when rates were levied in twenty-one parishes and the largest in 1630 when thirty-two parishes were obliged to tax themselves. In all, the considerable total of £16,645 12s was received by the overseers, of which £10,878 12s was derived from rates, £5124 19s from charitable income payable to the overseers, and £642 1s from uncertain sources, most of which, it seems safe to assume, was in the nature of voluntary contributions of one sort or another. The overseers paid out £16,246 9s for poor relief in the course of this decade, of which £5179 8s was dis-bursed in thirty-nine urban parishes, £8740 9s in 112 parishes in market towns, and £2326 12s in 100 rural parishes. We possess detailed infor-mation regarding the disposition of about 31 per cent of these dis-bursements. In all, £4983 5s was paid to 1891 poor householders, the average disbursement having risen once more to an annual stipend of £2 12s 8d, a considerably larger amount than that which charitable donors of the period reckoned sufficient to lend at least subsistence support to a rural family. It would seem prudent to conclude that in the course of this decade something more than 6100 families were sustained and protected by rates in those communities in which overseers' accounts survive. This was by no means an insignificant contribution to human welfare, but it was insignificant indeed when compared with the vast support lent to the society by the huge aggregates of wealth being vested by private benefactors to curb and control the wasting scourge of endemic poverty.

The next decade, 1631–1640, is of particular interest because the government was to undertake in these years a vigorous, a systematic, and certainly a persistent effort to secure the enforcement of the Elizabethan poor laws on a national scale. The years 1629–1631 were marked by still another, and a severe, agricultural depression, accompanied by heavy unemployment in a number of regions dependent for their prosperity on the cloth trade. A proclamation and official *Orders* were issued in September, 1630, establishing local authorities charged with the regulation, the pricing, and the distribution of local stocks of the food grains and with seeing that the poor were provided at reasonable rates.[1] Even earlier, in May, 1629, a proclamation had commanded that the poor laws be enforced, while the assize judges were instructed to make enquiry on their next circuit regarding local arrangements which had been effected.

The Privy Council was faced with a difficult problem of policy, since Parliament had recently been stormily dissolved and since the King had taken a resolution to rule without benefit of its counsel and without recourse to its taxing power. A period of arbitrary government was being ushered in, just at the moment when the Council was persuaded that the social needs of the nation required the full and rigorous enforcement of a system of law and administration which depended in the last analysis on the support of the justices of the peace, men principally drawn from the politically dominant class in the realm which had been so recently and so generally estranged. Furthermore, the Council was itself weak, was seriously out of touch with opinion in the realm at large, and was to undertake a gigantic task of local administration with an administrative mechanism that had fallen into sad decay in the generation that had elapsed since Elizabeth had brought the arts of local governance to a pitch of high excellence. None the less, the decision was taken, principally, it seems certain, on the strong advice of Archbishop Laud and Wentworth, both of whom were particularly insensitive to political opinion and both of whom suffered from the tendency to assume that when an order was issued, a blueprint carefully drawn up,

[1] *Orders appointed . . . for the preuenting and remedying of the dearth of graine and other victuall* (L., 1630), 2–3, 9, 11–13.

successful administration and execution followed as a consequence of fiat.[1]

This resolution was carried into formidable effect, involving the power and the attention of the whole Council, when in June, 1630, a special committee of the Privy Council was constituted as a commission for the poor, charged to bring fully into enforcement the *corpus* of the Elizabethan poor laws and to establish local commissions in areas where distress was particularly acute. Shortly afterwards, the conciliar committee divided itself for administrative purposes into six sub-committees responsible for regional areas coterminous with the several judicial circuits in order the better to follow in detail the progress of the social commitment which had been assumed.[2] This action was followed in January, 1631, by the drafting and publication of *Orders and directions* which recited and glossed in detail the existing statutes relating to poor relief and set out the method by which their enforcement was to be secured. All justices of the peace were required to form themselves into committees to ensure the administration of the law in each hundred and were to hold monthly meetings with the overseers, constables, and churchwardens who were charged with the ultimate responsibility for administration in the parishes. Neglect of duty was to be sternly punished and the justices of the peace were to render regular and detailed reports to the assize judges, who would in turn forward them to the Privy Council. The *Directions*, twelve in number, reviewed the principal terms of the Elizabethan legislation, setting out with clarity and no little eloquence the view that each community must assume full and unflinching responsibility for the care of its own poor.[3]

The Privy Council maintained continuous pressure on the justices of the peace to secure the enforcement of the poor laws from 1631 to 1638, during a period when the constitutional crisis was mounting steadily and the realm was drifting towards civil war. It must, indeed, have devoted a considerable proportion of its business time to a consideration of the enormous mass of returns that flowed in during these years from the harassed justices and to trying to secure at least formal returns from some eight counties which did not even deign to reply. There are upwards of 1200 of these returns from committees of justices responsible for individual hundreds.

An examination of these returns suggests that the Council was incredibly naïve in assuming that because a return had been filed the

---

[1] Lipson, *Economic history*, III, 450–451; Leonard, *Poor relief*, 150–154.

[2] *S.P. Dom.*, 1631, CLXXXII, 8, CLXXXIII, 60.

[3] *Orders and directions with commissions for the better administration of justice* (*BM Add. MSS.* 12, 496, f. 243); printed, with changes, as *Orders and directions* (L., 1630). We have followed the first text in this analysis.

law was being enforced. The great mass of the returns are on their face evasive, vague, or misleading and could have given the Council little more solid information than they give us. Yet these returns, save in a few instances, were filed and accepted as meeting the requirements of the ambitious, indeed, revolutionary, policy to which the Council had addressed itself. In many areas from which returns were faithfully made we have certain knowledge that overseers had not even been appointed, in far more that rates were not being levied despite the inference that they were. In almost half the returns we are told that there were no poor who stood in need, that incidental fines levied and devoted to the poor were sufficient, or that local charities were quite adequate to carry the burden. Many justices reported most confidently that rates were about to be levied, which the Council seems to have taken as sufficient assurance. Other returns were stiffly and arrogantly couched, saying almost nothing save that local needs were being met by local resources and methods. This great body of material conveyed little solid information to the Privy Council and suggests most strongly that the central government was almost completely out of touch with those responsible for local administration. Laud and Wentworth had set for the Privy Council a gigantic task of administration at a time when the sovereign was proceeding with a hazardous experiment in arbitrary government that was doomed at the moment of the first national crisis. The letters and demands flowing out from the Council were imperious, wordy, and assured in tone, but they commanded little of respect, nothing but vagueness of response, from men of high local station who had a generation earlier been the principal pillars of monarchy but who were now its estranged and sullen enemies. The structure of sovereignty in England had crumbled well before the convention of the Long Parliament.

This conclusion, derived from a study of this huge and amazing mass of evidence, is most abundantly confirmed by our independent assessment of the overseers' accounts for this tragic decade. Amounts flowing into the overseers' accounts and amounts disbursed by them had from 1571 forward been rising on a remarkably stable curve from decade to decade and little more than this occurred in the decade under discussion.[1] It almost seems, indeed, that the Council's frenzied efforts were without any substantial consequence at all. In a considerable number of parishes we do know that rates were for the first time imposed, but there is reason for believing that in part this was the result of local needs which would have been met in this manner, the fussy and nervous insistence of the Council notwithstanding.

In the course of this decade 434 parishes in England levied poor rates in at least one year, the smallest number of assessments occurring

[1] See graph of overseers' accounts overleaf.

ironically in 1634 when the activities of the Privy Council were at their height and the largest in 1638 when weary experience, disillusionment, and serious political crisis had caused the Council to abandon its efforts to secure an enforcement of the poor laws on a national scale. In all, the overseers rendered accounts for receipts of £26,947 11s during these years, of which £17,262 15s. was derived from rates, £1609 5s from uncertain sources, and £8075 11s from voluntary contributions. Of this total, £25,841 9s was disposed by the overseers for poor relief, £9769 4s in thirty-two urban parishes, £3186 3s in 246 rural communities, and the large sum of £12,886 2s in 156 parishes in market towns suffering seriously from the economic crisis which marked these years. We have been able to trace out the distribution of almost half (48·77 per cent) of the whole amount disposed by the overseers, a total of £12,603 5s having been provided for 5453 needy persons. This works out to an average distribution of £2 6s 3d annually to each poor man, slightly less than in the preceding decade, and would suggest that something over 1100 families were each year being maintained and succoured by public funds in those communities where overseers' accounts have been found.

We shall in the course of this work have frequent occasion to comment on the remarkable stability of English institutions, or, perhaps one

OVERSEERS' ACCOUNTS, 1560-1660

TOTAL DISBURSEMENTS ......
INCOME FROM POOR RATES ———

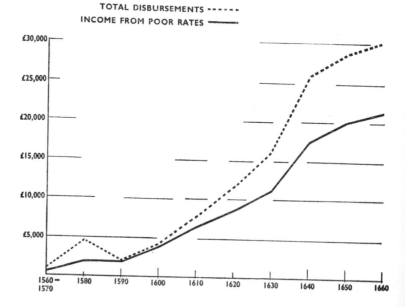

could as accurately say, English habits, during the revolutionary decades with which this study closes. Save when there was disruption caused by actual hostilities or the presence of large bodies of troops, life in a rural parish or a market town seems to have proceeded in the usual patterns and local institutions to have continued to function as they always had. We shall note that the flow of charitable funds continued, though with some abatement, during the whole course of these two decades and that charitable endowments continued to be properly administered under the watchful eye of the central government, the courts, and interested local bodies. There was serious economic dislocation in much of England during the period of hostilities, but there is abundant evidence that so far as poverty and unemployment were concerned the requirements of the two armies for men, for transport, and for supplies tended to absorb the unemployed and actually to lift the general level of wages. Army pay considerably exceeded that commanded by ordinary labour, and the official complaint from Hertfordshire that its waggons were being drained off at twice the pay offered locally suggests the kind of inflationary process at work in much of England during this interval. At the outset of this period the King had somewhat plaintively commended to the realm the Elizabethan code of poor law which his Council had failed to bring fully into effect,[1] while a renewed and extremely vigorous sovereign power under the Commonwealth and Protectorate intervened actively and steadily to secure the administration of the laws relating to charitable trusts and to lay on the local authority the ultimate responsibility for the care of the poor.[2]

Nor does it seem to be true, as has been so uniformly said, that the administration of the poor laws collapsed or was gravely impaired during these years. The remarkable fact is that the level of receipts and of disbursements carried into the overseers' accounts even during the troubled decade of civil war rose substantially as compared with that reached in the preceding decade when the whole weight of the government had been brought to bear on the justices of the peace and the parishes, while in the decade of the Commonwealth and Protectorate overseers' receipts and disbursements were to increase once more. This is only one of the many myths which need to be dispelled with respect both to the policy of the Cromwellian government and, more impor-

---

[1] *A proclamation commending the due execution of the laws made for setting the poor on work* (1640); in *S.P. Dom.*, 1640, CCCCLIV, 12, and printed in full in Rymer, Thomas, *Foedera* (L., 1704–1735, 20 vols.), XX, 407.

[2] *S.P. Dom.*, 1650, IX, 45 (May 3) 3; XI, 10 (September 7) 13; 1651, XV, 43 (March 29) 2; XVI, 16 (July 28); 1652, XXIV, 113 (August 27) 9; 1653, XXXVI, 86 (May 21) 24; XLIII, 366 (September 6); 1654, LXXIII, 16 (July 6) 8, 9; LXXIV, 100 (August 21); 1655, C, 42 (August 22) 5; C, 55 (August 29) 16; 1655–1656, CXXIII, 8 (January 2) 1; 1659, CCIV, 33, 35 (September 20) 15.

tantly, to the effect of the revolutionary period on English life and institutions.

In the decade of civil war, 1641–1650, rates were levied for poor relief for at least one year in 401 parishes, the heaviest incidence occurring in 1650 when forty-seven overseers' accounts have been found and the lightest in 1643 when thirty-four parishes laid taxes for the purpose. The period of the heaviest and most continuous warfare did clearly take its toll, since the £1947 10s disbursed by overseers in 1642 and the £2314 12s expended by them in 1643 was markedly less than in any other year in the period. For the whole decade £28,913 12s was recorded as received in the accounts of the overseers, of which £19,657 14s was gained by rates, £7613 8s from voluntary gifts, and £1642 10s from uncertain sources. The overseers for these years reported outlays for the succour of the poor totalling £28,451 7s, or about £2600 more than the amount we have noted in the preceding decade. By far the largest expenditure was in 117 parishes in market towns, which accounted for £14,507 8s 5d, or nearly 51 per cent of the entire sum, while £6249 7s was disbursed in 250 rural parishes, and £7694 12s in thirty-four urban parishes. We can account in detail for the expenditure of about 29 per cent of the whole amount, £8210 1s having been employed to provide stipends for 3470 poor families in the given years, or an average of £2 7s 4d for each pauper receiving his support from public funds. This amount, it will be observed, is not far off from the average subsistence payment made in each decade from 1611 onwards, a remarkable stability in such payments having been maintained despite a steadily mounting inflation and the admission of an ever-larger proportion of permanent pensioners to the relief rolls.

The amounts raised and disbursed for poor relief by the enforcement of the Elizabethan code were to increase modestly during the closing decade of our period when political stability had been restored and when the revolutionary government in its turn brought at least moderate, though hardly sustained, pressure to bear on the local communities to discharge their responsibilities by taxation if charitable funds in hand proved to be insufficient. During these years the substantial total of £31,288 9s was raised by the overseers in 456 parishes, of which £20,879 16s was derived from rates, £7975 9s from charitable sources, and £2433 4s from uncertain quarters. The overseers disbursed in all £30,061 13s, the largest sum being £11,585 spent on poor relief in ninety-six market towns, or an average annual outlay in these communities of slightly more than £120. A total of £8983 10s was spent for the needs of the poor in 324 rural parishes, while a somewhat larger outlay of £9493 3s has been noted in the accounts of urban overseers. For this decade, we have the particulars regarding disbursement of well over half (55·89 per cent) of the total outlay, £16,802 12s having been

paid to 5934 poor men and women, or an average stipend of £2 16s 8d
annually for each pauper. This outlay was somewhat higher than that
noted in the preceding decade, very much larger than the £2 5s 1d
which is the average overseers' disbursement during our entire period,
and is likewise substantially greater than founders of charitable endowments assumed, again in average terms, was required to lend subsistence
to a family for a year even in urban parishes. In part this rise may be
attributed to a still greater proportion of disbursements made to pen-
sioners, persons permanently deriving their support from public moneys,
by the substantial inflation marking this period, and, at least in part,
by a somewhat greater sensitivity to the needs of poor families, ranging
just a little beyond the concept of maintenance on the plane of bare
survival.

We may conclude, then, from substantial, though certainly incomplete evidence, that the Elizabethan poor laws were regarded as prudential by the government which enacted them and by later governments as well, save for the determined effort of the Privy Council to
implement this great legislation just prior to the outbreak of the Civil
War. It stood ready to be enforced in the event of great national emergency, but it was never brought fully to bear on social needs during our
period because the immense flow of private charitable funds dedicated
to the succour of the poor was, save for local and emergency exceptions,
almost sufficient to meet the basic needs as the age understood and
defined them. We have observed, however, that the law was gradually
brought more fully into effect as our period progresses, although in all
parishes where rates were levied they were regarded as no more than
supplementary to the permanent charitable provisions which private
donors were creating in every corner of England. But at no time in our
period were the sums raised by rates substantial or particularly significant when compared with the great amounts available as a consequence
of the ever-mounting endowments created by private generosity.

To lend further support to this conclusion we may take the year
(1650) in which the largest disbursements to the poor were made by the
overseers. In this year £4306 5s of payments are recorded, the funds
supporting the outlays having been derived from £3269 12s in rates,
£266 6s from uncertain sources, and £906 17s from voluntary contributions, or £4442 15s of income in all. If we may assume, and it is most
unlikely, that the revenues from uncertain sources were also from rates,
a total of £3535 18s was in this year raised by taxation in those parishes
in all parts of England about which we have certain knowledge. This
amount, and the somewhat larger amount paid out by overseers, may
properly be contrasted with the income available, and expended, in our
ten counties alone from the endowments which had by the close of our
period been established for household relief and for the support of

many hundreds of almshouses. The income disbursed for household relief in the parishes of our counties, and in other counties as their gift, was about £30,525 p.a., while for the support of almshouses massive endowments had been constituted yielding something like £20,870 to secure the full maintenance of those who were irrevocably derelict. In all, then, something over £51,000 was annually available for distribution by private trustees, city companies, parish officials, including overseers, and many other trustees, by a nation which had performed a kind of miracle in mustering great charitable wealth from most generous private sources in an heroic and largely successful effort to deal with a problem as old as history itself.[1] This resolution and this effort had been supplemented and strengthened by prudential legislation, by the setting forth of an ultimate public responsibility undergirding the private resolution, which had not in the course of our period to be brought fully into force and which in fact made relatively no more than slight direct contribution to the social needs of the age.

By the most liberal analysis of the data this would seem to suggest that in no year prior to 1660 was more than 7 per cent of all the vast sums expended on the care of the poor derived from taxation.[2] We believe that this is not far from the mark for England as a whole, in great areas of which rates for poor relief were never levied at all. But it is not, of course, true in those parishes for which overseers' accounts have been found in the ten counties with which we are concerned. Excluding, as we should, thirteen parishes in London and Middlesex which together possessed huge charitable endowments, in part vested for the relief of other areas, we have within our group of counties found overseers' records in seventy-nine market towns and rural parishes where in all 822 annual assessments were made for the care of the poor. A few of these were parishes well endowed for poor relief but which were obliged to levy rates for supplementary needs because of famine, fire, or acute economic distress. But this group of parishes generally were among the poorest in their respective counties, most of them being areas of social blight, as we shall describe them in the detailed county analyses in later volumes. They were, then, typically parishes with far less than average charitable resources, communities which were wanting in strong local leadership and often with no resident gentry. Nevertheless, taking in every instance the year (1650) in which the largest amount was raised by rates, even in this group of marginal parishes, the sums available for the needs of the poor from charitable endowments

---

[1] For a fuller discussion and elucidation of these estimates, *vide post*, 253–263.

[2] We have in our reckoning of the amounts available from charitable sources included only income from endowed (capital) funds. There was as well a steady flow of outright gifts and doles for immediate use, amounting, it may be noted, to £627 6s in our ten counties in the year 1650.

exceeded by slightly more than three times the amounts gathered by taxation for distribution by the overseers. It would seem, therefore, that the Elizabethan legislation was in a general sense prudential, and that broadly speaking it was invoked only in those areas in which private charity, for a variety of reasons, had failed to bring communities level with the realm at large in their social resources.[1]

Though, in general, it may be said that the poor laws were not invoked because they were not needed, because private charity bore almost the whole of the great burden of poor relief prior to 1660, it must also be said that they were enforced in any community only as a last resort, for these rates were extremely unpopular and they were most difficult to raise until time and experience had established local habits and until innumerable judicial decisions had fixed the pattern of their administration. In almost every parish where rates were levied there was a swarm of angry and outraged complaints regarding the rating methods, the probity of the overseers, and urgent denials that the poor were not already well provided. There are hundreds of complaints from overseers of outright refusals to pay assessments and many scores in which a rich parish simply declined to pay even a light assessment for the relief of another in the same hundred hard hit by plague or poverty. This enormous body of obdurate complaint flowed from the overseers to the justices of the peace, who did their best in quarter sessions to adjudicate in terms of local traditions and knowledge, often with scant regard for the crystal-clear prescription of statute law. But many cases they referred on to the assize judges or directly to the Privy Council, especially in the Laudian period when refusals to pay poor rates ordered from above took on some of the ugly political aspects of refusal to pay Ship Money rates in these same years. The life of a justice of the peace was hard in those hundreds where levies were made, that of the overseers intolerable and on occasion perilous. The countryside resisted these rates as best it could, though they bore but lightly upon the individual property owner, in part to be sure because they

[1] It should once more be emphasized that the figures we have used for amounts raised for poor relief are limited to the amounts set out in the overseers' accounts which we have found. These figures are necessarily incomplete, so any attempt to project them by computation to the whole of England would be pointless. There has, in any case, been far too much of wild conjecture on the whole subject. Willet (*Synopsis papismi*, 1220) believed that from £30,000 to £40,000 p.a. was being raised by taxation for poor relief in *ca.* 1613, certainly far too high an estimate. Thomas Ruggles, adducing no evidence whatsoever, suggests a figure of £188,811 p.a. in 1650 (*History of the poor*, L., 1793, 2 vols., I, 168–169). The first credible estimate is for 1696 when poor rates were probably yielding as much as £400,000 p.a., but this bears no relation to the realities for our period. The poor laws were widely enforced after 1660, as the flow of private charities began to diminish and as the economy became at once more complex and erratic.

were taxes, in part certainly because they were untraditional, but one senses even more importantly because for a parish to be rated was an admission of local failure to meet responsibilities which men of this age had come to agree they should freely and fully meet from their own resources as citizens of a Christian and a civilized community.

VI

The Impulse

1. *The problem of motives*

We have observed that broadly speaking the whole elaborate apparatus of the Elizabethan poor laws was never brought fully into operation at any time during the course of our era and, save for a brief period of fairly extensive trial under the somewhat excited direction of Archbishop Laud, was never generally tried at all. The burden of responsibility for the care of the poor and for the enlargement of social opportunity was borne by private charity which created massive endowments for the founding and fashioning of the basic institutions of the liberal society. The great *corpus* of Elizabethan law was, as we have seen, a prudential system, framed to protect the society and the state against the threat of social disaster which might have become very real indeed had not private men acted so quickly, so generously, and so intelligently as they addressed themselves to the mastery of the transcendent problems of their age. The state had taken the necessary resolution to move into a vast area of need when circumstances should require, but a whole system of ideas, of ideals, and of institutions which we describe as liberal resulted from the fact that a great outpouring of private wealth dedicated to social ends made any substantial sovereign intervention unnecessary. An historical decision of very great moment was perhaps unwittingly taken by private donors of all classes, but most importantly by those of the merchant élite, which initiated not only the fashioning of adequate social institutions for the nation but also the fashioning of an ethic of social responsibility which was to be the hall-mark of the liberal society. Very generally, one may say that the bulwarks raised by private generosity against poverty, disease, ignorance, and impotence remained sufficient until they were overwhelmed by the forces loosed by the Industrial Revolution, which in England and the western world made necessary the direct and ultimately the massive intervention of the state in order to ensure the welfare, perhaps the survival, of large masses of men chronically in danger from, when they had not been rendered permanent casualties by, the complex society which is the modern industrial economy. Surely it is not too much to say that our ideals and our social ethic are still largely an inheritance from the earlier age with which this study is concerned. Men of our generation do not fully realize that an immensely significant social revolution has occurred over the course of the past century which has left them all citizens of a welfare state. This encompassing historical reality must in turn require from our society an accommodation in ideals, in social and political theory, and doubtless in institutions which may well move it far from the bases upon which it has reposed since the seventeenth century. The Elizabethan poor laws were prudential; in a very true sense we may say that mankind did not have fully to impose them until our own generation.

We are now concerned with an analysis of the motives which, as it were, impelled men to save their society from the state, albeit with the almost frantic encouragement of the central authority. What, in brief, were the impulses which caused a relatively small group of private donors to undertake in the course of our period, one can almost say in a period of about two generations, such a vast burden of social responsibility for a society which stood in considerable peril? We are here concerned at bottom with an analysis of human motives, with an area of reality in which the historian moves with great uncertainty and without the sure guidance of neatly ordered fact. Our question, quite exactly put, is what caused men to perform essentially noble, self-sacrificing actions, and particularly why they were considerably more inclined to do so in the rather tightly defined interval of a century extending from the accession of Queen Elizabeth to the restoration of the monarchy than in any other period before or since. We do here concern ourselves with human motives, and about them we can never speak with comfortable assurance. This is true, of course, even when we seek coolly and dispassionately to examine the moving forces underlying our own actions, our own decisions, and most particularly those occasional deeds of ours which may be believed to embrace some elements of nobility. What really animates our action when we subscribe to a hospital fund, endow a scholarship, found a college, or give casual alms to a passing beggar? Such benevolent actions, we may suppose, are at bottom taken because we are subtly subject to the pressures of a culture which regards such actions as worthy. They are in one sense, therefore, not free actions at all, but are a tithe levied upon our means by the ethic of a society of which we are part and to which we all must in greater or lesser degree conform. But even if this be so the fact does not explain the true springs of our action, does not, as it were, elucidate and illumine the moment of decision. This most essential datum remains buried deep in the recesses of our nature, immune, perhaps happily, from the fumbling probing of the historian and, certainly happily, from the too arrogantly pitched enquiry of the psychoanalyst.

These difficulties of analysis, of arriving at understanding, are, need-less to say, enormously increased as we seek to assess the impulses which moved men to generous and noble actions in a much earlier age. Not understanding the wellsprings of our own actions carries no im-pressive certification for discovering the motives for action in another and very different era. Moreover, this difficulty is greatly increased by the fact that we are dealing with an interval of time in which there was a profoundly important and most massive shift in the structure of men's aspirations for their society, when many men were taking great charitable decisions which did not enjoy the general approbation of their society, when they were evidently moved by impulses of noncon-formity rather than of conformity. It is quite precisely this metamor-phosis in men's aspirations from the needs of the religious society to the requirements of the secular society that principally concerns us, with the result that we must probe for motives which ran against an ethic prevailing in the western world for a very long time. To pose this question more explicitly and in humble, and hence perhaps in the ultimately important, form, just why did it occur that the customary bequests from husbandmen in Somerset of a few pence for the needs of their parish church give way at about 1580 to equally customary legacies of a few pence for the parish poor? It was certainly not that there were suddenly more poor or that the church stood in less need. Something had happened to the motives, the moving aspirations, of very simple men in a remote county just as it had happened to richer and more socially sophisticated classes of men a generation or more earlier. In the broader sense, in terms of large masses of men, we believe we do understand what had occurred; we remain very uncertain indeed when we seek to discover the springs of action forming and then dictating the immensely significant decision in 1581 of John Broocke, husband-man, of Winford, Somerset, to leave 4s for the needs of the poor of his parish rather than to give modestly to the needs of his parish church as his ancestors had before him.

Yet it must be said that even in this area of historical concern we are not without impressive resources of knowledge. As we have already had occasion to say, men of our period were verbosely eloquent when the solemn moment came to draw their wills and to order their charities. In this deeply religious age men composed their wills and testaments in the sight of God and in a large number of cases they sought, perhaps as honestly and as fully as men have ever done, to explain and even to examine the motives which underlay and enforced their actions. Thus very typically indeed, a London merchant by will founding and endow-ing a grammar school in Lancashire not only explains at length the reasons for his zealous hatred of ignorance and illiteracy but tells us why he has chosen to found an important social institution in a particular and a remote community. The motives, the impulses, under-girding action are then commonly explicit in the wills and deeds of gift of these thousands of donors who were creating a new society in the image of their own aspirations, just as they may be said to be implicit in the multitude of smaller gifts for which only scant information survives.

2. *Metamorphosis of the mediaeval conception of alms*

Before turning more precisely to a consideration of the great moving forces which were to elicit and to order an immense outpouring of charitable wealth in our period, it will be well to review very briefly the principal historical movements which had created an environment in which the great metamorphosis of men's aspirations might occur. Thus we have observed that the decay of the mediaeval society created a social crisis which could not for long be ignored by sensitive and responsible men, while at the same time this very process of decay hastened the end of the mediaeval system of alms which had been inadequate for the needs of an earlier era and which stood irrelevant to the requirements of the sixteenth century. We shall have many later occasions to point out that few indeed of the truly charitable mediaeval institutions, the alms-houses, the schools, and all the rest, that survived at the close of the Middle Ages were harmed by the swift and ruthless process of the revolutionary movement which we call the Reformation. They were on balance rather strengthened, improved, and extended, principally by private charity, while generally speaking they were all wrenched free of ecclesiastical control as part of the violent process of secularization then under way in every aspect of English life and institutions.[1] The pitifully few remaining charitable assets were on balance nurtured and rendered more relevant to the needs of a new age. But, as we shall see in county after county, there were few indeed that had survived the long process of the death of an earlier society. Men of the sixteenth century had of necessity to begin to build their institutions *de novo*, and they built in accordance with the requirements of a new and a very different con-ception of social architecture.

It perhaps simplifies a process of social change far too much to say that men of the Middle Ages gave alms as an act of piety while men of the sixteenth century gave, and much more generously, under the dic-tate of social need. Yet the evidence runs most persuasively with the statement. Mediaeval alms were on the whole quite indiscriminately given, quite sentimentally disposed, without much reference either to the present need of the recipient or his future fate. The most perfectly typical forms of mediaeval alms were those given to beggars at the monastery gates and those disbursed wholly indiscriminately under the

---

[1] Tawney, *Religion and the rise of capitalism*, 217; Ashley, *English economic history*, II, 327.

terms of the will of a rich prelate or noble as funeral doles. This whole pattern of almsgiving, which was probably insufficient if not harmful even during the high Middle Ages, was coming to an end well before the Reformation and was almost forgotten a generation later. At the same time, we shall observe an immediate and an immense burgeoning out of benefactions for poor relief, secular in form and intent, addressed to the control, if not the cure, of poverty, and designed to relieve the conscience of a society which had come quite suddenly to regard poverty as a social evil and as a danger to the strength and well-being of the realm. We have in earlier pages discussed at some length the really rapid development of this new attitude which supplied one of the most important of the underlying motives for private charity.

3. *The changing pattern of aspirations: secularization of the charitable impulse*

In later pages we shall deal in detail with the profoundly important shift from men's concern with the needs of organized religion to the human needs which they saw in the world around them. But here it is well at least to note that this great translation in their interests and aspirations had the effect of immensely enlarging the sphere of their responsibility. The mediaeval church was in many senses an institution offering to men no more than a vicarious opportunity for the exercise of their philanthropic impulses. Alms, it was taught, were better distributed to the needy through the good offices of the church; the derelict were better provided for through hostels and hospitals administered and oriented by the ecclesiastical authority. The objects of the pious concern felt by donors were accordingly once removed from the act of generosity, while the effectiveness of ecclesiastical charity, subserving as it did the ends of faith, came with cause to be doubted by laymen quite untouched by heresy. In London, for example, education was for many years a closely guarded ecclesiastical monopoly, proof even against other ecclesiastical competition, with an inevitable freezing of the sources of rich and ready lay assistance for a need which had by 1500 reached a state of scandal. Merchant wealth for almost a century before the Reformation poured out from London in mounting streams for the founding of grammar schools in the provinces, with in most cases scarcely concealed efforts to secure these foundations as nearly as possible against clerical control. When the weight of ecclesiastical control was lifted in London itself by the revolution which began with Colet and ended with the Reformation, the task of forming the school resources of the great city was well begun within a generation and in terms of sixteenth century needs all but completed by the close of the second generation. The triumph of secularism had, then, its liberating aspects; it cleared the way for the free play of imagination and daring in meeting the needs of mankind; and it placed in the hands of men who were as bold as they were generous instrumentalities for the attainment of their aspirations for their own age and the age to come.

4. *The logic of the need*

Surely, too, the impulse of charity owed much to the ever-clearer evidence of grievous social need which marks the unfolding of the sixteenth century. We have previously dealt at length with this question,[1] having observed that aid was at once more urgently required than in earlier generations and that the fact of need was informed by a rapidly maturing social conscience. Because secularism triumphed with the Reformation it meant that the society had assumed a vast responsibility and concern which had been left in priestly hands before and that the forces of social evil and rot could no longer be ignored. This awareness of need, this increasingly sensitive concern, likewise owed much to the warm and persuasive eloquence of the great preachers of the Reformation, clustering around the heroic genius of Latimer, who angrily denounced Rome and the forces of poverty in the same breath and who set for Protestantism perhaps impossibly high standards of moral attainment in the very generation of its emergence. Latimer and his brethren were often ill-informed, always overly dramatic, and ever better moralists than social commentators, but they literally bludgeoned into the English conscience an awareness of new and pressing responsibilities which it was never quite to renounce again.

But even if he convicted the sixteenth century for depopulations which had mostly occurred in the fifteenth, Latimer none the less was profoundly perceptive in his understanding that men of his age must come to grips with an ancient evil which had appeared in new and sinister forms. We have seen that the sixteenth century was marked by an immensely important agricultural revolution and by the inevitable dislocations accompanying the rapid spread of industry and urbanization. New and marginal classes of men emerged, bereft of the sanctuary of land and instantly vulnerable to seasonal or cyclical unemployment. It was a poverty wanting in the possibility of any dignity; it was a creeping, mobile poverty that could never be quite confined to the region of its origin; and it was a poverty which bred the possibility of social disorders born of hopelessness. Contemporary observers who were at once responsible and unsentimental believed that there were forces loose in the land which might bring the realm to the brink of social disaster, and, as we have seen, Parliament in 1597 itself thought that this time had come. This awareness of acute need, need no longer sustained either by the community of the land or by the ministrations of the priest, supplied an immensely powerful impulse to charity. And it

---

[1] *Vide ante*, 56–76.

was private charity, flowing out as it did into every nook and corner of the land, which saved England at once from social disaster and from the necessity for the intervention of the state on a massive scale. The secular spirit of mankind won for itself a notable triumph in this first great trial of its strength and its sense of social responsibility.

5. *The confirmation of national policy*

The understanding which men of the sixteenth century came to have of large areas of national need was animated, as it was disciplined, by Tudor social and economic policy. The three great Tudors, whose reigns encompass more than a century of our period, all possessed an extraordinary sense not only of the needs of their age but of its historical direction. They assessed with rare wisdom the social and economic tensions of the century and then lent strong and intelligent support to those countervailing forces which would afford relief. Above all else, these great monarchs were extremely sensitive to all threats of disorder, to all those pressures which threatened the security and power of the Crown. It is very clear indeed that their steady concern with the eroding poverty of their age proceeded not from any sentimental concern for the poor but rather from an astute understanding that unrelieved and uncontrolled want constituted a grave threat to the stability of the realm. It is not too much to say that the Tudors viewed charity as a necessary aspect of public policy rather than as a requirement of Christian morality.

We have previously observed that the whole weight of Tudor policy was secular and that discreet but sustained support was lent by the Crown to a process of social revolution already well under way. Most of the institutions of the realm, including the church itself (one is almost tempted to say), were to be completely secularized in the course of the sixteenth century. Thus it was that the whole range of institutions wherewith the society was sustained and bettered were rebuilt when they were not freshly constituted by private and intensely secular charitable funds which flowed into channels opened up by national policy. Thus, for example, the pressing problem of poverty was transferred from the sphere of religion to that of secular social policy and came by the close of the century officially to be declared the responsibility of the whole body politic. The full authority of the Crown and the effective powers of its principal agencies were accordingly ranged in support of the impulse for private charity, which it was hoped might prove sufficient to bear the ever heavier social burdens of a new age.

The direct concern of the Crown with the social needs of our period is well illustrated by the increasing number of charitable briefs directly promulgated for a variety of worthy causes. These royal warrants for the collection of funds for specified charitable purposes were a secular replacement of the earlier papal briefs, perhaps the earliest example being that issued in the form of letters patent by Henry VIII to assist the prior and monks of Kirkby (Leics.) in raising funds for the rebuilding of their priory. We have counted in all some eighty-three of these royal warrants for general charitable purposes, excluding a considerable number granted for the relief of particular persons. The secular temper of the age is suggested by the fact that only twenty of these briefs authorized collections for the repair or rebuilding of churches, usually after a fire or some other local disaster, or for some more general religious need, most of these being concentrated after 1606. There were, as well, numerous briefs issued for the relief of persecuted Protestants abroad, by far the most important being the collection made in 1655 for the relief of the Protestants in the Vaudois and in Poland, when the huge sum of £51,532 17s 8d was raised in a national effort in which most intensive propaganda was employed. The largest number, thirty-one in all, were authorized to secure the relief of communities which had suffered from fire or to assist in the carrying forward of needed municipal betterments such as bridges, causeways, and havens. All the remainder were addressed towards some scheme of social rehabilitation, the relief of the poor in a particularly distressed community, or for miscellaneous public purposes.[1]

These charitable interventions of the state were, of course, relatively unimportant and occasionally most eccentric indications of national policy with respect to the expanding social needs of the national community. They were, in point of fact, no more than visible tokens of a vast intervention which the state had reluctantly undertaken for the social welfare of the nation in the slowly accumulating legislation which was at last forged into a system in the codifying statutes passed towards the close of the great Queen's reign. These laws, as we have noted, were designed as no more than emergency measures to be employed and implemented when the social fabric of the nation should be endangered by forces too powerful for policy to master or for private charity to ameliorate. They were posited on the assumption that the responsible, the dominant, social classes of the realm would in ordinary seasons bear the burdens not only of social relief but of social betterment; that private men would with their own means build a society according to the designs framed by their own aspirations. These vast obligations were

[1] It should be noted here that these collections, with the single but important exception of the moneys raised for the repair of St Paul's, have not been included in our totals save when the amount contributed from the counties with which we are concerned can be established. In only relatively few instances, in fact, are the particulars available regarding the amounts raised in these charitable canvasses. Excellent discussion of this whole matter may be found in Ping, L. G., *Raising funds for good causes during the Reformation* (L., 1936) and in Bewes, W. A., *Charity briefs* (L., 1896).

undertaken principally by two classes of men, the mercantile aristocracy and the gentry, classes which enjoyed the steady confidence and favour of the Tudors and on whose loyalty and devotion the whole edifice of Tudor power and policy had been erected. These relatively small classes of men, vigorous, articulate, and intelligent, possessed an astute understanding not only of the needs of their age but of the direction in which the forces of history sloped. In the sixteenth century we shall observe a steady translation of responsibility to these classes, to be followed in the seventeenth by an inevitable translation of power. The Tudors not only understood but they assisted this whole process of historical change, which to their tragic undoing the Stuarts almost blindly and uncomprehendingly resisted. Power, as history has so often demonstrated, flows inevitably to those unafraid to assume the burdens of responsibility.

B. THE GREAT MOVING IMPULSES

1. *The emergence of the Protestant ethic*

We have been dealing with the broader historical background from which the powerful impulses of private charity sprang during the course of our period and which framed and ordered men's aspirations for their age. We should now seek to analyse somewhat more specifically the great moving forces which evoked the immense outpouring of charitable funds and which, it is not too much to say, founded and brought to a remarkable maturity the basic social institutions of the liberal society. We shall have later occasion abundantly to demonstrate that the structure of men's aspirations became increasingly secular and that the institutions endowed as a consequence lent massive, perhaps decisive, support to the secular forces which were to master English policy well before our period closes. Yet it must be understood that the huge accumulations of charitable funds, the whole framing of the social institutions of the age, and the impulses which moved men were firmly and deeply rooted in the Protestant ethic which had itself been brought to an almost precocious maturity before the close of the sixteenth century. The Protestant Reformation in England, proceeding as it did quite independently from the decorous and prudent formulations of official statement, was in its nature revolutionary, in most important respects anti-clerical, and in its social consequences deeply imbued with secularism. This process of reformation affected the lay mind more profoundly than it did clerical and governmental policy, having as one of its most formidable aspects the earnest denunciation and repudiation of the whole Catholic apparatus of alms, of social inaction dominated by clerical policy, and of a generally conservative attitude towards broad areas of social responsibility. The surviving mediaeval social institutions were weak and attenuated indeed at the beginning of our period; the reformers were prone to deny with great eloquence that they had ever existed at all in any effective form. There is real and there is deep hatred of the Catholic social and cultural past in the great and persuasive preaching of Latimer, of Lever, and of Hooper in the first generation of Protestantism, which animates as well most evangelical preaching during the two generations that were to follow. There was hatred and there was also an historical repudiation. The preachers and the lay moralists alleged that there was a social, as well as a spiritual, vacuum in English life which must be filled by private charity and by a broad assumption of responsibility for an immense range of social needs.

Though the great preachers lent their aid and animated it with their zeal, the Protestant social ethic which was forged in the course of the sixteenth century was none the less profoundly secular in its spiritual concerns. It was encouraged and employed by an intensely secular government likewise preoccupied with the great social needs to which a deeply moved laity now addressed its energies and its wealth. The range of this really herculean effort was as broad as the society itself, though, as we have seen, it was from the outset to be concentrated on the succour of the poor by an immense widening of the base of social responsibility and the systematic relief of poverty by a variety of institutions wholly dominated by lay control and leadership.[1] The Protestant clergy, being Calvinist, could not argue that good works were necessary to grace, but they did hold with a most persuasive and sustained vehemence that good works were an authentic and a necessary fruit of grace categorically demanded of His saints by God. Thus the grounds so quickly and firmly established for the relief of poverty and the enlargement of social opportunity were moral in their nature, while public policy buttressed moral resolution by support springing from an intelligent appraisal of the requirements of civil order and well-being.[2] The Calvinist not only said but he believed that we are but stewards of wealth for which we are accountable to God and that our means must be so used as to 'tend to Gods glorie, and the salvation of our soules'. Indeed, a great preacher could hold that the fact of wealth and the necessity of charity are inseparable, for almsgiving 'is the best kinde of thrift or husbandry . . . it is not giuing, but lending, and that to the Lord, who in his good time will return the gift with increase'.[3] This view of charitable obligation was remorselessly and deeply etched into the English conscience by a host of Calvinist divines, of whom Perkins may again be taken as the exemplar, when in the language of the

---

[1] White, H. C., *Social criticism in popular religious literature of the sixteenth century* (N.Y., 1944), 255–285.

[2] Wright, *Religion and empire*, 152.

[3] Perkins, 'Of diuine or religious worship', in *Works* (1605), 862.

counting-house he presses the point that 'a man upon good securitie lends to another an 100. pounds, hoping for the principall with the increase at the yeares end: yet dare not he skarse deliuer an 100. pence to the poore members of Christ vppon the promise and bonde of God himselfe'.[1] So strongly and powerfully were men persuaded of this view of the requirements of stewardship that Edward Dering, a noted Puritan divine, could stoutly and consistently oppose the poor laws of the mid-Elizabethan period on the grounds that they tended to weaken the moral responsibility which wealth must bear for poverty and need. Men, he said, are made rich for no other reason than that they may give to the poor. This social responsibility, he maintained, was direct, was personal, and must not be vitiated by an effort to spread it over a whole polity. If men of substance decline to assume their moral duty by the voluntary support of their needy brethren, the poor should be assigned to them in direct proportion to their wealth.[2]

This view of the charitable responsibility of the substantial members of the society was well established within a generation after the advent of the Reformation and was generally accepted by the close of the sixteenth century. As we shall see, it was held with particular tenacity by those small but most powerful classes, the merchants and the gentry, which for complex reasons were steadily gathering wealth and a dominant position within the society as the rule of the Tudors wore on. In these classes particularly the habit of substantial charity, vested largely for secular purposes, got itself well established by the beginning of the Elizabethan period. Men of these classes had come to assume a large and an essentially aristocratic measure of responsibility which very few of their number failed generously to implement as they ordered their affairs towards the close of their lives. Thus it was that in the early seventeenth century the failure of a London merchant to settle some substantial and conspicuous charitable trust or gift was generally regarded as little short of shocking unless there had been a grievous wasting of the estate because of age, ill-health, or commercial misfortune. A powerful tradition of charitable responsibility had gathered strength within these two rich and aggressive classes which resulted in a golden stream of wealth that spread its way through the many channels of need opened during this remarkable period.

The importance of this phenomenon of habit, of the tradition of social responsibility, cannot be too strongly stated. We have observed in many hundreds of parishes that one substantial foundation of say

[1] Perkins, 'How to live', in *Works* (1605), 581.
[2] Strype, *Annals*, II, 279–281. Dering (1540 ?–1576) was educated at Christ's College, Cambridge, where he was highly regarded for his great learning. He became a famous preacher, but his increasingly fierce and critical turn of temper brought him into royal disfavour as early as 1570.

an almshouse would very quickly draw many other gifts either for the support of that institution or some other equally ambitious undertaking for still another need in the community. A grammar school founded in one parish would inevitably tend to inspire a similar foundation in a nearby community. Thus it was that these immensely important foundations spread by a kind of social osmosis from parish to parish across the face of England, establishing in the end an intricate network of helpful and healing social agencies which no man and no class had quite planned but which none the less expressed most perfectly the *ethos* of an age. So it was, too, that the habits of responsibility first assumed by the now culturally dominant classes, the merchants and the gentry, spread gradually amongst other classes in the society. We shall later see that the various classes of men accepted this intensely secular concern for the society with differing degrees of completeness, that their aspirations for the age underwent differing degrees of velocity of change, but it remains true that in general terms a most powerful and significant cultural revolution was under way which came to include all classes of the society as private charity first re-defined and then re-made the social institutions of the realm.

2. *The ambit of opportunity*

It is likewise most evident that from about the time of the Reformation onwards men were moved by a very strong urge to broaden the base of opportunity within their society. We shall see that well before 1540 the secularization of aspirations had begun, with at first a rapidly mounting concern for the outright relief of poverty, which men were coming quickly to realize was the most pressing social problem of the century. But though the flow of funds for poor relief was to continue to rise through the whole course of the next century, a considerable number of rich, perceptive, and highly sophisticated donors, particularly among the merchant aristocracy, began to sense that the crux of the problem was not so much the outright relief of the poor as the prevention of poverty itself through the enlargement of the ambit of social and economic opportunity. Very broadly, we may say that after 1580 enormous sums of charitable wealth came to be vested in schools and in scholarship foundations, in the conviction that poverty bred and perpetuated itself in the slough of ignorance, and in various schemes for social rehabilitation, in the warmly held persuasion that every honest and ambitious youth must be afforded the opportunity to gain a footing in a now intensely competitive and relatively complex economy. The motives of these men who were founding the basic institutions of the society in which we still live were complex, partly intuitive, and sometimes imperfectly stated, but it remains abundantly clear that they were moved by a fresh and confident conviction that men had learned how to master and to form the cultural environment in which they lived. They were confident and courageous men who in less than a century were quite literally to create a new England with their own incredible generosity. They were for the most part moved by sentiments of high morality and of great nobility as they addressed themselves to the task of remaking a society; their impulses were in the main drawn from the Protestant ethic in which they had been bred, though the form which their aspirations took was intensely, often fiercely, secular in its nature. As one reads the many hundreds of wills and deeds of gift with which these donors established the schools, the scholarship funds, and the hospitals of England he has the sense not only of the almost exalted confidence of these men in the efficacy of education and reasonable opportunity in curing the blighting problems of the age, but of a fervent patriotism as they so consciously sought to mould the England which they loved to the requirements which modernity had imposed on mankind.

3. *The literature of exhortation*

In our discussion of the impulses which evoked the great flood of charitable giving in the age with which we are concerned, we must now lend quite detailed attention to the vast body of tracts and sermons which may accurately be described as a literature of exhortation. From 1540 onwards, it is not too much to say, a drumfire of exhortation was maintained by which the moral obligation of charity was established, the generous men praised and the covetous condemned, and the whole righteous quality of Protestant good works extolled. It is of course difficult to assess the precise influence of these eloquent documents, for they quite as truly bespoke the moral temper of the age as they assisted in its creation, but we may at least be certain that they were widely read, much quoted, and represented the moral consensus of the last century of the era with which we are dealing. Most of these treatises were from the pens of clergymen, though we shall note that a remarkable number were written by laymen whose essential thought was in fact inseparable from that of their clerical confrères. It is likewise important to observe that no really significant distinction can be drawn between the thought of Puritan and more strictly Anglican authors, for all bear the indelible stamp of the rigorous Calvinistic ethic which, until Archbishop Laud's fatal intervention, may be said to have marked the whole of Anglican thought. Generally speaking, however, it is evident that most of these treatises, in so far as they were clerical, were from the pens of the evangelical wing of the church, which, whether Puritan or not, remained dominant in the formulation and statement of Anglican thought until about the time of the accession of Charles I.

Most of the tracts with which we shall deal were originally delivered as sermons, the power and fervour of which echo even in printed form. The hundreds of surviving sermons that deal so eloquently and compellingly with the moral obligation of charity represent but a tithe of the countless sermons preached on the same subject by now forgotten clergymen to languid squires in rural parishes throughout the realm and to harassed merchants and tradesmen in all the market towns and cities of England. All of England was in church on the Sabbath during our era, and the sermon was without doubt the most important single instrumentality for the moulding of thought, the forming of resolution. The sermons of our period were carefully hewn from Scripture; were in the main literate, skilful, and thoughtful; and possessed most persuasive power because they were preached by men whose faith was unmarred by the slightest scepticism. We may believe, then, that this considerable and persistent body of literature possessed great effectiveness in forming the Protestant social ethic in England and in shaping the social vision which generous and responsible laymen were so nearly to translate into institutional reality before our period was at an end.

a. *Prior to the Reformation*

It is notable that during the first interval (1480-1560) into which we may divide this extensive material, this literature of exhortation, there was almost nothing of any considerable consequence prior to the advent of the Reformation. Sermons and moral essays do survive in fair number from the first half-century of this period, but charity when treated at all is dealt with in a most formal and remote fashion, bearing neither on the problems of the age nor on the aspirations of the auditor or reader. Nor were the earlier years of the Henrician Reformation marked by any deep concern with the direct, the compelling, obligation of charity or any bold affirmation that England had broken cleanly with the mediaeval social past. But in the closing years of that great monarch's reign, as thought itself began to move in a massive and revolutionary fashion despite the angry prohibitions of an imperious ruler, and in the short but irrevocably decisive reign of his son, what can only be described as a transformation of social thought and of national aspirations visibly occurred. The great preachers and their lay colleagues in this brief period were angry, high-minded, and courageous men who not only denounced the social evils of the age but forged the essential elements of the Protestant ethic by linking it organically with social reformation. In spite of the exaggerations, the economic naiveté, and the godly wrath of these men, of whom Latimer was the greatest, they laid for ever on the English conscience a sense of the shame of poverty and a moral responsibility for the enlargement of the ambit of opportunity. These men, be it remembered, were in a brief period not only to make England a Protestant nation but were to shape an ethic which, refined and enlarged by the Puritanism which was their spiritual legacy, profoundly and permanently altered the English character and aspirations.

The ancient problem of the relation of the rich and poor, in a world presumably ordered by God's will and mercy, received considerable attention from the writers of this interval, but we shall confine our comment to the views of one whose work was published early in the period and another whose great influence was exerted at its close. The Carmelite friar, Henry Parker, in his *Dives and pauper* (1493), had the pauper say that though God is worshipped by both rich and poor, the poor man is spared the sin of covetousness and the temptation of riches and may well remain content with his lot.[1] But Dives, in the ensuing dialogue, points out that the rich man, if he be godly, may be even more blessed in that he possesses the means for precious acts of charity. Ideally, and by God's mandate, rich and poor are necessary to each other, though the poor remain protected from the consuming sins which may overwhelm the very rich.[2] With this the early Protestant, Thomas Becon, would agree, but the ideal relationship has, he strongly argued, been wholly destroyed by the covetousness of the few who have beggared the realm, famished the King's subjects, and laid waste the poor. 'As riches, so likewise poverty cometh from God; and both are to be taken thankfully, and not to be grudged at', but neither policy nor Christian morality can permit sinful and irresponsible rich men to disorder the Christian state, on which there reposes an obligation to protect all its members.[3]

The early reformers warmly insisted that the obligation of charity lies on all Christian men and may not be disavowed without separating oneself from the community of Christ. Christ was never more precise than in His command that we dispense alms, not only that the poor may be succoured but that the rich man may be purged of his devotion to worldly wealth and thereby joined in the love of God.[4] All the other Christian virtues are comprehended in charity, 'for yf men be chary-

---

[1] *Dives and pauper* (L., 1534?), 1–2. Parker was a Carmelite friar of Doncaster. Preaching at Paul's Cross in 1464, he violently attacked the episcopacy and the secular clergy for their arrogance and covetousness. He was imprisoned for a season by the Bishop of London, but was released upon recanting at Paul's Cross. He died in 1470, the work under discussion being published posthumously in 1493 and then republished in 1534 or in 1536 as a Reformation tract.

[2] *Ibid.*, 5–12.

[3] Becon, 'The fortresse of the faythfull' (1550), in *Catechism*, 601. Becon (1512–1567) is admirably treated in the article in the DNB.

[4] Lupset, Thomas, *A compendious . . . treatyse, teachynge the waye of dyenge well* (L., 1534); in Gee, J. A., ed., *Life and works of Thomas Lupset* (New Haven, 1928), 285–286. For a biographical memoir of this Christian humanist, *vide* the DNB.

table they shall not onely love God feare God, and serve God . . .
but also shal helpe . . . sucker and sustayne theyr poore neyghbours with
all theyr strength and myght'.[1] It is love of material possessions, of
wealth, which may most dangerously separate us from God, whereas
true charity disposes man favourably towards all other men for the sake
of God and His love for them. The Christian 'in visytynge the sycke,
in clothynge the naked, in feding the hungry, in refreshyng the pore,
in comfortinge the miserable', is joined in a fast love for God, is made
perfect in all virtues by the one transcendent virtue of charity.[2] We can
stand in no doubt with respect to the obligation of charity, for here the
Bible is clear and specific in its requirements on the man who would
call himself Christian.[3] The Christian obligation is simply that Christ's
flock must be fed. The community of Christ is an economic as well as a
spiritual polity in which distributions must be made to every member
according to his need. This is the commandment that lies upon us,
which neither the individual Christian nor the church itself can repu-
diate.[4]

The principal outlines of charitable exhortation, later to be so fully
and skilfully developed, were laid out during these tumultuous years
prior to the Elizabethan settlement of religion. These authors, almost
all being preachers with vehemently Protestant convictions, set out the
moral obligation of charity with arguments gathered from Scripture and
from the compelling realities of need which they observed in their own
society. Thus an anonymous pamphleteer writing in 1537 strongly
maintained that 'faith must declare it selfe by deeds of charite'.[5] It is
only when the rich man dedicates his wealth 'to the benefite of his
neighbours' that his wealth ceases to be hateful to God and without
danger to the soul of the owner. This dogma of the social responsibility
of wealth was unequivocally argued by the reformers of the period, as
they lashed out against covetousness, avarice, and oppression. Still
another anonymous author, writing in *ca.* 1548, stated the case very
bluntly indeed. 'How do we loue our neyghbour as our selues when we
put them out of their houses and lay their goods in the stretes?' Men
of this age, the author continued, lay the lash of oppression on their
poor brethren, exhibiting less care for the needs of poor men than they
do for their own dogs.[6] Such selfish and obdurate men, fastening as

---

[1] Conway, William, *An exortacion to charite* (L., 1550?), sig. A.ii.

[2] Lupset, *A treatise of charitie* (L., 1533), sig. C.4; in Gee, *Life and works*, 207–231.

[3] Conway, *Exortacion*, sig. B.iiii *et passim*.

[4] Becon, 'Preface' (1564), in Ayre, John, ed., *The early works* (Cambridge, 1843), 19–20.

[5] *A goodly treatise of faith, hope, and charite* (Southwark, 1537), lxxi.

[6] *The prayse and commendacion of suche as sought comenwelthes* (L., 1548?), 2–3.

they do on their own wealth, violate the clear and certain commandments of Scripture and are rebels against the social order which the
Christian religion has established.[1]

Thomas Becon, perhaps more notably than any other preacher of his
generation, established this pattern of charitable exhortation which was
in the course of the next century to receive such full and effective
development in England. Christ, he maintained, has laid upon us the
stark commandment to love our neighbours. This injunction rests with
clear and special severity upon all those who enjoy power and wealth.
Wealth possesses no other virtue than to be employed in the advancement of Christ's purposes and in the maintenance of His poor. 'Covet
not to reign alone in a town. Suffer other men to live by thee, yea, and
that of their own. . . . So let them hire thy farms that they may not be
impoverished . . . but rather enriched, that they may be the more able
virtuously to bring up their children in good arts and godly sciences,
to help their poor neighbours, to keep hospitality, and to bear the
charge of the commonweal for their portion.' We wield the power conferred by wealth only as stewards, and those who betray that trust will
certainly hang in hell.[2]

Our social duty is clear, Becon eloquently maintained, but men have
grown callous and faithless in the care which they lend to the poor
around them. 'Again, what unmercifulness reigneth among men at this
time! How slenderly are the poor members of Christ provided for now-
a-days!' The very fact of beggary, of hunger, stands as an awful indict-
ment on a society whose Christian duty it is to succour and maintain
the poor.[3] But the poor increase until 'they be almost innumerable',
weakening the structure of a society which has impiously declined to
assume its responsibilities towards the needy.[4] We have forgotten,
Becon thundered, that no Christian can live with his own wealth while
men and women hunger and suffer around him. 'Thus see we that all
good men have ever pitied the poor, and sought all means possible to
do them good. But the contrary is found among us now-a-days. For
men . . . are "the lovers of themselves", and not of the poor. . . . They
heap to themselves, they provide nothing for the poor. There be many
signs of the last day to be at hand; but this cold affection, and more
cold love, and most cold liberality toward the poor, prove evidently
that it is not far off.'[5] Our return to Christ, and our obedience to His
will, will not be confirmed or complete until we pledge our wealth to

[1] Coverdale, Myles, 'Confutation of the treatise of John Standish' (1541 ?),
in Pearson, George, ed., Remains (Cambridge, 1846), 366. For this great
preacher's career, vide the excellent article in the DNB.
[2] 'A pleasant new nosegay' (1542), in Early works, 222–226.
[3] 'The news out of heaven' (1541 ?), in Early works, 40.
[4] 'The fortresse' (1550), in Catechism, 583.
[5] Ibid., 584–587.

the relief of a poverty which is not consonant with a Christian society.[1]

The relief of conspicuous and wasting poverty, the reformers argued, is in fact simply the first, the basic, obligation imposed on the Christian by his faith. The true duty of the society runs far beyond this essentially emergency mending of the social fabric. There lies on us as well the necessity of building a world in which poverty will be prevented by better institutions and by a wider range of opportunity. 'It is not ynough . . . to geue onely meate, harbour, and clothing to suche as be in extreme necessite'; we must as well lend support to every agency of education and of social rehabilitation so that 'all those that be baptized in Christe, be uertuouslie brought up from their childehood, and taught good artes, that euerie one, accordyng to his portion' may make some contribution to the perfection of the Christian commonwealth.[2] Above all else, we must come to understand that poverty is spawned in ignorance and that it can be prevented only when youth is afforded the opportunities which education, apprenticeship, and the special leadership of an informed and learned clergy can supply. All these things charity can and must accomplish. The liberality of the rich, required for the salvation of the society as well as for the salvation of their souls, must not be postponed until death, but must rather inform and fructify the whole course of the lives of men of substance.[3]

The great and angry preachers of this early and intensely evangelical phase of the Reformation were deeply concerned with the whole complex problem of poverty, were disposed to connect the spreading evil of beggary with the derelictions of the ancient church, and were preaching a doctrine of far-reaching social reform as a concomitant of the religious revolution then under way. They were, as we have earlier suggested, laying the foundations of the Protestant social ethic during the course of these tumultuous years and they were fixing in the English social conscience a sense of responsibility, of very direct and immediate responsibility, for needs and for opportunities which men had never before fully recognized. Their social and economic philosophy was warm and generous, though it must be stressed that their understanding of the economic processes then transforming England was incredibly naïve and that their proposals were often so disingenuous as to betray a kind of utopian irrelevance. We should now notice at least briefly the social thought of a few of the principal of these remarkable, these attractive, and these somewhat dangerous men.

---

[1] Becon, 'The fortresse' (1550), in *Catechism*, 619.

[2] [Bucer, Martin], *A treatise how . . . christian mens almose ought to be distributed* (Printed abroad, 1557 ?), sig. B.4. Bucer was in England from 1549 until his death in 1551.

[3] Becon, 'A new catechism' (n.d., *ca.* 1553), in *Catechism*, 110–116, 306–307, 317–326, 390–393.

Thomas Starkey, who was perhaps the boldest and most original of them all, writing between 1533 and 1536, believed that England was under-populated, that far-reaching social and economic reforms were required if the realm was to attain its full vigour and strength, and that the state should lend its sovereign power to the amelioration of the condition of the poor. Nor should the government tolerate the wasting sin, the social crime, of idleness. The cure could only be attained if every child were required to learn a craft beginning at the age of seven, under pain of banishment if as an adult he could offer no useful skill to the society of which he was part. Starkey also preached the virtues of a closed economy in which practically all imports were prohibited and in which the manufacturers were regulated with a view towards increasing and sustaining employment. He likewise denounced the rising curve of land rents and all enclosing, which he seemed to regard as a deliberate assault on the well-being of the state and as the principal cause of poverty. He proposed that all rents be by law reduced to earlier, though unspecified, levels in the belief that in a few years 'we should have this miserable poverty taken away'. In such an economy all those who wished to do so and who were sturdy could find employment, while those who were truly impotent might be decently cared for as their need engaged the charitable instincts of a society which was at last Christian in fact as well as in name.[1]

The social thought of Henry Brinkelow, writing as he did about a decade later, was even bolder, while his suggestions for reform were at once more specific and more nearly within the realm of practicality. This former monk was an early convert to Protestantism and was perhaps the most courageously insistent of all the reforming group that the wealth of the ancient church be employed for worthy and bold social needs. In 1542 he lashed out against the citizens of London, one of whom he had become, for their shocking neglect of the poverty which they saw about them. 'O lord God how blynde be these cytezins which take so greate care to prouyde for the dead' by popish superstitions, while neglecting their bounden Christian obligation to relieve those in desperate want. Even supposedly responsible merchants leave from £6 to £12 yearly for superstitious masses for the dead while scattering only a few pennies on the Sabbath for the care of the derelict. 'Oh ye cytezyns if ye wold turne but even the profettes of your chauntryes and obbets to the fyndyng of the poare with a pollytique and godly provysyon where as now London beyng one of the flowres of the world as touchyng worldly richesse hath so many, yee innumerable of poare people forced to go from doare to doare and to syt openly in the streates bedgyng and many not able to do ere other but lye in their houses in

---

[1] Starkey, Thomas (K. M. Burton, ed.), *A dialogue between Reginald Pole and Thomas Lupset* (L., 1948), 73-79, 89, 95, 140, 143, *et passim*.

most grevouse paynes and dye for lack of ayde of the riche.' London, Brinkelow earnestly maintained, was disgraced and its very religion rendered suspect by its heartless want of concern for the plight of its swarming poor.[1]

In his more famous *Complaint of Roderyck Mors*, probably first published in 1545, Brinkelow dealt more generally and certainly more powerfully with the social needs and opportunities of his age. He believed that a true reformation in England must comprehend the ills of the society, and he argued with most courageous insistence that the expropriated monastic properties as well as the bishops' lands should be expressly devoted to this end. A portion of this wealth should be yielded to the Crown as income in order to relieve the poor and middling people of the realm from the burdens of taxation. But the great bulk of it should be devoted to the care of poor householders, in assisting poor maidens in their marriages, in loans to men who might thereby be rescued from poverty, 'and the reste to be employed uppon poor cities and townes and to their provision of the poor'. Almshouses should be founded in every substantial town for the succour of the derelict. 'Let physicyans . . . be founde in euery suche towne or cyte . . . to loke uppon the pore in that towne and in all others joyninge unto it', with stipends assumed by the community, and let grammar schools of high quality be founded in all urban centres which the able poor might attend without charge. These and other social benefits would relieve existing poverty, would go far towards curing ignorance and want in the next generation, and would create a fairer and a better England, all as an indirect, but infinitely beneficent, consequence of the great spiritual reformation then so well under way.[2]

These great propagandists of the Reformation, nourished as they were in its first warm and hopeful days, were evidently animated by a vision of a new social and economic order. They connected, quite naively and incorrectly, the social and economic ills which troubled and wasted their society with the Roman order which had just been overthrown, while they demanded that social reformation must proceed as a concomitant of the spiritual reformation which they believed to be at hand. For a revolutionary moment during the weak reign of Edward VI it did look as if an evangelical reformation of the church was imminent and that bold and far-reaching social reforms were to be undertaken as well. In this moment, and it was a truly dangerous one for the realm, the control of policy was almost lost by the Crown just as that policy

[1] Brinkelow, Henry, *The lamentacion of a Christian against the citie of London* (L., 1542), sig. A.iiii, B.iiij. Brinkelow had become a citizen and mercer of London. *Vide* DNB.

[2] Brinkelow, *The complaint of Roderyck Mors* (Geneva, 1545?, 1550), sig. F.iiij.

was perverted and vitiated by the violence of the reaction under Mary Tudor. Under Elizabeth, surely the greatest if not the most admirable of all English rulers, cold, remorseless, and prudent policy again came to prevail, with the result that the bounds of the Reformation were most modestly prescribed and the course of social reform was cautiously set by a government disposed to do no more than was necessary in order to adapt the society to the requirements of a new and a very complex age. But none the less the vision of the great reformers had stirred England; the aspirations which they had enunciated for their generation had come to animate the minds and consciences of many men; and these almost recklessly righteous men had contributed much to the forging of the Protestant ethic. In an ultimate sense, in fact, the Edwardian preachers and not Queen Elizabeth were to prevail.

Among the greatest of these preachers was Thomas Becon, whose eloquent delineation of the requirements of Protestant charity we have already discussed. Becon maintained that the charitable impulse was perverted by the Roman church which persuaded amiable but misguided men to pour funds into 'great monasteries for the bellied hypocrites, great colleges, chantries, and free chapels for soul-carriers and pur-gatory-rakers'.[1] All this golden flow of wealth, for so long dedicated to worthless and superstitious ends, must now be gathered and righteously employed for the cure of poverty in England. But this, he said, had not occurred. 'When', he asked, 'was the love of men ever so cold toward the poor?' Thus the recent risings (1549) in Norfolk and Devon were occasioned by true and desperate poverty, the real instigators being those covetous men who engrossed and enclosed the lands, who de-spoiled the poor, since they 'study not, as the true gentlemen do, to profit many, to do good to the country, to maintain the poor, to relieve the succourless, to nourish the weak, to cherish their needy tenants'.[2] There would be no true emancipation from popery until England had assumed the full measure of her Christian responsibility towards the poor and until the ignorance that gripped the nation had been dispelled by education. Ignorance, papistry, and poverty, Becon warmly argued, were links in the evil chain which had bound the nation. The urgently required, 'the next and only remedy is, that godly learned school-masters be placed with liberal stipends, to whom the christian youth may be committed' in order to gain some measure of understanding of the meaning of the Christian religion and the nature of the Christian commonwealth.[3]

These views were even more strongly urged by Thomas Lever in two remarkable sermons preached in London in 1550. Lever disavowed any teaching of economic egaliatarianism, for such a view would utterly

---

[1] 'The fortresse' (1550), in *Catechism*, 587.　　　　[2] *Ibid.*, 599.
[3] 'Preface' (1564), in *Early works*, 10.

destroy the 'misticall bodie of Christ' in which there are divers members having divers places and duties. But there devolves upon the Christian rich a heavy and an omnipresent duty of charity which in time of great necessity can only be discharged by the employment of capital assets for the care of the needs of Christ's congregation.[1] And it must be said since the Reformation that the Christian rich of England have been moved more by greed and by covetousness than by charity, as they have fattened on the wealth released from the grip of popery.[2] Even the merchants of London, whom God has endowed with great wealth, are not content with 'the prosperous welth of that vocacion to satisfye themselues and to helpe other, but their riches muste abrode in the contrey to bie farmes out of the handes of worshypfull gentlemen, honeste yeomen, and poore laboringe husbandes'.[3] Thus wealth has been employed for self-aggrandizement rather than for the advancement of God's kingdom and the succouring of His weak members.[4]

Lever, like all the strongly evangelical clergy of the Edwardian period, hotly maintained that the Reformation had been betrayed in the spoliation that had occurred in the disposition of the monastic and chantry properties. This wealth was meant by Parliament, and by godly men generally, to accomplish a great and a needed social reformation in the realm, 'that thereby suche abundaunce of goodes as was supersticiously spente upon vayne ceremonies, or voluptuously upon idle bellies, myght

---

[1] Lever, Thomas, *A fruitfull sermon . . . in Poules churche* (L., 1550), sig. B.iii. Lever (1521–1577) was ordained a priest in 1550. He sought refuge in Zurich during the Marian regime and was strongly preferred during the early Elizabethan period; but his increasingly radical Puritanism led to his deprivation in 1567. There is a biographical notice in the DNB.

[2] Lever, *A sermon preached . . . before the Kynges Maiestie* (L., 1550), sig. C.iii.

[3] Lever, *A fruitfull sermon*, sig. B.iiii.

[4] Robert Crowley, 'a very forward man for reformation', made the same point in most vigorous language. A merchant long abroad, he tells us, on his return looked for an ancient almshouse near his own home but found instead a great house on the site:

> Than, by the waye syde,
> hym chaunced to se
> A pore manne that craued
> of hym for charitie . . .

The beggar explained to the merchant that men of great riches had bought the old almshouse and the pensioners had been turned out.

> Lorde God! (quod this marchaunt)
> in Turkeye haue I bene,
> Yet emonge those heathen
> none such crueltie haue I sene.
> The vengeaunce of God
> muste fall . . . vpon these wicked men,
> and that verye shortelye.
>
> [Crowley, Robert (J. M. Cowper, ed.),
> *Select works* (L., 1872), 11–12]

come to the kynges handes to beare his great charges, necessarilie
bestowed in the comen wealthe, or partly unto other mennes handes, for
the better releue of the pore, the maintenaunce of learning, and the
settinge forth of goddes worde'.[1] But this wealth, which might have been
dedicated to godly and charitable uses, has in fact been looted by men
who are as evil as they are rapacious. These men, who have despoiled a
Reformation, must be compelled to make restitution if England is to
escape the awful vengeance of God.[2] In a sermon preached before the
King in 1550, Lever called upon the government itself to compel the
proper and the charitable use of this great wealth. 'The Kyng beareth
the slaunder' for what has occurred, while 'the poore feeleth the lacke,
but who hath the profit . . . I can not tell: but well I wot . . . that the
Act of Parliament . . . for the mayntenaunce of learnyng, and reliefe of
the poore, hath served some, as a most fyt instrument to robbe learnyng,
and to spoyle the poore.'[3]

b. The Elizabethan age

The stirring warmth of the preaching in the early and radical stage
of the Reformation in England gave way in the course of the Elizabethan period to a more temperate but a none the less most insistent
emphasis on the Christian obligation of charity. There are a great many
of these sermons and tracts; so we must needs be content with citing
only a few representative works which state the case of the rapidly
maturing Protestant ethic with some eloquence and certainly with deep
conviction. We shall deal first with a number of clerical utterances and
then turn to a consideration of a few of a larger number of lay tracts
which expounded the high necessity for charity in the same terms and
in very nearly the same language.

The whole position in this important matter is well set out in the
semi-official *Certaine sermons*, first published in 1563, in which charity
is represented as inseparable from the love of God.[4] God requires our
alms, though we are, as it were, officially assured that such acts of mercy
are profitable to us, for 'who so is liberall to the poore . . . shal . . .

---

[1] Lever, *A fruitfull sermon*, sig B.iiii.　　　　　　[2] *Ibid.*, sig. C.i.

[3] Lever, *A sermon preached . . . before the Kynges Maiestie*, sig. E.iii. Lever
continued, at some personal risk, to urge the issue even during the Elizabethan
period and after his deprivation. In 1572 he complained bitterly to Burghley
that the statute of 37 Henry VIII disposing of monastic property had been
systematically violated by rapacious men. The intention had been to foster the
universities and the hospitals of the realm, but the property had in fact been
treated as private spoil. (*S.P. Dom.*, 1572, LXXXVIII, 21.)

[4] *Certaine sermons appoynted by the Quenes Maiesty* (L., 1563), Sermons V,
VI; *The second tome of homelyes* (L., 1563), 'An homely of almes-dedes', 354,
362–363; also in *Certaine sermons . . . appointed to be read in churches* (L., 1676),
27, 30.

have sufficient for him selfe & evermore be without daunger of penury'. The admonition of generosity runs through the whole of the Bible, is an inherent part of Christian teaching, since alms given to the poor are really given directly to God. Nor is this all, for alms-deeds 'preserve . . . our soules in safetie . . . pourge the soule from the infection and fylthy spottes of sinne . . . as water quencheth burninge fire, even so mercy and almes resisteth and reconcyleth sinne'.[1] This view was further advanced by Thomas Drant, Vicar of St Giles Cripplegate, who urged his congregation to emulate the earth in its bounty. The Christian man 'should give his almes though he hath no more hope to recover it than he hath whiche casteth upon the face of the runnyng water'. Our fortune, he urged, has no meaning unless we use it for good works, 'and when as they themselves [the rich] will not bestow it upon the poore or to good use, then the common place will suck it up. The Kinges bench will suck it up and the Chancery will swallow it up. Therefore . . . geve accordyng to the necessitie of those that want, be plentifull unto the poore and follow the example of the liberall cloudes which let their water gushe uppon the face of the earth'.[2]

The Christian obligation of charity was stated with a warmth and intensity of conviction reminiscent of the great Edwardian preachers by Thomas White, Vicar of St Dunstan's in the West. The son of a Bristol clothier, White had inherited a large fortune which he was to expend upon notable charities in London and in his native city.[3] An Anglican clergyman with Puritan leanings, this founder of Sion College spoke with rare force and eloquence to one of the richest congregations in the city. The commandment of charity lies upon us as Christians with unequivocal clarity, White maintained, while Scripture commands us to give to the generality of the poor to the limit of our abilities. 'Surely there are many poore, and made many wayes, as well by their owne default as otherwise and as they are almost without number, so they are altogether without order. . . . Better care would be had both of them and for them, but in the meane season thou maist never dispise him to whom thou maist be like.'[4] The commandment is clean and clear, but England stands sinfully in the breach of that commandment. Charity has waxed cold at the very moment of reformation. 'As it is an argument of the whole worldes overthrowe when universally winter shall come ouer charitie, so is strõg as a conclusiõ of the cõfusion of ÿ citie that hath lost the heate of christiã loue and pittie: if thy enimy

---

[1] *Certaine sermons* (1676), 230–231, 233–237.

[2] Drant, Thomas, *A fruitfull and necessary sermon* (L., 1572), no pagin. The DNB provides a biographical notice of Drant.

[3] White's great charities will be discussed in later volumes of this study.

[4] White, Thomas, *A sermon preached at Paules Crosse 17 Nov. 1589* (L., 1589), 34.

hunger, feede him; but we are so farre out of charitie, that we would feede on him rather.'[1]

The steady emphasis placed by the clergy on the Christian obligation of charity became at once more specific and insistent as the Elizabethan reign drew towards its close and as the problem of dealing with poverty became more acute throughout the realm. Our alms must flow from us as an aspect of our faith, while our piety and our generosity must increase as a factor of our prosperity.[2] We must give generously and we must give thoughtfully, for to consider 'the necessities of men in giving, is much more acceptable thã to giue hand over hand'. We must order our charity, eschewing the wasteful and harmful tendency to scatter doles, thus helping to create a system of charity which will most effectively cure the ills of our society. And we must give during our own lifetime, to needs as we see them, rather than bestowing the whole of our charity in one massive bequest.[3] Though our charity should be intelligently and carefully ordered, it must none the less flow from our love of Christ and our sharing with Him a deep compassion for men who are sore and afflicted.[4] The obligation of charity is indeed nothing more than the obligation of mercy, and mercy must run in a flowing stream to both the souls and the bodies of our fellow men. Thus are condemned all those who 'seeme to pitie mens soules but not their bodies: they will instruct others, admonish them, forgive them and pray for them, but will not give them one penny to help them withall; being like unto a popish prelate who being asked a penny by a poor man, refused to give it but offered to blesse him, which the poore man refused because he thought that if it had been worth a penny he would not have given it to him'.[5] Our giving, then, must at once be well considered and animated by mercy; and it must be generous and joyous. 'Therefore . . . giue . . . and giue gladly . . . know that in the ende what thou keepest thou shalt lose . . . ere you dye, lay . . . forth for the profit of your poore brethren', exhorted that 'silver-tongued' Puritan divine, Henry Smith.[6]

The almost vehement insistence of the great Elizabethan preachers, and most particularly those of Puritan inclinations, on the obligation of

[1] White, Thomas, *A sermon preached at Pawles Crosse 3 Nov. 1577* (L., 1578), 60.

[2] Turnbull, Richard, *An exposition upon the canonicall epistle of St James* (L., 1591), Sermon 4, 31 ff.; Sermon 8, 81–84; Sermon 10, 97 ff. A graduate of Corpus Christi College, Oxford, in 1566, Turnbull was licensed to preach in 1576 and was Rector of St Pancras Soper Lane from 1582 until his death in 1593.

[3] Bird, Samuel, *Lectures* (Cambridge, 1598), 69. Bird was born in Essex and educated at Cambridge. For a season the schoolmaster at Lavenham, Suffolk, he became in 1580 the minister at St Peter's, Ipswich, where he served until his death in 1604. The DNB article confuses Bird with his son.

[4] Turnbull, *An exposition*, Sermon 12, 122; Sermon 10, 107, 116.

[5] Harrison, William, *Deaths advantage* (L., 1602), 20.

[6] Smith, Henry, *Sermons* (L., 1599), 509.

charity was firmly rooted in their view that we possess wealth only as stewards, though men afflicted with the dreadful sin of covetousness do persuade themselves otherwise. 'That which makes men so loth to giue is, because they thinke that it is their own, not considering that they are onely disposers of the manifold graces of God . . . as stewards.'[1] This view was also most eloquently expressed by Henry Smith, who complained that 'in this yron age, it is as hard a thing to perswade men to part with money, as to pull out their eyes . . . or cut off their hands'. 'I cannot but wonder,' he added, 'that men are so slow in giuing of almes . . . when the promises of God warrant them not to lose their reward.'[2] Wealth which serves no social end, which is not sanctified by compassion, is an evil to mankind and is destructive to its possessors. The rich must therefore share 'the overplus of their riches none of theirs, but the poores, whom they slay and murther, asmuch as in them lieth, when they detaine it: therefore, when they suffer the poore to perish; the naked to sterve; the needie to die for want of necessary succour', all this will in the final day 'stande up in judgement against them'.[3]

We have been examining no more than a sampling of a powerful, a moving, and a deeply persuaded body of sermons addressed to the obligations of wealth in a new economy and, in some senses, in a new society. These sermons reflect the charitable temper of the age and they must have made considerable contribution towards inspiring the impulse from which the burgeoning charities of the period sprang. They purposely exaggerated the covetousness of the age, while they evoked generosity by an almost conventional insistence that charity was as cold as it was deficient. These views are perfectly expressed in a work published in 1596 which held that 'in our time the charitie of most men is frozen up, so that it is now high time to blow up the dead sparkels of love, and to kindle the cold coales of charity'. To this task the anonymous author addressed himself with extraordinarily effective zeal. We dare not be idle in the doing of good, and the transcendent good is the giving of alms. 'Riches cannot make a man good, but men may doe good with them.' The times in England require the generality of private men of substance to dedicate their wealth to the needs of mankind, just as the state itself, the totality of men, must regard the whole of the wealth of the realm as a common stock with which hunger, sickness, and misery may be relieved. Both our hearts and our purses must accordingly be opened. 'If ye will in time distribute your money and wealth, with a ready and willing mind . . . ye shall not want God's assistance. . . . Seeing Christianity is not an idle profession, but a busie practice,

---

[1] Bird, *Lectures*, 15.   [2] Smith, *Sermons*, 499.
[3] Turnbull, *An exposition*, sig. Mm4v. For similar sentiments, *vide* Smith, *Sermons*, 502–503, 506–513.

alwaies occupyed in doing good; And seeing among all other good workes, distributing to the necessitie of other, is a speciall good worke, not onely comfortable to other, but also profitable to our selves, and acceptable to God.' There are too many poor in England and there remains too much wealth not dedicated to their succour. We must, as we contemplate the need about us, remember that 'the rich man is no more than Gods steward and the poore mans treasurer . . . give your money . . . and you shall have Gods treasures . . . rewards in this life and in the world to come'.[1]

Certain of the Puritan sermons of the Elizabethan period glow with a righteous anger most reminiscent of the Edwardian period. They denounced the social irresponsibility of the rich and laid out in specific, if exaggerated, fashion a bill of particulars of what must be accomplished before England could be regarded as a nation worthy to be called Christian. Thus Thomas White, while granting that there was general provision made for the poor in the city of London and while praising the generosity that had founded its hospitals, none the less blasted those men who were content with the achievements of their age. 'I would Christians would learne to be liberall for very shame . . . what say you, and the poore lye under euery wall, and crie under euery stall, and die in the streates in the tyme of the Gospell.'[2] True it is that London clothes many backs and feeds many bellies, 'but yet not withstanding the dead doe give more then those that are alive, and therefore if God will have the poore more provided for, I thinke hee must provide to take away more of the rich men'.[3] Christopher Hooke, in a sermon preached at St Paul's, spoke of the misery of the poor of London, who sought work which they could not find, as a blight on the conscience of all Christian men of the city.[4] The righteous indignation of these Puritan divines could on occasion pass the bounds of exhortation into sentiments disturbing to the government, as happened in 1603 when Richard Stock, a lecturer at St Augustine Watling Street, uttered words disrespectful to the lord mayor in a sermon preached at Paul's Cross. Stock alleged that most of the funds raised for poor relief were by assessments of fifteenths which bore more heavily proportionately on the artisan than on the merchant. Bluntly addressing the aldermen, Stock continued, 'You are magistrates for the good of them that are under you, not to oppress them for your own ease.'[5]

[1] *Three sermons or homelies to mooue compassion towards the poore* (L., 1596).
[2] White, *A sermon* (L., 1578), 61–62.
[3] White, *A sermon* (L., 1589), 39.
[4] Hooke, Christopher, *A sermon preached in Paules church* (L., 1603), no pagin.
[5] *Hist. MMS. Comm.*, *Salisbury Papers*, XII, 672. A native of Yorkshire, Stock (1569–1626) was educated at Cambridge and was incorporated at Oxford in 1595. He was appointed curate of All Hallows Bread Street in 1604 and served there as rector from 1610 until his death in 1626.

It will have been observed that even the most evangelical of these Protestant divines strayed very far indeed into those indefinable verges which delimit the doctrine of the necessity of good works. They were, it it is true, carefully orthodox in their view that good works were the inevitable and demonstrable concomitant of a state of grace, but so insistent were they on the high necessity of charity that the lay auditor must have been more persuaded by the argument of works than the more intangible and subtle complexities of grace. This stern insistence on good works from the elect may be illustrated by a sermon of Richard Curteys, Bishop of Chichester, who warned his congregation that we can never assure ourselves of God's mercy and favour unless we do our duty both to God and to our neighbour. 'God graunteth mercy to none, but to them that leade a godly and charitable life . . . except you doe good workes, you cannot assure your selues of Gods mercy . . . I . . . exhort you to good workes, that you may feele the favour and goodnesse of God thereby towards you.' And good works, Curteys went on to suggest, may in fact be precisely defined as fulfilling our obligation of charity. By this infallible test, it can only be said that England is not in a state of grace. There are hungry men in England, while there are wealthy landowners who have closed up their houses 'to take a chamber in some citie' to the complete neglect of the duty which they owe to their neighbours and dependents. God's curse is upon such men of property. 'Consider wherefore did God giue you such great store of riches, and large possessions in this life, aboue your brethren; was it not to doe good with them, and to helpe them that haue neede . . . I counsel you to study, to bee more carefull in relieuing the poore distressed members of Jesus Christ' against the 'great day of accompt' which all men will have for the stewardship of their wealth.[1]

This is powerful and effective preaching. It was, moreover, a kind of preaching heard all over England during this period when the velocity of charitable giving was mounting with an almost incredible rapidity. Such preaching without any doubt contributed most fruitfully towards creating a climate of social opinion from which the great benefactions of the Elizabethan era flowed. These preachers purposely exaggerated the want and misery left unattended in their era, just as they grossly underestimated the mounting flow of charitable funds being directed by private donors towards the relief and even the cure of poverty. But such almost poetic exaggeration is the price of eloquence and perhaps as well the price of warm and healing moral fervour.

The whole *corpus* of clerical literature dealing with the obligation of charity and with the social needs of the realm was well summarized at the close of Elizabeth's reign in a curious but a none the less impressive book, the *Oderifferous garden of charitie*, by Robert Allen, which man-

[1] Curteys, Richard, *The care of a christian conscience* (L., 1600), Sermon 4.

ages to treat the complex question with an evangelical zeal that is not wanting in an understanding of the very great accomplishments of the preceding half-century. Allen believed that the recently enacted poor laws constituted a landmark in the treatment of poverty. It was, for one thing, Christian law-giving. Above all, the laws had at last cleanly separated the worthy poor from the professional beggars and vagabonds, whose demands and artifices had prostituted the mercy of almsgiving, for 'that mercie was degenerated to the cruell and wastfull feeding and fostering of such an idle and wicked rout as . . . were altogether unworthy of any almes inso much as they were such, as utterly refused to work'.[1] This great accomplishment had had the happy effect of liberating and ennobling the impulse of almsgiving, of lending assurance to the donor that his charity would serve a worthy social and religious purpose. Poverty could now be genuinely and completely relieved. Even the quiet and unknown poor must be sought out and sustained in 'many a blind and unmercifull nooke in the land'.

Allen suggested that the church itself should strive to supplement and augment the worthy purposes which had now been undertaken by the secular authority. Each church in the realm should seek by voluntary contributions to build up a stock from which particularly needy poor men might be relieved and work found for those able to support themselves.[2] Not only does this proposal have practical virtue, Allen held, but it acknowledges that the church itself bears a direct obligation for alms which it does not wholly relinquish to the state.[3] All men should be encouraged to give generously to make their full measure of contribution towards the needs of their fellow men during the course of their lifetimes. The passage of the poor laws, Allen seems to hold, should be regarded as a commitment of the whole polity towards its minimum responsibilities of Christian decency, but many more areas remain to be opened and occupied by private charity. The poor have many needs beyond bare subsistence, persecuted Christians abroad need succour and a sanctuary in England, and the ministry of the church requires more than 'grudging and niggardlie' support. All these things and many more have been made possible since the great Elizabethan statutes emancipated charity by defining its obligations and separating the worthy from the unworthy poor.[4]

There is likewise a very considerable body of lay writing which urged the necessity for greater charitable giving and the requirement of a broader sense of social responsibility on the part of the whole realm in

---

[1] Allen, Robert, *The oderifferous garden of charitie* (L., 1603), Dedication. We have been unable to learn much concerning Allen's career. He was a clergyman, probably in London, and was the author of a number of religious works published between 1596 and 1612.

[2] *Ibid.*, 35–37.   [3] *Ibid.*, 14.   [4] *Ibid.*, 42, 77, 116, *et passim*.

terms not dissimilar from those which we have found in clerical thought during the Elizabethan era. This lay thought, only a tithe of which we can discuss, was on the whole more pragmatic, more concerned with social order, and less dependent on scriptural authority, yet it must be said that it most evidently proceeded from the same stratum of Calvinist morality. This writing, too, was essentially hortatory, reflecting a need of social reformation which, as we have seen, was transforming the institutions of England and vastly enlarging the ambit of opportunity for all classes of men.

These lay thinkers also laid stern emphasis on the Christian obligation of charity and the unforgivable sin of covetousness. 'Why doo wee so gape for rytches, why doo wee dedicate all our labour to uniust Mammon ?', William Fulbecke enquired.[1] Wealth must be regarded as a gift of God to be employed for His glory, but pride of riches and a covetous nature are destructive to a man and to his commonwealth. And the age, these moralists agreed, was too preoccupied with the winning of wealth for the mere sake of wealth. As one ballad writer put it:

> I read in ancient times of yore,
> That men of worthy calling
> Built almes houses and spittles store,
> Which now are all down falling;
> And few men seek them to repair,
> Nor none is there among twenty
> That for good deeds will take any care . . .[2]

The true Christians, the good men, 'seeke not to haue theyr names blazed by the trumpet of the common people . . . they do not hawke nor hunt for lucre and gaine, but if it please the Lord to place them in seates of honour, they take it as a free gift . . . charitablie dispensing their substaunce, to the use of their needie brethren, to the discharge of their owne want, and to the glorie of God'.[3] Our alms, our liberality, attest our love of God and our religious concern for our fellow men. As we are Christian and as we are civilized, so shall we assume responsibility for the needs of the world around us. In the beautiful and biblical words of Thomas Twyne, a physician at Lewes, Sussex, 'A mans almes is as a purse with him, and shall keepe a mans favour . . . and afterwarde . . . pay euery man his rewarde upon his head'; accordingly, 'Say not unto thy neighbour, goe thy way and come agayne, tomorow I wil giue thee, wheras thou hast now to giue him'.[4]

---

[1] *A booke of christian ethicks* (L., 1587), sig. C.4. Fulbecke's career is noted in the DNB.

[2] Collier, J. P., ed., *A book of Roxburghe Ballads* (L., 1847), 50.

[3] Fulbecke, *A booke*, sig. C.ii.

[4] Twyne, Thomas, *The garlande of godly flowers* (L., 1574), no pagin.

The lay thought of this period was by no means limited to rhetorical exhortation, to a calling on men to assume responsibilities which at least in the abstract were generally recognized and accepted. Many of these writers likewise held very specific views regarding the duty of the magistrate to intervene in order to frame a more equitable and merciful polity in which the poor would be relieved and opportunity broadened. Perhaps three of these treatises might be briefly examined in, as it were, a descending order of generality. They are typical of a substantial body of lay thought which lent strong impulse not only to the final and decisive intervention of the state in the problem of poverty late in the Elizabethan age, but to the even more significant burgeoning out of private charitable giving in the second half of the sixteenth century.

That extraordinarily versatile Elizabethan, George Whetstone, who had spent his own considerable patrimony in riotous living, in his *A mirour for magestrates of cyties* couched much of his distinctly Puritan advice to the magistrate in terms of reflections on the corruption and vices that had overwhelmed the Roman world.[1] Many of these same evils, the author held, afflict England, though they may be epitomized in the social irresponsibility of wealth in the land.[2] Such abuse, such want of concern for the needs of the poor in a commonwealth, Whetstone maintained in a later work, can only be corrected by the direct intervention of the magistrate, whose office it is to 'defende the poore and fatherlesse, and to see that such as bee in neede and necessitie, may haue right'.[3]

Far more specific and impressive were the recommendations of Andreas Gerardus, as very freely translated and applied to the English scene in 1572 by Henry Tripp, a London clergyman of the period. This work, which enjoyed considerable currency and which was much quoted, took the view that the relief of poverty was the joint responsibility of the secular authorities and of the church. The root of the sixteenth century problem, it was argued, was in the fact that the church had come gradually in earlier ages to neglect its basic responsibility for the care of its poor, with the consequence that the state had been obliged to move into a vacuum of social need. 'Magistrates, your integritie and diligence . . . shall neuer be approved of God or godly men, before you haue prouided a meane in your comõn wealth to releeue the poore, whiche are alway the greater part in any societie.' Nor is that all, for 'the citizens uniuersally desire, that beggers . . . may bee brought in order . . . and that the true povertie . . . maye be prouided for . . . and that some certaine way maye be prescribed for the right . . . disposing

---

[1] Whetstone, George, *A mirour for magestrates of cyties* (L., 1584), 1–23. For Whetstone's career (1544?–1587?), *vide* the DNB.

[2] *Ibid.*, 23–37.

[3] Whetstone, *The English myrror* (L., 1586), 223.

of the common almes'.[1] The problem of poverty, the author held with
prophetic correctness, could never be truly resolved until the rogues
and vagabonds were separated from the worthy poor, so that the full
and free flow of alms might be directed towards need that was real and
ubiquitous. Such a separation could not be made unless the state imposed substantial authority on local officers, who knew the facts and
who could see that all distributions were made to the worthy. Once the
true poor had been segregated, the whole of the charitable resources of
the commonwealth might be concentrated on the extirpation of the
shameful want and misery which afflicted it.[2]

Magistrates of all ranks were being advised by citizens of all degrees
during the troubled generation that preceded the passage of the great
corpus of poor laws towards the end of the Queen's reign. Thus in
1575 (?) John Hooker, the historian who was for almost a half-century
Chamberlain of Exeter, angrily rebuked the municipal authorities of his
native city as he observed 'what troupes . . . of children, boyes and elder
persons, lye loytering and floistering in every corner of the citie, but
more lamentable it is that no care, no order, nor redresse is had thereof,
which if it be not looked into in time, it will rebound to the peril of the
publique state of your citie'. There has been long discourse regarding
the problem of the poor in Exeter, but nothing of consequence has been
done to relieve the ill. Talk must yield to effective action, 'if you do
indeed tender the preservation of the common state of your citie and the
continuance of so honourable and ancient a common wealth'. Not only
must idlers, rogues, and vagabonds be driven out, 'but also the occasion
and breeding of them is to be cut of[f] whiche is that yong children may
be brought up and be instructed in honest arts'. Many measures Exeter
cannot effectively take alone, but there is much that she can do. Thus
all orphans must be given full protection of the law and provided for if
they have been left without means. Widows should and must receive
at least one-third of their husbands' estate, no matter what the provision
of the wills may be. Poverty, idleness, and vagabondage can be cured in
England only by the protection of children and by ensuring them some
measure of opportunity, whether this be undertaken by parental care or
in default of that by the community at large.[3]

The vexed problem of chronic and unrelieved poverty in the realm
constantly engaged the conscience and mind of responsible men during
the Elizabethan period. As we shall have later occasion to observe in
detail, conscience was to a degree relieved by the immense endowments

[1] Gerardus, Andreas (H. T[ripp], tr.), *The regiment of the pouertie* (L., 1572),
9, 11.

[2] *Ibid.*, 11–20, *et passim*.

[3] Hooker (alias Vowell), John, *Orders enacted for orphans within the citie of
Excester* (L., 1575 ?), 9–38.

which this half-century raised up for the succour of the poor and for the prevention of poverty by the creation of institutions which would enlarge for all men the area of social and economic opportunity. But these problems also engaged the attention of the idealists, the projectors, who though they thought of themselves as intensely practical men were in fact social reformers who pressed with great zeal for some social or economic panacea which they believed would cure the problems of the age. Some of these men held colonization to be the answer, rather more denounced enclosures as the cause of all the social woes of the era, while still others would simply make the rich generous and the poor thrifty by legislative fiat.[1] There is a considerable body of this literature which we cannot pertinently discuss here in detail, but some mention may at least be made of three representative documents which exhibit the strong demand of the age for sweeping social reform in quite different ways.

There survives in the Lansdowne Collection a most interesting manuscript treatise, addressed to the Queen, in which a grand design for the cure of poverty is laid out by 'John Easte'. The work, which seems to have been composed in *ca.* 1580, was entitled *A discourse how the poor may be relieved*, and is a curious mixture of practicality and vapoury idealism.[2] Easte maintained that the worthy poor, when relieved at all by parochial alms, were receiving doles of not more than 4d to 6d a week, which was simply not sufficient to support a family. Such poor men were inevitably forced into beggary and then into criminality. With rare astuteness, the author made the point there there was no clean separation between the worthy and the professional poor, because there was no general and adequate provision for the former. Many of the poor, yielding to pressures that were irresistible, were in the end executed as malefactors, which in itself was expensive to the realm, for Easte reckoned that at the least it cost society £100 to bring a man up to his maturity. The curse of poverty in England could only be cured by providing honest and remunerative work for all who wished it and by teaching all children some useful trade. Easte estimated, upon no authority save his own conjecture, that there were at least 200,000 paupers in England, whom, he reckoned, it would require £520,000 annually to support with a decency which would prevent them from falling first into beggary and then into criminal pursuits. Of this number, he believed about 50,000 were permanent charges on the society because of age or impotence, while another 50,000, though infirm, could, if work were to be had, earn at least a portion of their sustenance. All the

---

[1] *Vide ante*, 63–65, 71–72, for a discussion of certain of this literature, not all of this period, in a somewhat different connection.

[2] *Lansdowne MSS.*, XCV, 3 (n.d.). The manuscript is subscribed 'John Easte' on eighty-six sheets, though an endorsement in another hand suggests that it was probably written by Sir Thomas Smith.

rest could easily provide for themselves with some economic increment for the society to assist in the support of the 100,000 poor who were in whole or in part true wards of the realm.

The crucial question was, of course, precisely how work was to be provided for this large and scattered potential labour force. Here Easte, like all the social reformers of the age, had no particularly relevant suggestions to make, though he promised that 'I shall set forth what ordinances are to be made of how the people should be set and kept at work if I am so commanded'. Needless to say, the Queen never 'so commanded', but from the mass of the author's eloquent generalizations it is possible to see that he was thinking in rather muddled mercantilist terms. He strongly argued that the quality of English cloth must be improved and the export market regained, which he somehow thought could be accomplished if the export of wool were absolutely prohibited. The cultivation of flax should also be encouraged and a linen industry established. These quite unrealistic, and certainly uneconomic, suggestions, are the sum of Easte's 'revealed' solutions, though he does provide further particulars on the care of the poor. The author would have all sums collected for poor relief, whether from private sources or taxation, placed in the hands of local officials who would use the whole of it, save for amounts required for the succour of the aged and impotent, for providing workhouses and stocks on which the poor might be profitably set at labour. Such a plan, he maintained, would cure idleness and beggary and would afford training for the host of poor and neglected children who inevitably became charges on the society under the existing scheme of poor relief.

Easte's proposals, like so many made by the social reformers of the period, were laden with good intentions but made only very slight contribution to the solution of a problem with which the English society was struggling. For one thing, he thought of the realm as an economic entity, while it was in fact a political mass embracing many and diverse local economies in every stage of development and growth. Most of the social ills of the age had to be dealt with and cured parish by parish, region by region, which was the inevitable course private charity was taking. Thinking on the problems of the age in local terms, followed by actions designed to better conditions in a modestly defined area, was, then, at once more fruitful and hopeful. Such more practical thinking was set out in a memorandum of James Rither, a gentleman and a landowner in Harewood in the West Riding of Yorkshire, as he reflected on the ills of his community. His was a large and sprawling parish with at least twenty scattered hamlets, whose problems arose principally from the fact that most of the lands, to a value of five hundred marks annually, had once been held by the monasteries. Much of the land had been bought by the Gascoigne family, from which they created a demesne, leaving a large area of about eight thousand acres in commons, which was so poorly utilized and distributed that it simply could not support the commoners. Rither proposed that each household be assigned a freehold of three convenient acres of this land, that it be enclosed and that each household pay rent in the amount of a shilling annually, as well as light charges on certain pasture lands, in perpetuity, the whole of the income to be employed for the founding and maintenance of a school which would cure the ignorance of the community and provide the training and skills required if children were to be taught to support themselves. If this could be done, self-employment would be provided for the older generation, hope and opportunity for those to come. Rither had thought a great deal about the problems of his own community, and he had thought responsibly and sympathetically. 'What moves my compassion the more for these poor people is that I may have them for work at 2d a day and meat and in harvest for 4d a day, be it never so long, and if they were always thus set on work, they would live well. This shows they would do well with the assistance of superiors, and though this be agreed to of all those people and though by law I might enclose more to my private use, yet it needs higher powers if it is to be supported.'[1]

Rither's proposals, modestly conceived and thoughtfully related to the specific problems of a community which he fully understood, are impressive in the sense that they document the concern, the sense of responsibility, which the gentry as a class displayed for the difficult social problems with which their age had of necessity to deal. It is not too much to say, indeed, that men like Rither, among the gentry and the merchant aristocracy, were in the course of our period to attack problems and evils which had plagued mankind through the whole of Christian history with firm resolution, high courage, and with very great personal generosity. It was the concern of men like Rither, their brooding contemplation of the vexing and eroding social situations which lay about them, which supplied the impulse for their own charitable actions; or to put it in another way, which evoked private intervention on a grand scale in one of the most harassing problems that the western world has ever known.

One more instance of the thought of the social reformers of this age may be mentioned. Robert Hitchcock, soldier and projector, in 1580 propounded a somewhat grandiose scheme which he assured his readers would at once assist in the solution of the problem of poor relief and the better arm the realm against its enemies abroad. Despite the many laws enacted in the course of a century against vagabondage, such acts have not 'nor cannot banishe that pestilent canker out of this commonweale,

---

[1] *Lansdowne MSS.*, CVIII, 29. The document is undated but was probably written in the last decade of the sixteenth century.

by any degree, but that the same encreaseth daiely more & more, to the greate hurte and impouerishyng of this realme'.[1] This festering social problem the author proposed to resolve by creating a great fishing fleet on which the poor might be set at useful employment. He would dispose £1000 in each of the principal ports and £200 in each of the 225 lesser and decayed port towns of the realm, in order to provide a fleet of 400 fishing vessels, with appropriate gear, each of which would be manned by a professional master and twelve lusty beggars or poor men wanting employment. This plan would, Hitchcock argued, have the great merit of providing permanent work for a large number of unemployed persons, would greatly increase the diet of the realm, and would establish a sorely needed training school for deep-water mariners. Hitchcock felt certain that if the proposal were lent official approbation, the £80,000 of capital required could be raised by loans from substantial men in all shires, from men fearful lest the worsening poverty of the realm lead to riotous outbreaks not easily suppressed. 'Therefore the wise and wealthie men of this lande, had neede by greate discretion to deuise some speedy helpe herein, that this poorerer [sic] sorte of people, maie be sette to some good artes, science, occupacions, craftes and labours, by whiche meanes they might be able to relieue them selves of their greate nede and want.'[2]

This plan was of course quite impracticable, among many reasons because it would have bankrupted an already existing and considerable fishing industry, but it does suggest the deepening concern of men of many classes, and of many talents, with difficult social and economic problems which England was no longer prepared to leave to time, chance, and God's inscrutable will. This sense of buoyancy, of accomplishment, and of steady social purpose began about the middle of the Elizabethan period to replace the almost nervous uncertainty and despair which marks the writing of the social reformers of the Edwardian era. Perhaps one example of the substantial body of writing in this new and more hopeful mood might be discussed.

John Howes, who had served as a kind of bursar for Christ's Hospital, in two discourses, one written in 1582 and the other in 1587, described with understandable pride the immense contribution made in the course of a generation by the great London hospitals, which as we shall later note had been founded and supported by mixed private and municipal funds.[3] These institutions had been well and securely founded in a very brief period when responsible men in the city became persuaded that

---

[1] Hitchcock, Robert, *A pollitique platt* (L., 1580), sig. a.i.; also in Dunham and Pargellis, *Complaint and reform*, 276–292. There is a memoir of Hitchcock in the DNB.

[2] Hitchcock, *Pollitique platt*, sig. e.i.

[3] The founding of these institutions will be dealt with in a later volume.

bold and effective measures must be taken, and at once, to deal with the worsening problem of widespread and unattended poverty and want.[1] At the same time, Howes pointed out in his second discourse, much more remained to be done and further reformation should be undertaken. London is still harassed (1587) by rootless poor, in part because the municipal authorities are lax in enforcing their own ordinances and, more importantly, because 'London cannot releve [the whole of] Englande'. London, having the best and most enlightened policy for the care of the poor, has inevitably attracted wandering poor from the whole of the realm, 'so that London is but an hospitall, a place of releife' for the poor of the entire nation. This difficulty can never be wholly resolved, Howes felt, but many things can be done, such as providing distinctive badges for the true London poor, buying up and razing the evil slums which the paupers infest, and prohibiting under severe penalties all employers from importing poor country children as sweated labour. Further gains could be made, the author suggest. d, if more practical instruction were introduced in the curriculum of Christ's Hospital in subjects such as 'to wright divers kinds of hands', book-keeping, and playing musical instruments. Girls should be taught numerous trades, as well as the spinning to which they have traditionally been bound. The grammar schools should remain open to the children of the poor, but their curriculum might, Howes courageously suggested, also be enlivened and broadened by the inclusion of more practical and immediately useful disciplines. Hospitals and lodging places should be set up outside the walls for those afflicted with plague, the alley ways which breed crime and disease should be converted to open gardens, and fresh, cleansing water should flow through every street in the city, so that it may be 'the sweetest city in Cristendomme'.[2]

On this hopeful, confident, and proud note we may well close our discussion of the body of thought in the Elizabethan period which evoked and lent encouragement to the impulse of charitable action. At the very close of this reign, as we have seen, bold and effective action was taken by the whole polity to ensure that the state itself would intervene if now confident and responsible classes failed in attaining the grand design of social betterment towards which they were directing so much of their energy, their patriotism, and their substance. This great *corpus* of legislation had been occasioned by a brief and stunning period of acute social crisis, but men had by this time accumulated enough of experience and of resources to be reasonably confident that they possessed the means and the knowledge to relieve poverty and just possibly to cure it. This fact represented a very great gain for the spirit and the dignity of mankind.

[1] Howes, John, 'A familiar and frendely discourse' (1582), in Tawney and Power, *Tudor economic documents*, III, 415–420.   [2] *Ibid.*, III, 421–443.

c. *The early Stuart period*

The fruits of Elizabethan policy and thought were to be harvested in the early Stuart period when, as we shall shortly observe, the great outpouring of charitable funds in England was to occur.[1] During the course of this interval there was quite as much discussion of the problem of poverty and of ways to effect its cure as in the Elizabethan age, though it should be said that this literature of tracts and sermons wants something of the heat, of the troubled spirit, which enlivened the writing and preaching of the preceding generation. There is more of equanimity, less of anger; there is more of certainty, less of doubt regarding the ability of the society to handle its problems. Nor is there any substantial difference between lay thought and clerical in these later years in the treatment lent to the whole complex question of social reform, though it remains true that, until *ca.* 1630, most of the effective discussion of the meaning and the necessity of charity came from clergymen of Puritan leanings. It is also interesting to note than in the writing of the early seventeenth century there was far less hammering out of the arguments, buttressed by persuasive scriptural authority, for the religious obligation of almsgiving seemed to be taken for granted. There was instead more relatively unsupported exhortation to congregations and to readers to give, and that immediately and generously. It is perhaps not too much to say that charity had become the habit of the nation.

Only one work in the period seems to require separate comment, this being a rather ambitious and important book by George Webbe, who had long been Vicar of Steeple Ashton, Wiltshire, and who in the year his treatise was published was made rector of a rich living in Bath.[2] Webbe undertook a detailed and certainly an impressive discussion of the meaning of poverty and its significance within a Christian society in a treatment which was scriptural in its documentation, philosophical in its method and language. Contrary to the teaching of the schoolmen, Webbe maintained that poverty as such has no virtue whatsoever, it being a matter wholly indifferent in a religious sense.[3] Christ's blessing was on the poor in spirit, not on those who were poor in purse. The whole weight of scriptural teaching enjoins us to labour 'that we may have sufficient, not only to relieve our owne wants, but also to relieve the necessities of others'. Wealth, then, can provide both religious and social utility, when it is regarded as a blessing of God to be used for godly purposes. Hence, 'seeing riches are the instruments of doing good, and to this end are giuen vnto vs by God, that with them we may

---

[1] *Vide post,* 244–246.

[2] Webbe, George, *Augur's prayer* (L., 1621). There is a sketch of Webbe's career in the DNB. *Vide* also *Alumni oxonienses.*

[3] Webbe, *Augur's prayer,* 119.

doe good, and glorifie God, they are not wilfully to be reiected'.[1]
Wealth is in fact the necessary instrument of Christian charity, which
'requireth not only that we should doe good, but also that wee should
doe it well and by good meanes'.[2]

Not only is it true that poverty has no inherent virtue, but clearly it
is to be laboured against by the individual Christian and in so far as
possible extirpated by the society. The droves of beggars and vagabonds
infesting England are mediaeval survivals and our very human instinct
of casual alms perpetuates an ancient and an essentially irreligious vice.
Professional beggary in the realm must be proscribed in fact as well as in
law, and the wasteful and vicious habits which breed such unnecessary
poverty must be cured by religious courses.[3] But this kind of poverty
quite aside, 'pouerty . . . may befall a wise man, vertuous man, a faithfull man . . . Extreme pouertie and necessitie may befall the godly'.[4]
There are, and there will always be, worthy poor in the Christian society
who are its religious charges. Bishop Ridley, Webbe suggested with
great admiration, had perfectly defined these poor men in the glorious
days of the Edwardian Reformation as those who were poor because of
impotence or casualty. These 'are the poore of Gods making, and our
dutie in respect to them, is . . . to pittie them . . . comfort them . . .
relieue them, and support them in deeds'.[5]

These worthy poor are part of God's order for the Christian society,
possibly because if all men were rich there would remain none on whom
could be exercised the precious work of charity, which is an inherent
attribute of Christianity itself. The obligation of charity is laid upon us
absolutely, and lies as a first charge against the whole of our substance.
Yet, the author reflected, 'how hard-hearted and hard-fisted are the
men of our age to the fatherless and the widdowes, to the aged, maimed,
and decaied poore?' May God 'drop down more pittie . . . into our
frozen . . . hearts'![6] We are knit together as one society and our wealth
has neither sanctity nor title unless it be employed towards making the
whole of the society of which we are part a mean between riches and
poverty. Wealth, then, may be sought as a way to preserve ourselves
and our children from want, making it certain that we shall not ourselves burden our brethren, but it possesses Christian title only if we
understand that there lies on it a public and a religious charge as well,
which is the charge of charity.[7] 'If then our good God hath beene so
gracious . . . as to give vs a conuenient competency . . . let vs reckon
. . . *that wee have a goodly heritage*' and employ it as the needs of our
religion and our society require.[8]

Webbe in this impressive and carefully composed treatise sketched

[1] Webbe, *Augur's prayer*, 136.   [2] *Ibid.*, 111.   [3] *Ibid.*, 143–150.
[4] *Ibid.*, 154.   [5] *Ibid.*, 170–171, 178.   [6] *Ibid.*, 181.
[7] *Ibid.*, 211–214, 216, 222–223.   [8] *Ibid.*, 243.

broadly and systematically the consensus of responsible English thought on the whole complex problem of poverty and its treatment. It will have been observed that his argument was derived from and supported by proofs and conclusions drawn principally from Scripture. It may, in fact, be regarded as an adequate statement of the Protestant, and more specifically of the Calvinistic, position on the whole range of ethical and social problems raised by the hideous realities of poverty in the early modern world. Protestantism had been obliged to lend careful and immediate attention to this question because, by an irony of history, urbanization and the rise of capitalism made their effective appearance in the western world simultaneously with the Reformation. We are inclined, on the whole, to the view that the causative factors have been greatly overstated, indeed that both were probably the consequence of powerful forces at work in the society, but Protestantism had none the less speedily to frame an ethic which would not only explain its own position vis-à-vis the poverty with which it found itself confronted but to gather resources with which to relieve and if possible to cure a malignant social ill.

As we have suggested, the writers of the early Stuart period did not lay great stress on the religious obligation of charity, which they assumed was 'a doctrine obvious to all'.[1] None the less, they clearly and eloquently stated the view that this commandment of charity lies heavily upon us and that the Christian who ignores it stands guilty of oppressing the weak and the poor.[2] We must consider the needs of men around us with mercy and our alms must flow out almost as an act of religious worship as we seek with compassion to help those who stand in need.[3] Wealth is vested in us, if it be godly wealth, only that it may arm compassion in doing its effective and healing work among the poor. Our whole substance stands in trust to God, for we are but stewards who will seek to dispose our means in accordance with the clear knowledge of His purposes as revealed to us in Scripture.[4] We dare not forget that rich and poor are inextricably bound together in the Christian community, and that we despoil and lay waste this commonwealth when those with means do not lend their full support to the needs of

[1] Donne, John, 'A sermon preached in St Paul's . . . 1628', in Alford, Henry, ed., Works (L., 1839, 6 vols.), V, 183.

[2] Ibid., V, 187–188, 198; I, 185.

[3] Sibbes, Richard (A. B. Grosart, ed.), The complete works (Edinburgh, 1862–1864, 7 vols.), IV, 524–525; Scot, Patrick, A fathers advice or last will to his sonne, (L., 1620), sect. vi.

[4] Cooper, Thomas, The worldlings adventure (L., 1619), 15–16, 31–34; Church, Henry, The good man's treasury (L., 1636), 283–291 (we can discover little regarding this author, save that he appears to have been a layman); Layfielde, Edmund, The mappe of mans mortality (L., 1630), 38, 56; Donne, John (G. R. Potter and E. M. Simpson, eds.), Sermons (Berkeley, 1953–   , 10 vols.), II, 215–220; Donne, Works, III, 111–113

their poor brethren. For the rich man, wrote Francis Rogers, 'is like the elme-tree, the poore man is like the vine-tree: the elme under-proppeth the vine, and so causeth it to stand and beare fruit. . . . Euen so, the rich men by their almes vphold the poore, who otherwise would starue, and the poore men againe ouer-shadow the rich men with their prayers to God, whereby they doe the better flourish in this world, and liue foreuer in the world to come'. We are all children of God, commanded to care for each other, and so the wealth with which the few are blessed must be dispensed to sustain the worthy poor and to temper the extremes of excessive wealth and of bestial poverty.[1] Those men of substance who decline to assume the Christian obligations of alms, who husband their resources for their own sake, are guilty of the awful sin of covetousness and fully merit the punishment infallibly in store for them.[2] We are commanded to give, and we must give joyously, secure in the knowledge that thereby we lend succour to our weak brethren and support to Christ's kingdom on earth.[3] For those who submit gladly to the Christian discipline of giving generously in alms, the spiritual rewards are certain and their temporal estate will remain unharmed because they have done the will of God. Christian alms cannot in their nature be grudging, and they should not be postponed until the frightening moment of death; they should rather flow from our resources during the whole course of our lifetime as we earn the franchise of Christian men.[4]

The moralists of the early seventeenth century were, as we have said, able to assume that men of the age were reasonably persuaded of the religious necessity of abundant charity, and hence they tended to undertake by every artifice of logic and eloquence to exhort their readers to do their Christian duty. There is a considerable body of this literature of exhortation which we should now treat at least briefly. These writers, and particularly the preachers amongst them, were first of all concerned that men should possess some understanding of the social meaning of Christian charity, the place of charity in the nexus of human relationships. Thus William Whately, a rigorously Puritan divine, in preaching

[1] Rogers, Francis, A sermon of love (L., 1613), 33, 34-35, 40. (The son of Richard Rogers, Dean of Canterbury, Rogers was educated at Cambridge, where he proceeded B.A. in 1598 and B.D. in 1608. Ordained in 1604, he served as Rector of Trinity the Less, London, Vicar of Alkham, Kent, and Rector of St Margaret's, Canterbury. He died in 1638); Donne, Sermons, II, 213; Sibbes, Works, V, 178 ff., IV, 6 ff.; Wakeman, Robert, The poore-mans preacher (L., 1607), 7-17 (Wakeman was the son of a Worcester clergyman. He was educated at Oxford, where he was graduated B.A. in 1594; he held livings in Devon, where he was appointed Canon of Exeter in 1616. He died in 1629.)

[2] Layfielde, Mappe of mans mortality, 33; Donne, Sermons, II, 293-294.

[3] Rogers, Sermon of love, 34-35; Donne, Works, V, 513-518.

[4] Cooper, Worldlings adventure, 39; Sibbes, Works, IV, 524-525; Rawlinson, John, Mercy to a beast (Oxford, 1612), 48-49.

to his congregation after a great fire had all but destroyed their town (Banbury), took the view that the burdens laid upon those whose goods and fortunes were spared offered a perfect instance of the nature of Christian responsibility. 'Now let your abundance supply their wants, whom God hath therefore called to want, that he might giue you an occasion of declaring the abundance of your charitie. . . . Bountifull and mercifull actions are the best bargaines, and the best purchases. No fire shall be able to consume those riches, wherewith a man doth enrich himselfe by succouring those that are distressed.' Alms-deeds are thank offerings made to God. We must remember that all we keep from the poor, we in fact withhold from God in defiance of His goodness towards us.[1]

This view of the social meaning of charity was even more forcefully advanced by Robert Harris, an eminent preacher of decided Puritan persuasion, who stressed the fact that the distribution of poverty, want, and personal disaster among men proceeds from the inscrutable purposes of God.[2] But if these purposes are not clear to us, clear indeed is our own obligation of rendering help and of keeping intact the bonds of love and compassion with which the Christian commonwealth is knit together. Nor will simple alms suffice; the need in England is work for those who are prepared to work. 'Tis in vaine to speake of bringing downe markets unlesse there bee employment. Were barley at two shillings, if men haue not work tis all one: therefore you poore bee willing to worke for bread, you rich study to finde worke.' The answer that there is no work, no help that is consonant with dignity, simply will not suffice. 'Looke to your fields, were ditches scoured, marishes drained, lands ploughed in many fields, it would quite cost; looke to your high wayes, all the poore in the countrey bee scarce enow to gather and lay stones in them. . . . But we haue not to pay them. I answer once for all, better keepe them working than begging and wandring.' Kept they must be, and it is at once better for the poor and better for the whole society if useful work be contrived by every man of property who can assist.[3]

We lie, then, under an obligation of charity which is pervasive and which proceeds both from our duty as Christians and our responsibilities as citizens. We give to our fellow men who are in need, not only because we must but likewise because spiritual benefits accrue to us in the performance of what is almost a sacramental obligation. No man

---

[1] Whately, William, *Sinne no more* (L., 1628), 20–24, 41–43. The son of a mayor of Banbury, Whately was educated at Oxford. He was appointed lecturer at Banbury in 1604, vicar in 1610, serving until his death in 1639. The Banbury fire destroyed upwards of one hundred houses in the town.

[2] Harris, Robert, *Davids comfort* (L., 1628), 1–12. There is a DNB memoir of Harris.

[3] *Ibid.*, 24–25.

has been destroyed by his charity, while a great many have been eternally ruined by their own greed. 'Thy hearty zeale towards God, and thy
willing charity towards man, and both these, in secret, and without
noise', declared Sydenham, will conjoin to make man fully Christian.
To the rich God holds out, though only briefly, possibilities of grace
not enjoyed by most men.[1]

The flow of our charitable giving, the alms which we dispense,
should, then, be an inevitable concomitant of our faith. The truly
Christian man regards his store of wealth as subject to the requirements
not only of himself and his household, but the whole of the household
of Christ. Our giving must accordingly proceed from faith and from
righteousness. And it is a necessary attribute of the grace with which
God has mercifully endowed us. So, 'in heart wee should bee touched
with compassion . . . next with milde and kinde wordes to comfort our
distressed brethren . . . and thirdly (if we haue ability) to succour and
releeue them; and if power bee wanting in vs, yet let vs not omit the
two former, whereby wee are made partakers of others misery'. It is our
charity which unites us in the fellowship of the Christian society, its
rewards and blessings are quite as efficacious to those of us who can
give as to those of who must receive.[2]

Though all this is evident and necessary to our faith and to the
Christian society, the clerical moralists, one can almost say propagandists, held with forgivable exaggeration that their age was in fact one in
which the springs of charity were all but dry. As Whalley put it, 'the
charitie of our times is like feeble old age, blinde, or lame, or deafe, or
dumbe'.[3] The good works of the age, another writer held, were of little
worth or moment because men had been distracted from their true
duty by greed and self-seeking.[4] The great Puritan divine, Thomas
Gataker, advanced a more sophisticated statement of this theme, holding that his age was afflicted with 'a kind of negative Christianity', since
men had grown content with the 'omission of evill', forgetting that God
requires as well the positive virtues of piety, charity, justice, and equity.
It is not enough that the rich no longer rob and oppress the poor, for
on them lies as well the obligation of generous, joyous, and compassionate alms for the needy in Christ. What, he enquired, is 'more contrary

---

[1] Sydenham, Humphrey, *The rich mans warning-peece* (L., 1630), 37; Benson,
George, *A sermon preached at Paules-Crosse* (L., 1609), 46–48; Hildersham,
Arthur, *The doctrine of fasting* (L., 1633), 26, 65; Hildersham, *A sermon preached
in Ashby-Chappell* (L., 1633), 1, 18–19; Warren, John, *Domus ordinata* (L.,
1618), *passim*.

[2] Est, William, *The right rule of a religious life* (L., 1616), 212–216, 303; Gore,
John, *The poore mans hope* (L., 1635), 9–13, 20; Whalley, John, *Gods plentie* (L.,
1616), 22, 27, 41.

[3] Whalley, *Gods plentie*, 2.

[4] Benson, *Sermon at Paules-Crosse*, 44.

to Christianitie then an vtter want of charitie ? when as charitie is the badge or cognisance of Christ, and the very character of a Christian. . . . He is no Christian man therefore, he is scarce a man, that hath no compassion of other mens miseries. . . . It argueth a want of loue to Christ, when men haue no commiseration of the members of Christ, being in want or misery, in distresse, danger, or extremitie'.[1]

These writers agreed, as well, that the distribution of benefactions was best made during the lifetime of the donor. Not only are the spiritual rewards greater and society assured that demonstrable need is thus supplied with healing resources, but the habit of good works is thus ensured. Too many men, they held, were cold in their charity throughout their lifetime and then sought by a kind of impious purchase to gain grace by bequests which imposed no burden upon them and which afforded no joy in the fact of the gift. All this notwithstanding, the righteous man in ordering his affairs against his death, against the moment when he faces God, will make certain that the poor and needy are well provided for in his last will. 'You shall do well to testifie at the end when you are going to give up your account to God, that you are not lesse loving and pittifull to the poore than you have been before.'[2] As we contemplate the approach of death, we should regard our wealth as a storehouse, the whole of which we propose to distribute in such wise as best to help the Christian society and to meet the wishes of God from whom our wealth has come. Consequently, 'hee who maketh his will may obserue the will of God, that so the testament of man may agree with the testament of God'.[3]

At Paul's Cross, the most influential pulpit in England, in the city churches, in pulpits across the length and breadth of the realm, and in tracts warmly composed and eagerly read, this drumfire of exhortation to charity was steadily maintained throughout the early Stuart period. Many of these sermons were never printed, others have been lost, but a very large body of this literature remains, which we have endeavoured to present by a most cursory sampling of its still compelling rhetoric and logic. Surely this sustained and intensely evangelical effort made considerable contribution to the impulse towards charitable giving, offers at least a partial explanation for the tidal surge of giving which set in at about 1550 and which reached its flood during the first generation of the seventeenth century. We could provide many other examples of

---

[1] Gataker, Thomas, *A sparke toward the kindling of sorrow for Sion* (L., 1621), 28; also in *Certaine sermons* (L., 1637).

[2] Jones, William, *A briefe exhortation to all men* (L., 1612 ?), 16. Jones, a native of Northamptonshire, was educated at Eton and Cambridge. He was ordained in 1607. A Puritan, he served as a lecturer in the Isle of Wight.

[3] Warren, *Domus ordinata*, 19. Warren, an early graduate of Emmanuel College, Cambridge, was from 1610 until his death in 1628 Vicar of Great Clacton, Essex. He was a moderate Puritan.

moving exhortation, using every rhetorical device known to skilful divines,[1] but brief quotations from two must suffice.

John Rawlinson, in a sermon preached at St Mary Spittle, London, early in the period, took full advantage of the fact that among his auditors were many of the merchant élite of London. He reminded them that the 'Lord in the riches of his mercy, hath anointed [you] with the oyle of gladnesse, aboue your fellows', in no small part because of the tradition of this class of assuming heavy responsibilities for the poor in Christ. 'Yee are . . . sheepe cloathed with golden fleeces . . . And . . . thou fillest so many empty bellies, cloathest so many naked backes, lodgest so many houseless strangers, relievest so many maimed souldiers, providest for so many impotent creeples, and mainteinest so many fatherlesse orphans . . . Into these . . . channels . . . do the sylver-streames of your mercifull devotion runne.' But Rawlinson admonished the merchant élite because its members tended to dedicate their great charities by bequest. Surely, 'a blessed thing . . . it is, thus to do good, though it be but at your death. But, much more blessed should ye be in your work, not only in the sight of men, but of God himselfe, if in your life time ye would deale & distribute with your owne hands, that which ye cannot tell whether ye shall hold till your death; which indeed is to do good . . . to benefite others rather by your life, than by your death'. Further, that emulation among the great merchants which had borne such rich fruits should be extended to a godly rivalry for good works during the lifetime. One can almost hear the language of the counting-house, when in conclusion Rawlinson assured his congregation that 'he that is a benefactor to others, is a benefactor to his owne soule'.[2]

This was immensely powerful and beautifully skilful preaching. It so happens that Rawlinson was quite wrong, and may well have realized it, in his contention that merchant generosity was almost wholly confined to bequests, but he none the less was seeking by every possible appeal to open even wider the already vast flow of merchant generosity. His argument was couched in terms that would appeal to a rich merchant congregation, his admixture of flattery and rebuke was perfectly contrived, and his manifest fervour and dignity still animate the crumbling pages of his printed sermons. These great merchants attended their parish churches and they attended as a body the many special services such as that at St Mary Spittle. There were many Rawlinsons in London, merchant generosity had seen to that, and they preached to their auditors a fearless gospel of charity, of responsibility, and of a

[1] As, for example, Layfielde, *Mappe of mans mortality*, 12–33; Page, Samuel, *A sermon preached at the funerall of Sir R. Leveson* (L., 1605); Anyan, Thomas, *A sermon preached at Saint Marie Spittle* (Oxford, 1615); Whalley, *Gods plentie*.
[2] Rawlinson, *Mercy to a beast*, 48–49, *et passim*.

kingdom of Christ on earth which they most earnestly believed might be brought about by godly men.

The exhortation to charity was undertaken by William Whately in much more general terms and for a much wider audience.[1] We are assured, the author says, that those who give generously of their means for the relief of the poor will never want themselves.[2] Giving to the poor is a necessary Christian duty and it is required by God of all men, not only the rich, but the 'meane . . . in case they have any thing to spare'. The whole of the resources of a truly Christian society belongs to the whole of that society, the rich being but stewards for those who must be assisted and sustained.[3] It is accordingly 'fruitfull of thanks' to God to give alms; 'it is undoubtedly a duty which must justifie the truth of our religion . . . [and] whosoever professeth religion and is hard, miserable, niggardly, and cannot finde in his heart to give to the poore according to his meanes, that man looke he never so faire to the worlds eye and to his owne, pray he never so often . . . is but a hypocrite, a dissembler . . . a false hearted man'.[4] There can be no faith and no love in us without abundant and joyous works of mercy, and the riches which God may bestow upon us have no virtue unless we use them as stewards and servants of God.[5] So great and so heavy is the obligation of charity that rests upon us that our choice as stewards, as feoffees of Christ, is limited to how and for what purpose our alms shall be given. Of all the clear and irrevocable commandments of God, none lies more certainly upon us than that of charity.

So steady, so insistent, and so central was the statement of the religious necessity of charitable conduct, particularly on the part of the Puritan divines, that only subtle differences would seem to separate their views from those of the arch-enemy, the Church of Rome. It will have been noted that these clergymen were elevating the injunction of charity within the *corpus* of Protestant thought to a position which can almost be described as a doctrine of works. This matter deserves some further consideration. We shall accordingly attempt to discuss it quite specifically in terms of the writings of a number of representative clergymen, both Puritan and, shall we say, orthodox, who grappled honestly with what they fully realized was an embarrassing doctrinal dilemma.

Richard Reeks, a clergyman of Little Ilford, Essex, evidently moderately Puritan in persuasion, tells us flatly that faith and good works are inseparably conjoined, that the one provides the testimony of the other.[6]

[1] *Vide ante*, 183-184, for an earlier mention of this author and comments on another of his sermons.
[2] Whately, William, *The poore mans advocate* (L., 1637), 2-4.
[3] *Ibid.*, 9, 14.   [4] *Ibid.*, 20-23.   [5] *Ibid.*, 41-42.
[6] Reeks, Richard, *Faith and good workes united* (L., 1630), 7.

This was likewise the view of a far more famous preacher, Laurence Chaderton, chosen by Mildmay as the first master of Emmanuel College, who held that in the final day of judgment we shall all be judged 'according to the workes of loue and mercie' done in the course of our lives, when 'they which gaue unto his members meate, drincke, lodging, clothing, and visited the sicke and imprisoned, shalbe pronounced righteous and goe into life eternall. But the unmercifull, being voyde of these workes, shalbe pronounced cursed, and goe into everlasting fire'. This was putting it very strongly indeed, and Chaderton confessed as much. But 'workes are necessarilie required to the doing of the Fathers will . . . for the declaration of our faith, for the confirmation of our hope'.[1] This was the view, too, which John Donne advanced when he reminded his congregation that the good works which Christ commands are things hard and painful, things that 'are against the nature, and ordinary practice of worldly men to do'.[2] In fact, the obligations which the man of the reformed faith must shoulder are more difficult than those of the Roman Catholic, for he must understand that good works, abundant charity, are required of him, but 'without relying upon them, as meritorious'.[3]

Reeks sought to make the point that the reformed faith impelled men to undertake deeds of charity because they stood confident in their faith and because Protestantism stressed practicality as well as piety of faith and conduct. In fact, he carried this argument extraordinarily far, doctrinally quite dangerously far. God, he maintained, wishes 'doings rather than sayings'. The Christian religion 'consisteth in practice more then in theorie; being an occupation rather then a mere profession of doing good'. It is our doing good, or more bluntly, to use the dread phrase, our good works, by which we 'make our election certayne'.[4] We cannot, it is true, be saved by good works, yet we cannot be saved without them, 'as the necessary effects of that grace which brings glory . . . [for] a naked faith, is no true fayth'.[5] This insistence on the Christian obligation of charity had carried men of the strongest Calvinistic persuasion very far indeed towards a statement of a new, a reformed, doctrine of good works. Captious men would raise the cry of popery, but, as another clergyman put it, this is irrelevant so long as we understand that the generous giving of our substance 'for God's sake truly expresses our love for him'.[6] This teaching, whatever its doctrinal merits, evoked a most powerful response from the conscience and substance of England. We may well believe that this persuasion was

---

[1] Chaderton, Laurence, *A godly sermon preached at Paules Crosse* (L., 1580), sigs. C.ii, C.iii.

[2] Donne, *Works*, I, 161.   [3] *Ibid.*, I, 168.

[4] Reeks, *Faith and good workes*, 33.   [5] *Ibid.*, 37–40.

[6] Fleming, Gyles, *Magnificence exemplified* (L., 1634), 26–30.

generally entertained by laymen who were giving more of their substance than men had ever done before or, for that matter, than they ever were to give again.

We must have no fear of good works under the true and infallible certainty of the reformed faith. For now our 'workes of mercy are ioyned with righteousnesse and well doing', cried a Wiltshire divine with a kind of exalted certainty.[1] Under the Gospel we are blessed with a faith which 'cannot be separated from charity; but wheresoeuer it is it bringeth forth good works, to the praise and glory of God'.[2] Faith and charity have at last been perfectly conjoined and men need no longer fear the popish trap of works contrived and exacted by a selfish and venal clergy. So a Devonshire clergyman maintained, in an assize sermon in 1630, when he tells us that 'faith and charitie are like a paire of compasses, to take the latitude of our Christian profession, whiles faith, like the one foot, stands fixt in the centre of justification: charity, like th'other, must goe round in a continuall circle of beneficent operation; and delight to doe good'. It is from faith that we gain our justification, but it is from our charity that we attain our sanctification and the certainty of our election. It is 'faith, [that] having brought us home to Christ . . . leaves us . . . at the grave; but charity . . . doth never fall away . . . and keepes us company to heaven'.[3]

The difficult and tangled problem of Protestant good works, so to speak, was more systematically and impressively handled by John Squire, Vicar of St Leonard Shoreditch, in a sermon preached at St Paul's and dedicated to Sir Alexander St. John and his lady, 'of my poore parish', who were 'zealous of good workes'.[4] All good Christians, the preacher said, have ever, as they must, sought to walk that narrow way to heaven which is paved with good works. By the carrying out of good works alone can we make our election sure.[5] There can be no valid, no saving faith not illumined and accompanied by good works. 'I dispute not the distinctions, whether good workes bee . . . *sacrificia impetrantia*, to beg a blessing upon our King and kingdome, upon our families and persons: or whether they be onely *sacrificia eucharistica*, the tribute of our thankfulnes . . . But this I know, [they are] sacrifices wherewith God is pleased'.[6] Good works possess a transcendent goodness and flow inevitably from faith. This view, Squire maintained, did not throw the

---

[1] Parsons, Bartholomew, *A christians remembrance* (Oxford, 1636), 15.
[2] Reeks, *Faith and good workes*, 42.
[3] Foster, Thomas, *The scourge of covetousness* (L., 1631), 13–14.
[4] Squire, John, *Three sermons* (L., 1637), Dedication. Squire was a grandson of Bishop Aylmer and the son of Adam Squire, Master of Balliol. He was graduated from Cambridge in 1605, becoming vicar of the London parish in 1612. An orthodox Anglican, he was sequestered and imprisoned in 1643. He died in 1653, having kept a school at Richmond, Surrey, after his release.
[5] *Ibid.*, 95.   [6] *Ibid.*, 98–99.

reformed church into the trap of the doctrine of merits. Good works simply exhibit our love of God and all His children. The reformed church must and can teach that 'good workes are necessary to salvation, not in the act of justification, but in the worke of sanctification, without which there can be no salvation . . . Indeed we doe not, indeed we dare not avouch with the Jesuites of Rome . . . that heaven is the value, worth, and price of our workes . . . But if it can be proved, that the Protestant church doth hold dogmatically, that good workes are not necessary to salvation, I will turne papist'.[1]

The good works of the reformed church in England, so its clergy vigorously maintained, far exceeded those of the Romanists since such alms issued from a true comprehension of the conjunction of faith and works, rather than from the fear and the false expectation induced by the wholly wrong doctrine of merit. But it is England's shameful sin, the clergy held, that poverty still exists unsuccoured, misery and sickness unattended. 'Those that should bee eyes to the blinde, pluck out their brethrens eyes and make them blind, whilst they grinde their faces who should cheare them; and robb them of their garments who should cloath them. Where is mercy ? . . . Whilst men turne bread into stones . . . selling good land to build fine houses, turning the smoake that ascended the chimnies of their fore fathers . . . Whilst there is so much pride, so little pity, great feasts, little charity . . . small alms . . . where will you go to find out mercy ?'[2] Shame will be upon us until our wealth has relieved the suffering of the poor, until charity sustains the whole of the nation's need. Good works flow inevitably from the compassionate heart, for 'faith indeed is the life of a Christian but [charity] is the breath whereby he is known to live'.[3] The whole of England must experience the warming surge of compassion and be moved by it to abundant charity, before the Reformation may be regarded as complete in the realm. As another clergyman put it:

> Thou which with pitty in thy heart are moued,
> Towards the needy soule with care oppressed,
> Thou blest of God, of earthly men beloued,
> For helping of the orphan so distressed.
> Comforting widdowes, saluing sick-mans sore,
> Aiding the simple, with fall of thy store.[4]

[1] Squire, *Three sermons*, 103–104.
[2] Rogers, Nehemiah, *The good Samaritan* (L., 1640), 79. Educated at the Merchant Taylors' School and at Emmanuel College, Cambridge, Rogers was for many years Vicar of Messing, Essex. He was briefly (1642–1643) Rector of St Botolph Bishopsgate, London, but was sequestered. He regained an Essex living in 1648. He was the father of John Rogers, one of the most violent of all the Fifth Monarchy men.
[3] *Ibid.*, 119–121.
[4] West, Richard, *The court of conscience* (L., 1607), 'Charitable benefactor'.

The kingdom of Christ is not yet at hand in the land, despite the great gains made by men of the reformed faith.

We may well close our discussion of the literature of the early Stuart period dealing with the necessity of charity by at least a brief notice of a number of works which took a somewhat more secular view of the whole question of the relief of poverty. The authors of these works were men who at bottom looked forward to the cure and prevention of poverty and who took the view that this was the proper and the necessary goal for the Christian society. Both laymen and clergy made due contribution to this literature of social protest, which we may treat under several heads.

Numerous writers held that the principal cause for chronic poverty in the realm was the subtle but continuous oppression of the poor by the rich and powerful. In part this oppression had become quite unconscious, but it none the less had the effect of creating and perpetuating a marginal social and economic group within the English society, doomed to a state of hopeless poverty. Thus that stalwart Puritan divine, Thomas Adams, lashed out at grasping landlords who all too frequently ruined the customary economy of a community by their enclosing greed and then attempted to salve their guilty consciences by charitable courses. 'It is not seasonable, nor reasonable charitie, to vndoe whole townes by your vsuries, enclosings, oppressions, impropriations; and for a kind of expiation, to giue three or foure the yeerely pension of twentie markes: an almeshouse is not so big as a village.'[1] But of all these miscreants, the enclosing landlord is worst, for he is but a 'monstrous theefe' who 'steales away the poore mans liuing and life'.[2] Such cruel men who lay waste a countryside to assuage their greed must be moved by some powerful and sinful forces, mused another divine, Charles Richardson, who sought to analyse the acquisitive instinct of his age. The first of these forces, he concluded, 'is ambition, when men hauing gotten a deale of wealth together, giue many hundreth pounds, to buy one degree of honour after another, to make themselues great in the world, & I know not how many thousand poundes, to aduance their daughters in marriage, to make them ladies or great personages'. Still another impulse animates such ambitious and wasting men. Every man of fortune who has purchased an estate symbolizes his newly acquired degree of honour by sumptuous building, 'one of the vanities of this age'. Such men seek to build on a princely scale, with the result that 'not onely their owne tenants, but all the countrey about them shall bee tyred out' by their frenzied outlays. And then, the great house having been built, prodigal sums must be expended on its upkeep and its diet

---

[1] Adams, Thomas, *The white devil* (L., 1613), 35; also in *Workes* (L., 1629), 48.
[2] Adams, *White devil*, 47; and *vide* Powell, Robert, *Depopulation arraigned* (L., 1636).

while the poor of the community are plunged even deeper into poverty as the landlord exacts revenues for the support of his new estate.[1]

There is much angry and eloquent protest of this kind, and particularly in the years prior to 1630, of which a few more examples should perhaps be given. Thus a testy anonymous author agreed fully and most vehemently with Richardson and Adams in his analysis of the social evils of the age which bred and then perpetuated poverty. He held that the common lands of England were being consumed by grasping landlords. These men handle land as if no human beings were involved in its management and disposition. The rich invariably purchase large estates; such men 'get whole townes into their hands; and then dis-peopling the same by letting downe of houses and turning forth of tenants, they recover the commons from the poore, and make them their own'.[2] This having been done, these grasping landlords exploit their estates by systematic farming, with the result that a few farmers find work where scores were earlier supported. All this vaulting ambition, all this waste and corruption, has no other effect than to grind down the poor. 'Our monstrous pride', declared Adams, has turned 'hospitallity into a dumbe shew: that which fed the belly of hunger, now feedes the eie of lust . . . we make our selues the compounds of all nations: we borrow of Spaine, Italy, Germany, France, Turkie and all: that death when he robs an Englishman, robs all countries: where lies the wealth of England? in three places, on citizens tables, in vsurers coffers, and upon courtiers backes.'[3]

It would seem, Richardson lamented, that every powerful group in English life was involved in a malignant conspiracy to destroy the poor. Thus he lashed out at the lawyers as oppressors, with their spinning out of cases and their unconscionable bleeding of every client before his case was even brought to trial.[4] This complaint was bitterly shared by Arthur Warren, a poet who had himself known imprisonment for debt, when he wrote:

> What i'st to begge, but to be counted base?
> What i'st to borrow, but to be denide?
> When poore are trespas'd, they learne Ploydons case,
> And must for recompence content abide,
> Yet giue the rich but an uncourteous looke,
> It prooues a forfeit by their statute booke.[5]

Every hand, these moralists seemed to hold, was raised against the poor. Even the tradesmen, those men on the way up in estate, entrap and

---

[1] Richardson, Charles, *A sermon against oppression* (L., 1615), 11–12.
[2] S[parke], *Greevous grones*, 19.
[3] Adams, *White devil*, 17–18.
[4] Richardson, *Sermon against oppression*, 14–15.
[5] Warren, Arthur, *The poor mans passions* (L., 1605), no pagin.

defraud the poor with their lies, their cheats, and their smooth persuasion. They are engrossers, they speak falsely of quantity and of costs;
even training up their servants and apprentices to share in their essential corruption and deceit.[1] These are but 'little rich men', but they share
with the truly rich want of charity, guilt in the oppressing of the poor,
and that contempt for the poor which is itself the worst of all oppressions:

> Degrading vs with contumelius spelles,
> They touch, attach, and summon us with shames,
> To our discredit ring reprochfull bells,
> And catalogue us with inhumane names,
> Vagabonds, varlets, villaines, vassalls, slaues,
> Rogues, caterpillers, runnagates, and knaues.[2]

All this is, of course, reminiscent of the literature of protest, of
wrathful demand for reform, which had its clearest and most extreme
statement in the period of the Edwardian Reformation, but which, as we
have seen, had a continuous and effective history in English social
thought until it burgeoned out, once more in radical and vehement form,
as an aspect of the Puritan Revolution. This was essentially old-fashioned thinking, depending heavily on accepted but wholly outworn
axioms and symbols which possessed in the early seventeenth century
neither historical nor economic reality. Yet it seems evident that this
writing was persuasive and that the teachings which it propounded
were widely accepted. It was essentially moralistic in tone and it
undoubtedly supplied a significant impulse to charitable giving in this
as it had in earlier generations.

We should deal, in concluding our discussion of the literature of protest in this era, with at least a sampling of writers who were 'projectors',
men fanatically wedded to one course of reform, or to a single explanation of the woes of mankind, and who at least incidentally offered to
cure poverty by the prescription of panacea. Certainly one of the ablest
of all this group was Gerard de Malynes, the early economic theorist
who was often officially consulted on monetary problems during the
Elizabethan period.[3] De Malynes strongly argued that England could
never be truly prosperous or happy so long as great extremes of wealth
and poverty existed. The harmony and balance of the economy had been
destroyed by the 'dragon' of covetousness, which he identified as
monetary inflation. Until this dragon was loosed by unscrupulous
usurers, 'the inhabitants of this noble iland did liue by the naturall

---

[1] Richardson, *Sermon against oppression*, 17-23.
[2] Warren, *Poor mans passion*, no pagin.
[3] DNB; Beer, *Early British economics*, 106-113, 146, 149; Viner, Jacob,
Studies in the theory of international trade (N.Y., 1937), 5, 9, 17, 54, 61, 76.

richesse of the lands they were borne unto, or by the . . . riches they were bred vnto . . . euery man using . . . his own . . . Clergy men and magistrates did liue by their reuenues and pensions . . . gentlemen of their lands . . . merchants and citizens by their trade, artificers by their craft', while concord and justice reigned in the commonwealth.[1] With gross oversimplification, De Malynes blamed the monetary policy for the inflationary process, which as we have seen was certainly a significant cause of endemic poverty in England, holding that it amounted to deliberate and controllable devaluation.[2] Men have become quite mad in their thirst for money, with the result that charity is cold and 'brittle metall' is preferred to 'eternall treasure'.[3] Inflation he denounced as a monster which 'taketh away the chiefest comfort of the poore, which is the quietnesse of their minds, and deuoureth their gaine before it can be gotten'.[4] All this he would cure by a reform of monetary policy, just as another economic theorist of the period, Charles Gibbon, would relieve the poor and restore the harmony of the commonwealth by a complete reform of assessments in order more equitably to distribute the burden of taxation.[5]

Still other writers found the solution to the problem of poverty in some specific economic undertaking. There were many who believed that the principal reason for supporting the colonizing projects of the era was that the marginal classes in the society might thereby be relieved either by transportation or by the economic benefits accruing to the mother country.[6] Even more numerous were the projectors who believed that substantial relief, if not the cure, of worthy poverty could be gained by lending full governmental support to the fishing industry. Chief among these was John Keymer [or Keymor], whose treatise entitled *Observation made upon the Dutch fishing* appears to have been written in 1601, and which enjoyed considerable circulation and influence in the Jacobean period, though it remained unpublished until the time of the Restoration. Keymer held that England had simply resigned to the Dutch and other European nations a great and profitable fishing industry, which if revived and well supported could vastly improve the prosperity of the nation and go far towards the relief of its chronic

---

[1] De Malynes, Gerard, *Saint George for England* (L., 1601), 13.

[2] *Vide ante*, 72–74.

[3] De Malynes, *Saint George*, 19, 47.

[4] *Ibid.*, 71.

[5] Gibbon, Charles, *The order of equalitie* (Cambridge, 1604), 11–14, 17–20.

[6] This subject has been well and fully treated in L. B. Wright's *Religion and empire*, in which abundant documentation is provided, and need not be developed here. *Vide ante*, 71–72, however. Mention may be made of Donne's sermon preached before the Virginia Company in 1622 (*Works*, VI, 225 ff.) and of M[ichael] S[parke's] *Greevous grones* (L., 1621), in which this theme is well developed.

poverty.[1] The author maintained that all the mining industries of England, and the clothing industry as well, did not produce the economic benefits that would flow from a well-managed fishing industry. It would add strength of ships and seamen, but above all else it would give employment 'for all people, both young and old, for the keeping of them from begging and stealing, and other disorders'.[2] The benefits which Keymer envisaged were rich indeed, and the picture roseate, for he held that 'the trade of fishing is work-master to all other trades, and by that means the Dutch increase their farthings to pounds, and their pounds to thousands; and what fruitfulnesse is in their country and not a beggar there, every one getting his own living . . . the poor man, tho' he be blind and have but one hand, will get his own living sitting on a seat, with knitting and making of nets and hooks; every boy and wench, from ten and twelve years and upwards, will get their own living by winding hemp, spinning yarns, making twine and thread for nets'. Then and then alone, 'idlenesse, beggary, and penury, will be driven out of this land'.[3]

One projector, who signed himself 'Captain Baylie', combined two current enthusiasms when in 1625 he proposed linking a revival of the fishing industry with a huge undertaking for planting Virginia. Baylie believed that funds could be raised by subscription in every parish of the country—in fact, he had made trial proposals on his own authority —to finance the building and equipping of a fishing fleet which would employ as many as 10,000 young men, who would also be available to man the navy. The King was asked to build each year, from timber obtained from Virginia, two warships of 1000 tons burthen each for the defence of the fishing grounds and the sea routes to Virginia. At the same time, as many as 3000 poor were to be despatched each year to Virginia, with a grant of twenty acres of land, household and other necessary gear, and victuals for their first year. All this was to be financed by subscription from persons disturbed by the poverty so widespread in the realm, those refusing to subscribe to have their names 'recorded in a blank book'. If this were undertaken over a period of ten years, the coastal towns would be enriched by the fishing industry and by outfitting the Virginia fleet, while the resulting revival of trade 'will sett so many a work of all trades that I dare not sett downe'. The poor throughout the realm will either be relieved or transplanted, while even the prisons which 'are everlasting full & great store of bloud spilt in regard there is no way for them to expose themselves to live' will be

---

[1] 'John Keymer's observation made upon the Dutch fishing about the year 1601', in *A small collection of valuable tracts relating to the herring fishery* (L., 1751), 7.

[2] *Ibid.*, 33–34.

[3] *Ibid.*, 36.

emptied as such men, often vicious because of hopeless poverty, will be transported to Virginia.[1]

It may be said that a powerful and persistent pressure of informed opinion was concentrated on the problem of poverty and its relief during the whole of the early Stuart period. Steady support was lent to the charitable impulse which in the course of this era brought private benefactions to such a high plane both in amount and in quality of disposition. A climate of opinion had been created in which two rich and powerful classes particularly, the merchant aristocracy and the gentry, had assumed really immense burdens of responsibility which they were carrying with great dignity and a sense of social dedication. The literature which we have been considering undoubtedly made significant contribution to this great achievement of human generosity in the years 1601–1640, for it had established in the public mind at once the religious and the social necessity of bringing all possible resources to bear on the age-old problem of poverty. We have necessarily been content with presenting as evidence only a sampling of this literature. It is important to note here that we have been drawing from a much larger mass of material, including fifty-one published sermons urging the high necessity for charitable responsibility. Most significantly, it may be said that of this group of sermons, thirty-two were preached by clergy of undoubted Puritan persuasion and that another six of these ministers would seem from the biographical data available or from internal evidence to have been Puritan as well. This fact is remarkable when we bear in mind that throughout these four decades Puritanism lay under pressure of an increasing severity and that the printing press was in the later years of the period not available to men of a pronounced Puritan bias. We are not saying that this literature, essentially moralistic and evangelical as it was, was in any sense giving expression to a factional point of view, but rather that the great strength of the charitable impulse, at least in its social aspect, was to be found in the Puritan party. This remarkable preponderance of Puritans among the clerical writers considered was also accounted for by the further fact that the Puritan wing of the clergy tended, as it always had, to include most of the famous preachers of the church; and in an age when the published sermon was widely prized and read as a piece of literature, it was the sermon of a man with an established reputation as a popular preacher that tended to get published.

d The ferment of revolution

We turn now to our last period, the tumultuous years of intellectual ferment, social experimentation, and political dislocation which mark the Puritan Revolution. We are here considering only the treatment of

[1] *S.P. Dom.*, 1625, CLXXXIX, 36.

the problem of charity in the literature of the era, but a few more general remarks may be permitted as well. This was inevitably a period of serious economic dislocation, offset, however, by the demands for employment, including the armed services on both sides, of the war itself. There is no indication in our evidence of any considerable augmentation of poverty or of economic distress during these two decades, save for that caused by the physical impact of war itself, and we have earlier observed that there was very little slackening of parochial relief in those areas where charitable endowments were available or where rates had earlier been imposed for poor relief. The new and on the whole the most difficult problem of these two decades was the care of the war casualties, the thousands of wounded men, the widows and orphans, and the necessity for resettling into normal civilian pursuits men whose mature life had been spent in the camps and barracks. The formidable problem of handling the social wreckage of a sharp and lengthy civil war, then followed by the casualties from Cromwell's foreign adventures, tended to be solved by burdening existing institutions, hospitals, and almshouses, with of course serious dislocation of their normal services. But there was no breakdown of institutions, there was no social disaster, and, as we shall shortly suggest in detail, there was certainly no catastrophic falling away in the flow of funds from private charity, which in this interval, as in the past century, bore the principal responsibility for the care of the distressed.[1]

As we turn to the discussion of the extensive body of literature dealing with the whole complex problem of poverty and its relief, we may observe that there is remarkably little difference in either the quantity or the quality of thought, as compared with the two preceding generations, save that this period of free discussion and experimentation inevitably produced a larger and a more interesting proportion of schemes set out by 'projectors'. But so great was the momentum of discussion, so well established was the dogma of charitable responsibility, and so well sustained was the flow of charitable funds that the literature of the revolutionary period may on balance be regarded as a continuation of a stream of thought which had its rise in the troubled but hopeful days of the Edwardian Reformation. Some other writers on the revolutionary era have discovered a hardening of the attitude of a triumphant Puritanism towards the poor, a contempt for poverty, which we do not observe in the literature.[2] There is rather, as there had

[1] This general view, it must be said, differs substantially from that advanced by a number of social and economic historians who have dealt in some detail with the revolutionary period.

[2] We would mention in particular the views of Miss Margaret James (*Social problems and policy during the Puritan Revolution*, L., 1930) and of Professor Tawney (*Religion and the rise of capitalism*), which must, of course, carry great weight; but we believe that they have read the literature of the period 1640–

been for a century, a denunciation of rogues and vagabonds, harsh proposals for the handling of the unworthy poor, which possibly differ somewhat in intensity but by no means in substance from an attitude firmly fixed in the public and governmental mind for well over a century past. But the main stream of thought, which we believe to have been animated by Puritanism for more than two preceding generations in any case, remained relatively unaffected by the political and religious disaster which had overwhelmed the land. We should now address ourselves to the consideration of a small, but we believe representative, sampling of the extensive body of literature in this period which lent support and renewed strength to the already mature impulse towards charitable giving.

The preachers of the revolutionary era, like their brethren before them, lashed out at the coldness of their age, at the decline of charity, and the drying up of the springs of compassion. Thus the formidable Henry Symons saw a general decay of virtue in the commonwealth, but particularly denounced the rich, 'how few of them that are rich towards God . . . rich in faith . . . rich in good works' and the care of the poor.[1] Such men must repent, must open their hearts and purses freely and gladly if they are to stand before the last judge.[2] The age is cold, is wanting in compassion, urged another divine, for 'never had we more need to presse men to acts of charity, then in this iron age upon which we are cast'. At a time when need is so evident and so great, our 'mercy to the poor runs very low. Our forefathers . . . how bountifull and charitable were they; we have standing monuments of it in colledges, in hospitalls', while in this corrupt generation 'we are so farre from erecting such monuments of mercy, that we are rather for the pulling down of these, as being popish, unnecessary, and I know not what'.[3] Yet, since mercy is a debt owed by us to man by the command-ment of God, the author charged all men of substance to undertake the full measure of their responsibilities towards the poor and needy.[4]

1660 out of the century-long context in which it should be set and, more par-ticularly, that they have failed to note that the denunciations of the unworthy, the professional, poor were framed with a logic and usually in language that was a century old. No one in England ever liked idlers and rogues, or those thought to be such, the Puritans least of all.

[1] Symons, Henry, *The Lord Jesus his commission* (L., 1657), 19. A native of Kent, Symons was graduated from Cambridge in 1632. He was ejected in 1662 as Rector of Southfleet, Kent. [2] *Ibid.*, 32.

[3] Jacomb, Thomas, *Gods mercy for mans mercy* (L., 1657), 14–16. Jacomb (1622–1687) was educated at Melton Mowbray School, Leicestershire, and at Oxford, where he was graduated B.A. in 1643. He was Rector of St Martin Ludgate from 1647 until his ejection in 1662. An outspoken Presbyterian, he was imprisoned for a season for holding a conventicle in London, but was pro-tected by the Dowager Countess of Exeter, whom he served as chaplain.

[4] *Ibid.*, 17, 21–22.

The preachers of this period also urged in the terms so eloquently expounded for a century past the absolute obligation to charity which lay on the Christian conscience. We are commanded to give generously to all men who are in need, and we should with terror search our hearts when we repel the claims of men who stand in distress. Our alms should flow instantly and inevitably from the Christian mercy in our hearts, and we may be sure indeed that 'the poor mans hand is Christ's treasury, and there is nothing lost which is put there'. The charitable man will be blessed on earth as he is in heaven, 'so, whatsoever we give to the poor, we give to men, but Christ repayes it. We give it away in earth, but we meet it in heaven: we cast it away in this world, but find it in the world to come'. No society which calls itself Christian, which heeds the express commandment of God, dares be anything less than charitable, while the existence of unrelieved poverty in a state is a clear indication that the duties inherent in the Christian community simply have not been met. Our charity must be cheerful, it must be a first call on our own wealth, and it must flow from the reservoir of faith through the channels of humility.[1]

The Puritan clergy patiently insisted that we must not accept the commandment of alms as a kind of doctrinal abstraction without admitting it to our minds and hearts as an intensely personal responsibility. There can be no salvation unless we lend our obedience to this injunction of Christian charity, maintained Richard Younge, who gave specific examples of men who had well discharged their responsibilities by disposing from 10 per cent to 20 per cent of their incomes in alms.[2] Earlier piety had done much, had wrought great achievement of alms, another minister held in a sermon at St Paul's, but there remain the poor, the impoverished clergy, the children unapprenticed, and the sons of indigent men who deserve education but cannot attend the universities without help. 'Remember . . . it is your duty to consider the ability which God hath given you, to weigh the necessitous condition of the objects set before you, and accordingly to extend your bounty to the honour of God, the discharge of your consciences, the regaining of your credit, and the relief of the needy.'[3] The poor have an absolute claim on some generous measure of our wealth, a claim which transcends our man-made title. To withhold from the poor, accordingly, is to defraud them and, if we 'deprive them of the means where by their lives might have been preserved', to murder them.[4] Not only do we live

[1] Moore, John, *The crying sin of England* (L., 1653), 18 ff., 24, 27–30; Watson, Thomas, *A plea for almes* (L., 1658), 40–43, 49, 53–54, 59–60. Both men are noted in the DNB. Moore died in 1657; Watson was ejected at the Restoration, having been a pronounced Presbyterian.

[2] Younge, Richard, *The poores advocate* (L., 1654), 27–29.

[3] Hardy, Nathaniel, *The olive-branch* (L., 1658), 38.

[4] Younge, *Poores advocate*, 6.

under a stark prescription of charity, but we must needs learn to give joyously, in full confidence as an act of faith. 'He who hath no true charity, hath no true faith, no true wisdom, no well grounded hope, peace of conscience, or any other saving grace whatsoever'.[1]

When we have at last experienced the grace of alms freely and gladly given, of alms distributed as an act of mercy, our own mercy will be rewarded by the mercy of God towards us. God, Jacomb tells us, will 'return to the mercifull man what he gives to the poor . . . if God do not returne your mercy in the very kind, he will do it in some other way', for a benefaction to the needy 'is a loan to God, and he is a faithfull paymaster'.[2] This Presbyterian divine put it bluntly and forcefully in terms of the counting-house, when he wrote that 'charity to the poor 'tis your bill of exchange; pay down your money here, and you shall receive it again in glory'.[3] Infinite rewards, then, flow to us, once we have learned the meaning of mercy towards our unfortunate brothers in Christ. London merchants must have been moved indeed to have such certain assurance that 'works of mercy are all expended upon a mans self, he hath the comfort here, and the reward hereafter . . . laying up a foundation, a way to make our uncertain riches sure and stable'.[4] We dare not forget that, in truth, that which we possess has come from the 'deep places of the earth'; 'it is gift, it is not property; Gods, not yours; you are the fiduciaries, the despositaries onely'.[5] We betray the trust of God, just as we betray our own profession of Christian faith, when we seek to seal off our treasure against the needs of our brethren in Christ.

And, if these Puritan divines were blunt and categorical in expounding the personal obligation of charity and the ubiquitous rewards that flow from mercy, they were equally assured in treating the subject in its dreaded connection with the question of the necessity for good works. One suspects, in point of fact, that their evangelical zeal to inspire charity tended to master their orthodox qualms as they enunciated, and a powerful argument it is, what we can only regard as a Protestant doctrine of the merit of works. Good works, the merit of alms freely given, ensure us the reward of a tranquil conscience in this life and 'joy forevermore' in the life to come. They are 'seeds of glory' that follow us into heaven. When the angel of darkness cuts us down, preached Cartwright, 'riches they take wing and fly away . . . but our good works prove our close and faithful friends, they follow us still'.[6] Our works of mercy endure with a godly and compelling righteousness for all time to come, another divine would hold.[7] Our deeds of mercy will assuredly

---

[1] Younge, *Poores advocate*, 21–22.   [2] Jacomb, *Gods mercy*, 11.   [3] *Ibid.*, 24.
[4] Reynolds, Edward, *The rich mans charge* (L., 1658), 45. The career of this eminent moderate is noted in the DNB.
[5] *Ibid.*, 46–47.
[6] Cartwright, Thomas, *The good man's epitaph* (L., 1659), 15–16.
[7] Watson, *Plea for almes*, 3–8.

be blessed by God, for 'it is lawful to put out your monie to use, when you lay it out for good uses'.[1] Indeed, this preacher, if we read him correctly, would seem to say that good works may well be more important than faith itself in the attainment of salvation.[2] More cautiously and certainly with more of Calvinistic orthodoxy, the moderate Reynolds, in preaching before the Lord Mayor and Aldermen of London, suggested that though 'we dare not ascribe unto good works, any meritorious dignity, or proper causality, whereby they procure or produce salvation for us, yet such a necessity of them we ever acknowledge, as that without walking in the way of holiness, we shall not arrive at the Kingdom of Glory; without doing the will of God, we can never expect to receive the promises'. God commands good works, the acts of mercy, from us, and clearly the 'vertue of true saving faith' finds its outlet, its confirmation, in the good works that we do and leave behind us.[3]

We have been considering the thought of some of the greatest and most persuasive preachers that Protestantism has ever known. They were men who spoke with that unique confidence of infallible knowledge of faith which Calvinism alone among the Protestant dogmas has inspired, and they spoke in an age in which the learned clergy possessed a prestige perhaps never equalled before or since. They were pronouncing, with respect to the area of our interest, a quite remarkable doctrine of the social meaning and responsibilities of wealth. They loved to emphasize the fact that we are no more than feoffees of wealth, that we hold our substance from God as stewards and remain strictly accountable to Him for the wisdom and social generosity of its use.[4] It is when we have come fully to understand the nature and obligations of our stewardship that we have freed ourselves from the evil of wealth, for then we know that 'the poore mans hand is the rich mans treasury, what hee layes up there, he shall find in heaven: hee that feeds the hungry, puts bread into Christs owne mouth; hee that clothes the naked, puts a garment on Christs owne backe'.[5]

We must, then, come to comprehend that we hold our wealth in trust, that wealth has virtue only when it is disciplined by and dedicated to the service of God. Our wealth must serve the ends of our social responsibility, of our duty to God, our country, and our fellow men. As Reynolds phrased it, 'whereas worldly riches are onely . . . for the present time . . . being put into good works, they are . . . returnable into another country. A mans works will follow him . . . An house thus

---

[1] Watson, *Plea for almes*, 37.   [2] *Ibid.*, 30–43.

[3] Reynolds, *Rich mans charge*, Epist. Dedic.

[4] *Christs order* (L., 1644), 4; Marriot, Robert, *A sermon in commemoration of . . . Mistris Elizabeth Dering* (L., 1641), 22. Marriot, a graduate of Cambridge in 1630, was in 1641 Vicar of Lenham, Kent. He conformed after the Restoration, serving successively in two London parishes. He died in 1689, aged 81.

[5] *Ibid.*, 23.

founded, shall continue for ever'.[1] Christ did not forbid us to have or to gain wealth; this view betokens a complete misunderstanding of His precepts and teachings. But He did command us at our peril to dedicate our substance to His purposes, and He did warn us against the dreadful sin of covetousness, of seeking wealth for its own sake. How, then, shall we know 'those lawful means, which God gives for the getting of wealth?'[2] We are not only permitted, but we are required to gain sufficient substance to lend full support to our own needs and those of our family, and to provide for the 'necessity of our calling and condition of life; which admits a very great latitude, according to the various relations, and stations, which men hold, both in church and state'. But what imperils us in this world and the next is the insidious and wholly evil love of wealth for its own sake, for the 'covetous man is possessed . . . by his wealth . . . of all sinners [he is] most miserable . . . His end shall be, begger, and fool'.[3] We must come fully to comprehend, Reynolds taught, that wealth is but transitory, 'fit to buy some trifles with, but not to purchase an inheritance'. Our eternal, our true, estate is laid up in another world by the good works we leave in this life, with the consequence that our wealth has no moral meaning, no real meaning, save as it enables us to carry forward charitable, useful, and enduring works.

This seems to us to be a clear statement of the later Calvinistic position on the meaning and utility of wealth in the Christian society. Wealth must be dedicated to God's uses, for 'God hath given [riches] to us . . . to do good with . . . for the good of our souls, and the comfort of our poor brethren'. The right use for wealth, then, is to employ it as the 'material for good works', that we may discharge our lives profitably for the needs of other men.[4] God has in His wisdom given more to some men than to others for the sole purpose of imposing a larger measure of social responsibility, so held Samuel Richardson, the leading Baptist theologian. God will bless us in the act of giving. We must recall at all times that 'it is the will of God that there should not be any inequality of living among his people', and be guided by the understanding that 'it is not enough to do some good, or much good, unless we do all the good we can'.[5] Rich men have their wealth, Reynolds taught, 'as the sun hath

---

[1] Reynolds, *Rich mans charge*, 4–5.

[2] Ryves, Brune, *Two sermons* (L., 1652), 1–6. Ryves was educated at Oxford, where he proceeded B.A. in 1616. He was appointed Rector of St Martin Vintry in 1628 and Vicar of Stanwell, Middlesex, about 1640. He was a chaplain to the King, an Anglican, and a Royalist. He was rewarded at the Restoration by appointment as Dean of Chichester and of Windsor. He died in 1677, aged 83.

[3] *Ibid.*, 8, 11–14, 19–22.   [4] Reynolds, *Rich mans charge*, 30–31.

[5] Richardson, Samuel, *The cause of the poor pleaded* (L., 1653), no pagin. (cropped). Richardson was the most eminent and responsible of the Baptist thinkers of his generation (Jordan, W. K., *The development of religious toleration*

light, or the fire heat, to communicate unto others . . . the whole good that money doth . . . is while it is in motion', the sole justification for riches consisting in the good uses to which they may be applied.[1] We shall accordingly bear our wealth as a burden laid upon us, to be discharged according to God's clear purposes of charity, conducting our own lives and providing for our families with that frugality and charity of outlay which recognizes that wealth possesses no personal meaning for us.[2]

If the rich man, the Christian whom God has endowed with means to serve the ends of His will, understands all this, recognizes the nature of his responsibility, then may his wealth be put to an infinite variety of godly purposes, then will he be blessed. Surely, as one writer of the period puts it, 'there lyes before you the fairest of opportunities; never was there a fitter seeds-time for prayer and almes . . . that's your happinesse that you can give'. Many demands lie against our charity, many objects of mercy: 'old men and babes, widowes and orphans, many poore persons that want stocks to set them on work, that would faine be imployed if they knew how'; these are but instances of the good works which God requires.[3] And there are many other worthy objects of charity which make due claim on the divinely trusteed wealth which we hold. The schools and universities require support, the ministry is ill supplied in its necessary work, all the hopeful experiments in social rehabilitation need ever more capital, and there are about us poor and distressed Christian men and women who require our alms.[4] All these needs we must supply, all these responsibilities lie unfulfilled as a charge on our charity and conscience. All this we must bring about 'as in communion, as members one of another . . . with meekness . . . and facility . . . with mercy . . . as a debt of love . . . for the credit of our Reformed Religion, that the mouths of adversaries may be stopped, who falsely charge us with preaching and . . . professing a naked, empty, fruitless faith'.[5] All Christian men, whether their estates be large or modest, must set themselves at these great tasks, with an understanding that almsgiving cannot be regarded as a wasting of a man's estate. The only impediment to this great and godly, this necessary, achievement 'is the affection and passionate love, that we bear to our wealth, that lust . . . as the apostle cals it'. Surely, we as Christian men

in England, L., 1932–1940, 4 vols., III, 515–523). It is interesting that, Richardson aside, the sectaries gave little or no consideration to the great social problems which we have under discussion. This is doubtless principally explained by the fact that for most of these men such problems were unimportant because they were possessed of a vision of the Kingdom of Christ which they believed to be at hand.

[1] Reynolds, *Rich mans charge*, 31.   [2] Ryves, *Two sermons*, 28–38.
[3] Harris, Robert, *True religion* (L., 1645), Preface, 35.
[4] Reynolds, *Rich mans charge*, 33–37.   [5] *Ibid.*, 38–41.

of the reformed faith will come to understand that the 'final reward of almesgiving [is] a present coronet, and a future crown'.[1]

We have dealt all too briefly with a large and a very impressive body of clerical literature which in the course of the revolutionary era may be said to have brought to its maturity the Calvinistic teaching on the moral and social responsibility of wealth and to have assessed with great care and considerable nobility the nature of the Christian obligation of charity. Most, but by no means all, of these men were Puritans, as, in point of fact, they had been in the earlier periods with which we have dealt. It is noteworthy that the thought of this period on the whole complex and troubled problem of the relief of poverty was in no sense revolutionary, being linked solidly and organically with the thought of the past century as men sought to analyse and set down the obligation of the reformed faith towards problems which were ancient in their origin but which had become critical in a society undergoing a social and economic metamorphosis of revolutionary proportions. Any one of these sermons could with perfect propriety have been preached in the Caroline period; most of them would have been consonant with the mood of the late Elizabethan age. They represent, then, no sharp break with the past, but rather a maturing of a profoundly important body of Christian thought to which the best and most responsible minds in England had been lending prayerful attention for a full century.

But the revolutionary era was also marked by an immensely significant burgeoning out of lay thought on these difficult and complex matters of poverty, of want of opportunity, and the chronic wasting not only of human life but the resources of the state. The sectaries, who were lending fanatical but stimulating attention to religious questions during these years, were so engrossed with their spiritual vision, with the Kingdom of God which seemed to be at hand, that they gave but scant attention to the more pedestrian problem of poverty and the charity which might cure it. But there were other laymen who were almost completely secular in their interests and who demanded that the political and religious revolution be extended in the realm of social institutions. These men wished for as much boldness and experimentation in social problems and issues as had characterized the flow of events in the realms of faith and the constitution, but here they were to be halted by the solid social conservatism of Cromwell and the power groupings which he led and fused with such consummate skill. We shall now briefly discuss the thought and the recommendations of these laymen, all of whom were bold but none of whom, it is interesting to note, was an incendiary. Most of these men, and, as we have observed in earlier pages, there had been others before them, were 'projectors', men who believed they had found the solution for problems of vast com-

---

[1] Hammond, Henry, *The poor mans tithing* (L., 1657), 63–66, 73.

plexity by some single formula which they advanced with an admirable but occasionally tiresome persistence. The *corpus* of this thought is very large, and we must accordingly be content with a most modest, and we hope, representative sampling, particularly since it has already been well and thoroughly treated,[1] and since the principal emphasis of most of these writers is quite irrelevant to our problem.

A pamphleteer, Henry Peacham, a painter, musician, mathematician, and professional writer, among other attainments, sought rather early in the revolutionary period to discover 'the causes of our want and . . . generall scarcity', without, it might be added at the outset, propounding any very convincing analysis.[2] Peacham took the view that the principal difficulty in England arose from the fact that a relatively small number of men had accumulated vast estates which they 'brood over and watch . . . day and night', with the result that the necessities of countless men remain unrelieved. There are others who are simply misers, wholly withdrawing their money from circulation and hence making no contribution to the common needs of the realm. The land is impoverished, too, by sumptuous tastes and the conspicuous wasting of its resources, by foreigners who abuse their sanctuary in England by engrossing its wealth, by chronic losses of bullion in the East India trade, and by a general tightening of trade 'in these tickle times'. The result is that the opportunities open to a likely boy, a marriageable daughter, or a young man taking orders have been dangerously and uncharitably restricted.[3] God has ordained that there should be rich and poor, but it is also His injunction that the poor must be relieved and that the path of opportunity be left open and easy for the children of the poor whom 'God raiseth up, as by miracle . . . oftentimes to possesse the most eminent places either in church or commonwealth'.[4] All these benefits, all these social necessities, are retarded or destroyed when charity is withheld, when wealth is hoarded or employed for wholly personal ends.

One of the few legislative or policy changes of the revolutionary era which may possibly be attributed to the earnest recommendations of the many projectors was the establishment in 1647 of the Corporation of the Poor in London.[5] It was London wealth which principally prosecuted and won the Civil War and it was London which inevitably had to carry the chief burdens of social dislocation and the ever-mounting problem of caring for the casualties of the war. The institutions and the endowments accumulated over the past century, as well as the quite decentralized system of administering poor relief, were simply unable to carry

[1] In James, *Social problems and policy*.
[2] Peacham, Henry, *The worth of a peny* (L., 1647), 1.
[3] *Ibid.*, 6.　　　　　　　　　　　[4] *Ibid.*, 9.
[5] For a brief discussion of the legislative proposals and changes of this period, *vide ante*, 104–107.

the burdens in this period of emergency, and the Corporation was founded to cope with these pressing difficulties.[1] Rice Bush [or Buck], a pamphleteer about whom little can be certainly said, in a treatise published in 1649 claimed that the idea was first developed by him and his friends at a meeting called to discuss the urgent problem of poor relief and to consider modifying the London system by judicious borrowings from that prevailing in the Low Countries and such English towns as Norwich, Ipswich, and Dorchester, where there were no beggars.[2] Bush held that the difficulty was not so much the want of salutary laws, but rather a breakdown in the methods of administering and enforcing them. He further, and correctly, argued that the problem which London must face was genuine and widespread unemployment, whereas the weight of administrative effort and concern was steadily directed towards the punishment and control of vagrancy. The administration of the charitable resources of the city ought accordingly to be carried forward in relation to the state of trade, so that an already depressed industry be not further depressed by engulfing it with a flood of unwanted and unneeded apprentices. The worthy poor simply must be supported until employment can be opened for them, the sick must be cared for at municipal expense, and all fines laid against alehouses, drunkards, and the profane should be added to the resources from which relief is drawn.[3] Four additional workhouses should be erected in London, in which the poor might be gainfully employed, while funds should be raised, beyond amounts available from past charity and present taxes, by soliciting food and loans from householders, paying over all unclaimed legacies to the Corporation, and diverting the estates of childless couples to these worthy purposes.[4] If even these heroic measures will not suffice, the bells of London's churches, which he reckoned as worth £9660, should be melted down and the citizens persuaded for 'one year to forbear altering their apparell into other fantastick fashions', the saving to be paid into the stock of the Corporation.[5]

The Corporation as actually constituted bore only a somewhat casual relation to the ideal which seems to have been in Bush's mind.[6] The ordinance establishing it reposed authority in officers who were in effect the existing municipal officers. It was given somewhat wider powers to arrest and set at work all idle and disorderly persons, to levy taxes for the financing of work programmes, and was declared to possess all the powers of justices of the peace in punishing vagrants, binding out

[1] Ordinance, 17 December, 1647; in Firth and Rait, *Acts and ordinances*, I, 1042.
[2] [Bush, Rice], *The poor mans friend* (L., 1649), 3.
[3] *Ibid.*, 10–14. [4] *Ibid.*, 18–19.
[5] *Ibid.*, 20. [6] Leonard, *English poor relief*, 272–273.

apprentices, and affording relief for the poor. Some hundreds of poor were employed by the Corporation in spinning and weaving on stocks maintained at the Wardrobe and in the Minories, while a considerable number of additional orphans were brought under the charge of the city.[1] The municipal authorities in 1649 announced hopefully that they intended to put the poor at work on gear for the fishing trade, as well as other manufactures, in appealing to the clergy of London 'to stir up your hearers with the most religious and pressing arguments to so pious and charitable a work, that so this city might not be found guilty of such a neglect as not to provide for the poore'.[2] The Corporation continued to find itself short of funds and, perhaps almost inevitably, continued as well to expend most of its resources and energy on the curbing and punishment of vagrancy. In 1655 the governors of the Corporation put into the mouths of orphans being maintained by that body a persuasive, if improbable, plea for funds and support, employing all those arts which are known to modern advertising:

> These children orphans singing show,
> Though God's above, he dwels below,
> Who clothes their backs and bellies feed,
> And gave them fathers in their need.
> These father'd fatherless, their fathers bless,
> And warble forth their worth in thankfull verse . . .

> God is the poor mans God, who doth express
> Himself the father of the fatherless,
>   And men like gods themselves appear
>   To whom poor fatherless are dear,
>   Whose works of charity,
>   He suffers not to dye,
>   What thus they spend
>   To God they lend,
> Who will repay with glory in the end . . .

> This is the pure religion, and this
> By Gods appointment leads to lasting bliss;
>   When scarlet robes, and golden chains
>   Shall come to nothing, this remains,
>   When creature comforts faile,
>   Such works as these prevaile . . .

> You that have thus so well begun, go on,
> Finish your work, let no man take your crown,
>   Such works as these their workmen bless;
>   By spending thus, you shall increase,

---

[1] Gray, *English philanthropy*, 72–74.

[2] *Bute broadsides* (Houghton Library, Harvard University), I, 43 (February, 1649).

> This is Gods way of thriving,
> Thus give, and get by giving;
> What else you save
> Others may have;
> These works your selves shall find beyond the grave.[1]

The Corporation in its report and appeal in the same year stated that it was lending complete sustenance and education to about one hundred poor children and was 'ayming at the entertainment of some hundreds more'. Many hundreds of poor families were being supported at useful labour, 'none being refused or denied imployment that will come for it'. None the less, it must be concluded that the Corporation added only slightly to the resources already in being for the care of the derelict and that its work remained somewhat uninspired and inconsequential. Its contribution had been fully made by the time of the restoration of the monarchy.

It seems quite certain that the establishment of the Corporation inspired a proposal in 1649 by Peter Chamberlen, a prominent London physician and a 'projector' par excellence, for a really heroic attempt to deal with the problem of poverty. The poor constitute a heavy drain on the national economy, and they simply must be provided for whether by a debit or a credit against national resources. Hence he suggests that a national stock, or corporation, be formed whose assets would consist of the remaining royal and episcopal estates, all common lands and marshes, abandoned mines, tithe assessments for a period of three years, after which they would be eliminated, and certain other national resources. This huge capital wealth, most of which was quite unexploited, would be employed for the advancement of education, colonization, and above all to provide fruitful labour for the poor of England. These resources would be used for the 'benefit of the whole nation, by improving of lands that were never improved, by imploying of men that were not onely useles; but a burthen, through idleness, or want of imployment, and by converting them into good common-wealths-men . . . for the honour . . . and . . . strength of the nation'.[2] Chamberlen also advocated a public bank which he thought would revive trade, while he had every confidence that great national prosperity would at once result if the poor of the nation could be set on useful work.[3] No better use could be made of the public resources of the nation, since 'all riches

---

[1] *Bute broadsides*, I, 66 (1655).

[2] Chamberlen, Peter, *The poore mans advocate* (L., 1649), 3–5. The son of a barber-surgeon, Chamberlen (1601–1683) was educated at Cambridge and at Padua. He was admitted to Gray's Inn in 1631 and was successively physician to James I, Charles I, and Charles II. He was highly skilled in obstetrics, using forceps in deliveries. At one time, at least, he was a Baptist.

[3] *Ibid.*, 6–10.

whatsoever proceed from the labour and industrie of the poor . . . the more poor, the more hands, the more work, the more wealth'.[1] If such a plan, fired with boldness and imagination, were set in motion, within a few years England would discover that she had not a surplus but an acute shortage of labour.

Chamberlen's plan did possess great boldness, but it was of course sketched only in the broadest outlines and concealed by its warm enthusiasm the legal, the administrative, and the practical difficulties which would have been encountered in setting in motion even a segment of this grandiose proposal. But this kind of thinking was very much in the air during this period of revolution and swift change. Thus in the next year, 1650, an anonymous tract, almost certainly inaccurately attributed to John Keymer,[2] recommended the founding of a national stock, to be called the 'state merchant', to deal with all the problems of foreign trade, to lend support to the fishing industry, and to take measures to ensure the manufacture in England of all the principal fabricated commodities. This sober mercantilist tract urged that such measures were required to give employment to the poor of the nation, and that a revival of the cloth industry and a rebuilding of the fishing trade would alone absorb most of the surplus labour with which England was now plagued.[3]

One of the most sensible and thoughtful of all the many proposals for social and economic reform advanced in this period, which literally seethed with ideas, was that made by Adam Moore, of Somerset, whose work was published in 1653, but the preface of which indicated that it was written a generation earlier. Moore, daring to attack frontally the now venerable myth that all enclosures were harmful to the poor and to the economy, boldly proposed that the whole of the common land and the wastes of England be enclosed by legal means in order to provide a broader base for a society that had become overpopulated, whose resources of land had been consumed. The commons and wastes of England, he held, and quite correctly, were badly and most imperfectly exploited, surely because common rights were vested in them. They could never be improved or tilled until they were divided and placed under private ownership. Rights in common encourage idleness, subsistence living, and offer just enough of sustenance to support a marginal and a doomed class of rural paupers. Those who draw their living in part from common and waste lands will, of course, say: 'Here . . . we can keep a horse or a cow (if we have any), or if our estate will not reach to such a one, yet can we compass a goose or a swine, that in a yeer may yield us many a penny (God wot'.)', which means that a whole class of men, usually with large families, was accepting a life of penury, hard-

---

[1] *Poore mans advocate*, 13.　　　　　　　　　　[2] *Vide ante*, 195–196.
[3] I. D., *A clear and evident way for enriching the nations of England and Ireland* (L., 1650), 2, 10, 12, 15–16.

ship, and idleness.[1] Even the animals bred and raised by such men stood always in danger of starvation, while the breed could not be improved so long as herds ran in common.[2]

This system, Moore maintained, had always been hopelessly wasteful, and the nation could no longer afford such wastage of its resources, for 'the great increase of people in our dayes . . . cannot but compell us . . . to make the best use of our abilities for our relief and preservation'.[3] The best, the only, hope for England is by law to enclose such lands, allot them equitably under private ownership for tillage by men who, when they once find themselves masters of land of their own, will mend their idle ways and become self-supporting and self-respecting members of the commonwealth. Moore estimated, probably very conservatively, that there were upwards of 2300 square miles of waste and commons in England which might be profitably enclosed, which he optimistically reckoned could lend full support to something like 750,000 persons. Quite as important would be a great national effort to drain and then enclose the marshy areas and the fens of the nation, which he held were now completely useless to the economy. The canals would serve as enclosures, willows set on their banks would supply fuel and timber, and the rich lands thus brought under the plough would release exhausted upland areas which ought in any event to be returned to pasture.[4] Such enterprise would immediately absorb the labour of the working poor, who when the work was done would receive their due proportion of the land they had made available. Distributions in each county should be made by commissions of the most trusted inhabitants, who should take particular care to safeguard the rights of the worthy poor and who should vest specified tracts in all regions in the churchwardens for the perpetual care of the impotent poor.[5] Moore remained confident that even the most idle poor, once they experienced the benefits and joys of owning land of their own, would be animated by pride and industry in order further to improve their lot as self-respecting citizens of a more prosperous England. Thus, he concluded, 'we have now . . . from these few heads discovered a new plantation in our own continent . . . as for wealth and people, even another kingdome would seem to be gained unto us . . . the state enriched . . . poor and idle employed . . . provisions encreased . . . people multiplied, and the whole nation in power advanced'.[6]

Moore addressed the problem of the enclosure of commons and wastes with more reasoned sense than any writer had brought to bear before on the question. In fact, his views were widely adopted when many years later enclosures were generally undertaken, though his sensitive regard for the rights of the poor and his essentially reforming

---

[1] Moore, Adam, *Bread for the poor* (L., 1653), 6.   [2] *Ibid.*, 9.
[3] *Ibid.*, 12.   [4] *Ibid.*, 28.   [5] *Ibid.*, 35–36.   [6] *Ibid.*, 38–39.

approach to the whole tangled issue was to be quite neglected. His proposals were at bottom modest and they were wholly practical, save that he skirted round the central problem of costs and dismissed rather blithely the evident fact that a herculean administrative effort would be necessary if his plans were to be carried forward. But his scheme of social and economic rehabilitation remains within the ambit of the possible. This alone sets Moore quite apart from most of the social reformers of this interesting and seminal age when almost every idea known to the modern world managed to get itself before a somewhat bewildered generation for at least a moment of discussion.

But always the problem of the poor, and the nature of the obligation of the society towards them, stood central to the discussion. Thus a petition presented to the Council of Officers in 1659 proposed that all prisons be turned into workhouses, and that the revenues of the prisons combined with certain other funds be employed in a great effort to afford relief to all the poor.[1] Another author, while conceding that the relief of poverty was 'a laudable and necessary work', held that true reform could only come when education was more widely extended. Hence a national canvass of schools should be made in order to set all able students in the universities at public charge, so as to build a learned ministry and endow the nation with proficiencies which only education could supply.[2] William Sprigg, a fellow of Lincoln College, Oxford, on the other hand, argued that there were already so many schools and so many possibilities of attaining an education that the nation spoiled 'many a good plough-man to make a poor scholar . . . to keep our colledges thinly stock'd with half-witted stapish fellows'. The number of educated men, or at least of those 'thinly educated', far exceeded the professional opportunities available, Sprigg maintained, with the consequence that men of ability were made dangerously discontented and sought violent changes in the state and society.[3] He proposed rather that charity be confined to the more urgent task of supporting the poor in their great need and that tithes be wholly suppressed and all glebe lands annexed to workhouses for their endowment. He expressed himself as shocked that of all the episcopal lands expropriated by the state, none had been appropriated for setting the worthy poor on work, which

---

[1] *S.P. Dom.*, 1659, CCV, 24 (November 24).

[2] [Poole, Matthew], *A model for the maintaining of students* (L., 1658), Preface, 2–7, 15–18. A native of York, Poole (1624–1679) was educated at Emmanuel College. Rector of a London parish at the Restoration, he declined to conform and retired to Holland, where he spent the remainder of his life. He was a biblical scholar of some note.

[3] [Sprigg, William], *A modest plea for an equal common-wealth* (L., 1659), Preface, 65–68, *et passim*. A notable pamphleteer and a Parliamentarian, Sprigg was deprived of his fellowship at the Restoration. He was a brother to Joshua Sprigg, a clergyman of considerable reputation.

betokened 'the deafness of this uncharitable age to the cryes of the poor', and which stood as a crime and a black reproach to the Christian conscience of England.[1]

The greatest, and very probably the most influential, of all the many 'projectors' of the revolutionary era was without doubt the ubiquitous Samuel Hartlib, who had interesting and often most practical ideas on a great variety of topics. In 1650 he expressed himself as hopeful that Parliament was at last ready to undertake some really promising and well-conceived plan for the relief of poverty and, more particularly, for the care of poor children, and he proceeded, as was his wont, to instruct that assembly in precisely what ought to be done.[2] Parliament should attack this whole festering social problem with courage and energy. Thus he recommended that the waste and barren lands of the nation be improved at public expense and that the growing of such crops as tobacco be prohibited, while the planting of such labour-producing crops as hemp, flax, and roots ought by every inducement to be encouraged.[3] Indeed, a great 'work of reformation' must be set under way 'for the good of the poor', such as 'was never . . . performed in former ages in our nation'.[4] A clean and a full separation must be made between the incorrigibly idle and the large mass of the poor who are unable to labour or who cannot find employment. Facilities for setting the poor on useful work must be provided in every town and city in the land, all economic oppression of the poor under whatever guise must be stopped by law. The 'honest rich . . . and comfortles poor . . . wait for a reformation, as the thirsty ground for raine . . . and there is . . . great need for the Parliament to find out ways and means to preserve people from poverty' and to protect the weak from the strong. The flotsam of the society, those who simply decline to work, must be subjected to the salutary disciplines of the workhouse and if this does not effect their reformation, they should be summarily deported to the colonies.[5]

Hartlib's ranging and ingenious mind, informed as it was by a brooding sense of charity, was fertile with suggestions for the cure of the ancient evil of poverty. He called for some plan to ensure the universal education of poor children in the useful rudiments of knowledge until they were old enough to be apprenticed. More could be done in making available stocks of raw materials on which poor families might work in their own cottages, while the clergy could render great contribution by attending more effectively to the educational and spiritual needs of poor and neglected children. In fact, Hartlib's central preoccupation was

---

[1] *A modest plea*, 54–57.
[2] Hartlib, Samuel, *London's charity inlarged* (L., 1650). Hartlib was one of the most important of the social thinkers of the period. A full-length study of his thought and his place in his age is needed. There is a DNB notice.
[3] *Ibid.*, 22.   [4] *Ibid.*, 1.   [5] *Ibid.*, 8–10.

with the plight of poor children; his protest was against dooming them to the fate of their own parents by closing against them the door of education and the opportunity which it opens up for all men. This problem, he contended, was by no means insoluble. He estimated that for every grouping of a hundred children, something like £461 5s would be annually required to secure their lodging, their diet, their training in crafts, and the essentials of their education.[1] It was, he thought, a conservative estimate that children under proper supervision and training might, while learning useful trades and skills, produce goods to the value of £260 p.a. for each such unit. This outlay is a pittance indeed if it will preserve a hundred children from ruin, will offer to them the opportunity through their whole lifetime to become useful, decent, and self-sustaining men and women.

There was fervour, there was deep compassion, and there was hope in Hartlib's musings on what might be done in England to bring about the Kingdom of God on earth. All his writings display an ingenious and fertile mind, never, however, wanting in practicality and an adequate sense of the possible. But we should conclude with a truly utopian tract, more typical of much of the social thought of this amazing and in so many ways fruitful era when men caught for a moment a vision of a new social order. Hugh Peter, that remarkably versatile and gifted man, whose great abilities were flawed by weaknesses of character, in 1659 epitomized the utopian dreams of the social reformers of the revolutionary era in a tract entitled *A way propounded to make the poor . . . happy*. He proposed setting up, within the framework of the English society, an insulated community in which young and old, husbandman and scholar, might join in a truly Christian commonwealth. The society would maintain a London house in which from twenty to thirty of its artisan members would dwell, with shops for the sale of their wares, and a country house where 'husbandmen, handicrafts people are to live and work . . . mariners . . . to go forth to sea to trade and carry goods', and where several scholars should reside. All profits gained by the community, after sustenance was provided, were to be shared equally. The children of the rich and of the poor members, for goods were not to be held in common, were to be educated together in handicrafts, the arts, and the natural sciences. Medical care was to be furnished for the aged and the infirm. Indeed, 'there will be no need in our society to take any care, or to make provision for the aged time, or day of sickness, nor for children; for the aged will be better looked after than the young, the sick then the healthful, and the children after the death of their parents as before'.[2] The aim of the society will be to

---

[1] *London's charity inlarged*, 14–18.

[2] Cornelisson, Peter (pseud.), *A way propounded to make the poor . . . happy* (L., 1659). Most authorities agree in attributing this work to Hugh Peter.

banish all the evils that spring from both riches and poverty, and to provide a Christian and wholly tolerant sanctuary for all those that weary of
religious controversy. All this and more might be accomplished if men in
a spirit of Christian fellowship and humility would pool their resources,
their energy, and their good will. Indeed, Peter most persuasively set
forth the hope that such a settlement might be made in County Mayo,
where the assurance of lands had been given, though we must note that
within a year after the publication of the book the monarchy had been
restored and Hugh Peter had been done to death as a regicide.

4. *In praise of famous men*

We have been endeavouring to explore the impulses which prompted
so many men to give so generously of their means to the charitable needs
of England. We have in earlier pages suggested that the reasons for the
great outpouring of charitable endowments during the long interval,
1540–1660, were very complex indeed. In part this great generosity was
in response to apparent and pressing need; quite as truly, it is most
evident, men's growing sensitivity with respect to suffering and want
occasioned a greater perception of need, or, more accurately, a broader
definition of areas of need. We have just concluded a long discussion,
necessarily quite repetitious in its insistence on certain axioms and
attitudes, in which we have examined an enormous literature, principally comprised of sermons, in which the clergy and the moralists laid
before men with ever-mounting emphasis and conviction the Chistian
obligation of charity and a doctrine of the social and moral injunction
laid by God on wealth. This literature beyond any possible doubt
constituted one of the very important impulses towards charitable
giving; it was moving and hortatory; it assisted most significantly in
establishing a climate of opinion which engendered certain attitudes
and actions as an obligation of wealth; and it went very far towards
establishing habits of giving or of bequeathing among certain classes of
men. Most of these sermons were preached by clergymen of stalwart
Puritan persuasion. They were all preached with deep conviction, and
it must be remembered that they were addressed to living and to
susceptible human beings in the congregation before the pulpit. These
preachers were all essentially moralists, they were intensely evangelical,
and they were in the course of a century to hew out of Scripture and
historical experience an ethic which we can describe broadly as Protestant and much more specifically as Puritan.

We have reserved for separate discussion another considerable body
of published sermons from this period which were even more expressly
hortatory and which must have possessed an immense efficacy in
evoking the good works of alms from the congregations at hand and the
larger audiences which purchased and read these sermons. These were

the funeral sermons, the sermons in praise of famous men. It must be remembered that funeral sermons in this age were long, most carefully composed, and awaited with a kind of breathless uncertainty by the mourning family, since they could on occasion be brutally frank with respect to the demerits of the dead. These were funeral orations, or elegies, going far beyond the gentle and compassionate commentary of the offices provided by the Book of Common Prayer for the Burial of the Dead, and they were with few exceptions preached by clergymen who can certainly be identified as Puritans. Those with which we are concerned are funeral sermons for famous men and women as the Puritan mind and conscience had come to assess human values. In all of them it is the work of charity, the alms disposed, the grammar school founded, which is extolled as the abundant proof of grace in the life of the deceased person and the assurance of election among God's saints in the life to come.

It is most significant that in the main these sermons were preached over the bodies of merchants and their widows, faithful members of that class which had in the course of our period assumed such a vast measure of social responsibility within the English society. Moreover, when funeral sermons survive which annotate the virtuous lives of members of the nobility or gentry, it is not too much to say that they praise the dead for having possessed virtues and having disposed their wealth in a fashion becoming to a merchant. Most of the landed magnates so eulogized, it is also important to note, were in fact Puritans. The men so praised, whether of the merchant élite or of the gentry, were truly famous men because of their acts of charity; and such sermons firmly established their memories and their good works among the illustrious of a new age. In literally hundreds of wills, often of humble men and women in remote counties, bequests were left in acknowledged imitation of a famous London donor, to establish a school or an almshouse on a model prescribed by an earlier gift, or actually saying that the bequest had been inspired by an earlier and notable legacy. These sermons, then, possessed tremendous power of persuasion; no auditor or reader could possibly escape without at least a moment of earnest brooding on man's mortality and on a very personal death and funeral sermon that loomed in a not too distant future. The literature of these sermons is large, and deserves full analysis, but we must necessarily confine ourselves to a modest sampling, noting first certain of the relatively small number preached over the bodies of members of the landed classes and then a few of the much larger number preached to celebrate the good works of merchants. We should add that we have included in this body of material a certain number of 'elegies' and 'epitaphs', composed and published after the will of the dead man had been proved and the extent of his generosity made known, since these pieces were identical in their social and moral utility and were read with the same avidity by large audiences.

Though the always short-tempered Queen Elizabeth charged Francis Russell, Earl of Bedford, with subsidizing all the beggars in England with his profuse alms,[1] that Puritan gentleman and nobleman was to be so extolled for his charitable virtues as almost to create a myth of a generosity that flowed from the very fact of his Puritanism. So, too, the Earl of Huntingdon, Henry Hastings, was famous for his charity and his purchase of advowsons for Puritan clergymen, having somewhat impaired his estate by his deeds of mercy.[2] Of him a popular ballad was to say:

> To poore and to needie, to high and to low
> Lord Hastings was friendly, all people doth know;
> His gates were still open the straunger to feed
> And comfort the succorless alwaie in neede . . .
> He built vp no pallace nor purchaste no towne,
> But gaue it to schollers to get him renowne,
> As Oxford and Cambridge can rightly declare
> How many poor schollers maintained are there.
> No groues he inclosed, nor felled no woodes,
> No pastures he paled to doe himselfe good;
> To commons and countrie he liude a good friend,
> And gaue to the needie what God did him send.[3]

Similarly were the virtues of Sir Francis Walsingham praised in an *Epitaph* published shortly after his death in 1590. We are told that he was the 'cheefest stay' of all those who were in need and of the 'sincere preachers of Gods word'. Hence:

> Farewell Sir Francis Walsingham, that usurie sore didst hate,
> That still didst good to rich and poore that came unto thy gate.
> Farewell the comfort of the poore, that to them almes did give,
> Farewell the stay to souldiers good, while he on earth did live.
> Farewell the comfort of the court, and Londons dailie freend,
> Farewell to thee that for the poore thy letters farre would'st send.

[1] Scharf, George, *A descriptive . . . catalogue of the collection . . . at Woburn Abbey* (L., 1877–1878, 2 parts), I, 19–20. Bedford (1527?–1585) was extolled in his funeral sermon, preached by Thomas Sparks, for his many virtues. Before his death he had founded an almshouse at Watford and a free school at Woburn. By his will (PCC 45 Windsor 1586) he disposed £120 for the poor of four parishes, left £40 for road repairs at Woburn, £20 each to Oxford and Cambridge, and £20 p.a. for the use of two poor divinity students at Oxford.

[2] *Hist. MSS. Comm., Hastings Manuscripts*, II, 44–45.

[3] *The crie of the poore for the death of the . . . Earle of Huntington* (s.n., s.l., n.d.); in Lilly, Joseph, ed., *A collection of . . . black-letter ballads* (L., 1870), 228–231. Huntingdon (1535–1595) had decidedly Puritan leanings and was a supporter of the Huguenot emigrees. He endowed a school at Ashby-de-la-Zouche, gave £40 13s 4d p.a. for the schoolmaster and lecturer at Leicester, and lent generous support to Emmanuel College. Camden tells us that he 'much wasted his estate by a lavish support of these hot-headed preachers'.

Farewell the sutor for the poore, that seldome let thee rest,
Farewell the frend to fatherlesse and widdowes sore opprest.
Farewell the care for countries good, when corne was prisde so hie,
Farewell the knight that succourd'st those that then were like to die.
Farewell and thousand times farewell thou good and worthy knight,
That in the cause of poore and rich, full many a wrong didst right.
Farewell thou good and freendly knight to schollers poore and bare,
Of Cambridge and of Oxford to, of whom thou hadst great care . . .[1]

So, too, rather more than a decade later, Thomas Sackville, Earl of
Dorset, was praised in a funeral sermon preached by George Abbot, who
was himself an archbishop with more than a little of Puritan sympathies.
Abbot extolled Dorset, who had been married for fifty-three years and
who for thirty years had kept a great household of at least two hundred
persons, excluding workmen and 'other hired'. He had ever recognized
that the Christian obligation of alms lay as a charge against his estate,
and to perfect a life of charitable bounty had in his will left £1000 to
establish a granary at Lewes, £2000 for the creation of a stock of grain
that the poor of that town might be relieved in times of scarcity, and
£1000 for the building of a chapel at Withyham.[2]

Thus the great magnates of the realm were praised in those relatively
few instances when they were famed for their acts of charity, and more
precisely if their charities flowed from the convictions inherent in
Puritanism. More typical and far more numerous were the funeral
sermons of members of the gentry, again principally Puritan, who had
distinguished themselves by their good works. We are reminded in the
sermon preached over the body of Sir Richard Leveson, who died in
1605, that during our lifetime our Christianity must express itself in
alms, in good works which will still abide when we die. Yet in this day,
'good works live in exile from us'. We must take necessary steps, the
preacher concluded, to 'lay up if not your harvest, at least your gleaning
on the poor and they will bless you'.[3] Similarly, if we may for chronological convenience treat him as among the gentry, William Russell, a
son of the Earl of Bedford and an uncle of the Earl of Dorset, was in
1614 eulogized by the preacher of his funeral sermon for his continuous
liberality to the needy. 'Hee was . . . the hand of Christ to the poore,
who receiued his daily almes and his weekely allowance.' To learn

[1] Nelson, Thomas, *A memorable epitaph . . . for the death of Sir Frauncis
Walsingham* (L., 1590).

[2] Abbot, George, *A sermon at the funerall of the . . . Earle of Dorset* (L., 1608),
16–18.

[3] Page, *Sermon at funerall of Sir R. Leveson*, no pagin. A native of Bedfordshire, Samuel Page was educated at Oxford, where he was graduated B.A. in
1591. He was vicar of a Kentish parish for many years, dying in 1630. Sir Richard
Leveson was the son of Sir Walter Leveson of Shropshire; he served almost
continuously in the Spanish wars. He was made captain-general of an expedition
against Spain in 1601 and in 1604 was designated vice-admiral.

their needs he would enter the houses of poor men, and 'finding out the great want of labouring men: that shaming to begge, liued more miserably then ordinary beggers, hee would often giue them good summes of money'. Poor gentlemen he would assist by anonymous gifts. In his peroration the preacher lamented that more landed men of great substance did not emulate Russell's quiet example of charity. It is shameful that such men do not 'share their estate with the poore . . . whom now they passe by with scorne and contempt. How farre short of [the example of Lord Russell] come our great men, who doe spend more upon pictures in their houses, then they doe upon the poore, the images of God . . . when Christs starving members cannot get a crumme of bread at their gates'.[1]

The death of Sir Edward Lewkenor, High Sheriff of Suffolk, in 1618 afforded a perfect example of Christian charity, since his continuing generosity had laid a heavy charge on his estate and he died in debt, having in the last year of his life distributed 'more than £1000 more then ordinary'. In fact, so perfect was the opportunity that we have two treatises which profess to be his funeral sermon, which would seem to be gilding even a Puritan funeral lily. In any event both preachers agreed on Lewkenor's abundant generosity and on his deep conviction that he was no more than God's feoffee for his wealth. Sir Edward's house 'was full of hospitality and there was always a great crowd at his gate', for whom special provision was made three days in the week.[2] The second preacher, Bezaleel Carter, appealed to his auditors, 'Your selues can beare me record, how many of your poor people he cloathed with the fleeces of his sheepe, and what his custome was, for euery yeare of his life, to cloath one of your poore and naked ones'.[3] Nor was this all, for Lewkenor had erected a special building near his house, provided with a large table on which his abundant alms were disposed to the hungry.[4] But his sense of charitable reponsibility ranged far beyond his own gates, for 'every year he gave clothing to several towns for apparelling the poor', not to speak of 'his bountiful mind to other pious and religious uses, maintenance of learning, relieving of prisoners and the care of his poor neighbours oppressed with sickness'.[5] These are

---

[1] Walker, William, A sermon . . . at the funerals of . . . William Lord Russell (L., 1614). Russell (1558?–1613) was the fourth son of the second Earl of Bedford. He served as a soldier in the Dutch wars and as an administrator in Flushing and in Ireland. His estate was small, but legacies of £30 were left to the poor and £20 for the repair of his parish church (PCC 86 Capell 1613).

[2] Oldmayne, Timothy, Gods rebuke in taking from us . . . Sir E. Lewkenor (L., 1619), 27.

[3] Carter, Bezaleel, The wise king (L., 1618), 61.   [4] Ibid., 62–63.

[5] Oldmayne, Gods rebuke, 29. Lewkenor left considerable landed property in Suffolk, though his estates were burdened with debt. There were no charitable legacies in his will (PCC 42 Meade 1618). His principal seat was at Denham.

persuasive passages, describing an undoubtedly religious and charitable man, and they were calculated to move to emulation all men whether of the seventeenth century or our own.

Sir Anthony Rous, who had kept a generous house for more than forty years, was praised for his great charity by his minister, Charles Fitz-Geffrey, in a funeral sermon published in 1622. Rous, it was emphatically explained, was 'none of those lay-nonresidents, who build faire houses, and immediately flie from them into some cabbine in a towne or city, as if they feared their houses would fall downe upon their heads . . . his house for many years was the centre of charity and hospitality, wherein met the lines of poore and strangers, drawn from a large circumference round about him'.[1] So, too, we are told, Sir Francis Pile was a righteous man, one of the elect famous for his openhanded charity. He was in fact the soul of charity, 'for the poore round about him, his heart, his hand, and his gate was ever open to them, the widow and the fatherlesse, the lame, the impotent, the poore children of the neighbour parishes were relieved constantly at his gates . . . he hath dispersed and given to the poore, his righteousness endureth' for ever.[2]

Moving two decades forward, deep into the period of the Puritan Revolution, we may conclude with two more funeral sermons, the one for a gentleman of large estates and the other extolling the charitable virtues of two great Puritan peers. We are told by the two preachers who seem to have preached at the funeral of Francis Pierrepont, of Nottinghamshire, that the dead man had been constant in his generosity to the poor, which included an annuity of £12 he had vested in an almshouse in Nottingham. He had served his country and his community well, but above all he had lived with justice and integrity, had been 'an instrument of much good', and had exemplified those two rare charitable virtues of righteousness and mercy.[3] In this same year (1658) the two great peers, the Earl of Warwick and the Earl of Essex, were extolled by the notable divine, Edmund Calamy, for their many charitable virtues. Their deaths remind us that all men, great and humble, must die. Even the greatest of this world go forth from it with nothing,

[1] Fitz-Geffrey, Charles, *Elisha his lamentation* (L., 1622), 46. Sir Anthony Rous's fourth son was Francis Rous (1579–1659). Sir Anthony was himself a strong Puritan and was Sheriff of Cornwall in 44 Elizabeth. He had presented the living of Halton to Fitz-Geffrey, who was a poet of some little fame.

[2] Parsons, *Christians remembrance*, 35–36. Pile, who died in 1635, was a very rich landed proprietor in Wiltshire. His charitable bequests were modest, £20 being left the poor in four parishes where he held land and £1 to the use of Salisbury Cathedral (PCC 1 Pile 1635).

[3] Reynolds, William, and John Whitlock, *The vanitie and excellency of man* (L., 1658), Sermon I, 5, Sermon II (*The upright man*), 2–6. Pierrepont was possessed of a large estate in Lincolnshire and Yorkshire. He left £6000 each to his two daughters. He was a younger brother of the Marquis of Dorchester. (PCC 368 Wootton 1658).

naked before God, and they can leave nothing of enduring worth save the good works that they have accomplished during their lives. 'Greatnesse,' Calamy exclaimed, 'without goodnesse will be but as a great fagot to burne them the more in hell', with the consequence that the rich and powerful must the more 'labour to be righteous as well as rich, and great men to be good'.[1] Of the good works, of the faith and holy zeal of the Earl of Warwick there could be no doubt whatever. A pious and a good man, he had most carefully filled his inherited livings in the church, had supported many painful ministers of God's Word, and had been constantly 'merciful and charitable to the poor members of Jesus Christ'. His whole aim and purpose in a useful life had been to appear 'for God and for his cause and servants', even in the days when such courage and righteousness had been dangerous in the realm of England.[2]

We have examined a fair, and a typical, number of funeral eulogies addressed to the living over the bodies of landed gentlemen and magnates who in their lifetime had exhibited that quality of Christian mercy and charity which the age had come to expect and all but to require. These were principally Puritan gentry, and the preachers of these funeral sermons were with few exceptions Puritan as well. But there was now another gentry, that of commerce, which from 1540 onwards bore a far larger burden of social responsibility than did the gentry of land, a new aristocracy of trade whose ideals, whose convictions, and whose deeds of charity were quite literally transforming the social fabric of England. Inevitably, therefore, a far larger number of these funeral eulogies survive for men and women of this class, sermons designed not only to commemorate the great contributions made by the dead but to stir the auditors to equally laudable works. Almost all these sermons were preached by city clergy to extol the services and the alms of London merchants distinguished at once for their wealth and piety. We should now examine at least a few of the many of these published tracts.

In 1570 Alice Avenon, the wife of the Lord Mayor of London, Alexander Avenon, was extolled after her death for her many Christian virtues:

Unto the poor opprest with sickenesse, griefe and payne
To minister and give reliefe her hart was ever fayne,
The poore have lost a nurse to helpe their needie state.
The poore by almes and lyberall giftes to tender longe she sought.[3]

Just a decade later William Lambe, a very rich merchant and clothworker of London and one of the most generous of the benefactors of

---

[1] Calamy, Edmund, *A patterne for all* (L., 1658), 14, 15.   [2] *Ibid.*, 36–37.
[3] Phillips, John, *An epitaph on the death of the ladie maioresse* (L., 1570). This thrice-married lady was the daughter of a London mercer. Her first two husbands were mercers, but Alexander Avenon was an ironmonger who served at different times as president of three of London's hospitals and was lord mayor in 1569–1570. Alice Avenon left a bread charity for the poor of London.

his generation, died full of years and good works. In Thomas Fuller's words, he was a 'person wholly composed of goodness and bounty, and was as general and discreet a benefactor as any that age provided'. Abraham Fleming published two works memorializing Lambe in the year of his death. In the one, *An epitaph . . . upon . . . William Lambe*, the great merchant was praised for his abundant charity, 'for this he knew, by giving them, he lent unto the Lord'. In the second and larger work, *A memoriall of the . . . almesdeedes of . . . William Lambe*, Lambe was extolled as a rich and powerful merchant who had never lost his humility in the face of God. Will other rich men 'so die, that they may live in the Lorde ? Then let them be charitable and pitifull, liberall and bountifull'. The rich man need not despair of his election, if his heart is moved by pity and if he holds his wealth to dispose on works called good by God. Happily, 'the Lord hath reserved unto himselfe a remnant of rich men, in these latter daies . . . whose light shining to the worlde, and their good workes plentifully emploied to the benefitte of the comfortlesse, provoketh everie godly disposed person to glorifie our Father'. Such a man was William Lambe, whose record of good and noble charitable works Fleming then recited in detail.[1]

The undoubted virtues of Helen Branch, the wife of Sir John, late the Lord Mayor of London, and herself the daughter of a London draper, were commemorated in eloquent detail. She had been generous and persistent in her charities, particularly those centring on the needs of her own parish, St Mary Abchurch. The death of so generous and wise a benefactor was an occasion of regret and mourning for London and all the realm:

> You springs of arts, eyes of this noble realme,
> Cambridge and Oxford, lend your learned teares,
> To waile your own losse and to witnesse theirs:
> Tell, you that have the voice of eloquence,
> This bounteous ladie's large beneficence,
> First to your selves, for love unto your lore,
> Then severalie to everie kind of poore
> Within this citie: To the Drapers' Hall,
> To everie prison, everie hospitall,
> To lunatickes, and poore maides' marriages,
> And many other worthie legacies . . .[2]

---

[1] Fleming, Abraham, *An epitaph . . . upon . . . William Lambe* (L., 1580), *A memoriall of the . . . monuments and . . . almesdeedes of . . . William Lambe* (L., 1580). Lambe's will may be found in PCC 19 Arundell 1580. We shall deal at length with the career and the notable charities of this great merchant in the second volume of this study.

[2] Sylvester, Joshua, *Monodia, an elegie in commemoration of . . . Dame Hellen Branch* (L., 1594); in Grosart, A. B., ed., *The complete works* (Edinburgh, 1880, 2 vols.), II, 329–330. Dame Helen, who died in 1594, left not much more than £80 in charitable bequests, principally for the needs of the poor and for prisoners (PCC 31 Dixie 1595).

We may well reflect that all Elizabethan verse was not touched with poetic genius, but these lines none the less pay tribute to a woman of compassionate spirit and they do serve to commemorate those virtues which the merchant society had come to prize.

The great generosity and the innumerable social institutions already founded by the merchant aristocracy of London had come by the beginning of the seventeenth century to be a matter of justifiable pride, not only to its members but to the whole of the realm. These merchant princes were now famous men, of whom a certain pattern of charitable conduct was expected, on whom a very heavy weight of tradition already lay. Thus in 1601 an interesting tract recited with much pride and no little reverence the enduring works of men like Sir William Harper, Sir Thomas Rowe, and Sir Thomas Ramsay, whose munificence a generation earlier had raised up institutions which had great and continued value in the relief of poverty and in the enlargement of the circumference of opportunity for many men.[1] Such donors were now almost legendary, had become folk heroes, in a society which had framed new and most salutary social aspirations for itself, aspirations which it was rapidly translating into historical reality. These men took great pride in the achievements of their class, and from their pride flowed the necessity of an ever-enlarging charity as they came in their turn to emulate and to excel the pious deeds of their predecessors. Thomas Heywood sensed this psychological factor in merchant giving when he made a lord mayor, and a great merchant, describe with frank detail his humble origin and then reflect with pride that he had founded an almshouse and had contributed substantially towards the strengthening of the resources of a hospital.[2] In still another of Heywood's plays, the merchants of a preceding generation were introduced as principal characters. Sir Thomas Gresham was made, as it were, to will the Royal Exchange into being:

> . . . it angers mee
> That such a famous citie as this is,
> Wherein so many gallant marchants are,
> Haue not a place to meete in, but in this . . .
> Ile haue a roofe built, and such a roofe,
> That marchants and their wiues, friend and their friends
> Shall walke vnderneath it as now in Powles.[3]

---

[1] Jaggard, William, *A view of all the lord mayors of London* (L., 1601), no pagin. Nicholas Bourman [N.B.], in his *Epitaph upon the decease of . . . Lady Mary Ramsey* (L., 1602), also recited the great charities which Sir Thomas Ramsay's widow had carried forward in her own right and, it might be added, with her own money.

[2] Heywood, Thomas, *The dramatic works* (L., 1874, 6 vols.), I, 57.

[3] Heywood (W. W. Greg and M. Doran, eds.), *If you know not me* (Oxford, 1935), II, lines 544–553. The principal characters introduced in the two plays

In another even more perceptive passage Heywood introduced such great merchant donors as Gresham, Sir Thomas Ramsay, and Lady Ramsay, who were shown the portraits of famous merchant benefactors of a still earlier era.[1] The spirit of emulation, the determination to advance the good works of earlier merchant benefactors, and the great pride of status which animated these men was well and astutely portrayed by the dramatist. Lady Ramsay at once expressed her resolve to follow the example of those great charitable donors of the past who were merchant wives:

> Why should not I liue so, that being dead
> My name might haue a register with theirs . . .

while Gresham was made to say:

> Why should not all of vs being wealthy men,
> And by Gods blessing onely rais'd, but
> Cast in our mindes how we might them exceed
> In godly workes, helping of them that need . . .[2]

We have been noting a number of 'class epitaphs' which caught up and memorialized the great virtues and the incredible generosity of the merchant class in London. But it remains true that the individual panegyrics were probably more effective in their influences on other donors and in building by accretion not only the traditions of this remarkable social group but their fame as leaders in the society. Thus in 1612 Anthony Nixon dealt at length with the divers charities of Robert Dove, a merchant tailor who was actually of the second rank in terms of his wealth and generosity. Dove's generosity, the author urged, was so quick and so catholic that it flowed out in all the channels of need. His concern for the poor and the infirm was without stint, and he held in view the needs of all the great hospitals of London, for 'so did he but at Easter last, not three weekes before his happie departure out of this miserable world, send to each of . . . [them] thirtie and odde pounds a peece, to be imployed to the ease and comfort of such as were there detained'.[3] He was bountiful towards the miserable prisoners of the city, generous towards young tradesmen 'beginning to trade in their professions, to helpe them forward in the world'; towards needy students in the university, and towards aiding the education of the children in Christ's Hospital. Wherever he went, and at all times, he was deeply moved by the spectacle of men willing to work who could find no employment. 'If he had seene poore men addicted to labour, he

were Sir William Harper, Sir Thomas Rowe, Sir Thomas Ramsay and his wife, and Sir Thomas Gresham. All will be discussed in some detail in the second volume of this work.

[1] *Ibid.*, II, 760–843. [2] *Ibid.*, II, 844–849.
[3] Nixon, Anthony, *Londons dove* (L., 1612), sig. B⁴.

would set them on worke and cause them to be imployed to their better furtherance and encouragement. If he heard that any of his poore neighbours were decrepit or destitute of meanes to follow their professions, he would supply their needes' in order to save good and worthy men from slipping into the morass of hopeless poverty. He epitomized the virtues of a Christian and was an exemplar to the merchant community of which he was a part.[1]

The theme of social responsibility and the proud tradition of the mercantile aristocracy in assuming its full burden was stressed in the visitation sermon which the illustrious Puritan divine, Thomas Gataker, preached at Tonbridge, Kent, in 1620. The school there had been founded in the mid-sixteenth century by the great London merchant, Sir Andrew Judd, receiving fresh and generous support in 1620 from Judd's grandson, another great merchant, Sir Thomas Smith, who was in the congregation on the occasion of Gataker's sermon.[2] The preacher commended Smith for not having deferred his charities wholly to his deathbed, having made bounteous and wise provision for a noble purpose 'while you may yet surviving your owne donation, your selfe see things settled in a due course, and receive comfort by view of the fruit and benefit that may thereby redound both to church and commonweale'. The benefactions made during the course of our lifetime have a peculiar efficacy not only for the donor but move out to the recipient with warmth and compassion. It may indeed be said that the 'good done at our end is like a lanterne borne after us, that directeth them that come after us, but affordeth us little light; whereas the good done in our life time is like a light borne before us, that both benefiteth them and us also alike'. This great example set forward by Smith should stir many men the better to provide for the crying needs of education, in order that the church and commonwealth may be supplied with the ability and learning which they require. 'What a great mercy of God then is to this land,' Gataker concluded, 'that . . . stirreth up the hearts and minds of worthy men to establish such courses, whereby instruction and learning may be conveighed to us and our children.'[3]

The virtues of a dead merchant, very possibly Thomas Adams, were more modestly and subtly immortalized by John Donne in a commemorative service for a deceased parishioner. But Donne's sermon too takes its place in a considerable body of literature which was establishing not only the Christian obligation of charity but the particularly notable role of London merchants in building the charitable institutions

[1] *Londons dove*, sig. C² ff.
[2] The benefactions of these London merchants will be discussed in the second volume of this work.
[3] Gataker, Thomas, *Davids instructer* (L., 1620), Dedic., 11; in *Certaine sermons* (L., 1637).

of the realm. Though the man whose life the congregation had gathered to commemorate had been dead for some years, it might be assumed that his soul was in the hands of God, for the certainty of good works was in him. He had provided for his family, which is the first requirement laid on us, and had 'also distributed something to the poor of this parish, yearly, this day, and something to a meeting for the conserving of neighbourly love', as well as endowing the commemorative sermon. Surely, the meaning of this sermon was not to praise the donor, the dead man, but to afford an occasion at which others might be encouraged to follow the example of his charity. We may be sure that they 'who have left permanent examples of good works, [may] well be believed, to receive additions of glory and joy, when others are led by that to do the like'.[1] Our charity, Donne seems to be saying, possesses a virtue quite beyond the immediate benefits which it effects, for it provides the certain example which will encourage others to emulate good works and thereby bring the Kingdom of God nearer to hand.

The immense benefaction of Thomas Sutton, the founder of Charterhouse, must have created some difficulties in composition and presentation for Percival Burrell, the preacher at Charterhouse who in 1629 discharged his obligation of eulogizing that great donor. Sutton's charitable legacy was the largest ever made in England, but it was well known that he was not a particularly religious man, while it was held generally, if somewhat unjustly, that he was one of the most fiercely competitive and grasping men in a ruthlessly competitive age. None the less, the sobering and compelling fact remains that this great donor had created a matchless charitable legacy and that almost the whole of his huge fortune, however gained, had been left for a worthy and godly purpose. Burrell handled his problem with great skill and grace in the anniversary sermon, in which he described Sutton as 'a captaine worthy to lead the whole Christian world, for he loued the people of God, and built a synagogue for the God of all people'. The preacher stated that he had no intention of canonizing the founder, it was rather his purpose 'to inuite an imitation of his blessed magnificence'. The building of good works must flow from faith, and faith is attested by the good and pious works of those who acknowledge that 'Christ . . . is the chiefe cornerstone, the foundation of foundations'. Sutton was in point of fact a quietly generous man through his whole life, though his crowning glory was the building and endowing of Charterhouse, which 'no cunning advocate, no greedy lord could undermine'.[2] Almost two hundred needy persons were daily fed on Sutton's bounty, twenty-four scholars were maintained in the university by his generosity, and all England

---

[1] Donne, *Works*, V, 302-303.

[2] Burrell here refers to the efforts of Sir Francis Bacon to overthrow the will; *vide* Bacon, *Works* (L., 1838), I, 494 ff.

was the better for his life and the pious determination with which it closed.[1]

A few years later, in 1631, the charities of an humbler donor, William Fawcett, a member of a Norwich merchant family which had made substantial charitable contributions in Norfolk and Yorkshire, was praised at West Ham, Essex. Fawcett's own stewardship of his considerable wealth permitted the clergyman to express regret for 'the living corps, of those dead soules, that minde earthly things; who making gold to be their god in heaven, and honour, and pleasure their deitie on earth, expell the Lord of heaven and earth out of their hearts and habitations'. These are lost men, mired in the awful sin of avarice. God commands frugality, He requires diligence, and He does not condemn wealth as such, but lays special and rigorous burdens on those whom He has blessed with the fruits of substance. It is faith in Christ alone which imparts that humility, that generosity, and that compassion wherewith the rich may hope to enter the kingdom of heaven. 'Riches are the blessing of the Lord, and not to be contemned; it is the minde, and man, abusing riches is condemned . . . Heaven was never offended with any man, because hee had riches, but because he was had of riches; not as he was wealthie, but because he was wicked with his wealth'. We are but stewards of all our wealth, which we must as we are Christians dispose for the sustenance of our fellow men and for the glory of God. This understanding of the social responsibility for wealth was sensed by the dead man, who 'though mammon came thorow his fingers, yet hee washt his heart from the love of it. . . . For the space of this ten yeeres last past, his custome was at the yeeres end to take a survey of his temporall estate, which hee having briefly summ'd up in a sheete of paper; he made a godly prayer, and thanksgiving, which he annexed unto his account'.[2]

We should now move deep into the revolutionary period in our sampling of this rich and compelling body of elegiac materials and conclude with a few briefly noted funeral sermons for women donors, differing not at all in structure or argument from those of the earlier and more settled decades. Thus we may mention the sermon preached at the funeral of Lady Alice Lucie in 1648, who had for years instructed the porter at her gate to turn away no poor men. 'Everie week, in these times of scarcitie, shee sent manie loavs of bread to manie neighbour-towns; caussed her corn to bee sold in the markets by the smallest

---

[1] Burrell, Percival, *Suttons synagogue* (L., 1629), 1, 3, 7, 25. A detailed discussion of Sutton's foundation and his other charities (1611) will be provided in the second volume of this study.

[2] Layfielde, Edmund, *The soules solace* (L., 1633), 36, 48, 50–58, 63, 65, 71, 118 ff. The charities of this merchant and his equally generous brother will be discussed in later volumes of this study.

measures, that it might not exceed the poor's abilitie', while each Christmas she distributed alms and food in a large area. She had great compassion for the old and the infirm, employing many of them at tasks which they could still perform. All her actions displayed that her faith was compounded of love, recognizing that the rich are blessed only that they may 'bee rich in good works, readie to distribute, willing to communicate, so laying up in store for themselves a good foundation'.[1] Similarly, a merchant's wife of London, Honor Vyner, was praised in her funeral sermon for her great works of mercy, for her resolution to do good to the poor and not to gain pious renown for herself. Her charity 'ran with a still and silent stream' in the manner of deep rivers rather than babbling brooks.[2] So too was Lady Elizabeth Capell eulogized for her good works through a whole lifetime, which are 'the foundation to support us . . . in the time to come of our death . . . and the time to come of the last tribunall'. The preacher at her funeral confessed that he had himself been her almoner and that large sums had been given him for distribution to poor and distressed ministers and others. 'She did not drop, but pour out her alms . . . her gifts . . . came freely and readily flowing.' Lady Capell knew that all she had was from the bounteous hand of God and that her greatest joy and happiness had been derived from her ability to do good in His name. The merit of faith and of works was in her.[3]

5. To put the enemy to shame

We have dealt with a complex variety of impulses to charitable giving which moved men in the course of our period, some noble and intensely spiritual, others coldly secular and pragmatic. We have just concluded the examination of an interesting and large body of funeral and elegiac material in which clearly the Protestant ethic expressed itself, perhaps crudely and often in bad taste, but always effectively and powerfully. Fame among his fellows, enduring good works, and the promise of spiritual reward in the world to come awaited the rich merchant who disposed his fortune in the interests of mankind. Here was supplied the most persuasively compelling impulse towards charitable giving on a wide and generous scale; here was a bargain in terms of perpetuity in

---

[1] Dugard, Thomas, *Death and the grave* (L., 1649), 49–51. Dame Alice was the daughter of Thomas Spencer of Claverton. She resided in Warwickshire at the time of her death. No charities were listed in her will (PCC 125 Essex 1648).

[2] Spurstow, William, *Death and the grave* (L., 1656), 47.

[3] Barker, Edmund, *A sermon . . . at the funerall of . . . Lady Elizabeth Capell* (L., 1661), 24–25, 33. This lady was a grand-daughter of Baptist Hicks and the daughter and heiress of Sir Charles Morrison of Cassiobury, Hertfordshire. Her husband, Lord Capell of Haddam, was a Royalist leader who was executed by order of Parliament in 1649 after the siege of Colchester.

this world and the next. This is by no means to suggest that all or even most of the great charitable endowments of the merchants of London or of the gentry in the provinces were principally inspired by such crass and essentially self-preserving impulses, but rather that among a most complex congerie of motives, the structure of which we have sought to examine with some care, the possibility of becoming enrolled among generous and famous men, among the saints of God, could never have been wholly absent after about 1580. These munificent men, as we come to estimate them and seek to apprehend the impulses which moved them to actions of great compassion, were generally pious, genuinely concerned with the needs and the fate of their fellow men, and essentially noble in their deeds and in the impulses which animated them. But they remained human beings.

The donors of our period were also human in another sense. It must be said without doubt, as we conclude our examination of the well-springs of charitable action, that many of the benefactors of the age were moved to noble and generous actions in part at least in order to put the enemy to shame. These men were with very few exceptions not only Protestants; they were likewise Calvinists of extreme orthodoxy and rigour to whom Rome and all its works were anathema. Among all the reformed faiths, surely, only Calvinism showed no nostalgia for Rome, no trace of a cultural and spiritual inferiority complex vis-à-vis the ancient church. The Calvinist, and more especially the Puritan, in England opposed one system of infallibility with another equally infallible, and upon Rome and all its works he heaped not only his censure but his contempt. It was in part from this certainty of grace, this deep awareness of infallible conviction, that the enormous vitality of Calvinism during the first century of its pure estate sprang; it is equally from this glorious but vexing certainty of belief and purpose that the good works of the Calvinist flowed.

None the less, the English Protestant was throughout our period only thinly separated in time and environment from the ancient church and the monuments of its kind of charity. Not many years earlier its abbeys had been dispersed across the whole of the island, its hospitals and lazar houses were still remembered, and the universities which its prelates had founded remained, though transformed, as a reminder of a Catholic past. Nor did the Catholic controversialists across the Channel fail to taunt an aggressive but a still new faith with the good works of the ancient church and with the niggardly charity which should in logic have been the consequence of the Calvinist's repudiation of the Catholic doctrine of works. Then too, men's memory being short and their historical sense fallible, after perhaps two generations Protestants themselves had to a degree forgotten the ruin in which mediaeval social and charitable institutions stood at the close of the fifteenth century, the ruin which was monasticism when it disintegrated at the first touch of sovereignty. They forgot too that the good works of Catholicism were the accumulation of a half millennium and more, that it was against this background of an almost ageless past that the social accomplishments of Protestantism must be gauged. Nor could they realize, until the first glimmerings of historical and statistical awareness began to emerge in about 1610 that in the span of two generations Protestantism had in fact created in England a new social order and that in terms of effective charitable giving had outstripped by far the whole of the charitable accumulation of the mediaeval past.

Rome, then, the enemy of the faith, was never wholly absent from the merchant's mind as he ordered his charitable dispositions against the day of his death. Nor was it ever absent from the minds of the preacher and the moralist as they sought to bestir English Protestantism to a sense of its obligation and its destiny. In part this is a literature of bitter contempt for Rome, in part it consists of a purposeful exaggeration of the charitable achievements of the Catholic past in order to advance the good works of the age of the Gospel. Thus Bedel, preaching in 1571, exhorted his congregation to generous provision for the poor, 'for that is the gift that hath the promise of reward annexed unto it . . . what shall we have for helping the poore; surely blessing in this world, honor and deliverance . . . in the life to come'. This all Christian men of reformed faith must understand. Yet their charity seems weak and cold. 'Looke what . . . our fathers as fooles did lay forth . . . upon shameless friers . . . and fat bellyed monkes whose bellyes were their gods. . . . Where is the plentye of gold that garnished the erroneous church, the silver & jewels . . . geven forth to steckes and stones, the cloth that cloathed the pylgrime-god that felt no colde, the stocke that bought the candels to set before them, that had eyes and saw nought'. It is true that men of the past gave from the subjection of fear and to avoid the harshness of penalties which might be laid on their backs, but none the less they gave. We are discredited indeed if men moved by fear give more generously than those moved by the compelling reason of an implicit faith. 'Is this the life of Christians? Is this the fruite of our Gospell?' Bedel enquired, in concluding his moving sermon.[1]

The irascible Philip Stubbes, writing in 1593, upbraided his fellow Protestants for neglect of their charitable duty and sought, he says deliberately, to shame them into good works by reciting the fruits of the charity of the Catholic past. For this purpose he had made a tour of the kingdom, to find 'the ancient monuments which our good forefathers left us (hospitalls, spittles, almeshouses, churches, chappels, schools of learning, bridges . . . and the lyke) . . . some quite dissolved . . . and othersome so ruinatic and decayed, as if the first founders thereof were

[1] Bedel, Henry, *A sermon exhorting to pitie the poore* (L., 1572), no pagin.

now living . . . they would not take them for their owne'.[1] Protestants must, then, face up to the fact that the lives of their Catholic forbears were characterized by good works. He wondered, indeed, whether Protestantism has not been weakened by the doctrine that men are saved by grace alone, not understanding the fact that good works inevitably flow from a state of faith.[2] Good works possess their own inherent virtue, their great value to the society whether they are provided by a Catholic or by a Protestant, and too many of the visible good works of Protestant England are the inheritance of a Catholic past.[3] The Catholic doctrine of works is a hideous error, 'repugnant and contrary to the Word of God', while Protestant charity is grounded upon the very word of life, yet members of the reformed faith are not moved to exercise this clear and Christian duty.[4] The pressing and necessary task of Protestant charity is the clearing away of the evil of poverty, on which no more than a scant beginning has been made to the shame of England.[5] The very monuments of the generosity of a superstitious past in England, the evidences of a generosity springing from wrong or irreligious sources, should serve to remind every man of the true and reformed faith that there is a charitable duty to be done, and that quickly, if he is to be worthy of his title of Christian and Englishman.

This theme, developed in different ways and with persuasive effect, was set forth by numerous writers during the whole course of the last century of our period. Thus, to move into the seventeenth century, Laurence Chaderton reminded his congregation that 'the papistes, they alwayes cast in our teeth the great and famous hospitalitie of their nobilitie, and clergie, the buylding of abbies, monasteries, and nunneries, cathedrall churches, colledges, with many other outward works: which in deede are such as do stoppe our mouthes, and put us protestäts to silence'.[6] In these great and worthy works the Catholic past has exceeded the Protestant present, William Guild, writing in Scotland, would agree.[7] This fact should confound us, should make us examine with humility and trembling the faith and the grace which we as Protestants so earnestly profess. 'Where,' Chaderton enquired, 'is that Protestant that feedeth the hungrie, clotheth the naked, visiteth the prysoner and him that is sycke, that lodgeth the harbourless, without ceasing or beyng wearie of well doyng? I speake not this to iustifie the papistes, or to condemne all Protestantes, but to shewe howe rare the woorkes of mercie are amongest those that seeme to put all their ioye and felicitie in . . . Christ.'[8] Even Edward Waterhouse, writing when

[1] Stubbes, Philip, *A motiue to good workes* (L., 1593), Dedic.
[2] *Ibid.*, 37–40. [3] *Ibid.*, 77. [4] *Ibid.*, 96, 128.
[5] *Ibid.*, 89, 92. [6] Chaderton, *A godly sermon*, 52.
[7] Guild, William, *The humble addresse both of church and poore* (L., 1641), no pagin. [8] Chaderton, *A godly sermon*, 53.

Puritan power and certainty were at their zenith, purposely mixed the good works of the Roman with those of the apostolic past in contrasting the achievements of earlier ages with the failure of Protestantism to assume the whole of its evident charitable obligation. He confessed that 'for my part I judg faith by works, and if living charity appear, I will not judg that a dead faith which moved it. They must have somewhat to say in extenuation of other mens charities, who never mean to be renowned by any of their own'.[1] In point of fact the whole of the Christian past has been marked by works of charity which the reformed faith must not only emulate but immensely excel if it is by its fruits to justify and to glorify the truth and piety with which it is vested.

Persistent, skilful, and effective as this preaching was, the auditors, and the readers, were not left in any doubt that Catholic charity, impressive as it may have been, proceeded from sources inspired by fear, superstition, and compulsion. There may well have been good fruits, even though they grew on 'a poisoned vine'. The whole of this literature was, then, essentially hortatory; its purpose was to move men of the true faith, men of the era of the Gospel, to assume the whole of their Christian duty, to be mindful that works of charity could spring even from an erroneous faith. 'We must do good unto all, yet especially to the houshould of faith . . . they must haue . . . euen a double portion. If the almes of some fewe of the papists which are forwarder in giuing then their fellows, were examined by this rule, it would not dazle the eyes of some men as it doth.'[2] It remains compellingly true, and this we must never forget in our acts of charity, that 'a good worke maketh not a good man but a good man maketh a good woorke'.[3] It is upon this rock of doctrine and upon this understanding of the meaning of Christ's teaching that the whole great edifice of Protestant charity must be securely and eternally built.

But even the hortatory advantages of dwelling on the good works of the Roman Catholic past, the propaganda value of lashing out angrily at the 'coldness of charity in these times', could not restrain the pride which men began to have in the immense achievements made by private charity in the century that followed the Reformation. This pride was, as we shall point out in detail, wholly warranted by the historical facts. This sense of achievement grew in vigour and in confidence as the great accumulations of charity, secular though they were in form and aspiration, brought into being the principal social institutions wherewith the modern world was to be fashioned. In point of fact, even the most sanguine of the writers who dealt with this theme grossly underestimated the immensity of the achievement that had been wrought by

[1] Waterhouse, Edward, *A modest discourse* (L., 1655), 174.
[2] Bird, *Lectures* (1598), 19.
[3] *The testament of master W. Tracie* (Antwerp ? 1535), no pagin.

generous, responsible, and high-minded men in the age. In one sense this declaration of attainment, against the background of the past, was difficult for an age which loved to dwell with an almost self-conscious and stylized morbidity on the golden age that lay behind and on the evil and corrupt present. But facts spoke in compelling terms even to Elizabethan and Jacobean inclinations.

The first writer to emblazon the fact that 'our dayes are more happie and blessed than the dayes of our fore fathers', was Francis Trigge, writing, it may be noted, just a year after the defeat of the Armada. In his view, England lived in a blessed age of the Gospel in which men should have no regrets for a largely imagined past. Thus many mistakenly lament the destruction of the abbeys, commending their hospitality, their liberality, and their utility to the commonwealth. But the fact is that their generosity has been grossly overstated, and the charity of the Catholic past would have been impotent in supplying the needs of the poor in the recent past of England. They would not have been able 'to share I beleeve in our age, so great liberalitie towarde so manye as we have tryed these many yeares next going before, and especially this deare yeere last past here in England. The which deare yeare truely, I thinke the Lorde sent to this our England . . . [as a] proofe and tryall made of all men'. Englishmen of all classes and all estates were moved in that year of scarcity and want to vindicate their title as Christians and as Englishmen, to hold intact the fabric of the society by their private efforts springing from charity and compassion. 'These men gave more in their penurie, and even of their owne scarcitie and want than all these monkes of their aboundance and great superfluitie, neither of that yeare onely, but of everie yeare.' England may well be proud of the fact that no man is any longer permitted to perish from hunger, or to subsist upon funeral doles and scraps of charity, as far too many did in the vaunted days of the abbeys and, for that matter, as recently as in the reign of the Catholic Queen Mary.[1]

Protestant charity, it was held, was characterized by modesty and by the effective concentration of resources on pressing areas of human need, as contrasted with the vainglory and the great but empty monuments of the Catholic past. Catholic charity was fabricated of stone, whereas the charity of men of true faith gives men bread. But even in terms of the institutions built by charity, 'since the Gospel has enlightened the church, there have been more deeds of charity, colleges, schools, hospitals, etc., founded, than in the time of popery', one writer held, though these godly donors understood that holy works do not purchase our salvation.[2] Thus we discover in the manifold works of charity which spread over the whole of England 'the true miracles of our church' as

[1] Trigge, Francis, *An apologie or defence of our dayes* (L., 1589), 7–9.
[2] Wakeman, *Poore-mans preacher*, 25.

opposed to the papists, maintained another eloquent preacher.[1] The evidence of God's holy works is at every hand as true religion has been restored, 'witnesse your owne eies and eares this very day, heere at home amongst your selues', the preacher admonished his London audience, 'which may heare and see the multitudes of Christ his poore . . . most charitably and carefully releeued in your hospitals, to the great glory of God, the comfort of the poore and afflicted, and the eternall memorie of the worthy founders and benefactors of the same'.[2] Protestants might, indeed, held Robert Wakeman, as they reflected on the inestimable good wrought by London's hospitals alone, 'pronounce of London, for these her singular deedes of charitie, that her faith, and the fruit of her faith, her many good works, are famous throw the whole world: neither doe I thinke that any one citie hath given more worthy testimonies of a true and lively faith'.[3]

This great pride in the achievements of Protestant charity, in the great institutions built by the generosity of private men, found its finest and most persuasive documentation in the quiet but replete pages of John Stow's massive work of historical scholarship, *The Survey of London*. First published in 1598, the work constitutes a kind of eulogy of the good works of London's merchants, being the annal of an incredible and a sustained generosity which created not only a great urban society, but one whose benefits spread across the length and breadth of the land. This record of private generosity, of Protestant good works, is all the more impressive because it was in a sense quite unintended, for it is the throbbing genius, the *ethos*, of London that Stow is seeking to capture in his many pages. But the documentation is there in overwhelming abundance, in parish after parish, ward after ward, generation after generation. Stow pauses for no moralizing, he draws no conclusions, he raises no cry of triumph against the mortal enemy, Rome; the immense impact of the work is all the stronger for that. It is at bottom the account of a great and enduring work of civilization wrought by rich but inconspicuous men according to a design which they all held so clearly and so confidently for their city and their age. England read and she was proud as this great work surveyed the vast accomplishments which, in this 'time of the Gospel', had been wrought by a relatively small group of men of charitable disposition who, imbued with a deep and brooding sense of social responsibility, had built a culture as well as a city. Stow's whole emphasis, his whole preoccupation, was intensely secular, but men could scarcely help reflecting that his almost staccato recital of the record of London's

---

[1] Tynley, Robert, *Two learned sermons* (L., 1609), 68. Tynley (1562–1616) was a native of Kent. Educated at Oxford, where he was graduated B.A. in 1582, he served as Vicar of Witham, Essex, Canon of Ely (1603), and Canon of St Paul's (1608). He also held livings in Suffolk and in Cambridge.

[2] *Ibid.*, 67.   [3] Wakeman, *Poore-mans preacher*, 25.

generosity was after all the fruit of the reformed gospel. The ends which eloquence seek are sometimes the better attained without its distracting intervention. Though we shall never know, the fact that the total of London's truly vast generosity approximately trebled in the generation after the publication of this great book may not be unconnected with its appearance.[1]

Of a very different temper indeed was the long and eloquent recital of Protestant charity incorporated as an appendix to his popular *Synopsis papismi* by Andrew Willet.[2] This catalogue, which was to be widely read and quoted, was an exultant essay on the immense charitable achievement which had been wrought in England during the period of roughly sixty years extending from the 'settling of the Gospel' with the accession of Queen Elizabeth to about 1620, with particular emphasis on the vast charitable endowments created by London's generosity. Depending heavily and without acknowledgement on Stow's patient and unpretentious research, Willet cited first the charities of the Protestant sovereigns, then of the peerage, and then in closely packed pages the long annal of 'the particular gifts and workes of charity by divers worshipfull and well disposed citizens of London'. Though he did not examine wills and complains that the livery companies were unwilling to open their records for his perusal, Willet poured out a recital of giving which was perhaps all the more persuasive and impressive because it was wholly unsystematic in form. He was deeply persuaded that his record proved that 'the Gospell in the space of 60. yeeres hath brought forth more fruit, than twice so many of the late times of popery can shew', while he declared himself certain that more free schools and almshouses had been founded in this short interval than in the whole of the Middle Ages.[3] He therefore proposed to 'stop' the 'slanderous mouths' of all papists who held that the reformed faith was devoid of charitable works, and to lay out for all men to read a 'golden catalogue' of the good works that began to flow in a mounting stream directly the true religion had been well and securely established in the realm.

Willet took particular pride in the charitable giving of London, which he believed exceeded that of any city in the world, but even so he reminded his readers that the great generosity of the city was but typical

---

[1] We deal thus briefly and generally with Stow's work only because of the heavy dependence we shall have on it in our later treatment of London.

[2] The dating of this catalogue of charitable works presents certain problems. It did not appear in the earlier editions of the *Synopsis*, which was first published in 1592, but was certainly written by Willet some little time before his death in 1627. The appendix was dedicated to Sir Thomas Middleton, Lord Mayor of London in 1613–1614, while the preface to the reader was signed by Willet as from Barley, Hertfordshire, in 1613. There are, however, references to events later than 1613, and it seems probable that the book was completed in rough draft by Willet in 1613 and that minor additions were made prior to the posthumous publication in 1634 by the author's son-in-law.

[3] Willet, *Synopsis* (1634), 1219.

of the realm at large. His evidence would show that the charitable works of Protestants by far exceeded those of Catholicism in number, in greatness, and in quality, since 'theirs were done in the pride of their heart, in opinion of merit to purchase remission of sinnes', that of Protestants only to 'serve as testimonies of our faith'.[1] This proud record of generosity, of giving for socially useful purposes, affords abundant and irrefutable evidence that men of true faith and understanding need not be compelled and tricked into generosity by fear, by false promises or by the damnable teaching that salvation may be purchased by benefactions which simply serve the selfish ends of the priesthood. These gifts, large and small, were made by men and women moved to compassion because they understood the meaning of the Christian obligation of charity. He spoke with particular pride of Sutton's immense benefaction, it being 'the greatest gift, that these many hundred yeeres was giuen by any one man, to charitable vses, and I doubt whether the like can bee shewed to haue been done in this land in any age'.[2] But this was only the largest of a myriad of substantial benefactions, made in life or at death, which have so greatly advanced the cause of Christ in England and which have made of the realm a better place for Christian men to live in. He has, he tells us, spoken principally of donors 'now at rest in the Lord', but he knew as well of many men who with great modesty had carried out significant works of charity while still living, 'and their charity is so much the more commendable, because they are content to part with a portion of their wealth, before it leave them: whereas men dying, cannot carry their substance with them, they must leave it to the world'.[3] Even more, he confesses he simply has not had time or opportunity to note 'names that are not in this booke expressed', but these we may be sure are 'in Gods booke of remembrance registred'.[4]

It was Willet's conclusion that the city of London alone had in the space of two generations given upwards of £600,000 for charitable uses, while he felt certain that the two universities had been strengthened with benefactions totalling at least £360,000. He confessed that he had 'no auditers account in hand' and that his estimates were roughly gathered, for 'sometimes I doe but rove at the summe', but he was convinced that England had advanced far indeed in resolving her social and human problems as the teaching of the Gospel came to animate men's impulses and actions. Hence he would conclude that the 'slandrous objection of the papists' have been well answered, for these great acts of charity and mercy 'doe glister as pearles and the workers thereof doe shine as starres amongst us'.[5]

---

[1] Willet, *Synopsis* (1634), 1219.   [2] *Ibid.*, 1221, 1231.
[3] *Ibid.*, 1231.   [4] *Ibid.*, 1233.
[5] *Ibid.*, 1243. Willet's estimate is very rough and certainly incomplete. This matter will be fully discussed in the second volume of this study.

This work was an extremely important document in the history of ideas and in the history of social development in England. Though inexact, roughly cast, and almost casually written, it brought together, principally by borrowings from Stow, the long 'golden' catalogue of London's great generosity almost precisely as the full flood of that giving was attained. It was a proud and almost haughty review of the past generosity of the city and it most dramatically and accurately sensed that social forces of immense historical significance had somehow been freed in England at about the time of the great Queen's accession. Willet's explanation was arrogantly and simply stated: this noble annal of giving simply confirmed the inevitable good works of the Gospel, displayed fully and triumphantly what the elect could accomplish once released from the thraldom of Rome and its priesthood. Willet sets forth for all men to read the roster of the famous men of a new age, an age in which new classes were assuming an enormous measure of social responsibility and laying out the clear design of a new order of a society which they were building with their own wealth. It is our own reading of the evidence so abundantly provided in this amazing age that essentially secular aspirations were flourishing, were in fact triumphing. Willet construed the evidence to mean that he had witnessed in his own lifetime the triumphant climax of the accomplishments of the elect, the putting to shame of the enemy of the true faith. Whether he was right or wrong in his analysis, he had at the very least provided still another immensely powerful impulse for Protestant charity and had, almost as an afterthought, in a moving appendix to a tedious and otherwise quite unimportant controversial work, published a brief and sparse treatise of extraordinary historical significance.

As we have suggested, Willet's work was widely read and its main contention was very soon fully absorbed into the body of Protestant teachings in England. A few references will suggest how quickly and how effectively his argument was used by other preachers. Thus Thomas Anyan, in a sermon preached in London in 1615, in making the point that a good life is the inseparable 'companion' of faith, held that this very teaching of the reformed church in England 'hath brought forth so good fruit that since the first yeare of our late soveraigne Queene ... there haue beene more hospitalls, publicke schooles, libraries, colleges, and places for learning, built, adorned, and now in building, then ever were before in any one 60 yeares'.[1] Nor did John Donne hesitate to employ Willet's contention, and language, in one of his great sermons. The 'shamelesse slanderers' who have held that Protestantism is weak in charity because it disavows the teaching that salvation may be

---

[1] Anyan, *A sermon*, 37. A native of Kent, Anyan was graduated B.A. from Oxford in 1602. He served as President of Corpus Christi College from 1614 to 1629 and held numerous ecclesiastical preferments. He died in 1632.

gained by works, are confounded indeed when we reflect that 'there have been in this kingdome, since the blessed reformation of religion, more publick charitable works perform'd, more hospitals and colleges erected, and endowed in threescore, then in some hundreds of years, of superstition before'.[1] The great Puritan divine, Edward Reynolds, was more scrupulous in citing his authority in a sermon preached in 1658 before the Lord Mayor and Aldermen of London, when he indicated that he would 'press upon London the example of London' in his plea for even greater generosity in meeting the need which all men could see about them.[2] The same thesis, the same appeal to the generosity and the pride of London, had been earlier employed by the Bishop of London in calling for funds with which the restoration of St Paul's might be undertaken. The reign of King James was a proud age in which schools, libraries, colleges, hospitals, and other great works of charity were carried forward and completed. England may well be called the ring of Europe, and 'your city is the gem . . . there is yet one thing wanting vnto you, if you will be perfit, perfit this church'.[3]

All this exultation, this sense of an immense social task well done, was caught up at the end of this age in the writings of a good and a great man, a man in whom compassion for all humanity was instinct, Thomas Fuller. The well-springs of the flood of charity that had formed the social history of the previous century were not for the sophisticated Fuller so clearly marked as they had been for a Willet or a Reynolds, but he had an intuitive sense that a great social revolution had taken place, which had been carried through by private men moved by new aspirations that were not wanting in nobility. Fuller's mind broods over the great benefactions and the men, pious and profane, spiritual and worldly, who had made them. Fuller sensed, as an eminent historian in commenting on him and his genius has well said, that the age of which he wrote was the great era 'of collectivism, of social construction, of educational and charitable endowment. Of no age are the worthies still so vivid to us. In hundreds of parish churches we still see their marble or alabaster effigies . . . under great canopies, with their quarterings, their pedigrees and their children complacently grouped around them. . . . From whatever motive, they all, lawyer or merchant, peer or gentleman, Anglican or Puritan, founded something for that society of which none ever forgot his membership'.[4] These were the men of whom Fuller wrote, theirs the virtues which he celebrated in a homely and inimitable style.

---

[1] Donne, *Sermons*, II, 234. This sermon was preached in 1618 or 1619.
[2] Reynolds, *Rich mans charge*, 42. And cf. Waterhouse, *Modest discourse*, 251–255; Hakewill, George, *An answere. to a treatise* (L., 1616), 253.
[3] King, John, *A sermon at Paules Crosse* (L., 1620), 43–46, 55.
[4] Trevor-Roper, H. R., in *The New Statesman and Nation*, January 10, 1953, 42.

Fuller quite rejected the thesis, already persuasively advanced from opposite points of view and for different ends by both Catholic controversialists and extreme Protestant social reformers, that the Reformation had itself resulted in a spoliation of ecclesiastical properties held and administered for charitable purposes. He recited the good works effected by Henry VIII with much of the wealth that came into the hands of the Crown and dwelt at length on the broad foundations laid for English charitable institutions by his son.[1] On this base of royal policy, private charity began early in the reign of Elizabeth to raise the immense edifice of social institutions which was all but completed in the course of a century.[2] This great outpouring of generous wealth for the accomplishment of more good works than the world had ever known before proceeded, Fuller held, from a new and a very different understanding of the nature of alms from that which had inspired the faulty charities of the Middle Ages. Charity, since the advent of the Reformation, had not been 'parched up by the fear of the fire of purgatory, but kindly ripened with the sun'.[3] For a short time, Fuller quite correctly taught, Protestantism stood still, stunned and paralysed by the horrors of the Marian Counter-Reformation, almost barren of good works. But 'since her beginning to bear fruit, she hath overtaken her Roman co-rival, and left her fairly behind'.[4] Fuller would lay no prescription against the instinct to charity, professing to 'let the charitably minded do what, when, where, how, to whom, and how much God and their own goodness shall direct them'. But he wished that more donors would carry forward their good works during their own lifetime and he could not but deplore the fact that the great streams of charity of the past century had not watered such areas of need as Christian captives in the Barbary states, needy clergy, and servants who had spent their lives in the service of one family.[5] For the rest he was content as he recited in matchless prose the immense cultural and social achievements of the worthies of England. To an estimate of this great achievement we must now lend our own attention.

---

[1] Fuller, Thomas, *The church history of Britain* (L., 1837, 3 vols.), II, 116 ff., 252–259, 337, *et passim*.

[2] *Ibid.*, III, 91, 153, 235–242, 255, 260–261.

[3] Fuller, Thomas (P. A. Nuttall, ed.), *The history of the worthies of England* (L., 1840, 3 vols.), I, 52.

[4] *Ibid.*, I, 52.   [5] *Ibid.*, I, 49, 50–51.

VII

The Achievement

A. THE GENERAL SWEEP OF THE EVIDENCE

We have seen that, towards the close of the age with which we are concerned, thoughtful and perceptive men, observers like Stow, Willet, and Fuller, came to reflect with pride on the immensity of the achievement which had been wrought in England by private charity. And well they might, for in the course of these years the curse of poverty had been chastened, humane care had been arranged for the derelict, and the area of opportunity for aspiring youth had been enormously enlarged. A quiet but a veritable revolution had occurred during which private donors, men who held in view a vision of the future, had repaired the damage society had sustained from the slow ruin of the Middle Ages and had then laid firmly and surely the foundation of the liberal society of which we are the inheritors. It was a revolution too in which men's aspirations for their own generation and those to come had undergone an almost complete metamorphosis, as the essentially religious interests of the later Middle Ages yielded to social aspirations which were most aggressively secular and which wrested from the church the control and the direction of the institutions which lend care to men's bodies and tuition to their minds. The historical price the great donors of the sixteenth and seventeenth centuries exacted for the immense contributions which they made was the secularization of the society and its institutions.

We shall now examine in detail the achievements of private charity during our long period, dealing in all cases with the aggregates for our group of ten representative counties, and reserving a discussion of the materials for the individual counties for the later volumes of this work. As we have earlier warned, we shall inevitably refer to this sampling of ten counties as *All England*, though, as we have suggested, it seems evident that the area with which we are dealing included almost exactly one-third of the land mass of the realm, one-third of its parishes, a third of its population, and something like one-half of its wealth.[1] We are describing, then, a considerable fraction of the whole, but it remains a fraction.

[1] *Vide ante,* 26–29.

In the course of our period we have counted 34,963 private donors
who gave for charitable uses the enormous sum of £3,102,696 9s. These
donors were not evenly distributed among the ten counties under examination, almost two-thirds (64·88 per cent) of them having been concentrated in the three counties of Yorkshire, Middlesex, and Kent,
while of the total of charitable funds provided almost 61 per cent was
disposed by the incredible generosity of London's benefactors.[1] Further,
it will be observed that the average charitable benefaction differs
markedly in the various counties, ranging downwards from the almost
unbelievably high average of £255 12s 2d for London to the modest
£28 4s 6d for Yorkshire. This difference only in part reflects the relative
wealth of the several counties, for in certain areas, such as Yorkshire
and Kent, there was, for reasons to be discussed later, a very considerable, and certainly salutary, participation of humble classes of men in the
charitable history of the county, while in London there was almost no
contribution made by a rootless and fluid urban poor.

It will immediately be observed that, when London and Bristol are
taken together, these urban communities account for nearly two-thirds
(63·9 per cent) of the total of all charitable wealth provided in the ten
counties studied, which, as we have said, included a third of the land
mass of the realm and something like half of its wealth. Significant as
this is, it still understates the decisive quality of the urban contribution
to the charitable needs of the age, to the building of its badly needed
social resources, if we take into account the total of funds contributed
by other but smaller cities and market towns within the various counties
under review. Confining our listing to those urban communities contributing as much as £10,000 of charitable endowments, it appears that
urban England was to give very nearly three-fourths of the total of the
charitable wealth of the age.[2] This was of course a decisive contribution,
one which largely shaped the social growth of the period and which to

[1] County	Known donors	Per cent of whole	County total			Per cent of whole	Average benefaction		
			£	s	d		£	s	d
Bristol	531	1·52	92,042	6	0	2·97	173	6	9
Buckinghamshire	1722	4·93	88,152	6	0	2·84	51	3	10
Hampshire	1956	5·59	87,060	13	0	2·81	44	10	2
Kent	6662	19·05	251,766	12	0	8·11	37	15	10
Lancashire	939	2·69	103,753	5	0	3·34	110	9	10
London	7391	21·14	1,889,211	12	0	60·89	255	12	2
Norfolk	2714	7·76	177,883	11	0	5·73	65	10	10
Somerset	3629	10·38	116,531	16	0	3·76	32	2	3
Worcestershire	787	2·25	52,643	14	0	1·70	66	17	10
Yorkshire	8632	24·69	243,650	14	0	7·85	28	4	6
Totals	34,963	100·00	3,102,696	9	0	100·00	88	14	10

[2] See table at foot of the next page.

a large degree determined the future development of English life and institutions. In a quite overwhelming sense this vast contribution of £2,262,709 7s of urban wealth for the institutional needs of the realm is the measure of the immense social responsibility undertaken by the mercantile élite of England. This, then, was the contribution of a very small, but a rich and generous class, animated, whether in London or in Hull, by tightly disciplined and clearly held aspirations which men of this group were prepared to translate into historical reality by the substance of their own wealth. Here we find the clue to the social metamorphosis under way in England through the full span of our period.

It should be stated again that the great *corpus* of charitable funds accumulated by the society during the years under study were given both by bequest and by dispositions made during the lifetime of donors. Though the proportions are not precise, having been derived from an extensive sampling, something like 63 per cent (63·17 per cent) of the total of charitable wealth was vested by bequest, and the considerable remainder by living gifts.[1] Further, as we have pointed out, these funds were composed both of enduring capital gifts and of more casual, and in most cases, much more modest, gifts or bequests for immediate use. It is rather surprising, however, that of the vast total of charitable moneys with which we are concerned, the great mass, £2,551,880 19s in all, was left in the form of endowments in order to secure in perpetuity the charitable intentions of the donors. In all, therefore, rather more than 82 per cent of the whole of the charitable accumulations of the era were endowments, yielding, we should suppose, at least £127,600 p.a. for a great variety of salutary social uses by the close of our period.[2] This was, we need scarcely say, an immense capital sum, dedicated to specific charitable ends, while the income flowed out each year in a fruitful and life-giving stream. It is, as we have already indicated, quite impossible to measure this great wealth in modern terms or by modern standards. But some sense of the worth and meaning of the sum is suggested when we reflect that the charitable income available in our counties alone for good and healing causes at the close of our period

	£	s	d		£	s	d
London	1,889,211	12	0	Worcester	15,149	1	0
Bristol	92,042	6	0	Rochester	14,803	7	0
Norwich	53,018	5	0	Hull	12,218	15	0
Canterbury	48,605	2	0	Greenwich	12,143	15	0
York	26,067	9	0	Wells	11,560	7	0
Manchester	23,028	0	0	Basingstoke	10,920	19	0
Winchester	17,393	2	0	Bruton	10,286	1	0
Taunton	16,046	11	0	Faversham	10,214	15	0

[1] *Vide ante*, 23–25, for a fuller discussion of this matter.
[2] See first note on p. 243.

approximately equalled the whole of the royal revenues as they stood in 1540,[1] while the total capital value may very possibly have amounted to as much as 4 per cent to 5 per cent of the whole of the capital stock of England as it stood in 1660.[2]

These great funds were in the early decades of our long period accumulated quite slowly, the total provided by donors in the first six decades, which we may well regard as the closing years of the Middle Ages, having reached an aggregate of £525,595 1s, or a little less than 17 per cent of the whole of the accumulations during our period. The average rate of giving during this interval was thus of the order of £87,600 per decade (£87,599), with a particularly notable climax of giving in the first decade of the sixteenth century, when the substantial sum of £131,220 5s was provided for charitable uses.

The curve of giving fell very steeply indeed during that troubled decade 1541–1550 when the great King's health was quite as uncertain as were his religious intentions and during the first unsettled months of the reign of Edward VI, no more than £71,388 15s having been provided in these years by donors whose aspirations were beclouded by an almost overwhelming uncertainty. But in the decade following, despite the Marian interlude, the 'good works of reformation' quite literally poured out, when the astonishing total of £155,643 6s was given for a variety of uses, an amount not to be equalled, it may be observed, until the first decade of the seventeenth century. These gifts were principally made by men moved by the stirring pleas of the great preachers of the Edwardian Reformation, Latimer, Ridley, Hooper, and the rest, who were warm in their confidence, resolute in their demands on the reformed conscience, and fresh and humane in their view of the social

Vide ante, 24–25, for a more detailed analysis of these figures. We should here, however, provide a table setting out the full particulars:

County	Per cent capital	Total capital			Total outright			Grand total		
		£	s	d	£	s	d	£	s	d
Bristol	91·00	83,767	10	0	8,274	16	0	92,042	6	0
Buckinghamshire	82·40	72,631	17	0	15,520	9	0	88,152	6	0
Hampshire	80·09	69,722	18	0	17,337	15	0	87,060	13	0
Kent	81·35	204,799	14	0	46,966	18	0	251,766	12	0
Lancashire	76·83	79,709	16	0	24,043	9	0	103,753	5	0
London	82·60	1,560,422	16	0	328,788	16	0	1,889,211	12	0
Norfolk	80·96	144,019	2	0	33,864	9	0	177,883	11	0
Somerset	80·86	94,224	4	0	22,307	12	0	116,531	16	0
Worcestershire	80·51	42,381	7	0	10,262	7	0	52,643	14	0
Yorkshire	82·17	200,201	15	0	43,448	19	0	243,650	14	0
Totals	82·25	2,551,880	19	0	550,815	10	0	3,102,696	9	0

[1] Dietz, *English government finance*, 138–140.
[2] *Vide ante*, 26–29, for a discussion of this matter.

obligations of the Christian conscience. The almost heady achievement of this quite amazing decade is all the more remarkable when we reflect that of the total provided for charitable uses only a little more than 21 per cent was given during the tragic, the hopeless, reign of Queen Mary, even though her tenure of power occupied more than half of the decade.

During the Elizabethan period the curve of charitable giving in England mounted slowly, though very steadily, in no decade attaining the great heights of the Edwardian years. In average terms, something like £111,000 was provided in each of the four decades, but it was not until the second half of this interval that the flow of charitable benefactions began in an abundance springing from certainty of aspirations. In all, £445,672 19s was given for charitable uses during the Elizabethan era, this sum amounting to slightly more than 14 per cent (14·36 per cent) of the whole for our long period. It is most evident that the first half of Elizabeth's reign was marked by a ruthlessly competitive and acquisitive spirit on the part of the two classes, the merchants and the gentry, which were ultimately to bear such a heavy burden of social responsibility. As we have seen, mounting social and economic distress, the increasing concern and the steady policy of the government, and the sustained preaching of the necessity for liberality and charity were to have their full and mensurable effect only in the more mellow and certain period of the last two decades of the reign when truly large charitable aggregates began to be gathered, preparing, as it were, for the golden flow of charity in the four decades which we have called the early Stuart period.

In so many respects it may be said that the Elizabethan age enjoyed its full fruition in the next generation. This is true in the realm of domestic architecture, in letters, and in some respects in the history of thought, and it is certainly overwhelmingly true with respect to charitable giving and the assumption by the society of immense burdens of social responsibility. For one thing, it must be remembered that men who drew their wills, men who left large charitable bequests in the years 1601–1630, had on the whole reached their maturity and had formed their aspirations for their society in the preceding generation. Thus does the present always lie in debt to the past. Nor should we forget that the passage of the great Elizabethan social code at the close of the Queen's reign marks a kind of climax of discussion and decision with respect to the future of the society. In particular, as we have earlier pointed out, the passage of the acts defining charitable trusts lent an enormous and an immediately observable impetus to charitable giving, the fruits of which were to be gathered in the early Stuart period. The result was that the curve of charitable giving lifts with a really incredible steepness during the first four decades of the seventeenth century. In all, the huge total of £1,437,490 3s was provided for one or another charitable purpose during this relatively short interval, this amounting to somewhat more than 46 per cent (46.33 per cent) of the whole given for charitable uses during our entire period. The magnitude of this achievement is suggested when we say that in the one generation extending from 1611 to 1640 a larger total was provided for charitable needs than during the course of the long interval from 1480 to 1600. In average terms, approximately £359,372 was given in each of the decades of this period. During the two great decades 1611–1630, when the floodgates were fully opened, principally by merchant generosity, upwards of £853,270 was provided for charitable purposes by men and women of our ten counties, surely on a scale of giving never before equalled and probably never again, in relation to the assets of the society.

But the forces of disruption and uncertainty were at work in the society, or more exactly in the polity, and men's aspirations began once more to be clouded by irresolution and hesitancy. In the Laudian decade, 1631–1640, the charitable total fell away significantly, for it was clear that the tensions now wracking the realm could be relieved only by a formidable test of power between the opposed forces in the state. During the two decades of grave civil and religious dislocation, as was inevitable, the curve of charitable giving declined very steeply indeed. In this interval, if a small total which cannot be precisely dated may be included, £466,906 5s was disposed for charitable causes, this amounting to 15.05 per cent of the whole sum for our period. Steep as was this decline, there were still very large amounts being given in each decade, while the sum for these twenty years, it must be observed, somewhat exceeded that provided during the whole course of the Elizabethan age. Moreover, with the restoration of political stability under the Commonwealth and Protectorate, the trend of giving mounted upwards sharply once more, the most substantial total of £242,749 19s having been provided during the last decade of our age.

As we assess the data, then, our first conclusion is that the totals given for charitable uses in England held on a low but a remarkably level plane until the decade of the Edwardian Reformation. After a kind of precocious climax in that interval, the curve of giving began to rise steadily to its astonishing culmination over the full course of a generation in the early seventeenth century. There is the clear suggestion of gathering momentum as one examines the table or the curve herewith provided, a momentum which found its full expression in the incredible generosity which marks the years 1611–1640.[1]

When the data are analysed more closely and qualitatively, as it were, a second and even more significant conclusion may be drawn which provides the underlying thesis of this work. As we view our whole period, there was not only a most formidable and fruitful increase in

[1] See table on p. 246.

the amounts given by private donors for charitable uses, but there was a truly revolutionary shift in the charitable uses for which these amounts were given. Furthermore, it is evident that these two principal forces, the gathering momentum and the shift in men's aspirations, were inter-related, were in fact simultaneous. All our evidence would suggest that the second of these great social forces fed and animated the first: that as men's aspirations underwent swift and conclusive change, new and compelling areas of need were laid open, into which funds flowed as men became persuaded of the central significance for themselves and their society of the new good works to which they had set their hands and dedicated so much of their fortunes.

This great, and permanent, change in the structure of men's aspira-tions may be dated very clearly from the decade of the Edwardian Reformation, which for many reasons we are now persuaded was more conclusive in its effect on the English mind and faith than we had here-

Totals of charitable benefactions by decade intervals:

Decades	Decade totals					
	£	s	d	£	s	d
1481–1490	49,383	19	0			
1491–1500	75,472	19	0			
1501–1510	131,220	5	0			
1511–1520	81,868	12	0			
1521–1530	107,405	17	0			
1531–1540	80,243	9	0			
				525,595	1	0
1541–1550	71,388	15	0			
1551–1560	155,643	6	0			
				227,032	1	0
1561–1570	92,926	4	0			
1571–1580	105,980	2	0			
1581–1590	120,550	11	0			
1591–1600	126,216	2	0			
				445,672	19	0
1601–1610	210,058	2	0			
1611–1620	424,129	9	0			
1621–1630	429,141	1	0			
1631–1640	374,161	11	0			
				1,437,490	3	0
1641–1650	216,070	9	0			
1651–1660	242,749	19	0			
No date	8,085	17	0			
				466,906	5	0
Total	3,102,696	9	0			

These decade totals are presented as Curve 1 in the Appendix.

tofore supposed. A steep and a decisive decline in the amount and in the proportion of giving for religious purposes occurred in this period as men's concern turned with an almost frenzied zeal to a great variety of secular needs which they felt laid a heavier charge on their charitable resources than did the requirements of the church, whether Calvinist or Romanist. As we shall have frequent occasion to point out, these benefactions tended to be militantly and aggressively secular in temper and in purpose, though it by no means follows that the donors were not themselves men of the sternest possible piety. None the less, their gifts betray an evident anti-clericalism, a disposition to vest their endowments securely in trustworthy lay hands, and the explicit conviction that for too long the church in its institutional aspect had drained off far too large an increment of the social wealth of the community.

The cold logic of our curves would, indeed, suggest that these sentiments, this great metamorphosis, in men's aspirations, had begun in England well before the Reformation, for proportionately the amount being dedicated by the society for religious uses began to decline quite steeply and continuously after 1510. None the less, taking in view all the decades prior to the Reformation, the very large total of £281,158 15s was dedicated by pious donors to the various needs of the church, this amounting to somewhat more than 53 per cent of the whole amount given for charitable causes during this interval of sixty years. Another substantial total of £131,170 5s, this being almost 25 per cent of the whole, was provided, principally by the great prelates, for educational uses, which in this era were of course not only controlled by the ecclesiastical authorities but lent almost exclusive service to their needs. The relatively modest remainder was spread among the other great charitable heads, 13·33 per cent of the total being disposed for poor relief, 6·18 per cent for municipal uses, and an insignificant amount for the various instrumentalities of social rehabilitation.[1]

Reference to the table just cited will suggest at once, and that most compellingly, that an immense social and cultural revolution occurred during the interval of the Reformation, despite the frantic, and almost wholly unavailing, efforts of Mary Tudor to stem the tide of change. While, as we have noted, the average decade rate of giving increased during this brief interval, the amount and the proportion provided for the many needs of the church sank with an incredible velocity. In the long interval prior to the Reformation giving for religious causes had for each decade averaged very nearly £47,000, while in the years 1541–1560 it averaged somewhat less than £17,000. More significantly, the total of £33,526 5s designated for religious purposes amounted to not more than 14·77 per cent of the whole of charitable wealth for the

[1] *Vide* Table I (Appendix) and the accompanying bar graphs for the detailed analysis.

period. While this catastrophic decline in the support of ecclesiastical needs was taking place, there was a tremendous burgeoning out of support for all the great secular uses. Thus the interesting and hopeful outlays on the institutions experimenting with the possibility of the social rehabilitation of the poor commanded £68,589 17s of funds, or well over twice as much as was given for religious uses, while the £61,383 4s given for the direct relief of the poor in percentage terms (27·04 per cent) exhibited an interest in this pressing problem somewhat more than double in intensity that of the preceding period. The £48,320 9s given for educational uses amounted to about 21 per cent of the whole, a little less than in the decades prior to the Reformation, but with the extremely important difference that this substantial sum was principally dedicated to the founding of schools under firm secular control.

These very strong and compelling changes in the structure of English aspirations were not only confirmed but were rendered permanent in the course of the Elizabethan age. The great Queen did far more than lead her people and her age, she was herself in a complete sense identical with her people and her age. Intensely secular, concerned at bottom only with the substance of power, coldly suspicious of the clerical mind, she was the embodiment of a secularism which nearly destroyed the fabric of the church and the clergy which she had founded. Not only did the rate of giving for religious needs fall to slightly under £8000 for each decade of the period, but the £31,959 7s provided for these uses in this interval represents no more than 7·17 per cent of the great sum advanced for all charitable purposes in the course of the reign. In perhaps more meaningful terms, we observe in this remarkable period an intensity of interest in the needs of the church only one-seventh that exhibited in the years prior to the Reformation, and only half that shown during the two decades of the Reformation itself. In point of fact, less was given for religious purposes than for any other great charitable head, even the amount provided for municipal uses (£33,720 5s) somewhat exceeding that given for the totality of the needs of organized religion in the realm. Relatively, the care of the poor absorbed a much larger proportion (39·03 per cent) of all charitable funds, the £173,944 4s given for this purpose constituting a very real and demonstrably helpful contribution towards resolving the age-old problem of poverty and human misery. Another large total (£139,947 8s) was given for the pressing and hopeful uses of education, the proportion (31·40 per cent) devoted to this purpose in the Elizabethan period being greater than that observed in any other interval. Finally, the considerable sum of £66,101 15s was given for the prosecution of various experiments in social rehabilitation, this amount, it may be noted, being more than double that devoted to all religious needs. This, most evidently, was an age of almost complete secularism of aspirations on the part of men who were in the main

personally pious to a fault, and the most generous of whom were possessed of a piety tinged with an evangelical fervour most distasteful to
their Erastian and very probably sceptical sovereign.

It is only by comparison with the Elizabethan age that we may say
that the crying needs of the church gained some larger measure of support during the early Stuart period, when, as we have seen, the immense
outpouring of charitable giving was to occur in England. In part, this
modest revival occurred because most visibly the church was in process
of serious decay, in part because the Stuarts lent warm and continuous
support to the needs of the church, mounting to an almost frantic
appeal in the period of Archbishop Laud's dominance in the affairs of
church and state, and finally because comprehended within the substantial total afforded for religious needs there is a very large sum given
by Puritan laymen engaged in a formidably bold effort to capture the
church through its clergy. In all, £256,522 was provided for one or
another need of the church, this comprehending 17·85 per cent of all
charitable funds for the interval. This was modest indeed when contrasted
with the enormous total of £383,594 1s (26·68 per cent) given for the
various educational interests of the age. And it was quite dwarfed by the
huge total of £620,480 provided by countless benefactors for a frontal
assault on poverty, an amount which was singularly useful because
almost the whole was in the form of capital. Very substantial sums were
also disposed for the agencies of social rehabilitation (£119,340 15s) and
for municipal betterments (£57,553 7s), though it will be observed that
proportionately both these interests show a marked decline when
compared with the two preceding intervals.

In the course of the era of the Puritan Revolution the requirements
of the poor commanded a slightly higher proportion (43·58 per cent)
of the charitable wealth of England than in any preceding period, the
£203,485 18s so designated representing a huge further commitment to
the institutions with which poverty was being curbed in England. The
interest maintained in this tumultuous period in education was proportionately (27·94 per cent) slightly greater than in the preceding
interval (26·68 per cent), the total of £130,461 9s. given for this use
being almost as large as that provided during the Elizabethan age,
somewhat incorrectly famous for its foundation of grammar schools.
Interest in the maintenance of the church, even of the 'godly church'
which seemed now to be at hand, waned considerably, the 12·09 per
cent of all charitable funds dedicated to this purpose being sharply
lower than in the preceding era, though it should be remarked that in
this brief period a much larger total (£56,462 8s) was given for religious
uses than in the whole of the Elizabethan age. A substantial total of
£54,707 7s was provided for experiments in the rehabilitation of the
poor, this being 11·72 per cent of the whole, while proportionately the

£21,789 3s designated for municipal improvements represents a slight gain over the early Stuart interval.

In summary, we may note that taking our whole long period in view, it was the needs of the poor that commanded the bulk of men's benevolence, well over a third (36·40 per cent) of the whole of their immense charitable giving having been disposed for this worthy and certainly pressing need. The closely related interest in education, in the enlargement of the circumference of opportunity, remained remarkably constant through this period of almost two centuries, while on balance something more than a fourth (26·86 per cent) of all charitable funds were devoted to this fruitful purpose. Considerably less was given for religious uses, the total of £659,628 15s so designated amounting to not much more than a fifth (21·26 per cent) of the vast total wherewith men were altering and bettering the social institutions of their age. Almost half as much, 10·30 per cent of the whole sum, was risked by wise and often prescient donors on a great variety of essentially experimental undertakings in which the cure of poverty was sought, while rather more than 5 per cent (5·18 per cent) of all the charitable wealth accumulated during our period was disposed for the betterment of the fabric of the communities in which men lived.

These trends and the curves which document them reflect of course the aspirations of many thousands of individual donors, of numerous classes of men, and of widely separated areas of a society which was only then becoming homogeneous. We shall later comment in detail on the amazing differences in the structure of aspirations as we compare class with class, but we should now speak at least briefly of certain important differences among the counties under study. Thus we have just observed that for England donors of our period gave 36·40 per cent of all their charitable benefactions for the relief of poverty, whereas in the individual counties this proportion ranges from the 22·01 per cent devoted to this purpose in Lancashire to the incredibly high proportion of 52·04 per cent in Buckinghamshire.[1] We have no really persuasive

---

[1] Proportion of total charitable funds disposed for poor relief:

	Total			Per
	£	s	d	cent
Bristol	42,306	10	0	45·96
Buckinghamshire	45,872	13	0	52·04
Hampshire	36,002	4	0	41·35
Kent	102,519	7	0	40·72
Lancashire	22,836	7	0	22·01
London	664,608	14	0	35·18
Norfolk	60,075	6	0	33·77
Somerset	50,500	18	0	43·34
Worcestershire	23,115	17	0	43·91
Yorkshire	81,513	13	0	33·46

explanation for the preoccupation of the Buckinghamshire gentry with the needs of the poor, though in Lancashire it is clear indeed that the very small sum provided for poor relief reflects the almost fanatical interest of its donors in winning the county for the reformed faith and in remedying the pervasive want of educational opportunity in this then remote and backward shire. The proportion (35·18 per cent) designated by London donors for poor relief was, it will be noted, almost precisely that for England at large, while in Bristol, the other urban complex examined in detail, the proportion (45·96 per cent) devoted to the needs of the poor was exceeded only by that so disposed in Buckinghamshire.

Even cursory examination of the resources given for experiments in social rehabilitation in the several counties will suggest that these were a form of speculative undertaking most highly favoured by the merchant class throughout the realm. The aim of these donors was to destroy poverty by effecting its cure, and the merchants were prepared to stake very large sums indeed in these hopeful, aggressive, though often naïve, ventures.[1] Thus in London the amazingly large proportion of 13·32 per cent was devoted to this broad purpose, while in Bristol rather more than 10 per cent (10·42 per cent) was ventured. Almost as large a proportion (9·63 per cent) was dedicated to the ends of social rehabilitation in Norfolk, where the merchant aristocracy of Norwich was intensely interested in experiments of this kind. The remaining, and more typically rural, counties displayed markedly less interest in these appealing but novel undertakings, the proportion of total wealth so dedicated ranging from 2·66 per cent in Somerset to 5·94 per cent in Worcestershire.

The proportion of charitable funds devoted to the various municipal betterments in the several counties, on the other hand, suggests no sensible statistical pattern. These proportions range from the unbelievable low of 0·78 per cent for Somerset, which seemed even to despair of its notoriously evil roads, to the remarkably high 10·92 per cent in principally rural Hampshire. Norfolk likewise devoted a gener-

---

[1] Proportion of total charitable wealth designated for social rehabilitation:

	Total			Per
	£	s	d	cent
Bristol	9,592	1	0	10·42
Buckinghamshire	3,920	2	0	4·45
Hampshire	3,846	1	0	4·42
Kent	12,043	4	0	4·78
Lancashire	3,153	12	0	3·04
London	251,728	13	0	13·32
Norfolk	17,127	16	0	9·63
Somerset	3,101	2	0	2·66
Worcestershire	3,128	4	0	5·94
Yorkshire	11,805	17	0	4·85

ous proportion (10·58 per cent) of its charitable assets to municipal
uses, particularly to endowments intended to afford tax relief, while the
lusty and proud burghers of Bristol dedicated 9·10 per cent of their
charitable wealth for the betterment of the fabric of their city. London,
on the other hand, which had the most maturely developed tradition of
employing the taxing power for improvements today commonly carried
forward as a charge on the whole community, was little interested in
such outlays, only 4·95 per cent of its huge charitable aggregate being so
designated.[1]

Devotion to the need for the enlargement of educational opportunity
was, it is clear, most evenly dispersed among the several counties.[2]
The two exceptions are Lancashire and Yorkshire, both remote and
backward, into which there flowed very large benefactions from London
merchants, usually natives of the two counties, who were determined to
bring these regions level with the realm at large in terms of the educational resources which men had come to realize were essential if the
ignorance in which poverty bred was to be dispelled. In Lancashire, the
really staggering proportion of 41·79 per cent of all charitable funds was
dedicated to this worthy purpose, a far larger share, incidentally, than
was devoted there to any of the other great charitable causes. An extraordinarily large proportion of charitable wealth was likewise disposed

[1] Proportion of charitable wealth designated for municipal betterments:

	Total			Per cent
	£	s	d	
Bristol	8,378	5	0	9·10
Buckinghamshire	7,757	19	0	8·80
Hampshire	9,511	6	0	10·92
Kent	11,558	15	0	4·59
Lancashire	1,265	10	0	1·22
London	93,593	16	0	4·95
Norfolk	18,820	15	0	10·58
Somerset	905	15	0	0·78
Worcestershire	2,862	9	0	5·44
Yorkshire	6,121	11	0	2·51

[2] Proportion of charitable wealth designated for education:

	Total			Per cent
	£	s	d	
Bristol	19,635	7	0	21·33
Buckinghamshire	18,741	2	0	21·26
Hampshire	21,626	4	0	24·84
Kent	58,255	16	0	23·14
Lancashire	43,359	13	0	41·79
London	510,890	17	0	27·04
Norfolk	40,920	4	0	23·00
Somerset	30,158	7	0	25·88
Worcestershire	14,093	14	0	26·77
Yorkshire	75,812	8	0	31·12

for educational purposes in Yorkshire, the £75,812 8s dedicated to this constituting nearly a third (31·12 per cent) of the whole of the considerable charitable funds of that county. In the remaining counties the differences were remarkably slight, all falling within the narrow range of from 21·26 per cent in Buckinghamshire to the 27·04 per cent given for this great use in London.

By far the most striking and interesting of the differences in the charitable aspirations of the several counties is to be observed in the proportion of their charitable wealth which they disposed for the various religious needs of the age.[1] In Lancashire and Yorkshire the proportion devoted to religious uses far exceeded the nation's average of 21·26 per cent, principally because of 'missionary funds' flowing into these remote counties from London, most of which bore a distinctly Puritan stamp, and because the parochial structure of these two counties was at the outset of our period far from complete. In most revealing contrast to the 31·94 per cent of all charitable funds devoted to religious causes in Lancashire, such rural counties as Buckinghamshire (13·45 per cent) and Hampshire (18·46 per cent) gave only a slight proportion of their wealth for such purposes through the whole long course of our period. As we should expect, both the great urban complexes under study were coldly secular in their preoccupation, London giving 19·50 per cent of its immense charitable wealth for religious needs and Bristol no more than 13·18 per cent. These differences are extremely interesting and important: the quite complex causes, which reveal a great deal concerning the steady drift of the realm towards secularization of aspirations, will be considered in detail in later volumes, where the evidence for the several counties is examined.

B. THE GREAT CHARITABLE CAUSES

1. *The poor*

We have seen that in the whole course of our period the relief of poverty was by far the most significant of all the charitable concerns of donors.

[1] Proportion of charitable wealth devoted to religious uses:

	Total			Per cent
	£	s	d	
Bristol	12,130	3	0	13·18
Buckinghamshire	11,860	10	0	13·45
Hampshire	16,074	18	0	18·46
Kent	67,389	10	0	26·77
Lancashire	33,138	3	0	31·94
London	368,389	12	0	19·50
Norfolk	40,939	10	0	23·01
Somerset	31,865	14	0	27·35
Worcestershire	9,443	10	0	17·94
Yorkshire	68,397	5	0	28·07

To one or another kind of direct relief men and women of the age were to give the really immense total of £1,129,351 9s of funds, this amounting to somewhat more than 36 per cent (36·40 per cent) of all the charitable wealth disposed by the age.[1] But this great outpouring was not spread evenly through our period, men during the six decades prior to the Reformation having disposed no more than £70,058 3s for the several forms of poor relief, this being only about 13 per cent of the whole of their charitable giving. In proportionate terms, the intensity of interest in the plight of the poor was almost exactly doubled in the brief interval of the Reformation, donors of those years having provided £61,383 4s for the needs of the poor, or 27·04 per cent of all their benefactions. Significantly, the total amounts designated for this use rose steadily during the Elizabethan age, from £28,203 1s in the first decade of the period to £56,133 10s in the last, the most substantial total of £173,944 4s having been given during this interval of four decades, which amounts to upwards of 39 per cent of all charitable wealth and which represents a proportionate intensity of interest approximately treble that displayed in the later mediaeval decades.

The effects of the economic crisis occurring in the last decade of the century, the consequences of the general discussion of poverty associated with the passage of the Elizabethan poor laws, and, above all, the fruitful results of the enactment of the law defining and protecting charitable trusts were immediately and most dramatically evident in the first decade of the seventeenth century, when the large total of £104,492 19s was provided for the several agencies of poor relief, an amount approximately double that given in the last decade of Elizabeth's reign. Even so, this great achievement was no more than a harbinger of the immense generosity of the remaining decades of the early Stuart period, which reached its climax in the years 1621–1630 when £198,672 7s was provided for the succour of the needy. In these amazing four decades the staggering total of £620,480 was given for various forms of poor relief, this amounting to 43.16 per cent of the whole of the great sum designated for charity during these years and constituting well over half (54·94 per cent) the prodigious amount to be given for such uses in the whole course of our period. There was, inevitably, a falling away in the rate of giving for poor relief during the disrupted and uncertain years of the Puritan Revolution, but it should be observed that the most substantial sum of £203,485 18s provided in this brief interval represented 43·58 per cent of the whole of the charitable wealth of the period and was in fact a considerably larger sum than that given for this purpose in the whole course of the Elizabethan age.

Not only was there a steep and steady rise in the amounts provided

[1] *Vide* Table II and the accompanying curve (Appendix) for the details of the discussion.

for poor relief as our period progressed, but there was an extremely important change in the quality of the sums given. Thus in the first decades of our age, in certain precocious communities like London and Bristol until about 1520, and in more backward, or at least conservative, counties like Somerset and Yorkshire until about 1560, the rather slender sums given for such an important head as outright, or household, relief were in the main disbursed as doles, particularly in connection with funerals, for the immediate use of the recipients. But towards the middle of the century, as we have suggested, this typical, but on the whole wasteful, if not harmful, form of mediaeval almsgiving was superseded by endowments most carefully established and regulated, the incomes to be employed in perpetuity by responsible trustees for the relief of the poor under conditions set down with great care. In all, the wealth given for the purposes comprised under the head of *Outright Relief* was, taking our whole period in view, largely capital in form. The proportions range from about 77 per cent for such counties as Buckinghamshire, Hampshire, Somerset, and Yorkshire, to the remarkably high proportion of 90·05 per cent for Kent, while for our whole group of counties this proportion was 83·31 per cent of the whole amount.

The great sums devoted quite directly to the relief of poverty may for convenience be divided into those amounts which have been classified as having been given for outright relief, for general charitable purposes, or very specifically for the aged, and those endowments which were disposed for the founding of almshouses. The first grouping we may in turn regard as amounts disposed to assist the poor in their own houses, as household relief, when it was the intention to prevent the disruption of the family by applying such relief as might be necessary until employment could be found, illness cured, or a moral reformation of the wage-earner effected. Huge sums were disposed for this purpose during the course of our period, the £585,385 6s designated for outright relief alone constituting 18·87 per cent of the whole of the accumulation of charitable wealth and being by a fair margin the largest sum devoted to any single charitable purpose. There should be included as well in this grouping a most substantial total of £121,408 2s of endowments established for general charitable uses, at the discretion of the trustees, which as we have earlier noted were almost wholly devoted to household relief, at least during our period; and there was as well a sum of £5143 designated under rigorous restrictions for the household relief of aged persons of various sorts. In all, therefore, the massive total of £711,936 8s, comprising almost 23 per cent (22·95 per cent) of the whole of the charitable wealth of the realm, was dedicated by many thousands of donors for the household relief of the poor.

It is very evident that the care of the poor became the central social preoccupation of men of our period after about 1550. Funds devoted to this great purpose flowed into several channels, but, as we have just suggested, by far the largest amounts were dedicated to uses which we may fairly describe as household relief. These donors were principally intent on establishing endowments in the parishes, the income of which would be employed by trustees, who most typically were parish officials in various combinations, for the support at a subsistence level of needy and worthy poor, legally resident in the parish. Though these benefactions were evoked by the highest motives of generosity and compassion, they were not sentimental and they normally established stipends which could hardly have lent full support to a family even in a rural community. To put it bluntly, these charitable payments were designed to do no more than keep a family from starvation and really abject want, the intention being to supply every persuasion to the wage-earner to find full, or at the very least, supplementary employment. As we shall see, the really impotent and the derelict were carefully separated from the able-bodied poor, the unemployed, and were provided either with permanent pensions or, ideally, permanent sanctuary in almshouses.

As we have said, by no means the whole amount given for household relief was vested in the form of endowments, but after 1550 a very large proportion indeed was so disposed. In all, about 86 per cent of the whole of the wealth given for these purposes which we have grouped under the general head of household relief was settled as capital, with the consequence that the enormous sum of £608,142 9s was prudently and thoughtfully vested by donors in trusts which would lend care for the poor in perpetuity. This means, of course, that a very large annual income of perhaps £30,407 was by the close of our period available in the hundreds of parishes of which our ten counties were comprised for the relief of a poverty which the society had come to accept as its responsibility. This, as we have seen, was a far larger amount than was in any year assessed on these communities under the existing and wholly competent legislation, and it may well be that this great achievement in social responsibility was in part at least the consequence of the resolution of responsible men to assume this enormous load as an act of charity rather than as a requirement of law. In our more detailed studies of the several counties, we shall have occasion to observe that donors in most cases established the stipend, the rate of distribution, to needy families, in average amounts ranging from about £2 p.a. for the full support of a destitute family in such counties as Buckinghamshire, Hampshire, and Yorkshire, to £2 15s p.a. in London or £2 16s p.a. in Worcestershire. In all, it is our reckoning that these endowments for household relief lent full support, according to the standards of subsistence for the age, to nearly 13,000 families in these ten counties alone. It is quite futile to attempt any accurate estimate of the number of human beings thus protected from disaster, if not from starvation, because poverty was so frequently an aspect of old age in the early modern world, but surely it would be most conservative to assume that the family unit in average terms included at least 3·5 persons, which would in turn suggest that upwards of 45,000 men, women, and children (for poverty was also not uncommonly a consequence of a very high birth-rate) were at all times sustained by these great endowments. In other words, again in the somewhat deceptive terms of averages, something over four families were being supported in each of the 3033 parishes comprehended within the area with which we are concerned. Our evidence would in fact suggest that if these capital funds had been well and evenly distributed over the region under study, they would have been very nearly sufficient for the minimum purposes for which they had been established. Unfortunately, as our discussion of the counties will suggest, these great endowments tended to be concentrated in areas of ever-increasing opportunity, with the result that something like a third of all the parishes with which we are concerned were ill favoured indeed with these helpful and healing moneys. It was precisely here that private charity failed, here that real suffering could occur, and here that the ministrations required by law had in periods of economic crisis to be carried forward. But all the frailties and shortcomings notwithstanding, this is a record of magnificent achievement, of a sensitive assumption of a vast burden of responsibility by an age, and by classes, which had come to care deeply about the material fate of their fellow men.

The fruitful concern which donors of our age displayed for the relief of the worthy poor in their households was accompanied by a steadily mounting attempt to provide for the care of the hopelessly indigent, the permanent casualties of the society, in carefully constituted almshouse foundations. We shall want to consider this remarkable social achievement in some detail, since it not only added most impressive institutional strength to the efforts of individual men of this period to curb and control the evil forces of poverty in their society, but in a true sense may be said to delineate the whole structure of their conception of charity. In the course of time the term 'almshouse' has acquired a socially unpleasant connotation, with the result that we tend to forget that it is a noble word and that the men who founded the innumerable almshouses of the sixteenth and seventeenth centuries were moved by the highest instincts of piety and social concern.

There remained to men of the early modern world a still valuable, though sadly attenuated, mediaeval inheritance in numerous hospitals, a fraction of which had from the time of their foundation assumed the responsibilities which the sixteenth century came to associate with almshouses. Mediaeval hospitals performed a variety of functions, some having been founded for the care of the sick and infirm, others for the aged, for the insane, the lepers, the orphans, and still others for the care of the hopelessly poor and impotent. A most valuable study has listed 731 of these foundations made prior to 1547, of which it would appear that something like 640 were established before the beginning of our period.[1] It is most interesting to note that of the whole number, fully 73 per cent. were founded prior to 1350. The often inadequate local evidence in our counties at least would suggest that approximately half of the mediaeval foundations at some time in their history fulfilled those functions which the sixteenth century required of almshouses. Not only was the great movement of foundation at an end by 1350, but grave abuses and neglect had set in which an act of Parliament sought unsuccessfully to avert in 1414, the preamble stating that there were 'many hospitals . . . now for the most part decayed, and the goods and profits of the same, by divers persons, spiritual and temporal, withdrawn and spent to the use of others, whereby many men and women have died in great misery for default of aid, livelihood, and succour'. As our authority suggests, these abuses and neglects were manifold. Trustees frequently regarded these hospitals as private hostels; room and lodging covenants were frequently given or sold; and many of those under monastic control simply had their revenues expropriated. The fabric of these institutions was frequently permitted to fall into ruin, and, most serious of all, there were diversions of trust income to ecclesiastical or private uses on a very wide and a wholly shocking scale.[2]

It should be emphasized as well that a large proportion of these mediaeval foundations were at no time endowed, with the inevitable consequence that they disappeared at the first touch of neglect or abuse. Most of the remainder were never substantially endowed by the founders or later mediaeval philanthropists, and these too were ill-prepared to meet substantial neglect or maladministration. The unhappy result was that most of these great works of early mediaeval piety had either disappeared long before or were derelict when a new era opened in about 1480. Though we have no confidence that our data will hold for all of England, some further analysis of the facts as they do apply to our region may be of value. There appear to have been something like 262 hospitals founded in these ten counties prior to 1480, of which we are fairly confident 140 to 150 had at some time fulfilled the functions of almshouses. In 1480 not more than seventy-four of these institutions remained,[3] and of this number nearly half were either derelict or were

---

[1] Clay, R. M., *The mediaeval hospitals of England* (L., 1909), Appendix B.
[2] *Ibid.*, 212–225.
[3] The number of these almshouses was by counties:

Bristol	5	London	8
Buckinghamshire	4	Norfolk	10
Hampshire	4	Somerset	6
Kent	12	Worcestershire	2
Lancashire	0	Yorkshire	23 Total: 74

so badly managed that almost the whole of their usually scanty income was being diverted or employed for essentially administrative (or bureaucratic) purposes.

These, then, were the resources with which our period began, resources which had been materially strengthened even before the advent of the Reformation. The Reformation statute granting the hospitals to the Crown intended that 'the premisses [shall be] used and exercised to more godly and vertuous uses', that they should be reconstituted and not destroyed. In our counties at least this injunction was faithfully followed save in those rather rare instances where by long fact and tradition the whole of the income had been improperly diverted to monastic uses or for the support of chantries. In other words, in so far as these institutions performed the function of almshouses they were preserved and strengthened when they were vested in secular control, usually in the municipal authorities who had intervened to save them.[1] Further, as we shall note in detail in our study of the counties, almost all of these earlier foundations, having been reconstituted, and often refounded, were greatly strengthened in their endowments and in their good works within a generation after the Reformation. Among the many myths still clustering around the English Reformation, not the least is the one persuading us that the mediaeval hospitals were destroyed.

During the course of our period the enormous sum of £417,415 1s was vested by benefactors in almshouse foundations in the regions with which we are concerned. Since save for trifling sums this great total was in the form of capital gifts,[2] these new foundations of the early modern era were securely established, lending permanent and ever-increasing aid as the society sought to come to effective grips with the age-old problem of poverty. As the curve presented below will suggest,[3] the support lent to almshouse foundations gathered formidable momentum after 1540 as responsible men sought to link these establishments with the great endowments which they were simultaneously creating for the care of poor men in their own households. Even in the decades prior to the Reformation, steady and by no means insignificant support was lent to this worthy cause, with a notable sum having been vested for this purpose in the years 1501–1510. But new and powerful impetus was supplied to this development during the short interval of the Reformation, when the £22,432 18s so disposed fell but little short of the amount given in the six preceding decades. After a relatively inaus-

---

[1] This also seems to be the conclusion of Leonard (*English poor relief*, 208–209) and of Clay (*Mediaeval hospitals*, 227–243).

[2] The proportion of capital gifts for the support of almshouses ranges from 96·92 per cent in Hampshire to 99·91 per cent in Worcestershire. For the whole group of counties 99·30 per cent was in capital form.

[3] See p. 260.

picious beginning in the first of the Elizabethan decades, gifts for the founding of almshouses began to mount steadily and most impressively, with the result that for the whole interval of four decades the substantial total of £58,768 12s has been recorded. Great and fruitful as this capital was, it was but an earnest of the immense outpouring of wealth for this purpose during the first three decades of the seventeenth century. In the years 1601–1610, £48,157 15s was vested for this use, while in the next decade the really incredible total of £116,225 12s was given, principally by London donors, for the foundation of new almshouses or the strengthening of older endowments. In this one decade, in point of fact, somewhat more was provided for this charitable cause than in the whole of the long period extending from 1480 to the close of the sixteenth century. For reasons not wholly clear, the momentum of giving for almshouses slackened significantly and steadily for three successive decades after 1620, to rise again most abruptly in the final decade of the era of the Puritan Revolution. Among the explanations, which will be considered in greater detail in our county analyses, are the widespread persuasion that quite enough foundations had been made to lend succour to the really hopelessly indigent, the general pessimism which characterized the decade immediately preceding the outbreak of the Civil War, the dislocations of the decade 1641–1650, and the mounting interest in the prevention of poverty as contrasted with its relief. Be this as it may, surely this is an annal of a magnificent and a noble achievement wrought by private men who had become

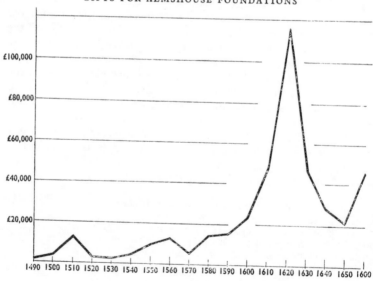

GIFTS FOR ALMSHOUSE FOUNDATIONS

increasingly sensitive to human suffering. The capital provided for almshouse foundations in the course of our period amounted to 13·45 per cent of the whole of the charitable wealth afforded by the age, being exceeded among the several charitable heads only by the benefactions made for outright relief (18·87 per cent) and by the great sums dedicated to the founding of schools (14·47 per cent).

There were, of course, considerable differences in the intensity of interest in almshouse foundations among the several counties.[1] Thus in Lancashire only £2122 4s was provided for almshouse foundations, this being a meagre 2·04 per cent of the whole of its charitable resources, a disinterest presumably accounted for principally by the persistent, one can almost say fanatical, devotion of its donors to the needs of education and of the reformed faith. In Hampshire, too, a remarkably low proportion (7·55 per cent) of all benefactions was dedicated to this use, largely because it was a rural county in which there was a particularly marked concern with the outright relief of the poor, to which it lent 32·27 per cent of all its charitable funds, a substantially higher fraction than that observed in any other county in England. For the rest, the proportions range within the more normally narrow limits of the 10·20 per cent to be found in Norfolk to the 25·24 per cent of all charitable wealth devoted to the founding and endowing of almshouses in Somerset.

This was indeed a momentous and a memorable achievement which charitable men had wrought with their own substance in England. We have observed that as our period began there were seventy-four surviving almshouses in the great region under study, of which almost half were in terms of performance of function derelict. In the course of our period 309 endowed foundations were made in our ten counties by private benefactors, including those mediaeval foundations which were reorganized and then adequately endowed. Moreover, donors resident in our counties had founded and endowed seventy-eight almshouses in other parts of England, while they had established as well seventy-one unendowed institutions within our group of counties. In all, then,

[1] The proportion of all charitable wealth vested in almshouse foundations in the several counties was:

	Total			Per
	£	s	d	cent
Bristol	16,677	13	0	18·12
Buckinghamshire	16,287	6	0	18·48
Hampshire	6,574	6	0	7·55
Kent	44,614	3	0	17·72
Lancashire	2,122	4	0	2·04
London	237,636	11	0	12·58
Norfolk	18,146	7	0	10·20
Somerset	29,413	13	0	25·24
Worcestershire	7,106	1	0	13·50
Yorkshire	38,836	17	0	15·94

these benefactors had permanently endowed 387 almshouses, while the seventy-one foundations without stocks, though usually ephemeral in the long range, were at least to serve the era under discussion with their fruitful and kindly works.[1]

There were wide and interesting differences in the views of founders with respect to the amount required to support an almsman with all the necessaries of life, and very frequently indeed with certain of the amenities, one is happy to say, ranging from the incredibly low average of £1 16s p.a. for Lancashire to the certainly comfortable £4 8s 7d p.a. for Buckinghamshire. London's donors, it may be observed, in average terms regarded £4 4s p.a. as a reasonable stipend for its own almspeople, while by their deeds of gift establishing an average of £3 10s 1d p.a. in the numerous almshouses founded by them in other counties. The wills and the deeds of gift for these many foundations stipulated that a total of 6389 almspeople were to enjoy full support in these establishments, a number certainly exceeded by the close of our period, as the founders' constitutions tended inevitably to be enlarged. This means, of course, that in not too meaningful average terms, endowments and institutions had been provided which secured in perpetuity the succour of rather more than two almspeople in every parish in the counties with which we are dealing. Even more impressively, it means, when we consider this immense achievement in relation to the provision made for household relief, that by the close of our period upwards of 51,000 unfortunate

[1] Analysis of almshouse foundations:

County	Number of certainly surviving mediaeval founda- tions, en- dowed and un- endowed	Number of endowed founda- tions, 1480–1660	Number endowed elsewhere by donors of the ten counties	Unen- dowed foun- dations	Alms- people to be supported	Average stipend pre- scribed		
						£	s	d
Bristol	5	9		1	160	4	5	0
Buckinghamshire	4	22		1	140	4	8	7
Hampshire	4	15			105	3	9	7
Kent	12	48		6 (?)	687	4	0	0
Lancashire	0	6	2	2	23	1	16	0
London	8	67		11	1600	4	4	0
London—for other counties			72		1100	3	10	1
Norfolk	10	35	4	6 (?)	1310	2	12	0
Somerset	6	35		11	343	3	10	9
Worcestershire	2	12		4 (?)	108	3	0	8
Yorkshire	23	60		29	813	2	7	9
Totals	74	309	78	71 (?)	6389			

beings were at all times being relieved in their homes or wholly supported by the great almshouse endowments vested by this most generous age. These donors, to quote one of them, had in truth 'wrought mightily the good works of the Lord'.

2. *Social rehabilitation*

Very closely connected with these massive outlays for poor relief were other large benefactions whose primary purpose, however, was the rehabilitation of the poor rather than their relief. These were in the main quite novel, and experimental, undertakings of men who were persuaded that poverty could never be mastered unless an attack should be made on its roots. Their gifts, then, were hopeful, were made by men prepared to take long and speculative risks to test their conviction that degrading poverty could be prevented if the ambit of opportunity were greatly enlarged, especially for the children of the poor. These donors, much of whose capital was inevitably wasted, were in fact precocious in their understanding of the true nature of the problem of poverty in the industrial society and they were opening up lines of experimentation which in the course of the next three centuries were to have most fruitful development. In the main, experimental ventures of this sort, quite untried and breaking sharply with the mediaeval conception of alms, were favoured by men accustomed to risk-taking on a large scale. It is therefore not surprising that the bulk of this capital was provided by merchant donors, though it does none the less seem quite extraordinary that almost 82 per cent of the whole amount should have been disposed by London and Bristol donors.

In the whole course of our period the substantial total of £319,446 12s was given for the various experiments in the social rehabilitation of the poor, this amounting to slightly more than a tenth (10·30 per cent) of the whole of charitable wealth. Only slight interest was displayed in such ventures in the decades prior to the Reformation, the £10,706 18s so provided amounting to only about 2 per cent (2·04 per cent) of the charities of the era, while of this total, it may be observed, almost exactly half was for the somewhat old-fashioned and sentimental purpose of marriage subsidies for poor but respectable young women.[1] But in the hopeful and boldly experimental period of the Edwardian Reformation there was an immense upsurge of interest in all sorts of measures designed to secure greater protection and opportunity for the poor, with the result that £68,589 17s was given for such uses in this short interval of two decades. During these years, in fact, somewhat more than 30 per cent of all charitable funds were designated for these uses. There was a steep falling away in this prodigious giving during the first

---

[1] *Vide* Table III and the accompanying curve (Appendix) for the particulars on which this general discussion is based.

decade of the Elizabethan age, when £17,283 4s was earmarked for
these undertakings in social betterment, but a glance at the curve
suggests that there was thereafter a steadily mounting interest in these
uses, reaching a new and a somewhat more fruitful climax in the last
decade before the outbreak of the Civil War, when £40,527 11s was
provided. In the course of the four decades comprising the early Stuart
period the very large total of £119,340 15s was given, almost wholly by
London and Bristol merchants, for various experiments, it being notable
that, marriage subsidies aside, each of the heads under which we have
gathered these charities received most substantial support. None the
less, this large sum must be set against the immense charitable outpouring of this remarkable period, it having comprised actually no
more than 8·30 per cent of the whole amount, a sharply lower proportion than that (14·83 per cent) observed in the Elizabethan era. The
total of benefactions for the several types of experiments dedicated to
social rehabilitation fell away only slightly during the revolutionary era,
the £54,707 7s given for these uses in this short interval amounting to
11·72 per cent of the whole sum given for all charitable uses. In fact,
it may be said that these bold and often fruitful undertakings, ventures
as it were with risk capital dedicated to worthy social ends, appealed
greatly to merchants and most particularly to merchants of staunch
Puritan persuasion.

Since the dominant interest in the various schemes for social rehabilitation was almost uniquely a burgher phenomenon, we shall reserve
full discussion of this most significant social development to our comment on the huge investment which London made in these undertakings.[1] We shall now, accordingly, content ourselves with relatively
brief and sparse statistical notes on the six heads under which a bewildering variety of bold and vigorous schemes has been grouped.

There was throughout our period a steadily growing concern with the
plight of prisoners, and more particularly prisoners for debt. It should
be recalled that prior to the Elizabethan period there were few prisons,
the principal places of detention being the common gaols, of which
there were perhaps as many as two hundred operated by diverse municipal or county authorities. They were mainly operated for profit, the
gaoler gaining his livelihood from fees exacted for all services and for
food beyond the 'county bread' which an Elizabethan statute at least
required for the care of convicted felons.[2] Conditions in local prisons,
as well as in the great London prisons which were reconstituted by
Elizabeth, were barbarous beyond description, suffering, starvation,
filth, and disease being chronic in all of them.[3] These conditions began

---

[1] In the second volume of this study.   [2] *14 Eliz., c. 5.*
[3] This situation will be discussed in some detail in the second volume of this
study.

in about 1560 to trouble the conscience of many men, most particularly because of the hopeless situation of hundreds of men imprisoned for debt, who if they could procure no help from family or friends were in a truly helpless condition. Merchants and tradesmen who were accustomed to speculative risks, and who were themselves from time to time in danger from their creditors, viewed this social need with a keen interest, seeking by their endowments to provide means by which respectable men imprisoned for small debts could be released and rehabilitated.

During the whole of our period the considerable sum of £38,967 13s was disposed for the relief of prisoners, this amounting to 1·26 per cent of the total of England's charitable wealth. It is most interesting to note that of this total the merchants of London and Bristol contributed the incredibly large proportion of 91 per cent (91·39 per cent), nearly the whole of which was in capital sums. Concern for the sufferings of prisoners was by no means wholly lacking even in the late mediaeval decades, £2099 6s having been given for this use prior to 1540, in the main for outright distributions to needy prisoners of all sorts. The concern of donors during the Reformation decades was also relatively slight, no more than £1209 15s having been contributed and again largely as outright largess. But a greatly heightened interest in the fate of prisoners for debt set in quite precisely at 1560, gathering momentum with every decade in the course of the next two generations. During the Elizabethan age the substantial total of £9222 9s, almost all being endowment, was vested for the relief and rehabilitation of prisoners, while in the course of the early Stuart era really large totals are noted in each decade, with a capital accumulation for the four decades of £19,846 17s for this wholly worthy purpose. There was widespread and vociferous interest in prison reform and in the amendment of the law relating to imprisonment for debt throughout the revolutionary years,[1] which was doubtless reflected in the large total of £5149 17s given by donors in the decade of the Civil War and in the very modest sum of £1439 9s provided in the decade of the Protectorate, when substantial reforms were carried through.

In all, upwards of £28,000 of the amount given by benefactors of our period for the relief of prisoners was in the form of endowments, thereby providing a superbly charitable income principally employed to secure the return of small debtors to their families and to useful and self-sustaining lives. Since the terms of the deeds of gifts vary in a most bewildering fashion, even when they are precise at all, it is not possible to suggest quantitatively the measure of the relief and the social good which flowed from an annual income of somewhat more than

[1] Niehaus, C. R., *The issue of law reform in the Puritan Revolution* (Harvard University, unpublished doctoral thesis, 1957), 100–105, 195–196, 222–223.

£1400 available to trustees for these uses. In general, donors instructed their trustees to use income for the redemption of prisoners for debts and charges in the range of from £2 to £5, and so one would suppose that at the very least as many as three to five hundred persons each year regained their franchise as respectable artisans and lesser tradesmen as a consequence of the sensitive response of many donors to one of the shocking ills of the age.

Much larger capital amounts (77·54 per cent) were vested, again principally by urban donors, for the creation of loan funds wherewith respectable poor men might on sufficient surety borrow at no, or at a nominal, interest rate, or, more commonly, from which young men who had completed their apprenticeships and who possessed no resources of their own, might secure the capital required as they began their callings as tradesmen, artisans, or merchants. During the years under study the massive total of £63,242 11s was provided by benefactors as capital for this worthy purpose. This large accumulation of risk capital was principally made for the benefit of worthy young men of London, £43,942 1s having been so designated. But it is most significant that considerable sums were likewise gathered in all save one of our counties, ranging from the £290 available in Hampshire to the £6833 1s which Norfolk afforded, principally, it might be noted, as a consequence of the generosity of Norwich merchants.[1]

These loan funds, all being capital, were an invention of our age, being increasingly favoured as instrumentalities of social rehabilitation as benefactors observed the immense social good, and the very few defaults, resulting as such capital was accumulated. We have noted no such endowment in the first decade of our period, but a beginning was made in the next, and relatively modest amounts were provided in the remaining decades of the period prior to the Reformation, with the result that a total of £2189 2s of this capital was available and at work by 1540. Substantially more was dedicated to this use during the two decades of the Reformation, while in the first years of the Elizabethan era the

[1] The amounts available for loans in the several counties, with the proportion as it relates to the total of charitable funds:

	Loan capital			Per cent of total charities
	£	s	d	
Bristol	5,118	0	0	5·56
Buckinghamshire	—			—
Hampshire	290	0	0	0·33
Kent	894	15	0	0·36
Lancashire	666	0	0	0·64
London	43,942	1	0	2·33
Norfolk	6,833	1	0	3·84
Somerset	877	0	0	0·75
Worcestershire	1,820	0	0	3·46
Yorkshire	2,801	14	0	1·15

impressive total of £10,967 was vested for the purpose. Very large amounts were in fact given in each of the Elizabethan decades, with the result that the total of £24,737 8s accumulated during these years slightly exceeded the amount to be provided in the early Stuart interval. The intense interest in this agency of social rehabilitation was well maintained during the revolutionary era, £9803 4s more of capital having been made available as an addition to the now large stock of loan moneys.

It should be emphasized that this substantial capital stock of £63,242 11s, representing as it did 2·04 per cent of the whole of charitable funds, was available under usually carefully ordered, but always generous, provisions, as capital in needed amounts for young men with no resources of their own who were of good character and who had by apprenticeship gained the requisite skills for the pursuit of their calling. It should be noted as well that this capital had been given wholly for this purpose, under the deeds of gift bearing either no interest for the period of the loan or at the most an uneconomic interest charge. These funds were established with a quite bewildering variety of conditions, but it may at least be said that donors seem generally to have agreed that a young man beginning his trading as a merchant in London required a capital stock of about £70, and a little more than £40 in the provincial cities, while something like £30 was thought to be the requirement for a young tradesman about to open his doors. Disregarding the amounts left specifically as emergency loans for the true poor, therefore, we may with some certainty assume that by the close of our period capital was freely available wherewith at the very least 800 to 1000 aspiring young men could be and were launched on trading careers. Our own reading of literally hundreds of wills in which merchants testify to the great good accomplished by these loan funds, as well as the clear evidence that very little of this capital was lost, attest the enormous social and economic value of this instrumentality of social rehabilitation. Nor was this all that had been made available for this general purpose. We have included under the heading of *The Poor* upwards of £29,000 of additional capital which the donors specified was to be lent to worthy but needy tradesmen on which, however, an economic interest rate was to be levied for distribution as poor relief. Great and viable resources had been established in an age of limited credit, no banking facilities, and harsh competitive trade for the benefit of young men who thereby escaped from the grip of poverty and who became not only men of responsible substance but almost invariably generous charitable donors in their own turn.[1]

Closely related in purpose and sentiment to the loan funds were the apprenticeship endowments established principally in the second half of

[1] These loan funds will be discussed much more fully in Volume II, since they were so classically a London invention.

our period. The rapid accumulation of these stocks after about 1590 was organically linked, it seems evident, with the development of social thinking and legislation on the whole matter. The system of apprenticeships had remained a voluntary guild instrumentality until by statute law in 1562 a period of seven years of service was established as the minimum for learning any craft or trade. The legislation was inspired in part by a resolution to raise the standards of industrial and commercial production and in part to bring still more force to bear in the general attack being made on the problem of poverty.[1] It was thought, too, that vagrancy might thereby be to a degree prevented, since justices of the peace were fully empowered to bind any unemployed or resourceless minor to any person qualified by law to accept an apprentice in trade or in husbandry, while in 1601 these local officials were vested with authority to bind at their own discretion the children of paupers, vagrants, or families overburdened with children. The legislation provided no really adequate machinery for administration, though in the towns and cities the existing companies undertook a fairly tight and efficient enforcement. In the rural areas enforcement was placed in the already tired hands of the justices of the peace, who, our evidence would most strongly suggest, did very little in applying the law until the zealous policy of the Privy Council prodded them into a reluctant activity in the reign of Charles I. The great weakness of the system as so rigorously prescribed by law lay in the unskilled trades and crafts where there were few traditions, low standards of workmanship, and no corporate bodies competent either to administer the training or to protect apprenticed children from exploitation masquerading in the guise of training.

In total, the benefactors of our counties provided the relatively modest sum of £38,729 6s for the support of apprenticeship schemes, this being 1·25 per cent of the whole of the charitable resources of our period, and approximately the amount, it may be observed, given for the amelioration of the lot of prisoners. Some small proportion of this sum was given outright for the binding of individual boys or girls, but a very large proportion indeed (98·18 per cent) was vested in the form of endowments. These endowments were of two kinds. By far the larger sum, amounting to more than three-fourths of the whole, was disposed to secure the binding of poor boys in recognized and named companies under the traditional requirements of these societies, while the lesser sum was vested, usually in parishes, simply to secure the binding of boys and girls to responsible persons who would provide them with some measure of training in domestic, craft, or agricultural skills. Though it is not possible to establish exact data, because of alternative choices frequently permitted by donors to their trustees, we can say that considerably more than half of the whole amount dedicated to

[2] Dunlop, O. J., *English apprenticeship* (L., 1912), 60–65.

apprenticeships was so disposed that likely boys from all parts of the realm might be admitted and sustained during the period of their apprenticeship in the various London companies, a training which, very properly, was highly regarded indeed and which opened wide the doors of opportunity for able and ambitious youths.

As a glance at the relevant table[1] will suggest, there was almost no interest displayed by donors in apprenticeship endowments prior to 1560 and only modest interest prior to 1590. The total of funds in hand for this use in the earlier years amounted to no more than £528 14s. But the last decade of the Elizabethan era witnessed a very sharp, a dramatic, rise in the intensity of concern with this mechanism of social rehabilitation, the substantial capital of £2683 being so disposed in these years. Somewhat lesser contributions were made during the first two decades of the early Stuart period, while enthusiasm for this charitable use mounted markedly during the years just prior to the Civil War (1621–1640), when a total of almost £12,000 of these funds was vested. Interest in these endowments reached its climax during the unsettled period of the Puritan Revolution when, despite most adverse political and economic conditions, the substantial total of £19,907 6s was disposed for a great many apprenticeship endowments, amounting to rather more than half of the whole capital provided for this use during our entire period. In part, of course, this does exhibit the Puritan persuasion that self-help was more salutary than outright relief of the poor, but the evidence of the many wills in which these sums were disposed makes it clear that these merchants were more often moved by the striking proof of the immensely useful work carried forward by such endowments over the period of their own lifetimes.

It is remarkable as we review the data more closely that over our period as a whole London donors remained relatively indifferent to these apprenticeship plans.[2] It is true that the £19,587 18s vested by

---

[1] *Vide* Table III (Appendix).

[2] The amounts and proportions given for apprenticeship endowments in the several counties are:

	Total			Per
	£	s	d	cent
Bristol	1,880	0	0	2·04
Buckinghamshire	855	0	0	0·97
Hampshire	1,733	6	0	1·99
Kent	3,580	0	0	1·42
Lancashire	854	6	0	0·82
London	19,587	18	0	1·04
Norfolk	4,984	0	0	2·80
Somerset	509	3	0	0·44
Worcestershire	666	10	0	1·27
Yorkshire	4,079	3	0	1·67
	38,729	6	0	1·25

London donors for this use amounted to slightly more than half the total, but in proportionate terms London gave considerably less than did donors in numerous rural counties. Much of London's generosity is included in the totals of other counties, but it remains true that as merchant benefactors looked back on their own careers, and most of them had come up from the provinces, they tended to assess as socially more valuable such charitable outlays as loan funds or education. This somewhat sceptical attitude prevailed among the group who were to exercise a dominant role in fashioning the structure of social institutions in England until, as we have suggested, the very close of our period when, having been persuaded of the good works done by these endowments, London began to vest large amounts for this worthy cause.

Though there are many variables, it is possible to say that in average terms a London benefactor took the view that about £4 15s was a sufficient stipend to secure the binding of an apprentice, while in the provinces £3 10s was regarded as a reasonable amount. In all, then, by the close of our period the income available from apprenticeship endowments was probably sufficient to secure training for a constant flow of something like 475 youths a year, drawn from a social and economic background in which there was no hope and transposed to an environment in which not only a livelihood in an honest calling but very great rewards indeed were opened up to aspiring youths. A most useful and demonstrably successful mechanism of social rehabilitation had been well advanced by the close of our period.

London donors likewise remained sceptical, in this case throughout our period, of the many schemes attempted in England, under the hortatory prodding of law and sermons, to provide work for the poor either in formally constituted workhouses or on stocks of goods distributed to cottage labourers. The first large-scale undertaking of this sort is to be observed at Bridewell, organized in London in the mid-sixteenth century, for the dual purpose of offering remunerative employment and subjecting sturdy vagabonds to the curative discipline of honest labour.[1] Houses of correction were enjoined by the statute of 1576, to be set up on the model of Bridewell, and it has been estimated that as many as two hundred were so founded, usually for short terms and at public charge.[2] For some little time there appeared to be a measure of hope in these institutions, but they gradually lost their essentially charitable purpose and well before the close of our period had become little more than places of detention and enforced labour for vagabonds and other rootless persons.

[1] The history of this important institution will be fully dealt with in the second volume of this study.

[2] Webb, Sidney and Beatrice, *English prisons under local government* (L., 1922), 12–13.

Consequently, a differentiation in purpose so far as charitable funds were concerned became clearly established early in the seventeenth century under which private donors lent their support to more carefully designed and disciplined workhouses, where the reputable unemployed could find gainful employment at simple but useful tasks, or gave money to schemes for carrying out such work in the homes of the poor. Few of these plans succeeded, or remained solvent, for more than a few years. The mercantile élite were persistently and correctly sceptical since they understood, as projectors and the Privy Council did not, that greater skill and training were required for such operations than could possibly be provided if they were to be self-supporting and, as witness a particularly persuasive example financed in Reading by London generosity,[1] they would bankrupt competitive private undertakings if they were in fact well organized. These practical difficulties and objections are well set out in a report made to an insistent Privy Council by the Deputy Lieutenants of Hertfordshire in 1620 on the effort made to establish 'the trade of the new drapery' in that depressed area. They had found it impossible to raise funds from the substantial men of the community in order to launch the undertaking, because of discouragement at the failure of a similar scheme in Hatfield not many years before where '£100 a year has been spent, yet few are instructed in the trade and the burdens of the poor there much increased'. In eight towns they had compelled contributions and a trial was made with the aid of a projector who offered assurances that the necessary skills could be learned in two or three weeks. The skills were in fact not mastered in twenty weeks, the poor could not earn enough for their own subsistence, and the whole community regarded this valiant effort as a failure.[2]

This brief discussion of an exceedingly complex subject, more fully dealt with in the counties, may at least have set out the principal reasons why workhouses and stocks for the poor failed to elicit substantial charitable support. In the whole course of our period £29,869 15s was vested for such uses, this amounting to no more than 0·96 per cent of the whole of English charitable wealth. Nothing at all was provided for this purpose in the decades prior to the Reformation, while it was 1570 before as much as £591 13s of capital had been accumulated. An earnest trial was made of what so evidently appealed in a most beguiling fashion to unpractical men in the decade 1581–1590, when the substantial sum of £3649 13s was disposed for these purposes. The results, as we have seen, were most discouraging, with the consequence that the total of such benefactions ranged in decade terms between the modest sums of £866 13s and £2144 for the next generation. The Privy Council brought intensive pressure to bear for another trial in the period

[1] This instance will be dealt with fully in the second volume of this study.
[2] *S.P. Dom.*, 1620, CXV, 13.

of Archbishop Laud's dominance, and the impressive total of £8455 10s was disposed for these uses in the last decade before the outbreak of the Civil War. The results, it may categorically be said, were unimpressive, but none the less the whole conception of self-help for industrious though unemployed men was to make a strong appeal to the Puritan mind and to the innumerable projectors who wrote during the period of its dominance. Consequently, another large charitable investment was made in these schemes during the decade of the Civil War, when £6730 9s was given for their support, with, however, a most precipitous decline of interest in the final decade when the £1287 so disposed reflects the ultimate discouragement of men with this appealing but wholly impractical form of social rehabilitation.

If London wealth remained stubbornly sceptical of the social benefits to be derived from workhouse schemes, it had no doubts whatever regarding the humane necessity of providing adequately, indeed generously, for the care of the sick. The mediaeval hospitals had offered some measure of relief for the helplessly ill, the craft guilds rather more, but with the opening of the sixteenth century there was practically no organized system of succour available for the treatment of illness, which was of course the handmaiden of poverty.[1] This shocking situation was eloquently denounced by the great Edwardian preachers and the civic conscience of London was aroused to carry through the organization and endowment of the immensely effective royal hospitals, which were not only to save the rapidly growing city from almost predictable social disaster but to establish models which the rest of England, and, for that matter, the western world was to follow.

In the course of our period the enormous total of £135,346 12s was provided for the support of hospitals or for the care of the sick in pesthouses or in their own homes. This great sum accounts for 4·36 per cent of all the charitable wealth accumulated in England. Though no county was wholly barren of such benefactions, it remains true that the warm and the sustained interest of London's donors in this charitable use accounts for the incredibly high proportion of 96·69 per cent of the whole sum.[2] Accordingly, we shall reserve detailed treatment of this extraordinarily interesting and important achievement of the age to our discussion in a later volume of London's charitable contribution, contenting ourselves here with a few generalized observations.

The all too evident needs of the sick and the ruinous connection of illness with poverty were by no means ignored in the long interval prior to the Edwardian Reformation, but men's instincts to be helpful were chilled and frustrated by the want of institutional agencies through

---

[1] Levy, Hermann, 'Economic history of sickness', *Econ. Hist. Rev.*, XIII (1943), 42–57, and XIV (1944), 135–160.
[2] See table on next page.

which their benefactions could be rendered socially useful. Thus in the first seven decades of our period the not insubstantial total of £1608 11s was provided, principally in London, for direct assistance to the sick in their own households, for pesthouses, or as stipends for physicians who would undertake the care of the deserving sick in specified parishes. The towering climax came in the following decade, 1551–1560, when the great London hospitals were founded, the enormous total of £61,428 19s having been given for their support and initial endowment. Though this great achievement dominates our whole period, it should be pointed out that the substantial sum of £4064 19s, almost the whole of which was endowment, was provided for the needs of the sick in the first Elizabethan decade, and that with the exception of one decade, the amounts disposed for the humane care of sick men rose steadily from interval to interval to reach a secondary peak of generosity in the decade just prior to the outbreak of the Civil War, when the substantial total of £12,511 12s was given, principally again by London generosity.[1]

The amount and the proportion designated for hospitals and other care for the sick was as follows for the several counties:

	Total £ s d			Per cent
Bristol	5	0	0	0·005
Buckinghamshire	320	0	0	0·36
Hampshire	171	10	0	0·20
Kent	1,994	1	0	0·79
Lancashire	30	0	0	0·03
London	130,872	17	0	6·93
Norfolk	740	4	0	0·42
Somerset	716	13	0	0·61
Worcestershire	100	0	0	0·19
Yorkshire	396	7	0	0·16
	135,346	12	0	4·36

[1]   GIFTS FOR HOSPITALS AND CARE OF THE SICK

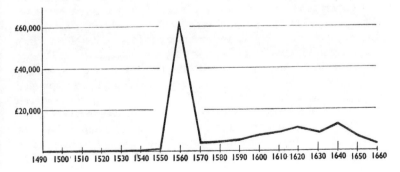

From 1560 onwards, the tradition was well established that every London merchant of substance left at least something to one or more of the London hospitals. While there were relatively few massive gifts, the accumulation of these bequests of from £10 to £100 was to bring most impressive and well-sustained resources to bear on the formidable task of providing medical care and sanctuary for the poor and securing their social as well as their economic rehabilitation once their cure had been gained.

Finally, in discussing the various agencies of social rehabilitation with which this confident and generous age experimented, we should comment at least briefly on what is statistically the least important. These were the various arrangements under which marriage subsidies were provided for poor but deserving young women, and rather rarely young men, who could bring no portion to the new household which they and the society wished to create. In total, only £13,290 15s was given for this interesting, if sentimental, use which in almost every particular refuses to conform to any sensible statistical pattern. This, perhaps, is what makes this relatively unimportant charitable head worth some comment. For one thing, these amounts were in four counties wholly given as direct gifts for immediate use by the recipients, while in two counties (Buckinghamshire and Kent) they were in large part vested as endowments. In three rural counties only trifling amounts were provided for this charitable use, while in two they had some real significance in the structure of charitable institutions. They tended to be established by sentimental gentry and their wives, yet by far the largest was endowed by a London merchant, and a bachelor at that, for the benefit of Welsh maidens, the difficulties of administration of which led his harassed company, which had been named trustee, to plead with intended benefactors 'never to leave portions to marriageable maidens, especially if they be Welsh'. Finally, this charitable use is remarkable for the fact that the curve of interest in it, while never significantly high, remains more nearly level than that for any other single charitable head. Thus £122 13s was given for this purpose in the first decade of our period, £65 in the last. It is true that there was a slight peak of interest in the decade 1531-1540 when the substantial total of £3559 10s was given for marriage portions, to be followed by a singularly level intensity of interest for almost a century until £2050 was given in the years just prior to the Civil War. But this scarcely affects the structure of giving for this use, which simply appealed through the years to a relatively small number of donors of all sorts, all classes, and all degrees of wealth. It is pleasant, indeed, to reflect on the persistence of this sentimental, yet doubtless useful trend of giving for still another outlay designed to assist in the social rehabilitation of young people.

3. *Municipal betterments*

A large and most diverse group of benefactions has been included under the several heads which we have gathered under the covering title of *Municipal Betterments*. The general nature of these gifts for essentially public uses has been previously discussed,[1] and we shall, of course, deal in some detail with this bewildering variety of useful benefactions in our treatment of the several counties. Broadly speaking, most of the gifts made for municipal improvements in our period were designed to strengthen and better the physical fabric of community life by lending support in areas which today, and long since, have been regarded as the province of government. One tends to forget how narrowly sovereignty defined the frontiers of its responsibility in this earlier age, how much it left to the discretion and generosity of private men.

In the whole course of our period private benefactions totalling £160,776 1s, or 5·18 per cent of the charitable funds of the age, were given by donors for municipal betterments. While not a great sum, amounting, for example, to not much more than was provided for the care of the sick and hospitals, it none the less represents a most substantial addition to the fabric of the community and was sufficient to add considerably to the amenities of life in the towns and countryside of the realm. It is remarkable, too, that though there were shifts from one sphere of interest to another, the curve of giving for this general purpose was on the whole steady and level throughout our long period.[2] The range of benefactions for this use by decade intervals extends from £4130 8s (1511–1520) to £24,178 14s (1611–1620). In the more meaningful terms of the proportion of funds given in each of our great intervals for municipal improvements, the spread is much narrower, extending from the 4 per cent so disposed in the early Stuart period to the 7·57 per cent given for such uses in the Elizabethan era.

It should be noted, however, that when we turn to the data for the several counties, considerable and interesting differences appear in the degree of intensity with which men addressed themselves to these municipal tasks.[3] Thus in counties like Lancashire, Somerset, and Yorkshire relatively little could be spared from the more urgent charitable concerns of the age for the amenities of community life. London donors also gave only modestly to municipal betterments, in this case undoubtedly because the city had made considerable progress in employing the taxing power for so many of the uses comprehended under this general head. In Bristol, on the contrary, the very high proportion

---

[1] *Vide ante*, 46–48.

[2] *Vide* Table IV (Appendix) and accompanying curve.

[3] *Vide* table on next page.

of 9·10 per cent of all charitable benefactions was disposed for municipal improvements by merchants who went far towards providing the city with its essential services before our era was ended. In Norfolk a slightly higher proportion of funds was given for these uses, principally by Norwich merchants who were likewise changing the physical aspect of their city while creating its social institutions.

Throughout our period remarkably sustained interest was exhibited by benefactors in the *general uses* of their communities: the building of town halls, the provision of corporate plate, endowments to secure the lessening of tax burdens, and a great variety of other gifts designed to make divers communities more attractive and agreeable places in which to work and live. In all save three decades, more than £1000 was given for such purposes, while the respectable total of £45,399 6s represents 1·47 per cent of the whole of the charitable funds of our age. The climax of interest in this particular need was, interestingly enough, attained in the decade of the Civil War, when the impressive total of £7299 was provided, with an earlier climax in the last decade of the Elizabethan interval, when £5652 16s was given for such uses. There were most striking differences in the degree of concern for these general municipal uses in the several counties, London, for example, devoting only a fraction of 1 per cent to such purposes, and Lancashire and Somerset no more than trifling amounts. In point of fact, this particular interest was very highly concentrated in Hampshire and Norfolk, which together supplied very nearly half the total for our whole group of counties.[1]

As we should expect, a large proportion of the considerable sums accumulated by the various companies and other trading societies under deeds of trust for their own or the public benefit was given by London donors for the uses of the great London livery companies. In all, the

Proportion of total charitable wealth disposed for municipal betterments in the several counties:

	Amount			Per
	£	s	d	cent
Bristol	8,378	5	0	9·10
Buckinghamshire	7,757	19	0	8·80
Hampshire	9,511	6	0	10·92
Kent	11,558	15	0	4·59
Lancashire	1,265	10	0	1·22
London	93,593	16	0	4·95
Norfolk	18,820	15	0	10·58
Somerset	905	15	0	0·78
Worcestershire	2,862	9	0	5·44
Yorkshire	6,121	11	0	2·51
	160,776	1	0	5·18

[1] See table on next page.

substantial total of £60,656 14s was provided by merchants and tradesmen explicitly for their companies, this amounting to almost 2 per cent
(1·95 per cent) of all the charitable wealth accumulated during our
period. Broadly speaking, we observe a steadily mounting interest in
such benefactions from the first decade of our period, in which £554 13s
was provided for this use, to the point of climax of such generosity in
the decade just prior to the outbreak of the Civil War, when the
impressive total of £9037 4s was provided. But even in the years prior
to the Reformation a total of £8945 10s had been given as endowments
for company uses, a rate of giving well sustained during the years of the
Reformation, when £3450 4s was given by benefactors, almost wholly
of London. Really substantial sums were accumulated by the companies during each decade of the Elizabethan era, £11,933 1s having
been so disposed over the four decades, while in the early Stuart
interval such gifts mounted steadily and rapidly to a total of £28,509 12s
for these years. There was, inevitably, a sharp diminution of such gifts
during the decade of the Civil War, but once political and commercial
conditions had been rendered more stable, such benefactions began to
rise rapidly again, with the result that the substantial sum of £5390 8s
was given in the closing decade of our period.

As has been noted,[1] all these benefactions were vested in the companies either for their own use—for the upkeep of their halls, for their
dinners and other ceremonial occasions, or for the carrying forward of
their own charities—or as owners in the public interest. These were
sums absolutely vested in the companies, which, as we shall point
out in detail in our discussion of London, were as well trustees for
immense capital which they administered for a great range of charitable
causes. This rapidly growing wealth undoubtedly expressed the understanding of donors that the livery companies had come to possess, well

The proportion of all charitable funds disposed for general municipal uses
in the several counties:

	Total £	s	d	Per cent
Bristol	3,955	0	0	4·30
Buckinghamshire	2,742	0	0	3·11
Hampshire	6,992	11	0	8·03
Kent	2,448	10	0	0·97
Lancashire	264	5	0	0·25
London	9,424	7	0	0·50
Norfolk	15,032	18	0	8·45
Somerset	321	6	0	0·28
Worcestershire	1,895	17	0	3·60
Yorkshire	2,322	12	0	0·95
	45,399	6	0	1·47

[1] Vide ante, 47.

before our period had closed, a semi-public status, and it certainly testifies to the immense prestige which they had attained as skilful and responsible trustees of huge aggregates of charitable capital held in the public interest. Inevitably, therefore, London merchant donors tended to make most generous provision for their own companies and very frequently for all the livery companies, with the result that giving for this charitable use was heavily concentrated in London. In all, London donors gave the large total of £56,511 1s for this purpose, or rather more than 93·17 per cent of the whole.

Still another considerable amount was accumulated in the course of our period for a great variety of purposes best described as public works, at least principally listed in earlier pages.[1] All these contributions for roads, bridges, harbours, streets, and the rest were in areas of need for which the state had as yet assumed only slight responsibility and which the church had declared to be proper objects for mediaeval piety.[2] In the course of our period the impressive total of £54,418 19s was disposed by private donors for public works of a most complex variety, though it should be noted that well over half (56·81 per cent) of the whole amount was for the building or the maintenance of roads which were not only generally in an incredibly poor state of repair but which were most severely retarding the commercial and industrial development of the nation. The whole sum given for this purpose was an aggregate of charitable giving of some thousands of donors, small bequests, particularly for highways, having by 1580 become traditional among all classes of substantial men in certain of the rural counties.

The support of public works by private donors was steadily maintained throughout our long period, the amount provided falling below £1000 in only one decade (1601-1610). In the years prior to the Reformation the substantial total of £14,207 14s was given by donors for the carrying forward of public works, a very large proportion of all the funds designated for municipal betterments having been given for this use. Almost half as much (£7013 7s) was provided for public improvements during the short interval of the Reformation, while there was a most noticeable and somewhat inexplicable lessening of interest in these needs during the Elizabethan age, when only £9347 12s was given. Substantial contribution to the bettering of public works was made in all save one of the four decades of the early Stuart interval, a total of £19,811 14s having been provided for the purpose, while in the period of the Puritan Revolution such benefactions fell away quite steeply, the total of contributions for these years having been £4038 12s.

When, however, we turn to the individual counties this record of

---

[1] *Vide ante*, 47-48.
[2] Wilkinson, T. W., *From track to by-pass* (L., 1934), 25, 31-32.

remarkably level interest in public works by no means appears.[1] In the rural counties of Buckinghamshire and Kent quite substantial proportions of all charitable wealth were given for the improvement of highways, while in Bristol £4349 18s, or 4·73 per cent of the whole, was designated for such needed purposes as building and clearing streets, bettering the water supply, and for the improvement of the harbour and docking facilities of that proud and aggressive city. London, while contributing slightly more than half of the total, none the less in the more significant terms of proportions lent a rather grudging and cautious support to such outlays which tended in any case to be fairly satisfactorily provided by the public authority. Donors in certain other rural counties, such as Hampshire, Somerset, and Lancashire, where the roads were notoriously bad, may well have felt that substantial improvements lay beyond the resources of private charity, for only modest proportions of their charitable wealth were assigned to the bettering of public facilities.

4. Education

English culture was at once moulded and transformed by the vast extension of educational opportunity which took place in the course of our period. This metamorphosis, revolutionary in its nature, was almost wholly the consequence of the sustained, the almost obsessive, determination of private donors to help able and aspiring children, however poor, and to open avenues for their educational progress extending from remote rural schools to and through the universities. It is not too much to say that private charity in the years under study literally founded a system of secular education in England, which at the close of our period was at once more competent and comprehensive than the nation was to possess again until deep in the nineteenth century. Men of our period were earnestly persuaded of the virtue and the necessity of education

---

[1] The proportion of total charitable wealth disposed in the several counties for public works was as follows:

	Amount			Per cent
	£	s	d	
Bristol	4,349	18	0	4·73
Buckinghamshire	5,015	19	0	5·69
Hampshire	217	2	0	0·25
Kent	7,936	15	0	3·15
Lancashire	1,001	5	0	0·96
London	27,604	8	0	1·46
Norfolk	3,282	13	0	1·85
Somerset	553	9	0	0·47
Worcestershire	944	19	0	1·79
Yorkshire	3,512	11	0	1·44
	54,418	19	0	1·75

and were prepared to spend heavily of their own fortunes in order to bring the requisite resources into being.

This preoccupation with the founding of a national system of education may be said to extend through the whole of our period, though it is of great importance to note that it was transformed and then made immensely stronger shortly after the full effects of the Reformation came into play. In general terms, the great donors prior to 1540 were rich and usually worldly prelates, quite as much princes of the state as of the church, who gave generously of their wealth for the strengthening of the universities, which in 1480 were by any standard of appraisal in a state of shocking decay. Then abruptly with the Reformation the whole emphasis swung to the foundation and endowment of grammar-school education, almost the whole of the burden being assumed by the mercantile aristocracy and the gentry, men whose aspirations were vigorously secular and who took most elaborate pains to vest their incorporations in lay hands. While still in the process of forming, and in their view completing, the structure of secondary education, these men, or their sons, began linking the schools which they had founded to the universities by rich and elaborate scholarship endowments and then moved to strengthen and revivify the universities themselves by the founding of new colleges and the augmentation of the meagre university endowments gathered as a consequence of mediaeval piety. The flow of gifts from these donors did not set in in full tide until there was assurance that the universities were safely and soundly Protestant, and then great and well-conceived benefactions, invariably carefully ordered, played a probably decisive role in the revolutionary process which brought about the secularization of the universities. We must recall that in the age of Henry VIII the university curriculum, and the whole environment, was regarded as neither appropriate nor quite respectable for the son of a squire or a merchant unless malevolent fate had disposed him towards the priesthood, while by the close of the Elizabethan era a very large proportion even of members of the House of Commons had at least been matriculated in the universities.

Our period was, then, deeply persuaded of the virtues and necessity of education, education for youth of all classes who wished it and who possessed the native ability to pursue a curriculum of considerable academic rigour. This persuasion was most firmly held by the mercantile élite, whose devotion to the cause of education for a period of about sixty years may with reasonable accuracy be described as fanatical. Though it is exceedingly difficult to assess any such great and complex cultural movement, the eloquent and we may believe wholly honest expression of purpose to be found in many hundreds of deeds of gift and wills establishing schools, setting up scholarship funds, or adding some further measure of strength to the universities do reveal the prime forces which moved men of this period to bring to fair completion a noble and an enduring work.

Above all, these benefactors believed that the enlargement of educational opportunity was the most effective instrumentality which the society could contrive in the endless and grim war it was waging on poverty. Poverty, hopeless poverty, they sensed was bred in ignorance, and it was ignorance against which their great endowments were set. To these men, then, the founding of a free school was inspired by motives not dissimilar to those which could as easily have led to the creation of an apprenticeship scheme or a loan fund to assist young merchants. It was an instrument of social rehabilitation which they were creating with their great generosity. They were determined that no boy with native ability infused with ambition should be denied opportunity and they sensed, certainly correctly, that education alone could break the shackles which bound whole classes of men. The testimony to this impulse, to this intention, is often moving and as often intensely personal. Thus scores of London merchants of humble provincial birth, who had won great wealth, when they came to set their worldly affairs in order, bethought themselves of the poverty and ignorance which had all but overwhelmed them. This explains, as they themselves so frequently confessed, why so many of them ordered the founding of a free school or a great scholarship fund in the home parish with which they had had few if any ties for a full generation. They remembered their own youthful hardships, the narrowness of the margin of their own emancipation, as they set out in poignant personal terms the motives which impelled them to make their foundation, sometimes quite unwisely, in that particular parish, as if to ensure for ever opportunity for boys not unlike themselves in this remembered corner of England. These were very human men, men not unlike ourselves, and they were good men, for the title of goodness is not weakened by the fact of sentimentality.

These great benefactors testify as well to a second important and exceedingly complex moving force as they created their endowments for the widening of educational opportunity. They were Protestants, and they were for the most part evangelical Calvinists of Puritan persuasion. They designed these foundations, whether a grammar school in Yorkshire or Emmanuel College, to assist in bringing about the Kingdom of God on earth and to levy holy warfare against the ignorance from which they so ardently believed popery specifically and untruth generally sprang. They believed confidently, if naïvely, that if all men were endowed with ability to read and to ponder the Word of God, not only would one truth, one transcendent truth, prevail, but that it would be the pure and complete truth not long since preached in Geneva. They were determined to bring about this miracle, which while it bred more sects than it united, which while it failed to evoke universal truth, was in due time to secure universal literacy. The depth of the passion of these men as they contemplated the good that must flow from vastly broadening the ambit of educational opportunity is very great and must be credited with absolute sincerity. Their aspirations were clear, firmly stated, and sufficient to move them to noble and immensely effective action. These men wished a learned clergy: in a half-century the institutions which they had founded had created one. They were appalled by lingering popery in the fastnesses of Lancashire and the West Riding, which they largely rooted out by the founding of grammar schools, scholarships, and lectureships, with the result that both regions, it may almost be said, moved from Rome to nonconformity without ever having been truly Anglican at all. These donors, most of whom were London merchants, knew precisely what they wanted, and they possessed the wealth and the firmness of resolution to implement their most formidable intentions. They were in many ways naïve, they narrowly failed in their determination to win England for Geneva, they doubtless overestimated the pragmatic benefits of education, but they none the less shaped the whole cultural development of the western world and set that development along lines which we even now pursue. These were men who wrought mightily.

The donors of our age brought immense resources to bear as they sought to attain the ends to which their aspirations were dedicated with such warm and persistent intensity. Thus in the course of our period the vast total of £833,493 12s was disposed for the several educational purposes, this amounting to nearly 27 per cent (26·86 per cent) of the whole of the charitable resources accumulated during the years under examination. Not only was this capital much larger than that devoted to the great purposes of social rehabilitation and municipal betterments combined, but it was also greatly in excess of the amount given for all religious purposes during the whole of our period. It was exceeded, and that very considerably, only by the huge sums mustered for the direct relief of poverty, the prevention of which, as we have seen, at least in part evoked these great educational endowments.

Benefactions for educational purposes commanded almost a fourth of all philanthropic funds even in the decades prior to the Reformation. During these six decades a total of £131,170 5s was given for such uses, or somewhat less than half the huge sum provided in these years for the needs of the church. The amounts so given during the first two decades of the period were relatively modest, but from 1501 to 1530 really substantial sums were given, principally, as we have suggested, by the upper clergy. The prime interest of these donors was in the universities, where several of them made great foundations, with the consequence that a heavy proportion of all their educational benefactions in this period were disposed for this use.[1] Thus in the years prior to the Reformation well over twice as much was given for university needs as to the foundation of schools. This disposition was precisely reversed during the brief interval of the Reformation, upwards of £29,000 being vested for school endowments as contrasted with rather less than £15,000 for augmenting the financial resources of the universities. In total, the most substantial capital of £48,320 9s was given during these two decades towards all educational needs.

Even larger sums were disposed by Elizabethan donors for educational uses, with the result that in the course of forty years the massive total of £139,947 8s was provided, this amounting to very nearly a third (31·40 per cent) of the whole of the charitable wealth of the era and contrasting most dramatically with the really trifling proportion (7·17 per cent) of charitable funds dedicated to religious needs in this incredibly secular era. It is significant too that of the great sum given for educational uses more than half was for grammar-school foundations, this capital of £72,736 13s considerably exceeding the total vested for schools in the preceding eighty years. The age of the foundation of the English grammar schools was at hand.

But the great, the prodigal, outpouring came in the early Stuart period, when in four decades the enormous total of £383,594 1s was provided for the several, and interrelated, educational uses. This sum far exceeded the total given in the whole of the preceding one hundred and twenty years, and, for that matter, there is reason to believe during the whole of the past two centuries. Moreover, almost 58 per cent (57·51 per cent) of this immense sum was given for grammar-school foundations, the £220,599 15s so provided accounting, as we shall shortly observe, for the settling of schools across the length and breadth of England. The climax of this great surge of giving for educational uses was attained in a most remarkable period of twenty years, 1611–1630, when the incredible total of £249,331 11s was provided, principally by London generosity, for this whole range of needs. In other words, very nearly 30 per cent of the vast sum given during the full course of our period for the founding of a system of education in the realm was vested during this brief interval.

There was inevitably a falling away in giving even for these uses during the period of the Puritan Revolution, though it should be noted that relatively a somewhat larger proportion of charitable wealth was so dedicated even than in the early Stuart era. In these years the large total of £130,461 9s was settled for educational uses, of which almost £90,000 was for still more grammar schools. In fact, one is dazzled by the vastness of the contribution of the early decades of the century, and

[1] *Vide* Table V (Appendix) and the accompanying curve for the particulars of this discussion.

hence inclined not to lend full credit to the amazing accomplishment of the revolutionary era, when almost as much was given for educational causes as during the whole of the Elizabethan age.

From 1550 onwards the interest of benefactors was to be concentrated on the strengthening, one can with fair accuracy say the founding, of grammar-school education in England. We have suggested that this almost obsessive preoccupation with the enlargement of educational facilities was the consequence of complex but most powerful motives to be observed particularly in the merchant class. There was, moreover, a considerable body of literature 'in praise of learning' which undoubtedly exercised some measure of influence, two examples of which may be mentioned, one drawn from a relatively early date in our period and the other from its close. William Kempe, writing in 1588 and dedicating his book to the mayor and burgesses of Plymouth, emphasized particularly the utility of learning. Some father, he tells us, 'will rubbe his forehead and . . . aske why . . . spend . . . goodes and possessions about that which cannot feede the belly, nor clothe the backe'. The answer, Kempe assures us, is simple and incontrovertible. It is learning alone that moulds a civilization, that separates man from barbarism, and it is learning alone that brings men to a knowledge of the Gospel requisite for salvation. Thus even the naturally endowed boy can neither 'aspire to heavenly blessing' or 'winne worldly felicitie' with 'his unlettered wit'. Hence any nation must seek to extend the benefits of education as widely as possible, for thus is the whole commonwealth strengthened and the Kingdom of God advanced. In terms of more local reference, the writer pointed out that Plymouth must regard its schools as its principal asset, for by them alone will the merchants, the 'maisters in the arte of nauigation', the magistrates, and the clergy be secured for the needs and services of the city. All of western England, he concluded, suffered from a still too straitened educational opportunity, which would be corrected only when there was to be found 'even in marchants shops, learning more plentiful then wares'.[1]

Similar if more eloquent sentiments were set forth in 1657 by the great preacher Edward Reynolds, in a funeral sermon for a schoolmaster of St Paul's School. Learning, Reynolds submits, is alone competent to discern truth and it is God's will that we should set ourselves to this high task. 'All good learning and wisdom is *per se*, and in its owne nature desireable, as an ornament and perfection to the mind, as a part of that truth whereof God is the author . . . all secular learning is the knowledge of Gods works . . . a small emanation from eternal verity'.[2] Learning is consequently essential not only to the state but to a truly religious com-

---

[1] Kempe, William, *The education of children in learning* (L., 1588), no pagin.
[2] Reynolds, Edward, *A sermon touching the use of humane learning* (L., 1658), 12.

munity, and any man who opposes its extension stands guilty of ignorance or malice.[1] In fact, so indispensable are the schools of England that the profession of the teacher must be made so respected and honoured that men of great learning will more often be attracted to the calling.[2] The schools of the nation are a precious asset, requiring even more of support and care if they are to carry forward a noble and a necessary work already well begun.[3]

There has been considerable and sustained controversy on the extent of the educational facilities in England just prior to the Reformation, and even more regarding the effect of the Henrician and Edwardian expropriations on existing school foundations. The principal authority apparently wrote as a somewhat extreme Protestant, but was choleric as he contemplated what the Reformation sovereigns might have achieved had they appropriated more of the monastic and chantry spoils to the strengthening of secondary education in the realm. The consequence, if the ten counties under study are in any sense typical, has been a gross over-estimate of the number of grammar schools actually in existence and functioning in say 1480, as well as a considerable exaggeration of the number of functioning schools closed as a result of the chantry confiscations. Though the statistics offered are confused, it seems evident that a most inexact appraisal of English grammar-school education results from the fact that it has been assumed that any school,

[1] Reynolds, *A sermon*, 23.   [2] *Ibid.*, 26.

[3] This general view was opposed by Bacon in the brilliant but servile brief prepared for the King when an outrageous attempt was made to break Thomas Sutton's great will. (This interesting and important case will be fully discussed in the second volume of this study.) Bacon opposed the founding of Charterhouse, among other reasons, because the proposed school would add still another grammar school where there were in fact too many. The numerous schools of the realm had, he held, drawn youths from trade and husbandry, with the result that there were 'more scholars bred, than the state can prefer and employ'. Consequently, Bacon would divert this portion of Sutton's huge bequest to the universities (*Works*, I, 495–496). This view had small impact on the circumstances to which it was so skilfully addressed and on English thought, though it was frequently and specifically rebutted. As one would suppose, it was most effectively answered by the gentle Fuller, who confessed that there had been some concern because of the 'multitude of schools' founded and supported in England by private generosity. Such men in effect argued that because 'the nursery is bigger than the orchard, the one breeding more plants than the other can maintain trees; and the land not affording sufficient preferment for them, learning is forced to stoop to mean courses, to make a livelihood' (*Worthies*, I, 45). This argument, Fuller maintained, was irrelevant and absurd because it dwelt on the occasional harm done to individuals, while ignoring the great and necessary good flowing into the whole society from the schools of the realm. In fact, one Scottish writer held that it was indispensable that schools be founded in every parish in the realm and that additional colleges be established 'in some the most eminent parts of the kingdome' to add to the inadequate facilities of the two universities (Cockburne, William, *Respublica de decimis*, Edinburgh, 1627, 4).

any intent to found a school, or any reference to monastic education is reckoned not only as a mediaeval school founded but as a school actually functioning at the close of the Middle Ages.[1] The evidence, at least in the counties under review, would seem rather to suggest that the number of mediaeval foundations in which lay children might gain instruction was limited indeed and that by 1480 most of these foundations had been gravely weakened or had been closed, while instruction for laymen was most uncommon in the monasteries.[2] Far more important in establishing the structure of mediaeval secondary education were the chantry schools, a considerable number of which were founded in our ten counties, with, however, hazardously small and restricted endowments. Unfortunately, chantry foundations rarely survived in any case for longer than a century, with the result that there were relatively very few functioning chantry schools in 1480, fewer still at the time of the Expropriation. Finally, our evidence, derived principally from local sources, would suggest that in these ten counties at least no school connected with or deriving support from a monastic foundation was permanently suppressed, though these schools were reorganized and did in most instances shortly gain adequate support as lay benefactors moved swiftly and effectively to sustain them with endowments. Further, the Chantry Commissioners took the most elaborate pains to protect existing schools, or more usually the informal and part-time services of a stipendiary priest, often searching valiantly and unsuccessfully for a school which the deed of gift suggested should exist but which had in fact long since lapsed. The educational function was ordinarily carefully separated, when it existed at all, from the uses now deemed superstitious, and then being re-founded was vested with properties representing the capital heretofore employed for educational purposes. All these matters will be discussed in detail in the later volumes of this study, but it may be suggested here that though a few existing chantry schools were closed as a result of the chantry confiscations, a larger number of lapsed or moribund schools were reinstituted. On balance, it would be our judgment that the spoliation of the monasteries and the expropriations of the chantry endowments benefitted rather than harmed the slender educational resources surviving from the Middle Ages.[3]

[1] Leach, A. F., *English schools at the Reformation* and *Schools of medieval England*.

[2] This view is also advanced by Rowse (*England of Elizabeth*, 491) and most convincingly by Miss Eileen Power (*Medieval English nunneries*, Cambridge, 1922, 261–270) in so far as the education of girls is concerned.

[3] We speak with some confidence, of course, only of the ten counties under study. The somewhat similar views of other writers who have comprehended the whole of England in their judgment should be noted: Watson, Foster, *The old grammar schools* (Cambridge, 1916), 46–47; 'Charity schools', *Westminster Review*, n.s., XLIII (1873), 450–472; Stowe, A. M., *English grammar schools in the reign of Queen Elizabeth* (N.Y., 1908), 9–20, 157–170.

Stretching as far as we can not only our definition of what a school must be but likewise what is implied in its actual function, we may say that in our ten counties there were thirty-four schools offering instruction to lay youth in 1480, of which, it should be noted, certainly two and probably four had closed for want of financial support before 1540.[1] This, then, was the meagre inheritance surviving from the Middle Ages. the foundation on which men began to build well and solidly even before the advent of the Reformation. In point of fact, the whole discussion of this question so exclusively in terms of the Reformation seems at once unfortunate and a little irrelevant because most clearly the aspirations of men for a vast enlargement of the opportunities for secondary education were deeply imbued a full generation before this great revolution occurred. The sentiments of most of these early donors were secular, they were often balked or constrained by a jealous ecclesiastical authority, and their educational interests were in large part derived from the humanistic, the Renaissance forces, which made a considerable and a too much neglected contribution to English life and thought in the course of the first of our time intervals.

During the long period 1480–1540, a total of £36,292 13s was vested by a considerable number of donors for the foundation of grammar schools or for the strengthening of existing institutions. The amounts given in the first half of this interval were relatively modest, but it seems clear that new and compelling forces were at work in the society from 1511 onwards to 1540 when decade totals ranging from £7379 12s to £10,062 4s were provided for this great and beneficent use. Some measure of the magnitude of the accomplishment of this early and neglected period may be gained when it is considered that this capital very nearly equalled the wealth being employed for the support of all existing grammar schools in our ten counties in 1480.[2] Significant and hopeful as was this achievement, it was quite overshadowed by the intensity of interest shown in school foundations in the brief interval of the Reformation, when the large total of £29,399 10s was provided for school foundations in every part of England. The curve of giving, it will be observed, rose most strongly and dramatically in the Edwardian years, when the quite astonishing total of £21,172 18s was vested for the enlargement and betterment of school facilities throughout the realm.[3]

This extraordinary generosity was, in fact, only scantly excelled in

[1] Again, we must reserve discussion of the particulars to the later volumes of this work.

[2] Few of the schools in 1480 enjoyed considerable endowments. The computation is made by adding to endowment values the capital worth implied in assured income from monastic, chantry, or other sources. It should be further noted that certain of the income values date from the time of the Expropriation and hence are probably only roughly accurate.

[3] See graph on next page.

any one of the Elizabethan decades, though the steadiness with which funds were poured into these foundations in this era accounted for the fact that during these years the large total of £72,736 13s was added to the educational resources of the nation. But as was to be the case in so many areas of generosity, this was only a prelude to the surging flood of benefactions in the early years of the seventeenth century. In the course of the early Stuart period the immense total of £220,599 15s was provided by benefactors, mostly of London, for the founding of schools in every quarter of the realm. The measure of this achievement is suggested when we reflect that of the vast total provided for school foundations during our whole period very nearly half must be credited to this generation of almost prodigal generosity, while, even more remarkably, well over a third (35·84 per cent) of the whole sum for our entire age was disposed in the space of two decades, 1611–1630. It is not too much to say that the basic structure of English secondary education as it was to exist for a very long time was literally created in the early Stuart period. It is in these years that we find the climax of this great movement, which was to bear such rich fruit in terms of social and cultural advancement and so vastly to enlarge the arc of opportunity in the realm. But it was by no means the whole of the contribution to be made during the course of our period. In the brief interval of the Puritan Revolution, distracted and torn as it was, the huge total of £89,870 17s was provided by a host of donors for the further extension and, as they confidently thought, the completion of secondary education in England. This great sum, it may be observed, far exceeded the total provided during the whole of the Elizabethan age, while in terms of yearly rate of giving for this most

GIFTS FOR GRAMMAR SCHOOLS

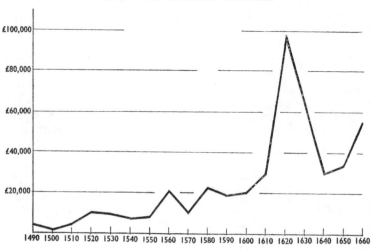

worthy cause it represents but a relatively slight diminution from that even of the early Stuart period.

In all, then, donors of our age gave of their substance the immense total of £448,899 8s for the creation of a national system of education in England. Beginning with most meagre resources from the mediaeval past, these men had greatly extended the whole range of opportunity for aspiring youths and had established educational resources which were on balance not to be substantially improved for all of two centuries. They had addressed themselves to this great undertaking with a steady purpose from the beginning of our period, with what can only be described as an obsessive concern after 1550. They had in the final reckoning devoted somewhat more than 14 per cent (14·47 per cent) of all their charitable giving to this one great purpose, almost the whole being in capital form, thereby ensuring for future generations the opportunities which they wished all English youth to enjoy.[1] Theirs was a very great and a salutary achievement which was to transform an entire culture.

Every county shared in this great charitable achievement, though by no means in equal proportions. Thus Buckinghamshire and Somerset, with relatively slender resources and deeply absorbed as they were with the problem of poverty, made proportionate contributions for this educational use which were well below the national average. Bristol dedicated a very large proportion (20·16 per cent) of all its charitable wealth to building its own magnificent system of schools while giving almost nothing for other educational uses. Lancashire, greatly aided by London wealth, vested the staggering proportion of 31·98 per cent of all its charities for this one purpose, bringing itself level and more with the rest of England by these heroic exertions of about a century. While London's immense generosity for educational uses was remarkably evenly spread over the several heads, its huge total contribution of £259,263 2s, given principally for the founding of schools outside Middlesex, accounts for the decisive proportion of almost 58 per cent (57·76 per cent) of the whole great sum dedicated by England for this use.[2] All classes shared importantly in this epical undertaking, but it was the merchant wealth of London, of Bristol, of Norwich, and even of the raw new towns of the West Riding that first conceived and then completed this grand design.

The great achievement is all the more impressive when we reflect on it in terms of the number of schools actually founded during the age. In this era, we must recall, £500 would build and endow a school of fair

---

[1] By counties, the proportion of the whole amount given for grammar schools which was capital in form ranges most narrowly from 99·11 per cent for Lancashire to 99·96 per cent for Norfolk.

[2] See table on next page.

strength; £1000 was quite sufficient for a school of notable resources. There were, as we have said, thirty-four functioning schools in our ten counties at the outset of our period, few of which were supported by endowments. In the course of our period a total of 305 schools was established and endowed in our counties, of which a large proportion were grammar schools and very nearly all institutions providing free tuition for needy boys. In addition, we have counted 132 schools which were founded and endowed by donors of this group of counties in counties other than that of the donor, almost all (123) being the munificent gift of London to other parts of the realm. In sum, then, we may say that benefactors resident in the counties under study founded and endowed a total of 437 schools prior to 1660. Nor was this by any means all. Donors of these counties also made some contribution to 105 additional schools within our area, to schools which often enjoyed a hopeful beginning, performed significant and treasured services to their communities, but which failed to attract endowments before the close of our period. Though we are concerned only with those schools to which charitable benefactions were made, it should also be recorded that there was a fair number of schools, several being at least for a season strong institutions, which were wholly supported by taxation levied by the community or by tuition fees exacted from parents. In summary, then, we may say that a total of 542 schools were during the years with which we are concerned either endowed or partially supported by private charity, while a much smaller but uncertain number were otherwise sustained in their work.[1] Furthermore, as we shall have occasion to point out in detail in our analysis of the county evidence, these foundations were distributed rather evenly and sensibly over the great area which we are studying, the foundations falling into a pattern before our period was out. In only two counties could a boy have lived at a distance

The proportion of total charitable wealth devoted to grammar-school foundations in the several counties was as follows:

	Amount £ s. d.			Per cent
Bristol	18,559	7	0	20·16
Buckinghamshire	6,789	2	0	7·70
Hampshire	9,850	11	0	11·31
Kent	28,308	18	0	11·24
Lancashire	33,185	9	0	31·98
London	259,263	2	0	13·72
Norfolk	20,865	0	0	11·73
Somerset	9,902	5	0	8·50
Worcestershire	13,602	18	0	25·84
Yorkshire	48,572	16	0	19·94
	448,899	8	0	14·47

[1] See table on page 291.

of more than twelve miles from an available grammar school in which he might have found free tuition under the terms of the founder's deed of gift. No city and no market town in all the ten counties lacked a school, while there were few really large villages without some place of instruction. Or to put it another way, there was by 1660 an endowed grammar school for something like each 6000 of the estimated population of this great area, one for each 4400 of population if the unendowed schools be added as well.[1] This was the achievement of our age; it was an achievement of which any age might well be proud.

Closely, often generically linked with these many grammar-school foundations were the scholarship funds and, occasionally, even the fellowship funds[2] which served to strengthen both secondary and highei

School foundations made in the group of ten counties, 1480–1660:

	Number endowed 1480–1660, including mediaeval schools refounded and endowed	Number founded but unendowed	Number of endowed schools founded in other counties
Bristol	3	0	0
Buckinghamshire	13	0	0
Hampshire	15	6 (?)	0
Kent	28	3	2 (?)
Lancashire	57	5	1 (?)
London	30	31 (outside	123
Norfolk	26	11 Middx.?)	2
Somerset	13	7	1 (?)
Worcestershire	20	4	0 (?)
Yorkshire	100	38	3
	305	105	132 (?)

The total of 437 endowed schools founded in or by these ten counties would, we believe, suggest that there must have been at least an equal number of grammar schools founded in the rest of England, assuming that we have in fact accounted for the whole of London's extra-mural foundations. Intensive local research would be required to determine the exact number, but it seems evident that all estimates of grammar-school foundations made during our period have been much too low.

[1] This computation assumes an increase of 30 per cent in the population of our area in the course of the interval 1600–1660 (vide ante, 26–27, 63).

[2] The distinction between 'scholar' and 'fellow' was not clearly marked in the sixteenth and seventeenth centuries, in official usage or in common speech. Not until 1440, in the statutes of King's College, was there mention of the transition from scholar to fellow, and the word 'scholarship', as applying to the status or emoluments of a student at a school, college, or university, seems not to have been used until 1535. Here and elsewhere in this work, we have kept the modern usage, meaning by 'scholarship' the funds supporting or helping to support a student in a school, college, or university, and by 'fellowship' the status or emoluments of a graduate fellow, one of the teaching or voting members of a college or university.

education and which created widespread opportunities for apt and aspiring students to proceed to the universities for the completion of their education. In many instances these endowments were vested in the universities for the benefit of particular schools, while the responsibility for stated visitations was placed upon the favoured college. In other cases, donors expressed a restrictive preference for boys from a named county or even a larger region, a testamentary device also not uncommon in the endowment of fellowships. Still other benefactors were more concerned with the strengthening of the resources of a particular college, consequently imposing no school or geographical restrictions on the scholars or fellows to be appointed to the foundation, though frequently describing in restrictive detail the qualifications of learning and character deemed desirable.

We know very little regarding the scholarship and fellowship resources of the universities in 1480, almost nothing about the scholarship funds of the few grammar schools then in existence. Just enough knowledge can be gleaned to lend some weight to the unsupported statement that such wealth in the hands of the universities was meagre in 1480, almost non-existent in the schools. On these scarcely outlined foundations, then, men of the early modern era began to build well and generously, moved as they were by the deep conviction that educational opportunities must be greatly extended and that they must be secularized. In the course of our period benefactors were to provide the enormous total of £145,055 7s for such worthy uses, this amounting to 4·67 per cent of the whole of the charitable wealth of the age. Furthermore, it should be noted that nearly the whole (97·89 per cent) of this massive sum was in the form of endowments, thereby ensuring permanent strength and vitality both to the grammar schools and to the universities which these funds served to link into a system of national education.

The undergirding of English education with scholarship and fellowship resources got modestly under way in the pre-Reformation years, during which the substantial total of £16,369 9s was vested for such purposes, of which, it may be noted, a large proportion was given in the single decade 1521–1530. This rate of giving was by no means maintained during the brief interval of the Reformation, the unsettling effect of the Henrician expropriations being suggested by the trifling total of £207 13s contributed in the years 1541–1550. Many, indeed most, of the scholarship funds in prior years had either been connected with chantry foundations or had been provided by clerics, with the result that a short interval elapsed before the flow of wealth gathered momentum in the secular foundations that followed. Then beginning with the rather cautious sum of £3125 17s disposed for these educational purposes in the first decade of the Elizabethan age, these endowments mounted almost steadily from decade to decade until the interval just prior to the outbreak of the Civil War, when the large capital of £29,965 5s was provided.

The whole amount given for scholarships and fellowships in the course of the Elizabethan age was £26,701 1s, a considerable and a most useful sum which was, however, quite dwarfed by the capital of £72,410 13s provided for these uses in the first four decades of the seventeenth century. So great was the interest of donors of the early Stuart period in such endowments, in point of fact, that about half the funds provided during the course of our whole period was disposed in this single interval. The intensity of interest in scholarship foundations, so largely centred in merchant donors, was well maintained during the brief interval of the Puritan Revolution, the £25,506 6s given during these years being but little less than the total for the much longer Elizabethan age.

Though at least some helpful contribution was made in each county towards creating this wholly magnificent structure of educational opportunity, there were marked differences in the intensity of dedication to this charitable cause.[1] Norfolk, Yorkshire, and Buckinghamshire devoted a substantially higher proportion of their charitable wealth to this purpose than did the generality of counties, the first two, moreover, principally with little help from London. But as was so often the case, the aspirations and the immense generosity of London were to lend decisive support to this great venture in extending so widely educational opportunities for the youth of the nation. London donors alone gave £92,465 8s for this purpose, or not far short of two-thirds (63·74 per cent) of the whole massive sum. Bristol, in the sharpest possible contrast, made only token contribution to this great need, being preoccupied as always with its own parochial concerns, for which it provided so lavishly.

[1] The proportion of total charitable funds devoted to scholarship and fellowship endowments in the several counties was as follows:

| | Amount | | | Per |
	£	s	d	cent
Bristol	473	0	0	0·51
Buckinghamshire	5,003	0	0	5·68
Hampshire	3,117	13	0	3·58
Kent	10,648	13	0	4·23
Lancashire	4,688	8	0	4·52
London	92,465	8	0	4·89
Norfolk	10,576	6	0	5·95
Somerset	3,655	10	0	3·14
Worcestershire	330	15	0	0·63
Yorkshire	14,096	14	0	5·78
Totals	145,055	7	0	4·67

We have sketched all too briefly and inadequately an historical achievement of very great significance, for by these generous benefactions the whole fabric of education in the realm was strengthened and secured, higher and secondary education firmly linked together, and the arc of educational opportunity vastly extended. These foundations and the stipends which they provided may seem small to us, but they were sufficient and often exceedingly generous for the time. Though we shall discuss them in some detail as in later volumes we consider the several counties, it may be said here that men of our age had created 487 new scholarships in the universities, with stipends ranging in a most bewildering fashion from 10s p.a. to one princely grant of £20 p.a. In average terms, these awards were set by their donors at £6 4s 1d p.a., which absorbed something like £3022 p.a. of the available income of about £7100 which had been established by this large group of benefactors. Moreover, in the course of our period gifts were made for the augmentation of existing stipends, with a total outlay for this purpose of £1014 7s p.a. as donors sought, principally in the seventeenth century, to mend the damage wrought on sixteenth century foundations by the eroding process of inflation. In all, then, 487 scholars were being supported in the universities before our period had closed as a consequence of the remarkable generosity of our age, a most substantial number indeed when we reflect that not more than 5400 students were matriculated at Oxford and Cambridge towards the end of James I's reign. Nor was this the full measure of the contribution of the age, since about £260 p.a. had been vested in scholarship endowments limited to the assistance of worthy students enrolled in the grammar schools founded during this period, while almost £2800 p.a. had been dedicated to the support, and augmentation, of upwards of 100 new fellowships in the two universities.

Even larger sums were given by donors of our period towards the support, the rejuvenation, and the enlargement of the two universities. Any accurate appraisal of the financial resources disposed by Oxford and Cambridge at the beginning of our era seems to be quite impossible to hew out of the jumbled quarry of fact and legend, but it is generally agreed that both universities were meagrely endowed and were in a far from flourishing academic state at the outset of the Tudor age. We have included in our reckoning a great variety of benefactions: the numerous and relatively rich new collegiate foundations, the augmentation of the resources of older colleges, the mending of old and the building of new fabric, the founding of professorships and lectureships, endowments for the general support of the universities, large sums dedicated to the strengthening, one should perhaps say the creation, of two great scholarly libraries, as well as the collections of several of the colleges, and, by no means unimportantly, the efforts, not favourably regarded by the older universities, to create quite new institutions of higher learning in the founding of Gresham College, Sion College, and the ill-fated Chelsea College. We shall deal with the particulars in our county treatments, though we should perhaps here note that the great benefactions which we have now to analyse are limited to those flowing in a golden stream from donors in the ten counties under examination.

In all, donors of our era vested the very large total of £231,195 10s in the universities, this accounting for the generous proportion of 7·45 per cent of all their charitable gifts. Some measure of the generosity of this contribution is suggested when we observe that the great sum was approximately the same as that devoted to all church building during our long period, and was considerably more than half as much as was provided for all the schemes of social rehabilitation by the burgher benefactors of the age.

As we have previously commented, the great and certainly the needed work of strengthening the resources of the universities was well begun in the period prior to the Reformation, when the substantial total of £78,335 8s was disposed, mostly by princely and prelatical gifts, for this purpose. Almost the whole of this large sum, be it noted, was concentrated in the generation 1501–1530, which may fairly be described as the age of Christian humanism in England, an age when it seemed for a tragically brief season as if the ancient church and its institutions might be preserved and reformed from within. Substantial, if sharply diminished, support was continued during the brief interval of the Reformation, a total of £14,793 1s being supplied for a variety of purposes, and by a considerable number of donors, for the augmentation of the resources of the two universities. The Elizabethan period witnessed the final shifting of responsibility into lay hands, but it was a responsibility not readily or generously assumed for a full generation, particularly by the great merchant donors who remained somewhat suspicious of both institutions until Emmanuel College and Sidney-Sussex College had been founded and their good works had become manifest, and who in any case were then devoting their charitable wealth with an almost obsessive absorption to the founding of grammar schools and the creation of scholarship endowments. The result was that in the whole course of the Elizabethan age not more than £40,384 was disposed by donors for the uses of the universities, only slightly more than half the great total given in the somewhat longer interval prior to the Reformation. But the tide of lay generosity turned towards the universities late in the Queen's reign, most substantial and well-sustained totals having been given, principally from London, in each of the first four decades of the seventeenth century. The total given for the strengthening of the universities during these years was the large sum of £86,334 11s, with a steep climax of intensity of concern in the years 1621–1630 when the huge capital of £39,491 was so disposed. The almost prodigal generosity of this period towards the universities, however, slackened dramatically indeed in the decade of Laud's dominance, when sternly Calvinistic London benefactors tended to withdraw their support as the Archbishop's pressure on the universities began to bear its fruit. Nor did this decline cease during the two decades of Puritan hegemony in England, when the modest £11,348 10s designated for the further strengthening of university resources should be contrasted with the huge total of £89,870 17s provided for grammar-school foundations and the £25,506 6s given for the endowment of scholarships.

When we turn to the counties, we observe most striking differences in the interest displayed in this great charitable need. London was, as usual, decisive in its support, though, as we have noted, the flood of its generosity was long delayed. London donors gave in all the immense capital of £154,591 5s for the advancement of higher education, this accounting for almost exactly two-thirds (66·87 per cent) of the whole sum and representing 8·18 per cent of all London's own enormous charitable wealth. Somerset contributed proportionately even more generously (14·16 per cent), though its impressive outlay of £16,495 12s was accounted for largely by Wadham's great foundation at Oxford. In contrast, such principally rural counties as Worcestershire and Lancashire gave most modestly indeed towards the support of university education, the latter certainly because little could be spared after the immense outlays made by its donors for grammar-school foundations. Bristol once more displayed its almost arrogantly intensive parochialism, contributing, as always, only a trifling sum for an extra-mural need. Bristol did immensely well for itself, but it had little to spare for the needs of the larger community which was England.

Finally, in our discussion of the resources vested by donors who blessed the England of our period with rich cultural and educational institutions, we must at least mention the gifts made to secure the founding of libraries, not including those of the universities. In all, the relatively modest capital of £8343 7s was provided for this purpose, principally, it should be noted, after 1600. In the early Stuart period £4249 2s was disposed for this charitable use, while almost as much (£3735 16s) was left during the two decades of Puritan supremacy. The amounts, then, were not large, but they did suffice to establish three public libraries, in Bristol, Manchester, and London, as well as to lend further support to the oldest public library in the realm, that at Norwich. Almost as importantly, donors of our period established eleven, very possibly twelve, small collections in grammar schools, parish churches, or cathedrals, with the express provision that they should be made available under proper restrictions for public use. Only a modest beginning had been made in this wholly new field of universal education, but it was a firm and a well-conceived beginning. This charitable outlay, quite as truly as the massive endowments for schools, for the universities, and for scholarship foundations, attests the warm and persistent devotion of men of this remarkable age to the conviction that poverty might be cured, the lot of mankind bettered, and the Kingdom of God attained by the extension of educational opportunity to all those who would receive it.

5. Religion

We have dealt at some length with the ever-broadening secular concerns of men of our period. Quietly, steadily, and irresistibly a profoundly important metamorphosis in men's aspirations had occurred which led them to devote their energies and their substance to the creation of new institutions having as their concern the fate of men in this world. As importantly, old institutions, such as the schools and the almshouses, were recast in a secular mould and then immensely enlarged and strengthened by lay donors who settled them on trustees moved by identical social aspirations. There were unmistakable evidences of this rising secularism, destined ultimately to master English culture, well before the advent of that exceedingly complex historical phenomenon which we call the Reformation. The Reformation itself was, in fact, partly a consequence of powerful and scarcely restrained forces of secularism and anti-clericalism deeply rooted in English thought. The great shift in men's aspirations, with which this study is at bottom concerned, has been fully demonstrated in the discussion of the several great secular charitable interests which were developed and exploited with such amazing generosity and such warm devotion by the men and women of our era. This, as it were, is the positive evidence with which we have been concerned. We now turn to a discussion of the religious charities of our age, to a depressing annal which exhibits all too starkly the negative evidence.

It may be suggested that the graphic evidence presented in connection with Table I tells us at a glance what happened over this period of almost two centuries, during this hinge period in the history of a great culture.[1] In the full course of our period donors disposed the substantial total of £659,628 15s for a great variety of religious uses, for maintaining the elaborate and essential offices of the church, this amounting to slightly more than a fifth (21·26 per cent) of all their charitable wealth. These benefactions were in total only a fraction of the great sums designated for the care of the poor and were far less than the capital provided for the several educational uses.

But far more important was the steep and irrevocable relative decline of men's interest in most pressing religious needs when measured

[1] *Vide* the bar graph submitted with Table I (Appendix).

against their immense contribution to the secular concerns of the age. Thus during the two generations prior to the Reformation they gave the very large total of £281,158 15s for various religious causes, this accounting for 53·49 per cent of all their charities and, even more significantly, constituting almost 43 per cent (42·62 per cent) of the whole amount which donors of our age were to provide for religious uses. This was a great achievement. One may reasonably suppose, indeed, that men in this era gave to the church roughly the resources required of their generosity for the carrying forward of its services and the due maintenance of its immense fabric. When, however, we examine the evidence in more detail, it becomes clear that the climax of giving for religious purposes was reached as early as the first decade of the sixteenth century, and that beginning most dramatically with the year 1510 there set in a steep and an irreversible decline, which was both absolute and relative, not arrested for a full century.[1] During the troubled decades of reformation and religious experimentation, as we should expect, giving for religious uses declined abruptly, the £33,526 5s provided in these years amounting to no more than 14·77 per cent of all charities, thus displaying proportionately far less interest in the needs of the church than in other of the great charitable heads such as poor relief (27·04 per cent), social rehabilitation (30·21 per cent), and education (21·28 per cent).

Even this slender and grossly inadequate support for the requirements of the church was in the course of the incredibly secular Elizabethan age to be in relative terms almost exactly halved. During this long and famous age only £31,959 7s was disposed by donors for religious uses, this constituting no more than 7·17 per cent of all charitable wealth, a smaller proportion even than was devoted to municipal betterments (7·57 per cent), and insignificant indeed when assessed against the Elizabethan preoccupation with the other great charitable uses. Still more significantly, the total designated for religious causes during the whole of this era was substantially less than the amount given in any, save one, of the decades of the two generations preceding the Reformation. This amazing, this truly revolutionary, shift in sentiment and aspirations was, as we should expect, most markedly an urban phenomenon, though the stark secularism of the age is fully and dramatically evident in every county in the realm. An immensely important and a permanent metamorphosis in the structure of men's aspirations had occurred as a consequence of the complex and powerful historical forces which this study seeks to analyse.

Elizabethan secularism was so intense and so sustained, as we shall see in county after county, that grievous damage was wrought by men's indifference to the fabric, the offices, and the ministry of the church. It

[1] *Vide* Table VI (Appendix) and the accompanying curve.

is ironical indeed that pious rectors and historians have for three centuries past blamed on the brief episode of Puritan hegemony the essentially irreparable damage done in the course of the reign of that great sovereign whose inscrutable personality only partially concealed an indifferent temper in religion, a coldly Erastian policy, and a basic contempt for the clerical mind. But in this respect, and this was true of her whole regimen, the mind and policy of Elizabeth reflected, always to an enhanced degree, the mind and the aspirations of her people. In this fact, indeed, consists the greatness of this illustrious ruler.

The church could scarcely endure if the intense, the almost contemptuous, secularism of the Elizabethan age were to persist. The Stuarts were pious sovereigns, deeply concerned with the needs of the church and alarmed by the stark secularism of their subjects. James, in an inept and erratic fashion, and Charles, under Laud's guidance, in a harsh and compelling manner, both sought to help the church in its great and manifest needs and endeavoured to create a climate of opinion which would restore the requirements of faith to the Christian conscience of their people. Though their efforts not only failed but assisted in bringing on the Civil War, there was a considerable relative and a very substantial absolute increase in giving for religious causes in the course of the early Stuart period. In all, £256,522 was disposed for the needs of the church, this amounting to 17·85 per cent of all charitable benefactions for the interval and exhibiting an intensity of concern somewhat more than double that of the Elizabethan period. It must, however, be said that a closer analysis of the data suggests that much of this increased concern for very real and certainly pressing religious needs was forced, and from Laud's point of view much of it was illusory. Relatively speaking, the benefactions provided in the first decade of the Stuart period were almost as starkly secular as those of the whole Elizabethan era, while nearly half the large total for the whole of the early Stuart period was concentrated in the single Laudian decade (1631–1640) when the really huge sum of £125,388 11s was disposed, principally by reluctant givers who were subjected to pressures which could approach *force majeure* in their intensity. The completion of the rehabilitation of St Paul's Cathedral had become for Laud a symbol of the success of his whole zealous but dangerously misguided policy, for he fully sensed the fact that the long Elizabethan and Jacobean neglect of the half-ruined fabric of the church was the national symbol for the cold and hard indifference of a great but an intensely secular age. Much of the huge sum raised for St Paul's, with the full majesty of sovereignty directing the effort, was, from the point of view of the principally Puritan merchants who made large but grudging contributions, given under a pressure which approached extortion, though we have, as we must, reckoned these as charitable contributions.[1] So, too, persistent but far less successful pressure was brought to bear on the counties of England to mend their crumbling fabrics, with the result that in this one frantic decade the large total of £85,438 6s was spent on church building in the whole of the area with which we are concerned, substantially more, it may be noted, than in the whole of the preceding century. But Laud, his sovereign, and his church, or more accurately his conception of the church, paid a terrible price not many months after this decade had closed for having lifted thus modestly the proportion of charitable benefactions dedicated to religious uses. Laud must himself have sensed the danger, for ominously enough during the early Stuart era the second largest sum, £46,253 12s, recorded for any religious use was dedicated to the endowment of Puritan lectureships, a movement bitterly opposed and finally throttled by the Archbishop. Laud and his government were barely able to restrain this movement; he knew full well that immense and resolute Puritan wealth stood ready, quite literally, to purchase the Church of England with coin of the realm. The interdiction of sovereignty had of necessity to be laid across the course of this resolution.

During the period of Puritan triumph, support for the various religious uses fell away considerably, though not dramatically, from the level so ruinously established in the early Stuart era. Donors of this period gave in all £56,462 8s to the church, this constituting 12·09 per cent of all charitable benefactions and very possibly representing the true measure of the intensity of the religious preoccupation. Puritanism, having gained by force of arms that which it could not purchase, showed itself essentially subject to the same social and historical pressures that had characterized English life and thought for a century past. The donors of this age, their wills would seem to testify, were deeply and genuinely pious men, but they were at bottom intensely secular in their aspirations for their own age and for the future of England; so perhaps was Puritanism itself.

The needs of the church were so multifarious, the traditional dependence on free gifts so great, the whole institutional organization of the church and its worship so complex, that we must needs examine the several heads under which we have reckoned benefactions, in order to assess more accurately the devastating effects of secularism in the England of our age. Though the total amounts were never large, it seems probable that the most sensitive of all the barometers of loyalty to the church and its offices were the gifts, usually made by bequest, for the general, the unrestricted, uses of the church and the support of its services. A most miscellaneous group of offerings has been gathered under this head,[2] such benefactions having been almost universal,

---

[1] This interesting and important matter will be fully discussed in the second volume of this study.   [2] *Vide ante*, 50, for a fuller listing.

usually in tiny sums, prior to 1530 in all counties and until about 1570 in several of the more completely rural provinces. The quite modest total of £40,763 15s was given for this use during the years under study, this amounting to no more than 1·31 per cent of all charitable funds, and providing in dubiously relevant average terms only slightly more than £13 8s for each of the many parishes comprehended in our group of counties during this long span of nearly two centuries.

Prior to the Reformation, or more precisely prior to 1530, these small but ubiquitous gifts had constituted an extremely important source of assistance in maintaining the offices of the church. Thus in the years before 1540 such contributions had attained the substantial total of £18,992, or upwards of £6 in average terms for the 3033 parishes with which we are concerned. Moreover, it should be emphasized, this contribution of late mediaeval piety accounted for nearly half the sum garnered for this significant use during the whole of our period. Such giving sloped off steeply after 1530, with little indication of renewed interest for almost three full generations.[1] In the twenty years of the Reformation, £3054 17s was provided for this use, while in the age of Elizabeth benefactions for general church purposes fell away abruptly and calamitously. The total given for this purpose in the course of these forty years was a trifling £2151 17s, or in average terms not much more than 14s for each parish in our regions.[2] Further, it will be observed that the curve for the whole interval was remarkably steady, each small decade total representing, so to speak, the irreducible minimum of concern on the part of humble and conservative benefactors, for the most part in rural parishes.

There was some measure of revival of interest in the general needs of the church during the early Stuart period, noted in both rural and urban

[1]

GIFTS FOR CHURCH GENERAL

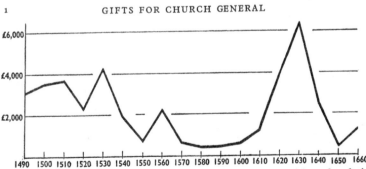

[2] An unsigned memorandum in the State Papers, composed in a decade in which in our ten counties the contribution for the general uses of the church totalled no more than £599 16s, in protesting against the sale of lands which of right were possessions of the church, complained bitterly of the want of support for the needs of the church (*S.P. Dom.*, 1593, CCXLIV, 68).

parishes, the total of such benefactions amounting to £14,239 19s, for this long interval. This interesting upswing was particularly marked in the two decades 1611-1630, when about £10,500 was given for this use, though it must be pointed out that relatively this whole development appears insignificant indeed when measured against the amazing charitable outpouring of this age for secular causes. During the Cromwellian period such benefactions fell away steeply once more, though hardly to the Elizabethan depths, the not very impressive total of £2324 5s having been provided during these years.

These interesting and significant trends are, as we shall see in our discussion of the several counties, to be observed in all parts of the realm, though there were substantial differences both in the time when secularism overcame the various communities and in the velocity of its momentum. Taking our whole period in view, the donors of London and Buckinghamshire gave relatively no more than trifling sums for this religious use, while those of Lancashire, Norfolk, Kent, and most particularly Somerset, gave quite substantially for this purpose, perhaps always more important symbolically than financially.[1]

We have included no head for gifts made for the support of monasticism in our period, having rather distributed such items to other appropriate categories of religious giving, all save one of which, prayers for the dead, persisted throughout our period. At the same time, we have recorded these benefactions with care and should comment at least briefly on the relatively slight support being lent to monastic institutions long before their expropriation was contemplated by Henry VIII and his ministers.

There is abundant evidence to suggest that English monasticism was in process of slow dissolution well before our period began. The great surge of foundations occurred in a relatively short period from the eleventh century to the early thirteenth, with few foundations being

[1] The proportion of all charitable wealth designated for the general uses of the church in the several counties was:

	Amount			Per
	£	s	d	cent
Bristol	1,702	2	0	1·85
Buckinghamshire	534	13	0	0·61
Hampshire	1,456	16	0	1·67
Kent	5,672	2	0	2·25
Lancashire	2,118	8	0	2·04
London	16,863	11	0	0·89
Norfolk	4,801	8	0	2·70
Somerset	3,794	5	0	3·26
Worcestershire	837	9	0	1·59
Yorkshire	2,983	1	0	1·22
	40,763	15	0	1·31

made in any part of England after 1325. Nor was that all, for a decline in the number of monks serving the existing establishments also set in during the fourteenth century, which by the opening of our era may have reduced by a full half the number of the regular clergy. The monastic life, for a variety of reasons, simply failed to attract sufficient priests, many small houses were of necessity abandoned, and many more in the early sixteenth century possessed so few brethren that the proper spiritual offices could not be maintained.[1]

These general observations are most precisely documented when we assess the support lent to the institution of monasticism by men of our age. In the course of two generations donors gave for various monastic uses £56,692 7s, of which it should be noted about 43 per cent was provided by royal benefactors for monastic purposes in London. These benefactions, swollen as they were by royal generosity, represented approximately a tenth of all charitable wealth disposed in the years 1480–1540, while it is noteworthy that in no county, London aside, was as much as 7 per cent of charitable giving directed to the needs of the many monastic establishments in the regions with which we are concerned. Moreover, when the purposes for which these funds were given are more closely analysed, it will be seen that of this total only a small amount (£6170 6s) was disposed for the general or free use of the monasteries and that no more than a trifling sum (£2720 5s) was vested directly for the support of the regular clergy. Rather more than half of the whole sum was disposed, for the most part in trusts, for the maintenance of prayers for the dead, while the grossly inadequate outlay of £18,576 16s was made for the support of the vast and the decaying fabric of the many monastic establishments to be found within our counties.[2]

This means that in average terms the whole great institution of monasticism in our region, with all its many services and needs, received a flow of sustaining funds of not quite £1000 a year. This support was totally inadequate when measured against the needs, trivial when assessed against the immense wealth with which an earlier age had established these monasteries. Using Savine's impressively careful data, we may estimate that the monastic institutions of our region possessed on the eve of expropriation capital resources of the order of £1,129,830, or something over 41 per cent of the monastic wealth of the whole realm. In the course of two generations men of our period contributed no more than an additional 5 per cent towards the sustenance of these numerous establishments, an amount far from sufficient to repair the

[1] Coulton, *Five centuries of religion*, III, 540–558; Snape, R. H., *English monastic finances in the later middle ages* (Cambridge, 1926), 20–22; Hughes, *Reformation in England*, I, 36–71; Holdsworth, *English law*, IV, 36–37.

[2] See p. 304.

Distribution of monastic benefactions, 1480–1540:

	Prayers			Clergy			Fabric			General			Total			Per cent of county total, 1480–1540
	£	s	d	£	s	d	£	s	d	£	s	d	£	s	d	
Bristol	5	0	0	6	0	0	626	13	0	501	7	0	1,139	0	0	6·77
Buckinghamshire	162	15	0	11	11	0				7	14	0	182	0	0	2·04
Hampshire	119	0	0	8	14	0	78	13	0	2	11	0	208	18	0	1·35
Kent	970	6	0	1960	17	0	868	19	0	982	7	0	4,782	9	0	6·42
Lancashire	153	14	0	24	3	0	194	19	0	421	17	0	794	13	0	3·57
London	23,884	12	0	194	9	0	15,420	8	0	2384	3	0	41,883	12	0	16·75
Norfolk	840	1	0	179	3	0	263	6	0	725	11	0	2,008	1	0	4·60
Somerset	401	10	0	12	4	0	702	10	0	676	10	0	1,792	14	0	5·80
Worcestershire	347	5	0	0	18	0	2	15	0	25	1	0	375	19	0	3·25
Yorkshire	2,340	17	0	322	6	0	418	13	0	443	5	0	3,525	1	0	6·86
Totals	29,225	0	0	2720	5	0	18,576	16	0	6170	6	0	56,692	7	0	10·79
	(51·55 per cent)			(4·80 per cent)			(32·77 per cent)			(10·88 per cent)						

ravages which time, fire, slow erosion, and maladministration had wrought on the fabric and on the endowment of English monasticism. In London alone, and there only because of royal generosity towards Westminster Abbey, was monasticism even maintained in its existing strength, while in six of our counties less than 2 per cent was added to monastic wealth by pious donors in the two generations prior to the Expropriation.[1]

Finally, it should be remarked that when we take our whole region into account the curve of support for monasticism declined steadily throughout our period, a dramatic and withering indifference charting a decline which there is reason to believe had set in well over a century before the accession of the Tudors. There were many and most complex causes for this decline of popular support for monasticism, a phenomenon which in a broad sense was quite as truly European as it was English. But among the most important of them, in our ten counties at least, were the fact that, despite its huge vested wealth, English monasticism was by the beginning of our era making only a slight social contribution to the pressing needs of the age by the distribution of alms, and the growing realization that such meagre alms as they did distribute were, because of their casual and undisciplined nature, probably on balance harmful. We shall examine this important question in detail in our discussion of charities in the several counties, but we may here suggest that the conviction was almost universally held, well before the Reformation, that English monasticism no longer served any important social function, while many responsible and devout men had come to question its spiritual efficacy. The springs of support for monasticism had dried up in England long before the Reformation; the whole institution collapsed at the touch of sovereignty.

[1] Relation of gifts to monasteries (1480–1540) to total estimated capital worth at the time of the Dissolution. (A multiplier of 20 has been used on Savine's estimates of income worth.)

	Capital worth			Gifts 1480–1540			Per cent of worth
	£	s	d	£	s	d	
Bristol	20,077	0	0	1,139	0	0	5·67
Buckinghamshire	21,236	0	0	182	0	0	0·86
Hampshire	103,751	0	0	208	18	0	0·20
Kent	137,948	0	0	4,782	9	0	3·47
Lancashire	33,975	0	0	794	13	0	2·34
London	230,678	0	0	41,883	12	0	18·16
Norfolk	103,605	0	0	2,008	1	0	1·94
Somerset	158,891	0	0	1,792	14	0	1·13
Worcestershire	80,981	0	0	375	19	0	0·46
Yorkshire	238,688	0	0	3,525	1	0	1·48
	1,129,830	0	0	56,692	7	0	5·02

While also subject to a notable decline, the flow of funds, whether capital or income, for the support of prayers for the dead exhibits no such withering as that which we have noted in our discussion of monasticism. There were few recorded chantry foundations in England prior to the beginning of the thirteenth century, but the late decades of that century witnessed a vast outpouring of funds for the endowment of prayers, the movement being greatly assisted by the rich foundation made in 1290 by Edward I on the death of his queen. The climax of benefactions for these foundations was attained in the fourteenth century, when several thousand were probably established, leading, as Coulton has put it, to a kind of 'liturgical bankruptcy', since cathedral churches, monasteries, and even parish churches had assumed on trust more precise obligations for masses for the souls of the dead than could possibly be fulfilled. The episcopal authorities were gravely concerned not only because of the neglect of the spiritual responsibilities thus undertaken, but because so large a proportion of religious benefactions was dedicated to the maintenance of stipendiary priests whose duties were at once light and not easily disciplined. The inevitable consequence was that in the course of the fifteenth century most of the earlier foundations simply disappeared, funds were devoted to other uses, and the whole institution of endowed prayers fell into considerable disrepute.[1]

Though the evidence is most uncertain, we may believe that the marked decline in the foundation of chantries which marks our period as contrasted even with the preceding century was occasioned by a widespread distrust of the church in its capacity as administrator of endowments in perpetuity rather than any substantial and heretical doubts concerning the efficacy of prayers for the dead. Very substantial sums, of capital and income, were dedicated by men and women of our period for the repose of their souls, but normally under terms and conditions which bespoke an almost complete distrust of the church as an administrator of trusts. Thus reversionary clauses were common, secular bodies, such as merchant companies, were constituted trustees, minute and binding instructions charged with suspicion were laid down, and increasingly prayers were linked almost incidentally to essentially secular foundations such as schools, almshouses, or university fellowships.[2] With the Reformation, of course, the whole question of the efficacy of such foundations became a matter of central doctrinal significance, priests being forbidden by law as early as 1529 to accept stipends for

---

[1] Cook, G. H., *Mediaeval chantries* (L., 1947), 8–9, 33–50, 58–60; Coulton, *Five centuries of religion*, III, 65–86.

[2] Wood-Legh, K. L., 'Some aspects of . . . chantries', *Royal Historical Society Trans.*, 4th ser., XXVIII (1946), 56–59; Cook, *Mediaeval chantries*, 58–59.

saying prayers for the dead, while in 1547 chantries were dissolved by law. It is most significant that Queen Mary's valiant and somewhat frenzied efforts to restore prayers for the dead failed almost completely, only slender capital sums being risked for this purpose by donors during these tragic years, while such prayers were absolutely and finally prohibited by the Elizabethan injunction of 1559.[1]

In total, the substantial sum of £149,656 11s was provided for prayers by donors of our period, amounting to 4·82 per cent of all benefactions. More pertinently, such gifts and bequests loom very large indeed in the years prior to the Reformation, when the massive total of £140,864 3s disposed for prayers represents more than a fourth (26·80 per cent) of all charitable wealth, greatly exceeding the amount provided for any other single charitable use and being almost exactly double the whole of the sum disposed under all heads for the succour of the poor. There are in all some thousands of these bequests, most donors of course having provided no more than a few shillings for a trental of prayers or an anniversary mass, or establishing a small capital sum to ensure an obit for a stated term of years. But, as we shall note in our discussion of the counties, a considerable number of these benefactions were very substantial indeed, being capital sums for the foundation of perpetual chantries. It is rather surprising that of the whole amount left for prayers the very large total of £124,152 13s, this being upwards of 80 per cent (82·96 per cent) of the whole, was in capital form. In other terms, these creations of our period were sufficient, had there been no attrition, to provide an annual income of perhaps £6000 for the support principally of stipendiary priests. Since the average stipend designated in these deeds of gift was £6 3s 9d p.a., this means

[1] The royal injunctions of Edward VI (1547) ordered a most important change from the traditional form of praying for the 'present felicity' of the dead to 'ye shall pray for all them that be departed out of this world in the faith of Christ that they with us, and we with them at the day of judgement, may rest both body and soule . . . in the Kingdome of Heaven' (Frere, W. H., ed., *Visitation articles and injunctions of the . . . Reformation*, 3 vols., L., 1910, II, 130). The Elizabethan injunction was even more strongly worded, requiring the clergy to do no more than to 'praise God for all those that are departed out of this life in the faith of Christ, and pray unto God that we may have grace so to direct our lives after their good example, that after this life we with them may be made partakers of the glorious resurrection' (*Ibid.*, III, 29). Archbishop Parker's *Articles* of 1560 warned the clergy that prayers for the dead were by law forbidden (*Ibid.*, III, 84), while the bishops were very specific in prohibiting their clergy from making 'the communion a mass of requiem . . . persuading the people to pray for the dead' (*Ibid.*, III, 167, 209, 289–290). Despite the pressure of the law and the persistent efforts of the bishops, it is interesting to note that at least some small amounts were left by will for a generation after the accession of Queen Elizabeth (the total is £201 7s) for prayers for the souls of the testators, without occasioning any difficulty in probate. Save for one in the Laudian period, these bequests disappeared after 1590.

that something like 1000 priests in England may well have received the whole or most of their support from these late and doomed foundations. The capital thus disposed, it is lamentable to report, approximately doubled that so painfully provided during our entire period for the support of the desperately poor parochial clergy of England. The whole of this capital for prayers was expropriated and was applied principally to a variety of secular uses. It seems tragic indeed that it could not have been disposed either by the donors or by the Crown to lifting the annual stipends of the parochial clergy of our ten counties, in average terms, by almost £2 p.a. each.

In no single respect, it may certainly be noted, did private charity fail more conspicuously than in bettering the status and the lives of the parish clergy. Broadly speaking, tithe income in the Middle Ages was sufficient to support the parochial clergy and the church fabric had it been solidly or even principally devoted to the central needs of the church and its worship. But in the course of the mediaeval period a large proportion of parochial revenues was appropriated for the support of monasteries, with the result that over broad areas no more than a miserly fraction of the whole of revenues derived from the parishes was in fact dedicated to the ministry of the church.[1] The expropriations of the era of the Reformation in no sense worsened an already serious situation, but, by vesting the impropriations as pieces of property in lay hands, did tend to fix the system irrevocably, it being probable that by 1560 somewhat more than one-third of all parochial revenues were lay possessions. The position of the parish clergy was further worsened when, at the Reformation, marriage, with its attendant responsibilities, was embraced by the great majority of their number, with no increases in stipend; even more serious was the steady erosion of the inflationary process against their fixed and very small incomes. Elizabeth displayed neither interest nor sympathy with the plight of the parochial clergy of the realm, though the always courageous Grindal warned her that 'this Church of England hath been by appropriations (and not without sacrilege) spoil'd of the livings, which at the first were appointed to the office of preaching and teaching. Which appropriations were first annexed to abbies, and after came to the Crown, and now are disposed to private men's possessions, without hope to reduce the same to the original institution. So that at this day, in my opinion, where one church is able to yield sufficient living to a learned preacher, there are at least seven churches unable to do the same.'[2]

[1] Henry Spelman (*English works*, L., 1727, 35) estimated that 3845 of 9284 parishes had been impropriated. In some areas conditions were wretched indeed; in Yorkshire, for example, 392 of 622 parishes were impropriated. Weever (*Ancient funerall monuments*, 194) estimated that 3236 parishes were impropriated.

[2] Kennett, White, *The case of impropriations* (L., 1704), 172.

It was not until the early Stuart period that any considerable secular concern was shown for the plight of the clergy. In the House of Commons the Puritan members particularly brought forward plans to better the lot of the parochial clergy, principally at the expense of the bishops and the cathedral clergy, who were also large holders of impropriations. As we shall see, the Puritan tactic was to secure more pulpits for earnest and godly preachers by the purchase or gift of impropriations and the founding of lectureships, but there was simultaneously an effort made by Archbishop Laud with the support of the King to persuade pious benefactors to return impropriations to the church from which they had originally been secured by the monastic foundations. This effort, which Bishop Kennett has traced out with care, was not impressively successful,[1] though the concern displayed by Laud and his followers undoubtedly did inspire capital gifts of considerably greater value designed to secure the augmentation of clerical income.[2]

During the whole course of our period £71,551 14s was disposed for the maintenance of the clergy by men concerned about their poor estate. Such contributions were relatively modest during the decades prior to the Reformation when £9291 15s was provided for this use, principally, it may be said, in testamentary gifts for named parish priests or sums to be divided amongst the monks of a particular religious house. Approximately the same intensity of interest was maintained during the short interval of the Reformation when £3626 10s was devoted to the augmentation of clerical incomes, with the important difference that a much larger proportion was in capital form. But even this modest flow of funds for the support of the parochial clergy all but dried up during the amazingly secular age that was to follow, the whole sum provided in the Elizabethan interval amounting to no more than £4253 6s. This really insignificant amount, given over a period of four decades, is all the more inadequate when we recall that this was precisely the period when the economic condition of the clergy was at its worst and that the government itself made no move to lend any assistance to well over half the parochial clergy of the realm, who simply could not live and carry on their ministry with the stipends available to them.

Substantial, though still modest, improvement in the status of the parish clergy was to occur in the early Stuart period. As agricultural prices rose steadily, the economic position of those of the clergy who possessed the whole of the glebes and the tithes rose accordingly,

[1] *Vide* Kennett's annotations in his own copy of *The case of impropriations*, preserved in the Bodleian Library. This source was brought to my attention by Christopher Hill's valuable *Economic problems of the church* (Oxford, 1956), to which remarks in this paragraph are also indebted.

[2] For examples, *vide* S.P. Dom., 1633, CCL, 57; 1637, CCCLXXII, 67; 1640, CCCCL, 36. For a typical statement urging the return of impropriated tithes, *vide* Squire, *Three sermons*, 105–107.

though, as we have suggested, these conditions applied to no more than a fraction of the clergy of the realm. Even more help was lent by a sharp rise in the contributions made during these years either by the return of impropriations or, and much more importantly, by the creation of endowments designed to secure the augmentation of the stipends of clergymen in particular parishes. In all, the substantial total of £37,540 4s was given during this interval for this desperately needed use, almost the whole of which was in capital form. This rate of giving was well maintained during the period of revolution, £16,839 19s having been vested as endowments to secure augmentations by men and women who were confident that the true gospel had at last triumphed.

Still, when we take our whole period in view, the contribution made by private donors towards the better maintenance of the parochial clergy was slight indeed. The total of £71,551 14s so provided amounted to no more than 2·31 per cent of the whole of the charitable wealth disposed in our era, while the amount did not greatly exceed the sums given for such relatively minor uses as loan funds or for company needs. Moreover, of the whole amount not more than £57,437 15s (80·27 per cent) was in the enduring form of endowments, which would suggest that at the close of our period, in average terms, something less than £1 p.a. had been added to clerical stipends in the parishes of our area. There were, of course, pronounced regional differences in the degree of interest exhibited in the needs of the parish clergy, such counties as Somerset and Worcestershire having made no more than token contribution to this great need.[1] In Kent, Norfolk, and Lancashire, on the other hand, far more substantial contributions were made, while in Yorkshire, where the economic status of the clergy was notoriously degraded, the really helpful total of £15,661 9s was contributed for the augmentation of stipends, this being 6·43 per cent of all the charitable wealth there disposed.

[1] The proportion of total charitable wealth devoted to the augmentation of clerical stipends in the several counties follows:

| | Amount | | | Per cent |
	£	s	d	of whole
Bristol	1,223	3	0	1·33
Buckinghamshire	1,625	10	0	1·84
Hampshire	1,693	12	0	1·95
Kent	8,718	17	0	3·46
Lancashire	2,425	15	0	2·34
London	34,822	0	0	1·84
Norfolk	4,279	15	0	2·41
Somerset	848	16	0	0·73
Worcestershire	252	17	0	0·48
Yorkshire	15,661	9	0	6·43
	71,551	14	0	2·31

Conjoined with the rather feeble interest in lifting the stipends of the parochial clergy by the endowment of augmentations was a far more powerful effort on the part of Puritan donors to raise the standards of preaching and the whole level of the clerical status by the foundation of lectureships within existing churches. Formidable and substantial as this movement was, it is apparent that Puritan generosity for this charitable use was restrained only by the suspicion of the governmental and ecclesiastical authorities, giving way in the Laudian period to a prohibition sanctioned by confiscatory power. This whole interesting movement, which deserves to be carefully studied from the rich materials available, seems to have had three principal aspects.

The first and certainly the most important motive on the part of the Puritan merchants who supplied most of these endowments was to secure a preaching clergy, particularly in those areas which had not been wholly won from Rome or in key pulpits where the Gospel according to Geneva could be most effectively preached by men carefully selected for their evangelical fervour. The case of John Shaw, a native of Yorkshire, comes to mind as typical. A graduate of Cambridge, where his Puritanism was freely expressed, Shaw was none the less licensed by Bishop Morton and in 1630 gained a lectureship at Brampton, Derbyshire, where he remained for three years. At the suggestion of friends he went to London, probably in 1633, where he knew 'there was at that time (and formerly had been) a custom for the merchants and other tradesmen that lived in London, so many of them as were al borne in the same county, to meet at a solemn feast (upon their own charges) . . . and then to consult what good they might do to their nativ county by settling some ministers (or some other good work) in that county'. Shaw preached before a number of merchants who were natives of Devonshire and these men in the next year settled him as lecturer in the market town of Chumleigh, where he remained for three effective years until Laud's attack on the whole system of lectureships under lay (and Puritan) control brought his ministry to an end.[1]

The second aspiration of the founders of Puritan lectureships was to secure for the church an able and a more learned clergy. We sometimes forget that only a relatively small proportion of the Elizabethan parochial clergy were as late as 1580 graduates of the universities and that their deficiencies became all the more glaring as the general level of literacy and education was almost precipitously raised by the cultural

---

[1] 'The life of master John Shaw', in *Surtees Society Publications*, LXV (1875), 126–129. It might be added that Shaw then returned to York, where he was appointed lecturer at All Hallows in the Pavement. He shortly collided with Archbishop Neile, who accused him of being a leader in the strong Puritan party in the city, but Shaw remained undisturbed under the protection of the Puritan Earl of Pembroke.

impact of the many grammar schools being founded in all parts of the realm. The lecturers appointed under the new endowments were, in general, learned as well as highly gifted men whose attainments were so conspicuous as to exert on the episcopal authorities an irresistible pressure to seek in turn to raise clerical standards generally. A swift and a most substantial betterment resulted as the flow of graduates from hundreds of new grammar schools to the newly strengthened universities set in, with the consequence that in as backward a county as Worcestershire, where in 1580 no more than 23 per cent of the clergy were university graduates, more than half were so trained in 1620, and nearly all (84 per cent) by the close of the early Stuart era.[1]

Finally, it may be suggested, these merchant donors in about 1625 joined their efforts in a common undertaking which the ecclesiastical authorities could only regard as a conspiracy to secure control of the clergy with the intention of converting the church by purchase into the Puritan mould. This interesting and most significant episode has been well and thoroughly discussed by earlier writers,[2] but we might here say that when judgment was rendered against the lay feoffees in 1632 those shrewd and determined men had already gained control of eighteen impropriations and eleven advowsons by the device of purchasing from lay impropriators and settling the legal power of appointment and the income thus gained under trust covenants firmly vested in lay and godly hands. Laud was very properly alarmed, since he was fully aware of the immense wealth that stood poised and ready to wrest power and the control of policy from him and his bishops. The endowment of lectureships did not come to an end in 1632, but any massive Puritan undertakings had for a season been frustrated. It is no wonder that Puritan hatred and distrust of Laud was after 1632 implacable.

Steadily restrained and opposed as was this charitable use, so powerful were the impulses that animated it that in the relatively brief span of about eighty years almost exactly as much was supplied, nearly all of it capital, for the founding of lectureships as was given during the course of our whole period for the maintenance of the parochial clergy.[3] In all, the substantial total of £70,267 18s was vested for the endowment of lectureships, this amounting to 2·27 per cent of the whole *corpus of*

---

[1] Hill, *Economic problems of the church*, 207. *Vide ibid.*, 239, for a most discerning comment on the general improvement in the intellectual standards of the clergy.

[2] Gardiner, S. R., *History of England* (10 vols., L., 1896-1901), VII, 258-262; Kirby, E. W., 'The lay feoffees', *Journal of Modern History*, XIV (1942), 1-25; Calder, I. M., 'A seventeenth century attempt to purify the Anglican church', *American Historical Review*, LIII (1948), 760-775; Parker, H. A., 'The feoffees of impropriations', *Colonial Society of Massachusetts, Publications*, XI (1906-1907), 263-277; Hill, *Economic problems of the church*, 252-263.

[3] See graph opposite.

charitable wealth accumulated during our period. The movement began
very modestly and tentatively towards the middle of Elizabeth's reign,
gathering momentum slowly but steadily with the result that a total of
£4307 16s was provided for the purpose by the close of the century.
Modest as was this sum, it is interesting to note that it slightly exceeded
the slender amount given during the whole course of the reign for the
augmentation of the stipends of the parochial clergy. The total disposed
for lectureships in the first decade of the next century rose abruptly
to £3436 and then almost quadrupled in the following decade, when
£12,823 7s was given. The climax came in the years just prior to the
legal decision which ran so catastrophically against the feoffees for impropriations, the very substantial total of £17,323 7s having been given
for lectureships in the years 1621–1630. There was a considerable,
though hardly an abrupt, falling away in the last decade before the outbreak of the Civil War, when £12,670 18s was dedicated to the founding of lectureships, though closer analysis reveals that a heavy
proportion of this sum was given in the first two years of the decade.
Giving for this godly purpose increased markedly in the decade of the
Civil War, to the impressive total of £15,066, and then declined steeply
when under the Commonwealth and Protectorate it seemed that the
church as defined by the godly was secure. The whole movement, then,
was effectively concentrated in a relatively brief period of forty years
(1611–1650) when the large total of £57,883 12s was vested for lectureships, this being 82·37 per cent of the whole amount so dedicated.

GIFTS FOR MAINTENANCE OF THE CLERGY AND
PURITAN LECTURESHIPS

MAINTENANCE OF THE CLERGY ————
PURITAN LECTURESHIPS ·······

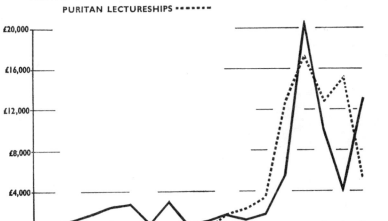

The support of Puritan lectureships was largely the contribution of London and provincial merchants who possessed the evangelical fervour and the considerable substance, and who had available the legal skills required to undertake a complex benefaction of this kind. London wealth was even more than commonly decisive in the establishment of these trusts, nearly 71 per cent of the whole amount having been given by its donors. Relatively heavy outlays for this charitable purpose were also made in Hampshire and Yorkshire, with a very substantial vesting of such endowments in Lancashire, where, as we shall see in a later volume, the founding of lectureships was importantly connected with the organized effort being made to wrest the county from Rome. In the remaining counties in our group, the interest displayed in this significant undertaking was very slight indeed.[1]

Doubtless one of the most sensitive of all indicators of men's loyalty to the church and devotion to its needs is the care which they give to its fabric. Under the large head of *Church Repairs*, as has been explained,[2] we have grouped a great variety of contributions for the repair of churches, the embellishment of their furnishings, and the provision of objects used in divine services. Generally speaking, such benefactions sprang from instincts of deep piety and reverence, though, when the fabric of a parish church was in really bad repair, moving secular instincts of local pride must likewise have been involved. It is with the analysis of the curve of this interest in the maintenance of church fabric that we are now concerned.

The exact nature of the responsibility for the care of church fabric was not well defined either at the beginning or at the close of our period, nor were attempts so to define it at all successful. Thus the duty of impropriators to maintain churches in repair was never legally established despite the persistent efforts of the bishops, the common law

---

[1] Proportion of total charitable wealth vested in Puritan lectureships in the several counties:

	Amount			Per cent
	£	s	d	of whole
Bristol	1,410	0	0	1·53
Buckinghamshire	404	0	0	0·46
Hampshire	2,200	0	0	2·53
Kent	1,724	14	0	0·69
Lancashire	4,963	14	0	4·79
London	49,744	10	0	2·63
Norfolk	1,920	0	0	1·08
Somerset	1,020	0	0	0·88
Worcestershire	520	0	0	0·99
Yorkshire	6,361	0	0	2·61
	70,267	18	0	2·27

[2] *Vide ante,* 51–52.

courts tending to set prohibitions against efforts to distrain these lay proprietors. Successive royal injunctions from 1536 to 1559 made it clear that the clergy were expected to employ a full fifth of their revenues towards the maintenance of the fabric of the chancels of their churches, while the parishes were required, if need be by rates, to maintain in decent repair the rest of the building and the churchyard.[1] It seems probable that rates were infrequently imposed for this purpose prior to 1560, the contribution of the clergyman and the pious benefactions of the parishioners being, save for disastrous occurrences, normally sufficient to meet the requirements of the magnificent gothic inheritance with which England was endowed.

But, as we shall see, lay interest in the maintenance of fabric fell away sharply and disastrously, while it is all too clear that efforts to impose rates were most vigorously resisted by the principal landowners of many parishes, men who were quite prepared to endure excommunication rather than spend their substance on the repair of structures which not infrequently their own ancestors had built.[2] The impropriators continued to resist all efforts to oblige them to assume responsibility, most parish clergy were too poor to meet the chancel dilapidations, and despite the exhortation in 1619 of all the bishops to parishioners to assume the burden as a charitable duty, no considerable interest could be aroused in the repair, much less the maintenance, of a rapidly disintegrating church fabric. The ruinous condition of hundreds, very probably thousands, of parish churches throughout England is abundantly testified to by every available source. Thus in Norfolk and East Suffolk, Bishop Redman's visitation of 1597 would suggest that almost one-seventh of the 806 churches of the diocese were in a state of disrepair ranging from 'decayed' to 'ruinous decay'.[3] At about the same date Philip Stubbes tells us that many churches were in a ruinous state, with roofs thatched with straw, chancels in decay, and windows and doors gone.[4] A generation later the full consequences of a half-century of almost complete neglect was summarized for Buckinghamshire in a survey of 116 churches, those of the larger towns being not included; of all these churches only three did not merit some censorious comment. In all, 107 of these edifices were in a state of serious decay and neglect, the almost oppressively certain evidence being not so much that poverty had prevented decent care of the fabric as that no one, clergyman or parishioner, had taken the trouble to make even minor repairs that

[1] Frere, *Visitation articles*, II, 11, 106, 122, 188, 262, 294, 336, 365, 402; III, 3, 13, 210, 221–222, 225, 255, 281–282, 285, 310–311, *et passim*.

[2] For instances, *vide S.P. Dom.*, 1635, CCLXXXVIII, 71; 1637, CCCLXXI, 90; CCCLXXII, 85; 1638, CCCCII, 31.

[3] Williams, J. F., ed., 'Bishop Redman's visitation, 1597', *Norfolk Record Society*, XVIII (1946).

[4] Stubbes, *A motiue to good workes* (1593), 80.

might at least have stayed the process of disintegration.[1] This condition, no worse in Buckinghamshire than in other regions, moved the always sagacious Thomas Fuller to confess that 'it grieves me to see the superstition of the former insult over the religion of this present age, bragging that she left us ten thousand churches and chapels, more or less, ready built, if we can find but repairers to keep them up'.[2] But 'the repairers to keep them up' were simply not forthcoming in the sternly secular age with which we are concerned.

In the whole course of our period private donors gave for the maintenance and repair of upwards of 3000 parish churches in the region under study the wholly insufficient total of £91,189 15s, this representing no more than 2·94 per cent of all charitable wealth. This amount, almost the whole of which was in the form of outright gifts,[3] in average terms supplied only £30 1s 4d over a period of almost two centuries for each of the churches in our ten counties, though the fact is that it was largely concentrated on about half the churches of the area. Even more significantly, most of the giving for this important and certainly pressing charitable use was concentrated in the years prior to the Reformation, when a total of £42,312 13s was provided for the care of the fabric of parochial and monastic churches, this being upwards of 46 per cent of the whole sum given throughout our long era. Even during these earlier years there were many ecclesiastical complaints regarding the neglect of fabric, but it seems probable that the average rate of giving of something over £7000 a decade so stubbornly maintained through this interval was at least scantly sufficient for the care of the fabric as well as permitting several counties to indulge in the craze for towers and porches which marked the era. During this interval of six decades very nearly £14 (£13 19s) was available in average terms for the care of the fabric of each of the 3033 parish churches and chapels of the huge region under discussion.

Private contributions for the maintenance of parish churches sank abruptly, dramatically, and significantly with the advent of the Reformation. In the years 1541–1560 the modest total of £5146 6s of contributions has been reckoned. But even this seems generous indeed when we turn to that unblushingly secular age which followed. During the whole course of the Elizabethan era, gifts and bequests for the maintenance of the church fabric sank to an average decade rate of giving of only slightly more than £1570. In this long period, no more than £6283 7s was disposed for this purpose, despite the now frantic com-

---

[1] S.P. Dom., 1637, CCCLXVI, 79; CCCLXIX, 59.

[2] Fuller, Worthies, I, 43.

[3] The proportion of gifts for church repairs which were outright ranged from 37·29 per cent for Buckinghamshire to 97·98 per cent for Kent. Buckinghamshire was unique in its disposition to vest such gifts in capital form.

plaints from responsible ecclesiastical officials that the church fabric of England was in a state of disintegration. Incredible as it may seem, only £2 1s 5d was provided, in average terms, for each church in our whole area, while there is reason for believing that a similar study of the whole of England would reveal an even lower rate of contribution.[1]

Nor was there any really substantial improvement, any real evidence of interest during the first decades of the early Stuart period, despite the desperate representations of the bishops and the active support of the central government. Though scores of churches were literally collapsing or being declared unsafe for worship, the curve of contribution for the now appalling need rose only very slowly from the £2922 5s given during the first decade of James's reign to the £6526 18s provided in the years 1621–1630. It is wholly accurate to say that over a span of ninety years the church fabric of the realm had been almost completely neglected by private donors, and this precisely during the years when,

[1]   GIFTS FOR CHURCH REPAIRS AND CHURCH BUILDING

CHURCH REPAIRS ▪▪▪▪▪▪▪▪   CHURCH BUILDING ▬▬▬▬▬

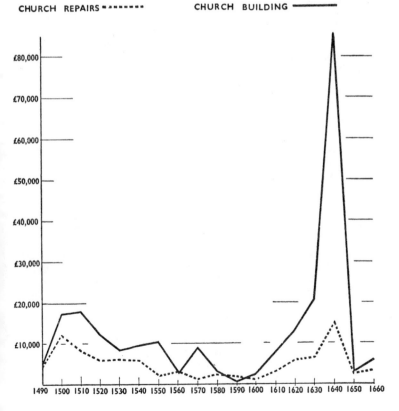

as we have pointed out, other resources were only inadequately available. This was the age when irreparable damage was done to many, perhaps most, of the churches of England, damage springing from a widespread and almost irresponsible indifference which was the fruit of Elizabethan secularism. Cromwell and the Puritans were on occasion responsible for changes in fabric and decoration which proceeded from their conception of worship, but, sentimental vicars and their descriptive leaflets notwithstanding, their brief inheritance and custodianship was of a gothic ruin on a national scale. It was this against which Archbishop Laud waged such a relentless and hopeless campaign, for his every move and every policy were suspect and stubbornly opposed precisely by those men who possessed vast substance which they were pouring into every area of secular charitable need. During the decade of his greatest power, it is true, the total given for church repairs rose abruptly to the considerable sum of £15,078 6s. But these 'gifts' in form were in fact often exactions. It was too little, it was too late, and it could not be sustained beyond the day of this strange man's fall. With the outbreak of the Civil War, contributions for the care of fabric fell steeply again to a level suggesting an intensity of interest roughly twice that of the Elizabethan era, but wholly inadequate for a still urgent need.

It may also be observed that there are most striking differences in the degree of intensity of interest in church repairs and maintenance among the several counties. The great urban areas, as we should expect, gave no more than really trivial proportions of their charitable substance for such uses, while in most of the rural counties, too, the amounts dedicated to this purpose were wholly inadequate.[1] Thus in Buckinghamshire, Worcestershire, and Yorkshire, where conditions were particularly bad, the proportion of funds given for this need ranged narrowly and most modestly from 2·78 per cent to 3·43 per cent of the whole. Only in

---

[1] Proportion of total charitable wealth given for church repairs in the several counties:

| | Amount | | | Per cent |
	£	s	d	of whole
Bristol	872	7	0	0·95
Buckinghamshire	2,958	4	0	3·35
Hampshire	2,967	0	0	3·41
Kent	19,138	9	0	7·60
Lancashire	5,802	4	0	5·59
London	33,601	12	0	1·78
Norfolk	13,004	13	0	7·31
Somerset	4,265	0	0	3·66
Worcestershire	1,806	6	0	3·43
Yorkshire	6,774	0	0	2·78
	91,189	15	0	2·94

Kent and in Norfolk, both counties having quite certainly an excess of churches, were substantial and just possibly scantly adequate amounts provided for the care of the magnificent fabric which both regions had inherited from the Middle Ages.

We may believe that this amazing and persistent neglect of the church fabric was in part due to the fact that the mediaeval frenzy of church building had left the nation endowed with more and very frequently with larger houses of worship than rural England needed or than it would support directly the sustained and effective pressure of the priesthood was lifted in the era of secularism which began well before the Reformation. This fact, too, may help to explain the relative indifference of donors during most of our period to the building of new churches in parishes where the ancient edifices had either become derelict because of long neglect or inadequate because of the natural growth of population. We have endeavoured, under difficulties earlier discussed, to arrive at rough estimates of amounts given during our period for the building of new churches, the rebuilding of old and decayed edifices, and improvements on existing churches which were so considerable as to amount to rebuilding rather than extensive repair.[1] It should be stressed that our lists, which will be fully discussed in the several county analyses in later volumes, include only new construction carried forward in whole or in part by voluntary contributions, there having been a few instances, to our knowledge, of building financed by rates prior to 1540.

Granted that the realm at large was over-churched in 1480, or perhaps more accurately in 1540, this was by no means the case in all parts of England a century later. For one thing, there was a steady and a most considerable increase in population during the whole of our period. Far more importantly, there was a very rapid growth of numerous market towns and not a few industrial and urban complexes, which resulted in acute strain on the existing parochial system and which really called for extensive new building. Further, as we shall stress in later volumes, the parochial structures of certain counties, most notably Lancashire and Yorkshire, were far from complete even in 1540, with the result that in such areas, also growing rapidly in population, there remained throughout our period a pressing need for new church or chapel building. Finally, the infirmities of gothic construction, the almost complete neglect of a century, and the inevitable destruction of fire, wind, water, and sea had simply wiped out a large number of churches which in most cases a truly pious age would have rebuilt. Though we have made no systematic study of the matter, our notes on building record quite incidentally the destruction or abandonment of 306 parish churches in the ten counties with which we are concerned during the course of this

[1] *Vide ante,* 33–34, 52.

period of almost two centuries. These churches, and doubtless many more of which we have no record, were destroyed and were not replaced.

The need was generally recognized, but attendance to it either in literature or in fact was at best perfunctory and insufficient. The Queen's homilies, published first in 1563, did call upon men to keep their churches in sufficient repair and declared it 'sinne and shame to see so manye churches, so ruinous, and so fouly decayed, almoste in euery corner', and reminded Christian men of their obligation to build new churches.[1] Two generations later a moderately Puritan writer, while deploring any decoration that smacked of popery, complained against the general decay of churches and the fact that pious donors neglected the pressing need for the building of new and comely places in which God might be honoured.[2] In fact, another writer suggested, the age was one far more notable for the pulling down than the putting up of churches, despite evident need and the example of the rich generosity of a former era.[3] When churches were destroyed or fell in final decay, even in quite large parishes or market towns, neither local efforts nor subscriptions taken over large areas were sufficient to secure the necessary funds even for the starting of the work of rebuilding.[4] Archbishop Laud applied a fanatical energy to the huge task of building and rebuilding, with, it must be said, almost no success whatever save for the symbolic triumph of completing the rebuilding of St Paul's. In point of fact, by far the most important contribution was to be made under the Commonwealth and Protectorate when numerous chapels, gaunt and severe though they usually were, were built principally at governmental expense in remote, neglected, and backward areas of the land. But despite the need, at no stage after 1540 did private donors concern themselves seriously with the task in hand. In the whole course of our period we have counted in our ten counties a total of 123 churches which were either built or rebuilt, as well as 79 chapels of ease which were constructed, almost wholly in Lancashire and Yorkshire, in areas now populous which were inconveniently distant from the parish church. Of this total of 202 places of worship added to the fabric of faith in England, more than half (104) were in Lancashire and Yorkshire, leaving an extraordinarily trivial accomplishment for all the remainder of a great and populous region. Taking our whole area into account, far fewer church edifices were built or rebuilt than we know by a most inadequate census to have been destroyed. Not only was the

---

[1] The second tome of homelies (1563), 'An homely for repayringe . . . of churches'; in Certaine sermons (1676), 163.

[2] Brinsley, John, The glorie of the latter temple (L., 1631), 15–19.

[3] Guild, Humble addresse (1641), no pagin.

[4] For examples: S.P. Dom., 1636, DXXXVI, 6–7; 1657, CLV, 44.

church fabric of England gravely damaged by the studied and persistent failure to lend it adequate maintenance, it was seriously diminished in this coldly secular age by failure to replace that which time and neglect had ruined.

During the long period under review it is true that the not inconsiderable estimated total of £236,199 2s was given for church building in England, this constituting 7·61 per cent of all charitable wealth and being slightly more than the amount contributed to the needs of the universities in this same interval. But it should be immediately observed that a large proportion (29·51 per cent) of the whole amount was provided by donors prior to the Reformation, the £69,697 7s given in these six decades having been sufficient to build well over half of all the new churches (chantry chapels not included) constructed during the whole of our era. Further, when this sum is added to the enormous total of £85,438 6s which Archbishop Laud raised and exacted in a single decade, principally for the rebuilding of St Paul's, it will be noted that close to two-thirds (65·68 per cent) of the whole amount provided by our age for church building may be attributed either to the completion of the fabric of the mediaeval church or to the desperate and historically eccentric achievement of the Archbishop. All the rest of our period remained starkly secular as it contemplated the need occasioned by the decay and even the destruction of a noble inheritance.

Men of our age had brought about a great and an enduring historical achievement as they translated their aspirations into institutional reality. We have seen that a profoundly significant and permanent shift had occurred in the structure of their aspirations as they came to contemplate and then to embrace the variegated secular needs of their age. It was not so much that they repudiated the religious aspiration, for they were godly and pious men, as that they lent such full and excited devotion to the support of new needs and new obligations that they came to neglect when they did not ignore the old. We have seen that men of our period addressed themselves with a persistent and intelligent intensity to the ancient problem of poverty, having by the close of our age erected effective and magnificently endowed institutions for its relief and cure. They had opened up whole areas of new opportunity by their bold and energetic experimentation with a great variety of schemes for social rehabilitation; they had beautified their cities and had made the whole of the realm a more pleasant and a better place in which to live by their own generosity. They had founded and had then endowed an impressive and a beautifully articulated system of education which ensured a vast extension of opportunity for all youth bright and ambitious enough to aspire to enjoy its benefits. They had, in sum, laid securely and deeply the foundations of the liberal society of which we are the inheritors, and they had embraced a body of aspirations for man and his society which still animate the best of thought and the best of action in the world which we have received from them. This, surely, is achievement enough for any age.

C. THE CHANGING STRUCTURE OF CLASS ASPIRATIONS

1. *Introductory comment*

We have sketched in broad terms the record of a great achievement wrought by private benefactors in England in the course of the early modern period. Though men and women of every class made some contribution to the rapid building up of the enormous total of this historically effective and immensely viable wealth, it remains true that most of the heavy burden of responsibility was assumed by a small group of donors who were members of two relatively very small classes, the merchants and the gentry. We shall now examine not only the measure of responsibility assumed by the several classes of men in the England of our age, but shall note with particular interest the quite different pattern of aspirations, and of fulfilment, as we move from class to class. We shall also be much concerned with the vitally important fact that in certain classes the whole structure of aspiration began to shift at an early date from an essentially religious preoccupation to a wide and pressing concern for a variety of secular needs, thereby establishing the pattern of charitable interest and giving which well before the close of our period was to be accepted, with varying degrees of completeness, by all classes of men. The merchants, and more particularly London's merchants, were almost prescient in their sense of the slope of history in this period and at a very early date indeed laid out and then began rapidly to implement a whole fabric of social institutions which were to bring about a cultural revolution in England. Other classes of men, we shall observe, yielded most slowly and grudgingly to the momentum of change set in motion principally by the merchants and the gentry.

Tudor and Stuart institutions were, then, largely shaped by two small and also relatively recent classes of men. The gentry and the merchants assumed during the course of our period an immense burden of social responsibility heretofore, in so far as it was borne at all, vested by society in older and powerfully placed classes. The Tudors, with a sure sense of history, reposed their government and policy in large measure on these new, these vigorous, and these most aggressive classes which were moving with great confidence and certainty towards translating their bold aspirations into social reality by prodigal outlays of their own substance. With responsibility, with the fluid wealth these classes disposed, there went as well the aspiration of power, which even before the close of the great Queen's reign was engendering friction and which was in little more than a generation to engulf the hapless Stuarts. These men were in fact creating an England which the Stuarts only dimly understood, and which, in so far as they did understand it, they disliked and intensely feared. Forces of change were powerfully under way in England from 1590 until 1640 which could not be brooked and which had in no small part been released and then most effectively directed by the great charitable foundations of these donors, animated as they were by strongly secular aspirations. Power is the inevitable concomitant of responsibility. These donors, drawn so largely in effective terms from the mercantile élite and the gentry, had as it were moved with their wealth, their generosity, and their vision, into vast social areas—those of poverty, of want of opportunity, and of want of knowledge—which lay as dangerous and forbidding wastes in the early modern society, and they had before our period was done rendered them fruitful by the great and enduring institutions which they created. They had, it is not too much to say, formed the shape of the modern world.

We shall need first of all to set out our definitions of the several classes of men before proceeding to an analysis of the extent and nature of their contributions. Thus we have included benefactions made by the Crown, by which is meant members of the royal family, seeking, we trust successfully, to limit such entries to those which actually came from the private fortune of the royal family. This means, of course, that we have intended to exclude those royal foundations which, as was so often the case during the period of the Reformation, amounted to no more than a redistribution of social assets, valuable and important as they may have been. Nor have we included as royal benefactions the many foundations named for the ruling monarch out of courtesy, when, as was usually the case, the charter was all that was supplied, and that usually at a fee. It might also be mentioned that we have in this one instance consciously introduced duplication into the donor count, since royal gifts tended to be substantial and were made in every county, with the result that the number of donors (thirty-six) under this head refers rather more accurately to the number of benefactions than to the actual members of the royal family (seventeen) who made charitable gifts.

The nobility offer no problem of definition and, as we shall later note, were in any event relatively unimportant in the contribution which they made to the development of the institutions of modern England. The gentry, on the other hand, were of very great importance indeed and raise several thorny problems of definition.

We have, for one thing, found it advisable to divide the class into two fairly well-defined groups, the upper gentry and the lower gentry, not only because their social position, their wealth, and their generosity show clear and clean evidences of differentiation, but because the structure of aspirations exhibited by the two classes is markedly different. By the upper gentry we mean simply the knights and their immediate families, whether the title of honour was obtained in effect by inheritance of a social status long enjoyed, for reward to a soldier or courtier, or, as was so common, by the lucrative practice of law. There is one exception: in the not insignificant number of cases when a great London merchant was elevated to the upper gentry after settling in his mature years on the estates he had purchased for such complex reasons, we have perhaps with some injustice to his memory and his thrusting ambition persisted in calling that man merchant who won his wealth in commerce. The upper gentry were, of course, a relatively small class at any given moment of reckoning, though our own fragmentary evidence would suggest that Wilson's rather offhand estimate of five hundred such families in 1600, which Professor Tawney seems to accept, sets the number somewhat too modestly.[1]

We have treated as members of the lower gentry those persons who so described themselves in their own wills or deeds of gift. This status we have also conferred on their widows and sons when they too left charitable benefactions. At bottom, Professor Tawney is certainly correct in suggesting that this was a class whose 'position [was] determined, not by legal distinctions, but by common estimation'.[2] It was a class firmly wedded to land, and it was a class of amazing fluidity of composition, being fed steadily from the yeomanry below, from whom in the lower ranges of wealth and status it cannot easily or sharply be separated. We have, in fact, seen a great many wills in which a testator in one place describes himself as a yeoman and in another as a gentleman, the uncertainty existing in his own mind because he and his family were at the point of a social translation which had not yet fully taken place. And we have seen other wills in which a man firmly describes himself as a gentleman whose executors or an officer of probate with equal firmness placed back in the yeomanry from which in common estimation he had not yet emerged. This class was likewise fed and enlarged throughout our period from the mercantile élite, with which it had ever stronger ties, from the professions, and from the younger sons of the upper gentry. It was a large class indeed as compared with the upper gentry, and clearly its numbers increased greatly during the course of our period. Wilson believed that something like 16,000 families were numbered in the class as early as 1600, while more recent research would seem to suggest that, in rural counties at least, between 2·6 per cent and 5 per cent of the total population was included in this class.[3]

---

[1] Wilson, *State of England*, 23; *Econ. Hist. Rev.*, XI (1941), 2–3.   [2] *Idem.*
[3] Tawney, A. J. and R. H., 'An occupational census of the seventeenth century', *Econ. Hist. Rev.*, V (1934), 47; Barley, M. W., 'Farmhouses and cottages, 1550–1725', *Econ. Hist. Rev.*, 2d. ser., VII (1955), 291. Tawney's figures are from Gloucestershire, those of Barley are from Nottinghamshire. Both, it should

Though it does not seem possible to be very precise regarding the size of the class at any given date, we can with confidence say that it increased greatly in the course of our period and that its whole structure was marked by an almost unbelievable fluidity. It was in so many ways a new gentry, usually rooted in monastic lands, if its members were relatively old; in land speculations, the law, trade, or the yeomanry if recent in status. We are told that nearly two-thirds of the gentry of Bedfordshire in 1620 were families unknown to the class in 1668,[1] while half the manors belonging to members of the class in Shropshire changed hands in the course of two generations. A member of a relatively old gentle family of the Isle of Wight noted in scathing and libellous detail how recent indeed was the status of the gentry of his neighbourhood, unless, be it said, they had at some stage intermarried with the Oglanders. One had begun life as an apprentice to a shoemaker, another was bred a serving man, another family 'were never written gentlemen till late', another had married as his second wife 'his maid, a poor wench', another had married a whore, another had purchased his estate with wealth gained as a merchant, and still another was the son of a man 'between a gentleman and a farmer'.[2] A later and more objective commentator on the amazing fluidity of this class tells us that in Staffordshire in the interval 1609–1669 half the land of the county had come into the hands of new owners; that whereas in 1609 there had been only three 'citizen owners', there were in 1669 three barons, four baronets, and twenty esquires who had purchased land with wealth made in trade.[3]

The lower gentry were, then, a thrusting and a highly mobile class, possessed of great toughness and resilience, and bound neither by firmly rooted traditions nor by entails. The more successful of them were in fact agricultural capitalists, close enough to the land to sense the new possibilities of exploitation and close enough to the people surrounding them to undertake, under Tudor tuition, a large measure of social responsibility. As we shall see, they were not even in relative terms particularly rich, but great prizes lay open for the abler and more adventurous members of this somewhat amorphous social group. They

be noted, do not differentiate between the upper gentry and the lower. Tawney's figures may be questioned because they do not seem to include a sufficient proportion of labourers and servants, an enormous class most difficult to assess in this or any other respect, while Barley's, depending on inventories, are certainly much too high (5 per cent) because the propertyless are not included. Our own efforts at a calculation, based on wills and inventories, were frustrated for the same reasons and are not included, though they run rather closer to the estimate (2·6 per cent) provided by Professor Tawney's useful calculations. We believe his proportions, as well as our own discarded estimate, to be too high.

[1] *Econ. Hist. Rev.*, XI (1941), 21–22.

[2] Bamford, Francis, ed., *A Royalist's notebook* (L.; 1936), 137–183.

[3] Degge, Simon, 'Observations upon the possessors of monastery-lands', in Erdeswicke, Sampson, *A survey of Staffordshire* (L., 1723).

had in the main attained gentility very recently, and their interest in arms, in elaborate houses, and the other symbols of status did not pass unnoticed by their contemporaries. It was principally of them that the always astute Gervase Holles wrote, in speaking of Lincolnshire, which he knew as a learned antiquary: 'There is nothing appeares to me more ridiculous or more nearly allied to a vulgar spirit then what I meet wth in most gentlemen of England, namely a vayne affectation to fly beyond the moone and to credit themselves . . . wth long and fictitious pedigrees. How many have wee that will confidently tell you their sirnames flourished even in the Saxon times. . . . How many have wee in Lincolneshire that will affirme themselves to have beene gentelmen there ever since the Normans' entrance, when I know there are scarse sixe families in the whole county that can make proofe they had one foot of land there the 20th yeare of K. Henry the third'.[1]

As we have suggested, the line of definition of status between the rich yeomanry and the lesser gentry was indistinct, often confusing men of the period with respect to their own position. It was, to put it bluntly, largely a matter of wealth and of aspiration, for many of the yeomanry preferred to retain their status. The yeoman class begins to emerge importantly at quite different dates in our several counties, but in all it had become by the middle of the sixteenth century a numerous and substantial rural middle class whose chief concern was with land.[2] The yeomen were in the main proprietors of freehold lands, though many, perhaps most of them, held copyhold or leasehold lands as well. Wilson thought that as many as 10,000 of them were really very substantial men, though their advantage as skilful and aggressive farmers was being lost as the lesser gentry turned with greater capital to the exploitation of their estates, while this same authority believed that there were an additional 80,000 families of the class holding more modest but still comfortable estates.[3] These were men who bore the brunt of the burden of local administration, serving as constables, churchwardens, and as overseers of the poor. They were, then, directly concerned with poverty, deeply conscious of the social threat which it contained, and were as a class early inclined to leave a large proportion of their benefactions to the relief of indigence.

Far below them in wealth and status were the husbandmen, an amorphously defined class embracing a very large proportion of the rural population in all counties. Few of them owned land, most of them were small tenant farmers, and in average terms at least they were separated by a wide economic gulf from their yeomen betters. Yet, as we shall see, they were by no means devoid of a sense of social responsibility, since

[1] Holles, *Memorials*, 3.
[2] Campbell, Mildred, *The English yeoman* (New Haven, 1942), 3–20.
[3] Wilson, *State of England*, 19.

some thousands of their tiny gifts and bequests have been included in the massive charitable funds accumulated in this age. Finally, there was a still more numerous class of agricultural labourers and servants, certainly the largest single social group in England. Unfortunately, we know little about the lives and aspirations of men of this class. We have watched for their gifts and bequests with particular care, but this was on the whole a class which did not draft wills because it had nothing to bequeath. This was in fact the very class in which poverty was endemic throughout our period, a class never far above the level of subsistence, and with scant resources to carry it through periods of economic difficulty. It was to the relief and sustenance of the agricultural poor that most of the prodigious national effort which we here describe was directed.

Since their status, their wealth, and their charitable, if not their spiritual, aspirations differed so markedly, we have also thought it well to divide the clergy into two classes, the upper clergy and the lower clergy. By the former, of course, we mean the bishops and, until the Expropriation, the great abbots and priors. For all purposes of computation, though with some slight degree of resulting inaccuracy, the lower clergy have been treated as a rural class, since upwards of 90 per cent of these donors were in fact residents of rural England.

Turning to the urban classes with which we are concerned, we have regarded as merchants those men who so describe themselves in their wills or in other pertinent documents. We shall deal much more fully with the sociology of the merchant class in our discussion of London, comprising the second volume of this work, but it may here be said that with rare exceptions these were men engaged in wholesale trade, though a considerable number of them were devoted to enterprises so extensive and diverse as to cause them to be more properly regarded as speculators and entrepreneurs. It was a small class, even in London, recruited constantly from the provinces, and marked from the earlier decades of our period by clearly and tenaciously held aspirations for the society and the age. It was in average terms a very rich class, and the wealth which it possessed gained enormous added power because it was fluid and disposable. This was the class which was to exercise a decisive influence in forming the basic aspirations of our age, translating them with prodigious generosity into historical reality by the enduring institutions which it founded. Merchant fortunes were quickly won, and could be as quickly lost, and were rarely indeed carried as trading fortunes through a second generation. Men of this group were still a little uncertain of their status, tended themselves to marry and all but to require their widows to marry within the class. Yet the very fact of their great wealth, the boldness of their vision, the massive generosity of their charities, and their willingness to assume an immense burden of social responsibility created for them the reality of status.[1] The age came rather quickly to sense that here was a new aristocracy, in fact socially and historically the most significant element of aristocracy in the realm. The mercantile élite quickly realized, too, the many points of identity in their own aspirations, in their conception of what England ought to be, with the gentry of the land. The merchants themselves bought lands as investments to ensure otherwise fragile fortunes, to secure the status wished by a wife or contemplated for a son, and their daughters, richly endowered, were prizes for whose dowry gentlemen and even the shrewdest of the peers might aspire. Apprenticeships in the London livery companies became valued opportunities for younger sons by gentlemen who now remembered that the great Queen herself had called Sir Martin Calthorpe and Sir Godfrey Boleyn kinsmen.[2] Gentility, it was pointed out, may well be bred in the counting-houses, for 'there are at this day not a few, whose . . . great-grandchildrens children are reputed amõg the oldest and best families of their shires, without any relation to London, which notwithstanding raised them'.[3] Both classes, merchants and gentry, were aggressive, articulate, secular in their instincts, and generous in their acceptance of new and uncharted areas of responsibility. Their interests and their aspirations ran together, said Henry Robinson, the astutest of the observers of the social and political revolution then under way, and in the merging of the aspirations of the gentry of the market place and of the land the future of England would be attained.[4]

A much larger urban class, though not notable for its charities, was the tradesmen. These men ranked far below the merchants in wealth, prestige, and civic pride, being a quite amorphous social group, usually without strong traditions or corporate organization. We have regarded as tradesmen all shopkeepers and retailers not of merchant rank, members of lesser companies, and members of a number of urban occupations such as innkeepers, brewers, and chandlers, who are not easily classified but who were solid members of the urban middle class. Closely related to them was still another urban group, which for want of more precise information we have described simply as 'additional burghers'. These were men, or very frequently their widows, who failed to describe themselves adequately in their wills or deeds of gift, but who are known to have held minor civic office, to have been en-

---

[1] It would lead us far astray to pursue this interesting point. For examples of the literature establishing the status of the merchant, *vide* Wilkinson, Robert, *The merchaunt royall* (L., 1607); Price, Daniel, *The marchant* (Oxford, 1608); Pemberton, William, *The godly merchant* (L., 1613); Preston, John, *Christ's reward* (L., 1655); Reynolds, Edward, *True gain* (L., 1657).

[2] Bolton, Edmund, *The cities advocate* (L., 1629), 8–10.

[3] *Ibid.*, 47.

[4] Jordan, W. K., *Men of substance* (Chicago, 1942), 218–220.

rolled as freemen of their cities, or whose wills make it clear that they were engaged in some sort of commercial activity. Both the average size of their charitable bequests and, more importantly, the structure of their charitable interests make it statistically evident that most of them were in fact tradesmen, with some admixture of small merchants who cannot be certainly identified.

We have also been particularly interested in gathering details concerning all the benefactions of the artisans and urban poor, a large and a rapidly growing class which our evidence would suggest constituted fully 80 per cent of the population of the provincial cities and possibly 90 per cent of the population of London. This is, of course, a population group offering most interesting comparisons with the husbandmen and agricultural labourers of rural England. These were the working men of the cities, the artisans, the industrial workers, the porters, the servants, and the floating mass of unemployed who throughout our period comprised a labour surplus in every city with which we have been concerned. Regrettably, we have learned relatively little about them or their aspirations, since they were on the whole rootless and propertyless men, too poor either to draw wills or to provide even nominal charitable gifts during their lifetimes.

Counted also as an urban group are the rising professional classes, centred principally on London but with smaller entities well established before our period was out in every provincial city and in numerous market towns. This group, as we shall note, was at once relatively numerous and extraordinarily generous. The largest number were lawyers, who were likewise on balance the largest donors, they being followed numerically by the physicians, public officials and civil servants, scriveners, notaries, apothecaries, teachers, parish clerks, administrators (as, for example, the full-time director of the affairs of a large almshouse), artists, scholars, and the rest.

Finally, we have a large group of donors, both urban and rural in composition, whom reasonably diligent and certainly extensive research simply failed to identify with respect to status. These benefactors comprise almost 19 per cent of all individual donors and have necessarily been described as 'unidentified donors'. A large proportion of them were women, who are extraordinarily difficult to identify if in their wills they clothe themselves in the eternal anonymity of the title 'widow' or 'spinster' and are equally vague with reference to their forbears and collateral relations. It may be said that the size and structure of gifts and bequests made by members of this group would suggest that in so far as they were urban dwellers they possessed the composite character of tradesmen and that the much larger number who were residents of rural parishes fall somewhere in this defining respect between the status of the yeomanry and the lower gentry.

2. *The means of grace*

Before turning to a study of the contributions and the patterns of social aspiration of the several classes, it will be well to say as much as we can regarding their wealth and their relative generosity as they drew upon that wealth for social purposes in which they believed. It must be emphasized that the assessments that follow are for no more than a very small fraction of donors in any one class and that for various reasons, with which we shall deal, they may not be typical either of those members of a social class who made charitable contributions or of the class as a whole. These assessments of the total wealth of the estates of donors of the several social classes are in the first place approximate, having been drawn from wills, which tended chronically to over-value property, and from inventories and inquisitions *post mortem*, which tended quite notoriously to under-value lands and chattels. It should also be pointed out that we are supplying average amounts derived from a long historical period in which the purchasing power of money was steadily declining. Further, our figures provide a reasonably reliable estimate only of the disposable estate, since we have had no reason to explore in the historical wilderness of entails. These data, then, attempt to assess only the disposable wealth available to donors, which, however, is socially and historically the effective and fruitful wealth of a man or of a class. Since the wealth of most merchants was in cash, inventories, and negotiable debts, though even the most prudent often died with 'desperate debts' to harry their executors, their assets are not only easily totalled but were easily liquidated, with the result that relatively we may somewhat exaggerate mercantile fortuntes. But we must hastily add that those whom we have treated as the 'great merchants' of London in average terms likewise held as much in landed wealth as did the upper gentry of four of the eight rural counties with which we are concerned. Finally, we should point out that these appraisals are of the estates of men drawn statistically from the oldest segment of the population, of men who normally at least had enjoyed sufficient time to put their affairs in order in contemplation of death. Thousands of the wills we have read indicate, frequently with precise amounts or values given, which we scarcely need say have not been included in estate values, that dowries have been settled on daughters, provision made for younger sons, trusts already established for wives, daughters, and other dependents, and personal gifts made to friends or apprentices. Many wills, too, make it clear that a once prosperous merchant or gentleman had in old age lost his grip on affairs and that the estate left was no more than a shell of a once considerable fortune. These data, then, do to some quite unknown but substantial degree tend to reflect the erosion which age and dispositions made in contemplation of death had brought to bear on their earlier maximum value.

Our figures for the estate values of peers making charitable bene-factions are too fragmentary to be of worth and hence will not be cited. The wealth disposed by only nine members of this class can be approxi-mated, this being much too small a sample, and much of the landed worth even for this small group was locked in entails which cannot be valued with any reasonable degree of accuracy. Our sparse data do, however, suggest an average true, or net, wealth for the nobility con-siderably more modest than most estimates we have seen.[1] There has been sustained and brilliant discussion of the tangled question of the

[1] The subject is most tangled in controversy, and we stand in great need of averages rather than of proofs adduced from easily available but individual instances. We do have good figures for 1436, the always careful Gray having estimated that in that year the average baronial landed wealth (and here and below we have converted to capital sums by applying the multiplier 20) was of the order of £17,300 (Gray, H. L., 'Incomes from land in England in 1436', Eng. Hist. Rev., XLIX, 1934, 622). A seventeenth century observer, Wilson, though he despaired of the problem, suggested as an average that the great magnates of his age might have possessed a total worth of about £100,000, while the lesser nobility, the barons and viscounts, disposed estates valued at a little more than £58,000 (State of England, 20–22). Reasonably reliable data from the later years of our period, prepared in connection with the work of the Com-mittee for Compounding, suggest an average worth for the estates of the Royalist peers of £30,290, the values for individual peers ranging widely and wildly from £340 for one impecunious earl to the great sum of £150,000, at which the worth of the Earl of Thanet was appraised (Klotz, E. L., and Godfrey Davies, 'The wealth of Royalist peers and baronets during the Puritan Revolution', Eng. Hist. Rev., LVIII, 1943, 218–219). Stone, who believes that the wealth of the nobility was declining absolutely as well as relatively in the Elizabethan period because of failure to deal with the inflationary process then under way, excessive standard of living, and chronic litigation, seems to set the 'average' at between £40,000 and £60,000 of capital worth for something like sixty of the Elizabethan peerage and holds that the whole class stood in considerable financial danger when it was saved by James's lavish favour and by aldermanic marriages (Stone, Lawrence, 'The anatomy of the Elizabethan aristocracy', Econ. Hist. Rev., XVIII, 1948, 19–20, 38, 40, et passim). Professor Trevor-Roper, in reply, agrees that the Elizabethan peerage was in real economic difficulties, but says that the noble families were saved by their tenacious disposition to hold their central estates in a rising land market, while he very correctly stresses the recuperative powers an estate possessed when the key lands were not sold (Trevor-Roper, H. R., 'The Elizabethan aristocracy', Econ. Hist. Rev., 2d. ser., III, 1951, 288–289). In a later and very valuable study of the estates of twenty-three peers of the period 1617–1642, he arrives at an average worth of about £169,000 for those included in the sample. The list, it should be said, tends to include a disproportionate number of the 'great peers' and for other reasons seems to be set too high (The gentry 1540–1640, L., 1953). It is our own very general conclusion that the estates of the peerage declined sharply in a relative sense and slightly in an absolute sense throughout the sixteenth century, rising very rapidly in the seventeenth century, when, it must be remembered, the peerage was on the whole a much larger and a very different body. The ex-tremely important point of the amazing fluidity even of the landed classes must always be borne in mind in these discussions.

wealth of the peerage and of the gentry in recent years, which has now reached the stage at which most extensive research of a quite dull but extremely important kind is required if further light is to be thrown on the matter. As we shall later point out, the nobility made only slight contribution to the social needs of England during our period, withdrew from responsibility which they had once assumed as a matter of class obligation, and were as a class relatively unimportant in the shaping of the course of modern social and cultural history. This may be because their wealth was locked in land and leases, because they had failed to adjust their wealth and standards of living to the requirements of a new age, or, and we think this, broadly speaking, more likely, because the whole slope of historical and social change ran counter to their own essentially cautious instincts. In any event, they left little of their wealth for charitable uses.

We feel on much more certain ground in our assessment of the wealth of the upper gentry who left charitable benefactions and whose estates can be appraised with fair accuracy. There were ninety-eight such estates in the course of our period, for which an average worth of £3484[1] may be established, while the median estate amounted to £3014. There are, it must be emphasized, amazing regional differences, the average worth of men of this class ranging from £1669 for Somerset and £1984 for Yorkshire[2] to the very substantial average total of £12,298 for Norfolk.[3] In fact, our evidence suggests both consistently and persuasively that any discussion of the wealth of any landed class, and most particularly of the gentry, is quite meaningless unless the approach is undertaken on a carefully established regional basis. Thus it seems clear that the average Yorkshire knight disposed rather less in wealth than did the squire of Buckinghamshire or Worcestershire. But wherever resident, men of this class were in average terms extremely well-to-do, were deeply sensitive to the needs of their communities, and if the estate values suggested by this probably inadequate sampling are valid, left the surprisingly large proportion of 7·12 per cent of the whole worth of their estates for charitable uses. Here again, however, there are extremely interesting and important regional differences, the upper gentry of Kent, who were so often non-resident, having left no more than 2·57 per cent of the total worth of their estates to charitable causes,

---

[1] For this and all other classes, save for husbandmen and yeomen, estate values have been reckoned to the nearest £.

[2] It should be said that the validity of these averages, and the same is true for the lower gentry, is weakened by the disproportionate number included from Yorkshire.

[3] For further details of this matter, *vide* Table VII (Appendix). It should again be remarked that for the upper gentry and all other classes we have been able to include in these estimates only the relatively small proportion of charitable benefactors whose estates can be accurately valued.

while those of Yorkshire and Somerset, surely among the poorest in England, left 10·77 per cent and 11·22 per cent respectively for charitable uses.

There are much fuller, and hence probably more reliable, data for the lower gentry. The estates of 342 of those who made charitable contributions during the course of our period have been appraised, the average estate being valued at the surprisingly low figure of £980, suggesting an average income of not more than £50 p.a. for members of the class. Even if the ubiquitous and relatively very poor Yorkshire gentry are wholly excluded from our computations, the average worth rises to only £1319. The median estate for the whole group may be valued at £1179. Among this class, too, there were marked regional differences, ranging from an average worth of £2565 for the relatively rich landed gentry resident at the time of their death in London and in Middlesex to the £699 for Lancashire and the £693 for Yorkshire. Referring again to our sampling of counties, the proportion of the total estates left to charity by men of this class may be set at 4·29 per cent of the whole, but again with quite an amazing range from the 1·60 per cent thus disposed by the tight-fisted Norfolk gentry to the extremely generous 13·78 per cent recorded for Kent.[1]

[1] Professor Gray suggests that the worth of members of the lower gentry in 1436 was considerably lower, in the range (again converting to capital amounts) of from £400 to £780, while that of the knights ran from £1200 to £3740 (*Eng. Hist. Rev.*, XLIX, 1934, 624–630). Hoskins tells us that in 1522–1523 in Devon only eight of the gentry of the whole county were assessed who held lands valued at £100 p.a. or more, the generality of the gentry, upper and lower, having landed estates worth from £50 p.a. to £100 p.a. (Hoskins, W. G., *Devon*, L., 1954, 82). Wilson was certainly wildly inaccurate in his offhand estimates of a worth of from £1000 to £2000 p.a. for the upper gentry and from £500 to £1000 p.a. for the squirearchy (*State of England*, 23–24). Sir John Oglander, a careful and accurate business man, tells us that in 1623–1624 he spent £450 9s 6d, which was more than any other man on the Isle of Wight could dispose, while in 1631 he recorded his outlay of £747 3s 5d in 'his own blood', since it far exceeded the worth of his estate (Bamford, *A Royalist's notebook*, 231–238). Professor Tawney proves that the gentry were acquiring land most aggressively during the whole period 1560–1640 but does not make it clear that this was a consequence of the rising wealth of the gentry rather than because the class itself was expanding very rapidly in numbers (*Econ. Hist. Rev.*, XI, 1941, 1–38). We believe that our estimates of wealth for both the upper gentry and the lower gentry may not be far off the mark in appraising their relatively modest wealth through the period as a whole. We are not so certain regarding the curve of that wealth because our sample when arranged in periods is inadequate and, even more importantly, because we cannot estimate the related curve of the inflationary process. But it is our impression that the wealth of both groups rose very steeply absolutely and only slightly relatively in the century 1540–1640. More important to the whole discussion is the fact that the class was amazingly fluid. When we speak of the gentry of 1640 we are simply not, with few exceptions, speaking of families who possessed that status in 1540. Moreover, the class itself expanded in numbers enormously during the course of this amazing

We have particulars regarding the estates of a large number (615) of yeomen who left charitable benefactions, though it will be observed that a disproportionate number of these appraisals are drawn from Somerset and Yorkshire, both being in our period relatively poor counties. In average terms these yeomen left estates valued at £181 12s 4d, a surprisingly substantial figure, while the median estate for members of the class was £164 3s 2d. Once again, the range was very wide when we scrutinize the data by counties, the yeomanry of Kent and Norfolk having possessed estates with the most comfortable average value of £415 9s 8d and £442 12s 9d respectively, while those of Somerset and Yorkshire were relatively quite poor. Thus in average terms it may be said that a Norfolk yeoman possessed a substance almost four times as great as that disposed by a yeoman of Somerset, while again in average terms the yeomanry of Norfolk and Kent were not much less prosperous than were the lesser gentry of such counties as Yorkshire and Lancashire. This fact once more suggests the great difficulty, the very real danger, in generalizing about data in our period, particularly for classes as amorphously defined as the gentry and the yeomanry. The yeomanry particularly, certainly more markedly than any other single class save the merchants, were rising rapidly in wealth and in status through most of our period. While they were no more than an emerging class in most counties before 1540, during the Elizabethan era yeoman estates possessed an average worth of £91 7s 9d, whereas in the early Stuart era the average value of their estates showed an amazing increase to £188 2s 4d. This was one class which both relatively and absolutely did well for itself during much of our period, though its decline had begun by the close of our age. This interesting, admired, and sturdy class assumed a considerable degree of social responsibility in every county with which we are concerned, our sampling suggesting that these men left 4·47 per cent of the whole worth of their estates for charitable causes, again with a quite wide range when we refer to the several counties. Thus the yeomanry of Norfolk, the most prosperous of the realm, left only 1·05 per cent of their wealth for charitable uses, they being even more cautious in their outlays than their betters among the lower gentry of the county,

century. Finally, we are strongly inclined to the view that after the period of digestion of monastic spoils and the profitable but speculative gains of laying land down to sheep grazing was past (*ca.* 1570), most of the gains in wealth made by particular members of the class were as a consequence of the influx of London wealth into the gentry and the growing tendency of members of the class, probably because their estates barely supported their standards of living, to indulge in speculative risks in ventures ranging from coal mining to the plantation of America. We are in this whole connection much impressed by Professor Trevor-Roper's statement that of the seventy-odd Elizabethan and Jacobean houses about which he knows the particulars only one was built from landed wealth, all the rest being monuments to success in trade or at the court.

while those of Kent, where the class was early and solidly established, disposed the very considerable proportion of 6·57 per cent of all their wealth for charitable causes.[1]

The enormous class which we have described as husbandmen gave little to charity, principally, we should suppose, because it was only scantly above the line of poverty. A far greater economic gulf separated the husbandmen from the yeomanry than separated the yeomanry from the lower gentry, though it must be emphasized that this was a rural class with some measure of status, of great respectability, and with sufficient substance to support itself, save in times of general hardship, and to make modest but extraordinarily interesting contributions for charitable causes which appealed to its conservative instincts. For England as a whole, the estates of members of this class have been assessed in average terms at £21 11s 6d, though it should at once be observed that this sum is considerably affected by the large number of these estates which we have found and valued in Somerset, where the class was badly off during the whole of our period, its average worth there being no more than £12 5s 6d. The class was also economically submerged in Kent, while in four of our counties the average worth of upwards of £30 suggests a much more comfortable status for a class which comprised a very large proportion of the total population of the realm.

But it was urban wealth, and more specifically London wealth, which was to be decisive in framing the pattern of social aspirations in the England of our period and in translating those aspirations into effective and enduring institutions. The merchant class, the smallest of all clearly defined social groups save for the peerage, was to assume an immense

[1] Wilson thought the yeomanry were declining as early as 1600, though he believed that there might well be 10,000 such families of rich yeomen disposing from £300 to £1000 yearly, while there might be as many as 80,000 with estates valued at from £300 to £500 (State of England, 19). These estimates are much too high; there certainly was a well-defined group of very rich yeomen, but of the 615 regarding whose estates we have precise knowledge there were only 11 with wealth of more than £1000. A careful recent estimate sets the value of the average yeoman estate at £176 10s in Leicestershire in about 1640 (VCH, Leics., II, 201), while Miss Campbell, having examined upwards of three thousand deeds relating to yeoman land purchases, tells us that 59 per cent of their land purchases involved sums of £100 or less, 78 per cent sums of £200 or less (English yeoman, 78). Though the analysis is not so applied, we should suppose that Barley's analysis of Lincolnshire estate inventories would most helpfully document the rise of the yeomanry in that region, where in 1540 only 4·4 per cent of all estates were valued at £100 or more, this proportion having risen to 8·2 per cent in 1605 and to 16 per cent in 1635 (Econ. Hist. Rev., 2d. ser., VII, 1955, 293). These figures, it should be noted, would certainly be substantially increased had the wills and inventories in the PCC and the PCY, where rich yeomen's wills tended to be proved, been consulted as well as those in the district registries.

burden of social responsibility and early to establish its leadership in laying out the course which English social and institutional history was to take. This was a class armed at once with firmly held aspirations and with the viable wealth necessary to give them full effect. Taking in view the whole of England, there were 569 merchant donors making charitable benefactions whose estates can be accurately valued, whose average estate may be appraised at £5815 7s 7d. This figure is, however, almost meaningless because of the vast difference in wealth existing between the average provincial merchant and that of his London confrère. But even the provincial merchant was in average terms a rich man, his estate during our period being worth £1428 3s 9d, an amount, it will be observed, considerably in excess of that of the lower gentry of the realm. But in London, taking into account both great merchants and lesser merchants, between whom there was a great economic difference, the average merchant fortune during our period may be set at £7780 2s 7d, or well over twice that of the upper gentry of England.[1] Very broadly speaking, it can be said, indeed, that in London the average estate of lesser merchants was somewhat less than but comparable to the wealth of the lower gentry, while that of the great merchants was not far off from the disposable wealth in the hands of the nobility of the realm. All this is of great social and economic importance, but of even greater social significance is the added fact that the merchants of this period, whether of London or of the provinces, were so prodigally generous. Of all the great wealth which they disposed, the merchants of England left more than a sixth (17·25 per cent) for charitable uses, not taking into account the great sums which so many of these donors had vested during their lifetimes. This telling proportion ranged widely, though it was always very high, from 6·12 per cent for a small group of Kentish merchants whose estates can be valued to an incredible 41·54 per cent for a larger group in Somerset, while the decisively important London proportion of the total worth of merchant estates vested for charitable causes was 16·76 per cent. No class in England, then, even approached these men either in disposable wealth, in clarity and aggressiveness of aspirations, or in generosity in seeking to attain the social ends which they held so tenaciously in view.

A great economic as well as social gulf separated the merchant aristocracy from the tradesmen, while, as we shall later note, there were also most pronounced differences in the aspirations held by these two urban classes. While it can be said that in average terms men of this class left estates valued at £587 10s 6d, it is more meaningful to point out that a London tradesman of our period, again in average terms, possessed an estate valued at £1463 1s 3d, of considerably greater value

---

[1] We here deal only very briefly with the subject of the merchant wealth of London, since it will be discussed in detail in the second volume of this work.

than the average estate of the lesser gentry, whereas a provincial shop-keeper left an estate valued at no more than £234 19s 9d, not consider-ably more than that of the average yeoman. It should at once be said, however, that in social terms this wealth was extremely important and viable, since a full eighth (12·46 per cent) of it was disposed for charit-able causes, it thus having possessed a social utility almost thrice that of the wealth of the lesser gentry or of the yeomanry.

We have far fewer data than we would wish regarding the value of the estates of artisans making charitable dispositions, our findings for London being particularly meagre. It should also be said that such figures as we do have tend to be drawn from the estates of skilled artisans and craftsmen who had been able not only to support their families but to build up modest competences. For all our counties, the average estate of an artisan may be valued at £43 4s 6d, or approximately twice that of the husbandman of the period. In such counties as Somer-set, Buckinghamshire, and Worcestershire the average values are very modest indeed, whereas in London and more particularly in Norfolk, where most of our estates are those of highly skilled mechanics connected with the cloth trade, the average far exceeds that of the country at large.

We may conclude this discussion with notes on the wealth of two other classes for which, regrettably, we have too little information to permit extended discussion. We have assessed the estates of 128 of the lower clergy, but the average of £224 6s 8d is really meaningless be-cause of the not infrequent instances of clergymen inheriting consider-able landed fortunes as scions of the gentry, or, as in London, which has been omitted entirely, of members of the clergy inheriting very large estates from merchant fathers or brothers. Our data for the professional classes are also far too scattered and meagre to permit useful discussion, though it may at least be said that of the seventy-six estates regarding which we have full information the average worth was relatively very high, £2548 19s 8d, and that of these the largest single group were lawyers and judges, twenty-two in all, whose estates pos-sessed an average worth of £2348 13s.

3. The measure of responsibility

We have dealt in an incomplete and perhaps inconclusive fashion with the means which the several classes of men disposed during our period. We have sought at least to measure roughly the amount of wealth, of disposable wealth, at hand, but the important concern for us is the intensity with which the various classes undertook the immense social responsibilities of the age. Here we have differences far more striking and far more important historically than wealth itself, which might be either socially sterile or immensely fruitful. Further, we have been con-cerned, in the discussion just finished, only with a relatively small

number of our many donors, those whose estate values could with some
reliability be established; we are now concerned with the flow of charitable funds from all our nearly 35,000 donors, in so far as they can be
grouped into the several social classes of which humanity was then
comprised. Of our 34,963 individual donors, the social status of 28,362,
or 81·11 per cent of the whole number, has been determined, there
being a residuum of 6601 who remain cloaked in social anonymity. It
is first of all significant that only about half (49·53 per cent) of our
donors were rural dwellers, though without any doubt the rural
population in the whole area under consideration comprised something like 80 per cent of the total population.[1] In other words, the
relatively small urban population of these regions contributed a far
larger, a most disproportionate, number of donors (31·47 per cent)
than did all the rural groups.[2] When this fact is further assessed in terms
of the extent of contribution, measuring the degree of responsibility
assumed, the disproportion is all the more startling, since a relatively
small urban class provided more than 62 per cent (62·46 per cent) of all the
charitable funds accumulated, as contrasted with about 21 per cent (21·52
per cent) which may certainly be attributed to the several rural classes.

   The powerful and effective intervention of the numerically tiny
merchant class of England in the social and cultural needs of the nation
is suggested immediately when we observe that they comprised more

[1] In the following table, R indicates Rural, U, Urban.

Class		Number of donors	Percentage of total benefactions	Percentage of all donors
			per cent	per cent
Crown		36	4·63	0·10
Nobility	R	192	4·02	0·55
Upper gentry	R	959	5·53	2·74
Lower gentry	R	3753	5·84	10·73
Yeomen	R	5144	1·49	14·71
Husbandmen	R	5079	0·09	14·53
Agricultural labourers	R	634	0·005	1·81
Upper clergy	U	175	4·97	0·50
Lower clergy	R	1561	4·55	4·46
Merchants	U	3679	43·17	10·52
Tradesmen	U	2640	4·82	7·55
Burghers	U	1557	2·91	4·45
Artisans	U	2087	0·28	5·97
Professions	U	866	6·31	2·48
Unidentified		6601	11·40	18·89
Totals		34,963	100·01	99·99

[2] It should be noted that throughout this discussion the benefactions of the
Crown and of all unidentified donors have been excluded.

than a tenth of the whole number of donors and gave the staggering proportion of 43·17 per cent of the whole immense sum accumulated for charitable uses during our entire period. It is sobering indeed to realize that they alone gave very nearly half the total which may certainly be ascribed to donors of known classes, and that they alone gave almost twice as much as all the rural classes of England combined. They are followed in importance by the gentry, which as an entity contributed rather more than 11 per cent (11·37 per cent), and they in turn by the clergy as a whole, which gave somewhat more than 9 per cent (9·52 per cent) of the whole charitable wealth. The rapidly growing and on the whole the comfortably rich professional classes gave most liberally in relation to their numbers, somewhat more than 6 per cent of the whole amount having been afforded by their great generosity. No other single group of men gave as much as a twentieth of England's charitable resources, it being remarkable that not only the professions but the tradesmen as well were to give substantially more than the 4·02 per cent of charitable wealth provided by a nobility which had all but abandoned the social responsibility it was traditionally supposed to bear. There remains something more than 11 per cent of the aggregate of charitable wealth given by men of uncertain status of whom it can only be said that the larger number were rural dwellers.

When we seek to measure the differing degrees of social responsibility of men of our age, even by relatively refined groupings of social classes, we still speak somewhat inexactly of the process by which social change was accomplished in England. Men gave as individuals, disciplined normally by the aspirations of the class and the generation to which they belonged, though in the whole of this essay we have said little about them as individuals, reserving this emphasis for the discussion in subsequent volumes. Yet there were very great differences in the scale of giving by individual donors, as wealth, intensity of aspiration, and purposefulness determined whether a benefaction would be nominal at best or quite sufficient to endow an almshouse or a loan foundation. We have accordingly analysed the 'depth of giving' of donors of known social status in three of our counties, London, Somerset, and Yorkshire, in which are to be found almost exactly half of all donors and which together contributed upwards of 72 per cent of the charitable wealth accumulated in the England of our period. There were in all 17,450 of these donors, who together gave the enormous total of £2,057,709 13s of charitable capital, or the very substantial average sum of £117 18s 5d for each benefactor.

Yet the great mass of these gifts, from donors of every class, fell within the range of 1d to £9 19s. Though the total of gifts made within these limits amounted to only slightly more than 1 per cent (1·04 per cent) of the immense whole of charitable wealth provided in these three counties, this was the measure of the charitable benefactions made by almost two-thirds (65·22 per cent) of all donors.[1] This is to say that a very large group of 11,381 gave in all no more than the relatively unimportant total of £21,363 10s towards the charitable needs of the age. Such was the measure of generosity and participation of great numbers of men drawn from all classes, though a gift of £9 19s might represent only a token gift for a nobleman and the life savings of a husbandman. It is interesting to note that here are to be found more than a fifth (21·88 per cent) of all donors of the upper gentry, upwards of 58 per cent of the lower gentry, and about 55 per cent of the lower clergy. Included in this category, as we should expect, are almost 87 per cent of all yeoman donors and nearly all (99·57 per cent) husbandmen. Somewhat surprisingly, we find among these relatively very modest donors well over a fourth (27·81 per cent) of all merchant donors, closer analysis suggesting that these were men, often quite rich, who honoured the rigorously charitable tradition of their class with only token contributions and who, unless the smallness of their bequests could be explained by reverses of fortune or estates encumbered with obligations, were despised for the fact by their contemporaries.

A relatively small proportion (7·72 per cent) of all donors made gifts or bequests in the next range of generosity extending from £10 to £19 19s, the total of such benefactions constituting somewhat less than 1 per cent (0·82 per cent) of the whole of the charitable resources of these counties. It is interesting to observe, though, that the measure of the generosity of nearly 73 per cent (72·94 per cent) of all donors, men and women of all classes, is to be found within the range of the most nominal gift of a penny or so to just short of £20, though the total amount of their charity accounts for somewhat less than 2 per cent (1·86 per cent) of the great sum with which we are concerned.

In the next range of giving, amounts between £20 and £99 19s, we find a large proportion of capital sums, of endowments some hundreds of which survive to the present day. These were, in terms of seventeenth century purchasing power, substantial charities, quite sufficient to ease materially the burden of poor relief in a rural parish, to found a modest scholarship, or to create a useful loan fund. There were 2437 donors making such gifts, the total of their benefactions accounting for slightly more than 5 per cent of all the charitable wealth disposed by these counties. It is significant that between a fifth and a fourth of all donors of such classes as the lower gentry, the merchants, the tradesmen, and the professional groups are to be found in this range of generosity.

The next range of giving, in amounts of from £100 to £499 19s, in-

---

[1] For this discussion *vide* Table VIII (Appendix, pp. 378–381), where the depth-of-giving data are set out for these three counties in a composite table, and where bar graphs are also presented.

cludes very considerable endowments indeed, this being quite sufficient to found a modest almshouse, to create a substantial apprenticeship foundation, or fully to provide for the relief of the poor in most rural or village parishes in England. There were in all 1650 such donors in these three counties, composing not much short of a tenth (9·46 per cent) of the whole number, while the total of their benefactions represented about a sixth (16·91 per cent) of all the charitable funds under discussion. It is interesting to observe that nearly half (46·24 per cent) of the donors giving within this range were merchants and that five notably generous classes, the merchants, the lower gentry, the tradesmen, the burghers, and the professional groups, account for upwards of 82 per cent of these most substantial benefactions. In fact, it may here be pointed out that so economically formidable was the capital sum of £500 in the England of this period that somewhat more than 96 per cent of all our donors gave smaller benefactions.

A man must needs have been very rich indeed to provide an endowment of from £500 to £999 19s for charitable uses, since it will be recalled that the average total wealth even of the lower gentry of the realm probably did not exceed the larger of these amounts. These were sums ample enough to found a large almshouse, to establish a well-endowed grammar school, or to create a lectureship foundation even in London; yet there were in all 311 such donors, comprising 1·78 per cent of the whole number, who together gave the very large total of £212,743 15s for various charitable uses, this amounting to about a tenth (10·34 per cent) of the whole sum. It is most significant that of these donors rather more than half (51·13 per cent) were merchants, as compared with an eighth (12·54 per cent) who were drawn from the upper and lesser gentry combined. As importantly, of this group of large benefactors, who were creating institutions with their generosity that were to remake England, nearly four-fifths (77·81 per cent) were members of the several urban classes. Here we discover the true centre of gravity of socially important wealth in England, here we discover the true pillars of the new society which was being built by the incredible generosity of this period.

All this is even more fully revealed as we analyse the social origins of the great benefactors, the pillars of the society, who created charitable endowments of £1000 or more. There were 323 such benefactors in these three counties, accounting for only a tiny proportion of all the donors in these regions. In all, this very small group of men and women gave the staggering total of £1,353,555 15s, or close to two-thirds (65·78 per cent) of the whole of the charities of the counties under consideration. The charitable endowments disposed by these donors were truly huge, amounting in average terms to the great sum of £4190 11s 6d, capital sufficient for the creation of renowned and enduring institutions. In fact, we may well say that this relatively very small group of donors were to create the institutions of modern England and that it was their aspirations which were to be decisive in determining the whole slope of social and cultural history in the modern world. These great donors were predominantly, of course, drawn from the merchant aristocracy, there having been 189 merchant benefactors, or somewhat more than 58 per cent of the whole number. The second largest number, thirty in all, were members of the several professional classes, a considerably larger number, incidentally, than we have recorded for the great and lesser gentry combined. Something more than four-fifths (80·50 per cent) of all these great donors, who so decisively shaped the development of modern institutions, disposed urban wealth, which was aggressive, intensely secular, highly viable, and disciplined by certainty of aspiration. Though many thousands of men and women had made their due contribution, often at great sacrifice, it remained for this small group of donors to provide the ultimately important resources required for the completion of the grand design which men held so tenaciously and courageously for the betterment of the world in which they lived.

4. The aspirations of the several classes of men

We have been examining in some detail the quantitative contributions of the several social classes, and of individual donors within those classes. But of equal importance is what may be described as the qualitative interests of the several classes, since here is revealed the whole structure of aspirations held by these groups, aspirations which were in quite differing degrees to be translated into institutional reality. We shall note that there were profoundly different views held of the needs of mankind by the various social groups, just as we shall later observe markedly different rates of velocity of change in aspirations among them. We shall now comment rather fully on the commitments made by the various social classes to the several great heads under which we have grouped their charitable benefactions, with some remarks as well on significant regional differences as they may appear.[1]

---

[1] It would be tedious indeed to comment on the individual charitable heads, the tables for which were too cumbersome to present. Reference to Table X, where the broad aspects of the contributions of the various classes are submitted, will be helpful in following this discussion. It will also be recalled that taking all donors and all classes into account the *all-England* totals and distributions were as follows:

Poor	Social Rehabilitation	Municipal Betterments	Education	Religion
£1,129,351 9s	£319,446 12s	£160,776 1s.	£833,493 12s	£659,628 15s
(36·40 per cent)	(10·30 per cent)	(5·18 per cent)	(26·86 per cent)	(21·26 per cent)

The table, in necessarily abbreviated form, on which this discussion is based is presented as Table X (Appendix).

The nobility, who accounted for no more than a modest 4·02 per cent of all charitable wealth in our period, were also on the whole eccentric in the range and quality of their interests and distributions. An extremely high proportion (52·68 per cent) of all their benefactions were dedicated to poor relief; only the very poor classes of the society gave in proportion as much for this purpose. In three rural counties, in fact, their devotion to this cause was so great that upwards of 68 per cent of all their giving was for the succour of the needy, with the extraordinary proportion of about 91 per cent so provided in Kent. Though members of the nobility made a number of great almshouse foundations, the peers in general were far too often inclined to follow mediaeval precedents by leaving large sums to be distributed as funeral doles or as immediate alms on a vast scale, such distributions, as we have frequently noted, possessing only slight social utility. The second great concern of the nobility was with the strengthening of the educational resources of the nation, to which they gave almost a fourth (25·63 per cent) of all their charitable funds, or only slightly less than the national average. Their interest in this regard was heavily concentrated on the needs of the universities, over-matched only by that of the upper clergy and the professional classes. The interest of the class in the new and extremely important experiments in social rehabilitation which characterized the age was relatively most modest (2·97 per cent), while their want of concern for municipal betterments, absorbing only 1·27 per cent of all their charitable funds, was rivalled only by the husbandmen and the upper clergy. Somewhat surprisingly, the proportion (17·45 per cent) of their charitable wealth devoted to religious uses was markedly lower than that of the realm at large, with, however, a quite high proportion of their total charitable wealth having been designated for chantries (6·03 per cent) and church building (5·42 per cent). We may conclude that on balance the nobility of this period were remarkable for neither the extent nor the quality of their benefactions. Distrusted and harassed by the Tudors, their estates locked in entail and too often poorly managed, bound to standards of living and housing which could impose very heavy debits on their resources, this was a class which had surrendered not only the prime responsibilities for the social order but the determination of the future course of social history to newer, more vigorous, and infinitely more generous classes of men.

One such class was the upper gentry, a relatively small social group in the England of this period, who were to contribute in all £171,658 9s of charitable wealth, or 5·53 per cent of the whole great total for the society. To the needs of the poor the great gentry gave rather more than 36 per cent of all their charitable resources, with a particularly heavy concentration of funds for the endowment of poor relief in their own parishes. Their concern for this great need was almost precisely of the intensity of the nation at large (36·40 per cent), but from county to county exhibited a rather wide spread of from about a fourth (24·08 per cent) given for this use in Lancashire to the amazingly high proportion of three-fourths (76·82 per cent) in Worcestershire. These men devoted almost exactly a third (33·66 per cent) of their benefactions to the betterment of the educational resources of the nation, considerably more, it will be noted, than the proportion for the realm at large (26·86 per cent), with their contributions about evenly divided between the universities and the founding of grammar schools in their own communities. They were only cautiously interested in schemes of social rehabilitation (4·87 per cent), while proportionately their concern with municipal betterments (2·02 per cent) was not much greater than that of the nobility. Their devotion to the needs of the church, to which they gave 22·80 per cent of all their funds, was roughly comparable to that of the society at large, with, however, a persistent and old-fashioned tendency to endow chantries and prayers generally (8·60 per cent) that considerably exceeded the contributions made for this purpose by the nation as a whole. In several counties, most notably in Hampshire, Lancashire, and Norfolk, a very substantial proportion of the gifts of the upper gentry were dedicated to religious needs, while in one, Buckinghamshire, where there was a considerable infusion of London blood and wealth in the class, the upper gentry were throughout our whole period resolutely secular in their aspirations, no more than 8·43 per cent of their benefactions having been made for religious uses.

The structure of aspirations exhibited by the lower gentry differs markedly from that which we have just analysed of their greater and richer brethren. The lesser gentry comprised a large and a substantial body of donors whose benefactions totalled £181,092 7s, or not quite 6 per cent (5·84 per cent) of the whole of the charitable wealth of England. Since, broadly speaking, as we descend in the social scale for both rural and urban groups, concern for the needs of the poor increases in a most marked fashion, it is not surprising that men of this class devoted a substantially larger proportion of their charitable wealth to this worthy purpose than did the great gentry. In all, they gave the large total of £80,619 1s to this use, this being 44·52 per cent of their total benefactions, with a particularly heavy concentration on endowments for parochial relief. In five of our counties the preoccupation of the gentry with the needs of the poor was so great that well over half of all their gifts were for this use. The gentry disposed relatively modest sums for municipal improvements (2·97 per cent), while only slightly more (3·85 per cent) was given for experiments in social rehabilitation; the founding of apprenticeship endowments and the setting up of workhouses both had some measure of interest for them. They devoted far less of their capital wealth to education (23·35 per cent) than did the upper gentry, exhibiting quite steadily a slightly greater interest in the founding of schools than in the strengthening of the universities. Their devotion to the church and its needs, to which they gave about a fourth (25·31 per cent) of all their charitable wealth, was slightly more intensive than that of the nation at large, with a notably high proportion of their funds having been given for prayers (11·00 per cent) and for church repairs. It should be said, however, that in this one respect there were notable differences in the intensity of interest among the lower gentry in the various regions, the proportion of total charitable wealth devoted to religious needs ranging from an incredibly low 6·91 per cent for Buckinghamshire to the 42·29 per cent for Yorkshire. But the gentry in all counties were substantial and responsible men, deeply concerned with essentially local needs, whether it was the care of the parish poor or the fabric of the parish church, and exhibiting throughout the realm a remarkably homogeneous and disciplined concern for the welfare of the society to which they were to make such a variety of contributions.

We have observed that the gentry in its lower social and economic strata merged with the yeomanry from which so many of its members had sprung. Be that as it may, the composite aspirations of the yeomanry differed markedly and significantly from those of the gentry. The yeomen, comprising as they did the largest group of donors for any single class, made what can only be regarded as a modest charitable contribution, the £46,114 14s afforded by them constituting only 1·49 per cent of the charitable wealth of the realm. Their preoccupation was with the needs of the poor, among whom they lived in the closest contact and whose affairs they ordered so directly. Far more than half (56·52 per cent) of all their charitable resources were given for the care of the needy, this proportion rising to above two-thirds in two of our counties. It is also significant that almost the whole of their contribution was disposed for direct household relief, the £1194 13s given by the class for almshouse endowments representing but 2·59 per cent of the sum of their charities. Yeomen made only slight contribution (2·63 per cent) to the schemes for social rehabilitation, though proportionately they made the largest commitment (6·29 per cent) of any rural class to municipal betterments, their particular concern with highway repairs bespeaking the struggles they had had with the wretched rural roads of the age. Relatively, their gifts for the advancement of education (14·41 per cent) suggest an intensity of interest only half that of the nation as a whole, since in general schools were being founded for them rather than by them. None the less, they did contribute the not inconsiderable total of £5943 18s for the founding or strengthening of schools, with more modest amounts for scholarships and libraries. The very existence of universities must have been little more than a remote report to most of them, the class having contributed precisely £1 to their support in the whole course of our period. The yeomanry, finally, were only mildly concerned with the religious needs of the age, to which they gave no more than a fifth (20·16 per cent) of all their charitable funds, with, it might be added, a fairly even distribution among the numerous heads of religious interest.

There were almost as many donors drawn from the ranks of the husbandmen as from the yeomanry. We have, therefore, a very large and probably representative sampling from this huge class, which, as we have earlier suggested, was separated from the yeomanry by a broad social and economic gulf. So too the aspirations of the two classes are amazingly dissimilar. In all, the 5079 husbandmen with whom we are concerned contributed the relatively tiny sum of £2815 15s to charitable uses, this being no more than 0·09 per cent of the charitable resources of the nation. A very large proportion (44·45 per cent) of the whole sum was left or given by these poor and humble men for the maintenance of the church which so many other classes of men had all but abandoned. This warm support was continuous throughout our period, was principally directed towards tangible and everyday needs such as church repairs (11·79 per cent) and the general uses of the church (19·90 per cent), and was consistently strong in every county of England, save in the singularly secular county of Buckinghamshire. These were humble, conservative, and certainly deeply pious men, the pattern of whose aspirations and whose basic interests changed only slowly and reluctantly as our period progressed. They were concerned, too, with the needs of the poor, to which they gave a large proportion (50·43 per cent) of all their charitable wealth, almost the whole amount being in the form of direct alms. Together, the needs of the poor and the requirements of the church absorbed almost the whole (94·88 per cent) of their tiny and we may be sure most carefully considered bene-factions, the needs of education, for example, commanding somewhat less than 2 per cent (1·92 per cent) of their funds. There is historical irony in the fact that they regarded with disinterest the founding of a system of education which was in due time to redeem their class.

We turn now to the clergy, with the preliminary observation that the difference in the structure of aspirations between the prelates and their humbler brethren was so strikingly great as to suggest not only wholly different modes of life and thought but very nearly different vocations. There were 175 of these upper clergy, bishops and abbots, who in the course of our period contributed the relatively very large total of £154,194 3s to charitable causes, this constituting 4·97 per cent of the whole of the social wealth of our era. These were, then, on the whole great gifts, the average benefaction of £881 2s 2d being higher than that of any other social group, the Crown aside. The structure of aspirations displayed by these gifts is all the more interesting because, broadly speaking, the fact of the Reformation changed the complexion of prelatical charitable giving scarcely at all, save that Protestant bishops were much poorer than the great prelates who had preceded them. The most arresting fact is that the upper clergy throughout our period exhibited but slight concern for the needs of the poor, the 10·04 per cent of funds disposed for this purpose suggesting an intensity of interest only one-third as great as is to be observed in the most nearly comparable lay social group. Furthermore, such wealth as was afforded for the care of the poor was principally devoted to the founding of almshouses, no more than the really tiny proportion of 3·63 per cent of all their charitable wealth having been disposed for direct alms or for endowments to provide household relief. This inevitably suggests not so much inhumanity in the great clergy, for surely the grim struggle with poverty was the central social problem of the age, as preoccupation with other matters and a want of understanding of the mood and the direction of thought in the England of this age. The central aspiration of the great clergy was in fact the strengthening of the educational resources of the nation, to which they devoted the amazing proportion of 63·45 per cent of all their charitable giving, only two other social groups even rivalling them in this intensity of interest. Thus they gave almost nothing (0·76 per cent) to the fabric of their communities and only modestly (2·50 per cent) to the experimentations fruitfully under way in social rehabilitation, which might well have possessed some measure of interest for them. Most surprisingly, perhaps, they devoted only a slightly larger proportion of their charitable giving than the nation at large to the needs of the church, which they could describe so movingly and eloquently in their tracts and sermons. Here their principal concern was of course inevitably with church fabric, with repair and new building, which together absorbed 13·75 per cent of all their charitable funds. It is especially noteworthy that they gave markedly less than most rural classes to secure prayers for the repose of their own souls (4·01 per cent), this being in fact less proportionately than that so provided by all classes save for the merchants, who tended to be at once prudent and anti-clerical, and the professional classes, which were not untinged with scepticism. The great clergy of England, throughout our period, werè among the most secular of all classes in an increasingly secular age.

The lower clergy likewise made a substantial total contribution to the social needs of England, their gift being £141,080 4s and representing 4·55 per cent of the charitable wealth of the realm. Very few of the 1561 of the lower clergy who made contributions were rich men, and so their bequests were in the main modest, the average gift of £90 7s 7d being relatively quite high only because of large benefactions made by a few members of the class who had inherited considerable fortunes from merchant fathers. The pattern of their social interests was very different indeed from that of their great confrères, though the lower clergy too devoted a large proportion (44·00 per cent) of their wealth to the advancement of educational opportunities. Their generous gifts were spread remarkably evenly to grammar schools, to the universities, and to scholarship foundations, to which last they gave more in proportion (13·16 per cent) than any other class in England. Though they gave far more both proportionately and absolutely towards poor relief than did the prelates, the 26·33 per cent of their wealth dedicated to that great and central need of the age leaves them, none the less, after the bishops, the most insensitively concerned class in the realm. This is difficult to understand, since they worked and lived closely with the poor, exhorted their congregations to acts of charity, and could not have escaped from the harsh realities of the problem with which all classes of the realm were engaged. Further, their proportionate support for plans of social rehabilitation (2·29 per cent) and their undertakings for municipal improvements (4·27 per cent) were far less substantial than was afforded by the generality of donors. Finally, they gave to the church in its great need no more than 23·10 per cent of all their gifts, this being in fact slightly less than the measure of support (23·24 per cent) afforded by the bishops and abbots, their interests being spread rather evenly among the several religious uses, but with a high proportion (6·20 per cent) of their resources being dedicated to the prayers for the dead so meagrely sustained by the bishops. All the clergy, whether the great or the parochial, did lend continuous and certainly valuable support to the needs of education, but they did so by separating themselves to a notable degree from the main stream of English life and thought. Even in their central preoccupation with education, they disposed funds which were slight indeed when compared with the massive and decisive support which the small but very rich and very generous merchant class brought to bear.

The benefactions of the merchant class were to be dominant, indeed decisive, in the settling of the social aspirations of modern England, not only because of their enormous scale but because they were on the whole so perfectly ordered and disposed as trusts creating permanent institutions. Then, too, there was social weight in their gifts which lent to them an enhanced value and power, because the merchants sensed more quickly than any other class, save possibly the professions, and this means largely the lawyers, the slope of English life and needs. Finally, the merchant class, whether of London, Bristol, or a dozen provincial towns, to a most remarkable degree showed the same aspirations at the same time, introducing thereby a class solidarity, an articulate expression of purpose, and a social leverage which enabled them to create great and pervasive institutions as if from a blueprint which all merchant donors seem to have held in mind. The enormous total of £1,339,498 18s was provided for charitable uses by this relatively very small body of men, comprising the incredibly high proportion of 43·17 per cent of the whole of the charitable wealth of the realm. Not only was this prodigious sum almost seven times as great as the total provided by the next most generous class, the professions, but it considerably exceeded the combined contributions of the whole of rural England, and England was still overwhelmingly rural in population and predominantly rural in wealth.

The merchants were generously and continuously concerned with the needs of the poor, to which they devoted 40 per cent of all their charitable wealth, though it should be noted that they gave more circumspectly and thoughtfully than the other typically urban classes. They gave little indeed in direct alms, marshalling their resources in huge capital aggregates, carefully vested and ordered, which were designed to afford permanent succour to classes of men whose personal security was marginal in the new economy which the merchants were themselves creating. They displayed as well a lively and a sustained interest in the experimentation designed to secure the rehabilitation of the salvageable poor, to which they devoted the very considerable proportion of 14·23 per cent of all their charities, bearing, in fact, the amazing load of 60 per cent (59·66 per cent) of the total outlay for such undertakings in the whole of the great area with which we are concerned. Their concern with municipal betterments was relatively modest, 6·92 per cent of their wealth being disposed for such uses, most of these prudent men preferring to bring into being capital sums and institutions rather than to undertake useful but perishable outlays. They dedicated almost exactly a fourth (24·95 per cent) of all their charitable wealth to strengthening, one can almost say to founding, the educational resources of the realm, though in this respect the intensity of their concern was markedly less than that displayed by the clergy and the professional groups. But there was one important difference, since the merchants concentrated their benefactions principally on grammar-school foundations, to which they devoted 18·16 per cent of all their charities, a far larger amount than they disposed for any other single charitable cause except the household relief of the poor (18·64 per cent).

All this left little indeed for the requirements of religion, the total of their contribution to this vast area of need amounting to no more than 13·91 per cent of all their benefactions. This establishes the merchants as decidedly the most secular of all social classes in England, save for the professions, and lends an immensely powerful secular bias to the whole of their massive social contributions. This is all the more pronounced when we consider that by far their strongest single religious concern was with the founding of Puritan lectureships (3·54 per cent), gifts distrusted or actively opposed by the ecclesiastical authorities of the realm. This pervasive and aggressive secularism was, as we shall see, characteristic of the class even in the late mediaeval period, their dispositions for prayers (3·04 per cent), for example, being substantially less than those of any other class in the society. There was at no time much of heresy in the class—they were too unenthusiastic for that—but there was, long before the advent of the Reformation, a deep and an unconcealed anti-clericalism in the temper of the class. The merchant fraternity embraced Protestantism almost at once, and it was a Protestantism from the beginning tinged with Puritanism. They were as a class deeply pious men, but theirs was a lay view of the church and of Christianity, which they translated into intensely secular aspirations.

The tradesmen comprised a large donor group, whose substantial charitable contributions of £149,642 19s seem small only when contrasted with the immense generosity of the merchants. Their philanthropy amounted to 4·82 per cent of the whole for England, being somewhat less but still comparable to the contributions of such classes as the upper gentry, the lower gentry, and the upper clergy, while it was well over three times as great as the amount contributed by the yeomanry. The charitable interests of the class were well defined and were less determined by the formidable preoccupations of the mercantile aristocracy than might be supposed. Thus they gave a much greater proportion (49·06 per cent) of their wealth for relief than did the merchants, with a particular concern for household and parochial relief, to which they dedicated relatively nearly twice as much of their gifts (35·73 per cent) than did their richer neighbours (18·64 per cent). It is interesting, too, that they gave a slightly higher proportion (15·22 per cent) of their wealth to the many schemes for social rehabilitation than did their merchant contemporaries, displaying a particularly active interest in the establishment of loan funds and the support of hospitals. They were likewise considerably more disposed to make outlays for municipal betterments, to which they devoted 8·43 per cent of their charities, this being by some margin the highest proportion given by any class for such uses. Quite significantly, the tradesmen were relatively unconcerned with the building of the educational resources of the nation, designating no more than 12·61 per cent of all their funds for this use, thereby exhibiting an intensity of interest only half as great as that which moved the merchant donors. Further, their concern for education was in most cases intensely local, substantial gifts (£9759) having been made for grammar schools in their own communities and for scholarship funds (£8436 17s), but with no more than a nominal contribution (£257) for the strengthening of the universities. In their general attitude towards religious needs alone was the structure of their aspirations closely comparable to that of the merchant aristocracy, the tradesmen having disposed an almost identical and certainly slight proportion (14·68 per cent) of all their charitable wealth for this purpose.

The whole structure of charitable contributions made by the imperfectly identified class which we have called 'additional burghers' suggests, as we have previously indicated, that most of them were in fact tradesmen, as does the average amount of their benefactions. In all, men of this group gave £90,223 4s for the various charitable uses, or 2·91 per cent of all charitable wealth. The spread of their interest was so closely comparable to that of the tradesmen that no detailed comment is required, save to say that they gave a slightly greater proportion of their means for poor relief than did the shopkeepers and likewise displayed considerably less interest in various outlays for municipal betterments.

We have been especially interested in assessing the structure of aspirations displayed by the considerable body of artisans whose gifts and bequests have been recorded. There were 2087 of these men, principally skilled workmen, who comprise 5·97 per cent of all donors but whose total contributions represent no more than 0·28 per cent of the charitable whole. None the less, the average charitable benefaction (£4 3s 4d) made by this group is surprisingly high, while the sturdy social independence displayed by them in London, Bristol, Norwich, and in the industrial towns of Kent and the West Riding is of considerable significance. As we should expect, they were considerably more concerned with the needs of the poor, to which they devoted 57·49 per cent of their whole contribution, than was any other urban group. Almost all their wealth was disposed not as outright alms but in the more enduring and efficacious form of modest augmentations to existing parochial endowments for household relief. They likewise disposed an amazing proportion to the bold and hopeful experimentation under way in social rehabilitation, relatively almost twice as much, it might be added, than any of the more cautious rural classes. Nor were they without civic pride, for they bestowed 5·49 per cent of all their gifts on a great variety of municipal improvements. They were not, however, substantially interested in the schools being founded for the cultural emancipation of their own children, devoting no more than 5·67 per cent of their gifts for this use, and almost the whole of that modest sum for the support of scholarships. It is most interesting to observe that these humble but evidently independent men were consistently more generous towards meeting the needs of the church than any other urban class, they having dedicated 23·72 per cent of all their benefactions to such uses, this being, in fact, slightly greater than the proportion so vested by the generality of men (21·26 per cent) in our period. Perhaps the nature of their callings explains the fact that their religious concern was very heavily concentrated on the repair and maintenance of the church fabric, to which they devoted the amazing proportion of 9·85 per cent of all their charitable gifts, suggesting an intensity of concern for the churches, which they so evidently loved, something like six times that of their merchant employers. Surely it is significant that this one concern, this intensity of interest, was exceeded only by that of a somewhat comparable rural class, the husbandmen.

One of the most interesting, homogeneous, and generous of all the social classes in the England of our period was comprised of men of the several professions, including, as we have earlier noted, a fair number of professional administrators and public officials. By far the most numerous group were the common lawyers, who were not, however, conspicuously more generous than the class as a whole and whose own cultural and social aspirations were remarkably similar to the other professional groups here included. This class was still relatively small, its 866 donors accounting for no more than 2·48 per cent of all benefactors, but it was at once rich and very generous, the average contribution working out to the high figure of £225 18s. This small but cohesive social group, in fact, contributed the enormous total of £195,630 9s to charitable causes, this being 6·31 per cent of the whole of the charitable wealth of England and an amount substantially exceeding that disposed by any other single social group save, it need scarcely be said, the merchants.

The structure of social aspirations held by the class differs markedly and consistently from all others. Thus these men gave a slighter proportion (32·82 per cent) of all their wealth for the relief of the poor than did any other social group except the clergy. They were particularly dubious regarding endowments for the household relief of the poor, devoting most of their funds for this general purpose to the founding and endowing of almshouses, to which they gave a proportion (18·91 per cent) of their charitable wealth exceeded only by that vested by the nobility. As essentially prudent men, they were conspicuously disinterested in the experiments in social rehabilitation (3·47 per cent) and in the various needs of their municipalities (3·56 per cent), though the class was of course urban. The class was, however, throughout our period almost fanatically devoted to the strengthening and extension of educational opportunity, to which it devoted almost half (49·49 per cent) of all its charitable wealth, a proportion exceeded only by that given by the upper clergy. Themselves products of the universities, with skills forged by education, they vested very large sums for all educational uses, but were moved by particularly generous sentiments towards the universities, to which they gave £62,568 2s, a far larger sum, and, we should add, a far larger proportion than that so disposed

by any other social group in the England of our period.[1] This was a
class animated by clearly and aggressively defined aspirations for the
age, and these aspirations were intensely secular. The professional
group gave no more than a tenth (10·67 per cent) of all their wealth for
the various religious needs, suggesting a cold and stark secularism
shared by all the powerful urban groups but scarcely rivalled by any
save the merchants (13·91 per cent). These were men, like the merchants, who knew precisely what they wanted the world to be and who
possessed the fluid wealth as well as the conviction and generosity to
bring it into being.

There remains for brief comment a considerable sum, £353,573 16s,
representing upwards of 11 per cent of all charitable wealth, which was
given by donors of uncertain social status, of which there were 6601, or
by persons quite unknown who have not been counted as individual
donors at all. These last were with few exceptions contributors to the
large total of £153,385 17s given by unknown donors for church building in the England of our age, this being comprised principally of
amounts raised by voluntary subscriptions in an individual parish, in
groups of parishes, or in great areas where royal briefs were issued.
Also remaining is a substantial total of about £200,000 contributed to
various charitable uses by persons of uncertain social status, but whose
names are known and who have been reckoned as donors; such benefactions tended to be small, were rarely designed to found institutions,
and were very heavily concentrated (£64,952 1s) under the head of the
outright relief of the poor.

Though women are hardly a social class, we might appropriately
conclude our analysis of the structure of class aspirations with some
comment on their charitable interests. This subject will be treated in
detail in our discussion of the several counties; so our remarks here will
be limited to certain general conclusions which may be drawn from the
data. In all, there were 4699 women donors who made gifts or bequests
for charitable uses during the course of our period, they having constituted the most substantial proportion of 13·44 per cent of all donors.
It should at once be added that this total considerably understates the
participation of women in the social and economic life of the period,
since this is the number of women who made individual benefactions,
the numerous joint gifts, doubtless often inspired by the wife, having in
all cases been credited to the husband. Though the number of women

---

[1] The amounts and proportions contributed for the strengthening of higher
education by other social groups making significant gifts were:

	£	Per cent
Upper clergy	37,604	24·39
Nobility	28,100	22·54
Upper gentry	26,714	15·56
Merchants	25,591 14s	1·91

making personal contributions was proportionately slightly higher in London (14·88 per cent) and Bristol (15·44 per cent), it is significant indeed that in all regions, rural and urban, the proportion of women donors was spread in the amazingly tight range of from 11·28 per cent for Lancashire to the 15·44 per cent noted in Bristol.[1]

These women were drawn from all ranks of the society, though, as we should expect, there are relatively few who may certainly be identi-fied as possessing the status of artisans or husbandmen. Something over half the total number were widows, very often of uncertain status; a considerable number were spinsters; and a surprising number, about a fourth of the whole, were married women who, with their husbands' consent, disposed or bequeathed property of their own right. The largest number were drawn from the yeomanry, with women of the lower gentry almost as numerous, though it is important to observe that in relation to the number of men donors women of the merchant and tradesman classes were even more numerous.

This considerable body of women donors contributed the substantial total of £272,167 8s to various charitable causes, this representing not quite 9 per cent (8·77 per cent) of the whole of the charitable wealth of the realm. Though we have seen that proportionately the number of women donors varied only insignificantly from county to county, this was by no means true with respect to the sum of their contributions. Here we discover remarkable variations, ranging from the very low proportion of 3·92 per cent in rural Hampshire to the amazingly high proportion of 13·01 per cent in even more solidly rural Buckingham-shire. Most interesting, however, is the fact that in remote and pre-sumably backward Yorkshire women donors accounted for 12·55 per cent of all the charitable wealth of the county, while in London women gave no more than 9·14 per cent of its immense charities. For England as a whole, of course, the data under discussion suggest that women controlled and disposed nearly 9 per cent of all wealth, a proportion which must in point of fact be considerably understated, for one thing because we have conclusive evidence that women were not relatively so charitably inclined in the disposing of their wealth as were the gener-ality of men in the era. The conclusion follows that women possessed far more of disposable wealth and certainly far greater independence of judgment than has commonly been supposed. The ultimate test of ownership, after all, is the ability to bequeath wealth or to give it away.

The women of our era, some of whom rank among the really great and farsighted donors, gave in a pattern which suggests not only indepen-dence of judgment but a maturity of understanding which we find very impressive indeed. Thus they devoted upwards of 44 per cent of all their charitable funds to the various forms of poor relief, concentrating

[1] *Vide* Table IX (Appendix) for the details on which this discussion rests.

this considerable sum principally on endowments to secure household aid in their own parishes. Here, too, however, there were quite astonishing regional differences, from the very low proportion assigned to this use in Lancashire (21·21 per cent) and Norfolk (33·03 per cent), to the incredibly high proportion (85·55 per cent) so vested by women donors in Buckinghamshire. But, as compared with the generality of benefactors, women donors were on balance much more substantially committed to the care of the poor than were their husbands and fathers.

Women donors had but scant interest in financing municipal improvements of any kind, the modest 2·63 per cent devoted to this purpose suggesting an intensity of concern only about half as great as that displayed by all donors (5·18 per cent). At the same time, they exhibited a most lively interest in the experiments under way for the social rehabilitation of the poor, to which they gave the impressive proportion of 10·94 per cent of all their funds, this being in fact slightly greater than the proportionate interest exhibited by donors in general. In such diverse counties as London, Worcestershire, Lancashire, and Bristol, this dedication to new and hopeful methods of dealing with the ancient problem of poverty was particularly marked.

The contributions made by women donors to the educational needs of the realm were only slightly less proportionately than for the generality of donors, nearly 24 per cent of all their charitable wealth having been disposed for this use. But here there were great regional differences, ranging from the insignificant 5·65 per cent so provided in Buckinghamshire to the really massive proportions observed in such counties as Lancashire and Norfolk.

Most surprising, however, is the fact that women donors were as a group far more determinedly secular in the pattern of their aspirations than the benefactors of the era as a whole. They gave in all no more than a modest 18·07 per cent of their wealth for religious needs, thereby establishing themselves as far more implacably secular than any of the large rural social classes and comparably as secular as the great urban groups. In county after county the proportion of their benefactions made for religious uses fell sharply under that noted for the county as a whole. Their interests were in the main centred on the needs of mankind in this world, to which they made due and considerable contribution in their own right and in their own way.[1]

---

[1] A careful and full-scale study of the realities of the position and wealth of women in this period would be most rewarding. For too long we have mistaken the law, what was supposed to be the status, for the reality. Particularly important is the undoubted fact that women gained immensely in status during the period of the Civil War and the ensuing era of unsettlement, when their husbands were away in military service or prudent exile. In every county, significantly, the charitable benefactions of women rose sharply in proportion during these years. The most valuable of several discussions of the legal position of

5. The velocity of change

The several classes of men in the England of our period not only assumed different degrees of social and historical responsibility and displayed different patterns of social aspiration, but they yielded in a quite varied fashion to the dominant pressures of the era. Certain social groups from the beginning offered abundant evidence of deep concern for the material needs of mankind, displaying a secularism of aspiration that became more steadily pronounced until it was all but complete, while other classes yielded only slowly and incompletely to the new and dominant forces of the age, the degree of their participation and the relative extent of their contributions becoming ever slighter. We should now lend brief attention to this most significant difference in the velocity of change amongst the several social classes. This we may perhaps best do by establishing curves which compare the proportion of total charitable contributions given to religious uses in the several intervals with the proportion dedicated to the relief of the poor. For this purpose we have added the amount given for poor relief strictly defined to the amount vested for experiments in social rehabilitation. We shall also limit ourselves to a consideration of certain of the social classes, setting out the full data more elaborately in an appended table.[1]

The upper gentry in the years prior to the Reformation displayed but slight concern with the needs of the poor, to which they contributed about an eighth (13·23 per cent) of all their benefactions, while the needs of the church commanded about 69 per cent (68·78 per cent) of their charitable resources. The class responded immediately and sensitively to the impact of the Reformation, since in the short interval from 1540 to 1560 the proportion of gifts made for religious uses fell away by almost two-thirds, while that devoted to poor relief increased by a factor of five. The metamorphosis of aspirations for the class was substantially completed during the course of the Elizabethan era, when the proportion of gifts made for religious uses declined to a meagre 9·89 per cent of the whole, while that vested for the needs of the poor held approximately steady at 60·38 per cent of the whole.

The lesser gentry in our earliest interval disposed a slightly higher proportion of their charitable wealth (14·11 per cent) for the relief of the poor, and also a somewhat greater fraction (70·12 per cent) for religious uses. The class yielded more slowly than did the great gentry to the dominant forces of the age, it having disposed a still generous 44·62 per cent of its charitable contributions for religious needs during

women in this period is E., T., *The lawes resolutions of womens rights* (L., 1632). The best recent treatment may be found in Dame Doris Mary Stenton's *The English woman in history* (L., 1957), which, however, somewhat neglects the rapid betterment of the social and economic position of women in this period.

[1] *Vide* Table XI (Appendix pp. 385–387).

the course of the Reformation, while the support of the poor in this interval commanded no more than a third (32·76 per cent) of its resources. With the lesser gentry lagging approximately twenty years behind the upper gentry in historical responsiveness, the change in the structure of aspirations was even more radical during the Elizabethan era, when the amount provided for the care of the poor rose very steeply to 63·21 per cent of the whole, while that given for the multifarious needs of the church declined abruptly to a trifling 8·71 per cent of the charitable dispositions made by the class in this era.

The yeomanry as a class reacted even more slowly to the pressures of the age, and then with a kind of violence of shift in aspirations that makes them particularly interesting. At the outset they displayed a firm conservatism, disposing four-fifths (80·75 per cent) of all their charitable wealth for the several religious uses, while the needs of the poor in their communities commanded no more than 12·21 per cent of the whole. The proportion disposed for poor relief rose most abruptly in the course of the Reformation era to about half of the whole (50·49 per cent), while the devotion of the class to religious needs declined only moderately in relation to most classes, to 42·18 per cent of their total contribution. But in the course of the Elizabethan era a most radical adjustment of class aspirations was to occur, the proportion of contributions for all religious purposes falling precipitously to not much more than a twentieth (5·18 per cent) of the whole, while almost 60 per cent of the sum of yeoman charitable wealth was dedicated to the needs of the poor. For this class relative stability in the structure of aspirations was not to be attained until the early Stuart era, the proportion of gifts made for the benefit of the poor rising very steeply again to 74·19 per cent of the whole amount, while contributions to the uses of the church rose only most modestly to 8·37 per cent of the whole.

Though their charitable contributions were in weight and consequence slight indeed, the husbandmen, certainly the most conservative social class in England, are extremely interesting as one watches the slow metamorphosis of the structure of their social aspirations. This process, as the curves presented below will suggest, was to require the whole of our long period.[1] Even at the outset, these humble men, mostly illiterate and infinitely cautious, contributed the incredibly high proportion of 91·25 per cent of all their charitable total for one or another religious use, quite the highest for any class in the society, while to the needs of the poor, among whom so many of them were on occasion numbered, they gave not much more than 5 per cent of their charitable total. The slow process of change had clearly begun during the Reformation interval, when about a third (33·84 per cent) of their benefactions were disposed for poor relief, but they as a class still gave not far

[1] See graph on next page.

from two-thirds (62·16 per cent) of all their wealth for the support of the church. In the course of the Elizabethan era, this relatively very slow metamorphosis continued, almost 70 per cent of the benefactions of the class having been disposed for the needs of the poor, though the husbandmen continued to give rather more than a fourth (26·75 per cent) of their small but hard-won charitable sums for the support of the church, suggesting an intensity of concern and loyalty twice as great as that of the next most conservatively committed class. The process of change in aspirations was not completed among these men and women until a century after it had occurred among the richer and more sophisticated social classes, the proportion of charitable wealth designated for religious uses at last falling sharply to 11·72 per cent during the early Stuart years, when the extremely high proportion of 85·08 per cent of all charitable sums contributed by the class was given for the needs of the poor. The pattern of aspirations of men and women of this class had changed slowly and cautiously over the course of more than a century, but in 1640 it stood complete.

We have already had occasion to observe that the clergy were singularly modest in their support of religious causes through the whole course of our period. If we may confine our attention to the lower clergy, we note that a most pronounced shift in the pattern of clerical

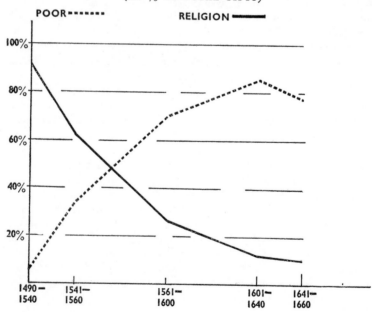

GIFTS BY HUSBANDMEN FOR POOR AND RELIGION
(IN % OF TOTAL GIFTS)

interest does take place, but with less violence, since the devotion of
the class to educational needs was steadily maintained in every interval.[1]
Thus in the decades prior to the Reformation, the clergy disposed a
relatively modest 45·42 per cent of their charitable benefactions for
ecclesiastical uses, while sparing no more than a shockingly low 4·24
per cent for the needs of the poor. The preaching zeal of the reformed
clergy had its effect, since, in decided contrast to every other social
group in England, the proportion of wealth the lower clergy gave to
religious uses rose substantially during these years to 56·50 per cent of
the whole, while contributions to the requirements of the poor rose
slightly to about an eighth (12·57 per cent) of all their gifts. The clergy
reacted much as did other men to the harsh secularism of the Elizabethan era, only 13·86 per cent of all their charitable wealth being
disposed for religious causes, while almost a third (32·73 per cent) of
their funds was given for the care of the poor. The economic as well as
the social plight of the clergy during these years is most dramatically
suggested by the fact that in the course of these four decades their
charitable benefactions amounted to no more than 3·61 per cent of the
whole of their gifts during our entire period, whereas other classes were
giving in a range of from 9·58 per cent to 25·03 per cent of the whole of
their contributions. Proportionately, however, the devotion of the lower
clergy to the needs of the church continued to fall slowly but steadily
for the remainder of our period, to the 9·38 per cent so given in the
early Stuart interval and 7·41 per cent during the unsettled years of
revolution, while benefactions for the care of the poor tended to mount
modestly until the Civil War was at hand.

The merchants, who as a class were to exercise a dominant role in

[1]

GIFTS BY THE LOWER CLERGY
FOR POOR, EDUCATION, AND RELIGION
(IN % OF TOTAL GIFTS)

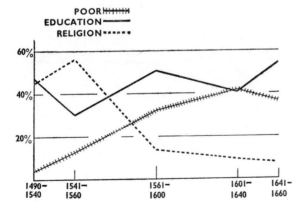

POOR
EDUCATION
RELIGION

shaping the aspirations and the institutions of England, not only because of the massive weight of their gifts but because of their qualitative strength, even in the years prior to the Reformation clearly and most precociously displayed a pattern of interest which other groups were to adopt from one to two generations later. During these early decades no other class was even remotely comparable in understanding the needs of the poor and the claims which they laid against the conscience of the age. The merchant aristocracy devoted 30·23 per cent of its charitable wealth to this cause. Moreover, of all lay classes, save for the nobility, the merchants were the most completely secular, having disposed even in these early years no more than the relatively very modest proportion of 48·38 per cent of their benefactions to the uses of the church. The impact of the Reformation was immediate and, it seems clear, welcome. Merchant contributions for spiritual causes fell abruptly to a slender 8·40 per cent of the whole, while quite as significantly the proportion of merchant wealth disposed for the succour of the poor rose at once to 58·73 per cent, a remarkably level curve thereafter being maintained through the next century, the merchants having early reached a mature assessment of the measures which they wished to take in the assault the whole society had now launched on an ancient evil. The Elizabethan era, however, saw an all but complete withering of merchant interest in the needs of the church, the incredibly tiny proportion of 3·16 per cent of their huge benefactions in this era having been devoted to spiritual uses. During the early Stuart interval this proportion rose modestly to 11·93 per cent of the whole, levelling off at about this amount for the remainder of the period.[1] These men had, then, been strongly secular in their aspirations from the outset of our period, and they quickly and confidently cast the pattern of their intentions in final form just as

1

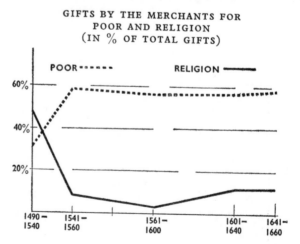

GIFTS BY THE MERCHANTS FOR
POOR AND RELIGION
(IN % OF TOTAL GIFTS)

POOR ------   RELIGION ———

60%

40%

20%

1490—   1541—   1561—   1601—   1641—
1540   1560   1600   1640   1660

their immense wealth began to flow so bounteously towards charitable ends. Their decision, taken so early and so irrevocably, was to be decisive as well for the social and institutional development of England.

D. ENGLAND BECOMES A NATION

The great charitable wealth whose origin and disposition we have sought to trace was principally important, of course, because of the immense good which flowed from it, not only to human beings of the period but to all the generations that have followed. These benefactions in their totality are perhaps principally significant, in social terms, because they betoken a new and ever-widening sensitivity on the part of a culture towards human suffering and want. It is not too much to argue, surely, that the ultimate virtue of any culture in any age may best be measured in precisely these terms, and, if that be so, the men and women of the era with which we have dealt had wrought a mighty and an enduring achievement.

But there is another aspect of achievement on which we should here comment at least briefly, leaving our fuller and documented discussion to the counties and most particularly to London. Most of the gifts and bequests which we have recorded were inevitably and surely properly made to meet local needs, to cure ills which men saw about them, and to enlarge the ambit of opportunity in a parish or village beloved because the donor was himself part of the stuff of its being. There was, however, an ever-increasing number of men who took a larger view, who in their dispositions sought to assess the needs of the whole nation or to bring relief and opportunity to distant parts of the realm where the economy was strait, where local leadership was wanting, or where the whole culture was backward. The charitable giving of our period was in consequence a most important solvent of the parochialism which marked the English society at the outset of our long period. The Tudors were skilful and persistent in their efforts to weld a nation out of its parts and by their policy and more particularly by the system of local administration which they created were to go far towards the attainment of this end. But the steady flow of charitable funds from parish to parish, county to county, and region to region was doing this beneficent work as well, an aspect of social and cultural change which Elizabeth recognized and powerfully assisted in the enactment of the poor laws which sought to define and to enforce the interdependence of all communities one with another. The problems with which she was struggling and the problems to which private donors were addressing themselves were, it came to be understood, national in scope and could be resolved only if the nation itself should be considered as a community. Out of the economic and social travail of the sixteenth century a nation was born.

Prior to the Reformation, giving for charitable purposes outside the donor's own parish, or the parish in which he was a landowner, was with few exceptions limited to monastic contributions, and even these, as we have seen, were relatively insignificant. Such occasional benefactions, too, were rarely made save by members of the nobility, the upper gentry, and the great clergy, social groups which themselves tended to possess relatively limited local ties. But shortly after 1540 a mensurable and certainly significant flow of charitable funds from numerous classes and in the main for intensely secular purposes set in from one region to another, with most fruitful and interesting results. This breaking down of the almost fierce parochialism which had characterized the England even of the early sixteenth century was greatly stimulated by the royal briefs which, beginning in the reign of Henry VIII, not only authorized but lent direct governmental encouragement to the solicitation of funds on a national scale for communities which had been grievously hurt by pestilence, fire, or economic disaster. As an example, in 1585 a national collection was authorized for the relief of Nantwich, Cheshire, which had recently suffered from a disastrous fire, the damage from which could not be repaired from local or regional resources. The Queen set herself down for a very large gift of £1000, while a member of the Privy Council and the Dean of St Paul's lent their names as starting subscribers with more modest gifts of £20 and £10 respectively. London and Middlesex followed, with gifts for this distant community totalling a little more than £717, while benefactions were reported from twenty-three additional counties, ranging from £8 from Rutland to £77 13s 5d from Surrey, from fourteen bishoprics, from twenty-one cities, and from the two universities, a total of £3142 0s 8d having been raised by a national effort to secure the rehabilitation of a single, and remote, community.[1]

We should not, of course, lend undue emphasis to the development of this concern for the nation as a social entity, for understandably and very properly the interests of most donors remained centred on needs with which they were well acquainted and on the improvement of communities of which they were themselves part. Most of the flow of extra-mural funds was, it should also be said, from parish to parish within the capacious entity which the county remained throughout our period. We possess no accurate estimate of the value of such gifts, but certainly most of the larger institutional foundations after 1580, and particularly the grammar schools and almshouses, were established for the benefit of a grouping of parishes and in not a few instances for very large areas within the favoured counties.

We can, however, measure accurately the endowments created within one county for the benefit of another, having, it should be noted,

[1] *S.P. Dom.*, 1585, CLXXXIV, 22, 23.

excluded from our listings all gifts to universities, which may more properly be regarded as gifts for the benefit of the whole nation and which by 1660 had attained the massive total of £231,195 10s, this representing 7·45 per cent of the whole of the charitable wealth accumulated in the course of our period.

In all, extra-county gifts during our age reached the very large sum of £623,302 19s, this being 20·09 per cent of the whole of the charitable wealth of the nation. These gifts were made to remedy needs of all sorts in other counties, though they were principally dedicated to the founding of schools and hospitals, to affording household relief to the poor, and to the establishment of lectureships. A glance at the accompanying table will at once suggest that there were quite amazing differences from county to county in the survival of parochialism.[1] Thus Bristol, urban community though it was, remained almost perversely parochial, bestowing no more than 0·79 per cent of all its great charitable wealth on the needs of other regions, while bringing to an almost precocious fruition its own magnificent social and institutional resources.[2] The western region generally seems to have remained parochial in its outlook, Somerset also bestowing less than 1 per cent of its considerable charitable wealth on other parts of the realm. But in the mature and relatively more prosperous southern counties such as Buckinghamshire, Hampshire, and Kent, very liberal proportions of their wealth were disposed to an amazing number of distant counties. Rich and generous Norfolk yet remained relatively insular in its interests, bestowing no more than 2·40 per cent of its charities on communities in twenty other

---

[1] Extra-county benefactions:

County	Number of counties and countries benefitted	Amount		Percentage of county total
		£	s	Per cent
Bristol	12	735	4	0·79
Buckinghamshire	17	4,275	16	4·85
Hampshire	24	7,434	14	8·54
Kent	33	10,566	14	4·20
Lancashire	14	2,266	7	2·18
London	45	584,741	8	30·95
Norfolk	20	4,277	19	2·40
Somerset	15	1,019	5	0·87
Worcestershire	14	1,635	5	3·11
Yorkshire	35	6,350	7	2·61
		623,302	19	20·09

[2] The parochialism of Bristol could be documented in many ways. In the collection for Nantwich (*vide ante* 362), for example, Bristol, though the third city of the realm, gave only £8 2s, an amount exceeded by fifteen other communities, including such relatively small towns as Bury St. Edmunds, which gave £53 15s 6d, Sandwich with £13 10s 3d, and King's Lynn with £12.

counties, though it should be added that no county in England was better supplied by the close of our era with endowments for groupings of
its own parishes or for the benefit of the county at large.

Though the solvent of charitable giving was weakening the hard shell
of parochialism in all the counties of the realm, it was in London that
this process was to be completed in the course of our period. London,
in fact, viewed the problem of poverty and the closely related problem of
want of opportunity as essentially a national matter, with a full understanding that no effective or abiding improvement could be gained unless
the whole of the community which was the nation was nurtured with
life-giving streams of charity. Hence it was that there poured out from
London, mostly from her great merchant donors, the vast sum of
£584,741 8s, or not far short of a third (30·95 per cent) of the whole of
her prodigious charitable capital. The scale of this giving is suggested
by the fact that for the other nine counties in our sampling nearly a
fourth (23·55 per cent) of all their charitable resources were supplied
by London generosity, and we may safely assume that for the whole of
the realm something like this formidable proportion prevailed.

We shall in the next volume of this study discuss in detail this incredible and fruitful generosity, which knew no parochial bounds, but
we may here make at least a few general comments on the decisive
influence which London wealth had in determining the aspirations of
the age, and also in establishing the structure of its institutions. This
merchant wealth founded and endowed seventy-two almshouses in all
parts of the kingdom, and it created and endowed 123 schools across
the length and breadth of the realm, as well as augmenting the resources
of scores of existing but meagrely furnished schools. It intervened
decisively in order to change the whole social and religious structure of
a county like Lancashire, and it lent important aid to Yorkshire as that
remote and heretofore backward county lifted itself in the course of a
century level with the rest of the nation. These great funds, disposed
throughout England, were then so singularly important not only
because of their sheer mass, but because they were carefully designed,
shrewdly vested, and set on tasks which needed badly to be done in
areas which could not with their own resources quite lift themselves
into modernity.

Thus it was that one great London donor, after investigation and
reflection which would lend credit to a great modern charitable
foundation, established a charitable trust the income of which was to
afford carefully defined and skilfully administered poor relief in 219
parishes spread over more than half the counties of England and Wales.
Most of these parishes Henry Smith had never seen, their people he
had never known. But in this very fact is somehow embedded the
kernel of true and abiding charity, just as in his great and pervading

generosity is to be found the essence of an understanding that the community which was England was one. Smith, and the great and generous merchant class of which he was an exemplar, was concerned with humanity, with the prevention and cure of suffering, which he could only know vicariously in his own age and in ages yet to come. Surely he, the London merchants like him, and the many thousands of small and humble benefactors whose acts of mercy we have also sought to memorialize, were in fact God's vicars among men.

APPENDIX

CURVE I

TOTALS OF CHARITABLE BENEFACTIONS BY
DECADE INTERVALS

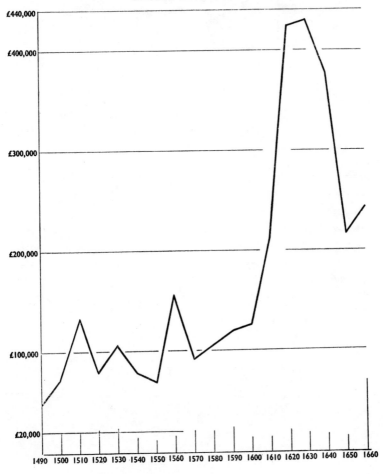

TABLE I

CHANGING STRUCTURE OF ASPIRATIONS

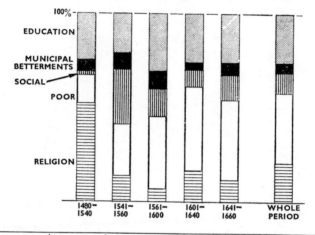

Interval	Poor	Social Rehabilita- tion	Municipal Better- ments	Education	Religion	Total
	£ s	£ s	£ s	£ s	£ s	£ s
1480–1540	70,058 3 (13·33%)	10,706 18 (2·04%)	32,501 (6·18%)	131,170 5 (24·96%)	281,158 15 (53·49%)	525,595 1 (16·94%)
1541–1560	61,383 4 (27·04%)	68,589 17 (30·21%)	15,212 6 (6·70%)	48,320 9 (21·28%)	33,526 5 (14·77%)	227,032 1 (7·32%)
1561–1600	173,944 4 (39·03%)	66,101 15 (14·83%)	33,720 5 (7·57%)	139,947 8 (31·40%)	31,959 7 (7·17%)	445,672 19 (14·36%)
1601–1640	620,480 (43·16%)	119,340 15 (8·30%)	57,553 7 (4·00%)	383,594 1 (26·68%)	256,522 (17·85%)	1,437,490 3 (46·33%)
1641–1660	203,485 18 (43·58%)	54,707 7 (11·72%)	21,789 3 (4·67%)	130,461 9 (27·94%)	56,462 8 (12·09%)	466,906 5 (15·05%)
TOTALS	1,129,351 9 (36·40%)	319,446 12 (10·30%)	160,776 1 (5·18%)	833,493 12 (26·86%)	659,628 15 (21·26%)	3,102,696 9

TABLE II

POOR RELIEF

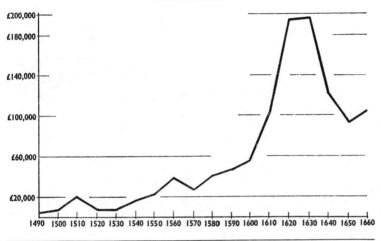

Interval	Outright Relief		Almshouses		Charity General		Aged		Total	
	£	s	£	s	£	s	£	s	£	s
1480–1490	2,518	4	1,531	3	1,301				5,350	7
1491–1500	4,650	13	3,558	12	351	11			8,560	16
1501–1510	5,208	17	12,829	15	1,878	7	100		20,016	19
1511–1520	3,104	11	3,044	17	2,168	10			8,317	18
1521–1530	4,454	15	2,543	4	1,491	13			8,489	12
1531–1540	9,802	19	4,646	4	4,873	8			19,322	11
Sub-total	29,739	19	28,153	15	12,064	9	100		70,058	3
1541–1550	12,996	19	9,807	19	365	14	1		23,171	12
1551–1560	21,280	15	12,624	19	4,305	18			38,211	12
Sub-total	34,277	14	22,432	18	4,671	12	1		61,383	4
1561–1570	16,916		5,379	18	5,907	3			28,203	1
1571–1580	26,552	3	14,110	13	744	6	100		41,507	2
1581–1590	30,265	10	15,675	18	2,158	3	1		48,100	11
1591–1600	31,218	4	23,602	3	1,217	13	95	10	56,133	10
Sub-total	104,951	17	58,768	12	10,027	5	196	10	173,944	4
1601–1610	51,586	14	48,157	15	4,618	10	130		104,492	19
1611–1620	76,047	14	116,225	12	2,917	14	2,017		197,208	
1621–1630	82,801	12	47,560	9	67,244	16	1,065	10	198,672	7
1631–1640	85,096	18	28,984	16	5,325		700		120,106	14
Sub-total	295,532	18	240,928	12	80,106		3,912	10	620,480	
1641–1650	60,073	9	21,484	4	12,198	3	450		94,205	16
1651–1660	57,741	9	45,547		2,220	13	483		105,992	2
No Date	3,068		100		120				3,288	
Sub-total	120,882	18	67,131	4	14,538	16	933		203,485	18
Totals	585,385	6	417,415	1	121,408	2	5,143		1,129,351	9

TABLE III

SOCIAL REHABILITATION

Interval	Prisons		Loans		Workhouses and Stocks		Apprenticeship Schemes		Sick and Hospitals		Marriage Subsidies		Total	
	£	s	£	s	£	s	£	s	£	s	£	s	£	s
1480–1490	105	5							488	9	122	13	716	7
1491–1500	229	8	100						35	6	407	14	772	8
1501–1510	432	7	974				0	13	212	2	511	2	2,130	4
1511–1520	175	3	66	15					98	12	343	18	684	8
1521–1530	148	10	200						202	9	352	2	903	1
1531–1540	1,008	13	848	7					84		3,559	10	5,500	10
Sub-total	2,099	6	2,189	2			0	13	1,120	18	5,296	19	10,706	18

1541–1550	390 8	1,070	60 13		487 13	699 5	2,707 6
1551–1560	819 7	2,289 7	326 13	3	61,428 19	1,015 5	65,882 11
Sub-total	1,209 15	3,359 7	386 13	3	61,916 12	1,714 10	68,589 17
1561–1570	1,130 8	10,967	205	73 8	4,064 19	842 9	17,283 4
1571–1580	2,337 12	3,256 15	1,363 8	249 13	4,704 13	587 18	12,499 19
1581–1590	2,149 17	5,077 13	3,649 13	202	5,414 8	232 6	16,725 17
1591–1600	3,604 12	5,436	866 13	2,683	6,892 10	110	19,592 15
Sub-total	9,222 9	24,737 8	6,084 14	3,208 1	21,076 10	1,772 13	66,101 15
1601–1610	4,448 13	4,512 13	1,692 6	1,880	8,801 6	1,100	22,434 18
1611–1620	4,737 2	7,880 14	2,144	1,753 16	10,846 12	555	27,917 4
1621–1630	4,541 16	5,262	3,036 13	6,083 10	8,850 10	686 13	28,461 2
1631–1640	6,119 6	5,498 3	8,455 10	5,893	12,511 12	2,050	40,527 11
Sub-total	19,846 17	23,153 10	15,328 9	15,610 6	41,010	4,391 13	119,340 15
1641–1650	5,149 17	4,563	6,730 9	7,369	7,014 19	50	39,877 5
1651–1660	1,439 9	5,220 4	1,287	12,458 6	3,207 13	65	23,677 12
No date		20	52 10	80			152 10
Sub-total	6,589 6	9,803 4	8,069 19	19,907 6	10,222 12	115	54,707 7
TOTALS	38,967 13	63,242 11	29,869 15	38,729 6	135,346 12	13,290 15	319,446 12

TABLE IV
MUNICIPAL BETTERMENTS

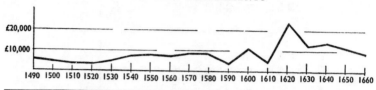

Interval	General Uses		Companies for Public Benefit		Parks		Public Works, Roads, etc.		Total	
	£	s	£	s	£	s	£	s	£	s
1480–1490	1,193	8	554	13	30		4,470	17	6,248	18
1491–1500	1,849	6	721	17			2,695	5	5,266	8
1501–1510	1,666	17	953	19	54	2	1,504	3	4,179	1
1511–1520	698	10	1,442	3			1,989	15	4,130	8
1521–1530	1,190	5	2,753	3			1,166		5,109	8
1531–1540	2,665	8	2,519	15			2,381	14	7,566	17
Sub-total	9,263	14	8,945	10	84	2	14,207	14	32,501	
1541–1550	2,269	17	852	4	5		4,631	3	7,758	4
1551–1560	2,473	18	2,598				2,382	4	7,454	2
Sub-total	4,743	15	3,450	4	5		7,013	7	15,212	6
1561–1570	4,313	13	2,090	17	12		2,433	7	8,849	17
1571–1580	1,624	1	4,383	19			2,593	9	8,601	9
1581–1590	837	2	2,266	16			1,561	11	4,665	9
1591–1600	5,652	16	3,191	9			2,759	5	11,603	10
Sub-total	12,427	12	11,933	1	12		9,347	12	33,720	5
1601–1610	763		3,336	5			780	12	4,879	17
1611–1620	2,804	13	9,018	16			12,355	5	24,178	14
1621–1630	2,084	8	7,117	7			4,625	11	13,827	6
1631–1640	3,380		9,037	4	200		2,050	6	14,667	10
Sub-total	9,032	1	28,509	12	200		19,811	14	57,553	7
1641–1650	7,299		2,424	19			2,733		12,456	19
1651–1660	2,573	4	5,390	8			1,265	12	9,229	4
No date	60		3				40		103	
Sub-total	9,932	4	7,818	7			4,038	12	21,789	3
TOTALS	45,399	6	60,656	14	301	2	54,418	19	160,776	1

TABLE V — EDUCATION 373

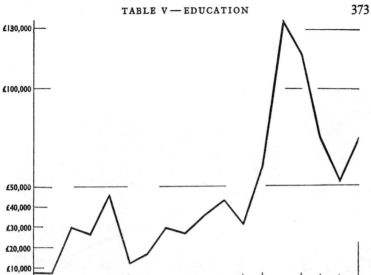

Interval	Schools		Colleges and Universities		Libraries (Non-University)		Scholarships and Fellowships		Total	
	£	s	£	s	£	s	£	s	£	s
1480–1490	3,894		2,767	10			499	13	7,161	3
1491–1500	1,200		1,694	14			4,519	13	7,414	7
1501–1510	4,230		24,075	7	60	14	1,808	7	30,174	8
1511–1520	10,062	4	15,791	1	100		1,943	2	27,896	7
1521–1530	9,526	17	30,384	10	4	7	6,372	16	46,288	10
1531–1540	7,379	12	3,622	6	7	14	1,225	18	12,235	10
Sub-total	36,292	13	78,335	8	172	15	16,369	9	131,170	5
1541–1550	8,226	12	9,263	1	30		207	13	17,727	6
1551–1560	21,172	18	5,530		30		3,860	5	30,593	3
Sub-total	29,399	10	14,793	1	60		4,067	18	48,320	9
1561–1570	10,377	6	13,760	13	32		3,125	17	27,295	16
1571–1580	22,647	3	7,220		83		6,393	19	36,344	2
1581–1590	19,171	17	16,789	1			8,902	3	44,863	1
1591–1600	20,540	7	2,614	6	10	14	8,279	2	31,444	9
Sub-total	72,736	13	40,384		125	14	26,701	1	139,947	8
1601–1610	30,314	18	16,010	15	111	12	14,354		60,791	5
1611–1620	97,774	9	19,634	7	222		15,462		133,092	16
1621–1630	63,118	17	39,491		999	10	12,629	8	116,238	15
1631–1640	29,391	11	11,198	9	2,916		29,965	5	73,471	5
Sub-total	220,599	15	86,334	11	4,249	2	72,410	13	383,594	1
1641–1650	33,345	6	6,636		835	12	12,732		53,548	18
1651–1660	55,387	18	4,712	10	2,900	4	12,749	6	75,749	18
No date	1,137	13					25		1,162	13
Sub-total	89,870	17	11,348	10	3,735	16	25,506	6	130,461	9
TOTALS	448,899	8	231,195	10	8,343	7	145,055	7	833,493	12

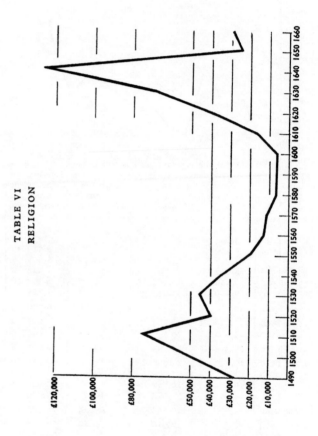

TABLE VI
RELIGION

Interval	Church General £	s	Prayers £	s	Church Repairs £	s	Maintenance of Clergy £	s	Purian Lectureships £	s	Church Building (Estimated) £	s	Total £	s
1480–1490	3,109	8	16,703	16	4,387	19	779	8			4,926	13	29,907	4
1491–1500	3,515	19	19,881	9	12,274	14	514	10			17,272	8	53,459	8
1501–1510	3,730	18	43,710	15	8,282	5	1,172	12			17,823	3	74,719	13
1511–1520	2,351	17	19,116	18	5,660	16	1,703	10			12,007	6	40,839	11
1521–1530	4,331	12	25,623	10	6,015	16	2,420	14			8,223	14	46,615	6
1531–1540	1,953	3	15,827	15	5,691	19	2,701	1			9,444	3	35,618	1
Sub-total	18,992	17	140,864	3	42,312	13	9,291	15			69,697	7	281,158	15
1541–1550	788	6	6,090	7	2,071	15	731	1			10,342	18	20,024	7
1551–1560	2,266	11	2,512	4	3,074	11	2,895	9			2,753	3	13,501	18
Sub-total	3,054	17	8,602	11	5,146	6	3,626	10			13,096	1	33,526	5
1561–1570	659	5	72	14	1,141	14	468	13			8,952		11,294	6
1571–1580	438	8		15	2,223		1,077	3	267		3,021	4	7,027	10
1581–1590	454	8	6	8	1,794	1	1,599	3	1,771	13	570		6,195	13
1591–1600	599	16			1,124	12	1,108	7	2,269	3	2,340		7,441	18
Sub-total	2,151	17	79	17	6,283	7	4,253	6	4,307	16	14,883	4	31,959	7
1601–1610	1,272	14			2,922	5	1,734	11	3,436		8,093	13	17,459	3
1611–1620	4,104	16			5,910	6	5,538	17	12,823	7	13,355	9	41,732	15
1621–1630	6,423	10	70		6,526	18	20,574	14	17,323	7	21,093	2	71,941	11
1631–1640	2,438	19	70		15,078	6	9,692	2	12,670	18	85,438	6	125,388	11
Sub-total	14,239	19	70		30,437	15	37,540	4	46,253	12	127,980	10	256,522	
1641–1650	487	19			2,431	10	3,927	1	15,066		3,070		24,981	11
1651–1660	1,372	14	40		3,273	19	12,792		4,640	10	6,022		28,101	3
No date	464	11	40		1,304	5	120	18			1,450		3,379	14
Sub-total	2,324	5	40		7,009	14	16,839	19	19,706	10	10,542		56,462	8
TOTALS	40,763	15	149,656	11	91,189	15	71,551	14	70,267	18	236,199	2	659,628	15

T

AVERAGE WORTH OF CERTAIN SOCIAL GROUPS (1480–1
TO CHARITABLE

County	Upper Gentry			Lower Gentry		
	Number	Average Worth	Per cent to Charity	Number	Average Worth	Per Ch
		£			£ s d	
Bristol						
Buckinghamshire	6	5,796		4	2,210	
Hampshire	4	4,113		4	1,802 10	
Kent	14	5,176	2·57	30	1,097	13
Lancashire				14	699	
London	6	2,722		16	2,565	
Norfolk	7	12,298	5·92	32	1,377	1
Somerset	18	1,669	11·22	53	1,040	2
Worcestershire				4	2,024	
Yorkshire	43	1,984	10·77	185	693	3
TOTALS	98	3,484	7·12	342	980	4

County	Merchants			Tradesmen		
	Number	Average Worth	Per cent to Charity	Number	Average Worth	Per t Cha
		£ s d			£ s d	
Bristol	47	1,921	27·00	18	148 9 1	5
Buckinghamshire						
Hampshire				4	359 18 0	
Kent	8	1,226	6·12	10	570 14 5	7
Lancashire	14	2,325		4	505 9 0	
London	393	7,780 2 7	16·76	91	1,463 1 3	14
Norfolk	26	1,335	13·92	21	391 0 8	4
Somerset	16	899	41·54	38	252 6 2	15
Worcestershire	4	1,153				
Yorkshire	61	1,066	24·97	131	179 2 8	7
TOTALS	569	5,815 7 7	17·25	317	587 10 6	12

PROPORTION OF GROSS VALUE OF ESTATES DISPOSED
ELECTED COUNTIES

	Yeomen			Husbandmen		County
nber	Average Worth	Per cent to Charity	Number	Average Worth	Per cent to Charity	
	£ s d			£ s d		
I	75 0 0					Bristol
16	390 10 0		12	30 18 10		Buckinghamshire
12	268 4 9		18	35 12 4		Hampshire
18	415 9 8	6·57	18	18 14 4		Kent
66	195 13 9		42	50 5 9		Lancashire
						London
36	442 12 9	1·05	8	38 1 0		Norfolk
47	117 13 5	3·52	335	12 5 6		Somerset
14	241 13 3		8	26 16 0		Worcestershire
05	148 0 3	5·70	205	28 10 2		Yorkshire
15	181 12 4	4·47	646	21 11 6		TOTALS

	Artisans				County
umber	Average Worth	Per cent to Charity			
	£ s d				
5	49 3 2				Bristol
7	12 9 5				Buckinghamshire
					Hampshire
I	84 13 0				Kent
28	41 0 0				Lancashire
46	68 0 0				London
14	101 10 1				Norfolk
11	6 3 5				Somerset
3	18 5 0				Worcestershire
73	25 17 6				Yorkshire
188	43 4 6	5·83			TOTALS

TA

DEPTH OF GIVING: ALL KNOWN DONORS OF TH

(SUMMARY TA

Total No. of Donors	Class	No. Donors	Gifts £0 0s 1d to £9 19s	No. Donors	Gifts £10 to £19 19s	No. Donors	Gif £20 £99 1
			£ s		£ s		£
18	Crown	1	2			2	74
119	Nobility	13	59	7	82	38	1,315
416	Upper Gentry	91	383 16	65	799 15	130	5,973
1772	Lower Gentry	1032	2,981 5	224	2,766 13	342	14,741
2539	Yeomen	2204	4,343 10	119	1,477 19	178	6,56
3927	Husbandmen	3910	1,481 12	12	139 15	5	146
192	Agricultural Labourers (Yorks. only)	190	44 3	1	10	1	20
75	Upper Clergy	5	19 15	5	57	7	337
747	Lower Clergy	413	1,141 6	91	1,226 6	122	5,739
3121	Merchants	868	3,129 16	359	4,591 6	783	35,441
1781	Tradesmen	929	2,637 17	210	2,596 7	400	17,102
1021	Burghers	446	1,775 4	155	1,901 14	259	10,694
1091	Artisans	1045	1,865 10	23	268 13	20	816
631	Professional	234	1,498 16	77	938 9	150	6,184
17,450	TOTALS	11,381 (65·22 per cent)	21,363 10 (1·04 per cent)	1,348 (7·72 per cent)	16,855 17 (0·82 per cent)	2,437 (13·97 per cent)	105,153 (5·11 per ce

NTIES: LONDON, SOMERSET, AND YORKSHIRE
GRAPHS)

No. Donors	Gifts £100 to £499 19s	No. Donors	Gifts £500 to £999 19s	No. Donors	Gifts £1000+	Total Contributions
	£ s		£ s		£ s	£ s
6	1,166 7	1	653	8	120,750 6	122,646 6
31	8,170 11	14	9,839 14	16	69,438 7	88,904 19
95	19,148 7	22	14,848 11	13	31,018	72,171 17
48	27,470	17	11,027 8	9	29,499 14	88,486 8
36	6,137 5	1	540	1	2,180	21,243 2
						1,767 19
						74 3
27	7,042 12	13	8,808 3	18	82,849 4	99,114 1
91	18,163 3	14	9,293 1	16	69,889 7	105,452 14
63	172,010 15	159	112,397 6	189	812,085 11	1,139,656 9
91	39,310	31	20,244 7	20	28,858 9	110,749 1
43	26,264 9	15	8,992	3	4,600	54,228 5
2	200	1	696 11			3,847 7
17	22,954 7	23	15,403 14	30	102,386 17	149,367 2
50 46 cent)	348,037 16 (16·91 per cent)	311 (1·78 per cent)	212,743 15 (10·34 per cent)	323 (1·85 per cent)	1,353,555 15 (65·78 per cent)	2,057,709 13

DEPTH OF GIVING

LONDON—SOMERSET—YORKSHIRE
(PER CENT OF TOTAL CONTRIBUTIONS AND DONORS
IN CATEGORIES OF SIZE OF GIFT)

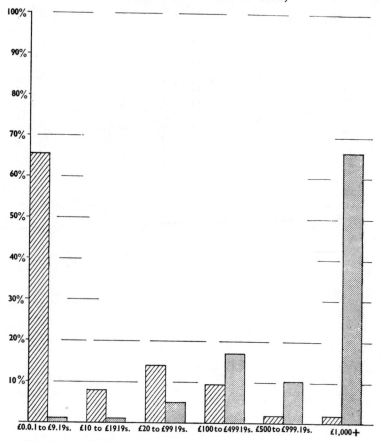

Of each pair of columns, the left-hand column represents % of donors
and the right represents % of contributions

DEPTH OF GIVING

LONDON—SOMERSET—YORKSHIRE
(PER CENT OF TOTAL NUMBER OF DONORS AND TOTAL
CONTRIBUTIONS IN SIX CATEGORIES OF SIZE OF GIFT)

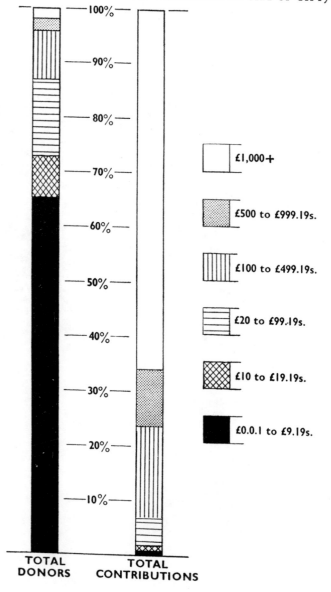

£1,000+

£500 to £999.19s.

£100 to £499.19s.

£20 to £99.19s.

£10 to £19.19s.

£0.0.1 to £9.19s.

TOTAL
DONORS

TOTAL
CONTRIBUTIONS

TA

STRUCTURE OF GIV

County	Known Donors	Women Donors	Per cent of all Donors	Total Contributions by Women		Per cent of Whole	Poor	
				£	s		£	s
Bristol	531	82	15·44	6,976	4	7·58	4,043	11
							(57·96 per cen	
Bucks	1,722	232	13·5	11,466	7	13·01	9,809	12
							(85·55 per cen	
Hampshire	1,956	238	12·17	3,415	4	3·92	1,883	10
							(55·15 per cen	
Kent	6,662	837	12·56	13,833	2	5·49	6,961	9
							(50·32 per cen	
Lancashire	939	106	11·28	6,579		6·34	1,395	6
							(21·21 per cen	
London	7,391	1,100	14·88	172,635	5	9·14	71,505	4
							(41·42 per cen	
Norfolk	2,714	352	12·97	16,849	5	9·47	5,564	19
							(33·03 per cen	
Somerset	3,629	531	14·63	7,028	5	6·03	2,866	12
							(40·78 per cen	
Worcs	787	100	12·71	2,795	9	5·31	1,987	6
							(71·09 per cen	
Yorkshire	8,632	1,121	12·99	30,589	7	12·55	14,968	8
							(48·93 per cen	
TOTALS	34,963	4,699	13·44	272,167	8	8·77	120,985	17
							(44·45 per cen	

WOMEN DONORS

Social Rehabilitation	Municipal Betterments	Education	Religion	Totals
£ s	£ s	£ s	£ s	£ s
571 6	40	1,350	971 7	6,976 4
8·18 per cent)	(0·57 per cent)	(19·35 per cent)	(13·92 per cent)	
351	198 18	648	458 17	11,466 7
3·06 per cent)	(1·73 per cent)	(5·65 per cent)	(4·00 per cent)	
60	217 7	412	842 7	3,415 4
·76 per cent)	(6·36 per cent)	(12·06 per cent)	(24·66 per cent)	
377 10	495 14	2,328 13	3,669 16	13,833 2
2·73 per cent)	(3·58 per cent)	(16·83 per cent)	(26·53 per cent)	
620	22 9	2,280 3	2,261 2	6,579
·42 per cent)	(0·34 per cent)	(34·66 per cent)	(34·37 per cent)	
25,547 18	5,277 3	42,788	27,517	172,635 5
·81 per cent)	(3·05 per cent)	(24·78 per cent)	(15·95 per cent)	
616 17	261 10	7,658 19	2,747	16,849 5
3·66 per cent)	(1·55 per cent)	(45·46 per cent)	(16·29 per cent)	
514 3	88 10	1,109 12	2,449 8	7,028 5
·31 per cent)	(1·26 per cent)	(15·78 per cent)	(34·84 per cent)	
310	61	274	163 3	2,795 9
·09 per cent)	(2·18 per cent)	(9·80 per cent)	(5·84 per cent)	
806 18	487 8	6,237 5	8,089 8	30,589 7
·64 per cent)	(1·59 per cent)	(20·39 per cent)	(26·45 per cent)	
29,775 12	7,149 19	65,086 12	49,169 8	272,167 8
·94 per cent)	(2·63 per cent)	(23·91 per cent)	(18·07 per cent)	

TABLE X

STRUCTURE OF CLASS ASPIRATIONS

Class	Poor	Social Rehabilitation	Municipal Betterments	Education	Religion	Total Contributions
	£ s	£ s	£ s	£ s	£ s	£ s
Crown	27,304 9 (19·00 per cent)	54,026 (37·61 per cent)	2,173 (1·51 per cent)	29,112 3 (20·27 per cent)	31,028 2 (21·60 per cent)	143,643 14
Nobility	65,669 7 (52·68 per cent)	3,700 (2·97 per cent)	1,581 13 (1·27 per cent)	31,961 (25·63 per cent)	21,751 4 (17·45 per cent)	124,663 4
Upper Gentry	62,916 3 (36·65 per cent)	8,358 9 (4·87 per cent)	3,460 6 (2·02 per cent)	57,780 9 (33·66 per cent)	39,143 2 (22·80 per cent)	171,658 9
Lower Gentry	80,619 1 (44·52 per cent)	6,972 2 (3·85 per cent)	5,382 11 (2·97 per cent)	42,280 18 (23·35 per cent)	45,837 15 (25·31 per cent)	181,092 7
Yeomen	26,062 8 (56·52 per cent)	1,211 11 (2·63 per cent)	2,901 5 (6·29 per cent)	6,644 14 (14·41 per cent)	9,294 16 (20·16 per cent)	46,114 14
Husbandmen	1,419 19 (50·43 per cent)	13 13 (0·48 per cent)	76 8 (2·71 per cent)	54 2 (1·92 per cent)	1,251 13 (44·45 per cent)	2,815 15
Agricultural Labourers	119 17 (72·75 per cent)	0 14 (0·42 per cent)	0 11 (0·33 per cent)		43 13 (25·49 per cent)	164 15
Upper Clergy	15,484 14 (10·04 per cent)	3,872 7 (2·50 per cent)	1,165 2 (0·76 per cent)	97,839 1 (63·45 per cent)	35,832 19 (23·24 per cent)	154,194 3
Lower Clergy	37,151 8 (26·33 per cent)	3,233 18 (2·29 per cent)	6,029 15 (4·27 per cent)	62,070 11 (44·00 per cent)	32,594 12 (23·10 per cent)	141,080 4
Merchants	535,712 13 (39·99 per cent)	190,589 5 (14·23 per cent)	92,632 9 (6·92 per cent)	334,203 18 (24·95 per cent)	186,360 13 (13·91 per cent)	1,339,498 18
Tradesmen	73,412 6 (49·06 per cent)	22,776 19 (15·22 per cent)	12,619 18 (8·43 per cent)	18,868 19 (12·61 per cent)	21,964 17 (14·68 per cent)	149,642 19
Burghers	49,022 19 (54·34 per cent)	10,526 3 (11·67 per cent)	2,877 1 (3·18 per cent)	13,066 17 (14·47 per cent)	14,730 4 (16·33 per cent)	90,223 4
Artisans	5,000 19 (57·49 per cent)	663 19 (7·63 per cent)	477 13 (5·49 per cent)	493 3 (5·67 per cent)	2,063 17 (23·72 per cent)	8,699 11
Professions and Public Officials	64,211 19 (32·82 per cent)	6,781 1 (3·47 per cent)	6,959 14 (3·56 per cent)	96,813 4 (49·49 per cent)	20,864 11 (10·67 per cent)	195,630 9

TABLE XI

CHANGES IN THE STRUCTURE OF CLASS ASPIRATIONS

Interval	Poor	Social Rehabilitation	Municipal Betterments	Education	Religion	Totals and % of Whole Contribution made in the Several Periods
	£ s	£ s	£ s	£ s	£ s	£ s
Nobility 1480–1540	3,578 16 (10·56%)	45 (0·13%)	893 7 (2·63%)	18,967 (55·97%)	10,406 5 (30·71%)	33,890 8 (27·18%)
1541–1560	813 6 (46·45%)	45 (2·57%)	153 6 (8·76%)	40 (2·28%)	699 7 (39·94%)	1,750 19 (1·40%)
1561–1600	8,989 1 (38·49%)	1,130 (4·84%)	420 (1·80%)	11,187 (47·90%)	1,630 (6·98%)	23,356 1 (18·74%)
1601–1640	42,398 (76·98%)	2,240 (4·07%)	105 (0·19%)	1,767 (3·21%)	8,567 12 (15·56%)	55,077 12 (44·18%)
1641–1660	9,890 4 (93·41%)	240 (2·27%)	10 (0·09%)		448 (4·23%)	10,588 4 (8·49%)
TOTALS	65,669 7 (52·68%)	3,700 (2·97%)	1,581 13 (1·27%)	31,961 (25·63%)	21,751 4 (17·45%)	124,663 4

	Poor	Social Rehabilitation	Municipal Betterments	Education	Religion	
	£ s	£ s	£ s	£ s	£ s	£ s
Upper Gentry 1480–1540	4,180 16 (12·85%)	123 11 (0·38%)	483 6 (1·48%)	5,374 5 (16·51%)	22,388 14 (68·78%)	32,550 12 (18·96%)
1541–1560	3,464 13 (60·08%)	130 17 (2·27%)	157 (2·72%)	631 (10·94%)	1,383 8 (23·99%)	5,766 18 (3·36%)
1561–1600	8,485 14 (51·60%)	1,444 18 (8·78%)	265 (1·61%)	4,624 6 (28·12%)	1,626 5 (9·89%)	16,446 3 (9·58%)
1601–1640	30,312 17 (34·16%)	4,822 10 (5·43%)	1,713 (1·93%)	40,445 11 (45·57%)	11,449 13 (12·91%)	88,743 11 (51·70%)
1641–1660	16,472 3 (58·51%)	1,836 13 (6·53%)	842 (2·99%)	6,705 7 (23·82%)	2,295 2 (8·15%)	28,151 5 (16·40%)
TOTALS	62,916 3 (36·65%)	8,358 9 (4·87%)	3,460 6 (2·02%)	57,780 9 (33·66%)	39,143 2 (22·80%)	171,658 9

	Poor	Social Rehabilitation	Municipal Betterments	Education	Religion	
	£ s	£ s	£ s	£ s	£ s	£ s
Lower Gentry 1480–1540	5,137 5 (13·68%)	161 7 (0·43%)	2,815 10 (7·50%)	3,105 11 (8·27%)	26,331 11 (70·12%)	37,551 4 (20·74%)
1541–1560	2,047 18 (31·10%)	109 1 (1·66%)	599 6 (9·10%)	890 (13·52%)	2,937 18 (44·62%)	6,584 3 (3·64%)
1561–1600	15,397 8 (57·96%)	1,394 13 (5·25%)	962 13 (3·62%)	6,496 7 (24·46%)	2,313 3 (8·71%)	26,564 4 (14·67%)
1601–1640	41,992 18 (55·43%)	3,000 1 (3·96%)	405 12 (0·54%)	22,193 (29·29%)	8,166 13 (10·78%)	75,758 4 (41·82%)
1641–1660	16,043 12 (46·32%)	2,307 (6·66%)	599 10 (1·73%)	9,596 (27·71%)	6,088 10 (17·58%)	34,634 12 (19·12%)
TOTALS	80,619 1 (44·52%)	6,972 2 (3·85%)	5,382 11 (2·97%)	42,280 18 (23·35%)	45,837 15 (25·31%)	181,092 7

TABLE XI—*cont.*

CHANGES IN THE STRUCTURE OF CLASS ASPIRATIONS

Interval	Poor	Social Rehabilitation	Municipal Betterments	Education	Religion	Totals and % of Whole Contribution Made in the Several Periods
	£ s	£ s	£ s	£ s	£ s	£ s
Yeomen 1480–1540	756 8 (11·74%)	30 12 (0·47%)	453 6 (7·03%)		5,203 14 (80·75%)	6,444 (13·97%)
1541–1560	1,045 12 (47·77%)	59 9 (2·72%)	160 12 (7·34%)		923 7 (42·18%)	2,189 (4·75%)
1561–1600	6,693 13 (57·98%)	154 17 (1·34%)	1,911 10 (16·56%)	2,186 12 (18·94%)	597 13 (5·18%)	11,544 5 (25·03%)
1601–1640	10,844 7 (69·98%)	653 (4·21%)	269 3 (1·74%)	2,431 6 (15·69%)	1,297 13 (8·37%)	15,495 9 (33·60%)
1641–1660	6,722 8 (64·38%)	313 13 (3·00%)	106 14 (1·02%)	2,026 16 (19·41%)	1,272 9 (12·19%)	10,442 (22·64%)
TOTALS	26,062 8 (56·52%)	1,211 11 (2·63%)	2,901 5 (6·29%)	6,644 14 (14·41%)	9,294 16 (20·16%)	46,114 14
Husbandmen 1480–1540	27 11 (3·81%)	10 5 (1·42%)	25 6 (3·50%)		658 7 (91·25%)	721 9 (25·62%)
1541–1560	178 7 (33·83%)	0 1 (0·01%)	21 1 (3·99%)	0 1 (0·01%)	327 15 (62·16%)	527 5 (18·73%)
1561–1600	407 12 (69·59%)	0 17 (0·15%)	18 10 (3·16%)	2 1 (0·35%)	156 14 (26·75%)	585 14 (20·80%)
1601–1640	569 4 (84·71%)	2 10 (0·37%)	9 9 (1·41%)	12 (1·79%)	78 15 (11·72%)	671 18 (23·86%)
1641–1660	237 5 (76·67%)		2 2 (0·68%)	40 (12·93%)	30 2 (9·73%)	309 9 (10·99%)
TOTALS	1,419 19 (50·43%)	13 13 (0·48%)	76 8 (2·71%)	54 2 (1·92%)	1,251 13 (44·45%)	2,815 15
Lower Clergy 1480–1540	1,282 11 (3·89%)	114 9 (0·35%)	1,095 5 (3·32%)	15,513 5 (47·03%)	14,982 (45·42%)	32,987 10 (23·38%)
1541–1560	1,908 4 (11·65%)	150 6 (0·92%)	138 16 (0·85%)	4,930 7 (30·10%)	9,256 8 (56·50%)	16,384 1 (11·61%)
1561–1600	1,341 13 (26·38%)	323 1 (6·35%)	121 11 (2·39%)	2,595 3 (51·02%)	704 19 (13·86%)	5,086 7 (3·61%)
1601–1640	24,046 13 (38·42%)	2,365 2 (3·78%)	4,552 3 (7·27%)	25,754 16 (41·15%)	5,870 1 (9·38%)	62,588 15 (44·36%)
1641–1660	8,572 7 (35·67%)	281 (1·17%)	122 (0·51%)	13,277 (55·24%)	1,781 4 (7·41%)	24,033 11 (17·04%)
TOTALS	37,151 8 (26·33%)	3,233 18 (2·29%)	6,029 15 (4·27%)	62,070 11 (44·00%)	32,594 12 (23·10%)	141,080 4

TABLE XI—cont.

CHANGES IN THE STRUCTURE OF CLASS ASPIRATIONS

Interval	Poor	Social Rehabilitation	Municipal Betterments	Education	Religion	Totals and % of Whole Contribution made in the Several Periods
Merchants	£ s	£ s	£ s	£ s	£ s	£ s
1480–1540	29,737 (23·31%)	8,830 5 (6·92%)	15,844 4 (12·42%)	11,426 (8·96%)	61,716 17 (48·38%)	127,554 6 (9·52%)
1541–1560	23,796 6 (42·90%)	8,782 7 (15·83%)	6,601 9 (11·90%)	11,631 14 (20·97%)	4,660 18 (8·40%)	55,472 14 (4·14%)
1561–1600	68,479 5 (31·85%)	52,498 1 (24·41%)	19,036 7 (8·85%)	68,210 16 (31·72%)	6,803 (3·16%)	215,027 9 (16·06%)
1601–1640	313,269 12 (45·28%)	76,202 10 (11·01%)	38,230 10 (5·53%)	181,630 7 (26·25%)	82,564 17 (11·93%)	691,897 16 (51·65%)
1641–1660	100,430 10 (40·25%)	44,276 2 (17·74%)	12,919 19 (5·18%)	61,305 1 (24·57%)	30,615 1 (12·27%)	249,546 13 (18·62%)
TOTALS	535,712 13 (39·99%)	190,589 5 (14·23%)	92,632 9 (6·92%)	334,203 18 (24·95%)	186,360 13 (13·91%)	1,339,498 18

Interval	Poor	Social Rehabilitation	Municipal Betterments	Education	Religion	Totals and %
Tradesmen	£ s	£ s	£ s	£ s	£ s	£ s
1480–1540	4,145 17 (23·25%)	132 14 (0·74%)	2,857 15 (16·03%)	464 17 (2·61%)	10,227 (57·36%)	17,828 3 (11·91%)
1541–1560	5,926 4 (49·09%)	2,052 19 (17·01%)	1,794 17 (14·87%)	877 (7·26%)	1,422 (11·78%)	12,073 (8·07%)
1561–1600	11,231 13 (51·01%)	3,496 11 (15·88%)	1,568 15 (7·12%)	4,664 7 (21·18%)	1,057 (4·80%)	22,018 6 (14·71%)
1601–1640	35,748 14 (50·75%)	14,344 19 (20·36%)	4,303 9 (6·11%)	8,221 13 (11·67%)	7,822.15 (11·11%)	70,441 10 (47·07%)
1641–1660	16,359 18 (59·97%)	2,749 16 (10·08%)	2,095 2 (7·68%)	4,641 2 (17·01%)	1,436 2 (5·26%)	27,282 (18·23%)
TOTALS	73,412 6 (49·06%)	22,776 19 (15·22%)	12,619 18 (8·43%)	18,868 19 (12·61%)	21,964 17 (14·68%)	149,642 19

Interval	Poor	Social Rehabilitation	Municipal Betterments	Education	Religion	Totals and %
Artisans	£ s	£ s	£ s	£ s	£ s	£ s
1480–1540	481 5 (24·71%)	61 7 (3·15%)	159 16 (8·20%)		1,245 11 (63·94%)	1,947 19 (22·39%)
1541–1560	255 16 (53·95%)	27 3 (5·73%)	28 6 (5·97%)	2 (0·42%)	160 18 (33·93%)	474 3 (5·45%)
1561–1600	780 10 (71·46%)	172 14 (15·81%)	73 3 (6·70%)	27 9 (2·51%)	38 7 (3·51%)	1,092 3 (12·55%)
1601–1640	2,276 6 (67·11%)	325 5 (9·59%)	174 3 (5·13%)	57 12 (1·70%)	558 7 (16·46%)	3,391 13 (38·99%)
1641–1660	1,207 2 (67·30%)	77 10 (4·32%)	42 5 (2·36%)	406 2 (22·64%)	60 14 (3·38%)	1,793 13 (20·62%)
TOTALS	5,000 19 (57·49%)	663 19 (7·63%)	477 13 (5·49%)	493 3 (5·67%)	2,063 17 (23·72%)	8,699 11

INDEX

GEORGE ALLEN & UNWIN LTD

London: 40 Museum Street, W.C.1

Auckland: 24 Wyndham Street
Bombay: 15 Graham Road, Ballard Estate, Bombay 1
Bridgetown: P.O. Box 222
Buenos Aires: Escritorio 454–459, Florida 165
Calcutta: 17 Chittaranjan Avenue, Calcutta 13
Cape Town: 68 Shortmarket Street
Hong Kong: 44 Mody Road Kowloon
Ibadan: P.O. Box 62
Karachi: Karachi Chambers, McLeod Road
Madras: Mohan Mansions, 38c Mount Road, Madras 6
Mexico: Villalongin 32–10, Piso, Mexico 5, D.F.
Nairobi: P.O. Box 4536
New Delhi: 13–14 Asaf Ali Road, New Delhi 1
Ontario: 81 Curlew Drive, Don Mills
Philippines: 7 Waling-Waling Street, Roxas District, Quezon City
São Paulo: Caixa Postal 8675
Singapore: 36c Prinsep Street, Singapore 7
Sydney, N.S.W.: Bradbury House, 55 York Street
Tokyo: 10 Kanda-Ogawamachi, 3-Chome Chiyoda-Ku

MORAL EDUCATION IN CHRISTIAN TIMES

E. B. CASTLE

'On no account must you miss this book. It is tremendous fun. I doubt whether I have enjoyed anything quite so much since Trevelyan's *Social History* or Russell's *History of Western Philosophy*. . . . It has stimulated me more than any similar work I have had to read in ten years.' This is how our adviser described this remarkable book. In Professor Castle's hands the history of education—the long struggle of the best theory and practice against conservatism and brutality—has colour, immense interest, and depth.

The views of philosophers and pioneers are contrasted with actual practice in the schools of England and Western Europe from early Christian times to the present day—a range of thought from St. Augustine to John Dewey, from Vittorino to Montessori, from Mulcaster to Thring, and practices so divergent as those of Joseph Lancaster and A. S. Neill. He covers moral education and discipline in both school and home.

'This is a masterly survey of educational ideals from the Christian Fathers to the not-so-Christian father-figure of the most modern "progressive head".' *Western Mail.* *Demy 8vo. 30s. net*

THE ENGLISH WOMAN IN HISTORY

LADY STENTON

Lady Stenton has attempted the ambitious task of surveying the position of Englishwomen in the society of their day from the earliest down to modern times. No historian has ever undertaken a survey of this kind before. During her study of this subject, which arose out of her work on medieval records, and has extended over a considerable period, Lady Stenton has discovered a great deal of new information, correcting much that has been generally accepted in the past.

The first chapter deals with the Anglo-Saxon woman, and here, Lady Stenton has been able to draw on the knowledge of the author of *Anglo-Saxon England*. The Anglo-Saxon heritage is displayed in her treatment of the countrywoman and the townswoman. The effect of the Norman Conquest on their position in Feudal England; the influence of the Renaissance, including the effect of the personality and achievements of Queen Elizabeth I on the intellectual relationships between men and women; and the impact of the Reformation on the position of women in society are recorded with admirable clarity. A chapter on morals and manners describes the shifting pattern of relationships between men and women discernible through the ages. Then the long story of the rise of the independent woman carries the narrative into modern times.

'A book of outstanding scholarship seasoned with wit and charm.' *International Women's News.* *Illustrated. Sm. Royal 8vo. 35s. net*

GEORGE ALLEN & UNWIN LTD

Preface

THIS BOOK has two fundamental purposes. One is to provide a resource (there are too few) for the growing number of courses that focus specifically on state and local public management. The other is to enrich introductory public administration courses. In this book the functions of public management are "brought home" to students through cases, games, exercises, and background readings. Here students *experience* some of the challenges of public management in familiar local and state contexts.

The materials here are organized in eleven chapters that cover the principal concepts and processes of pragmatic public management. The use of cases is hardly new to the fields of business and public administration. But good cases on contemporary state and urban management are still neither plentiful nor widely available. The cases in this book treat states as well as large and small localities across the United States, from Massachusetts to California to Florida. They deal with the principal functions of state and local governments — human services, criminal justice, environmental protection, transportation, education, recreation, public works, and health care, as well as general management.

This text has a number of potential uses:

1. It can provide the basis for a course devoted to state and local administration, urban administration, or city management for students in public administration, political science, urban studies, public policy, or management. Other courses to which the book is relevant are sometimes titled Case Studies in Public Administration or Problems in Public Administration. It can also be used in institutions where elements of the public service are organized into separate academic programs; criminal justice, social work, health care, and educational administration are examples.
2. It can accompany a standard textbook in an introductory course in public administration or public sector management. The state and local setting of the materials often facilitates student comprehension of the issues. Actually "working at" public administration results in better understanding.
3. It can be used in connection with governmental internships or similar field work courses. The text is uniquely suited to fit in with the experiential nature and learning design of such courses, which are increasingly popular. Such course work may be sponsored by a college or university, or by a governmental jurisdiction through a management internship or fellowship program.

4. It can be used to help upgrade governmental employees in in-service training or continuing education programs.

A comprehensive *Instructor's Manual* is available from St. Martin's Press, 175 Fifth Avenue, New York, N.Y. 10010. It contains an analysis of each case and suggestions for the classroom use of each chapter. In addition, the *Instructor's Manual* has a section with supplemental cases and exercises that may be duplicated locally for classroom use. The exercises have been carefully structured to develop both knowledge and skills. They have been extensively classroom tested and work well with a wide range of students.

Many individuals have been essential in the preparation of these materials. I am especially grateful to my students at Bernard M. Baruch College, City University of New York, who tested various versions of these materials. I have also had the benefit of using some of these chapters in connection with the New York City Summer Management Intern Program, the Urban Fellows Program, the University Year for ACTION, and the City University of New York Seminar/Internship in New York City Government.

Some of the items included here were supported in part by a grant from the Chancellor's Fund for Curricular Diversity, City University of New York, awarded to Professor David Bresnick and myself. This early encouragement and support was essential in developing the materials and is gratefully acknowledged.

In the final revision of the manuscript, St. Martin's Press commissioned six reviewers who teach public administration in different sections of the country to comment in detail on the volume as a whole, its organization, and its contents. Their anonymous suggestions were quite helpful to me in the text's final editing. At St. Martin's Press, Tom Broadbent and Bert Lummus, as well as the entire staff, have offered encouragement and demonstrated their commitment not only to this project but also to publishing a wide range of innovative materials for the education of public managers in the United States. Michael Weber and Charles Thurlow were enormously helpful in preparing this book for publication.

I am also indebted to Pauline Blacker, Pauline Brownsten, and Pearl Schwartz, as well as to Katherine Curtis, for their assistance in manuscript preparation and other office work. Beatrice Bussey ably assisted in reading the galleys. In addition, Antoinette Georgiades, Neville Rosemin, and Lynn Alston were always ready to assist in duplicating materials.

Frederick S. Lane

Note to the Student

EACH OF THE ELEVEN CHAPTERS in this book opens with three sections. The first, *Pre-Class Preparation*, alerts you to the readings in the chapter and tells you precisely what to do with the case(s) or game which is the key to the chapter. There usually are questions to be answered or a problem to be solved to help you focus your work. You should remember that each case included here is designed to serve as a basis for analysis and class discussion, not necessarily to exemplify either effective or ineffective handling of an administrative situation.

The second section, *Procedure for Class Meeting* (which your instructor may choose to alter), requires you to articulate your ideas and recommendations and defend them in discussion with other course participants.

The third section, *For Additional Information*, offers further reading suggestions. These carefully selected references may aid you in completing an assignment. They may also be valuable if you encounter a particular subject again in a more advanced course or while you are working in a state or local government agency. The availability of some of these references in inexpensive paperback editions is also noted.

Contents

Managing State and Local Government:
Cases and Readings

Introduction: Understanding Public Management

Frederick S. Lane

BILL DONALDSON IS Cincinnati's city manager.

When a Congressional committee held hearings on how cities could cut costs, ward off taxpayer revolts, and still deliver vital public services, Donaldson was one of the first witnesses.

Donaldson has had a colorful career. He began as a theological student in Toronto, worked nights as an embalming clerk in Denver, and later served as city manager of Scottsdale, Arizona, and of Tacoma, Washington.

While its sister city Cleveland was heading for bankruptcy and tax increases in the late 1970s, Cincinnati imposed no new taxes and held its budget increases to about half the rate of inflation. Although Cincinnati had always been somewhat conservatively as well as professionally managed, the results were not always so successful.

In 1975 Cincinnati was headed for a $15 million deficit, having overestimated its tax revenues and underestimated the rate of inflation. The city council asked Cincy's citizens to increase the payroll tax; they said no.

Enter William V. Donaldson. Donaldson stopped hiring new city employees as a short-term measure, although some replacements were subsequently allowed.

The longer-term Donaldson/Cincinnati approach focused on the following:

- motivating city employees
- developing a set of productivity measures to appraise the performance of city agencies
- getting more citizen volunteers to help out, especially in their own neighborhoods
- promoting Cincinnati's economic development, to increase the fiscal health of the city

For example, Cincinnati's highway maintenance bureau rescheduled its work crews and substituted labor-saving trucks, with the assistance of a labor-management committee. The bureau wound up increasing the work it accomplished in spite of personnel cuts.

1

Donaldson tried to get city employees to participate in developing new approaches toward effective management. "If they're going to have to run it," he said, "they'd better be part of developing it."[1]

And Bill Donaldson is only one example. There are approximately 12 million public employees in state and local government in the United States. They are organized into some 80,000 different units of government. It is the important challenges and issues of state and local management which are the subjects treated in this text.

What Is Public Management?

Management is the process of organizing and maintaining human and fiscal resources toward the attainment of group goals.

Just as biological organisms do, human organizations exist in an environment — political, social, and economic — which shapes and influences the organizations' activities. Organizations are adapting to a constantly changing environment. Maintaining a healthy public organization is often not an easy task. As we enter the 1980s, we are acutely aware that managing change is one of the fundamental challenges of public management.

The utilization of management resources — principally people, organization, and money — is a critical management responsibility. In a period of "steady state" or shrinking resources, this is even more difficult.

In all this, organizations, public and private, seek to be purposive — that is, to accomplish certain goals or purposes in an efficient and effective way. This normally requires careful planning as well as the day-to-day management of the operations of an organization. As part of this, the activities and results of organizational activity need to be monitored and evaluated to ensure that the organization is indeed on its intended course.

Students almost always ask, "What is the difference between *public* management and *business* management? Isn't management just about the same no matter in what type of organization it occurs?" The answer to this question is not simple, but it is important.

Many Americans believe that business organizations are more effective than public organizations. Evidence does not confirm (or deny) this contention. We do know that they are very difficult to compare at all because management in government differs fundamentally from management in business.

Public management is unique in five principal ways:[2]

1. The first of these is the *lack of a profit measure*. The "bottom line" which exists for a private firm — its statement of profit or loss — does not exist in government. While the profit measure does not tell us

all we might like to know about a company, it is a useful single measure. It facilitates quantitative analysis, including the comparison of one company's record with another. Imagine how helpful it would be to public managers and citizens generally if such a measure existed in government.

Related to the absence of a profit measure is the problem of profit motive ("making money"). The pressures for efficiency and cost reduction may not be as great or the results as quantifiable in government.

Beyond this, goals in public agencies are often vague and unclear. Even where specified, they may be numerous and conflicting, and there may be widespread disagreement and lack of commitment to them throughout the organization.

Even when there is clarification and agreement on an agency's goals, it is often difficult to measure results. Public agencies are often unable to determine when and if their performance is effective.

2. Public management is different from business management with regard to *ownership and control*. In government, authority is frequently fragmented. To begin with, the American constitutional framework prescribes three separate branches of government — executive, legislative, and judicial. Each has devices, or "checks and balances," limiting the others' authority. Power is structurally divided. This pattern repeats itself at almost all levels of government in the United States.

Most public organizations also exist in a more turbulent environment than business organizations. External groups are constantly and often intensely attempting to influence public agency goals and activities. Politics is the way environmental demands are made known to the public agency; for a business, this is much more a matter of economic choice by consumers.

Regular elections mean that top public management personnel periodically turn over. Beyond this, these top executives also carry the short-term time perspective of the politician with them, even when they are in office for a relatively long time.

Public organizations are open to public visibility and scrutiny far more than businesses. With visibility come public expectations of honesty, fairness, and responsiveness. In all this, agency goals, unlike those of business, are determined largely by "outsiders."

Finally, a permanent cadre of employees is somewhat insulated from the control of top management. Civil service procedures were originally designed to protect public employees and the management of public agencies from the excesses of politics and political patronage.

3. The *marketplace* plays a smaller role in public organizations. Government departments are often monopolistic in the sense that they have no competitors. Police and fire services, for example, engage in no market competition.

The way consumers or clients affect private businesses is well known: you either buy their products or seek their services or you don't. Client groups—industries, farmers, other interests—often affect the public agencies which serve them, but in government, client or consumer influence may sometimes be quite weak, as in schools and colleges, hospitals and mental institutions, or police and welfare departments.

4. Public organizations tend to be *service organizations.* Some private businesses are service providers, but private manufacturing, wholesale and retail sales, and construction make up the overwhelming majority of business employment. Goals tend to be less tangible (but no less important) in service-oriented government agencies. At the same time, services mean that government agency expenditures are largely for people's salaries. Government is what economists call a "labor-intensive" enterprise. People are obviously less easily controlled and deployed than capital and materiel, as in business production.

Another characteristic of service organizations is a failure to understand fully the task involved, *how* to actually accomplish the desired results. Declining scores on the Scholastic Aptitude Test ("College Boards") suggest that we don't really know exactly how to teach people to read or write. Similarly, we don't seem to be improving our ability to rehabilitate criminals, to "heal" mental patients, or to prevent crime.

5. Public agencies tend to be *dominated by specialists and professionals.* Specialists, like doctors and engineers, often dominate federal as well as state and local agencies. Management in such agencies is further complicated because many professions, such as college teaching, have a tradition of autonomy. (Professors even maintain control over their own time, except perhaps for time spent teaching.)

One result of the dominance of specialists is the secondary status often accorded to the generalist manager, who plays a much more fundamental role in private enterprise. Somewhat belatedly, new attention is now being paid to attracting and promoting generalist managers and administrators in government.

Regarding "management," then, management *in government* is a unique, much more complex and often more difficult process than is normally found in business.

These distinctive features have important implications for the role of the public manager. In goal setting and planning, public managers have less flexibility and independence. Goals may be harder to specify and more diverse. Planning involves a variety of influences and greater complexity; long-range planning is much more difficult.

Regarding the selection, motivation, and control of employees, public administrators also experience greater restraints. Difficulty in measuring results means additional difficulties in appraising employee performance as well as organizational effectiveness.

The Challenges of State and Local Management

Despite the term's increased popularity, this text refrains from referring to the "public sector." *Government* is far too important to be thought of only as a sector of the economy. This book focuses on the management of state and local government, which is also unique in its own way. While most textbooks in public administration and public management stress the federal level, state and local management is especially important. This is true for a number of reasons:

- State and local government has grown in size and complexity. Of the 15 million (civilian) governmental employees in the United States, 12 million are in state and local government. State and local management today goes far beyond the nineteenth-century notion of simple housekeeping and distribution of patronage.
- State and local agencies are closer to people and have higher visibility. These public employees have been characterized as "street-level bureaucrats." (If your garbage is not picked up on the scheduled day, everybody in the neighborhood knows it.)
- Beyond physical proximity there is also the "intimate" nature of state and local agency activities—education and health care, welfare and recreation, police and fire protection, even sewerage and water supply. Most of these affect the quality of our lives directly.
- Finally, it is the state or local agency which actually delivers most governmental services, even if they are funded by the federal government. As one local manager keeps saying to me, "This is the only place in American government where we actually do what needs to be done to help our clients."

The 1980s promise new as well as familiar challenges for state and local administrative agencies. The first of these is inadequate resources. State and local managers in recent years constantly talk about not having the resources they need to solve the problems for which they were established.

A second challenge is the threat to the traditional authority of public administrators. Even if there is a small chance of actual physical danger, there is an increasing threat to the manager's control over the potential work-related circumstances: consider the problems of policemen in high crime areas, teachers in urban schools, and social service administrators in welfare centers. State and local managers are often called insensitive, racist, unprepared to work with certain classes of clients, or resistant to new approaches.

Third, public employees sometimes have to cope with ambiguous or even contradictory work expectations. The cop on the street knows what the department's SOP (Standard Operating Procedure) says, but he also knows what his precinct captain told him, what other officers at the station are thinking, and what various publics expect. These do not always fit neatly together.[3]

Fourth, there are allegations of an inability to perform the required service delivery tasks: allegations of inefficiency, ineffectiveness and inequity.

Finally, there is the feeling of inadequate accountability on the part of state and local agencies. State and local managers must function in an increasingly turbulent political environment.

Managing state and local government today requires new understandings, new skills, and new approaches if the expectations about government at its most basic level are to be fulfilled. For the 1980s, this is what public management is all about.

An Experiential Approach

The question now is, "How *do* we increase understanding of public management and prepare individuals to be state and local managers?"

These individuals basically require three kinds of skills:

- analytical skills, to recognize and solve an ongoing series of organizational problems
- interpersonal skills, to work with others in human organizations and to coordinate and influence their joint efforts
- technical skills, to accomplish tasks in a particular policy area, such as transportation, criminal justice, human services, or environmental protection[4]

Increasingly, educational programs are relying on experiential approaches, along with traditional cognitive learning, to promote deeper understanding of the knowledge necessary and improved development of the skills essential for contemporary public management. After all, most learning in life is based on experience.

One experiential approach is the use of cases in public management education. The use of cases is especially effective in building analytical and interpersonal skills:[5]

1. Cases provide a sense of what public management is, a sense of realism, a kind of "understanding."
2. Cases increase student awareness of the particular context or setting in which management occurs—whether that setting be the organization's broader external environment or its own internal climate. They become more sensitive in diagnosing problems, the causes, and the relationships to other organizational activities.

3. Case analysis promotes the development of clear, logical, and analytical thinking. This includes, where necessary, manipulation of data and quantitative methods.
4. Cases force students to make decisions and plan for implementation of programs. This also encourages self-reliance and a sense of responsibility on the part of the future manager.
5. Cases require students to present and articulate their ideas and recommendations, orally and in writing—important skills for any manager.
6. In case presentation and discussion, students learn about working with others and group dynamics. Beyond this, they also increase self-awareness about their own attitudes, perspectives, and skills.
7. Learning to use the case method sensitizes students to the place of uncertainty in management and to the need for relevant and reliable information.
8. Cases allow students to "test," with the assistance of an instructor, theoretical and conceptual material, and to assess its value. In this way they can work toward generalizations about public management.
9. Finally, it is my experience that the case method greatly increases student interest and enthusiasm about public management.

Case analysis, then, is a solid first step toward administrative problem solving and good management. This volume combines cases with readings, relying on a certain amount of preparation to ensure that a student is ready to tackle the problems or situations raised in the case(s) that follow.

Cases were chosen for inclusion here in order to promote familiarity with the strategies public managers often use to solve problems, to influence others, and to bring about planned change and improvement in governmental organizations. While any case is necessarily something of an abstraction and simplification of real world events, and while cases are necessarily limited in length, the information and data presented in these cases is normally comparable to that which many state and local managers actually possess on their jobs.

A second experiential technique, which is a natural extension of case discussions, is simulation gaming. Here students play out the roles of various organizational actors. They not only represent their own interests and perspectives, but they experience those of a wide range of participants—supervisors, subordinates, public executives, and clients. Gaming is often no better than the case method at building generalizations on the part of the student, but it seems especially effective in developing interpersonal skills and practical techniques. Here students are much more likely to try out risk-taking behavior or new approaches to management. And with only a modest amount of exposure, students rapidly develop into excellent "gamesmen." This volume also offers the potential for gaming the public management process.

In all this, the goal should be clear: to increase and enhance understanding of public management, its dynamics and complexities.

NOTES

1. Neal Peirce, "Cincinnati Sets the Style," *The News World* (August 23, 1978), p. 15A. Peirce's column is syndicated throughout the United States by the Washington Post Company.
2. This builds on earlier work in this area, principally: Robert N. Anthony and Regina Herzlinger, *Management Control in Nonprofit Organizations* (Homewood, Ill.: Richard D. Irwin, Inc., 1975), ch. 3; Paul Appleby, *Big Democracy* (New York: Alfred A. Knopf, 1945), pp. 1–10; Joseph L. Bower, "Effective Public Management," *Harvard Business Review* (March–April 1977); Michael H. Moskow, *Strategic Planning in Business and Government* (New York: Committee for Economic Development, December 1978), ch. 3; Hal G. Rainey, Robert W. Backoff, and Charles H. Levine, "Comparing Public and Private Organizations," *Public Administration Review* (March–April 1976), and David Rogers, *Can Business Management Save the Cities?* (New York: The Free Press, 1978), ch. 2.
3. These first three are based on Michael Lipsky, "Street Level Bureaucracy and the Analysis of Urban Reform," in *Neighborhood Control in the 1970's: Politics, Administration, and Citizen Participation*, edited by George Frederickson (New York: Chandler Publishing Company, 1973), pp. 103–115.
4. Adapted from Robert L. Katz, "Skills of an Effective Administrator (with Retrospective Commentary)," *Harvard Business Review* (Sept.–Oct. 1974).
5. While this volume does not seek to teach the "technical" knowledge and skills in the many policy areas managed by states and localities, it does deliberately expose the student to a wide range of these, from human services to environmental protection to law enforcement.

Politics and Public Management

A dministrative agencies represent only one actor in the public policymaking process. There are many others: citizens, interest groups, political parties, the media, chief executives, legislative bodies, and the courts. All of these other actors influence the political setting in which state and local agencies function.

Part One is designed to examine, and let the student experience, the relationship between politics and public management and the give-and-take between public managers and other policymaking actors.

1

Participative Policymaking

PURPOSE

The purposes of this chapter are:

— to examine the place of the various participants in the formation of public policy;
— to explore the impact of the political setting on management in state and local government, and
— to introduce the key elements in public management.

CONTENTS

Reading
   Gordon Chase, "Managing, Compared"

Game
   "Participative Policymaking"

Instructions

Pre-Class Preparation

If you did not read the Preface and Introduction, go back and read them before beginning this chapter.

The reading in this chapter will help you understand the material presented here. Make sure you read it before proceeding.

Read carefully the General Information Sheet, with Budget, for the "Participative Policymaking" game.

Procedure for Class Meeting

The class will be divided into groups of six or seven members. Each group will play the same game simultaneously. A public school setting was chosen so that all participants, regardless of education or experience, could relate to the situation.

Each class member will be assigned a role to play in each group. In this exercise, portray the attitudes and feelings you would associate with the *role* you are playing, *not* your own personal beliefs.

For Additional Information

This text focuses on the *management* of state and local government. To fully understand the functioning of states and localities, the student needs to draw upon the perspectives of political science, economics, sociology and history (at least). The following carefully *selected* works are recommended to the student without an understanding of state and local government. This list is far from all-inclusive, nor is it meant to be. It is intended to serve as an introduction, although a solid introduction, to state and local government.

Regarding *state* government, the following provide an overview:

Alan K. Campbell and Roy W. Bahl, eds., *State and Local Government: The Political Economy of Reform* (New York: Free Press, 1976).

Robert Caro, *The Power Broker* (New York: Random House, 1974). Paperback edition available.

Thomas R. Dye, *Politics in States and Communities,* 3rd ed. (Englewood Cliffs, N.J.: Prentice-Hall, 1977).

Douglas M. Fox, *The Politics of City and State Bureaucracy* (Pacific Palisades, Calif.: Goodyear, 1974). Paperback edition available.

Herbert Jacob and Kenneth N. Vines, eds., *Politics in the American States,* 3rd ed. (Boston: Little, Brown, 1976).

Kenneth T. Palmer, *State Politics in the United States,* 2nd ed. (New York: St. Martin's, 1977). Paperback edition available.

Ira Sharkansky, *The Maligned States: Policy Accomplishments, Problems, and Opportunities,* 2nd ed. (New York: McGraw-Hill, 1978). Paperback edition available.

Martha Wagner Weinberg, *Managing the State* (Cambridge, Mass.: MIT Press, 1977). Paperback edition available.

Regarding *localities,* their politics, economics, and overall development, see:

John C. Bollens and Henry J. Schmandt, *The Metropolis: Its People, Politics, and Economic Life,* 3rd ed. (New York: Harper & Row, 1975). Paperback edition available.

Edwin Eames and Judith Granich Goode, *Anthropology of the City* (Englewood Cliffs, N.J.: Prentice-Hall, 1977). Paperback edition available.

Charles N. Glaab and A. Theodore Brown, *A History of Urban America* (New York: Macmillan, 1967). Paperback edition available.

William Gorham and Nathan Glazer, ed. *The Urban Predicament* (Washington, D.C.: Urban Institute, 1976). Paperback edition available.

John J. Harrigan, *Political Change in the Metropolis* (Boston: Little, Brown, 1976). Paperback edition available.

Samuel P. Hays, "The Politics of Reform in Municipal Government in the Progressive Era," *Pacific Northwest Quarterly,* LV (October 1964), pp. 157–169. Also, Bobbs-Merrill Reprint H-408.

Harold Hochman, ed., *The Urban Economy* (New York: W. W. Norton, 1976). Paperback edition available.

Herbert Kaufman, "Administrative Decentralization and Political Power," *Public Administration Review,* XXIX (Jan.–Feb., 1969), pp. 3–15.

William A. Schultze, *Urban and Community Politics* (North Scituate, Mass.: Duxbury Press, 1974). Paperback edition available.

Clarence N. Stone, Robert K. Wheelan, and William J. Murin, *Urban Policy and Politics in a Bureaucratic Age* (Englewood Cliffs, N.J.: Prentice-Hall, 1979). Paperback edition available.

Charles Tilly, ed., *An Urban World* (Boston: Little, Brown, 1974). Paperback edition available.

Douglas Yates, *The Ungovernable City* (Cambridge: MIT Press, 1977). Paperback edition available.

There are certain periodicals and reference works which might be of particular value in connection with this text. At a minimum, students should "touch" each one of these to get a feel for its content:

Administration and Society
Book of the States
The Bureaucrat
County and City Data Book
County Yearbook
Good Government
Harvard Business Review
Intergovernmental Perspective
International Journal of Public Administration
Midwest Review of Public Administration
Modern County Government
Municipal Yearbook
National Civic Review
Nation's Cities Weekly
Policy Analysis
Policy Sciences
Policy Studies Journal
Public Administration Review (the premier journal in this field)
Public Interest
Public Management
Public Personnel Management
Public Policy
Publius
Southern Review of Public Administration
State Government
State and Local Government Review
Urban Affairs Quarterly

In addition, three states now have regular journals concerning their internal governmental activity. These are the *California Journal, Illinois Issues,* and *Empire State Report* (New York).

Managing, Compared
Gordon Chase

As . . . NEW MAYORS (and governors) choose administrators to run government agencies, many of us wonder how we should judge the managers. Inevitably, we measure the performance of public officials against that of the private sector, in spite of the late political scientist Wallace Sayre's warning that "business and government administration are alike in all unimportant respects."

In fact, managing effectively and efficiently in the public sector is not only unlike managing in business, it's harder.

Take the question of goals. While the goals of a private firm are set by its executives and board of directors, the goals of a public agency are frequently determined by outsiders like legislatures, pressure groups and the news media. The implications? Roy L. Ash, Director of the Office of Management and Budget until 1975, after heading Litton Industries, put it this way: "Just imagine yourself as chief executive officer where your board of directors is made up of your employees, customers, suppliers and competitors. How would you like to run that business and try to be effective?"

As one consequence, the choice of goals is likely to be less realistic in the public sector. In business it's often said that it's smart to apply large resources to limited objectives. But in government, it's the reverse.

Public managers are frequently forced to apply limited resources to unlimited objectives because of pressures from outside power groups that lead to doing a little something for everybody and raise expectations beyond the capacity of government to deliver.

Moreover, the public manager's dealings with outside power groups are frequently rough, public and damaging to his personal reputation. After a year as Deputy Mayor for Finance of New York City, Kenneth Axelson, a senior vice president at J. C. Penney, noted that it's different in the corporate world, "where a man may be criticized but rarely discredited."

Another problem is structure. Private managers generally have great flexibility in how they organize their firms while public-agency heads can often only change the structure of their organizations significantly through lengthy legislative activity. Moreover, public managers must deal with three levels of government (including checks and balances within each level), frequently with no clear lines of authority, and with enormous opportunities for confusion, duplication and waste.

There are also differences in process that work to the responsible public manager's disadvantage. Public managers cannot measure results by how much money their organizations earn, making the evaluation process more difficult. Also, government's budget process — use the funds by year's end or lose them — provides a powerful incentive for agency heads to spend their appropriations more quickly than the merits might dictate.

Finally, the "people" problems are different. Few public-agency heads, or their key aides, can count on more than four years in any given job. But most important programs in the public sector take many more years to implement. This is also true of the private sector, but there the executive has time, like George Romney who said it took him 14 years to develop the compact car and get it accepted by the American market.

And then there is the pay problem. J. Henry Smith, who recently was New York City's Human Resources Administrator, noted that only he and his first deputy made over $40,000 in a public agency of 25,000 people, and that he didn't know where he could find executives markedly superior to the ones he had for the kind of money he could offer.

At lower levels, private firms have great flexibility compared to public agencies, which can't compete financially with business in recruiting for critical middle managers or rewarding outstanding performance on the job. Moreover, public agencies are usually constrained by unions and antique, irrelevant civil service systems that are outside of management control in many respects. Commenting on these restraints, Mr. Smith noted: "You can't say 'Here's a problem, so let's move this group of people in to deal with it.' The mobility of our work force is nil."

There is even an "atmospheric" problem that adversely affects public-sector employees. Mr. Axelson suggests that a company like J. C. Penney urgently requires continuity and takes particular care in developing and communicating its objectives to its people. And because its employees know the company would not shift gears without repeating the process, they feel secure: "They know if the game plan changes," he said, "they'll have the opportunity to change with it." Unlike the government, where continuity rarely exists, "the system doesn't work to double-cross the individual."

PARTICIPATIVE POLICYMAKING: A SIMULATION GAME

GENERAL INFORMATION

Today you are a member of the Advisory Council to the local Board of Education in a Rocky Mountain state. The Advisory Council was set up to advise the School Board on the annual budget. This Council represents diverse community interests: taxpayers, teachers, parents, School Board members, principals, and even students.

The time is now. Attached is the School Board budget for the current year, which is just about over. The budget is for the ninth grade only and not the whole school system to facilitate the purposes of this game.

Next year's budget must be *cut* by $100,000 because the State Legislature cut back on state aid to public education at its recent session. School taxes (local property tax) were raised last year in this largely middle-class suburban community, and were approved only narrowly by the voters after a heated campaign. There is a general feeling in the community that the School Board should not try to raise taxes again in these financially depressed times.

Your committee's job is to recommend to the School Board which programs to cut and by how much. You may increase the funding for some projects if you wish, and you may also add programs. You may also change goal statements.

The total number of students in the ninth grade—both this year and projected for next—is 400. While the school district operates several elementary and intermediate schools (through grade eight), it has only one high school, which includes grades nine through twelve. The per pupil cost this year was $2,000. The total budget for ninth grade this year was $800,000. If you need data not furnished, make assumptions.

The school has maintained a goal of one grade-level advance for 80 percent of its students in academic subjects each year. It was announced at the last School Board meeting that, based on the results of standardized achievement tests, the school did not meet its goal this year.

While only a (clear) majority vote is necessary for the Advisory Council to make its recommendations to the Board, the School Board seeks a broader consensus on this important, controversial, and well-publicized issue.

The School Board did not designate a chairperson of the Advisory Council, leaving it up to the Council's members to select their own chairperson.

THE SCHEDULE FOR THIS GAME IS AS FOLLOWS:

1. Convene a meeting of the Advisory Council and select a chairperson.
2. Discuss the changes you want to make in the ninth grade budget for next year.
3. Vote on the formal recommendations the Advisory Council desires to make to the School Board.

The assistance of Dr. Richard Montesi in adapting this simulation is gratefully acknowledged.

Note: For Steps 1–3, you have a time limit of approximately 30 minutes (the *actual* time limit will be set by your instructor).

4. Critique and evaluation of simulation and lessons learned.

BUDGET

The costs below include teacher salaries, books, equipment and supplies, and administrative overhead. Teacher salaries (including benefits) make up approximately 80% of costs.

No.	Subject and Goal	No. of Student Hrs.	No. of Teacher Hrs.	Cost This Year	Cost Next Year
1	80% of the students in the class will advance one grade-level in reading skills and English language knowledge as measured by a standard test.	90,000	3,000	$150,000	$_____
2a	80% of the students will advance one grade level in math (algebra) as measured by a standard test.	90,000	3,000	$200,000	$_____
2b	95% of the students will "like" math as well at the end of the year as they did when they entered as measured by attitude questionnaires, homework done, etc.				
3	80% of the students will advance one grade level in biology as measured by a school developed test.	60,000	2,000	$140,000	$_____
4	80% of the students will show the ability to examine social issues critically as indicated by a school developed test.	90,000	3,000	$140,000	$_____
5	All students will be provided with education on tobacco, alcohol, and narcotics. Effectiveness measured by sampling the tobacco and alcohol purchases at local stores and narcotics by several indicators, e.g., reported use, arrests, anonymous questionnaires, etc.	22,500	750	$ 40,000	$_____

No. Subject and Goal	No. of Student Hrs.	No. of Teacher Hrs.	Cost This Year	Cost Next Year
6 All students will be provided with a comprehensive family living course including sex education. Effectiveness will be estimated by the number of unwanted pregnancies reported among schoolage girls, VD reports, sampling of local medical community, etc.	22,500	750	$ 50,000	$_____
7 All students will be provided with an exposure to art forms by two field trips to city art museums and an audio-visual course in art appreciation.	22,500	750	$ 15,000	$_____
8 80% will rank above 50 percentile on President's physical fitness scale.	22,500	750	$ 65,000	$_____
TOTAL	420,000	14,000	$800,000	$700,000

Advisory Council vote on recommended budget: ____ in favor, ____ opposed

ROLES FOR PARTICIPATIVE POLICYMAKING

A description of the role you will play in the simulation is shown below. Please study the interests associated with *your role* and *try to represent this person's interests responsibly,* using the best judgment, sincerity and good will you can bring to it.

1. SCHOOL BOARD MEMBER

You want to get reelected. You like holding this position in your community.

Your reelection depends on your pleasing the taxpayers and parents of your school district by representing their interests in this group. Although you realize that objective tests cannot measure all the goals of the school, you know that the school is judged externally on the basis of student performance on standardized tests.

You hold the principal directly responsible for the school's poor performance this year.

2. HIGH SCHOOL PRINCIPAL

You hold a masters degree in educational administration.

You would like to see the school have better community relations. It would help if there were:

—a lower incidence of pregnancy among students,

—less drug use, and

—less vandalism in the neighborhood in the immediate vicinity of the school.

The school did not meet its goal of 80 percent student advance this year. The actual figures were:

Math	72 percent
English	41 percent
Social Studies	58 percent

You are convinced that your job depends on making those 80 percent marks next year.

3. HIGH SCHOOL ENGLISH TEACHER
(President of Teacher Union)

You want smaller classes. Thirty students are too many.

The facilities for the math and science teachers are so much better than those for others that conflict frequently arises.

Teachers want to have time off to take courses to improve their skills.

Teachers in the school district have generally been well treated and well paid, although the School Board has encountered increased financial difficulties in recent years. The current two-year contract expires at the end of this year, and negotiations are already underway for a new contract; little progress has been made to date. Inflation and the cost of living have been rising, and you feel teachers want a solid salary increase. The individual you narrowly defeated for the union presidency has been hinting about running against you when you are up for reelection next year, suggesting to some teachers that you have been ineffective.

4. TAXPAYER
(No Children in School)

You are concerned about the growing element of the student body which is experimenting with drugs.

Your best friend's daughter got pregnant last year. You would like to see the high school do something about student morals.

You are anxious to eliminate the frills from the curriculum. You learned from books. Why do students today need a $5,000 leased computer terminal to learn math?

5. PARENT
(Active in PTA)

You are anxious for your son to get into a good college and into medical school.

You are aware that there are many students in the school who will not go on to college, and you feel they should be prepared to enter the world of work upon graduation.

The general feeling of the PTA is that the home should be responsible for education directly related to values of the students, like sex, drugs, and health.

6. STUDENT
(Representing the High School Student Council)

Not all the students in the school will go on to college. They should be prepared to go into the world of work, if that is their goal, after graduation.

If they wish, students should also be prepared to do the work in the better colleges.

Most kids feel they don't know enough about drugs.

Some students strongly and vocally oppose having sex education in the school. Others find it their only source of reliable information.

You made your reputation in eighth grade by leading a sit-in in one of the junior high school cafeterias, because of what you called the "slop" they served.

7. PARENT/BANKER

You are a high prestige member of the community; that is why the School Board asked you to serve on the Advisory Council. Your membership gives the group increased legitimacy, both with the Board and in the District.

To be honest, you haven't thought much about the state of your district's public schools in the last few years. You don't bring any particular set of preconceptions to the Council, although you have the vague notion that the traditionally solid high school has been slipping lately.

You have a daughter who will be entering the ninth grade next year.

(*Note*: If your group has only six participants, this role may be eliminated.)

Management Resources: People, Organization, Money

I n the administration of government agencies, there are three essential resources — the "building blocks" of public management: people, organization, and money. Part two examines each of these.

We start with people, analyzing both human behavior in public organizations and the personnel systems which have so much to do with influencing that behavior. Even with logical structures, sensible procedures, and adequate funds, it is *people* who make things happen. Understanding and working with other human beings is the most important task of a manager.

The design or structure of administrative agencies is also important. It shapes the potential for managerial effectiveness in many ways.

And in the 1980s it goes without saying that money (or the lack of it) is a critical ingredient in public management. Fresh attention is necessary to how funds are budgeted and expended, for what purposes, and with what effect.

2

Human Behavior in Organizations

PURPOSE

The purposes of this chapter are to examine the nature of organizational behavior and its motivational base, and to introduce approaches to improving organizational effectiveness.

CONTENTS

Readings

Harry Levinson, "Asinine Attitudes toward Motivation"

"Management Diagnosis Chart"

Peter F. Drucker, "What Results Should You Expect? A Users' Guide to MBO"

"The Use of 'Staff Papers' in Public Management"

Cases

"Who Authorized This Trip?"

"The Chief"

"Chris Logan—City Engineer"

Instructions

Pre-Class Preparation

The readings in this chapter will help you understand the material presented here. Make sure you read them before proceeding.

1. Read "Who Authorized This Trip?" What is your reaction to the bureaucratic rules which seem to be prevalent? Are such rules and procedures necessary in large public organizations? How might this incident affect Paul's attitude ("psychological contract") toward working for this public organization in the future?

2. Read the case, "The Chief," and respond to the questions below:

   a. How do the formal organization and the "informal" organization, taken together, affect managerial behavior at Southwestern Arsenal?

b. Discuss the motivational aspects and leadership roles of the actors in the various interpersonal encounters in the case.

c. Assess the likely result when the chief finally reports to Brown for his reprimand.

3. In "Chris Logan — City Engineer" we see a portrait of a local manager.

a. What kinds of stress and conflict does Chris experience in his job? How does he resolve them?

b. Engineers are professionals. How is managing with professionals different or more difficult?

Procedure for Class Meeting

Classwork will involve the analysis of cases and discussion of organizational behavior.

For Additional Information

Organizational psychology and behavior are nicely introduced in:

Harold J. Leavitt, *Managerial Psychology,* 4th ed. (Chicago: University of Chicago Press, 1978). Paperback edition available.

H. Joseph Reitz, *Behavior in Organizations* (Homewood, Ill.: Richard D. Irwin, Inc., 1977).

Edgar H. Schein, *Organizational Psychology,* 2d ed. (Englewood Cliffs, N.J.: Prentice-Hall, 1970). Paperback edition available.

Regarding the participative management movement, see especially:

William B. Eddy, W. Warner Burke, Vladimir A. Dupre, and Oron Smith, eds., *Behavioral Science and the Manager's Role* (Washington: NTL Learning Resources Corporation, 1969). Paperback edition available.

Rensis Likert, *The Human Organization* (New York: McGraw-Hill, 1967).

Douglas McGregor, *The Human Side of Enterprise* (New York: McGraw-Hill, 1960).

William G. Scott, "Organization Government: The Prospects for a Truly Participative System," *Public Administration Review,* XXIX (Jan.-Feb. 1969), pp. 43-53.

Regarding the impact of participative management on public administration, also see Frank Marini, ed. *Toward a New Public Administration* (Scranton, Pa.: Chandler Publishing Company, 1971), especially chapters 3, 4, 5 and 11.

Regarding organization development (OD), see:

Warren Bennis, *Organization Development: Its Nature, Origins, and Prospects* (Reading, Mass.: Addison-Wesley, 1969). Paperback edition available; one of the excellent Addison-Wesley series on Organization Development.

Wendell L. French and Cecil H. Bell, Jr., *Organization Development* (Englewood Cliffs, N.J.: Prentice-Hall, 1973).

Robert T. Golembiewski and William B. Eddy, *Organization Development in Public Administration* (New York: Marcel Dekker, 1978).

Public Administration Review, XXXIV (March/April 1974). "Symposium on Organization Development."

Southern Review of Public Administration, I (March 1978). "Perspectives on Public Sector OD Symposium."

Robert A. Zawacki and D.D. Warrick, eds., *Organization Development: Managing Change in the Public Sector* (Chicago: International Personnel Management Association, 1973). Paperback edition available.

As for MBO (Management by Objectives), the most lucid introduction is in Anthony P. Raia, *Managing by Objectives* (Glenview, Ill.: Scott, Foresman, 1974). Paperback edition available.

Also see:

Public Administration Review, XXXVI (Jan./Feb. 1976). "Symposium on MBO in the Public Sector."

Paul Mali, *Managing by Objectives* (New York: Wiley, 1972).

George S. Odiorne, *Management by Objectives* (New York: Pitman Publishing Co., 1965).

The Bureaucrat, II (Winter, 1974). "Forum on MBO in the Federal Government."

Some other useful materials on organizational behavior include:

Chris Argyris, *Integrating the Individual and the Organization* (New York: Wiley, 1964).

Jameson W. Doig, "Administrative Oversight and Control," *Policy Studies Journal,* V (Autumn, 1976), pp. 86–96.

H. George Frederickson and Charles R. Wise, eds., *Public Administration and Public Policy* (Lexington, Mass.: D.C. Heath/Lexington Books, 1977). Especially Part I.

Frederick Herzberg, "One More Time: How Do You Motivate Employees?," *Harvard Business Review,* XLVI (Jan.–Feb., 1968), pp. 53–62.

Eric A. Nordlinger, *Decentralizing the City: A Study of Boston's Little City Halls* (Cambridge, Mass.: MIT Press, 1972). See "The Boston Bureaucracy" (Ch. 3).

Carl R. Rogers and F.J. Roethlisberger, "Barriers and Gateways to Communication," *Harvard Business Review,* XXX (July–Aug., 1952), pp. 28–34.

David Sirota and Alan D. Wolfson, "Pragmatic Approach to People Problems," *Harvard Business Review,* LI (Jan.–Feb., 1973), pp. 120–128.

Asinine Attitudes Toward Motivation

Harry Levinson

What this noted psychologist calls "the great jackass fallacy" is an unconscious managerial assumption about people and how they should be motivated. It results in the powerful treating the powerless as objects and in the perpetuation of anachronistic organizational structures that destroy the individual's sense of worth and accomplishment. And it is responsible for the "motivational crisis" that afflicts many large organizations. The author argues that in today's climate of increased pressure on organizations to become more responsive to both their members and society, it is particularly incumbent on managers to recognize the effect of the jackass fallacy on their thinking and to counter its effects in their organizations. Then he offers some suggestions for taking the first steps in this direction. [While Levinson primarily discusses private corporations, his perspectives are also quite relevant to public organizations.]

IN SPITE OF THE CORPORATE EFFORTS to promote smooth management-employee relations, events like these continue to happen:

- The top management of a large manufacturing company discovers that some of its line employees have embezzled a five-figure sum while their superiors stood by unperturbed. The executives are dumbfounded. They had thought that the supervisors were loyal, and that they themselves were thoughtful and kindly.
- An airline purchases a fleet of hydraulic lift trucks for placing food aboard aircraft at a large New York terminal. Although these trucks cost hundreds of thousands of dollars, they sit disabled on the airport apron. Maintenance employees and technicians occasionally glance at them contemptuously as they go about their work in sullen anger. Management is dismayed that these employees seem unresponsive to its cost-reduction efforts.
- Large companies, seeking new products, acquire smaller companies. Almost invariably, the successful managements of the acquired companies are soon gone and no new products are forthcoming. The larger organizations only increase their size and managerial burdens, and the hoped-for advantages evaporate. While this happens repeatedly, executives do not seem to learn from such failures.

When these events are looked at psychologically, their underlying causes become evident.

In the *first case*, the manufacturer renegotiated its labor contract every two years. Obviously, the appropriate person to do so was the vice president in charge of labor relations. But the people who carried out the contract and knew the employees best were the first-level supervisors; no one asked them what should be in the contract and what problems they had in implementing it. By its actions, management communicated to the supervisors that they did not matter much.

Furthermore, the union let grievances pile up just before the contract came up for renewal every two years, knowing full well that, to get a contract, management would settle the grievances in the union's favor. But the supervisors were the ones who bore the brunt of the grievances, since they carried out the terms of the contract. When management gave in, the supervisors felt that they had been undercut. In effect, these people were being told that they were stupid, that they had nothing useful to contribute to policy making, and that their job was to do as they were told. So they stood by during the stealing — if management did not care about them, why should they care about management?

In the *second case*, the issue for the airlines was much the same. A purchasing officer had bought the trucks, complete with sophisticated electronic controls. What was more natural than the purchasing officer doing the buying and getting the best? But he failed to check with the mechanics and technicians who kept the trucks operating. After all, what did they know about buying, and who asks technicians anyway?

Had he asked them, he would have learned that sophisticated electronic controls were fine for Los Angeles and Phoenix, where the weather was dry and mild, but that they failed repeatedly in New York, where the trucks were exposed to variable and sometimes harsh weather. No matter how hard the technicians worked, they could not keep the trucks functioning. Like the supervisors in the previous example, they felt that they were being exploited and contemptuously treated. Ultimately, they gave up trying to keep the trucks going. Seeing how much money the company had wasted on the trucks, they had little incentive to economize in their own small ways.

In the *third case*, what happens most frequently in merger failures is that the parent (note the use of that word) company promises the newly acquired company that there will be no changes. But changes are soon forthcoming, and the first of these is likely to be in the area of accounting control systems. Obviously, controls are necessary, and, just as obviously, many small companies do not have sophisticated controls. But they tend to be flexibly innovative for that specific reason. When controls become the central thrust of management, creative people who need flexibility leave, and the parent company is left with a corporate shell. The communication to the acquired company is that it is stupid and unsophisticated and therefore the parent must control it more rigidly.

Each of the foregoing problems would be dismissed in most organizations simply as a "failure in communications." Many psychologists would advocate dealing with such difficulties by participative management. Yet beneath that glib "explanation," and unresponsive to that ready "remedy," lies a fundamental unconscious management attitude that is responsible for most contemporary management-labor problems and for what is now being called a "crisis in motivation." I call this attitude the great jackass fallacy.

Later in this article, I shall describe the fallacy in detail and offer some suggestions for correcting it. But first let us explore in more depth the motivational crisis that it has precipitated.

Motivational Miasma

The crisis takes many forms, and its effects are easy to spot. Here are just a few examples:

- Companies are repeatedly reorganized on the advice of management consultants, but to little avail in the long run.
- New managerial devices, such as the four-day workweek and putting hourly people on salary, are loudly touted for their effect on employee motivation and morale, but the old problems soon reappear.
- Efforts to enrich jobs by giving employees more responsibility show encouraging results, but these disappear when employees seek to influence company policy and then are turned down by management.
- Business and nonprofit organizations alike are burdened by job encumbrances that result from union-management compromises.
- Increasing numbers of middle managers, engineers, teachers, and hospital personnel turn toward unionization.
- Many people in managerial ranks resign in favor of new jobs that pay less but offer greater individual freedom and initiative.

Most executives with whom I come in contact cannot understand why people do not respond to their efforts to sustain effective organizations, why people seemingly do not want to work, and why people want to leave apparently good organizations. Executives faced with these problems are often confused, angry, and hostile to their own people. The terms of office of chief executives, particularly those in educational and governmental administration, become shorter as the managerial frustrations increase.

The crisis in motivation has long been evident to students of organization, and they have offered problem-plagued executives a wide range of theories to cope with it. Suffice it to say that, by this time, thousands of executives are familiar with these theories. Many have taken part in managerial grid training, group dynamics laboratories, seminars on the psychology of management, and a wide range of other forms of training. Some have run the full gamut of training experiences; others have embraced a variety of panaceas offered by quacks.

Disappointing Remedies

The results of the aforementioned theories have not been impressive. While some companies have put them into practice with a degree of success, most have either given up their efforts as too simplistic for the complexity of organizational phenomena or have simply failed in their attempts.

There are, of course, many reasons why the remedies have failed. For one thing, executives often feel unqualified to apply the concepts. And in that feeling they are frequently right. Managers who have had little or no previous exposure to the behavioral sciences, let alone any formal training in this area, can get only the barest introductory knowledge in a brief training program. An executive would not expect a person to be able to design a complex building after a week-long training program in architecture; yet both the executive and the people who train him often expect that he will be a different person after he attends a one-week sensitivity-training laboratory.

Furthermore, it is one thing to learn to become more aware of one's own feelings; it is quite another to do something different about managing them, let alone about managing those forces that affect the feelings of other people. If everyone who had experienced psychotherapy were by that fact an expert therapist, there would be no shortage of such healers. Experience is not enough; training in a conceptual framework and supervised skill practice is also required. Many executives who have expected more of themselves and of such training have therefore been disillusioned, despite the benefits that have often resulted from even such brief experiences.

Would longer training help? Not much. Unlike marketing executives who implement marketing programs, and experts who install financial control systems, behavioral scientists (with the exception of certain kinds of psychotherapists) are not themselves expert in *doing*. While many know about the theories, and some of them practice what is called organizational development, they do not themselves change organizations. Instead they usually help people to think through alternative action possibilities and overcome communications blocks to working out their own solutions. Since most behavioral scientists are not skilled in changing organizations, then, they are not in a position to teach executives how to change them.

Power and fear   Another reason why solutions to motivation problems do not work is that many executives are fearful of losing control of their organizations. The new theories have confronted executives with the need to distribute power in their organizations, which in turn raises questions about their authority and right to manage.

A recent study of 400 top executives in Europe indicates that they feel menaced by these new theories.[1] Most see themselves in the middle of an unsettling transition in management styles. They report that they can no longer use the authority of position; instead, they must gain their position by competition with subordinates and defend that position each step of the way. Of those interviewed, 61% spontaneously indicated that their primary problem is personnel management. Almost all of these executives have leadership problems.

Many businessmen are threatened when they must stimulate people to participate in making organizational decisions and invite people to express themselves more freely. When an executive's whole life thrust has been to obtain a position of power and control, he finds it particularly threatening to witness his power eroding as older methods of control and motivation become less effective.

Coupled with the fear of losing control is the fact that a disproportionate number of executives are characteristically insensitive to feelings. Some people, for example, pursue executive careers to obtain power over others as a way of compensating for real or fancied personal inadequacies, or as a reaction to an unconscious sense of helplessness. They are neurotically driven, and their single-minded, perpetual pursuit of control blinds them to their own subtle feelings and those of others.

Furthermore, many executives have engineering, scientific, legal, or financial backgrounds. Each of these fields places a heavy emphasis on cognitive rationality and measurable or verifiable facts. People who enter them usually are trained from childhood to suppress their feelings, to maintain a competitive, aggressive, nonemotional front. They are taught to be highly logical, and they seek to impose that kind of rationality on organizations.

As a result, they simply do not understand the power of people's feelings, and all too often they are incapable of sensing such feelings in everyday practice without considerable help. They are like tone-deaf people who, attending an opera, can understand the lyrics but cannot hear the music. Such executives are typified by a company president who was a participant in a seminar on psychological aspects of management. Halfway through the first lecture, he broke in to say, "You have already told me more about this subject than I want to know." Although he stayed to the end of the program, he simply could not grasp what was being taught.

All of these reasons, coupled with the inadequacies of contemporary motivational theory itself, explain much of the gap between theory and practice. In time, with new knowledge and better training experiences, most of the gap may be overcome. But the fact remains that much more effort could be applied now. This brings us to that unconscious assumption about motivation to which I referred earlier, one held particularly by executives in all types of organizations and reinforced by organizational theories and structure.

Fact and Fallacy

Frequently, I have asked executives this question: What is the dominant philosophy of motivation in American management? Almost invariably, they quickly agree that it is the carrot-and-stick philosophy, reward and punishment. Then I ask them to close their eyes for a moment, and to form a picture in their mind's eye with a carrot at one end and a stick at the other. When they have done so, I then ask them to describe the central image in that picture. Most frequently they respond that the central figure is a jackass.

If the first image that comes to mind when one thinks "carrot-and-stick" is a jackass, then obviously the unconscious assumption behind the reward-punishment model is that one is dealing with jackasses who must be manipulated and controlled. Thus, unconsciously, the boss is the manipulator and controller, and the subordinate is the jackass.

The characteristics of a jackass are stubbornness, stupidity, willfulness, and unwillingness to go where someone is driving him. These, by interesting coincidence, are also the characteristics of the unmotivated employee. Thus it becomes vividly clear that the underlying assumption which managers make about motivation leads to a self-fulfilling prophecy. People inevitably respond to the carrot-and-stick by trying to get more of the carrot while protecting themselves against the stick. This predictable phenomenon has led to the formation of unions, the frequent sabotage of management's motivation efforts, and the characteristic employee suspicion of management's motivational (manipulative) techniques.

Employees obviously sense the carrot-and-stick conception behind management's attitudes and just as obviously respond with appropriate self-defending measures to the communications built around those attitudes. Of course, there is much talk about the need to improve communication in organizations. All too often, however, the problem is not that communication is inadequate but, rather, that it is already too explicit in the wrong way. When employees sense that they are being viewed as jackasses, they will automatically see management's messages as manipulative, and they will resist them, no matter how clear the type or how pretty the pictures.

Perpetual Power Gap

Since the turn of the century, numerous different philosophies of management have appeared, each emphasizing a different dimension of the management task and each advocating a new set of techniques. Although these philosophies differ from each other in many respects, all are based on reward-punishment psychology. For example, most of the contemporary psychological conceptions of motivation take a reward-punishment psychology for granted; they advocate trust and openness among employees and managers, but at the same time they acknowledge that the more powerful have a natural right to manipulate the less powerful.

As long as anyone in a leadership role operates with such a reward-punishment attitude toward motivation, he is implicitly assuming that he has (or should have) control over others and that they are in a jackass position with respect to him. This attitude is inevitably one of condescending contempt whose most blatant mask is paternalism. The result is a continuing battle between those who seek to wield power and those who are subject to it. The consequences of this battle are increased inefficiency, lowered productivity, heightened absenteeism, theft, and sometimes outright sabotage.

Bureaucratic Badlands

The problems resulting from the jackass fallacy are compounded further by bureaucratic organizational structures. Such structures are based on a military model that assumes complete control of the organization by those at the top. In pure form, it is a rigid hierarchy, complete with detailed job descriptions and fixed, measurable objectives.

The bureaucratic structure requires everyone at every level to be dependent on those at higher levels. Hiring, firing, promotion, demotion, reassignment, and similar actions are the prerogatives of superiors who can make decisions unilaterally. In short, one's fate is decided by a distant "they" who are beyond his influence and control.

Under such circumstances, the subordinate person becomes increasingly defensive. He must protect himself against being manipulated and against the feeling of helplessness that inevitably accompanies dependency. Rank-and-file employees have long done so by unionization; managerial and professional employees are beginning to follow suit, and this trend will continue to grow.

While the bureaucratic structure, with its heavy emphasis on internal competition for power and position, is often touted as a device for achievement, it is actually a system for defeat. Fewer people move up the pyramidal hierarchy at each step. This leaves a residual group of failures, often euphemistically called "career people," who thereafter are passed over for future promotions because they have not succeeded in the competition for managerial positions.

Most of these people feel resentful and defeated. Often they have been manipulated or judged arbitrarily. They are no longer motivated by competitive spirit, because the carrots and the sticks mean less. There is little need, in their eyes, to learn more; they simply do as they are told. They usually stay until retirement unless they are among the "deadwood" that is cleaned out when a new management takes over.

Executives new to a company or a higher-level job like to think of themselves as being effective in cleaning out such deadwood or trimming the excess managerial fat. Some take to that task with great vigor. Unfortunately, the consequences are more negative than enthusiastic executives like to recognize. In one large company, for example, management hoped that the 40-year-olds would respond with unbridled enthusiasm when the 50-year-olds were cleaned out. But the younger men failed to respond, because they saw that what was happening to the older men would be their likely fate ten years hence.

Bureaucratic structure, with its implicit power-struggle orientation, increases infighting, empire building, rivalry, and a sense of futility. It tends to magnify latent feelings that the organization is a hostile environment which people can do little to change, and it bolsters the jackass fallacy. Little wonder that many young people do not want to get caught up in such situations! Since 90% of those who work do so in organizations, most young people, too, must do so. But they would rather be in organizations that provide them an opportunity to demonstrate their competence and proficiency than in organizations that test their ability to run a managerial maze successfully.

A Formidable Challenge

The great jackass fallacy and the bureaucratic organization structure present major obstacles to organizational survival. They are essentially self-defeating if what an executive wants from employees is spontaneity, dedication, commitment, affiliation, and adaptive innovation.

As I have already indicated, many executives try to cope with the pathology of the system by introducing such new techniques as group dynamics and job enrichment. These are simply patches on the body politic of an organization. There is no way to integrate them effectively. When people are asked to express their feelings more freely and to take on greater responsibility, they soon come into conflict with power centers and power figures in a system geared to the acquisition of power. The latter soon cry, "Business is not a democracy," and disillusionment sets in once again, both on the part of managers who tried the new techniques and on the part of subordinates who were subjected to them.

Unless the fundamental assumptions of management (and behavioral scientists) about motivation are changed, and unless the organizational structure is altered to match these changed assumptions, the underlying jackass fallacy will remain visible to those who are subjected to it. Despite whatever practices the organization implements, people will avoid, evade, escape, deny, and reject both the jackass fallacy and the military-style hierarchy.

If the executive grasps the import of what I am saying, shudders uncomfortably, and wants to do something about the problem, what are his alternatives? Is he forever doomed to play with psychological gimmicks? Is he himself so much a victim of his assumptions that he cannot change them? I do not think that he necessarily is. There are constructive actions that he can take.

The First Steps

Anyone who supervises someone else should look carefully at the assumptions he is making about motivation. He must assess the degree to which carrot-and-stick assumptions influence his own attitudes. For example, an executive might argue that if he tried to be nice to people, the stick would be softened. But even then he would merely be exhibiting paternalistic kindness. As long as his assumptions about people remain unchanged, his "being nice" is only a disguised form of carrot-and-stick which seeks to increase loyalty by creating guilt in those who are the recipients of his managerial largesse. His first priority should be to change his way of thinking about people.

After honestly and frankly facing up to one's own assumptions about what makes people tick, the next step is to look at one's organizational structure. Most organizations are constructed to fit a hierarchical model. People assume that the hierarchical organizational structure is to organizations as the spine is to human beings, that it is both a necessity and a given. As a matter of fact, it is neither a necessity nor a given.

I am arguing not against the distribution of power and control, but, rather, that this distribution need not take one particular form. Every executive should ask himself: "Is my operation organized to achieve a hierarchical structure or is it structured to accomplish the task it must do?" If it is organized more to fit the model than to fit the task, he should begin exploring more appropriate organization models.[2] To do otherwise is to invite trouble — if it has not already started.

Conclusion

It is time for business leaders to enter a phase of more serious thinking about leadership and organizational concepts. They must do so on behalf of their own organizations as well as on behalf of society. The issue I have been discussing is critically important for society as a whole, because society increasingly is made up of organizations. The less effectively organizations carry out the work of society, the greater the cost in money and in social paralysis. The latter leads to the kind of demoralization already evident in organizations as well as in problems of transportation, health care delivery, education, and welfare.

Furthermore, we are in the midst of a worldwide social revolution, the central thrust of which is the demand of all people to have a voice in their own fate. Business leaders, many of whom have international interests and see the multiple facets of this thrust in a wide range of countries, should be in the forefront of understanding and guiding these social changes into productive channels. By applying new principles of motivation to their own organizations, they are in a position not only to sustain the vitality of those organizations but, more important, to keep them adaptive to changing circumstances.

In addition, the progressive changes that executives institute in their own organizations can then become the models for other institutional forms in a given culture. Not the least of the advantages of being on the frontier is that executives and corporations avoid the onus of being continuously compelled by angry or apathetic employees to change in ways which may be destructive to both the business and the people involved.

But leading is more than a matter of pronouncing clichés. Leading involves an understanding of motivation. It is to this understanding that business leaders must now dedicate themselves. And the way to start is by countering the great jackass fallacy in their own organizations.

NOTES

1. Frederick Harmon, "European Top Managers Struggle for Survival," *European Business*, Winter 1971, p. 14.
2. Paul R. Lawrence and Jay W. Lorsch, *Organization and Environment: Managing Differentiation and Integration* (Boston, Division of Research, Harvard Business School, 1967).

Management Diagnosis Chart

THE CHART ON THE NEXT PAGE is adapted from a technique developed by Rensis Likert, director of the Institute for Social Research at the University of Michigan, to analyze management styles. Anyone — executive or employee — can use it to make his own diagnosis. Check the appropriate answers, using the guide marks to shade your emphasis. After the first question, for example, if your answer is "almost none," put the check in the first or second notch of the "none" box. Regard each answer as a sort of rating on a continuous scale from the left to the right of the chart. When you have answered each question, draw a line from the top to the bottom of the chart through the check marks. The result will be a profile of your management. To determine which way management style has been shifting, repeat the process for the situation as it was three, five, or ten years ago. Finally, sketch the profile you think would help improve performance. Likert has tried the chart on a number of business executives. Most of them rated their own companies about in the middle — embracing features of System 2 and 3. But nearly all of them also believe that companies do best when they have profiles well to the right of the chart, and worst with profiles well to the left.

	SYSTEM 1 Exploitive Authoritative	SYSTEM 2 Benevolent Authoritative	SYSTEM 3 Consultative	SYSTEM 4 Participative Group
LEADERSHIP How much confidence is shown in subordinates?	None	Condescending	Substantial	Complete
How free do they feel to talk to superiors about job?	Not at all	Not very	Rather free	Fully free
Are subordinates' ideas sought and used, if worthy?	Seldom	Sometimes	Usually	Always
MOTIVATION Is predominant use made of 1 fear, 2 threats, 3 punishment, 4 rewards, 5 involvement?	1, 2, 3 occasionally 4	4, some 3	4, some 3 and 5	5, 4, based on group set goals
Where is responsibility felt for achieving organization's goals?	Mostly at top	Top and middle	Fairly general	At all levels
COMMUNICATION How much communication is aimed at achieving organization's objectives?	Very little	Little	Quite a bit	A great deal
What is the direction of information flow?	Downward	Mostly downward	Down and up	Down, up and sideways
How is downward communication accepted?	With suspicion	Possibly with suspicion	With caution	With an open mind
How accurate is upward communication?	Often wrong	Censored for the boss	Limited accuracy	Accurate
How well do superiors know problems faced by subordinates?	Know little	Some knowledge	Quite well	Very well
DECISIONS At what level are decisions formally made?	Mostly at top	Policy at top, some delegation	Broad policy at top, more delegation	Throughout but well integrated
What is the origin of technical and professional knowledge used in decision making?	Top management	Upper and middle	To a certain extent, throughout	To a great extent, throughout
Are subordinates involved in decisions related to their work?	Not at all	Occasionally consulted	Generally consulted	Fully involved
What does decision-making contribute to motivation?	Nothing, often weakens it	Relatively little	Some contribution	Substantial contribution
GOALS How are organizational goals established?	Orders issued	Orders, some comments invited	After discussion, by orders	By group action (except in crisis)
How much covert resistance to goals is present?	Strong resistance	Moderate resistance	Some resistance at times	Little or none
CONTROL How concentrated are review and control functions?	Highly at top	Relatively highly at top	Moderate delegation to lower levels	Quite widely shared
Is there an informal organization resisting the formal one?	Yes	Usually	Sometimes	No—same goals as formal
What are cost, productivity, and other control data used for?	Policing punishment	Reward and punishment	Reward, some self-guidance	Self-guidance, problem solving

What Results Should You Expect?
A Users' Guide to MBO

Peter F. Drucker

MANAGEMENT BY OBJECTIVES (MBO) has a longer history in governmental institutions than most of its present-day practitioners realize. The basic concepts are strongly advocated by Luther Gulick and his associates in the mid and late '30s, in their studies of the organization and administration of the federal government. Yet, the concept of management by objectives and self-control originated with the private sector. It was first practiced by the DuPont Company after World War I. By the mid-'20s, Alfred P. Sloan, Jr., of General Motors used the term "Management by Objectives and Self-Control" systematically and with great conceptual clarity.

Yet today MBO seems to have become more popular in public service institutions than it is in the private sector; it is certainly more discussed as a tool of the public, especially the governmental administrator.

There is good reason for this popularity of MBO in the public sector. Public service institutions need it far more than any but the very biggest and most complex businesses. Public service institutions always have multiple objectives and often conflicting, if not incompatible objectives. While no institution, including business, has truly satisfactory measurements, the measurements generally available to government agencies and other public service institutions, especially in the budget area, rarely have anything to do with performance and goal attainment. Even a fairly small governmental agency, such as one of the smaller and less populous states or a medium-sized city, is a "conglomerate" of greater diversity and complexity than even ITT.

The resources of public service institutions are people, and the outputs are rarely "things." Therefore, direction toward meaningful results is not inherent in the work or in the process itself. Misdirection, whether by the individual employee or by the administrator, is at the same time both easy and hard to detect. Public service institutions are prone to the deadly disease of "bureaucracy"; that is towards mistaking rules, regulations, and the smooth functioning of the machinery for accomplishment, and the self-interest of the agency for public service.

Public service institutions, in other words, particularly need objectives and concentration of efforts on goals and results—that is management. These are, of course, precisely the needs management by objectives and self-control (MBO) promises to satisfy. But the same reasons which make MBO potentially so productive for the public service institution also make it only too easy for the institution to mistake MBO procedures for the substance of both management and objectives. Indeed, they may encourage the fatal error of misusing MBO as a substitute for thinking and decision making.

Therefore, the administrator in the public service institution needs a "users' guide." He needs to know whether he uses MBO correctly or whether he misuses it. He needs to know, above all, the results MBO yields if used properly. That, I am afraid, is what few of the texts and manuals spell out. Yet only when these results have been achieved has MBO really been applied.

MBO is both management by *objectives* and *management* by objectives. What is needed, therefore, are two sets of specifications—one spelling out the results in terms of objectives and one spelling out the results in terms of management.

What Are Our Objectives? What Should They Be?

The first result, and perhaps the most important one which the administrator needs to aim at in applying MBO, is the *clear realization that his agency actually has no objectives*. What passes for objectives are, as a rule, only good intentions.

The purpose of an objective is to make possible the organization of work for its attainment. This means that objectives must be operational: capable of being converted into specific performance, into work, and into work assignments. However, almost no public service agency has operational objectives. To say our objective is "the maintenance of law and order" or "health care" is operationally a meaningless statement. Nothing can be deduced from these statements with respect to the goals and the work needed. Yet these statements are already a good deal more operational, more nearly true objectives, than is commonly found in the objectives statements of public service agencies.

The first result to be expected from management by *objectives* is the realization that the traditional statement of objectives is inadequate, is indeed in most cases totally inappropriate. The first work to be done is to identify what the objectives should or could be.

The moment this question is raised however, it will also be realized—and this is the second result to be obtained—that *objectives* in public service agencies are ambiguous, ambivalent, and multiple. This holds true in private business as well.

The hospital, while complex, is still a very small institution compared to most governmental agencies. Yet its objectives are by no means clear. "Health Care" sounds plausible, most hospitals have nothing to do with health care. They are concerned with the treatment and care of the sick. Clearly, the most intelligent and most effective way to produce health care is the prevention of sickness, rather than its treatment and cure. To the extent that we know how to provide health care it is not, bluntly, the task of the hospital at all. It is done by public health measures such as vaccination, providing pure drinking water, and adequate treatment of sewage. Hospitals, in effect, are the result of the failure of health care, rather than agencies to provide it.

Yet even if the hospital defines its objectives very narrowly, as do the hospitals in the British Health Service, as the "treatment of the sick" (repair of damage already done), the objectives are still cloudy. Is the hospital, as in the traditional concept of the American community hospital, the private physician's plant facility and an extension of his office? Is it, in other words, the place where the physician takes care of those patients whom he cannot take care of in his own office or in his own private practice? Or should the hospital as so many American hospitals have attempted, be the "health care center" for the community, through such activities as the well-baby clinic, counselling service for the emotionally disturbed and so on? Should the hospital also become the substitute for the private physician and provide the physician's services to the poor—the objectives of the out-patient department in the American big city hospital today? If the hospital defines its function as care of the sick, what then is the role and function of the maternity service? Giving birth to a baby is, after all, no sickness, but a perfectly normal and indeed perfectly healthy occurrence.

Similarly, when the police department tries to make operational the vague term "maintenance of law and order" it will find immediately that there is a multiplicity of possible objectives—each of them, ambiguous. "Prevention of crime" sounds very specific. But what does it really mean, assuming that anyone knows how to do it? Is it, as many police departments have traditionally asserted, the enforcement of all the laws on the statute book? Or is it the protection of the innocent lawabiding citizen, with respect both to his person and to his property? Is it safety on the streets or safety in the home, or is it both? Is the primary task the eradication and prevention of corruption within the police force itself? The latter may sound quite peripheral, if not trivial. Yet, in a recent major study of the job of chief of police, sponsored by one of the agencies of the federal government, the experienced police chiefs guiding the study maintained that to rid police forces of corruption was the first, and most important, objective in maintaining law and order.

In attempting to reduce pious intentions to genuine objectives, the administrator will invariably find that equally valid objectives are mutually incompatible or at least, quite inconsistent.

The classical example is the American farm policy of the last 40 years. Strengthening the American farmer was the stated objective from the beginning, before New Deal days. Does this mean protecting the family farmer? Or does it mean making the American farmer efficient, productive, and capable of world market competition? Congress, in writing farm legislation, has always used rhetoric indicating that the purpose of farm policy is to protect and preserve the small family farmer. However, the actual measures then enacted to achieve this purpose have primarily been aimed at making farming a more efficient, more productive, and more competitive industry, in which the small family farmer has practically no place and may indeed be an impediment to the attainment of the goal.

Thus the most important result of management by *objectives* is that it forces the administrator into the realization that there cannot be one single objective, notwithstanding the language of policy statements, whether acts of Congress or administrative declarations. To call realization of this fundamental problem a result of management by *objectives* may seem paradoxical. Yet it may be the most important result, precisely because it forces the administrator and his agency to a realization of the need to think and of the need to make highly risky balancing and trade-off decisions. This should be one of the results management by *objectives* strives for, which have to be attained if MBO is to be an effective tool which strengthens the performance of the institution.

The next area in which management by *objectives* has to attain results is that of *priorities* and *posteriorities*.

Public service institutions, almost without exception, have to strive to attain multiple objectives. At the same time each area of objectives will require a number of separate goals. Yet no institution, least of all a large one, is capable of doing many things, let alone of doing many things well. Institutions must concentrate and set priorities. By the same token, they must make risky decisions about what to postpone and what to abandon — to think through posteriorities.

One basic reason for this need to concentrate is the communications problem, both within the institution and among the various external publics. Institutions which try to attain simultaneously a great many different goals end up confusing their own members. The confusion is extended twofold to the outside public on whose support they depend.

Another cogent reason for concentration of goals is that no institution has an abundance of truly effective resources. We have all learned that money alone does not produce results. Results require the hard work and efforts of dedicated people; such people are always in short supply. Yet nothing destroys the effectiveness of competent individuals more than having their efforts splintered over a number of divergent concerns—a function of the frustration that results from giving part-time attention to a major task. To achieve results always requires thorough and consistent attention to the problem by at least one effective man or woman.

Finally, and this may be the most important factor, even a unitary, or a simple goal often requires a choice between very different strategies which cannot be pursued at the same time; one of them has to be given priority, which means that the other one assumes secondary status or is abandoned for an unspecified time.

One example of this dilemma, which is familiar to every experienced administrator, is the educational policy in developing countries. That a trained and schooled population is desirable, and is indeed a prerequisite for social and economic development, would be accepted by practically all students of development. However, should primary emphasis be given to the education of a small, but exceedingly capable, elite? Or should the main drive be on "mass literacy"? Few countries can pursue both goals simultaneously—they must make a choice. If the first course is followed there is the risk of educating people to be highly skilled and at great expense to the country. The consequences are that the society cannot utilize the expertise it has paid for and cannot provide meaningful jobs for those individuals. The result is then a "brain drain" in which the potentially most productive, most expensive resources of a poor country leave to find opportunities elsewhere for the application of their knowledge.

If the second alternative is being followed, there is the risk of educating large masses of people who are no longer satisfied with traditional employment and/or traditional subsistence standards of living. These people cannot find the jobs they have been trained for and have been led to expect, simply because institutions capable of employing them do not emerge, and the leadership is missing.

To set priorities is usually fairly simple, or at least seems politically fairly simple. What is difficult and yet absolutely essential, is the risk-taking and politically dangerous decision as to what the posteriorities should be. Every experienced administrator knows that what one postpones, one really abandons. In fact, it is a sound rule not to postpone but to make the decision not to do something altogether or to give up doing something. For in strategy, timing is of the essence. Nothing is usually less productive than to do ten years later what would have been an excellent and worthwhile program ten years earlier.

If an illustration is needed, the fate of so many of President Johnson's programs would supply it. What made so many of these programs fail is not that they were the wrong programs, or even that they were inadequately supported. They were, in large measure, five or ten years too late. These programs had been postponed, and when the time came to do them, that is when Congress was willing to consider them after long years of resistance, they were no longer the "right" programs.

In addition, public service institutions find "abandonment of yesterday" even more difficult than businesses. Business, of course, does not like to abandon. The product or service that no longer serves a purpose, no longer produces results, no longer fulfills a major need, is usually also the product or service which the people now at the top have spent the best part of their working lives to create and to make succeed. However, in business enterprise, the market eventually forces management to face up to reality and to abandon yesterday.

The Ford Motor Company held onto the Edsel as long as it could — far longer than economic reality justified. The American public had abandoned the Edsel long before Ford management was willing to accept the verdict. Eventually, however, even a very large, strong, and stubborn company had to accept reality.

No such pressure exists as a rule in the public service institution. Indeed, if we had had ministries of transportation around in 1850 or 1900 we might now have in every country major research projects, funded with billions of dollars, to reeducate the horse. In any public service institution, whether government agency, hospital, school, or university, any activity and any service almost immediately creates its own constituency: in the legislature, the press, or the public. Yet nothing is quite as difficult to do as to maintain the moribund. It requires greater energies, greater effort, and greater abilities to sustain an obsolete program than to make effective the responsive and productive program.

Thus, the public service agency is always in danger of frittering away its best people as well as a great deal of money on activities which no longer produce, no longer contribute, have proven to be incapable of producing, or are simply inappropriate.

Therefore, essential to management by *objectives* in the public service agency is the establishment of priorities, decisions concerning areas for concentration.

Equally essential is the systematic appraisal of all services and activities in order to find the *candidates for abandonment.* Indeed it is wisdom in a public service agency to put each service and activity on trial for its life every three or four years and to ask: if we had known what we now know at the time we established this service, would we have gotten into it? If the answer is no, one does not say, what do we have to do to make it viable again? One does not even say, should we consider getting out of it? One says, how fast can we get out?

Goals of abandonment and schedules to attain these goals are an essential part of management by *objectives*, however unpopular, disagreeable, or difficult to attain they might be. The great danger in large institutions, especially in public service institutions, is to confuse fat with muscle and motion with performance. The only way to prevent this degenerative disease is a systematic procedure for abandoning yesterday, setting specific and courageous goals for abandonment.

In this respect, the Budget Reform Act of 1974 may represent the biggest step forward in public administration in many decades, though it still remains to be seen, of course, whether the act will produce the desired results. This Act entrusted the General Accounting Office with the duty of appraising existing programs and projects in the federal service based on their suitability, stated objectives, and appropriateness.

But will the Congress that wrote the Act be willing to face up to its abandonment implications?

The next results are *specific goals,* with specific *targets,* specific *timetables* and specific *strategies.* Implicit in this is the *clear definition of the resources* needed to attain these goals, the efforts needed, and primarily the *allocation* of available resources—especially of available manpower. A "plan" is not a plan unless the resources of competent, performing people needed for its attainment have been specifically allocated. Until then, the plan is only a good intention; in reality not even that.

Finally, management by *objectives* needs to bring out as a clear result of the thinking and analysis process, how performance can be *measured* or at least *judged.*

It is commonly argued that public service institutions aim at intangible results, which defy measurement. This would simply mean that public service institutions are incapable of producing results. Unless results can be appraised objectively, there will be no results. There will only be activity, that is costs. To produce results it is necessary to know what results are desirable and be able to determine whether the desired results are actually being achieved.

It is also not true that the activities of public service institutions cannot be measured. "Missions" are always intangible, whether of business enterprise or of social service institutions.

Sears Roebuck and Company defined its mission in the '20s as being the "buyer for the American Family." This is totally intangible. But the objectives which Sears then set to accomplish this mission (e.g., to develop a range of appliances that most nearly satisfy the largest number of homeowners at the most economical price) was an operational objective from which clear and measurable goals with respect to product line, service, assortment, price, and market penetration, could be derived. This in turn made possible both the allocation of efforts and the measurement of performance.

"Saving Souls" as the mission of a church is totally intangible. At least, the bookkeeping is not of this world. However, the goal of bringing at least two-thirds of the young people of the congregation into the church and its activities is easily measured.

Similarly, "health care" is intangible. But the goals for a maternity ward which state that the number of "surprises" in delivery must not be more than two or three out of every hundred deliveries; the number of post-partum infections of mothers must not exceed one-half of one per cent of all deliveries; eight out of ten of all premature babies born live after the seventh month of conception must survive in good health are not intangible, but fairly easy to measure.

To think through the appropriate measurement is in itself a policy decision and therefore highly risky. Measurements, or at least criteria for judgment and appraisal, define what we mean by performance. They largely dictate where the efforts should be spent. They determine whether policy priorities are serious or are merely administrative doubletalk. For this reason it needs to be emphasized that measurements need to be measurements of performance rather than of efforts. It is not adequate, indeed it is misleading, to use measurements that focus on efficiency of operation, rather than on the services the agency delivers to somebody outside, whether another public service agency or the public. Measurement directs effort and vision. One of the central problems of public service agencies, indeed of all organizations, is the tendency to direct efforts and vision towards the inside, that is towards efficiencies, rather than towards the purposes on the outside for which every public service institution exists.

With measurements defined, it then becomes possible to organize the *feedback* from results to activities. What results should be expected by what time? In effect, measurements decide what phenomena are results. Identifying the appropriate measurements enables the administrator to move from diagnosis to prognosis. He can now lay down what he expects will happen and take proper action to see whether it actually does happen.

The actual results of action are not predictable. Indeed, if there is one rule for action, and especially for institutional action, it is that the expected results will not be attained. The unexpected is practically certain. But are the unexpected results deleterious? Are they actually more desirable than the results that were expected and planned? Do the deviations from the planned course of events demand a change in strategies, or perhaps a change in goals or priorities? Or are they such that they indicate opportunities that were not seen originally, opportunities that indicate the need to increase efforts and to run with success? These are questions the administrator in the public service agency rarely asks. Unless he builds into the structure of objectives and strategies the organized feedback that will force these questions to his attention, he is likely to disregard the unexpected and to persist in the wrong course of action or to miss major opportunities.

Organized feedback leading to systematic review and continuous revision of objectives, roles, priorities, and allocation of resources must therefore be built into the administrative process. To enable the administrator to do so is a result and an important result, of management by *objectives*. If it is not obtained, management by *objectives* has not been properly applied.

What Is Management? What Should It Be?

Management by objectives, similarly, has to attain a number of results to be properly applied.

The first result is *understanding*. *Management* by objectives is often described as a way to obtain agreement. But this is gross oversimplification. The decision which MBO identifies and brings into focus: the decisions on objectives and their balance; on goals and strategies; on priorities and abandonment; on efforts and resource allocation; on the appropriate measurements, are far too complex, risky, and uncertain to be made by acclamation. To make them intelligently requires *informed dissent*.

What MBO has to produce as the first *management* result is understanding of the difficulty, complexity, and risk of these decisions. It is understanding that different people, all employed in a common task and familiar with it, define objectives and goals differently, see different priorities, and would prefer very different and incompatible strategies. Only then can the decision be made effectively.

The decisions to be made are also of such complexity and of such importance that the responsible administrator would not want to make them without understanding them. The full complexity of any issue can only be understood on the basis of informed dissent. "Adversary proceedings" are not the best way, as a rule, to make these decisions. Informed dissent is essential where people of good will and substantial knowledge find out how differently they view the same problem, the same mission, the same task, and the same reality. Otherwise, symptoms rather than the underlying problem will be attacked; trivia rather than results will be pursued.

It is almost 50 years since Mary Parker Follett applied the early insights of perception psychology to point out that people in an organization who seem to differ on the answers usually differ on what the right question is. The issues, with which the administrator in the public service institution deals, are of such complexity and have so many dimensions that any one person can be expected to see only one aspect and only one dimension rather than the total concept.

However, effective action requires an understanding of complexity. It requires an ability to see a problem in all its major dimensions. Otherwise, a maximum of effort will produce no results, but more commonly wrong and undesired results.

Management by *objectives* is an administrative process rather than a political process. This makes it all the more important to focus on understanding as the first management result — bringing out the basic views, the basic dissents, the different approaches to the same task and the same problem within the organization.

The major departments of the federal government that have been created in the last 20 years: the Department of Defense, the Department of Health, Education, and Welfare, (HEW), the Department of Transportation, and the Department of Housing and Urban Development (HUD) are commonly criticized for being ineffectual as well as administrative labyrinths. They are often contrasted, to their detriment, with older agencies such as the Department of the Interior or the Department of Agriculture, which, it is alleged, are so much more effective. The reason usually given for the lack of effectiveness of these newer agencies is "lack of direction" or "internal division." What made these older agencies effective, especially in the New Deal days when they reached a peak of effectiveness, was however, the intelligent use of informed dissent on the part of the men who led them. Harold Ickes in Interior or Henry Wallace in Agriculture took infinite care to produce informed dissent within the organization and thus to obtain understanding for themselves and to create understanding for their associates. Thus, when decisions on goals and priorities were made unilaterally by the top man himself, and by no means democratically, they were understood throughout the organization; the top man himself understood what alternatives were available as well as the position of his people on them.

Similarly, the Japanese system of "decision by consensus" is often cited these days as an example for the American decision maker. However, the Japanese do not make decisions by consensus, rather they deliberate by consensus. The seemingly long gestation period of a decision in Japanese organizations is devoted to bringing out the maximum understanding within the organization and to enabling those who are going to have to participate in the subsequent action to express their own views of the issue and their own definitions of the question. Consequently, they find out where their colleagues and associates stand, what they feel, and how they feel. Then a decision can be reached which the organization understands, even though large groups within it do not necessarily agree or would have preferred a different decision. Perhaps the greatest strength of the Japanese process is that priorities can actually be set and be made effective.

The second management result of management by objectives is to produce *responsibility* and *commitment* within the organization; to make possible *self-control* on the part of the managerial and professional people.

The advocate of MBO likes to talk about participation. This is a misleading term, or at least an inadequate term. The desired result is willingness of the individual within the organization to focus his or her own vision and efforts towards the attainment of the organization's goals. It is ability to have self-control; to know that the individual makes the right contribution and is able to appraise himself or herself rather than be appraised and controlled from the outside. The desired result is commitment, rather than participation.

For this reason the usual approach of MBO towards goal-setting for the individual or for the managerial component is inadequate and may even do damage. Usually MBO says to the individual manager, here are the goals of this institution. What efforts do you have to make to further them? The right question is, what do you, given our mission, think the goals should be, the priorities should be, the strategies should be? What, by way of contribution to these goals, priorities, and strategies, should this institution hold you and your department accountable for over the next year or two? What goals, priorities, and strategies do you and your department aim for, separate and distinct from those of the institution? What will you have to contribute and what results will you have to produce to attain these goals? Where do you see major opportunities of contribution and performance for this institution and for your component? Where do you see major problems?

Needless to say, it is then the task of the responsible administrator to decide. It is not necessarily true, as so many romantics in management seem to believe, that the subordinate always knows better. However, it is also not necessarily true that the boss always knows better. What is true is that the two, subordinate and boss, cannot communicate unless they realize that they differ in their views of what is to be done and what could be done. It is also true that there is no *management* by objectives unless the subordinate takes responsibility for performance, results, and, in the last analysis, for the organization itself.

The next results are *personnel decisions.* As stated earlier, MBO requires allocation of resources and concentration of effort. *Management* by objectives should always result in changing the allocation of effort, the assignment of people and the jobs they are doing. It should always lead to a restructuring of the human resources towards the attainment of objectives. It is not true, though administrative routine believes it, if only subconsciously, that every existing job is the right job and has something to contribute. On the contrary, the ruling postulate should be: every existing job is likely to be the wrong job and needs to be restructured, or at least redirected. Job titles may be sacred and in every large organization there is an unspoken, but fervent belief that the Good Lord created section chiefs. In reality, job substance changes with the needs of the organization, and assignments, that is the specific commitment to results, change even more frequently.

Job descriptions may be semi-permanent. However, assignments should always be considered as short-lived. It is one of the basic purposes of managerial objectives to force the question, what are the specific assignments in this position which, given our goals, priorities, and strategies at this time, make the greatest contribution?

Unless this question is being brought to the surface, MBO has not been properly applied. It must be determined what the right concentration of effort is and what the manpower priorities are, and convert the answer into personnel action. Unless this is done there may be objectives but there is no management.

Similarly important and closely related are results in terms of *organization structure*. If the work in organizations over the last 40 years has taught us anything, it is that structure follows strategy. There are only a small number of organization designs available to the administrator.[1] How this limited number of organization designs is put together is largely determined by the strategies that an organization adopts, which in turn is determined by its goals. *Management* by objectives should enable the administrator to think through organization structure. Organization structure while not in itself policy, is a tool of policy. Any decision on policy, that is any decision on objectives, priorities, and strategies, has consequences for organization structure.

The ultimate result of *management* by objectives is *decision*, both with respect to the goals and performance standards of the organization and to the structure and behavior of the organization. Unless MBO leads to decision, it has no results at all; it has been a waste of time and effort. The test of MBO is not knowledge, but effective action. This means, above all, risk-taking decisions.

The literature talks about MBO often as a "tool for problem solving." However, its proper application is as a means of problem definition and problem recognition. Perhaps even more important, it is a means of problem prevention.

Thus, MBO is not a procedure to implement decisions, a systematic attempt to define, to think through, and to decide. Filling out forms, no matter how well designed, is not management by objectives and self-control. The results are!

MBO is often called a tool of planning. It is not the same thing as planning, but it is the core of planning. MBO is usually called a management tool. Again, it is not all of management, but it is the core of management. It is not the way to *implement* decisions on policy, on goals, on strategies, on organization structure, or on staffing. It is the *process* in which decisions are made, goals are identified, priorities and posteriorities are set, and organization structure designed for the specific purposes of the institution.

It is also the process of people integrating themselves into the organization and directing themselves towards the organization's goals and purposes. The introduction of MBO into public service institutions, especially into governmental agencies during the last few years, may thus be the first step towards making public service institutions effective. So far it is only a first step. What has been introduced so far, by and large, is the procedure, and there is danger in procedure being mistaken for substance. Yet the great need of the public institution is not procedure. Most of them have all the procedures they need—the great need is performance. Indeed, performance of the public service institution may be the fundamental, the central, need of modern society. Management by objectives and self-control should help fill a good part of this need. However, its success depends upon the administrator: in applying MBO he or she must obtain the right results, both with respect to *objectives* and to *management*.

NOTE

1. Peter F. Drucker, *Management: Tasks; Responsibilities; Practices* (New York: Harper & Row), 1974), chapters 41-48.

The Use of "Staff Papers" in Public Management

Many public agencies have a standard format for briefing other managers, often top executives, about pending problems or decisions. This is referred to here as a "Staff Paper," although the name varies from agency to agency.

The format for staff papers is not universally applicable to all problems, but most issues do fit into this framework. This could range from sophisticated, quantitative program analysis to simply describing, say, a problem in coordinating two different bureaus in a given agency. This problem solving approach is also useful in analyzing the public management cases contained in this book.

Suggested Content of a Staff Paper

1. *What is the Problem?*
   a. What seems to be the real problem? Relate this to program or agency goals.
   b. What appear to be the causes of the problem? To what extent are they currently known?
   c. What is the specific population (e.g., clientele groups, etc.) affected? If other than the general public, identify their special characteristics such as age group, race, income class, special needs, geographical location, etc. Some quantification should be attempted.
   d. What is the magnitude of the problem? How widespread is it now? How large is it likely to be in future years? Some quantification is desirable here as well.

2. *Objectives and Evaluation Criteria*
   a. Toward what public objectives should programs for meeting the problem be directed? Sought here are the *fundamental* purposes, not the immediate (physical) outputs.
   b. How can estimates of progress against these objectives be made? Identify the appropriate evaluation criteria (i.e., measures of effectiveness). If these do not seem directly measurable, indicate the "proxies" that might be used.

3. *Current Activities and Who's Involved*
   a. What specific activities (outputs) are currently being undertaken by this agency or jurisdiction that are relevant to the problem? Identify each such current program and, to the extent possible, provide current costs and their current estimated impact relative to the criteria in 2(b). Indicate the number in each beneficiary group identified in 1(c) that is currently being served. If possible, project these into the future. Again, some quantification should be included here.
   b. What other agencies of the government, what other sectors of the community, or other levels of government, in addition to this agency or jurisdiction, are involved in attempting to meet the problem?
   c. Include any other facts relating to the problem or its solution.

4. *Political and Other Significant Factors*
   a. Are there major political factors that seem to affect the problem?

b. Are there any unusual resource or timing limitation problems of special significance.

5. *Alternatives*

What alternative programs, activities, or strategies should be considered for solving the problem? Analyze the nature, characteristics, advantages, and disadvantages of each in depth.

6. *Conclusions*

State your conclusions based on foregoing analysis of the problem, factors relating to the problem, and alternatives to meet the problem.

7. *Recommendations for Action*

a. Present recommendations for administrative action. These must be in consonance with the conclusion(s).

b. Sometimes the next recommended step is for additional study. The principal purpose of the paper here is largely to raise a particular problem as an issue of importance. In these cases, recommendations as to the timing and scope of the follow-up analysis should be made, whether this will be a "quick response" or "in-depth" study, and whether there are any major data problems associated with such a study.

c. Sometimes a Staff Paper will recommend a new agency directive or written policy. In these cases, a draft of such a policy is frequently attached.

Attachments (if any)

a. Appendices may be attached which furnish supporting analysis, illustrations, raw data, etc.

b. It is often necessary to coordinate such work with other individuals or offices, and sometimes this should be in writing. Concurrences or nonconcurrences by other individuals or organizations in a particular agency or jurisdiction may also be included here. If someone else doesn't concur in your analysis and/or your action recommendations, you may want to respond to those comments here as well.

'Who Authorized This Trip?'

Robert Lasson and David Eynon

Paul Revere didn't work for nothing. . . . Official records in the archives of the Massachusetts State House show Revere submitted an expense account for 10 pounds 4 shillings for services performed as a messenger during the first two weeks of the American Revolution. He was paid by the Massachusetts House of Representatives.

— THE BOSTON GLOBE

Scene: Colony Counting House

CLERK: *(Looking up from sheet of foolscap)* A marvelous ride, Mr. Revere! Might I have your autograph for my lad? He's ——

REVERE: Of course. *(Scribbles with clerk's quill)* Will it take long to process my expense account?

CLERK: Not at all, sir. A question or two and . . . *(Scans the sheet of foolscap, raises eyebrows at bottom line)* Who authorized this trip, incidentally?

REVERE: The Sons of Liberty. Sam Adams. John Hancock.

CLERK: A copy of your travel orders should be attached, Mr. Revere, but we'll waive that. Was public transportation available?

REVERE: At that hour? I was lucky I had my own horse.

CLERK: You didn't avail yourself of one of the official Post horses at the Green Dragon Tavern?

REVERE: The Postmaster was a Tory. His suspicions ——

CLERK: Use of a privately owned horse requires supervisory authorization, Mr. Revere. If John Hancock will sign your ——

REVERE: John Hancock will sign anything.

CLERK: And this trip destination, "Every Middlesex village and farm." Couldn't you be more specific?

REVERE: How about "Lexington-Concord and return"?

CLERK: Much better. Now, under "Time," this "hour of darkness and peril and need" sounds . . . well, inexact.

REVERE: Late P.M. to early A.M.?

CLERK: That's the ticket! Oh, and for "Purpose of Trip," might we say something less . . . literary than "the fate of a nation"?

REVERE: Dissemination of mobilization instructions?

CLERK: Excellent. By the way, was any personal business conducted en route?

REVERE: We took a 10-minute break—but we're only asking straight time for the whole tour, even though it was after hours.

CLERK: Admirable. Now these "expenses for horse" break down to two shillings per day. Were you figuring the horse by the mile—or per diem?

REVERE: He eats either way. Two shillings daily.

CLERK: I take it, then, you didn't employ a livery stable that offers government rates? And you didn't get three bids to —— *(Brushes aside question)* Pshaw! Enough of these petty technicalities, Mr. Revere. You made a gallant ride, and you deserve your expenses, which come to . . . *(Runs quill deftly through several items and corrects bottom line figure)* 13 shillings and sixpence in Continental currency—or one Spanish milled dollar.

REVERE: *(Clutching chit offered by clerk and staring in disbelief)* Thirteen and six! That won't even cover what the ride did to my suit! What are all these deductions?

CLERK: *(Using feather end of quill to tick off items)* There's your withholding, of course. City wage tax. The horse's pension. Wear and tear on the highway.

REVERE: Thirteen and six! I could have stayed home and made teapots for thirteen and six!

CLERK: Well, Mr. Revere. For an unauthorized trip outside business hours on privately owned transportation, you're doing pretty good.

REVERE: Thirteen and six! I could have been soldering tankards at five times that rate!

CLERK: Yes. On your way home, could you drop this off with the sexton at the Old North Church? It's a summons for a fire code violation. Someone's reported two lanterns in the belfry.

The Chief
George Eddy and Jerry Saegert

"I NEVER THOUGHT that b—— would try a stunt like that!" angrily exclaimed Alex Brown striking his desk with a clenched fist so hard that he winced momentarily. Startled by the outburst, Anne Stevens looked up from her desk nearby where she had been trying to type the minutes of the last Safety Council meeting. Astonished and concerned by this unexpected action from her boss, Mr. Brown, Anne realized that something quite serious must have occurred in the Plant Manager's office after Mr. Brown had rushed there when Mr. Arrowsmith called over the office intercom. She had always regarded Mr. Brown as a quiet and fairly restrained type of person who never "blew his top." She believed most people would agree with her view of Mr. Brown as a competent and highly motivated individual whose considerable energies were devoted to developing ways to increase the efficiency of the office of Plant Safety Officer at Southwestern Arsenal.

As his secretary, Anne knew Mr. Brown was experimenting with some new approaches that he was confident would resolve a number of problems created by the newly organized firefighter-guard force at Southwestern. For the past several weeks, Mr. Brown had been trying to define responsibilities and authorities of several new supervisory positions in this force, which was an amalgamation of two formerly separate organizations — a security force and a firefighting force — that had existed for several years. Selected to head this new combination was William Sprague, who had been the Chief of the Fire Department at Southwestern almost since the inception of that organization at the commencement of World War II. An aggressive, outspoken person, Sprague's substantial physique seemed particularly consonant with a brusk, authoritarian manner.

Constructed in the early 1940s, Southwestern Arsenal was typical of scores of industrial plants the federal government built to produce explosives of all sorts and to load, assemble and pack (lap) a great variety of small arms, artillery shells, and bombs. Encompassing some 15,000 acres of relatively flat and treeless terrain, this installation was divided into two principal areas; one devoted to administrative purposes and the other designed to provide the extensive areas needed for working with explosives. Each area was separately fenced with entrance and egress controlled by guards of the internal plant security force. Activities in the explosive operational areas were closely supervised and performed in accordance with detailed, written procedures commonly referred to as Standard Operating Procedures (SOPs).

Because of the potential catastrophic results which might ensue from a fire involving explosives, the plant firefighting personnel required special knowledge of the important characteristics of explosives and principal chemical reactions to high temperatures associated with conflagrations. Training and drills for such personnel received continuous emphasis, and frequently the Plant Manager, Henry Arrowsmith, either participated himself or observed in the company of the Safety Officer. Supplementing these drills, detailed critiques were held with the objective of improving subsequent performance. During World War II, all firefighting was the responsibility solely of the Fire Department, while the separate Guard Force concerned itself with the aspects of physical security of the administrative and operational areas of Southwestern. Not considered qualified to fight fires involving explosives, the guards did get some training in the subject of explosives characteristics and were expected to assist the Fire Department during emergencies.

After the war, Southwestern continued in production — the majority of such government facilities were closed and most were sold — under the same general management, although the scope of its activities were substantially reduced and there was considerable turnover of personnel. Included in the numerous organizational realignments necessitated by the significantly lessened need for the plant's products, was the decision to merge the Guard Force with the Fire Department. Shortly after the Plant Manager, Mr. Henry Arrowsmith, chose Mr. William Sprague to become the chief of this new organization of some 50 men, Mr. Alex Brown joined the staff as the Plant Safety Officer. After reviewing the organization chart as shown in Figure 2-1, Mr. Brown realized his arrival was coincidental with probably the maximum degree of turbulence engendered by the considerable shifting and reassignment of both former guards and firemen.

Following his initial meeting with Chief Sprague, a tour of the fire-fighter-guard facilities and an opportunity to talk with most of the supervisors and men on duty, Mr. Brown began to assess what he had observed. When he first visited the central station, located about the middle of the Restricted Area, Mr. Brown noticed that Mr. Arrowsmith was in the kitchen pouring himself a cup of coffee. Each station had sleeping quarters, a small kitchen and eating area, an office, supply and armory facilities, general equipment area, washing and toilet facilities, and an area that could be used for a variety of purposes, such as for conferences or meetings, a classroom, and the like. Operated on a 24-hour basis, there always was a coffee pot brewing.

"Hello, Alex," greeted Mr. Arrowsmith, "I see you are making the rounds. What do you think of our setup?"

"I think I've seen just about everything that's under the Chief's control, Hank. Of course, I'm still trying to sort things out, but it shouldn't take long. Already, I can appreciate this reorganization of security and firefighting elements requires a 'new look' in a lot of aspects," replied Mr. Brown, as he concluded with a comment that he thought that the realignments would place a premium on flexibility in attitudes.

"Well, okay, Alex," Mr. Arrowsmith noted as he got up to leave, "I've got to get back to the office. It sure makes a nice break to get out in the area and stop off here and shoot the bull with the Chief. It'll soon be hunting season again, so I'll be out here a lot."

As the chief walked out to the car with Mr. Arrowsmith, Mr. Brown noted that the conversation seemed quite informal and jovial. He wondered how often the Plant Manager visited the station and

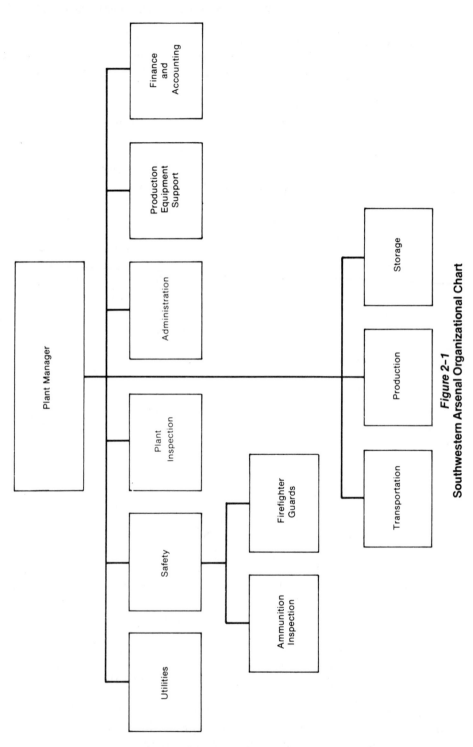

Figure 2-1
Southwestern Arsenal Organizational Chart

what sort of relationship existed between them. Recalling that each time the Chief had come to visit him in the Administrative Area, some six miles distant, the Chief had yet to come on his own initiative. Further, that he either stopped by Hank's office before coming to see him or went there right after Mr. Brown had concluded their discussion about some matter on firefighting or security.

Soon after Mr. Brown had proposed a major change in the training schedule to the Chief, the subject was mentioned by Mr. Arrowsmith. Surprised at first by the extent of Hank's knowledge of some of the details which he had not discussed with the Plant Manager, Mr. Brown quickly learned that the Chief had spoken to Hank about it, voicing various apprehensions of certain provisions. Mr. Arrowsmith told Mr. Brown that he had agreed with several of the Chief's concerns. Due to the manner in which Mr. Arrowsmith related his conversation with the Chief, Mr. Brown was convinced that the Plant Manager did not know these were matters that originated with the Safety Officer, not the Chief. "Yeah, Alex, I told him the idea to increase the amount of time spent on security training by 40 percent was screwy," remarked Mr. Arrowsmith offhandedly. "Afer a bit, the Chief said he had to agree with me."

It was about this time that Mr. Brown recognized with growing irritation that the Chief seemed to be getting more disputatious on changes or innovations that Mr. Brown proposed. As he reflected on the past three sessions with the Chief, Mr. Brown had to note that the Chief disagreed with every new idea the Safety Officer suggested was worth trying out. He gathered that while the Chief did not say so directly, he managed to convey the impression he felt these recommendations were absurd. The Chief began to emphasize that since his long tenure as the Fire Chief had run smoothly, there was no need to get tangled up in schemes of questionable merit. Clearly, the Chief was nettled by what he believed was meddling in his affairs by a newcomer who had not been at Southwestern when "things were really tough" and who furthermore had probably never even held a fire hose in his hands.

Even Hank suggested that perhaps he was pushing the Chief too hard, and that Mr. Brown should give him a little more time to adjust to the requirements of the new firefighter-guard organization. The hunting season had commenced, and Mr. Brown learned that the Plant Manager spent several hours every day "out in the area". While some of these hours occurred right after daybreak, and thus were before the normal working day started, it seemed apparent that Mr. Arrowsmith stopped at the firefighter-guard station at least once every day for coffee and conversation. Mr. Brown was convinced the Chief always managed to be present when the Plant Manager appeared. Not a hunter himself, Mr. Brown never went out with Mr. Arrowsmith, who did not lack for company. Usually he took the mayor of Midvale, a small town nearby, as his guest.

"That must be quite a chore, Hank, to clean all those birds you seem to shoot so expertly," Mr. Brown remarked at the height of the season.

"Oh, hell, Alex, I don't do that!" exclaimed Mr. Arrowsmith, "the Chief always takes care of it for me."

Some four months after he assumed the duties of the Safety Officer, Mr. Brown was dismayed to recognize that whatever changes he had succeeded in getting implemented in the firefighter-guard organization had been "by direction". It no longer seemed possible to discuss matters of importance with the Chief, who never failed to find something wrong with anything new or different—Mr. Brown concluded—and who had become so intractable that Mr. Brown was weary in his repeated attempts to get the Chief to focus on central issues instead of personalities. Even the relatively simple matter of determining the vacation schedule for supervisory personnel had become a contentious matter. The schedule the Chief had presented bothered Mr. Brown as he believed it unduly "favored" the supervisors with the longest tenure, giving them a disappropriate share of the most desirable vacation periods and simultaneously leaving the force largely under the newest and least experienced hands. After a heated discussion, the Chief reluctantly agreed to modify the schedule, but remained vague concerning his own plans.

Pointing to the wall calendar, Mr. Brown remarked that there were several periods available to the Chief. "Just let me know when you want to take off, Chief," Mr. Brown declared as the Chief got up to leave. "Yeah," replied the Chief and departed.

Mr. Brown picked up the latest training schedule and tried to concentrate on those portions that pertained to leadership and the general aspects of how to improve supervision. Based on his observations of the firefighter-guard organization Mr. Brown was convinced the supervisory personnel, both relative newcomers as well as most of the "old-timers," were significantly deficient in performance in that capacity. Technically, they seemed to be reasonably proficient, and the continuing program to upgrade the force in this respect had progressed without major difficulty. He had spoken at length on leadership matters with the Chief, but since the latter had not shared his concern about such an emphasis, Mr. Brown went ahead and prepared a detailed and comprehensive program. At the time of the session on the vacation schedule, Mr. Brown had just concluded the last details, including lesson plans and the preparation of reference material he proposed to hand out for further study by the firefighter-guard supervisory personnel. Scheduling himself as the instructor for the majority of the lessons, Mr. Brown believed he had developed something significant that was long overdue.

Still smarting over his last discussion with Hank Arrowsmith about the Chief who had complained again directly to the Plant Manager over a matter that Hank seemed disposed to regard as minor but was considered by Mr. Brown as most important, Alex was astounded by this contention:

"The Chief says you are trying to get him, Alex," Hank began, "He claims you've never stopped attacking him since the day you first arrived. He does not understand why this is happening as he has done his job for years without prior criticism. Then you appear and nothing is right? Why? Suddenly he figures it out. You are trying to act like your father!"

"What?"

"Let me finish, Alex," continued Hank Arrowsmith. "That's the way the Chief looks at it. He thinks you are so impressed with your father's methods that you can't help imitating him."

"You've got to be kidding, Hank. He's never even met my father, who has never been to Southwestern. I know that my father is fairly well known as a forceful plant manager elsewhere . . . but to imitate him; that's fantastic! And for what . . . I'm not trying to 'get' the Chief—unless you regard trying to persuade him to follow reasonable instructions as something intolerable. I've given him every chance to cooperate, Hank, and he has chosen to fight me instead."

"Now, Alex, I don't think it's quite that," interjected Hank.

"Yes it is, Hank. The Chief has decided that he's going to override my authority and that he doesn't have to listen to anyone but you! It's now gotten to the point that it's either him or me. . . ."

Mr. Arrowsmith had risen from his chair while Mr. Brown was speaking agitatedly. Now he went over to the window, turning his back to Mr. Brown in silence. After a few minutes of waiting for Mr. Arrowsmith to turn around, Mr. Brown abruptly left the office.

When he returned to his own office, Mr. Brown required some moments to regain his composure. Finally he picked up the telephone and dialed the number of the central firefighter-guard station.

"I want to speak to the Chief," he said to the person who answered.

"Golly, Mr. Brown, I thought you knew."

"Knew what?"

"That he's gone on vacation."

"Oh . . . ah, yes. Must've forgot." He hung up fuming.

The day the Chief returned he found a message to report to Mr. Brown's office right away. Just as he started to leave the central station, the telephone rang. He picked it up and recognized Hank Arrowsmith's voice: "Say, Chief, glad you're back. I've got an errand I'd like you to run for me. It's quite important and you'll have to go right now."

"Sure, Mr. Arrowsmith, just tell me what you want and I'll be on my way."

"I feel like a damned fool, Chief, but I know I can count on you. You see, I just realized that when I sent my suit to the cleaners in Midvale this morning I forgot to take out the master key I have to all the gates at the plant. . . . You've got to get it back immediately and quietly without tipping anybody off what the key is. Got it?"

"I understand, Mr. Arrowsmith. I'll get it, you can be sure. Don't worry about a thing. I'm on my way."

Wondering what was keeping the Chief, Mr. Brown reread the letter of reprimand he had prepared to give him as soon as he arrived.

It was the strongest disciplinary letter he had ever written, and he thought grimly it would probably lift the Chief right out of his chair.

Chris Logan—City Engineer
Dorothy N. Harlow and Ellen Kimmel

FOR TEN MONTHS Christopher Logan had been the acting City Engineer-Public Works Director of Culligan City, Florida. He had had the title of Assistant City Engineer-Public Works Director during the first five years with the city, but no one had the title now. Before coming to the city, he had been for twelve years an engineer with the Florida State Department of Transportation. He had substituted "years of experience in a responsible position" for an engineering degree to become eligible to take the state exam, and six years ago he became a registered engineer.

Chris had memberships in both the American Society of Civil Engineers (ASCE) and the Florida Engineering Society (FES). As his wife was President of the FES Auxiliary, he attended most of the monthly meetings and occasionally went to some of the ASCE meetings as well.

The City Engineering–Public Works Department office was located in the city hall. Among the thirty-nine subordinates who reported to Chris there were two or three secretaries and four graduate engineers. These engineers had all passed the first part of the state professional registration examination but still needed to accumulate four years of experience before taking the second half.

Some engineering turnover occurred. Last year one man went to Saudi Arabia. Chris Logan had helped write civil service examination questions when the position was filled again. The Personnel Department advertised the opening in professional journals and the local newspapers. The new staff engineer had been selected by the department from among those who had made the five highest scores on the examination.

Chris Logan had responded to the question, "What do you do?" by saying,

> I am an engineer for Culligan City—because it is my profession. I am an engineer even though I use my engineering background and training in the administration of an engineering department.

An Interview with Chris Logan

Following are excerpts from an interview with Logan conducted by a college professor looking for classroom material.

Q: What kinds of activities occur in your department?
A: This department is responsible for the design and construction of public work type projects which include roads, storm drainage systems, sewers, water systems and recently added is the gas system. We also design and construct recreation projects such as tennis courts and related parking areas. We perform large maintenance projects on city buildings such as roofs. We have a plumbing system replacement over in the city jail going on at the present time. We also control, at least I have to check and make sure that our consulting engineers who are doing the major sanitary treatment sewage plants, are performing as required. So they are technically under my control.

This was a different group of people from Logan's thirty-nine subordinates. These consulting engineers were hired by the city to do specific things—in this particular case to design roughly $20 million worth of sewage treatment plants.

Q: Would you care to discuss the department generally?
A: We actually perform the surveying required for our projects, then do the design and drafting work to draw up the plans and our engineers prepare the specifications for the projects. We advertise and let the bid on the construction projects—$3.5 million last year— and then we inspect and lay out the construction projects. It is a

survey layout sort of thing: we inspect and also, to some extent, test the materials used in the projects. And, of course, we supervise payments to the contractor.

At the same time, another of our responsibilities is to respond to citizen complaints. This department is very heavily involved in annexations of additional property to the city. As city engineer, I act in the capacity of an advisor to the city manager and the city commission on any engineering-related matter. I am required to attend all commission meetings and, of course, all related functions that go with that. I also act as advisor in an engineering context for all other city departments that require engineering, which is a very broad term. The Parks and Recreation Department, for example, requires plans and estimates on its park properties which are extensive. They occasionally require vertical elevations, horizontal alignment and so on for their various projects such as ball parks. We also assist them in making estimates for budgeting.

The Traffic Engineering Department looks to us to construct sidewalks, to revise intersections, to perform surveying work perhaps related to alignment of streets. Although the Traffic Engineering Department is responsible for intersections, we design and build the intersections in this department. They design the traffic aspects of the intersection. For example, they might say, "We need an intersection with 12 foot lanes, with 25 or 50 foot radius. We need to have a storage area at least 500 feet long. Now you build it." We take their needs and design the drainage, the pavement type and thickness, and so on. And we actually make it fit the property that we have to build on. They are looking at the project as if they were up in an airplane and looking down on it, and saying how the traffic is going to move and what widths and lanes are required, and so on. And we take that and translate it into something on the ground. It's a cooperative effort you might say. It absolutely is. We work very closely together.

Q: Do you get along well with the traffic department?

A: Yes, as a matter of fact, we get along well with all the departments.

Q: Do you deal more with the traffic department than you do with any other department?

A: There are several others which I did not mention. The Utilities Department is responsible for the water and sewage systems billing, minor maintenance of the water system, and control of the sewage treatment plants. In other words, they actually run them. Now, they look at us to build related facilities. For example, I am doing some gas repair work at the present time. They also control the gas system. They would look to us for performing the construction work related to new systems and additions to the present system. In major maintenance work such as replacement of an entire system and related work, we would serve as their engineer. They would say, "O.K., we would like to move a line from here to here. Here's what we would like to do. You do it." We would supervise the construction. I must say that that's in a period of transition right now, because we have just "inherited," so to speak, the gas construction and have not actually performed any of this type of work.

Although Logan was describing the relationship with other departments, the crew that actually did the construction work was that of an outside contractor. Any project over $5,000 had to be advertised and usually resulted in hiring outside contractors to do the work. The city crews were not designed for construction. They were primarily responsible for maintenance of existing systems. Major new construction and major maintenance was done by outside contractors.

Q: Is the City ever criticized for being in competition with private industry?

A: We have been on occasion. But it is our system and it is our construction and we can build it if we want to. In competition with private industry means that we would be competing with them for money, which we are not. We are not going out, for example, and bidding against them on other jobs. That would be competition. We have work that has to be done. It can either be done by the city forces or we can hire someone else to do it. But it is our system and we can build it if we want to. And I don't really feel that it is in competition with private industry. That's like saying that in your home, if you want a door put on your cabinet, you have two options: you can put the door on your cabinet or you can go out and hire a carpenter to put it on. You certainly are within your rights to put your cabinet door on, and you are not in competition with private industry. You are simply doing something that needs to be done in your own facility. You might decide that it would take you forty hours, and it might take someone else two hours who had the proper equipment. If you consider your time valuable, it would cost less to hire someone outside to do it. And we use that philosophy a lot. There are many times when it would take our crews and tie them up from maintenance and keep them from doing the things that they need to do, so we simply contract for it.

Q: What is your view of departmental conflict?

A: One thing that can cause conflict between departments is having different goals. What might be very important to me might be nothing for someone else. For example, we had a pre-construction conference this morning for plumbing fixtures for the jail. Now that was probably one of the most important things to the jail system and police system that you can imagine — not having a commode in one of the jail cells. Very important to them. It is insignificant to us in our $3.5 million construction program. You are talking about $10,000 worth of fixtures. It is totally insignificant to us, and I'm sure that on occasion they have been upset with us because we haven't given this the attention that they think it deserves. So, we are serving the police department in that we are providing engineering for their facilities, and we are doing it at our convenience not theirs. There is a possibility for conflict if your goals and objectives are different and/or if something is more important to you than it is to another department.

Q: How does one go about resolving those issues? I'm sure it must happen occasionally.

A: That's one thing the administration does — or tries to do. For example, if a department director is unhappy with the status of one of his projects, he can always go to the assistant city manager to whom he is assigned and say, "This guy is just not doing me right. I need all of us to sit down and talk about it, because what is important to me is not important to him. And it's not getting done the way I think it should be." I've done that before. We have said, "O.K., we realize that this is most important to your department, but we have five departments that we are working for — in addition to our own systems that we are trying to improve and maintain."

Construction projects in drainage, for example, were strictly the responsibility of Logan's department. In this particular case he was talking about major streams from five or six major basins in the city. Each of these basins ultimately connected into a stream which flowed into the bay or gulf. The maintenance of those streams and development of the pipes and bridges crossing them were his responsibilities. So in addition to working for the other departments and the administration, he also had his own responsibilities. He said he would like to think that these responsibilities were at least equal to those of the other departments.

Q: How do interdepartmental priorities break down?

A: We have sat down with directors before and said, "Look, we have eighty-seven projects to accomplish this year, and you have one that you have just come up with that you want done right now. We have your other projects scheduled at various times during the year along with all the other projects. If you want to bump one of your projects — either completely out or change the schedule on your projects — then we'll try to work this one in. But we are not going to continue to do all of your projects and take someone else's project and throw it aside in order to shove in a different one for you." We have had to tell them this in no uncertain terms, because in any organization you have aggressive people and non-aggressive people. The non-aggressive ones will say, "Here's my list and do the best you can," and aggressive ones will say, "Here's my list, I'll be back next week and give you an additional list. I'll be back after that with another list, and I want you to do my stuff and let everyone else's go," which of course we cannot do. It's human nature. The squeaking wheel strategy sometimes works. At the beginning of this year we set a program trying to allocate space as best we could to each department.

Q: When you set it up, did you go to each and ask for their priorities?

A: Yes, then we made our own priority list based on what their priorities were. The unfortunate thing is that priorities change. Even during the year.

Q: What is your connection with and relationship to the building department?

A: There's no actual connection except that sometimes we advise them. Yet we have similar activities. For example, when the sanitary sewer line is on private property, it is inspected by the building department. We pick it up at the point it leaves private property and comes onto public property. It is our responsibility to oversee and inspect the construction that occurs within the public right-of-way.

Q: And so you would do the same kind of building inspection for sewage and whatever, on public property that the building department does on private property?

A: Yes.

Q: It is fairly clear, but isn't there a chance of disagreement as to where one department's authority stops and the other one picks up?

A: We work very closely and get along very well with all of the public directors. We assist them and they assist us. For example, building is going to inspect our plumbing project at the jail on which we opened bids and had a pre-construction conference about, this morning. As an assistance to us they are going to actually inspect that for us because we are not plumbing fixture inspectors. It can go both ways. If they feel, after looking at something that has been designed by an engineer or an architect, that they need engineering assistance determining if it is structurally adequate, such help is provided by us. Not long ago a swimming pool was to be built in the Ocean Park Estates subdivision very near the sea wall. They asked us to review the plans and approve it for construction because it might cause structural failure in the sea wall. As it turned out, there were problems. We made the suggestions for corrections. The corrections were made and approved by us. We inspected it and they proceeded with the pool construction. So it's a related and interconnected operation.

While we do not have a direct connection with the building department, we do have an association with them. The building department controls the Certificates of Occupancy of buildings. If we are having problems with the public works system related to any structure, we can request building to hold Certificate of Occupancy, and they will do so. Again, this is just a cooperative effort. We are trying to accomplish an excellent public works system for the city, and all the other departments work with us to try to do this.

Q: Are you saying that one way they do this on an unofficial basis is when you asked them to hold up on the occupancy of the building? They have a little more muscle than you do so they can help you get done what you need done?

A: That's right. It isn't written anywhere, so it is not necessarily an official procedure. It's just a thing we use in order to accomplish the things that we have to do.

Q: The building department, because of such opportunities as this, is more of an enforcement agency than you are?

A: Yes. The occupancy itself is really the important goal of the developer. Without that he really has nothing. If he cannot occupy his building, he does not have anything because to have an empty building is nothing but a liability.

Q: My guess is that once they are in that building, the chance of getting them to do something after that is nearly impossible.

A: Yes. Experience has shown that once they occupy the building they no longer are responsive to anything, unless they just happen to feel like they want to do it. And we have not been able to force them out. Taking it to court is just a time-consuming waste of effort.

Q: You probably have something to do with the legal department, too.

A: We work closely with the legal department because of several things: (1) The property acquisitions are handled through this (Logan's) department. We have a registered real estate broker who acts as our right-of-way agent and is a part of this department. He acquires rights-of-way and property, and he also acquires all of the park property, for example. If a fire station needs property to build an addition, he acquires the land. We than assist the fire department by drawing up the basic area needs. They use that information to go to an architect and say, "O.K. this is what we are thinking about, now can you give us a price for the design work based on what we have done." But you see, we have already done a great deal of design work before they ever get to the architect.

Q: And then once the architect is through, you put it out on bids. Does the contractor then construct the building to meet the building department's inspection regulations?

A: Right, and they are inspected just like private facilities.

Q: And when they are through, to whom does the building belong?

A: The building then belongs to the Fire Department. The Building and Maintenance Department of the City which is a part of Central Services will do the maintenance. They take care of it after we have done our job.

Q: How do you spend your time?

A: That's very difficult to say. It varies, of course, depending upon the workload we have. I would say that probably 95 percent of my own time is spent in administration and 5 percent in engineering. There are times when special projects come along that require more attention than that, but primarily I am an administrative officer. Some days, for example, I spend all of my time with customers. I spend a lot of time with budgeting functions—who has money to do what? This morning I have been on the phone twice regarding budgeting. In the pre-construction conference, for example, it came up (and I conduct all the pre-construction conferences myself), that some additional work may be needed to be done. The building and maintenance supervisor was there, and he said he had been having problems. "In addition to installing the gold plated johnnies there (they are stainless steel and are located in the security cells), I have been having trouble with valves and I would like to get them replaced at the same time." This was not a part of the contract, and I did not know if we had money available. I called someone in budgeting to see how much money we actually had. As it turned out we did have money, so we ordered the valves.

How do I spend my time? A large portion of time I spend going through my paperwork, handling mail, and trying to perform jobs requested by other departments. It is not uncommon for me to write five to ten letters a day, sometimes more and sometimes less, but an average of ten; I receive approximately twenty to fifty telephone calls a day. Of course I receive mail each morning that has to be reviewed and information is either dispersed to other persons for work or I have to sit and assign the duties myself. At the present time I do not have an assistant. Consequently, most of the work that I would delegate to an assistant I must do myself.

I normally work from 8:30 in the morning until 6:00 at night and occasionally I take work home. But that's a workaholic problem that I have to deal with. Right now I am preparing for two court appearances next week representing the city in a condemna-

tion suit, and we are now finishing the acquisition of some property. It is very important that I prepare the maps, which are being
done under my direction, and I must make sure that we have all
the information. It could make a difference of some $200,000. It is
very important that I be prepared for that even if I must let some
of the other paper work go.

The second court case that I have to attend to next week is related to some drainage problems. The drainage structure was constructed by the developer, and it has caused damage to a downstream property owner. The downstream property owner is suing
the developer, who is at the same time bringing the city in as a party to the suit. I must go in defense of the city's position. Those are
some of the things I am doing right now. I have also just finished
the budgeting process trying to outline capital improvement for
next year's projects. Some 2.5 million worth of just plain drainage
and construction projects. We also required each department director to come up with the various projects they need done around
the city.

Q: Do you put some sort of priority on these cases?

A: Not at this point. It is a question of "here are the things that need
to be done, and here is how much they cost." Later on in the budget hearings they will be prioritized. We will decide which ones are
the most important. There is rarely enough money to do everything that we would like to. At this time raising taxes is not very
popular.

Q: How much time do you figure you spend with your own department people as opposed to outside?

A: I don't spend nearly as much as I would like to with the internal organization. Day-to-day, face-to-face contact probably takes up 10
percent of my time.

Q: Now take the other 90 percent and divide it — if you can — with the
state, county people, other department heads, the public, etc.

A: O.K., another 10 to 15 percent for outside contact. Much of that is
spent with persons in the administration. I've been working very
closely with the assistant city managers, for example, working on a
sewer agreement for one small neighboring town. I've done two or
three things related to that this morning. So, much of my outside
contact is really with other persons in the city. Very little of it is
with property owners, etc. A small percentage is spent with the
outside. The other 75 percent I'm here at my desk working trying
to respond to letters, make sure that my projects are going correctly, doing administrative sort of work related to my budget, responding to complaints, handling directions from administration,
planning the work that has to be done, and actually seeing that it is
done.

Q: Out of the departments in the city, which ones do you spend the most time with?

A: Probably parks and recreation and traffic engineering.

Q: And as a final question to this interview, what is your biggest problem?

A: If it were two years ago I would have a different answer than I do now. Functioning in an acting position for ten months as I have, one of my biggest problems is making sure that the work all gets done — because we do have an extremely large number of assignments for an Engineering Department. We are expected to do many, many things related to all of the activities in the City and must see that they all get done. This is one of the biggest problems. Two years ago I would have said that our biggest problem was trying to get our programs approved and get funding for everything that we wanted to do. That is not as big a problem now. The budgeting process has changed for one thing, and we do seem to get our projects funded. We do have a good direction also in the sense that our master drainage plan is finished. So on a whole, I'm fairly optimistic that this department is now accomplishing and can continue to accomplish its mission and goals.

With a pleasant smile, Logan stood up, shook hands with the professor, and left the office for a late lunch.

3

Personnel Management and Employee Relations

PURPOSE

The purpose of this chapter is to familiarize students with common issues related to public personnel systems which affect the management of state and local government.

CONTENTS

Readings

    Richard P. Shick, Rose Williams Boyd, and Barry Bader, "Civil Service Systems: A Short History"

    "Elements of a Modern Personnel Program"

    Jay F. Atwood, "Collective Bargaining's Challenge"

Game

    "County Hospital"

Cases

    "Missing Raise"

    "Why California Fires So Few Incompetents"

    "Collective Bargaining in Madison"

Instructions

Pre-Class Preparation

If you did not read "The Use of 'Staff Papers' in Public Management," go back and read it now. The framework will help in case analysis throughout this volume. Then proceed with the readings for this chapter.

1. Do *NOT* read *anything* about the "County Hospital" game before coming to class. This is the only time in this volume when it is better to come to class unprepared — and no cheating please.

2. Regarding the "Missing Raise" case, be prepared to answer the following:
   a. What management "errors" did you see?
   b. How have events altered John's attitude (or "psychological contract") toward working at Central State University?
   c. Assume you are Fred Massie. What do you do now?

3. Read "Why California Fires So Few Incompetents." Why does it seem so difficult to terminate unsatisfactory public employees? What can be done about this? How is this problem affected by the trend toward participative management?

4. Prepare a response to each of the questions below based on the "Collective Bargaining in Madison" case.
   a. How did a "divided management" structure affect Madison's response to the firefighter union's demands?
   b. Public employees are often highly organized and influential in state and local government. How does this affect contract negotiations? How might this affect day-to-day agency management?
   c. With the growth in importance of formal employee relations, how might this function be restructured in Madison's city government?

Procedure for Class Meeting

The "County Hospital" game will be explained in class.

Case discussion and further exploration of the importance of state and local personnel management and labor relations.

For Additional Information

There are currently four standard textbooks dealing with public personnel management. These are:

N. Joseph Cayer, *Public Personnel Administration in the United States* (New York: St. Martin's, 1975). Paperback edition available.
Felix A. Nigro and Lloyd G. Nigro, *The New Public Personnel Administration* (Itasca, Ill.: F. E. Peacock, 1976).
Jay M. Shafritz, Walter L. Balk, Albert C. Hyde, and David H. Rosenbloom, *Personnel Management in Government* (New York: Marcel Dekker, 1978).
O. Glenn Stahl, *Public Personnel Administration*, 7th ed. (New York: Harper & Row, 1976).

Public Personnel Management, formerly *Public Personnel Review*, is the principal journal in this area. Some solid articles from *Public Personnel Management* have been collected in Jay M. Shafritz, ed., *A*

New World: Readings on Modern Public Personnel Management (Chicago: International Personnel Management Association, 1975). Paperback edition available.

In addition, three unusually good readers deal with public personnel systems. These are:

Robert T. Golembiewski and Michael Cohen, eds., *People In Public Service: A Reader in Public Personnel Administration*, 2nd ed. (Itasca, Ill.: F. E. Peacock, 1976).

Charles H. Levine, ed., *Managing Human Resources: A Challenge to Urban Governments* (Beverly Hills, Cal.: Sage Publications, 1977). Paperback edition available.

Frank J. Thomspon, ed., *Classics of Public Personnel Policy* (Oak Park, Ill.: Moore Publishing Company, 1979). Paperback edition available.

The literature on public employee unionism and collective bargaining has started to keep pace with developments in state and local government. See:

Alan Edward Bent and T. Zane Reeves, *Collective Bargaining in the Public Sector: Labor-Management Relations and Public Policy* (Menlo Park, Cal.: Benjamin/Cummings, 1978). Paperback edition available.

Characteristics of Agreements in State and Local Governments, July 1, 1975 (Washington: Bureau of Labor Statistics, U. S. Department of Labor, Bulletin 1947, 1977).

Paul F. Gerhart, *Political Activity by Public Employee Organizations at the Local Level: Threat or Promise* (Chicago: International Personnel Management Association, 1974). Paperback edition available.

Raymond D. Horton, David Lewin, and James Kuhn, "Some Impacts of Collective Bargaining on Local Government: A Diversity Thesis," *Administration and Society*, VII (Feb. 1976), pp. 497-516.

Labor-Management Relations in State and Local Governments: 1976 (Washington: Bureau of the Census, U. S. Department of Commerce, and Labor-Management Services Administration, U. S. Department of Labor, State and Local Government Special Studies No. 88, April 1978).

Jerry Lelchook and Herbert J. Lahne, *Collective Bargaining in Public Employment and the Merit System* (Washington: U.S. Government Printing Office, April 1972).

J. Joseph Loewenberg and Michael H. Moskow eds., *Collective Bargaining in Government* (Englewood Cliffs, N.J.: Prentice-Hall, 1972). Paperback edition available.

Marvin J. Levine and Eugene C. Hagburg, *Public Sector Labor Relations* (Los Angeles: West Publishing Company, 1979).

David Lewin, Peter Feuille, and Thomas A. Kochan, eds., *Public Sector Labor Relations: Analysis and Readings* (Glen Ridge, N.J.: Thomas Horton and Daughters, 1977). Paperback edition available; the most sophisticated collection to date.

Seymour Z. Mann, "Bargaining and Labor Relations: Issues and Trends in the Public Sector," *National Civic Review*, LXVII (Sept. 1978), pp. 352-357.

Public Sector Labor Relations: Recent Trends and Developments (Lexington, Kentucky: The Council of State Governments, 1975). Pamphlet.

Questions and Answers on Contract Administration: A Practioner's Guide (Bloomington, Ind.: Midwest Center for Public Sector Labor Relations, School of Public and Environmental Affairs, Indiana University, n. d., c. 1978). One of a series of helpful pamphlets.

Sterling Spero and John M. Capozzola, *The Urban Community and Its Unionized Bureaucracies* (New York: Dunellen Publishing Co., 1973). Paperback edition available.

Harry H. Wellington and Ralph K. Winter, Jr., *The Unions and the Cities* (Washington: The Brookings Institution, 1971). Paperback edition available.

Specifically regarding the state of performance appraisal practices, see:

Hubert S. Feild and William H. Holley, "Performance Appraisal: An Analysis of State-wide Practices," *Public Personnel Management*, IV (May-June 1975), pp. 145–150.

Kenneth J. Lacho, G. Kent Stearns, and Maurice F. Villere, "A Study of Employee Appraisal Systems of Major Cities in the United States," *Public Personnel Management*, VIII (March-April 1979), pp. 111–125.

Other relevant materials include:

Peter Allan and Stephen Rosenberg, "Establishing a Personnel System for Managers: The New York City Approach," *Public Personnel Management*, VII (July-Aug. 1978), pp. 236–242.

Winston W. Crouch, *Guide for Modern Personnel Commissions* (Chicago: International Personnel Management Association, 1973).

Winston W. Crouch, ed., *Local Government Personnel Administration* (Washington: International City Management Association, 1976).

Dennis L. Dresang, "Public Personnel Reform: A Summary of State Government Activity," *Public Personnel Management*, VII (Sept.-Oct. 1978), pp. 287–294.

Myron D. Fottler and Craig Norrell, "State Government Personnel Directors: A Comparative Analysis of Their Background Characteristics and Qualifications," *Public Personnel Management*, VIII (Jan.-Feb. 1979), pp. 17–25.

Good Government, LXXXVII (Spring 1971). Contains a "Survey of Current Personnel Systems in State and Local Governments."

A Model Public Personnel Administration Law (Washington: National Civil Service League, Nov. 1970). Pamphlet.

Selma J. Mushkin and Frank H. Sandifer, *Personnel Management and Productivity in City Government* (Lexington, Mass.: D. C. Health/Lexington Books, 1979).

E. S. Savas and Sigmund G. Ginsburg, "The Civil Service: A Meritless System?," *The Public Interest*, No. 32 (Summer 1973), pp. 70–85.

Raymond A. Shapek, "Federal Influences in State and Local Personnel Management: The System in Transition," *Public Personnel Management*, V (Jan.-Feb. 1976), pp. 41–51.

Frank J. Thompson, *Personnel Policy in the City: The Politics of Jobs in Oakland* (Berkeley: University of California Press, 1975).

Deil S. Wright, Mary Wagner, and Richard McAnaw, "State Administrators: Their Changing Characteristics," *State Government*, L (Spring 1977), pp. 152–159.

Civil Service Systems: A Short History

Richard P. Shick, Rose Williams Boyd, and Barry Bader

THE CIVIL SERVICE SYSTEMS that predominate among today's state and local governments are products of a century of reform that goes back to the 1870's. It was then that civil service reformers began agitating Congress to dump the spoils system and create a permanent federal career "merit" service, with appointments based on functional job requirements rather than on the basis of political ties. Progress was slow and frustrating until, on July 2, 1881, a dramatic event galvanized public opinion against the spoils systems of politically-based appointments to federal jobs.

Infuriated that he'd been denied the consulship to Paris because his faction of the Republican Party was feuding with the President, Charles A. Guiteau shot President James A. Garfield. While Garfield lay in a coma dying, the civil service reformers met to map plans for rallying public and Congressional support to end the spoils system. Spearheaded by New York's reform group, they formed the National Civil Service Reform League, later to become the National Civil Service League. Sixteen months later, their efforts resulted in Congressional passage of the Pendleton Act, signed into law by President Chester A. Arthur on January 16, 1883.

Intended to prevent the ravages of the spoils system from ever again threatening Constitutional government, the Act set down the basic principles of merit employment that still exist today:

1. Positions are filled by "an objective method for assessing the relative fitness of an applicant." This means that jobs are to be filled by open, practical examinations that test the applicant's "fitness for the job" in terms of the knowledge, skills, and abilities needed to perform the job tasks required.
2. Employees are retained on the job as long as their performance is adequate.
3. Promotions are made on the basis of practical "fitness," also, based on assessments of their performance of the job tasks to which they have been assigned.

The concept of "merit" employment means, simply, that a governmental employee should be hired on the basis of ability to perform the job, rather than partisan or other political considerations. Elimination of political standards for hiring was intended to make government employment (traditionally a source of highly-prized jobs) accessible to *all citizens* willing and able to perform the tasks required by the job. Additionally, the intent was to serve the cause of governmental efficiency and economy by attempting to assure job competency, as well as to prevent the majority party from obtaining total control over the machinery of government.

Once hired, a public employee must be protected from arbitrary firing, if functional, job-related standards are to prevail over political considerations. For this reason, the second basic component of merit employment is *tenure*. Tenure is not meant to guarantee an *incompetent* employee a job. In fact, incompetence was another basic criticism of the spoils system.

In order to find employees "fit for the job," an administrative machinery had to be created to recruit, screen, hire, and serve the day-to-day employment needs of government workers. This administrative machinery is called a "personnel system," or a "civil service system." Where employees are hired, retained, and promoted on the basis of merit, it is often called a "merit system."

Because they so mistrusted elected officials, the old civil service reformers did not believe that anybody who was elected could be trusted to set the kind of objective, job-related hiring standards necessary for "merit" governmental employment. So, they devised the "civil service commission" as an independent regulatory agency that would both set policy and supervise the administration of the merit system. The Pendleton Act established the bi-partisan U.S. Civil Service Commission.

Only about 10 percent of the 130,000 federal workers initially were covered by the new merit system in 1883. Today, over 90 percent of the two million federal civilian workers outside the U. S. Postal Service are covered. Even while Congress debated the 1883 law, civil service reformers pressed their case among state legislatures and city councils. In the New York state legislature, Republican Assemblyman Theodore Roosevelt managed a reform bill which was signed into law by Democratic Governor Grover Cleveland (also a League Board member) on May 4, 1883. New York's was the first state civil service merit law. Massachusetts followed suit in 1884. Both laws covered municipal as well as state employees.

Despite large scale education and lobbying efforts, no other states passed a merit system law until Wisconsin and Illinois did so in 1905, Colorado in 1907, New Jersey in 1908, and Ohio in 1912. Meanwhile, New York in 1894 became the first state to incorporate the merit system into its state Constitution. The move was hailed at the time, but since proved a hindrance to modernization efforts.

Cities, too, were jumping on the bandwagon. Some became part of their state merit system, including 24 Massachusetts municipalities. Others, such as Chicago, San Francisco, and Los Angeles had separate merit systems. In 1926 Murray Seasongood was elected Mayor of Cincinnati in a campaign that ousted the local spoils machine. A member of the National Civil Service League since 1904 and an NCSL National Board member since 1921, Seasongood was termed "a hell-raiser *par excellence*" and directed most of his fury towards ridding the city of the last vestiges of the spoils system.

The tide of civil service reform carried through the 1920's and 30's with renewed vigor, joined by a new movement: "Scientific Management." Finite yardsticks, like time and motion studies and standardized written examinations were supposed to supplant human judgments. Spurred by research conducted by the U. S. Army, employers began examining for "job fitness" with a whole range of general intelligence tests and other standardized written instruments. These "scientific instruments" were hailed as a boon; for they were thought to allow totally "objective" examination of candidates, selection of only the "best qualified," defined in terms of the highest scorers, and easy ranking of the order of candidate scores for the purpose of certification.

Standardized written tests won wide acceptance by public employers who needed convenient, inexpensive, and "merit" methods of ferreting through the hordes of applicants left unemployed during the depression. Unfortunately, although the tests certainly were neutral in the sense that they were impersonal and non-partisan in their effects on applicants, they did not necessarily adequately examine for the job-relatedness of the applicants' knowledge, skills, and abilities. Thus, many if not most civil service written examinations failed to fulfill the fundamental merit system requirement of examining for functional, practical, or job-related fitness for the job. Instead, by their very nature as written tests, they emphasized verbal and mathematical skills to a degree not always needed by the jobs to be filled.

Still, it was thought that the "best qualified" applicants in terms of those with the highest examination scores would make the "best" employees, regardless of whether successful applicants were over-qualified or whether they had demonstrated qualifications other than those actually needed for the job.

In 1939, the federal government reinforced the reform drive by requiring states and localities receiving certain federal grant-in-aid funds, such as unemployment and public assistance, to adopt merit systems to cover the employees in state and local government whose jobs were paid for out of federal funds. (The National Civil Service League had recommended this requirement.) After World War II, states and localities continued to adopt merit systems and to use "scientific" screening tools to select and promote employees.

Further refinement of Army screening and job placement techniques, together with other developments within the personnel and manpower systems of the U. S. government and private sector employers pointed towards the practicality of implementing job-related employee selection devices that would enable true "merit" employment by more accurately testing for the ability to perform the job.

In 1970, the League conducted a survey of the nation's 568 largest public employers with 500 or more employees, in order to identify the extent of merit system practices. A total of 55 percent of the jurisdictions responded. Eighty-five percent indicated that they had some form of a merit system. Both written tests and credentialism are common. Entry level office workers have to take written tests in 88 percent of the jurisdictions and 94 percent require at least a high school diploma. Sixty-one percent said they used written tests to select entry level professional staff. Eighty-eight percent require at least a grammar school education for unskilled workers. Sixty-three percent of the merit systems surveyed also had independent civil service commissions, a reflection of the 1883 desire to protect the public service from partisan political abuses. Fearing that newly-elected politicians might decimate the career service, most state and local civil service reformers followed the federal example and established independent civil service commissions and a set of complex rules and regulations designed to make the political manipulation of the hiring process very difficult.

Civil Service Today

The civil service merit systems of today mirror to a large extent what the reformers of 1883 tried to accomplish. However, changes in American society have placed new demands on public personnel systems and some parts of the old civil service systems cannot bear the burden. Although merit *principles* apply today as much as ever, some common merit *practices* are in fact failing to measure up to their original intent.

This is not to imply that all civil service systems are bad, or that all are failing. But, in its work around the country with over 500 state and local jurisdictions, the League has found that the following problems are commonplace:

1. The traditional split of authority between an executive personnel department and an independent civil service commission often causes uncoordin-

ated, inefficient personnel management. Appointing authorities cannot get people with the kinds of qualifications they need to perform the job.

2. Minority group members and women often are not employed at levels commensurate with their skills, apparently because traditional civil service qualification and examination requirements over-emphasize formal education and experience, unrelated to the knowledge, skills, and abilities actually needed to perform the job.

3. Tenure provisions coupled with a lack of job performance and employee evaluation standards make it difficult for management to maintain high productivity and eliminate "deadwood."

4. The drive to protect employees from political pressures — and the public from politicized employees — has at times strayed into over-zealous limits on personal freedom.

5. Lack of due process and impartial adjudication of employee grievances and adverse actions undermines employee morale and performance.

6. The emergence of public employee unions requires a whole new apparatus for employee relations and dispute settlement, as well as new management attitudes towards the rights and duties of public employees, which many jurisdictions lack.

7. Making changes in civil service procedures often consumes months or years of arduous red tape, including hearings, legislative approval, and referenda.

Why Do Civil Service Systems Resist Change?

An unsophisticated observer might wonder why any government would tolerate a civil service system that is inefficient, quagmired in red tape, screening out minorities and women, generally not able to predict applicant nor measure employee performance reliably. After all, employees are the foundation of government. They perform the necessary tasks and deliver the services. Wages and benefits take the lion's share of most governmental budgets. The reason is that, despite their drawbacks, civil service systems may meet practical political needs. The spoils system was knocked down but not out by the several reform movements that have swept over it.

New Haven, Connecticut, is one case in point, but not unique. There, split authority between the civil service commission and personnel department, compounded by inadequate staffing, low funding, and poor communications, resulted in a system that, in the 1960's, was unable to examine and certify applicants fast enough to fill vacancies. Instead, department heads made "temporary appointments" which were later rubber-stamped into permanent status by the compliant civil service commission. The "merit" system functioned in name only.

Why did the city officials allow this situation? Primarily because it met political needs. Party leaders could send job seekers to department heads who had the authority to make "emergency appointments." Some department heads relished their power of appointment, unfettered by civil service rules. Political patronage continued in the old line departments while the mayor (who served from 1954 to 1969) gave his attention to the new "redevelopment agencies" he was using to cure the city's urban ills.

When a new mayor came into office in 1969, he recognized that the patronage strengthened political forces who were not necessarily *his* allies. He also saw the system as an impediment to effective government. Thus, it was in the new mayor's self-interest to stem temporary appointments and institute some civil service reforms.

The lesson from New Haven for civil service reformers is that a commitment from top level management is the single most important prerequisite for reforming the system. If the chief executive feels that the present system best serves his or her interests, then change will be virtually impossible, unless there are legal aspects conducive to court intervention or sufficiently broad forces at work in the legislature to override executive resistance.

If the executive believes that reform strengthens his or her power, then reform becomes far more feasible. Chief executives make things happen. They have wide discretionary powers over budgets and appointments, including civil service commission appointments, and almost always possess great power in their political party. Enlistment of the support of the chief executive of a city, county, or state is key to successful civil service reform.

Because most public employees work for the executive branch of government and because the personnel department is most often an executive staff agency, civil service modernization is of most concern to the executive branch. But, the other two branches of government also play important roles. The legislature is responsible in the first place for any civil service or merit employment law. Through its budgetary process it authorizes the money to pay for administration of the personnel system, and usually authorizes the number of positions and any changes in the classification and pay system.

While many of the most important civil service changes can be made by the executive and/or civil service commission in terms of civil service rules and regulations and administrative policies, the legislature can influence civil service change. Where the executive and/or civil service commission is reluctant to make changes, the legislature often can mandate them by changing the law. Or, it can appropriate (or withhold) money for civil service modernization, such as programs for validating selection procedures.

The President of the legislature, or key committee chairmen, like appropriations, or personnel, or civil service, can wield great power over civil service modernization. Their cooperation may be just as important as that of the Chief Executive, particularly where changes in the law are required to facilitate personnel administration reorganization and certainly where a change in the structure of the civil service commission is proposed.

The judiciary also plays an important role. It was the U. S. Supreme Court, for instance, that mandated selection instrument validation in all instances where selection procedures have an adverse impact on classes of persons protected by the Civil Rights Act of 1964.

Conceivably, the courts can also influence civil service change through their decisions on the legality or Constitutionality of proposed and existing civil service laws, policies, and/or administrative practices.

Like most other aspects of American government, each of the three branches of federal, state, and local governments has a potential influence over both the existing, or any proposed policy or administrative changes.

But, the executive and/or civil service commission has the most discretion in the administration of civil service policies and, therefore, is the single most important link in the policy chain.

The role of extra-governmental influence also is important. None of the three branches of government exists in a vacuum. Public interest groups may influence elected officials and, through them, appointed officials. Governmental officials with power to influence civil service modernization often act on the basis of their own perceptions of constituency demands for civil service change—or the *status quo*. Where an elected official feels strongly that existing employees are important to his or her re-election, any demands for civil service change, or for the *status quo*, may be reinforced or countermanded by the official's perception of the electoral influence of a public interest group. . . .

Elements of a Modern Merit Personnel Program

THE FOLLOWING ARE GENERALLY CONSIDERED to be the principal elements of a modern program of merit personnel administration for a jurisdiction with at least 500 employees or thereabouts. Depending on the needs and preferences of particular jurisdictions, some of these elements will be specifically authorized in law while others will be based on general statutory authority.

- Provision for *equal employment opportunity applicable to all personnel actions* without regard to political affiliation, race, color, national origin, sex, age, religious creed, marital status, or physical handicap.
- A plan for systematic *job analysis* involving collecting data and making certain judgments about the nature of individual jobs to provide a basis for such things as classifying positions, developing minimum qualification requirements, constructing job-related tests, identifying training needs, and reviewing individual performance. Job analysis is a major component of affirmative action for equal employment opportunity. The courts have specifically cited job analysis as a required basis for qualification standards and written tests.
- *Grouping or classification of positions* by occupation according to similarities or differences in duties, responsibilities and qualification requirements.
- A realistic *pay system* tied to sound job analysis and position classification which assures equity within the system and comparability with pay offered by other employers in the same labor market area for similar work.
- Job related *minimum qualification requirements* which describe the nature and amount of experience, training, knowledges and skills needed for successful performance as well as a means for determining that applicants possess such requirements.
- *Recruiting, examining, rating certification, and selection procedures* which reach all parts of the labor market; which apply the established qualification requirements in a fair, job-related fashion in testing and selecting the best-qualified persons from among all eligible candidates; and which make special affirmative action provisions for assuring equal opportunity to members of minority groups, women, and those disadvantaged by educational, economic, physical or social handicaps.
- A *placement* system which not only assures the sound initial placement of new employees, but also provides for follow-up and for remedial placements.
- An adequate *probationary period* which must be satisfactorily completed before permanent tenure or status is conferred.
- A continuing *performance evaluation* system providing employees and managers feedback aimed at strengthening employee and organizational performance.
- An *incentive awards* program which provides recognition for exceptional performance and successful ideas for improving operations.
- A *training and career development program* which, among other things, fills the gaps between the qualifications required for the positions in question and the qualifications possessed either by employees already in, or on the career ladder for such positions or by outside candidates for such positions; which prepares employees to meet the future needs of the public service; and which keeps the public service up-to-date in its use of modern techniques, technology, and equipment.

- A *promotion* system which provides for fair and objective consideration of eligible employees for the promotion opportunities which arise; and which assures that selection for promotion is job-related and based on merit, not political or personal patronage or racial or other favoritism.
- Provision for lateral *transfers and reassignments* of employees among different agencies or parts of agencies and for *details* and *temporary duty* assignments to meet short-term needs.
- Provision for *reprimands, suspensions, demotions, and removals* of employees for disciplinary reasons or unsatisfactory performance.
- Objective and effective *appeals and grievance* systems for employees.
- A *labor-management relations* provision which enables employees to be involved in personnel policies and practices affecting their employment consistent with merit principles, the preservation of management rights and the protection of the public interest.
- An orderly and fair method of making necessary *cutbacks in the work force* due to budget reductions, decrease in work load, reorganizations, or other reasons.
- Fringe benefits, such as *age and disability retirement, group life and health insurance, vacation and sick leave, paid holidays, and employees' compensation for job-connected injuries and sickness.*
- An *occupational safety and health program* and provision for employee counseling and guidance services.
- A statutory or executive code of *ethical conduct* for all public service personnel which includes prohibitions against conflict of interest, nepotism and political coercion.
- A system of *policy, regulatory, and operational issuances* published by the central personnel agency for the direction and guidance of employing agencies of the government.
- A system of *personnel records, reports, and statistics* as needed for legal or personnel management purposes.
- Provision for *personnel planning, overall program planning and continuing program evaluation* which recognizes the critical role of effective personnel management in the delivery of government services to the public.
- A sound basic *public personnel law*, positive *support from top management, adequate financial resources* for essential personnel operations, and *competent professional personnel staffs* both in the central personnel agency and in the line departments.

All of this must operate within the context of an open employment environment where the procedures and information necessary to administer the program are available to applicants and employees.

Collective Bargaining's Challenge
Jay F. Atwood

THE EMERGENCE OF COLLECTIVE BARGAINING in the public service may be characterized as the single most significant development in the field of public personnel administration during the past decade. Evidence of this development is found in four trends: (1) increasing membership of public employees in unions; (2) enactment of collective bargaining laws covering public employees by an increasing number of public jurisdictions; (3) effectuation of countless written agreements or contracts by public employers and employees; and (4) increased incidence of work stoppages and other concerted activities by public employees.

As a consequence of this development, public managers are confronted with the challenge it generates as an administrative reality. In this "real world" context, the public manager is faced with the dilemma of rising employee expectations to participate in decisionmaking and of continuing public expectations for responsible and economical management of public organizations.

How does the public manager cope with this dilemma? As with most complex and controversial public policy issues, there is no simple panacea. Nevertheless, there must be a starting point. The one this article suggests is the identification and description of some five imperatives (*i.e.*, facts which compel attention or action) that provide an initial frame of reference for the public manager to meet this challenge.

Recognizing the Distinctive Nature of Public Sector Labor Relations

Even though the claim of comparability between private and public sector labor relations continues to be set forth,[1] an experiential analysis demonstrates that it is a myth. There are certain characteristics which make public sector labor relations distinctive.

Public Employees More Highly Organized

Notwithstanding certain highly publicized union recognition controversies (*e.g.*, Memphis and Charleston, among others) and the relatively high incidence of work stoppages attributed to recognition disputes in the public sector, evidence exists that public employees are more highly organized than their counterparts in private industry.

For instance, in 1974 at the federal government level, approximately 57 percent of all nonpostal employees were represented by unions; 88 percent of all postal employees; 82 percent of all "blue collar" (wage grade) employees; and 48 percent of all "white collar" (general schedule) employees.[2] For the Canadian federal government, the percentage of employees organized is a near universal 99 percent.[3] In New York state and local government (which has had an enabling law only since 1967), about 90 percent of the eligible public employees have organized.[4] Moreover, approximately 65 percent of all municipal employees in the U.S. are represented by employee organizations[5] and more than one-third of all public employees in the U.S. are represented in exclusive bargaining units.[6]

Contrast these percentages with the less than 28 percent of all private employees in nonagricultural establishments who have organized and opted for collective bargaining.[7] Consider also the fact that private sector organizing efforts have been legally sanctioned for over 35 years, whereas most public agency labor relations enabling laws have occurred only within the past 10 years and are not universal.

The public service is generally characterized by less visible and intense management opposition to employee organizing efforts and in representation elections. Sam Zagoria, a former member of the National Labor Relations Board, has described this attitudinal difference between the two sectors as follows:

> The potential for public union growth is enhanced by the attitudes of elected officials, who, by virtue of their office, are often thrust into the role of public employer. Unlike their private employer counterparts — some of whom are still fighting the statutory right of employees to decide whether they want a union to represent them or not — these public employers, accustomed to representing many and varied segments of society, do not as often look on unions as the enemy when employees choose them.[8]

Political Context of the Relationship

In the public sector, the political implications of labor relations are pervasive, simply because the negotiating process culminates in the allocation of public resources which is a political decision involving elected representatives.[9] As Horton has cogently observed: "The allocation of public money and the fixing of public and managerial policies, two major functions of the labor relations process, are central political acts in any organized society . . . the labor relations process inevitably is political."[10]

Characteristics of this political milieu which bear directly upon the labor relations process include:

Pressure to settle. Public officials are more susceptible than private employers to public (hence, political) pressure to settle a negotiating dispute. The high visibility of public services, ready accessibility of public officials, and sole-source character of most public services contribute to the generation of this public pressure. Such pressure stems from the reality that these public officials run periodically for reelection to their current office or for election to a higher office. As has been observed, ". . . voters will tend to choose political leaders who avoid inconveniencing strikes over those who work to minimize the costs of settlements at the price of a strike."[11] Or as Cook concluded in an analysis of New York City labor relations ". . . public labor relations are fundamentally determined and carried out under the law of politics and that consequent settlements are political acts."[12] Although the New York situation is certainly more highly publicized, similar circumstances in microcosm surround countless settlements and occasional impasses in public jurisdictions throughout the country.[13]

Political clout of public employee unions.   Since public employer-employee agreements or contracts are ultimately consummated in the political decision-making process and not at the bargaining table, the incentive for an employee organization to influence successfully that process is considerable. Consider the impact that a well-organized public employee union can exert on a local government election (usually characterized by a relatively small voter turnout) and subsequent influence on the politically oriented decisionmaking process. One San Francisco union leader has very candidly stated the public employee unions' stake in the local governmental electoral process:

> Many members might wonder why should a labor union get itself involved in politics? . . . The action of the Mayor and the Board of Supervisors has a great effect on the material well-being of these employees for the next four years. At the first of the year, these three unions will be in a bargaining process with the same supervisors and mayor. Obviously, if liberal and labor-minded candidates win the election, the job will be much easier in bargaining and the benefits much greater.[14]

Symbiotic relationship between elected officials and unions.   A mutual benefit relationship can and has evolved between public officials and a particular employee organization. The relationship between the City of Los Angeles' Department of Water and Power and the International Brotherhood of Electrical Workers, Local 18, which represents many of its employees, is illustrative. Local 18 has been characterized as the "political arm" of the department as a result of its support since the 1930s. Initially, this support was given in a bond election for the embryonic department and more recently in a city charter election which, had it been successful, would have curtailed the administrative independence of the department. Management of the department has generally provided very generous compensation and employee benefits for its employees. Indeed, after the defeat of the proposed charter amendment, the department increased its monthly contribution to the employees' retirement fund to such a degree that the Los Angeles City Council president was prompted to describe it as ". . . a pretty good method of rewarding their employees for their opposition to the charter."[15] The potential impact of this type of symbiosis upon the electoral process has been identified by Horton in his study of labor relations in New York City government. He found that:

> In return for 'special attention' at the bargaining table and elsewhere municipal unions offer two commodities highly valued by the public official in electoral trouble: labor peace and their own electoral support in the form of endorsements, campaign workers and money, and membership votes.[16]

Work stoppage as a political weapon.   With the private sector collective bargaining model, the work stoppage is utilized as an economic weapon by the union to secure an agreement with the employer. As a counterweapon, the employer has the option of imposing an economic sanction against the employees in the form of a lockout. The theory is that the employer weighs the economic consequences of a work stoppage against the cost of meeting the economic demands of the employees. Conversely, a threatened or actual work stoppage by a group of public employees may not necessarily have economic consequences or costs for either the public jurisdiction or the public employees involved. Such a work stoppage unavoidably has political consequences. The employees utilize the political consequences of a work stoppage or other job action as leverage to gain their objectives rather than relying solely on the economic consequences, which may very well be nonexistent.

Diffused Authority of Public Management

"Who is the employer?" can be a perplexing problem in a public agency whereas this issue is virtually nonexistent in the private sector. In the private sector, management is an identifiable, unified entity which has authority to bargain and to commit the organization in attempting to reach an agreement with an employee representative. In the public sector, on the other hand, not only is there the bifurcation between the executive and legislative branches of government, particularly at the federal and state levels, but there may be autonomous entities within the executive structure as well, each with authority to establish some term or condition of employment.[17]

Absence of Economic Market Constraints

A most insightful statement which captures the fundamental difference between the two sectors in the traditional economic context has been written by Samuel Krimsley in an arbitration decision:

> Instead of arguing that its contribution to the wealth of an enterprise is equivalent to that of the capital and expertise of management, the police are discussing their contribution to the fabric of society, which prevents a large city from deteriorating into an anarchistic lawlessness. Instead of management arguing, in effect, that labor is an economic commodity purchased similarly to the raw materials used in manufacture and its right to control the commodities it purchases, the city discusses its fiscal responsibilities to the taxpayers and the historically proven need to manage the city without being controlled by the employees.[18]

In the 1967 strike by the United Federation of Teachers against New York City, ". . . the teachers emerged with a contract giving them an average 20% increase in salary and benefits, as well as a voice in the determination of school policy. The board saved at least $6 million. In an economic sense, for the two parties most involved, there were few if any costs, and possibly some very real benefits."[19]

Limits on Scope of Bargaining

Perhaps the key point in establishing the scope of bargaining in the private sector is the fact that ". . . the actual scope of bargaining is left to evolve out of the relationship of the parties under the administrative authority of the National Labor Relations Board."[20]

This is not the case in the public sector. The existence of alternative or competing methods of determining the terms and conditions of employment is unique to the public sector. This constraint is largely external to the bargaining relationship because it falls within the province of entities who may not be a party to the bargaining, such as civil service commissions, retirement boards, etc.

The Western Assembly pinpointed the distinctiveness of the public sector in this respect when it reported that "the question whether public employees should be permitted to bargain over issues of public policy has no exact analogue in the private sector."[21]

Existence of Merit or Civil Service Employment Systems

Many of the traditional terms and conditions of employment which are established through the bilateral decisionmaking process in private industry are established unilaterally by either the legislative body or independent boards and commissions in the public service.

Legal protection of individual public employee rights related to the employment relationship are often built into the system. For example, such matters as employee selection, tenure, punitive actions, appeal rights, performance appraisal, merit salary adjustment, transfer, reinstatement, demotion, layoff, promotion, and other employee status issues are usually provided by statute or quasi-legislative rules in a public jurisdiction. Moreover, such employee benefits as retirement, vacation allowance, holidays, premium overtime pay, night-shift pay differentials, travel and per diem allowances, employer contributions to health and welfare insurance premiums, leaves of absence, etc., are typically included in the statutes governing public employment.

As a result of this overlapping, a contest for hegemony over employment relations matters is generated between civil service systems and collective bargaining. The ultimate outcome of this contest is as yet undetermined. One view holds that they are inherently incompatible[22] whereas another believes that an accommodation can be found.[23]

Greater Reliance upon Arbitration of Interest Disputes

In private industrial relations, the use of arbitration as a means of resolving interest or bargaining disputes is rare. It is generally viewed as a threat to free collective bargaining since, so the argument goes, resorting to a third party to make a binding decision as to the terms of the agreement is inimical to the "give-and-take" bargaining process.

Arbitration as a bargaining impasse settlement technique has received a better reception in the public sector. In fact, more experimentation with a variety of such techniques has occurred in the public service. Twelve states currently mandate compulsory arbitration of negotiating disputes for certain public employees; twelve other states and the District of Columbia permit voluntary arbitration upon request of either one or both parties to the dispute. Due to public health and safety considerations, compulsory arbitration is more frequently made applicable to disputes involving police and fire fighters.

These several distinctions summarized above are significant because of the implications they have for the implementation and administration of a collective bargaining process, in terms of both its structure and dynamics, in the public service. In other words, if the private sector model cannot suitably be transplanted wholesale into the public sector, then other models which reflect the distinctiveness of the governmental environment must be conceived. Recognizing this fact is the first imperative for the public manager.

Responding Proactively
to a Changing Environment

The paramount message heralded by public employee relations in recent years is that employees desire a change in the decisionmaking processes used in determining their terms and conditions of employment. Public employees generally are no longer content to allow management, no matter how benevolent, to determine conditions of employment in a unilateral, paternalistic fashion.

This discontent is yet another facet of the turbulent environment which confronts the public manager. Gawthrop has characterized the ". . . external sociopolitical environment of the bureaucrat . . ." as one where ". . . instability has replaced stability, uncertainty has replaced predictability, and complex patterns of rapid change are becoming institutionalized."[24] To compound the problem, this external uncertainty has been joined by an equally uncertain internal environment. Public employees, no less than the client groups which they serve, are organizing their efforts to exert their influence. The rise of collective bargaining in public employment is a highly visible reflection of this pressure for change. Indeed, what better example is there of the "politics of confrontation" than an illegal public employee strike?

Unfortunately, public management's response to this overtly expressed desire for change by public employees has, for the most part, been reactive rather than proactive. Rather than taking a positive stance and assuming the role of a "change agent" by initiating a process of planned change, they have tended to rely upon the paternalistic pattern that resists the notion of increased employee participation in decisions affecting terms and conditions of employment. They tend to be wedded to a set of values that are being questioned.

In response to this behavior on the part of bureaucratic and political leadership, the employees have opted for the adversarial approach embodied in the private industrial collective bargaining model. In an organized fashion, they have been relatively successful in securing passage of legislation in most states which grants organizing and bargaining rights akin to those which pertain to employees in the private sector. Now, they are pressing their claim on the national level for these rights through statutes which would mandate collective bargaining for every public jurisdiction.

Public management's unwillingness or inability to foster a climate and to evolve a structure for joint decisional processes with employees (apart from the adversarial, ritualistic collective bargaining model) reflects a lack of responsiveness to a changing situation. When employees, particularly professional employees with a sense of commitment to the well-being of their clients, want to participate in and influence the decisions which concern their working situation, such an opportunity to utilize this resource should be exploited in a positive sense. Powerlessness regarding influence upon general management policies, employment conditions, and the immediate work process has been identified as one of the major contributors to the feeling of "alienation" by workers.[25] It behooves public managers to mitigate this feeling of powerlessness by finding suitable methods for participation. It is imperative that public management recognize the rising employee expectations for participation and work towards a suitable means of providing for it. The forms this takes is of secondary importance. Primary emphasis should be on evolving a philosophy and administrative style that deals with this imperative.

Understanding the Fusion of Politics and Administration

In simpler times, public administration theory held that administration (*i.e.*, the functions of the executive) and politics (*i.e.*, the functions of the legislature) could be neatly dichotomized. The latter's role was to determine matters of public policy whereas the former executed that policy in a nonpolitical fashion. More sophisticated analysis, however, challenges this Wilsonian theory. Caiden expresses the more modern view that, "The two overlap, and in many instances are fused. . . . The politics-administration distinction is not a dichotomy but a continuum; between the two extremes, there are various gradations of fusion."[26]

Public managers should be alert to attempts to characterize labor relations as a managerial or administrative function that deals exclusively with so-called "management prerogatives". If labor relations is cast in these specious terms, then it follows that bargaining is distinguishable from policy decisions, which are reserved for the politically elected officials. Such a view, however, does not coincide with the premise that public managers have an active political role in public administration.

It is imperative that public managers understand this fact because of its ramifications upon the way decisions are made in government. If, as Kleingartner suggests, bargaining results in a "genuine redistribution of authority" in the "everyday management in the public sector",[27] then public managers must assess the alterations to the process that stems from a bilateral relationship.

One example will suffice in demonstrating the relevance of this imperative:

> . . . after a 12-hour strike by fire fighters in Newark, New Jersey, state urban aid funds originally authorized for the poor were diverted to salary increases. This situation clearly illustrates not only an imbalance in the political process, but also a conflict in the development of appropriate governmental priorities.[28]

Balancing Pluralistic Interests in Our Political Society

In the allocation of public resources (which is the essence of the political decisionmaking process), the various pluralistic interests are in competition for these limited resources. In our democratic system, the goal is to achieve some rough semblance of equity in this competition.

This means that power is fragmented among these several groups and any redistribution of such power among the groups will potentially upset the equilibrium of the political decisionmaking process. In terms of public employee relations, the public manager must recognize the impact of a shift of power to the organized public employees through conventional collective bargaining power tactics.

Hampton cautions against this potential power shift resulting from public employee strikes:

> If Federal employees were able to withhold their services in addition to engaging in the accepted methods of political activity of private interest groups, it could not only result in the reallocation of national resources in their favor but also could leave competing private interest groups at a permanent and substantial disadvantage.[29]

Some observers of public employee relations have noted that there are more parties at interest in the negotiating process than the two—labor and management—which exist in the conventional private sector bilateral relationship. They postulate that public service bargaining may better be characterized as trilateral (where the public constitutes the third party at interest) or even multilateral.[30]

This is an illusive concept to describe, let alone operationalize. Nevertheless, the public manager's obligation to be responsive to the public interest or social equity is not lessened by the difficulty of definition or implementation. All too often, as Newland has noted:

> . . . collective bargaining agreements in the public sector have the appearance of a conspiracy between two giants to solve their mutual problems at public expense; the parties have found their narrow organiza-

tional reasonableness, but not always in terms that are just to the public.[31]

It is incumbent upon the public manager to strive to answer the questions of "Who represents the public interest at the public bargaining table?" and "How can multiple interests be accommodated?"

Avoiding the "One-Best-Way" Trap

Public managers have frequently pursued the false god of the "one-best-way". Whether cast in the form of scientific management, bureaucratic organizational design, POSDCORB, planning-programming-budgeting system, etc., the tendency has been to take an idea, a process, an organizational structure, or a system which enjoys some success in a particular environment and to claim universality in application. Experience has demonstrated that such universality is a fallacy. As a result, much energy and resources are lost trying to fit or force the latest technique into every situation.

We seem to be headed down this well-used track once again by applying the same type of specious reasoning to public employee relations. Formalized employer-employee relations systems created thus far in public agencies are coming from the same mold; that is, the private sector collective bargaining paradigm. Indeed, there is a strong effort now to force the public sector even more completely into this "one-best-way" approach by amending the National Labor Relations Act to encompass public employees. What little innovation which exists now in the various state enabling laws would be lost as well as any future opportunities to experiment in the social and political laboratories afforded by the fifty states.

In some very pertinent comments, Newland advises against the mindless adoption by the public service of ". . . a rigid model of collective bargaining formulated by doctrinaire unionists of an earlier generation". He equates the adoption of the "rigid model of collective bargaining" with the ". . . one-best-way orientation of scientific management and classical organizational theory . . ." which represent for him, ". . . worn-out philosophies of certainty and singular truth." He believes that ". . . variety as an approach is more realistic in our dynamic, plural society".[32]

Newland is disenchanted with the notion of a single truth whether enunciated by advocates of the now-questioned traditional public personnel administration "principles" or the outdated conflict model of labor economics. He opts for variety and multiple truths in the public personnel function. Experience in the practice of public personnel administration tends to support his perspective.

The fifth imperative, then, for the public manager is to pursue multiple options and approaches in public employee relations and, conversely, to avoid becoming locked into a single, universal approach.

Summary

The intent of this article has been to set forth some of the more critical imperatives for public managers who are confronted with the rising expectations of public employees for participation in decisions which affect them in their employment. A dilemma for the public manager is generated by the desirability of expanding the degree of participation by employees in these decisions, while retaining the viability of representative government, including public accountability of management. This dilemma has been aptly captured by Mosher in the following:

> Participation in decisions affecting public policy by any group of citizens (including employees) not politically representative of the whole or responsible to such political representation may, in theory, and sometimes in practice, collide with that central premise of American governance . . . a polity resting ultimately on majority control through political representatives.[33]

Living with, if not completely resolving, this dilemma generated by the participation of public employees in decisions formerly reserved solely to public managers poses a now and future challenge. In developing such a *modus vivendi*, the public manager ought to begin with a comprehension of the five imperatives set forth.

NOTES

1. See, for example, A. Bilik, "Close the Gap: NLRB and Public Employees", *Ohio State Law Journal* 31 (Summer 1970): 456–489.
2. *Government Employee Relations Report (GERR)*, Reference File 71 (May 5, 1975): 201.
3. H. W. Arthurs, *Collective Bargaining by Public Employees in Canada: Five Models* (Ann Arbor: Institute of Labor and Industrial Relations, University of Michigan, 1971), p. 31.
4. National Governors' Conference, *1970 Supplement to Report: Report of Task Force on State and Local Government Labor Relations* (Chicago: Public Personnel Association, 1970), p. 31.
5. *GERR*, Reference File 32 71 (no date): 501.
6. *The Emergence of Public Sector Collective Bargaining* (Washington, D.C.: U.S. Civil Service Commission, n.d.), p. 7 (Mimeographed).

7. *Labor Relations Yearbook, 1970* (Washington, D.C.: Bureau of National Affairs, Inc., 1971), p. 501.

8. S. Zagoria, "The Future of Collective Bargaining in Government," in *Public Workers and Public Unions,* ed. by S. Zagoria (Englewood Cliffs, New Jersey: Prentice-Hall, Inc., 1972), p. 161.

9. For a very comprehensive analysis of this issue, see C. W. Summers, "Public Employee Bargaining: A Political Perspective," *Yale Law Journal,* 83 (May 1974): 1156-1200.

10. R. D. Horton, *Municipal Labor Relations in New York City: Lessons of the Lindsay-Wagner Years* (New York: Praeger Publishers, 1973), p. 123.

11. H. H. Wellington and R. K. Winter, Jr., "Structuring Collective Bargaining in Public Employment," *Yale Law Journal,* 79 (April 1970): 847.

12. A. H. Cook, "Public Employee Bargaining in New York City," *Industrial Relations,* 9 (May 1970): 267.

13. See, for example, K. Ocheltree, ed., *Six Strike Stories,* Public Employee Relations Library No. 20 (Chicago: Public Personnel Association, 1969); and J. A. Grimes, *Work Stoppages: A Tale of Three Cities* (Washington D.C.: Labor-Management Relations Service, 1970).

14. *Service Union Reporter* (October 1971), pp. 1, 12.

15. Boyarsky, "City Workers Make Their Power Felt at the Polls," *Los Angeles Times* (January 31, 1971), Sec. B, p. 1.

16. Horton, *Op. cit.,* p. 134.

17. See, generally, M. Derber, "Who Negotiates for the Public Employer?" in *Perspective in Public Employee Negotiation,* ed. by K. Ocheltree (Chicago: Public Personnel Association, 1969), pp. 52-58.

18. Fraternal Order of Police Lodge 1 and City of Pittsburgh, AAA File No. 55-30-0128-71, November 4, 1971, as quoted in *GERR* 433 (January 3, 1972): B-4.

19. J. A. Belasco, J. A. Alutto, and F. Green, "A Case Analysis of Negotiation Behavior in an Urban School System," *Education and Urban Society* 2 (November 1969): 34.

20. Vial, "The Scope of Bargaining Controversy: Substantive Issues vs. Procedural Hangups," *California Public Employee Relations,* No. 5 (November 1972), p. 14.

21. Western Assembly, *Collective Bargaining in American Government,* Report of the Western Assembly, Carmel, California (May 11-14, 1972), p. 4. (Mimeographed).

22. J. F. Burton, Jr., "Local Government Bargaining and Management Structure," *Industrial Relations* 11 (May 1972): 138.

23. F. A. Nigro, "Collective Bargaining and the Merit System," in *Unionization of Municipal Employees,* ed. by R. Connery and W. Farr (New York: The Academy of Political Science, Columbia University, 1971), p. 67.

24. L. C. Gawthrop, *Administrative Politics and Social Change* (New York: St. Martin's Press, 1971), preface.

25. Special Task Force to the Secretary of Health, Education and Welfare, *Work in America* (Cambridge, Massachusetts: The Massachusetts Institute of Technology Press, 1973), p. 22.

26. G. E. Caiden, *The Dynamics of Public Administration: Guidelines to Current Transformations in Theory and Practice* (New York: Holt, Rinehart and Winston, Inc., 1971), pp. 99-100.

27. A. Kleingartner, "Collective Bargaining Between Salaried Professionals and Public Sector Management," *Public Administration Review* 33 (March-April 1973): 171.
28. S. S. Boynton, "Industrial Collective Bargaining in the Public Sector: Because It's There?" *Catholic Law Review* 21 (Spring 1972): 525.
29. R. E. Hampton, "Federal Labor-Management Relations: A Program in Evolution", *Catholic Law Review* 21 (Spring 1972): 508.
30. See, generally, M. McLennon and M. Moscow, "Multilateral Bargaining in the Public Sector" in *Collective Bargaining in Government: Readings and Cases,* ed. by J. J. Lowewenberg and M. Moscow (Englewood Cliffs, New Jersey: Prentice-Hall, Inc., 1972), pp. 227-234; and P. Feuille, "Police Labor Relations and Multilateralism," *Journal of Collective Negotiations in the Public Sector* 3 (Summer 1974): 209-220.
31. C. A. Newland, "Collective Bargaining and Public Administration: Systems for Changing and the Search for Reasonableness," in *Collective Bargaining and Public Administration,* ed. by K. O. Warner, Public Employee Relations Library No. 34 (Chicago: Public Personnel Association, 1971), p. 15.
32. C. A. Newland, "Variety: A Public Personnal Approach," *Public Personnel Review* 28 (October 1967): p. 231-233.
33. F. C. Mosher, "The Public Service in the Temporary Society," in *Organizational and Managerial Innovation: A Reader,* ed. by L. A. Rowe and W. B. Boise (Pacific Palisades, California: Goodyear Publishing Company, Inc., 1973), p. 313.

COUNTY HOSPITAL: A ROLE PLAYING EXERCISE

GENERAL INFORMATION

Today we are going to take an inside look at the management of a large county hospital.

The class will divide itself up into groups of three persons. In each group there will be:

- one person playing Dave Jones, the Administrator (head) of County Hospital
- one person playing Chris Marshall, the Budget Director of County Hospital
- one observer, who will report back to the class on what happens when Jones and Marshall meet in conference

THE SCHEDULE FOR THIS GAME IS AS FOLLOWS:

1. (About 5 minutes.) Individuals playing the role of Dave Jones should read and familiarize themselves with their description which follows. Individuals portraying Chris Marshall should familiarize themselves with that role. But read only *your* role, *not* the other person's. The observer should read both role descriptions.
2. (About 15 minutes.) Jones and Marshall should hold their conference and explore pending management issues fully.
3. (At least 15 minutes.) Each observer should report on what transpired in their group. Then the broader issues raised by this game (revolving around performance appraisal) should be discussed.

ROLE OF DAVE JONES, ADMINISTRATOR, COUNTY HOSPITAL

You have just asked Chris Marshall, Hospital Budget Director, to come to your office for a conference. Marshall is a key member of the hospital's staff. In most respects, you regard Marshall as an ideal administrator and analyst. Chris is highly motivated, hard working, intelligent, and displays great initiative and unquestionable integrity. Under Marshall's guidance, new projects have increased steadily and the quality of budget analysis seems to have improved. Moreover, as so often happens in close working relationships, Chris is a personal friend.

You have called Chris to your office to discuss a problem which has been bothering you for the last year. Despite Chris's many virtues, there is one major problem. Younger managers and analysts in the budget office refuse to work for Marshall. Many have not stayed in Marshall's unit more than six months. They complain that Chris is authoritarian and never allows them to handle any problem on their own. Marshall is constantly looking over their shoulder and tells them exactly how to conduct even the most trivial aspects of their job.

You would like to appoint Marshall to the vacant position of Deputy Hospital Administrator. Chris has a masters degree in public administration, specializing in health care management, and is well qualified for the position. At the same time, you are afraid that you may have to *terminate* (or at least transfer) Marshall for the good of the hospital. You have spoken to Chris several times in the past about this problem, and you feel that you have made it clear that the promotion depends upon Chris's having trained a successor—someone to take over his current job when Chris is promoted.

Recently, so many bright young people have left the office that you are determined that Chris must either reverse this trend or leave himself. (You are a little behind in your paperwork and you are not aware of any memoranda Chris may have sent you lately. If Chris mentions a memo, say that you have not had a chance to read it yet.) At this point, Chris enters your office in answer to your call.

ROLE OF CHRIS MARSHALL, M.P.A.*,
BUDGET DIRECTOR, COUNTY HOSPITAL

You have just been notified that your boss, Dave Jones, the Hospital Administrator, wants to see you in his office. As you walk to his office, you wonder what Dave wants to see you about. It might be one of two things.

Maybe Dave is going to promote you to Deputy Administrator. Several times in the past year he has indicated he was thinking along these lines. As Dave put it, if you could prove yourself as Budget Director, the job would be yours. Well, your record certainly indicates you deserve the promotion! Productivity has never been higher and you have guided the budget office to a solid solution of every problem which has come up. You are damn proud of your many accomplishments, particularly in working on the latest budget.

Or Dave might want to respond to your memorandum of last week on recruitment of supervisors and trainees for the budget office. You have recommended (1.) offering substantially higher salaries in hopes of attracting better quality personnel, and (2.) instituting some sort of improved personnel testing program to weed out incompetent and irresponsible applicants.

Although you are very proud of your accomplishments, the one problem that bothers you is the quality of lower and middle managers and analysts in your unit. You have lost several of these people lately, but you were glad to see most of them go. Most of them were sullen, irresponsible, and not very bright. Most were already in jobs over their heads, and none had potential for promotion.

It has been a constant drain on your energies trying to improve the performance of these subordinates. No matter how much coaching, pleading, encouraging, and threatening you do, it seems as if you have to double-check all of their work to be sure it is done correctly. Through your watchfulness you have corrected mistakes that would have cost the county many thousands of dollars.

Dave Jones is an old personal friend, and you have enjoyed working for him. At this point you enter Dave's office.

---

*In case you did not know, an M.P.A. is a Master of Public Administration graduate degree, similar to the M.B.A. in business administration.

Missing Raise
John R. Schermerhorn, Jr.

IT WAS LATE FEBRUARY IN 1975, and John Lloyd had just completed an important long-distance telephone conversation with Professor Fred Massie, Chairman of the Department of Management at Central State University.* In the conversation John had accepted an offer to move from his present position at Private University, located in the East, to Central in the Midwest, as an Assistant Professor. After replacing the telephone receiver, John turned slowly to his wife Marsha and the following conversation ensued.

JOHN: "Well, it's final."

MARSHA: "Oh, hon, it's been a difficult decision, but I know it will work out for the best."

JOHN: "Yes, however, we are leaving many things we like here."

MARSHA: "I know, but remember, Professor Massie is someone you respect a great deal and he is offering you a challenge to come and introduce new courses at Central. Besides, he will surely be a pleasure to work for."

JOHN: "Marsha, we're young, eager, and a little adventurous. There's no reason we shouldn't go."

MARSHA: "We're going dear."

Early Fall, 1975

John Lloyd began the fall semester eagerly. The points discussed in his earlier conversations with Fred were now real challenges and John was teaching new undergraduate and graduate courses in Central's curriculum. Overall, the transition to Central had been pleasant. The nine other faculty members in the department were warm in welcoming him, and John felt it would be good working with them. John also felt comfortable with the performance standards that appeared to exist in the department. Although it was certainly not a "publish- (and count the numbers) or-perish" situation, Fred had indicated to John in their interview discussions that research and publications, along with teaching and service activities, would be given increasing weight in future departmental decisions. This was consistent with John's personal belief that a professor should live up to each of these responsibilities. Although there was some conflict evident among the faculty over the weighting of these performance areas and the standards applying to each, John felt a sense of consensus that the multiple responsibilities should be respected.

*Central State University and all persons named in this case are fictitious.

April, 1976

It was spring vacation and John was sitting at home reflecting upon his experiences to date at Central. He was pleased. Both he and Marsha had adjusted very well to midwestern life. Although there were things they both missed from their prior location, she was teaching in a very pleasant school and they found the rural environment of Central's location very satisfying. The move to Central was also working out well for John in the professional perspective. Student feedback on his fall semester courses had been very positive, he had presented two papers at a recent professional meeting, and he had just been informed that two of his other papers would be published by a journal. This was a good record and John felt satisfied. He had been working hard and it was paying off.

May, 1976

The spring semester had recently ended and John was preoccupied. It was time, he thought, for an end-of-the-year performance review by Fred Massie and to learn what his pay raise would be for the following year. This anticipation had been stimulated by a recent meeting of the College faculty in which the Dean indicated a 7% raise pool was available, but that he was encouraging department chairpersons to distribute this money differentially based on performance merit. John had listened closely to the Dean and liked what he heard. This means, he surmised, that Central is really trying to establish a performance-oriented reward system. Such a system was consistent with John's personal philosophy and, indeed, he taught such reasoning in his courses.

Throughout May John kept expecting to have a conversation with Fred Massie on the above topics. One day, the memo presented in Exhibit 3-1 (see pages 101-102) appeared in his faculty mailbox.

John read the memo with mixed emotions. Initially, he was upset that Fred had obviously made the pay raise decisions without having spoken with John about his performance first. On the whole, though, John felt good because he was sure to be one of those receiving a 9 + % increase. "Now," he mused to himself, "it will be good to sit down with Fred and discuss not only this past year's efforts, but my plans for next year as well."

John was disappointed — Fred did not contact him for such a discussion. Furthermore, John found himself frequently involved in informal conversations with other faculty members who were speculating over who received the various pay increments.

June, 1976

One day Carl Block, another faculty colleague, came into John's office and said he had asked Fred about his own raise and learned not only that he personally had received a $7 + \%$ increase, but that the two $9 + \%$ increases had been given to senior faculty members. John was incredulous. "It can't be," he imagined, "I was a top performer this past year. My teaching and publications records are strong, and I feel I've been a positive force in departmental matters in general." Still, John felt Carl could be mistaken and waited to talk the matter out with Fred.

A few days later another colleague reported to John the results of a similar conversation with Fred. This time John exploded internally. He felt he deserved a top raise. He had come to Central to work hard—he did—and he deserved just reward. The next day John received a written notice on his pay increment from the Accounting Office. His raise was 7.2%. That night, after airing his feelings with his wife, John telephoned Fred at home and arranged to meet with him the next day.

The Meeting

Fred Massie knocked on the door to John's office and entered. The greetings were cordial. John began the conversation by saying, "Fred, we've always been frank with one another and now I'm concerned about my raise. I thought I had a real good year, but I understand that I've received just an average raise." Fred Massie was a person who talked openly and John could trust him. He responded to John's inquiry in accord with this summary:

> Yes, John, you are a top performer. I feel you have made great contributions to the Department. The two $9 + \%$ raises went to correct "inequities" that had built up over a period of time for two senior people. I felt that since the money was available this year that I had a responsibility to make the adjustments. If we don't consider them, you received one of the three top raises, and I consider any percentage differences between these three very superficial. I suppose I could have been more discriminating at the lower end of the distribution, but I can't give zero increments. I know you had a good year. It's what I expected when I hired you. You haven't let me down. From your perspective I know you feel you earned an "A," and I agree. I gave you a "B + ." I hope you understand why.

John sympathized with Fred's logic and as usual felt good having spoken with him. Although he wasn't happy, he did see Fred's position. His final comment to Fred was this. "You know, it's not the absolute dollar value of the raise I didn't get that hurts—$350 more and I would have been tickled pink. It's the sense of letdown. For example, I recently turned down an extensive consulting job that would have paid far more than the missing raise merely because I felt it would require too many days away from the office. I don't see my colleagues making those kinds of choices."

July, 1976

In the course of a casual conversation Carl mentioned to John that he heard where two of the faculty receiving 4 + % raises had complained to the Department Chairman and the Dean, and had received additional salary increments. "Oh great," John responded to himself, "I thought I had put this thing to rest." He knew that this information would bother him and rekindle the irritation he had felt earlier.

Approximately three weeks later, John, Fred, Carl, and another colleague were in a meeting with the Dean. Although the meeting was on a separate matter, something was said which implied that Carl had now received an additional pay increment also. John confronted the Dean and learned that this was the case. Carl had protested to the Chairman and the Dean, and they raised his pay further on the justification that an historical inequity in his salary had been overlooked. Fred was visibly uncomfortable as a discussion ensued on the whole issue of how salary increments should be awarded and what had transpired in the department in this respect. After a time Fred left to attend another meeting. John and the others continued to discuss the matter with the Dean and the conversation became increasingly heated. Finally, they each rose to terminate the meeting and John felt compelled to say one more thing. To the Dean he said, "It's not that I'm not making enough money. But, I just don't feel I received my fair share—especially in terms of your own stated policy rewarding faculty on the basis of performance merit."

With that remark John left the meeting and, as he climbed the stairs to his office, said to himself, "Next year there will be no turning down consulting jobs because of a misguided sense of departmental responsibility."

Exhibit 3-1

MEMORANDUM

May 21, 1976

TO: Fellow Faculty

FROM: Fred

RE: Raises for Next Year

The Dean has been most open about the finances of the College as evidenced by his detail and candor regarding the 1977 budget at the last faculty meeting. Consistent with that philosophy I want to provide a perspective on raises and clarify a point or two.

The actual dollars available to our department exclusive of the chairman total 7.03%. In allocating those funds I have attempted to reward people on the basis of their contribution to the life of the Department and the University, as well as professional growth and development. In addition, it was essential this year to adjust a couple of inequities which had developed over a period of time. The distribution of increments was the following:

5% or less 3	7 + % − 9% 3
5 + % − 7% 2	More than 9% 2

Why California Fires So Few Incompetents
Darlene King Mercier

Is IT IMPOSSIBLE TO FIRE a state Civil Service employee? Not impossible — but very difficult, according to many department representatives and the attorneys who handle firing cases. The reasons for that difficulty range from human nature to red tape.

Take a look at the figures: In 1976, there were about 110,000 Civil Service employees working for the state. In that same year, there were only 175 formal dismissals. Other punitive actions were more numerous — suspensions, demotions, salary cuts, official reprimands, denial of merit pay hikes, transfers, medical terminations and so on. Also, many employees resign or take early retirements rather than wait to get fired.

But the state Civil Service system, at least in theory, is supposed to hire, retain and promote on the basis of employee merit. Why should it be so difficult to remove incompetent workers from such a system? Here are some of the reasons:

Supervisors are either not aware of the procedures necessary for punitive actions or are lax in enforcing those procedures. Some supervisors are inadequately trained, some are simply reluctant to be the "bad guy." A supervisor with a less than competent employee — especially in small departments where the supervisor is close to the employees — may find it easier to "work around" that employee than to initiate formal action that would become a permanent part of the employee's personnel file.

"Working around" an incompetent employee expands the problem, because the longer the employee works in state service with a "clean record," the more difficult it is for subsequent supervisors to build up a solid punitive action case, barring blatant misconduct. State Personnel Board summaries of punitive actions indicate that

most employees are dismissed for various kinds of misconduct, such as drunkenness on duty, insubordination, misuse of state property or inexcusable absence without leave. Rarely is "incompetence" the cause. Personnel officers and attorneys agree that misconduct is easier to identify and document than incompetence.

As Dan Keller, personnel officer at the Department of Motor Vehicles, points out, competence is "very difficult to measure, especially at the management level where decision-making, judgment, organization, ability to meet deadlines and respond to upper management and creativity" are criteria for job effectiveness.

Loren McMaster, chief counsel for the California State Employees Association, suggests another reason for the small number of dismissals for incompetence. Many incompetents, he says, are removed during their probation period. Yet the statistics don't suggest a pattern of major probationary housecleaning. From March 1976 through March 1977, the state posted 8,530 new hirings, all of which were probationary. During the same period, 11,286 employees were promoted and also placed on probation,. Yet during the same year, only 231 probationary employees were rejected and released. McMaster adds that many newly hired employees who are aware they will not be retained after probation elect to resign and thus aren't included in the rejection statistics.

Another reason department representatives cite for the difficulty in firing a Civil Service employee is the so-called "Skelly procedure." This procedure was named for a California Supreme Court decision which held that a permanent public employee's job is "property" under the Fourteenth Amendment due process clause. Thus, before that employee can be discharged or suffer other disciplinary action, he or she must be accorded "due process" which includes the following rights: to be informed in writing of the charges, to be given all materials upon which the charges are based, to be given an opportunity to present his or her side of the controversy, to be represented by a person of his or her choosing, and to have a decision rendered on whether or not disciplinary action will be taken and the degree thereof.

The disciplinary action becomes effective only after all those steps are followed. Designed to minimize the risk of error in the initial removal decision, the process has its critics. Attorney Frank Iwama, former deputy attorney general and now a private attorney, feels the Skelly procedure presents another roadblock for the state in the disciplinary procedure. Another deputy attorney general, Tal Jones, sees it differently. He says the Skelly procedure has had the positive effect of weeding out unwarranted cases or those with insufficient evidence. Eliminating the weak cases at this point saves time and money, Jones says.

The appeals process also plays a large part in the punitive action story. Most punitive actions are appealed to the State Personnel Board, and the number of appeals has risen in the past 15 years. For example, in 1960, only about half of all dismissals were appealed to the hearing office of the State Personnel Board. In the 1976 calendar year, by contrast, 75 percent of all dismissals were appealed. There seem to be two major reasons for the rise: People generally are more willing to question decisions; and the California State Employees Association and other employee groups have been increasingly aggressive in areas like punitive actions. The CSEA recognizes that the firing of a civil servant is, in McMaster's words, a "professional death sentence," and it wants to be sure the firings that do occur are justified.

If an employee requests an appeal, the hearing office of the State Personnel Board sets up a case number and file, gathers all pertinent documents and holds a hearing with the employee and the employee's counsel in attendance. The hearing officer then presents his decision to the board and the board can accept or reject that decision. If the board accepts the decision but the employee doesn't, the employee can request a rehearing. The request for rehearing is usually denied unless there has been some blatant error. Then the employee has the option of appealing the decision to the state Superior Court and, if necessary, to the Appellate Court and California Supreme Court.

Few cases ever go as far as the Supreme Court, the Skelly case being a notable exception. But cases do go to Superior Court and, according to CSEA's McMaster, this is due to problems with the State Personnel Board's hearing process. McMaster's chief criticism is that, even though the hearing officers are attorneys, they deal more with the factual questions of the case than the legal questions. The hearing process is given the status of a trial court but the decisions don't always reflect this, he says. McMaster feels that the cases that are won by CSEA have to be won in court instead of before the board, which requires a greater investment of time and money than should be necessary. State employees who do not belong to the CSEA and who can't afford to hire a private attorney for this long legal process find themselves at a disadvantage.

While there is general agreement that the SPB does uphold most of the punitive actions of the state departments, attorney Iwama thinks the cases which go as far as the SPB hearing office are solid ones, and that this explains the large number of cases upheld. McMaster's solution to the appeal problem is third-party arbitration. He believes the interests of the state and employees would be best served by an independent hearing body rendering a final and binding decision. Deputy Attorney General Jones defends the thoroughness and fairness of the State Personnel Board and considers third-party arbitration to be "anti-merit system." Allowing negotiation would defeat the basic purpose of the Civil Service system which is supposed to have the "same rules for everyone," Jones says.

The people who deal with disciplinary actions say they don't want to jeopardize the rights of civil servants, but only want the system to work the way it is supposed to. It is clear to them that one major area needs attention — that of supervisor awareness and enforcement of disciplinary procedures.

One department may serve as an example of how the system can work. It's generally agreed that the California Highway Patrol presents the best investigation packages to the attorney general's office in punitive action cases and that they lose few of their cases. This is partly explained by the fact that the CHP is a law enforcement agency itself. But Captain Jim Cole of CHP Internal Affairs believes that the department is serious about "doing their own housecleaning."

If other state departments followed the CHP example, there probably would be more dismissals of incompetent employees, fewer cases of "working around" them, and less "shuffling" of them from one department to another.

Collective Bargaining in Madison
Thomas A. Kochan

THIS (CASE) . . . WILL CONSIDER the dispute between the city of Madison, Wisconsin, and Local 311 of the International Association of Firefighters (IAFF) that grew out of the negotiations for the 1969 labor agreement. The format of the chapter will be as follows: the provisions of the Wisconsin state statute covering collective bargaining by municipal employees will be outlined in the first section; the second section will contain a brief description of the decision-making structure in the city as it related to this particular dispute; the chronology of events during the dispute will be presented in section three. . . .

Summary of the Municipal Collective Bargaining Statute

The basic legislation that enumerates the rights of municipal employees to organize or join labor organizations and which regulates the nature of bargaining in municipal employment was passed by the Wisconsin legislature in 1959. The major provisions in the law are as follows:

1. Municipal employees have the right to organize and affiliate with labor organizations of their own choosing and to be represented by such organizations in negotiations with the municipal employer on questions of wages, hours, and working conditions. The law further protects the employees' right to refrain from any such activities.
2. Municipal employers are prohibited from interfering with, coercing, restraining, encouraging, or discouraging participation of employees in a labor organization or in the exercise of an employee's rights under the law.
3. Municipal employees are prohibited from coercing, intimidating, or interfering with the legal rights of another employee under the law or of attempting to induce a municipal employer to do so.
4. The Wisconsin Employment Relations Commission (WERC) is authorized to: (a) handle cases involving prohibited practices and collective bargaining unit determinations under the law, (b) function as a mediator in disputes between municipal employees and their employers at the request of both parties, and (c) initiate fact finding procedures if after a reasonable period of negotiations a deadlock exists and either party or both parties request fact finding, or where an employer or a union fails to meet and negotiate at reasonable times in a bona fide effort at settlement.
5. All agreements between municipal employers and a labor organization representing a majority of employees in the bargaining unit must be reduced to writing. Agreements are binding only if express language to that effect is included.
6. Strikes by municipal employees are expressly prohibited.
7. Discipline and discharge cases that are covered in state or local civil service regulations are excluded from the fact finding procedures.

Decision-Making Structure in the City of Madison

The City of Madison, which has approximately 170,000 residents, has a mayor-council form of government. The mayor is elected at large and serves a two-year term of office while the 22 members of the city council are elected on a ward basis and also serve two-year terms. Decision-making responsibility concerning labor relations with uniformed personnel (police and firemen) is officially divided among six different individuals or groups. These groups and their official roles as they were structured in 1968 are outlined below.

The Mayor

The mayor is the chief executive officer of the city. State law prescribes that as one of his executive responsibilities, he "shall be the head of the fire and police departments." The mayor has the power to appoint the members of the Police and Fire Commission and department heads such as the fire chief and the personnel director. All of his appointments are subject to the approval of the Common Council. The mayor also holds the power of veto over council decisions.

The Common Council

The powers of the city councils are enumerated in state statutes as follows:

> . . . the council shall have the management and control of city property, finances, highways, navigable waters, and the public services, and shall have the power to act for its commercial benefit and for the health, safety, and welfare of the public. . . .

Another section of the statute governing municipal corporations places in the hands of the council the authority over compensation issues in the police and fire departments. The broad role provided for the council indicates the amount of discretion it enjoys in the decision-making process. It is generally accepted as the central decision-making unit in the city government. As such, it retains the ability to make the final decision on any changes that affect the city ordinances, including changes in civil service provisions and bargaining agreements.

The Police and Fire Commission, the Fire Chief, the Personnel Director, and the Bargaining Committee

The original intent of the legislature in making it mandatory for each city to establish a board of police and fire commissioners was to be construed ". . . as an enactment of statewide concern for the purpose of providing a uniform regulation of police and fire departments." The boards were given specific jurisdiction over the recruitment, promotion, and disciplinary actions in the department. The members are appointed by the mayor for a term of five years with one commissioner's term expiring each year.

The fire chief is appointed by the Police and Fire Commission. He serves as chief administrative officer in the fire department and reports to both the mayor and Police and Fire Commission.

The personnel director is the chief administrative officer for the civil service system. Part of his duties involve representing the city in the negotiation of collective bargaining agreements. He is appointed by the mayor, subject to the approval of the Common Council. He reports directly to both the mayor and the Personnel Board.

In this dispute, the Common Council Bargaining Committee was composed of five aldermen who were appointed by the mayor. The basic function of this committee was to work with the personnel director in direct negotiations with Local 311. The committee was to bring any tentative agreement reached with the union to the council as a whole for final approval.

In addition to the above six individuals or bodies, another public commission, the City Personnel Board, became directly involved in the firefighters' dispute. The personnel board is charged with overseeing the civil service system in the city and, as such, has no jurisdiction over issues involving police and fire department personnel. However, in this particular case, the Common Council specifically authorized the board to conduct a reclassification analysis of the positions in the fire department and to submit its recommendations to the Common Council. Therefore, because of this authorization, a seventh city body became involved.

Chronology of the Dispute

It has already been noted that parity between the salary levels of police and firefighters was the main issue in the dispute between the city and the union. In order to place this issue in perspective, the historical background of the parity controversy as it developed in the city will be outlined.

Like most cities in the country, Madison had a long tradition of paying equal salaries to police and firefighters at comparable classification levels in the two departments. City officials generally agreed that, prior to 1967, the Madison firefighters set the basic wage pattern through informal bargaining and lobbying with the city council and that the police association then followed the pattern set by the firefighters.

In 1963, the city commissioned the firm of Griffenhagen-Kroeger to make a comprehensive study of the civil service salary structure, this study being the first of three that brought the issue of the relationship of police and firefighters' salaries to the forefront in the city's attention. As part of their report, the consultants recommended that the traditional parity relationship be maintained.

Also in 1963, a special study of police and fire department compensation programs was undertaken for the city by the Public Administration Service. In contrast to the Griffenhagen-Kroeger report, this firm recommended that police salaries be set approximately 10 percent higher than the corresponding classifications in the fire department.

The relationship of the police and fire salaries again became the subject of a study in 1966. This time a "blue ribbon" citizens' committee was appointed by the mayor to study the relationship of police and firemen's salaries. The members of this committee were unable to reach a consensus and submitted both a majority report which favored the continuation of the parity tradition and two separate minority reports which favored an increase in police salaries relative to those of firefighters.

These three studies provided the background to the controversy over the parity issue that surfaced in the 1968 labor negotiations. They indicate the degree to which the parity issue was already a source of historical controversy in the city.

Labor Negotiations in 1967

The outcome of the 1967 negotiations between the city and the four city employee organizations had several important implications for the 1968–69 firefighters' dispute. Prior to the initiation of negotiations in 1967, the four unions established a tentative agreement to negotiate as a coalition with the city's bargaining team. However, during an early bargaining session, the Madison Professional Policemen's Association (MPPA) became dissatisfied with the joint efforts and withdrew to bargain separately. Subsequently, the firefighters and the other two unions reached an agreement with the city, while the policemen's association and the city submitted their unresolved dispute to fact finding. This greatly angered the firefighters since they saw fact finding as a threat to the traditional parity relationship. The basic wage recommendation of the fact finder called for acceptance of the pattern set by the firefighters, but more importantly, the report recommended that a long-term fact finding study be undertaken to revamp the entire salary structure in the police department. The fact finder also recommended that the police classification system be "broken out" of the overall classification system of the city and that police bargaining be conducted separately in order that "those problems which relate specifically to police officers can be dealt with individually and expeditiously."

The long-term report of the fact finder was submitted to the city council in the summer of 1968, and its recommendations for a sizable wage boost were adopted by the city and the MPPA as a substitute for wage bargaining for the 1969 contract. Consequently, prior to the initiation of bargaining between the city and the firefighters in 1968, the wage package for the police association had already been determined.

Original Request for Firefighter Reclassification

One other significant event took place prior to the beginning of negotiations in 1968. In April of that year, while the police study was in progress, the president of the firefighters' union sent a letter to the mayor requesting a reclassification study of firefighters' positions be started immediately. This request was subsequently referred to the Common Council, which in turn referred the issue to the Personnel Board, the Personnel Department, the Police and Fire Commission, and the Common Council Bargaining Committee. The Personnel Board agreed to make such a study by January 1969. This request for a reclassification analysis was to play a major role subsequently in the dispute under study.

Bargaining for the 1969 Labor Agreement

Negotiations began between the city and Local 311 in August 1968. The city bargaining team was composed of the personnel director and five members of the Common Council Bargaining Committee. In addition, the fire chief participated in the negotiations as an adviser to the city bargaining team on issues that related to the operation of the department. Any tentative agreement reached between the bargaining team and the union had to be submittted to the council as a whole for final approval. It had been agreed that the mayor would stay completely out of negotiations; therefore, the basic bargaining strategy and policy decisions were left to the discretion of the bargaining team. The personnel director was to keep the mayor informed of the team's decisions. No consultations were held with any of the other city officials in the process of determining the bargaining team's position on issues raised in negotiations.

The initial demands submitted by the firefighters called for their wages to be tied to 90 percent of the prevailing wages of the licensed trades in the state. The city, however, refused to bargain on this premise, and after two futile negotiation sessions, the firefighters' chief negotiator publicly charged the city with refusing to bargain in good faith and suggested that a mediator be called in. The city's negotiators refused. Several more bargaining sessions were held in September, but negotiations remained bogged down over the skilled trades issue. At this point negotiations were suspended and the city bargaining team suggested the use of fact finding. The union, in turn, rejected this proposal and restated its demands for a mediator.

During this time the firefighters began threatening to engage in a non-emergency work stoppage. After hearing the union negotiators discuss this possible tactic on a local television news program, a city councilman initiated a discussion of the threatened action at a meeting of the council. Several members of the council bargaining committee also participated in the discussion. This represented the first time during the dispute that a bargaining issue was publicly discussed before the council.

A week later, the union formally voted to halt all non-emergency duties by November 1 if "satisfactory results" could not be achieved by negotiations prior to that date. This move set off a series of discussions among various city officials. The fire chief gave his assessment of the state of bargaining during a meeting of the Police and Fire Commission. It was also reported that the mayor called several members of the Police and Fire Commission, the fire chief, and the personnel director together to discuss the situation.

During this time, negotiation sessions were again being held, but discussions remained deadlocked over whether mediation or fact-finding should be requested. The lack of progress prompted the union to vote to begin immediately the non-emergency work stoppage previously scheduled for November 1. The city then agreed to mediation, and although several sessions took place during the following week, the slowdown continued for ten days. On the seventh day of the slowdown, a number of union members began calling in sick. At this point, the mayor entered the dispute by calling an emergency meeting of the Common Council to request its permission to seek a temporary restraining order to halt the firefighters' limited strike action. His request was approved and the restraining order calling for the firemen to refrain from "striking under any guise whatsoever, including mass absenteeism for sickness," was obtained in Circuit Court. Under the advice of their attorney, the firefighters agreed to abide by the court order, and they returned to work. At the same time, however, the union issued a new threat to call a full scale strike by November 15 if its demands were not met. By this point, the discussion had moved away from the skilled trades wage formula and the parity issue was openly acknowledged as the basic impediment to an agreement.

When the firefighters returned to their normal duties, the fire chief added his voice to the widening dispute. He held a group meeting of on-duty firefighters in an attempt to persuade them of the inappropriateness of any further strike action. He also publicly stated his full support of the firefighters' demand for parity with the police, and his statements were reported in a newspaper article which compared his reasons for supporting the parity concept with statements of the personnel director which outlined the basic arguments of those who opposed the union demand.

The judge who issued the restraining order suggested that the parties once again return to the bargaining table and offered to act as an additional mediator if the parties so desired. The parties did hold several negotiation sessions in the next several days, this time with the mayor as a direct participant. At one point, the mayor, who in his own view was attempting to act as a mediator between the bargaining team and the union, suggested a settlement which would have given the fire-fighters parity. The city bargaining team, however, rejected the mayor's proposal. Meanwhile the union leaders threatened to introduce a resolution to the city council as a whole that would have called for a pay increase for firemen equal to that granted to the police. They also stated to reporters that they were considering taking the issue to the citizens of Madison to seek their support. The chief union negotiator was quoted as saying, "We also wish that people would put pressure on the mayor and the aldermen. We honestly feel we have the people's support."

A compromise agreement was finally reached on November 9. At a mediation session in the court chambers of the judge who issued the restraining order, the city bargaining team accepted a compromise offer suggested by the union that called for an increase in wages short of that granted to the police, along with an agreement to have the Personnel Board conduct the reclassification study originally requested by the union in April. The city bargaining committee also agreed to recommend that the council set aside sufficient funds to cover the costs of any salary changes which might be recommended by the Personnel Board. The city council and the union membership both approved this agreement and the threatened strike was averted.

The Reclassification Study and the Strike of 1969

In accordance with the November 9 agreement, the city personnel board instructed the personnel director to conduct a study of fire-fighter positions and to submit a report along with his recommendations to the board. The personnel director's report, presented to the board in February 1969, recommended no change in the basic salary level for firefighters over that which was agreed to in bargaining. The personnel board, however, voted to reject the report of the personnel director and submitted a recommendation to return to the "relationship existing prior to the 1968 negotiations between the city and other bargaining units," *i.e.*, a return to parity.

As the Common Council debated the conflicting recommendations of the Personnel Board and the personnel director during a series of meetings in February and March 1969, various city management officials, including a representative of the Personnel Board, the fire chief, and the mayor, argued before the council in support of the parity recommendation, while the personnel director and the chairman of the Police and Fire Commission spoke in favor of the personnel director's recommendation. The chairman of the Police and Fire Commission also questioned the legality of the personnel board's action in reclassifying uniformed personnel and indicated that he felt such action was under the jurisdiction of the Police and Fire Commission.

After a lengthy council debate of the issue, a final vote was taken in which the Personnel Board's recommendation was rejected. Immediately after the vote was taken, the firefighters went out on strike.

The strike lasted for three days, ending only after a 52-hour marathon bargaining session between the union and the Common Council. The final agreement called for an hourly wage increase for the firefighters which brought them to within one cent an hour of policemen's wages. The following "amnesty clause" was also included in the agreement to end the strike:

> IT IS AGREED that all legal proceedings commenced by the city presently pending against the Union and its members shall be dismissed without prejudice and without costs. It is further agreed that all causes of action whatsoever by the City which may arise or have arisen as a result of the negotiation and the strike by Union members in March, 1969, are hereby waived.
>
> Consistent with appropriate Wisconsin Statutes, it is the express policy of the City that it will not directly or indirectly commence an action that will in any way discipline any member of the Union or any employee represented by the Union for having participated in the events leading to the said strike or the participation therein or for any conduct in connection therewith.

The Suspension of the Union President

Several months after the end of the strike, a citizen of the City of Madison filed a complaint with the Police and Fire Commission charging the president of the firefighters' union with leading an illegal strike and requesting the board to conduct a disciplinary hearing on the charge. The board agreed to hear the complaint and subsequently found the union president guilty of the charge and suspended him from his position in the fire department for six months. Although the commission was aware of the amnesty clause in the bargaining agreement, it argued that (1) such a clause was illegal, and (2) the commission was not a subordinate body of the city council and, therefore, was not bound by the agreement. The union then appealed the commission's ruling to the Circuit Court and succeeded in getting the commission's decision reversed and the union leader reinstated in his job.

The action of the Police and Fire Commission served as the final chapter in the chronology of events in the lengthy dispute between the city and the firefighters. . . .

4

Organization Structure

PURPOSE

The purpose of this chapter is to explore the aspects of administrative organization in state and local government, focusing on the issues associated with reorganization.

CONTENTS

Reading
> Frederick C. Mosher, "Some Notes on Reorganizations in Public Agencies"

Case
> "Organizing Human Services in Florida"

Instructions

Pre-Class Preparation

Read "Some Notes on Reorganizations in Public Agencies." Then read and analyze the case, "Organizing Human Services in Florida," and respond to the questions below:

1. What were the reasons for reorganization in Florida?

2. Which were the key actors, roles, and interrelationships in Florida's reorganization of its Department of Health and Rehabilitative Services?

3. How does the political setting influence administrative reorganization? Why does reorganization almost always seem to become so politicized?

4. How will the intended beneficiaries of human services in the State of Florida fare through the change process?

5. What problems in implementing the new pattern of organization might be anticipated?

6. If you were a state official in another state, what lessons could you learn from the Florida experience?

Procedure for Class Meeting

Discuss "Organizing Human Services in Florida" and governmental administrative organization generally.

For Additional Information

An outstanding collection on government reorganization is Frederick C. Mosher, *Governmental Reorganization: Cases and Commentary* (Indianapolis: Bobbs-Merrill, 1967).

The literature on organizational structure and organization design is nicely summarized in Jay R. Galbraith, *Organization Design* (Reading, Mass.: Addison-Wesley, 1977).

President Carter's interest in reorganization is the current thrust in a long history of federal government reorganization. The highlights of the politics of federal government organization may be found in the following:

Harold Seidman, *Politics, Position, and Power: The Dynamics of Federal Organization*, 2d ed. (New York: Oxford University Press, 1975). Paperback edition available; probably the best place to start.

Tyrus G. Fain, ed., *Federal Reorganization: The Executive Branch* (Ann Arbor, Mich.: R.R. Bowker, 1977). A compendium in Bowker's Public Document Series.

Harvey C. Mansfield, "Reorganizing the Federal Executive Branch: The Limits of Institutionalization," *Law and Contemporary Problems,* XXXV (Summer 1970), pp. 461–495.

Herbert Emmerich, *Federal Organization and Administrative Management* (University, Ala.: University of Alabama Press, 1971).

Rufus E. Miles, Jr., *A Cabinet Department of Education: Analysis and Proposal* (Washington: American Council on Education, 1976). Paperback edition available.

Still focused on the federal scene but somewhat more bureaucratic in their focus are:

Anthony Downs, *Inside Bureaucracy* (Boston: Little, Brown and Company, 1967).

Herbert Kaufman, *Are Government Organizations Immortal?* (Washington: The Brookings Institution, 1976). Paperback edition available.

With regard to local government organization, the work of the National Municipal League and the International City Management Association should not be ignored. *National Civic Review* and *Public*

Management, the journals of these two organizations, respectively, often treat organizational issues. Also see:

Model City Charter, 6th ed. (New York: National Municipal League, 1964). Paperback edition available.
Richard J. Stillman, *The Modern City Manager: A 1971 Profile* (Washington: International City Management Association, 1971). Pamphlet.

Important broader works include:

Louis C. Gawthrop, *Bureaucratic Behavior in the Executive Branch: An Analysis of Organizational Change* (New York: The Free Press, 1969).
Gerald Caiden, *Administrative Reform* (Chicago: Aldine, 1969).

There has been a significant amount of state level reorganization in recent years. For example, see:

George A. Bell, "States Make Progress with Reorganization Plans," *National Civic Review,* LXI (March 1972), pp. 115–119, 127.
Elizabeth H. Haskel and Victoria S. Price, *State Environmental Management* (New York: Praeger, 1973). Paperback edition available. Focuses on reorganization of state environmental agencies in nine states.
Neal R. Peirce, "State/Local Report: Structural Reform of Bureaucracy Grows Rapidly," *National Journal,* VII (April 5, 1975), pp. 502–508.

The organization of government in the United States is based on a federal system. Intergovernmental relations influence the formation of public policy as well as its implementation. Some key works on federalism and intergovernmental relations include:

George F. Break, *Intergovernmental Fiscal Relations in the United States* (Washington: The Brookings Institution, 1967). Dated but still valuable.
Martha Derthick, *New Towns In-Town: Why a Federal Program Failed* (Washington: The Urban Institute, 1972). Paperback edition available.
Daniel J. Elazar, *American Federalism: A View from the States,* 2d ed. (New York: Thomas Y. Crowell, 1972). Paperback edition available.
Parris N. Gendening and Mavis Mann Reeves, *Pragmatic Federalism* (Pacific Palisades, Cal.: Palisades Publishers, 1977). Paperback edition available.
Thomas H. Kieffer, *The Political Impact of Federal Aid on State and Local Governments* (Morristown, N.J.: General Learning Press, 1974). Paperback edition available.
Martin Landau, "Federalism, Redundancy and System Reliability," *Publius,* III (Fall 1973).
Jerome T. Murphy, "Title I of ESEA: The Politics of Implementing Federal Education Reform," *Harvard Educational Review,* XLIC (February 1971), pp. 35–63.
Gary Orfield, "Federal Policy, Local Power, and Metropolitan Segregation," *Political Science Quarterly,* LXXXIX (Winter 1974–75), pp. 777–802.
Michael D. Reagan, *The New Federalism* (New York: Oxford University Press, 1972). Paperback edition available.

James L. Sundquist, with the collaboration of David W. Davis, *Making Federalism Work* (Washington: The Brookings Institution, 1969). Paperback edition available.

Deil S. Wright, *Understanding Intergovernmental Relations* (Scituate, Mass.: Duxbury Press, 1978). Paperback edition available; unusually good synthesis.

Anyone studying intergovernmental problems should become familiar with the work of the Advisory Commission on Intergovernmental Relations. Publications of the ACIR include: *Improving the Federal Grants Management* (1977), *The States and Intergovernmental Aids* (1977), and *Pragmatic Federalism* (1976).

Regarding the impact of revenue sharing, see:

Richard P. Nathan, Allen D. Manvel, Susannah E. Calkins, and associates, *Monitoring Revenue Sharing* (Washington: The Brookings Institution, 1975).

Richard P. Nathan, Charles F. Adams, Jr., and associates, *Revenue Sharing: The Second Round* (Washington: The Brookings Institution, 1977). Paperback edition available.

Regarding the administration of human services, a useful compendium is Wayne F. Anderson, Bernard J. Frieden, and Michael J. Murphy, eds., *Managing Human Services* (Washington: International City Management Association, 1977).

Some Notes on Reorganizations in Public Agencies
Frederick C. Mosher

STUDENTS OF PUBLIC ADMINISTRATION as well as the majority of our educated citizenry have long associated and even identified the word *reform* in the administrative realm with *reorganization*. There is ample etymological justification for such an association. *Reform* has literal origins in the giving of new or different form to something; and, in treating organizational matters, new form signifies new organizational structure. *Reform* has a strong normative connotation: as a noun, it signifies "change for the better"; as a verb, "to change from bad to good." *Reorganization,* though somewhat more restricted and precise in its definition, has come to acquire nearly the same meaning in American culture, both in its descriptive and in its normative senses. For a good many decades, American students—and probably the citizenry in general—have relied upon reorganization as a principal tool as well as symbol of administrative improvement, i.e., of reform. At least since the advocacy of the strong-mayor system before the turn of the century, municipal reform has been nearly synonymous with improvement in administrative structure—the commission plan, the council-manager plan, and, more recently in large cities, the mayor-administrator plan. A parallel emphasis has occurred in the states and the national government during the last half-century, beginning with the report of the Taft Commission in 1912 and 1913 and including in its sweep the wave of state reorganizations begun during the ensuing decades and renewed after World War II, as well as the studies of the Brownlow Committee and the two Hoover Commissions. The proposals of most of these groups emphasized the realignment of powers among agencies and officials and the rearrangement of functions and activities. Most of these studies aimed to promote "economy and efficiency" and were so justified; indeed, one or the other, or both, of these words found their way into the names of many of these commissions.

Faith in reorganization as an important instrument of administrative improvement is exhibited at governmental levels well below these sweeping jurisdiction-wide surveys—in individual departments and agencies, divisions, sections, field offices. Efforts to reorganize at these levels are less generally known to the public, but they are a common event in the official lives of most bureaucrats and, over the long pull, they may well have more impact than those more widely heralded. It is probable that such internal efforts to reorganize occur most frequently in new agencies whose programs, procedures, and personnel are still in flux, like the Office of Economic Opportunity; in agencies whose programs are controversial and vulnerable, like that whose current name is the Agency for International Development; and in those operating in a situation of high pressure and rapid change, such, for example, as the military departments during wartime and Cold War time, or the National Aeronautics and Space Administration. Overt efforts at reorganization seem to have been less frequent among those older agencies which are more or less protected from political exposure and from rapid changes in demands, in environment, and in technology. But even among these they do occur. In fact, reorganization in one or another agency and of one kind or another is a common though sporadic phenomenon in governments at all levels.

It is somewhat surprising that there has been so little dispassionate and objective analysis of public reorganizations. Many practitioners and many students of public administration have taken part in studies and in decisions intended to bring about reorganization. But rather few have looked back systematically at their experience and the experience of others in order to relate their efforts to the context in which they were working and to assess the effects of their efforts in the ongoing process of administrative development.

More specifically, there has been rather little objective treatment of three aspects of reorganization: (1) the underlying reasons and occasion for it in the changing context within which an agency or a group of agencies operates; (2) the process whereby it is carried out (or fails); (3) the appraisal of its actual effects on the operations of the agencies concerned. Although students of administration have contributed a great deal of thought and imagination to the bringing about of reorganization, they have devoted little scholarly attention to the totality of the process or to the later assessment of effects. Most of our work has been normative and prescriptive—a description of what is, followed by a prescription of what should be. It is typically represented by the familiar "before" and "after" charts—two still pictures lacking in the dimension of motion, of the dynamic process whereby the "after" supersedes the "before."

Yet the study of reorganization processes has a particular value for students of organization in general. As anyone who has survived a reorganization process—and this includes most of us—well knows, major organizational change or just the threat of change can be a traumatic experience in the career of an agency and in the lives of many of its members. It brings to the surface the aspirations, the anxieties, the conflicts, the motivations which are in more normal times submerged or sublimated—not easily recognized by observers of day-to-day administrative operations. From it we may be able to note and analyze attitudes and responses that are only faintly detectable during more normal times.

The paragraphs that follow contain some tentative observations and hypotheses which are directed principally to the first two questions above (the reasons for and the process of reorganization). They are based upon three principal sources of information. First are the previous writings in this field, admittedly few and thin although there are prominent exceptions. Second are my own observations and experiences with reorganizations in government. Third and perhaps most important are my interpretations of a series of about one dozen case studies of governmental reorganizations which were carried on under the auspices of the Research Committee of the Inter-University Case Program and the Institute of Governmental Studies of the University of California, Berkeley. These cases were focused upon efforts, successful and unsuccessful, to reorganize governmental agencies at national, state, and municipal levels of government. Although their primary intent was to test the empirical validity of the hypothesis of participation as an effective instrument in bringing about success in organizational change, they shed much light upon the reorganization process in general.[1]

Incremental Change and Episodic Change

Organization itself is an essentially static concept implying regularized behaviors, rules and roles, activities and relationships. It relies heavily upon predictability of actions and responses; and it implies a considerable degree of continuity and stability through time. It is interesting to note that even those organizations whose business it is to bring about change in the matters with which they deal and in the world around them are often, if not usually, internally stable and appear resistant to internal change. Thus a university, a good part of whose mission is the enlargement of knowledge, the improvement of research method, and the transmission of new knowledge and method to students, may be among the most conservative of institutions so far as its internal policies, rules, and relationships are concerned. The same is often true of research laboratories, of psychiatric clinics, and of government budget offices. Change is their business, but within themselves is a remarkable stability.

Yet it is a commonplace of most observers of governmental organizations in the United States — and of observers of private organizations as well — that change occurs over time within organizations, sometimes very dramatically. Its pace and dimensions vary enormously among different agencies and within the same agencies at different times. The expectability of organizational change has come to be nearly a hallmark of our society, sharply distinguishing it from many of the so-called primitive societies in which a significant institutional change was — and in some places still is — a threat to the social structure and to the survival of the culture.

Paul Appleby, in one of the earliest and still one of the most insightful essays on the subject, distinguished between two types of organizational change.[2] These he labeled, respectively, *constant* change and *episodic* change. The first, which is herein referred to as *incremental* change, has to do with the daily and weekly modifications in organizations, the continuing adjustments, none of which are conceived as "reorganizations" although many are consciously and purposefully planned and carried out. They include, for example, the shift of recruitment standards, the reclassification of a position, the promotion of an incumbent, the expansion or contraction of a budget, the addition of a new activity, the opening of a field office. More important and more subtle than these official and structural modifications are the changes in the members of the organization and in their relationships — their attitudes toward their jobs and toward organizational purpose, their developing skills, habits, and work ways, the routinization and modification of procedures, and others. Finally, there are changes arising from outside the organization, from the dynamics of the social context in which it works which are the sources of changing policies, changing emphasis in programs, changing clientele relationships, and many others.

Over the course of years, such incremental modifications in the workings of an organization can be and perhaps usually are enormous, even though no one of them would qualify as a "reorganization" in the usual sense. Like members of a growing family, the members of the organizations themselves are perhaps least likely to notice such changes and their impact as they happen, but an observant visitor or consultant who comes back after two or three or five years is often struck by the transformation that has occurred in his absence. Such alterations over a period of time are as significant as any which consciously planned reorganizations might bring about, but some elements in every organization are more resistant to incremental change than others, leading over the years to internal maladjustments between the elements which have responded rapidly and easily to dynamic forces and those which have not. Among the latter may be included work habits, attitudes, particularly of older personnel toward their agency and their jobs, long-established routines, and venerable traditions. Thus, paradoxically, it is the cumulation of small changes which periodically creates the requirement for comprehensive and systematic efforts.

Among government agencies in particular the difficulty of modifying the legal basis for programs and procedures in constitutions, statutes, charters, and regulations is often a major source of organizational lag. In other words, what Appleby has referred to as *episodic* reorganization may be best understood as a requisite periodic process to bring obsolescent elements in the organization up to date. In fact it may be postulated that every organization should undergo such an episodic reorganization as a matter of course every few years, its frequency dependent upon the nature and severity of such lags. It is this kind of episodic change, herein referred to simply as *reorganization*, to which we address ourselves. As distinguished from incremental change, it is characteristically planned, intended, and to some degree comprehensive. It is viewed by its participants not as an adjustment but in fact as a reorganization.

Underlying Reasons for Reorganization

Examination of the reorganization cases referred to earlier suggests that this kind of partial obsolescence was an underlying reason for reorganization in almost every instance. They arose from a failure or partial failure of the organization to respond to the dynamics of new times in one or more of six different dimensions. The first of these was simply *growth* — growth in size, growth in workload, growth in scope, etc. There has been an unfortunate absence of research on the effects of growth upon organizational structure, especially in government agencies.[3] It is a matter of common observation that large organizations are structured differently than small ones, even when their objectives and functions are exactly the same. For example, a growing organization, initially organized on a functional basis, must at some point move to a unitary structure (on the basis of clientele or geography or materials dealt with) because of the multiplying difficulties of communication and coordination and the congestion of procedures as among different related functions. Growth must certainly be a major underlying reason for decentralization and regionalization of both decision-making and operations. It may be noted also that the reverse process, contraction, can usually be expected to have the opposite effect upon structure.

A second source of obsolescence is the failure to respond adequately to *shifting problems and needs* in the area of activity in which the agency is operating. Public programs in the international field and in social and economic fields at home are replete with examples of this. In the field of public health the emergence of environmental health problems and of chronic disease are gradually surpassing in importance the more traditional emphasis upon sanitation and communicable disease. The mushrooming growth of metropolitan areas is having tremendous impact on virtually all domestic programs of government and indirectly upon their organization structures. The transformation of our foreign policy and the international programs to carry it out since World War II has been virtually total, and the repeated efforts to reorganize our foreign policy agencies are basically a structural response to rapidly changing demands.

A third source of obsolescence, usually related to the second, is *changes in the role of government* itself, both in the field of activity in which an individual agency operates and in the larger arena of governmental activities that are related to that field. Such changes in turn are a reflection of governmental response to the dynamics of the social and economic context within which governments operate. Thus, the growing responsibilities of cities in the fields of transportation (airports, freeways), of physical development (housing, urban renewal, open spaces), and of social development (the poverty program, civil rights) have almost everywhere created organizational maladjustments, giving rise to needs for reorganization. The explosions of the responsibilities of the national government in the past three decades have given rise to even more striking organizational obsolescence in almost every field—economic programs, social and welfare programs, military programs, natural resource development, science, research, and education. Our national response to new problems and new programs has, at least since the beginning of the New Deal, been typically opportunistic. New agencies are set up for each new problem area— the alphabet agencies of the New Deal, the hodge-podge of war agencies, more recently the Peace Corps and the poverty program's Office of Economic Opportunity. Later, when the emergency has subsided, or at least the new programs have matured from the stage of newness to one of "normalcy," we undertake the arduous business of integrating them with older ones where logic might have dictated their location in the first place.

The history of federal bureaus, many of which long antedate the great depression, illustrates another kind of obsolescence: that arising from the *changing shape and character of the administrative structure in general*—and outside of the internal functioning of the individual bureaus themselves. Some were initially established as independent units, at least partially because there appeared at the time no appropriate department in which to house them. Others were located in departments which, at the time, were clearly the most appropriate places for them. But over the course of decades, the accepted missions and scope of the departments changed and the berths became increasingly awkward to the point, in a few instances, of absurdity. Good examples of this phenomenon are provided by the older bureaus which were brought together under the canopy of the Federal Security Agency, later the Department of Health, Education, and Welfare:

Bureau	Department of Origin	Date of Origin
Public Health	Treasury	1798
Office of Education	Interior	1867*
Food and Drug Administration	Agriculture	1907†
Children's Bureau	Labor	1912‡

*The Office of Education was originally established in 1867 and became part of the Department of the Interior in 1869.

†Carried on under various titles from 1907 to 1930 when it received its current title.

‡Originally in the Department of Commerce and Labor, the Bureau moved to the newly separated Department of Labor in 1913.

The original location of each of these bureaus was entirely proper and logical in terms of the then current roles and structures of the then federal departments.

A fourth source of organizational obsolescence, actual or potential, is the *development of new technology, new kinds of equipment,* and *new knowledge* which are applicable in the performance of agency activities. The introduction of automated equipment and automatic data processing is best known in this category today. Very often, the decision to install new equipment of this sort occasions a simultaneous major reorganization; or sometimes, after halting efforts at incremental adjustments, a major reorganization follows. The effects of automation appear to be in some ways opposite and counteracting to the effects of growth cited above. By mechanizing routine decisions, automation changes the kinds of decisions that must be made by human minds as well as the kinds of processes that must be carried on by human hands. The role of top and middle management, and the introduction of management specialists and programmers, so alter ongoing individual functions and relationships that a major reorganization becomes almost inevitable.

A fifth source of organizational obsolescence is the *changing qualifications of personnel* in the fields of operation in which an agency works. This arises principally from changes in the educational system and its reflection of new and enlarging knowledge in different fields that are relevant to an agency's responsibilities. These changes in education may themselves be a response to changing problems and needs (second item above) of government agencies and may be initiated or stimulated by the agencies themselves. There is evidence that a good many of the professional schools in the United States were developed in response to such emerging governmental needs. Two of the best examples are the fields of forestry and agricultural sciences, but more recently we may cite social welfare, foreign area specialization, nuclear physics, and many specialized fields devoted to health research. In several of the cases of reorganizations cited earlier an underlying motivation was to enhance the qualifications, the stature, and the prestige of some of the professional personnel—biologists and wild life experts for fish and game wardens, psychiatrists in the field of mental health, public health officers, and others.

Finally, organizational obsolescence may arise from *actions taken by higher echelons* of a department or government or by higher levels of government. These may take the form of basic policy and program changes or of reorganizations, initiated and sometimes enforced from above, which make the current structure obsolescent in terms of the total organizational context. Thus, a basic change in structure at the headquarters of an agency may have the effect, directly or indirectly, of forcing a complementary reorganization in its field offices. Likewise, higher levels of government, through new and changed grant-in-aid programs, have brought about fundamental organizational changes in the recipient jurisdictions, sometimes making a reorganization a condition of receiving the grant. Reorganizations thus encouraged or imposed from above have had, over the years, enormous impact upon the structures of states, counties, cities, and districts in such fields as highways, welfare, public health, and education.

Goals of Reorganization

In the foregoing section I have suggested that "episodic" reorganizations are a response to organizational obsolescence which has not been met by incremental adjustments; and I have cited six sources of such obsolescence which appear to be frequent. Reorganizations, however, may not be perceived in the general and impersonal terms indicated above by those who sponsor them. Nor are they usually perceived primarily as efforts to achieve greater economy and efficiency in the narrow and traditional senses of those terms. It would appear that the majority of reorganization efforts stem from the initiative of the top management of individual agencies—departments and bureaus and major divisions. The reorganization objectives of these officials may for convenience be classified in four major categories.[4]

First and most frequent are goals related to the *changing of operating policies and programs,* and frequently the expansion of the scope and extent of programs. In some instances, the goal is to implement or to make feasible a shift in program emphasis already decided upon; in others, its aim is to shift the loci of power in such a way as to facilitate desired program changes later. In either case the basic goals have to do with the broad directions and extensiveness of the substantive operations of the agency.

A second category of goals is directed toward the *improvement of administrative effectiveness* in the carrying out of existing agency responsibilities. In a good many instances, the improvement of administration is seen as a corollary or a secondary objective to accompany changes in program. And in very few cases is the improvement of administration omitted from the stated goals of an aspiring reorganizer. The administrative objectives may themselves be classified in five main categories: (1) increased control at the top and thus presumably better-coordinated operations, (2) decentralization of decision-making and operations, (3) increase in productivity and/or improved quality (efficiency), (4) reduction of costs in carrying on going programs (economy), and (5) the application of administrative principles.

It is interesting that among the cases referred to earlier the goal of economy was dominant only once, and then in connection with the installation of automated equipment. And efficiency, as defined above, also occurred only once as a dominant objective. "Administrative principles," though usually advanced in terms of economy and efficiency, appear to carry some independent force of their own: only seldom could any clear-cut relationship be established between organizational performance and principles such as clear-cut lines of authority and responsibility, symmetry and propriety of the organization chart, and limited spans of control. It was not a dominant goal in any case, though it was a secondary aim and provided justification in many of them.

A third type of goal for reorganization has to do more or less specifically with *personnel*, their qualifications, their welfare, their job satisfaction, their advancement, and in a few instances the removal or alleviation of individual personnel problems. As has already been indicated, reorganization is often seen as a device whereby qualifications and the performance of personnel can be upgraded. The realignment of activities and responsibilities is sometimes helpful in this regard and, in instances where there is some type of position classification system, it is virtually essential. In some reorganizations a major objective is the elimination of sources of employee unrest and unhappiness or, more positively, the enhancement of opportunities for advancement of individuals and groups and the enlargement of jobs. In fact some reorganizations are a direct response to employee demands of this kind. While comprehensive reorganizations to eliminate individual personnel problems are seldom so acknowledged, it appears that many are used in part for this purpose.

Finally, reorganizations are sometimes undertaken in response to, or in anticipation of, *criticism or threat* from the outside — whether another agency of the administration, the legislature, or pressure interests. Our studies suggest that such stimuli are fairly frequent provocations for organizational surveys, sometimes initiated and conducted from outside the agency itself, sometimes carried on from within to forestall outside action. They may explain the high frequency of reorganization efforts in agencies like AID whose programs are constantly under criticism. Such reorganization efforts are essentially protective or defensive in nature.

The Setting of Agency Reorganizations

A reorganization is by definition a change or a set of changes in a going system of relationships established and internalized over a period of time. That is, the organization which is to be changed has a history. It is here hypothesized that every such complex organization includes among its members individuals and groups whose ambitions, aspirations, and views of organizational purpose are in some degree at variance with one another. There are within each such organization, at least in latent form, *tensions* in the relationships among its different members.[5] There are also frequently links between such internal tensions and the groups and individuals outside the organization who are concerned with its activities — in the executive branch, in the legislature, among clientele and other pressure groups. Some of these external tensions often parallel and support some of the internal ones. That is, there are individuals and groups outside, whose views and influence can be expected to coincide with those of some organizational members and who can exercise their influence in appropriate directions when the occasion arises.

In the other direction, outsiders may call upon allies within the organization to gain bureaucratic support. Intraorganizational tensions within many agencies are a kind of mirror of continuing tensions of competing groups within the government and in the society as a whole. Among some of the embattled agencies which have little articulate external support and are laboring under a barrage of external criticism the tension may exist between organized external groups and the agency as a whole. Such a situation may contribute to the drawing together of the agency internally and the consequent reduction in the virulence of the internal tensions which might otherwise be expected. In the absence of issues or crises, tensions of these kinds may normally be considered to be latent and inactive. They rise to the surface when a particular problem or action out of the ordinary run of things activates them. A reorganization or a threat to reorganize is usually such an event in so far as it promises or proposes a shift in power over agency purpose and over the relative status and advancement opportunities of different individual groups. In fact reorganization may be a particularly useful time to study an organization for this very reason; it permits an examination of the underside of the iceberg.

The study of a number of reorganization efforts reveals certain common and expectable types of tensions, even in organizations having vastly different purposes and activities. Thus complex public organizations typically include two or more different professional groups vying with each other for influence, recognition, and status. This situation differs from that discussed in much of the literature on private business where stress is laid upon the tension between management and worker on the one hand or between management and professionals on the other. In many or most public agencies management itself at the very top is normally a professional group in a functional field such as public health, psychiatry, forestry, and military. This top professional group seems usually to be the one whose field of specialism is historically identifiable with the overall function of the agency. But there are always other professions or sub-professions also engaged in agency work — administrative support officers such as budget, supply, personnel, legal officers, and usually operating personnel in related professional fields such as engineers, nurses, librarians, etc. Almost every reorganizational proposal involves or at least suggests a shift in the going power and status situations as among these different professional groups.

Another expectable kind of tension usually closely related to the first arises from different views as to organizational purposes and the relative emphasis to be given in the agency program to different kinds of problems. As indicated earlier, shifting emphases on purpose are perhaps the principal goals of reorganization as seen by their initiators.

A third common type of tension is that between higher and lower echelons of an agency: the pull of the higher level to maintain or enhance control and power over the lower *versus* the pull of the lower echelon for a greater degree of autonomy and self-control. This centrifugal-centripetal tension occurs both within the agency and perhaps at every level thereof, and between the agency as a whole and outside groups such as the chief executive, his staff agencies such as the budget bureau, and the legislature. It is closely related and sometimes identical with another type of tension: that between individuals and groups seeking to maintain or preferably enlarge programs and those seeking to restrain or contract programs.

Finally there is the kind of tension frequently found within agencies between those favoring the established and secure ways of doing things and those desirous of innovation and change. This is the well-known conflict between the old and the new, the conservative and the liberal. It is likely to be found among different groups of personnel: the senior *versus* the junior, the old *versus* the young, the high seniority *versus* the low seniority.

There are clearly a number of other kinds of tensions found in different kinds of organizations, such as tensions between management and labor, tensions between members of elite career services and others not so favored, tensions between political officers and career officers, tensions arising out of educational attainment, social and religious groups, sex and race differences, and personality clashes. But the ones listed above appear to be more or less generic and predictable in almost every organization and for the purposes of this discussion to be fundamental elements in the situations in which reorganizations are attempted. In our study of individual reorganization cases we found that almost every reorganization attempt had a considerable background in the agency's recent history. In most cases there had been one or more earlier efforts to reorganize and most of these earlier attempts were only partly successful or were truly unsuccessful. The themes of the subsequent reorganizations were usually fundamentally similar to the earlier ones and the kinds of continuing tensions revealed were also similar.

The Reorganization Process

Reorganizations which are undertaken by and within individual agencies for the most part follow a fairly standard sequence of steps: (1) a spark, (2) a study leading to the development of a plan, (3) consideration, negotiation, and decision, (4) a study or studies on how to put the plan into effect, and (5) implementation. The sequence is not pursued religiously in every instance. Where the basic decision (step 3) is negative, the last two steps, of course, do not occur. Sometimes the initial planning includes a fairly detailed plan for implementation and the fourth step is omitted. And in a few instances there is no study at all where prior information is considered to be adequate for the decision. Each of these steps is discussed briefly in the succeeding paragraphs.

The Spark

Most organizations in the normal course of events operate in what may be considered to be a condition of dynamic equilibrium. That is, those individuals and groups who desire a major change in one direction are balanced against those desiring no change or desiring a change in the other direction. Or the desirability of the change, even when the bulk of persons concerned would favor it, is more than overbalanced by the upset and the dangers implicit in a major reorganization. One may therefore ask why in such a situation is reorganization undertaken? What is it that upsets the equilibrium of continuity and stability? The answer seems to be some particular event or combination of events which temporarily unhinges the equilibrium and makes possible the serious consideration of basic organizational change. This I have labeled a "spark." The spark need not be directly related to the organization's inner structure. And it appears from our review of reorganization cases that the spark is more often than not ignited from outside the agency itself; that is, although the main problems and the main tensions encountered in reorganization may be internal, their ignition is usually consequent upon some external event beyond the control of the agency or any of its members.[6] Our cases suggest that the most frequent kind of spark is a change in leadership at the very top of an agency. This may be the consequence of an election of a new chief executive or it may result from the retirement or resignation of the agency's head. In any case, it appears that a successor for at least a temporary period following his appointment has a freer hand, a "honeymoon period," for the consideration of organization changes. In fact, in many instances he is expected by both his superiors and his subordinates to bring about such changes, and in a few instances his own appointment is conditioned on the understanding that he will reorganize.

A second kind of spark is a significant change in the agency's budget by the legislature or by the executive budget agency.

A third is a criticism or a threat to the agency or to a major part of it from the outside — the chief executive or his staff, a legislative committee, or outside pressure groups. A major mistake or calamitous event in agency operations may give rise to outside criticism which in turn ignites a spark for reorganization.

Illustrative of the reorganization sparks in the case studies were the following: (1) replacement, on the retirement of an agency head, by his erstwhile deputy, (2) appointment of a new agency head from outside following the election of a new governor, (3) refusal by central budget agency to consider a proposed budgetary increase until a major reorganization study had been made, (4) protest by an organized clientele group against a proposed increase in fees, conveyed to a legislative committee which thereupon ordered a study, (5) proposal by a chief executive's staff unit that a particular division be transferred from one department to another, and (6) suggestion by leaders of a legislative committee that they would require by law that an agency set up a new bureau to handle certain kinds of activities. Most interesting for our purposes is that, whereas the situation, the problems, and the tensions which reorganizations confronted were largely internal and had existed and been recognized for some time, the ignition of efforts to do something about them in almost every instance came from some event outside the agency in question.

Reorganization Studies

The initial gestation of thinking and negotiation as to whether a reorganization attempt should be undertaken and the scope of studies leading to such projected reorganization is usually carried on by the top agency executive and a small coterie of officials and advisers close to him. Where he feels it advisable to obtain informal approval in advance from above and outside the agency — its superior executive, the budget bureau, the personnel office, the appropriate legislative committee — representatives of these groups are consulted. At this stage, however, the discussions are typically a closely guarded secret within a small, narrowly circumscribed number of officers. The decisions made at this stage — as to the "givens" and the constraints within which the study is to be made, the methods to be pursued, the problems on which the study is to focus, and perhaps most of all who will make the study—are crucial. For they to a substantial extent determine the kinds of recommendations which will be forthcoming and the degree to which such recommendations will prove to be feasible of accomplishment. In fact, it is probable that most skilled administrators can predict in advance the general nature of recommendations that will emanate from a study on the basis of the way it is set up.

Thus a study may be purely exploratory with no prior instructions as to directions and focus; it may be specifically directed to the solution of particular problems, itemized in some detail; or it may fall at some point on the continuum between these extremes. It may be limited to the consideration of possible actions which appear to be politically and administratively feasible to the boss; it may be initiated with instructions to seek the best possible answers without any regard to their practicability;[7] or it may fall somewhere on the continuum between these two extremes. With regard to scope, it may be sweeping, covering all aspects of an agency operation; it may focus only on certain elements of structure, policy, and procedure; or it may be comprehensive with the exception of certain areas of operation which are declared "off limits." Finally it may be directed to the determination of the goals and objectives for the organization to pursue in the future, or it may be limited to the problems of implementing goals that are already decided. In all of these dimensions, the initiatory decision of the authority who sets the study under way to a substantial extent predetermines the nature of the study and the report which it will produce.

Just as important is the prior determination of what individuals or groups will participate in the study and in what ways. Accompanying this question and often of major significance are the prior determinations as to whom the report will be addressed to; in what form and with what specificity it will be prepared; how much time will be permitted for the study; and at what stages and to whom the copies of the written report, if any, will be made available.

It is useful to consider different kinds of study groups as falling on a continuum between those completely outside the organization concerned and presumably outside its direct control and influence on the one hand, and those completely inside the organization and immediately subject to the control and influence of the top line officials. At the extreme outside end of the continuum might appear a commission of private citizens established under authority of a legislative body or the chief executive, or a legislative investigating commission, or a mixed Hoover-type commission. At the extreme inside end of the continuum might be a study conducted by the principal executive himself without any assistance. In between would lie a variety of arrangements such as the use of private consultants, outside staff agencies, inside staff agencies, and line personnel. A hypothetical pattern of possible arrangements for organization studies is shown below.

Outside-Inside Continuum of Reorganization Study Groups in Rough Order of Relationship to Agency Studied

Outside

private citizen groups, established and reporting to superior executive and/or legislature
legislative committee or group responsible to it
mixed or "Hoover Commission" group
private consultant, engaged by and reporting to legislative body or to chief executive or his staff
private consultant, engaged outside of agency by superior and reporting to him
government staff agency without agency invitation and reporting above or outside agency

Intermediate

private consultant working with agency officials on agency invitation and reporting to agency head
outside staff agency, working with agency officials on agency invitation and reporting to agency head

Inside

agency staff personnel, reporting to agency head
agency line officers, temporarily relieved of operating responsibilities, with or without assistance of staff personnel
agency line officers, working part-time on reorganization problems concerning their particular line responsibilities
agency head, with or without assistance of his immediate aides

The observation of a number of cases of reorganization study groups suggests certain hypotheses with regard to the expectable consequences of their location on the "outside-inside" continuum. Those relatively far toward the outside extreme are likely to (1) take longer and cost more, (2) be more comprehensive, (3) be more objective in considering agency program and welfare, (4) lay more emphasis on structural arrangements and administrative principles and less emphasis on substantive, program considerations, and personnel, (5) result in longer and more elaborate reports, (6) be more extreme and radical in recommendations, (7) require an "inside" follow-up study to consider problems of practicability and implementation, and (8) be more imitative of other like organizations in the same field of activities.

Studies conducted by groups or individuals near the "inside" end of the continuum are likely to (1) be less elaborate and less expensive, (2) result in shorter and more focused reports (sometimes they are not even written), (3) pay more attention to the problems of political and administrative feasibility, (4) give more emphasis to implementation and to the probable impact of organizational changes upon the welfare of personnel, (5) pay more attention to substantive policies and program and less to administrative principles, (6) be more focused on specific and known problems rather than covering the universe, and (7) be easier and quicker to implement.

There is of course a wide variation arising from special circumstances with respect to different types of studies, but these generalizations would appear to have validity. It should be noted however that studies conducted by outside groups, presumed to be immune from the influence or bias of the officials and personnel of the agency concerned, often have certain distinctive characteristics. Where a study is initiated primarily in response to external criticism, the presumed objectivity of a completely outside survey group has obvious advantages, at least from the standpoint of those who initiated it. Likewise, when an administrator is reasonably assured that the study group's basic recommendations will accord with his own objectives and when his aim is to gain the support of power centers beyond the limits of his agency (such as the chief executive or the legislature or pressure groups) the aura of objectivity provided by a reputable outside survey group may greatly strengthen his hand in his search for external support. In such situations the purely inside study might be useless or even negative in its impact. Not infrequently, in fact, outside surveys are sought for the primary purpose of providing an administrator objective and professional support to do what he wanted to do in the first place.

There seems to be an almost infinite variety of methods and style in the conduct of organization surveys, more than can be fruitfully described here. Suffice it to point out that the methods employed have a very substantial impact in at least two major ways: first, in the accuracy, validity, and wisdom of findings and recommendations; and second, in the acceptability and persuasiveness of the recommendations, which in turn depend partly on the relevance and the invulnerability of the findings.

The Reaching of Decision

Normally, following the receipt of a survey report there is a considerable period of discussion, negotiation, and consideration before a decision is made. This gestation is likely to be more prolonged if the report and its recommendations were prepared in secret and if they were prepared by a relatively outside group. It is not unknown, however, for individual recommendations to be discussed and put into effect during the course of the survey itself, especially when the study is conducted by an inside group.

Final decisions are typically made by the principal executive in the agency, usually with the advice of his immediate aides and subordinates and often following discussions and clearance with superior officers, superior staff agencies, and legislative representatives. At this stage of deliberation, the question of political and administrative feasibility appears to be at least as important as that of desirability. And like the initiatory decision discussed above, discussions at this stage, as well as the study report itself, seem usually to be held on a confidential basis within a limited circle of top officials. In the cases of sweeping recommended changes the decision is seldom totally affirmative. Some recommendations are usually turned down, modified, or delayed. Particularly sensitive questions may provide the occasion for further and more intensive study and the establishment of new and more specialized study groups.

Implementation

The reaching of a basic decision to reorganize is only the beginning of a long and arduous series of tasks. These may include: the drafting of legislation, new regulations, instructions, and manuals, and a variety of other directives; the revision of budgets and personnel classifications; reassignments of personnel; and, perhaps most important and most difficult of all, the education and training of personnel as well as of outsiders as to the new ways of doing things and the reasons for doing them differently. When the initial study has given little attention to the requisite steps for implementation—as outside studies usually do—the preparation for implementation gives rise to a new planning process which is more or less formalized and is typically conducted on an inside basis under the immediate direction of line officials.[8] The planning for implementation must comprehend in great and specific detail the duties and relationships of individual positions, the reactions and capabilities of individual people, the locations of equipment, furnishings, supplies, and people, and a host of other matters. It is therefore ordinarily more arduous and time-taking than the initial study. In fact, the total process of implementation, including its planning and replanning, is a matter of months and sometimes years. It often settles into the ongoing process which was referred to earlier as incremental change.

The machinery established for planning implementation and for the implementation itself—they are sometimes inseparable—is often elaborate, involving a variety of committees and subcommittees, task forces, staff meetings, special study groups, trial or demonstration runs, etc. At these stages more than any other does a reorganization give rise to employee participation in planning and in action. Indeed, some participation is almost by definition inevitable since ultimately the individuals whose routines and behaviors are to be changed must participate in bringing about the changes. But the nature and style of the participation, the degree to which ideas and suggestions are invited, accepted, and considered, vary a great deal. The cases suggest that a substantial degree of participation in the planning and carrying out of the implementing steps is generally conducive to willing and even enthusiastic employee acceptance of a reorganization. But, of course, from the standpoint of top management, extensive participation at this stage, as at any other, has its dangers. It provides disaffected individuals and groups, of whom there normally are some, the opportunity to plant road-blocks and sometimes to nullify the intent of proposed organizational changes.

In fact, the process of giving effect to the plan is the "cutting edge" of a reorganization, an aspect too often overlooked in organizational study. It provides the test of the plan—its wisdom, its practicality, its acceptability—a test of the administrators who are seeking change, and a test of the employees themselves. It is here that substance and intent may give way to form and title; that unanticipated costs of change appear and may be purposively magnified by dissidents; that the goals of change may be misinterpreted both within and outside the agency, sometimes with damaging—even disastrous—results to the agency's program.

The Effectiveness of Reorganization: A Concluding Note

The assessment of the success of reorganization efforts is a hazardous business in most, but not quite all, cases. Results are seldom objectively measurable—in terms of either the values achieved or the costs entailed. And the comparison of what happened as a consequence of the effort and what would have happened had it not been made is at best hypothetical. It would seem, at first glance, that one could easily identify the total failures—reorganization studies which were made and abandoned in the files. In fact, it would appear that such "failures," complete or substantial, are more frequent than "successes." But such a verdict is often itself doubtful, even where the recommendations are at the time ignored or repudiated. I once conducted a study of a large division and presented my recommendations in some detail to its chief. He thanked me for the suggestions, said he didn't agree with them, and filed them away. Several months later he was replaced, and his successor almost immediately unburied the proposal and put almost all of it into effect. A more frequent consequence of an unsuccessful reorganization effort is that it provides a precedent and guidelines for future reorganization studies and for incremental changes carried on during the months and years which follow it. This is probably a common result of many of the sweeping outside studies of organization when the administrator deems it unwise to proceed at once. Often he will use the study as a road map for subsequent piece-by-piece changes in law, in budget, in personnel, in assignment, etc. Under such circumstances, it would be inaccurate to attribute total failure to the study, even though its immediate effects were nil.

Another kind of difficulty in assessing the success of efforts to reorganize arises from the cost side of the equation. All such efforts entail some costs, but only a part of the costs are measurable. An organizational survey alone may itself be accurately costed, particularly if it is contracted out in a consulting firm — at five, or fifty, or one hundred thousand dollars. This fee will of course not include the incidental costs of staff time and other charges incident to the study, most of which are not susceptible of specific valuation. Potentially more significant are the hidden costs of putting proposed changes into effect in terms of work, of retraining, of morale, of time from regular duties, of separations and new hiring, etc. Such costs are hardly measurable and seldom even estimated. In fairness, one should observe that there are often values in reorganization of the same kind — increased motivation of personnel, better morale, new and better qualified people — which are equally difficult to quantify.

Perhaps the greatest difficulty in appraising the success of reorganization efforts is the fuzziness and the controversiality of the criteria, the yardsticks, against which to measure. Earlier paragraphs of this discussion should have made clear that reorganization is seldom an end in itself. Rather it is a means to the accomplishment of other ends such as change in policy and program, or greater operating efficiency, or the increasing satisfactions of personnel, or the quieting of outside criticism. One may accept the goals of the initiators and sponsors of reorganization, who are usually the heads of the agencies themselves, as the criteria against which to judge — as was done in connection with the cases referred to earlier. Or one may substitute his own criteria, his own view of the public interest in the functional area of the agency studied. The former seems the wiser course in the assessment of reorganizational efforts, in so far as the goals may be reliably determined. The public interest, however reasonable and specific it may be to each of us individually, is a vague, even mystical guide for an entire polity. Judgments on the merit of reorganizations which have to do with policy and program—and these apparently include the majority of them—can hardly escape the underlying difficulty of the "policy sciences," as some have dubbed them, the problem of social values in a democratic society. Who is to determine what is good and what is bad?

This is not to be construed, however, as an argument against systematic organizational review and assessment. The acceleration of change in our society and in the world makes ever more necessary rapid change in our government. As has been suggested in earlier paragraphs, incremental adjustments can seldom keep pace with these dynamic demands on every front. It is likely that planned reorganizations—"episodic" changes, as Paul Appleby labeled them—will occur with increasing frequency in the future. Perhaps they will be put on a regular, expected, and scheduled basis. Such an arrangement might at the same time increase their prospects of effectiveness and diminish their costs.

NOTES

1. The agencies which these cases concerned include: (1) *national government*—the Agricultural Research Service, the Public Health Service, a defense research and development laboratory and the Children's Bureau; (2) *state governments*—Division of Architecture, Department of Employment, Fish and Game Department, Highway Patrol, Personnel Board, and a psychiatric clinic; (3) *city government*—health department, City Clerk, and certain other departments. The cases, together with an analytical commentary by this author, are published in Frederick C. Mosher, *Governmental Reorganization: Cases and Commentary* (Indianapolis: Bobbs-Merrill, 1967).

2. "The Significance of the Hoover Commission Report," *The Yale Review*, Vol. 39, No. 1 (September 1949), pp. 2–22.

3. One of the relatively few examples was the study, reported by Mason Haire, of the structure consequence of growth in four private businesses. ("Biological Models and Empirical Histories of the Growth of Organization," in Mason Haire, editor, *Modern Organization Theory* (New York: John Wiley & Sons, 1959.) See also the study, described by Bernard P. Indik, on "The Relationship Between Organization Size and Supervision Ratios" *Administrative Science Quarterly*, Vol. IX, No. 3 (December 1964), pp. 301–12.

4. I distinguish organizational (or reorganizational) goals from individual motivations, although the latter of course condition and provide part of

the base for the former. Herbert A. Simon has recently written: "By *goals* we shall mean value premises that can serve as inputs to decisions. By *motives* we mean the causes, whatever they are, that lead individuals to select some goals rather than others as premises for their decisions." "On the Concept of Organizational Goal," *Administrative Science Quarterly*, Vol. IX. No. 1 (June 1964), p. 3.

5. A tension is here understood as a quality of a relationship among people or among identifiable groups of people centering around one or more issues on which there is underlying and continuing disagreement.

6. As a well-known example of this phenomenon on a very broad scale one might cite the reexamination and reorganization of school systems all over the United States which was begun immediately after the Russians launched Sputnik.

7. Such an instruction is said to have accompanied President Johnson's "marching orders" to his various task forces during the fall of 1964.

8. Although consulting firms as well as staff offices sometimes conduct implementation studies.

Organizing Human Services in Florida
Laurence E. Lynn, Jr.

An Overview

ON JUNE 3, 1975, Florida Governor Reubin Askew signed into law a far-reaching attempt to integrate and decentralize human services delivery. Figure 4-1 charts the previous organization structure; figure 4-2 shows the new organizational arrangements.

The act calls for the delegation of line authority over the delivery of HRS [Health and Rehabilitative Services] services to eleven district administrators, who will report directly to the newly created Assistant Secretary for Operations. The categorical service divisions, such as the Division of Mental Health, have been abolished along with their operational control over service delivery. Categorical program identity has been retained only in the form of program offices reporting in strictly a staff capacity to the Assistant Secretary for Program Planning and Development; functions of the program offices include program planning, monitoring, and evaluation.

The new Secretary of HRS, William J. "Pete" Page, explains the significance of the change at the client level as follows. To obtain services under the old HRS structure, "you're likely to have [had] to go to half a dozen different offices and two or three different towns. You're likely to [have heard] a lot of 'come back next Thursday, that's when so-and-so will be here.' " Under the new setup, Page says, each of the more than two million Floridians who obtain HRS services annually will report to a local office for referral to a case manager, who will assure that the individual gets as many of the agency's services as he or she needs. "The client in the past had to make the system work," he said. "Now the system takes the responsibility for making the system work for the client."[1]

The district administrator will appoint a district manager for administrative services and may appoint district managers for social services and health services. He must create district programs that parallel statewide programs and are based on statewide objectives and policies, but client support services are to be consolidated and managed by the district administrator.

To insure citizen and consumer access to human services managers, each district is to have an advisory council of citizen members appointed by the governor. There will also be subdistrict councils designated by the district council and composed of district council membership. Finally, each district will have a human rights advocacy committee with the important responsibility of "protecting the constitutional and human rights of any client within a program or facility operated, funded, or regulated by the department."

A significant change mandated by the act relates to how departmental resources are budgeted. Formerly, resources were allocated to the program divisions and within them to program activities. For example, the Division of Mental Health budget was further apportioned to mental hospitals, drug abuse programs, community mental health programs, and the like, and, within community mental health programs, to community mental health services, public education services, development of mental health manpower, and the like. The act budgets for four entities: the Office of the Secretary, the Assistant Secretary for Program Planning and Development, the Assistant Secretary for Administrative Services, and the Assistant Secretary for Operations. The latter's budget is to be further broken down by district, thus creating a district-oriented, rather than a program-oriented, budget system. Within each district, funds are budgeted by program, with the programs defined in the traditional way. The secretary will approve and may amend all budgets, and he can transfer up to five percent of an approved district operating budget. The district administrator, with the prior approval of the secretary, can transfer up to 10 percent of the district operating budget among the various programs of the district.

Another important change relates to departmental program evaluation. In 1970 the legislature authorized creation within HRS of a Division of Planning and Evaluation. This office was to assist the sec-

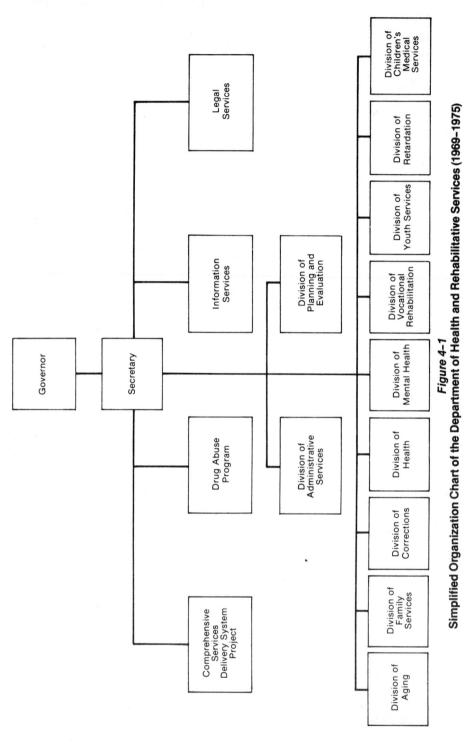

Figure 4–1
Simplified Organization Chart of the Department of Health and Rehabilitative Services (1969–1975)

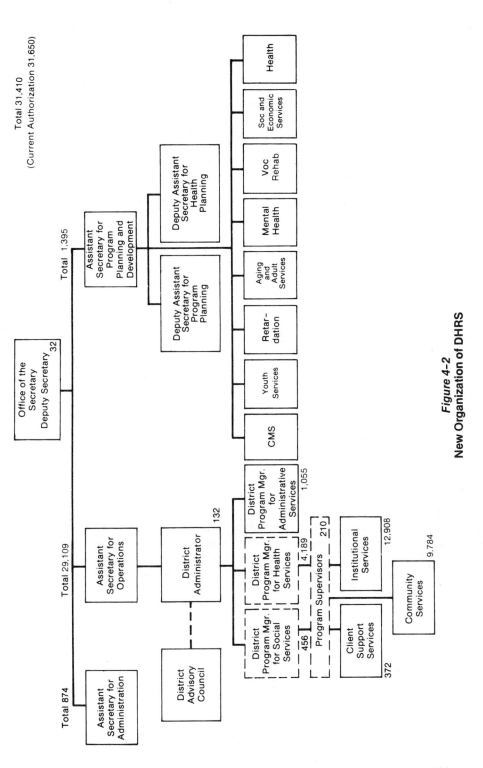

Total 31,410
(Current Authorization 31,650)

Office of the Secretary
Deputy Secretary 32

Total 1,395

Assistant Secretary for Program Planning and Development

Deputy Assistant Secretary for Program Planning

Deputy Assistant Secretary for Health Planning

CMS

Youth Services

Retar-dation

Aging and Adult Services

Mental Health

Voc Rehab

Soc and Economic Services

Health

Total 874

Assistant Secretary for Administration

Total 29,109

Assistant Secretary for Operations

District Administrator 132

District Advisory Council

District Program Mgr. for Administrative Services 1,055

District Program Mgr. for Health Services 4,189

District Program Mgr. for Social Services 456

Program Supervisors 210

Client Support Services 372

Institutional Services 12,908

Community Services 9,784

Figure 4-2
New Organization of DHRS

141

retary in setting developmental priorities and allocating resources through the development of comprehensive planning and program evaluation capabilities.

Section 5 of the 1975 reorganization act upgrades the role of evaluation and analytic studies on departmental decision-making. It directs that "a comprehensive program evaluation system shall be established which shall encompass all major programs of the Department of Health and Rehabilitative Services. The department shall establish measurable program objectives and performance criteria for each program it operates. Such a system of evaluation shall require all programs to develop identifiable goals which are quantifiable whenever practicable and to estimate the cost of attaining such goals in advance. Studies of the relative cost and effectiveness of departmental and alternative programs shall be conducted. The department shall develop a program evaluation schedule and shall evaluate at least twenty percent of its programs annually. The department shall submit these evaluation schedules and reports to the secretary, who within thirty days of receipt shall transmit copies of the schedules and reports to the appropriate substantive committees of both houses of the legislature for review. When possible, the department's management information system shall provide the basic information for program evaluation studies."

Viewing Reorganization According to Policy Objectives

To policy-makers, reorganizing an executive agency is not simply an issue of how to improve the effectiveness or efficiency of agency operations and services.[2] Though their rhetoric may suggest that "responsiveness" or "efficiency" or "quality" are the issues, advocates of reorganization often have any of several other objectives in mind.

For example, proposing reorganization may represent a symbolic declaration of intent to challenge entrenched interests, to take the initiative on behalf of those seeking to change or "shake up" the system. It may represent a more specific political challenge to specific vested interests, a means of putting these interests and their protectors on the defensive and of eroding their power and credibility. It may represent an attempt to gain greater control over an existing organization and its resources by mandating change and then controlling or influencing the steps necessary to carry it out, *e.g.*, the filling of new positions, the reallocation of payroll and budgets, the definition or refocusing of organizational missions. Depending on the form it takes, reorganization may be seen as a way to increase the scope of an agency's responsibilities and enlarge its budget and personnel, as a way to weaken or eliminate competing organizations, or as a way of increasing the visibility and apparent priority of an agency's missions and programs. Reorganization may signal a desire to "do something" about a problem when it is not clear what should be done.

Viewing reorganization in this context has three important and related implications. The first is that different parties to the issue can be expected to react to reorganization depending in large measure on whether they believe they stand to gain or lose by it. The second is that the actual resolution of the issue can be expected to depend on the relative political power of the actors involved in the decision. The third, related to the above two, is that a reorganization proposal is unlikely to become a serious issue at all unless a relatively powerful political actor sees sufficient advantage in it to warrant sustained advocacy.

These ideas will be explored further in the next three sections, which describe how three parties to the HRS reorganization proposal — the legislature, the mental health community, and the governor's office — viewed the issue.

The Legislature

Reapportionment and Reform   A useful starting point for describing recent legislative developments in human services decision-making in Florida is the United States Supreme Court's "one man, one vote" decision (*Baker v. Carr*) in 1962. This decision was the beginning of the end for Florida's "Pork Chop Gang," a group of rural legislators and business lobbyists who largely controlled the Florida legislature. These business interests were so strong that they were often referred to as Florida's "third house." On at least one occasion a private lobbyist actually took the chair at a meeting of a legislative committee. The "Pork Choppers" consistently blocked attempts to amend Florida's 1885 constitution, which called for a biennial 60-day calendar (44 working days).

Beginning in 1966, younger, more liberal Democratic legislators began challenging the control of the "Pork Choppers." At the end of that year, moreover, a constitutional revision commission was appointed to develop a proposal for revising the outdated Florida constitution. It was in 1967, however, five years after the *Baker v. Carr* decision, that a three-judge federal panel broke the hold of the "Pork Chop Gang" by ordering reapportionment of the Florida legislature. Almost overnight, many of the "Pork Choppers" were replaced by young, aggressive, and predominantly Democratic lawmakers from the cities and suburbs. These lawmakers, seeking issues to establish their power and taking advantage of the fact that the governor,

Claude Kirk, was a Republican, took the initiative in pressing for the reform of state government.

Among the first acts of the post-reapportionment legislature was the adoption in 1968 of the new state constitution proposed by the constitutional revision commission. This new constitution was ratified by Florida voters by a three-to-two margin in November, 1968. During the next few years, through this and other measures, the entire lawmaking environment was modernized. For example, the legislature henceforth was to meet annually, committee work was no longer to be conducted in secret, the keeping of records was required, and fulltime staff services were provided for legislative committees. Public understanding of and access to the legislature and the quality of legislative activities in Florida were dramatically improved. These improvements led to a number four ranking among all U.S. legislatures—behind California, New York and Illinois—in the 1971 Committee Report by the Citizens Conference on State Legislatures.[3] The Eagleton Institute of Politics concluded that Florida was setting a "standard of excellence for representative assemblies throughout the nation."

An example of this excellence has been the growing competence of the Health and Rehabilitative Services Committee of the Florida House of Representatives. Chaired until 1975 by a physician who became an expert on Florida human services administration, then by an energetic and ambitious young attorney from Miami, and now by an activist female legislator, the Committee has won two awards for excellence in legislative representation from the National Conference of State Legislative Leaders (now known as the National Conference of State Legislatures).

Of particular note is the committee's development of a capacity for independent program evaluation.[4] It was a 1974 program evaluation, *Florida's Correctional System: A Preliminary Evaluation,* that earned national recognition for the committee (and led to reorganization of the state's correctional program in 1975).

Two pieces of legislation are indicative of how the post-reapportionment legislature has been seeking to reform state government. In 1967, after years of trying, a group of legislators succeeded in moving through the legislature the now famous "Government in the Sunshine" Act. The act states that all meetings of public boards and bodies to which the law applied must be held in public, public notice of such meetings must be given, and minutes are to be kept.

In 1974, the legislature took on what one legislator referred to as the "phantom government." Prior to that time, state agencies could establish rules and regulations without a public hearing. Often these rules appeared to contradict if not to contravene the intent of the legislature. Licensing boards, under the guise of insuring professional skills, were being operated as closed societies. Yet the only recourse anyone with a grievance had was to the courts.

To rectify these situations, the legislature passed the Administrative Procedures Act without a dissenting vote. This act established a joint Administrative Procedures Committee in the legislature. Now, following an agency's publication of new rules and regulations, any party with a substantial interest can request a public hearing. Then the rules and regulations must be sent to the Administrative Procedures Committee, where they are reviewed to see if the promulgating agency has the necessary legislative authority to issue them.

The act also established an independent Division of Administrative Hearings in the Department of Administration, but insulated it from control by the executive branch by requiring that its budget be submitted directly to the legislature. (Workmen's compensation, unemployment compensation, driver's licenses, and welfare are exempted from these processes.) Before the act was passed, for example, an appeal of a licensing decision had to be made to the body that had made the decision in the first place. Now it is independently reviewed.

Former state Senator Louis de la Parte of Tampa, who played a key role in the evolution of the state's human services agency, summed up the situation in the legislature:

> "The post-reapportionment period brought about a radical realignment in the balance of legislative and executive powers and rising expectations among legislators as to what constitutes the proper exercises of legislative responsibility. Frequently programs enacted and funded were not properly implemented. This prompted the legislature to spell out its intent, in the most exact terms conceivable, and subsequently to hold those executive agencies accountable for implementation. To do less, from the legislative perspective, is to abandon its responsibility. Who is a better articulator of state needs and the means available to meet those needs?"

Reorganization Prior to 1975   The 1968 constitution required simplification of the structure of state government through the consolidation of overlapping, duplicative, and overly fragmented functions and agencies. Accordingly, in 1969 the legislature created the Department of Health and Rehabilitative Services (HRS). Human services agencies, many of which had originally been independent and had reported directly to the governor and an elected cabinet, which sat as the Board of Commissioners of State Institutions, were grouped under a secretary appointed by the governor, and confirmed by the senate; they became known as divisions of the Department of HRS.[5] The new line divisions were corrections, family services, health, mental health, retardation, vocational rehabilitation, and youth services. (In 1973 two more line divisions were added: aging and children's medical services.)

The intent of the legislature was to create a fully integrated human services delivery system to insure adequate communications among service providers and between consumers and providers, complete coordination of service delivery consistent with individual or family needs, and better response to actual community circumstances. Its objectives were both better services and efficiency—getting maximum value for dollars spent. However, the legislature made two key compromises when creating HRS. First, under pressure from provider groups and from the agencies themselves, the Tallahassee-based program divisions were permitted to retain line authority over local program administration. Second, the division directors were to be appointed by the governor, subject to senate confirmation, not by the secretary of the department. These two compromises helped guarantee that the program divisions would retain substantial autonomy within the newly created department.

As time went on, the maintenance of program autonomy proved to be a source of irritation to many legislators intent on achieving integrated human services. A lightning rod for the legislature's unhappiness with departmental administration was the Comprehensive Services Delivery System (CSDS) Project. In 1969 the U.S. Department of Health, Education, and Welfare (HEW) decided to initiate 10 sophisticated pilot projects to develop and demonstrate, within limited geographic areas, computer-based, comprehensive social services delivery systems. Florida applied for and secured one such project for Palm Beach County.

The CSDS project in Palm Beach County was to redress the chronic administrative problems of duplicative services, uncoordinated case handling, duplication of staff and manpower, and poor access. It was to operate as a one-stop, integrated service center that might become the model for all Florida state service delivery and the basis for an administrative restructuring of HRS itself. All divisions were to participate in the common service delivery effort. (The Division of Youth Services, then headed by O. J. Keller, refused to participate in the project. Later, Keller was forced to step down as Secretary of HRS by the senate, which had become distrustful of his administrative abilities and of his willingness to carry out the intent of its reorganization.) CSDS top staff consisted of a representative of each of the divisions and was headed by a general project manager. However, coordination and cooperation among these representatives were to be voluntary. The project manager was given no clear-cut line authority over the semiautonomous units under him.

In the view of many legislators, the CSDS project was a notable failure. Knowledgeable legislators need only mention the name CSDS to signal their chief complaint about HRS: "all powerful" division directors create fiefdoms within the department and resist any effort to cooperate in the delivery of services. One senate staff member recalls visiting the CSDS project at the height of a controversy with the telephone company. The telephone company was refusing to bill each service division separately. Then because the CSDS staff could not agree on who would pay the bill, the bill was not paid at all. Even the department's own evaluation of the project concluded that "voluntary cooperation of semiautonomous divisions was inadequate to accomplish the integration of services."

As early as 1972, Representative Richard Hodes, chairman of the Health and Rehabilitative Services Committee of the Florida house, began thinking of measures that would improve the ability of the Secretary of HRS to manage his department. By 1973 it was becoming increasingly clear to others that the performance of the department was not living up to expectations. In Hodes' view, for example, the department could not provide "reasonable answers to reasonable questions," *e.g.,* how many clients were being served, how much money was being spent, the amount of expenditures for direct services and for administrative costs. Hodes introduced a reorganization bill that would have grouped the program divisions under three deputy secretaries.

Though the governor and the department opposed the proposal, two important rescue operations were mounted. First, at the urging of the department, the legislature passed a measure that made the Secretary of HRS responsible for appointing program division directors. This was to allow the secretary greater control in the coordination of his department.[6] Second, Governor Reubin Askew appointed O. J. Keller, director of the Division of Youth Services, as Secretary of HRS, replacing Emmett Roberts, who had agreed with the governor that "a change in leadership is now in order." This was a popular move with most legislators in the senate. De la Parte, for example, a long-time supporter of youth programs and an admirer of Keller, warmly supported the nomination, and the senate confirmed Keller unanimously. Representative Hodes was dubious, however. In terms of budget documentation and authentication, he had found Youth Services under Keller an "impossible division" to work with.

Whatever revival of hope for the department occurred in 1973 as a result of these measures was sharply dissipated in 1974. There was no evidence that the department was taking the reorganization issue seriously. Many legislators were frustrated by HRS recalcitrance, and a bill to abolish the department altogether, sponsored by Representative John Culbreath, almost passed the house. Louis de la Parte played the key role in the legislature. By then President *pro tem* of the Florida senate, de la Parte was widely regarded as the "father of HRS" for the role he played during the 1969 conference committee that approved a single department of HRS instead of three separate ones. He had been influential in persuading O. J. Keller to come to Florida in the first place. He was a good friend and admirer of the governor. He believed the time had come to carry out what he regarded as the original intent of the legislature in creating HRS. Said de la Parte:

> "There is very little doubt that the present organizational structure of the department encourages the arbitrary pigeonholing of clients, discourages communication and the pooling of resources among divisions, and creates costly duplication of effort. Further this 'confrontation' of divisions frustrates attempts by the private sector and other state and local governmental entities to acquire knowledge of and tap the comprehensive services available within the department."

Following unsuccessful efforts to persuade Keller that reorganization and further decategorization of service delivery was necessary, on April 22, 1974, de la Parte introduced a bill calling for a thoroughgoing reorganization of the department. In an open break with Keller he proposed creation of 11 service regions, each headed by a regional director who would have line authority over service delivery in his or her region. The categorical program divisions in Tallahassee, which at the time had the line authority over service delivery, would be abolished and replaced by three Deputy Secretaries: for Administrative Services, for Program Development, and for Regional Services. The regional directors would report to the secretary through the Deputy for Regional Services. In addition, de la Parte's proposal called for central intake and case management in each region. Instead of being bounced from place to place, each client would have a single caseworker, total client needs would be monitored and assessed, and regional directors would have the authority to solve service delivery problems.

The bill led to an epic and at times confusing fight in the Florida legislature. The bill passed the senate but with an amendment, labeled "crippling" by de la Parte and an unfortunate "mistake" by its own sponsor, that allowed implementation to be delayed for a year. In the house, Hodes had reintroduced his bill, strongly preferring it to the de la Parte proposal, which, in his mind, would have created regional "fiefdoms" in place of categorical program "fiefdoms." The department supported neither proposal, but, with the governor's backing, Keller finally agreed to support a compromise that would create the 11 service regions and the central intake, diagnostic, evaluation, and casework management operations in each region, but would leave the program divisions and their authority largely intact. In the end, the compromise bill was voted down by the House Government Operations Committee, to which it had been referred. Observers offered numerous reasons for the negative vote: too much discretion left to the secretary, poor legislative craftsmanship, insufficient time allowed in the bill for planning prior to implementation, and intense opposition lobbying of the medical, nurses, pediatric, mental health, mental retardation, cerebral palsy, epilepsy, and other associations.

By the end of 1974, however, it was clear that the legislature was determined to reorganize HRS. Funds had been appropriated to HRS to be used in developing a reorganization proposal. On October 15, 1974, Dempsey Barron, president-designate of the 1975 Senate, announced a "massive onslaught" against governmental bureaucracy. Of HRS, which he described as the "monster of all state bureaucracies," he said, "We're pouring $400 million annually into this bureaucratic haystack and as the money sifts down it is eaten up by government before it reaches the people it is designed to help."

Though de la Parte had already decided not to run for reelection, before the year was out, help for proponents of de la Parte-style reorganization came from another quarter. In August, 1974, the Governor's Management and Efficiency Commission, a blue ribbon group of Florida businessmen appointed by the governor to advise him on making Florida government more efficient, recommended that HRS be reorganized along lines similar to those contained in de la Parte's original senate proposal. Their recommendation, and the prestige behind it, helped form a strong foundation for the legislature's successful 1975 reorganization effort.

The 1975 Legislative Reorganization   Impatient with the lack of progress toward services integration by HRS, and with opposition from special interest groups, both houses of the Florida legislature passed major HRS reorganization bills within days after convening in April for the 1975 legislative session. In preliminary committee sessions, the Department of HRS had opposed both bills and Secretary Keller had submitted a proposal of his own patterned after the Hodes proposals of 1973 and 1974. However, most legislators considered Keller's plan a "poor effort" to appease division directors and at the same time to offer legislators what he thought they wanted. Basically, in the view of these legislators, HRS lacked the motivation to reorganize. Only the legislature could initiate reorganization. In the view of House HRS Committee Chairman Barry Kutun, who replaced Hodes in 1975, "They (HRS) could never do internally what we could do externally." The governor and many in his office appeared to concede that the legislature would have its way, and chose to work toward a reorganization bill that would preserve as much as possible of the governor's and the secretary's discretion over departmental management.[7]

The matter was not settled without considerable controversy and compromise. The house and senate versions of the reorganization differed in several important respects, and these differences had to be resolved. For example, the house bill retained program offices at the state level to oversee policy and program development and had the regional administrators report directly to the Secretary of HRS; the senate bill eliminated program officers altogether and had the regional administrators responsible to an Assistant Secretary for Operations. Both the house and senate bills created a new department centered around corrections and offender rehabilitation. However, the house version transferred that portion of the Division of Youth Services dealing with juvenile offenders from HRS to the new department, whereas the senate left all youth services in HRS. In general, the house bill was quite detailed in providing statutory specifications for HRS management. The senate bill, on the other hand, was patterned after the less detailed de la Parte/Governor's Management and Efficiency Commission proposals; Senate HRS staff consulted frequently with former commission members.

The legislature in general and the senate in particular had several points of apparent leverage with the governor. The first was an environmental reorganization bill, prepared by Senate President Dempsey Barron's personal staff, which proposed to merge the state's four environmental agencies into one super-agency responsible to the governor and the cabinet. This proposal would have weakened Governor Askew's control over Florida's pollution control and land use programs, and he strongly opposed it. The second was Governor Askew's commitment to the reconfirmation by the senate (required by law) of O. J. Keller as HRS Secretary. The third was a series of incidents that put HRS in a bad light with the legislature and the public. One involved an individual acquitted of murder by reason of insanity whose subsequent convalescent release and employment as an armed guard raised an outcry against the "coddling" of criminals. Another involved a lease for additional office space that appeared to many to be both unnecessary and signed according to questionable procedures.

The governor chose to negotiate with the senate over its version of the bill and seek its passage by the entire legislature. The final bill specified that hard-core delinquents accused of specific crimes such as rape, murder, or robbing were to be tried as adults and retained in a Youthful Offender Division of the new Department of Offender Rehabilitation, whereas youths charged with lesser offenses were to remain under the jurisdiction of the Division of Youth Services in HRS; it created three Assistant Secretaries — for Program Planning and Development, Administrative Services, and Operations—with regional administrators reporting to the Assistant Secretary for Operations, in line with the senate bill; it retained program offices at the state level, in line with the house bill, and retained from the house bill a provision for state and district Human Rights Advocacy Committees; and it mandated regional budgeting, also in accordance with the house version. It was during this session that HRS Secretary Keller was forced to step down by the senate.

The Mental Health Community

A different view of the problems associated with delivery of human services in Florida is provided by study of the mental health community.

Florida was one of the first states to begin construction of community mental health centers under the Mental Retardation Facilities and Community Mental Health Centers Construction Act passed by Congress in 1963. In subsequent years, Florida moved from an institutional system to a successful community-based system in which 18 community mental health centers and some 50 state- and locally-funded community mental health clinics were supervised by the Florida Division of Mental Health. Resident patients in state hospitals per 100,000 civilian population declined from about 170 in fiscal year 1965 to less than 85 in fiscal year 1974. In the same period the number of patients treated in community mental health facilities grew from 20,000 to 120,000.

However, to many in the mental health community, several executive, legislative, and judiciary initiatives made the task of directing the design and delivery of mental health services increasingly complex. For example, from 1965 to 1969, the Commissioner of Mental Health reported directly to Florida's governor and cabinet, sitting as the Board of Commissioners of State Institutions. The cabinet consisted of the Secretary of State, the Commissioner of Agriculture, the Commissioner of Education, the Treasurer, the Comptroller, and the Attorney General, all of whom possessed equal votes in the determination of basic state policy. This situation was quite satisfactory to mental health professionals, who felt that their advice was heard and acted on directly by elected, and sympathetic, state officials.

In 1969, the reorganization of state executive agencies by the legislature changed this arrangement. As noted previously, the Division of Mental Health was placed under the jurisdiction of the Secretary of HRS. From the division's point of view, this new arrangement meant that a new layer of bureaucracy had been interposed between the director (formerly commissioner) and the mental health professionals, on the one hand, and the highest policy-making authority, on the other. Had there been assurances that the secretary would be a physician—health professionals repeatedly sought such assurances—such objections would probably not have arisen. However, the likely outcome, in their view, was a significant diminution of the influence of professionals in mental health policy-making.

Complaints about departmental personnel administration were typical. Professional service agencies have always had problems with state personnel administration. However, such problems seemed to many to get worse under the new department. Approval of personnel authorizations was often subject to lengthy delays, both within the department and at the state's Department of Administration. A division request to classify a position as requiring a Ph.D. with three years' experience might have been revised to call for an M.S. with two years' experience. Animal handlers might receive higher pay than psychiatric aides. The Division of Corrections could be permitted to offer a job two grades higher to someone with the same qualifications.

There were further problems. As a division, mental health experienced the problems of being too closely allied with social service divisions and, in fact, felt itself insensitively treated by HRS. One often-cited example of objectionable treatment—and an example meriting special attention—was the decision to transfer prisoners from HRS's overcrowded correctional facilities into mental health facilities. The first such transfer occurred early in 1974. At this time the state prison system was overcrowded; conditions had deteriorated to the point where the Division of Corrections was under suit for failure to provide adequate housing for its inmates. At the governor's request, the Secretary of HRS tried to find some form of alternate housing for prisoners. Governor Askew eventually accepted the secretary's proposal to place prisoners in some facilities of one of the mental hospitals. The Division of Mental Health offered no objections to this measure, as the facilities were some of the oldest in the state and were not being occupied by mental patients at the time.

However, from the division's perspective, a dangerous precedent had been set. Soon after, the Department of Administration recommended that an entire hospital—the G. Pierce Wood Memorial Hospital at Arcadia—be transformed into a prison facility. The division strongly objected. A compromise resulted in the decision to transfer only a portion of the facility—the central portion—to the Division of Corrections. The hospital's recreation facilities, including the swimming pool, would have been at the disposal of the inmates. Some of the mental patients began to be transferred to other buildings.

The citizens of Arcadia and the Mental Health Association filed suit against the governor and the Secretary of HRS, claiming that the transfer was illegal. (Ironically, the Division of Mental Health was a party to the defense, due to its relationship to the parent HRS agency.) The court's decision confirmed the governor's and secretary's right to make such transfers. However, a class action suit subsequently filed on behalf of a patient in the Arcadia facility culminated in a decision that the transfer of prisoners violated the rights of mental patients to quality care, free from stigma and in a therapeutic environment. Transfer of prisoners to this hospital was barred. This decision has been appealed, but it is expected to be upheld. Meanwhile, the Division of Corrections has decided not to use this facility.

Incidents such as "Arcadia" served in many observers' minds not only to reveal the disadvantages of the Division of Mental Health's close association with HRS, but also to highlight the dangers associated with legislative reorganization. If mental health were abolished as a division, many officials argued, the community might have less confidence that there would be an effective agent to fight such decisions.

In addition, the legislature made new and complicated demands on the Division of Mental Health. For example, in 1972 Florida passed the Baker Act. This act revised existing state laws relating to the civil commitment of the mentally ill and set up an additional budget category for mental health. The act was intended to develop and improve receiving and community treatment facilities, make hospital admission voluntary whenever possible, and guarantee individual liberty and human rights for mental patients. Despite the laudable intent of the bill, many mental health professionals objected to the provisions for legal safeguards and court involvement in what they perceived to be essentially medical adjustments. Also, some were worried about what they regarded as "unworkable requirements" of the act and the greatly increased workload in the division, for which the legislature had provided no additional resources.

In 1971, the legislature passed the Comprehensive Alcoholism Prevention, Control, and Treatment Act (the Myers Act). This act, which was first implemented in 1975, was designed to transfer activity with respect to alcoholism from the criminal justice system to a medical/rehabilitation system to be administered by the Division of Mental Health. The act, however, contained a rather detailed specification of the treatment programs: "Professional supervision means one professional working with a maximum of six (6) alcoholism counselors if in daily personal contact and providing direct supervision on a minimum basis of an hour per week per supervisee; or one professional working with a maximum of three alcoholism counselors located in separate facilities and providing direct supervision on a minimum basis of two hours per week per supervisee." Such detailed legislative intervention into professional service management was not welcomed by mental health professionals.

Further frustration for the division was created by procedures under which the state receives federal funds for the financing of mental health services. Prior to 1971, Florida's mental hospital services had been financed by state appropriations. Beginning in 1969, however, the federal government began giving strong encouragement to states to utilize federal matching funds under various titles of the Social Security Act to finance social services. As a result, the Florida legislature now bases its appropriations for mental health on projections of earnings under these titles. As services are delivered during the year, the Division of Mental Health is responsible for providing reports and work sampling for review at various levels of state government. This documentation is submitted to the HEW regional office in Atlanta, and eventually the federal government reimburses the state for the delivery of services. The red tape, uncertainty, and nonprofessional scrutiny of division activities was regarded as a clear procedural setback from the simpler days of direct state appropriations, even though the division received greater funding.

Finally, the division was worried by the implications of recent litigation that might affect the way the division provided care in both state and community facilities without guaranteeing the availability of resources to bring about such changes. For example, the United States Supreme Court recently ruled in *Donaldson v. O'Connor* that nondangerous mental patients who are involuntarily committed have a constitutional right to be either treated or released. Such rulings, mental health professionals worried, might force mental hospitals to dump patients back into society because budget constraints prohibit the delivery of (as yet undefined) "adequate care."

The upshot of such developments was that mental health required more funds to operate a high-quality mental health care system than the legislature was accustomed to providing. Staff had to grow by leaps and bounds to keep up with recent legislation, and this rapid growth drained its resources. Legislative developments in Florida seemed to the mental health community to demonstrate the tendency of state legislatures to make new and complicated demands on state agencies — demands that had radical implications for budgeting, personnel, and services — without facing up to the price tag attached to such demands.

Not surprisingly, mental health professionals were unhappy with the legislature's 1975 reorganization of HRS. This opposition did not stem from opposition to regional administration *per se*. Beginning with the 1970 Florida Community Mental Health Act, division operations were being decentralized. The 1970 act established 23 mental health boards serving 23 districts within the state. These boards have been responsible for contracting with appropriate public and private organizations for mental health facilities or services. The district board has been responsible to the division for the soundness of programs, priorities, and services and for the legality of local contracts negotiated for these services.

However, to improve the relationships between the division and the district boards, the division developed a regional structure that allocated each of the 23 districts into one of four basic areas, each served by one of the four state hospitals to insure the integration of the community system with the hospital system. Each mental health board within the jurisdiction of a regional office was to have a program staff consisting of a program coordinator and one specialist each in drug abuse, alcoholism, and mental health. Thus, each of the 23 mental health board districts would have a team of four professionals with an overall regional director and a small staff at the state hospital. Though this system of regional offices had yet to prove itself — some legislators were suspicious that it would further dilute the accountability of the division to elected officials — the 1975 reorganization, with its structure of 11 districts, brought implementation to a halt.

Doubts about the reorganization in the mental health community went much deeper than irritation at the scrapping of the division's regionalization plans, however. Many saw the prospect that deprofessionalization and politicization would be pushed to their ultimate limits. A completely regionalized administration of human services would expose mental health programs to an unhealthy and perhaps costly competition among the regions. As one observer explained, the most important coin in local politics is "payroll," not "services." Local politicians want jobs, facilities, and funds coming into their areas. Under the legislature's regional system, the opportunities for political manipulation are legion.

"The district hospitals and offices have to be located somewhere," said one mental health professional. "This means several millions worth of payroll and several institutions coming into an area. Before there were bureaucratic layers which prevented political manipulation. Now local politicians may be able to bargain with each other about where offices will be located and what comes into each area."

Some mental health officials also worried that reorganization would discourage highly qualified professionals from joining Florida's system, assuming that such professionals would be unwilling to work as program staff with no authority in Tallahassee or under a "city manager" type at the local level. In short, the mental health community saw the reorganization as a distinct threat to the delivery of quality mental health care in response to patient needs.

The Governor's Office

Florida's most recent governors, Republican Claude Kirk, who left office in 1971, and Democrat Reubin Askew, who took office in 1971 and was reelected in 1974, have initiated, encouraged, or gone along with a variety of steps to enhance executive control over human services policy and delivery. Their measures have been influenced by their convictions concerning the role the governor should play in policy-making, by the Florida legislature's active interest in the regionalization and integration of services delivery, and by financial and moral support for comprehensive planning and services integration from several recent HEW officials.

Nevertheless, what Florida's recent governors have been able to accomplish has doubtless been limited in part by the fact that Florida's 1968 constitution left the governor relatively weak institutionally. Only about one-third of the heads of state departments are directly responsible to the governor, another one-third are elected, and the remaining one-third report to the governor and the elected cabinet as a collegial body. This factor, in addition to others, limits the governor's ability to carry out his policy agenda, and forces him to carefully husband his political resources. Hence, the governor's office seems to have been caught between legislatively-initiated pressures for regionalization/integration/decategorization, on the one hand, and the strong preference for voluntary cooperation and coordination among the separate service divisions in HRS, on the other. Moreover, the influence of the federal government has been notably inconsistent. While HEW officials such as Secretary Elliot Richardson and Under Secretaries John Veneman and Frank Carlucci have personally supported the efforts by Florida governors toward achieving more responsive and efficient services delivery with less federal red tape, Congress and the federal program offices in Washington have been largely unsympathetic.

Executive Management Reforms   Governor Kirk appointed James Bax, a strong believer in services integration, as the first Secretary of HRS. Together, they persuaded HEW Secretary Robert Finch to approve in 1969 the CSDS Project in Palm Beach County. Though Bax had his problems—his request for a larger staff to run the department offended legislators who thought that reorganization meant savings—he earned respect for his knowledge and commitment to effective services delivery.

Reubin Askew also took an interest in furthering services integration, and he took steps to enhance his role in human services policy-making as well. Following discussions with HEW Secretary Richardson, who was seeking to develop national support for services integration, Askew obtained (under the Intergovernmental Personnel Act) the services of David Beecher, Acting Commissioner of HEW's Community Services Administration in Washington, D.C., to assist Florida in exploring ways to plan more effectively for, manage, and integrate human services programs.[8] It was Askew's contention that the multiplicity of programs in HRS hindered him in establishing his own priorities and effectively following the progress of the department. Moreover, observers contended that relatively few issues were even reaching him, and that when they did, they often had been filtered through the Department of Administration and arrived with a budget officer's bias.

On behalf of the governor, Beecher helped institute a series of management reforms of the type that Richardson was actively employing as Secretary of HEW. One such reform was a management conference system modified by Beecher from the one used by Richardson. Askew would meet regularly—say, once a month—with his senior advisers on HRS policies, programs, and budgets. The agenda for these meetings would consist of a limited number of important issues of concern to the governor. Preceding such meetings were meetings of the Clearance Council, whose function was to prepare the agenda for the management conferences. In deciding what should go to the governor, council members, who included key HRS aides and staff of the governor, were forced to negotiate with one another, and to winnow from the list of potential issues those they could decide themselves or that would prove embarrassing if brought before the governor unresolved. The governor's staff sought to force council members to do adequate staff analysis before proposing an item for the agenda, insuring that the members were prepared for the meetings. Once an agenda was decided on, the governor's aides were responsible for preparing an agenda book containing appropriate backup papers and materials.

From observers' accounts, the process has had several results:

1. Before the process was begun, officials in the Budget Division of the Department of Administration, affectionately known as the "Fiscal Fascists," held a disproportionate number of high cards vis-à-vis the program people. Once the division began to see that they had to account to the governor for their positions, a number of smaller matters began to be ironed out in a mutually satisfactory way.
2. The governor began to develop a personal agenda of priority items on which he became quite knowledgeable, thus adding to the effectiveness of his leadership.
3. The morale of the program people was lifted by their regular access to decision-makers and the improvement in their relative bureaucratic strength.

The governor's interest in services integration, his staff's expertise in management-by-objectives processes, and the department's growing experience with CSDS and computerized case management were pulled together in 1972 into a single effort of planning and analysis: the Comprehensive Services Planning and Management Improvement Project (known as CSP). One outcome of this project, though apparently not a major goal, was to be a departmental reorganization plan. However, this project, the progress of which was being inhibited by the lack of strong interest on the part of the department's leadership, was virtually halted in 1973 following the replacement of Emmett Roberts by O. J. Keller as Secretary of HRS. Keller, with little knowledge of and no commitment to CSP, let it lapse.

At Beecher's urging, the department also began to develop a structured management-by-objectives system. Each program division was to define operational objectives for its activities and to track its progress toward their attainment. However, development of the system was temporarily sidetracked by the 1975 reorganization battle and the pressures to implement the new organization.

Reorganization   By most accounts, Governor Askew has brought unusual knowledge and personal commitment to the task of overseeing the administration of human services programs and budgets in Florida. In a traditionally conservative state in which support for human services brings few political rewards, Askew has consistently supported high-quality professional services designed to meet the needs of the whole person. He has been concerned, however, that organizational arrangements aimed at breaking up categorical program fiefdoms through regionalization and services integration do not end up creating new, regional fiefdoms under which the creation of a high-quality service system serving the whole state would be hampered by parochial, "pork chop" politics.

Askew also believes in obtaining the services of high-quality, dedicated public servants and supporting them. In Keller he believed he had found such a man to lead the Department of HRS. He viewed Keller as a genuine servant of the people, dedicated to giving the best services to the whole person and to creating and maintaining high-quality human services. De la Parte describes Keller as totally committed, non-malicious, determined to do good. It turned out, however, that Keller's views about the way the department should be organized differed from those of de la Parte and others in the legislature.

Legislative critics of HRS had been somewhat mollified in 1973 by promises that the department would submit a reorganization proposal. In 1974, in the absence of a strong departmental direction to produce a carefully crafted plan, departmental staff, realizing the mood of the legislature, put together a reorganization proposal that, by the admission of those involved, was hastily drafted and too steeped in tradition. Nevertheless, this was the departmental plan that was discussed with the legislature. Though legislative leaders were unhappy with it, the principal alternatives, the de la Parte bill and a compromise version of it, could not be enacted. However, the HRS appropriation included funds for HRS to use in consulting with program officials and service providers throughout the state and coming up with a comprehensive reorganization plan for the 1975 session.

The Askew administration formed an Executive Steering Committee for Reorganization chaired by Deputy Secretary of HRS E. W. Sandberg and consisting of the division directors or their representatives. All CSP material was turned over to this committee. The executive committee studied a wide range of reorganization alternatives, from one that retained strong program division control to one that was patterned after the de la Parte proposal. In the end the committee endorsed a reorganization proposal patterned after the Hodes proposals of 1973 and 1974 that retained the program divisions, grouping them under three substantive deputy secretaries who would exercise strong statewide oversight and review. It also created a system of HRS area coordinators to oversee services delivery, with certain "pragmatic exceptions" to enable the department to deal with constraints on the use of federal funds, county health issues, and statewide institutions that did not lend themselves to local management integration.

According to HRS Secretary Keller, the proposal embodied ". . . what I thought made sense, [which was] to have a coordinator in each of the regions with a small staff. That person would be the eyes and the ears for the Secretary . . . someone to head off crises, someone who could deal with the judges, someone who could create a stronger link between the state agency and its different divisions and the private agencies . . . someone who could also coordinate service so that you could combine intake services, office space, and transportation facilities—in other words, someone who could make better use of the resources."

Keller's objections to the legislature's proposals had centered around a lack of accountability, confusing lines of authority, and the possible erosion of professional expertise in specialized programs. He feared that the introduction of generalists at the decision-making level would tend to dilute the programs and also inhibit the department's capability to attract top quality professionals. Keller used his work in Youth Services to demonstrate his point: "When in 1967, I came to this state, it was with the firm understanding that in the youth corrections field, I'd be able to implement my ideas if I could sell them. I did sell them . . . and it worked." However, as the legislature intended to separate operational and planning functions, Keller feared that "the top people in those specialty areas will not come to a state where they cannot directly implement the program." Keller also worried that the regional manager, who would be responsible for hiring the specialists, would not be equipped to "get the right people for the right programs," since it takes a certain expertise and familiarity with the program merely to evaluate an applicant's suitability.

Integration under a regional system proved to be the most discouraging aspect of legislative reorganization for Keller. Under this arrangement, he argued, program officials would be responsible for planning only, thus eliminating accountability. Keller illustrates the potential problems as follows:

> "I'm the Secretary and I'm sitting in Tallahassee. Up to this time I have been able to say to my division directors located around this lake, 'You're the Mental Health expert . . . it's your program, now what's happening, why is a hospital blowing up in Miami?' The future could be, I bring in my director and he says, 'You know, I wrote the plan, I wrote the policies and those damn people down there in Hollywood, South Florida, they don't follow it. I put it on paper. I've been down there; I've pulled. I've told them that they had all the wrong people. . . .' So then I call the District Administrator down there and say, 'I've been talking to my director and he says he wrote the plan and you people aren't following it down there.' 'Oh,' he says, 'those crazy goddamned people in Tallahassee will put anything on paper. They don't have to run the program. I've got to run it.' And then he might add, 'Look, how many programs have you given me to handle down here, nine? Why pick on me just because they have a problem at the mental hospital? Look at the good job I'm doing for you in Drug Rehab.' So you see how it could get to be."

Thus the program model appeared to Keller to be the only one that guaranteed professional control, from the planning level to the delivery of service. As a professional himself, Keller resented the taint on professionalism that was widespread in the legislature. Said Keller:

> "Their feeling is that the State divisions are really kind of bad guys, that the division heads are power hungry chiefs of principalities, all of them guarding their own little fiefdoms. . . . I haven't found that to be true, but maybe I am in my own dream world. I thought the division directors were on the whole very cooperative, and if I asked them to do something, they really tried to solve some of the serious problems."

As many observers and officials point out, the opportunities for political manipulation and/or "empire building" would be far greater under the regional system than under the division system; with authority located in the regional offices, there would be nothing to prevent local co-optation of the whole system and inappropriate competition between regions. They state that, while the divisional organization focuses attention on a comprehensive state program plan, the regional structure would shift that focus to the amount of payroll and facilities coming into each district. The regional structure, then, would be antithetical to the original justification for a statewide service organization — that is, to provide a nonparochial authority that would be accountable for all aspects of plannning and operation.

In earlier discussions with his committee on reorganization, Askew had ruled out approaches that he viewed as unresponsive to the legislature's desires for services integration at the local level. He took a personal hand in drafting the final proposal of the steering committee and offered it to the legislature with his endorsement. His objective was to use this proposal as a basis for negotiating a mutually satisfactory arrangement with the legislature in 1975. In December, 1974, he asked the incoming Lieutenant Governor, James H. Williams, to meet with the legislative leadership and thrash out reorganization issues prior to the beginning of the 1975 legislative session.

By then, however, it was much too late for patient compromise. The senate, the house, and their respective HRS committees had new, aggressive, and, by most observers' accounts, politically ambitious leaders who were in no mood to make deals with the governor prior to introducing their own proposals. Moreover, the senate and house were far apart in their views on reorganization. When the 1975 session opened, HRS Committee Chairmen Jack Gordon in the senate and Barry Kutun in the house introduced comprehensive HRS reorganization plans.

The governor's office analyzed the two bills, and Askew, accompanied by Beecher, met individually with the committee chairmen to discuss their proposals and his. When it became clear that the Askew administration would be unable to get its own proposal to the floor of the legislature, Beecher was assigned the task of working with key legislators of both houses to insure that the reorganization that finally emerged from the conference committee was as close as possible to one that the governor could live with. Moreover, as political temperatures on the issue rose, Askew himself chose not to get into open warfare with the legislature except on a limited number of specific issues about which he felt most strongly. For example, the department and specifically Keller, who under Florida law had to be reconfirmed by the senate in his job as secretary, were under intense political fire from the legislature. Askew wanted to be able to support Keller's reconfirmation personally without having the entire reorganization question tangled up in the raw politics of that confrontation.

As the 1975 legislative session approached its end, Beecher worked with the legislature, helping to engineer the compromises that would produce a workable department. A successful compromise from the governor's perspective was that concerning the treatment of juvenile offenders. On the other hand, a provision backed by the governor's office that would have had regional directors appointed upon the recommendation of the state program officer—a feature thought necessary to attract the best people to the state program offices—was excluded from the final bill.

On the whole, the governor's office professes considerable satisfaction with the outcome. Because Askew has three years more to oversee departmental activities, he feels he has the time to get the right people into key positions and make the new organization work. Upon signing the final measure passed by the legislature, Governor Askew said:

> "People problems will not go away overnight. We should have no illusions that these are perfect pieces of legislation, but they are better than what we had before. They will improve our management and consolidate our delivery of social services. They will take the department closer to the people it serves." . . .

NOTES

1. *Tallahassee Democrat.* September 28, 1975.
2. For further discussion of these ideas, see Harold Seidman, *Politics, Position, and Power.* New York: Oxford University Press, 1975.
3. Citizens Conference of State Legislatures (now Legis 50). *The Sometime Governments.* 1971.
4. See Mark Lincoln Chadwin, "The Nature of Legislative Program Evaluation," *Evaluation*, Vol. 2, No. 2, 1975, pp. 45–49.
5. This outcome, a compromise between the Florida house and senate, settled two intensely contested issues. The first was over whether the governor or the elected cabinet should have primary executive control over health and rehabilitative services administration. The "strong governor" model favored by the house was adopted. The second was over whether human services should be incorporated into a single department or into three separate departments dealing with health, social and rehabilitative services, and youth and adult correctional services. The single comprehensive department favored by the senate was finally adopted.
6. Neither Emmett Roberts, secretary of the department when the measure was passed, nor Keller, his successor, ever used this authority to remove and replace a division head. Whether their power to do so enhanced their control over their organization is unclear.
7. One observer notes that physician lobbies muted their views on reorganization during 1975 because of warnings by legislative leaders that they would receive less than satisfaction on the all-important issue of rising malpractice insurance rates if they fought the legislature on reorganization.
8. Beecher became acting head of the agency following the departure of Bax, who had left Florida to become head of CSA. While Bax was head of CSA, Beecher had been his deputy.

5

Governmental Budgeting

PURPOSE

The purposes of this chapter are to familiarize students with the processes and issues of public budgeting and to develop a working knowledge of various approaches to budget formulation.

Reading
> Lewis Friedman, "City Budgets"

Cases
> "Sunset Hills"
> "Zero-Base Budgeting in Wilmington"

Instructions

Pre-Class Preparation

Read Friedman's "City Budgets" carefully before proceeding to the cases.

1. Read the "Sunset Hills" case, and respond to the questions below:
   a. What is your evaluation of the strengths and weaknesses of the two principal approaches to public budgeting—line-item budgeting and program budgeting?
   b. How might the budgetary process be different depending on which of the two budget formats is used?
   c. Are you an advocate of program budgeting? Why or why not?
   d. What can we learn about trends in financing public education in Sunset Hills from these budget materials?

2. Read carefully "Zero-Base Budgeting in Wilmington." What was the actual impact of ZBB on budgetary outcomes in Wilmington?

Procedure for Class Meeting

Discussion of the Sunset Hills and Wilmington cases, and the importance of budgeting in state and local government.

For Additional Information

Individuals without previous familiarity with public budgeting would greatly benefit from:

Augustus B. Turnbull III, *Government Budgeting and PPBS: A Programmed Introduction.* (Reading, Mass.: Addison-Wesley, 1970). Paperback edition available.

The classic description of budgeting in the federal government is contained in Aaron Wildavsky, *The Politics of the Budgetary Process,* 3rd ed. (Boston: Little, Brown, 1979). Paperback edition available.

A useful guidebook on state-level budgeting is:

S. Kenneth Howard, *Changing State Budgeting* (Lexington, Kentucky: Council of State Governments, 1973). Paperback edition available.

Another useful volume, this one a collection, is Fremont J. Lyden and Ernest G. Miller, eds. *Public Budgeting: Program Planning and Evaluation,* 3rd ed. (Chicago: Rand McNally, 1978). Paperback edition available.

Other summary works of high quality include:

J. Richard Aronson and Eli Schwartz, eds., *Management Policies in Local Government Finance* (Washington: International City Management Association, 1975).

Albert C. Hyde and Jay M. Shafritz, eds., *Government Budgeting: Theory, Process, Politics* (Oak Park, Ill.: Moore Publishing Company, 1978).

Fred A. Kramer, *Contemporary Approaches to Public Budgeting* (Cambridge, Mass.: Winthrop Publishers, 1979).

Thomas D. Lynch, *Public Budgeting in America* (Englewood Cliffs, N. J.: Prentice-Hall, 1979).

Lennox L. Moak and Albert M. Hillhouse, *Concepts and Practices in Local Government Finance* (Chicago: Municipal Finance Officers Association, 1975).

One important subject which has not to date had sufficient systematic study relates to the impact of federal funds on state budgeting and, in turn, the effects of federal and state funds on local budgeting. For an introduction to this, see:

George E. Hale and Marian Lief Palley, "The Impact of Federal Funds on the State Budgetary Process," *National Civic Review,* LXVII (November, 1978), pp. 461–464, 473.

Peter A. Pyhrr's contributions to the idea and practice of zero-base budgeting have been especially important. These are developed in:

Peter A. Pyhrr, *Zero-Base Budgeting: A Practical Management Tool for Evaluating Expenses* (New York: Wiley, 1973).

———, "The Zero-Base Approach to Government Budgeting," *Public Administration Review*, XXXVII (Jan.-Feb. 1977), pp. 1-8.

Other helpful material on ZBB is listed below:

The Bureaucrat, VI (Spring 1977), "Symposium on Zero-Base Budgeting." See especially the articles by Taylor and Broadnax.

Logan M. Cheek, *Zero Based Budgeting Comes of Age* (New York: AMACOM, 1977).

Donald F. Haider, "Zero-Base: Federal Style," *Public Administration Review*, XXXVII (July-Aug. 1977), pp. 499-507.

John D. LaFaver, "Zero-Base Budgeting in New Mexico," *State Government*, XLVII (Spring, 1974), pp. 108-112.

George S. Minmier and Roper Hermanson, "A Look at Zero-Base Budgeting: The Georgia Experience," *Atlanta Economic Review*, XXVI (July-Aug.1976), pp. 5-12.

John Rehfuss, "Zero-Base Budgeting: The Experience to Date," *Public Personnel Management*, VI (May-June, 1977), pp. 181-187.

Peter C. Sarant, *Zero-Base Budgeting in the Public Sector* (Reading, Mass.: Addison-Wesley, 1978). Paperback edition available.

Allen Schick, "The Road from ZBB," *Public Administration Review*, XXXVIII (March-April, 1978), pp. 177-180.

James D. Suver and Ray L. Brown, "Where Does Zero-Base Budgeting Work?" *Harvard Business Review*, LV (Nov.-Dec. 1977), pp. 76-84.

United States Senate, Committee on Government Operations, Subcommittee on Intergovernmental Relations, *Compendium of Materials on Zero-Base Budgeting in the States* (Washington: U.S. Government Printing Office, 1977).

Based on his experience in Georgia, President Carter began ZBB in the federal government in May, 1977. The Office of Management and Budget's instructions and President Carter's rationale may be found in the *Federal Register*, May 2, 1977, Part VII.

An earlier attempt at innovation in budgeting was PPBS — The Planning, Programming, Budgeting System. The rise and fall of PPBS in the federal government are described in the following:

Alan Schick, "The Road to PBB: The Stages of Budget Reform," *Public Administration Review*, XXVI (Dec. 1960), pp. 234-258.

———, "A Death in the Bureaucracy: The Demise of PBB," *Public Administration Review*, XXXIII (March-April 1973), pp. 146-156.

Local government problems are nicely covered in:

Arnold J. Meltsner, *The Politics of City Revenue*, (Berkeley: University of California Press, 1971). Paperback edition available.

James A. Maxwell and J. Richard Aronson, *Financing State and Local Governments*, 3rd ed. (Washington: The Brookings Institution, 1977). Paperback edition available.

Intergovernmental aspects are treated in:

Kenneth Hubbell, ed., *Fiscal Crisis in American Cities: The Federal Response* (Cambridge, Mass.: Ballinger, 1979).

Two good summaries of city financial problems are:

Richard P. Nathan and Paul R. Dommel, "The Cities," in *Setting National Priorities: The 1978 Budget,* edited by Joseph A. Pechman (Washington: The Brookings Institution, 1977). Paperback edition available.
George E. Peterson, "Finance," in *The Urban Predicament,* edited by William Gorham and Nathan Glazer (Washington: The Urban Institute, 1976), pp. 35-118. Paperback edition available.

Since the New York City fiscal crisis, municipal bonds and local government financial statements have been given a second look. Two useful publications in this regard are:

Understanding Local Government Financial Statements: A Citizen's Guide (New York: Price Waterhouse and Co., Office of Government Services, 1976). Paperback edition available.

Understanding the Market for State and Local Debt (Washington: Advisory Commission on Intergovernmental Relations, 1976). Paperback edition available.

Also see:

Sidney Davidson, David O. Green and associates, *Financial Reporting by State and Local Government Units* (Chicago: Graduate School of Business, University of Chicago, 1977). Paperback edition available.

The New York experience has been an important one. An insightful early description of what occurred in New York is presented in:

Donna E. Shalala and Carol Bellamy, "A State Saves a City: The New York Case," *Duke Law Journal,* Vol. 1976 (No. 6) (January 1976), pp. 1119-1132.

One type of state and local agency which has been praised for its financial management practices is the public authority. There are over 7,000 public authorities in the U.S. which spend over $24 billion annually. For a careful study of these public organizations, see:

Annmarie Hauck Walsh, *The Public's Business: The Politics and Practices of Government Corporations* (Cambridge, Mass.: MIT Press, 1978).

Finally, increasing attention is also being given to budget administration. For a good understanding of these issues, see:

George E. Hale and Scott R. Douglas, "The Politics of Budget Execution: Financial Manipulation in State and Local Government," *Administration and Society,* IX (Nov. 1977), pp. 367-378.

Allen Schick, "Contemporary Problems in Financial Control," *Public Administration Review*, XXXVIII (Nov.-Dec. 1978), pp. 513-519.

City Budgets
Lewis Friedman

The Budget Is Everything

EVERY YEAR, with fanfare, city governments announce their budgets. Newspapers dutifully fill their pages with detailed explanations of where taxpayer money is going. Commentators provide behind-the-scenes analyses of how the budget was put together and try to explain what it all means. Editors write to praise or criticize spending policy. Then, like a tiger lily, the budget disappears from public view only to reappear the following year at the same time, in the same form.

Most people find the budget uninteresting, unexciting, even unimportant — understandably. Who needs several pounds of thin, over-sized pages replete with charts and graphs full of fine-printed numbers with little explanation of what the figures really mean? Citizens conclude the budget is better left to the professional accountants who have mastered the arcane bookkeepers' language and have become custodians of the municipal pocketbook.

What difference does it all make? What goes into the budget and what comes out appear unconnected. The bureaucracy goes on. Once a program starts it rarely ends. Government continually spends more, achieves less. Public dissatisfaction grows and faith in government declines. You can't fight City Hall.

The Budget Is Public Policy

But the budget is important. The budget is money. New York's Mayor Beame says: "The budget is everything." The allocation of financial resources among municipal service areas is a statement of public policy. Every government activity ultimately means money. The single common denominator, the budgetary bottom line, tells all. As Milwaukee Mayor Henry Maier says: "The budget is the World Series of Government."

Every expenditure decision is made in a situation of scarcity. Proposals for extended funding of existing or new programs almost always exceed available funds. Revenues grow but rarely as fast as demands for more services.

Budgets are always created within a restricted financial environment. Decisions are costly. Funds granted to one department must be denied to another. The value of each dollar spent is measured not only by the benefits obtained, but by what has to be given up. The return of every dollar is its opportunity cost, sacrificed alternatives. The question is: "How shall we decide whether to allocate dollars to activity A or activity B?" So budgeting is a choice among competing and alternative programs. How is the choice made between guns and butter, police and social workers? We cannot have everything.

An Economic Model of Budget Choices

A common approach to this question applies the market model of the economic system. Decisions are based on individual citizen-consumer preferences. The combined welfare of society's individual members is then regarded as "the public interest."

In this approach, each dollar spent should provide the same value to all, and not provide benefits to some at the expense of others. This normative standard is called a Pareto Optimal solution.

Such a solution to budget making, however, would be Utopian. Spending decisions are not made on the basis of such abstract criteria or on the basis of their "merits," because there is no agreed-upon standard to judge the value of any government activity or program. It is impossible to merge individual value preferences. As long as interests and goals differ, concepts of good government will also differ. But these very disagreements are the raw material of the political process. If everyone agreed which public wants and needs should be funded, government might be unnecessary.

A Political Approach to Budget Choices

Our political model of the budget-making process follows the broad outlines of the market place but incorporates the unique features of public organization. The individual *votes*, instead of indicating his preference through dollar purchases. In place of competition among firms and products, political parties and individuals seek public office. The value of services provided is measured not by profits but by the political support they provide. Political rationality and economic rationality are not necessarily the same.

The political party is a group of office seekers who band together under a common label for mutual advantage. Whatever personal reasons one office seeker may have for running for office, one's major goal is to win the election and then be re-elected. A successful politician is one who wins. In order to satisfy his office-seeking ambition, the politician must obtain voter support by proposing policies that provide benefits to the electorate.

Government resources are distributed to this end. Expenditures are increased only to the point where the vote gained by the additional dollar spent is more than cancelled out by the vote lost by the additional dollar taxed. The budget is established where the trade-off between spending money and raising revenues is equal.

Budget-making is a political process conducted in the political arena for political advantage. It is not the exclusive province of financial experts but is of legitimate and vital concern to the wider circle of political actors. The budget lies at the heart of the political resource allocation process.

As Wildavsky writes (1964, p. 4):

> If politics is regarded in part as conflict over whose preferences shall prevail in the determination of national policy, then the budget records the outcomes of this struggle. If one asks who gets what the government has to give, then the answers for a moment in time are recorded in the budget. If one looks at politics as a process by which the government mobilizes resources to meet pressing problems, then the budget is a focus of these efforts.

The dollar and cents figures of the budget record who gets what, when, and how. In the political struggle, who wins and who loses, who receives the benefits and who bears the costs are reflected in governmental appropriations. The spending pattern is a statement of society's value priorities, the relative importance attached to different activities. Public goals are documents in the way government spends its money.

Special Features of Municipal Budgeting

To understand how municipal budgeting works, the larger governmental process must also be examined. Since it is only one specific arena of government decision making, it takes on and reflects the properties of the organizational setting. Often the study of budgeting has ignored the differences between national, state and local government. Although studies indicate much consistency, evidence suggests dissimilarities as well. Four unique features of immediacy of the urban government setting distinguish the budgetary process from state and national decision making:

- intergovernmental relations
- fiscal atrophy
- the balanced budget requirement
- insulation from external pressure

Intergovernmental Relations

Government authority in the United States is divided geographically. However, national, state and local government do not enjoy distinct spheres of jurisdiction, but are inexorably intertwined. Consequently, fiscal and program decisions made at one level directly affect government at another level.

City-State Relations   States constitutionally dominate cities. Cities are creatures of the state and have no rights of self-government except those explicitly granted them. Although many cities possess considerable amounts of local autonomy in what has been called "home rule," they are still subject to state supervision, if not direct involvement, in their internal affairs. This subordinate relationship has the following effects on municipal budgeting:

1. *Mandated actions and costs.* Functioning as administrative units of the state, cities are often required by law to carry out state responsibilities and state programs. Cities often bear the costs of such programs without the freedom to choose whether to participate or not.
2. *Restricted authority.* States can also tell cities what *not* to do. Many state constitutions limit the scope of local fiscal authority. State law defines taxable sources as well as rates. In New York City, for example, the property tax is limited to 2.5 percent of the five-year moving average value of taxable real estate. Limitations are also placed on state ability to borrow funds for capital improvements—in New York City 15 percent of the above.

   Review. States must often approve city programs before they can be initiated. This provides the opportunity for a state to interfere in the affairs of localities within its borders.
4. *Required Budgetary Procedures.* State constitutional superiority affects the organizational arrangement of local budget-making. The requirement for a formal public hearing, limitations on the power of a city council to reduce but not add to executive recommendations or vice versa, the inability of a city council to modify revenue estimates, exact dates of the budget calendar, types of expenditure classification employed in budget forms, and type of accounting system are often all state-determined.

Dependence on Grants-in-Aid   Money raised by the federal government and state governments is distributed to lower-level governments through both narrow and broad-purpose grants-in-aid. Usually federal programs require matching percentage contributions by recipients.

Critics contend that such money transfers distort local spending priorities. Some programs might never be undertaken if their cost did not seem to be "free" or a bargain. For example, highways have cost cities only ten cents on the dollar. So highways have been built instead of needed mass transportation facilities. Other critics charge that external funds replace locally raised funds — they do not add money, but simply substitute for local efforts.

The complexity of local spending patterns makes it difficult to disentangle the determinants of expenditure outlays. Two effects on the local budget can, however, be identified. First, earmarked funds reduce local government discretion. While the administration of programs is usually local, the purse strings are controlled elsewhere. Operating regulations, distributive formula and funding level changes often leave the municipality holding the bag — an empty one at that. Governments carelessly embark on programs, dazzled by the short-term benefit. If locally popular programs are curtailed, the government is politically compelled to continue funding them from municipal revenues, to honor past policy commitments. Indirect unforeseen costs fall to the cities. After a highway is built, a city must maintain it alone.

Outside funds can also fragment the local budget and diminish fiscal control over the bureaucracy. Departments with earmarked external funds obtain fiscal independence from central city authorities. The same is true of independent authorities, special districts and user-financed activities.

Fiscal Atrophy

The revenue constraint plays a key part in budgeting as cities continually find themselves in a fiscal straightjacket. Governments can only spend the funds they have. Resource capabilities of urban governments depend on two factors: the adequacy of the tax base and citizens' willingness to pay taxes.

A community's resources are limited by area business. If business moves out of the central city, the tax base declines. Annual rises in government purchases and employee salaries commonly outstrip city revenue growth. As Meltsner and Wildavsky write of Oakland, California (1970, pp. 324-326):

> The main problem city officials try to solve every year is simply to find sufficient revenue to maintain their current payroll. Their problem is that the city's budget increases at a faster rate than the tax base. Fiscal atrophy is the city chronic malady . . . The local property tax, the main source of revenue for cities, is exhausted in a political if not an economic sense. The common perception among officials is that we cannot raise the property tax rates. Taxpayers complain that the tax rate is too high.

How much do elected officials believe city residents are willing to pay for government services? Often, not a cent more.

This does not necessarily indicate the community is without resources, only that they are unavailable to government. Budget makers do not feel they can raise property taxes higher than they are.

Fiscal atrophy motivates cities to look for outside funds and focuses attention on costs rather than benefits. Budgets are cut to find available revenues and preserve tax rates.

Balanced Budget Requirement

The municipal budget must be balanced. Deficit spending, the hallmark of national government, is simply prohibited. For every dollar spent in the general fund, operating budget, an equal dollar has to be raised through taxation. Cities cannot borrow to finance current expenses.

The legal requirement forces an explicit linkup between revenues and expenditures. Taxation and spending decisions are made together. The budget exists as a comprehensive and unified document, income on one side, outlay on the other.

Consequently, a definite upper spending limit exists. The total budget is not simply the sum of individual department budgets, but has a ceiling independent of its component requests. Every expenditure decision has an explicit tax implication.

Insulation From External Pressure

Municipal budget-making is isolated from external pressure. Public participation is often too little, too late, and fulfills only democratic ritual. Wildavsky reports that national officials serve their clientele and constituency (1964, p. 65):

> . . . everywhere and at all times in the budgetary system. The need for obtaining support is so firmly fixed a star in the budgetary firmament that it is perceived by everyone and uniformly taken into account in making the calculations upon which strategies depend.

Logically, however, this does not appear to be the case. In the political clash of budget making, community interest groups have negligible impact upon spending. The system includes and reflects only the bureaucrats' and elected officials' concerns.

Crecine writes (1969, pp. 189, 191, 192, 216):

> The presence of external influence or pressure in the political sense was not detected in the budget formation process. . . . influentials play a very minor role in the formulation of municipal operating budgets . . . and play a very minor role in the gross allocation of governmental resources . . . budgets in municipal governments are reasonably abstracted documents bearing little direct relationship to community pressures . . . the-

ories that assume the city budget is the result of some kinds of external event do not prove to be consistent with the process uncovered in this study.

Interest groups are either uninvolved or uninfluential in the municipal budget process.

In the first case, the budget process is isolated from external pressure. Interest groups are simply not involved in budgeting and believe they lack the fiscal information and expertise to articulate demands. Often interest groups fail to appreciate the significance of budgeting as policy-making device. They do not understand the connection between expenditure and service delivery.

In the second case, group demands can be articulated, but do not necessarily influence authoritative decision-makers. Groups are involved, but powerless.

Often they fail to utilize the most effective channels of influence. By the time the formal public hearing occurs, it is generally too late to influence spending preferences. By that time the budget is usually set and immutable.

The public budget hearing should not be the place to present a first claim on the budget, but a tactic of political pressure. It should bring out the troops — show the political muscle that would provide the rationale for budget demands articulated earlier to be accepted. The most effective strategy for budgetary influence is to include additional items at the department level. Often interest groups are only able to prevent exclusion of items already in the budget. The city council may not be able to add to the executive's budget. Even if it can, the departments still have to implement such budgets; if they are opposed to a last-minute addition, they will place obstacles in the way of its implementation.

One of the few powerful interest groups are government employee unions. Since most local government spending goes toward workers' salaries and benefits, these interest groups can directly influence spending choices.

The Budget Cycle

Budget-making is a traditional function of government that can be broken down into related stages of preparation, formulation, adoption, and execution.

Preparation Revenue Estimation

The central finance office's first job is to estimate available revenues for the coming fiscal year. Economic conditions in a city and hence the yield of municipal revenue are enormously difficult to forecast accurately. The record of unanticipated federal deficits attests to the hazards of such a process.

Innumerable delays in federal and state appropriations add to local revenue estimating problems. Program changes, new money, and termination of old programs permit local government to estimate revenue only tentatively and to subject estimates to revisions all year.

These uncertainties allow room for strategic manipulation of estimates. But conservative administrators try to underestimate revenues and overestimate expenditures. The budget must stay in balance: a deficit would require expenditure reduction, or specially authorized loans to finance the debt until the next fiscal year. Such a crisis would certainly damage a city's credit standing. To run out of money would bring the charge of fiscal mismanagement, while a surplus would concern few.

Departmental Decision Making   The way municipal departments prepare spending requests varies depending upon the size and complexity of their operation, as well as the importance they attach to budget making. It can range from an elaborate set of procedures involving departmental budget office meetings, to the simple procedure of department head completing the required documents alone.

The latter situation is most prevalent. The budget is seen as a necessary, albeit dull ritual. Budget forms are not related to department activities. They neither define nor control the services actually provided to the public. The mechanism for securing money from authorities in control seems a bothersome diversion — vast amounts of meaningless paperwork.

Executive Formulation

Initial department spending figures arrive at the central finance office to be checked for mathematical accuracy and other technical considerations. Then they are transferred to the executive, which actually allocates funds among the departments.

The position of the budget office in local governments varies. But rarely is it analogous to the influence and prestige of the Office of Management and Budget (OMB), formerly Bureau of the Budget, in Washington. Whether a budget office or an individual budget officer exists depends upon the size of a city and its expenditures. Budget review is not thought to require organizational independence. The formulation of executive budget recommendations may simply be the ad hoc responsibility of his immediate staff and individuals from the finance office. Usually, few people work on the budget. The average is 19.2 people per city over the 88 cities we surveyed. The number varies widely depending on city size. Only 17 cities (19 percent) are above average. The median is only 8 employees (38 above, 38 below and 8 exactly at that number). In 6 cities no one worked solely on the budget, 5 cities have only one person, 9 cities have only 2 and 4 cities have only 3 people.

The ratio of budget staffers to all city employees ranges widely. In eleven cities the ratio is 1 percent, in 16 it is less than one-tenth this ratio, .1 percent or less. The bulk of cities, 43, are between .1 percent and 1 percent. In six cities there are no budget officials and eight offered no response to the question.

If such an office exists, however, it does not form an independent element in the budget-making cycle. Crecine, in his study of Detroit, Cleveland, and Pittsburgh, reports that only Detroit has a unit that even resembles the federal OMB, in that local budget officials exert power only at some specified point in the cycle. Municipal departments interact so closely through the year that the budget office influences decisions before requests are formally submitted for review, in the second stage of executive budgeting.

The layers of executive deliberations over departmental requests begin with a mayoral staff preliminary screening. Usually interaction is informal; only large cities hold formal hearings, with prepared testimony and structured interrogation.

The chief executive becomes personally involved afterward. He reviews the decisions made by his staff and resolves any outstanding issues. He may choose to meet with all departments again. More often he serves as a court of appeals for departments dissatisfied with the initial budget formulated by the staff.

Legislative Adoption

Next, the city council formally adopts the budget. Only the legislative branch can legally appropriate public funds.

Organizational arrangements for this review of the executive budget also vary widely. The municipal legislative process is different from that of Congress. A Finance Committee exists in less than 40 percent (34) of the cities we surveyed and even here the entire city council often considers the budget together sitting as a committee of the whole. Contact with departments can entail their formal appearance or simply their presence to answer specific questions. Public hearings often are required, before the budget is passed into law.

Execution

The budgeting process does not end with ratification but continues through the entire year as funds are disbursed.

The central finance department integrates the separate bookkeeping functions under executive direction. Budget implementation, as discussed under the "control orientation" below, is designed to guarantee that funds are spent according to legislative intent and that sufficient funds are available to pay bills.

The legislature receives financial reports and must authorize certain forms of transaction throughout the year. An independent accountant submits a post-audit to the legislature at the end of each year.

Summary: Budgetary Cycle Characteristics

Compared to the ad hoc nature of other political policy-making arenas, the regularity of the budgeting cycle is extremely important.

Its repetitiveness institutionalizes roles for its participants. Year in and year out, the same individuals carry out the same duties, interact in the same channels, face the same problems and make the same kinds of decisions. Each actor understands his own responsibility because he has fulfilled it before and will fulfill it again.

Budget-makers have their own world view. Inundated in an endless flow of paperwork, moving forms from one desk to another, continuously checking and rechecking the accuracy of figures and their compliance to the law and accounting rules, the budget-maker sees government as a series of dollar and cents signs, and as journals and ledgers to be kept. Any consideration which cannot be expressed as a number is ignored. Policy goals—the ends to which these purchases are only the means—fall from view. The relationship of money spent and delivery of services often goes unexamined.

The sequence of budget decisions is geared to the inexorable passing of the calendar. When budget time arrives, the rush of deadlines dominates activity and the midnight candle is burnt at both ends. The artificial division of time into the fiscal year creates a narrow, short-run perspective.

Since the activity of government is continuous, the time frame of the budget should also be. However, present procedures encourage the idea that each year is independent of the one before and the one following. The deadline rush allows room neither for retrospection nor investigation of what is happening to the money.

Budget making is an example of what has been called a programmed decision. Since the same situations recur annually, participants' responses also recur. Decision making becomes routinized, standard operating procedures develop and innovative problem solving is minimized.

Budgeting exemplifies bureaucracy: it is orderly and regular. It illustrates a Gresham's Law of Organizations: "Routine drives out planning." Routine also drives out analysis and evaluation.

Existing criteria of successful budgeting focus on the methods employed rather than the substance of the choice made. They do not examine where the money went but only how it got there. A "good" budget in practice is one which completes all mechanical operations accurately, on time, in accordance with the law, minimizing disagreements and satisfying all participants. COMP does not endorse this view. Later we will propose other criteria.

Budget Roles

Each actor in the budget process plays a distinct part in the sequence of decisions. Each role is an interdependent element in a network of reciprocal relationships. One's action triggers another's expected reaction. The division of labor simplifies and limits rules. Each participant represents a single set of interests, values, and spending objectives and no one else's. "Partisan advocacy" in budgetary conflict is like the adversary system in a court of law. Issues neglected by one are considered by another.

Departments Are the Spenders

The departments' role is that of the "spenders." Departments seek more money than they received in the previous appropriation ordinance, and more than they are currently spending. The financial output of the first state of decision making is expansionary. In Friedman's study (1974) of 14 Michigan cities, the sum of all departmental requests increased 21 percent. Three-quarters of all the individual departments sought up to 49 percent or more.

The department head assumes the position of advocate. He promotes and defends his programs in the competition over distribution of scarce, costly resources. Each department provides a different, often conflicting service to the community. Naturally, each wants to expand the scope of its activities, and improve its financial position within the organization.

But departments are more than self-aggrandizing and imperialistic, for their directors are professionals, uniquely competent to evaluate service wants and needs. Their institutional position and personal values combine to create a genuine commitment to their departments' policy objectives. They believe in the importance of what they do.

They lay claim to its significance as a vital community service. Burk-head writes (1956, p. 249):

> Very often, what looks like an overweening ambition may turn out to be responsive administration. The government official who seeks to expand his program may do so because he sees the need, because he would like to do a better job, because he is close to the beneficiaries of his programs operations.

The best way for a department head to fulfill his expectations is to adopt an aggressive, expansive posture and promote the financial position of his department.

The Executive Is the Economizer

The executive (and budget office) role is that of "economizer" or cutter. Charged with the responsibility to unify the separate departmental budget requests, he or she is compelled to regulate departmental growth in the face of enthusiastic advocacy. The executive becomes cynical—departments always want more, the executive thinks, whether they need it or not. He or she takes a hard line and says no. The executive reduces the budget as quickly as the departments request raises. In 14 Michigan cities, the executive reduced total departmental requests by an average of 11 percent. Over three-quarters of individual department budgets are decreased by amounts ranging up to 24 percent of original requests.

The executive must balance the budget. Since initial expenditure requests almost always exceed estimated revenues, for no other reason the budget must be cut. This does not mean the executive opposes budget growth. The budget he recommends to the legislature is almost always higher than the current one. In the 14 cities his recommendations were 10 percent more than expenditures previously appropriated. Three-quarters of the departments, about the same number that first sought increases, obtained them at the end of the second decision-making stage. The role of the municipal chief executive is analogous to Schick's description of the governor's (1971, p. 267):

> . . . he directs the pace of spending increases and program expansion by deciding which of the programs proposed by the agencies and by his own office shall be included in the budget. As gatekeeper the governor rarely looks back at programs that have already passed through the gate; his attention is focused on those programs that have not previously gained approval.

By means of his review, the executive exerts his own policy judgment by choosing among requests and initiating his own spending alternatives. Budget formulation provides the opportunity to implement his own programs and assert leadership over the course of government.

The Legislature Is the Overseer

The city council oversees the administration. In the U.S., the job of legislature has come to be less policy initiation than a chance to respond to others' proposals. As the administrative branch of government proposes, the legislature disposes.

In the course of reviewing the budget it checks the departments' and the executive's decisions. Since only the legislature can appropriate, it can judge the pace and direction of the yearly increment of expenditures and either increase or decrease spending. By so doing, it not only monitors previous budget decisions, but also determines spending policy.

As councilmen go over the budget's "line by line" purchases, they affect not only spending, but agency operations as well. Burkhead writes (1956, p. 189): "The legislature's review of the executive's budget provides a major occasion for the examination of the character and quality of administrative actions." Often the amateur and part-time municipal legislature can analyze and evaluate public policy only through this detailed review. Through their mastery of specifics they monitor programs.

Frequently critics charge city councils with abrogating policy-making responsibilities by concentrating on line item details. Such a viewpoint, however, creates an artificial distinction between policy making and policy implementation. Details affect the substance of policy. They are inseparably linked. The legislature's budgetary review not only ensures proper execution of appropriations and prevents administrative transgression, it also influences the course of bureaucratic policy.

On the national level, the fiscal impact of this oversight role provides the motivation for a negative response to the modestly expansive recommendations of the executive. The Congress serves as a "watchdog of the Treasury" and as a "guardian of the Public's purse," but at the local level this legislative role is more than a budget cutting position. This is made evident in the 14-city Michigan study, where adherence to this role orientation is more closely associated with the absolute size of the changes made than it is with reductions. Although the average of all the cities is a slight decrease in the executive's budget of 2 percent, the response of the city councils ranges from no modification in three cities to slight additions in three others. Increasing the budget is as legitimate a legislative role as decreasing. Only when the city council makes no changes at all is it not fulfilling its part in the budget-making sequence.

The explanation of this pattern of spending behavior derives from the balanced budget requirement that cities alone face. Because of that legal contract, any legislative change in the equilibrium of revenues and expenditures previously established by the executive represents the exercise of the legislative role. The executive in this situation defends the integrity of his recommendations against any imposed alteration.

Consequently, in the final measure of the budgetary process, the change in appropriations from one year to the next, expenditure levels still increase. The budget finally approved by the city council in these cities is generally higher than current spending, although it is considerably below initial requests and somewhat lower than executive recommendations. The exercise of legislative oversight is not a negative orientation to spending that only seeks to limit the rate of annual growth or even eliminate it entirely. More fundamentally, it serves as a mechanism for legislative participation in the budget making process. As long as it has a part to play the city council is satisfied.

Budget-Making Influence

The opposing roles budget participants play and their conflicting spending behavior highlight the importance of their influence. Each actor stands in the way of another's objectives. The spenders try to inhibit the negative behavior of those who review their budgets. The cutters use their influence to reduce the spenders' budgets. Who wins and who loses depends on the influence each has on the others' decisions.

For each actor to obtain what he wants, someone else's budget choices must be altered. The spending preferences of the strong emerge from the municipal budgetary process.

According to past municipal budgeting studies the executive, be he elected mayor or appointed professional manager, occupies the central position in the structure of budgetary influence. The departments are on one side and the legislature is on the other (see Figure 5-1), with the executive at the fulcrum of the system. Crecine concludes (1969, p. 38):

> In summary, the municipal budget is the mayor's budget in which the mayor's policies dominate the department totals and city-wide wage and tax policies. The council and department heads have surprisingly little to say about municipal resource allocation on a macro level.

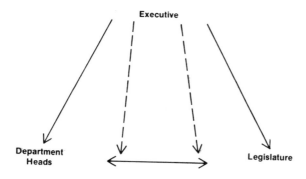

Figure 5-1
Structure of Budgetary Influence

Similarly Meltsner and Wildavsky write (1970, p. 344) of the manager of Oakland, California:

> He is the key figure in making most of the decisions . . . the city manager reviews all the budget and, for the most part, makes the decisions. He guides the city council in its considerations. He feels that it is his budget. And he uses it to make his influence felt throughout city government.

Budget reformers in the early twentieth century vested budget authority with the chief executive.

Before that, budget responsibility was divided between the legislature and departments. The departments prepared their own budgets and submitted them independently to the legislature which individually appropriated funds. No central finance office even existed to impose a uniform accounting system. Today, the executive consolidates departmental requests into a single whole in his own recommendations to the legislature. In this way the executive assumes primary influence in the sequence of budgeting.

Financial functions such as treasurer, comptroller, assessor, purchaser, along with budgeting, are consolidated into a single executive-appointed department of finance (see Figure 5-2). No financial officials (such as treasurer and comptroller) are elected independently under the new model. This feature is generally accepted, as only 18 percent of the cities (16/88) report an independently elected financial officer. Similarly, under the new reform model no boards or commissions stand between executive and the departments. Half of the cities (45/88) accept this practice. Under the strong executive model, the budget director's appointment does not require the advice and consent of the legislature. Also, the executive has an item veto over expenditures—a practice followed in half of the cities (41/88).

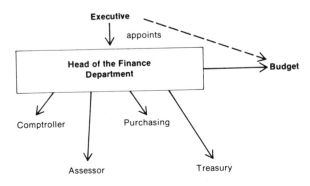

Figure 5-2
Budgetary Organization

But we must get beyond procedural formalities to see how the budgetary process really works. Not all chief executives are powerful enough to make such a structure work. Caputo reports that in the four cities he studied, departments, executive, and the legislature share equally in the determination of expenditure outputs. He writes (1970, p. 11):

> It is possible to conclude that no one participant (or group of participants) can formally or informally dominate the budgetary process. In the four cities (I) studied, no one individual or municipal body has absolute formal authority over budgetary decisions. This was insured by (a) diffusing ultimate authority; (b) creating a process during which a variety of individuals would be participating; . . . In addition to these factors, informal relationships developed among the participants which prevented one individual or municipal group from gaining absolute control over the budgetary process.

Anton describes still another pattern of influence in two of the three Illinois cities he studied. The legislature makes most budget decisions. The executive (1964, p. 18):

> . . . does not suggest policies to deal with identifiable problems, nor does he provide detailed information . . . [The council] considers the budget in a series of lengthy public meetings, with the entire council sitting as a committee-of-the-whole . . . the council invites individual department heads to testify, and the stage is set for the kind of political bargaining.

To understand structural differences and the executive's particular position, its formal and informal elements can be identified. The executive can change others' behavior as he officially reviews the departmental requests and as the legislature goes over his recommendations. The record is the less direct and less apparent exercise of influence to inhibit the transmission of spending proposals he opposes. The executive tries to constrain the departments' expansionary requests before they are actually submitted as the legislature seeks to exclude items from the executive's budget.

An executive-centered system is closed to departmental pressure. During the second stage of budget formulation the meeting that takes place between executive and departments simply notifies the departments of unilateral cuts. As Crecine (1969, p. 37) says:

> A series of executive budget hearings or review sessions are held before the mayor's budget is submitted to the council. . . By the time the mayor's budget reaches this stage, most of the mayor's decisions have been made and there is very little money left, if any, to allocate. Oftentimes these sessions are used to explain to department heads just why no funds are available to grant their particular request.

In a decentralized influence structure, the departments can sell their ideas to an executive susceptible to such pressure. Spending changes are not imposed. The departments themselves are allowed to determine where their budgets cuts could be made. They bargain, negotiate, and compromise. The executive's legislative recommendations emerge from an adversary process of mutual accommodation.

The legislature's formal influence depends on the extent to which they independently evaluate the pace and direction of annual spending increases. When it depends on executive recommendations, the legislature is a "rubber stamp." In Crecine's three cities (1969), the council approved the mayor's budget almost exactly as submitted in virtually every case; but an influential legislature assumes an autonomous position by extensively reviewing the budget. Such actions influence municipal spending policy considerably.

The final interaction between departments and legislature comes at the time of budget adoption. Significantly, the executive's dominance derives extensively from his ability to limit such direct contact.

Department heads cannot make an "end run" to appeal to the city council to restore executive cuts. Sometimes they do not even appear before the legislature. (In 25 percent of the cities they don't.) When they do, as agents of the executive they are compelled to support executive recommendations.

Nor does the legislature ever see initial spending requests. In one third of the cities only executive budget recommendations are forwarded to the legislature. Executive control over information is assured. It would be easier for the legislature to restore what was previously eliminated if it knew what the departments originally wanted. Without these alternative figures, the legislature must devise new alternatives.

Actors can also use informal influence to inhibit spending proposals before they become part of the official record. Challenges to the most powerful actors' preferences are suppressed before public discussion. The weaker actor, who could only lose by raising unlikely demands, does not make them at all. Overt conflict is muted. The question becomes not only "what was requested and refused?" but also "what was prevented from ever entering the decision making arena?" The departmental budget-maker must therefore make and pick up cues about what to request. The department head must estimate what will be acceptable to those who review the budget, and then ask for what is possible and probable in the context of executive and legislative spending preferences.

Behind the scenes, communication is a mechanism of informal influence. Formal meetings are not the only interaction between the three major sets of actors. Discussions occur through the year as those with influence continually express their preferences. Such contact between the executive and the legislature occurs in half of the cities. The executive gets to know legislative priorities before he officially transmits his own spending recommendations.

Executive-Legislative Influence During Budget Execution

The executive implements the appropriation ordinance adopted by the city council, which again reveals the pattern of budget making influence. Authority flows from the legislature to the executive and from there to the departments. Because the executive holds authority over his administrative subordinates, he is held accountable to the legislature for the proper implementation of the budget. As Burkhead (1965, p. 84) says:

> . . . a two-way pattern of responsibility, centering on the executive. One line of responsibility runs from the executive to administrative agencies. The executive must be charged with general supervision of administrative affairs; executive authority must be able to control administration. Only then is it possible for the executive to prepare a financial plan; only then it is possible to execute the plan as adopted by the legislature. The second line of responsibility in a budget system runs from the executive to the legislature. In every democratic government the legislature may approve or reject the proposals of the executive; in some governments the legislature may also modify executive proposals. In the exercise of this authority the legislature must be able to hold the executive accountable — both for the execution of last year's financial plan and for the comprehensiveness of this year's program.

The Power of the Purse, once the hallmark of legislative supremacy, has fallen to the executive and departments as legislative budget influence diminishes. The bureaucracy has gained the discretion to disregard legislative intent. The executive can *reprogram* funds. While reprogrammings might conform to the contours the legislature appropriated, they may not have been mentioned in the original appropriation. The executive can also transfer funds between accounts within departments, without legislative approval in 77 percent of the cities (68/88), and among departments without approval in 19 percent of the cities (17/88). *Contingency funds* are also usually provided to cover emergencies. The executive, in one quarter of the cities, can disburse these monies without legislative concurrence (20/86). *Impoundment* is executive refusal to spend funds for specific projects as appropriated by the legislature. The legislature's ineffectiveness in determining spending policy is now accurately seen as a sign of weakness. As Schick writes (1974, p. 217):

> The power of the purse is a barometer of legislative vigor and purpose, reflecting the ups and downs in the long contest between the Congress and the President for control over spending. To the victor has gone not only financial power but governmental supremacy as well. When the legislature has succeeded, it has been able to function as an independent and effective body; when it has failed, the legislature has been little more than a debating club, bereft of a significant voice in governmental policy-making.

Before we can suggest changes in legislative decision-making and their interaction with the executive to recapture lost influence over spending, we must recognize that structural modifications alone will not permit the legislature to reclaim its diminished power. True, a part-time, amateur legislature is no match for a professional bureaucracy, but the city council often lacks even the will to assert itself.

Nevertheless, several institutional changes can be suggested to restore legislative supremacy over the Power of the Purse.

Information control is a crucial resource of influence in today's complex world. The legislature is often severely disadvantaged concerning fiscal data. It has a problem obtaining crucial information without relying on the executive branch itself to provide it.

Departmental requests and back-up data represent an independent body of information highly relevant to the legislature. Their timely presentation to the legislature — possibly concurrent with their original presentation to the executive — could enhance the legislature's position within the budgetary sequence.

The legislature needs staff to aid it in digesting and interpreting such information. In only half of the cities (48/88) does the city council have any staff whatsoever.

The legislature can also reassert itself by enhancing supervision of the administrative branch (oversight) through such non-statutory techniques as hearings, investigations, committee reports, floor debates and informal ad hoc meetings (a letter, a call, a field trip). While not legally binding, they often are effective in expressing guidance, advice and warnings over the course of budgetary policy.

The legislative oversight role is also acted out through a post-audit of financial transactions. An independent year-end audit can verify that accounts and transactions have been legally recorded according to accepted accounting principles and as authorized by the legislature. Such is the case in three-quarters of the cities (66/86).

The independent status of this audit is most important. Those who maintain the books throughout the year cannot be expected to review and judge their own decisions. Such an audit should be made by a city-council-selected C.P.A. firm, an appointed auditor, or a state agency.

The Spenders

Each actor tries to satisfy his own particular spending objectives, not only through influence, but also by following certain budget-making strategies. These "rules of thumb" place proposals in a favorable light as they justify either seeking increases or imposing reductions.

The spender's basic strategy is to *Always Ask for More*. No action is more fundamental to the expansionary position of the advocates than continual pressure for increases. It follows that they should *Never Ask for Less than they Already Have*. Only by seeking more can they fulfill the mutual expectations of the system of budget roles. If they don't provide the thrust for expansion, then others, acting out their own cutting role, will decrease spending below current expenditures. After all, if the spenders who are supposedly committed to expansion reduce their request it suggests that even this amount of money might be too high and unnecessary.

Instead, spenders *Should Not be Afraid of Being Cut*. You can't get an increase without asking for one. The more one seeks the more one winds up with in the end. If you don't ask for it, no one else will. The spenders won't get all of it, and in fact will experience what seem to be larger cuts as a result. But these percentage reductions are made to a larger base figure so the outcome is still larger than if more modest budgets were submitted. The first alternative keeps this process completely outside of executive control. Although the audit supplements available information and functions as staff aid, the legislature rarely uses the reports. They do not provide an effective resource for legislative influence and need to be reinvigorated.

Another strategy is to *Use Up All Current Funds*. Any significant lapse, or surplus at the end of the fiscal year, should be avoided. If existing appropriations are not spent, apparently too much has been appropriated. Additional funds, above a figure that already seems too large, then are not required. The result is a cut and not an increase as desired.

Padding budget proposals is a favorite spenders' strategy. Since cuts will certainly be imposed, a budget is submitted that can be reduced. "Fat" is added so the cutting expectations of others will be fulfilled. Spenders attempt to offset and neutralize the detrimental impact of such reductions by anticipating such cuts in initial proposals.

Always Claim a Fair Share of the Annual Growth in the Budget. Each department is entitled to a fair share of the annual increment of funds. Some mathematical formula of "equity" is devised, or at least proposed. Something extra is automatically received each year, regardless of other consideration, because funds are allocated with this notion of fair share in mind.

The budget is often divided into two parts. The first is additional funds to maintain existing service levels in the face of inflation. The second expands levels of service and opens new activities. These two parts of the budget are treated differently. Existing program and funding commitments undergo only cursory review. Deviations are subject to more searching deliberations. Spenders can adroitly manipulate the supplemental expansion of their budgets to appear to be part of the base. Spenders *Mask the Appearance of Increases for New Programs* by presenting them as outgrowths of current activities.

Another spenders' strategy is the *Wedge*, which emphasizes the smaller start-up costs of a program in its early years. Higher expenditures needed in later years are hidden and total costs are under-estimated. Once the foot is in the door, the story goes, no matter how small the initial allocation, by the time expenses have ballooned, it is too late to curtail the program. Previous political support and built-in costs guarantee its continued funding. After all, eliminating the program would waste the money already spent, and admit previous error.

Faced with inevitable cuts, spenders sometimes suggest cuts which will be rejected or have to be replaced later in the year. This is known as the strategy of the *Sore Thumb*. Consequently if the proposed cuts are rejected, others must bear the burden of imposing reductions. If the cuts are made but have to be replaced later, the spenders do not lose anything after all.

A variation of this strategy manipulates a priority list of projects to be increased. The most desirable programs are placed in the middle of the list, rather than at the top. If the most popular program is listed third, it implies those above are more worthwhile. Its success, therefore, improves the chances of the first and the second.

The *Appeal to National Standards* established by professional associations of educators, librarians, hospital workers, police etc. is a spenders' strategy. These appear to be objective measurements of the quantity and quality of necessary services. These standards of performance, however, are really subjective, essentially arbitrary statements of goals and nothing more than a mask for the demands of a particular interest group.

In any event, they justify additional funds whether a city finds itself above or below prescribed levels. They are a double-edged sword. If the city finds itself below the levels, money is claimed in order to catch up. If the city finds itself above them, more money can be claimed to maintain this superior position. In either case, an appeal to civic pride supports the spenders' expansionary budgets.

The absence of such measures of performance can also be useful to the spenders. If *It Can't Be Measured*, little "hard" data exist to support claims for additional funds, then only the subjective evaluation of the decision makers can assess spending requests. The spenders need not expose themselves to the damaging evidence of extravagance, inefficiency or ineffectiveness these measures may appear to show.

The Cutters

Cutters also formulate counter-strategies. Several simply double-think spenders' strategies. Reductions are imposed when spending proposals are below current levels, when a surplus is present, and when padding is thought to exist.

But as the basic strategy of the spenders is always to ask for more, so those who review the budget *Always Cut Something*. No budget emerges unscathed. It is the only way budget reviewers can fulfill expectations of their role.

Cutters focus attention on additions to the base of existing spending as they *Reduce Increases*. These increases most readily trigger the budget cutters' negative response. The larger the growth first proposed, the larger the reduction subsequently imposed. The best opportunity to restrain the budget is to stop something before it begins.

No Item is Too Small for elimination. Cutters go over the budget line by line. Often cost-of-purchase details are the most important considerations in spending. The way mundane items are handled provides a good indication of the way more complex ones are.

Delay is an all-pervasive, multi-faceted strategy. Expenditures can always be postponed, if for no other reason than to find something to cut. Several procedures can accomplish this. One is *Further Study*. Additional information and reports can always be required. This, of course, takes time, often from one budget year to the next. Uncertainty about future conditions may then make the *Initial Allocation Unnecessary*. Through a deficiency amendment to an appropriation ordinance or by shifting funds from other accounts, money can be made available, if it is needed after all. But in the initial adoption, such monies can be saved and cut.

Finally proposals can be deferred or cut because *Money Cannot Be Spent* by the end of the budget year. Purchasing and staffing delays make appropriation of some of the monies unnecessary. This is particularly true of capital improvements and their operating expenses. Inevitable construction delays postpone the opening of such facilities. Less operating money is needed for the entire year than first thought. In fact, delays can be *imposed*, just to stretch the costs incurred across another budget year.

Another strategy is to *Eliminate Interdepartment Competition* and by so doing eliminate the incentive to submit expansionary budgets. Competition among spenders for scarce funds is inherent in the budgetary process. But if reviewers recognize it and minimize its disruptive effects, they can keep down the rate of spending growth. The cutters adopt "arbitrary allocative rules that maintain the relative positions of members of the organization" (Cyert and March, 1963, p. 260). Such conflict reducing strategies are:

Fair Share. By cutting the spenders so each maintains a fair share of the total, the incentive to seek more and upset the balance is reduced.

Balance Out. If an increase is given to one department one year then the next year is another department's turn.

Do Not Set A Precedent. Proposals are not accepted for one spender that have consequences for others. The claim that if it is given to one it has to be given to all is an excuse for giving none.

Budget reviewers can establish a priority among accounts to focus attention on expenses. The greater the possibility that an item can be deferred without adversely affecting ongoing operations, the more likely it is to be cut. Thus new personnel, capital outlays, equipment, maintenance, operating supplies and materials, and then existing personnel (first non-administrative and then administrative employees) are typically considered in descending order of importance. Each new person hired represents a moral commitment, since cities are reluctant to fire employees. Personnel accrues many hidden costs—such as fringe benefits, supplies, maintenance for performance of duties. Administrative overhead expenses are less important than direct services to the public. Travel contracts, for example, will be reduced before fire and police expenses.

Incrementalism

How do department heads, executives and legislatures make budget choices? Two models of this decision making process have been proposed: "synoptic" and "incremental."

Under the synoptic process, the values involved in a specific decision are clarified and objectives are decided. Then these values and objectives are ranked together in order of importance. Actors consider alternative ways to achieve the desired aim. Then the consequences of each alternative are considered. The best solution, one that maximizes the value to be achieved, is selected. Such a series of steps identifies specific means to reach agreed-upon ends. "Rationality" reigns. The principles of this budget making process have been summarized by Lindbloom (1961) from the writing of Smithies:

1. Governmental objectives should be as clearly and explicitly defined as possible;
2. Alternative policies should be explicitly regarded as alternative means toward the achievement of objectives;
3. Specifically, expenditure decisions should be made explicitly and deliberately in the light of all objectives they are intended to achieve;
4. In the interests of a rational comparison of alternatives, final expenditure decisions should not be made until all claims on the budget can be considered;
5. Revenue and expenditure decisions should be deliberately coordinated;
6. For each expenditure, some systematic and deliberate appraisal of benefits and costs should be made; and
7. Policy making, including budgetary policy making, should achieve a unified policy.

The synoptic model of budgeting has been criticized, however, as being less an empirical description of how spending choices are made than a normative statement of how they *should* be made. Public officials do not adhere to the tenets of such a cognitive process. Instead they *Muddle Through.* In order to manage complexity, diminish uncertainty, and minimize risk, they follow a set of "aids to calculation." These standard operating procedures identify the alternatives to be considered, analyze their suspected consequences, and then select one that highlights the "incremental" character of the decision-making process.

Our limited problem-solving capabilities, as well as limited information, preclude an exhaustive search for all alternative paths to a goal. Such limitations also preclude a comprehensive analysis of all consequences. Knowledge of society is too incomplete to predict the impact of public policies upon the environment they are intended to affect.

Besides, the problem is often ambiguous. Multiple and conflicting objectives change in importance as decisions are made. Values and goals cannot be isolated in advance and placed in a clear-cut order. Social preferences are inherently incomparable. Means and ends are so intimately intertwined that it is impossible to separate the desirability of any objective from how it is going to be achieved. Often we do not know the priority of what is desired until we find out what can be accomplished.

Consequently, the decision-making process is no longer deliberate, comprehensive and analytical. Instead, it is partial, short range, and pragmatic. Choices are made along the margins. The search for alternatives and the evaluation of their consequences is limited to those few who can at least partially agree on basic values. All but the immediately identifiable alternatives are neglected; all but their most relevant consequences are ignored.

Spending choices are not made on the basis of the worth of an activity, but according to financial considerations. Consequently, debate over values and preferences is minimized. It is not necessary to agree on the worth of a program to decide how much money can be allocated in any year. Budget-makers bargain and compromise as each recognizes that the budget must be adopted every year, even if some object to the way funds are spent.

Decisions are not comprehensive or coordinated, but remedial and serial. The budget is considered in fragments. Simultaneous means ends analysis does not examine the interrelationship of departments. Choices are not "all or nothing" but tentative adjustments to an existing situation based on the familiar and past experience. One adjusts for unforeseen consequences as one goes along. One is satisfied by a continuous series of small steps away from the problem, rather than accomplishment of the ideal solution.

Directly translated into budgeting, the incremental process means policy commitments of current programs and their spending levels are not reconsidered in the annual cycle of budget review. Existing appropriations are accepted as the legitimate base of funding. Previous decisions are not reexamined every year. They belong to the agency. From this starting point the budget for the next year is made. Decisions are based on a narrow range of differences—the increment from one year to the next, and in 72 percent of the cities (63/87) the budget forms themselves demarcate and explain the increase above the level of spending in the previous year. Wildavsky writes (1964, p. 13):

> . . . the men who make the budget are concerned with relatively small increments to the existing base. Their attention is focused on a small number of items over which the budgetary battle is fought.

The future is an extension of the present as the present is a continuation of the past. Historical continuity and consistency in spending levels is the hallmark of incremental budgeting. Totals from one year to another are stable as appropriations expand steadily albeit modestly.

Reform

Budget reform is a perennial concern among those interested in government. Ideas to change the organization and procedures of preparation, formulation, adoption and execution of the budget are a favorite topic because of the varied purposes budgets serve as an arena of government decision-making. The different participants each have their own particular interests, values, and goals despite varying pay-offs from budgeting. The alternative functions of the budgetary process can be grouped under the headings: *Control, Management,* and *Planning.*

Control

Control orientation is the traditional mode of budgeting. In many ways it corresponds to the incremental process of decision making. Historically and logically the first order of budgeting is to guarantee fiscal accountability. As originally defined by Schick (1966, p. 4), this approach is the ". . . process of enforcing the limitations and conditions set forth in the budget and appropriations, and of securing compliance with the spending restrictions imposed by central authorities." Government operates within the rule of law and the disbursement of money abides by legal restraints.

Given the financial mismanagement evident at the turn of the century, it was only natural that the first aim of reformers was to eliminate graft and restore public confidence in the honesty of government officials. Public officials were made strictly accountable for funds under their control by limitations on their discretion to spend. Consequently, the control orientation focuses upon the following range of issues: "How can agencies be held to the expenditure ceiling established by the legislature and the chief executive? What reporting procedures should be used to enforce propriety in expenditures? What limits should be placed on agency spending for personnel and equipment?" (Schick, 1966, p. 246).

This view of budgeting is distinctively negative—it aims to curb government spending. Decision-makers are cost conscious and see themselves as "Watchdogs of the Treasury" and "Guardians of the Public Purse." Thus the evaluative criteria of budgeting is economy. The goal is to save money and hold the line on annual spending growth. Consequently it is basic to the incremental objective to minimize deviations from the base of existing spending. This reinforces executive responsibility to see that the budget stays in balance without supplemental appropriations, as it supplements the city council's oversight of administration role.

This control orientation can be broken into several principles of budget organization.

The first principle is the *Annual Budget*. By restricting the obligation to authorize funds one year at a time, a regular opportunity for supervision and control over the activities of the spenders is ensured. Multi-year authorizations would diminish this control by granting autonomy to the bureaucracy at the expense of elected public officials.

The budget process must be *Comprehensive*. One all-inclusive document fully records the complete financial transactions of government. All special purpose funds (capital, reserve, bond, federal, custodial, trust, etc.) must be included and are so listed in 70 percent of the cities (59/86). State and federal grants-in-aids which grant a degree of autonomy must at least be perused, if not actually deliberated (75 percent, 64/87, do so). Independent authorities and special districts which have their own taxing and debt-incurring power must also be included. Enterprise funds, which are supported by user fees and service charges, must also be reported and reviewed, and are included in 91 percent of the cities (78/86).

Comprehensiveness also enhances the *Unity* of the budget. With all the parts integrated, the full impact of government upon the community can be understood and evaluated. The spillover effects of special governments upon the expenditures of the general government can now be assessed. The executive and legislature are ultimately responsible for all government activities since they created them.

Appropriations Must Be Detailed. Expenditures are to be authorized individually purchase by purchase and are so categorized in over 90 percent of the cities (82/86). The costs of government purchases ultimately make up the goods and services delivered by the agencies. The items bought are classified into literally thousands of items, such as wages and salaries, supplies, equipment, repair and maintenance, etc.

Each Transaction Must Be Identified. Legislative appropriations are not a mandate to spend, only authority to do so. They do not automatically require that the money provided be spent. Instead they are upper limits on what can be expended. Before a contract is signed and any funds are actually disbursed, the central finance department under the direction of the chief executive must approve. This is called a pre-audit, and occurs in 71 percent of the cities (61/86). Such approval is required for (a) filling a personnel vacancy or adjusting a salary (not from the personnel department, but from the finance or budget office), (b) regular purchases for which a system of vouchers and requisition forms exists, (c) extraordinary purchases costing more than a certain dollar limit, (d) travel, contractual agreements, equipment and so forth. Almost any item the government buys is under the central finance office's supervision. Such techniques not only guarantee the legality of expenditures, but assure that money is actually available for its payment.

Another technique of budget control is an apportionment or allotment system followed in 44 percent (39/86) of the cities. This is a scheduling of the actual outlay of funds over the year by month or quarter to ensure that money is available for the entire year. Expenditure disbursements are spaced out so they are not used up by the end of the year. This system is designed to reduce the need for a deficit and supplemental appropriation.

One objective of the control orientation is saving money. Tax increases may be forestalled not only by cutting expenditures at budget adoption time but also by applying control techniques throughout the year. Savings are forced upon the departments, either explicitly or as the direct outgrowth of control. All the paper shuffling and layers of approval delay the actual obligation of funds and thus in the short term save money. If it takes three months to replace an employee, one quarter of a salary is saved. The consequence is underspending.

Control orientation is narrow. Flexibility is sacrificed to excessive, cumbersome red tape. The finance office gets lost in the picayune minutiae of dollars and cents. The result is an incremental budget process that sees budgeting as a mechanism to control government costs and the budget document merely as its financial record, rather than a mechanism to manage delivery of services or plan what should be done. The long-term consequence of reliance solely on control to cut costs is to add to municipal costs by preventing efficient operation of services.

In recent years, attention has been called to the inadequacy, if not breakdown in government control over spending. The principles of the Annual Budget, Comprehensiveness, Detail and Individual Identification are not observed with as much care as they may have been in the past and as some may prefer. Dissatisfaction with the growing level of governmental expenditures, the accompanying increased taxes, deficit spending at the federal level and the fiscal crunch on local government, plus the actual pattern of allocations among departments-service areas have again made budget control the focus of current reform. Spending outputs are difficult to adjust because they are locked in by past decisions ostensibly beyond anyone's influence. The amount and pattern of money spent are determined by institutional procedures and practices other than the regular sequence of budget making, and are not subject to review. In 1974 only 44 percent of the federal budget was included in Congressional appropriation bills and only 60 percent of the authority to spend required any Congressional action. The situation is often not much more flexible at the local level.

These practices have been called "backdoor spending" and take several forms. *Permanent Appropriations* provide authority to spend for a specified or unspecified period of time a definite or indefinite amount derived from basic programmatic legislation. No further action is required in the budgetary process, which has been completely bypassed.

Borrowing Authority is granted to departments to obligate funds which have been obtained from borrowing. *Contract Authority* is granted to departments to sign contracts involving the direct obligation of funds. While subsequent budgetary action is required to liquidate the contract, little real control remains. Obligations incurred must be met.

Mandatory Spending is another technique of backdoor spending more common at the local level. Here payment levels established in programmatic legislation constitute an obligation binding upon the government. Although appropriations are required to finance the program, the amount of funds required is not determined by the budget but by statutory benefit levels. *Earmarked Revenues* are similar. Funds derived from specific revenue sources are mandated to specific purposes.

Unexpended Balances are authority to carry what is left over from previous years forward to subsequent years. In 1974, without further approval, $304 billion remained with U.S. government departments from unobligated funds.

However, it is a misnomer and conceptual error to characterize spending as uncontrollable. Backdoor spending derives from legislatures' delegation of fiscal autonomy to the executive branch of government. But what was given away can be taken back, if with more difficulty.

Furthermore, the budget is not so much uncontrollable, as irreducible. Well-entrenched programs and activities are politically costly to change. Barber writes (1966, p. 38):

> In a good many cases, however, the reasons for categorizing an item as uncontrollable are not clear. The borderline between expenses which are irreconcilably committed, those which are thought to be difficult to change without disrupting essential services are not well defined. Often the members (of the city council) seem to be referring not to some fixed commitment but to a general consensus among themselves that changing an item would be undesirable.

Spending represents accepted policy. If a program's values and goals enjoy widespread political support, pressure to reconsider its activities and expenses is small.

One way to restore the principle of budget control is to alter the annual decision making cycle. Funds would be authorized and appropriated on a multiyear basis. Each department would assume its funds to automatically continue. When the department desires an increase or decrease, it submits a request. Deliberations are spread out. If the tyranny of the annual cycle ended, the legislature could devote more attention to analyze and evaluate local programs.

Management

The all-inclusive function of management is the chief executive's responsibility whether he is appointed city manager or an elected mayor. He or she uses the budget to achieve operational direction over the activities of subordinates. Budgeting is not just a statement of finances but is the link between mobilization of funds and attainment of programmatic objectives. Schick notes (1966, p. 244) the budgetary process now means the ". . . programming of approved goals into specified projects and activities, the design of organizational units to carry out approved programs and the staffing of these units and the procurement of necessary resources."

Under what is often called Performance Budgeting, the amount and kind of government activities undertaken and services rendered are highlighted. Traditional line-items do not reveal anything about the end-products. Knowing how much is spent for salaries, supplies, maintenance and repair does not reveal much about the actual delivery of services. How many police cars are patrolling the streets? How many children are in school? How many tons of garbage are being collected? How many patients are being treated in the hospital?

To answer these questions line items of expenditure are rearranged into activities or jobs to be done. Three quarters of the cities (64/87) have reorganized financial data into this format. Police stations can be demarcated budget units, or the police department can be compartmentalized into crime prevention control, investigation and apprehension, traffic control, emergency service, communications, and so forth. New information is devised to measure such activities—some quantified indication of work accomplished evaluates service delivery. In 70 percent of the cities (62/87) narrative statements about the purpose of individual programs are included to focus attention on what agencies seek to do with their funds.

When the evaluative criteria of budgeting shift away from economy to efficiency, government is accepted as a community problem and the sole object is no longer solely to save money. The question becomes: "What does the community get from its taxes?"

Efficiency is the relationship between cost and the quantity and quality of the end product. But what is most often represented as an efficiency measure — amount of work done, such as tons of garbage collected, in fact simply measures the output of government actitivy. Only 30 percent of the cities (26/88) undertake any efficiency measures at all. Yet merely simple, workload figures counting an identifiable product is meaningless. Input must also be included — how much effort went into bringing about the desired result?

The evaluation standard of efficiency is used to maximize government productivity by either decreasing the cost of raw materials or by increasing results. Of two alternatives costing the same, the one that yields the greatest results will be selected. Given the same results, the one costing the least will be chosen. The objective is to "Get the biggest bang for the buck."

Efficiency is not a mechanism to decide what programs and goals should be pursued. It is not an assessment of value of benefits provided in relationship to costs. To conclude that more funds should be spent on fire protection than on police because the former is more efficient would be absurd. One cannot even choose between high cost and high results and low cost and low results within the same program, if they display the same efficiency ratio.

Accepting the goals of the organization, efficiency relates services of existing agency operations in relation to their cost. Efficiency is a tool of management to direct the delivery of services to the public by eliminating such common maladies as duplication, red tape, overstaffing and so forth. But once a particular course of action is chosen, efficiency criteria are crucial in evaluating alternative paths to its end.

The effect of management-orientation on bureaucratic routine is to decentralize execution procedures from the central finance department to the departments themselves. Central supervision and surveillance, budgetary detail, and the use of nonfiscal controls all go down. Departments gain the authority to enter obligations without prior clearance. Departmental cost consciousness and internalized self-control substitutes for central surveillance. Performance orientation rejects the notion that without central direction, departments abuse their spending authority. Instead it proposes that once released from interference, departments gain incentive to improve performance. Spending rules are viewed as legitimate and rational, and complied with voluntarily. Instead of being concerned with the desirability of particular items of expense, departmental personnel focus attention upon the larger and more inclusive issue of performance.

Under a Post Control System, central surveillance takes place after the fact. Agencies have spending discretion but must report their expenses and achievements periodically. The budget office periodically checks actual performance against the estimated work program established.

Central review concentrates upon variances from the original plan. Intervention occurs only in special cases such as overspending, emergencies, evidence of misuse of funds etc. But day to day spending decisions are made by departments without clearance.

Techniques of Managerial Budgeting

The desire to use the budget as a tool of management to improve government efficiency has coalesced into a movement for productivity in government. Several foundations, "think tanks," and government agencies are jointly sponsoring research and conferences to promote such concerns throughout all levels of U.S. government. Several techniques can be identified:

Operations Research. Operations Research techniques analyze repetitive tasks like scheduling, inventory, replacement of equipment, assignment of men and equipment. Because of their routinization, such tasks can be viewed through mathematical techniques of modeling, simulation, queueing, sequencing, game theory and linear programming. For example, in fire departments a system of variable responses to alarms can be instituted. Instead of automatically responding to all calls with the same apparatus, different patterns are devised that consider frequency of calls and likely fire hazard. Location of police and fire stations can be arranged to correlate service demand and traffic patterns so every point is equidistant from a response. Instead of assigning the sanitation department work force evenly over a six-day period, staff scheduling can consider day to day variations in accumulation of waste. Since there is no collection on Sunday, Monday is naturally a heavy work day; logically more men should be assigned to it. The use of such techniques, in one form or another, is reported in just over half of the cities (44/84).

Network Analysis. Network techniques ensure that activities take place according to schedule. Information reporting systems are geared to the completion of a task on a calendar date, or in sequence (process flow chart). Gnatt Charts, Milestone Charts, Program Evaluation and Review Techniques (PERT) and Critical Path Methods (CPM) all fall into this category. Network analysis can be most effectively employed to simplify work such as payment of purchase orders to vendors, processing personnel forms and paying salary checks, and completing capital construction items. They eliminate unnecessary detail, consolidate steps and suggest where labor saving machines could be put to the best use.

Cost Accounting   Financial information may be generated for management rather than control purposes. Such accounting is independent of and subsidiary to techniques discussed earlier for recording government expenditures, as it does not provide a complete picture of all transactions. Its goal is to assess the actual cost of a specific operation. Thus it provides a fundamental basis for performance budgeting's calculation of efficiency by providing output per unit of input. This is a figure of the unit cost, the total expense of an end-product, and is reported in 56 percent of the cities (49/87).

Assignment of managerial responsibility to organizational subunits comes with this measure. Cost centers identify places that perform agency work and the key individuals in charge, so they can be held responsible for accomplishing tasks and incurring costs.

The traditional post audit made to the city council can expand to consider performance. Instead of simply being concerned with accounting accuracy, it can investigate management and delivery of services. The Government Accounting Office, an arm of Congress, is spearheading such a reorientation of the post audit function nationally. More local audits will incorporate this focus in years to come. The audit as a city council tool to fulfill budget-making responsibilities will be reinvigorated.

Planning

Planning is a budgeting approach that seeks to apply a synoptic model of decision-making. Its primary recent exemplar is the Planning Programming Budget System (PPBS), but a planning orientation does not require specific PPBS jargon or methods. With the growth of public activity, the purpose of the budgetary process has again expanded, this time to include policy objectives and identification of alternative programs. The budget is used to set public goals, then translate them into activities and dollars.

Budgeting as strategic planning determines the most appropriate action for achieving a desired state of affairs. The budget's concern turns to: What are the purposes of the city government? What is it trying to do, for whom and why? What services should be provided?

Traditional budgeting has always looked back; planning's perspective is turned toward the future. Schick contrasts incremental "process politics" with a planning or system perspective (1969, p. 138):

> System polities tend to have a prospective bias; budgeting is regarded as the allocation of money to obtain some future value (the outcome or objective). This year's budget, in system terms, is an installment in buying that future.

The budget becomes not just a dollar statement of what government does, but a process to stimulate deliberate examination of the fundamental purposes of spending. Budget questions no longer revolve around saving money or increasing output, but around determining what should be done.

The Planning approach to budgeting strives to supplant the most fundamental feature of incremental decision making and thus contrasts with the control and management approaches. It does not consider existing spending and program levels to be above annual review. Programs and policies of the past no longer continue unquestioned.

As planning proposes to achieve specified purposes, particular programs become intermediate steps, not ends. Planning evaluates whether these purposes are worthwhile and their funding should be continued or curtailed. Thus the appropriate budgeting criteria on effectiveness. Such measures are found in less than 30 percent of the cities (25/86).

Government policy can be regarded as a response to demands, a perceived need, or a problem arising from the environment in which the political system operates. Effectiveness studies are made to discover what works. Effectiveness differs from efficiency. The value of the program itself is assessed. The efficiency of an activity can be improved but the program still may not achieve its goals or be a worthwhile public purpose.

PPBS

The comprehensive, planning approach heavily influenced the movement toward the Planning, Programming, Budgeting System (PPBS) which swept the governmental landscape in the 1960s. PPBS is an attempt to close the gap between planning and budgeting. It represents synoptic decision making in:

- Specification of objectives — identification and examination of fundamental aims of an activity. Thus it is output oriented, rather than considering cost of resources of the control or the incremental process. Specific activities are then related to the goal and a statement of goals is found in 60 percent of the cities (52/87).
- Planning — identification of the long range implications of present decisions. This is achieved by multiyear estimation of expenditures (only one-quarter of the cities do so, 22/86) and program outputs (41 percent of the cities do so, 35/85).

These decision process features are institutionalized in the PPB system through formal procedures to replace the incremental budgeting routine:

- Program Structures, a basic change in the type of information available to decision makers. Control orientation emphasizes line-item. Management emphasizes activity categories. Planning emphasizes program data, rearranging line items according to objectives. Functionally related activities which cut across existing organizational lines, either complementary or competing activities, are grouped together. This organization of information facilitates comparison among alternative means to an objective. It ends the serial and remedial incremental process by instituting a comprehensive view and is evident in close to 60 percent of the cities (51/87).

- Program Memorandums, relatively brief summaries of reasons for an agency decision on a major issue. These state the problem, the alternatives considered, evaluation of alternatives and recommendations and justification for action.
- Special Analytical Studies, more detailed studies which analyze a particular problem in advance of the PM's.
- Program and Financial Plan, five year projections of funding needs and service outputs of a program. They provide the future view absent in traditional incremental budgeting. Total cost and all relevant component costs, both direct and indirect, are to be included.

Is PPBS just old wine in new bottles as some critics claim? Certainly PPBS is not the only system to provide opportunities for planning and analysis, and there is nothing new under the sun. But it is important as a budgetary reform, because it is a system. It formally brings together planning, programming (analysis) and budgeting. As Schultze says (1968, pp. 77):

> One way of defining PPB is simply as a system for bringing analysis to bear on program decisions. Analytic efforts that stay outside of the stream of decisions remain just that — analytic efforts, not instruments for shaping decisions. The crucial element of PPB is that it operates through the budget process. It seeks to bring analysis to bear on decisions by merging analysis, planning, and budgetary allocation. It is a decision structure, and therefore must relate to other elements of the decision process.

The systematic features of PPBS are crucial. They are established as a regular feature of the budgetary process, and are not dependent upon good will, force of personality or the capabilities of any single individual. The systematic features of PPB provide a better framework for analysis and planning for the purpose of affecting resource allocation decisions. Both were meant to have greater importance in budget choices.

The separate elements of PPBS are not novel. Their integration into a coordinated system, however, is of fundamental importance. The whole, in this case, is greater than the sum of the parts.

Zero-Base Budgeting — The Newest Reform

The election of Jimmy Carter to the Presidency focused attention on the latest example of budgetary reform — zero-base budgeting (ZBB). ZBB is yet another challenge to the traditions of incremental-control budgeting. It is an attempt to have the budget process serve the purposes of management and planning.

By 1976, the National Association of State Budget Officers found that ZBB had been adopted in eleven states. In addition, another six used some but not all of its components. Its appeal seemed so pervasive that the NASBO researchers reported: ". . . state interest in ZBB probably has not reached its peak. It is possible that as many as one-half of the states will be involved in some ZBB activities before the end of the decade."

The individual component of ZBB are not unique; budgets could always have been put together from a "zero-base." What is different and significant about ZBB is the particular way it puts together various analytic and evaluative techniques to provide a results-oriented, priority-setting budget process. As a result, ZBB merits serious consideration.

Ideally, the first step in zero-base budgeting is the identification of *decision units*. Decision units represent the arrangement of financial information. They are the base of the system and can be devised according to programs, organizational units, or responsibility or cost centers. What is necessary is that they are self-contained units that are susceptible to a budget decision.

Decision packages are next devised for each decision unit. These contain all the relevant information necessary for a zero-base budget choice. Each decision package identifies the mission of the decision unit, the activities by which this goal(s) is obtained, the benefit(s) expected (in terms of effectiveness as well as productivity measures), alternative means of achieving the goal(s), in addition to the usual fiscal and other resource information.

Several decision packages are prepared for each decision unit that present alternative levels of expenditures and service delivery performance. In theory, five packages could be prepared:

1. a *zero* spending package that describes the consequences of not funding the decision unit;
2. a *minimum* funding package which presents the legally mandated level, or the point below which it is no longer viable or feasible to continue operations;
3. a *reduced* level, somewhere below current outlays;
4. the *current service level*, which is the cost of continuing existing services into the next year, and
5. one or more *increased* spending and performance levels.

The number of alternatives could be reduced for the sake of simplicity. In practice, decision packages have been established as a percentage of current funding, such as 75 percent, 90 percent, 110 percent, 125 percent, etc. *But at least one decision package must be below the current level of spending for ZBB to be said to exist.* This is the fundamental meaning of ZBB and the change it introduces in the way the budget is put together; alternatives below the base of current spending are explicitly formulated.

The last step in the ZBB process is the *ranking of decision packages.* This is the priority setting process of budgeting. Here the several decision packages of each decision unit are compared to each other and placed in order of preference. The total size of the budget is determined by starting off with the highest priority (rank #1) and including successively lower priorities until the cumulative cost of these packages reaches a pre-determined level of spending.

ZBB does not actually call for the formulation of the budget from scratch each year. It does not really challenge the right of existence and the funding base of programs. ZBB does not require a ground-zero review that assumes no legal mandates, no history, no past commitments, and no political support. However, it does *not* accept that the base of spending will be accepted and continued without an assessment of program performance and policy priorities. In this way, it is a reform of the incremental process of traditional line item budgeting. This is what is so unique about ZBB.

ZBB calls for a participative budgeting process instead of the top-down centralization of an earlier reform — PPBS. Authority and responsibility are decentralized. Peter Pyhrr, its developer, writes that, "ZBB requires the participation of managers at all levels of each organization . . . and is a tool for agency or division use and requires active administration and participation of operating managers."

Decision packages are to be formulated at the "gut level" of the organization. Since it is those who are in charge of daily operations who actually incur the costs and deliver the services, they should participate in the budgetary process. The assumption here is that not only are line managers often the best informed, but — given the opportunity, responsibility and incentives — they would choose to be economical, efficient, and effective. Thus, ZBB seeks to promote the involvement of program management in budgeting as a way to foster their commitment and motivation to organizational goals and organizational performance. According to Minmier's study of ZBB in Georgia, department budget analysts, ". . . generally (61 percent) believe that there was a greater degree of involvement in budget formulation by first line supervisors" than before.

ZBB is primarily an instrument of the executive, associated with his or her preparation of the budget. This does not have to affect the legislative appropriation process in form or content, although there is also no reason why the legislature cannot take advantage of the executive's analysis of alternative decision packages and rankings. The legislature can decide to use the ZBB framework or to ignore it. However, unlike PPB, the format of the adopted budget and appropriation ordinance does not have to be recast in a decision unit format.

The interest in ZBB is partially an outgrowth of the current financial stringency of government. The mismatch between available resources and expenditure demands is not a temporary "crisis" that can be muddled through by marginal adjustments of tax and spending policy. It seems to require, along with other changes, a fundamental review of existing program commitments. ZBB can be used for this purpose. It can identify decision units (activities and programs) that are not well managed, that do not achieve their mission, and that are of low priority.

At the same time, expenditure reductions are not necessarily a consequence of ZBB. Dollar savings will be obtained only if saving decisions are made. The formulation and ranking of alternative decision packages does not inherently translate into cost reductions. In Georgia, for example, "there is substantial evidence that there has been no appreciable reallocation of financial resources as a direct result of employing ZBB." In New Jersey, total state spending declined after the implementation of ZBB, but several observers conclude that it would be difficult to attribute the change in spending outputs to the use of ZBB.

It seems fair to conclude that to expect ZBB to be a money-saving device is to misinterpret its purpose. ZBB will probably not lead to program termination as much as to the redirection of funds within and among activities and programs according to considerations of efficiency, effectiveness, and priorities. In any event, ZBB and its associated techniques of analysis and evaluation reflect the tradition of reform as it incorporates the management and planning function of public budgeting.

Capital Budgeting

Up to now, we've examined the municipal budget as it relates to locally raised revenues to support operating expenses. But another form of local government activity involves capital expenditures. The differences between these two budgets lie in the nature of the item purchased, the method of financing, and the accompanying decision-making process.

The Item Purchased

Operating expenses are depleted in a single year. Capital outlays purchase goods, which are not so quickly used up. Capital items have long-range returns, a useful life span, and even a physical presence over an extended time period. In a private business, they would be considered investments in the future—depreciable additions to the fixed assets and net worth of the enterprise.

Generally, in government, they are physical facilities or projects that need to be constructed. Thus schools, hospitals, libraries, police and fire stations etc. are capital items, along with streets and highways, water supply, storm drains and sewage mains.

Capital items are relatively expensive. The cost of some particular building—a single line item in the budget—could involve up to tens of millions of dollars. Compare this to items costing only hundreds of thousands of dollars. They are "lumpy," nonrepetitive and extraordinary compared to the regularity of the purchase of operating expenses.

These characteristics of capital outlays, however, are not as simple as they seem. Their demarcation from operating expenses is often the subject of controversy. The definition of a capital outlay is not universally agreed on. How should office furniture and equipment be classified? Are they long-term, or immediately consumable items? What about renovations and maintenance of existing facilities? Is a cycle of police cars or of fire truck replacements a capital item or not?

Thus the capital budget, for strategic reasons we shall discuss, has become a grab bag of items which on the surface seems capital, but on closer inspection are at best only marginally related to a pure form of capital outlays.

Financing

The capital budget is further defined from the general fund budget by its method of financing. For the most part, cities rely upon bond issues to pay for such items. In other words, capital purchases are not supported on a pay-as-you-go basis, as is the expenses budget, but through deficit financing. The nature of the purchase supports this method of payment. Since the future community residents will use the item, it seems appropriate that current population should not bear the full burden. Consequently, costs are stretched over years by the repayment of bonds.

Sometimes part of current revenues is put aside to pay for capital outlays. But in 1970, according to a national survey, 63 percent of capital items were purchased through borrowing. Twenty percent were supported from the general fund. The remaining 17 percent came from federal grants. Some revenues, especially water and sewer facilities, are often financed through special assessments, so only particular users bear the cost of such projects. The bond market opens vast funds not otherwise available to local government.

Although state constitutions and local law limit indebtedness any city can incur, the restrictions are not as tight as those on general revenue sources. Most cities have sufficient funds to finance desired capital improvements.

The absolute amount of debt incurrable is generally tied to the total assessed value of property. Since the value of property continually increases, so does the amount of debt incurrable. To expand the calculation base and provide greater borrowing capacity, property assessments and the state "equalization ratio" are open to manipulation. The amount of money actually borrowed each year rarely comprises the full amount allowable. The unused portion provides a cushion for future years.

Borrowing procedures are often designed to increase debt incurring capacity. Often a down payment out of operating budgets is required for each project so the total cost of the project is less than the amount of funds borrowed. The term of the bonds is often less than the full life of the facility. The city replenishes its debt as it goes along.

State law exempts certain activities from constitutionally prescribed limits. Borrowing for such activities as Pollution Control, Job Development, Housing, Water and Sewage Project is excluded. Special authorities and public corporations can be set up with their own borrowing capacity. Revenue producing projects may be exempt from any constraints.

The political and financial consequences of this method of financing and the munificent financial environment of capital projects makes them appear to be almost free. Capital budget decisions appear to be less directly tied to the property tax rate and other local taxes than operating expenses. While the operating budget is constrained, the capital budget continues to expand.

This financial strategy has two effects. Without a rigid definition of capital expenditures financial decision-makers have an incentive to transfer operating expenses into the capital budget. When operating costs are spread out over a number of years, opposition to such expenditures is minimized and greater flexibility exists as more money is available.

But this apparent costlessness is illusory. There ain't no such thing as a free lunch. The result of such practices is increasingly large interest charges that must be paid out of operating expenses. The city may find itself in a vicious circle, where constraints on general funds push spending into the capital budget which further decimates the operating budget. This practice also costs more since the bonds of independent authorities, not backed up by the "full faith and credit" of the government, have higher interest rates.

Second, its apparent costlessness provides an incentive for overexpansion of such debt. Cities see the financial ease of highway construction and buildings and fail to address less tractable areas like social welfare and human development. The fiscal drain of such facilities on the operating budget is often forgotten. Once the initial investment in schools, hospitals, libraries is made these facilities have to be operated and maintained every year. Furthermore, once the facility exists, city officials must develop programs and adopt policies that make use of it.

Decision-Making Process

The capital budget is also subject to a different decision making process. While it is most often presented to the legislature at the same time as the operating budget, choices are made with different considerations in mind.

Howard writes (1973, p. 241): ". . . the planning emphasis has been more widely appreciated and recognized in capital budgeting than in operating budget systems." An awareness of the importance of capital purchase planning stems from the nature of the item. Decision-makers must anticipate the future and prepare for it—if a school is needed this year, it is already too late to do anything about it. The capital budget cannot make serial and remedial adjustments to existing situations because the result will not be evident until the future when the need may no longer exist.

A five year projection into the future, called a Capital Improvement Program, can be instituted as part of a city's Master Plan. This relatively long-range plan is part of City Planning Theory. Along with zoning power, construction of city facilities should shape and guide private community development decisions. Such improvements can affect land use and physical shape of the city through deciding where and what kinds of activities should be spatially located.

Research and analysis can provide such a forward look. Population movements and residential mobility are consequences of the location of schools, parks and streets. Projects to cycle the replacement of existing physical facilities must also be planned.

The capital budget process includes an actor not previously present, the Planning Commission. The Planning Commission has authority over the establishment of a master plan, zoning controls and the capital improvement plan, and is supposed to be "above" politics. The voluntary, nonpartisan nature of this planning function is ensured by overlapping and extended terms of office. It serves as an overhead, coordinating function providing a comprehensive viewpoint of the physical and social development of the community. The planning commission functions as a broad-based, deliberative body concerned with the entire city, not narrow constituencies.

Such an independent structural position, however, has other consequences. Since the planning commission lacks a constituency, it is isolated from community support and thus, powerless. To redress this situation, a movement to end its independence and place the planning commission within the executive is spreading. Planning and coordinating are integral parts of executive responsibility. Under such a system the capital improvement plan and budget travel from commission to the executive and then to city council, instead of being forwarded directly to the legislature.

For the planning function to be effective and important, the plan has to be followed and implemented in actual projects funded. For the most part, however, past studies have revealed a considerable gap between the plan and the legislatively approved budget.

In practice, the Capital Improvement Plan often carries little weight. Projects are listed in the plan but not funded. The capital budget is not a systematic, integral step in the implementation of a long range program. The capital budget represents programs, activities, and projects, not plans.

The plan is not binding on the legislature, and the planning commission is not powerful enough to make it so. Many projects are included to satisfy political pressure; money not allocated supplies symbolic rewards to community interests with no cost other than falsely fed expectations. At the same time, many projects are built that are not part of the plan. This does not represent a change in the plan or needs, however, but a response to other decision-making criteria, especially when different interest groups are strong enough to satisfy their desires in more tangible ways.

Departments also influence the capital improvements policy. The planning commission often only rearranges the priority of projects among the departments and judges the specific desirability of a project. The initiative rests with the lowest level of the organization, the operating units, who prepare their own capital budget without central direction.

Departments possess considerable discretion in the implementaion of the capital budget through the year. Often they are granted a lump sum for street repairs, renovation of existing buildings etc. which allows rearrangement and substitution of projects not within the plan. The capital improvement plan is only a statement of goals — goals often not implemented.

Not only must the plan be funded, but the budget must be executed, and the projects built. Often this is not the case. Budgeted projects never get built or more often are built so late that the relevance of planning is questioned. Here we have a question of control and management over the capital budget process.

The process of executing the capital budget is complex. Many separate steps come between initial funding, construction and actual use.

So many individuals and agencies are involved, so many points of decision and delay exist that only the strong emerge. A typical set of decision making steps involves:

- Study
- Site Selection and Acquisition (title search, condemnation, relocation, demolition, zoning modifications).
- Planning and Design (engineering and architectural studies and designs and their approval by city agencies)
- Construction (letting of contracts, inspections, payments)
- Financing (floating bonds and authorization that funds are available)

The result of such procedures and accompanying rules and regulations is innumerable delays. From the start to finish, a project often takes up to ten years. Such delays cast into question the validity of the initial plan. By completion date, it may no longer be needed. Schools may be built despite a decline in the birth rate or highways despite evidence of a fuel shortage and changing land or travel preferences.

Inordinate delay makes a shambles of cost estimates and the ability to finance the remaining projects approved in the capital budget and plan. Construction costs have skyrocketed. A waste treatment facility estimated at $100 million five years ago is built today for $300 million.

Consequently new managerial control techniques called "Project Management" are needed to expedite construction. This includes management information systems to ensure that projects are completed on time, according to estimates and according to plan.

Politics of Capital Budgeting

One problem of capital budgeting as a planning device is that little support for planning exists in government, especially in the legislature. Legislators are more concerned with pragmatic, short range considerations—especially immediate electoral support. The legislature and executive rearrange the priorities of professional planners and initiate unplanned projects to gain electoral support. Each wants credit for neighborhood improvements. In fact, the legislature often pays attention to the capital budget rather than the operating budget, since it is more politically malleable. Burkhead writes (1965, p. 185): ". . . the most difficult budgetary decisions faced by the mayor and the city council will involve the construction or acquisition of new facilities, not the expenses recorded in the operating budget." Capital projects are visible. This conflicts with rational planning.

Legislatures prefer many small projects rather than a few large ones. That way all members can point to some project in their own district. Capital budgeting represents traditional legislative pork-barrel, log-rolling politics.

The capital budget process—because of the nature of the items purchased, their physical presence and impact upon community development—provides an excellent vehicle to examine the prospects of opening up the budget decision-making process to the greater involvement and influence of the public. Can the capital budget process be decentralized to allow for greater community control?

Today, people want to shape their own lives and take part in governmental decisions that affect their living conditions. Government is regarded as too remote, unresponsive, and unaccountable to the clients it supposedly serves. The electoral process seems unable to control government and decide the course of public policy.

Several changes in the capital budget process could help decentralize decision-making. Public hearings as they are now conducted are usually a sham. But the sequence of decisions can be altered. Hearings should and could be held earlier in the cycle of decision-making, possibly at the time of departmental budget formulation or at the latest during executive review. By the time legislative deliberations begin, it is too late. Citizen committees could provide continuous community representation throughout the year, and not just as advisory sounding boards.

Hearings could also be held in affected neighborhoods. This would make it easier for local groups to participate and remove the geographic and psychological distance between the people and the government downtown.

Data could be placed in an understandable format, with spending broken down geographically. The local community should be able to evaluate planning commission proposals and devise its own alternative. The community needs an independent source of information, staff and other resources to play an autonomous part in the decision-making process.

Communities could initiate their own proposals with the approval of existing government officials. But only powerful communities would be able to satisfy their own preferences. Local communities could establish their own priorities, e.g., more schools vs. more parks. They could also select the location of certain types of projects, e.g., what streets are to be repaired. More fundamentally, with independent decision making authority communities could have their own budget and make choices without central review.

REFERENCES

Anton, Thomas J., *Budgeting in Three Illinois Cities.* Commission Papers of the Institute of Government and Public Affairs, University of Illinois. Urbana: University of Illinois Press, 1964.

_____, The Politics of State Expenditure in Illinois. Urbana: University of Illinois Press, 1966.

_____, "Roles and Symbols in the Determination of State Expenditures," Midwest Journal of Political Science, 11:1 (February, 1967), pp. 27-43.

Appleby, Paul, "The Role of the Budget Division," Public Administration Review. 18:3 (Summer, 1957), pp. 156-159.

Bachrach, Peter and Baratz, Morton, Power and Poverty: Theory and Practice. New York: Oxford University Press, 1970.

Barber, David, Power in Committees: Experiments in the Governmental Process. Chicago: Rand McNally, 1966.

Borut, Donald J., "Implementing PPBS: A Practioner's Viewpoint," in John P. Crecine, ed. Financing the Metropolis: Public Policy in Urban Economics. Beverly Hills: Sage Publications, 1970, pp. 285-310.

Browning, Rufus P., "Innovative and Non-Innovative Decision Making in Governmental Budgeting," in Ira Sharkansky, Policy Analysis in Political Science. Chicago: Markham Books, 1970, pp. 304-334.

Buchanan, James, Public Finance in Democratic Process. Chapel Hill: University of North Carolina Press, 1967.

Burkhead, Jesse, Governmental Budgeting. New York: John Wiley & Son, 1956.

Caputo, David, "Normative and Empirical Implications of Budgetary Processes," prepared for delivery at the 65th annual meeting of the American Political Science Association, Los Angeles, California, 1970.

Crecine, John P., Governmental Problem Solving: A Computer Simulation of Municipal Budgeting. Chicago: Rand McNally, 1969.

Cyert, Richard M. and March, James G., A Behavioral Theory of the Firm. Englewood Cliffs, New Jersey: Prentice-Hall, 1963.

Davis, Otto A., Dempster, M.A.H., and Wildavsky, Aaron, "A Theory of the Budgetary Process," American Political Science Review, 66:4 (December, 1966), pp. 529-547.

Downes, Bryan, and Friedman, Lewis, "Local Level Decision Making and Public Policy Outcome: A Theoretical Perspective," in H. Hahn, ed., Urban Politics and People, Vol. 3. Beverly Hills: Sage Publications, 1972.

Eyestone, Robert, The Threads of Public Policy: A Study of Policy Leadership. Indianapolis: Bobbs Merrill and Company, 1971.

Fenno, Richard, Jr., The Power of the Purse: Appropriations in Congress. Little, Brown and Company, 1966.

Friedman, Lewis, Budgeting Municipal Expenditures: A Study in Comparative Policymaking. New York: Praeger, 1974.

Howard, S. Kenneth, Changing State Budgeting. Lexington, Kentucky: Council of State Goverments, 1973.

Key, V.O., "Lack of a Budgetary Theory," American Political Science Reviews, 34:6 (December 1940), pp. 1137-1144.

Lee, Robert, and Johnson, Ronald, Public Budgeting Systems. Baltimore, Md.: University Park Press, 1973.

Lewis, Verne B., "Toward a Theory of Budgeting," Public Administration Review, 12:1 (Winter, 1952), pp. 42-54.

Lindblom, Charles, "Decision Making and Taxation and Expenditures," in Public Finances: Needs, Sources and Utilization: A Conference, National Bureau of Economic Research. Princeton: Princeton University Press, 1961), pp. 295-323.

MacMahon, Arthur, "Congressional Oversight of Administration: The Power of the Purse," Political Science Quarterly. 58:2 (June-September, 1943), pp. 161-190, 380-414.

Meltsner, Arnold J., *The Politics of City Revenue*. Berkeley: University of California Press, 1971.

———, and Wildavsky, Aaron, "Leave City Budgeting Alone: A Survey, Case Study and Recommendations for Reform," in John P. Crecine, *Financing the Metropolis: Public Policy in Urban Economics*. Beverly Hills: Sage Publications, 1970, pp. 311–358.

Minmier, George Samuel, *An Evaluation of the Zero-Base Budgeting System in Governmental Institutions*. Atlanta: Georgia State University, School of Business Administration, Publishing Services Division, Research Monograph No. 68, 1975.

Moak, Lennox L. and Killian, Kathryn W., *A Manual of Techniques for the Preparation, Consideration, Adoption and Administration of Operating Budgets*. Chicago: Municipal Finance Officers Association of the United States and Canada, 1963.

Morton, T. Gregory, *A Statistical Analysis of Municipal Bond Ratings*. Unpublished doctoral dissertation, Syracuse University, 1973.

———, and Renshaw, Edward F., "Some Questions on State and Local Government Credit Ratings," *The Daily Bond Buyer*, June 24, 1974, pp. 11–17.

Mushkin, Selma, "PPB in Cities," *Public Administration Review*, 29:2 (March-April, 1969), pp. 167–177.

National Committee on Governmental Accounting. *Governmental Accounting, Auditing and Financial Reporting*. Chicago: Municipal Finance Officers Association of the United States and Canada, 1968.

Pyhrr, Peter A., *Zero-Base Budgeting: A Practical Management Tool for Evaluating Expenses*. New York: John Wiley, 1973.

Reilly, James F., "Municipal Credit Evaluation and Bond Ratings Diagnosis," in *Financing Municipal Facilities*, Vol. 1. Washington, D.C.: U.S. Government Printing Office, 1968.

Riehle, Robert C., "Moody's Municipal Ratings," *Financial Analysts Journal*, 24 (May-June, 1968).

Rubinfeld, Daniel, "Credit Ratings and the Market for General Obligation Municipal Bonds," *National Tax Journal*, March, 1973.

Schick, Allen, "Control Platform in State Budget Execution," *Public Administration Review*, 24:2 (June, 1964), pp. 97–106.

———, "The Road to PPB: The Stages of Budget Reform," *Public Administration Review*. 26:4 (December, 1966), pp. 243–258.

———, "Systems, Politics and Systems Budgeting," *Public Administration Review*, 29:2 (March/April, 1969), pp. 137–151.

———, *Budget Innovation in the States*. Washington, D.C.: Brookings Institution, 1971.

Schultze, Charles L., *The Politics and Economics of Public Spending*. Washington, D.C.: Brookings Institution, 1968.

Sharkansky, Ira, "An Appropriations Sub-Committee and Its Client Agencies: A Comparative Study of Supervision and Control," *American Political Science Review*, 66:3 (September, 1965), pp. 622–628.

———, "Four Agencies and an Appropriations Sub-Committee: A Comparative Study of Budget Strategies," *Midwest Journal of Politics*, 93:4 (December, 1965), pp. 254–281.

———, "Agency Requests, Gubernatorial Support and Budget Success in State Legislatures," *American Political Science Review*, 64:4 (December, 1968), pp. 1220–1231.

———, and Turnbull, Augustus G., "Budget Making in Georgia and Wisconsin: A Test of a Model," *Midwest Journal of Political Science* (November, 1969), pp. 1141-1162.

Smith, Wade, Interview, *The New York Times,* April 2, 1972, Section 3.

Smithies, Arthur, *The Budgetary Process in the United States.* New York: McGraw Hill, 1955.

Steiss, Alan, *Public Budgeting and Management.* Lexington, Mass.: D.C. Heath & Co., 1972.

U.S. Senate, Subcommittee on Budgeting, Management, and Expenditures of the Committee on Government Operations, *Improving Congressional Control over the Budget: A Compendium of Materials.* Washington: Government Printing Office.

Wildavsky, Aaron, *The Politics of the Budgetary Process.* Boston: Little, Brown and Company, 1964.

Zisk, Betty, *Local Interest Politics: A One Way Street.* Indianapolis: Bobbs Merrill, 1973.

Sunset Hills
Richard L. Montesi

Background

The Sunset Hills School District, with an area of approximately 6.8 square miles and an estimated population of 5,000, is located within easy commuting distance of a large metropolis. It is primarily residential in character but in recent years has experienced a rapid growth in commercial and industrial valuations.

Residential development consists mainly of single family homes in the middle-to-upper price ranges. Commercial and industrial enterprises are centered in industrial parks and office building complexes. Residents find employment at these commercial and industrial facilities in the district or commute to a major city, where they are employed in executive positions.

The school district serves approximately 1,000 students in grades prekindergarten through twelve. Facilities are located on a single, twenty-five acre site. The facilities accommodate the prekindergarten through eighth grade program, and secondary students, grades nine through twelve, attend two neighboring high schools on a tuition basis.

The district also conducts a twelve month community recreation program for all residents and a six week summer day camp for youngsters four to fourteen years of age.

The district employs approximately 65 full-time and 25 part-time staff members (professional and civil service), and an equal number of summer employees.

Program Budgeting

In December 1978, the Sunset Hills School Committee directed the administration to prepare the 1979–1980 budget in both line-item and program format. The emphasis was to be on specific programs or subjects of instruction and supporting services.

Exhibit 5-1 is a summary of the 1979–1980 budget in line-item format. Exhibit 5-1A provides the details for one major line-item, Regular School (Code 2110).

Exhibit 5-2 is a summary of the 1979–1980 budget in program format. Exhibits 5-2A and 2B provide more detail in terms of specific programs and services.

Exhibit 5-3 is a multiyear estimate of expenditures for the reading program.

Exhibit 5-1
Sunset Hills School District 1979-1980 Budget

Code	Function	1978-79 Budget	1979-80 Budget
1010	Board of Education	$ 6,200	$ 7,450
1040	District Clerk	600	600
1060	District Meeting	800	800
1240	Superintendent's Office	69,600	73,600
1310	Business Office	45,450	47,550
1320	Auditing Services	3,000	3,000
1325	Treasurer	1,050	1,050
1420	Legal Services	13,300	13,300
1620	Operation & Maintenance	281,700	288,400
1670	Printing & Mailing	2,100	2,100
1680	Data Processing	14,500	15,600
1910	Insurance	15,000	16,600
1950	Assessments & Taxes	20,500	20,500
1964	Property Tax Refunds	-0-	15,000
1981	Administrative Charges - Special Education	15,850	17,000
	TOTAL GENERAL SUPPORT	$ 489,650	$ 522,550
2010	Supervision	$ 50,750	$ 44,950
2110	Regular School	1,702,250	1,711,400
2250	Handicapped Programs	63,800	99,100
2255	L.D. (Learning Disabilities) Programs	-0-	35,050
2270	PSEN (Pupils with Special Educational Needs) Programs	50,100	51,450
2610	Library & Audio Visual	44,150	39,850
2805	Attendance Services	3,450	3,500
2810	Guidance Services	27,700	45,000
2815	Health Services	30,050	31,700
2820	Psychological Services	32,800	23,500
2855	Athletics	16,500	20,500
	TOTAL INSTRUCTION	$2,021,550	$2,106,000

Exhibit 5-1 (Continued)

Code	Function	1978-79 Budget	1979-80 Budget
5510	District Transportation	$ 79,200	$ 88,400
5540	Contract Transportation	119,300	131,500
	TOTAL PUPIL TRANSPORTATION	$ 198,500	$ 219,900
7140	Community Recreation	$ 49,300	$ 44,450
7310	Youth Program (Summer Day Camp)	107,600	99,950
	TOTAL COMMUNITY SERVICES	$ 156,900	$ 144,400
9010	State Retirement	36,000	38,000
9020	Teachers' Retirement	234,000	264,000
9030	Social Security	75,600	83,000
9040	Workmen's Compensation	10,400	14,400
9045	Life Insurance	5,000	4,000
9050	Unemployment Insurance	21,000	5,000
9060	Health Insurance	49,000	49,000
9070	Union Welfare Benefits	4,600	9,400
9530	Inter-Fund Transfers (Cafeteria)	10,000	19,000
9711	Debt Service	375,175	365,375
	TOTAL UNDISTRIBUTED	$ 820,775	$ 851,175
	TOTALS	$3,687,375	$3,844,025

Exhibit 5-1A

1979–80 Budget Regular School

Code	Function	1978–79 Budget	1979–80 Budget
2110-100	Teachers' Salaries (PreK & Kindergarten)	$ 53,300	$ 56,800
120	Teachers' Salaries (Grades 1–6)	418,500	403,600
130	Teachers' Salaries (Grades 7–8)	358,700	401,200
132	Professional Development Program	25,000	25,000
133	Teacher Assistants	28,300	25,400
140	Substitute Teachers	12,500	14,400
160	Aides, Clerical	11,300	12,400
164	Aides, Cafeteria-Playground	11,000	12,000
165	Monitors	16,300	16,400
	TOTAL PERSONAL SERVICES	$ 934,900	$ 967,200
2110-400	Equipment Purchase	$ 2,600	$ 7,700
406	Equipment Rental	5,600	5,600
408	Equipment Repairs & Maintenance	1,000	1,000
410	Travel & Conferences	1,700	1,700
414	Program Development	2,000	2,000
416	Field Trips & Environmental Education	4,000	9,000
417	Special Activities	1,000	2,000
450	Materials & Supplies	34,850	30,350
472	Tuition - High Schools	602,000	642,800
472	Tuition - Summer School	5,500	3,000
480	Textbooks	8,700	7,200
490	Special Services	98,400	31,850
	TOTAL OTHER EXPENSES	$ 767,350	$ 744,200
	TOTAL REGULAR SCHOOL	$1,702,250	$1,711,400

Exhibit 5-2
1979–80 Budget by Program, Summary of Expenditures by Program

	1979–80 Budget	Percent of Total
INSTRUCTIONAL PROGRAMS		
Basic Education	$1,086,100	28.25
Special Education	185,600	4.83
Tuition Pupils	645,800	16.80
TOTAL INSTRUCTIONAL PROGRAMS	$1,917,500	49.88
INSTRUCTIONAL SUPPORT PROGRAMS		
Learning Resources	39,850	1.04
Pupil Personnel Services	103,700	2.70
Plant Operation & Maintenance	288,400	7.50
Pupil Transportation	219,900	5.72
Food Service	19,000	.49
District Management	279,100	7.26
TOTAL INSTRUCTIONAL SUPPORT PROGRAMS	$ 949,950	24.71
COMMUNITY SERVICES	144,400	3.76
EMPLOYEE BENEFITS	466,800	12.14
DEBT SERVICE	365,375	9.51
GRAND TOTAL	$3,844,025	100.00

Exhibit 5-2A

1979–80 Budget by Program Summary of Expenditures by Program

Code	Function	Total Budget	Percent of Total Budget
	INSTRUCTIONAL PROGRAMS		
	Basic Education		
01	English	$ 133,200	3.46
02	Reading	171,300	4.46
03	Science	81,450	2.12
04	Health	75,000	1.95
05	Mathematics	120,600	3.14
06	Social Studies	82,100	2.14
07	Physical Education	77,300	2.01
08	Gifted & Talented	29,100	.76
09	Foreign Languages	59,600	1.55
10	Home Economics	42,500	1.10
11	Industrial Education	40,350	1.05
12	Art	56,700	1.47
13	Music	60,000	1.56
00	Non-Program	56,900	1.48
	Total Basic Education	$1,086,100	28.25
21	Special Education	185,600	4.83
22	Tuition Pupils	645,800	16.80
	TOTAL INSTRUCTIONAL PROGRAMS	$1,917,500	49.88

Exhibit 5–2A (Continued)

Code	Function	Total Budget	Percent of Total Budget
	INSTRUCTIONAL SUPPORT PROGRAMS		
23	Learning Resources	$ 39,850	1.04
24	Pupil Personnel Services	103,700	2.70
31	Plant Operation & Maintenance	288,400	7.50
41	Pupil Transportation	219,900	5.72
51	Food Service	19,000	.49
61	District Management	279,100	7.26
	TOTAL INSTRUCTIONAL SUPPORT PROGRAMS	$ 949,950	24.71
71	COMMUNITY SERVICES	144,400	3.76
81	EMPLOYEE BENEFITS	466,800	12.14
91	DEBT SERVICE	365,375	9.51
	GRAND TOTAL	$3,844,025	100.00

Exhibit 5-2B
1979–80 Budget by Program, Summary of Expenditures by Program with Allocation by Object

Code	Function	Certified* Salaries	Non-Certified* Salaries	Other Expenses	Total
	INSTRUCTIONAL PROGRAMS				
	Basic Education				
01	English	$107,800	$12,200	$ 13,200	$ 133,200
02	Reading	145,400	13,200	12,700	171,300
03	Science	71,500	-	9,950	81,450
04	Health	66,900	-	8,100	75,000
05	Mathematics	112,700	-	7,900	120,600
06	Social Studies	77,000	-	5,100	82,100
07	Physical Education	68,000	-	9,300	77,300
08	Gifted & Talented	22,000	-	7,100	29,100
09	Foreign Language	53,400	-	6,200	59,600
10	Home Economics	32,700	-	9,800	42,500
11	Industrial Education	29,800	-	10,550	40,350
12	Art	44,300	-	12,400	56,700
13	Music	50,600	-	9,400	60,000
00	Non-Program	14,400	40,800	1,700	56,900
	Total Basic Education	$896,500	$66,200	$123,400	$1,086,100
21	Special Education	74,300	14,500	96,800	185,600
22	Tuition Pupils	-	-	645,800	645,800
	TOTAL INSTRUCTIONAL PROGRAMS	$970,800	$80,700	$866,000	$1,917,500

Exhibit 5-2B (Continued)

Code	Function	Certified* Salaries	Non-Certified* Salaries	Other Expenses	Total
	INSTRUCTIONAL SUPPORT PROGRAMS				
23	Learning Resources	$ 30,200	-	$ 9,650	$ 39,850
24	Pupil Personnel Services	82,100	6,100	15,500	103,700
31	Plant Operation & Maintenance	-	124,700	163,700	288,400
41	Pupil Transportation	8,000	64,700	147,200	219,900
51	Food Service	7,000	12,000	-	19,000
61	District Management	88,900	48,800	141,400	279,100
	TOTAL INSTRUCTIONAL SUPPORT PROGRAMS	$ 216,200	256,300	$ 477,450	$ 949,950
71	COMMUNITY SERVICES	-	109,000	35,400	144,400
81	EMPLOYEE BENEFITS	-	-	466,800	466,800
91	DEBT SERVICE	-	-	365,375	365,375
	GRAND TOTAL	$1,187,000	$446,000	$2,211,025	$3,844,025

*"Certified" indicates professional teachers; "non-certified" means other staff, like aides, secretaries, custodial staff, etc.

Exhibit 5-3
Multiyear Financial Plan, Program: Reading; Levels: PreK-8

Object	1978-79	1979-80	1980-81	1981-82
1. Salaries (Certified)	$137,400	$145,400	$154,200	$164,400
2. Salaries (Non-Certified)	12,500	13,200	14,200	15,000
3. Equipment	800	5,600	1,000	1,200
4. Supplies & Materials	1,700	1,900	2,100	2,300
5. Textbooks	1,400	2,100	1,700	2,000
6. Workbooks	1,500	1,700	1,900	2,100
7. Other Expenses	1,200	1,400	1,500	1,600
8. Total	$156,500	$171,300	$176,600	$188,600

Zero-Base Budgeting in Wilmington

David W. Singleton, Bruce A. Smith, and James R. Cleaveland

IN RECENT YEARS, governments at every level have shown growing interest in adopting progressive management techniques. These techniques are in stark contrast to such factors as tradition and political considerations, which have historically played a central role in governmental management. The rapid growth in governmental expenditures in recent years, and the fiscal crises confronting many governmental units, have contributed significantly to the growing interest in adopting these modern approaches to management.

As in the private sector, the fundamental area of management in the public sector is the planning-budgeting-accountability process. Consequently, it is in this area that a large share of public sector management concern and improvement has taken place. Executive budgeting, performance budgeting and the program planning and budgeting system (PPBS) all represent innovations—and advances—in this field.

One of the major drawbacks in most budgeting systems is their primary focus on the increases from year to year in various accounting categories, with little systematic regard for programmatic priorities and results. A relatively new approach to planning and budgeting—zero base budgeting—aims to overcome this drawback by subjecting all proposed activities and expenditures to the type of intensive scrutiny normally reserved for proposed new programs. Zero base budgeting, or ZBB, originated in the private sector and has been little used in the public sector. This article presents a case history of its implementation in the municipal government of Wilmington, Delaware.

With a resident population of 80,000, and a daily commuter influx from the suburbs of another 60,000, Wilmington is far and away Delaware's largest city, and its commercial hub. The City also houses half of the state's welfare recipients, a quarter of the senior citizens, a quarter of the persons with incomes below the poverty line, and nearly a third of the crime—although it represents only 15 percent of the state's population. Since 1960, the city's resident population has declined 17 percent.

For fiscal 1976, Wilmington's general operating budget was $34.8 million, of which $9.1 million was an operating subsidy to the local school district. In addition, the city operates separate funds for its water, sewer and Marine Terminal operations, totaling $11.3 million in Fiscal 1976, and administers another $10.2 million annually in federal, state and private grant funds. The city's capital budget for Fiscal 1976 amounted to $12.5 million.

Wilmington's governmental structure, under home-rule charter, is characterized as "strong mayor-council" form. The present Mayor, Thomas C. Maloney, has held office since 1973. During that time, Maloney has established a national reputation for fiscal restraint, limiting the growth in the city's operating budget to only 18.9 percent for all four of his budgets combined—compared to 16 percent annually under his predecessor. A mainstay of Maloney's approach has been improved management of resources, and dramatic productivity improvements in a variety of city services.

In their continuing review of the planning-budgeting-accountability process in Wilmington, Mayor Maloney and his staff had identified a variety of disadvantages with the existing process—a fairly typical, although heavily detailed, line-item approach. Among the more significant difficulties were:

Insufficient Information: The existing budget process provided little useful information about the nature and level of services provided, the reason for providing the service, the beneficiaries of the service, or the resources needed to provide a specific level of service.

Existing Level Assumed: In general, the budgeting process took as given the level of funding from the current year, and focused almost entirely on the increase sought for the coming year. Expenditures included in previous budgets usually required no significant justification.

No Trade-offs: Although the city did not have sufficient resources to fund all services at the requested—or even current—level, there was no meaningful process available to make choices and trade-offs among the city's different services on anything even approaching a cost/benefit basis.

Impact of Change Unclear: There was no mechanism to predict the impact of significant changes in the funding of particular services, and no systematic way to identify the absolute minimum level of service (if any) which the city must provide. Similarly, there was no way to project the likely benefits of significant funding increases in a particular service.

Although these problems are relatively common to all levels of government, they were exacerbated in Wilmington's case by the severe and continuing fiscal problems which beset Wilmington and so many of America's older cities:

Little or no growth in existing revenue sources, coupled with a high level of inflation and excessive unemployment.

Locked-in union wage settlements in the 5–7.5 percent range.

Relatively "fixed" expenses, such as pensions, debt service, insurance, and the public school subsidy, consuming roughly half the available revenues.

Continuing demands for new programs (or continuation of programs formerly federally funded), particularly social services.

Strong aversion to any tax increases, which tend to accelerate the erosion of the city's tax base.

As a result of these concerns, members of Mayor Maloney's staff were attracted by the concept when they learned of the successful use of ZBB in the private sector.[1] After further research, discussions with a consulting firm having considerable ZBB experience, and consultation with city officials in Garland, Texas, one of the few public jurisdictions which had utilized ZBB, a decision was made in the late autumn of 1975 to promptly implement ZBB in Wilmington.

In most organizations, the one type of budget request certain to receive intensive screening and analysis is the one that proposes to establish a new service. It is likely to be reviewed as to desirability and need for the service, beneficiaries of the service, reasonableness of proposed costs, potential future implications, and availability of funds—often in terms of relative priority of all proposed new services. Zero base budgeting aims to apply this same type of process, in a more sophisticated manner, to all proposed expenditures.

Essentially, ZBB seeks to accomplish this through a process which divides all proposed activities (and expenditures) into cohesive units of manageable size, subjects them to detailed scrutiny, and ultimately establishes a rank-order of those units which, given unlimited resources, would be funded. A selected level of expenditure is then matched against the final rank ordering, and if funds are not sufficient to cover the entire listing, lowest priority items are left unfunded until the cumulative total of the funded priority list exactly matches the level of funding that is available. The final priority list, balanced with available funds, then becomes the budget.

ZBB is a sophisticated management tool which provides a systematic method of reviewing and evaluating all operations of the organization, current or proposed; allows for budget reductions and expansions in a planned, rational manner; and encourages the reallocation of resources from low to high priority programs. Because of the nature of the process involved, ZBB also tends to have some important fringe benefits, such as involving more managers in the budgeting process, providing more information and options to decision makers, and establishing a systematic basis for management by objectives and priorities.

The foundation of ZBB is a four-step analytic process. Conceptually, the steps are:

1. *Establish Budget Units:* A budget unit is a grouping of existing or proposed activities which might be identified as a "program." It may consist of only one distinct activity, as in the case of trash collection in Wilmington's budget, or it may consist of a group of closely related activities, as in the case of Wilmington's recreation program. In nearly every case in Wilmington, the budget units were smaller than a department, consisting of the previously established divisions within most departments. As a result, the budget units did not create a new and unfamiliar organizational structure, and each budget unit had a readily identifiable manager.

2. *Divide Budget Units into Service Levels:* Since the variety, quantity and quality of service to be provided is usually a more realistic question than whether or not a given budget unit will be funded at all, each budget unit is divided into several alternative levels of service. In most cases in Wilmington, this began with a level at about half of current, and advanced in steps through a slightly reduced level, the current level, and a possible expanded level. Each level represents a forecast of the cost and service consequences of operating at that level. In Wilmington's budget, the 61 budget units were eventually divided into a total of 194 service levels, with from 1 to 7 levels per budget unit.

3. *Analyze Service Levels:* Given the relatively small size, and programmatic cohesiveness of the budget units and the service levels, it is then possible to analyze each segment of the proposed budget in considerable detail. The need to provide a given level of a particular service may be explored. Potential alternative approaches to meet a particular need may be identified. The manpower and other costs proposed to provide a given level of service may be examined for reasonableness. A given level of marginal cost may be compared to a given marginal increase in the quality or quantity of service.

4. *Priority Ranking of All Service Levels:* Following the analytic progress, all of the potentially desirable service levels from all of the budget units, as revised and finalized, are rank-ordered into a single list. The basic concept is that a given service level is ranked higher than all of the service levels that would be foregone, if necessary, to

make available the funds for that given service level. Meanwhile, a level of expenditure (typically the projection of revenue from existing sources) is selected. Since, generally, revenues are not sufficient to cover the entire list, the priority rankings determine which service levels will be funded and which will not.

In practice, the ZBB process is considerably more complex than this conceptual framework. Wilmington's experience with ZBB, in chronological order, is presented in the following sections.

Following Mayor Maloney's decision in the late autumn of 1975 to implement ZBB in Wilmington, a variety of planning and decision-making became necessary. In recognition of the priority ascribed to the project by the Mayor, two members of the Mayor's staff were, from the outset, given essentially full-time responsibility for ZBB. Also, a consulting firm was retained to assist.

The first step was the development of a detailed timetable, from the starting point in mid-November, 1975 to the charter-mandated City Council submission date, April 1, 1976. From the outset, it was recognized that the schedule was tight, with little allowance for slippage.

The major milestones of the schedule were:

Task	Completion
Determination of Agencies to be included	December 5
Review and Approval of Budget Manual	December 12
Training Program	December 19
Preliminary Departmental ZBB Submissions	January 16
Final Departmental ZBB Submissions	January 30
Departmental Hearings	February 27
Preliminary Ranking and Revenue Estimate	March 5
Mayor's Approval of Final Ranking	March 19
Presentation of Budget to Council	April 1
Approval of Budget by Council	June 1

A fundamental decision was the comprehensiveness of the ZBB process. The possibility of including only some departments or only certain expenditures (such as personnel costs) was discussed. However, the ranking process which culminates ZBB was judged to be far more meaningful if all requests competing for the General Fund were ranked competitively.

While Wilmington's water, sewer and Marine Terminal funds are maintained independently of the General Fund, it was decided to include all of these funds in the ZBB process—although they would be ranked separately. This was done both to strengthen the overall resource allocation process, and also because any year-end surpluses in these funds are transferred to the General Fund, thus giving expenditures in these funds a direct impact on the General Fund.

Likewise, federal and state grant funds, which had never previously been included in the budgeting process (except for federal revenue sharing) were to be included. In each case, federal and state grant funds were to be identified as such, but shown as part of the relevant budget unit and service level. The inclusion of grant funds would provide significant additional information, not previously available to decision-makers in a systematic manner. In many cases, this data would show major activities which had been little known to decision-makers because they used no city funds. In some cases, the data identify critical areas with heavy dependence on grant funds, which might have to be assumed by city funds upon expiration of the grants.

The major exclusion from ZBB was to be the operating subsidy to the local school district. In view of the limited time available, the relative autonomy of the Board of Education, and the fact that the bulk of the schools' funding comes directly from state appropriations, it was considered infeasible to include the schools in the first implementation of ZBB.

The other significant exclusion from ZBB was to be so-called "fixed" expenses. Due to the lack of short-term control and discretion over these expenditures, items such as pensions, debt service and insurance were omitted from the process.

Once the extent of inclusion in ZBB had been determined, it was necessary to identify budget units. In the great majority of cases, budget units were selected to correspond with the established divisions within city departments. Thus, for example, Wilmington's Public Works department was divided into 11 budget units, corresponding to its 11 divisions, Planning and Development was assigned four budget units matching its established divisional structure, and the Auditing and Treasurer's Departments were each assigned one budget unit, since there were no established divisions within those departments. In a few cases of very large divisions with highly varied functions, budget units were established to subdivide the established divisions. Thus, in the Department of Public Safety, the police and fire divisions were sub-divided into, respectively, six and three budget units.

A critical step in the planning process was the development of forms. The unique needs of every jurisdiction make it improbable that any set of standardized forms can be used for ZBB. In Wilmington's case, consideration was given to such local factors as past budget practice, accounting system needs, availability of data and other factors in developing ZBB forms. Where possible, the forms were designed to resemble the previously used budget forms. A total of seven forms were designed and utilized, although later experience suggests that the process can and should be somewhat simplified, with the number of forms reduced.

The final planning step was the preparation of a budget manual, containing ZBB instructions as well as traditional data, such as salary scales, hospitalization insurance premiums, and submission deadlines. Although it was recognized that the manual would have to be supplemented with training and technical assistance support, the manual did serve a useful purpose as the only written compendium of ZBB forms and instructions.

Recognizing the need for technical assistance, a team of nine budget analysts was assembled from the Mayor's Office, the Finance Department, the Department of Planning and Development and City Council's staff. All had past experience in fiscal analysis. After a period of intensive training, one of the budget analysts was to be assigned to each city department, to assist them in responding to the demands of ZBB.

With these steps completed, ZBB was ready for presentation to the city's departments for implementation.

The impending implementation of ZBB was formally announced to Wilmington's department heads by the Mayor in late November, 1975. Although—as with any radical departure from the past practice—there was some criticism and resistance, cooperation and support from the departments generally proved to be excellent.

Actually, the first involvement by most departments had been in early November, when the city's consultants met with department heads to gather their impressions of the former budget process, suggestions to improve the process, and sufficient information regarding departmental operations to identify budget units. This information was all used in developing Wilmington's ZBB format.

Following the formal announcement, department heads and budget unit managers (usually division managers) were split into two workshops, of about 25 participants each, for training. Each group received two half-day training sessions, at which budget manuals and forms were also distributed. The first session was an orientation to ZBB concepts and general procedures, while the second session was used to review specific instructions in the manual and to discuss samples of completed forms.

The first major process for departments—the preliminary analysis—focused largely on the definition of service levels. As the most radical and fundamental concept of ZBB, it is essential that service levels be soundly developed. Departments were given some guidance in defining service levels, but functioned largely on their own. For each service level of each budget unit, departments were asked to submit basic information as shown in Exhibit 5-4.

PRELIMINARY

B-2 SERVICE LEVEL DESCRIPTION

Department Planning & Develop.	Division Development	Budget Unit Development

Rank 3	Service Level Title Extensive Planning & Development Activities

Describe Services Provided and Activities Performed in this Service Level

Update Urban Renewal plans and the comprehensive plan for areas of the city, and prepare zoning ordinance amendments. Prepare plans for the expenditure of Community Development funds and coordinate the execution of those plans. Prepare designs for simple capital improvement projects. Develop housing programs and initiate downtown business improvement projects.

Briefly Describe Resources to be Used in this Service Level

1 Senior Planner
1 Community Development Coordinator
1 Renewal Technician
1 Draftsperson
  Total Personal Services $57,797
"CURRENT LEVEL"

	Est. Fiscal 1977	
	City	Non-City
No. Pos.	2	2
Cost	$29	$29

Rank	Service Level Title

Describe Services Provided and Activities Performed in this Service Level

Briefly Describe Resources to be Used in this Service Level

	Est. Fiscal 1977	
	City	Non-City
No. Pos.		
Cost		

Exhibit 5-4

Some departments felt that a reduced service level might be misconstrued as a recommendation to operate at that level, and resisted proposing reduced levels. As a result, all budget unit managers were instructed that service levels represented options, not recommendations, and the first level must not exceed 40-60% of the current expenditure level. Generally, a second level below current service was to be proposed, then the current level, and finally an improved level of service (when desirable), yielding a recommended minimum of four service levels. In fact, budget units ultimately submitted averaged three service levels each.

The structuring of service levels is cumulative. If a given service level is funded for a department, those that precede it will also be funded — although those that follow will not necessarily be funded. This assumption means that the costs for each level are costs to be added to prior levels in a department in order to produce the higher level of service.

Service levels vary either the quantity or the quality of a department's operations, or both. For example, in firefighting, the first service level might either: *Quantity Variation* — Reduce by 50% the number of fire companies, but maintain manning on each company as at present. *Quality Variation* — Maintain the same number of fire companies as at present, but reduce by 50% the manning on each. *Both* — Reduce both the number of companies and the manning on each by 25%.

Service levels were devised in all of these manners in Wilmington. Sanitation, in Public Works, varied primarily the frequency, and thus the quality, of service:

Level 1: Once weekly pick-up at curb
Level 2: Twice weekly pick-up at curb
Level 3: Pick-up from rear or side yard, plus special services and school pick-ups (current level)

The department apparently did not see sufficient marginal improvement to show possible service expansion to a fourth level (which could have been three times a week pick-up).

Other departments defined service levels largely in terms of the quantity of services provided on a prioritized basis, holding quality relatively constant. For example, the police patrol division budget unit in Public Safety divided current and proposed services into six levels:

Level 1: Basic patrol and preliminary investigation of major crimes
Level 2: Preliminary investigation of all criminal complaints; response to priority non-criminal calls

Level 3: Follow-up on all criminal and non-criminal calls; operation of jail and selective parking enforcement

Level 4: Increased parking enforcement; full-service response to non-criminal calls

Level 5: Additional patrols, school crossing guards (current level)

Level 6: Expansion of patrol, parking enforcement and school crossing functions

Here, the department saw sufficient marginal improvement to show expansion to a sixth service level.

Whatever the approach, the objective was to show the department's assessment of what services should be provided if only a certain level of funding was available.

Once levels were defined, an estimated cost for each level was calculated. This did not prove to be difficult, since the bulk of the costs were personnel and fringe benefits, which could be readily correlated with the manner in which personnel were divided among the levels. The service levels and costs, along with certain additional data and a preliminary ranking by the department head were submitted by the departments in mid-January, 1976. This provided the Mayor's staff with an estimate of the total budget, and an opportunity to discuss possible revisions in the service level structure and priority rankings with the departments. As a result of this process, several significant revisions were made.

In the latter part of January, departments completed the detailed final service level descriptions, as shown in Exhibit 5-5. In addition to the information reported in the preliminary phase, more precise data and certain supplemental information were required for the final submission.

A unique feature of ZBB is the "program measures" reported for each service level. Up to seven measures could be selected for each budget unit, which would be repeated for each service level and reflect the increasing quality or quantity of services provided at each higher service level. Unfortunately, many departments had not accumulated such data, and were unable to provide the desirable level of documentation of program measures. However this process has established a foundation for future years, and has led to efforts by several departments as well as the Mayor's staff to begin the accumulation of more useful data.

The final service level description was accompanied by a detailed line item listing of all costs associated with that service level, including personnel, fringe benefits, materials, supplies, and equipment. These forms resulted in a considerable bulk of paperwork and a significant work-load to the departments, although the work was more time consuming than onerous.

B-3	SERVICE LEVEL ANALYSIS				RANK: 5

RANK: 5
Department 2 of 15
Division 1 of 4
Budget Unit 1 of 4

Department Planning	Division Prog. Anal. & Admin.	Budget Unit Program Analysis	Service Level Title Administrative, Budgeting, Plan & Grant Preparation	Bud Acct # 01-17-00

Describe Services Provided and Activities Performed in this Service Level
- general administration of the Dept. of Plan. & Devel.
- preparation of the Criminal Justice Plan
- preparation of the Capital Budget
- preparation of federal & state grant applications
- collection of data & other pertinent information necessary to complete the above mentioned tasks
- Fiscal management of Department Federal Grants
- Collection & dissemination of facts about the City
- Secretarial support for above functions

SUMMARY BUDGET DATA ($ 000's)

	This Serv. Level		Cumulative*	
	City	Non-City	Total	% FY76
No. Bud. Pos.	4	2	4	80
Pers. Serv.	86	38	86	96
M.S.E.	47	39	56	110
Total	142	77	142	101

Justification of Need for this Service Level

Preparation of the Criminal Justice Comprehensive Plan is required by contract #10-07-000-01-76 with DARC.
Preparation of the Capital Budget and program is an essential activity of city government. Section 5-700(e) of the City Charter states that the Department of Planning will prepare and submit the capital budget and program to the Planning Commission.
The city benefits substantially from the use of federal and state funds obtained by grant applications. Fiscal & operational management of federal grants is necessary for effective and efficient utilization of funds. In order for the above mentioned functions to be completed effectively, data collection and analysis must be carried out. Overall department administration of the varied activities is necessary for effective management and control.

PROGRAM MEASURES

Description	This Serv. L	Cumulative	
		Total	%FY76
1. Federal Grants prepared	7	7	100
2. Value, Federal Grants	3,900	3,900	74
3. Special studies	1	1	NA
4. Capital Budget prep	1	1	100
5. Criminal Justice Plan	1	1	100
6. Program Budgets Prep.	0	0	0
7. Programs Evaluated	0	0	0

Describe and Justify Resources Required in this Service Level
1 Planning Director - needed for overall administrative control and expertise for all divisions and special projects.
1 Grants & Contracts Manager - needed for fiscal management of federal grants, other financial matters in department, and maintenance of census data and other Management Information Systems.
1 Criminal Justice Coordinator - prepares criminal justice plans and serves as expert on crime trends in Wilm.
1 Program Analyst)- It is necessary to have these two people to prepare capital budget
1 Director of Program Analysis) & assist in data collection for other activities.
1 Clerk Stenographer III - Secretarial functions for above-mentioned professionals.
Contractual/other services: $87,645
Materials/supplies: $5,950   Equipment: $1,000
*Cumulative for City funds only.

Exhibit 5-5

In addition to the service level and line item listings, each department also submitted a departmental priority ranking of all budget units and all service levels within the department. A running cumulative total was included to show the amount required to fund the department to a particular priority level. Also, departments were asked to include a memorandum indicating the rationale for the order of prioritization selected.

The focus then shifted to the Mayor's staff for the preparation of the city's consolidated budget.

The Mayor's Office review of departmental budget submissions began with a preliminary assessment of the city's financial position. Departmental general fund requests,[2] including requests for new or expanded services, amounted to $19.9 million, an increase of 15.6 percent over the existing budget. With a 1-2 percent revenue growth likely, requests would exceed revenues by roughly $2.6 million.

Wilmington's ZBB process presented a number of alternatives, which could be used singly or in combination to deal with the $2.6 million gap: 1) Raise taxes to increase revenues; 2) Reduce the cost of providing a specified level of service; or 3) Not fund lowest priority service levels.

The first alternative is generally least desirable. For policy reasons, it was ruled out in Wilmington at this time.

The second alternative is generally most desirable, in that it tends to represent an increase in efficiency or productivity. In practice, this approach is most similar to traditional budgeting, with the prime emphasis on large or unusual expenditures, and expenditures showing significant increases from the current budget. Ultimately, Wilmington was successful in reducing the departmental budget requests by approximately $900,000, or 4.5 percent, through these line-item cuts.

Once revenues are established, and the cost of each service level has been reduced as much as possible, the third alternative — prioritizing — comes into play. This alternative represents the unique characteristic of ZBB. For Wilmington, this provided the mechanism for identifying $1.2 million in departmental requests that were of lowest priority, and would not be funded.

A major portion of the administration review process was consumed by departmental budget hearings. Each department was afforded a session of 3–6 hours duration, attended by both members of the Mayor's staff and representatives of City Council Finance Committee. At the hearings, discussions focused on opportunities to reduce the cost of providing a specified level of service, as well as on the rationale for the structuring of the service levels and the prioritization of the department's service levels. Numerous minor changes in the costs of service levels were made at the hearings, generally with the consent of the department head. Changes in prioritization were not made at the hearings, although areas of disagreement with a department head's rankings were identified. Budget hearing discussions also covered program measures, beneficiaries of the service, involvement of grant funds and marginal cost of increasing service levels.

The consensus of both departmental officials and members of the Mayor's staff was that with the introduction of ZBB, the hearings provided a more comprehensive and penetrating view of a department's activities than hearings in previous years. Specifically, the basis for proposed expenditures was usually related much more directly and rationally to services provided than in the past. Also, more discussion of the value of specific services, and the need for specific services, was possible.

Separately from the hearings, members of the Mayor's staff also reviewed the departmental submissions for completeness, clarity, arithmetic accuracy, and other largely technical considerations. This process, along with the hearings, resulted in minor adjustments to the total cost for most of the service levels.

Formal ranking of priorities is the crucial and distinctive step in ZBB. A variety of criteria may be used, both formally and informally. Some criteria are relatively general, probably applicable to any jurisdiction, while some are more related to local goals and objectives. Key criteria considered in Wilmington include:

Importance of the service level in terms of the perceived health, welfare, safety and satisfaction of city residents
Statuatory, charter, and contractual commitments met by the service level
Potential consequences of not providing the service level
Federal and state funds received dependent on a particular expenditure of city funds
Informal assessment of the quality of the service provided
Cost effectiveness of the service level
Preference, where feasible, to direct services to the public over administrative costs

The final analysis and ranking process began with the decision to lump together a group of services identified as essential, without further prioritization. Little benefit was seen in discussing whether the most fundamental service levels of police, fire or sanitation service is more important. Clearly, all of these services will be provided, at least, at the first level of service. Thus, 34 of the 196 service levels were lumped together as a "basic" group, and ranked above all other services. Since most budget units had developed a first service level of 40 to 60 percent of the existing funding level, the total cost of the "basic" group amounted to $10.0 million.

After isolating the "basic" group, $9.0 million in requested service levels remained, as against only $7.8 million in forecasted revenue. Efforts focused on analysis and ranking of the 162 service levels remaining.

Numerical ranking of 162 separate items is quite difficult — particularly when the 162 items are as varied as the service levels in Wilmington's budget. Consequently, the process began by dividing the remaining service levels into four groups: High priority; Medium priority; Low priority; and Service levels not to be funded for policy reasons.[3]

The initial ranking of the remaining service levels showed that revenues were sufficient to cover the entire "high" and "medium" priority groups and part of the "low" priority group. Service levels undesirable for policy reasons were ranked below the "low" priority group, but were effectively eliminated from further consideration.

With the number of service levels to be ranked now reduced to groups of manageable size, all of the service levels in each group were then numerically prioritized. For the "high" and "medium" groups, this was somewhat academic, since revenues were sufficient to fund all of the service levels in the group. However, it was judged important to establish these rankings as the first organized, comprehensive statement of the City's priorities.

For the "low" priority group the specific numerical ranking was of critical importance. Of the 56 service levels within the group, funds were sufficient for only about half. After rankings were assigned, a cumulative funding total was calculated to determine the point at which revenues were exhausted. An analysis of the rankings showed that many of the service levels below the cut-off point were new or expanded levels of service, although 21 levels of service currently being provided also fell below the cut-off. Two levels of new or expanded service ended up above the cut-off.

The compete rankings, as proposed by the Mayor's staff, were then presented to the Mayor for his consideration. The Mayor directed a number of minor changes, but generally expressed satisfaction with the priority order. However, the Mayor was concerned that a number of existing service levels involving incumbent employees fell below the cut-off, necessitating immediate lay-offs and service cutbacks.

As an alternative, the Mayor's staff developed a factor known as "special attrition." A factor had already been allowed for normal attrition, representing funds that would not be spent for salaries and fringe benefits during the period positions remain vacant between incumbents. Now, in order to avoid layoffs and abrupt service cutbacks, an additional factor was calculated representing anticipated savings from positions which would be left unfilled for the balance of the fiscal year when they become vacant. Although this may still entail modest service cutbacks, unless compensating productivity increases are achieved, they would occur on a scattered basis throughout the year. While the exact positions to be left vacant could not be identified, past turnover experience indicated that the savings budgeted for "special attrition" were reasonable and attainable.

Following the addition of "special attrition" and minor priority adjustments, the ranking was finalized. No layoffs would be required, although some existing services without incumbent personnel still fell below the cut-off. All told, the "basic" group and ranks 1-110 were shown as funded; ranks 111-162 were shown as not funded.

With the completion of prioritization the budget was then ready for final housekeeping details, printing and submission to City Council.

In a radical departure from most jurisdictions which have implemented ZBB, Mayor Maloney decided that the Council should receive the actual ZBB documentation. Other jurisdictions using ZBB have recast their budget in traditional format for legislative consideration and public distribution. Although this decision was sure to significantly increase the complexity of City Council's work, Mayor Maloney regarded Council's involvement in the actual ZBB process as critical.

City Council's exposure to ZBB had actually begun at the very start of the City's involvement. The Councilmen were thoroughly briefed before the decision was made to adopt the process, and had registered their support by adoption of a resolution. In addition, Council's Finance Committee Chairman and a staff member had attended all of the departmental hearings.

Council's consideration of the completed ZBB budget began with an orientation session, devoted to both the process and the output of ZBB. The ZBB budget represented such a total departure from past budgeting practice—in process as well as appearance—that a thorough orientation was essential.

As in past years, Council then proceeded to hold public budget hearings for each department. The hearings, which lasted from one to three hours each, repeated some of the discussion from the administration's budget hearings, but primarily served as a forum for the discussion of concerns of particular relevance to the Councilmen. Several departments used the hearing to appeal either a ranking or a line item cut made earlier by the administration. In a number of cases, members of the public or city employees raised questions about specific items in the budget. Members of the Mayor's staff attended all of the hearings, and were often asked to explain the rationale behind the prioritization of a particular service level.

Prior to the hearings, Council agreed that no actual changes in the rankings would be discussed until all of the hearings were complete and all comments were heard. This avoided moving service levels up and down the ranking until all the hearings were completed and the Council could put all the levels in perspective.

Initially many of the Councilmen approached the budget much as they had approached past budgets. Most of the discussion concerned the incremental changes to line-items. However, as the hearings proceeded, greater and greater attention focused on ZBB considerations. The rationale for a particular ranking, for example, was discussed more and more frequently. Much interest centered on the federal and state grant funds—information which the Council had never before had available in a systematic manner. There was also steadily increasing discussion of program measures and the marginal costs associated with a higher level of service.

One problem was the greatly expanded amount of paperwork. As part-time City officials, many of the Councilmen had difficulty finding the time to digest the large volume of information on a department prior to the hearing. The line-item budget detail, a 1000-page document, was simply too heavy and bulky to be readily taken home for review.

At the conclusion of the hearings, Council's staff checked with all the Councilmen to determine what changes in the administration's budget should be considered. After all had been polled, only five changes were proposed. Three proposed changes concerned service levels, with a total cost of $15,000, which had been ranked below the cut-off point but which Council wished to see funded. One change was a line-item cut of $6,000 within a funded service level, which the department head had argued for convincingly. The final proposed change of $8,000 was a service previously provided which the department involved had not included in their budget submission.

The latter proposal was most easily resolved by the administration's commitment to continue the service with personnel under a federally-funded Summer Youth Program, thus not requiring any additional City funds.

Council met at some length to consider possible rerankings to accommodate the other desired additions to the budget. The process proved difficult. Every service level suggested for deletion, as a trade-off, had its own supporters among the Councilmen. Most of the service levels just above the cut-off point included incumbent personnel, whom the Councilmen were not anxious to see laid off. A tax increase was seen as unpalatable.

Ultimately the small amount involved in the desired changes proved decisive. Council recommended to the Mayor that the four service levels in question be reranked to include them in the budget, and that all service levels then be reduced by 0.1 percent to provide the needed funds. Since extensive line-item cutting had already been undertaken, the Mayor accepted the recommendation only with the understanding that the 0.1 percent savings would be achieved through attrition, by slightly increasing the time a position remained vacant between incumbents. Council agreed, and the appropriate rerankings were made. With these changes, the Council soon thereafter gave its approval to the entire budget.

Generally, City Council appears to have found ZBB preferable to the City's former process. A major reason appears to be that Council now gets more information, and more useful information, than they have ever had before. The ranked service level format, although not legally binding on the Mayor, provides Council with a strong moral commitment as to what services will be provided—whereas the old process had provided only a commitment as to what the line-item expenditures would be. Many Councilmen have expressed a desire to continue the ZBB process in future years and possibly expand it to other areas, such as the operating subsidy to the school district and the City's capital budget.

It is important to establish the context in which zero base budgeting was adopted in Wilmington. Essentially, it represented a logical step forward in a well-established process of fiscal restraint and improved management of resources. It followed earlier experimentation with other budgeting innovations, particularly program budgeting. It drew heavily on analytic and management staff resources which had been developed over an extended period. And it relied on the cooperation and support of the Mayor, City Council, and city department heads. The process and the results could differ significantly in a different context.

Insufficient time has passed to assess fully ZBB's impact on Wilmington. However, a number of conclusions may be drawn as to the benefits already derived, and the disadvantages.

On the positive side a key accomplishment has been the detailed identification of all the services provided by the city—regardless of funding source. Such information was never previously available in systematic form. Once identified, all programs and expenditures were reviewed to a level of detail usually reserved for proposed new programs.

Also beneficial is the establishment of a systematic prioritization of the City's services. This establishes a firm foundation for future years when the City's financial situation may require extremely difficult decisions, and helps assure that those decisions will be based on a well-developed set of priorities.

The ZBB process itself was beneficial, in that it involved nearly all management personnel in the budgeting process, considerably more than in the past. Also, as a planning and budgeting process, ZBB involved these personnel in a far more comprehensive resource allocation process.

The ranking of federal and state grant funds establishes a mechanism for identifying the importance of these funds to the City and anticipating the future demands to replace these funds with City funds when they expire. In effect, Wilmington has adopted a comprehensive planning and budgeting process for all its resources.

The statement of priorities and program measures by department heads serves as an excellent basis for a management by objectives program. In the past, the City's approach to management by objectives had been more general, making performance assessment more difficult. With the level of specific detail provided by ZBB, performance against objectives can be measured much more quantitatively.

ZBB has also involved City Council more meaningfully in the budget process. Specifically, it has given them a better picture of the issues involved and a direct involvement in the tradeoff process inherent to budgeting. Potentially ZBB could serve to very significantly increase the role of the legislative branch of government by providing more effective control of the planning and resource allocation process.

ZBB also has significant disadvantages. Foremost is the large increase in the time, effort and paperwork required. Increased time devoted to the budget by City personnel, the need for consultants in the initial implementation, and increased printing costs probably resulted in a net increase of 100 percent in the cost of preparing the budget. The increased effort, and the high level of detail required, caused numerous complaints, especially from Department Heads. Particularly in the cases where a service is already rather well known to the City administration and City Council, such complaints are understandable.

The large size of the first service level in most budget units—40 to 60 percent of current spending—may also have provided an opportunity to effectively shelter costs which might, if listed as separate service levels, be more seriously questioned. In a number of departments it appeared that overhead-type costs were unduly heavy in the initial service level, although if more time had been available, this could have been addressed by revisions in the proposed service levels.

Another limitation is the underlying assumption that the specified level of funding must be provided in order to obtain the specified level of service. Past experience suggests that improvements in efficiency and productivity may enable a specified level of service to be provided even with reduced funding levels. While the knowledge that reducing the cost of *each* proposed service level enables more service levels to be funded tends to encourage economy and stimulate productivity improvement, the stimulus may not be sufficiently strong to produce the desired results. Thus, it is desirable to undertake separate measures to promote efficiency and productivity in combination with the implementation of ZBB.

Wilmington's experience with ZBB has generally been quite positive and seems likely to lead to further use of ZBB in Wilmington. Combined with a variety of measures geared to improved organization effectiveness and economy, ZBB appears to be making a significant contribution. While ZBB would not necessarily prove beneficial in every jurisdiction, its implementation is certainly worthy of consideration.

NOTES

1. Peter A. Pyhrr, "Zero Base Budgeting." Harvard Business Review, Nov.-Dec. 1970, pp. 111-121. *Zero Base Budgeting: A Practical Management Tool for Evaluating Expenses.* New York: John Wiley & Sons. 1973.
2. Excluding fixed costs and the operating subsidy to the schools, which were not included in ZBB. These items were budgeted at $17.1 million.
3. For example, a proposed change in water billing procedure that would initially result in serious cash flow problems.

## PART THREE

Managing Public Programs and Agencies

A s perhaps never before in American history, the 1980s have brought with them a public concern for improved performance in the management of government at all levels. More than ever, state and local agencies are asked to clarify their goals, improve the quality of their decision making, and assess the effectiveness of public programs.

Ask a public manager how he or she does this, and the answer increasingly is, "I plan. I analyze. I implement. And I evaluate." It is through these steps that public managers attempt to ensure that their agencies meet their goals and objectives with the available resources.

This is what Section Three is all about: planning, analyzing, implementing, and evaluating—the "guts" of agency and program management.

6

Planning

PURPOSE

The purpose of this chapter is to examine the problems and benefits of goal-setting and planning in public management.

CONTENTS

Reading
   Bertram M. Gross, "Planning: Developing Purposefulness"

Case
   "Metropolitan Tulsa Transit Authority"

Instructions

Pre-Class Preparation

When you have considered carefully the material in "Planning: Developing Purposefulness", read the "Metropolitan Tulsa Transit Authority" case and respond to the questions below:

1. Overall, how would you judge the MTTA's planning process? In what ways could planning have been improved?

2. If you were on the staff of the MTTA at that time, what additional information would you have sought as part of the planning process?

3. The case here obviously occurred before there was any shortage of gasoline. How might an "oil crisis" have affected the MTTA's plan?

Procedure for Class Meeting

Discuss the case as well as the concept and practice of planning.

For Additional Information

Two key works in the planning field are:

George A. Steiner, *Top Management Planning* (New York: Macmillan, 1969) and *Strategic Planning: What Every Manager Must Know* (New York: Free Press, 1979).

Also see:

Robert N. Anthony, *Planning and Control Systems: A Framework for Analysis* (Cambridge: Division of Research, Harvard Business School, 1965), especially Chapters 1 and 2.
William I. Goodman and Eric C. Freund, eds., *Principles and Practices of Urban Planning*, 4th ed. (Washington: International City Management Association, 1968).
Charles L. Hughes, *Goal-Setting: Key to Individual and Organizational Effectiveness* (New York: American Management Association, 1965).
Erik Jonsson, Mayor, "Goals for Dallas," *Nation's Cities* (November 1970).
Donald N. Michael, *On Learning to Plan—and Planning to Learn* (San Francisco: Jossey-Bass, 1973).
Aaron Wildavsky, "If Planning Is Everything, Maybe It's Nothing," *Policy Sciences*, IV (June 1973), pp. 127-153.

Planning: Developing Purposefulness
Bertram M. Gross

A PLAN OR A PROGRAM is a sequence of future actions to which a person, unit or organization is committed. In its simplest form planning is the process of making, changing, or coordinating such plans. Planning by administrators is a process of promoting planning by people, units, and organizations and weaving various plans together into a common purpose pattern. In essence, therefore, administrative planning is purposeful action to develop purposefulness.

As a more structured form of administrative decision-making, planning is the subject of many preceding chapters and all sections of this chapter. Thus the global matrix of organizational purposes is merely a way of setting forth in an analytical hierarchy the various performance purposes that enter into plans. The previous discussions have dealt with the conceptual and dynamic aspects of each category separately. The task of this section is to deal with the process through which these various purposes are woven together into action sequences.

Many concepts of planning, unfortunately, are little more than special forms of the fallacy that "in good administration everything runs smoothly and easily," liberally seasoned with myths of central omnipotence. Many planners see themselves enthroned on a divine chair high in a hierarchial heaven, with the rules of reason (as they expound them) carried out by lesser people. If, in their ignorance, politicians, workers, and "line administrators" do not cooperate, they must be "educated." And if they will not be educated, this goes to show the depths of man's ignorance and the perversity of the world.

In actual practice planning is much more complicated. A combination of decision-making and communication, it is bedevilled by all the difficulties of both. The first element in the planning-activation-evaluation circle, planning may largely determine the effectiveness of the other two. It often yields plans that can never be activated or that serve as obstacles to — or even substitutes for — action. Underplanning and neglect of planning may readily be replaced by utopian planning or overplanning. The best laid schemes of men as well as mice "gang aft agley." Those succeeding today may create the rigid routines that prevent rational planning tomorrow.

Let us now define planning more specifically as the process through which (1) some people, who may be called the "planners," (2) commit themselves or others to (3) some representation of future action. Each of these phases confronts administrators with serious problems.

The Planners

In a very fundamental sense the only nonplanner in an organization is the mythical person who operates entirely in accordance with plans laid down by others, ingrained habits and — when neither plan nor habit dictate his acts — total spontaneity. Even assembly-line workers moving in accordance with the choreography of time-and-motion engineers have a minor leeway in planning their movements (and may indeed develop anti-plans to frustrate the engineers). In a much larger sense all skilled workers and technical and professional employees, and administrators do some planning — even though it may be very short range — for the use of their own time. All administrators and many technical and professional employees do some planning for the activities of other people. The potentially most important planners in any organization are its top executives and upper-level bureaucrats. As [Harlan] Cleveland has pointed out in connection with foreign affairs planning, "The most usable end product of planning is not a paper, but a person thoroughly immersed in the subject — a person whose mind is trained to act, having taken everything into account, on the spur of the moment. And that is why the ultimate decision maker must himself participate in the planning exercise. A busy boxer, training for the bout of his life, cannot afford to let his sparring partners do all his daily calisthenics for him".

The administrator, however, is often so pressed by immediate problems that he has little time to invest in longer-range planning. Besides, he will usually lack the technical abilities and knowledge necessary for many aspects of planning. The typical solution to this problem is to establish specialized planning positions or planning units. This step may long be deferred by ignorance or resistance. When taken, it may readily lead to a number of typical "planner problems."

First, the planning specialist or planning unit may readily become seriously disengaged from the operations of the organization. This is particularly likely in the case of highly professional planning personnel whose professional "lingo" separates them from the rest of the organization and whose major aspiration is recognition by professional peers outside the organization. Under such circumstances the specialized planning unit may serve as little more than a symbolic substitute for long-range planning or a rationalization for the failure to develop long-term plans.

Second, when the planning specialists try to come to grips with realities, they are apt to meet serious resistance from "line" administrators. The very administrator who got them going in the first place may be too busy to listen to their proposals. If he listens, he may not understand them. If he understands them, he may reject them. If he accepts them, they still have to cope with other administrators. The opposition to Frederick Taylor by the operating managers of Bethlehem Steel was not the last occasion of vigorous resistance to planning specialists. Many administrators regard it as a personal insult that a planning specialist may come up with ideas as to how *they* should perform their work. The feeling of resentment may be particularly deep if they suspect that the specialist is correct. It may be still deeper if the specialist has obtained his ideas from the line administrator without giving him due credit.

Third, as planning processes become more sophisticated, the number of specialized planning positions and units increases. Engineers, budgeters, accountants, personnel officers, lawyers, economists, operations researchers, and many others all start developing a variety of plans. When the planners deal with entirely separate activities or when one set of planners achieves monopolistic control over a certain field of activity, competition among the planners may be avoided. In many areas, particularly when the specialized planners merely deal with single aspects of the same operation, such competition becomes unavoidable. Under these circumstances, the administrator may try to cope with the problem by setting up a super planning position, unit, or committee to coordinate the planners. This device will rarely settle matters. The most it can do is help structure a situation which can be handled only by his active personal participation.

"In any democratic structure," write Simon, Smithburg, and Thompson [in their text, *Public Administration,* 1950] concerning government organizations, "specialized long-range planning units must always remain the most vulnerable units in the administrative organization." The same statement may be made about any specialized planning unit set up to initiate major changes in a private corporation. In both cases vulnerability is increased by a widespread tendency to ignore the planning functions of others in the organization and to develop ultraprofessionalized delusions of grandeur. On the other hand, it must be recognized that many a so-called "planning office" is merely a relatively harmless fact-gathering or fact-analysis unit parading under a more honorific title.

The Commitments

Commitment to a future course of action is a very personal matter. Many people will not commit themselves quickly or very far to plans that they themselves have not had a part in developing. The imposition of legitimate sanctions to back up such plans may lead to a significant amount of commitment under duress. But this may be counterbalanced to some extent by noncommitment in the form of open or latent opposition.

Under such circumstances it is only natural to find many activities that often masquerade as full-fledged plans but nonetheless fall far short of genuine commitments.

Precommitment steps

Here we find the collection of information, its processing and interpretation. One or all of these survey activities may be the exclusive function of planning advisers or specialized planning units.

Usually based on a survey, the forecast goes one step further. It suggests, with varying degrees of confidence, the nature of probable future situations or sequences. It may even indicate the varying desirability of different developments, but without reaching the stage of proposing objectives.

The next step is the actual proposing of objectives. This may be done in terms of full sequences from the immediate to the distant future, of longer-range objectives or of more immediate steps toward achieving already accepted objectives. In any case, this is a long step beyond the mere making of forecasts, a step which involves considerable risks for individuals and units that prefer to "stick to the facts." Some may try to define an in-between area by limiting themselves to an identification of alternatives and an analysis of the advantages and disadvantages of each.

Formal Decision

Here a plan of action is formally accepted by those in the appropriate positions of high authority—a President, a board of directors, a central committee, a national legislature, or a municipal council. But this does not necessarily mean commitment even by those who have formally made the decision. The ratification of proposals for new programs may be a mere gesture—as is often the case of economic development plans formally adopted by national governments and land use plans embodied in municipal ordinances.

As we look back over precommitment and formal decision activities, we see immediately that each of them may contribute substantially to the process of developing organizational purposefulness. Hence any one of them may be called "preplanning." When all of them are found together the result may even be called "quasiplanning." Yet to the extent that they do not lead to genuine commitment, the more appropriate designation would be "pseudoplanning."

Central or Broad Commitment

Here we come much closer to purposefulness and action orientation. Indeed, if we accept the myths of central omnipotence, we have arrived; the will of the masters is the will of the organization. Yet, as has already been demonstrated in previous chapters, this is an acceptable hypothesis only in small or extremely weak organizations. Commitment by those in the highest positions of formal authority is an extremely favorable condition for the development of organizational purposefulness. Under certain circumstances (there are some who would say all circumstances) it may even be an essential condition. But it is never sufficient. The commitment of the top decision-makers must also be internalized as part of the desired objectives of those individuals and groups with a significant degree of power throughout the organization. This, in turn, usually implies a two-way relation: namely, that the commitments of the top decision makers also reflect the perceived interests or objectives of many others in the organizations.

Overcommitment

In turn, overcommitment is both the fruit of past plans and a barrier to the making of current and future plans. When a plan is thoroughly "sold" to all who are involved in its operations, it tends to take on a "life of its own." The sunk costs invested in the development of purposefulness may make its scrapping, or even any major change, seem inordinately expensive—as in the case of a battleship which is half constructed. All the logic at a certain level of rationality and, more important, all the social power that has been mobilized work toward doing what was planned even if the planners themselves have changed their minds. In *The Guns of August* Barbara Tuchman shows how both sides in World War I became the prisoners of defective war plans that had been worked out years ahead of time by their general staffs. "Once settled," VonMoltke told the Kaiser with respect to the Schlieffen Plan, "it cannot be altered." Although Kitchener disagreed violently with France's Plan 17, he was forced to accept it because "with the troops already on the water . . . , it had to be accepted because there was no time to make another."

The Action Sequences

We turn now to the sequence of actions to which flexible or rigid commitments may be made. Here the typical difficulties involve the use of planning documents, the extent of detail and the nature of long-range plans. . .

The Script and the Play

Some form of planning document is essential in all but the simplest of plans. The written word is valuable in recording the actions that are to be taken and the reasons for them. Without it, there is no possibility of supplementing the defective memory of people and of providing effective communication among them, particularly on details. This value may increase when supplements are provided in the form of tables, charts, diagrams, and pictures. Well constructed and sharply presented planning documents provide an ideal way of recording action sequences that could not otherwise be communicated.

The planning documents may also be largely designed to swell professional pride or impress external sources of support. This is often the case with the "master plan"—whether a master plan for a new or expanded factory, urban redevelopment, or economic development. Yet, the master plan can never express the major elements of purposefulness; by the time these points are written down and doublechecked, they are out of date. A master plan can only be up to date when it represents a "planner's" vision upon which little or no action is being taken. If the master plan is beautifully printed, with elaborate charts, tables, and pictures, one may be sure that it does not represent what is going on or that—as is often the case—nothing is going on.

Details

The extent of detail in a plan, whether or not recorded in a document, is subject to serious limitations. An organization's general plan can include little more than selected generalities or meaningless detail that will weigh oppressively upon operating units or be ignored by them. The meaningful detail can be developed and kept current only by subordinate units. When we look at plans at these lower levels, the same phenomenon reappears. In absolute terms, of course, a plan such as a train schedule, a production schedule, or a procedure for placing purchase orders may seem unbelievably detailed. The amount of detail usually fades, however, when placed against the tremendous complexity of daily operations. Train schedules are limited to departure and arrival times; they do not include the number of passengers to be carried to each destination. If the plan is that the train move only when filled, this would mean an abandonment of prior scheduling of departures and arrivals. Production schedules often concentrate on quantity and speed at the expense of quality. If quality is to be emphasized, speed may have to be sacrificed. At any rate, no preplanning of quality attributes can afford to be anything but extremely selective among all the many possible quality specifications that may have to be included. Purchase procedures, in turn, no matter how detailed, can never hope to prejudge the quantities to be purchased or the prices to be paid. The former is left to specific purchase programs, the latter to negotiation. In all of these cases, it should be noted, the important element is the *strategic* nature of whatever detail is included.

Time Change

Myopia and utopia provide two simple ways of avoiding the selection of strategic details. The myopic plan concentrates entirely on certain aspects of the immediate future. Strategy is rendered impossible by the inability to appreciate the broad reality of the present or to be concerned at all with the future. The utopian plan concentrates upon remote situations with no attention to the intermediate sequences that are necessary to bring them about. Or else it is based upon commitments to desired situations that are simply impossible to obtain. In this latter case, the elaboration of presumed methods of attaining the unattainable may serve to make the plan more plausible, even though not a bit more feasible. The fact that a plan may be utopian need not prevent its reaching the stage of central decision and commitment. National political leaders often make "pie in the sky" promises as the only way to distract attention from current suffering. While such promises may lead to bitter disillusionment, they may also start the wheels going around on more realistic planning processes.

A more sophisticated avoidance of strategic selection is sometimes found in the use of comprehensive long-range projections. In a business organization these may take the form of projected income statements and balance sheets, with special attention to sales forecasts, expenses and revenues for all products. In national economic planning organizations they usually take the form of projections of major items in the national economic accounts. Yet such projections are usually too general to be operational objectives. Their importance derives from two uses. First, they provide considerations that may be used in developing a strategic decision. Second, they may help in evaluating the consequences of a strategic decision. The strategic acts themselves, however, cannot possibly be comprehensive. They are rather a set of very incomplete segments of the future—those selected segments which are regarded as having significant causative power.

Even in the longest-range planning, however, the most strategic details are those relating to the present and the short-range future. The most critical part of any plan is its link with the present. "The object of planning . . . is to decide what should be done now in light of the best present estimate of how the future will look. Planners think about the future in order to act wisely in the present" (U.S. Senate Subcommittee on National Security Staffing and Operations, 1963, p. 5). Flexible commitments to long-range objectives are significant only because they serve as a guide to the present. This guide is particularly important when the current action may itself be a long, drawn-out affair or may have serious future implications. It is also important when the long-range objectives serve to mobilize support for current actions. . . .

Metropolitan Tulsa Transit Authority
M. M. Hargrove

THE TULSA BUS SYSTEM was operated several years by Missouri-Kansas-Oklahoma Transit Lines. The number of passengers carried annually had declined steadily with a resultant drop in the profitability of the operation. During the summer of 1968, a strike occurred which caused the M-K-O management to conclude that the settlement terms undoubtedly would remove profit possibilities permanently from their Tulsa operation. They communicated their conviction to the Mayor and Commissioners and surrendered their franchise.

On August 2, 1968, the Metropolitan Tulsa Transit Authority, a trust, was created "to plan, establish, develop, install, repair, enlarge, improve, maintain, equip, finance and refinance, operate, and regulate public transportation systems and facilities either within or without the territorial boundaries of the city of Tulsa," and to perform other related functions described in the Trust Agreement and Indenture.

The Mayor and City Commissioners met to consider staffing the MTTA. It was evident that the MTTA must have close liaison with the Commissioners because, by law, only the Commissioners could expend municipal funds and, in turn, were held responsible for the activities and functions provided by such expenditures. Accordingly, two Commissioners were named to the Authority along with five additional citizens. The trustees named were:

Mr. Robert LaFortune, Street Commissioner and Chairman (Later, Mr. LaFortune was elected mayor.)
Mr. Jack O'Brien, Finance Commissioner. (When Mr. LaFortune became mayor, Mr. O'Brien became the chairman.)
Mr. Rex Ball, architect and president of Downtown Tulsa Unlimited.
Mr. Fenelon Boesche, attorney.
Dr. M. M. Hargrove, Dean and, later, Trustees Professor, University of Tulsa.
Mr. A. E. McMillan, Director, North Tulsa YMCA.
Mr. James Robinson, Republic National Bank, later, National Bank of Tulsa, and an attorney.

The trustees were without prior experience in operating a mass transportation system. They faced many serious problems. The most urgent problem was to settle the strike and reestablish passenger service. Also, there was the problem of evaluating, recruiting, and developing a competent operational staff. Obviously, it was necessary to contract to purchase the rolling equipment, repair equipment, and supplies; to write an agreement about the acquisition of the maintenance garage; and to decide how to maintain the buses.

After these and similar problems were settled, the trustees were determined to take a longer look into the future operations of the Tulsa transit system. Some of the commitments being considered extended for many years into the future. Longer range planning was a necessity. For example, the buses acquired already had an average age of ten years. A new fleet would commit the community for a decade. Then, what kind, what size, how many, and at what cost should the contemplated buses be?

A special committee appointed by the Authority settled the strike rather quickly. The drivers and employees were given a substantial increase in pay and new fringe benefits. When the buses returned to the streets, it was found that the net effect of the two-month cessation of service was a reduction in the ridership of nearly 40 percent.

Planning

In an effort to generate the information needed to make wise, long-range decisions, the MTTA requested that the Tulsa Metropolitan Area Planning Commission (1) undertake a study of the immediate and short-range (1970-1974) transit needs in Metropolitan Tulsa, and (2) begin planning for a subsequent study of Tulsa's long-range (1974-1990) transit requirements. The basic purpose of this activity was viewed as the development of answers to the following questions:

1. What specific actions were to be taken in the immediate future (1970-1974)? What annual net costs would they generate? To what extent would these net costs be defrayed by financial assistance under the federal Urban Mass Transportation Act of 1964, or under other federal financial aid programs?
2. Beyond serving the needs of nondrivers and drivers without cars, what other Metropolitan Tulsa objectives were advanced by alternate, higher levels of transit service scheduled for long-term (1974-1990) implementation?
3. What portion of Metropolitan Tulsa's transportation needs—year by year to 1990—were to be met by transit?
4. How much restructuring of the transit system was required in order to meet these needs efficiently? What net annual costs were involved for each alternative and to what extent were these to be defrayed by federal or other external assistance?

The first focus, of course, was upon question Number 1, above, and it was to provide the foundation for considering longer range, public transportation issues.

To give authority, experience, and guidance to the first study, the services of Barton-Aschman Associates, Inc. of Chicago, Illinois were secured. The officials of the City of Tulsa Metropolitan Area Planning Commission and the Tulsa Department of Education all combined to develop the resulting plan. Also, the citizens of Tulsa who rode the buses on January 22, 1970 contributed by completing a survey card explaining their use of transit that day.

Basic Data

Basic information was generated by the study. It was revealed that the number of passengers carried annually by the buses declined from 9,077,000 in 1960 to 1,807,600 in 1969, an average yearly decrease of

9 percent. During the same period, annual revenue decreased from $1,584,487 to $655,035, an average decrease of 6 percent. Much of the decline in ridership and revenue resulted from the two-month strike when nearly 40 percent of the ridership was lost.

Revenue passengers, gross revenue and operating ratios were not available for the fiscal years ended June 30, 1965, 1966, 1967 and 1968 as this period was under the operation of the M-K-O. However, the downward trend in revenue passengers was determined to be as presented in Table 6-1.

Table 6-1
Decrease in Revenue Passengers, 1960-1969

Year	Revenue Passengers	Percent of 1960 Volume	Percent of 1964 Volume
1960	9,077,000	—	—
1964	5,871,000	64.7	—
1969	1,807,600	19.9	30.8

The average weekday revenue passengers in 1969 were estimated to number 6,700, and 1,000 of these (15.9 percent) were required to transfer under the route network in force.

This drop in riders was accompanied by a drop in gross revenue. This unfavorable trend was determined to be as presented in Table 6-2.

Table 6-2
Decrease in Gross Revenue, 1960-1969

Year	Gross Revenue
1960	$1,584,487
1964	1,337,349
1969	655,035

The sources of revenue for 1969 were determined to be as presented in Table 6-3.

Table 6-3
Passenger Revenue

Type	Amount	Percent of Total
Basic fares	$582,305	88.9
Transfer charges	13,908	2.1
Other shoppers	295	.1
School routes	58,526	8.9
Total	$655,034	100.0

The fare structure was confined to cash fares only. The system was divided into three fare areas: inner, middle, and outer, with respective fares of thirty, thirty-five, and forty cents. The average fare paid was thirty-four and four-tenths cents. The transfer charge was five cents.

The fare for students was twenty cents, restricted to school days and during the time period when students travelled to and from school. No reduced fare was offered to children; they paid the regular fare.

Bus Routes

The MTTA furnished service on ten regular routes. All routes were oriented to the central business district, but only three routes terminated in the central business district. The other seven were through routes and terminated in outlying residential areas. Each had a loop at each end; a few were rather long. Two lines also had branches on one of the outer ends, over which alternate trips were operated. This provided a service to areas otherwise unserved, but cut the frequency of service on the branches to half of that of the main lines.

The combined round-trip mileage of the lines routed through the central business district ranged from 22.9 to 36.4 miles. These routes were considered reasonable, although they were somewhat longer than those normally found in transit systems. The policy of routing through the central business district, which provided service demands about equally on each side of the area, was beneficial to the riders. Also, this policy reduced the number of vehicular movements making a loop in the congested central district.

The average speed of the buses ranged from 10.0 to 15.2 miles per hour. These speeds compared favorably with those of cities of similar size and were considerably higher than the speeds in larger cities. Since no layover time at the outer terminals was provided, the speed represented the overall vehicle speed.

The level of service on weeekdays was limited to a frequency of about thirty minutes during the rush-hour periods and a frequency of about sixty minutes during the non-rush hours. Some lines did not operate at all during the midday periods.

Saturday service was scheduled at an hourly frequency, except on the route serving the black district, which was scheduled on a half-hourly frequency, and on four other branches, which were scheduled on headways of two hours. No service was furnished on Sundays or holidays.

During an average day when school was in session, 6,000 regular rider trips and an additional 2,000 school rider trips were made on the MTTA. Of the regular rider trips, nearly 90 percent were made before 9:00 A.M. and after 3:00 P.M. An on-board transit survey indicated that nearly 60 percent of all daily transit trips were made to and from the central business district.

Most of the regular riders lived in the area which was immediately north of the central business district. This area was commonly referred to as the Model Cities Area. It was a low-income black district. These were necessity riders who generally had no other means of transportation available.

Characteristics of Metropolitan Tulsa

In order to determine the public transportation needs of the Tulsa Metropolitan area, it was necessary to determine the basic demographic and land-use characteristics. The socioeconomic data considered to be most important to transportation planning were as follows:

1. Tulsa had evolved into a medium-sized metropolis with a population of slightly over 325,000 now and 500,000 expected by 1975.
2. The one-time highly specialized petroleum-oriented economy had become diversified over the years with a broad economic base.
3. Tulsa had one of the nation's highest ratios of autos to population, with 467 cars for every 1,000 persons in 1969. It was projected that the number of autos would continue to increase from 202,000 in 1969 to over 320,000 by 1990.
4. Multifamily living units had been a minor proportion of the total housing units in the Tulsa metropolitan area, but the construction of multifamily units was expected to average between 40 percent and 50 percent of annual starts between 1969–1990.
5. In 1969, 167,000 persons were employed in the metropolitan area. An expansion of 64 percent, or 90,000 people, was anticipated by 1990, bringing the total employed to 257,000.

Comparable Transit Data and Trends

The decline in transit patronage in the Tulsa area was to a level far below that of comparable cities in the region. The decline had continued until the system actually served only a fraction of the citizens of the metropolitan community. And, only four of the ten bus lines operated continuously throughout the day. The shrinking system became the equivalent of one typically operated in a city half the size of Tulsa. In 1969, Tulsa had one of the lowest ridership ratios in the entire United States, when about six transit trips per capita were made.

Tulsa had been called the "Los Angeles of the Midwest." Like Los Angeles, it had a low-density population and was geared to the automobile for its primary mode of transportation. Expressways, arterial streets, and available parking facilities in the central business district had contributed to the steady decline of transit patronage and promised to continue the decline.

Historically, the automobile had begun to have an impact on the national transit industry in the 1920s. During this period, the streetcar, commuter trains, and rapid transit carried a peak number of passengers on a per capita basis. The tire and gasoline rationing during World War II caused a sharp increase in transit ridership. Annual transit rides per capita dropped rapidly after the war. The trend still appeared to be downward. Concurrently, the trend of more and more cars per capita had moved ever upward.

Transit Policy Guidelines

The Tulsa Metropolitan Area Planning Commission developed a set of "policies" to guide the planning of the transit system. These guides recognized that the transit needs, problems, and potentials cut across all facets of the community, such as commerce, housing, land-use, the Model Cities program, schools, and zoning. In developing these policies, the following issues were considered:

1. What type of environment did Tulsa want?
2. What kind of communities did Tulsa want?
3. How did the transportation system influence the environment and the community of Tulsa?
4. How was the transportation system influenced by the environment and the community of Tulsa?
5. What was to be required of public transportation in Tulsa?
6. What was to be the "balance" between public and private transportation in Tulsa?
7. What was to be the "balance" between the resources allocated to local transportation and other public services in Tulsa?

Generally, the Tulsa Metropolitan Planning Commission related several primary goals of the future to public transportation as a part of its study. One consideration was the provision for increased and more equitable accessibility to employment and, also, to recreational opportunities. Another consideration was efficiency and economy in the use of public funds. Specifically, the short-term future (1970–1974) operation of the MTTA's bus transit system was to meet the needs of those citizens whose travel requirements were not likely to be met except by bus service. Particularly, the service was to be directed to those who depend upon public transportation for employment, education, and health-related travel. And, the transit system was expected to provide the highest quality service possible within the resources allocated to public transportation.

As a consequence of the "policy" framework, certain service "standards" were adopted with operating characteristics expressed in quantifiable terms when possible. For the standards which did not lend themselves to quantitative measurements, qualitative guidelines were established.

1. *Routing Standards.* To the greatest extent possible, routes were to be developed so that they were within one quarter mile of those citizens requiring service, and routes were to be designed so that the majority of passenger origins and destinations were directly connected.

2. *Loading Standards.* The ratio of passengers to bus seats was not to exceed one-to-one during the base service hours (midday and night) and not to exceed 1.3:1 during the peak (rush) hours.

3. *Frequency of Service Standards.* The rush period frequency of service was to be scheduled so that the loading standards were not exceeded and so that the maximum interval between buses did not exceed thirty minutes.

   The off-peak period frequency was to be cut back—severely, if necessary, or even discontinued altogether—if it proved significantly uneconomic to operate. It was hoped that a maximum sixty-minute interval between buses could be scheduled and maintained.

4. *Frequency of Transit Stops.* The spacing of transit stops was to provide relatively high convenience to the riders and at the same time to minimize the decrease in trip speed.

5. *Trip Speed.* The average schedule speed was to be fifteen to eighteen miles per hour exclusive of end-of-the-line recovery time.

6. *Dependability.* Dependability was considered a crucial measure of the quality of the transit service. It included schedule adherence, freedom from trip interruption due to breakdowns, and continuity of service during bad weather. Steps were to be taken through the maintenance of the buses and training programs for drivers to increase dependability.

7. *Range of Special Services.* Many community events required special transit service. The system was to be flexible enough to respond to these special needs.

8. *Fare Structure.* The fare structure was to be maintained at a relatively low level so that the use of basic transit service was not discouraged because of the price.

9. *Availability of Information.* Information regarding schedules and routes was to be made available on the buses, at major stops, and through the mail. When the buses were operated on wide headways (infrequently), it was considered imperative to have timetables available to the riders.

10. *Vehicle Design Amenities.* Design amenities were measured in a practical way by the age of the bus. The current standard accepted by the industry for average fleet age was seven and one-half years. An additional standard important in Tulsa in determining the quality of the bus was air conditioning.

11. *Vehicle Cleanliness.* The buses were to be well maintained and present a clean, inviting appearance inside and out.

12. *Passenger Stop Convenience.* Passenger shelters were to be located at major transfer points or at any stop in the system where people congregated while waiting for a bus.

13. *Responsiveness to Passenger Communications.* The MTTA was to actively seek ideas, opinions, and recommendations from its patrons and to develop procedures for immediate response to complaints and questions from its riders.

14. *Operating Costs per Bus Mile.* All possible steps were to be taken by MTTA to reduce the operating costs of the system while maintaining services at a relatively high level.
15. *Environmental Contamination.* Bus operations affected the environment in many ways, such as air pollution, sight, sound, and vibration. Air pollution was considered the most serious. An obvious guideline was that buses were to emit a minimum of pollutants into the atmosphere.

Labor Force

Full-time employees of MTTA as of May 1970, numbered seventy-four, including fifty-one bus operators and three supervisors, seventeen maintenance men, and three in general administration. Also, an employee of the city auditor's office devoted one-half of his time to MTTA duty.

The ratio of full-time employees to revenue vehicles was 1:64. This ratio was among the lowest of transit operations of similar size. Concern was felt that the operation was understaffed, certain necessary functions were not receiving appropriate attention, and that, perhaps, certain functions were not being performed at all.

The labor contract with the Amalgamated Transit Union, Division 892, became effective June 1, 1970 and was scheduled to expire on May 31, 1972. The contract was expected to increase the operating expenses by $135,000 during the two-year period. Increases of fifteen cents per hour, fringe benefits including one additional holiday, sick leave, and vacation allowances were provided in the contract. The hourly rates were now consistent with those in cities of a similar size in the same general area.

Maintenance Practices

Bus interiors were cleaned and exteriors washed on a daily basis. The buses were inspected as they entered the garage for midday storage and were kept reasonably clean. The storage area was roofless and the ground was covered with crushed rock which generated considerable gray dust during dry weather.

The maintenance department developed a preventive maintenance program based on the inspection of certain parts after each 2,000 miles of operation with a more thorough inspection after each 24,000 miles. Nineteen items were checked at the 2,000-mile interval and fifty-one items at the 24,000-mile interval. This program was not as extensive as that of some systems, but it kept maintenance costs at a reasonable level. The maintenance expense experience for 1969 is presented in Table 6-4.

Table 6–4
Maintenance Expenses, 1969

Item	Amount	Cost Per Mile
Revenue Equipment		
Labor	$ 68,869.31	$ .0556
Materials	30,549.25	.0246
Total	$ 99,418.56	$ .0802
Other Expenses		
Shop and garage salaries	18,302.44	$ .0148
Tires and tubes	10,274.56	.0083
Servicing equipment	3,475.49	.0028
Other expenses	14,504.64	.0117
Grand Total	$145,975.69	$ .1178

All of the buses were manufactured by GMC in 1957, 1960, and 1961. They were powered by diesel engines and had a seating capacity of forty-five persons. The average age of the buses was ten years. A desirable average age was considered to be seven and one-half years or less. Newer units usually resulted in reduced maintenance cost and had greater passenger appeal. The maximum scheduled requirement was forty-one units, leaving four buses as spares. This was considered sufficient for a fleet of this size. Six of the oldest buses were not air conditioned. All the others were.

Survey Reveals Ridership Characteristics

In Tulsa, as in most cities, public transit was used primarily by people traveling to and from work. On January 22, 1970 a survey was made of the riders to determine the following information:

1. Purpose of trip
2. Reason for using public transit
3. Distance walked to public transit
4. Hourly distribution of patronage
5. Occupation
6. Age and sex

Of all riders, 92 percent rode at the peak periods—before 9:00 A.M. and after 3:30 P.M.—and were going to or from work. The second largest volume of trips was 6 percent and represented students going to and from school. This last percent was understated somewhat as survey cards were not distributed to the youngest riders.

After the morning peak hours and during the base period of operation, there was a shift in the distribution of trip purposes. Work trips still dominated, however, and accounted for 70 percent of the total off-peak trips. Shopping, the second highest, was the purpose of 15 percent of the midday riders. The predominance of work trips in both the peak and off-peak periods produced a relatively constant volume of patrons during the weekdays.

It was found that the majority of the riders had no alternate transportation available. These necessity riders accounted for 60 percent of the ridership. Some did not possess a driver's license; others did not have access to an automobile. The remaining 40 percent of the riders were choice riders with alternate means of transportation available. Since this percentage of choice riders was several times larger than that of comparable systems, there appeared to be relatively good potential for increasing ridership through improved service and equipment. The choice riders were sensitive to fare and service changes, and, it was concluded, they could be lost if fares increased or services decreased.

The largest group of necessity riders was located in the black area immediately north of the CBD. The choice riders were generally more predominant in white areas to the south and the southeast of the CBD.

Over one-half (55 percent) of the riders lived within two blocks of a transit stop, and 85 percent of the riders walked no more than four blocks to board a bus. Generally, the service was considered to include the population residing within one-quarter mile of each side of the line.

The existing ridership was made up of clerical personnel (27 percent), household personnel (15 percent), and service personnel (14 percent). This was partially accounted for by the fact that the CBD had an abundance of clerical and sales jobs and, thus, was the principal destination of riders.

Nearly 20 percent of the riders were under fifteen or over sixty-five years of age. This segment of riders was regarded as necessity riders. The largest number of riders (40 percent) were in the age bracket of forty-five to sixty-five. Females accounted for approximately 70 percent of the patronage. Twenty-five percent of all riders were females between the ages of forty-five and sixty-four. The age and sex distribution reflected the existence of a significant number of clerical and household workers who ride the MTTA system.

Considerations

From time to time in formal meetings and in informal conversations, the trustees enumerated and stated problems and convictions about the transit operations and the future. Some of these ideas are given below.

1. A primary goal to guide the development of public transportation in Tulsa was to provide increased and more equitable accessibility to employment and educational opportunities. A sector of the city was locked into poverty unless these citizens moved freely to jobs and schooling.

2. Health maintenance of the people depended, in many cases, on cheap and reliable transportation to the doctors' offices, hospitals, medical centers, etc.

3. Public funds available for city services were in short supply, and it was mandatory for Tulsa to achieve efficiency and economy in the use of public funds. From September, 1968 to March, 1971, the cash subsidy from the general fund amounted to almost $400,000. A concern was expressed as to how much the city could afford to subsidize public transportation.

4. Excellent progress had been achieved in the past several years in improving the trafficways of Tulsa. Had the planning been forward-looking enough to provide for the needs when the population doubled? What were these needs to be?

5. An application was submitted to the Federal Government for $1,000,000 to acquire new buses. Favorable action on the application was anticipated. What actions would follow if the application was refused? The citizens had failed previously to approve a bond issue for purchase of new buses.

6. An additional general administrator and a secretary were needed in the general office. How much could be added to the payroll when the deficits were mounting?

7. Public relations had been generally neglected. What kind and how much should be done in public relations activities?

8. A recurring refrain in the thinking of all was what does the long-term future hold for mass transit?

9. The bus problem was not defined in its proper perspective. The total problem was transportation—private and public. Private transportation flourished in Tulsa because of the available, cheap parking in the downtown area. The net incomes from public parking lots should be applied against deficits in public transportation.

10. The City of Tulsa could not afford to continue such a costly service for so few users. Serious considerations should be given to the elimination of public transit.

11. New buses, innovative services, courteous personnel, and acceptable schedules would attract choice riders.

12. It is a proper function of municipal government to provide transportation even at a substantial deficit which must be charged to the general fund and passed to nonusers in the taxation process.

Exhibit 6-1
Metropolitan Tulsa Transit Authority Balance Sheet, December 31, 1970

ASSETS		
Current Assets		
Cash in Bank	$ 8,561.24	
Shoppers Fare Fund	101.70	
Dispatchers Fund	4,000.00	
Drivers Fund	3,500.00	
Accounts Receivable	4,959.35	
Prepaid Insurance	10,820.00	
Total Current Assets		$ 31,942.29

Exhibit 6-1 (Continued)

Fixed Assets

Revenue Equipment	$630,000.00		
Res. for Depr.-Rev. Equip.	176,221.59	453,778.41	
Service Car & Equip.	$ 250.00		
Res. for Depr.-Service Car & Equip.	112.54	137.46	
Shop & Garage Equipment	$ 14,954.63		
Res. for Depr.-S & G. Equipment	7,643.25	7,311.38	
Furniture & Equipment	$ 4,997.12		
Res. for Depr.-Furniture & Equipment	2,271.44	2,725.68	
Miscellaneous Equipment	$ 17,510.00		
Res. for Depr.-Miscell. Equip.	9,192.68	8,317.32	
Total Fixed Assets			$472,270.25

Deferred Assets

Parts Inventory	$ 18,140.55
TOTAL ASSETS	$522,353.09

LIABILITIES

Current Liabilities

Notes Payable M.K.&O.	$ 85,421.11	
Accounts Payable	7,629.69	
Accrued Interest	1,293.51	
Wages Payable	16,943.01	
FICA	-0-	
Federal Withholding Tax	-0-	
State Withholding Tax	614.05	
Insurance	(119.95)	
Equipment Deposit	864.20	
Pension - Employees	257.04	
Total Current Liabilities		$112,902.66

Long Term Liabilities

Notes Payable M.K.&O.	225,021.45

Deferred Liabilities

Advances - City of Tulsa	352,275.00
TOTAL LIABILITIES	$690,199.11

Unappropriated Surplus

Earned Surplus—Deficit, June 30, 1970	$ 85,920.89	
Earned Surplus—Deficit, 7/1/70 thru 12/31/70	81,925.13	(167,846.02)
TOTAL LIABILITIES & UNAPPROPRIATED SURPLUS		$522,353.09

Prepared by,
Wayne K. Meyer
Internal Auditor

Exhibit 6-2
**Metropolitan Tulsa Transit Authority Statement of Income & Expenses for
Month Ended, December 31, 1970**

Item	December 1969	December 1970
REVENUE		
Operating Revenue		
Passenger	$54,244.25	$ 47,824.91
Charter	784.17	1,097.50
Vending	21.47	12.90
Advertising	110.00	700.00
Other — Transfers	1,118.30	994.70
Other — Shoppers Fare	295.00	-0-
Total Operating Revenue	$56,573.19	$ 50,630.01
Other Income	18.41	453.31
Summer Youth Transportation Program —		
Federal Grant	-0-	567.50
TOTAL REVENUE	$56,591.60	$ 51,650.82
EXPENSES		
Equipment & Garage Expense		
Shop & Garage Salaries	$ 2,847.60	$ 2,356.25
Co. Portion — Shop & Garage Employees Health Ins. Pro.	-0-	9.20
Repairs to Shop & Garage Equipment	-0-	30.75
Operations & Maint. — Service Equipment	48.06	51.95
Repairs — Shop & Garage Buildings	-0-	583.03
Utilities — Shop & Garage	613.58	512.18
Other Shop & Garage Expense	256.65	53.76
Towels & Uniforms	167.55	208.31
Total Equipment & Garage Expenses	$ 3,933.44	$ 3,805.43
Transportation Expense		
Drivers Wages	$24,597.98	$ 24,690.15
Co. Portion — Drivers Health Ins. Program	-0-	329.20
Fuel for Revenue Equipment	2,377.27	2,421.87
Oil for Revenue Equipment	85.80	42.90
Labor — Repair to Revenue Equipment	4,756.73	5,550.17
Co. Portion — Mechanics Health Ins. Program	-0-	64.40
Material — Repair to Revenue Equipment	2,179.54	2,938.37
Servicing of Revenue Equipment	242.00	46.01
Tires & Tubes — Revenue Equipment	95.29	322.81
Other Transportation Expense	35.00	44.00
Total Transportation Expense	$34,369.61	$ 36,449.88
Traffic Solicitation & Advertising Expense		
Tariffs & Schedules	$ 51.23	$ -0-
Advertising	(20.00)	-0-
Total Traffic Solicitation & Advert. Ex.	$ 31.23	$ -0-

Exhibit 6-2 (Continued)

Item	December 1969	December 1970
Insurance & Safety Expense		
P. L. & P. D. Insurance	$ 3,018.27	$ 3,219.51
Physicals	24.00	-0-
Workmens Compensation	555.27	462.87
Fire & Theft	-0-	-0-
Service Car & Equipment	-0-	-0-
Felonious Assault	-0-	-0-
Total Insurance & Safety Expense	$ 3,597.54	$ 3,682.38
Administrative & General Expense		
General Office Salaries	$ 4,446.40	$ 4,690.00
General Office Employees Expense	35.00	52.50
General Office Supplies	122.26	248.99
Outside Auditing	1,450.00	350.00
Other General Expense	131.15	113.40
General Office Employees Death Benefit Ins.	-0-	119.42
General Office Employees Pension Company Portion	-0-	-0-
Uncollectible Revenue	-0-	-0-
Social Security Tax	1,570.52	1,793.75
Total Administrative General Ex.	$ 7,755.33	$ 7,368.06
Depreciation Expense		
Revenue Equipment	$ 6,569.50	$ 6,569.50
Service Car & Equipment	4.22	4.69
Shop & Garage Equipment	280.41	278.06
Furniture & Equipment	80.74	87.63
Miscellaneous Equipment	328.31	328.31
Total Depreciation Expense	$ 7,263.18	$ 7,268.19
Operating Rent		
Interest on Note	$ 2,380.02	$ 1,563.87
Rent for Shop & Garage Space	2,200.00	2,200.00
Total Operating Rent Expense	$ 4,580.02	$ 3,763.87
TOTAL EXPENSES	$ 61,530.35	$ 62,337.81
NET OPERATING LOSS	$(4,938.75)	$ (10,686.99)

Exhibit 6-3
Metropolitan Tulsa Transit Authority Statement of Income & Expenses,
Year to Date, December 31, 1970

Item	July–Dec. 1969	July–Dec. 1970
REVENUE		
Operating Revenue		
Passenger	$313,216.81	$278,569.08
Charter	15,948.23	17,479.64
Vending	150.83	270.86
Advertising	4,615.00	2,957.74
Other — Transfers	6,913.95	6,290.10
Other — Shoppers Fare	295.00	-0-
Total Operating Revenue	$341,139.82	$305,567.42
Other Income	1,470.65	858.99
Summer Youth Transportation Program-		
Federal Grant	7,037.50	4,775.00
TOTAL REVENUE	$349,647.97	$311,201.41
EXPENSES		
Equipment & Garage Expense		
Shop & Garage Salaries	$ 16,942.61	$ 13,881.15
Co. Portion-Shop & Garage Employee		
Health Ins. Pro.	-0-	24.05
Repairs to Shop & Garage Equipment	-0-	151.35
Operations & Maint.-Service Equipment	446.32	335.57
Repairs-Shop & Garage Buildings	628.00	642.47
Utilities-Shop & Garage	3,207.95	3,412.11
Other Shop & Garage Expense	2,255.68	1,225.52
Towels & Uniforms	673.92	1,023.74
Total Equipment & Garage Expense	$ 24,154.48	$ 20,695.96
Transportation Expense		
Drivers Wages	$144,824.92	$154,003.63
Co. Portion-Drivers Health		
Ins. Program	-0-	811.25
Fuel for Revenue Equipment	14,727.58	14,552.41
Oil for Revenue Equipment	1,984.26	1,422.90
Labor-Repair to Revenue Equipment	28,527.54	35,016.67
Co. Portion-Mechanics Health		
Ins. Program	-0-	168.35
Material-Repair to Revenue Equipment	16,935.28	21,008.46
Servicing of Revenue Equipment	1,536.45	1,733.31
Tires & Tubes-Revenue Equipment	5,337.80	5,747.40
Other Transportation Expense	31.30	538.32
Total Transportation Expense	$213,905.13	$235,002.70
Traffic Solicitation & Advertising Expense		
Tariffs & Schedules	$ 2,227.93	$ 788.25
Advertising	370.40	-0-
Total Traffic Solicitation & Advert. Ex.	$ 2,598.33	$ 788.25

Exhibit 6-3 (Continued)

Item	July–Dec. 1969	July–Dec. 1970
Insurance & Safety Expense		
P. L. & P. D. Insurance	$ 20,028.04	$ 22,301.06
Physicals	104.00	143.33
Workmens Compensation	3,501.75	2,451.44
Fire & Theft	213.00	213.00
Service Car & Equipment	813.00	950.00
Felonious Assault	236.50	180.00
Total Insurance & Safety Expense	$ 24,896.29	$ 26,238.83
Administrative & General Expense		
General Office Salaries	$ 26,001.98	$ 27,032.25
General Office Employees Expense	268.04	210.00
General Office Supplies	414.53	967.01
Outside Auditing	3,200.00	3,200.00
Other General Expense	3,559.61	857.34
General Office Employees Death Benefit Ins.	-0-	708.47
General Office Employees Pension Company Portion	-0-	115.26
Uncollectible Revenue	175.00	-0-
Social Security Tax	10,203.38	10,094.00
Total Administrative & General Ex.	$ 43,822.54	$ 43,184.33
Depreciation Expense		
Revenue Equipment	$ 39,417.00	$ 39,417.00
Service Car & Equipment	25.32	28.14
Shop & Garage Equipment	1,653.06	1,668.36
Furniture & Equipment	484.44	508.43
Miscellaneous Equipment	1,969.86	1,969.86
Total Depreciation Expense	$ 43,549.68	$ 43,591.79
Operating Rent		
Interest on Note	$ 15,260.96	$ 10,424.68
Rent for Shop & Garage Space	13,200.00	13,200.00
Total Operating Rent Expense	$ 28,460.96	$ 23,624.68
TOTAL EXPENSES	$ 381,387.41	$ 393,126.54
NET OPERATING LOSS	$ (31,739.44)	$ (81,925.13)

7

Policy and Program Analysis

PURPOSE

The purpose of this chapter is to introduce students to modern analytic techniques, exploring the place of systematic, rational analysis of public policies and programs in governmental decision making.

CONTENTS

Readings
    Jacob B. Ukeles, "Policy Analysis: Myth or Reality?"
    Harry P. Hatry et al., "A Checklist for Assessing Program Analyses"

Cases
    "Swimming Pools"
    "Emergency Ambulance Service (A)"
    "Emergency Ambulance Service (B)"

Instructions

Pre-Class Preparation

After studying both the Ukeles and the Hatry selections, read the case "Swimming Pools" and respond fully to the following questions:

1. What are the alternative service delivery mechanisms in the Swimming Pools case, and what are the benefits and costs of each alternative?

2. Based on the information presented in the case, what method of providing swimming opportunities for the model cities neighborhood would you recommend?

3. If you were the responsible Dade County, Florida, official, what additional information would you want before making a final decision?

Regarding the set of cases dealing with emergency ambulance service, *first*, read the case "Emergency Ambulance Service (A)," and:

1. Define the system and/or systems involved;
2. Specify possible objectives and output measures;

3. Formulate alternative ways of achieving the objectives;

4. Suggest the analytic approach you would use to evaluate each alternative.

Then, read "Emergency Ambulance Service (B)." In your capacity as a special assistant to the mayor, you have been asked to *evaluate* the actual analysis performed, paying particular attention to:

The scope of the analysis

The objectives and effectiveness measures chosen

The alternatives considered for analysis

The analyst's methodology

The usefulness of the analysis as an aid to better decision making

Procedure for Class Meeting

Class discussion will focus on policy and program analysis and the utility for state and local public managers.

With regard to the benefit-cost approach to providing swimming opportunities, which class members favor which alternatives? Why?

How is the approach to analyzing the emergency ambulance service problem different from that used for swimming pools? How are the approaches similar?

In each case, what role did your analysis play in your final recommendation for action?

For Additional Information

Policy analysis is nicely introduced in:

Duncan MacRae, Jr., and James A. Wilde, *Policy Analysis for Public Decisions* (North Scituate, Mass.: Duxbury Press, 1979). Paperback edition available.

Regarding benefit-cost analysis, see:

Robert Dorfman, ed., *Measuring the Benefit of Government Investments* (Washington: The Brookings Institution, 1965).

Jesse Burkhead and Jerry Miner, *Public Expenditure* (Chicago: Aldine-Atherton, 1971). Chapter 7, "Benefit-Cost Analysis," offers a clear and cogent explanation.

T. R. Durham, *An Introduction to Benefit-Cost Analysis for Evaluating Public Programs* (Croton-on-Hudson, N.Y.: Policy Studies Associates, 1977), paperback.

Evaluation and Analysis to Support Decisionmaking (Washington: U.S. General Accounting Office, 1976), paperback.

Eva C. Galambos and Arthur F. Schreiber, *Making Sense Out of Dollars: Economic Analysis for Local Government* (Washington: National League of Cities, November, 1978). See especially chapters 5 and 6. A paperback edition of this useful treatment, funded by the Office of Policy Development and Research, U. S. Department of Housing and Urban Development, is available.

Robert H. Haveman and Julius Margolis, eds., *Public Expenditure and Policy Analysis*, 2nd ed. (Chicago: Rand McNally, 1977). Paperback edition available.

Regina Herzlinger, "Costs, Benefits, and the West Side Highway," *Public Interest*, No. 55 (Spring 1979), pp. 77-98.

Harley H. Hinrichs and Graeme M. Taylor, *Program Budgeting and Benefit-Cost Analysis: Cases, Text, and Readings* (Pacific Palisades, Cal.: Goodyear Publishing Co., 1969). Paperback edition available.

E. J. Mishan, *Cost-Benefit Analysis* (New York: Praeger, 1976). Paperback edition available.

Henry Peskin and Eugene P. Seskin, eds., *Cost-Benefit Analysis and Water Pollution Policy* (Washington: Urban Institute, 1975).

Edith Stokely and Richard Zeckhauser, *A Primer for Policy Analysis* (New York: Norton, 1978). See especially chapters 9 and 10. Paperback edition available.

Victor A. Thompson, *Decision Theory, Pure and Applied* (New York: General Learning, 1971). Paperback edition available.

For a nontechnical, easily read introduction to the *systems approach* generally, see:

C. West Churchman, *The Systems Approach* (New York: Dell, 1968). Paperback edition available.

A good introduction to systems analysis can be found in:

Chester Wright and Michael D. Tate, *Economics and Systems Analysis* (Reading, Mass.: Addison-Wesley, 1973). Paperback edition available.

Applying Systems Analysis in Urban Government: Three Case Studies (Washington: International City Management Association, 1972). Paperback edition available.

A related useful volume is:

Philip M. Morse, ed., *Operations Research for Public Systems* (Cambridge, Mass.: The MIT Press, 1967).

For a critique of systems analysis in government, see:

Ida Hoos, *Systems Analysis in Public Policy* (Berkeley: University of California Press, 1972).

The journals *Policy Sciences, Public Policy* and *Policy Analysis* contain related studies and analyses.

Also see:

Russell L. Ackoff, *Redesigning the Future: A Systems Approach to Societal Problems* (New York: Wiley, 1974).

Guy Black, *The Application of Systems Analysis to Government Operations* (New York: Praeger, 1968).

Robert Boguslaw, *The New Utopians: A Study of System Design and Social Change* (Englewood Cliffs, N.J.: Prentice-Hall, 1965). Paperback edition available.

Garry W. Brewer, *Politicians, Bureaucrats, and the Consultant: A Critique of Urban Problem Solving* (New York: Basic Books, 1973).

Jack Byrd, Jr., *Operations Research Models for Public Administration* (Lexington, Mass.: D.C. Heath/Lexington Books, 1975).

Alvin W. Drake, Ralph L. Keeney, and Philip M. Morse, *Analysis of Public Systems* (Cambridge: MIT Press, 1972). Solid collection of examples.

Economic Analysis Handbook (Washington: Government Printing Office, June 1975). Paperback edition available; developed by the Department of Navy, Naval Facilities Engineering Command, Facilities Planning and Real Estate Group.

Ida R. Hoos, "Systems Techniques for Managing Society: A Critique," *Public Administration Review*, XXXIII (March-April 1973), pp. 157–164.

G. J. Kelleher, ed., *The Challenge to Systems Analysis: Public Policy and Social Change* (New York: Wiley, 1970).

Arnold J. Meltsner, "Bureaucratic Policy Analysts," *Policy Analysis*, I (Winter 1975), pp. 115–131.

Selma J. Mushkin, "Policy Analysis in State and Community," *Public Administration Review* (May/June 1977), pp. 245–253.

Stuart S. Nagel with Marian Neef, *Operations Research Methods* (Beverly Hills, Cal.: Sage Publications, 1976). Part of Sage's Quantitative Applications in the Social Sciences Series.

Nation's Cities, January 1972.

Public Administration Review, XXXIX (Jan./Feb. 1979). "Symposium on Policy Analysis in State and Local Government."

Public Management, August 1973.

E. S. Quade, *Analysis for Public Decisions* (New York: Elsevier, 1975). Outstanding text.

Richard S. Rosenbloom and John R. Russell, *New Tools for Urban Management* (Boston: Division of Research, Harvard Business School, 1971).

Frank P. Scioli, Jr., and Thomas J. Cook, *Methodologies for Analyzing Public Policies* (Lexington, Mass.: D. C. Heath/Lexington Books, 1975).

Henri Theil, John C. G. Boot, and Teun Kloek, *Operations Research and Quantitative Economics: An Elementary Introduction* (New York: McGraw-Hill, 1965).

Michael J. White, *Management Science in Federal Agencies* (Lexington, Mass.: D.C. Heath/Lexington Books, 1975).

Aaron Wildavsky, "The Political Economy of Efficiency: Cost-Benefit Analysis, Systems Analysis, and Program Budgeting," *Public Administration Review*, XXVI (Dec. 1966), pp. 292–310.

Walter Williams, *Social Policy Research and Analysis* (New York: Elsevier, 1971).

Robert E. D. Woolsey and Huntington S. Swanson, *Operations Research for Immediate Application: A Quick and Dirty Manual* (New York: Harper & Row, 1975).

Policy Analysis: Myth or Reality?

Jacob B. Ukeles

IN THE SEPTEMBER 1967 ISSUE of *Public Administration Review,* Yehezkel Dror called for the development of a new professional mission called policy analysis.[1] In May 1974, the National Association of Schools of Public Affairs and Administration (NASPAA), in issuing its first guidelines for member schools, identified policy analysis as one of five major subject areas which should be included in all public affairs programs.[2] Thus in only seven years, policy analysis moved from proposition to reality, from a "fringe" idea to a central place in official public administration thinking. This rapid acceptance of the legitimacy of policy analysis is one of the most remarkable developments in modern public affairs.

The purpose of this article is to present an overview of policy analysis that may shed some light on its growth. The article is divided into two parts: (1) current views of policy analysis — what it is and what its intellectual and pragmatic roots are; and (2) an assessment of the state of policy analysis — how these problems might enhance American governance.

Current Views of Policy Analysis

What Is Policy Analysis?

Policy analysis can be defined as the systematic investigation of alternative policy options and the assembly and integration of the evidence for and against each option. It involves a problem-solving approach, the collection and interpretation of information, and some attempt to predict the consequences of alternative courses of action. The fundamental purpose of policy analysis is,

> to facilitate the reaching of sound policy decisions. . . . It may include the examination of problems, issues, legislation or proposed legislation, positions of politically accountable leadership, programs of agencies, policies of private sector organizations, or any subject of significance which calls for attention and decision-making. It calls for analysis of underlying assumptions and their implications; information gaps; internal inconsistencies; conflicts with other goals, policies, programs; political consequences; impacts on society, the economy, the environment; problems of administrative implementation; institutional aspects; problems of coordinating interdisciplinary impact; the hypothetical alternatives, with

disqualifying reasons for those ruled out; realistic alternatives, with pros and cons of each; and evaluation, oversight, and follow-up requirements and procedures.[3]

While the activities identified with policy analysis have been associated with public policy making throughout the history of governance, it is only relatively recently that analysis has been *formally* associated with public decision making. Current developments in policy analysis have been fed by two sources: empirical and theoretical.

The Empirical Roots of Policy Analysis

In foreign affairs and defense, policy planning has evolved over a long period of time; the Policy Planning Council in the State Department and war gaming in the Pentagon are but two of many examples in this area. In the domestic arena, post-depression and war-time planning and analytic activity were widespread in such areas as price control, scarce resource allocation, etc.; thus the spillover from war planning to domestic planning was substantial.

In the post-war era, the increasing scope of the federal government and the increasing complexity of domestic problems led to increased investment in research and analysis in conjunction with the massive federal highway program and the anti-poverty program. In the mid-1960s this effort culminated in the attempt to install a planning-programming-budgeting system in the entire federal governmental system.

As urban problems began to receive more attention, some federal investment was directed towards developing analytic capacity at the local level. For example, the Community Renewal Program, funded by HUD in the early '60s, produced not only the widely publicized systems analysis disasters in San Francisco and Pittsburgh, but also less-well-known, highly effective policy analytic staff work directly linked to housing and renewal policy making in New York and Detroit.

In various cities around the country, city planners, systems analysts, MBAs, economists, and lawyers began to experiment with new ways of approaching urban policy problems that transcended the limitations of their own disciplinary models. Without necessarily using the term "policy analysis," they developed styles of working in government that fit the definition of policy analysis given above.

The Theoretical Roots of Policy Analysis   At the same time that there was a pragmatic response to the increasing need for better information to support complex public problems and programs, there was, quite independently, substantial ferment in the thinking about public decision making. In 1951 Harold D. Lasswell and D. Lerner edited a volume entitled *The Policy Sciences.* In his introductory essay, Lasswell expressed his view that:

> A policy orientation has been developing that cuts across the existing specializations. The orientation is twofold. In part, it is directed toward the policy process, and in part toward the intelligence needs of policy. The first task, which is the development of a science of policy forming and execution, uses the methods of social and psychological inquiry. The second task, which is the improving of the content of the information, and the interpretations available to policy makers, typically goes outside the boundaries of social science and psychology.[4]

Remarkably little happened for the next ten to 15 years in the evolution of the policy sciences idea; in 1971 Lasswell was still describing his ideas as "A Preview of Policy Sciences."[5] A great deal of thinking, however, was going on in and around political science and economics that was germane to this thesis. Partly based on their success in influencing defense planning, Rand thinkers wrote widely in the 1950s and early 1960s on the need to apply systems analysis to public problems.[6] In effect, they were promoting the need to expand rationality in the public sector.

At the same time, Lindblom and others were arguing that the rational model was ill-suited to a political environment which was characterized by "muddling through" and that, in fact, the incremental model of decision making was more suited to democratic pluralist norms.[7] Schultze attempted to define some middle ground between *laissez-faire,* political decision making and rational, goal-oriented, systematic analysis as a basis for policy decisions.[8]

But the great impetus for the development of such a middle ground was provided by Yehezkel Dror, first in a brief comment on Lindblom's famous "muddling through" article, and more completely in his 1967 article which called for the development of a new professional role in government service, "the policy analyst." In his *Public Administration Review* article, Dror made three major points:

1. Systems analysis with its classical emphasis on quantitative tools and an economic view of the world could be of only limited utility in government;
2. Policy analysis should combine proven methods of systems analysis with qualitative methods and full awareness of the special characteristics of political phenomena; and
3. Policy analysis should be institutionalized as a new professional role in government to contribute to aggregate policy making without preempting the functions of politicians and line executives.

While many of those who subsequently wrote about policy analysis subscribe to Dror's view, a variety of other views have also surfaced. Some of the differences revolve around these issues:

(1) *Is policy analysis normative or positive?* The seeds of this dichotomy were identified by Laswell in his initial definition of the policy sciences in 1951: "The policy sciences are concerned with knowledge *of* and *in* the decision processes of the public and civic order."[9] Many of those who identify their activity as policy analysis are in fact involved in the analysis of policy making. Studies such as Allison's three models of the Cuban missile crisis are in a positive mode, i.e., they describe and explain how policies are made.[10] Such activity is not essentially directed towards indicating how policies should get made or what knowledge would lead to better policies in some sense. Policy analysis in the normative mode is analysis *in* policy making, designed not to increase understanding but rather to improve the process of policy making as well as the content of the policies that are made.

(2) *Is policy analysis an activity or a profession?* Even among those who agree that policy analysis is designed to serve in policy making, there is a wide disparity of views. Some view policy analysis as an activity carried out by many different disciplines and researchers. Thus, anyone engaged in the collection of evidence bearing on alternative policy options is viewed as engaging in policy analysis. Others have viewed policy analysis as a subject matter relating to the training and practice of the public affairs generalist. As such, it is identified with a particular set of knowledge and skills that public administrators or public affairs generalists might employ in the course of their work. Still others, like Dror, have seen the need to establish policy analysis as a professional role with its own underlying discipline. This does not mean that only professional policy analysts engage in policy analysis. What it does mean is that those who practice policy analysis need to develop a professional identity in order to cope with the pressures and frustrations of doing analysis in the public sector. The activity is most likely to flourish, improve, and become established if it is taught and practiced as a separate and identifiable field.

(3) *What is the role of the analyst?* Even among those who agree on the need to establish policy analysis as a professional mission, there are several views as to what the role of the policy analyst should be. There are some, like Wildavsky, who see the purpose of policy analysis as enriching the adversary nature of American public policy making by raising the level of dialogue through greater information. Analysts in such a system become advocates of the views of their principals. Others have talked about the analyst as helping central decision makers, those executives in the policy-making system on whose desk "the buck stops." The analyst is seen as balancing competing interests, values,

and information. Still others see the policy analyst as a quasi-independent actor within governmental policy making. Schultze, for example, writes of the need for a "rationality advocate" within the otherwise disjointed, interest-based, political, policy-making process."[11] It is too soon to tell which view will come to dominate in the future or whether in fact any one view of policy analysis will dominate. For the immediate future, certainly many different approaches will co-exist side by side.

Policy analysis is an activity faced with an essentially hostile environment in the classical policy-making process in the United States. The complex processes of negotiation and bargaining whereby policy is made have been well-documented in the literature. In such a fragmented, rapidly moving process, it is not obvious what kind of analysis can be done and how it should bear on decision making. The political nature of data in policy making, very short time spans for research, and relatively little staff resources all place a premium on "shooting from the hip," as opposed to careful thought and systematic weighing of options.

For those who can foresee an evolving profession, there are added difficulties. The policy analyst faces substantially more competition for the role of staff expert than might be imagined. The systems analyst and economist compete for the analyst title. The lawyer in government is a generalist-expert of long standing with strong credentials as a vigorous professional who is at home with political phenomena. Beyond these professional roles the political policy-making system has generated its own expertise. The staff person who is an expert in political negotiation, has a keen sense for anticipating voter reaction, and can help maintain a position of power is invaluable to any policy executive. Although it might be argued that the latter are policy analysts as well, in practice the politician-advisor and the analyst-advisor are likely to come from different backgrounds, to claim different expertise, to use different processes to arrive at conclusions, and to be highly competitive for staff positions. Where political advisors and policy analysts co-exist within the same structure, they compete for the ear of the decision maker.

Each of the different policy-making subsystems is likely to have its own traditions of credentials and expertise. The M.D. in health, the engineer in environmental control, the lawyer in criminal justice historically dominate planning and administration in their respective fields.

Despite these difficulties, policy analysis seems to be flourishing. There are new journals—*Policy Analysis, Policy Sciences, Urban Analysis*—and new emphases in older public affairs journals—*Public Policy, Public Administration Review, Public Interest.* There are new graduate programs, specifically in policy analysis, as well as many public affairs programs with a reorientation to policy analysis. The subject has been explored by congressional committees (1973, 1976) and special units have been defined by the National League of Cities and the National Governors Conference. Think tanks and governmental research agencies have increasingly begun to define their activities in terms of policy analysis. In the recent transition to a Carter Administration, policy analysis was featured as the task of one of the four major transitional efforts.[12]

The increasing scope of public policy and the complexity of the issues have apparently generated the need for relatively unbiased information produced in close proximity to decision making. Future development and continued growth will depend on creative solutions to two basic problems that affect the state of policy analysis: (1) the knowledge base, and (2) the methodology for policy analysis.

An Assessment of the State of Policy Analysis

Policy analysis has failed to develop a unique methodology specifically appropriate to public sector policy problems. Analysts have borrowed the methods of systems analysis, yet the rational model which underlies systems analysis and operations research rests on a structure of cognitive demands that are overwhelming even in relatively simple problems, as Schoefler pointed out in great detail two decades ago.[13] In summary form, the rational model structures analysis in four steps: (1) identify objectives; (2) identify all possible courses of action relevant to achieving objectives; (3) predict the probable consequences of alternative courses of action; and (4) select that alternative which maximizes the attainment of objectives. The costs in time and manpower, and the requirements for knowledge and understanding of relationships to implement this model are immense for most public policy problems. It is safe to assume that in 90 to 95 per cent of the policy problems likely to involve a practicing policy analyst, the policy problem would be long since resolved by the time the requirements of the rational model could be met. Most analysts, of course, are aware of this and make no attempt to collect all the alternatives, quantify all the objectives and predict all the consequences of alternatives. They had to adjust their own expectations to the realities of time and data limitations. The inclination in the literature is to attack analysts for not being systematic enough, rather than to attack the rational model for not being relevant to policy analysis. Over the coming years active debate among competing analytic models is needed if the field is to develop. One such general model for policy analysis included the following elements:

Step One: Assess the policy-making environment within which the analyst and the relevant decision maker(s) are operating.

Step Two: Identify the policy question or problem needing resolution.

Step Three: Identify policy alternatives appropriate to the policy-making environment and the decision maker(s).

Step Four: Identify criteria that are relevant to choosing among alternatives.

Step Five: Using assumptions and limited information, assess the pros and cons of each alternative in terms of the relevant criteria.

Unlike the rational model—where the purpose of analysis is to maximize the achievement of objectives, or in other words to select the best possible alternative—the purpose of policy analysis may be merely to screen out the worst possible alternatives.

A second important methodological challenge of the next several years involves the identification of different classes of policy problems that lend themselves to different versions of the basic analytic model. Such a concept was noted in 1966: "distinctions need to be made among types of decision problems and the sort of analytic techniques appropriate to each."[14] The development of operations research took a leap forward with the identification of analytic submodels each corresponding to a basic class of business operations (production-inventory, reliability, etc.).

In the same way, policy analysis needs to define basic classes of policy problems. Such a classification should lend itself to a construction of useful analytic sub-models. In one of many possible approaches to this problem, policy problems and the relevant analytic tools were sorted into four categories: issue analysis, program analysis (design and evaluation), multi-program analysis (resource allocation), and strategic analysis.[15] This sequence of classes is distinguished by (1) increasingly complex policy questions, (2) a decreasingly politicized but increasingly imprecise policy-making environment, (3) a wider range of alternatives, (4) increasingly broad criteria, and (5) increasing lead time and resources to do the research that links alternatives and criteria.

Issue analysis defines the class of policy problems where there is a relatively specific policy choice (e.g., should a particular type of economic enterprise receive a tax abatement) and a highly politicized environment with a clearly defined role for a policy executive *vis-à-vis* the issue. The range of alternatives is effectively defined by the political arena; relatively narrow criteria apply (e.g., time, cost, political feasibility, and limited definitions of effectiveness), and there is likely to be an extremely limited time for data gathering and analysis. Assessments of probable consequences of alternatives thus are likely to be highly conjectural. Given such a problem, an analyst must rely on tools such as decision trees to clarify and sort, crude approximations based on existing data sources, careful interviewing of actors in relation to the problem, and previous studies.

At the other extreme, strategic analysis defines a class of policy problems where the policy problem is very large, e.g., an economic development strategy for a region. The policy-making environment is diffuse and likely to involve many decision makers as users of the analysis. Alternatives developed in such an environment should be more wide ranging, involving search methods designed to generate alternatives and broad criteria focusing on short and long-range costs and the probable effectiveness and impact from a variety of points of view. Such problems are likely to have substantial lead times for research, the opportunity to generate primary data through surveys, etc., and to apply more sophisticated mathematical techniques including model building. Program analysis (e.g., the design of a manpower training program) and multi-program analysis (e.g., resource allocation among different manpower programs) involve policy problems and appropriate analytic tools of intermediate complexity and scope. Even if real world policy problems do not fit neatly into one of these four categories—and they do not—the analyst equipped with a set of such paradigms has a structure to help decide how to approach a real policy problem and generate a useful solution. While there are dangers in too rigid an approach—the tendency to make the problem fit the model instead of vice-versa—the needs for systematic approaches to qualitative analysis seem at this point to outweigh the dangers of rigidity.

A third methodological issue is the need for better, specific tools of analysis. Particularly in relation to middle-range problems—program and multi-program analysis—substantial improvements are needed in the approach to criteria definition, particularly in effectiveness analysis. It has been widely recognized in the theoretical literature of economic analysis that one person's benefit can be another person's cost. Or in more formal language, there is no known measure of inter-personal utility, and therefore no known method of aggregating individual utilities. Yet it has not been clear what one is to do with this critical insight; systems analysts continue to talk about a public policy objective and measuring the effectiveness of alternatives in obtaining an objective. Yet clearly in a pluralist society there is no unitary definition of the public interest.

Even in public policy areas with a relatively developed history of quantitative analysis of costs and benefits, such as water resource development, one does not need to probe very deeply to discover that the benefits of irrigation and the benefits of water supply tend to fall unequally on different groups. The choice between dam proposal A, which yields more irrigation, and dam proposal B, which yields more water supply, is in effect a choice between two groups. Policy analysts, with a heightened sensitivity to the political arena, should be careful to explicate the groups that are impacted by a policy alternative. New tools need to be developed to generate and present effectiveness analysis with group impact differentiation built in. A critical tool should be client analysis: differentiating groups in the population with relatively homogeneous intra-group interests and needs.[16] Groups are ordered by the degree to which they are likely to be affected by a decision. Trade-offs are constructed on the basis of the net benefits and losses to the most highly impacted groups. One of the benefits of client analysis is that it allows the analyst to focus attention on groups who are not particularly vocal in the political arena.

It is too soon to tell whether policy analysis is merely a passing fad or a vigorous new development in public affairs. The field appears to have staked out a useful middle ground between those who have condemned political policy making as irrational, and those who have scoffed at the irrelevency of research and analysis in the political arena. The concepts appear to be right; only high standards of practice will make the idea of policy analysis meaningful.

NOTES

1. Yehezkel Dror, "Policy Analyst: A New Professional Role in Government," *Public Administration Review*, Vol. 27, No. 3 (September 1967), pp. 197–203.
2. The other four subject areas are: political, social, and economic context; analytic tools (quantitative and non-quantitative); individual/group/organizational dynamics; and administrative management processes. *Guidelines and Standards for Professional Masters Degree Programs in Public Affairs/Public Administration* (Washington, D.C.: NASPAA, 1974).
3. Norman Beckman, "Issues in Implementing Policy Analysis Guidelines for Public Administration," paper prepared for NASPAA Annual Conference, April 3–6, 1975, Chicago, Illinois.
4. H.D. Lasswell, "The Policy of Orientation," in D. Lerner and H.D. Lasswell (eds.), *The Policy Sciences* (Stanford, Calif.: Stanford University Press, 1951), p. 3.
5. H.D. Lasswell, *A Pre-View of Policy Sciences* (New York: American Elsevier Publishing Co., Inc., 1971).
6. David Novick (ed.), *Program Budgeting* (Cambridge, Mass.: Harvard University Press, 1965).

7. Charles E. Lindblom, *The Intelligence of Democracy: Decision Making Through Mutual Adjustment* (New York: The Free Press, 1965).
8. Charles L. Schultze, *The Politics and Economics of Public Spending* (Washington, D.C.: The Brookings Institution, 1968).
9. Lasswell, 1951, p. 1.
10. Graham T. Allison, *Essence of Decision* (Boston: Little, Brown, 1971).
11. Schultze, p. 96.
12. Hedrick Smith, "Carter Striving for Fast Action on His Budget, *The New York Times*, Nov. 17, 1976, 1, 1:2.
13. Sidney Schoeffler, "Towards a General Definition of Rational Action," *Kyklos*, Vol. VII (1954), pp. 245–271.
14. Ruth P. Mack in Samuel B. Chase, Jr. (ed.), *Problems in Public Expenditure Analysis* (Washington, D.C.: The Brookings Institution, 1966), p. 220.
15. Such a classification of policy problems was used over a five-year period in the training of prospective policy analysts and was found relatively successful in equipping graduate students with the orientation and skills to operate in relation to a bewildering array of policy problems.
16. Janet Reiner, "Client Analysis of Program Evaluation; the Onondaga County Evaluation," *COM Reader*.

A Checklist for Assessing Program Analyses

Harry P. Hatry, Louis Blair,
Donald Fisk, and Wayne Kimmell

Definition of Issues and Problems

1. Does the analysis clearly identify the specific problem being addressed?
2. Are the specific clientele groups that are involved explicitly identified? Are estimates made of the future size of each of these clientele groups?
3. Are appropriate evaluation criteria identified? Do these criteria cover unintended, as well as intended, effects? Do they cover negative occurrences as well as positive? If any of these effects were subsequently ignored in the analysis, were reasons given for their not being used?
4. Are estimates of the *future* need provided?

Alternatives

1. Are alternatives presented?
2. If alternatives are presented, are they real alternatives and not merely added to be rejected out of hand?
3. Are the alternatives specific enough to be evaluated?

Estimating Program Costs

1. Are all appropriate costs included? Are employee benefits included, as well as direct salaries?
2. Are possible costs of other departments or agencies, as well as the agency being considered, included? (For example, an increased police force might lead to additional jail and court requirements.)
3. Are true incremental costs identified for each alternative? Does the analysis avoid arbitrary cost-accounting adjustments? For example, are fixed costs properly distinguished from variable costs?
4. Are future costs included, as well as current costs?
5. Are imputed costs distinguished from actual cost outlays? For example, are imputed dollar values for travel time saved distinguished from actual cost outlays?
6. Are other scarce resources identified (in addition to dollars)? For example, is there likely to be a significant shortage of trained personnel needed to successfully implement the proposed alternative?

Estimating Effectiveness

1. Is each of the appropriate evaluation criteria evaluated (even if only in a qualitative way) so that the objectives are adequately covered, or are some objectives and evaluation criteria neglected and only data used that are easily available?
2. Are multiple measures of effectiveness used? Does the analysis avoid a premature combining of measures of effectiveness into a single index of effectiveness, thereby hiding individual measures?
3. Are data on the measures of effectiveness provided for each relevant population subgroup?
4. Are likely changes in the mix (and "difficulty") of the clients to be served, and in the environment in which the program will have to operate, considered in making effectiveness estimates?

Treatment of Uncertainty

1. Is there some indication of how accurate or inaccurate the key numbers and assumptions are?
2. Is some indication provided of how sensitive the study findings are to the major basic assumptions?

The Time Problem

1. Are relevant future costs and benefits estimated and their time periods indicated?
2. Do the estimates cover a long enough time period to provide a fair comparison among alternatives?

3. If discounting is used, are the undiscounted figures also presented?*
4. If discounting is used, are the proper caveats shown to indicate the considerable technical uncertainties as to the appropriateness of any given discount rate?

Selecting the Preferred Alternatives and Solutions

1. Are the costs and effectiveness estimates compatible with each other? That is, are they based on the same assumptions and data?
2. Are the cost and effectiveness estimates of each significant alternative summarized and presented together clearly?
3. Do the analysts leave major value judgments to the political decisionmaking process?
4. If recommendations are made, do the results recommended follow from the analysis, or do they merely fall back upon unsubstantiated opinions?

Implementation Feasibility

1. Does the analysis imply any recognition of possible implementation difficulties? Does it consider the effects of likely implementation problems on the costs and effectiveness of the various alternatives?

Documentation

1. Is the report clear, concise, understandable, and usable by a decision maker? Does it have a reasonably brief, clearcut summary?
2. Are the assumptions clearly identified in the document? Can the reader understand how the analysis used data and translated them into cost and effectiveness estimates?
3. Have all affected agencies had the opportunity to review and comment on a draft report prior to formal issuance?

Swimming Pools
Graeme M. Taylor

IN JULY, 1968, A TEAM OF THREE ANALYSTS representing the Dade County (Florida) Park and Recreation Department, the Department of Housing and Urban Development, and the Dade County Community Relations Board were conducting an analytic study to determine the

*Discounting is a technique sometimes used to reflect the time value of monetary inputs. It has been used to represent the economic opportunity cost for removing funds from the private sector.

best method of providing swimming opportunities for residents of
Dade County's Model Neighborhood. The decision to undertake this
analysis had been made following a request by residents of Brownsville
(a community within the Model Neighborhood) for construction of a
swimming pool in Brownsville.

Data Gathered for the Study

Admission fees for pools operated by Dade County were 15 cents per
day. The team had gathered the following information on the use of
three County pools.

Neighborhood Pool	Average Daily Attendance (Summer)	Population Living within 1½ Mile Radius of Pool	Type of Neighborhood
Bunche Park	150	18,000	Poor; black
Richmond Park	200	5,750	Upper-middle; black
Cutler Ridge	350	10,000	Upper-middle; white

The population of the Model Neighborhood, as determined by a
1964 study, was 75,000; it was expected that this would rise to 80,000
by 1985. The area of the rectangularly-shaped Model Neighborhood
was nine square miles, consisting primarily of single-family dwellings
on small lots. The population was predominantly black; average family income was $3,000.

National recreation organizations had issued "rules of thumb"
concerning the percentage of the population living near a pool that
would use the pool on an average day; these estimates ranged from 1
percent to 5 percent. Various standards had been established for the
minimum acceptable surface area of water per swimmer per day,
ranging from fifteen square feet to thirty square feet, with nineteen
square feet approximating Dade County's own experience. It was estimated that a mile and one half was the maximum practical distance
that any potential swimmer would walk to use a pool.

The analytic team had gathered cost information on two sizes of
swimming pools—"standard" and "olympic."

Standard: A standard pool had 5,000 square feet of water surface, and would
require a total of two acres of land. Construction costs were estimated at
$127,900, including equipment. Operating expenses, including life-
guards' wages, were estimated at $20,800 per year.

Olympic: An olympic pool would be 11,700 square feet, and would require
five acres of land. Construction and equipment costs were estimated at
$278,900, and annual operating expenses at $39,100.

Land costs in the Model Neighborhood area were estimated at $120,000 per acre, including acquisition, demolition, and relocation. Each acre of land, on average, contained property returning $656 per year in property taxes to Dade County. The "life" of a pool was estimated to be seventeen years.

It was possible to construct a pool at each of three locations in the Model Neighborhood area, selected such that all residents would be within a mile and one-half radius of a pool. Several other sites were available. Six pools, for example, could be located so that all residents of the Model Neighborhood would be no more than two-thirds of a mile from a pool. County-operated swimming pools were normally open from March 15 to November 15.

Bus Swimmers to Crandon Park

Another possibility considered by the analytic team was to bus swimmers to Crandon Park, a Dade County beach park located approximately an hour's bus ride from the Model Neighborhood area. This would operate each day during the four summer months, and on twenty weekends during the remainder of the year, for a total of 162 days of operation. Crandon Park contained a zoo, various amusement rides, and other attractions such as miniature golf and skating. Buses and drivers could be hired for $44 per bus per day; each bus could carry seventy-two passengers. It was considered desirable to have one adult recreation leader for every thirty children; the leader's wages would be $18.25 per day. Admission to the beach and all amusement attractions was free. The beach was supervised by lifeguards employed by the County: it was anticipated that no additional lifeguards would be necessary if children were bused from the Model Neighborhood. Public transportation operated between the Model Neighborhood area and Crandon Park; however, service was limited and several changes were necessary.

Emergency Ambulance Service (A)
Richard J. Gill and Graeme M. Taylor

THE CITY OF NEW YORK has been providing emergency ambulance service to residents, visitors, and transients since 1870. In 1967, the Department of Hospitals provided round-the-clock service with 109 ambulances, and responded to over a half million calls.

Organization

The city was traditionally divided into forty-nine hospital districts for the purpose of emergency ambulance operation.

In each of seventeen districts, emergency ambulance service was operated by a municipal hospital, while in the remaining thirty-two districts, private hospitals operated the service under contract to the Department of Hospitals. The organization of the department's ambulance service is indicated in Figure 7-1. Table 7-1 summarizes ambulance deployment.

Table 7-1
Operation of Emergency Ambulances in New York City

Boroughs	Hospitals (Districts)		Ambulances		Actual Reported Tours* Per Week	
	Private	*Municipal*	*Private*	*Municipal*	*Private*	*Municipal*
Manhattan	10	4	18	15	394	294
Bronx	1	4	1	14	21	259
Brooklyn	10	6	15	23	301	392
Queens	8	2	11	6	224	126
Richmond	3	1	4	2	84	42
Sub-Total	32	17	49	60	1,024	1,113
Grand Total	49		109†		2,137	

*A tour is an operational ambulance for 8 hours (one ambulance can operate $3 \times 7 = 21$ tours/week).

†109×3 tours/day $\times 7$ days/week = 2289 possible tours per week. (Note: "actual reported tours" do not agree with this theoretically possible figure.)

The ambulances in each district were based at the hospital, with the ambulance attendants reporting to the head of nursing, and the drivers to the garage foreman. Until 1942, a hospital intern had been assigned to each ambulance, but since then trained attendants were used. Ambulance attendants were typically nurse's aides who were given additional training and paid an extra $240 per month for duty on ambulances. The position was non-competitive and did not require an examination. In 1967, 40 percent of the ambulance attendants were female.

The drivers normally had no medical training, and were classified as "motor vehicle operators" in the city's civil service scheme. They were permanently assigned to a specific hospital garage although they reported to the Department of Hospitals rather than to any specific hospital administrator. Their work schedule differed from the attendant's schedule. Neither attendants nor drivers were paid overtime.

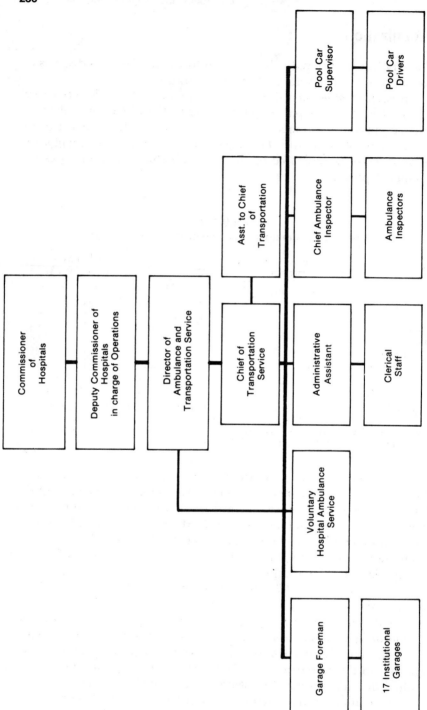

Figure 7-1

Organization Chart, Department of Hospitals, Ambulance and Transportation Service

Operation

A typical call for service originated with the police department. The police dispatcher determined the hospital district in which the emergency was located, and contacted the hospital garage by telephone. At the same time, he also dispatched a police officer to the scene. The police officer's main role was to render emergency aid prior to the arrival of the ambulance, and to gather necessary information regarding the incident. In cases of illness, he sometimes assisted in moving the patient into the ambulance.

At the hospital garage, the ambulance dispatcher (foreman) assigned the call to a particular ambulance. The ambulance could communicate with the police dispatcher by radio to report its status and receive information; there was no radio communication with the hospital. (Sometimes an ambulance would be reassigned to a more urgent call while en route.)

Upon arrival at the scene, the ambulance either picked up the patient to be taken to the hospital (after administering necessary first aid) or, if no action was necessary, notified the police dispatcher of its availability for assignment to another call.

The patient was taken to the hospital's emergency facilities where appropriate treatment was administered. Upon completion of a standard form (requiring such information as patient's age, nearest relative, address, and telephone number), the patient was formally accepted by the hospital and the ambulance was released.

Table 7–2 summarizes emergency ambulance calls in 1967.

Costs

The Department of Hospitals annually entered into contracts with voluntary (private) hospitals to supply emergency ambulance service. The hospitals were paid on the basis of the number of calls handled. In 1967, the city contracted for forty-nine ambulances from thirty-one hospitals at a cost of approximately $1.87 million. All operating costs including purchase of the ambulance(s) were borne by the private hospitals; they were reimbursed $35,000 annually for up to 3,500 calls, $37,500 for 3,501 to 5,000 calls, and $40,000 for over 5,000 calls.

The city spent approximately $4.3 million in 1967 to operate emergency ambulances attached to municipal hospitals.

Table 7-2
1967 Emergency Ambulance Calls in Thousands

	Emergency Room Only	Admissions	Unnecessary	DOA	Other Hospital	Not Removed	Other	Total Calls*
Manhattan								
Municipal	31.7	16.3	10.6	2.3	10.8	3.6	1.2	75.4
Private	38.1	10.8	12.7	3.6	23.7	4.1	0.8	88.8
Total	69.8	27.1	23.3	5.9	34.5	7.7	2.0	164.2
Bronx								
Municipal	42.1	10.6	12.6	2.2	12.1	2.9	0.3	81.1
Private	1.3	0.6	0.5	0.3	1.6	0.3	0.0	3.9
Total	43.4	11.2	13.1	2.5	13.7	3.2	0.3	85.0
Brooklyn								
Municipal	53.9	18.3	14.1	2.8	10.2	4.8	1.0	102.0
Private	35.7	7.4	11.4	2.7	17.5	3.6	1.6	75.1
Total	89.6	25.7	25.5	5.5	27.7	8.4	2.6	177.1
Queens								
Municipal	12.9	7.0	3.5	1.4	1.5	1.2	0.1	27.1
Private	14.7	3.5	4.2	2.0	15.2	2.4	0.2	39.2
Total	27.6	10.5	7.7	3.4	16.7	3.6	0.3	66.3
Richmond								
Municipal	0.0	0.0	0.0†	0.0†	0.2	0.0†	0.0	0.2
Private	2.9	2.4	0.7	0.5	1.8	0.9	0.1	8.6
Total	2.9	2.4	0.7	0.5	2.0	0.9	0.1	8.8
Whole City								
Municipal	140.6	52.2	40.7	8.7	34.9	12.6	7.5	285.8
Private	92.7	24.7	30.1	9.1	59.9	11.3	2.0	215.7
Total	233.3	76.9	70.8	17.8	94.8	23.9	9.5	501.5

*Totals may not add due to rounding.
† Less than 51.

Emergency Ambulance Service (B): Simulation and Cost-Effectiveness Analysis of New York's Emergency Ambulance Service

Richard J. Gill and Graeme M. Taylor

This case contains a report by Dr. E. S. Savas, Deputy City Administrator, Office of the Mayor, City of New York, on the analysis which he performed of the City's emergency ambulance service.

Introduction

EMERGENCY AMBULANCE SERVICE has been provided by the City of New York to residents and visitors since 1870. With the growth of the City, the service is now available to approximately ten million persons daily, twenty-four hours a day, every day of the year. In 1967, the City's ambulance service responded to more than half a million calls for emergency assistance — an increase of more than 43 percent in the past decade. This growing work load, together with an increasing concern about the adequacy and responsiveness of the system, led to a request by Mayor Lindsay to Dr. T. W. Costello, Deputy Mayor-City Administrator, to analyze the service and to recommend and implement significant improvements.

Scope of the Study

Emergency Medical Care—An Overview

Viewed in perspective, the emergency ambulance service fits within a more general framework of an overall emergency medical care system. Such a system is composed of the following subsystems, with the first two comprising what is usually considered the ambulance system:

1. Communication
2. Transportation
3. Medical treatment

In addition, one can consider that preventive health care also enters into the total picture, for it clearly affects the requirements for and the nature of an emergency medical care system. For instance, improved preventive health measures and their ready availability to the community through neighborhood Health Care Centers can be expected to reduce the demand for emergency care.

Communication Subsystem   This subsystem includes the means by which aid is summoned for a patient and the procedure for screening, assessing, and establishing priorities for such calls. It also encompasses the requirements and means for communicating among dispatchers, ambulances, and hospitals, and possibly even for contacting the Doctors' Emergency Service, Poison Control Center, etc.

Transportation Subsystem   This subsystem includes the means for conveying a patient to the medical facility, or for transporting medical facilities (doctor, first-aid attendant, oxygen, resuscitation equipment, stomach pump, antidotes, etc.) to a patient. Elements within this subsystem include such factors as the boundaries of ambulance service districts, the locations of ambulances and hospitals, and the number of ambulances. Other elements might involve the use of sirens and express lanes, the design and construction of ambulances, the location of first aid stations, devices for carrying people down stairs, etc.

Medical Treatment Subsystem   This area encompasses the nature, speed, and adequacy of emergency medical treatment, in terms of the qualifications of personnel, their prompt availability, the organization, procedures, and equipment in an emergency room, the equipment carried on an ambulance, the possible utility of first aid stations, etc. Improvements in the transportation subsystem could be vitiated, for example, if no doctor were available immediately after the patient is carried into the hospital.

Systems Analysis of the Emergency Ambulance Service

In light of the urgent need to improve the ambulance service itself, no effort was made initially to examine the prevention or treatment subsystems. For the purposes of this report, the communication subsystem can likewise be ignored. The major effort was focused instead on particular elements of the transportation subsystem. Specifically, a quantitative analysis was made of the geographic distribution of emergency calls in the most severe problem area of the city, and the number and placement of ambulances needed to service these calls effectively. The merits of a proposed satellite ambulance station were examined in detail.

Systems analysis of a problem involves four classical steps:

1. Defining a specific objective which is to be achieved by the solution
2. Formulating alternative ways of reaching that objective
3. Establishing explicit criteria for evaluating the alternatives
4. Selecting the best alternative, in terms of the criteria

Objective   The concept of "improved ambulance service" can be described quantitatively by two related performance measures:

1. Response time—the period between receipt of a call at the ambulance station and arrival of an ambulance at the scene
2. Round-trip time—the period between receipt of a call at the ambulance station and arrival of the assigned ambulance at the hospital with the patient.

Both of these related parameters are important from the public service point of view. Prompt arrival of an ambulance and trained attendant on the scene saves lives, reduces suffering, and produces confidence in the service on the part of the general citizenry. Round-trip time is the vital parameter in those cases where the patient requires prompt professional medical treatment in the emergency room of a hospital.

The objective that was adopted was to decrease the response time in the Kings County Hospital district of Brooklyn. (It follows from the above definitions that a decrease in response time produces the same reduction in round-trip time.) However, no numerical target (*e.g.*, a five minute reduction in response time) could justifiably be set unless it were possible to relate time savings to the saving of lives. No such study has been reported and to tackle this problem was well outside the initial scope of the project. This remains an important topic for future medical research.

Alternatives   Three alternatives that were considered initially were the following:

1. Redistribute the existing ambulances in the district by locating some of them at a satellite garage
2. Increase the number of ambulances at Kings County Hospital
3. A combination of the above two alternatives

Criteria   Both the cost and the effectiveness of the alternatives were considered. Costs include the capital and operating costs of additional ambulances and of a satellite garage. Effectiveness was measured in minutes of average response time and also in the percentage of calls whose response time exceeded a certain level.

The Problem

Figure 7-2 portrays a typical district which is served by a hospital, indicated by H in the figure. Under the present mode of operation, the ambulances serving that district are all stationed at the hospital. The dots on the map indicate the location and relative numbers of emergency calls from different points throughout the district. Calls are not uniformly and randomly distributed throughout the area. Due to varying population density and socio-economic characteristics, certain subsections of the district exhibit rather dense clustering of dots; there is a high demand for ambulance service from those areas.

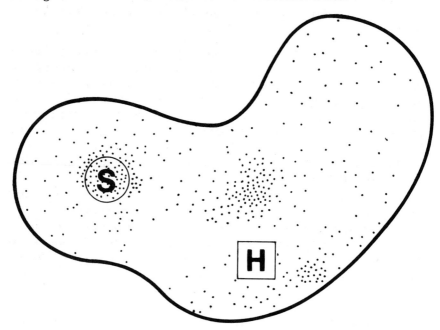

Figure 7-2
General Representation of an Ambulance District, Showing
Location of Hospital (H) and Satellite Garage (S) and Showing Points
Where Calls Were Made

A superficial look at Figure 7-2 suggests that a substantial improvement in ambulance service could be achieved by the relatively simple expedient of stationing ambulances at a satellite garage in the middle of one of the clusters, for example, at point S. Such a garage could consist of ordinary commercial garage space, or the garage of a police station or firehouse. Proponents of this idea reasoned that an ambulance located at the satellite could pick up a patient in that vicinity and deliver him to the hospital in half the time that it would take an ambulance from the hospital to go and pick up that patient and return with him to the hospital; they envisioned a 50 percent reduction in round-trip time. However, a closer look shows that the situation is not so simple. In the first place, not all the time that elapses is travel time; various delays contribute to the total round-trip time (Figure 7-3) and these would not be reduced by locating the ambulances elsewhere. Secondly, the ambulances will be called upon to service calls from anywhere in the district, not only those in the immediate vicinity of their satellite station, and it is difficult to forecast an improvement in handling those calls. Finally, the round-trip time is very sensitive to the frequency of calls; for example, infrequent calls from the area around the satellite can be assigned to waiting ambulances and in this case a substantial improvement would be realized. However, as the frequency rises, the ambulances would be spending more and more time shuttling back and forth between the hospital and the high-demand area around the satellite, calls would queue up to await an available ambulance, and in this case it would make no difference whether the busy ambulance were nominally stationed at the satellite, at the hospital, or at any point in between.

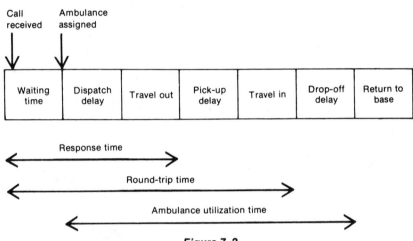

Figure 7-3
Sequence of Events during a Call, Showing Time Relationships

This qualitative analysis clearly shows that the picture is not so simple as appears at first glance, and that the level of service depends in a complex way on the following five major factors:
1. Geographic distribution of calls throughout the district
2. Frequency of calls
3. Number of ambulances in the district
4. Location of hospital
5. Location of ambulance garage(s)

Given the complexity of this system, no intuitive estimate can provide a sound guide. Nevertheless, the basic idea of a satellite station, that is, to put the ambulances where they are needed, is a sound one that warrants a detailed, quantitative analysis in order to provide valid estimates of the improvements to be expected.

The Approach

In light of the fact that the level of service is a complicated function of five variables, conventional computational approaches and simple mathematics will not suffice. Instead the ideal analytical tool to use in this case is computer simulation. This is the method of choice where there are many interrelated factors, where the expected effects are complex, and where trial-and-error experimentation is costly or impractical. This definition describes the ambulance system perfectly.

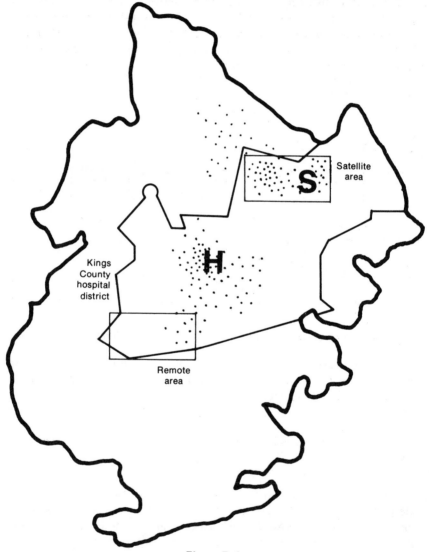

Figure 7-4
Map of Brooklyn Showing Hospital District and Areas near Hospital and Satellite

The ambulance service system in the Kings County Hospital district was simulated on a digital computer using a mathematical model of the system. A map of the district, as it was in August, 1966, appears in Figure 7-4; the hospital is located at H and the proposed satellite is at S. About 175,000 calls were simulated, corresponding to almost four years of operation of that hospital's ambulance service. Attention was focused on the peak load period, the 4 p.m. to midnight shift. The inter-arrival time was set at 7.28 minutes, which characterizes the peak load period in an average month of 4570 calls. (This number of calls is 15 percent greater than the actual observed monthly load, to allow for the predicted future load.) General and technical details concerning the simulation appear elsewhere.[1] A general flow diagram of the model appears in Figure 7-5.

Results of the Simulation

Effect of a Satellite

The number of ambulances serving the Kings County Hospital district was retained at seven and the effect of a satellite station at the location indicated in Figure 7-4 was simulated. Figure 7-6 shows what happens to the average round-trip time and average response time in the district as the seven ambulances are redistributed between the hospital and that satellite in various proportions.

The first thing to notice is that the times decrease continuously as the ambulances are removed from the hospital, one by one, and placed at the satellite garage. In fact, if there are seven ambulances available to service the Kings County district, the optimum way to use them is to have all seven located at the satellite and none at the hospital. In other words, the satellite is at a better location for the hospital than is the hospital itself, at least in terms of ambulance service. This finding should not be interpreted as an argument for moving the hospital. A constructive conclusion is that redrawing of hospital district lines as well as redeployment of ambulances may be in order.

The second conclusion to be drawn from Figure 7-6 is a disappointing one: the average round-trip time is reduced a mere 5 percent, from thirty-three to thirty-one and one-half minutes, which is far less than the 50% improvement which seemed so obvious at first glance. (This reduction of one and one-half minutes applies to the average response time as well, and constitutes an 11 percent improvement over the existing time of thirteen and one-half minutes.) This negative finding was not unexpected, in light of the discussion under the heading "The Problem" above.

296

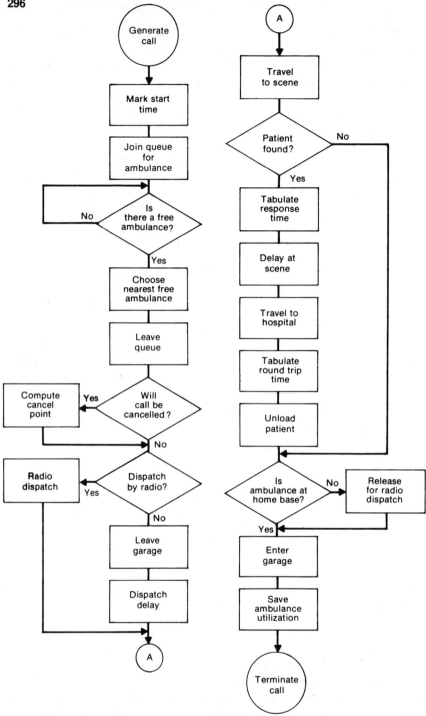

Figure 7-5
Flow Diagram of Ambulance Service Mode

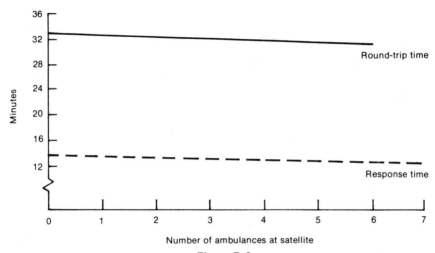

Figure 7-6
Effect of Satellite on Service with a Total of Seven Ambulances in the System

Effect of Additional Ambulances

In this case, the effect of placing additional ambulances at the hospital was studied. The results are evident in Figure 7-7. Average response time drops by 0.3 minutes as the number of ambulances stationed at the hospital is increased from seven to ten, but thereafter virtually no improvement occurs no matter how many ambulances are added. Only one reaches the "elbow" of the curve, one is operating on a plateau, and additional ambulances are wasted.

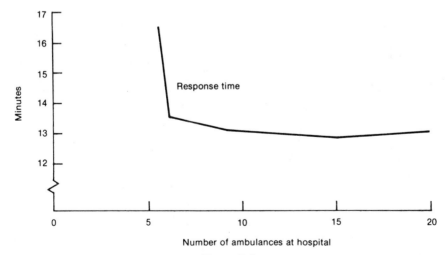

Figure 7-7
Effect of Additional Ambulances at the Hospital on Response Time

Waiting Time   The reason for this effect becomes clear upon inspecting Figure 7-8. The solid line shows the average waiting time as a function of the number of ambulances at the hospital. Waiting time is the period between receipt of a call at the ambulance station and assignment of an available ambulance to that call (see Figure 7-3). Waiting time constitutes one identifiable segment of the response time. As more ambulances are added to the system, the waiting time drops essentially to zero and the response time therefore levels off (as in Figure 7-7) at a value which depends almost exclusively on the travel time. Travel time, in turn, is a fixed characteristic of a given district and depends upon its geometry (size and shape, and the location of its ambulances) and its traffic (routes and conditions).

Ambulance Utilization   The dashed line of Figure 7-8 shows how ambulance utilization declines as more ambulances are added. (Utilization is the fraction of time that an ambulance spends on a call; see Figure 7-3 for a graphic definition.) The increase in idle time (decreased utilization) is the price paid for reducing the average waiting time, that is, for assuring that an ambulance will be available for prompt assignment when a call comes in.

It should be noted that the minimum response (at the "elbow" of Figure 7-7) which is achieved when the waiting time approaches zero (in Figure 7-8) corresponds to a utilization of 42 percent. This compares to the actual current utilization of about 60 percent.

This utilization factor is an important indicator of service, and be-

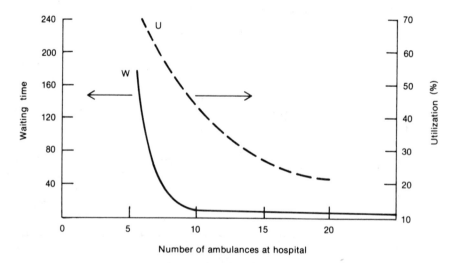

Figure 7-8
Effect of Additional Ambulances on Waiting Time and on Ambulance Utilization

cause it is relatively easy to measure, it can be used to manage the ambulance system. For example, given the existing boundaries for Kings County Hospital (and no satellite), this analysis shows that if utilization is greater than 42 percent, improved service can be obtained by adding ambulances. On the other hand, if utilization is less than 42 percent, ambulances can safely be released from the district without fear that the level of service will be degraded. Furthermore, simple arithmetic suffices to calculate how many ambulances to add or remove in order to arrive at the 42 percent utilization figure.

Economy of Large Districts   Figure 7-9 displays the relationship between work load (in calls per month) and "ideal utilization" (the utilization corresponding to negligible waiting time, *e.g.*, 42 percent). The significant observation here is that ideal utilization is not constant and independent of the load; as the load increases, the ideal utilization rate also increases. In essence, this says that if the load were to be doubled, one would need less than twice as many ambulances in order to continue providing ideal service. This result has important policy ramifications. It means that a group of small districts, each with a small load and one or two ambulances, requires more ambulances to provide a given level of service than would be required if the districts were consolidated into a single large district with the ambulances pooled under a unified command in that district. The same effect is achieved by ignoring district lines and simply assigning the nearest available ambulance.

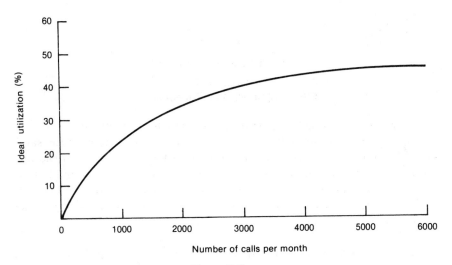

Figure 7-9
Relationship between Ideal Ambulance Utilization and Work Load

Figure 7-9 could be used to adjust the number of ambulances in the Kings County Hospital district as the work load fluctuates over time. With minor modification, the data could also be used to guide the staffing patterns at the three work shifts.

Effect of Satellite with Additional Ambulances

The number of ambulances serving the district was increased to ten and their effect, with a satellite, was simulated.

Figure 7-10 shows the results for various distributions of the ten ambulances between the hospital and the satellite. The corresponding curve for seven ambulances, taken from Figure 7-6, is also displayed here for comparative purposes.

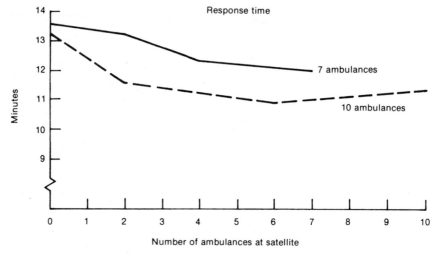

Figure 7-10
Effects of Satellite on Response Time

The most important feature to observe is that the response time drops to a minimum of 10.9 minutes (with six ambulances at the satellite and four at the hospital), a reduction of 19 percent from the pre-existing 13.5 minute average. When more than six ambulances are at the satellite, the service gets worse; the area near the satellite becomes oversaturated with ambulances, just as too many ambulances at the hospital also wastes resources.

Service in Subareas   Up to this point, the discussion has centered on average response time for the entire district. The question can be raised whether certain subareas of the district will experience a *decline* in service, a decline which might be masked in the district average because of a more-than-compensating improvement in service in the subarea near the satellite. Accordingly, the remote subarea and the satellite subarea indicated by the two rectangular areas on the map of Figure 7-4 were examined. The results are shown in Figure 7-11. As would be expected, the satellite subarea has better service than the district average; with the six ambulances at the satellite station, the satellite subarea has an average response time of 10.1 minutes, a 21 percent improvement over its pre-existing value of 12.8 minutes.

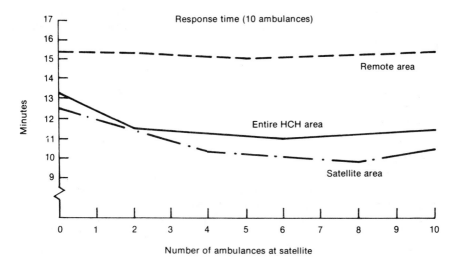

Figure 7-11
Effect of Satellite on Service to Remote Area and to Area near Satellite

Even for the remote subarea, however, it was gratifying to note an improvement of 6 percent over the pre-existing situation, a drop from 16.1 to 15.1 minutes when the ambulances are divided 4:6 between the hospital and the satellite.

Proposed System

On the basis of the simulation results it was concluded that the proposed satellite station, with additional ambulances, could be justified as an immediate way to realize substantial improvements. This satellite was in fact placed in operation on a pilot basis. However, it was felt that further improvements were possible.

In the section "Effect of a Satellite," it was brought out clearly that Kings County Hospital is not particularly well situated with respect to the district that its ambulances service. Undoubtedly, this is true of many other districts in the city as well. This suggests that one source of improvement would be to redistrict the city, taking into consideration the locations of the hospitals and the distributions of calls in order to draw more rational district boundaries.

In considering this suggestion, however, a different and more fundamental recommendation emerged. Simply stated, *ambulances ought to be stationed where the patients are*, without regard to hospital locations, and *an ambulance ought to bring a patient to the nearest appropriate treatment center*, without regard to the ambulance's home station. In other words, the transportation and the treatment subsystems should be separated ("de-coupled"). The problem can therefore be stated as:

1. Where to locate ambulances so that they reach patients promptly
2. Where to deliver patients

Location of Ambulances

Practically speaking, this recommendation to divorce the transportation service from the treatment service means that ambulances should be operated centrally, for example, by the Department of Hospitals. They should be distributed throughout the city in accordance with the observed demand, and they should be redistributed periodically as the geographic pattern of demand changes due to changes in the population. Hospitals are relatively permanent installations with no mobility and therefore it makes little sense for the transportation service to be attached so inflexibly to such facilities.

These statements should not be interpreted to mean that ambulances should not be stationed at hospitals; if the distribution of calls indicates that a particular hospital is well-situated to serve as an ambulance station, of course it should be used as such.

Furthermore, it is evident that to reduce response time ambulances should be completely dispersed; that is, rarely should there be two or more ambulances stationed at one location. The simulation showed clearly how the response time improves as existing ambulances from one station are apportioned properly among two stations to put them closer to high-demand areas. Further dissemination will result in further improvement, and the maximum decentralization, one ambulance per station, will probably produce the maximum improvement. This statement is in no way inconsistent with the earlier statement concerning the economy of large districts. The crucial point here is the elimination of the entire concept of districts as far as the transportation subsystem is concerned. The nearest available ambulance will be assigned to a call, without regard to any real or hypothetical district boundaries. In fact, this approach is completely equivalent to making the entire city a single district and having all the ambulances serve that district. This is in perfect harmony with the comments about the savings associated with large, multi-ambulance districts.

Satellite garages, provided they entail only short-term commitments in terms of leases and amortization of capital conversion costs, offer one relatively inexpensive way to provide a more rational dispersion and distribution of ambulances, as has been shown. However, a further extension of this concept is suggested. It is not at all clear that ambulances must be inside a garage while awaiting assignment. Just as there are taxi stands, bus stops and reserved parking places in front of hotels, consulates, hospitals, and post offices, one can conceive of on-the-street ambulance stations. Besides permitting optimal placement of ambulances, this would reduce costs, increase the visibility of the service, and probably reduce the dispatching delay. (On the other hand, additional unnecessary calls might be generated by virtue of the high visibility.) The problem of comfort facilities for the ambulance crew can be handled in the same way that it is handled for radio patrolmen, bus drivers, sanitation men, and taxi drivers. The problem of keeping warm in a standing ambulance in the winter should be surmountable; at worst it will be necessary to keep the motor running, although recognizing the cost in gasoline, noise, and air pollution.

Dispatching of ambulances in such a highly decentralized system must be performed centrally, as it is now, by the communications bureau of the police department, but without going through an intermediary dispatcher at a garage. This capability exists today. Each ambulance is already equipped with a two-way radio and is in communication with the police dispatcher. The forthcoming computer-based command-and-control system ("SPRINT") at the Communications Bureau will enable the ambulance dispatcher to provide even closer, minute-by-minute control over the status and activity of each ambulance in the city system. Furthermore, SPRINT can automate the process of selecting and assigning the nearest available ambulance to each call, despite the wide dispersion of ambulances among many individual locations.

In addition, by employing statistical estimates for the length of time that an ambulance is assigned to a call, the computer might even be able to advise the dispatcher whether to assign a call immediately to a relatively distant but available ambulance, or to wait a few minutes for another ambulance, currently on assignment, that is likely to become available at a location sufficiently close to the point of demand to warrant a brief delay in making the assignement.

Supervisory control, as distinguished from dispatching, would be exercised by the Department of Hospitals by matching information reports on each call from the police dispatcher, the ambulance crew, and the hospital emergency room. SPRINT makes such detailed reporting practical, and such reporting is strengthened by the accurate and prompt feedback on ambulance service that the public provides when it calls in to complain that no ambulance has yet arrived on the scene. This opportunity for feedback control, which is absent in the case of routine preventive police patrol and in the case of sanitation trucks, minimizes the need for on-site supervision. However, such supervision, if deemed necessary, could be performed by a borough commander driving around on inspection in a sedan, in the manner of a district sanitation superintendent.

This tentative recommendation for garage-free satellite operation requires more careful evaluation to determine its feasibility and to see if any necessary functions of a garage have been overlooked. For example, some garage space would still be needed for parking excess ambulances during low-load shifts. In any event, an ambulance from a street station will have to be driven back to a garage at shift change. Refueling and minor maintenance could be performed there. Locker facilities at that garage enable the attendants to change into uniforms and store personal belongings, just as they do now.

Delivery of Patients

The above recommendations, when implemented, will tend to minimize the response time — the time required for an ambulance to reach the scene. The next question is where to deliver the patient so as to minimize round-trip time. The ideal answer is to deliver him to the nearest appropriate treatment center. (The general phrase "treatment center" is used here in order to leave open the possibility of providing some types of emergency medical care at neighborhood health clinics or first-aid centers. The term "hospital" will be employed for the sake of convenience, although the above option should be borne in mind.) The appropriateness of a hospital as a delivery point for ambulance patients depends on the following major factors:

1. Adequacy of its emergency room
2. If not a municipal hospital, its selectivity in terms of "interesting cases," a patient's economic resources, and other possible factors
3. Capacity or bed availability

One area of possible improvement lies in the first factor. If study shows that average round-trip time in an area could be reduced by bringing patients to a hospital which is not qualified at the present time solely because of inadequate emergency room facilities, the possibility, cost, and effectiveness of upgrading those facilities should be explored. (If such a hospital is too small to accept many emergency patients it should not be considered, as the *average* round-trip time will not show a marked improvement.)

The second factor, a non-municipal hospital's policy of selectivity, is outside the realm of practical systems analysis. Existing hospital district lines in some cases result from such selection criteria. Analysis can serve to identify those hospitals whose participation, or fuller participation, in the system would substantially improve the emergency ambulance service, thereby providing some direction for policymaking officials to negotiate and otherwise bargain with the private institution to secure its participation on mutually acceptable grounds.

It is the third factor, hospital capacity or bed availability, which presents the greatest problem. For the most part, the whole concept of a hospital's ambulance district is a crude attempt to match the hospital's capacity with the expected number of emergency cases in an area. Because it is such a round approximation, patients are sometimes re-transferred elsewhere when there is no space, and, conversely, overcrowding occurs despite available beds at a nearby hospital. The ideal situation would be for the central dispatcher to have up-to-the-minute information on the actual number of beds available in each hospital in the system. In that case the following ideal sequence of events would occur:

1. The dispatcher assigns the nearest available ambulance to a call.
2. After picking up the patient, the ambulance driver informs the dispatcher whether hospitalization is required and if a specialist or particular equipment is needed immediately upon arrival at the hospital (to the extent that he is able to make such determination).
3. If a hospital bed is required, the dispatcher determines the nearest hospital with an available bed.
4. The dispatcher instructs the ambulance to proceed to that hospital.
5. If the driver has requested special aid to be on hand, the dispatcher so advises the hospital.

The Department of Hospitals has already started developing a computer-based bed inventory system covering the municipal hospitals. Depending on the implementation timetable of various recommendations, the inventory could be made available initially to "its ambulances" and then, as decentralization of ambulances is carried out, the dispatcher at the Communications Bureau would receive this information, probably by telephone. When SPRINT is in operation, on-line input from the various municipal hospitals to the SPRINT computer can be considered. Extension of such an inventory system, where it does not yet exist, to non-municipal hospitals which provide emergency service would be encouraged.

Increased Availability of Ambulances

The simulation study showed that the combination of adding ambulances in a district and shifting ambulances closer to the point of demand produces improved service. The discussion here centers on low-cost means for increasing the effective number of ambulances. The alternative of simply buying more ambulances is an obvious one that will be excluded from the discussion.

Improve Screening of Calls   About 15 percent of all calls turn out to be "unnecessary," according to a recent statistical study of New York's emergency ambulance service.[2] More diligent efforts by personnel at the communications bureau to question the caller before deciding to dispatch an ambulance is likely to reduce substantially the number of cases where ambulances are sent out on unnecessary calls. (This is the procedure followed in Baltimore, where only 8 percent of the calls turn out to be unnecessary.) By decreasing ambulance utilization in this way, service on true emergency calls will be improved.

Overtime Pay   Because drivers and attendants do not receive pay at overtime rates, crews are said to be reluctant to accept assignments a few minutes before their normal quitting time. If this is true, it would seem that the marginal cost of overtime labor is an inexpensive way to buy, in effect, more ambulances. In addition, by being able to offer overtime pay, an employee finishing one shift can be induced to work a second shift if his relief man fails to report to work. Such absenteeism effectively results in ambulances out of service.

Interchange of Crew Members   At present, ambulance attendants report to the nursing service in hospitals while the drivers are responsible to a garage foreman. This divided allegiance results in inflexible scheduling; for example, it is not possible to shift crews from one garage to another when there is a local shortage. Furthermore, if only a driver reports to work at one hospital, and only an attendant at another, pairing the two men to provide one ambulance, instead of keeping two ambulances idle, is administratively awkward. By divorcing the ambulance service from the hospital itself, the resulting centralized authority over crew members should simplify the handling of such problems.

The suggestion has also been made to provide the same training for both driver and attendant. This will permit complete interchangeability and, together with the change in policy on overtime pay, will result in fewer ambulances standing idle due to personnel absences.

Patient Acceptance Procedures On certain classes of calls (*e.g.*, psychiatric cases), the ambulance crew must wait at the hospital, after delivering the patient, for an inordinately long time before the ambulance is released and becomes available for reassignment. A change in the admission/acceptance procedure in such cases will increase the effective availability of ambulances.

Cost-Effectiveness Evaluation

Effectiveness

Average Response Time Several simulation runs were conducted with ambulances stationed at various points in the district in order to compare the proposed system of dispersed ambulances to the other alternatives. The results are summarized in Table 7-3.

Table 7-3
Average Response Time

Alternatives	7 Ambulances		10 Ambulances	
	Average Response Time (minutes)	*Percent Improvement*	*Average Response Time (minutes)*	*Percent Improvement*
a. All ambulances at hospital	11.9	0		
b. Optimal allocation of ambulances between hospital and one satellite	10.2	14	9.3	22
c. Totally dispersed ambulances	9.7	18	8.4	30

It is clear that the dispersed system is superior to the other alternatives in terms of the improvement attainable; for example, ten dispersed ambulances will reduce the response time by 30 percent (from the base case) whereas the same ten ambulances distributed in optimal fashion (4:6) between hospital and satellite will produce only a 22 percent improvement. (Due to an adjustment in the mathematical model, the absolute values of the response times are not identical to the values shown on the figures and discussed earlier for identical ambulance configurations. This improvement does not change the earlier conclusions nor do they alter significantly the percentage improvements.)

Reduction of Long Delays The average response time in itself is insufficient to portray the effect of the alternatives on reducing the frequency of those unfortunate occurrences where a patient waits for an excessively long time before an ambulance appears. Because of the great desirability of reducing the fraction of calls which are subject to long delays, the effect of the alternatives on this factor was also examined. The findings are summarized in Table 7–4. Again, the dispersed pattern of operation is best by far: ten dispersed ambulances can be expected to reduce this fraction by 69 percent compared to a 48 percent reduction with a satellite.

Table 7–4
Fraction of Calls with Response Time Greater Than Twenty Minutes

	7 Ambulances		10 Ambulances	
Alternatives	Fraction	*Percent* Improvement	Fraction	*Percent* Improvement
a. All ambulances at hospital	.099	0		
b. Optimal allocation of ambulances between hospital and one satellite	.073	26	.051	48
c. totally dispersed ambulances	.065	34	.03	69

Inasmuch as mathematical models never duplicate the real world exactly and because of statistical uncertainties in the findings, it is felt that although the absolute fractions of delayed calls, shown in Table 7–4, are not necessarily accurate, the relative improvements shown for the alternatives are indeed meaningful.

Costs

The simulation results presented in the preceeding section were devoted exclusively to portraying the effectiveness of the different alternatives. Now the reverse side of the coin, the costs, must be examined. Table 7–5 displays the capital and operating costs for the various resources required. Using Table 7–6, which indicates the staffing patterns, the costs shown on Table 7–6 can be combined to reflect the incremental costs involved in going from the present configuration to each of the three alternative configurations; these are shown in Table 7–7.

It is assumed that:

1. On-the-street stations, with zero cost, are used for the dispersed ambulance systems.
2. Equivalent levels of supervision are employed for all alternatives, thus permitting accurate and fair comparisons to be made.
3. Shift-to-shift staffing patterns are the same for each alternative, as shown in Table 7–6.

Table 7-5
Estimated Costs

	Purchase Price	Annual Cost	Total Annual Cost*
I. Vehicle (ambulance)	$5,700	$ 950	$ 950
Ambulance (6 yr. life)	4,900		
Equipment (6 yr. life)	800		
II. Vehicle (supervisory)		3,040	3,040
Sedan (2 yr. life)	2,000	1,000	
Equipment (5 yr. life)	200	40	
Maintenance & supplies		2,000	
III. Vehicle maintenance and supplies		1,958	1,958
Maintenance and repair supplies		657	
Mechanics' labor		505	
Gasoline and oil		296	
Oxygen and medical supplies		500	
IV. Ambulance crew		14,505	72,525
Motor-vehicle operator		8,175	
Salary		6,500	
Overhead (22%)		1,430	
Uniform (allowance)		65	
Food allowance		180	
Attendant		6,330	
Salary		5,000	
Overhead (22%)		1,100	
Uniform (issued)		50	
Food allowance		180	
V. Garage		13,600	13,600
Rent		12,000	
Heat		1,100	
Light		300	
Telephone		200	
VI. Garage staffing		14,516	72,580
Foreman		9,395	
Salary and overhead		9,150	
Uniform and food allowance		245	
Clerk		5,121	
Salary and overhead		4,941	
Pool allowance		180	
VII. Cruising supervisor		9,395	46,975

*For three shifts per day, seven days per week. Allowing for vacations, illnesses, etc., five crews are required to staff three shifts per day, seven days per week.

Cost Effectiveness

The cost effectiveness of alternative ways to reduce response time and to reduce excessive delays are shown in Tables 7-8 and 7-9. The dramatic superiority of the dispersed configurations is self-evident; eight dispersed ambulances (alternative D) are as effective as ten ambu-

Table 7-6
Deployment of Ambulances

Alternative	Tour 1 E	Tour 1 T	Tour 2 E	Tour 2 T	Tour 3 E	Tour 3 T	Total No. Ambulances In System	Additional Ambulances	Total Tours*	Added Tours
Seven ambulances (original pattern)	6	0	7	2	7	0	9	—	20	—
Eight ambulances	6	0	7	2	8	0	9	0	21	1
Nine ambulances	6	0	7	2	9	0	9	0	22	2
Ten ambulances	6	0	7	2	10	0	10	1	23	3

E = Emergency service   T = Transfer service
*Does not include transfer service.
Note: A tour is defined here as an 8-hour work period for each of seven days.

Table 7-7
Incremental Costs of Alternatives

Alternative	Annual Cost	Monthly Cost
(A) 7 ambulances with a satellite Garage Garage staffing	$86,180 13,600 72,580	$ 7,182
(B) 10 ambulances with a satellite Garage and garage staffing Additional ambulance Maintenance and supplies Ambulance crews (5)	161,613 86,180 950 1,958 72,525	13,468
(C) 7 ambulances dispersed Cruising supervisor and vehicle	16,700 16,700*	1,400
(D) 8 ambulances dispersed Cruising supervisor and vehicle Ambulance crews (1-2/3) (to staff one seven-day tour)	40,800 16,700* 24,100	3,400
(E) 9 ambulances dispersed Cruising supervisor and vehicle Ambulance crews (3-1/3) (to staff two seven-day tours)	64,900 16,700* 48,200	5,408
(F) 10 ambulances dispersed Cruising supervisor and vehicle Additional ambulance Maintenance and supplies Ambulance crews (5) (to staff 3 seven-day tours)	92,133 16,700* 950 1,958 72,525	7,700

*Because a supervisor can cover 20–30 ambulances, a district of 7-10 ambulances requires only one-third of his time; hence, only one-third of the cost is charged to this district.
Note: The cost of a dispersed system does not include credit for savings due to staff, space, and equipment reductions at the base garage.

lances in a satellite system (alternative B) at about one-fourth the incremental cost per call. This is a significant conclusion and a compelling argument for a dispersed system. Furthermore, the relative ranking of the alternatives is clear and unambiguous even though the actual dollar figures in the cost/effectiveness columns of the tables may not be accurate enough for budgetary or accounting purposes.

Table 7–8
Cost Effectiveness of Alternative Ways to Reduce Response Time

	Alternative	Effectiveness: Minutes Saved	Cost: $ Per Month	Cost/ Effectiveness: $ Per Minute	Cost: $ Per Call
(A)	7 ambulances with a satellite	1.7	7,182	1.16	1.96
(B)	10 ambulances with a satellite	2.6	13,468	1.42	3.68
(C)	7 ambulances dispersed	2.2	1,400	.17	.38
(D)	8 ambulances dispersed	(2.6)	3,400	.36	.93
(E)	9 ambulances dispersed	(3.0)	5,408	.49	1.48
(F)	10 ambulances dispersed	3.5	7,700	.60	2.10

Note: Figures in parentheses are obtained by interpolation.

Table 7–9
Cost Effectiveness of Alternative Ways to Reduce Excessive Delays

	Alternative	Effectiveness: Percentage Points Reduced Below 20 Minutes	No. Calls Per Month Reduced Below 20 Minutes	Cost: $ Per Month	Cost/ Effectiveness: $ Per Call Reduced
(A)	7 ambulances with a satellite	2.6	95	7,182	75.50
(B)	10 ambulances with a satellite	4.8	176	13,468	76.50
(C)	7 ambulances dispersed	3.4	125	1,400	11.20
(D)	8 ambulances dispersed	(4.6)	168	3,400	20.20
(E)	9 ambulances dispersed	(5.8)	222	5,408	24.40
(F)	10 ambulances dispersed	6.9	252	7,700	30.60

Note: Figures in parentheses are obtained by interpolation.

These tables give the policy maker the opportunity to make an enlightened choice as to the degree of improvement he wishes to aim for, and the most efficient (least expensive) way to achieve that objective. Work is now under way to examine other areas of the city and to take the administrative steps necessary to translate these analytical findings into public policy.

NOTES

1. Gordon, G., and K. Zelin, A Simulation Study of Emergency Ambulance Service in New York City, Tech. Rept. No. 320-2935, March, 1968, IBM Corporation.
2. Dimendberg, D. C. "An Analysis of the Ambulance Service." Department of Hospitals, City of New York, June, 1967.

8

Implementation

PURPOSE

The purpose of this chapter is to familiarize students with the complexity and problems associated with implementing governmental programs, including the design, strategy, human relations, coordination, and monitoring aspects of program management.

CONTENTS

Readings

Walter Williams, "The Implementation Process"

David I. Cleland, "Project Management: Understanding Project Authority"

H. Sheldon Phelps, "Managing with PERT"

Case

"Model Cities Sanitation Project"

Instructions

Pre-Class Preparation

Study the Williams, Cleland, and Phelps readings and then read "Model Cities Sanitation Project."

Assume you are Steve Rank. You have scheduled a conference with Tom Yost a few days after the revised "Project Plan" for the BMCSP was distributed. Yost enters your office and sits down. "Tom," you say, "I just wanted to make sure to go over with you some of the lessons about program design and implementation in urban administration learned from the Bronx Model Cities Sanitation Project . . ." (Finish Rank's observations yourself.)

Procedure for Class Meeting

Discussion will consider the lessons learned from "Model Cities Sanitation Project" and general problems associated with implementing and managing public programs.

For Additional Information

The problem of implementing public programs is rapidly getting new attention. Useful recent works are:

Eugene Bardach, *The Implementation Game: What Happens After a Bill Becomes a Law* (Cambridge, Mass.: MIT Press, 1977). Unusual in its focus on state-level issues.

Jeffrey L. Pressman and Aaron B. Wildavsky, *Implementation* (Berkeley: University of California Press, 1973). Paperback edition available.

Jeffrey Manditch Prottas, "The Power of the Street-level Bureaucrat in Public Service Bureaucracies," *Urban Affairs Quarterly*, XXXIII (March 1978), pp. 285-312.

Public Policy, XXVI (Spring 1978). Symposium Issue on implementation.

Martin Rein and Francine F. Rabinovitz, "Implementation: A Theoretical Perspective," in *American Politics and Public Policy*, ed. by Walter Dean Burnham and Martha Wagner Weinberg (Cambridge, Mass.: M.I.T. Press, 1978), pp. 307-335.

Donald S. Van Meter and Carl E. Van Horn, "The Policy Implementation Process: A Conceptual Framework," *Administration and Society*, VI (February 1975), pp. 445-488.

Walter Williams and Richard F. Elmore, eds., *Social Program Implementation* (New York: Academic Press, 1976).

Public management learned a great deal from the experience of NASA, the National Aeronautics and Space Administration. This experience with project management is described in great detail in Leonard R. Sayles and Margaret K. Chandler, *Managing Large Systems* (New York: Harper & Row, 1971).

Also see:

David I. Cleland and William R. King, eds., *Systems, Organizations, Analysis, Management* (New York: McGraw-Hill, 1969). Paperback edition available.

_____. *Systems Analysis and Project Management*, 2d ed. (New York: McGraw-Hill, 1975).

Additional information about the use of PERT and CPM may be found in:

Anthony James Catanese and Alan Walter Steiss, "Programming for Governmental Operations: The Critical Path Approach," *Public Administration Review*, XXVIII (March/April 1968), pp. 155-167.

Richard I. Levin and Charles A. Kirkpatrick, *Planning and Control with PERT/CPM* (New York: McGraw-Hill, 1966). Paperback edition available.

F. K. Levy, G. L. Thompson, and J. D. Wiest, "The ABCs of the Critical Path Method," *Harvard Business Review*, XLI (Sept./Oct. 1963), pp. 98-108.

Robert W. Miller, "How to Plan and Control with PERT," *Harvard Business Review*, XL (April 1962), pp. 93-104.

Jerome D. Wiest and Ferdinand K. Levy, *A Management Guide to PERT/CPM* (Englewood Cliffs, N.J.: Prentice-Hall, 1969). Paperback edition available.

Other broadly relevant works include:

Robert Anthony, "Closing the Loop between Planning and Performance," *Public Administration Review*, XXXI (May/June 1971), pp. 388-398.

Stephen K. Bailey and Edith K. Mosher, *ESEA: The Office of Education Administers a Law* (Syracuse: Syracuse University Press, 1968).

James M. Banovetz, ed. *Managing the Modern City* (Washington: International City Management Association, 1971).

Timothy W. Costello, "Psychological Aspects: The Soft Side of Policy Formation," *Policy Sciences*, I (Summer 1970), pp. 161-169.

Robert T. Golembiewski and Alan Kiepper, "MARTA: Toward an Effective Open Giant," *Public Administration Review*, XXXVI (Jan./Feb. 1976), pp. 46-60.

Willis D. Hawley and David Rogers, eds., *Improving Urban Management* (Beverly Hills, Cal.: Sage Publications, 1976 [1974]). Paperback edition available.

Michael Lipsky, "Standing the Study of Public Policy Implementation on Its Head," in *American Politics and Public Policy*, ed. by Walter Dean Burnham and Martha Wagner Weinberg (Cambridge, Mass.: M.I.T. Press, 1978), pp. 391-402.

James L. Mercer and Edwin H. Koester, *Public Management Systems: An Administrator's Guide* (New York: AMACOM, 1978).

Brian Rapp and Frank M. Patitucci, *Managing Local Government for Improved Performance* (Boulder: Westview Press, 1977). Paperback edition available.

John W. Sutherland, ed., *Management Handbook for Public Administrators* (New York: Van Nostrand Reinhold, 1979).

In some ways, the Model Cities case is also a study in participatory administration (or the lack of it). "Participatory administration" has two meanings. First, there is increased participation by the "members" or employees of an organization (which is touched on here as well as treated in Chapter 2). Second is the growing demand by clients to participate in public agency decision making which affects their lives. Regarding increased client and citizen participation in government agency decision making, see:

Saul D. Alinsky, *Rules for Radicals* (New York: Random House, 1971). Paperback edition available.

Alan A. Altshuler, *Community Control: The Black Demand for Participation in Large American Cities* (New York: Pegasus, 1970). Paperback edition available.

Sherry R. Arnstein, "A Ladder of Citizen Participation," *Journal of the American Institute of Planners*, XXXV (July 1969), pp. 216-224.

Richard L. Cole, "Citizen Participation in Municipal Politics," *American Journal of Political Science*, XIX (November 1975), pp. 761-781.

D. Stephen Cupps, "Emerging Problems of Citizen Participation," *Public Administration Review*, XXXVII (Sept./Oct. 1977), pp. 478-487.

Norman I. Fainstein and Susan S. Fainstein, *Urban Political Movements: The Search for Power by Minority Groups in American Cities* (Englewood Cliffs, N.J.: Prentice-Hall, 1974). Paperback edition available.

George Frederickson, ed. *Neighborhood Control in the 1970's: Politics, Administration, and Citizen Participation* (New York: Chandler Publishing Company, 1973).

Daniel P. Moynihan, *Maximum Feasible Misunderstanding* (New York: Free Press, 1969).

Walter A. Rosenbaum, "The Paradoxes of Public Participation," *Administration and Society*, VIII (November 1976), pp. 355-384.

Hans B. C. Spiegel, ed., *Citizen Participation in Urban Development*, 3 vols., (Fairfax, Va.: Learning Resources Corporation).

William H. Stewart, Jr., *Citizen Participation in Public Administration* (University, Ala.: Bureau of Public Administration, University of Alabama, 1976).

John Strange, "The Impact of Citizen Participation on Public Administration," *Public Administration Review*, XXXII (September 1972), pp. 457-470.

Orion F. White, Jr., "The Dialectical Organization: An Alternative to Bureaucracy," *Public Administration Review*, XXIX (Jan./Feb. 1969), pp. 32-42.

Closely related to citizen participation is decentralization in urban areas. Decentralization and the management of decentralized cities or counties is nicely covered in the following:

Allen H. Barton et al., *Decentralizing City Government: An Evaluation of the New York City District Manager Experiment* (Lexington, Mass.: D.C. Heath/Lexington Books, 1977).

Robert L. Bish and Vincent Ostrom, *Understanding Urban Government: Metropolitan Reform Reconsidered* (Washington: American Enterprise Institute, 1973). Paperback edition available.

Mario Fantini and Marilyn Gittell, *Decentralization: Achieving Reform* (New York: Praeger, 1973). Paperback edition available.

Stephen J. Fitzsimmons, Barbara C. Sampson, and M. Brigid O'Farrell, *Guidance Manual to Providing Neighborhood Services* (Boulder: Westview Press, 1977).

Howard W. Hallman, *Neighborhood Government in a Metropolitan Setting* (Beverly Hills, Cal.: Sage Publications, 1974). Paperback edition available.

Howard W. Hallman, *The Organization and Operation of Neighborhood Councils: A Practical Guide* (New York: Praeger, 1977).

Eric Nordlinger and J. Hardy, "Urban Decentralization: An Evaluation of Four Models," *Public Policy*, XX (Summer 1972), pp. 359-396.

Elinor Ostrom et al., *Community Organization and the Provision of Police Services* (Beverly Hills, Cal.: Sage Publications, 1973). Paperback edition available.

Albert J. Reiss, Jr., "Servers and Served in Service," in *Financing the Metropolis*, edited by John P. Crecine (Beverly Hills, Cal.: Sage Publications, 1970), pp. 561-575.

Reshaping Government in Metropolitan Areas (New York: Committee for Economic Development, 1970). Paperback edition available.

While there are increased calls in metropolitan areas for decentralization, the student should not forget the pressures for metropolitan-wide reform and the steps toward increased sub-state regionalism. In this connection, the work of the Advisory Committee on Intergovernmental Relations is critical. See, for example, *Regionalism Revisited: Recent Areawide and Local Responses* (Washington: Advisory Commission on Intergovernmental Relations, 1977). Paperback edition available.

The Implementation Process
Walter Williams

IMPLEMENTATION IS FIRST AND FOREMOST a bureaucratic and political problem. Bureaucratic and political factors—not conventional technical or methodological problems per se—represent the main near-term deterrents to more effective implementation. By this I certainly do not mean that powerful techniques exist in the implementation area, but rather that considerably better results could be achieved with our present limited tools if political and bureaucratic factors fostered rather than impeded implementation activities. Further, technical questions often seem almost trivial when compared to such issues as whether or not political jurisdictions will cooperate or whether a teachers' union will be in favor of implementing a new idea.

Conceptualizing the Implementation Process

The general nature of the implementation process and the interrelationship of technical factors with bureaucratic and political ones can be explored through a discussion of Figure 8-1. Whether what is to be implemented is a detailed program package or a general directional guide, those who wish to get "it" into the field almost certainly will have to penetrate through bureaucratic/political layers in trying to reach the final set of actors—those who manage the treatment or service, those who deliver it, and those who receive it. Generally speaking, the higher the proposer/initiator/funder is in the hierarchical chain, the denser and more complex will be the bureaucratic/political layers that must be worked through. But things are not much simpler at the local level. Whether the impetus for a proposed educational innovation comes from the national level or out of a city school superintendent's office, the bureaucratic/political layers to be confronted will be relatively dense.

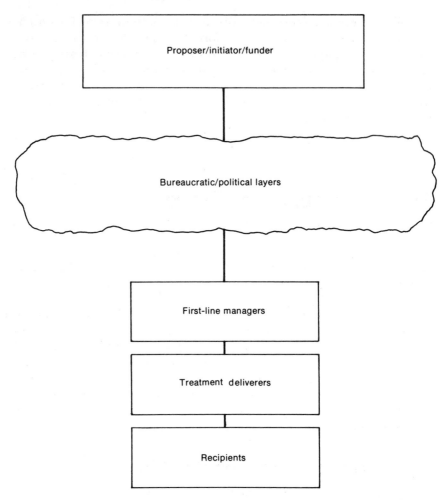

Figure 8-1
An Implementation Paradigm

The most vexing problems in the implementation process are less likely to derive from big political or philosophical issues than they are from more narrow problems arising from jurisdictional disputes. The person trying to initiate changes—be he or she a federal program director, or a governor, or a mayor—will often find specific directions blunted or subverted by lower-level bureaucrats trying to protect their turfs. These problems are the bane of any administrator, whether a U.S. commissioner of education or a local school superintendent, who must work with a hierarchical bureaucracy. As Pincus has observed in his work on factors associated with public school innovation, change is likely "when the innovation is perceived as favorable with respect to the current status and organization of the bureaucracy (because in a self-perpetuating nonmarket system, these bureaucratic values become socialized and tend to dominate other criteria; or in other words, the bureaucratic costs are the real costs of the system).[1] This does not mean that the public school district is a Machiavellian jungle of bureaucratic intrigue (at least I hope it does not), but rather that it is a complex social phenomenon not comprehended without a detailed study of its institutional functioning.

The bureaucratic/political layers in Figure 8-1 may contain a multitude of actors including, in an educational innovation, persons at different levels in a federal agency, personnel in state offices of education, the upper levels of a local school system, and a school principal. These actors stand between the initiator and those most directly involved in the treatment — in the education example, a supervisory teacher, a classroom teacher, and the students. By portraying the bureaucratic/political layers in this manner, I do not mean to imply the absence of technical issues. Indeed, many of the issues encountered as one works through politics and the bureaucracy may have a high technical content. Nor is it implied that once an innovation reaches the final actors, only technical concerns will be found. This should be apparent to anyone who has observed the opposition of classroom teachers to various kinds of innovation.

Figure 8-1 is meant to illustrate the perhaps obvious but nevertheless critical point that even after an innovation makes it through the various bureaucratic and political layers, formidable barriers may still remain. On the basis of recent experience, mainly in the field of education, I include in the figure a key element in implementation, labeled "first-line managers." These managers include administrators with direct responsibility for working with the treatment deliverers to see that the project is implemented and carried out. They may play a crucial intermediary role, as Neal Gross and his associates observed after their study of a failure to implement a new teaching approach in a small school:

> Subordinates may be unable, or find it difficult, to make changes in their role performance unless management conforms to a set of expectations that subordinates "have a right to hold" for its performance. More specifically, subordinates have a right to expect management (1) to take the steps necessary to provide them with a clear picture of their new role requirements; (2) to adjust organizational arrangements to make them compatible with the innovation; (3) to provide subordinates with necessary retraining experiences, required if the capabilities for coping with the difficulties of implementing the innovation are to develop; (4) to provide the resources necessary to carry out the innovation; and (5) to provide the appropriate supports and rewards to maintain subordinates' willingness to make implementation efforts.[2]

Finally, Figure 8-1 includes the recipients of the treatment, frequently a forgotten element when bureaucrats and treatment deliverers lock horns. Successful innovation requires a recipient who is both able to benefit from a treatment and willing to receive it — and knowing whether an intended recipient in fact has these qualities demands more than merely understanding his or her plight or deficiencies as perceived by professionals. This is vividly illustrated in recent efforts to "upgrade" children's television. As Tom Shales has observed: "A sad fact of children's TV reform is that while all the educational consulting and pro-socializing is going on, children still tend to prefer junk when they plop themselves down in front of a TV set. . . . Getting children to like what's good for them — or what some people think is good for them — could well be the hardest job ahead, then, for the children's TV reformers."[3] Shales cites some viewing statistics in which quality shows are pitted directly against the likes of a "Deputy Dawg" cartoon rerun. The outcome was 85 percent for junk and 15 percent for quality. One obvious explanation is that kids want to relax at home and do not want the busman's holiday of more schoollike offerings. The recipients whose welfare is ostensibly the main thrust of the innovation simply cannot be expected to accept passively what is offered.

Responsibility for Implementation in the Federal Social Agency

In the case of a major program in a large social agency, the multitude of layers and actors involved in the implementation process is striking, perhaps even appalling. With so many complex layers of power and authority, it is easy to lose the sense of direction that steers one toward the basic goals of the organization. What could be more obvious and fundamental than the fact that decisions need to be implemented, and that inattention to implementation will almost certainly be fatal? Yet a fantastic amount of bureaucratic foliage so obscures the way that social agencies can lose sight of this. *Responsibility for implementation tends to slip between the cracks.* Almost everyone assumes that specification and implementation are somebody else's task. Higher-ups see implementation as being a lower-level responsibility; but the lower levels look to higher echelons for specification and guidance.

Another reason why implementation slips between the cracks is that social agencies rarely deal directly with the building of implementation capability or see it as a separate activity. *The agency's program offices are concerned with operating what is in place, not with future large-scale implementation questions.* No separate staff is charged with *direct responsibility* for improving the capability to mount complex new programs. Instead, activities that may increase implementation capacity primarily *derive* from ongoing attempts to improve present operations. No one denies the importance of implementation, yet everyone has reasons why their office cannot or should not undertake it. When implementation responsibilities ever do get picked up, it is usually by a lower-echelon unit which cannot avoid them. Without an emphasis on implementation in general or a specific concern for capacity building, programs still get into the field—but through a process that is usually sloppy and poorly thought through.

Top Management: The Key to Implementation Success

Weaknesses in the agency implementation process may stem from more basic causes that relate to the fundamental issue of management responsibility. Recent work by the Urban Institute's program evaluation studies group highlights this point. On the basis of its earlier findings that the results of federal evaluation in the social areas have had a most limited impact on policy,[4] the group asks: "Why have those in charge of programs and those who evaluate them not been able to join their efforts in a way that leads more frequently to significant improvements in program performance?"[5] The group argues that the failure of evaluation results to have a material impact on policy derives from three prime causes:

Lack of Definition: the problem addressed, the program intervention being made, the expected direct outcome of that intervention, or the expected impact on the overall society or on the problem addressed are not sufficiently well defined to be measurable.

Lack of Clear Logic: the logic of assumptions linking expenditure of resources, the implementation of a program intervention, the immediate outcome to be caused by that intervention, and the resulting impact are not specified or understood clearly enough to permit testing them.

Lack of Management: those in charge of the program lack the motivation, understanding, ability, or authority to act on evaluation measurements and comparisons of *actual* intervention activity, *actual* outcomes, and *actual* impact.[6]

The first two causes flow from the basic failure to specify in terms that have clear operational meaning either the program objectives or the treatment and its relationship to the objectives. The Urban Institute group points to the vagueness of language in federal legislation and guidelines, where so much of what is said is cast in terms of "vaporous wishes" and almost meaningless phrases of guidance such as "improved local capacity" or "accessibility of services."[7] Just as with implementation, the process of evaluation runs into trouble because of specification failure. The parallel is hardly surprising. Both activities require a degree of concreteness—otherwise they become rather meaningless, futile exercises. Without a reasonable specification of objectives or of the treatment package, it is small wonder that evaluators flounder, struggling to create hard objectives out of vaporous wishes, or that implementers have developed massive regulations addressing mainly financial and administrative concerns.

Finding that clear specification is a necessary condition for sound outcome-oriented evaluation is hardly startling. What is less obvious is that the responsibility for determining definitions and the logic of treatment is not the responsibility of evaluators but of program management. The fundamental point, of course, is not that evaluators should be absolved of all blame for the shoddy work of the past. Rather, it is that evaluators can do little if program management either does not want evaluation or is not willing to exercise its responsibilities in developing specifications. Precisely the same thing is true for implementers. The attitude of management is the first and by far the most important factor in improving implementation. *Wanting better implementation will go a long way toward achieving it.* But "wanting it" does not mean that top-level management can simply mouth platitudes about the need for good implementation. Rhetoric is not enough. Management must make the hard choices required to institutionalize implementation as a critical part of programmatic activity.

Earlier experience with the Planning, Programming, Budgeting (PPB) System well illustrates the management issues involved. Separate surveys by the General Accounting Office and the Bureau of the Budget (now the Office of Management and Budget) were conducted three years after the start of the 1965 effort to implement PPB throughout the federal government. The surveys found that only three of sixteen domestic agencies had implemented a PPB system successfully, as measured by policy analysis becoming an important part of agency decision-making. In a summary article based on the findings of the two surveys, Marvin and Rouse observed: "The attitude of the agency head has been the single most important factor in the development of a PPB system and its integration with the agency decision-making system."[8] Agency heads who got relatively sound analysis accorded their central analytic offices (1) high status (generally assistant secretary rank or the equivalent), (2) direct responsibility and authority for carrying out analysis, and (3) sufficient personnel positions, in terms of both numbers and high civil service grades, to allow for the development of a viable analytic staff. The agency head was willing to make the basic changes in structure and status needed to get good analysis.

The changes needed for improved implementation may be even more difficult to make than those for policy analysis because the implementation process moves so widely and deeply in an organization. But if management has a hard task, it also has the power to start in the right direction. If it is willing to make basic structural changes, the biggest hurdle will have been passed. To say this does not deny that techniques are important or that developing technical capability in the implementation area is a critical prerequisite for improvement. Rather, the point is that the management commitment is more important. Not only that, but management's unwillingness to face up to the problems of implementation will so doom implementation efforts that technical improvements will probably have little or no effect. Finally, techniques are available for making real improvements in implementation — but, again, only in the presence of a strong commitment on the part of management.

Policy Analysts and Implementation

A central analytic office with responsibility for implementation analysis and assessment may be a key link between the agency's decision-making and implementation processes.[9] But if so, a lot of changes are needed. Elsewhere I have argued that the relatively good central analytic offices in the social agencies have both improved the basis of decision-making and had a significant influence on agency decisions.[10] The influence has generally been on people at the top of Washington's decision-making process — the agency head and the staffs of the Office of Management and Budget (OMB) or the White House. The analysts's *modus operandi* has been to produce a document, a policy analysis report, and to see that it moves up through the decision-making structure. In this milieu the big payoff is for good ideas and sound reasoning *without* a great deal of detail. Indeed, those at the top of the decision-making structure do not have time for programmatic detail — and they might not be comfortable with it even if they did. However, approval by the agency head and OMB does not magically convert a document's decisions into words that all will follow. Dollars and slot levels, of course, impel action, but action does not necessarily flow from a document's verbiage, however much lauded by the agency head and OMB. Implementation stands in the way. This simple truth has been very hard for analysts to comprehend.

To see how far removed central analysts have been from implementation — from both the agency's process itself and their own problems of getting action on approved decisions — let us speculate about some of the issues they would need to face in order to move toward a meaningful concern with implementation problems. It seems fair to generalize that analytic staffs in the past have been naive about the complexity of converting fairly abstract social policy concepts into terms useful for field operation. Policy analysis can include a step in which a decision document's relatively brief recommendations (e.g., more remedial education) are converted into detailed operational-type instructions. However, this detail is not a necessary condition for the high-level decision-making phase, so the step is best viewed as a separate activity beyond decision-making.

Reasonable specification is only one of the problems that a central analytic office must face if it is to have a marked effect on implementation. The analyst must address a number of other questions as well: How capable is the national office of developing guidelines or regulations for operating units and assisting the regional or local offices in carrying out these instructions? How capable are regional staffs of aiding in the implementation of a new policy? Is there clear responsibility for transmitting implementation information, and are there established lines of communication for such transmission? Basically, these are questions of linkages, from the top to the bottom of the implementation process, that concern capability, responsibility, and the analyst's own ties to the process.

Of critical importance for the central analyst in the implementation process may be his or her office's formal ties to the preparation of guidelines by the headquarter's staff. It is through these guidelines, not through the formal policy analysis report, that the field staff finds out about decisions. But what role should the analyst take here? One possibility is that the analyst should be responsible for judging whether what has been written in the guidelines is reasonable in terms of what was decided earlier. Such a determination is a straightforward matter, it would seem, until one confronts the reality of a large federal agency. Agency guidelines and regulations are often set out in massive documents or sets of documents prepared by many actors. A new program—especially if it has an established date set by law—may be in the field long before the final guidelines and regulations are issued. Does it really make sense to give an analyst the responsibility for passing judgment on these documents? If so, what is to be the process for changing those documents whose specifications are judged to be poor, and who is to be responsible for getting the new wording translated into action?

At the heart of the issue of implementation capability is the fundamental question of responsibility. Certainly it is reasonable to argue that the analysis of implementation capability should be carried out by an independent office, separate from the program bureaus *and* the central analyst, which reports directly to the agency head. *Yet the assessment of implementation capability seems to be so integral to any policy analysis underlying a decision that removing the responsibility from the central analyst would create a severe problem.* In making a set of programmatic recommendations, an analyst ought to answer for their implications, including the prospects for successful implementation. It seems almost frivolous to specify a set of complex programmatic actions without also considering in some detail the requirements for the implementation of those actions. . . .

NOTES

1. Pincus, "Incentives for Innovation in the Public Schools," *Review of Educational Research*, Winter 1974, p. 120.
2. N. Gross, J. Giacquinta, and M. Bernstein, *Implementing Organizational Innovations: A Sociological Analysis of Planned Educational Change* (New York: Basic Books, 1971), pp. 200-201.
3. Tom Shales, "Children's TV: Breaking the Snare," *Washington Post*, 19 May 1974.
4. See: Joseph S. Wholey et al., *Federal Evaluation Policy* (Washington, D.C.: The Urban Institute, 1970); and Garth M. Buchanan and Joseph S. Wholey, "Federal Level Evaluation," *Evaluation*, Fall 1972, pp. 17-22.
5. Pamela Horst et al., "Program Management and the Federal Evaluator," *Public Administration Review*, August 1973, p. 300.
6. *Ibid.*, p. 301.
7. I note only a few terms; the reader may have other favorites. For additional Urban Institute choices, see Horst et al., "Program Management," p. 303.
8. Keith E. Marvin and Andrew M. Rouse, "The Status of PPB in Federal Agencies: A Comparative Perspective," in U.S. Congress, Joint Economic Committee, *The Analysis and Evaluation of Public Expenditures: The PPB System*, vol. 3 (Washington, D.C.: U.S. Government Printing Office, 1969), p. 808.
9. This section will focus mainly on bureaucratic and political issues. In the following section I will address more technical issues concerning the policy analyst and implementation.
10. See my *Social Policy Research and Analysis* (New York: American Elsevier, 1971), p. 189, and "The Role of Social Scientists outside the Government in Social Policy," Public Policy Paper No. 7, mimeographed (Seattle: University of Washington, Institute of Governmental Research, August 1974), p. 10.

Project Management: Understanding Project Authority

David I. Cleland

THAT TODAY'S MANAGER MUST BE ABLE to deal with change is nowhere more evident than in the development and acquisition of major military and industrial products. Project management — molding the organization around a specific task or project—is the concept that has been developed to deal with situations where production and marketing strategy for new products do not fit into a purely functional type of organization.[1] The concept of the project manager is relatively new, and his authority is, as yet, unclear. Contemporary literature, which is incomplete in its study of the project manager's *modus operandi,* defines the manager's role but contains little information concerning the authority patterns in project management. It is the purpose of this article to examine the authority of the project manager, particularly in contrast to that of the traditional bureaucratic manager.

Why Project Management?

The need for project management is illustrated by the organizational activities of the engineering aspect of a research and development department. This is the area where the original effort on a project is made; yet, with many projects on hand, it is extremely difficult for the functional manager of engineering to cover both the project and the other efforts. One individual, therefore, is appointed to achieve management unity for each of the projects. Thus, two complementary management organizations exist within the operation: the *vertical* traditional organization and the *horizontal* project organization. Eventually, a matrix structure will extend across such functions as manufacturing, finance, contract management, engineering, and procurement.[2] The resulting organization will not consist of a single matrix and a single functional organization but rather of many matrices, even of a hierarchy of matrices. Such a structure reflects the impact of technological change on the corporate structure and its functions. Moreover, it points up the need to provide a management structure around a specific task with commensurate lateral and horizontal relationships.

What Is Authority?

Authority is required to accomplish the work of the manager. No philosophy of authority, however, can tell the manager how to proceed in specific cases, but it can give him a conceptual framework on which to base his thinking. Although most commentators agree that the authority patterns in an organization serve as both a motivating and a tempering influence, they are divided in the emphasis placed on a given authority concept. In general, the concept of authority is in a period of transformation, changing from the bureaucratic hierarchal model to a participative and persuasive one. While early theories of management regarded authority as a gravitational force that flowed from the top down, recent theories view it as a force to be accepted voluntarily, and which moves both vertically and horizontally. The elements of participation and persuasion in the authority relationship are products of modern organizations and reflect the influence of the democratic and scientific revolution in contemporary society.

Although authority is the key to the management process, it is not always used in the same way. The standard definition of authority is a "legal or rightful power, a right to command or to act." As applied to the manager, authority is the power to command others to act or not to act. It provides the cohesive force for any group and is created because of the group effort. In the traditional theory of management, authority is a right granted from a superior to a subordinate. But where does this right originate? Every manager obtains his formal authority as a delegation from the next higher level. The ultimate source of formal authority (as contrasted to other types of authority) lies in the right to private property[3] in our society, or in the charismatic power of a hierarchal role.[4] In theory, authority is still concentrated at the top of the organization and is delegated in the scalar chain to subordinate organizational elements. It is used in resolving intraorganizational disputes, in making basic strategic decisions affecting the whole organization, and in establishing overall policy for the organization. Barnard tempers this traditional view by recognizing the rights of the contributors (members) of the organization to accept or reject an order given by a higher official in a formal organization.[5]

Traditional theory has never considered that the sources and uses of authority are ever manifested outside the boundaries of the parent organization. This viewpoint, therefore, ignores the authority patterns that exist between managers and technicians in different organizations. Nor does the traditional view recognize the impact of the reciprocal authority relationships existing between peers and associates. With the exception of functional authority, the traditional view presupposes some superordinate-subordinate relationship in the organizational arrangement.

Power

Power is a concept frequently associated with authority. It is defined as the ability to unilaterally determine the behavior of others, regardless of the basis for that ability.[6] Authority provides power that is legitimately attached to the organizational position; it is delegated by job descriptions, organizational titles, standard operating procedures, and related policies.

Influence

Influence, on the other hand, is authority assumed without the legitimacy of an organizational position. An individual may exercise influence in his environment simply because he has knowledge and expertise. There is little doubt that a duly appointed superior has power over his subordinates in matters involving pay, promotion, and effectiveness reports, and that this delegated power functions unilaterally, from the top down. A manager's authority, however, is a result of his power and his influence combined so that subordinates, peers, and associates alike willingly accept his judgment. This combination of power and influence emphasizes both the project manager's legal rights and the personal effectiveness of his organizational position. Fayol uses this approach in defining the manager's authority as follows:

> Authority is the right to give orders and the power to exact obedience. Distinction must be made between a manager's official authority deriving from office and personal authority, compounded of intelligence, experience, moral worth, ability to lead, past services, etc. . . . personal authority is the indispensable complement of official authority.[7]

Project Authority

To understand the concept of project authority, one must first understand the framework of the project environment, which points up the salient differences between the role of the project manager and the traditional functional manager. (See Table 8–1.) While these differences are possibly more theoretical than actual, they do exist and they affect the manager's *modus operandi* and philosophy. Such comparison highlights a singular characteristic of the project manager — his role in managing activities that include extensive participation by organizations and agencies not under his direct (line) control.

The exercise of authority in the day-to-day conduct of a project is far removed from the organic power of the chief executive. Decisions are made constantly and their success depends upon the integration of delegated and assumed authority by the functional and project managers. In the project environment, the real basis of a man's authority (or perhaps better, his influence) is his professional reputation among his peers and associates. A man gains this type of authority only through recognition of his accomplishment by the other members of his environment, not by policy documentation, however extensive.

A significant measure of the project manager's authority springs from his function and the style with which he performs it. Thus the project manager's authority is a combination of *de jure* and *de facto* elements in the total project environment. In this context, his authori-

Table 8-1
Comparison of Functional and Project Viewpoints

Phenomenon	Project Viewpoint	Functional Viewpoint
Line-staff organizational dichotomy	Vestiges of the hierarchal model remain, but line functions are placed in a support position. A web of authority and responsibility relationships exists.	Line functions have direct responsibility for accomplishing the objectives; the line commands, staff advises.
Scalar principle	Elements of the vertical chain exist, but prime emphasis is placed on horizontal and diagonal work flow. Important business is conducted as the legitimacy of the task requires.	The chain of authority relationships is from superior to subordinate throughout the organization. Central, crucial, and important business is conducted up and down the vertical hierarchy.
Superior-subordinate relationship	Peer to peer, manager to technical expert, associate to associate relationships are used to conduct much of the salient business.	This is the most important relationship; if kept healthy, success will follow. All important business is conducted through a pyramiding structure of superiors-subordinates.
Organizational objectives	Management of a project becomes a joint venture of many relatively independent organizations. Thus, the objective becomes multilateral.	Organizational objectives are sought by the parent unit (an assembly of sub-organizations) working within its environment. The objective is unilateral.
Unity of direction	The project manager manages across functional and organizational lines to accomplish a common interorganizational objective.	The general manager acts as the head for a group of activities having the same plan.
Parity of authority and responsibility	Considerable opportunity exists for the project manager's responsibility to exceed his authority. Support people are often responsible to other managers (functional) for pay, performance reports, promotions, and so forth.	Consistent with functional management; the integrity of the superior-subordinate relationship is maintained through functional authority and advisory staff services.
Time duration	The project (and hence the organization) is finite in duration.	Tends to perpetuate itself to provide continuing facilitative support.

ty has no organizational or functional constraints, but diffuses throughout and beyond the organization, seeking out the ideas and the people it needs to influence and control.

In its total sense, project authority is the legal and personal influence that the project manager exercises over the schedule, cost, and technical considerations of the project. Project authority exists within the legitimacy of the project; it extends horizontally, diagonally, and vertically within the parent organization and radiates to outside participating organizations. Traditional line-staff relationships are modified in the project environment since a line functional manager (such as a production manager) now gives advice, counsel, and specialized support to the project manager. Project authority unifies all organizational activities regardless of where they are located.

One derivative of formal authority is functional authority. At first glance, it might appear that *functional* authority and project authority are one and the same. Functional authority is defined as the legal right to act or command with respect to specific activities or processes, in departments other than the manager's parent department. It is a small slice of the authority of some line manager and relates to particular phenomena in the organization, such as the authority of the personnel officer to prescribe certain grievance procedures. The project manager's authority vastly exceeds any that could be delegated under the concept of functional authority.

Project authority also determines how project requirements are to be met within planned schedule, technology, and cost restraints. The work of the project manager varies in accordance with the type and degree of authority vested in him. At one extreme, the project manager may serve as a project coordinator — an assistant to the general manager. At the other extreme, he may run his program with a degree of authority that denies the functional executive any significant right of appeal.

The project manager does not have unilateral authority in the project effort; he frequently negotiates with the functional manager. This relationship may be described as a "deliberate conflict," in which the project manager determines the *when* and the *what* of the project activities whereas the functional managers, in supporting many different projects in the organization, determine *how* the support will be given. Heretofore, the functional manager has tended to have total authority within his function, with the exception of specific restrictions from his superiors. These negotiations provide an opportunity to achieve trade-offs (checks and balances) between project performance, delivery, and cost objectives.

Current literature in organization theory has noted that informal and persuasive processes modify bureaucratic authority today. Under the bureaucratic theory, the line was assumed to be the one center of authority. In the project environment, no such clear-cut line of authority exists except for nonprofessional support people. The professionals do not form an authority structure in the regular sense of the term.[8] Various modifications to the formal authority structure exist, even in those organizations considered to be bureaucratic. Effective authority in the project environment depends on manifestations other than the legal ones. The most effective authority of the project manager is seldom autocratic, but rests on his ability to build reciprocity in his environment, to create and maintain political alliances, and to resolve conflict between the functional managers. The authority relationships in the project environment set the essential reciprocal elements as: (1) the sources of project authority; (2) the conceptual framework; and (3) the results of project authority. Unilateral decisions, dogmatic attitudes, and resort to the authority of a hierarchal position are inconsistent with the analysis of technological phenomena that occurs in the project environment. Instead, the project manager's job is to search for points of agreement, to criticize, to think reflectively, and only then to take an authoritative position based on the superiority of his knowledge. This is the basis for his authority, not his organizational position. Table 8-2 presents a model of project authority.

How Much Project Authority?

The project manager works across functional (parent company) and organizational (outside organizations) lines to bring together activities required to accomplish the objectives of his specific project. In the traditional bureaucratic organization, authority relationships are based on the vertical hierarchy. The project manager, on the other hand, is concerned with the flow of work in horizontal and diagonal relationships. The problems of motivation that exist for the traditional vertical manager are compounded for the project manager because the traditional leverages of hierarchal authority are not his to use. For example, the people working on a given project may be paid and promoted by the functional manager, not their supervisor on the project. However, if the project manager must act as the focal point for major project decisions and considerations, he must be given adequate authority to accomplish these objectives.

Several authors have commented on the efficacy of the project manager's authority. Peck and Scherer claim he has no legal basis to resolve interfunctional disagreements.[9] Ramo adds that project managers do not have substantial, well-delegated, clearly defined responsi-

Table 8–2
A Model of Project Authority

Sources of Authority	To Accomplish
De jure (legal)	Master schedule changes
Organizational charter	Assign project work priorities
Organizational position	Relax (or increase) performance
Position description	requirements
Executive rank	Authorize overtime budgets
Policy documents	Effect contract changes
Superior's right to command	Reallocate funds
Delegated power	Make vs. buy decisions
The hierarchal flow	Initiate work in
De facto (real)	support areas
Technical knowledge	Redirect project effort
Maintenance of rapport	Configuration changes
Negotiation with peers,	Bring subcontracted
associates, and so forth	work inhouse
Building and	Hire additional people
maintaining	Release people as
alliances	project declines
Project manager's focal position	Reward project
The informal organization	contributors
The deliberate conflict	Redirect project budget
The resolution of conflict	Readjust target cost

Framework of
Authority

Determine project
  requirements
Provide organizational and
  functional mobility
Participate in major management
  and technical decisions
Collaborate in staffing
  the project
Participate in budgeting,
  funding, and scheduling
Select the project team
Maintain project
  team integrity
Create project plans
Prescribe project
  information system
Select project
  organizational form
Serve as prime
  customer liaison

bilities nor commensurate authority.[10] These views, while only a sample, reflect the consensus about the project manager's authority. They are not an accurate reflection of the project manager's authority, however, since they consider only the legal aspect, which is, admittedly, important, but not complete. His other source of authority, the *de facto* source, is equally or even more important.

The project manager, it appears, must be a distinct type of specialist, a man with a broad perspective of the total organizational system, who can also unify the many activities involved in his project. Thus, he must have the authority to decide to abandon the hierarchal model of management completely and to establish closely coordinated and integrated teams or task forces to circumvent chains of command; these teams may contain within themselves personnel with a complete heterogeneous collection of skills. The project environment is indeed a radical departure from Max Weber's bureaucracy, where business was carried out "according to calculable rules and 'without regard for persons'."

But rearranging the compartments and shifting the lines on the organizational charts do not create adequate authority to accomplish project objectives. Participants in the project organization at all levels must modify, negate, add to, and reinforce the legal authority that emanates from a given arrangement of positions. The project manager accomplishes his objectives by working with personnel who are largely professional. Consequently, his use of authority must be different from what one would expect to find in a simple superior-subordinate relationship. For professional people, project leadership must include explanations of the rationale of the effort as well as the more obvious functions of planning, organizing, directing, and controlling.

Authority in project decisions may be indifferent to the hierarchal order of affairs. In many cases, the decisions that executives in the higher echelons reserve for themselves amount to nothing more than approving the proposals made by the project manager. The role played by these line-and-staff managers can easily deteriorate to one of delay, debate, investigation, coordination, and veto.

Upper-echelon executives may be in a more precarious position than they realize. The folklore of functional management includes the image of the powerful executive who sits at the head of a highly organized, tightly run, organizational pyramid, and runs things from the top down. In project management, the vertical organization still plays an important role, but this role is largely to facilitate project affairs and ensure that the proper environment is provided for those participating in the project.

Project management proves that "simply being in an executive hierarchy does not mean that one can freely direct those below him."[11] High level officials in an organization are more dependent on their subordinates and peers than traditional theory will admit. So many complex decisions are made in the course of a large project that one individual, acting unilaterally, cannot hope to have sufficient time to make a thorough analysis of all the factors involved. The decision maker in project management must depend on many others to provide analysis, alternatives, and a recommended course of action.

In sum, project authority depends heavily on the personality of the project manager and how he sees his role in relation to the project environment. His authority is not necessarily weak because it is not thoroughly documented and because it functions outside the parent organization and between the participating organizations. The project manager is in a focal position in the project endeavors, which allows him to control the flow of information and to have superior knowledge of the project. The scope of power and control exercised by the project manager may be virtually independent of his legal authority.

Documenting Project Authority

The project manager should have broad authority over all elements of the project. Although a considerable amount of his authority depends on his personal abilities, his position will be strengthened by the publication of documentation, such as a policy manual, policy letters, and standard operating procedures to establish his *modus operandi* and his legal authority. They should delineate his role and prerogatives in regard to:

1. His focal position in the project activities
2. The need for a deliberate conflict between the project manager and the functional managers
3. The need for his influence to cut across functional and organizational lines to achieve unanimity of the project objective
4. Active participation in major management and technical decisions to complete the project
5. Collaboration (with the personnel office and the functional supervisors) in staffing the project
6. Control over the allocation and expenditure of funds and active participation in major budgeting and scheduling deliberations
7. Selection of subcontractors to support the project and the negotiation of contracts
8. Rights in resolving conflicts that jeopardize the project goals
9. Voice in maintaining the integrity of the project team during the complete life of the project*

*A project has a distinct life cycle, moving from concept formulation and definition to acquisition and operation. This cycle begins with a concept feasibility analysis, progresses through market definition and production, and ends when the project is obsolete or nonexistent in its intended environment.

10. Establishment of project plans through the coordinated efforts of the organizations involved in the project
11. Provision for an information system for the project with sufficient data for the control of allowable cost, schedule, and technical parameters
12. Provision of leadership in the preparation of operational requirements, specifications, justifications, and the bid package
13. Maintenance of prime customer liaison and contact on project matters
14. Promotion of technological and managerial improvements throughout the life of the project
15. Establishment of a project organization (a matrix organization) for the duration of the project.

Some organizations have already taken positive steps in creating policy documents that outline the legal authority of the project manager. For example, Department of Defense Directive 5010.4, dated May 4, 1965, establishes the legal authority of the project manager throughout Department of Defense operations. In the defense industries, General Electric's Heavy Military Electronics Department has issued specific instructions concerning their "program managers."

The role of the project manager will be crucial and challenging in the years ahead. Not only will project management continue to facilitate the development and acquisition of major military weapons, but the techniques will continue to spread in the nondefense industries as well. Project management will change the relationships found in the traditional pyramid organizational structures. Authority in the project environment flows horizontally, diagonally, and vertically. Technical competence, persuasion, negotiation, reciprocity, alliances, and the resolution of deliberate conflict are some of the means that the project manager can use to augment his legal authority to accomplish project objectives. Thus, effective authority of the project manager is political as well as hierarchal.

NOTES

1. See David Cleland, "Why Project Management," *Business Horizons* (Winter, 1964), pp. 81–88.
2. For a discussion of this concept see John F. Mee, "Matrix Organization," *Business Horizons* (Summer, 1964), pp. 70–72.
3. Ralph C. Davis, *The Fundamentals of Top Management* (New York: Harper & Brothers, 1951), pp. 281–322.
4. Victor A. Thompson, *Modern Organization* (New York: Alfred A. Knopf, 1961), p. 77.
5. Chester I. Barnard, *The Functions of the Executive* (Cambridge: Harvard University Press, 1938), p. 163.
6. For example, see James D. Thompson, "Authority and Power in 'Identical' Organizations," *The American Journal of Sociology*, LX (November, 1956).

7. Henri Fayol, *General and Industrial Management* (London: Pitman, 1949), p. 21.
8. For a discussion of the authority structure in professional organizations, see Amitai Etzioni, "Authority Structure and Organizational Effectiveness," *Administrative Science Quarterly* (June, 1959).
9. Merton J. Peck and Frederic M. Scherer, *The Weapons Acquisition Process* (Cambridge: Harvard University Press, 1962).
10. Simon Ramo, "Management of Government Programs," *Harvard Business Review* (July–August, 1965).
11. Herbert A. Simon, Donald W. Smithburg, and Victor A. Thompson, *Public Administration* (New York: Alfred A. Knopf, 1950), p. 404.

Managing with PERT
H. Sheldon Phelps

PERT (Program Evaluation and Review Technique), like systems analysis and several other management innovations, was first developed for governmental programs but then was more rapidly utilized in business management. While the article here focuses on the private sector manager, PERT and CPM (Critical Path Method) are readily applicable and useful in managing state and local agencies.

SINCE ITS DEVELOPMENT a few years ago, the system known as PERT has come into increasingly widespread use, but there are still many companies that are not taking the fullest advantage of this valuable technique. For one thing, there seems to persist a belief that PERT is limited to use in weapons-system projects and research-and-development programs, even though it has been amply demonstrated that it is an effective tool for the fundamental planning of *all* nonrepetitive tasks.

Another related reason for failure to utilize PERT fully is that key people in the organization are often unfamiliar with the technique and its uses. No matter how well grounded top management may be in the principles and practice of PERT, the system will only be effective when managers at all levels understand at least the fundamentals of its operation. Moreover, this understanding often enables them to suggest worthwhile applications for PERT that might otherwise have been overlooked.

It isn't necessary to be a mathematician to grasp the basic facts about PERT; a discussion of the fundamentals of the system and how it works will familiarize managers with this valuable technique for planning and controlling the conduct of the company's business.

New Problems, New Tools

Even in the past, when products were less complex and technological breakthroughs less frequent, it was difficult to look far enough into the future to determine whether progress to date was sufficient to meet schedules, and unforeseen critical problems often cropped up to bring progress to a complete halt while solutions were being devised. In today's fast-moving economy, we can no longer afford such "unavoidable" breakdowns. Problems must be recognized in advance and either eliminated or planned for—and the important thing is that we now have the tools to do this job.

Among management's new tools are those utilizing what is called "network logic." The best-known of these systems is PERT, developed by the Navy Special Projects Office in 1958.

PERT is not intended to be a production-control tool; this function can be performed far more economically by other methods. It is primarily designed for use in complex projects in which it is difficult to keep track of progress in all areas, and it provides the timely information that will enable managers on all levels to act on specific problems before they halt or disrupt the entire operation.

Program Planning

Because PERT is often used for extremely complicated programs, the system can become quite complex in practice, but the principles behind it are simple. It involves three phases: (1) program planning; (2) evaluation of physical progress; and (3) management action.

The first requirement of the PERT system is planning, which must be done well in advance of the initiation of the project or task. The network logic of PERT and similar systems makes it essential to develop a detailed plan that depicts the way the program will actually be accomplished, rather than a way in which it might be accomplished.

To begin with, the objective of the program must be defined specifically, taking into consideration the scope and magnitude of the project and the money, manpower, and time available to do the job. Then a logical arrangement of the steps necessary to reach the objective can be outlined.

Planning Elements

In developing this plan, PERT uses three basic planning elements: events, activities, and networks.

- *Events* (sometimes called "mileposts" or "milestones") are the links in the chain of activities leading to the over-all objective. Events are described by such words as *complete, issue, begin,* and *approve.* Events are *not* indicated by such words as *conduct, design, prepare,* or *develop,* since these words indicate that work is being accomplished and thus represent activities.
- *Activities* are efforts required to achieve an objective of the over-all plan. Activities may be (1) tasks representing people doing work, (2) information

being transmitted, or (3) constraints on the completion of other events in other paths or segments of the total task. A constraint, in effect, tells everyone associated with the plan that event B cannot be completed and its ensuing events cannot begin until event A has been completed.
• *Networks* are illustrations that reflect the logical flow of work to be performed. Events are indicated on a network by circles or squares, and activities are indicated by a line joining two events. (See Figure 8-2.)

Constructing the Network

The first step in constructing a PERT network is to define the end objective. Next, the major areas of endeavor that will contribute to the accomplishment of the plan must be determined. The functional areas that will be involved in the project (design, drafting, tooling, production control, testing, purchasing, manufacturing, etc.) should be listed.

The major events (mileposts) that must be accomplished prior to achieving the main objective must then be determined and laid out with their associated activities in network form. This can be done in the following fashion:
• Write the description of the end objective near the right margin of a large piece of paper, centered vertically.
• Determine which major events must be completed just prior to the completion of the objective, and write them to the left of the end event.
• Indicate, by drawing a line, the work to be done between events.
• Determine which events must be completed prior to the accomplishment of each of the events listed, and record them and their associated activities another step to the left.
• Repeat the process until the beginning event is reached, making sure that all major areas of endeavor, with their events, activities, and constraints on other segments of the plan, are represented on the network.
• Lay out the network so that all activity lines flow from left to right. They may cross one another, as long as they can be followed easily.
• When the network has been laid out, assign event numbers, starting with the beginning event and numbering each event in the order in which it must be completed.

Reviewing the Plan

When this has been done, analyze the network to determine whether it represents a logical development of the task. Review the plan with the individuals responsible for performing the jobs outlined, and working with each area of responsibility, expand the preliminary plan by developing subcharts in sufficient detail to enable first-line supervision to understand, manage, and evaluate their portion of the program.

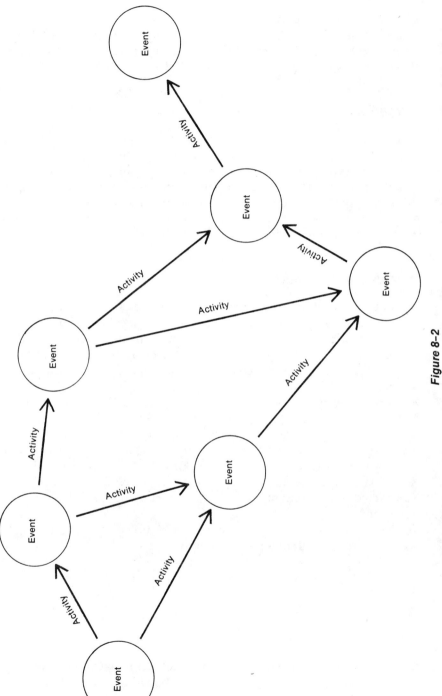

Figure 8-2
PERT Diagram Depicting Basic Elements. Idea adapted from John C. Karmendy and Thomas P. Monahan, "The Critical Path Method Applied to GAO Reviews," *GAO Review* (Spring, 1978), pp. 66–72.

The plan may disclose failure to follow existing company procedures or practices. If so, this must be recognized and steps taken to modify the affected procedures, but be sure that the plan really reflects the way the job will be accomplished.

Time-Estimating

The next major step is time-estimating the activities involved. The PERT technique uses three time estimates: optimistic time, most likely time, and pessimistic time. The person who will perform the task is usually best able to give realistic time estimates, and the process gives him an opportunity to express the degree of uncertainty involved. All three time estimates should be made on the basis of the standard work week, without considering the possibility of overtime.

Evaluating Progress

From these estimates, the *expected time* needed to complete each activity can be computed. This is done by adding the optimistic time, the pessimistic time, and four times the most likely time, then dividing by six. The *expected completion date* of each activity is the sum of its expected time and the expected times of all preceding constraining activities.

The allowed completion date is the latest date an activity can be completed without delaying the entire project. The most meaningful and widely used method of determining allowed completion dates is based on the establishment of a tentative schedule date for the completion of the over-all objective. Working backward along each constraining path from this point, the expected time for each activity is subtracted, establishing the allowed completion date for the predecessor event.

The difference between the expected completion date and the allowed completion date for each activity is called *slack*, and it may be either positive (when the expected date is earlier than the allowed date) or negative (when the expected date is later than the allowed date).

Problem Areas

Paths with negative slack or with no slack ("zero" slack) indicate areas of difficulty—present or potential—in reaching the end objective within the specified amount of time. Any slippage along the path with the greatest amount of negative slack—the most critical path—will result in an equal amount of slippage in the completion of the end objective.

Paths with positive slack indicate areas where activity may be allowed to slip until the slack has been reduced to zero without causing any delay in the project. The start of such activities may be delayed, or a lower level of effort may be expended on them, and the additional manpower can be transferred to more critical activities. The object, of course, is to reduce all negative slack to zero so the over-all objective can be attained on schedule.

The results of all this planning, networking, time-estimating, and computing must be analyzed and put into a form that can be used by management at all levels—summary information for top management, and detailed information for first-level supervision. Because today's management must manage by exception, the analysis must indicate in a simple and concise manner the problems requiring action. (See Figure 8-3.)

Analysis of the Plan

These are the major areas to be covered by this analysis:
- *Outlook.* What do the data say in terms of meeting program objectives? What are the specific problems?
- *Replanning.* What are some possible solutions? Is there a "best" solution?
- *Management action required.* Specifically, what corrective action is needed?
- *Impact of changes.* If corrective action is approved and initiated, what will be its effect? What side effects may have an impact on the project?

Management Action

As work on the project progresses, the plan must be updated continuously—usually, every two weeks. Data are collected from those responsible for each activity, activities in progress are re-estimated, and future activities are replanned to reflect program delays or technological breakthroughs. Special attention is given to activities with negative slack. Any activities no longer required are deleted, and new activities that have become necessary are added.

The new plan is then analyzed as before, new problems are defined, and corrective action is initiated. Each group is then given the information it needs to accomplish the objective or objectives for which it is responsible.

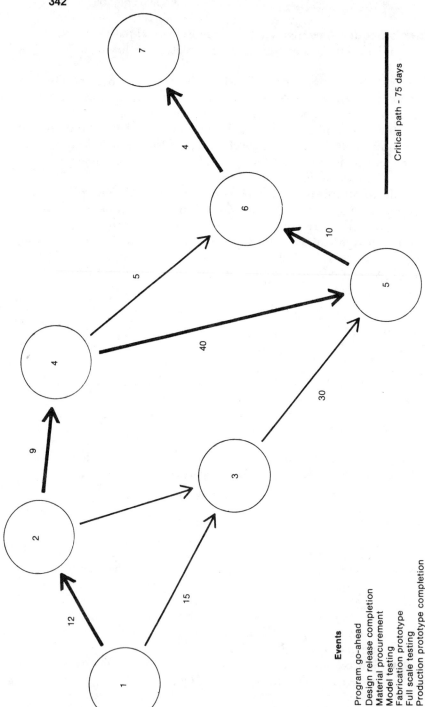

Critical path - 75 days

Events

1 Program go-ahead
2 Design release completion
3 Material procurement
4 Model testing
5 Fabrication prototype
6 Full scale testing
7 Production prototype completion

Figure 8-3

Simplified PERT Diagram of Process Necessary to Construct Prototype of New Missile. From Daniel D. Roman, "The PERT System," *Journal of the Academy of Management*, V (April, 1962), p. 58. Diagram indicates *expected completion time*, in days, of *activities* represented.

Solving Tomorrow's Problems

The discipline that PERT provides can be of outstanding value to management at all levels. In fact, if management goes no further than the initial phases — planning the network and estimating the time required for each activity — it will have realized more than half of the benefits of the PERT system, for it will have an accurate roadmap of the way the company intends to do business. Utilized to the fullest — with a continual evaluation of progress and problems as work on the project progresses — it has enabled many companies to recognize and solve future problems before they arise to disrupt company operations.

Model Cities Sanitation Project*
John R. Russell

MR. STEVEN RANK of the New York City Project Management Staff (PMS) had just reread Miguel Herrera's memo of July 7, 1970. Copies of the memo, Exhibit 8-1, had gone to a long list of recipients, including Mayor John Lindsay. Herrera was Neighborhood Director of the Bronx Model Cities Program and as such was responsible for the Bronx Model Cities Sanitation Project (BMCSP). A Project Plan for the BMCSP (the cover letter for this Project Plan is presented as Exhibit 8-2), had recently been distributed by Rank and it was this event that triggered Herrera's memo. In the memo Mr. Herrera expressed astonishment at the procedures used by Rank and accused him of being inaccurate, discourteous, and unprofessional. Rank wondered if the PMS response to Herrera was adequate and how to avoid a reoccurrence of this type of embarrassing situation in the future.

The Project Management Staff (PMS)

The PMS had been in operation since early 1968. Over 25 staff members were engaged in various types of management activities. A current recruiting description of the PMS included the following comments:

> The Project Management Staff is a high level group of experienced project managers and professional management consultants attached to the

Exhibit 8-1

MEMORANDUM

TO: Mr. Steven O. Rank   DATE: July 7, 1970

FROM: Miguel Herrera   RE: Bronx Model Cities
                                                   Sanitation Program

I received the copy of your Project Plan for the Bronx Model Cities Sanitation Program.

It astonished me that you would put together such a report without having once touched base with my office.

The report contains several critical omissions which give a completely misleading impression of where the program stands in the Bronx.

To name one, your Plan calls for June 26, 1970 (coincidentally the date of your Report) as the start-up date for implementation of the Program, thus leaving the impression that nothing has happened prior to your Day One. In fact, however, implementation of our Program began more than two months ago. Since then, and prior to June 26, we achieved the following:

— Hired and trained all Project Directors and supervisory staff
— Hired and trained staff for the educational component
— Completed a comprehensive survey of every vacant lot in the Hunts Point section of Model Cities from which priorities will be determined
— Recruited all Sanitation Aides (who are now undergoing training)
— Arranged for temporary space in all three areas of the Model Neighborhood
— Requisitioned permanent space
— Requisitioned supplies and equipment
— Pushed through the purchase order for our trucks and loaders
— Made temporary arrangements for trucks and heavy equipment until permanent trucks arrive
— Arranged some community meetings as part of the educational program

These are all steps that were arranged by and occurred in the Bronx Neighborhood while your report was being prepared downtown. The report could have presented a complete and accurate picture if your staff had bothered to touch base with us. We deserve at least that much, if only as a matter of courtesy, or as the most elementary step of professionalism.

cc: Report distribution

Exhibit 8-2

To: Honorable John V. Lindsay   *cc:* Griswold Moeller
Honorable Richard R. Aurelio   Hugh Marius
Honorable Timothy W. Costello   Miguel Herrera
Honorable Frederick O'R. Hayes   Jay Kriegel
Honorable Donald H. Elliott   David Grossman
Honorable Joseph Williams   James Cavanaugh
Honorable Jerome Kretchmer   Ronnie Eldridge
Steven Isenberg
Michael Ainsley
Horace Morancie
Wittie McNeil
Steven Lambert
Leonard Mancusi
Joseph Magucha
Biaggio Leggio

From: Steven O. Rank

Date: June 26, 1970

....

Subject: Project Plan for the Bronx Model Cities Sanitation Program

Attached is the Project Plan for the Bronx Model Cities Sanitation Program. This plan is based on the program narrative, developed by the Bronx Neighborhood Office. It outlines the background, objectives, responsibilities, resource requirements and time schedules for implementation of the Bronx Model Cities Sanitation Program.

As discussed in the attached plan, the Education and Initial Cleanup element of the program calls for hiring sixty Community Aides by July 31. These aides will begin initial cleanup activities by placing refuse in plastic bags for weekly pickups with rented trucks.

The Sidewalk Sweeping aspect will commence on August 28. A Full Vacant Lot and Backyard Cleanup Program will begin on November 13, when twelve purchased trucks become available.

We request that all concerned parties review this Project Plan. Should you have any comments or suggestions, would you kindly provide them by July 8. Otherwise we will assume you are in agreement with this Plan and committed to accomplishment of each task and its scheduled date.

Mayor's Office and reporting, through the staff director, to the Deputy Mayor and the Mayor. The main function of the Project Management Staff is to work with and assist the various City agencies in the development, planning, and implementation of high priority projects and programs. Most projects assigned to the Project Management Staff are large, complex, have severe time constraints, and require the coordination of activities of more than one City agency.

Projects are under way covering such areas as: Model Cities, air pollution abatement, drug addiction, hospital renovations, economic development, day care and other pre-school programs, experimental sanitation programs, parks maintenance and operations, housing, lead poisoning control, neighborhood government and stabilization programs, municipal services, and police.

A second function of the staff is to engage in assignments to upgrade the operation and management of City administrations and agencies. Assignments and the roles of staff members are similar to that of the traditional management consultant. Typical projects include: Planning the expansion of facilities, installing and designing computer systems, designing and implementing operating control systems, planning organizational changes, planning and establishing new City agencies, installing maintenance management systems, improving budget and payment.

A third function of the Project Management Staff is to perform special research and staff work in response to requests by the Mayor, the Deputy Mayor, or the Director or Deputy Director of the Budget.

Finally, the Project Management Staff provides a training ground and a source of management talent for the City agencies.

The position of the PMS in the municipal organization was formally that of a staff group reporting to the director of the Bureau of the Budget and acting as the implementation arm of the Program Planning and Budgeting Staff who were responsible for the identification of issues requiring concentrated and rigorous attention by the administration. In practice, however, the staff director reported to the mayor and the deputy mayor whose influence was often called upon to lubricate the bureaucratic machinery.

The Bronx Model Cities Sanitation Program (BMCSP)

The Bronx Model Cities Sanitation Program fell under the aegis of the Federal Model Cities Act of 1966. This act provided federal and city funds for comprehensive area-centered projects in housing, physical redevelopment, welfare, education, manpower, health, sanitation and other areas of social concern. New York City had designated three areas of the city as Model Cities areas. This case involves the Bronx area program.

Originally, the organization for Model Cities included a central administrative and decision-making body known as the Model Cities policy committee composed of the administrators of the city planning agency, the Human Resources Administration, the Housing and Development Authority, the Bureau of the Budget, and the Housing Authority. This body had responsibility for coordinating and integrating city services in each of the Model Cities areas as well as for allocating funds, approving program plans, and filing for state and federal grants. The Model Cities administration was established in early 1970 to replace the Model Cities policy committee. Planning in each of the areas was done under the authority of a local Model Cities policy committee elected by residents of the area. Planning and implementation were designed to involve widespread citizen participation. The city received a one year, $65 million federal grant for the Model Cities Program in July 1969. City administrators hoped to obtain another, larger grant upon completion of the first.

In addition, each area had a neighborhood director appointed by the Model Cities administration from a list of candidates supplied by community leaders and representatives. The neighborhood director had responsibility for assuring full and effective participation by neighborhood groups and assisting the local Model Cities policy committee in planning, coordinating, and integrating the area's city services.

The Bronx Model Cities area consisted of 300 residential blocks comprising about six percent of the borough's land area, one-third of which was devoted to streets and highways. The area, with 450 people to the residential acre was characterized by high density, a growing and rapidly changing population estimated at 320,000 in 1970, and poverty. Many of the Bronx families were receiving welfare assistance and unemployment was a critical problem.

Physical deterioration, obsolescence, poorly maintained housing and accumulated wastes were features of the Bronx Model Cities neighborhood. The rapidly growing population, in an almost unchanging physical infrastructure, had placed severe strains on public services. Many tenement buildings lacked superintendents and an adequate number of garbage cans. Bulk refuse, litter and garbage had accumulated in many vacant lots, back yards and alleyways. An active street life by residents, partially stimulated by the lack of adequate public play space, had created serious problems of street litter.

Since regular sanitation collections at curbside were not adequate to meet the neighborhood sanitation needs, the BMCSP was initiated. The stated over-all goals were: (1) to reduce and eventually eliminate unsanitary conditions which existed in the Bronx Model Cities neighborhood, (2) to improve the results of continuing services in the area,

(3) to decentralize program operations and involve residents in planning for and delivering sanitation services.

Mr. Tom Yost, a twenty-nine year old MBA, was the PMS member assigned as project manager for BMCSP. Yost's job was to work with and assist a number of agencies in planning and implementing BMCSP. Typically, once a project was operational, PMS people were no longer involved. Yost worked with the Model Cities Administration, Environmental Protection Administration, Bronx Model Cities neighborhood office, Model Cities central office, and Department of Sanitation.

Yost also had responsibility for developing and distributing the "Project Plan," a fifty-page document. Contents included background and introduction to the program, definition and objectives, the organization and approach, resource requirements, and implementation activities and schedule. A modified PERT-CPM network diagramming the education and initial cleanup element (Figure 8–4) was also included. In addition, milestone charts indicating those events which the PMS had designated as milestones and the responsible agency were contained in the "Project Plan."

The project was divided into three program elements with objectives stated for each as indicated by the following excerpts from the "Project Plan":

> The education and cleanup campaign element aims at removing accumulated wastes and informing residents about means to maintain a clean environment.
> Specific objectives were:
>
> —To begin removing refuse from vacant lots and backyards by July 1970.
> —To initiate an educational program using four education instructors by July 1970.
> —To hire 60 community residents as community aides by July 1970.
> The sidewalk sweeping and alternate side compliance element called for sweeping sidewalks and enforcing alternate side parking regulations.
> Specific objectives were:
>
> —To initiate sweeping sidewalks by community aides on a regular basis by August 1970.
> —To assure that street curbs are free of vehicles when they are scheduled for sweeping by enforcing alternate side parking regulations by August 1970.
> The full vacant lot and backyard cleanup program element was designed to clean vacant lots and backyards through the efforts of community aides and with the use of heavy equipment.
> Specific objectives were:
>
> —To intensify the vacant lot and backyard cleanup program with the use of heavy equipment by November 1970.

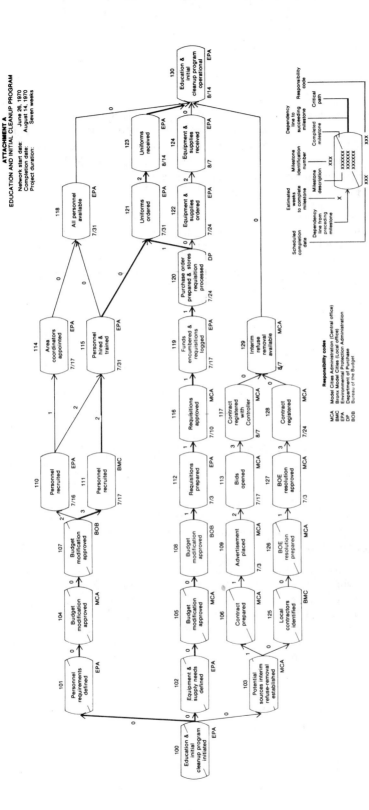

Figure 8-4
Network in Original Project Plan

— To set up decentralized program operations in three field office sites by November 1970.

Miguel Herrera, who was 29 and a graduate of a well-known law school, had been appointed Bronx neighborhood director in early March 1970 after the Bronx committee had worked for a year developing the plan and program submitted for funding in 1969.

Herrera commented on the sanitation project situation he confronted upon his appointment:

All the agency approvals had been obtained and it was just a question of coordination. But there are certain steps which take a long time — such as equipment deliveries which, in the case of the trucks, takes up to nine months. Therefore, when I took over we had to check back to make sure all of the paper work essential to expediting deliveries had been completed. I found out that even this had not been done and took immediate steps to submit the necessary purchase orders and provide for temporary rentals where necessary. It was also necessary to recruit, hire, and train the men who were to do the actual cleanup and perform sundry other tasks elemental to the program.

Herrera commented on Yost's entry into the project:

In late April or early May the fellow assigned to work on the project came in and said that someone downtown (I don't know who or why) had decided BMCSP needed project management and he was going to be working on it.

It wasn't a matter of someone being assigned formally with an introductory explanation. Yost merely presented himself saying he had been assigned to the project by the project management team. I heard nothing officially until about a month later.

[Casewriter's note: Herrera had encountered the PMS previously from his former position in the mayor's office.]

Herrera continued:

I said fine so long as I was kept informed of their activities and had an input into what they produced. About a month later I learned from an informal source that a meeting had been set up to include the Department of Sanitation and the Model Cities central staff to discuss the BMCSP "Project Plan" studies. And while it's only hearsay, the same source told me it had been suggested that a representative from the Bronx attend but that the PMS response was, "No, we don't want to get the neighborhood director involved yet." As it turned out I understand the meeting was never held.

Mr. Gregor Malloya, Deputy Director and Counsel for the Bronx Model Cities area commented:

Not having representatives from the neighborhood put the central staff in a bind as they didn't know much about the program as it stood in a specif-

Exhibit 8-3

Selected Text, Original Project Plan

V. IMPLEMENTATION ACTIVITIES AND SCHEDULE

1. GENERAL IMPLEMENTATION ACTIVITIES

(1) *Implementation of the overall program will occur over the next five months.*

The target completion dates for each phase of the program are as follows:
- Education and cleanup program - August, 1970
- Sidewalk sweeping and alternate side compliance program — August, 1970
- Fully implemented vacant lot and backyard cleaning program — November, 1970

When the Program is fully implemented, its operation will include all the elements described in this Project Plan: cleanup activities, sidewalk sweeping, education and enforcement of sanitation codes and alternate side parking regulations.

The schedule calls for hiring all Community Aides during the initial cleanup phase of the Program. Their work assignments will depend on the availability of equipment.

(2) *The major implementation activities for the establishment of the Education and Cleanup Program falls into four areas.*

The major activities to set up the education and cleanup portion of the Program are:
- Arranging for trucks and drivers on a temporary basis.
- Obtaining equipment, including:
  - Uniforms
  - Plastic bags
  - Small tools
- Obtaining temporary office space.
- Recruiting and assigning three area coordinators.
- Hiring and training other personnel, including:
  - 3 program directors
  - 6 program supervisors
  - 6 crew chiefs
  - 60 community aides
  - 6 secretary-typists
  - 3 office machine operators
  - 4 education instructors

Exhibit 8–3 (Continued)

(3) *Implementation of the Sidewalk Cleaning and Alternate Side Compliance Program consists of obtaining equipment and supplies, and hiring personnel.*

The major activities of the sidewalk cleaning and alternate side compliance portion of the program are:
- Arranging for transportation of vacuum sweepers on an interim basis.
- Obtaining equipment, including:
  • Sidewalk vacuum sweepers, additional bags
  • Motor scooters
- Assigning 3 sanitation inspectors
- Hiring personnel, including:
  • 1 maintenance man
  • 2 maintenance helpers
  • 3 watchmen

(4) *Implementation of the Full Vacant Lot and Backyard Cleanup Program requires obtaining heavy equipment, garage and storage space, permanent office space, and hiring personnel.*

The major activities required to fully implement the Vacant Lot and Backyard Cleanup Program are:
- Obtaining equipment, including:
  • 12 dump trucks
  • 2 front end loaders
  • Office furnishings
  • Office equipment
  • Maintenance supplies and equipment
- Obtaining garage space
- Obtaining 3 offices
- Assigning 1 Department of Sanitation garage foreman
- Hiring personnel, including:
  • 4 sanitation officers
  • 40 sanitationmen
  • 1 maintenance man
  • 2 maintenance helpers

2. DETAILED IMPLEMENTATION SCHEDULE

Attachments A, B, C at the end of this report present a network plan for the Education and Cleanup Program, the Sidewalk Sweeping Program, and the Full Vacant Lot and Backyard Cleanup Program respectively.

Attachments D, E, F are milestone charts for the same three phases of the Program. These charts indicate the agency responsible and target completion date for each significant task required to complete the project.

ic neighborhood. The PMS had called in the central staff technical assistant to the Bronx to represent our neighborhood and he quite understandably did not know enough to be a reliable information source.

Herrera continued:

Even at the time I was somewhat disturbed that these meetings were being held and the project being developed during an entire month without anyone letting us see what they were doing or coming to me to talk about it. It wasn't until a week prior to the distribution of the "Project Plan" that Yost told me he had completed a first draft and was going to forward it to me for review. When the report arrived I was not only disturbed that this massive document had been prepared without my once having been consulted to check figures, statistics, policy statements and accuracy, but I was even more disturbed that the plan neglected to include a number of things which had been done and contained several misleading statements. It gave a false impression of where the project stood simply because they weren't able to know of the things which had happened without talking to me. They may have talked to the people on the staff but one of what may be described as my managerial failings is that I'm not always able to keep my staff up-to-date.

From reading the "Project Plan" first-hand one would get the impression that the BMCSP had not really started and that the start-up date was June 26, 1970 — the date of the "Project Plan" submission. For at least two months before that a whole lot of things had happened. We had already hired the supervisory staff. We had ordered all the equipment and we had hired and were in the process of training all the sanitation aides. None of this was recorded in the "Project Plan."

If you sit down carefully enough, and are smart enough and have the understanding of those flow charts and plans and whatnot, you are able to get a little better understanding — but who is! Besides, even in those diagrams, all of the completed activities were not recorded.

The day after I sent that letter, which was quite a missive, Tom called me for the first time. Even so simple a thing as asking me if the network was an accurate picture of what had happened would have prevented this problem. I told Tom of my complaints and he agreed that it was a mistake not to let me approve the first draft before circulating it to everyone, including the mayor, all of whom saw it before I did.

We can't have managers not touching base with the people they're doing the management for and doing it in some ivory tower far removed from where things are really happening.

Some people see PMS representatives as young upstarts, who want to be controversial, producing status reports incriminating to administrators without giving them so much as a glance at the first draft. They seem to think this is what project management is all about.

It may be effective but only in getting people to mend their fences and guard their rears . . . but to start thinking creatively . . . no. It doesn't spur long-range planning which is the long-term objective of management. Other administrators say, "Why should I work with a guy who's supposed to be providing a service but instead is producing reports damaging to me?"

Tom Yost commented on the BMCSP, and Miguel Herrera's memo:

> May 15 was the original Project Plan deadline. That original deadline slipped because the job was bigger than we anticipated. Also, we were working on the Central Brooklyn program and we had to balance the priorities. Developing the plan was time-consuming . . . it involved a lot of reconnaissance work . . . meeting and talking with people—estimating, writing, working out sensitive issues, and so on. People would go on vacation and we'd have to wait for them.
>
> Most things have to be done through existing agencies. The problem has been getting the bureaucracy to move, so most of our time has been spent with them rather than the community groups.
>
> We had been fearing a garbage incident of some kind. The first incident came in late May in the Central Brooklyn area. This is an area where the program had been operational for some time.* We had to get the program moving and I knew the Project Plan was the most effective tool I had for monitoring. Without established deadlines the only way to control is informally. In the absence of a Project Plan what we did do was to isolate long lead-time items and get them moving.
>
> We were under tremendous time pressure . . . anxious to get the Project Plan out so we could start pushing through the bureaucracies. I did review the plan with the Central Model Cities office and the Department of Sanitation. In the interest of saving time I did not review it carefully with the Bronx. I felt we had a pretty good grasp of the program, but they were upset. It was important that neighborhood thinking be reflected in the plan. I made a big mistake by not making sure it was . . . besides I didn't do a good enough stroking job. Even though all the facts were right, it nevertheless wasn't enough.
>
> What Herrera said in the "nasty gram" wasn't really true because we did consult with him. I met with Miguel once, and again several times with his people. The program is so simple you don't have to wrestle with the concepts. The problem is pushing it through the bureaucracies. It takes a good deal of human effort to get people to work for you.
>
> Originally I intended to send the Project Plan to Herrera and ask him to review it. We decided at the last minute to send it to the mayor and ask the agencies for comment. I feel this was a mistake. We should have stuck to the initial plan. We made the decision in about one minute at the very last because we wanted to get the plan out as quickly as we could.
>
> It's not unusual for Herrera to send that kind of memo, but it is unusual for PMS to receive one. He is probably admired now by many

---

*There had been a public demonstration over garbage conditions in the Brooklyn area in May.

neighborhood directors. You just can't afford to bypass people . . . you need to have their support.

According to Steven Rank:

We were running behind on this one, the program was highly visible, and I was feeling pressure to let the mayor know we were making progress on it. In June, the City had spent $32 million of the first grant. I asked Yost if he had reviewed the "Project Plan" with everyone concerned and he said yes. Being assured those bases were covered, I decided to change our distribution plans at the last minute. One of the hardest things about this business is getting our project managers to keep everyone involved.

On August 13, 1970, in response to Herrera's objections, a revised "Project Plan" was issued. The revised plan was accompanied by the covering letter included as Exhibit 8-4, a modified network diagram for the "Education and Initial Cleanup Program," and a revised set of "Milestone Charts." The covering letter also noted that the first monthly status report (dated July 26) was being issued concurrently with the revised Project Plan.

Exhibit 8-4

TO: Honorable John V. Lindsay   CC: Herb Elish
       Honorable Richard R. Aurelio   Hugh Marius
       Honorable Timothy W. Costello   Miguel Herrera
       Honorable Frederick O'R. Hayes   Jay Kriegel
       Honorable Donald H. Elliott   David Grossman
       Honorable Joseph Williams   James Cavanagh
       Honorable Jerome Kretchmer   Ronnie Eldridge
                                                           Steven Isenberg
                                                           Horace Morancie
                                                            Wittie McNeal
                                                             John Forrer
                                                            William Ling
                                                          Steven Lambert
                                                         Leonard Mancusi
                                                               Bob Aten
                                                         Joseph Magucha

FROM: Steven O. Rank

DATE: August 13, 1970

Subject: Revised Project Plan for the Bronx Model Cities Sanitation
          Program

Attached is a revised project plan for the Bronx Model Cities Sanitation Program. The primary purpose for issuing this revised plan is to meet the

Exhibit 8-4 (Continued)

objections raised by the Bronx Model Cities Office. They felt that the original project plan gave the impression that nothing had been done prior to the issuance of the plan on June 26, 1970. Objections were also raised because the Bronx Office did not have an opportunity to review the plan before it was issued.

While we did discuss the Bronx Sanitation Program at length with representatives of the Bronx Model Cities Office, we neglected to provide them with an opportunity to review the final written document before it was issued. This was an error on our part for which we apologize.

Section V of the plan has been amended to recognize activities completed prior to June 26, 1970. By including completed activities in the text of the plan, emphasis is given to those activities which were indicated as completed in the milestone charts in Appendices D, E, and F of the original plan.

The Department of Sanitation comments are also noted, recognizing their inability to store equipment at Sanitation locations until Model Cities is able to provide storage space. The project plan was revised to reflect this. Other comments were discussed with the Department of Sanitation, but required no change in the project plan.

The effective date of this revised project plan is the same as the original plan, June 26, 1970. The first status report, dated July 24, is also attached. Status reports will be issued monthly until the program is fully implemented.

Attach.
/fe

9

Program Evaluation

PURPOSE

The purpose of this chapter is to explore the conceptual and methodological issues in assessing the performance of public programs.

CONTENTS

Readings

Joseph S. Wholey, "The Role of Evaluation and the Evaluator in Improving Public Programs"

Harry P. Hatry, Richard E. Winnie, and Donald M. Fisk, "How to Design a Program Evaluation"

Case

"The Summer Youth Program"

Instructions

Pre-Class Preparation

Read Joseph S. Wholey, "The Role of Evaluation and the Evaluator in Improving Public Programs" and Harry P. Hatry, Richard E. Winnie, and Donald M. Fisk, "How to Design a Program Evaluation" before proceeding to the case.

1. In the "Model Cities Sanitation Project" case, in the last chapter, no attention seems to have been given to a plan for evaluating the program. Assume the project has not yet started. Develop a complete program evaluation scheme for the project.

2. Read "The Summer Youth Program" case and respond carefully and fully to all of the questions below.

    a. As we have learned, the political setting is important in state and urban management. What was the impact of the political environment on the District of Columbia Summer Youth Program?

b. From the point of view of effective program management, what in your judgment were the two biggest shortcomings in the management of the program? Trace the difficulties encountered. Were these recognized by the managers and staff involved?

c. Were the programs meaningful, or did the Neighborhood Planning Councils "cop out" and do the most expedient things — recreation programs?

d. It is not easy to evaluate public programs, especially when little "hard" data are available. Evaluate the program evaluation carried out by the consultants and presented in the case.

e. Does the use of the twenty Neighborhood Planning Councils suggest the importance of decentralization and citizen participation in urban administration, or does it speak more to protecting vested interests and political bases than to anything else?

f. As Joe James asks at the end of the case, "O.K. my smart consultant, tell me what I should do next year!" Assume you are the consultant, what do you say to James?

Procedure for Class Meeting

Discussion of program evaluation will refer specifically to the "Model Cities Sanitation Project" and "The Summer Youth Program" cases.

For Additional Information

A relatively simple but most helpful publication is Harry P. Hatry, Richard E. Winnie, and Donald M. Fisk, *Practical Program Evaluation for State and Local Government Officials* (Washington: Urban Institute, 1973). Part of this study is excerpted in this chapter.

Other recent and solid additions to the evaluation literature include:

Peter Rossi, Howard E. Freeman, and Sonia R. Wright, *Evaluation: A Systematic Approach* (Beverly Hills: Sage Publications, 1979).

Joseph S. Wholey, *Evaluation: Promise and Performance* (Washington: The Urban Institute, 1979). Paperback edition available.

Program Evaluation and Analysis: A Technical Guide for State and Local Governments (Washington: Office of Policy Development and Research, U. S. Department of Housing and Urban Development, November, 1978).

Sage Publications, Beverly Hills, California, has published an eight volume "Program Evaluation Kit" by individuals associated with the Center for the Study of Evaluation, Graduate School of Education, University of California, Los Angeles. Topics of the individual monographs include establishing goals, design, measurement, and report preparation. All are available in paperback.

An extensive compendium is:

Marcia Guttentag and Elmer L. Struening, eds., *Handbook of Evaluation Research*, 2 vols. (Beverly Hills: Sage Publications, 1976).

The journals, *Evaluation, Evaluation Quarterly,* and *Evaluation and the Health Professions* contain useful, timely articles and other features. Also see *Evaluation Studies,* an annual review, published by Sage.

In terms of methodology, probably the clearest statements of the issues on research design are:

Donald T. Campbell, "Reforms as Experiments," *American Psychologist,* XXIV (April 1969), pp. 409–429.
Thomas D. Cook and Donald T. Campbell, *Quasi-Experimentation: Design and Analysis Issues for Field Settings* (Chicago: Rand McNally College Publishing Company, 1979). Paperback edition available.

Other useful publications include:

Clark C. Abt, ed., *The Evaluation of Social Programs* (Beverly Hills: Sage Publications, 1977).
Louis H. Blair and Alfred I. Schwartz, *How Clean Is Our City?* (Washington: Urban Institute, 1972). Paperback edition available.
Francis G. Caro, ed., *Readings in Evaluation Research,* 2d ed. (New York: Russell Sage Foundation/Basic Books, 1977).
Lawrence P. Clark, *Designs for Evaluating Social Programs* (Croton-on-Hudson, N.Y.: Policy Studies Associates, 1976). Paperback.
Bernard P. Donnelly, "Cheap Shots and Costly Pay-offs: A Plea for Purpose in Public Programs," *Public Administration Review,* XXXVII (March/April 1977), pp. 181–186.
A Guide for Local Evaluation (Washington: U.S. Government Printing Office, n.d.). Paperback edition available. This was produced by the Office of Evaluation, Community Planning and Development, U.S. Department of Housing and Urban Development, primarily for use in HUD-sponsored programs.
Harry P. Hatry, *et al., How Effective Are Your Community Services? Procedures for Monitoring the Effectiveness of Municipal Services* (Washington: Urban Institute with the International City Management Association, 1977). Paperback edition available. An important publication and most useful handbook.
R. A. Levine and A. P. Williams, Jr., *Making Evaluation Effective: A Guide* (Santa Monica, Cal.: RAND, 1971). Paperback edition available.
Sar A. Levitan and Robert Taggart, *The Promise of Greatness* (Cambridge: Harvard University Press, 1976). Paperback edition available.

Measuring the Effectiveness of Basic Municipal Services: Initial Report (Washington: Urban Institute and International City Management Association, 1974). Paperback edition available.

David Nachmias, *Public Policy Evaluation: Approaches and Methods* (New York: St. Martin's, 1979). Paperback edition available.

James E. Prather and Frank K. Gibson, "The Failure of Social Programs," *Public Administration Review*, XXXVII (Sept./Oct. 1977), pp. 556-564.

John Van Maanen, *The Process of Program Evaluation* (Washington: National Training and Development Service Press, 1973). Paperback edition available.

Carol H. Weiss, *Evaluation Research: Methods of Assessing Program Effectiveness* (Englewood Cliffs, N.J.: Prentice-Hall, 1972). Paperback edition available. A helpful primer.

Robert S. Weiss and Martin Rein, "The Evaluation of Broad-Aim Programs: Experimental Design, Its Difficulties, and an Alternative," *Administrative Science Quarterly*, XV (March 1970), pp. 97-113.

Richard E. Winnie and Harry P. Hatry, *Measuring the Effectiveness of Local Government Services: Transportation* (Washington: Urban Institute, 1972). Paperback edition available.

One section of the evaluation literature has to do with citizen feedback, normally through sample surveys of citizens. In this regard, see: Kenneth Webb and Harry P. Hatry, *Obtaining Citizen Feedback: The Application of Citizen Surveys to Local Governments* (Washington: Urban Institute, 1973). Paperback edition available.

Another aspect of the evaluation issue has to do with urban indicators, or the assessment of relative well-being in a particular urban area. On this, see:

Raymond A. Bauer, ed., *Social Indicators* (Cambridge: MIT Press, 1966). Paperback edition available.

Harvey A. Garn et al., *Models for Indicator Development* (Washington: Urban Institute, 1976). Paperback edition available.

Most of the work on program evaluation is concerned with the "outcomes" (or benefits or effects) of service delivery. "Outcomes" are represented by the impact of an agency's activity on a *client*. "Outputs" are the activities themselves, the goods or services an agency makes available for use by clients. Thus, in education, for example, teaching is an output, while learning is an outcome. There is a segment of the evaluative literature concerned with outputs in terms of who benefits or who potentially benefits from these. This idea may be found in:

Peter B. Bloch, *Equality of Distribution of Police Services: A Case Study of Washington, D.C.* (Washington: Urban Institute, 1974). Paperback edition available.

Frank S. Levy, Arnold J. Meltsner, and Aaron Wildavsky, *Urban Outcomes* (Berkeley: University of California Press, 1974). Paperback edition available.

Robert L. Lineberry, *Equality and Public Policy: The Distribution of Municipal Public Services* (Beverly Hills: Sage Publications, 1977). Paperback edition available.

William H. Lucy, Dennis Gilbert, and Guthrie S. Birkhead, "Equity in Local Service Distribution," *Public Administration Review*, XXXVII (Nov./Dec. 1977), pp. 687-697.

Astrid E. Merget and William M. Wolff, Jr., "The Law and Municipal Services: Implementing Equity," *Public Management*, LVIII (August 1976), pp. 2-8.

Public Administration Review, XXXIV (Jan./Feb. 1974), Symposium on Social Equity and Public Administration.

A final current topic related to program evaluation revolves around the idea that public programs should terminate periodically unless they are specifically assessed and renewed by the legislative branch of government. An excellent introduction to the sunset idea can be found in:

Bruce Adams, "Sunset: A Proposal for Accountable Government," *Administrative Law Review*, XXVIII (Summer 1976), pp. 513-542.

Allen Schick, "Zero-Base Budgeting and Sunset: Redundancy or Symbiosis?," *The Bureaucrat*, VI (Spring 1977), pp. 12-32.

Making Government Work: A Common Cause Report on State Sunset Activity (Washington: Common Cause, 1978).

On sunset, also see:

Robert D. Behn, "The False Dawn of the Sunset Laws," *The Public Interest*, No. 49 (Fall 1977), pp. 103-118.

Edgar G. Crane, Jr., *Legislative Review of Government Programs* (New York: Praeger, 1976).

James Davidson, "Sunset—A New Challenge," *The Bureaucrat*, VI (Spring 1977), pp. 159-164.

Evaluating Federal Programs: An Overview for the Congressional User (Washington: General Accounting Office, 1976). Paperback edition available.

Genevieve J. Knezo and Walter J. Oeszek, "Legislative Oversight and Program Evaluation," *The Bureaucrat*, V (April 1976), pp. 37-51.

Legislative Program Effectiveness Review Unit (LPER). House Fiscal Agency, State of Michigan, *LPER Program Memorandum Number 4: A "Sunset" Law in Michigan* (East Lansing, Mich.: LPER, 1976).

National Civic Review, LXVII (March 1978). Symposium.

State Government, IL (Summer 1976). Symposium on "Sunset."

Sunset Laws: A Tool for Reappraisal of Government Programs and Regulations (Albany: Temporary State Commission on Management and Productivity in the Public Sector, State of New York, 1977).

United States Senate, Committee on Government Operations, Subcommittee on Intergovernmental Relations, *Government Economy and Spending*

Reform Act of 1976—Hearings (Washington: U.S. Government Printing Office, 1976).

United States Senate, Committee on Government Operations, Subcommittee on Intergovernmental Relations, *Government Economy and Spending Act of 1976—Report* (Washington: U.S. Government Printing Office, 1976).

The Role of Evaluation and the Evaluator in Improving Public Programs

Joseph S. Wholey

A NUMBER OF PEOPLE HAVE ASKED me to talk and write on "The Role of Evaluation and the Evaluator." I have real trouble doing that.

One problem is that the word "evaluation" seems to cover everything from multi-million-dollar social experiments to one-day site visits.

Second, many people think that evaluation can help others; few think that evaluation will help them do their own job better.

Finally, to many people, evaluation is an activity that produces long, inconclusive reports that are never used for anything. In fact, the most frequent complaint about evaluation, both from evaluators and from their intended audience, is that evaluations aren't useful or aren't used.

What, then, is evaluation — and what is its role?

We define *evaluation* as systematic measures and comparisons to provide specific information on program results for use in policy or management decisions.[1]

By definition, then, the role of evaluation is to provide feedback on program results for use by policy makers and program managers. But policy makers and managers *already* get plenty of informal feedback on program results. Evaluation may be too costly or too time-consuming to help the busy policy maker or manager enough to be worth his time and attention.

In point of fact, evaluation is seldom sufficiently timely, relevant, and conclusive to provide useful feedback to decision makers.

A number of observers have noted that unrealistic expectations have often been raised about the results that can be achieved by evaluation because:

- Many programs are operated without a clear and agreed-upon statement of the objectives of the program, expressed in measurable terms. (In such cases, one cannot expect evaluation studies to answer the crucial question as to whether the program is meeting its objectives.)

- Many programs operate on a very limited scale, providing resources to meet only a small fraction of the need. Frequently, evaluation studies seem to be inconclusive regarding the impact of the program. (In such cases, it is not the evaluation study that is inconclusive; it is the program impact that is inconclusive.)[2]

The *good news* for today is that some evaluation processes are available that:

- Are relatively simple and inexpensive,
- Promote fruitful interaction and communication between evaluator and intended user of evaluation information, and
- Provide information useful for policy formulation and program management.

We have found at least two ways in which evaluators can help policy makers and program managers who are willing and able to direct their programs to some specific objectives; I'd like to share these with you today.

A Role for Evaluation in Policy Formulation and Communication

It is often very difficult to get agreement on policy directions, either within large organizations or between organizations.

Evaluators can help identify, document, and clarify the most important objectives of a project, a program, or an agency, documenting or helping develop agreed-on measures of success which can then be used in communicating policy directions and managing for results.

In many programs, of course, just spending the money is the objective. In a good many other cases, however, the program is intended to produce certain activities, outcomes, or impacts beyond the spending of money—and evaluators can help those in charge to agree on what is to be accomplished.

The best example I have seen of this evaluation role was in the planning for Cincinnati's Community Sector Team Policing Program, where evaluators helped police department planning personnel to specify measures of process and outcome corresponding to department objectives. Some of those measures were then used from time to time in managing the program.[3]

We have been excited to find that evaluators can communicate with decision makers. One useful technique is to contrast the decision makers' broadly stated program goals with the absence of measurable objectives and plausible links between program activities and objectives.[4] Through close interaction with policy makers and program managers, evaluators can then help decision makers to focus on achievable objectives and to specify their needs for information on the results of program activities.

By getting reactions to suggested measures and comparisons, evaluators can help secure and document agreement (or disagreement) on measurable program objectives and can clarify the feasibility and costs of measuring progress toward objectives and of testing hypotheses relating program activities to program objectives.

Documenting the extent to which there exist (a) agreed-on measurable objectives, (b) plausible, testable hypotheses linking program activities to objectives, and (c) intended uses for evaluators' feedback and helping policy makers and managers to define program objectives in measurable terms (processes we have called "evaluability assessment" and "program design") are among the most valuable services that evaluators can provide. Like evaluation itself, these pre-evaluation efforts are justified to the extent that policy makers and managers desire the direction and accountability that exist in an evaluable measurable program.

These types of interaction can be useful whether or not an evaluation of the program is carried out. Many programs would profit from participation by an evaluation specialist during the early planning and implementation stages.

Interaction among management, evaluators, and subordinate organizational units will be required to ensure that measurable objectives and specific measures and data collection procedures are defined appropriately. Such definitions of objectives and measures of progress can be important in ensuring that a public agency is in a position to properly manage implementation of its most important programs.

A Role for Evaluation in Program Management

Evaluators can provide managers with current information on resources expended, activities implemented, and results achieved, comparing actual program performance with some fixed or relative standard while the program is in progress. When program performance is judged inadequate, management can take corrective action; e.g., in funding or refunding decisions or redirection of program activities.

A number of potentially useful tools for monitoring federal, state, and local programs have been developed and tested:

- Relatively inexpensive, systematic *telephone surveys* of random samples of relevant federal/state/local program staffs and recipients of program services, from which one can obtain statistically reliable objective and subjective data on what services are actually being delivered by the program (to what extent are process objectives being met?) and what are staff members' and recipients' attitudes toward and experiences with those services (to what extent are output objectives being achieved?);

- *Signaling systems* that present information on which local projects are performing "extremely well" or "extremely poorly," displaying the relative performance of projects that are comparable from the managers' perspective;
- Comparisons of *actual project performance with expected project performance,* using information obtained from site visits, from project reporting systems, or from anonymous surveys.

The results have shown the power and potential utility of relatively inexpensive performance monitoring systems:

- In the Cincinnati Police Division, surveys of police officers', citizens' and aides' attitudes and experiences reversed a tentative decision to kill the Community Service Aide (police paraprofessional) Program.[5]
- In the Cincinnati Police Division, anonymous surveys of patrolmen and first-level supervisors were used to determine whether planned delegation of authority was actually in effect; *telephone surveys* of businessmen and households were used to determine whether hoped-for changes in police behavior, citizen attitudes, and crime rates had occurred.[6]
- In a health education demonstration program, *telephone surveys* of federal regional office staff members, state agency staff members, local Community Action Program staff members, and Head Start project directors and Head Start teachers were used to determine whether the planned program had been implemented and to learn the attitudes, opinions, and experiences of those involved in the program.[7]
- For the national Legal Services Program, a highly structured *site visit* data-collection schedule and site visit reporting format were developed to obtain observers' *subjective appraisals* of the quality of services delivered by each Legal Services project and effectiveness of those services in meeting national program goals.[8]
- In the District of Columbia, *observers' ratings* of the cleanliness of streets and alleys (based on comparisons with reference photographs) were used to monitor the effectiveness of the Sanitation Department.[9]
- In a child health care demonstration program, *quarterly progress reports* on health services required by each child and health services delivered to each child were used to monitor individual projects.[10]
- In the Atlanta Public Schools, the *relative achievement levels* of children in schools serving children from similar socioeconomic backgrounds were compared in monitoring the overall effectiveness of individual schools.[11]

If you haven't read John Waller's *Monitoring for Government Agencies*[12] (in fact, if you haven't read it in the last week or so), I strongly urge you to spend some time on it.

How Evaluators Can Play a Stronger Role

Since evaluation has so seldom been useful (not sufficiently conclusive, relevant, and timely to be used), the prudent evaluator will *interact with and involve potential users* of the information in order to estimate which evaluations are worth the cost of implementation.

In our experience, the evaluations that can be done in a non-experimental program are usually quite simple. Talking to potential users about how and whether they would use the evaluation information that can be provided helps focus limited evaluation resources on important, answerable questions.

Frequently, the evaluator has to *create a market* by showing himself or herself useful in small, simple ways early in the game. (If an evaluator can't produce *something* useful in the first six months, he or she's not going at his or her job right!)

Evaluation is a relatively new product — experience tells us that this particular product hasn't been used very much to date. Just as with other new products, evaluation programs need *market research* to determine consumer attitudes toward and experiences with their products in particular, the uses made or not made of their products, the reasons for use or non-use, and consumer views on how the products could be made more useful.[13]

We have found it extremely helpful to go back to customers to measure their satisfaction with, and use of, evaluation products after they have had opportunity to review and react to the evaluations. By formally or informally monitoring his own success, the evaluator can pick up clues as to how he can enhance the value of his services.

In 1973, The Urban Institute's Program Evaluation Group went back to our customers to get their appraisal of the utility of our past products. We identified demands for evaluations that more closely fit the short time constraints faced by policy makers — and demands for inclusion of narrative/anecdotal data as a part of, or companion to, quantitative evaluations.[14] By interacting with their customers, other evaluation groups can get their own clues as to what types of information are needed, wanted, and likely to be used in their own environment.

Conclusion

For many years evaluators and administrators have been meeting in conferences and workshops.

Sometime in this, the Bicentennial Year (or very soon thereafter!),

I'd like to see an evaluation conference in which all the papers have the same title:

"How Evaluation Was Used in Improving the Programs in Our Agency."

This could be a three-day conference, two-day conference, or a one-day conference. In my judgment, the specific focus on *use* would do a lot for evaluators — and for citizens and taxpayers throughout the country.

NOTES

1. The word "we" is used more than editorially. Many of the thoughts expressed here result from interaction with colleagues at The Urban Institute over the last several years, including, in particular, Peter Bloch, Garth Buchanan, Sumner Clarren, Pamela Horst, Dona Kemp, Joe Nay, John Scanlon, Richard Schmidt, Alfred Schwartz, Leona Vogt, John Waller, Donald Weidman, Bayla White, Thomas White, and Richard Zamoff.
2. Joseph S. Wholey, et al., "Evaluation: When Is It Really Needed?" *Evaluation Magazine*, Vol. 2, No. 2 (1975), pp. 89-93.
3. See the series of reports by Alfred Schwartz and Sumner Clarren on evaluation of Cincinnati's Community Sector Team Policing Program (Washington, D.C.: The Urban Institute, 1974-76).
4. See Pamela Horst, et al., "Program Management and the Federal Evaluator," *Public Administration Review*, Vol. 34, No. 4 (July/August 1974), pp. 300-308; and Joseph S. Wholey, et al.
5. Alfred Schwartz and Sumner Clarren, *Evaluation of Cincinnati's Community Sector Team Policing Program* (Washington, D.C.: The Urban Institute, final report, in draft).
6. Alfred Schwartz and Sumner Clarren, *Evaluation of Cincinnati's Community Sector Team Policing Program: A Progress Report* (Washington, D.C.: The Urban Institute, March 1975).
7. Richard Zamoff, et al., *Evaluation of Head Start Experience with "Health That's Me" in the Second Year* (Washington, D.C.: The Urban Institute, September 1973).
8. Hugh Duffy, et al., *Design of an On-Site Evaluation System for the Office of Legal Services* (Washington, D.C.: The Urban Institute, 1973).
9. Louis Blair and Alfred Schwartz, *How Clean Is Our City?* (Washington, D.C.: The Urban Institute, October 1972).
10. Leona Vogt, et al., *Health Start: Final Report of the Evaluation of the Second Year Program* (Washington, D.C.: The Urban Institute, December 1973).
11. Bayla White, et al., *The Atlanta Project: How One Large School System Responded to Performance Information* (Washington, D.C.: The Urban Institute, March 1974).
12. John Waller, et al., *Monitoring for Criminal Justice Planning Agencies* (Washington, D.C.: The Urban Institute, August 1974, and U.S. Government Printing Office, March 1975), revised and reprinted as *Monitoring for Government Agencies* (Washington, D.C.: The Urban Institute, February 1976).

13. See Richard Schmidt, et al., *The Market for Evaluation Services in the Department of Health, Education, and Welfare* (Washington, D.C.: The Urban Institute, May 1974).

14. John W. Scanlon, *Urban Institute Program Evaluation Staff Self Assessment,* Urban Institute working paper, June 1973 (unpublished manuscript, in draft).

How to Design a Program Evaluation
Harry P. Hatry, Richard E. Winnie, and Donald M. Fisk

What Is the Program All About?

In this [section] three elements of program evaluation are discussed: (1) identification of program objectives, (2) identification of the associated evaluation criteria (or "measures of effectiveness") for which data will be sought, and (3) identification of the relevant population segments or clientele groups on which the evaluation should attempt to measure impacts. Because these elements are interrelated, they are discussed together. In practice they can and probably should be undertaken jointly. These basic steps apply to both annual effectiveness status monitoring of major program areas and to individual program evaluations.

Officials requesting a program evaluation should make sure that all relevant objectives, criteria, and clientele groups are included in the evaluation and that the evaluation will be sufficiently comprehensive.

The following sections discuss some principal points in making these selections.

Identify People-Oriented Objectives and Evaluation Criteria

Criteria should reflect potential impacts on citizens and the community (or state). Unfortunately, even among some professionals there is a tendency to concentrate on: workload measures such as tons of garbage collected, number of cases handled, or number of persons processed at intake; or immediate physical measures such as number of acres of playground (perhaps per 1,000 population) or number of hospital beds (per 1,000 population).

These data may be useful for explaining certain aspects of a program's success or lack of it, but in themselves they say little about the extent to which citizens and the community are helped. The objectives and evaluation criteria should include the public conditions that the public programs are designed to affect (e.g., the objectives and evaluation criteria should encompass potential effects on citizen health, public safety, the quality and perceived satisfaction of citizens with recreational opportunities, street cleanliness, etc.).

Objectives and Evaluation Criteria Should Explicitly Consider Unintended Consequences of Programs— Particularly Negative Effects

Examples of unintended results of programs that need to be examined are the following:

- Major new road-building programs may result in significant noise and air pollution and community disruption.
- Urban renewal or housing code enforcement programs may reduce the amount of low-income housing available in a community.
- New recreational programs for youth may also bring increased street litter and street crime to the neighborhood.

The point is that for any program, an explicit objective should be to reduce the program's negative consequences. This is generally neglected. Objectives are usually expressed as intended, beneficial effects. But most programs also tend to have some negative effects and specific evaluation criteria should cover each negative effect.

The purpose of their explicit inclusion is not to retard progress, but to place the program's overall worth in proper perspective, and to design programs that reduce such negative consequences.

More Than One Objective and Evaluation Criterion Need To Be Considered

Rarely are a single objective and a single evaluation criterion sufficient to describe the impacts of a program. Inevitably a program involves numerous objectives, and numerous evaluation criteria will be needed to measure their effects.

Evaluation Criteria Should Not Be Rejected Because of Apparent Difficulties in Measuring Them

Evaluation criteria (as well as objectives and clientele groups) should be identified without concern initially with how or whether they can be measured. There are often ways to at least partially measure the more qualitative, subjective types of evaluation criteria (such as use of ratings, rankings, and other procedures which can be quite useful and appropriate if undertaken in a systematic way).

Too Many Objectives, Criteria, and Clientele Groups Are Better than Too Few

It is probably better initially to err on the side of including too many objectives, evaluation criteria, or clientele groups than to eliminate some that might be important when examined more closely. Neither public officials nor program evaluators should eliminate a potential evaluation criterion (or clientele group) on the basis of their own personal observation.

Program Effects on Individual Population Groups Should Be Distinguished

Different groups may be affected by a program in different degrees. It is important to identify such groups and to collect evaluation criteria data reflecting program impacts on them. An "average" crime rate or "average" family income for a government, as a whole, will not adequately reflect possible major differences that may exist among segments of the population. The following points should be considered:

- Each program will have some groups that are the *intended* beneficiaries, i.e., clients of the service.
- Each program is likely to have certain other groups that, though not intended beneficiaries, are nevertheless affected significantly by the program. These effects may be detrimental or beneficial.
- The citizens of the community or state considered as a whole often comprise a category that should be explicitly identified.
- In some cases, *future* citizens may be an important group to consider explicitly because their interests are closely related to the program.

Possible Sources for Identifying Relevant Objectives, Criteria, and Clientele Groups

Although it is rare to find program objectives, criteria and clientele groups neatly described and packaged, a variety of sources may provide important clues to what these are:

- Legislative statements relating to objectives and evaluation criteria. These are usually available on state and federally originated programs; at best, partial sources.
- Expressions made by legislators or citizens at hearings before a local council, in the press, or by organized citizen groups.
- Program personnel will often be aware of many unintended as well as intended consequences, both beneficial and negative, as well as the various population segments that appear to have been affected.
- Government officials themselves. (It may be argued that too explicit a statement of objectives may at times be politically dangerous. There may be

hidden agendas which, for one reason or another, may not be appropriate to identify. Nevertheless, in most program evaluations, evaluation criteria and objectives can and should be explicitly identified. If there is too much "hidden agenda," the formal program evaluation is likely to lack utility and should not be attempted in the first place.)

Always Include Dollar Cost as One Criterion

Although the literature on program evaluation does not always include cost analysis as part of evaluation, it is clear that state and local governments will want to know what the program has cost. Program costs can then be compared to effects and these figures can also be used to derive estimates of likely future costs if the program is continued. Estimating costs is more complex than generally recognized. . . .

Comparison: The Name of the Game

This [section] discusses the next major step in undertaking a program evaluation—how to estimate what changes can be attributed to the program being evaluated rather than nonprogram factors.

The material in this chapter does not, in general, apply to annual effectiveness status monitoring of major program areas since attributing change due to specific programs is too ambitious an undertaking for status monitoring. (Data from status monitoring, however, can sometimes be useful for individual program evaluations.)

Ideally, we would like to compare what "actually happened" to what "would have happened if the world had been exactly the same as it was except that the program had not been implemented." Since it is impossible to determine exactly what "would have happened if . . . ," the problem is to use procedures that approximate this.

This chapter presents in a simplified manner five "evaluation designs" or approaches for identifying and quantifying program effects due to the program.

1. *Before vs. after program comparison.* Compares program results from the same jurisdiction measured at two points in time: immediately before the program was implemented and at some appropriate time after implementation.
2. *Time trend projection of pre-program data vs. actual post-program data.* Compares actual post-program data to estimated data projected from a number of time periods prior to the program.
3. *Comparisons with jurisdictions or population segments not served by the program.* Compares data from the jurisdiction where the program is operating with data from other jurisdictions where the program is not operating.

4. *Controlled experimentation.* Compares pre-selected, similar groups, some of whom are served and some of whom are not (or are served in different ways). The critical aspect is that the comparison groups are pre-assigned before program implementation so that the groups are as similar as possible except for the program treatment.
5. *Comparisons of planned vs. actual performance.* Compares actual, post-program data to targets set in prior years—either before program implementation or at any period since implementation.

The major function of program evaluation is to identify those changes in the values of the evaluation criteria that can be reasonably attributed to the program. A major problem is that other factors, such as the simultaneous introduction of other related programs or unexpected external events may have occurred during the time period covered by the evaluation. These other factors, and not the program being evaluated, may have been the significant reason for the observed changes in program results.

All but the first and fifth designs include explicit provision for "controlling" for at least some of these other factors. Nevertheless, *in all cases there should be an explicit and thorough search for other plausible explanations of change.* Abnormal weather conditions, other public or private programs with coincidental objectives, special characteristics of the served population not originally recognized, and many other factors may also cause changes in the evaluation criteria data. The designs are now discussed in more detail.

Evaluation Design Number 1: The Bargain Basement Evaluation—Before vs. After Program Comparison

Other than Number 5, this first type or design is the simplest and cheapest type of evaluation. It identifies changes brought about by the program as differences between the values of the evaluation criteria measured before and an appropriate period after the program's introduction. (See Figure 9–1, Design 1.) Of the first four designs, it is probably the most common, but is least capable of separating the effect of program activities from other influences.

Steps   The steps in this evaluation design are:

- Identify relevant objectives and corresponding evaluation criteria.
- Obtain the values of these criteria as they existed before the program's introduction and for the period since introduction.
- Compare the "before" and "after" program data to estimate changes brought about by the program.
- Look for other plausible explanations for the changes. If there are any, estimate their effect on the data or at least identify them when presenting

Design 1

*Before vs. After
Program Comparison*

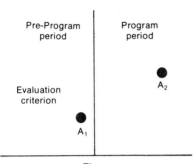

Time
$A_2 - A_1$ = Estimated Program Effect

Design 2

*Time Trend Projection
of Pre-Program vs.
Actual Post-Program Data*

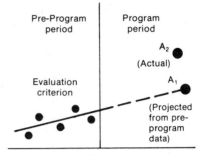

Time
$A_2 - A_1$ = Estimated Program Effect

Design 3

*Comparison with Other Jurisdictions
or Other Population Segments*

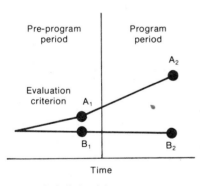

Time

Jurisdiction A has program;
Section B, the Comparison Jurisdiction,
does not.
$(A_2 - A_1) - (B_2 - B_1)$ = Estimated Program
Effect
(or rate of change might be used rather than
the absolute amount of change)

Design 4

*Controlled Experimentation
Comparison of Pre-Assigned Similar Groups
Only One of Which Is Served by the Program*

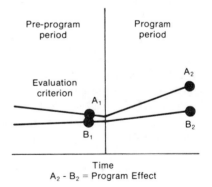

Time
$A_2 - B_2$ = Program Effect

Figure 9-1
Illustrations of Evaluation Designs

the findings. (This last step is often neglected. It is, however, a vital step to making this design credible.)

Types of Application This design often is the only type which is practical when available time and personnel are limited. It is most appropriate when the program's duration is short and of narrow scope. Such circumstances make it less likely that nonprogram related factors that might also affect the evaluation criteria will occur during the period encompassed in the evaluation. It is also appropriate where conditions measured have been fairly stable over time (and are not, for example, likely to be distorted by seasonal changes), and where there is reason to believe such stability will continue during the evaluation period. Otherwise, "before" vs. "after" program comparisons using such data may reflect short-term fluctuations rather than program-related changes.

> In 1971 the Washington, D.C. Operation Clean Sweep evaluation used this design. This intensive street cleaning program extended over a nine week period. No other major changes were expected which would affect the output criteria. Neighborhood cleanliness was measured just before and just after the program using a visual inspection system and a survey of citizens' perceptions. The "before" conditions were believed to be typical of conditions prior to Clean Sweep and not of a seasonal nature.
>
> An example at the state level is a state of Pennsylvania 1970 evaluation of vocational education and training programs in state prisons. Pre-prison jobs and earnings were compared to post-prison jobs and earnings indicating that in-prison education and training resulted in negligible impact. In addition, post-prison jobs seldom were in line with prison training.

This evaluation design contains the implicit assumption that the values for the evaluation criteria that existed just before the program was instituted are the best available estimates of what the values would have been without the new program.

This design (as well as the others) will generally be more effective if the evaluation can be planned prior to program implementation. Such pre-planning will permit a special data collection effort to provide adequate evaluation criteria. For example, the Operation Clean Sweep evaluation noted above required special inspections of street cleanliness before as well as after the program. Such "before" data could not have been collected after Clean Sweep had taken place. Seldom will data normally collected by a government be fully adequate for this type of evaluation.

Cost Except for Design Number 5, this is the least expensive of the five designs. If based solely on data already collected by the jurisdiction, its cost is likely to be quite low. Special data collection will increase the costs, depending on the collection procedures used. The Operation Clean Sweep evaluation involved special inspections of streets and a small telephone survey, both before and after the program. These added several thousand dollars cost to the evaluation, but were the backbone of the evaluation.

Evaluation Design Number 2: Time Trend Projection of Pre-Program Data vs. Actual Post-Program Data*

This design compares *actual* post-program data on the evaluation criteria with projections for the criteria based on data from previous years. Changes caused by the program are identified as the differences between present-day conditions as they actually are and as they were estimated to be by the projections if the program had not been instituted. (See Figure 9-1, Design 2.)

Steps

- Identify relevant objectives and corresponding evaluation criteria.
- Obtain data on each of the criteria at several intervals prior to the program and after implementation.
- Using statistical methods and the data from pre-program years make projections of the values of the criteria to the end of the time period covered by the evaluation.
- Compare the actual and projected estimates as to the amount of changes resulting from the program.
- Look for plausible explanations for changes in criteria other than those resulting from the program. If there are any, estimate their effect on the data or at least identify them when presenting the findings.

Types of Application   This design is useful where there appears to be an underlying trend (upward or downward) over a period of time that would seem likely to have continued if the new program had not been introduced. However, if data for prior years are too unstable, statistical projections may not be meaningful. Or, if there is strong judgmental evidence that underlying conditions have changed in very recent years, data on prior years should probably not be utilized.

For example, crime or accident statistics may rise and fall for individual years, but when many years are considered together a trend

---

*In some situations, projections based on factors other than time trends may be appropriate. For example, the population mix may have changed significantly over the period covered by the evaluation. Rather than using the pre-program values of the evaluation criteria, e.g., crime rates, projections of the crime rates might be made based on the latest mix. These projections would then be compared to those that actually occurred after the crime prevention program was introduced.

may be apparent around which annual statistics vary. Simple comparison of data from one "before" year to post-program data may be influenced by extremes and thereby be misleading. The projection of this trend to the time of the evaluation and comparison with post-program results will indicate whether or not the trend has been altered by the new program.

> This design was used in an evaluation of the Indianapolis "Police Fleet Plan." The plan calls for providing marked police cars to policemen for their full-time use. For the evaluation, traffic accident and crime rates for individual types of crimes (especially those most likely to be deterred by added police cars) were obtained for each of the six years prior to the new plan. A statistical projection was made and compared to the crime rates that occurred after the plan's implementation.

The availability of data on more than one time period since program implementation would also provide considerably more evidence that a significant trend change had occurred.

Cost   This design requires two added elements that increase the costs relative to Design Number 1: technical expertise to undertake the statistical projections, and added data collection for prior years. The latter requires special attention to see that the data collected for prior years is compatible with current data.

Evaluation Design Number 3: Comparisons with Other Jurisdictions or Population Segments Not Served by the Program

This design compares the values of the evaluation criteria in the jurisdiction having the program with those of other, similar jurisdictions which do not have the program. (See Figure 9-1, Design 3.) If the other jurisdictions show similar changes, it is possible that factors other than the introduction of the new program were significant. Similarly, this design can be used if comparison population segments *within* the jurisdiction, but not served by the program, can be identified.

Steps   The steps in this evaluation design are:

- Identify relevant objectives and corresponding evaluation criteria.
- Identify other similar jurisdictions where the program is not operating (or population segments within the jurisdiction not served by the program).
- Obtain data on each of the criteria in each of the jurisdictions (or for each of the population segments being compared) from before implementation of the program to the time of evaluation.

- Compare the changes in the values of the criteria for jurisdictions where the program does not exist with those from the jurisdiction where the program is operating. Compare both rates of change as well as amount of change.
- Look for plausible explanations for changes in criteria other than the program. If there are any, estimate their effect on the data or at least identify them when presenting the findings.

Types of Application   This design protects somewhat against attributing change to a specific program when external factors that affect many local governments (or other population segments within the jurisdiction) are responsible for bringing about the change.

> For example, in the Indianapolis Police Fleet Plan, such factors as the introduction of a new ignition lock system nationally, at about the same time, could have significantly affected auto theft crime rates. Selected comparisons with other jurisdictions and the nation as a whole for the time period indicated that Indianapolis' auto theft rate was going down while other parts of the country continued to go up. This strongly suggests that the national ignition lock program was not a significant factor in explaining the Indianapolis reduction.
>
> Another example: the evaluators of a strict speed enforcement program by the state of Connecticut used this design. The Connecticut program was evaluated partially on its effectiveness in reducing the number of traffic fatalities (per 100,000 population). While initial inspection of the data indicated a decline in fatalities coinciding with the introduction of the program, evaluators could not exclude the possibility that other nonlocal factors such as improved vehicle safety, national safety advertising, or general widespread weather conditions may have caused the decline. To test this, Connecticut's fatality rate was compared with fatality rates in neighboring states. This comparison showed that Connecticut's fatality rate declined relative to the neighboring states, thereby indicating that some factor, unique to Connecticut, was having an effect on fatality rates. . . .

The preceding paragraphs discuss comparisons with other jurisdictions. It is also possible to identify comparison groups *within* the jurisdiction. Considerable caution needs to be exercised in identifying the comparisons and interpreting the findings.

> For example, a recent evaluation of treatment programs of drug addicts in Dade County, Florida, compared the effectiveness of the various types of treatment programs—both methadone and residential therapeutic communities. An essential element was the need to consider apparent differences in characteristics of the clients—such as age, sex, extent of addiction, and arrest records and motivation as indicated by screening done by each program—to see whether the clients were at least roughly "similar." (Motivation and personality differences are much more difficult to

identify and would be better handled in the controlled experiment with clients assigned randomly to different types of treatment programs. But this is not likely to be popular in situations such as this.)

Without random assignment of recipients to the various groups (as called for in Evaluation Design Number 4) the groups may in reality be significantly different.

For example, as indicated in the drug treatment evaluation just noted, persons voluntarily enrolling in training or treatment programs of any kind are likely to have different motivations and different personal characteristics than those who do not volunteer. The program may have skimmed off the "cream" of the persons needing training or treatment. In the future, similar programs may have much less success in dealing with those less highly motivated.

Nevertheless, even if comparison groups differ in important characteristics, the information on relative apparent program effects for the different groups is still likely to be useful to public officials.

If the evaluation is designed before program implementation, this would also permit variations of the program to be tried and evaluated.

Special Problems   Identification of comparable jurisdictions (or similar population segments within a jurisdiction) is a particularly difficult problem. Nearby jurisdictions and those with similar population characteristics are the most likely to be useful for comparison. In addition, the values of the evaluation criteria should preferably be roughly similar and have similar recent trends. The characteristics which determine the choice of jurisdictions will vary with the program being evaluated. Ultimately, this choice is based on the evaluator's judgment of what nonprogram related factors might influence the program's effectiveness.

Evaluators of the Connecticut program, for example, were concerned with selected jurisdictions that had traffic conditions similar to Connecticut. Neighboring states were therefore selected for comparison because of similar climate and culture (attitudes and reactions of drivers).

Consequently, although this design helps to control for some important external factors, it is generally not a fully reliable measure of program effects. It is best used along with other designs.

Use of this design for interjurisdictional comparisons depends on the availability of comparable data on the evaluation criteria from other jurisdictions. Limited availability of comparable data may be a difficulty. The type of data collected and the precision with which they are collected are likely to vary among jurisdictions.

Cost   This design includes two elements not included in the first two evaluation designs:

Effort will be needed to identify similar jurisdictions. If standard categories are adequate (such as similar population size, proximity, etc.), the cost is small. However, if jurisdictions are selected for a particular combination of characteristics or to insure that a similar program does not exist in comparison jurisdictions, the cost of determining the appropriate comparison jurisdictions will be higher.

Effort is also needed to collect comparable data from these other jurisdictions. If the evaluation relies on a standardized data source (e.g., uniform crime reports), the costs of data collection will be small. If special data collection efforts are required (to gather or verify data), the cost may be considerably higher.

Evaluation Design Number 4: The Cadillac of Program Evaluations—Controlled Experimentation

This evaluation design is by far the most "powerful." Unfortunately, it is also by far the most difficult and costly to undertake. It assesses the effectiveness of a program by systematically comparing specific changes in two or more carefully separated groups: ones in which the program is operating and others in which it is not. This design can also be used to try variations of a program to determine which is most effective; thus, resulting in more groups to be compared.

Steps   The basic evaluation design consists of the following steps:*

- Identify relevant objectives and corresponding evaluation criteria.
- Select the groups to be compared, i.e., the "control" and the "experimental" groups. Members of the population of interest (or a probability sample of that population) are usually assigned randomly (in a "scientifically" random manner) to the groups. It is vital to select groups that have similar characteristics with regard to their likelihood of being effectively "treated" by the program.
- Measure the pre-program performance of each group using the evaluation criteria.
- Apply the program to the experimental but not the control group.
- Monitor the operation of the experiment to see if any actions occur that might distort the findings (such as the behavior of program operators toward one of the groups). If appropriate and possible, such behavior should be adjusted, or if not, at least identified and its impact on the eventual findings explicitly estimated.

*This report does not attempt to discuss the many technical steps in experimental design which can become quite complex, especially when many program variations are included in the experiment.

- Measure the post-program performance of each group against the evaluation criteria.
- Compare the pre- vs. post- changes in the evaluation criteria for the groups.
- Look for plausible explanations for differences between the two groups due to factors other than the program. The randomization called for in the second step above protects against this to a great extent. Nevertheless, there remains the small possibility that some event, perhaps occurring during the experiment, by chance affects one group and not the other in some special way.

Types of Applications Traditionally, Design Number 4 has been suggested for use in evaluating programs that are directed towards specific individuals, e.g., health or manpower training programs. This design should be considered for a variety of "treatment" programs such as health, drug or alcohol abuse, corrections, rehabilitation, and training. However, it is not likely to be appropriate when large capital investments are necessary.

However, an important variation of this for local government purposes is the comparison of different geographical areas of a community. Many programs can be split geographically. They might be initially introduced in some geographical areas of a community and not in others. For state evaluations, a program might be introduced in some counties and not in others. For example, new crime, traffic control, firefighting, or solid waste collection procedures might be (and often are) initially tried out in a few areas of the jurisdiction. Areas with similar characteristics would be identified (relative to the program being introduced), and some of the areas would then be randomly designated as program recipients.

> For example, a neighborhood policing program might be introduced on an experimental basis. Matched pairs of police sectors would be identified. The members of each pair would be selected on the basis of similar population and crime characteristics. One member of each pair would then be selected at random (e.g., using a table of random numbers) to be part of the program.

If the trends in the evaluation data before the new program was introduced were similar in both areas — but after the new program was operated, improvements were considerably larger in the areas with the program — this would provide considerable evidence for attributing the change to the program. A specific example may clarify how this type of evaluation (see Figure 9-1, Design 4) would be applied to a new public program or activity:

> A local government is considering installation of high intensity street lighting to combat neighborhood crime. Before spending large sums for

this purpose, it decides to test whether the street lighting program will actually reduce crime and traffic accidents. A number of geographical areas within the jurisdiction are identified which have similar characteristics (crime and accident rates; land use; population density; traffic patterns; family income). Some of these areas are then randomly selected for installation of the new lighting. The number of crime incidents and traffic accidents in each area are identified for the past two years.

After a period of time, perhaps six months or a year, the rates of crime and accidents in the test and non-test areas are examined and compared.

Other plausible explanations for changes in criteria other than the new lighting program, such as events that may have occurred in some areas and not in others, should be considered. If a significant reduction in crime and accidents in the areas with new street lighting occurred and no other explanations are identified, the change can be attributed with some confidence to the new program. An expansion to other areas would then seem appropriate. If there are no significant reductions in crime or accidents, future expansion would seem wasteful.

Special Problems For this fourth evaluation design (and its variations), certain factors can make the observed results unrepresentative of the program's future effects. The possibility of these influences should be considered when analyzing results of an evaluation using this design.

- Members of an experimental group may respond differently to a program if they realize they are being observed as part of an evaluation. This influence is commonly known as the "Hawthorne effect." Appropriate procedures, such as notification of control group members that they are also part of an experiment can help reduce the problem.
- If the experimental group is only one part of a jurisdiction, response to the program might differ from what it would be if all parts of the jurisdiction were receiving the program. (For example, crime control programs, if instituted in one part of a city or state, might merely move criminal activity to other locations. Crime in the experimental areas would show a marked decrease, but the jurisdiction as a whole might experience no change.)
- If persons are allowed to volunteer for membership in the experimental group, the two groups are not likely to be comparable. A self-selected group will probably be more receptive to the program and thus may not be typical of the whole target population.
- In some situations, political pressures may make it impractical to provide a service to one group in the jurisdiction and not to others. This resistance will probably be less where the government tests variations rather than merely using an "all or nothing" allocation of program resources.
- Similarly, concern with equal distribution of service among population groups may limit the ability of governments to provide a service to one group while withholding the same service from another group elsewhere in

the jurisdiction. This problem is less acute if the proposed program is not regarded as beneficial. (However, if everyone thinks the program is beneficial, there is usually no need to experiment.)

- It may also be considered morally wrong by some to provide a government service temporarily when the service could cause dependency of clients and make them feel worse off after the benefits are cut off. This problem may be partly overcome by advanced explanations of the experiment.
- One problem concerns the administrative control of the service—a service-oriented group or a research group. Use of the latter will minimize evaluation problems by maintaining the intent of the experimental design. However, such a group may not have a full understanding of service delivery problems.

Cost   Use of this design generally costs considerably more than the other designs because of:

- Greater amount of time required to plan, conduct, and analyze data from the evaluation.
- Higher level of analytical and managerial skill required for planning and undertaking the evaluation and analyzing the results.

This design also implies an indirect cost due to temporary changes in the way the program operates so that different types of program benefits are received by experimental and control groups.

Design Number 5: Comparisons of Planned vs. Actual Performance

In addition to comparing measurements from one time period to the next or for different groups, another type of comparison can also be useful. This is the comparison of actual results against planned or targeted results. This is a fairly straightforward approach and perhaps should not even be labeled a "design." Preparation of plans for the next year or two is often done in state or local governments, though generally based on measures of workload and population served rather than on measurements of the effects of services. In addition, it appears that *after-the-fact* comparisons of how the program did relative to what it had planned to do are still surprisingly rare.

Steps   The steps in this evaluation approach are:

- Identify relevant objectives and corresponding evaluation criteria.
- Set specific goals or targets for these criteria for specific time periods.
- Obtain data after the time period on actual performance.
- Compare the actual performance to the targets.
- Look for plausible explanations for changes in the criteria other than the program. If there are any, estimate their effect on the criteria or at least identify them when presenting the findings.

Types of Application   If a government establishes goals or targets that are expressed in terms of effectiveness measures, such evaluations can be undertaken. Targets should be established for specific achievements for specific time periods.

> For example, the goal of a vocational rehabilitation program might be to "rehabilitate" a certain number of people in each disability category in the next year. (The term "rehabilitate" will need to be defined as specifically as possible.) A cost target should also be set.

Actual performance at the end of the year should be compared against the targets that were set. This design, like Design Number 1, provides no direct means to indicate to what extent the change in values of the effectiveness criteria can be attributed solely to the new program. As with the other evaluation designs, evaluators should explicitly look for other plausible explanations, other than the programs, as to why the targets have been met, exceeded, or not met. In the vocational rehabilitation example, there may have been a large number of unusually difficult cases within a given disability category that were not considered in the plan (that is, the type of clientele changed significantly).

Today most state and local governments probably use on occasion a variation of this evaluation design. Currently this approach is generally used to compare actual program performance to *implied* rather than *explicit* targets.

Many times much can be learned from a careful systematic examination of a program and even its immediate, short-term consequences — even though a more elaborate evaluation design is not used. This is best explained by illustration.

> In 1968, the evaluators of the state of Michigan's Student Guaranteed Loan Program were surprised to discover the extent to which the loans were going to middle rather than lower income families. This was discovered by arraying and tabulating family data from loan applications.
>
> Another example is the examination of Nashville's existing system for pre-court disposition of neglected or dependent children. It was found that 60 percent of the children temporarily placed in the county's childrens home were returned to their own homes as soon as the court acted, suggesting excessive reliance on institutional care.
>
> This discovery led to corrective action to provide short-term, noninstitutional, emergency care.

This evaluation approach can be used widely and regularly once provision is made for regular collection of the data needed for measuring evaluation criteria. Setting targets each year for one or more years in advance can be readily done. Consequently, this approach is particularly useful for annual evaluations of programs that have existed for a number of years (where "before-program" data may not be of much utility).

Special Problems   This approach requires that appropriate, realistic goals or targets be established for the evaluation criteria. Such goal-setting may not be taken seriously if the evaluations are not used seriously. If used seriously, the establishment of targets is likely to become an important issue. Higher level officials as well as program managers should participate in setting targets. The targets set should explicitly encompass all key program effects. If the targets are met or exceeded by actual performance, this would be evidence for maintaining or expanding the program. Conversely, if the targets are not met, this should raise questions about the program. As usual, reasons for high or low performance, including nonprogram factors, should be considered in making future program decisions.

This design implicitly assumes that the targets set are the best available estimates of what actual accomplishment should be. Deviations from the targets should be carefully examined.

A major concern is that this design should not be used to encourage haphazard evaluations or to discourage use of the tougher but more meaningful approaches described in the earlier discussions of other designs.

Cost   This type of evaluation is likely to be the least expensive. Costs will depend primarily on the cost of any additional data gathering required for the evaluation criteria selected. Target-setting cost is likely to be small.

Additional Considerations—All Evaluation Designs

Three additional considerations need the attention of program evaluators:

Seldom Can One Be Absolutely Certain a Change Was Brought About by a Specific Progam   Almost always there is a small chance that other factors caused the change. Even in controlled experiments (Design Number 4), it would not be feasible to control for all conceivable factors that might be important. Often it will not be possible to attribute the effects solely to the program that is being evaluated.

A classic and recent example of this is Washington, D.C., where a drop in the reported crime rate occurred. During the period, several major program actions occurred, including: major increases in the number of policemen, build-up of a large drug addict treatment program, and extensive new street lighting in some portions of the city. In addition, some believe that various social conditions had changed in the city over the time period. Some of these effects could be partially isolated, e.g., the street lighting effects presumably would occur in some areas and not others, but others would be extremely difficult, if not impossible, to extract.

However, decisions concerning government programs are inevitably made under conditions of considerable uncertainty which evaluations can reduce but not eliminate.

In addition, even though it is not possible to isolate the effects of the program from others introduced about the same time, if the evaluation indicates significant benefits to the community, this should be important information and government officials may feel there is no need to break up a "winning combination."

In all cases it is crucial that the users of program evaluations insist that evaluators look for other plausible explanations for changes in the evaluation criteria before attributing changes to the program being evaluated.

Can Projections Be Made from the Evaluation Findings? The purpose of evaluations is to help guide future government actions. Even where the evaluation indicates with considerable certainty that a program had a significant effect in the past, some circumstances can make projection of evaluation findings treacherous. These include:

- Where only partial implementation of a program is evaluated, the findings may not be fully applicable to full scale implementation.
- Where special quality personnel (or special, demonstration-only equipment) are used in the program being tested but may not be available in the post-test period or for full-scale implementation, the degree of success may be due to these special capabilities and not be fully obtainable in the future.

Were Only Short-Term and Not Long-Term Effects Measured?
Over the long run, major problems may begin to appear (e.g., ground water pollution in a solid waste disposal land-fill, possible medical side-effects from prolonged use of high doses of special drugs to combat other illnesses, etc.). This type of problem is a good reason for requiring periodic follow-up.

The dilemma is that governments often cannot wait for long periods of time before making relevant decisions. Where decisions cannot be delayed, intermediate findings should be provided. However, the dangers involved in interpreting such findings should be made explicit.

Choice of an Evaluation Design

Selecting an evaluation design depends on the timing of the evaluation (if the evaluation is decided upon after the program has already been implemented, Design Number 4 will not be possible), the dollars available, and the accuracy desired.

The first four designs discussed above are progressively more expensive, with the fourth usually considerably more expensive than the others. The first three and the fifth can often be accomplished with but a very few man-months of analytical effort — the amount depending heavily on the amount of special data collection required. The fourth design will likely take many calendar months and possibly years. (It could well take several man-years of special effort to design, monitor, and analyze the findings.) The designs are also progressively more effective in providing substantial evaluation information; the fourth providing, by far, the most reliable results.

The designs presented above are not either/or choices. Some or all of the first three are, in fact, often used together.

Recommendations

1. *Whenever possible, utilize the most precise evaluation, Design Number 4.* However, its likely cost and special characteristics mean that a local government should probably use it very selectively. A state government, because of the more wide-scale application of its programs and the availability of more resources, should be more often able to use this design. Opportunities to use geographical areas as control groups as well as groups of individuals for experiments should be explored.
2. *Where Design Number 4 is not feasible, use Designs 1, 2, and 3 in combination.* That is, the evaluation would look at "before" vs. "after" values for the criteria, undertake projections for selected criteria where prior year data were available, and search for similar jurisdictions or similar population segments in the jurisdiction that have not been served by the program. The findings of all of these would be jointly considered in drawing conclusions. The additional costs of using Designs 2 and 3, in tandem with Design Number 1 should, in general, not be great and the added meaningfulness of the resulting information should be well worth the added cost.
3. *Avoid using Design Number 1 alone except as a last resort.* Evaluation Design Number 1 is a very weak evaluation tool. However, in combination with Designs 2 and 3 it becomes more meaningful.
4. *Make extensive and regular use of Design Number 5 (planned vs. actual) based on setting targets for individual evaluation criteria.* This should be done as a supplement to the other designs as well as the evaluation approach when the other designs are not feasible.

The Dirty Job—Data Collection

Data collection is often considered merely a dirty job in program evaluation (or in any type of analysis). However, it probably consumes the greatest amount of time and effort.

Government officials normally avoid getting too involved with the details of data collection. However, there are several points which require their attention, and occasionally cause many moments of anguish. This chapter focuses on major points that should be of most concern to sponsors and users of program evaluations.

Most of the discussion applies equally to data collected for both regular effectiveness status monitoring and individual program evaluations. Regular effectiveness monitoring requires standard procedures so that data can be collected routinely and are comparable from year to year. Individual program evaluations may require tailor-made data collection procedures and can involve elements that might not be feasible on a regular basis.*

The data to be collected is determined by following the steps described earlier. (1) Program objectives and evaluation criteria suggest what data can best indicate program effectiveness. Identification of relevant clientele groups suggests the type of data disaggregation that will be needed. (2) The evaluation design indicates specific time periods and for what specific groups data are required.

We have identified five sources of data:

- Existing records and statistics.
- Interviews with clients which in some cases involve citizens at large.
- Ratings by professionals.
- Other special data collection procedures.
- Experiences of other governments.

The Summer Youth Program
Edward J. Cherian

IN THE 1960S THE LOCAL political, economic, and social climate of Washington, D.C. was clearly undergoing change, as it was in other major cities with large minority populations. The youthful black power movement was growing increasingly militant. "Colored" became negro, which became black as the preferred name for black Americans. And black was now beautiful, and proclaimed as such. Black Washingtonians also wanted their "fair share" of economic and social equality.

---

*Individual program evaluations should also provide the basis for a regular ongoing system of data collection. Once the development and testing of measures have been achieved, collection becomes more routine. In turn, individual program evaluations will be improved by the availability of comparable data collected over time.

For the third consecutive year, the federal government provided funds to the District of Columbia for the purpose of conducting a summer program for the district's underprivileged youths. The funds were provided to the Youth Programs Unit of the D.C. government. In a city with a population of 750,000 people and a public school system enrollment of approximately 150,000, the 1968 D.C. Summer Youth Program was unique for three important reasons. First, the city which had experienced racial street riots (officially termed civil disobedience) had only three months before initiation of the summer program. Second, it was decided that in order to offer program activities which better satisfy the needs of the community, community members were to have a substantial role in the program planning and operations. This decision would not only allow the community to identify its own needs and develop programs to meet these needs but also insure greater community involvement in the summer program. Third, the federal government insisted that an independent evaluation be conducted to determine the effectiveness of the more than $2 million to be spent this summer. Accordingly, the D.C. government contracted with a consulting research organization to evaluate the 273 program activities funded by the Youth Programs Unit. (Figure 9-2 presents the 1976 D.C. organization, indicating a change in organizational name of the Youth Programs Unit.)

In June, 1968, the consultants met with Joe James, Director of the Youth Programs Unit, and his staff of two professionals assigned to the planning and conduct of the summer program. Joe James, a young ambitious professional, came from a background in the District of Columbia's Recreation Department to head up the Youth Programs Unit. Although James did not have a plan with specific goals, objectives, sub-objectives, activities, etc., he was committed to the concept of community inputs in the design of program activities. He was under great pressures. It was late: a plan had not been developed "because everybody spent the last three months trying to keep the city from burning." The Mayor's Office was committed to a "cool summer" and ostensibly did not care what summer activities were funded as long as the District of Columbia did not emulate the April riots or those experienced by several other cities. "I had good programs last year and I'll fund some of those again," said James. Also, some informal neighborhood street leaders, who had followings of youth, expected programs of their choosing to be funded this summer.

To facilitate community involvement, the District of Columbia was divided into four districts which contained a total of twenty neighborhood areas identified by population concentrations. Each neighborhood area was represented by a community group, called a Neighborhood Planning Council (NPC). The councils consisted of

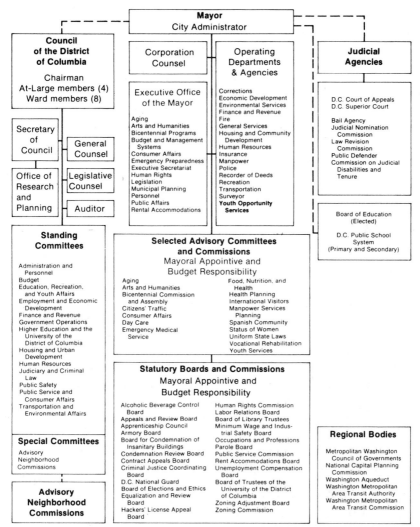

Figure 9-2
Organization of the District of Columbia Government

members elected by the community, through whom it was hoped community participation would be enhanced. Funds were allocated to each area dependent upon the number of youths from low-income families* in that area. Within the limitation provided by the amount of funds available and with the requirement that programs provide

*The federal government's property index was utilized: that is, a family of four whose annual income is $3,600 or less is considered low-income, with a scale of increasing family size to increasing income.

"wholesome activities," NPCs were allowed full leeway to develop their own activities to meet the needs of their specific youth populations; 273 activity programs were funded within the twenty areas during the summer of 1968.

But the city was tense; small racial incidents seemed to be magnified in the news media. Black residents were fearful of their own neighbors and began tagging their cars with "soul brother" stickers in hope that the identification would prevent damage. In a community that had ostensibly achieved racial peace years before, with low unemployment, with a large percentage of the labor force in white-collar and stable government jobs, a vocal and youthful Black Power movement was surfacing.

The Summer Effort

All public service programs operate with constraints on time and money, and the Summer Youth Program was no exception: activities were late getting started, and center locations and staff were slow in coming together and making their existence known to the community.

Add to this the tense racial environment and the perception of hostility that many youths expressed toward the establishment (i.e., District of Columbia and federal governments), and the constraints appear quite formidable.

Table 9-1 represents the original fund allocation, the supplemental fund allocation,* and the number and percentage of participants and staff actually observed participating in summer youth activities.

Tables 9-2 and 9-3 present the fund allocation, staff, and participants as a function of program activity type. Since the NPCs were permitted to determine the nature of the program best suited to the needs of youth in their areas, this table may reflect the needs of the employment and mixed (multipurpose) programs. It may be noted that 68.9 percent of the total funds were allocated to recreation programs, 13.0 percent to education, 7.7 percent to employment, and 10.4 percent to mixed programs.

Because the Summer Youth Program was conceived and implemented in a highly decentralized style, no central publicity or announcement was utilized in initiating the program. Recruitment was most frequently accomplished by staffs spreading the word and/or canvassing individual neighborhoods door-to-door. The efficiency of decentralized recruitment did, of course, vary from program to program, but a more systematic recruitment effort may have included some youths indicating an interest in the Program.

*Additional funds were provided late in the summer to the D.C. Youth Program Unit from the Office of Economic Opportunity.

Table 9-1
Total Allocations, Observed Staff, Observed Participants by Neighborhood Planning Council Area, Summer 1968

	Available Funds		Total Allocation		Observed Participants		Observed Staff	
	Original Allocation	Special Allocation	Amount	Percent	Number	Percent	Number	Percent
TOTAL	$2,036,263	$101,519	$2,137,782	100.0	21861	100.0	3395	100.0
Area 1	30,516	3,355	33,871	1.6	331	1.5	45	1.3
2	10,629	2,150	12,779	.6	55	.3	8	.2
3	18,112	2,795	20,907	1.0	404	1.8	11	.3
4	7,895	1,800	9,695	.5	209	1.0	7	.2
5	76,073	6,200	82,273	3.8	717	3.3	111	3.4
6	17,450	2,610	20,060	.9	345	1.6	38	1.1
7	22,860	3,415	26,275	1.2	400	1.8	34	1.0
8	115,999	5,453	121,452	5.7	2055	9.4	178	5.2
9	125,025	4,285	129,310	6.0	1214	5.6	221	6.5
10	136,473	3,600	140,073	6.6	1209	5.5	198	5.8
11	110,405	4,826	115,231	5.4	1244	5.7	196	5.8
12	24,046	1,850	25,896	1.2	845	3.9	165	4.9
13	33,979	1,750	35,729	1.7	275	1.3	29	.9
14	83,223	5,414	88,637	4.2	2140	11.0	411	12.1
15	267,246	12,044	279,290	13.1	2345	10.7	381	11.2
16	269,238	8,767	278,005	13.0	1724	7.9	396	11.7
17	92,339	2,575	94,914	4.4	872	4.0	164	4.8
18	297,099	13,440	310,539	14.5	2699	12.3	404	11.9
19	168,400	7,740	176,140	8.2	1408	6.4	191	5.6
20	129,256	7,450	136,706	6.4	1100	5.0	207	6.1

Table 9-2
Total Programs, Fund Allocation, Staff and Participants by Type of Program Activity, Summer 1968

Type of Program	Program Activities		Original Allocation		Total Staff		Participants	
	Number	Percent	Amount	Percent	Number	Percent	Number	Percent
TOTAL	273		$2,036,263		3,395		21,861	—
Administration	3		11,359		23			
Total minus admin.	270	100.0	2,024,904	100.0	3,372	100.0	21,861	100.0
Preschool	43	15.9	214,574	10.6	465	13.8	2,401	11.0
Youth center	81	30.0	823,561	40.7	1,360	40.3	8,359	38.2
Teen center	40	14.8	294,757	14.6	408	12.1	3,299	15.1
Multicenter[1]	10	3.7	163,204	8.1	249	7.4	1,671	7.6
Block and street camps	37	13.7	187,204	9.2	403	12.0	2,425	11.1
Work skills	14	5.2	95,836	4.7	108	3.2	517	2.4
Job development/ employment	7	2.6	58,405	2.9	61	1.8	298[2]	1.4
Beautification	4	1.5	14,675	.7	51	1.5	205	.9
Culture/science/ art center	12.4	4.4	69,169	3.4	85	2.5	588	2.7
General recreation and athletics		1.5	36,086	1.8	62	1.8	407	1.9
Other	18	6.7	67,433	3.3	120	3.6	1,691	7.7

[1] Includes 8 multipurpose centers and 2 preschool–youth center combinations.
[2] This figure is an estimate of the average number of weekly job referrals and does not mean the same as number of participants in other programs.

Table 9-3
**Fund Allocation, Number of Program Activities, Number of Participants and
Observed Staff by Type of Program, Summer 1968**

Allocation	Amount	Percent
Total allocation	2,036,263	
Administration	11,359	
Total, minus admin.	2,024,904	100.0
Education	262,373	13.0
Recreation	1,394,583	68.9
Employment	156,228	7.7
Mixed	211,720	10.4

Number of Program Activities	Number	Percent
Number of programs	273	
Administration	3	
Total, minus admin.	270	100.0
Education	55	20.4
Recreation	175	64.8
Employment	21	7.8
Mixed	19	7.0

Number of Participants	Number	Percent
Total participants	21,861	100.0
Education	2,876	13.1
Recreation	16,040	73.4
Employment	872	4.0
Mixed	2,073	9.5

Number of Observed Staff	Number	Percent
Total observed staff	3,395	
Administration	23	
Total, minus admin.	3,372	100.0
Education	533	15.8
Recreation	2,312	68.6
Employment	207	6.1
Mixed	320	9.5

The Evaluation Efforts

The design and conduct of a meaningful evaluation was an equally
difficult problem, greatly hampered by the lack of specific program
objectives against which a traditional evaluation construct could be
developed. To meet the problems inherent in examining programs *in
vivo*, the consultants chose to carry out interviews with the various persons connected with the program activity and to compare their attitudes. The following populations were interviewed: program participants, the neighborhood participants, the Neighborhood Youth
Corps,* program directors and senior aides (adult staff), non-partici-

*Originally an OEO-funded program for low-income youths, now funded by the U.S.
Department of Labor. Both in-school youths 14–21 years old and out-of-school youths
16–22 years old may participate for full-time or part-time employment.

pant youths, Neighborhood Planning Council chairmen and members, and the D.C. Youth Programs Unit staff.

Data collected from the summer programs was tabled and organized and thirty-five representative sample sites were selected. The sample of program activities was weighted to be representative of the total population of program activities underway. Field informants* then visited each selected site for the purpose of aiding data collection. Subsequently, field informants revisited all 273 sites to validate initial data collected and to insure that data which was dependent upon estimates was sufficiently reliable.

Seventy-four participants in the 1968 Summer Youth Program were interviewed at the thirty-five sample sites. Participants (forty-five males and twenty-nine females) were chosen at random and interviewed at their centers. Ages of interviewees ranged from seven through eighteen, with the greatest number being between fourteen and fifteen. The average age is somewhat older than that of the total population due to the fact that pre-school age children (for obvious reasons) were not interviewed. Despite this, the age distribution of the sample participant population does reflect the emphasis of the Summer Youth Program on youths fifteen and under.

Program Participants in 35 Sample Sites
Sample Interviewed

Age	7-10	11	12	13	14	15	16	17-18
Number	6	7	11	9	11	13	10	7

Seventy-one youths who did not participate in the Program were selected and interviewed at random from the neighborhoods surrounding the thirty-five sample sites. The sample included fifty-three males and eighteen females, with ages ranging from eight to nineteen (average 15.4 years). The average age of the group is similar to that of the program participants sample.

Program Non-Participants
Sample Interviewed

Age	8-10	11	12	13	14	15	16	17-19	No response
Number	3	2	2	7	3	17	9	24	4

With program operations, participants, and staff constantly changing, it was difficult to gather observations representative of on-going events. This resulted in differences in sample populations and,

*The term *informant* is used here in an anthropological sense, that is, an individual able to serve as a bridge between two dissimilar populations.

hence, in determining numbers of participants and staff members. In the case of participants, many of the activities did not require attendance records and, therefore, some evaluation results contain estimates based on the average number of youths being served at various sites. With respect to staff, the problems of recruitment and hiring as well as job maintenance resulted in the need for an estimate of onboard staff as opposed to any fixed number obtained either at the initiation or termination of a program activity.

Initially, field activities of the evaluation effort were directed by Barbara Jones, a senior research associate of the consultant's organization who by training and experience was well qualified for such an effort. Barbara, raised in a white middle-class family, had completed undergraduate and graduate degrees in psychology and had spent several years working for the State of California Juvenile Delinquency Program. She designed a project to examine each of the 273 summer program activities in terms of:

1. fiscal allocations,
2. number of participants,
3. number of staff members,
4. types of activities, and
5. general observations.

Based on this initial examination, thirty-five program activities representative of all types of summer programs were selected for in-depth examination in different geographic areas. In addition, NPC chairmen, co-chairmen, youth representatives, and staff members from the Youth Program Unit were interviewed to determine interactions between various organizations, in particular, community youths' attitude toward the existing D.C. government structure.

To best collect information from the population of participating youths, the evaluation consultants decided to recruit, train, and utilize resident youths as interviewers. Accordingly, ten youths ranging in age from fifteen to twenty years were selected and trained as field informants. To carry out the evaluation, a storefront field office, central to the target areas, was rented and equipped. After orientation and training, the field informants conducted initial site visits at all 273 programs, while themselves participating in program activities to maximize their relationship with program participants.

The first successful applicant informers were mostly from middle-class families, college bound, dressed in coat and tie; 40 percent were white. With this team, Barbara found it difficult to initiate discussions with street youths and the virtually all-black staff. (The District of Columbia's population is 72 percent minority [mostly black] as is 97 percent of the public-school population.)

Barbara was replaced by Boris Frank, a black psychiatric social worker and lifelong D.C. resident. "I'm not going to advertise for no kids with ties—I can find who I need by taking my coat off and hanging out at the right street corners." Frank retained two of the original group of field informants and recruited eight street-smart youths—"thugs," said Frank. Data collection forms and questionnaires were prepared covering various types of program participants to be interviewed:

1. *The site validation form* was used to gather data at each of the 273 programs.
2. *The program participant form* was used to gather in-depth information at thirty-five centers from youths who participated in programs.
3. *The NYC staff form* was used to gather in-depth information from youths working as staff members at the thirty-five programs examined in depth.
4. *The program directors and senior aides form* was used to gather in-depth information from adult staff members.
5. *The non-participant form* was used to interview non-participating youths for comparison purposes.

In addition to these structured interviews, senior staff from the consultant's organization interviewed NPC chairmen, co-chairmen, and youth representatives, as well as members of the Youth Program Unit staff. (Such interviews were more sophisticated, sometimes structured, sometimes unstructured.)

An in-depth analysis was performed at thirty-five sample centers. The centers chosen reflected the distribution of activities in the total Summer Youth Programs by geographic location and by type of program activity. Sample centers were chosen in all four NPC districts covering sixteen NPC areas. In Table 9-4 a comparison of the distribution of sample centers with the total Summer Youth Program by activity type is presented. Interviews were held with program participants, Neighborhood Youth Corps (NYCs), senior aides, adult staff, and center directors to determine attitudes toward the program.

The data from program participants, NYCs, and senior staff members indicates a strong identification between NYCs and program participants, rather than between NYCs and senior staff. To verify this finding, a comparison of future employment aspirations of NYCs and program participants was performed as a means of obtaining an indication of similarities between these two populations. Program participant data was derived from site validation forms and NYC data from the NYC interview format. Responses were coded according to the nine *Dictionary of Occupational Titles* job classifications and indicate an extremely high degree of correlation between the future aspir-

Table 9-4
Comparison of Sample Programs and Total Programs
by Type of Summer Program

Type of Program Activity	Total Summer Youth Program		Sample Sites	
	Number	*Percent*	*Number*	*Percent*
TOTAL	270	100.0	35	100.0
Preschool	43	15.9	6	17.0
Youth center	81	30.0	9	25.0
Teen center	40	14.8	4	11.0
Multicenter	10	3.7	1	2.8
Block and street camps	37	13.7	3	8.5
Work skills: skills workshop	14	5.2	2	5.7
Job development/employment: Job centers, employment odd jobs	7	2.6	3	8.5
Beautification	4	1.5	1	2.8
Culture/science/art: Youth adv. center, art skills, arts and crafts	12	4.4	3	8.5
General recreation and athletics	4	1.5	1	2.8
Other	18	6.7	2	7.4

ations of youths in the NYC program and youths participating in summer activities. Staff members also frequently appeared to accept the NYCs as program participants rather than as younger and less experienced co-staff. Many cited NYCs as beneficiaries of the summer program activities along with program participants. Indeed, the NYCs frequently seemed to see themselves as program participants.

An attempt was made to identify attitudes on the part of the various population groups involved in summer activities, and to identify the impact of developing (or not developing) plans for summer programs. Table 9-5 presents these attitudes.

Interview Responses

Perhaps the most interesting dimension of understanding the 1968 Summer Youth Program was the response of program participants (and some nonparticipants) to specific questionnaire items. Seventy-four program participants of the 1968 Summer Youth Program were interviewed at the thirty-five sample sites. Participants were chosen at random and interviewed at their centers. The sample population included forty-five males and twenty-nine females from the ages of seven to eighteen—the greatest number being between fourteen and fifteen.

Table 9-5
Attitudes of Four Populations towards Purpose of 1968 Summer Youth Program*

Sample Population	Total		Positive		Neutral		Somewhat Negative		Negative		To Give Teens Work		Don't Know & No Response	
	#	%	#	%	#	%	#	%	#	%	#	%	#	%
Program participants	74	100	17	23	10	14	40	54	3	4			4	5
NYCs	59	100	13	23	8	14	29	46			6	11	3	5
Program directors and senior aides (adult staff)	49	100	25	51	22	45			1	2			1	2
Nonparticipant youths	43	100	11	24	13	31	13	31	6	14				

*Key: Positive: To benefit youths
Neutral: To give youths something to do and some place to go
Somewhat Negative: To keep youths off the streets (riot control)
Negative: Expresses hostility towards program, e.g., anti-black

"What do you think about the activities in the program?" (74)

Very good program		Program OK		Program poor		No response	
#	%	#	%	#	%	#	%
24	34	43	58	3	4	3	4

"What don't you like about this program?" (74)

Nothing disliked		Something disliked	
#	%	#	%
55	74.3	19	25.7

"What, in particular, don't you like about the program?"
(20; 2 responses by one youth)

Inappropriate		Insufficient or inadequate		Other		
Schedule	Staff	Facilities	Equipment	Activities	Participants	Other
2	4	2	2	4	6	2

"What activities would you like to see next year?" (74)

More of same		Something not offered now*		More jobs	
#	%	#	%	#	%
66	89	6	8	2	3

*Activities specified: horseback riding, fishing, golf.

"Have you learned from the program?" (74)

Learned something from program		Learned nothing		No response	
#	%	#	%	#	%
63	84	6	8	5	7

What was learned from the program?" (63)

Specific skill		Character improvement, e.g., get along with others, assume responsibility, etc.		Other		Not specified	
#	%	#	%	#	%	#	%
33	53	20		32	7	11	6	10

"Why are there summer programs?" (74)

Positive: to benefit youth		Neutral: give kids some place to go, something to do		Somewhat negative: kids off streets; riot control		Negative: hostile; to take advantage of people; anti-black		Don't know		N R	
#	%	#	%	#	%	#	%	#	%	#	%
17	23	10	14	40	54	3	4	2	3	2	3

"What problems have you had in administering the programs?" (49)

Problems	No problems
30	19

"Specify": (55, multiple responses)

Equipment	Facilities	Staff	Activities	Planning	Security
15	4	6	3	2	2

Comm. with NPC	Money and red tape	Counseling and orientation for NYCs	In-program discipline	Comm. involvement	Other
4	7	2	3	2	5

"Why is there a summer program?" (49)

Positive: benefit youth	Somewhat negative: keep youths off street	Negative: free baby-sitting	No response
25	22	1	1

In reference to goal orientation, a more revealing response was obtained which required the respondent to specify the goals of his or her particular program.

"Does your program have specific goals, and if so, what are they?" (49)

Yes	No	No response
46	3	0

Goals stated in *specific terms*: e.g., expose youths to various team sports; teach them graphic arts; teach children to do one thing for themselves

Goals stated in general *non-action oriented terms*: e.g., help children; keep youths off street

Over 70 percent of the respondents felt that the purpose of the program was to "keep us busy and out of the way for the summer"; 58 percent that the program was set up as a riot control measure. It should be noted that despite the youths' feeling that the program was not set up to benefit them directly, they were eager participants and felt they had benefited from their summer's experience. This response, then, by the youths may not reflect negative attitudes towards the program itself but may instead be directed to the youths' perception of the general purposes of the program.

In light of the fact that the NYCs were closest in age to the program participants, they usually communicated with them more successfully than any other staff members, and thus they were able to influence their perceptions substantially. Had the NYCs understood the purpose of the program more clearly, the participants might also have gained a greater understanding, enabling both groups to derive more benefit from the program.

Forty-nine senior staff members were chosen at random at the sample sites and interviewed. The sample population consisted of twenty-one males and twenty-eight females ranging in age from eighteen to forty-three. Of the forty-nine adult staff members, thirty-six were residents of the neighborhoods surrounding the centers.

Over half of the staff were able to enunciate program goals in such a way as to direct the course of program activities, but *none* of the staff interviewed could verbalize specific goals for the Summer Youth Program as a whole.

Seventy-one youths who did not participate in the Summer Youth Programs were selected at random from neighborhoods surrounding the thirty-five sample sites and interviewed. The sample nonparticipant youth population included fifty-three males and eighteen females. Ages of interviewees ranged from eight to nineteen and averaged 15.4 years. The average age of the group is similar to that of the program participants sample.

"Do you know about Summer Youth Programs?" (71)

Yes		No		Misinformation		No response
#	%	#	%	#	%	
43	61	20	28	8	11	0

"Do you know about Summer Youth Programs? If so, what do they provide?"
(43, multiple responses)

Recreation programs	Employment placement and training	Education and pre-school
40	5	4

Cultural enrichment	Art and home economic skills	Type of information not specified
4	5	2

"If known, why not interested?" (37)

Hostile: won't participate in anti-black or baby programs		Working, going to school, family responsibilities	
#	%	#	%
5	13.5	14	38

Has to find job or job training		Interested		Nothing there of interest	
#	%	#	%	#	%
10	27	1	2.7	7	19

"What program activities, jobs, etc., would you have participated in?" (71)

Activities available		Activities not available		Don't know	
#	%	#	%	#	%
49	70	5	7	4	5.7

Won't participate in whitey or baby programs		None; no time		No response	
#	%	#	%	#	%
4	5.7	6	6.7	3	3.3

Activities desired: 2-post office jobs, 2-"Pride," 1-Army

"Why are there Summer Youth Programs?" (43)

Positive: beneficial		Neutral: gives youths something to do and some place to go	
#	%	#	%
11	24	13	31

Somewhat negative: riot prevention, keep youths off streets		Negative: anti-black; take advantage of people	
#	%	#	%
13	31	6	14

Despite the fact that both participating and nonparticipating youths indicated that what they wanted was what was offered, hostility to the Summer Youth Program in general was evidenced. Many of the same youths who stated that the program activities offered what they wanted also felt that the Summer Youth Program was a *buy out,* a kind of riot control. Summer programs have long been sought after and provided in middle-class neighborhoods without the onus of riot control or copping-out. Clearly, the youth in D.C. wanted the same kinds of services. A frequent suggestion to alleviate this attitude was that the programs be extended to a year-round effort.

In October, 1968, Joe James conducted a review of the summer's activities after reading the consultant's final report. He was displeased. "OK my smart consultant, tell me what I should do next year!"

## PART FOUR

Managerial Challenges for the 1980s

The climate of the 1980s stresses two principal managerial challenges to state and local agencies. The first of these, productivity improvement, has a long history in public management. Productivity essentially means getting more while paying less: to obtain the same level of services with fewer funds expended, or a higher level of services for the same amount of funds. Productivity means increasing the effectiveness and efficiency of agencies through better management. It means remembering all of the "tricks" we've learned so far in this text, as well as a few others.

Taxpayer "revolts," dissatisfaction with government, a troubled economy, and the economic decline of certain cities and regions have brought a final, somewhat unique and often very difficult challenge to public managers: the management of "decline" and cutback management. Since World War II public managers have had very limited experience in this. It was certainly easier to manage agency expansion or even a "steady state." But cutback management is part of state and local administration in the 1980s; we will have to learn quickly.

These two challenges, productivity improvement and cutback management, are introduced in Part Four, the final section of this volume.

10

Productivity Improvement

PURPOSE

The purpose of this chapter is to examine modern approaches to promoting efficiency and effectiveness in the delivery of governmental services.

Reading:
  John S. Thomas, "So, Mr. Mayor, You Want to Improve Productivity..."

Cases:
  "Productivity and Safety in Solid Waste Collection — Feather Bedder I?"
  "Productivity in Palo Alto"

Instructions

Pre-Class Preparation

Be prepared to apply what you know from the first three parts of this book as well as John S. Thomas's "So, Mr. Mayor, You Want to Improve Productivity. . . ."

1. Read the case, "Productivity and Safety in Solid Waste Collection — Feather Bedder I?" Answer the questions below:
   a. Based on this case, how do you feel about the state of effective public management in Sonora?
   b. Productivity improvements often require improved technology. What problems may be associated with new technology in urban administration based on this case?
   c. How important is employee and employee union participation in productivity efforts?
   d. Was Sonora measuring productivity improvements adequately?

2. Read the case "Productivity in Palo Alto." Carefully evaluate the performance of Palo Alto's productivity program. If you were a key manager in your own municipality, what could be learned from Palo Alto which could be used (productively) in your city?

Procedure for Class Meeting

Discussion will involve cases and problems in implementing productivity programs.

For Additional Information

Perhaps the most useful, state-of-the-art review of productivity concepts, programs and potential is George J. Washnis, ed., *Productivity Improvement Handbook for State and Local Government* (New York: John Wiley, 1980). This was funded by the U. S. Department of Housing and Urban Development.

An especially useful bibliography on the subject is contained in:

Public Productivity Review, I (no. 4). *Public Productivity Review* is published quarterly by the Center for Productive Public Management, John Jay College, City University of New York, 445 W. 59th Street, New York, N.Y. 10019.

Other useful materials are:

Walter L. Balk, *Improving Government Productivity* (Beverly Hills, Cal.: Sage Publications/Administrative and Policy Studies Series, 1975). Paperback edition available.

Edgar G. Crane, Bernard F. Lentz, and Jay M. Shafritz, *State Government Productivity: The Environment for Improvement* (New York: Praeger, 1976).

Edward H. Downey and Walter L. Balk, *Employee Innovation and Government Productivity: A Study of Suggestion Systems in the Public Sector* (Washington: International Personnel Management Association, 1976).

The Guide to Management Improvement Projects in Local Government (formerly the *Jurisdictional Guide to Productivity Improvement Projects*). Published bi-monthly with an annual update by the International City Management Association, 1140 Connecticut Ave., N.W., Washington, D. C. 20036.

Frederick O'R. Hayes, *Productivity in Local Government* (Lexington, Mass.: D. C. Heath/Lexington Books, 1977). Excellent coverage of innovative jurisdictions.

Marc Holzer, ed., *Productivity in Public Organizations* (New York: Dunellen, 1975). Paperback edition available.

Improving Productivity in State and Local Government (New York: Committee for Economic Development, 1976). Paperback edition available.

Theodore Levitt, "Management and the 'Post-Industrial' Society," *Public Interest*, No. 44 (Summer 1976), pp. 69–103.

Public Administration Review, XXXII (Nov.–Dec. 1972), and XXXVIII (Jan.–Feb. 1978). Symposia on Productivity in Government.

John Ross and Jesse Burkhead, *Productivity in the Local Government Sector* (Lexington, Mass.: D.C. Heath/Lexington Books, 1974).

E. S. Savas, *The Organization and Efficiency of Solid Waste Collection* (Lexington, Mass.: D.C. Heath/Lexington Books, 1977).

Francis X. Tannian, *Productivity of City Services* (Newark, Del.: University of Delaware College of Urban Affairs and Public Policy, 1977).

Anthony R. Tomzinis, *Productivity, Efficiency, and Quality in Urban Transportation Systems* (Lexington, Mass.: D.C. Heath/Lexington Books, 1975).

Joan L. Wolfe and John F. Heaphy, eds., *Readings on Productivity in Policing* (Washington: Police Foundation, 1975). Paperback edition available.

Technological improvement is often a part of productivity programs. For a good overview of this, see:

The Struggle to Bring Technology to Cities (Washington: Urban Institute, 1971). Paperback edition available.

Robert K. Yin, Karen Heald, and Mary E. Vogel, *Tinkering with the System: Technological Innovations in State and Local Services* (Lexington, Mass.: D. C. Heath/Lexington Books, 1977).

One application of technology in urban administration relates to the use of the computer and management information systems. For an excellent brief overview, see:

Kenneth L. Kraemer and John Leslie King, *Computers, Power and Urban Management: What Every Local Executive Should Know* (Beverly Hills, Cal.: Sage Publications, Administrative and Policy Studies Series, 1976). Paperback edition available.

Another useful introductory treatment can be found in:

Bonita J. Campbell, *Understanding Information Systems: Foundations for Control* (Cambridge: Winthrop Publishers, 1977). Paperback edition available.

So, Mr. Mayor, You Want to Improve Productivity . . .

John S. Thomas

WHO'S IN CHARGE OF GOVERNMENT PRODUCTIVITY in your town, Mr. Mayor? You are, and if you don't believe it, you may turn out to be right—after the next election. The electorate may choose someone who promises to be more productive with their tax dollars.

Improving productivity means giving the taxpayers more services for their tax dollars, or giving them the same services for fewer tax dollars. It is the path between tax increases and service reductions. It is not easy to find, and it will not lie in exactly the same direction in every city. So we have written this *article* to help you find the path to greater productivity in your city.

Our emphasis is on organization and management. Without them, you leave productivity to chance — which will work against you nearly as often as for you — or to outside forces, such as traveling salesmen promoting new asphalt spreaders or computer remote-job-entry terminals. Without an organized analytical approach, neither you nor the people whose support you want can ever be sure that your city is getting its money's worth.

A Modest Proposal

We propose systematic analysis of every government function. Don't wait for technological revolutions to make the need for change obvious. Don't depend solely on the imagination of career employees looking for ways to solve problems they have found particularly vexing. Of all the ways to address the productivity issue, systematic analysis holds the greatest promise of speeding improvement on every front by bringing to the surface needed changes which have long gone unnoticed. And it is a means of achieving greater accountability from your managers.

There are functions in every city that have never been exposed to a methodical study, one that deals in depth with the management system, the information processing system, the operational system, and the performance of the employees. When was the last time your building inspection or sewer maintenance work practices were analyzed in detail? Is your water department staffed by more or fewer people than those in comparable cities? How well does the productivity of the city motor pool compare with that of local commercial garages?

Most public officials don't have the answers to these questions and dozens like them because they haven't thought about their operations in the context of productivity. And they haven't used analytical staff to find out how money is spent, how work is done, or what results are achieved. A well executed, comprehensive improvement program can demonstrably increase the quality and quantity of services and hold down costs, or, in short, raise productivity.

Sustaining an organized improvement program requires dedication to productivity as a priority concern of your administration, continuing attention and hard work on the part of your managerial organization and whatever analytical staff you assign to the program, and a considerable measure of cooperation from your employees and their representatives. But most of all, it requires your leadership and support.

Myths, Misconceptions, and Risks

As we proceed through this *article*, we will cite a number of opportunities and techniques for productivity improvement already proven successful in some cities. Don't hesitate to copy others' successes. Your electorate is as interested in results as in originality. But because not every example will be applicable to the unique characteristics of your city, we have tried to abstract some general principles you can apply to your situation. And this *article* tries to help you organize these principles into a productivity program. But before we get into the details, let's take note of a few of the myths, misconceptions, and risks traditionally associated with productivity improvement.

Myths One myth is that somehow productivity improvement is inherent in the American economic system and work ethic, so that there is no need to "program" improvement efforts. But recent events have badly shaken these assumptions and expectations. . . . This lagging productivity coupled with rising inflationary pressure has helped retard the growth of the GNP and weakened the international competitive posture of the United States.

Productivity has become a national concern, and we have come to see that it is not part of the Bill of Rights. Productivity gains are the direct result of the collective actions of government, industry, and workers. And productivity gains in the public sector contribute to the national welfare as much as gains in the private sector. As government services consume a larger and larger share of our resources, it becomes imperative that public officials focus on productivity improvement.

Another myth suggests that productivity is fine for manufacturing industries, whose activities are easily measured, but has little meaning for services. Just look at the wide variations in tons per man for solid waste collection from city to city, and you'll suspect that some are more productive in providing service than others. (See Figure 10-1.) In reality, there are too many examples of real productivity gains in a broad spectrum of government services to give credence to this myth.

Misconceptions Possibly the most prevalent misconception is that organized labor opposes any effort to improve productivity. Organized labor is understandably protective of the wages and benefits won for its members at the bargaining table. While there are occasional contractual provisions that may seem restrictive, such provisions usually involve legitimate concerns about job safety or unreasonable hardship or burdens on the employee. The leaders of public employee unions who oppose productivity *per se* are indeed a small minority. After all, increased productivity is rapidly becoming the key to wage increases without the unpopular measure of tax increases.

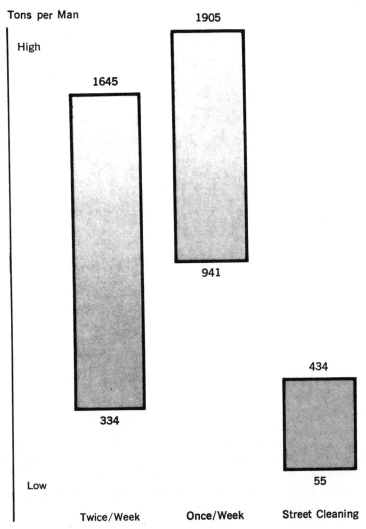

Figure 10-1
City to City Variations in Sanitation Productivity

Risks   There are some risks connected with a productivity program. There is a risk of breakdown in service if changes are not adequately planned or managed. Serious misunderstandings can arise in bargaining, but usually they can be avoided through careful preparation and effective communication. There is personal risk to you as mayor in terms of your credibility if you embark on a highly publicized program that ultimately yields little. On the other hand, the political risk of doing nothing about productivity is real if failure to act means deteriorating services or raising local taxes.

If your productivity program is successful, the rewards to you personally are whatever you are willing to make of them, but to the taxpayer the benefits are clear and unequivocal. Maximum productivity in municipal operations is not an option, it is an imperative. It reflects the right of every taxpayer to get every ounce of service from every dollar he provides.

Planning Your Productivity Program

Before embarking on your productivity program, you'll have to make some decisions about its scope, structure, and content. Few if any of these decisions will be irreversible, so avoid getting bogged down in endless planning sessions, debates about administration, organization, reporting mechanisms, philosophical concepts, and the like. Extensive planning isn't necessary, but consider the following:

- Scope of Your Program and Selecting Priorities
- Organizing Your Program
- Resource Requirements
- Involving Labor and Others
- Role of the Chief Executive

Scope of Your Program and Selecting Priorities

There are no broad management decisions you can take which will simultaneously increase productivity on all fronts. Whatever theoretical generalizations we may make, practical productivity gains are achieved in the delivery of particular goods and services, and different problems have different solutions. The computer that simplifies paper flow in tax collection will not clean the streets or inspect restaurant kitchens. Thus, while you eventually want your productivity program to embrace all city functions, you must begin with specific operations or specific problems.

Where do you start? Remember that poor productivity is often not a visible problem. Here are some criteria for conducting your search for a good starting point:

- Operations where large numbers of employees perform essentially repetitive tasks. Improvement of such operations is likely to yield large benefits.
- Functions continually faced with large backlogs of work. The backlogs themselves are symptomatic of problems to be solved.
- Operations where visible problems exist. Improvements will also be highly visible.
- Availability of new techniques or technology already proven practical elsewhere.

• Receptivity of the operation's managers to new ideas coupled with an ability to follow through.

Productivity pertains to both goods and services, and it pertains to both quantity and quality. More service and better service are both important objectives of your program. An increase in the number of tons of refuse collected per man-day represents a gain in productivity. So does eliminating missed collections or improving the cleanliness of your streets. Your search for a good starting point should include qualitative as well as quantitative improvements.

If at first you don't succeed, you've started in the wrong place. And you may not get to try, try again. Early failures make future efforts more difficult, if not impossible, so it is particularly important that your initial efforts succeed. And initial successes become valuable sales points in gaining the acceptance and support needed to expand your program. Thus, probability of success is perhaps the most important criterion in selecting your starting point.

Organizing Your Program

Your natural instinct may be to place the administrative responsibility for your productivity program in an existing staff organization such as budget, personnel, or labor relations. Resist that instinct. Don't delegate the responsibility for productivity, certainly not at the beginning of your program.

Productivity improvement is one of the more sensitive and difficult new programs you're likely to attempt. The very term "productivity improvement" implies criticism of present methods. So the program will require all the persuasive powers you can muster. You must show your personal determination to see the program through until others have become dedicated enough to maintain the momentum.

Keep the administration of the productivity program as close to you as possible for the first year or two and you'll increase the likelihood of success. Assign it to your deputy or assistant, or borrow the best staff assistant you can find in your government to work directly under you. His key duties will include documenting and promulgating decisions; determining reporting requirements and seeing that they are met; arranging meetings; advising you when policy decisions are necessary; and generally monitoring all activities to see that the program is moving on schedule.

Fixing administrative responsibility in a key official directly responsible to you is the first organizational step. The second is lining up your analytical talent. The most successful productivity improvements usually result from assigning competent analysts to the program on a fulltime basis.

Every government operation should at some time be subjected to in-depth studies using the systematic techniques commonly employed by industrial engineers, systems analysts, and accountants, techniques such as work-load balancing, time study, flow-charting, and systems design.

Labor-intensive operations are particularly susceptible to industrial engineering analysis. This approach frequently leads to improved planning, scheduling, and delivery of services. Information processing operations offer the greatest opportunities for systems analysis and application of computer technology. Typical targets for operations research techniques are functions that involve complex cause and effect relationships that are not clearly understood. Examples would be the impact of police deployment patterns on crime rates or the impact of housing regulations on housing availability.

In addition to technical analytical skills, your senior analysts should possess leadership and negotiating qualities. They must demonstrate an ability to apply their technical skills to the practical problems confronting your line managers, and they must gain the confidence and respect of the line organization. The analyst whose opinion on garbage collection will be listened to is the analyst who has gone out on a garbage truck. Your analysts should serve as catalysts to stimulate serious thought and discussion within the operating organizations about ways to improve service.

As you begin to organize your program, you will need to decide whether these analysts should be part of a central organization (an Office of Productivity?) providing assistance to operating departments, or whether they should be decentralized, reporting directly to their respective department heads. An important criterion in this decision is the level of skill and experience of the analytical people. There is a severe shortage of senior analysts who can achieve success without strong organizational support. And there is considerable risk in placing junior analysts in operating departments where they may become discouraged by nonreceptive managers.

Where you can find a good match between a self-sufficient analyst and a receptive line manager, by all means decentralize and hold your department heads responsible for getting results. Otherwise, you should create a central analytical staff and give it your personal attention and support, particularly during its first year.

Resource Requirements

The skilled analysts of whom we have been speaking are the primary resource needed for your productivity program. Whether they must be added or reassigned depends upon whether such people are now working in your city government. But it is essential to assign analytical talent specifically to the productivity program.

What kind of people and skills are we talking about? We have referred to some of the skills, those of industrial engineers, systems analysts, accountants. People with training in business administration should be considered. But in the absence of any specialized training, you should be looking for people with disciplined and logical minds, capable of working a problem through to its conclusion, and people with creative imaginations who can ask penetrating questions and break free of traditional ways of viewing problems. Ideally, you will be able to form an analytical team combining many of these capacities.

Creating your own analytical staff will enable you to provide your line organizations with technical assistance when they need it. Recognize that any organization has difficulty designing, approving, and implementing changes while still discharging its regular duties. Don't ask your department managers to set improvement goals without providing them with the resources necessary to meet their goals; otherwise, their failures will outnumber their successes.

Finding new and better ways of delivering services requires a great deal of effort and attention. New ideas must be sought out, carefully tested, and evaluated, and proposed methods and procedures must be worked out in precise detail. When changes are actually made, operations must be closely monitored to determine whether the benefits expected are in fact realized. Furthermore, modifications are often necessary to accommodate unforeseen problems. All of this requires a considerable amount of time of many people in the organization and must compete with a host of other tasks necessary in managing day-to-day operations. The assistance of the special analysts can keep the productivity improvement changes from being submerged by the very real concerns of the daily routine.

How many analysts are we talking about? Obviously, creation of an analytical staff more costly than anticipated savings is the very antithesis of productivity improvement. But we are not really talking about very many people. A couple of rules of thumb: Plan for one or two analysts for each improvement project for a period of three to six months; aim for an analytical staff capability of at least five analysts for every 1,000 employees. Manufacturing industries, whose operations are often less complex than government's, spend as much as one percent of sales on this type of analytical capability.

Productivity improvement should not be viewed as a crash program, or as a one-time effort, or as the exclusive responsibility of a specialized office or department. Rather, it is a continuing priority responsibility of all departments to find more efficient ways to deliver services.

You and your analytical staff should be evangelists of productivity in your government, convincing everyone in every department that productivity is his responsibility. And the analytical staff is your special resource to help everyone meet this responsibility.

While we are placing great emphasis on the development of analytical capacity, it is important to recognize that the knowledge of the employee is an under-utilized resource for productivity improvement. He knows the details of his operation and can often suggest practical changes to improve productivity. Or he can create an illusion of increased productivity without substantial change.

Involving Labor and Others

If you have already been thinking about a productivity program, you should also have been discussing it with your staff, council members, and employee representatives. If not, start today. Don't rely entirely on your own organization; ask for help from local business leaders, universities, and public interest groups. And talk to your union leaders to elicit ideas, to gain their understanding and then their cooperation. They can be particularly helpful in suggesting ideas and approaches that will help gain employee acceptance. Initial reactions are often somewhat negative, but don't become discouraged. These early discussions allow others to become participants in the program as their responses are taken into consideration during the program's formative stages.

Role of the Chief Executive

Don't expect anyone to take the initiative for you. Most line managers haven't been trained to search aggressively for new methods or to make use of outside technical or business management skills to stimulate ideas. More typically they assume a passive role, evaluating whatever proposals happen to come their way. In this kind of environment, you must supply the enthusiasm and the leadership until those below you have been converted.

Prepare yourself. Be sure that you understand the productivity concept well enough to explain it persuasively. Get a few examples worked out clearly in your mind: Look at successful new ideas in other cities, or, for that matter, successful old ideas. You must believe — before you can expect any of your staff to believe — that productivity can be increased in all departments of your government.

Time after time, your determination is going to be tested by your own staff. You must be able to respond effectively and convincingly to any department head or supervisor who says: "We're always looking for improvements, but meanwhile we're doing the best we can." Or perhaps: "Sure we have a big backlog, but what do you expect after last year's budget cuts?" Or: "Everybody knows that we have no control over the amount of work that comes in." Or: "Yeah, I know. Isn't that what we used to call [insert name of city's last management improvement program]?"

Recognize such answers as defensive postures rather than reasoned positions, and press on for facts, real problem identification, and real improvement. Accept the *status quo* only if it is demonstrably the best way, instead of the way it's always been.

One of your major tasks will be to overcome your people's natural instinct to procrastinate, especially their desire to set aside productivity improvement because it is not critical to keeping the governmental machinery churning daily. Productivity requires a longer range perspective than the ordinary tasks. Most productivity efforts take months of persistent effort before they pay off, and thus they are at a disadvantage in competing for staff attention with the daily crises of fires, floods, crimes, zoning, consumer complaints, and auditor reports.

How can you keep a productivity program moving in this environment? Insist on specific commitments from your department heads. Spell out and commit activities, time schedules, responsibilities. Always obtain specific agreements at the end of each meeting as to the next steps: what is to be done, who is to do it, and when results should be ready for review. Agree on the dates for follow-up meetings and hold those meetings. Commitments may not always be met, but don't accept postponements without renewed commitments.

And keep talking. First you'll convince yourself, and then you'll convince everyone around you, that you're really serious about productivity, and that productivity is worth being serious about.

In sum, be the executive: prepare yourself; manage your program; think, talk, and act productivity.

Implementing the Program

All too often, bureaucracy seems to be long on planning and programming but short on execution. Whatever your plans and organization, you have no productivity program unless it has actual impact on the delivery of services or the cost of those services. Translate your plans into action by concentrating efforts in the following major areas:

- Systematic Analysis
- Adopting Improved Technology
- Matching Resources with Demands for Services
- Scheduling of Work
- Evaluating Proposals

Systematic Analysis

Serendipity is the name of a rock group, not of a management system. There is no doubt that you or some of your staff will occasionally discover some ways to improve things that you weren't looking for. But luck comes in two kinds, good and bad, and some of your unplanned gains are going to be offset by unplanned losses. So don't rely on random circumstances to feed your productivity program. Plan your search for productivity improvement opportunities in a systematic fashion.

The following tasks are involved in systematic analysis:

- Define the objective
- Obtain the facts, identify all alternatives
- Estimate costs and benefits of each alternative
- Select the best alternative, design a model
- Specify criteria for measuring progress

Executing all these tasks may be more than is required for many of your operations, and we won't treat all of them in detail here. But the list contains some points we would like to highlight.

Clear statement of operational objectives is indispensable to good management. The definition should be realistic, translatable into specific work products, attainable with resources available, and as quantifiable as the nature of the work allows. A welfare department's objectives would include timely payment to all eligible recipients. A police department can set priorities for response times. A health department can set both qualitative and quantitative objectives for its inspection service.

Failure to define objectives clearly causes a myriad of problems. In one sense, the point seems obvious: How can a manager proceed towards an objective when he doesn't know what it is? But the problem is not usually that no objective is stated, but that the stated objective is not managerially useful. It may provide no fixed base for planning, such as the frequently heard "maximum service at minimum cost." It may not be translatable into terms of work products. If a prosecutor is to achieve "justice," should he work for more or fewer prosecutions, convictions, guilty pleas, cases closed? Or the objective may not be attainable, such as "elimination of all crime in the city," and therefore not a realistic guide for managerial decisions.

If analysis of all alternative means of attaining an objective seems to be too ambitious, start with the one you can see, that is, the way things are being done now. Have your analysts gather factual data by observing and recording what a typical employee does during each work shift, how he performs each task, and how long each task requires. Frequently used techniques for this are the time-and-motion study, work sampling, and predetermined methods/time standards. The results help identify and measure losses in productivity and their probable causes. It is this type of first-hand observation that most often will indicate the nature of needed improvements. Figure 10-2 sets forth some of the typical cause and effect relationships uncovered by these approaches (see page 418).

If there is a great deal of idle time, for instance, then scheduling may need to be improved, or perhaps the crew size is too large for the operation. If each employee spends an hour or more each day filling out reports, the information requirements may be too extensive or complex. The possibilities are almost unlimited, but the point is that a thorough study of the present use of manpower will usually pinpoint the problems to be given priority attention and often suggest the nature of the solution as well.

Manpower utilization studies are primarily concerned with the job content and performance of each employee. They can be building blocks in broader systems analyses, which look more at the interrelationships between functions in the operating system. Systems analysis will be concerned with the flow of information, the sequence of activities, the interrelationships of activities and their effect on the whole system. Systems analysis is usually characterized by flow diagrams that trace information flow and the sequence of activities from start to finish. These diagrams are one example of how a model of an operating system can be developed. And they aid in identifying opportunities to simplify record keeping, expand the use of communications and data processing, reduce response times, eliminate duplication.

These analytical approaches to productivity enable you to deal with facts rather than opinions, and with reasons, not excuses. After you obtain solid, accurate facts, your key to creating improvements is systematic questioning. Nothing should be taken for granted. Each activity should be subjected to the penetrating questions such as "Why is it done, what does it accomplish, how could it be done easier?" Ideally, the end-product of every analytical study is an operating system that:

- Utilizes the most cost-effective technology available
- Applies the lowest cost mix of skills required to perform the work
- Avoids or minimizes non-productive time of each employee

Adopting Improved Technology

The electorate that put you in office did not expect you to invent a trash compactor, design a snow plow, or build a computer. But it does expect you to see that your city is as technologically up to date as its resources will allow, and that means that you have a continuing obliga-

Figure 10-2
Common Problems of Low Productivity and Indicated Corrective Actions

Problem	Possible Corrective Action	Illustrative Examples
Sufficient work not available or workloads unbalanced	Reallocate manpower	Housing complaint bureau schedules revised and temporary help employed during peak winter season.
	Change work schedules	Mechanics rescheduled to second shift when equipment is not in use.
	Reduce crew size	Collection crew size reduced from 4 to 3 men.
Lack of equipment or materials	Improve inventory control system	Inventory reorder points revised to reduce stock-out occurrences.
	Improve distribution system	Asphalt deliveries expedited to eliminate paving crew delays.
	Improve equipment maintenance	Preventive maintenance program instituted.
	Reevaluate equipment requirements	Obsolete collection trucks replaced.
Self-imposed idle time or slow work pace	Train supervisors	Road maintenance foremen trained in work scheduling, dispatching, and quality-control techniques.
	Use performance standards	"Flat rate" manual standards adopted to measure auto mechanics' performance.
	Schedule more work	Park maintenance crews mobilized and work scheduling system installed.
Too much time spent on non-productive activities	Reduce excessive travel time	Permit expiration dates changed to reduce travel time of health inspectors.
	Reevaluate job description and task assignments	Building inspectors trained to handle multiple inspections.
Excessive manual effort required	Mechanize repetitive tasks	Automatic change and toll collection machines installed and toll collector staffing reduced.
Response or processing time too slow	Combine tasks or functions	Voucher processing and account posting combined to speed vendor payments.
	Automate process	Computerized birth record storage and retrieval system installed.
	Improve dispatching procedures	Fire alarm patterns analyzed and equipment response policies revised.
	Revise deployment practices	Police patrol zones redefined to improve response time.
	Adopt project management techniques	Project control system installed to reduce construction cycle.

tion to see that your city departments are adopting whatever technology will improve their productivity.

Some technological changes simply substitute machines for men or one machine for another. The typewriter replaced the pen, and the electric typewriter replaced the manual typewriter, but all are forms of enabling a person to place words on paper. Other forms of technological improvement supplant entire processes. Airplanes have almost completely replaced trains in the transportation of passengers over long distance. It is hard for the layman to predict what form of technological change is going to take place next.

Whether or not you can develop new technology, you can do several things to accelerate the rate of adoption of known techniques and products to upgrade your own productivity.

First, be sure that your department heads and their technical staffs are continually informed about new developments and applications. You have a right to expect career professional managers to be knowledgeable of the technology in their field. They should subscribe to appropriate trade journals and maintain communications with manufacturers and suppliers to be sure that these sources understand your particular needs.

Your staff should also actively search out other jurisdictions where new techniques are being tried. Known disparities in the costs of providing the same services in different communities suggest that there should be a greater exchange of information. Do you need park benches less vulnerable to vandalism? Can you mechanize bulk refuse collection? Are you plagued with false alarms? Does it take too long to dispatch a patrol car? These questions have already resulted in technological improvements in some jurisdictions.

Matching Resources with Demands for Services

Resource allocations often follow patterns established years ago though demand characteristics have changed over time. As a result, employees sometimes lack work and other times cannot cope with massive backlogs. A typical example is the tax accountant, whose workload suddenly multiplies in the first quarter of each year.

Do your police and fire deployment policies match periods of high crime and fire incidence? Are mechanics available when equipment is not in use? Are vacations scheduled during periods when demands are low? Every department has unique demand characteristics that should be reexamined periodically, and manpower deployments should be modified to match the demands.

On the other hand, there are many government functions whose demands can be controlled or substantially influenced by the administration. In these situations it may be easier to smooth the flow of work than to establish abnormal work schedules. Activities keyed to expiration or renewal dates, such as permits and inspections, are of this type. Not only can these dates be rearranged to smooth the work flow, but they can also be organized according to geographical location to improve the efficiency of the work force well beyond what random demand patterns allow.

Another aspect of the resource question is the crew size required to perform activities where two or more people are assigned to work as a team, such as two-man patrol cars, inspection teams, or highway repair crews. Such groups are often overstaffed to accommodate absenteeism, unforeseen problems, or perhaps habits carried over from times when more manual effort was required. All such group activities should be reexamined, but don't rely on opinions to determine proper crew sizes. The contribution of each crew member and the consequences of a reduction can be determined factually and accurately through careful analysis.

Scheduling of Work

How often have you heard, or perhaps yourself said, that the big problem in government operations is the quality of first line supervision? Time and again this group has incurred the brunt of criticism regarding the poor quality of work and low efficiency of government employees. Is this criticism valid, and if so, what can be done about it? This question bears careful consideration because it gets at the very heart of the day-to-day productivity of most public employees.

Let's consider the perspective of the typical supervisor. Chances are that he is conducting himself in a manner very similar to the way he was supervised by his predecessor. Has anyone assisted him in developing a systematic way to schedule work so that it can be performed efficiently, or to develop performance standards so that he knows how much work his employees should do each day? Or is he expected to be his own industrial engineer and systems analyst?

The key point is that in contrast to industry, government expects too much of its first line supervisors and doesn't reward them for doing what it expects. The absence of systematic work planning and scheduling is prevalent throughout government organizations. It is perhaps the greatest opportunity for productivity improvement. The very existence of a carefully prepared work schedule is the personification of effective management, for it defines what is to be done, by whom, and how much work is expected. Consequently, your productivity program will fall far short of its potential unless it aims at designing systems to organize, schedule, and dispatch work routinely and in a manner that will utilize the available resources most effectively.

Evaluating Proposals

Often you will be called upon to arbitrate between those who recommend improvements and others who resist them. A lot of time and effort will be wasted if your organization is unable to move beyond this point.

How can you gauge whether a thorough study has been performed and sound recommendations presented? The following line of questioning will help you determine the depth of the analysis and the appropriateness of the proposals.

- Does the analysis show a clear understanding of the purposes of the operation under study? Do the people in the operation share this understanding?
- Does the study show what percentage of time highly skilled personnel devote to clerical or other lesser skilled tasks?
- Has the study team compared the present performance level of the employees with what should normally be achieved? If it is low, what is proposed to improve it?
- Is the study team knowledgeable about the latest technology and have they evaluated its applicability?
- Has a profile of the demands for services been constructed and matched with the deployment of resources?

If you and your analysts are asking enough of the right kind of questions, you are going to find that path to productivity improvement.

Managing Projects

While we can state a general theoretical definition of productivity — the relationship between resources used and results achieved — and can make general recommendations on how to organize a productivity program, a generalized management approach will not in itself achieve the productivity improvements you are after. Practical implementation of productivity concepts will require quite different steps in different governmental activities. Trash collection must deal with the number of residences and businesses to be served; data processing must concern itself with data collection instruments and report requirements; a motor pool must keep vehicles in service. Each activity presents its own definitional and analytical problems.

To make sure each project has undergone a thorough analysis, and to keep track of your productivity program on all fronts, you and your productivity program manager should adopt a project management approach. It has several key elements:

- Project Coordinators
- Work Plans
- Status Reports
- Management Response to Problems
- Evaluation

Project Coordinators

For each productivity improvement project, assign a project coordinator. His duties will be to see that project work plans are prepared; to keep informed as to progress made and problems encountered; to see that the appropriate line managers are also kept informed and to respond promptly when problems need to be solved or decisions have to be made.

Generally, these coordination duties can be handled on a part-time basis, or conversely, several projects can be handled by one full-time coordinator. Project coordinators should be responsible to your productivity program manager.

Work Plans

Insist on having a work plan prepared for each project, for without it you will have no effective means of getting specific commitments and of monitoring progress. Each work plan should contain the following:

- Statement of objectives
- Scope of project
- Description of the tasks to be performed
- Identification of the individuals (by name) who will be responsible for completing each task
- Completion date of each task

These work plans need not be lengthy; rather they should be concise and to the point. Aside from the obvious benefit of enabling you to track progress and measure performance, the written work plan yields other advantages.

Writing the work plan increases the likelihood that it will be carefully thought out. "Writing maketh the exact man." Careful definition of the scope and objectives of the plan should make it more realistic and help avoid misunderstandings.

Insist that the plan state what specific results are to be achieved, and see that they are stated as quantitatively as the nature of the work allows. Quantitative outputs are very important to evaluation, to which we shall return in a moment. And they clarify managerial responsibilities, continually focusing attention on the project's main objective.

Status Reports

Periodical status reports should reflect the status of both the overall project and the specific tasks within it. Is the project on schedule? Are the tasks being completed on time? If not, why not? Is there some defect in the plan? Are the resources adequate? Are the individuals failing to perform their tasks?

Be sure the status reports are prepared and distributed regularly to interested parties at all levels of the organization. Knowing that reports pinpointing responsibility will be circulated is an added incentive for meeting schedules.

The information from the individual project status reports can be summarized to enable you to stay on top of all the productivity projects with a minimum of effort. Monthly summaries will be sufficient. They should be prepared by all department heads and addressed to you. Your productivity program manager should provide a standard format so that reports from all departments can be readily reviewed.

An aggressive productivity program will flush many difficult problems to the surface, and when your reporting system brings them to your attention, you should discuss and resolve them with the responsible program managers. If your reporting system is not identifying problems, then you should be concerned that your productivity program is not getting the results you want.

Management Response to Problems

You will have demonstrated your leadership by establishing the productivity program in the first place. You must continue to show your leadership and your commitment to productivity by resolving problems as they arise in your productivity projects. In addition, stir things up each month by selecting one or two projects that are behind schedule and demanding to know exactly what is being done about them. If necessary, bring all the participants together and debate the issues until a specific decision is reached and specific action agreed upon.

Evaluation

Project status reports tell you whether or not projects are being carried out. But you still need to know whether the project is any good. To make that judgment, you need data on the specific results being achieved.

As noted earlier, the place to start worrying about this problem is the project plan. The plan should identify quantitative output units that will best measure progress toward the project's objectives. For example, if your police department has a project to relieve uniformed patrolmen of routine clerical assignments that confine them to the precinct house, count the number of patrolmen or man-hours per week reassigned to patrol duty. If the health department aims to reduce the time to fill requests for birth certificates, then average processing time would be an appropriate unit of measure.

Properly chosen output measures are very valuable management tools. They enable you to establish project targets and to monitor progress towards them. They also give you a concrete way to determine whether the project improvements are up to your expectations.

Evaluative data can be reported concisely using a format such as that shown in Figure 10-3. Quarterly evaluative reports should be sufficient, although you may prefer to see them each month.

PRODUCTIVITY PROGRAM PROGRESS REPORT

AGENCY ______

PROGRAM/FUNCTION	UNIT OF MEASURE	FY 1972–1973	FY 1973–1974 TARGET			FIRST QUARTER			SECOND QUARTER			THIRD QUARTER			FOURTH QUARTER			REMARKS
						JULY	AUG	SEPT	OCT	NOV	DEC	JAN	FEB	MAR	APR	MAY	JUNE	
				MONTHLY	TARGET													
					ACTUAL													
					% OF TARGET													
				YEAR TO DATE	TARGET													
					ACTUAL													
					% OF TARGET													
				MONTHLY	TARGET													
					ACTUAL													
					% OF TARGET													
				YEAR TO DATE	TARGET													
					ACTUAL													
					% OF TARGET													
				MONTHLY	TARGET													
					ACTUAL													
					% OF TARGET													
				YEAR TO DATE	TARGET													
					ACTUAL													
					% OF TARGET													
				MONTHLY	TARGET													
					ACTUAL													
					% OF TARGET													
				YEAR TO DATE	TARGET													
					ACTUAL													
					% OF TARGET													

PAGE ___ OF ___

Figure 10-3
Productivity Program Progress Report

Labor Relations

From all that we have said so far, you can see that productivity improvement must affect and involve the employee. Therefore, it is inevitable that the issue of productivity will thread its way into your relationship with labor and eventually into the collective bargaining process.

Because of the weight given to precedents in labor relations, the initial practices with respect to what is bargainable, how the bargaining is conducted, and how disputes will be settled can have longstanding consequences. You should be quite conscious of these potential consequences as you begin your productivity program, and you should be particularly concerned about maintaining good channels of communication between management and labor. The key issues to consider fall into the following categories:

- Job security
- Job satisfaction
- Collective bargaining
- Wage incentives

Like the business executive, you are responsible for effective use of financial resources. But, as a public official, you are also obligated to consider the social consequences of your employment and personnel practices. While your productivity program addresses your responsibility as custodian of public funds, you should also be sensitive to a number of serious employee concerns, the foremost of which is job security.

Job Security

Will your employees believe that a productivity improvement program threatens their job security? They certainly will, because productivity improvement often means reallocation or reduction of resources, and manpower is your major resource.

Historically, manpower dislocations have resulted from technological innovations and other productivity advances. For instance, expanding use of computers has increased the need for data processing skills and reduced the need for manual and clerical skills. And in trash collection, larger equipment and automated systems have reduced the number of sanitation workers needed. Employees are aware of this process, particularly as it has taken place in their own kind of work, and their perception of it is likely to differ from yours.

Consider this example. Suppose that your park department is now understaffed, as many park departments are. Mechanized litter cleanup equipment or a more efficient manpower deployment may free resources which you can shift to park maintenance functions that are presently neglected. But what happens if you shift these newfound resources to some altogether different city activity? What to you is a reallocation of resources then becomes, to the employees directly affected, a reduction in force.

Keep in mind that a single layoff can have devastating personal consequences for the individual involved and can undermine the morale of the remaining workers. Fear of losing jobs can be the dominant force that motivates employees to resist improvement efforts. Unfortunately, the mere mention of the word productivity is often sufficient to stir thoughts of budget cuts and layoffs.

The goal of your program is to increase productivity, not to reduce the work force. And you cannot tell at the outset exactly what course of action will increase productivity in any given case. The solution may be redesign of work methods or reassignment of tasks. It may be change in the flow or sequence of the work. Or it may be to add resources where a unit has not been able to keep pace with increasing demands.

When overstaffing does turn out to be the problem, there are alternatives to layoffs: employees should be retrained and reassigned to other programs within the scope of their interests and capabilities; and where staff reductions are necessary, they can often be made through normal attrition. It is useful to remember in this context that many productivity improvements have been necessitated by the impossibility of recruiting people to perform additional tasks.

Actual experience in local government indicates that productivity improvements rarely result in layoffs because the alternatives just discussed usually suffice. To the extent that you make use of them, you can mitigate your employees' fears and gain their cooperation.

Admittedly, productivity poses difficult labor relations problems. New approaches and new solutions are needed, and you and your peers are going to have to find them. You may need to reappraise your civil service regulations, and devote more time and money to training and development programs that will broaden employee skills and enhance their economic value. You may also need to go beyond the annual budget cycle in planning manpower requirements. In the long run, better planning of staffing levels, job skills, and educational requirements can help alleviate these difficulties. Your productivity program can be immensely helpful in determining the real manpower needs of each department.

The responsibility for employee welfare doesn't fall entirely on your shoulders, though. Leaders of public employee unions have an equal share of responsibility in this matter. They can be particularly helpful in removing some of the constraints imposed by narrowly prescribed seniority rules. Retraining and reassignment concepts are of little practical use where employees lose all of their seniority when moved from one department to another or one bargaining unit to another.

Job Satisfaction

The employee becomes self-confident when he knows that he can routinely meet the requirements of his job. Improving productivity means change, and change arouses feelings of insecurity and fears of the unknown. Be sure to involve as many employees as possible in discussions about new ideas or new methods before they are implemented, and reassure them that they will be able to acclimate to a different way of working. And make sure all of the employees receive adequate instruction, and formal training if necessary, in their new tasks.

Productivity can be beneficial to the employee in several ways. The most important is that it is the measure of the worth of his services to the public. Productivity gains are gains in his value and grounds for increases in compensation. Furthermore, greater productivity should result in greater ease, safety, and efficiency in the performance of the job, and these are important elements of job satisfaction. Of course, the greatest element of job satisfaction is the feeling that the job is worth doing, and any job worth doing is worth doing better.

Collective Bargaining

Collective bargaining of wages, employee benefits, and working conditions is a complex phenomenon that is as dependent on local circumstances as it is on general economic conditions, and productivity improvement will be but one of many issues to be considered. Nevertheless, the productivity program can provide you the information you need about how work is actually performed and how you want to modify it. Wherever work schedules, deployment patterns, and other work rules are constraints to greater efficiency or work quality, you will be better prepared to negotiate these issues. Whether or not proposed changes need to be negotiated, always discuss them with employee representatives before you implement them. And be willing to accept suggestions that don't adversely affect your primary objectives.

From organized labor's point of view, productivity represents an opportunity for employees to share the economic benefits of greater productivity. And they will also expect a voice in how change takes place.

You represent the public interest in collective bargaining, and you should continually strive for recognition by labor of their public responsibility to cooperate in productivity improvement efforts. Find common grounds where both management and labor share similar objectives and your program should move forward without major confrontation.

Recognize, however, that collective bargaining alone will not make your organization more productive. In the final analysis management must still define the work to be done, and how, when, and by whom, it is to be done. It is still your responsibility to effectively manage all of the resources at your disposal — capital, labor, materials, supplies, and services. And you cannot bargain away that responsibility; the public holds you accountable for the results.

Wage Incentives

Productivity is often linked to employee motivation, and wage incentives have long been used in industry to motivate employees to higher performance. The subject will almost certainly arise during the course of your productivity program. But proceed with caution.

There are many pitfalls in using public funds for incentive pay purposes. Can the integrity of an incentive plan be maintained over the long haul as policies change and technology advances? Will the data upon which payments are based be recorded or verified by participants or by nonparticipants? Can quality be controlled where earnings are based solely on the quantity of work done? And what will be the consequences as inequities arise between incentive and nonincentive jobs? These are difficult questions, indeed, and there is little precedent to guide you.

The National Commission on Productivity and Work Quality has recently reported on several approaches being tried in State and local governments around the country.[1] These haven't yet stood the test of time. So assign a member of your staff to search out the various approaches being tried; to identify the problems encountered; and to determine what benefits are being achieved.

Incentives can increase employees' receptivity to change, and they can motivate employees to be more effective in executing the tasks that are assigned to them by their supervisors. On the other hand, you cannot depend on individual workers to develop new technology, coordinate delivery of services involving many different jobs, or determine how and when each task should be performed. In short, there are many techniques to increase productivity, and a wage incentive program is but one.

Wage incentives should only be considered after work methods and practices have been carefully analyzed and the best practical methods of operation developed and installed. Methods improvements should come first. So don't wait to decide about wage incentives before you begin your productivity program.

Producing for the Public

Governmental productivity is inescapably a political responsibility. After all, what we are discussing here is how public officials spend public funds to deliver public goods and services—the most fundamental purposes and activities of government.

But productivity as such is not a salient political issue to most people, and it won't be unless basic services fail or become too expensive. Nevertheless, public confidence in the capabilities of government to perform its functions is not as strong as it should be. The citizen is aware that government is the fastest growing sector of the economy, but he is not convinced that benefits are growing as fast as outlays. A survey for the National Commission on Productivity and Work Quality shows that public opinion rates government workers as far less productive than many other groups of workers in the economy (see Figure 10-4). Improving productivity can be a means of improving confidence in your government. How do you get public interest in and support for productivity in the absence of a crisis?

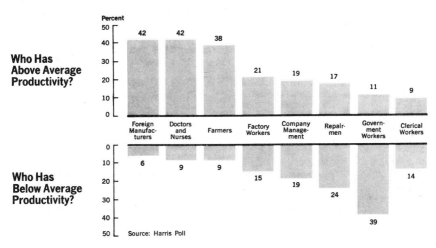

Figure 10-4
Public Opinion Regarding Relative Productivity of Various Groups of Workers

Obviously, the public has to know about your program before it can support it. And it has to see some tangible results before it can get very excited. This suggests a careful laying of the foundations for public support. Until your program has produced some demonstrable benefits, limit your public statements to comments about the need for improving productivity and your intentions to do whatever is necessary to achieve it. Show your understanding of the significance of the concept. But don't oversell a program before it has any real substance.

When you begin your productivity program, invite your local reporters to a background briefing, but again, don't oversell. Your objective at this point is to give them a basis for understanding how you intend to proceed and what you hope to achieve, telling them in effect how you want to have your administration evaluated.

Making specific plans and subsequent evaluation reports public entails some risk, but planning, evaluation, and problem solution are creditable enterprises and the public should be aware of them. Also, contrast the risks of candor to the risks of remaining silent about recognizable problems. You can also use the visibility of the program as additional motivation for the employees involved. Publicizing specific data on performance, provided it is reliable and identifies problems as well as achievements, will enhance the credibility of the program.

Favorable results, of course, are by far the best marketing device. Document and publicize specific, tangible examples of productivity gains. Give credit to those who have achieved the gains. Employee awards — promotions, raises, commendations, certificates of achievement — are an excellent means of drawing attention to productivity improvement while simultaneously recognizing outstanding work.

Arrange public demonstrations of technological improvements such as new fire fighting equipment, communications systems, or crime prevention techniques. Make use of every opportunity for public education. Let the public know how its cooperation can help cut costs or improve services. And you and your staff should include comments on the program whenever you address local public interest groups.

Your basic message is always the same. Your government is serious about managing the public resources efficiently. Productivity improvement shows your dedication to giving the public the most for its money.

NOTE

1. *Managing Human Resources in Local Government: A Survey of Employee Incentives,* National Commission on Productivity, October, 1973.

Productivity and Safety in Solid Waste Collection—Feather Bedder I?

Willard T. Price

THERE HAS BEEN A GROWING AND WIDESPREAD ATTENTION to productivity questions in the management of public sector functions. The City of Sonora is interested in improved productivity in a highly labor-intensive activity such as solid waste collection, where their goal is better cost-effectiveness performance and, hopefully, a reduced or stable cost of service for its citizens.

A breakthrough in this function is likely to result from mechanization of collection services with the concomitant reduction of labor force for each collection route. Sonora is located within a metropolitan area where other smaller communities have been national innovators in mechanization and who have been arguing that improvements in productivity have resulted. Their data indicates that collection costs have been approaching $4.00 per month per home for twice-a-week collection via rear-end loading trucks with crew sizes of three persons. But new mechanized front-end or side-loading trucks with only a driver have reduced costs to $2.50 per month per home. Sonora's previous system of collection has been the classic rear-end solid waste trucks, using a driver and two collection workers, but Sonora felt an obligation to its citizens to experiment with presently available equipment.

Sonora selected a side-loading truck equipped with a hydraulically operated arm extending from the right side of the truck which can be extended to pick up curb side refuse containers. The arm extends, grasps the container, empties its contents into the truck, and then returns the container to the curb. This arm is controlled by the driver from the right side of the vehicle so as to facilitate viewing the containers and operating the arm near parked automobiles. To allow for one-man operation the vehicle is designed to be driven from the right side during travel on the collection route. When transiting to a transfer station or disposal site the vehicle is operated from the normal left seat.

The City established a large test area to determine the cost-effectiveness of the newly configured vehicles and to provide a basis for expanding the system to the entire community. Of course, the test caused a decreased labor force in that area and affected personnel were either attrited or shifted to other sections or units. This effect appeared quite acceptable because it was relatively mild and because there was slack elsewhere in the community. Some workers were shifted to other solid-waste-collection routes, some were moved to other maintenance activities in other departments, and, fortunately, some retired or found other employment outside of the city.

Then one day, while a driver was completing a collection route with the new equipment, he failed to see a small girl crossing the street as he was pulling away from a pick-up point. His vehicle ran over the girl, resulting in her death.

The driver of the equipment involved in the incident was charged with manslaughter. In the trial his attorney based the defense on the assertion that the equipment had dangerous design defects which made its operation unsafe, thus the responsibility for the death of the girl must fall on the equipment rather than the driver. The attorney argued the faulty design prevented the driver from seeing the girl. The prosecutor countered by stating the driver to be criminally liable because he consented to drive the vehicle with the knowledge of its defects. While the County Superior Court acquitted the driver, other operators feared they would be subject to manslaughter charges in any subsequent death-related accidents.

After the court acquitted the driver, an attempt by the operator's union to establish a second operator in each truck was rejected by the City. Naturally the other drivers remained quite anxious regarding the legal risk involved in continuing to operate the new vehicles. They felt so strong about the situation that approximately 70 drivers filed a suit to enjoin the City from operating with less than two people and from withholding pay or taking disciplinary action against drivers who refuse to operate the trucks.

The questions before the court were reduced to the following:

1. Is the equipment safe with one man?
2. Would two men (or women) improve that safety?
3. Can the Court constrain the City from administrative or disciplinary actions against drivers who refuse to work during the litigation?

In this injunction hearing the plaintiffs argued that

1. The poor visibility from the right side would be enhanced by a second driver.
2. One-man crews over long routes creates excessive fatigue.
3. City regulations require drivers to engage in dangerous movements which could be lessened by employee discretion.
4. Vehicle maintenance fell below recommended standards.
5. The route design included certain routes with excessive cul de sacs, narrow alleys, and other hazards.
6. The braking system on the right side, which was hand-operated, was inferior to normal foot brake.

7. The one-man crew provided danger to employees because regulations do not allow drivers to leave disabled vehicles or to go inside of private residences.

Since this legal action is a temporary injunction or restraining order, it will be necessary for the City to argue before the court why the injunction should not be made permanent and the City prevented from operating the one-man collection equipment. The City was forced to quickly decide how it would defend the safety of this equipment. What standards were appropriate in this situation? What governmental requirements, either manufacturing or operational, are applicable? How can one distinguish the inadequacies of the equipment from the negligence of the operator?

In an attempt to support a defense, the City began to contact a variety of individuals who would have information and who might testify in the case. First, another community in the local area which had been an early innovator with one-man collection equipment was asked to provide some input regarding the safety of these equipments. Their response indicated that research reports on mechanization of solid waste collection established that the new equipment was able to meet the same safety standards of all other similar municipal equipment operated by a single driver. They added that one of the principal purposes of mechanization was to enhance the safety of solid waste collection because of the reduction of crew size and container handling.

Second, it seemed appropriate to contact the manufacturer of the equipment, clearly expecting that they could provide reports supporting the safety of their product. The manufacturer was quick to suggest that many other cities across the country were using the same equipment and had experienced improved safety records. This equipment, according to the manufacturer, was providing a badly needed improved safety performance in solid waste collection — a program which has classically led other municipal service activities, as well as industrial activities, in incidence of on-the-job injuries.[1]

Finally, selected university faculty were approached for their knowledge of research in the field which might shed further light on the safety question. The City was advised to contact the National Commission on Productivity which has become an advocate for innovations in collection methods so as to enhance public sector productivity.[2] Other faculty, interested in the federal government's Occupational Health and Safety Act (OHSA) program, were quick to point out that the municipal equipment are not included in OHSA requirements so that the City would have to look elsewhere for legal standards.

With these inputs, the City prepared arguments which concluded that the collection vehicles were as safe as any other equipment which operated solely with a driver, such as dumptrucks, street sweepers, or mail trucks and the safety burden must necessarily be placed on the operator.

Some specific data introduced included the following arguments about the new equipment's safety performance:

1. Over 300 cities are presently operating this particular piece of equipment with a one-man program.
2. The safety record of the equipment compares favorably with the three-man rear-loading vehicles. During the last fiscal year, Sonora's comparative data is as follows:

Item	One-Man Vehicles	Three-Man Rear Loaders
Miles driven	731,293	635,226
Accidents with vehicles or persons	23	26
Accidents with injury or death	1	0
Personal injuries per 100,000 miles — 72% less for one man v. three man		

3. The one-man vehicles' safety performance in third-party accidents was comparable with the National Safety Council's statistics for passenger-type motor vehicles.
4. One area of safety problems statistically were in total accidents. These included "fender-bender"-type accidents with inanimate objects such as fences, telephone poles, etc. During the last fiscal year, the one-man crews had 86 such accidents, although the vast majority were minor.

During the deliberations, the court concluded there were a "number of obvious changes which can be made to insure greater safety to the public." Even the City Attorney acknowledged communication problems between the drivers and management. The evidence indicated that employee safety recommendations had been ignored and the Sanitation Department had failed to provide the drivers with copies of its own safety regulations. During the hearing the City added a "simple mirror" to the left side of the truck which virtually eliminated a significant blind spot.

In justifying his decision, the judge stated that since "virtually all vehicles have blind spots and other potential hazards, the burden is on the plaintiffs to prove that the one-man operations pose excessive threat to the public. Since the court heard expert witnesses give both pro and con arguments for the safety of the equipment, it is the opinion of the court that Plaintiffs have failed to sustain their burden that the one-man crew poses excessive danger or that the city Council abused its discretion by refusing to implement the two man crews. The evidence introduced at the hearing overwhelmingly demonstrates that one-man operations in Sonora and elsewhere are not hazardous to public safety." The essence of the Court's judgment is that "many of the existing problems can be alleviated without a second man and it is *doubtful* whether the second man could improve the safety record."

While losing the court fight, the union recalls they were aware of the experiment and did not receive any grievance requests from their membership and did not lodge a formal position with the City prior to the beginning of the test. But, as they reflected on the situation after the incident, they realized they had not fully participated in the decision to implement one-man equipment, and the fact that none of their members were terminated as a result of the initial experiment was not sufficient justification for their exclusion.

The City's continuing position is that the goal of improved cost-effectiveness would be seriously damaged by a return to larger crew sizes. At the same time, the City will assure the union that there will be no layoffs as the City moves toward additional one-man crews, wherever extra crew members can be utilized in other jobs throughout the community. The City believes the citizenry would not stand for a second man in those vehicles designed to save the taxpayers' money on solid waste collection. As a result, the City Manager directed the Personnel Director to disregard his previous request to prepare a position description and to set a salary range for a new position to be called Feather Bedder I!

NOTES

1. See the cover story on injury frequency rate in *APWA Reporter*, Feb. 1972.
2. National Commission on Productivity, *Opportunities for Improving Productivity in Solid Waste Collection*, 1973. Also see the International City Management Association's *Refuse Report*, Mar/Apr 1975 on pioneers in mechanized collection.

Productivity in Palo Alto
Frederick O'R. Hayes and Daniel Rubin

PALO ALTO IS A SMALL CITY WITH A STABLE POPULATION just under 60,000. The community has a high average level of both affluence and education. The city budget for 1975–1976 provides for expenditures of $15.7 million. The city also manages five utilities (refuse, electric, water, gas, and sewer) with aggregate 1975–1976 expenditures of $23.3 million including $4.3 million in surplus funds used to help finance the city's regular budget.

The city has been prudently managed. It has no indebtedness and routinely finances capital improvements from current revenues and reserves. For the first time in recent years inflation, a slowing economy, and energy conservation (because of the impact on utility revenues) have eliminated General Fund financing for the Capital and Street Improvement Funds.

This is scarcely an augury of serious future financial problems. Palo Alto continues to be able to finance an extensive range of services for its residents within a moderate tax structure. It faces no financial problems that demand a strong effort to secure early and significant gains in productivity.

Service Management System

Palo Alto's major citywide productivity effort is the Service Management System (SMS), a sophisticated program budgeting, evaluation, and management information system conceived in 1973 largely at the initiation of City Manager George Sipel. In addition, there is a handful of analysts in a few city departments working on efficiency and effectiveness projects of interest related to SMS objectives.

The proposal to Housing and Urban Development that brought in first-year funds for the SMS project described its goals as follows: ". . . to improve the City's decision-making capabilities by delineating techniques in which output and effectiveness of the delivery of municipal services and their impact upon the community can be measured, evaluated and enhanced."[1] In practice, this was seen as involving everything from improved needs assessment (as through citizen surveys) and work with departments developing operational objectives and output measures, through to specific impact analyses and encouraging the City Council to make its decisions in a more rational-evaluative manner.

The Service Management System is an integrated, program budgeting and management reporting system. It employs a program structure with five major program categories, thirty-nine programs, 125 subprograms, and nearly 400 subprogram elements. This basic program structure is outlined in Exhibit 10-1. Goals are established for each of the categories including subprogram elements. The goals are, with few exceptions, concrete and specific and are stated in quantitative terms wherever feasible.

Exhibit 10-1
Palo Alto Program Structure

I.   Personal and Property Safety
To create an environment in which people can live, move about safely and feel reasonably confident that they and their property are protected from criminal harm and the hazards of fire and natural and man-made disasters.
- A. Animal Services
  1. Animal Control
  2. Animal Care
  3. Spay and Neuter Clinic
- B. Police
  1. Support Services
  2. Field Services
  3. Research and Training
  4. Police Community Services
  5. Investigative Services
  6. Administration and General
- C. Fire
  1. Fire Suppression
  2. Fire Prevention
  3. Fire Training and Research
  4. Paramedics
  5. Administration and General
- D. Transportation (partial)
  1. Traffic Operations

II. Community Health and Environment
To promote healthy, attractive environmental living conditions enhanced by safe, clean, and reliable utility service with minimum hazards of water, air, noise, and surface (visual) pollution.
- A. Light and Power
  1. Engineering
  2. Systems Acquisition and Construction
  3. Customer Relations
  4. Operations and Maintenance
  5. Energy Conservation
- B. Water
  1. Engineering
  2. System Acquisition and Construction
  3. Operations and Maintenance
  4. Water Transmission Operations
- C. Gas
  1. Engineering
  2. System Acquisition and Construction
  3. Operations and Maintenance
- D. Sewer
  1. Engineering
  2. System Acquisition and Construction
  3. Operations and Maintenance
- E. Waste Water Quality Control
  1. Treatment and Disposal
  2. Industrial Waste Treatment
- F. Refuse Management
  1. Solid Waste Disposal
  2. Collection and Customer Services
  3. Recycling

Exhibit 10-1 (Continued)

G. Inspectional Services
   1. Building Code Enforcement
   2. Zoning Standards and Municipal Code Enforcement
H. Planning
   1. Comprehensive Plan
   2. Development Monitoring
   3. Special Studies
   4. Inter-governmental Coordination
   5. Housing
   6. Environmental Control
   7. Administration and General
I. Streets (partial)
   1. Street Cleaning
J. Parks (partial)
   1. Parkway Maintenance
   2. Street Tree Planting and Maintenance
   3. Electric Line Clearing
   4. Utility Landscaping

III. Individual Development and Enjoyment

To promote individual self-development and to provide all citizens, to the extent practicable, with a variety of leisure opportunities which are accessible, safe, physically attractive, and enjoyable.

A. Library
   1. Bibliographical Services
   2. Readers Services
B. Recreation
   1. Parks and Playgrounds
   2. Physical and Sports
   3. Enrichment and Social
   4. Aquatics
   5. Special City Wide Events
   6. Administration and General
C. Arts
   1. Performing Arts
   2. Visual Arts
   3. Administration and General
D. Nature and Science
   1. Instruction
   2. Exhibits and Collections
   3. Maintenance
   4. Administration and General
E. Social Services
   1. Community Relations
   2. Senior Adult Community Resources Coordination
   3. Community Drug Abuse Project
   4. Child Care Services
   5. Registration
   6. Facilities Rental
F. Parks (partial)
   1. Parks and Grounds Maintenance
   2. Golf Course Maintenance
   3. Administration and General

IV. Transportation

To provide multi-mode access to desired destinations in a safe, quick, comfortable, and convenient manner for all segments of the community without causing major harmful side effects.

Exhibit 10-1 (Continued)

A. Streets (partial)
   1. Street Maintenance
   2. Sidewalk Maintenance
   3. Traffic Control
   4. Traffic Signal and Street Lighting
   5. Storm Drains
   6. Administration and General
B. Transportation (partial)
   1. Transportation Planning
   2. Administration and General
C. City Treasurer (partial)
   1. Parking
   2. Parking Enforcement
   3. Civic Center Garage

V.   General Administration and Support Services
To formulate City policy to effectively meet community needs and assure implementation through effective and efficient management and support services.

A. City Manager
   1. City Council
   2. Staff and Organization Development
   3. Inter-governmental Relations
   4. City Manager's Time Priorities
B. City Clerk
   1. Meetings and Minutes
   2. Elections
   3. Council Support
   4. Records and Filing
C. City Controller
   1. Resource Utilization and Control
   2. Data Processing
   3. Systems Development
   4. Administration and General
D. Budget and Resource Analysis
   1. Program Evaluation and Operations Analysis
   2. Budget Preparation and Administration
   3. Legislative Analysis and Research
E. Reproduction and Mailing
   1. Reproduction
   2. Mailing
   3. Administration and General
F. Purchases and Stores
   1. Purchasing
   2. Delivering
   3. Stores
   4. Administration and General
G. Communications
   1. Operations
   2. Maintenance
H. Building Maintenance
   1. Repair/Maintenance/Construction
   2. Janitorial Services
I. Equipment Maintenance
   1. Equipment Repair, Maintenance, and Operations
   2. Equipment Replacement
J. Real Estate
   1. General Real Estate Services
   2. Property Management

Exhibit 10–1 *(Continued)*

K. City Treasurer (partial)
  1. Cashiering
  2. Customer Service — Office
  3. Customer Service — Field
  4. Meter Reading
  5. Administration and General
L. Personnel
  1. Recruitment and Selection
  2. Employee Development
  3. Safety, Health, and Workmen's Compensation
  4. Classification and Pay
  5. Employee Relations
  6. Employee Services
M. Public Works Administration
  1. Budget Analysis and Special Studies
  2. Management Development in the Public Works Organization
  3. Develop and Monitor Affirmative Action in Public Works
N. Streets (partial)
  1. General Field Services
O. Parks (partial)
  1. General Field Services
P. Engineering
  1. Engineering Office
  2. Surveying
  3. Inspection

Source: *City of Palo Alto 1975–76 Program Statements,* pp. i–vi.

For each subprogram, SMS provides for a set of performance measures. Targets are set for the year for each item covered by a performance measure. The agencies report quarterly to the city manager on performance and a semi-annual report is prepared by the city manager to City Council. Exhibit 10–2 shows how one subprogram, investigative services in the Police Department, is presented in the semiannual report.

The semiannual report to the Council is submitted as a companion volume, *Program Statements,* to the annual budget. Beginning with the 1976–1977 budget, the budget and the program statements will be integrated into a single presentation.

The performance measures cover a number of different aspects of program operation including unit costs, cost recovery rates, workload,

Exhibit 10–2
Goals, Objectives, and Performance Measures for Palo Alto Police Investigative Services Subprogram

Subprogram: Investigative Services

GOAL: To provide an accurate, legally sound basis for discovery resolution and disposition of criminal cases; to utilize community resources as an alternative to the justice system for Juvenile offenders; and to provide other administrative support functions.

Exhibit 10-2 (Continued)

a. *Element: Follow-up Investigations*
  1. To maintain an overall clearance rate of Part I offenses of twenty (20) percent so as to correspond with the national average, and to increase the number of Part I offenses cleared to correspond with the probable numerical increase in those offenses.
  2. To increase clearances of burglaries to twenty-five (25) percent by 1976, and to increase the number of burglary clearances so as to correspond with the probable increase in burglaries.
  3. Through a federally-funded program, enter into the second year (Phase II) of alternative police investigatory procedures for rape. Phase II will concentrate on evaluating the first year's efforts and training for Palo Alto officers as well as other law enforcement personnel in Santa Clara County will begin. The end results will be aimed at increasing the number of reported rapes, while providing for a more modern and humane approach by the investigator in dealing with victims of rape.
b. *Element: Fraud*
  1. Maintain police involvement in the prevention and investigation of consumer fraud through the use of referrals and our own fraud investigators. To increase the number of reported consumer frauds by 25% through public awareness of our availability for such a service.
c. *Element: Juvenile Operations*
  1. To continue the partial funding of a professional social services worker so as to increase counseling capabilities and provide for on-going family crises counseling. Because on-going counseling is not currently provided, we are unable to judge how many individuals and families would benefit. Such a measurement will be developed after our first year's experience.
  2. To reduce the repeat rate of multiple offenders of W & I code Section 601 by twenty-five (25) percent through the use of a social worker.
  3. To continue efforts in diverting youths (as defined in Section 601 of the W&I Code) who are first-time offenders, from the justice system to local agencies by increasing the diversion rate to ninety (90) percent.
d. *Element: Special Investigations*
  1. To provide effective narcotics enforcement, concentrating primarily on illegal production and sales by exploring the feasibility of providing person-power to the county drug enforcement task force or by not providing person-power but utilizing the county's enforcement capabilities.

Performance Measures	Actual 1972–73	Actual 1973–74	Target 1974–75	Target 1975–76
Part I clearance rate	9.3%	14.0%*	20%	20%
Part I numerical clearances	N/A	380 *	445	500
Burglary clearance rate	14%	19.8%*	20%	25%
Burglary numerical clearances	N/A	184	180	200
Number of reported rapes	N/A	18	11	36
Rape clearance rate	N/A	44.4%*	45%	40%
Rape numerical clearances	N/A	8%*	5	16
Percent of 601 arrests diverted	58%	73%	75%	90%
Recidivism rate of first-time 601 offenders	N/A	42.9%	40%	35%
Number of consumer fraud cases referred or investigated	N/A	10	20	30

Source: *City of Palo Alto 1975–76 Program Statements*, pp. 10–12.
*Calendar Year Figures.

program results, citizen attendance or program usage, user evaluations of programs, response times, service frequencies, program variety, and others. Some of these measures directly reflect the characteristics of agency performance, but many deal with phenomena where agency control is limited or nonexistent. The targets vary accordingly from presumably achievable management objectives to estimates of external factors.

Performance measures and targets were determined initially on the basis of "best professional guess." It is contemplated that, with experience, irrelevant and weak measures will be weeded out and new better measures added.

The Service Management System in Palo Alto is, primarily, an information system rather than a structure for program analysis. Its value depends on the usefulness of a systematic information flow to program heads, department directors, the budget staff, the SMS staff, the city manager and the City Council in decisionmaking. It is hoped that these data will uncover otherwise buried problems in performance as well as changes in needs and demands.

The work of the Service Management System is supplemented and supported by a program evaluation effort. Most important from the longer range perspective is the commitment of the SMS staff to design an evaluation component for each significant new program undertaken by the municipal government.

Evaluation studies have been undertaken in several areas. These include: the Fire Department's paramedic program; a contract drug abuse program; the teen coffee house; child care services; the operation of a senior citizen center; and the Police Department's burglary prevention program.

The Citizen Survey

The SMS team's citizen survey, administered experimentally in 1974 to a sample of 600 Palo Alto residents, can be regarded as a supplement to the information gathered through departmental performance measures. The survey's purpose was described as follows:

> In simple terms, the survey's purpose is to provide for a citizen's evaluation of Police and Recreation services in Palo Alto. In addition, certain factual usage and incident data will be collected. Furthermore, for the first time, there will be systematic data available on non-use of public services and the citizen's reasons why. All this information will be combined with existing departmental data to provide a more comprehensive citizen-oriented evaluation. Data on nonuse may highlight correctable deficiencies and unmet needs.[2]

Besides basic demographic information (age, sex, race, income, housing type and location, length of residency), the sixty-five-item personal-interview survey included questions regarding:

General perceptions: overall satisfaction with city services, neighborhood and downtown safety, respect for police, summary evaluations of police, and recreation performance in several progam areas.

Measures of service quality for city handling of complaints, information and service requests; for contacts with police; and for participation in park and recreation programs. Quality measures included courtesy, speed of response, correctness of information, and (for recreation facilities) convenience, safety, and cleanliness.

Crime victimization, including whether actually reported and reasons if not.

Extent of use for a list of recreation facilities and programs, with reasons for non-use (interest, convenience, health, cost, quality, etc.) where this was the case.

Palo Alto previously had made fairly extensive use of both special purpose planning surveys and more traditional means of community input: public meetings, contact with associations, comments channeled through Council members or city officials. The rationale for a survey stressed the sporadic and often unrepresentative nature of such special-occasion information. By contrast, "if standardized and conducted annually," a survey could "more routinely collect citizen input that represents the total population, in a usable clear format" that would allow year-to-year tracking of "broad effectiveness trends within the city."[3]

The actual use of the pilot-year survey, however, does not suggest early accomplishment of this goal. The sample survey was tabulated and analyzed, and some relatively minor effects can be attributed to it: new signs directing patrons from busy tennis courts to others nearby that might be less crowded; deferral of building two more courts at a particular site; a decision not to go ahead with plans for a central complaint bureau. But with the end of HUD funds, which paid for the 1974 survey, there has been no move to continue the venture on a regular basis. Consequently, quality measures introduced in the survey have not been carried over into the system of "Program Statement" performance measures.

Initiation

The idea of a citywide Service Management System, coordinated with budget preparation, originated in informal discussions between Palo Alto City Manager George Sipel and management consultant Richard Hughes. Sipel was not a newcomer to Palo Alto; he had been city manager since 1972 and assistant city manager before that.

The city previously had been involved in operation audits in several areas including police, inspections, and purchasing, and in the beginnings of PPBS development. In addition, a few departments had analytic staff. Sipel—a strong believer in the fruits of systematic analysis—felt that the time was ripe for a comprehensive effort at rationalizing many community decisions.

Part of the impetus to go ahead derived from Sipel's knowledge that federal funds would almost surely be available for the experiment. The HUD regional office had already approached the city to solicit an application for "701" planning funds. Application resulted in a grant of $40,000 for 1973-1974, to be matched by about $25,000 in locally contributed services. This made it possible to finance the additional positions and supporting consultant services without using local funds.

Sipel also was encouraged to proceed with plans for the SMS by the City Council's established interest in analysis and evaluation. In particular, the Council's Finance and Public Works Committee had expressed a desire to review all city departments systematically and in depth, apart from the pressure of budget hearings, at the pace of a few departments per year. The Council majority was, in fact, receptive, despite some specific opposition to the federal funds ("boondoggle," "strings attached") and the absence of visible direct community service in the project.

Developing the Program

Detailed planning for the SMS was conducted by Hughes (then with Booz, Allen, and Hamilton) under a $12,000 consulting contract. Hughes' role at this point involved advice on implementation as well as technical expertise in designing the system. Except for a $7,000 contract with Diridon Research Corporation of San Jose for administration of the citizen's survey later that year, all other development of SMS was done by city staff.

A two-person Service Managment System staff was created within the Budget and Staff Services Department to take over the task of planning and coordinating the system. To serve as SMS Director, Sipel recruited George Barbour from the International City Manager's Association, where he had been overall project director of their productivity efforts, including a performance measurement project in St. Petersburg, Florida, and Nashville, Tennessee. Ed Everett, the sole operations analyst, came with community experience as a VISTA volunteer and analytic training at Princeton's Woodrow Wilson School.

The city had other assets relevant to SMS in the several small pockets of analytic talent. The Department of Budget and Staff Services had one budget analyst in addition to Director Clayton Brown, who himself had been a program analyst in Phoenix prior to coming to Palo Alto and had performed master's degree research on PPBS. This staff had been involved in reviewing various budget systems in other cities, as well as early stages of implementing PPBS stemming from a commitment in 1969.

Police Chief James Zurcher had actively supported the use of a civilian analyst added to the department's staff in 1969 by his predecessor in keeping with the recommendation of a Booz-Allen-Hamilton consultant (Hughes). When the Service Management System was created in 1973, this position — coordinator of research and training — was occupied by its third incumbent, James Hudak, with training in economics and public policy and experience in municipal government cost accounting. Hudak and his predecessors helped establish a Police Information System, adapted for Palo Alto use a model by which investigative time is allocated to burglaries on a point system, and successfully argued for changes in shift hours to improve patrol density during peak crime hours. These and other projects varied in success and reception, but Chief Zurcher's enthusiasm about rational decision making was enhanced rather than diminished during the period.

The Utilities Department has had two analysts since 1974, both permanently funded by the city as of the 1975–1976 budget. One analyst is employed in Public Works. Their experience has been a major asset to the survey components of SMS.

Palo Alto also has used outside assistance. The city participated for a time in the Public Technology, Incorporated (PTI) program and used the PTI fire station locator model to analyze fire-fighting needs before withdrawing this year dissatisfied with benefits. In addition, a strong relationship exists with Stanford University.

Barbour's strategy was to first develop a model approach to the Service Management System in two departments. This permitted a start to be made with the most interested and cooperative department heads. More important, Barbour and Everett could, with this limited initial application, provide substantial assistance to each of the two agencies. The agencies chosen were the Police Department and the Recreation Department. The first was especially important given the highly favorable orientation of the Police Chief and the short but significant history of the use of analyses in the department.

In the second year, the Service Management System manual was to be prepared and SMS extended to all the agencies of the city government. It was hoped that the experience with the two pilot agencies would make the extension to the remaining agencies relatively easy.

Two approaches were used to improve departments' analytic capabilities and their understanding of the Service Management System.

An initial task has been for SMS staff to train departmental staff. The SMS team conducted a two-day training session for all police sergeants and lieutenants to familiarize them with the format of the system's new reporting by quantified objective and to give them some sense of what might be found by manipulating these data. Similar training for key staff was conducted in Planning, Public Utilities, and Public Works. A more extensive training apprenticeship was also developed, in which the first participant, from Public Utilities, spent three months as an assistant on analytic projects. All these variants play on the same theme of personal indoctrination by SMS analysts, and all increase the pool of department staff potentially receptive to the centrally located analysts and their ideas.

Another approach used by Sipel involves his personal approval of new analyst candidates, and annual contracting on all analyst positions between the city manager and Department Directors in which roughly 25 percent of each analyst's time is reserved for projects of interest to Sipel, either in the home department or elsewhere in the city, on which they report directly to Ed Everett. This, in effect, aims at a split loyalty for the analyst between his departmental supervisors and the manager's priorities.

Internal Accommodation and Implementation: Relations of SMS to Departments

Despite strong backing from City Manager Sipel and at least moderate enthusiasm from the City Council, the SMS faced major obstacles in winning cooperation from the city's departmental officials. SMS required of the departments an onerous data collection effort and, at the same time, raised the threat of new hurdles to be cleared in the budget process. The pressure was intensified by an exceedingly ambitious schedule for implementation.

Initial plans called for development of a citywide program structure the first year, complete with goals, performance criteria, and quantified objectives down to the level of departmental "subprogram units." All departments were to file 1974–1975 budgets based on these program formulations. In addition, the SMS staff would work intensively with two departments the pilot year, making models of them. It was anticipated that full implementation citywide could be achieved the second year, with far less SMS staff assistance needed in other departments after a year's experience and the examples of the two pilot departments had taught them what the process was all about.

The extreme optimism of this timetable was soon evident. By the publication of the *SMS Handbook* reporting pilot year achievements in July 1974, implementation had been rescheduled over a five-year period. And a year later, the five-year schedule had been scrapped.

Police

Police Chief Zurcher involved his department at his own initiative. He was enthusiastic about the analyst position he inherited on assuming the job, and he was convinced of the usefulness of better management information. Participating as an SMS pilot department represented a chance for assistance in reaching his own objectives. Confident of benefits, he was comfortable with a large contribution of police staff time: over 550 hours (mostly from Jim Hudak) as opposed to 130 hours from the other pilot department, Recreation.

However, interest in SMS within the department was strictly limited to the chief and a few of his top staff. Most officers responded to the system with apathy or with mild irritation and cynicism about this new "paperwork exercise." For example, even though objectives and measures were being discussed as the coming basis for budgets, an attempt to set up an internal police committee to advise on the objective-setting process met with negligible interest. Practical discussions on objectives and measurement did take place—for example between Hudak and patrol officers searching for a workable stand-in for "street crime"—but they tended to depend on initiation and continued pressure from above.

Even among those high police officers whose administrative responsibilities made SMS a potentially useful management tool, interest was far from uniform. The importance of personal predisposition toward analysis is neatly illustrated by the two captains heading the Investigations and Uniform Services Divisions during that pilot year. After the chief and Hudak, these two were probably the most taken with SMS. However, the response from the investigations captain was clearly more intense, and Hudak compensated by spending more of his own time with Uniform Services as the two divisions developed measures and objectives. At first it appeared that the difference stemmed from the more frenetic problems of day-to-day administration in Uniform Services. But a year later, when the two captains had reversed duties as part of a rotation system, the two divisions' relative involvement in analysis shifted along with their leaders.

The Police Department made outstanding use of the chance to draft measures and, largely as a result, prepared "unquestionably . . . the best departmental budget submitted"[4] for 1974–1975.

However, use of the sytem since then has not been consistent. The first year, Chief Zurcher's personal interest was high and provided the impetus for a few top aides to do the hard work involved in initial development. By the end of the year, though, his interest had passed on to other matters. City Manager Sipel, noticing the difference, pressured him to improve the department's compliance with the reporting system just established. In essence, a stronger coordinator was needed — pulled in fewer directions than Zurcher, but higher in status than Hudak and his successor (who has little proclivity for quantitative analysis) as Research and Training Coordinator. The gradual decline in collection and use of information also reflected an upsurge of resistance to the task of collecting data, the usefulness of which was not clear beyond doubt.

Parks and Recreation

Parks and Recreation was chosen as the other pilot department to provide a contrast with Police. Although the Department lacked sophisticated analytical staff, George Barbour's work at ICMA had familiarized him with research from the Urban Institute and elsewhere, which lay the groundwork for output and effectiveness measurement in recreation. Also, he felt confident of his ability to provide strong support when it came to developing parameters and objectives. Finally, Recreation Director Keith Bruns, while not excited about the project, would make a conscientious effort at implementation.

From their first discussions with Bruns, in which he was asked if he wanted in, Sipel and Barbour offered the lure of some special purpose surveys to meet Recreation's immediate needs. This was an effective move. In fact, Bruns' recollection of those early contacts focuses on surveys. His apprehension about the Department's effectiveness being rated through a citywide sample survey was offset by general confidence in the services he provided. The offer of SMS help in running smaller surveys — to evaluate the use of the municipal golf course and expansion proposals for a neighborhood park — resonated with his sense of practical planning. Once he decided to go along with the project, he took it seriously and made it clear to his recreation supervisors that he expected them to do the same.

But Bruns was never struck with the value of SMS on its merits the way Zurcher was in Police. A lack of clarity about the nature and uses of the system probably contributed to his underestimation of the amount of energy it would require.

Given the lack of departmental expertise in analysis, Barbour's familiarity with a useful literature, and Bruns' unclear notion of what good objectives would look like, the two SMS staff spent more time with Parks and Recreation than with Police the first year. However, the involvement of middle-level Parks and Recreation staff was stronger and incrementally more important than was the case in Police. The interaction between Barbour and Recreation staff was successful enough that Bruns does not now sense any depth of resistance to using the reporting system devised. Even though it is energy consuming to collect the data, the only complaint he could pinpoint (with one major exception) involved not the overall utility of this quantity of data, but the appropriateness of a particular measure.

The one notable incident of Recreation staff resistance to SMS objectivication involved a newly established teen coffee house program. Fearing that initially low attendance would lead to budget cuts, the supervisor-counselors who ran that program refused for three quarters to file quarterly reports. Instead, they wrote to City Manager Sipel and the Council, claiming that quantified measures of success were inappropriate and inviting them instead to come for a visit to assure themselves subjectively of the program's essentiality and quality. Interestingly, after the program was better established and drawing more kids, resistance to reporting attendance was dropped.

SMS and the Budget: Citywide Objectives and Performance Measures

In addition to the close attention to Police and Recreation, the SMS staff gave limited assistance to all other departments during 1973–1974 in formulating program organization, measures, and objectives to be used in budget preparation. This more cursory exercise was not expected to produce results of consistently high quality. And as expected, some participating departments did not understand, or were unwilling to treat seriously, the charge. But at the end of the pilot year, the SMS staff made the following assessment: "The early involvement of the total City in the project, while cumbersome initially and putting a severe strain on the limited resources available, was clearly a good decision. Now, in the follow-on years of implementing SMS, the formats, style, and terminology are known city-wide and the early indoctrination is being reinforced through usage."[5]

The themes of familiarity and indoctrination sounded here are echoed in descriptions of analytic training for department staff and other SMS components. Careful groundwork was seen from the start as crucial to educating department officials, Council members, even the city manager to use the system effectively as an evaluation and management tool. For example, the initial sketching of program structure for the whole city was performed unilaterally by SMS staff. This was done "to expedite the process," and represented no more than a necessary dictation from above—ultimately, from the city manager's office—of a scheme that was going to cross-cut department lines and inevitably step on some toes. But it is worth mentioning that not everyone bought into this concept merely by following directives on a new reporting and budget preparation format. Even Recreation Director Bruns was uncomfortable with the lumping of "his" teen center counseling program with those of other departments.

The nexus between SMS and Palo Alto's budget process is so close that Barbour himself concedes the system can be viewed as "nothing more than an elaborate program budget process."[6] In the fall of 1973 all departments were instructed to prepare goals, objectives, and performance criteria as a "backdrop" for the 1974–1975 budget. Late that year, Sipel and Budget and Staff Services Director Brown held a series of meetings with top department staff to review the material prepared and discuss directions prior to preparation of draft budgets.

The process this first year had some characteristics of a formal exercise. Programs discussed in the prebudget sessions had not yet been costed out in most cases, and "decisions" made on a program budget basis were likely to be risky. In addition, the review of budgets by the Council's Finance and Public Works Committee followed quite traditional lines, with most discussion centered on work force and dollar requirements.

The SMS staff's plans for 1974–1975, as conceived following the first year's experience, involved greater synchronization between budget and objective preparation deadlines and an effort to provide better selected material to the Council (less financial detail, more reminders of objectives and outcomes) to nudge them in the direction of evaluation.

The Second Year: Public Works

This scenario was interrupted, however, by a major disruption in the relations between SMS and a key department. The Public Works Department was under fire for both sidewalk repair policy and chronic failure to meet schedules for funded capital improvements. The Department responded to the latter criticism by setting up a new position of Manager of Capital Projects, which was filled by police analyst Jim Hudak. SMS staff, under pressure from the City Council to show direct payoff from analysis, shifted their plans for work in Public Works to include not only improving the performance measures and objectives but also cost savings analysis. Sidewalk repair was to be the first component of this study. The analysis that ensued led to a budget cut of one position for Public Works. It was a small victory for productivity but a setback in establishing the credibility of SMS staff within departments.

The Director of Public Works was irate with the results. Other planned studies there were cancelled and further involvement with SMS was limited strictly to completion of the sidewalk study. As a result, Sipel placed the department off limits for the SMS staff with the proviso that the Public Works director would undertake with his own staff analyses of two pressing program needs—the programming of street repairs and the improvement of park maintenance.

The Department of Utilities also decided to do the analytic job internally. A new department director is learning the ropes, and the department has two highly regarded analysts to work on its problems.

The friction with DPW is no gain to the implementation of SMS, but one might argue that performing the analysis within the department is simply another way of skinning the same cat. However, both Barbour and Everett believe strongly that program analysis cannot be effective unless it is centralized. They are joined in this view by Clay Brown, the director of Budget and Staff Services. The argument rests both on the greater technical competence possible in a central unit and on the absence of the protective and defensive attitudes of the line departments. There is a directly contrary argument—made by Jim Hudak—that analysis cannot become an effective guide to program management until it is done in the departments.

Meanwhile, the SMS staff has put in place its basic system of performance measurement and reporting. It has limitations and imperfections, but it exists. It is buttressed by the commitments of at least a few departments to undertake program analysis.

The basic problem goes beyond the conflict with Public Works. It is that a majority of the department heads are not much interested in, or inclined to use, performance measurement and program analysis. City Manager Sipel, who "grooves on measurement and analysis," is reportedly disappointed that it has produced no comparable reaction in department heads who were largely selected by him. The limited acceptance by the heads of the operating agencies, if it continues. would seem certain to slow the rate of progress and reduce the usefulness of the system.

The Unions

Municipal employee unions have not been dramatically strong in Palo Alto, compared to, say, Eastern cities. For example, the Palo Alto Police Officers Association, representing 100 officers, is not a local unit in any national or international union. The Association has proved neither highly resistant to change nor interested in discussing, pro or con, the department's experiments with analysis and management information systems. Police officers have preferred to respond individually—with apathy, cynicism, or moderate cooperation—rather than en masse through the agency of union policy. Palo Alto's police ranks have been passing through a period of heavy turnover, and the force is now younger than most, better educated (median education three years of college), and better sexually integrated (14 percent of sworn officers are women). The significance of these changes for unionization are uncertain.

The city's fire fighters are more strongly unionized. The union is a local of International Association of Fire Fighters. Changes affecting the duties of work of fire fighters are cleared with the union, but this seems to have raised no obstacles to change thus far. More problems may be likely in the future.

Most of the remaining city employees are members of the Service Employees International Union (SEIU). The union went out in July 1975 on a one-month strike. Although the major stakes were wage and fringe related, an expansion of bargaining units to include many seasonal park employees was also at issue—a realm in which the city would lose much flexibility to alter programs and reassign personnel. Clearly, the potential for union stands antithetical to productivity measures is here in evidence.

SMS Director Barbour became intimately involved in labor relations, including the negotiations in the SEIU strike, through a new responsibility for analyzing every proposal to determine its costs and implications for productivity. The rapid escalation of leave provisions for city employees—educational leave and a guaranteed monthly three-day weekend as well as traditional sick and vacation provisions—had made this particularly useful. Comprehensive costing-out was an unprecedented procedure, and the unions lacked information and preparation to respond with detailed "counter analysis." In addition, the city's bargaining agents themselves were shocked at the magnitude of the costs implied by apparently simple proposals. Current negotiations with the fire fighters will be aided by Everett, using the cost analysis model developed by Barbour.

City Council

The early attitude of the Council toward the SMS proposal has been described: general approval tempered with a few reservations about the dangers of losing autonomy in federal programs and getting caught up in overhead activities providing little public service benefit. With the end of the one-year HUD pilot grant and the consequent increase in local costs, concern with the cost-effectiveness of analysis itself became more important.

When the Finance and Public Works Committee expressed its interest in gradual review of the directions of departments, SMS with its federal subsidy seemed to most members a good way to help this happen. Whether the Council's view of the review sessions matched the perceptions of the SMS staff, however, is unclear. "Now, for the first time," said Barbour of the first year's meetings with Recreation and Police, "the discussion was not the number of people to be employed or put in the street for patrol, but what impact these specific objectives were going to have on response time, on the crime rate, or the accessibility to recreational programs."[7] But Recreation Director Bruns recalls that many of the Council's questions related more to the choice of effectiveness measures than to the objectives of his department; the SMS as well as Recreation was under scrutiny. Similarly, the Committee's budget hearings that year, in which citywide use of objectives and effectiveness reporting was first introduced, followed usual lines of cost and staffing debate.

The Council's desire to put SMS to work for *it* was evident the second year of the program. The original SMS model called for setting priorities for intensive SMS staff work with the departments on the basis of a rating scheme that assigned points for the size of departmental budgets, the number of citizens served, the magnitude of current operating problems, and an assessment of the Council's interest (as perceived by top administrators). This list was revised substantially, however, in response to political pressures such as the Council's desire to examine sidewalk repair operations right away.

When it came time to prepare the 1974–1975 budgets, Council support of the SMS project had diminished to the point that there was initial resistance to including Project Director Barbour's salary. The Council was unwilling to rely on long-term benefits of program budgeting. Pressure was applied, in effect, for the system to earn its keep with immediate payoff projects such as the sidewalk analysis, Palo Alto-Stanford University fire consolidation, and involvement in labor bargaining. Whatever the relation of cause and effect, these new missions have gone hand in hand with a reduction in the trust of departmental officials for the SMS staff, and a slackening of work on the improvement of objectives and performance measures for the SMS.

Achievements and Prospects

The achievements of the Service Management System proper, to date, are not negligible: use of objectives and output measures as a matter of course in all budgets; a requirement of budget modifications for all changes in level of service; and familiarization of city administrators and Council members with the intent, mechanics, and vocabulary of the system. In the two departments that received most careful attention, the improved information is at least partly responsible for a few identifiable changes: (1) operation of a high school swimming pool shown to have low usage was terminated; (2) construction of two planned tennis courts was deferred in a park development; and (3) a reduction was made in the budget for the Department of Public Works sidewalk repair program. Of course, the new data may make a contribution to the decision-making process without necessarily determining the results. For example, the city manager pointed out to the City Council that the approval of a proposed new park in the eastern part of the city ran counter to the citizen survey data showing that the unmet needs for parks were almost entirely in the western sector of Palo Alto. The Council nonetheless approved the eastern city park under strong neighborhood pressure — motivated in part by the fear that the land would otherwise be preempted for low-rent public housing.

George Barbour sees broader implications in the SMS data — for example, the evidence of changing demography on the demand for city services. The demand for child-serving activities is declining in library, recreation, and other programs. At the same time, there is an increasing demand for recreational and educational programs for adults. But these insights have yet to have a significant impact on program decisions. Similarly, Barbour sees, in the citizen survey, the negative attitudes toward police of citizens who have been stopped or ticketed. To him it suggests the possible need to improve on police behavior — but the Police Department does not see it as a serious problem.

Budget and Staff Services Director Clay Brown could not identify, after the first full year of the Service Management Systems, a single major program decision based primarily on SMS data. Nor was there any indication of dramatic improvement in the targeted program measures. The lack of impressive results is disappointing but scarcely surprising at this early stage of the process.

The job of using the Service Management System data is substantially more difficult than the work that went into its development. The data tend not to provide answers but to suggest questions that in turn, demand some significant effort in further fact-finding analysis. This would, without doubt, strain the capacity of the small number of program analysts working for the city.

The limited acceptance of information systems and analyses by line officials is a major impediment. Both the hostility toward second guessing by the city's top staff units and the disinterest in analysis are very common problems. They are, at the same time, very real problems that, unless corrected, will limit the impact of SMS. It may be that SMS can make its greatest contribution by the pressure it can place upon the agencies through the budgetary process. This frankly adversary process can conceivably lead to a situation where the agencies see the need for a more analytic posture, if only to better defend themselves.

The SMS staff completed two evaluation studies in the fiscal year 1973-1974 and three more in the first half of 1974-1975. The studies have provided some important inputs to program decision making.

One completed evaluation reached favorable conclusions with respect to a drug abuse prevention and treatment program operated by a private group under contract with the city. Despite the supportive evaluation, the City Council elected not to renew the contract apparently because council members looked askance at the counterculture attitudes and political activism of the group that managed the program. The teen coffee house program was also favorably viewed with, however, a recommendation for some reduction in the program budget.

The study of child care services recommended a continuation of the program with the existing contractor, Palo Alto Community Child Care. Among the specific recommendations accepted by the City Council and the PACCC board were the development of better cost and effectiveness measures of component elements of the program and more adequate information on program impact on parent employment.

The most complete cost-effectiveness evaluation is that done for the Burglary Prevention Program. The program functions through crime prevention meetings with small groups of householders or businesses in burglary affected areas and through security checks of specific buildings. During the 1974-1975 fiscal year, there was one household burglary for every thirty-two residences in the city; in residences covered by the program, the rate was one burglary per fifty-one homes. One out of every twenty-two businesses covered by the program was burglarized compared to the one out of six businesses citywide. The average averted burglary saves an estimated $400 in property losses and $167 in investigation expenses. The savings from an estimated 57 burglaries averted were, then, $32,319, compared to a program cost of $46,560. The net costs of $14,241 represent about $250 for each averted burglary, an interesting lesson in the economics of a *successful* anticrime program. Yet, interestingly, the analysis recommends an expanded program using lower cost personnel and utilizing the Burglary Probability Factor to focus work more on areas with high burglary prospects. But, ultimately, the cost of the program must be partially justified by intangible benefits from "improved community relations, communications and public safety awareness."

The Palo Alto budget credited the SMS effort with savings in the last six months of the prior fiscal year of $47,000, attributable chiefly to the cuts in the sidewalk repair program. A new overtime scheduling program in the Fire Department saved $9600 in the last quarter of the same fiscal year, with expected full year savings of $43,000.

For 1975-1976, the budget established a target for savings of $118,000. This was based on the assumption that the city should realize annual savings in each year of 2.5 times the amount of its own funds in the financing of SMS. This was clearly responsive to the City Council view that the SMS unit must earn its keep by analyses that lead to budget reductions.

The press for concrete money-saving performance may be regarded as a symptom of the insecurity of SMS. Clearly, the city manager's strong support and interest were not sufficient to generate the needed City Council support beyond the initial trial period. The goal that an analytic staff develop annually savings equal to 2.5 times its own costs is by no means unreasonable, but the developing situation placed the SMS staff under special tensions that made the task more difficult.

First, the maintenance and improvement of the Service Management System required staff time with little or no resulting contribution to budget cutting. In addition, the agency cooperation needed for most effective development of SMS was likely to be jeopardized by the increasing focus of the SMS unit on budget reductions.

Second, the unit was hobbled by the inconsistencies in strategy between the Council and the manager. The Council demanded an aggressive program to effect productivity savings—while the manager responded to departmental complaints by placing some of the prime targets for such savings off limits to the SMS staff.

Third, the resignation of George Barbour in September 1975 to enter private consulting practice deprived SMS of its one experienced hand—although it was understood from the inception that Barbour would leave after the system was functioning and that no replacement would be recruited.

In the autumn of 1975, the future of the program seemed very much in doubt. Less than a year later, the effort seemed to have weathered the crisis and secured the support necessary for its continuance.

In December, City Manager Sipel delivered an annual performance report to the City Council and to the city. He was able to report (in addition to the savings in sidewalk repair and fire fighters' overtime) such successes as the reduction in power usage from a projected 734,000 megawatt hours to 728,000 mwh, a cut in average police emergency response time from a projected three minutes to an actual of 2.8 minutes, and the completion of 306 low- and moderate-income housing projects compared to the 244 estimated.

Palo Alto was under rising fiscal pressure. One reason was the continuing effect of inflation on city costs. Another special problem arose from the failure in the courts of Palo Alto's attempt to prevent development in its foothills area through use of zoning powers. The resulting acquisition costs of $7.5 million for the first group of affected properties virtually eliminated the city's accumulated reserves.

In this climate, City Manager Sipel understandably began to take a tougher line with his department heads. He proposed to cut city employment by fifty jobs over a five-year period and to make the reductions where he found them appropriate unless the departments developed acceptable alternatives. In addition, the moratorium on SMS involvement in Public Works and Utilities had expired without either department having effected any productivity improvements.

Sipel next introduced a "productivity contract" with each of his department heads and any future salary increases will be pegged to their performance of that productivity contract. By June 1976, contracts had been developed for half of the team.

At the same time, Ed Everett and the SMS staff were proving increasingly useful to the city. They had, for example, become regular and valued participants in the city's labor negotiations. Most important, they had provided the extensive analysis that made it possible to carry to fruition the long-discussed merger of the fire forces of the city and Stanford University. The merger was a major coup for the SMS staff. Over a seven-year period, the joint personnel savings to the university and the city will aggregate about $3 million. The city estimates its own annual savings after the seven-year period at $550,000.

In addition to the consolidation, SMS staff work resulted in the following 1975–1976 savings:

1. $10,500 annually from the determination of minimum fire department (preconsolidation) staffing levels;
2. Half of the $3200 annual increase in revenue from a new method of billing participating communities for sewage treatment costs;
3. $16,200 a year from work performance standards for janitors;
4. $9,300 a year for thirteen years from a financial analysis of an automatic library circulation system;
5. $30,300 a year from changes recommended in management of city hall pool cars.

Three studies have not yet been implemented. These include a marketing study of the industrial waste system with recommended savings of $17,600; new sick leave policies expected to save $82,500; and the proposed sale of surplus city property with an expected yield of $375,000.

Work is continuing on analyses of police scheduling, utilization of police vehicles, utility meter replacement, and a plan to consolidate the Stanford and Palo Alto communications center.

The staff is still small. At the time Barbour left, Everett was assigned two positions for analysts, one to be filled by rotation from other city departments, the other to be filled with an employee funded from federal funds under the Comprehensive Employment and Training Act (CETA). Subsequently, the CETA job was converted to a permanent city position, and an additional position was requested in the 1976–1977 budget.

NOTES

1. Quoted in *Palo Alto Service Management System Handbook,* July 1974, p. 44.
2. Ibid., p. 40.
3. Ibid., p. 40.
4. *SMS Handbook,* "Executive Summary," p. x.
5. Ibid., p. 46.
6. Ibid., p. 25.
7. Ibid., p. 2.

11

Cutback Management

PURPOSE

The purpose of this chapter is to familiarize students with problems and adaptive strategies necessary to manage public organizations under conditions of declining budgets and/or declining demands for agency services.

CONTENTS

Reading
Charles H. Levine, "Organizational Decline and Cutback Management"

Case
"L.A.P.D. in the Wake of Proposition 13"

Instructions

Pre-Class Preparation

After studying the reading, "Organizational Decline and Cutback Management," read the case "L.A.P.D. in the Wake of Proposition 13" and respond carefully to the questions below:

1. How did the L.A.P.D. confront the challenge of cutback management right after Proposition 13 was approved?
2. Based on organizational behavior revealed in the case, how is the police department likely to respond in the future?
3. What is unique about "cutback" in public management, and what are some strategies to cope with this?

Procedure for Class Meeting

Class discussion will focus on the Los Angeles Police Department case and the special problems of managing declining public organizations.

For Additional Information

Although systematic treatment is fairly recent, the literature related to cutback management continues to grow rapidly. The key collection so far would appear to be contained in *Public Administration Review*, XXXVIII (July–Aug. 1978), which has a special symposium on this subject.

Other materials on this subject include:

Eugene Bardach, "Policy Termination as a Political Process," *Policy Sciences*, VII (June 1976), pp. 123–131.

Robert D. Behn, "How to Terminate a Public Policy: A Dozen Hints for the Would-Be Terminator," *Policy Analysis*, IV (Summer 1978), pp. 393–413.

Robert P. Biller, "On Tolerating Policy and Organization Termination: Some Design Considerations," *Policy Sciences*, VII (June 1976), pp. 133–149.

James M. Cameron, "Ideology and Policy Termination: Restructuring California's Mental Health System," in *The Policy Cycle*, ed. by Judith V. May and Aaron B. Wildavsky (Beverly Hills: Sage Publications, 1978), pp. 301–328. Paperback edition available.

Peter deLeon, "A Theory of Policy Termination," in *The Policy Cycle*, ed. by Judith V. May and Aaron B. Wildavsky (Beverly Hills: Sage Publications, 1978), pp. 279–300. Paperback edition available.

Charles H. Levine, "More on Cutback Management: Hard Questions for Hard Times," *Public Administration Review*, XXXIX (March–April 1979), pp. 179–183.

John J. McTighe, "Management Strategies to Deal with Shrinking Resources," *Public Administration Review*, XXXIX (Jan.–Feb. 1979), pp. 86–90.

Public Administration Review, XXXVIII (Nov.–Dec. 1978). Symposium on Budgeting in an Era of Resource Scarcity.

A more general work, and a provocative one, is:

Richard Rose and Guy Peters, *Can Government Go Bankrupt?* (New York: Basic Books, 1978).

The older industrial cities of the Northeast and Midwest have experienced serious decline in recent years. Cleveland, Detroit and New York are examples. Materials related to government action there include:

Advisory Commission on Intergovernmental Relations, *City Financial Emergencies* (Washington: U.S. Government Printing Office, 1973).

Roger E. Alcaly and David Mermelstein, *The Fiscal Crisis of American Cities* (New York: Vintage Books, 1977 [1976]). Paperback edition available.

Herbert J. Gans, "Planning for Declining and Poor Cities," *Journal of the American Institute of Planners* (Sept. 1975), pp. 305–307.

William Gorham and Nathan Glazer, eds., *The Urban Predicament* (Washington: The Urban Institute, 1976). Paperback edition available.

Because of the declining birth rate and other factors, public schools and institutions of higher education were among the first to confront cutback problems. In this regard, see:

Carnegie Foundation for the Advancement of Teaching, *More Than Survival: Prospects for Higher Education in a Period of Uncertainty* (San Francisco: Jossey-Bass Publishers, 1975).

Frank R. Kemerer and Ronald P. Satryb, *Facing Financial Exigency: Strategies for Educational Administrators* (Lexington, Mass.: D.C. Heath/Lexington Books, 1977).

Lewis B. Mayhew and Associates, *Educational Leadership and Declining Enrollments* (Berkeley: McCutchin Publishing, 1974).

For an overview of the police function, the focus of this case, see:

Gerald E. Caiden, *Police Revitalization* (Lexington, Mass.: D.C. Heath/Lexington Books, 1977).

Daniel Cruse and Jesse Rubin, *Determinants of Police Behavior: A Summary* (Washington: U.S. Government Printing Office, 1973). Paperback; one of a series of publications from the U.S. Department of Justice, Law Enforcement Assistance Administration, National Institute of Law Enforcement and Criminal Justice.

Terry Eisenberg, Deborah Ann Kent, and Charles R. Wall, *Police Personnel Practices in State and Local Governments* (Washington: Police Foundation, with the International Association of Chiefs of Police, in cooperation with the Educational Testing Service, 1973). Paperback edition available.

Robert M. Fogelson, *Big-City Police* (Cambridge: Harvard University Press, 1978).

Bernard Garmire, ed., *Local Government Police Management* (Washington: International City Management Association, 1977).

Harvey A. Juris and Peter Feuille, *The Impact of Police Unions: Summary Report* (Washington: U.S. Government Printing Office, 1973). Paperback edition available.

Peter K. Manning, *Police Work: The Social Organization of Policing* (Cambridge: MIT Press, 1977).

Muir, William Ker, Jr., *Police: Streetcorner Politicians* (Chicago: University of Chicago Press, 1977).

Patrick V. Murphy and Thomas Plate, *Commissioner: A View from the Top of American Law Enforcement* (New York: Simon and Schuster, 1978).

Elinor Ostrom, Roger B. Parks, and Gordon Whitaker, *Patterns of Metropolitan Policing* (Cambridge: Ballinger Publishing Company, 1978).

Thomas A. Reppetto, *The Blue Parade* (New York: Free Press, 1978).

O. Glenn Stahl and Richard A. Staufenberger, eds., *Police Personnel Administration* (Washington: Police Foundation, 1974). Paperback edition available.

Charles E. Silberman, *Criminal Violence, Criminal Justice* (New York: Random House, 1978).

James Q. Wilson, *Varieties of Police Behavior: The Management of Law and Order in Eight Communities* (New York: Atheneum, 1970 [1968]). Paperback edition available.

Organizational Decline and Cutback Management

Charles H. Levine

GOVERNMENT ORGANIZATIONS ARE NEITHER IMMORTAL nor unshrinkable.[1] Like growth, organizational decline and death, by erosion or plan, is a form of organizational change; but all the problems of managing organizational change are compounded by a scarcity of slack resources.[2] This feature of declining organizations—the diminution of the cushion of spare resources necessary for coping with uncertainty, risking innovation, and rewarding loyalty and cooperation—presents for government a problem that simultaneously challenges the underlying premises and feasibility of both contemporary management systems and the institutions of pluralist liberal democracy.[3]

Growth and decline are issues of a grand scale usually tackled by only the most brave or foolhardy of macrosocial theorists. The division of scholarly labor between social theorists and students of management is now so complete that the link between the great questions of political economy and the more earthly problems of managing public organizations is rarely forged. This bifurcation is more understandable when one acknowledges that managers and organization analysts have for decades (at least since the Roosevelt Administration and the wide acceptance of Keynesian economics) been able to subsume their concern for societal level instability under broad assumptions of abundance and continous and unlimited economic growth.[4] Indeed, almost all of our public management strategies are predicated on assumptions of the continuing enlargement of public revenues and expenditures. These expansionist assumptions are particularly prevalent in public financial management systems that anticipate budgeting by incremental additions to a secure base.[5] Recent events and gloomy forecasts, however, have called into question the validity and generality of these assumptions, and have created a need to reopen inquiry into the effects of resource scarcity on public organizations and their management systems. These events and forecasts, ranging from taxpayer revolts like California's successful Proposition 13 campaign and financial crises like the near collapse into bankruptcy of New York City's government and the agonizing retrenchment of its bureaucracy, to the foreboding predictions of the "limits of growth" modelers, also relink issues of political economy of the most monumental significance to practices of public management.[6]

We know very little about the decline of public organizations and the management of cutbacks. This may be because even though some federal agencies like the Works Progress Administration, Economic Recovery Administration, Department of Defense, National Aeronautics and Space Administration, the Office of Economic Opportunity, and many state and local agencies have expanded and then contracted,[7] or even died, the public sector as a whole has expanded enormously over the last four decades. In this period of expansion and optimism among proponents of an active government, isolated incidents of zero growth and decline have been considered anomalous; and the difficulties faced by the management of declining agencies coping with retrenchment have been regarded as outside the mainstream of public management concerns. It is a sign of our times—labeled by Kenneth Boulding as the "Era of Slowdown"—that we are now reappraising cases of public organization decline and death as exemplars and forerunners in order to provide strategies for the design and management of *mainstream* public administration in a future dominated by resource scarcity.[8]

The decline and death of government organizations is a symptom, a problem, and a contingency. It is a symptom of resource scarcity at a societal, even global, level that is creating the necessity for governments to terminate some programs, lower the activity level of others, and confront tradeoffs between new demands and old programs rather than to expand whenever a new public problem arises. It is a problem for managers who must maintain organizational capacity by devising new managerial arrangements within prevailing structures that were designed under assumptions of growth. It is a contingency for public employees and clients; employees who must sustain their morale and productivity in the face of increasing control from above and shrinking opportunities for creativity and promotion while clients must find alternative sources for the services governments may no longer be able to provide.

Organizational Decline and Administrative Theory

Growth is a common denominator that links contemporary management theory to its historical antecedents and management practices with public policy choices. William Scott has observed that ". . . organization growth creates organizational abundance, or surplus, which is used by management to buy off internal consensus from the potentially conflicting interest group segments that compete for resources in organizations."[9] As a common denominator, growth has provided a criterion to gauge the acceptability of government policies and has defined many of the problems to be solved by management action and organizational research. So great is our enthusiasm for growth that even when an organizational decline seems inevitable and irreversible, it is nearly impossible to get elected officials, public managers, citizens, or management theorists to confront cutback and decremental planning situations as anything more than temporary slowdowns. Nevertheless, the reality of zero growth and absolute decline, at least in some sectors, regions, communities, and organizations, means that management and public policy theory must be expanded to incorporate non-growth as an initial condition that applies in some cases. If Scott's assertions about the pervasiveness of a growth ideology in management are correct, our management and policy paradigms will have to be replaced or augmented by new frameworks to help to identify critical questions and strategies for action. Put squarely, without growth, how do we manage public organizations?

We have no ready or comprehensive answers to this question, only hunches and shards of evidence to serve as points of departure. Under conditions and assumptions of decline, the ponderables, puzzles, and paradoxes of organizational management take on new complexities. For example, organizations cannot be cut back by merely reversing the sequence of activity and resource allocation by which their parts were originally assembled. Organizations are organic social wholes with emergent qualities which allow their parts to recombine into intricately interwoven semi-lattices when they are brought together. In his study of NASA's growth and drawdown, Paul Schulman has observed that viable public programs must attain "capture points" of public goal and resource commitments, and these organizational thresholds or "critical masses" are characterized by their indivisibility.[10] Therefore, to attempt to disaggregate and cutback on one element of such an intricate and delicate political and organization arrangement may jeopardize the functioning and equilibrium of an entire organization.

Moreover, retrenchment compounds the choice of management strategies with paradoxes. When slack resources abound, money for the development of management planning, control, information systems, and the conduct of policy analysis is plentiful even though these systems are relatively irrelevant to decision making.[11] Under conditions of abundance, habit, intuition, snap judgments and other forms of informal analysis will suffice for most decisions because the costs of making mistakes can be easily absorbed without threatening the organization's survival.[12] However, in times of austerity, when these control and analytic tools are needed to help to minimize the risk of making mistakes, the money for their development and implementation is unavailable.

Similarly, without slack resources to produce "win-win" consensus-building solutions and to provide side payments to overcome resistance to change, organizations will have difficulty innovating and maintaining flexibility. Yet, these are precisely the activities needed to maintain capacity while contracting, especially when the overriding imperative is to minimize the perturbations of adjusting to new organizational equilibriums at successively lower levels of funding and activity.[13]

Lack of growth also creates a number of serious personnel problems. For example, the need to reward managers for directing organizational contraction and termination is a problem because without growth there are few promotions and rewards available to motivate and retain successful and loyal managers — particularly when compared to job opportunities for talented managers outside the declining organization.[14] Also, without expansion, public organizations that are constrained by merit and career tenure systems are unable to attract and accommodate new young talent. Without an inflow of younger employees, the average age of employees is forced up, and the organization's skill pool becomes frozen at the very time younger, more flexible, more mobile, less expensive and (some would argue) more creative employees are needed.[15]

Decline forces us to set some of our logic for rationally structuring organizations on end and upside down. For instance, under conditions of growth and abundance, one problem for managers and organizational designers is how to set up *exclusionary* mechanisms to prevent *"free riders"* (employees and clients who share in the consumption of the organization's collective benefits without sharing the burden that produced the benefit) from taking advantage of the enriched common pool of resources. In contrast, under conditions of decline and austerity, the problem for managers and organizational designers is how to set up *inclusionary* mechanisms to prevent organizational participants from avoiding the sharing of the *"public bads"* (increased burdens) that result from the depletion of the common pool of resources.[16] In other words, to maintain order and capacity when undergoing decline, organizations need mechanisms like long-term contracts with clauses that make pensions non-portable if broken at the employee's discretion. These mechanisms need to be carefully designed to penalize and constrain *"free exiters"* and cheap exits at the convenience of the employees while still allowing managers to cut and induce into retirement marginally performing and unneeded employees.

As a final example, inflation erodes steady states so that staying even actually requires extracting more resources from the organization's environment and effectuating greater internal economies. The irony of managing decline in the public sector is particularly compelling under conditions of recession or so called "stagflation." During these periods of economic hardship and uncertainty, pressure is put on the federal government to follow Keynesian dictates and spend more through deficit financing; at the same time, critical public opinion and legal mandates require some individual agencies (and many state and local governments) to balance their budgets, and in some instances to spend less.

These characteristics of declining public organizations are like pieces of a subtle jigsaw puzzle whose parameters can only be guessed at and whose abstruseness deepens with each new attempt to fit its edges together. To overcome our tendency to regard decline in public organizations as anomalous, we need to develop a catalogue of what we already know about declining public organizations. A typology of *causes* of public organizational decline and corresponding sets of *tactics* and *decision rules* available for managing cutbacks will serve as a beginning.

The Causes of Public Organization Decline

Cutting back any kind of organization is difficult, but a good deal of the problem of cutting back public organizations is compounded by their special status as authoritative, non-market extensions of the state.[17] Public organizations are used to deliver services that usually have no direct or easily measurable monetary value or when market arrangements fail to provide the necessary level of revenues to support the desired level or distribution of services. Since budgets depend on appropriations and not sales, the diminution or termination of public organizations and programs, or conversely their maintenance and survival, are political matters usually calling for the application of the most sophisticated attack or survival tactics in the arsenal of the skilled bureaucrat-politician.[18] These strategies are not universally propitious; they are conditioned by the causes for decline and hoped-for results.

The causes of public organization decline can be categorized into a four-cell typology as shown in Figure 11–1. The causes are divided along two dimensions: (a) whether they are primarily the result of conditions located either internal or external to the organization, or (b) whether they are principally a product of political or economic/technical conditions.[19] This is admittedly a crude scheme for lumping instances of decline, but it does cover most cases and allows for some abstraction.

Of the four types, *problem depletion* is the most familiar. It covers government involvement in short-term crises like natural disasters such as floods and earthquakes, medium length governmental interventions like war mobilization and countercyclical employment programs, and longer-term public programs like polio research and treat-

Figure 11-1
The Causes of Public Organization Decline

	Internal	External
Political	Political Vulnerability	Problem Depletion
Economic/ Technical	Organizational Atrophy	Environmental Entropy

ment and space exploration — all of which involve development cycles. These cycles are characterized by a political definition of a problem followed by the extensive commitment of resources to attain critical masses and then contractions after the problem has been solved, alleviated, or has evolved into a less troublesome stage or politically popular issue.[20]

Problem depletion is largely a product of forces beyond the control of the affected organization. Three special forms of problem depletion involve demographic shifts, problem redefinition, and policy termination. The impact of demographic shifts has been vividly demonstrated in the closing of schools in neighborhoods where the school age population has shrunk. While the cause for most school closings is usually neighborhood aging — a factor outside the control of the school system — the decision to close a school is largely political. The effect of problem redefinition on public organizations is most easily illustrated by movements to deinstitutionalize the mentally ill. In these cases, the core bureaucracies responsible for treating these populations in institutions has shrunk as the rising per patient cost of hospitalization has combined with pharmaceutical advances in anti-depressants and tranquilizers to cause public attitudes and professional doctrine to shift.[21]

Policy termination has both theoretical import and policy significance. Theoretically, it is the final phase of a public policy intervention cycle and can be defined as ". . . the deliberate conclusion or cessation of specific government functions, programs, policies, or organizations,"[22] Its policy relevance is underscored by recent experiments and proposals for sunset legislation which would require some programs to undergo extensive evaluations after a period of usually five years and be reauthorized or be terminated rather than be continued indefinitely.[23]

Environmental entropy occurs when the capacity of the environment to support the public organization at prevailing levels of activity erodes.[24] This type of decline covers the now familiar phenomena of financially troubled cities and regions with declining economic bases. Included in this category are: market and technological shifts like the decline in demand for domestic textiles and steel and its effect on the economies and quality of life in places like New England textile towns and steel cities like Gary, Indiana, Bethlehem, Pennsylvania, and Youngstown, Ohio;[25] transportation changes that have turned major railroad hubs and riverports of earlier decades into stagnating and declining economies; mineral depletion which has crippled mining communities; and intrametropolitan shifts of economic activity from central cities to their suburbs.[26] In these cases, population declines often have paralleled general economic declines which erode tax bases and force cities to cut services. One of the tragic side effects of environmental entropy is that it most severely affects those who cannot move.[27] Caught in the declining city and region are the immobile and dependent: the old, the poor, and the unemployable. For these communities, the forced choice of cutting services to an ever more dependent and needy population is the cruel outcome of decline.[28]

Environmental entropy also has a political dimension. As Proposition 13 makes clear, the capacity of a government is as much a function of the willingness of taxpayers to be taxed as it is of the economic base of the taxing region. Since the demand for services and the supply of funds to support them are usually relatively independent in the public sector, taxpayer resistance can produce diminished revenues which force service reductions even though the demand and *need* for services remains high.

The *political vulnerability* of public organizations is an internal property indicating a high level of fragility and precariousness which limits their capacity to resist budget decrements and demands to contract from their environment. Of the factors which contribute to vulnerability, some seem to be more responsible for decline and death than others. Small size, internal conflict, and changes in leadership, for example, seem less telling than the lack of a base of expertise or the absence of a positive self-image and history of excellence. However, an organization's age may be the most accurate predictor of bureaucratic vulnerability. Contrary to biological reasoning, aged organizations are more flexible than young organizations and therefore rarely die or even shrink very much. Herbert Kaufman argues that one of the advantages of organizations over solitary individuals is that they do provide longer institutional memories than a human lifetime, and this means that older organizations ought to have a broader range of adaptive skills, more capacity for learning, more friends and allies, and be more innovative because they have less to fear from making a wrong decision than a younger organization.[29]

Organizational atrophy is a common phenomenon in all organizations but government organizations are particularly vulnerable because they usually lack market generated revenues to signal a malfunction and to pinpoint responsibility. Internal atrophy and declining performance which can lead to resource cutbacks or to a weakening of organizational capacity come from a host of system and management failures almost too numerous to identify. A partial list would include: inconsistent and perverse incentives, differentiation without integration, role confusion, decentralized authority with vague responsibility, too many inappropriate rules, weak oversight, stifled dissent and upward communication, rationalization of performance failure by "blaming the victim," lack of self-evaluating and self-correcting capacity, high turnover, continuous politicking for promotions and not for program resources, continuous reorganization, suspicion of outsiders, and obsolescence caused by routine adherence to past methods and technologies in the face of changing problems. No organization is immune from these problems and no organization is likely to be afflicted by them all at once, but a heavy dose of some of these breakdowns in combination can contribute to an organization's decline and even death.

Identifying and differentiating among these four types of decline situations provides a start toward cataloging and estimating the appropriateness of strategies for managing decline and cutbacks. This activity is useful because when undergoing decline, organizations face three decision tasks: first, management must decide whether it will adopt a strategy to resist decline or smooth it (i.e., reduce the impact of fluctuations in the environment that cause interruptions in the flow of work and poor performance); second, given this choice of maneuvering strategies it will have to decide what tactics are most appropriate;[30] and third, if necessary, it will have to make decisions about how and where cuts will occur. Of course, the cause of a decline will greatly affect these choices.

Strategic Choices

Public organizations behave in response to a mix of motives—some aimed at serving national (or state or local) purposes, some aimed at goals for the *organization as a whole,* and others directed toward the particularistic goals of organizational subunits. Under conditions of growth, requests for more resources by subunits usually can be easily concerted with the goals of the organization as a whole and its larger social purposes. Under decline, however, subunits usually respond to requests to make cuts in terms of their particular long-term survival needs (usually defended in terms of the injury which cutbacks would inflict on a program with lofty purposes or on a dependent clientele) irrespective of impacts on the performance of government or the organization as a whole.

The presence of powerful survival instincts in organizational subunits helps to explain why the political leadership of public organizations can be trying to respond to legislative or executive directives to cut back while at the same time the career and program leadership of subunits will be taking action to resist cuts.[31] It also helps to explain why growth can have the appearance of a rational administrative process complete with a hierarchy of objectives and broad consensus, while decline takes on the *appearance* of what James G. March has called a "garbage can problem"—arational, polycentric, fragmented, and dynamic.[32] Finally, it allows us to understand why the official rhetoric about cutbacks—whether it be to "cut the fat," "tighten our belts," "preserve future options," or "engage in a process of orderly and programmed termination"—is often at wide variance with the unofficial conduct of bureau chiefs who talk of "minimizing cutbacks to mitigate catastrophe," or "making token sacrifices until the heat's off."

Retrenchment politics dictate that organizations will respond to decrements with a mix of espoused and operative strategies that are not necessarily consistent.[33] When there is a wide divergence between the official pronouncements about the necessity for cuts and the actual occurrence of cuts, skepticism, cynicism, distrust, and noncompliance will dominate the retrenchment process and cutback management will be an adversarial process pitting top and middle management against one another. In most cases, however, conflict will not be rancorous, and strategies for dealing with decline will be a mixed bag of tactics intended either to *resist* or to *smooth* decline. The logic here is that no organization accedes to cuts with enthusiasm and will try to find a way to resist cuts; but resistance is risky. In addition to the possibility of being charged with nonfeasance, no responsible manager wants to be faced with the prospect of being unable to control where cuts will take place or confront quantum cuts with unpredictable consequences. Instead, managers will choose a less risky course and attempt to protect organizational capacity and procedures by smoothing decline and its effects on the organization.

An inventory of some of these cutback management tactics is presented in Figure 11-2. They are arrayed according to the type of decline problem which they can be employed to solve. This collection of tactics by no means exhausts the possible organizational responses to decline situations, nor are all the tactics exclusively directed toward meeting a single contingency. They are categorized in order to show that many familiar coping tactics correspond, even if only roughly, to an underlying logic. In this way a great deal of information about organizational responses to decline can be aggregated without explicating each tactic in great detail.[34]

The tactics intended to remove or alleviate the external political and economic causes of decline are reasonably straightforward means to revitalize eroded economic bases, reduce environmental uncertainty, protect niches, retain flexibility, or lessen dependence. The tactics for handling the internal causes of decline, however, tend to be more subtle means for strengthening organizations and managerial control. For instance, the management of decline *in the face of resistance* can be smoothed by changes in leadership. When hard unpopular decisions have to be made, new managers can be brought in to make the cuts, take the flak, and move on to another organization. By rotating managers into and out of the declining organization, interpersonal loyalties built up over the years will not interfere with the cutback

Figure 11-2
Some Cutback Management Tactics

	Tactics to Resist Decline	Tactics to Smooth Decline
External Political	(Problem Depletion) 1. Diversify programs, clients and constituents 2. Improve legislative liaison 3. Educate the public about the agency's mission 4. Mobilize dependent clients 5. Become "captured" by a powerful interest group or legislator 6. Threaten to cut vital or popular programs 7. Cut a visible and widespread service a little to demonstrate client dependence	1. Make peace with competing agencies 2. Cut low prestige programs 3. Cut programs to politically weak clients 4. Sell and lend expertise to other agencies 5. Share problems with other agencies
Economic/ Technical	(Environmental Entropy) 1. Find a wider and richer revenue base (e.g., metropolitan reorganization) 2. Develop incentives to prevent disinvestment 3. Seek foundation support 4. Lure new public and private sector investment 5. Adopt user charges for services where possible	1. Improve targeting on problems 2. Plan with preservative objectives 3. Cut losses by distinguishing between capital investments and sunk costs 4. Yield concessions to taxpayers and employers to retain them
Internal Political	(Political Vulnerability) 1. Issue symbolic responses like forming study commissions and task forces 2. "Circle the wagons," i.e., develop a seige mentality to retain esprit de corps 3. Strengthen expertise	1. Change leadership at each stage in the decline process 2. Reorganize at each stage 3. Cut programs run by weak subunits 4. Shift programs to another agency 5. Get temporary exemptions from personnel and budgetary regulations which limit discretion

Figure 11-2 (Continued)

	Tactics to Resist Decline	Tactics to Smooth Decline
	(Organizational Atrophy)	
Economic/ Technical	1. Increase hierarchical control 2. Improve productivity 3. Experiment with less costly service delivery systems 4. Automate 5. Stockpile and ration resources	1. Renegotiate long term contracts to regain flexibility 2. Install rational choice techniques like zero-base budgeting and evaluation research 3. Mortgage the future by deferring maintenance and downscaling personnel quality 4. Ask employees to make voluntary sacrifices like taking early retirements and deferring raises 5. Improve forecasting capacity to anticipate further cuts 6. Reassign surplus facilities to other users 7. Sell surplus property, lease back when needed 8. Exploit the exploitable

process. This is especially useful in implementing a higher level decision to terminate an organization where managers will make the necessary cuts knowing that their next assignments will not depend on their support in the organization to be terminated.

The "exploit the exploitable" tactic also calls for further explanation. Anyone familiar with the personnel practices of universities during the 1970s will recognize this tactic. It has been brought about by the glutted market for academic positions which has made many unlucky recent Ph.Ds vulnerable and exploitable. This buyers' market has coincided neatly with the need of universities facing steady states and declining enrollments to avoid long-term tenure commitments to expensive faculties. The result is a marked increase in part-time and non-tenure track positions which are renewed on a semester-to-semester basis. So while retrenchment is smoothed and organization flexibility increased, it is attained at considerable cost to the careers and job security of the exploited teachers.

Cutback management is a two-crucible problem: besides selecting tactics for either resisting or smoothing decline, if necessary, management must also select who will be let go and what programs will be curtailed or terminated. Deciding where to make cuts is a test of managerial intelligence and courage because each choice involves tradeoffs and opportunity costs that cannot be erased through the generation of new resources accrued through growth.

As with most issues of public management involving the distribution of costs, the choice of decision rules to allocate cuts usually involves the tradeoff between equity and efficiency.[35] In this case, "equity" is meant to mean the distribution of cuts across the organization with an equal probability of hurting all units and employees irrespective of impacts on the long term capacity of the organization. "Efficiency" is meant to mean the sorting, sifting, and assignment of cuts to those people and units in the organization so that for a given budget decrement, cuts are allocated to minimize the long-term loss in total benefits to the organization as a whole, irrespective of their distribution.

Making cuts on the basis of equity is easier for managers because it is socially acceptable, easier to justify, and involves few decision making costs. "Sharing the pain" is politically expedient because it appeals to common sense ideals of justice. Further, simple equity decision making avoids costs from sorting, selecting, and negotiating cuts.[36] In contrast, efficiency cuts involve costly triage analysis because the distribution of pain and inconvenience requires that the value of people and subunits to the organization have to be weighed in terms of their expected *future* contributions. In the public sector, of course, things are never quite this clear cut because a host of constraints like career status, veteran's preference, bumping rights, entitlements, and mandated programs limit managers from selecting optimal rules for making cuts. Nevertheless, the values of equity and efficiency are central to allocative decision making and provide useful criteria for judging the appropriateness of cutback rules. By applying these criteria to five of the most commonly used or proposed cutback methods—seniority, hiring freezes, even-percentage-cuts-across-the-board, productivity criteria, and zero base budgeting—we are able to make assessments of their efficacy as managerial tools.

Seniority is the most prevalent and most maligned of the five decision rules. Seniority guarantees have little to do with either equity or efficiency, *per se*. Instead, they are directed at another value of public administration; that is, the need to provide secure career-long employment to neutrally competent civil servants.[37] Because seniority is likely to be spread about the organization unevenly, using seniority criteria for making cuts forces managers to implicitly surrender control over the impact of cuts on services and the capacity of subunits. Furthermore, since seniority usually dictates a "last-in-first-out" retention system, personnel cuts using this decision rule tend to inflict the greatest harm to minorities and women who are recent entrants in most public agencies.

A *hiring freeze* is a convenient short-run strategy to buy time and preserve options. In the short run it hurts no one already employed by the organization because hiring freezes rely on "natural attrition" through resignations, retirements, and death to diminish the size of an organization's work force. In the long run, however, hiring freezes are hardly the most equitable or efficient way to scale down organizational size. First, even though natural and self selection relieves the stress on managers, it also takes control over the decision of whom and where to cut away from management and thereby reduces the possibility of intelligent long range cutback planning. Second, hiring freezes are more likely to harm minorities and women who are more likely to be the next hired rather than the next retired. Third, attrition will likely occur at different rates among an organization's professional and technical specialities. Since resignations will most likely come from those employees with the most opportunities for employment elsewhere, during a long hiring freeze an organization may find itself short on some critically needed skills yet unable to hire people with these skills even though they may be available.

Even-percentage-cuts-across-the-board are expedient because they transfer decision-making costs lower in the organization, but they tend to be insensitive to the needs, production functions, and contributions of different units. The same percentage cut may call for hardly more than some mild belt tightening in some large unspecialized units but when translated into the elimination of one or two positions in a highly specialized, tightly integrated small unit, it may immobilize that unit.

Criticizing *productivity criteria* is more difficult but nevertheless appropriate, especially when the concept is applied to the practice of cutting low producing units and people based on their *marginal product* per increment of revenue. This method is insensitive to differences in clients served, unit capacity, effort, and need. A more appropriate criterion is one that cuts programs, organization units, and employees so that the *marginal utility* for a decrement of resources is equal across units, individuals, and programs thereby providing for *equal sacrifices* based on the *need* for resources. However, this criterion assumes organizations are fully rational actors, an assumption easily dismissed. More likely, cuts will be distributed by a mix of analysis and political bargaining.

Aggregating incompatible needs and preferences is a political problem and this is why *zero base budgeting* gets such high marks as a method for making decisions about resource allocation under conditions of decline. First, ZBB is future directed; instead of relying on an "inviolate-base-plus-increment" calculus, it allows for the analysis of both existing and proposed new activities. Second, ZBB allows for tradeoffs between programs or units below their present funding levels. Third, ZBB allows a ranking of decision packages by political bargaining and negotiation so that attention is concentrated on those packages or activities most likely to be affected by cuts.[38] As a result, ZBB allows both analysis and politics to enter into cutback decision making and therefore can incorporate an expression of the *intensity of need* for resources by participating managers and clients while also accommodating estimates of how cuts will affect the *activity levels* of their units. Nevertheless, ZBB is not without problems. Its analytic component is likely to be expensive — especially so under conditions of austerity — and to be subject to all the limitations and pitfalls of cost-benefit analysis, while its political component is likely to be costly in political terms as units fight with each other and with central management over rankings, tradeoffs, and the assignment of decrements.[39]

These five decision rules illustrate how strategic choices about cutback management can be made with or without expediency, analysis, courage, consideration of the organization's long-term health, or the effect of cuts on the lives of employees and clients. Unfortunately, for some employees and clients, and the public interest, the choice will usually be made by managers to "go along" quietly with across-the-board cuts and exit as soon as possible. The alternative for those who would prefer more responsible and toughminded decision making *to facilitate long-run organizational survival* is to develop in managers and employees strong feelings of organizational loyalty and loyalty to clients, to provide disincentives to easy exit, and to encourage participation so that dissenting views on the location of cuts could emerge from the ranks of middle management, lower level employees, and clients.[40]

Ponderables

The world of the future is uncertain, but scarcity and tradeoffs seem inevitable. Boulding has argued, "in a stationary society roughly half the society will be experiencing decline while the other half will be experiencing growth."[41] If we are entering an era of general slowdown, this means that the balance in the distribution between expanding and contracting sectors, regions, and organizations will be tipped toward decline. It means that we will need a governmental capacity for developing tradeoffs between growing and declining organizations and for intervening in regional and sectorial economies to avoid the potentially harmful effects of radical perturbations from unmanaged decline.

So far we have managed to get along without having to make conscious tradeoffs between sectors and regions. We have met declines on a "crisis-to-crisis" basis through emergency legislation and financial aid. This is a strategy that assumes declines are special cases of temporary disequilibrium, bounded in time and space, that are usually confined to a single organization, community, or region. A broad scale long-run *societal level* decline, however, is a problem of a different magnitude and to resolve it, patchwork solutions will not suffice.

There seem to be two possible directions in which to seek a way out of immobility. First is the authoritarian possibility; what Robert L. Heilbroner has called the rise of "iron governments" with civil liberties diminished and resources allocated throughout society from the central government without appeal.[42] This is a possibility abhorrent to the democratic tradition, but it comprises a possible future—if not for the United States in the near future, at least for some other less affluent nations. So far we have had little experience with cutting back on rights, entitlements, and privileges; but scarcity may dictate "decoupling" dependent and less powerful clients and overcoming resistance through violent autocratic implementation methods.

The other possible future direction involves new images and assumptions about the nature of man, the state and the ecosystem. It involves changes in values away from material consumption, a gradual withdrawal from our fascination with economic growth, and more efficient use of resources—especially raw materials. For this possibility to occur, we will have to have a confrontation with our propensity for wishful thinking that denies that some declines are permanent. Also required is a widespread acceptance of egalitarian norms and of anti-growth and no growth ideologies which are now only nascent, and the development of a political movement to promote their incorporation into policy making.[43] By backing away from our obsession with growth, we will also be able to diminish the "load" placed on central governments and allow for greater decentralization and the devolvement of functions.[44] In this way, we may be able to preserve democratic rights and processes while meeting a future of diminished resources.

However, the preferable future might not be the most probable future. This prospect should trouble us deeply.

NOTES

An earlier version of this paper was presented at the 1978 Annual Meeting of the American Society for Public Administration, Phoenix, Arizona, April 12, 1978. I wish to thank the following people for providing valuable comments about that draft: Pierre Clavel, Pat Conklin, Richard Cyert, Paul Gallagher, Eugene Lewis, Laurence O'Toole, Nancy Petrovic, Sam Postbrief, Allen Schick, Frank Sherwood, Fred Thayer, Richard Schramm, and Dwight Waldo.

References to "this symposium" in the notes below refer to *Public Administration Review*, XXXVIII (July/August, 1978), Symposium on Organizational Decline and Cutback Management, edited by Charles H. Levine.

1. The intellectual foundations of this essay are too numerous to list. Three essays in particular sparked my thinking: Herbert Kaufman's *The Limits of Organizational Change* (University, Alabama: The University of Alabama Press, 1971) and *Are Government Organizations Immortal?* (Washington, DC: The Brookings Institution, 1976) and Herbert J. Gans, "Planning for Declining and Poor Cities," *Journal of the American Institute of Planners* (September, 1975), pp. 305-307. The concept of "cutback planning" is introduced in the Gans article. My initial interest in this subject stemmed from my work with a panel of the National Academy of Public Administration on a NASA-sponsored project that produced *Report of the Ad Hoc Panel on Attracting New Staff and Retaining Capability During a Period of Declining Manpower Ceilings.*

2. For an explication of the concept of "organizational slack" see Richard M. Cyert and James G. March, *A Behavioral Theory of the Firm* (Englewood Cliffs, N.J.: Prentice-Hall, 1963), pp. 36-38. They argue that because of market imperfections between payments and demands "there is ordinarily a disparity between the resources available to the organization and the payments required to maintain the coalition. This difference between total resources and total necessary payments is what we have called *organizational slack.* Slack consists in payments to members of the coalition in excess of what is required to maintain the organization. . . . Many forms of slack typically exist: stockholders are paid dividends in excess of those required to keep stockholders (or banks) within the organization; prices are set lower than necessary to maintain adequate income from buyers; wages in excess of those required to maintain labor are paid; executives are provided with services and personal luxuries in excess of those required to keep them; subunits are permitted to grow without real concern for the relation between additional payments and additional revenue; public services are provided in excess of those required. . . . Slack operates to stabilize the system in two ways: (1) by absorbing excess resources, it retards upward adjustment of aspirations during relatively good times; (2) by providing a pool of emergency resources, it permits aspirations to be maintained (and achieved) during relatively bad times."

3. See William G. Scott, "The Management of Decline," *The Conference Board RECORD* (June, 1976), pp. 56-59 and "Organization Theory: A Reassessment," *Academy of Management Journal* (June, 1974) pp. 242-253; also Rufus E. Miles, Jr., *Awakening from the American Dream: The Social and Political Limits to Growth* (New York: Universal Books, 1976).

4. See Daniel M. Fox, *The Discovery of Abundance: Simon N. Patten and the Transformation of Social Theory* (Ithaca, N.Y.: Cornell University Press, 1967).

5. See Andrew Glassberg's contribution to this symposium, "Organizational Responses to Municipal Budget Decreases," and Edward H. Potthoff, Jr., "Pre-planning for Budget Reductions," *Public Management* (March, 1975), pp. 13-14.

6. See Donella H. Meadows, Dennis L. Meadows, Jorgen Randers, and William W. Behrens III, *The Limits to Growth* (New York: Universe Books, 1972); also Robert L. Heilbroner, *An Inquiry into the Human*

Prospect (New York: W. W. Norton, 1975) and *Business Civilization in Decline* (New York: W. W. Norton, 1976).

7. See Advisory Commission on Intergovernmental Relations, *City Financial Emergencies: The Intergovernmental Dimension* (Washington, D.C.: U.S. Government Printing Office, 1973).

8. Kenneth E. Boulding, "The Management of Decline" *Change* (June, 1975), pp. 8-9 and 64. For extensive analyses of cutback management in the same field that Boulding addresses, university administration, see: Frank M. Bowen and Lyman A. Glenny, *State Budgeting for Higher Education: State Fiscal Stringency and Public Higher Education* (Berkeley, Calif.: Center for Research and Development in Higher Education, 1976); Adam Yarmolinsky, "Institutional Paralysis," *Special Report on American Higher Education: Toward an Uncertain Future* Vol. 2, *Daedalus* 104 (Winter, 1975), pp. 61-67; Frederick E. Balderston, *Varieties of Financial Crisis*, (Berkeley, Calif.: Ford Foundation, 1972); The Carnegie Foundation for the Advancement of Teaching, *More Than Survival* (San Francisco: Jossey-Bass, 1975); Earl F. Cheit, *The New Depression in Higher Education* (New York: McGraw-Hill, 1973) and *The New Depression in Higher Education—Two Years Later* (Berkeley, Calif.: The Carnegie Commission on Higher Education, 1975); Lyman A. Glenny, "The Illusions of Steady States," *Change* 6 (December/January 1974-75), pp. 24-28; and John D. Millett, "What is Economic Health?" *Change* 8 (September 1976), p. 27.

9. Scott, "Organizational Theory: A Reassessment," p. 245.

10. Paul R. Schulman, "Nonincremental Policy Making: Notes Toward an Alternative Paradigm," *American Political Science Review* (December, 1975), pp. 1354-1370.

11. See Naomi Caiden and Aaron Wildavsky, *Planning Budgeting in Poor Countries* (New York: John Wiley& Sons, 1974).

12. See James W. Vaupel, "Muddling Through Analytically," in Willis D. Hawley and David Rogers (eds.) *Improving Urban Management* (Beverly Hills, Calif.: Sage Publications, 1976), pp. 124-146.

13. See Richard M. Cyert's contribution to this symposium, "The Management of Universities of Constant or Decreasing Size."

14. See National Academy of Public Administration *Report* and Glassberg, "Organizational Response to Municipal Budget Decreases."

15. See NAPA *Report* and *Cancelled Careers: The Impact of Reduction-In-Force Policies on Middle-Aged Federal Employees,* A Report to the Special Committee on Aging, United States Senate (Washington, D.C.: U.S. Government Printing Office, 1972).

16. See Albert O. Hirschman, *Exit, Voice and Loyalty: Responses to Decline in Firms, Organizations and States* (Cambridge, Mass.: Harvard University Press, 1970); also Mancur Olson, *The Logic of Collective Action* (Cambridge, Mass.: Harvard University Press, 1965).

17. The distinctive features of public organizations are discussed at greater length in Hal G. Rainey, Robert W. Backoff, and Charles H. Levine, "Comparing Public and Private Organization," *Public Administration Review* (March/April, 1976), pp. 223-244.

18. See Robert Behn's contribution to this symposium, "Closing a Government Facility," Barry Mitnick's "Deregulation as a Process of Organizational Reduction," and Herbert A. Simon, Donald W. Smithburg, and Victor A. Thompson, *Public Administration* (New York: Knopf, 1950) for discussions of the survival tactics of threatened bureaucrats.

19. This scheme is similar to those presented in Daniel Katz and Robert L. Kahn, *The Social Psychology of Organizations* (John Wiley & Sons, 1966), p. 166, and Gary L. Wamsley and Mayer N. Zald, *The Political Economy of Public Organizations: A Critique and Approach to the Study of Public Administration* (Lexington, Mass.: D.C. Heath, 1973), p. 20.

20. See Schulman, "Nonincremental Policy Making," and Charles O. Jones, "Speculative Augmentation in Federal Air Pollution Policy-Making," *Journal of Politics* (May, 1974), pp. 438-464.

21. See Robert Behn, "Closing the Massachusetts Public Training Schools," *Policy Sciences* (June, 1976), pp. 151-172; Valarie J. Bradley, "Policy Termination in Mental Health: The Hidden Agenda," *Policy Sciences* (June, 1976), pp. 215-224; and David J. Rothman, "Prisons, Asylums and Other Decaying Institutions," *The Public Interest* (Winter, 1972), pp. 3-17. A similar phenomena is occurring in some of the fields of regulation policy where deregulation is being made more politically feasible by a combination of technical and economic changes. See Mitnick, "Deregulation as a Process of Organizational Reduction."

22. Peter deLeon, "Public Policy Termination: An End and a Beginning," an essay prepared at the request of the Congressional Research Service as background for the Sunset Act of 1977.

23. There are many variations on the theme of Sunset. Gary Brewer's contribution to this symposium, "Termination: Hard Choices-Harder Questions" identifies a number of problems central to most sunset proposals.

24. For two treatments of this phenomena in the literature of organization theory see Barry M. Staw and Eugene Szwajkowski, "The Scarcity-Munificence Component of Organizational Environments and the Commission of Illegal Acts," *Administrative Science Quarterly* (September, 1975), pp. 345-354, and Barry Bozeman and E. Allen Slusher, "The Future of Public Organizations Under Assumptions of Environmental Stress," paper presented at the Annual Meeting of the American Society for Public Administration, Phoenix, Arizona, April 9-12, 1978.

25. See Thomas Muller, *Growing and Declining Urban Areas: A Fiscal Comparison* (Washington, D.C.: Urban Institute, 1975).

26. See Richard P. Nathan and Charles Adams, "Understanding Central City Hardship," *Political Science Quarterly* (Spring, 1976), pp. 47-62; Terry Nichols Clark, Irene Sharp Rubin, Lynne C. Pettler, and Erwin Zimmerman, "How Many New Yorks? The New York Fiscal Crisis in Comparative Perspective." (Report No. 72 of Comparative Study of Community Decision-Making, University of Chicago, April, 1976); and David T. Stanley, "The Most Troubled Cities," a discussion draft prepared for a meeting of the National Urban Policy Roundtable, Academy for Contemporary Problems, Summer, 1976.

27. See Richard Child Hill, "Fiscal Collapse and Political Struggle in Decaying Central Cities in the United States," in William K. Tabb and Larry Sawers (eds.) *Marxism and The Metropolis* (New York: Oxford University Press, 1978); and H. Paul Friesema, "Black Control of Central Cities: The Hollow Prize," *Journal of the American Institute of Planners* (March, 1969), pp. 75-79.

28. See David T. Stanley, "The Most Troubled Cities" and "The Survival of Troubled Cities," a paper prepared for delivery at the 1977 Annual Meeting of the American Political Science Association, The Washington Hilton Hotel, Washington D.C., September 1-4, 1977; and Martin Shef-

ter, "New York City's Fiscal Crisis: The Politics of Inflation and Retrenchment," *The Public Interest* (Summer, 1977), pp. 98-127.

29. See Kaufman, *Are Government Organizations Immortal?* and "The Natural History of Human Organizations," *Administration and Society* (August, 1975), pp. 131-148; I have been working on this question for some time in collaboration with Ross Clayton. Our partially completed manuscript is entitled, "Organizational Aging: Progression or Degeneration." See also Edith Tilton Penrose, "Biological Analogies in the Theory of the Firm," *American Economic Review* (December, 1952), pp. 804-819 and Mason Haire, "Biological Models and Empirical Histories of the Growth of Organizations" in Mason Haire (ed.) *Modern Organization Theory* (New York: John Wiley & Sons, 1959), pp. 272-306.

30. For a fuller explanation of "smoothing" or "leveling," see James D. Thompson, *Organizations in Action* (New York: McGraw-Hill, 1967), pp. 19-24.

31. For recent analyses of related phenomena see Joel D. Aberbach and Bert A. Rockman, "Clashing Beliefs Within the Executive Branch: The Nixon Administration Bureaucracy," *American Political Science Review* (June, 1976), pp. 456-468 and Hugh Heclo, *A Government of Strangers: Executive Politics in Washington* (Washington, D.C. The Brookings Institution, 1977).

32. See James G. March and Johan P. Olsen, *Ambiguity and Choice in Organizations* (Bergen, Norway: Universitetsforlaget, 1976); and Michael D. Cohen, James G. March, and Johan P. Olsen, "A Garbage Can Model of Organizational Choice," *Administrative Science Quarterly* (March, 1972), pp. 1-25.

33. See Charles Perrow, *Organizational Analysis: A Sociological View* (Belmont, Calif.: Wadsworth Publishing Company, 1970) and Chris Argyris and Donald A. Schon, *Theory in Practice: Increasing Professional Effectiveness* (San Francisco, Calif.: Jossey-Bass, 1974) for discussions of the distinction between espoused and operative (i.e., "theory-in-use") strategies.

34. For extensive treatments of the tactics of bureaucrats, some of which are listed here, see Frances E. Rourke, *Bureaucracy, Politics, and Public Policy* (second edition, Boston: Little, Brown and Company, 1976); Aaron Wildavsky, *The Politics of the Budgetary Process* (second edition, Boston: Little, Brown and Company, 1974); Eugene Lewis, *American Politics in a Bureaucratic Age* (Cambridge, Mass.: Winthrop Publishers, 1977); and Simon, Smithburg and Thompson, *Public Administration.*

35. See Arthur M. Oken, *Equity and Efficiency: The Big Tradeoff* (Washington, D.C.: The Brookings Institution, 1975).

36. For a discussion of the costs of interactive decision making see Charles R. Adrian and Charles Press, "Decision Costs in Coalition Formation," *American Political Science Review* (June, 1968), pp. 556-563.

37. See Herbert Kaufman, "Emerging Conflicts in the Doctrine of Public Administration," *American Political Science Review* (December, 1956), pp. 1057-1073 and Frederick C. Mosher, *Democracy and the Public Service* (New York: Oxford University Press, 1968). Seniority criteria also have roots in the widespread belief that organizations ought to recognize people who invest heavily in them by protecting long time employees when layoffs become necessary.

38. See Peter A. Pyhrr, "The Zero-Base Approach to Government Budgeting," *Public Administrative Review* (January/February, 1977), pp. 1-8;

Graeme M. Taylor, "Introduction to Zero-base Budgeting," *The Bureaucrat* (Spring, 1977), pp. 33-55.

39. See Brewer, "Termination: Hard Choices—Harder Questions"; Allen Schick, "Zero-base Budgeting and Sunset: Redundancy or Symbiosis?" *The Bureaucrat* (Spring, 1977), pp. 12-32 and "The Road From ZBB" *Public Administration Review* (March/April, 1978), pp. 177-180; and Aaron Wildavsky, "The Political Economy of Efficiency," *Public Administration Review* (December, 1966), pp. 292-310.

40. See Hirschman, *Exit, Voice and Loyalty,* especially Ch. 7, "A Theory of Loyalty," pp. 76-105; Despite the attractiveness of "responsible and toughminded decision making" the constraints on managerial discretion in contraction decisions should not be underestimated. At the local level, for example, managers often have little influence on what federally funded programs will be cut back or terminated. They are often informed after funding cuts have been made in Washington and they are expected to make appropriate adjustments in their local work forces. These downward adjustments often are also outside of a manager's control because in many cities with merit systems, veteran's preference, and strong unions, elaborate rules dictate who will be dismissed and the timing of dismissals.

41. Boulding, "The Management of Decline," p. 8.

42. See Heilbroner, *An Inquiry into the Human Prospect;* also Michael Harrington, *The Twilight of Capitalism* (New York: Simon & Schuster, 1976).

43. For a discussion of anti-growth politics see Harvey Molotch, "The City as a Growth Machine," *American Journal of Sociology* (September, 1976), pp. 309-332.

44. Richard Rose has made a penetrating argument about the potential of governments to become "overloaded" in "Comment: What Can Ungovernability Mean?" *Futures* (April 1977), pp. 92-94. For a more detailed presentation, see his "On the Priorities of Government: A Developmental Analysis of Public Policies," *European Journal of Political Research* (September 1976), pp. 247-290. This theme is also developed by Rose in collaboration with B. Guy Peters in *Can Governments Go Bankrupt?* (New York: Basic Books, 1978).

L.A.P.D. in the Wake of Proposition 13
Jeffrey I. Chapman

ON JUNE 6, 1979, the ordinarily quiet world of public administrators in the State of California was severely shaken. On that day an overwhelming majority of the voters supported the Jarvis-Gann Initiative—Proposition 13 on the ballot. This initiative was designed to change the basic revenue system of local governments by drastically cutting property taxes. This property tax revolt, as the media described it, marked a watershed in local government finance and threatened an overhaul of local revenue systems and a temporary dislocation of public expenditures until the necessary adjustments could be made.

The Background of Proposition 13

The property tax in California had long been considered, as elsewhere in the United States, a mainstay of local government finance. Although California's reliance on the property tax had declined consistently over the previous decade, at the time of Proposition 13 it still accounted for 33 percent of county and 21 percent of municipal revenues — percentages close to the national yields. Yields had been consistent, easy to predict, and little affected by cyclical trends in the economy. Not surprisingly, local governments perceived this tax as the bulwark of their revenue systems.

The California property tax revolt was not, however, unanticipated. As the annual surveys of the Advisory Commission on Intergovernmental Relations indicate, the general public regards the local property tax as the "worst" tax; in the Western half of the counry, almost 45 percent of the population have consistently considered it the most unfair of all taxes.

The reasons for a negative citizen attitude toward the property tax are easily understood. It is the one tax that is clearly visible: income taxes are most often withheld, sales taxes are paid only in marginal amounts on most purchases, but property taxes are typically due in large, semi-annual, lump-sum payments. Further, unlike other taxes, property taxes are voted upon and the citizen perceives a direct relationship between what is extracted and what is received in return. Since surveys indicate that many people believe that government is inefficient and wasteful and that a good deal of "fat" could be trimmed without harming essential public services, they naturally feel overtaxed. This was especially true in California, where the State enjoyed a large and growing revenue surplus generated by high income and sales tax receipts.

Furthermore, Californian household values had increased rapidly. These increases resulted from increased demand for single family dwellings and a relatively static supply of buildable land. In many of the major urban counties, average annual property value appreciation was close to 20 percent. Currently, homes in Orange County and the areas around San Francisco, Los Angeles, and San Diego are rated among the most expensive in the United States, at 25 to 45 percent above the national average. County assessors typically reassess at three year intervals, and, with each assessment, huge increases in the assessed market values of properties are not unusual. Had California's local governments taken this increase in the tax base into account and lowered the tax rate, which they did not, the property tax liability of any household would have changed very little. Instead, counties had typical yearly increases ranging 11 to 13 percent in property taxes collected, and municipalities saw annual increases of 9 to 13 percent for two decades. While the state legislature debated how best to use the surplus, homeowners demanded property tax relief.

The Jarvis-Gann Initiative

Property tax revision had been under consideration since the passage of relief measures for senior citizens in 1967, which were followed by other relief measures and renter credits. Proposition 13, the Jarvis-Gann Initiative, advocated the twentieth and clearly the most far reaching change in the property tax law in eleven years.

In 1977, the state legislature considered twenty-five property tax relief bills and, although none had been enacted, they had raised expectations of immediate relief. Howard Jarvis, executive director of an apartment owners association, and Paul Gann, a retired real estate broker, took advantage of the legislature's indecision and division, and exploited public expectations of relief. Their initiative quickly gained nearly 1.3 million signatures, twice the number needed to qualify for the ballot, and presented the voters with their fourth chance in ten years to limit property taxes.

The Jarvis-Gann initiative included five separate but related proposals:

1. to limit the *ad valorem* property taxes to 1 percent of the full cash value of the property
2. to establish as the basis for full cash value the appraised value as of March 1, 1975, with any property changing ownership or newly constructed after 1975 being assessed at the new market value
3. to allow a maximum 2 percent increase in market value each year
4. to force a two-thirds vote of the members of each house of the Legislature for additional non-property taxes
5. to allow cities, counties, and special districts to impose special non-property taxes by a two-thirds vote of the qualified electors within that district

The state's legislative analyst estimated that passage of the initiative would result in a loss of about $7 billion in local property tax revenues.

Despite dire warnings of government collapse, state bankruptcy, mass unemployment, and tremendous reductions in public services should the proposition succeed, it was enthusiastically received as a measure that would "save the American Dream" of home ownership. It was portrayed as a taxpayer's revolt against wasteful government spending, excessive taxation, and non-productive bureaucracy. Hastily, its opponents put forward more moderate alternative proposals, but the proposition's success was virtually guaranteed by the spectacle of the political establishment trying to overcome its obvious embarrassment and the announcement of new assessments that threatened to double or triple many property taxes. Proposition 13 gained almost two-thirds of the popular vote (63 percent) and clearly many homeowners turned out only to vote for this measure.

Surveys taken after the election indicated that a high proportion of voters believed that government at all levels was inefficient. Eighty-four percent believed that the federal and state governments were inefficient; 64 percent believed that county government was inefficient, and 55 percent believed city government to be inefficient. Furthermore, 38 percent of the voters believed that even a 40 percent reduction in revenue need not result in any significant reduction in government service levels. If cutbacks were necessary, voters indicated that welfare should be the prime target. The least popular service areas for budget cuts were the fire and police departments. Only 8 percent believed that police department and law enforcement agencies should be cut back, while 6 percent believed that fire department budgets should be reduced.

Given the magnitude of the victory — until a month before election day, it had been touch and go — the political establishment could not ignore the message. Former opponents switched sides and became champions of reduced government spending and tax relief. The State Legislature decided to implement Proposition 13 as expeditiously as possible, and within three weeks Governor Brown had endorsed and signed the bill into law. What helped this turnaround was the discovery that the previously anticipated state surplus of $3 billion would be double that, and the state could allocate some $5 billion to local jurisdictions, replacing some 85 to 90 percent of the expected loss in property tax revenues during the next year.

Government Response

The legislative response to Proposition 13 consisted of four parts. The first was a determination of the allocation of property tax revenues that could be collected under the 1 percent limit. The second was the establishment of an emergency loan fund. The third was the determination of the level of state assistance to cities, counties, special districts, and school districts. (See Table 11-1. All tables are at the end of the case, beginning on page 493.) The fourth was a provision concerning state and local government employee pay increases.

The allocation of the approximately $4.3 billion of property taxes collected within the new limits was distributed among jurisdictions that collected property taxes on a pro-rata basis. In order to receive these monies, a jurisdiction was required to levy its taxes at the full 1 percent rate.

The emergency loan fund was allocated $900 million, and owing to a number of restrictions it has never been used. Only as a last resort could the state loan from the emergency fund and local borrowers were required to repay emergency loans within one year. The amount that could be loaned was limited to 50 percent of the property tax revenues collected by the local agency or jurisdiction in 1977–1978 and the repayment of the money borrowed would constitute a first lien on the agency's or jurisdiction's tax revenues and other incomes.

Two hundred and fifty million dollars went to the cities. The basis for apportionment was a city's proportional property tax loss. If a city had run a surplus, its share was reduced by one-third of the surplus in excess of 5 percent of the city's total 1977–1978 revenue. Cities were required to use the state assistance to ensure continuation of the same level of police and fire protection that had been provided in 1977–1978. However, cost savings can be implemented if such steps do not impair the protection provided.

Counties received $1.48 billion in state assistance. Of this assistance, $1.05 billion involved the state's takeover of Medi-Cal, SSI, AFDC, and the food stamp program, all of which had previously been county responsibilities. The remaining amount was a block grant based on the proportional property tax loss of each county (counties were also "punished" for running large surpluses). Priority use of this block grant was to ensure the continuation of police and fire protection at the 1977–1978 level.

One hundred twenty five million dollars went to special districts, through the county boards of supervisors. This was later augmented by about $30 million. Special districts had to go to the supervisors for their allocations. Districts that used non-property tax revenues (i.e., user charges) had a lower priority for funding than other districts. Punishment for running surpluses was again included in the allocation formula.

Public schools received $2 billion in state aid. The aid varied from district to district according to a sliding scale, with low-spending districts guaranteed 91 percent of their 1978–1979 budget and high-spending districts assured of 85 percent of their budgets.

Finally, the legislature mandated that no funds would be available to any local agency that provided a cost of living increase for local public employees or welfare recipients in excess of that provided for state employees. Since the legislature and the governor decided that state employees were to get no increase, the law limited salary increases for all public employees to zero. However, this provision did not preclude merit increases, promotion, transfer, or fringe benefit changes. The bargaining arena obviously shifted.

In summary, the state replaced about 90 percent of the lost revenue. However, the state aid did not come free. The state mandated certain expenditure patterns and also interfered with the wage-setting process. Because of this, there has been a clear centralization of local government finance.

Administrative Reaction

Administrative reaction to Proposition 13 fell into four distinct phases. The first preceded its passage: until a month before election day, many public officials felt confident that the initiative would not pass; similar measures in the past had failed. According to the polls, public opinion was divided but leaning toward passage, and a considerable number of the voters were undecided. Because a large sector of the electorate was made up of public employees who knew the hazards of the initiative, the administration was confident that more moderate measures would have greater appeal and that a sense of public responsibility would prevail. The political establishment, the mass media, and the labor movement all endorsed the more moderate alternative, Proposition 8, and apart from the usual noises from the conservative right, there seemed no overwhelming ground swell of support for Proposition 13. The administration only went through the motions of announcing contingency plans and warned about the irresponsibility of the Jarvis–Gann Initiative. When it became clear that they had misjudged public opinion, it was too late; they could only await the inevitable.

By May 1979, a month before the election, the campaign for and against the initiative had become intense, expensive, and bitter. Governor Brown enthusiastically endorsed the legislative alternative and actively campaigned against Proposition 13. He utilized the projections of economic models to predict chaos for the California economy, arguing that an unemployment increase of nearly 450,000 persons was possible.

Local politicians also became involved in this second phase. In particular, the Los Angeles County Board of Supervisors decided to endorse the state alternative. After this decision, they then asked the county assessor to release the new property values for homeowners before the June 6 election. This was about six weeks earlier than they had been released previously. The county assessor, a political appointee who was entering his first electoral race, decided to follow the wishes of the supervisors and released the new assessments. These were again extraordinarily high for many sections of the county and gave a strong impetus to the pro-Jarvis people. From that time on, public opinion began to shift strongly towards the Jarvis Initiative.

The third phase began with the passage of Proposition 13 and was basically concerned with the reactions of officials, who resented the proponents of Proposition 13 and the public that had supported it. With some panic they sought retribution. How could the public do this to them? How were they to continue to govern, to provide essential services, to meet their obligations? Surely the citizens realized that services were going to have to be cut back. In the heat of the moment, some public officials condemned, threatened, and predicted all kinds of negative results. Tempers cooled when it was recognized that a great many public officials had also voted for Proposition 13 for much the same reason as everyone else — property taxes were very high, governments had come to take taxpayers too much for granted, and the opportunity was there to tell a procrastinating establishment that long-needed governmental reform was past due. The public had to be accommodated. Spiteful actions would primarily hurt those groups most dependent on public services and least able to protect themselves politically.

As it was beyond most local jurisdictions to find immediate sources of revenue, they could only reduce expenditures. New programs were cut back; contemplated programs were put on back burners. Staff levels were frozen, no new hiring was to take place, and vacancies would not be filled unless absolutely necessary. Plans were hastily improvised to reduce expenditures. Economy and retrenchment schemes were put into effect as quickly as could be arranged. Such measures, however, could only be "too little, too late." Commitments could not be reduced to a level at which the new property taxes would cover their expense and the lead time for more severe overhauls of public services was months, not weeks.

However, relief was at hand. The third phase was speedily concluded by state passage of financial relief measures. The state discovered sufficient revenues on hand to maintain existing expenditure patterns for at least a year on a modified basis. Forecasts of drastic cuts proved to be untrue. Reality meant cuts of 10 percent rather than calamity, long-term hardship, and panic. The shortfall could for the most part be met by economy and retrenchment measures already in effect. The good years had ensured some slack, perhaps more than would ever be necessary. The facts appeared to sustain the popular contention that government was inefficient and that public bureaucracy could be reduced considerably without a substantial suspension of public services.

During the fourth phase, dating from mid-July 1978, most public agencies started adjusting activities, at least for 1978–1979, to the new realities of Proposition 13 and the subsequent state measures.

Nonetheless, there were still public agencies that had claimed for years that they were starved for resources, that they had used their resources as economically and efficiently as could have been expected, and that they could not function effectively with high costs *and* cuts in resources.

Adjustment to Proposition 13 varied greatly among agencies. As Tables 11–2 and 11–3 (pages 494–495) indicate, cities and counties did lose a great deal of property tax revenues. Yet the cities were able to increase their fees, service charges, and other taxes by nearly $82 million, and thus the share of locally raised revenues remained about the same, although total city revenues fell by more than 6 percent. The counties actually showed a net increase in revenues of about 2 percent, which reflected the nearly 66 percent increase in state aid. It might be noted that the share of locally raised county revenues had fallen from one-half to about one-third of the total, with a potential consequent loss of local control over services to be delivered.

Expenditures increased for both cities and counties, despite the low or negative growth in revenues, as shown in Tables 11–4 and 11–5. Aggregate city expenditures increased by almost 4 percent, while county expenditures rose by 9.5 percent. This occurred because of the drawing down of local surpluses or other revenue-producing budgetary techniques. It is interesting to note that the public safety component of the budget did not show the greatest growth in either cities or counties, although this was the one service area in which the legislature had required maintenance at previous levels. (See pages 496–497).

The L.A.P.D. and Proposition 13

Although it might appear that the passage of Proposition 13 only troubled public officials during the third phase, between June 6 and mid-July 1978, when the state devised a temporary solution, the situation within each public agency was far more complicated. One such agency is the City of Los Angeles Police Department.

The L.A.P.D. has for some decades been the pride of the City, consistently rated as one of the finest, if not the finest, police department in the country. In its time, it has been rehoused, reequipped, reorganized, scientifically managed, favored, and protected. It has earned a high degree of autonomy and its Police Protective League has been one of the strongest pressure groups in the City, gaining for department personnel enviable conditions of employment. It has enjoyed widespread public and political support, and in the past decade the public has yet to defeat any proposition in support of the department.

As a labor intensive service, the L.A.P.D. was particularly vulnerable in its budget dependency. Increases in manpower, new technology, and mobility, coupled with a remuneration formula that has given L.A.P.D. officers one of the highest pay rates and most generous pensions in the country, made it an expensive department to operate. Its budget had to pass through many steps—the police chief, the board of police commissioners, the mayor, and the city council. Further, the governor and the state legislature, after the passage of Proposition 13, also began to take an interest in police department finance. Proposition 13 showed up the differences of opinion among these actors.

The mayor of Los Angeles, although a retired police officer, had consistently argued since taking office in 1972 that the department received too much money. Yet he was careful to insist that, after the passage of Proposition 13, he was following the police chief's recommendation to cut back almost 1,100 officers. The police chief was new, having just been appointed from within the department, and he felt obliged to protect the department and retain the loyalty of his staff. He did not want to shoulder alone the blame for the cutback. Both the mayor and the chief fought publicly over the extent of the cutback and how funds should be allocated within the department.

The city council, mindful of public support for the police, tried to minimize the cutback, but still insisted that economies could be made by cutting out the police band and thinning out senior ranks. It also suggested a trade off between the cutback and frozen remuneration. The Police Protective League filed suit against the city government to prevent a wage freeze maintaining that the city was illegally withholding a 8.3 percent anticipated wage increase. If the protective league was successful, there was the threat that the city would be required to forego all state aid.*

Meanwhile the board of police commissioners, a weak citizen board appointed by the mayor to supervise the L.A.P.D., used the budget dispute to strengthen itself against the police chief and the department by suggesting alternative resource allocations within the department. At the state level, the legislature and the governor insisted

---

*In February 1979, the courts held that the wage freeze was not legal.

that if there were to be a state bail out, police services should be maintained at their former level, at the cost, of course, of freezing wage rates.

Thus, as far as the L.A.P.D. was concerned, Proposition 13 undermined what had appeared on the surface to be harmonious relations between all the parties concerned. As long as the money for the L.A.P.D. had been there, everybody had worked together to claim the credit. Now that the money was no longer guaranteed, each participant was putting forth his own solution, trying to put the blame for unpopular measures on somebody else, and claiming credit for ensuring that the level of police service would be maintained.

Tables 11-6 and 11-7 (pages 498-502) represent only a few of the nine police budgets prepared during the Jarvis turmoil. The September 1978 revised budget reflects the cuts that were made in response to Proposition 13. It shows that there was an approximate cut of 6.5 percent in salaries, a 6.5 percent drop in general expenses, and a tremendous drop of 84.5 percent in equipment purchases. Following Proposition 13, the total police appropriation was 7.6 percent less than was initially approved in April 1978.

The principal L.A.P.D. cut in the salary category was the total elimination of general overtime and the cutting by about 50 percent of the overtime allowed for police officers. If service needs remained constant and if police were no longer allowed overtime pay, then, by law, they would necessarily receive compensatory time off. There was, therefore, a real reduction of sworn officer time in the field.

The principal expenditure in the equipment category was for the addition of eighty three-wheel motorcycles. No replacement of the current capital stock of transportation equipment was undertaken during 1978-1979.

Table 11-7 illustrates the programmatic breakdown of the budget appropriations for four points in time: the original pre-Jarvis adopted budget, the revised budget of September 1978, the estimated expenditures of the department at the end of the 1978-1979 fiscal year (June 30, 1979),* the amount requested by the police department for 1979-1980 during the budget negotiation process, and the amount proposed by the mayor's office, prior to City Council amendments, in April 1979. There was a continuation of the cutting of expenditures, and a proposed cut in positions authorized across all programs. Most of the proposed drop, however, was in the area of traffic control, and basically consisted of moving the crossing guard function to the department of transportation. (This move was later rescinded by the City Council and, along with the allowance of more overtime pay and

*As estimated in April, 1979.

other changes, it brought the department budget up to about $213 million.)

Table 11–8 (page 503) examines the historical pattern of authorized positions in the department. The L.A.P.D. was cut back in 1978–1979 to pre-1973–1974 levels for sworn, civilian, and total authorized personnel. It might be noted that although the City Council did restore some positions for 1979–1980 against the mayor's recommendations, the department continued to see a reduction in labor resources, with a total drop of 5 percent and a greater decline in civilian than in sworn personnel.

However, as Table 11–9 (page 503) indicates, the police department had a large number of vacancies and was able to absorb many of the cutbacks by not filling currently unfilled slots. For example, there was a net drop of only 125 civilians when the department was obliged to reduce civilian employment by 445, since they had 325 unfilled positions. Further, since the department elected to reduce its labor force by attrition, many of these reductions did not occur immediately. By the end of fiscal year 1978–79, there were still thirty-six civilians that were employed above the budgeted level.

The same was generally true for the sworn employees. Although this group was budgeted for a reduction of 353 positions, the actual number of officers that had to be let go through attrition was considerably less, since there were already 278 vacancies.

However, the types of staff cutbacks were significant. As soon as the state bail-out plan was announced, about 200 officers, almost all of whom were from the upper ranks, retired from the department. Most of these were not patrolmen but experienced investigators. Many of those interviewed indicated that they would not have retired without the incentive of Proposition 13; they feared loss of money and benefits. After thirty years service, an L.A.P.D. officer can retire on 70 percent of salary with future, uncapped cost of living increases. To continue would have meant working for only 22.5 percent more (additional salary less 7.5 percent pension contribution), and possibly losing the sick pay bonus which could be as much as $7000. Many of the vacancies at the end of the 1978–1979 fiscal year were the result of these resignations.

The second type of labor cutback was the total elimination of new recruits during 1978–1979. There were no academy classes, and the usual 100 or so new officers, most of whom would serve by patrolling the streets, were not added to the force. This suspension of classes allowed academy instructors to resume other police duties; however, there was not a one-for-one street replacement. It was determined that during fiscal year 1979–1980 there would be some hiring on an as needed basis and that some training would be restored.

The state bail-out plan mandated that while expenditures for public safety could be cut, service levels would not be reduced. Given the extent of the budget reduction, it is interesting to ask the question of what impacts on service level did occur because of the reduced funds.

The L.A.P.D. identified several functions that were claimed to be essential to police services. None of the following divisions was to be cut:

- Robbery/Homicide
- Bunco/Forgery
- Records/Identification
- Communications
- Administration/Narcotics
- Metro Division
- Footbeats
- Investigative Support
- Burglary/Auto Theft
- Investigative Headquarters

The only entire program to be cut out of the budget was the student worker program. All other programs had at least some support.

However, as Tables 11-10, 11-11 and 11-12 (pages 504-505) indicate, there were cutbacks in the department, and it might well be determined that service levels were not as high as they had been previous to the initiative. These tables, derived from a police department report to the City Council Finance Committee, indicated that life in the city (and in the department) was not as secure as it had once been. Arrests, crimes, and accidents rose in the immediate post-Jarvis era. There were 200 fewer police officers deployed in operations, and only after a departmental realignment was the number of detectives in operations approximately what it had been in mid-1978.

The police department also identified some specific examples of declines in support services; these can be seen in Table 11-12. In particular, the potential for delay in an investigation greatly increased. Although citizens were not necessarily aware of these usually internal delays, over time the impact of delays on the ability of the police to respond to crime became noticeable.

However, in terms of response to emergency calls, police service levels did not fall. Yet, for the non-emergency call, response time increased and service levels fell (see Table 11-13, page 506). It is clear that the state mandate was not honored in spirit.

The Police Department is only one part of the criminal justice system. The rest of the system suffered much heavier cuts. The state decided not to take over the responsibility of court financing, and the counties were forced to make changes in courtroom usage and other court facilities.

County jails as well as county and city public defender offices had their budgets reduced. So, although the police segment of the criminal justice system may have succeeded in avoiding the drastic future that was initially promised by Jarvis-Gann, the rest of the system did not survive as well.

In all this, it is important to recognize the state centralized control over city expenditure patterns. By acting as a large city council, the state legislature intruded on local revenue decision making as well as on local expenditure allocations. To get state funds after Proposition 13, cities could not have large surpluses and were required to ensure full police protection. The eventual implications of this, not only for the criminal justice system but for all city budgetary decision making, are potentially enormous, if still not totally clear.

Table 11-1
Initial Bail Out Assistance*

	(in Millions of Dollars)
Cities	$ 250.
Counties	
(1) State assumption of mandated costs:	
(a) Medi-Cal	$ 418.
(b) SSI/SSP	168.
(c) AFDC	437.
(d) Food Stamp Administration	21.
	$1,044.
(2) Block grant assistance	436.
Total to counties	1,480.
Special districts (allocated by county boards of supervisors)	125.
Special districts, "unmet needs" funds to be distributed by State Department of Finance	37.
Public schools, K–12, block grant	2,000.
County offices of education	65.
Community colleges	240.
TOTAL	$4,197.

*In addition, an emergency loan fund of $900 million was established. Intended to smooth any cash flow crises that developed, none of this fund was ever used.

Source: A Study of the Local Government Impacts of Proposition 13 (California State Department of Finance, Sacramento, Cal.).

Table 11-2
City Revenue Summary (372 Cities Reporting)

	1977-78 Actual ($ millions)	Percent of Total Revenue	1978-79 Budgeted ($ millions)	Percent of Total Revenue	Percent Year-to-Year Change
Local					
Property tax—					
Current	$ 972.6	19.9	$ 422.6	9.5	−56.5
Prior and					
penalties	30.0	0.6	13.1	0.3	−56.3
Property tax Total[b]	$1,002.5	20.6	$ 435.8	9.8	−56.5
Sales and use tax	804.0	16.5	856.7	19.4	+6.5
Other local taxes	505.1	10.4	557.8	12.6	+10.4
Fees, fines, charges	567.6	11.6	604.6	13.7	+6.5
Other local revenue	431.4	8.8	484.3	10.9	+12.3
TOTAL, LOCAL[b]	$3,310.6	67.9	$2,939.2	66.4	−11.2
State/County					
SB 154 Assistance	—	—	185.7	4.2	—
Other state and county	609.0	12.5	558.9	12.6	−8.2
TOTAL, STATE/ COUNTY	$ 609.0	12.5	$ 744.6	16.8	+22.3
Federal					
Revenue sharing	$ 178.5	3.7	$ 188.0	4.2	+5.3
Anti recession fund	56.0	1.1	14.9	0.3	−73.4
Other federal	724.5	14.9	540.1	12.2	−25.5[a]
TOTAL, FEDERAL[b]	$ 959.0	19.7	$ 743.0	16.8	−22.5
Total reported revenue[b]	$4,878.7	100.0	$4,426.7	100.0	−9.3[a]
Less, other federal	−724.5	—	−540.1	—	—
GRAND TOTAL REVENUE	$4,154.2	—	$3,886.6	—	−6.4

General Fund revenue from new or increased taxes, fees, and service charges levied after June 6, 1978: $81.6 million.

[a]Many cities incorporate special Federal grant funds into their budgets only as these funds are received throughout the year. Thus comparisons of total 1977-78 *actual* revenue and 1978-79 *budgeted* revenue are distorted by this factor.

[b]Totals do not add due to rounding.

Source: See Table 11-1.

Table 11-3
County Revenue Summary (58 Counties Reporting)

	Actual 1977–78 ($ millions)	Percent of Total	Budgeted 1978–79 ($ millions)	Percent of Total	Percent Year-to-Year Change
Local					
Property Tax, current	$2,877	32.5	$1,441	16.0	−49.9
Property tax, prior and penalties[a]	58	0.7	50	0.6	−13.1
Property tax, Total	$2,935	33.2	$1,491	16.6	−49.2
Sales and use tax	$ 218	2.5	$ 226	2.5	+4.0
Other revenues and transfers	1,280	14.5	1,312	14.6	+2.5
TOTAL, LOCAL	$4,433	50.2	$3,029	33.7	−31.7
State[b]	$2,073	23.4	$3,438	38.1	+65.8
Federal					
Exclusive of project grants	$1,771	20.0	$1,825	20.2	+3.1
Project grants	493	5.6	595	6.6	+20.7
TOTAL, FEDERAL	$2,264	25.6	$2,420	26.8	+6.9
All Other Sources	77	0.8	130	1.4	+68.8
TOTAL REVENUES	$8,847	100.0	$9,017	100.0	+1.9
Revenues generated by new or increased county fees, charges, and levies since June 6, 1978					$22.1 million

[a]Prior year property taxes are the amounts which were *due* in a prior year but which will be *collected* in the current year.

[b]The Medi-Cal and SSP portions of the SB 154 "buy-out" were not reflected in many county budgets on the reasoning that Medi-Cal and SSP are State programs. These programs remain county responsibilities and, in any case, are needed to insure comparability between the two budget years. These amounts are included in these reports and add $313 million 1978–79 revenues from the State. If this State aid is excluded, overall county revenues would have shown a 1.6 percent year-to-year *decrease*.

Source: See Table 11-1.

Table 11–4
City Expenditure Summary (372 Cities Reporting)

	1977–78 Actual ($ millions)	Percent of Total Expend-itures	1978–79 Budgeted ($ millions)	Percent of total Expend-itures	Percent Year-to-Year Change
General Government					
Administration	$ 556.1	12.8	$ 571.5	12.6	+ 2.8
Nonadministration	738.7	17.0	746.6	16.5	+ 1.1
Libraries	103.3	2.4	93.8	2.1	− 9.2
Parks, Recreation	424.0	9.7	390.7	8.6	− 7.9
Building Regulation	59.3	1.4	61.2	1.4	+ 3.2
Fire Protection	467.6	10.7	467.3	10.3	− 0.1
Police Protection	865.5	19.9	878.5	19.4	+ 1.5
Other Public Safety	28.8	0.7	31.2	0.7	+ 8.3
Public Works	942.6	21.6	1,014,1	22.4	+ 7.6
Contributions to					
Enterprises	31.1	0.7	19.9	0.4	− 36.0
Other	138.1	3.2	243.6	5.4	+ 76.4[b]
TOTAL					
EXPENDITURES[a]	$4,355.0	100.0	$4,518.5	100.0	+ 3.8

[a]Some cities included contingency funds or other undistributed special funds (e.g., federally funded capital improvement projects) in this budget category. In many cases, as these funds are spent during the year, expenditures will be allocated to other budget categories. Most of the aggregate year-to-year increase in this category appears to result from this budgeting practice.
[b]Columns do not add due to rounding.
Source: See Table 11-1.

Table 11-5
County Expenditure Summary (58 Counties Reporting)

	Actual 1977-78 ($ millions)	Percent of Total	Budgeted 1978-79 ($ millions)	Percent of Total	Percent Year-to-Year Change
General Administration[b]	$1,566	18.1	$1,757	18.6	+ 12.2
Public Protection	1,647	19.1	1,752	18.5	+ 6.4
Public Ways and Facilities	413	4.8	566	6.0	+ 37.0[c]
Health and Sanitation	1,199	13.9	1,257	13.3	+ 4.8
Public Assistance[d]	3,389	39.2	3,745	39.6	+ 10.5
Education, Libraries	34	0.4	30	0.3	- 11.8
Education, Other[e]	13	0.1	9	0.1	- 30.8
Recreation and Cultural	137	1.6	113	1.2	- 17.5
Debt Service	44	0.5	47	0.5	+ 6.8
Contributions to Enterprises	74	0.9	77	0.8	+ 4.1
Other	122	1.4	107	1.1	- 12.3
TOTAL	$8,638	100.0	$9,461	100.0	+ 9.5[a]

[a]Increases were reported by 48 of 58 counties.

[b]Many counties budget all or part of their Federal revenue sharing, antirecessionary, other grant funds, and a variety of reserve funds in this account; hence, any major change is usually not due to an increase in county "administrative" costs.

[c]Some counties commonly budget larger expenditures for public ways and facilities than are actually spent. Generally this reflects an optimistic forecast of potential Federal subventions.

[d]The Medi-Cal and SSP portions of the SB 154 "buy-out" were not reflected in many county budgets, but are included here. See footnote on Table 11-3 for further detail.

[e]Excludes County Superintendent's Office, which is reflected in the Education portion of this report.

Source: See Table 11-1.

Table 11-6
Police Department Budgets: 1976-77 to 1978-79

This Department has the duty and power to enforce the penal divisions of the City Charter, the ordinances of the City, and the laws of the state and the nation for the purpose of protecting persons and property and for the preservation of the peace of the community. To these ends the department engages in patrol, prevention of crime, investigation of reported crimes, apprehension of suspects, the gathering and presentation of evidence, detention of unarraigned persons, regulation of traffic, investigation of traffic accidents, custody of property, and such staff services as are necessary to engage in these activities.

EXPENDITURES AND APPROPRIATIONS

	Expenditures 1976-77	Estimated Expenditures 1977-78	Budget Appropriation 1978-79	Revised 1978-79 Budget 9/12/78
Salaries				
General	$ 33,660,563	$ 36,000,000	$ 36,568,943	$ 33,655,862
Police Officers	155,299,611	167,120,000	167,518,401	160,264,971
Marksmanship Bonus	86,562	97,000	97,250	92,388
Unused Sick Time	2,288,034	2,412,000	2,462,297	2,339,182
To Be Employed as Needed	1,386,036	1,487,000	1,704,199	1,604,199
Overtime—General	358,594	500,000	562,988	—
Overtime—Police Officers	5,190,706	4,923,000	5,109,435	2,554,717
TOTAL SALARIES	$198,270,106	$212,539,000	$214,023,513	$200,511,319*
Expense				
Printing and Binding	$ 392,469	$ 475,000	$ 504,566	$ 443,794
Traveling Expense	96,015	136,000	175,200	175,200
Ammunition and Tear Bombs	158,333	195,000	194,780	169,196
Contractual Services	579,777	638,000	227,517	198,619
Field Equipment Expense	1,705,827	1,965,000	2,162,491	2,067,777
Institutional Supplies and Expense	313,074	340,000	370,270	370,270
Petroleum Products	2,336,847	2,480,000	2,604,862	2,477,219
Traffic and Signal Expense	115,578	205,000	167,525	167,525
Transportation Expense	20,024	23,000	23,112	23,112
Secret Service	256,012	305,000	305,000	305,000
Uniforms	188,544	255,000	246,952	184,476
Reserve Officers Expense	51,040	50,000	90,000	90,000
Office and Administrative Expense	507,682	680,000	730,393	644,217
Operating Supplies and Expense	184,333	229,000	252,747	226,315
TOTAL EXPENSE	$ 6,905,555	$ 7,976,000	$ 8,055,415	$ 7,542,720

Table 11-6 (Continued)

Equipment

	Actual 1976-77	Budget Appropriation 1978-79	Revised 1978-79 Budget 9/12/78
Furniture, Office and Technical Equipment	$ 852,321	$ 199,172	$ 155,389
Transportation Equipment	2,256,206	3,297,017	336,000
Other Operating Equipment	93,428	165,393	76,351
TOTAL EQUIPMENT	$ 3,201,955	$ 3,661,582	$ 567,740
TOTAL POLICE	$208,377,616	$225,740,510***	$208,621,779***

SOURCE OF FUNDS

	Actual 1976-77	Estimated 1977-78	Budget Appropriation 1978-79	Revised 1978-79 Budget 9/12/78
General Fund	$205,877,616	$222,496,939	$223,240,510	$206,121,779
Traffic Safety Fund (Schedule 3)	2,500,000	1,473,123	2,500,000	2,500,000
Off-highway Motor Vehicle Fund (Schedule 17)	—	12,938	—	—
TOTAL FUNDS	$208,377,616	$223,983,000	$225,740,510	$208,621,779

*No salary funds are to be used for the Police Motorcycle Drill Team.

**No funds are to be used for the Police Band.

***Any reduction in the level of funding for the Public Disorder and Intelligence Division which is reflected in the budget for this department as it is finally adopted shall not act to reduce the level of effort against organized prison gangs in Los Angeles.

Table 11-6 (Continued)

SUPPORTING DATA

DISTRIBUTION OF 1978-79 APPROPRIATIONS BY PROGRAM

Program	Salaries	Expense	Equipment	Special	Budget
Crime control	$134,005,702	$ 93,804	$ 2,990	—	$134,102,496
Traffic Control	22,761,479	21,800	4,881	—	22,788,160
Technical support	31,250,542	7,357,005	544,504	—	39,152,051
General administration and support	12,493,596	70,111	15,365	—	12,579,072
	$200,511,319	$7,542,720	$567,740	—	$208,621,779

DISTRIBUTION OF 1978-79 TOTAL COST OF PROGRAMS

Program	Authorized Regular Positions	Budget	Support Program Allocation	Related Costs	Cost Allocated to Other Budgets	Total Cost of Program
Crime control	6,052	$134,102,496	$ 43,685,854	$114,153,416	—	$291,941,766
Traffic control	1,193	22,788,160	8,045,269	20,088,237	—	50,921,666
Technical support	2,316	39,152,051	(39,152,051)	—	—	—
General administration and support	666	12,579,072	(12,579,072)	—	—	—
	10,227	$208,621,779	$ —	$134,241,653	$ —	$342,863,432

Source: Los Angeles City documents.

Table 11-7

Police Department Program Budget Summary

	Total All Police Department Programs	Crime Control	Traffic Control	Technical Support	General Administration and Support
DIRECT PROGRAM COST					
1978-79 Adopted Budget	$225,740,510	$142,032,567	$24,974,585	$44,559,149	$14,174,209
1978-79 Revised Budget 9-12-78	208,621,779	134,102,496	23,188,160	38,752,051	12,579,072
1978-79 Estimated Expenditures	209,968,000	133,211,000	23,093,000	41,299,000	12,365,000
1979-80 Amount Requested	220,808,951	138,534,754	24,446,424	45,566,625	12,261,148
1979-80 Proposed Budget	$203,717,306	$132,828,242	$17,213,414	$41,535,280	$12,140,370
RELATED COSTS					
Support Program Distribution	—	$ 47,519,053	$ 6,156,597	$(41,535,280)	$(12,140,370)
1979-80 Total Related Cost(s)	$186,515,441	162,451,590	24,063,851	—	—
1979-80 Total Cost of Program(s)	$390,232,747	$342,798,885	$47,433,862	$ —	$ —
Change from 1978-79 Direct Program Cost: Adopted Budget					
Amount	$ (22,023,204)	$ (9,204,325)	$ (7,761,171)	$ (3,023,869)	$ (2,033,839)
Percentage	(9.8)	(6.5)	(31.1)	(6.8)	(14.3)
Change from 1978-79 Direct Program Cost: Revised Budget					
Amount	$ (4,904,473)	$ (1,274,254)	$ (5,974,746)	$ 2,783,229	$ (438,702)
Percentage	(2.4)	(1.0)	(25.8)	7.2	(3.5)

Table 11-7 (Continued)

POSITIONS					
1978–79 Budget Regular Positions	10,227	6,051	1,194	2,316	666
1979–80 Proposed Regular Positions	9,172	5,701	764	2,147	560
Change from 1978–79 Regular Positions	(1,055)	(350)	(430)	(169)	(106)
BASIS FOR CHANGES FROM ADOPTED BUDGET					
Obligatory: Proposition 13	$(19,433,789)	$ (8,013,858)	$ (2,272,861)	$ (6,823,360)	$ (2,323,710)
Obligatory: Other	3,273,741	167,867	721,881	2,367,991	16,002
Workload	—	—	—	—	—
Other	(5,863,156)	(1,358,334)	(6,210,191)	1,431,500	273,869
Service Level	—	—	—	—	—

Source: Detail of Department Programs, 1979–80, City Administrative Officer, City of Los Angeles.

Table 11-8
Police Department
Authorized Positions

	Sworn	% Change	Civilian	% Change	Total	% Change
1970/71	6999		2391		9390	
1971/72	7155	2.2	2480	3.7	9635	2.6
1972/73	7017	− 2.0	2755	11.1	9772	1.4
1973/74	7459	6.3	2942	6.8	10401	6.6
1974/75	7390	− 1.0	2855	− 2.9	10245	− 1.5
1975/76	7440	1.0	2912	2.0	10352	1.0
1976/77	7442	0	2876	− 1.2	10318	0
1977/78	7411	0	2717	− 5.5	10128	− 1.8
1978/79	7369	− 1.0	2858	5.2	10227	1.0
1979/80	7101	− 3.6	2614	− 8.5	9717	− 5.0

Source: Police Department Documents and Author's Calculations.

Table 11-9
Authorized Positions, Vacancies, & Reductions*

	1978/79 Authorized	Vacancies	Reductions
Civilians			
Clerks	57	0	4
Clerk-Steno.	170	14	23
Clerk-Typists	816	64	81
Traffic Officers	355	94	55
Mechanics	151	5	0
Adm. Assist.	113	13	25
Other	1196	135	257
TOTAL	2858	325	445
Sworn			
Chief/Deputy	14	1	1
Commander	22	3	2
Captains	90	11	10
Lieut.	232	(2)	15
Sergeant	891	41	56
Invest.	1256	79	44
Police Off.	4864	145	225
TOTAL	7369	278	353

*All layoffs will occur by attrition. There is redeployment to take care of reductions in some departments. Thus actual employment is somewhat greater than authorized less the sum of vacancy and reductions.

Source: Police Department Documents.

Table 11–10
Service Level Measures—Crime and Arrests

	Jan–Mar 1978	Jan–Mar 1979	Change
Arrests	9,398	10,744	+ 14.3%
Part I Crimes	57,500	65,257	+ 13.5%
Traffic Accidents	19,266	20,418	+ 6.0%
Injury Traffic Accidents	8,377	8,696	+ 3.8%

The increases for 1979 come on the heels of an increase of 8.4% in Part I Crimes, an increase of approximately 7.4% in traffic accidents and a decrease of 1.8% in arrests in 1978 as compared to 1977. ("Part I Crimes" is the FBI label for the most serious crimes.)

Source: Police Department Report to City Council.

Table 11–11
Service Level Measures—Office of Operations Deployment

	1977–78	1978–79	Change
Police Officer Ranks			
August	4,327	4,211	− 116
September	4,294	4,228	− 66
October	4,336	4,199	− 137
November	4,342	4,159	− 183
December	4,341	4,142	− 199
January	4,324	4,124	− 200
February	4,297	4,107	− 190
March	4,311	4,112	− 199
Detective Ranks*			
August	867	776	− 91
September	860	777	− 83
October	853	793	− 60
November	856	806	− 50
December	851	801	− 50
January	851	801	− 50
February	847	844**	− 3
March	856	849**	− 7

*Reflects Departmental Realignment.

**Does not include detectives assigned to narcotics, vice, and intelligence.

Source: Police Department Report to City Council.

Table 11-12
Service Level Measures—
Examples of Difficulties in Service Delivery
Resulting from Loss of Support Services

Field Officer Impacts:

1. Officers have to wait longer to contact the Department's Vehicle Processing Unit Research and Investigation. Delays up to one hour and fifteen minutes have been reported.
2. Reductions in Property Division have increased the waiting time to book evidence.
3. There are now no garage attendants on the evening watch in sixteen areas, resulting in delays in servicing vehicles.
4. Field officers securing crime scenes must wait longer for Special Investigation Department and detective personnel to arrive at the scene.

Detective Impacts:

1. Detectives must now wait longer at crime scenes for photographers (up to one hour additional delay) and fingerprint experts.
2. Scientific analysis of evidence is delayed. It now takes three days to analyze narcotic evidence while only one day was required previously.
3. There are delays in scheduling polygraph examinations and obtaining fingerprint comparisons and it now takes ten days to obtain comparisons of questioned documents where only four days were previously needed.
4. Backlogs in Research and Investigation have resulted in delays in entering identifiable stolen property in the Automated Property System. Consequently the identification of pawned stolen property is delayed, resulting in delayed apprehension of offenders and delaying the recovery of stolen property.
5. Detectives now must duplicate needed criminal record summaries themselves, and the waiting time to obtain these criminal record summaries has increased from an average of three to an average of twenty minutes.
6. Air Support Division has now been forced to diminish special flights to assist detectives in maintaining surveillance in certain cases. The increased workload has caused investigative surveillance activities in general to be diminished significantly.
7. Clerical reductions have increased the amount of time needed to prepare and distribute investigative reports, thereby delaying the dissemination of information within the Police Department.
8. Intelligence Divisions are becoming less able to actively seek information on organized crime and potential threats to public law and order. The Labor Relations Division is having difficulty monitoring labor disputes and maintaining liaison with the 480 local labor unions.
9. There are delays in processing personnel complaints against Police Department employees because of a loss of investigators and clerical support.
10. Detectives must now wait longer to discuss and file criminal cases with the City Attorney and District Attorney owing to personnel reductions in these offices.

Table 11-13
Service Level Measures—Response Time

The department has been able to maintain service levels for the highest priority (emergency) calls for service (Priority 1 calls). Service levels for Priority 2 and Priority 3 radio calls have decreased indicating that citizens are waiting longer for police units in non-emergency situations. The following table shows the immediate impact of Proposition 13 on service levels in responding to citizen calls for service. (Service level is defined as the percentage of time a police unit can be dispatched within the Department's goal for Priority 1, 2, and 3 calls. The goal for Priority 1 call is 3 minutes. The goal for Priority 2 and 3 calls is 5 minutes.)

Call	1977–78	1978–79	Change
Priority 1	84.1	85.2	+ 1.3%
Priority 2	55.8	50.4	− 9.7%
Priority 3	35.7	32.0	− 10.4%

ACKNOWLEDGMENTS (continued from p. iv)

George Eddy and Jerry Saegert, "The Chief." Copyright © 1976 by George Eddy and Jerry Saegert of the University of Texas at Austin. Reprinted by permission. Distributed by the Intercollegiate Case Clearing House, Soldiers Field, Boston, Mass. 02163. All rights reserved to the contributors.

Dorothy N. Harlow and Ellen Kimmel, "Chris Logan—City Engineer." Presented at a Case Research Association Workshop and distributed by the Intercollegiate Case Clearing House, Soldiers Field, Boston, Mass. 02163. All rights reserved to the contributors.

Richard P. Shick, Rose Williams Boyd, and Barry Bader, "Civil Service Systems: A Short History." From *How to Modernize Your Public Personnel/ Civil Service System.* Copyright © 1976 by the National Civil Service League. Reprinted by permission.

"Elements of a Modern Merit Personnel Program" reprinted from *Guide to a More Effective Public Service: The Legal Framework* (Washington, D.C.: U.S. Civil Service Commission, Bureau of Intergovernmental Personnel Programs, 1974).

Jay F. Atwood, "Collective Bargaining's Challenge." Reprinted by permission from *Public Personnel Management,* January–February 1976.

"County Hospital: A Role Playing Exercise." Adapted from an exercise in Douglas T. Hall et al., *Experiences in Management and Organizational Behavior.* Copyright © 1975 by John Wiley & Sons, Inc.

John R. Schermerhorn, Jr., "Missing Raise." Copyright © by John R. Schermerhorn, Jr. This case was prepared by Dr. John R. Schermerhorn, Jr., as a basis for class discussion rather than to illustrate either effective or ineffective handling of an administrative situation. Distributed by the Intercollegiate Case Clearing House, Soldiers Field, Boston, Mass. 02163. All rights reserved to the contributor.

Darlene King Mercier, "Why California Fires So Few Incompetents." From *California Journal,* December 1972. Reprinted with permission of the *California Journal.*

Thomas A. Kochan, "Collective Bargaining in Madison." Excerpted from Thomas A. Kochan, *City Employee Bargaining with a Divided Management* (Madison: Industrial Relations Research Institute, University of Wisconsin, 1971).

Frederick C. Mosher, "Some Notes on Reorganizations in Public Agencies." From *Public Administration and Democracy: Essays in Honor of Paul H. Appleby,* edited by Roscoe C. Martin (Syracuse, N. Y.: Syracuse University Press, 1965), pp. 129–50. Reprinted by permission of the Publisher.

Lawrence E. Lynn, Jr., "Organizing Human Services in Florida." Reprinted (and adapted slightly) from *Evaluation* magazine. Copyright © 1976 by permission of the copyright holder, Minneapolis Medical Research Foundation, Inc.

Lewis Friedman, "City Budgets." © 1974 by the Council on Municipal Performance (COMP). Reprinted by permission. This chapter is excerpted and revised by the author for this text from COMP's Municipal Performance Report #4, *City Budgets.* For the full report and information on many other related publications, write to COMP at 84 Fifth Avenue, New York, N. Y. 10011.

Richard L. Montesi, "Sunset Hills." Copyright © 1979 by Richard L. Montesi. All rights reserved.

David W. Singleton, Bruce A. Smith, and James R. Cleaveland, "Zero-Base Budgeting in Wilmington." © 1976 by the Municipal Finance Officers Association of the United States and Canada. Reprinted from the August 1976 *Governmental Finance*. This article was originally titled "Zero-based Budgeting in Wilmington, Delaware."

Bertram M. Gross, "Planning: Developing Purposefulness." Reprinted with permission of Macmillan Publishing Co., Inc., from *The Managing of Organizations*, Vol. II, pp. 774–781. Copyright © 1964 by The Free Press, a Division of The Macmillan Company.

M. M. Hargrove, "Metropolitan Tulsa Transit Authority. Copyright by M. M. Hargrove. Reprinted by permission. Distributed by the Intercollegiate Case Clearing House, Soldiers Field, Boston, Mass. 02163. All rights reserved to the contributor.

Jacob B. Ukeles, "Policy Analysis: Myth or Reality?" Reprinted from *Public Administration Review*, XXXVII (May–June 1977). © 1977 by the American Society for Public Administration, 1225 Connecticut Avenue, N. W., Washington, D.C. All rights reserved.

Harry P. Hatry, Louis Blair, Donald Fisk, and Wayne Kimmell, "A Checklist for Assessing Program Analyses" (originally "An Illustrative Checklist for Assessing Program Analysis"). Reprinted from Harry P. Hatry et al., *Program Analysis for State and Local Governments* (Washington, D.C.: The Urban Institute, 1976). Reprinted with permission.

Graeme M. Taylor, "Swimming Pools." This case was prepared by Graeme M. Taylor, Management Analysis Center, Inc., with the cooperation of Dade County, Florida, on behalf of the Ford Foundation and the State-Local Finances Project, George Washington University. It is intended for class discussion only, and certain names and facts may have been changed which, while avoiding the disclosure of confidential information, do not materially lessen the value of the case for educational purposes. This case does not purport to be a statement of policy by the county involved. The author wishes to acknowledge his debt to Gloria Grizzle, Budget and Analysis Division, Dade County, and J. Robert Perkins, Chief, Planning and Research, Park and Recreation Department, Dade County, for their cooperation and assistance in the preparation of this case.

"Emergency Ambulance Service (A)" and "Emergency Ambulance Service (B)" are based on a report prepared for the mayor of New York by Dr. E. S. Savas, Deputy City Administrator. The report is entitled "Emergency Ambulance Service," March 8, 1968. The case was prepared by Richard J. Gill, Management Analysis Center, Inc., under the supervision of Graeme M. Taylor, on behalf of the Ford Foundation and the State-Local Finances Project, George Washington University. These cases are intended for class discussion only, and certain names and facts may have been changed which, while avoiding the disclosure of confidential information, do not materially lessen the value of the cases for educational purposes.

Walter Williams, "The Implementation Process." Excerpted from "Implementation Analysis and Assessment." © 1975 by the Regents of the University of California. Reprinted from *Policy Analysis*, Vol. I, No. 3, pp. 545–554, by permission of The Regents.

David I. Cleland, "Project Management: Understanding Project Authority." Reprinted from *Business Horizons* (Spring 1967). Copyright 1967 by the Foundation for the School of Business at Indiana University. Reprinted by permission.

H. Sheldon Phelps, "Managing with PERT." Reprinted, by perimission of the publisher, from *Management Review* (October 1962). © 1962 by American Management Association, Inc. All rights reserved. "Simplified PERT Diagram" reprinted by permission of Daniel D. Roman.

Joseph S. Wholey, "The Role of Evaluation and the Evaluator in Improving Public Programs." Reprinted from *Public Administration Review*, XXXVI (November–December 1976). © 1976 by the American Society for Public Administration, 1225 Connecticut Avenue, N.W., Washington, D.C. All rights reserved.

Harry P. Hatry, Richard E. Winnie, and Donald M. Fisk, "How to Design a Program Evaluation." Reprinted from *Practical Program Evaluation for State and Local Government Officials* (Washington, D.C.: The Urban Institute, 1973). Reprinted with permission.

Edward J. Cherian, "The Summer Youth Program." Copyright © 1976 by the Research Foundation of the State University of New York. This case, originally titled "District of Columbia Summer Youth Program," was prepared by Edward J. Cherian as part of a joint project by the State University of New York at Albany and Rensselaer Polytechnic Institute to develop case materials on the delivery of service at the state and local government levels for use in graduate programs in public administration. The project has been made possible by an institutional grant from the United States Office of Education under Title IX, Parts A and C, of the Higher Education Act of 1965, as amended, and was directed by Professor Donald Axelrod, State University of New York at Albany, and Professor William Wallace, Rensselaer Polytechnic Institute. All names appearing in the case are fictional.

John S. Thomas, "So, Mr. Mayor, You Want to Improve Productivity . . ." (Washington, D.C.: National Commission on Productivity and Work Quality in cooperation with the Ford Foundation, 1974).

Willard T. Price, "Productivity and Safety in Solid Waste Collection—Feather Bedder I?" Copyright by Willard T. Price, Ph. D. Distributed by the Intercollegiate Case Clearing House, Soldiers Field, Boston, Mass. 02163. All rights reserved to the contributor.

Frederick O'R. Hayes, and Daniel Rubin, "Productivity in Palo Alto." Reprinted by permission of the publisher, from Frederick O'R. Hayes, *Productivity in Local Government* (Lexington, Mass: Lexington Books, D. C. Heath and Company, copyright 1977, D. C. Heath and Company).

Charles H. Levine, "Organizational Decline and Cutback Management." Reprinted from *Public Administration Review*, XXXVIII (July–August 1978). © 1978 by the American Society for Public Administration, 1225 Connecticut Avenue N.W., Washington, D.C. All rights reserved.

Jeffrey I. Chapman, "L.A.P.D. in the Wake of Proposition 13." © 1979 by Jeffrey I. Chapman.